Encyclopedia of Nautical Knowledge

Encyclopedia
of Nautical Knowledge

by

W. A. McEWEN and A. H. LEWIS

Cornell Maritime Press

Cambridge Maryland

ISBN 0–87033–010-1

Library of Congress Catalog Card Number: 53—9685

Manufactured in the United States of America

Copyright © 1953, by Cornell Maritime Press

All Rights Reserved

*"They that go down to the sea in ships, that do busi-
ness in great waters; these see the works of the LORD,
and His wonders in the deep." (Psalm 107: 23–24)*

PREFACE

That a single volume devoted to the task of enumerating and clarifying the multitude of terms and phrases involved, with appropriate comments on their use and pertinent information under the heading of *Nautical Knowledge,* represents a bold step in abridgment or encompassment of a vast field in the affairs of men will be appreciated fully by those in any way concerned with the Sea and all the name conveys in a realm of her own.

It is believed, however, that such a book, if but scratching the surface of maritime lore in its broadest range and sense, should be complete on the practical side, sufficient on the theoretical, with a smattering of the historical, where weight of the particular caption demands it. Adherence only to a curt definitive wording has been left to the lexicographers.

The *Encyclopedia,* therefore, is aimed at meeting a demand for a compendium of nautical information that maintains on the even keel of consistency a treatment of each term or subject in harmony with the relative importance thereof. This may be verified by a cursory inspection of its pages.

A word regarding use of the *hyphen:* In compound terms, any rigid following of a rule may not be upheld, in view of the many differences of taste and opinion among authors, printers, and the dictionary-makers. For example, *main-royal, main royal,* and often *mainroyal,* are considered equally proper as naming a particular sail; also, *main-royal-clew, main royal clew,* and *mainroyal clew,* as designating a part of such sail. However, it is believed good usage, where further combining obtains, to connect *all* words comprising an *adjectival* group, as in the following terms: *Port-main-royal clew; starboard-mainroyal clew; weather-main-topsail brace; starboard-wing-propeller-shaft housing; port-main-deck-stringer angle-bar; lee-mizzen-topgallant-backstay dead-eye.*

Grateful acknowledgment must be expressed for much valuable help from a wide selection of books consulted during compilation of the *Encyclopedia.* To mention a few: *New Oxford, Merriam-Webster's, Chambers',* and *Winston's* dictionaries; *Knight, Nicholl, Riesenburg,* on seamanship; *Bowditch, Dutton, Norie,* on navigation and nautical astronomy; with different U.S. Navy and Coast Guard publications and, also, the many reliable sources of biological lore covering the ocean's principal birds, fishes, mammals, and vegetation.

In view of the recent changes in arrangement of the *Nautical Almanac* made to conform to present-day advancement in navigational practice, in which the use of *right ascension* no longer is considered necessary, the reader's attention is called to the text in the *Encyclopedia* under SIDE-REAL for an explanation of the *"sidereal hour angle"* as employed in indicating the places of Stars in the *Almanac.* Also see remarks under ASCENSION.

KEY TO ABBREVIATIONS

Abbrev.	*abbreviated*
A.S.	*Anglo-Saxon*
Cf.	*confer; compare; refer to*
Dan.	*Danish*
Dial.	*dialectal*
Dim.	*diminutive*
Du.	*Dutch*
Esp.	*especially*
Fr.	*French*
Gael.	*Gaelic*
Ger.	*German*
Gr.	*Greek*
Heb.	*Hebrew*
Hind.	*Hindustani*
Ice. (Old Norwegian)	*Icelandic*
It.	*Italian*
L.	*Latin*
LL.	*Low Latin*
Lit.	*literally*
M.E.	*Middle English*
Nor.	*Norwegian*
O.Fr.	*Old French*
Pers.	*Persian*
Pl.	*plural*
Port.	*Portuguese*
Pron.	*pronounced*
Russ.	*Russian*
Sp.	*Spanish*
Specif.	*specifically*
Sw.	*Swedish*
Teut.	*Teutonic*
W.	*Welsh*

Encyclopedia
of Nautical Knowledge

A. International Code *burgee* or swallow-tail flag, white and blue vertically divided, which, hoisted singly, denotes *"I am undergoing a speed trial"*; and, as a towing signal, shown by towing vessel, *"Is the towing hawser fast?"* or, by vessel towed, *"Towing hawser is fast."* Its uppermost place in a four-flag hoist, or *geographical signal,* distinguishes such signal as that denoting the name of a place. Also, in a two-flag hoist, or urgent or important signal, as upper flag it indicates signal concerns *abandoning* vessel, an *accident,* or *afloat* and *aground.*

A1. (*A-one*). A rating-mark given a vessel in a classification society's records, generally indicating first class condition. Lloyd's uses this mark for classifying equipment, as distinct from hull ratings. Steel hulls are classed 100-A1, 90-A1, etc., according to condition at latest survey. The very best. *See* CLASS.

A.A. Always afloat: Abbreviated form of phrase used in charter-parties when referring to a stipulated port of discharge, as in "or as near thereto as she can safely get, being *at all times afloat.*"

A.B. (*Able-bodied*). Abbreviation used in crew lists and shipping articles for rating of *able seaman. See* SEAMAN.

A.B.S. American Bureau of Shipping. *See* BUREAU.

ABACK. Backward against the mast; said of a square-rigged vessel, or of her sails, when the wind is acting on the forward side of and flattening the latter against her masts, thus tending to drive the vessel astern. **All a. forward,** a call (as from the lookout) indicating that the head sails are *aback.* **Braced a.,** said of yards hauled around so that their sails are *laid aback.* **Flat a.,** in such position that the wind acts at nearly a right angle with the fore side of square sails. **Laid a.,** reversed, as sails, to give a ship sternway. **Taken a.,** caught by a sudden change of wind resulting in sails drawing from the opposite side to that for which trimmed. In maneuvering, yards may be purposely braced to lay sails, especially topsails, *aback* or *to the mast.* However, when through faulty steering, a sudden change of wind, or other unforeseen circumstances in

heavy weather, a vessel is taken or caught *aback,* consequences may be disastrous.

ABAFT. Toward a vessel's stern; behind; back of; aft of; opposed to forward of; as, *abaft the mainmast.* **A. the beam,** relative bearing of any object lying outside a ship in any direction abaft that of right angles to her fore-and-aft line.

ABANDON SHIP. Order given for all on board to leave a stricken vessel by boats or other means available, there being no hope of her survival.

ABANDONMENT. Act or state of being abandoned; relinquishment of damaged property to its insurers, party insured claiming total loss. Abandonment is possible in cases of shipwreck, capture, seizure, vessel posted missing, constructive loss, and circumstances of catastrophic nature.

ABEAM. At right angles, laterally, to a vessel's fore-and-aft line; directly abreast a ship's side and in line with her deck-beams; as, *we had the wind abeam.*

ABERRATION. A small periodical displacement in position of a heavenly body, due to relative motions of Earth and body, combined with progressive motion of light from such body. **Annual a.,** that due to motion of Earth in her orbit. **Diurnal a.,** that due to rotation of Earth on its axis. **Planetary a.,** that due to a planet's orbital motion during the time required for its light to reach the earth. **Constant of a.,** greatest apparent annual displacement of a star from its mean position, or 20.47 seconds of arc.

ABOARD. Upon or in a vessel; on board; as, *our captain came aboard.* **All a.,** call or order to go aboard. **To fall a.,** to strike or come against another vessel's side; to foul. When ships encounter one another at an obtuse angle or broadside on, such collision is known as an *aboardage;* degree of proximity or contact is implied by **close a., hard a. To get a.,** to get close alongside, or foul of, a vessel. **To go a.,** to enter or go upon a vessel; go on board; embark. **To haul the tacks a.,** to haul weather clews of courses close down; set the courses. **To have the port** (or **starboard**) **tack a.,** to sail on the port (or starboard) tack; have the wind from port (or starboard) side. *With port tacks aboard* signifies a sailing-vessel's yards are braced so that the port lower corners. or tacks, of her courses are hove down forward and to windward; or, when a ship is sailing *close-hauled on the port tack*. To **keep the land** (or **coast**) **a.,** to keep within sight of shore while sailing more or less parallel with a coast-line. To **lay a.,** to run a vessel close alongside of another for boarding, as for combat or capture.

ABOUT. Around, in motion; round, in revolution or rotation; as, *he brought the ship about*. The situation of a sailing-vessel immediately after she has changed her course by going about and standing on the other tack. **A. ship,** a command to the crew to prepare for tacking, to take their stations for stays. **Ready a.,** same as *about ship*. To **bring a.,** to put the ship on another tack. To **cast a.,** to tack; wear ship. To **come a.,** to go on another tack; to turn; change; come round; as, *the wind will come about from west to east; the ship came about*. To **go a.,** to take a different direction, as a ship in tacking. To **heave a.,** to put a vessel on another tack suddenly. To **put a.,** to alter one's course to the opposite direction.

ABOVE DECK. On deck; also, honestly; openly; above board.

ABOX. Said of a vessel when her head yards are braced aback, after sails remaining full, so that head and after yards are actually trimmed for opposite tacks. By this procedure, ships used to maintain a proximate position while *gamming* at sea, or when awaiting a pilot. **Brace a.,** to lay the head yards *abox*.

ABRAHAM (or **ABRAM**), To Sham. To pretend illness. A slang expression dating to Shakespeare's time, when "*Abraham-men,*" a class of sturdy beggars who simulated lunacy, wandered about the country in a disorderly manner. Rigors of old-time shipboard life often caused men to *sham Abraham*.

ABREAST. Opposite; abeam of; by the side of; over against; at right angles to. Lying or moving side by side, as ships with stems equally advanced. **Abreast of** and **abreast with** are used to indicate a vessel's situation with respect to another object, the latter being on a line with her main beam; as, *a ship was abreast of the light. Of* and *with*, however, often are omitted. **Line a.,** squadron formation in which ships form a line abeam or abreast of one another.

ABRID. A bushing-plate around a hole in which a pintle works; a pivot-hole sleeve.

ABSENCE FLAG; ABSENT FLAG. Small square blue signal flag, flown from the starboard spreader of a yacht, signifying that her owner is not aboard.

ABURTON. Stowed athwartships or crossways in a vessel's hold; as casks, cases, pipes, rod-iron, etc. laid end to end.

ABYSM; ABYSS. (Gr. *abbussos*). An unfathomable depth, gulf, chasm, or space. **Abysmal,** of or pertaining to oceanic depths; as *the abysmal deep;* also, *abyssal*.

ACCELERATION. Rate at which velocity of a body increases per unit of time. The force with which the earth attracts a freely falling body, or an acceleration of velocity in falling of 32 feet per second, very nearly; this is known as *acceleration of gravity*. In navigation, acceleration is a correction made to figures of *mean time* in order that they may be raised or stepped up to terms of *sidereal time*. **A. of fixed stars,** apparent excess of diurnal motion of stars over that of the sun, or their earlier transit each day by a mean solar interval of 3 min. 55.91 secs. **A. of moon,** increase in moon's mean motion about the earth, amounting to about 9 seconds of arc in a century. **A. of the tides,** more commonly referred to as **priming of tides,** means shortening of the tide interval. Time interval between corresponding tides on successive days is ordinarily 24 hrs. 51 min., but is decreased by about 13 min. when moon, earth, and sun are nearly in a straight line, as at full and new moon, being then most favorably situated for producing highest tides.

ACCESS HOLE. An opening through a bulkhead, deck, or casing, to enable a person to reach work or gear.

ACCOMMODATION. Quarters or compartments on board ship for protection and convenience of crew, passengers, emigrants, or cattle. **A. ladder,** portable flight of steps leading down a ship's side, for access to or from a quay or a boat alongside; a stair slung at a gangway.

ACCON. French name for a small, open, flat-bottomed lighter or mud-scow used in the Mediterranean; also, *acon*.

ACCOUNT. Latitude (or longitude) by account; latitude and/or longitude deduced from courses and distances sailed since last position obtained by observation. To **go on the a.,** archaic slang for decision or act of a sailor to turn pirate.

ACCUMULATOR. A secondary or storage battery or cell. An elastic section in a trace or in a chain or rope used in dredging, or in sweeping for mines, to prevent parting by too sudden strain. A strong steel tank or cylinder, connected by piping to an air-compressor, for storage of compressed air used in starting Diesel engines, firing torpedoes, etc.

ACHERNAR. (Ar. *akhir al nahr*, end of the river). A first magnitude star in the group *Eridanus*, about 30° from the south pole in about 1 hr. 35 min. of right ascension.

ACKMAN. An old sailor's name for a fresh-water or river thief.

ACLINIC. Having no inclination or dip; situated where the compass needle does not dip. **A. line,** an irregular, variable line encircling the earth near the equator, where a magnetic needle has no dip; the *magnetic equator*.

ACOCKBILL. Said of a ship's yards when they are tipped up at an angle with the deck; also, of a ship's anchor when it hangs at the cathead, or by a chain over the bow, ready for dropping.

ACON. *See* ACCON.

ACORN. A small ornamental piece of wood sometimes fixed on the point of a spindle above a masthead vane. A solid acorn-shaped piece of metal used to finish off tops of uprights in a railing constructed of piping or rod iron. **A.-shells,** commonly and incorrectly called *barnacles, balanus,* or genus of *Cirripedes* in the class *Crustacea,* which, however, are allied to the true *barnacle, q.v.* **A.-point,** fore-sight or muzzle-sight of a gun.

ACOUSTIC CLOUDS. Areas of atmosphere through which sound is impeded, deflected, or stopped. Such a condition accounts for occasional erratic projection of fog signals.

ACROSS, To moor. To secure a vessel by anchors dropped on each side of a stream.

ACROTERIUM. (*Gr.,* = *summit*) An ornament, often gracefully curved and elaborately carved, surmounting prows and/or sterns of ancient vessels, especially those of Mediterranean history. It was customary for the victors in naval combats to take them as trophies. Also, *akroterion, acrostolium.* (Cf. *Aplustre*).

ACT. Generally, in legal parlance, an unpredictable event stipulated against or covered by a contract of affreightment or a marine insurance policy; exercise of power or result of such as affecting a marine adventure. **A. of God,** an inevitable event brought about by operations of nature, unmixed with human agency or negligence; applied broadly to damage due to lightning, hurricanes, tidal waves, earthquakes, etc. Any accident to a vessel, such as is caused by wind and/or weather, over which her master has no control. Under such circumstances, insurance is adjusted by *particular average,* where each loss is settled separately; *see* AVERAGE. **A. of hostility,** as pertaining to international relations, a warlike act; an act against a vessel or her interests which justifies resistance with force. **A. of man,** that of a vessel's master in sacrificing spars or furnishings, or in jettisoning of cargo, either wholly or in part, in order to save the remainder. In such instances, vessel, cargo, and freight share the loss proportionately, or according to their values; *see* General a. *in* AVERAGE.

ACTIVE SERVICE. Naval term for current employment in the service; "on the active list." Also, service before an enemy in time of war.

ADJUSTMENT. Of averages; *see* **General a.** *in* AVERAGE. Of a compass; *see* COMPASS. Of a sextant; *see* SEXTANT.

ADMEASUREMENT. Process of ascertaining various dimensions, capacities, and tonnage of total spaces in a vessel as required for official registration.

ADMIRAL. (O.F. *amiral;* M.E. *amiral;* from Ar. *amir-al-bahr,* commander of the sea). Title of highest rank of naval officer; commander-in-chief of a fleet. First English admiral was William de Leyburn, appointed *"Admiral of the Sea of the King of England"* by Edward I in 1297 and whose post was not that of a commander, but embraced those general and extensive powers afterwards associated with title of *"Lord High Admiral of England,"*— that is, administrative functions now vested in the Lords Commissioners of the Admiralty and judicial authority belonging to the present Admiralty Division of the High Court of Justice. England's Lord High Admirals are said to have been of royal blood, except Earl of Berkeley, who was a commander at 20, a vice-admiral at 27, and First Lord of the Admiralty at 38. Queen Anne (*1702–1714*) acted as Lord High Admiral of England, following death of her consort, who had held that title. Title of admiral (*amiral*) was introduced into France by Louis IX (*1226–1270*), the "St. Louis" of the Crusades, and for a time this rank was equivalent to that of a Marshal of France. Its great powers were reduced by Richelieu (*1585–1642*) but nevertheless enormous until the first Revolution. In 1805, Napoleon bestowed the honorary title of *"Grand Admiral"* on Murat (*1771–1815*). In the United States navy, creation of the *a.* grade was urged by John Paul Jones in a letter to Robert Morris in 1776, and the proposal was echoed by prominent citizens for nearly a century afterwards, but was opposed, it is said, because of its seemingly royal and authoritative flavor. Highest naval rank during this period was that of Captain. An act of Congress July 16, 1862, provided for nine grades of commissioned officers and authority to appoint nine *rear-a's* on the active list and another nine on the reserve or retired list. First *rear-a's* were selected for distinguished service; afterwards, vacancies were filled by regular promotions. In 1864, the President was authorized to appoint one *rear-a.* as a *vice-a.* to have equal status in rank with that of a lieutenant-general of the army. This new position was given to Rear-Admiral David Farragut. Then, in 1865, another bill made Farragut a full *a.* and permitted one *vice-a.* and ten *rear-a's.* Rear-Admiral David Porter thereupon became *vice-a.* and, upon Farragut's death in 1870, *admiral,* with the *vice-a.* post going to Rear-Admiral Stephen C. Rowan. In 1875 Congress decided that ranks of *a.* and *vice-a.* should not be filled by promotion. For all practical purposes this meant that these grades would die with Porter and Rowan. Another Act, in 1882, reduced *rear-a's* on the active list to six. The Navy was, in this period, threatening to become extinct. In 1899, the President was once again empowered to appoint an *a.*, the selection being Rear-Admiral George E. Dewey, who held the rank until his death in 1917. The Navy Personnel Act of 1899 increased *rear-a's* to 18 in number, but rank of *vice-a.* remained in disuse until 1915, when the *Naval Appropriation Act* provided that commanders-in-chief of Atlantic, Pacific, and Asiatic fleets should have rank of *a.* on such duty, with their seconds in command graded as *vice-a's.* In the following year, the *Chief of Naval Operations* was accorded rank and pay of an *a.* The office of *vice-a.* is probably of equal lineage with that of *a.* In England, the terms "lieutenant-admiral" and "lieutenant of the Admiralty" were in use for some years until they were supplanted by "vice-a. of England" in 1672; by "vice-a. of Great Britain" in 1707; and by "vice-a. of the United Kingdom" in 1801. The office was vacated in 1876 and revived by Edward VII in 1901. Admirals of all grades are often referred to as *flag officers,* from their privilege to fly a special flag indicating rank of such officer in command; traditionally, an *a.* carries his flag at the main, *vice-a.* at the fore, and *rear-a.* at the mizzen masthead. An admiral's ship, a flagship, sometimes is referred to as *The Admiral.* Along the east coast of England, title of *a.* is given by fishermen to one who, by their choice, is recognized leader of their fleet. Among riggers, largest size of *fid* is called *the a.* **A. anchor,** *see* ANCHOR. **A.'s barge,** formerly a smartly kept and handled boat pulling ten or twelve oars, which "served for state and ease, as for carrying the generalls, admiralls, and prynce captains." In modern times, a large, heavy motor-boat, resembling a small pleasure cruiser, used as a ferry or pleasure-boat by important personages. **A.-shell,** a richly colored cone-shell (*Conus ammiralis*). **A.'s march,** short and lively tune played by a ship's band when an admiral receives "honors" coming aboard or leaving a vessel. **A.'s walk,** private balcony or promenade sacred to an *a.* Until within the past quarter century it was customary in the design of even the mightiest British battleships to have a quaint little balcony around the vessel's stern, so that the great man might have a place in which to privately pace and ponder. **A.'s watch,** second dog watch (*6 to 8 p.m.*); period in which the admiral is supposed to amble up to the bridge with his after-dinner cigar for a final inspection of the world before darkness sets in. **Land-a.,** in British navy, one of that rank whose duties confine him to shore. **Lord High A.,** title of former head of naval administration in Britain. **Port-a.,** a British commander-in-chief of a naval port. To **tap the a.,** to steal from casks of liquor by means of a gimlet and a straw; also, to *suck the monkey.*

ADMIRALTY. **Board of A.,** a department of the British government entrusted with management of all matters concerning the navy. It is comprised of *Lords Commissioners* (originally two civil or political lords and four naval or sea lords) who decide collectively on important questions. The *First Lord,* who is always a cabinet minister—and who necessarily resigns when the prime minister resigns—besides having general control, is responsible for all business of the *A.*, the other board members acting as his assistants in various duties divided among them. *Department of A.,* in functioning under Board of *A.,* is in direct supervision of a wide variety of naval bureaus, activities, etc. To it belongs a hydrographer, directors of transports, victualling, ordnance, navy contracts, ship construction; an accountant-general, with assistants, clerks, and other subordinate officials; also termed *Admiralty Department.* It is also the term for that branch of jurisprudence or of the judiciary that takes cognizance of maritime affairs, civil and criminal. The name of a building housing officers of *British A. Department.* **A. coefficient,** also termed *Admiralty constant,* in naval engineering and architecture, a formula employed in determining horsepower required to propel a vessel of given displacement at a certain speed; *see* COEFFICIENT. **A. court,** one having jurisdiction over maritime matters, civil and criminal. In United States, admiralty jurisdiction is vested in district courts, subject to revision by circuit *Court of Appeals* and *Supreme Court,* and extends to cases of salvage, bottomry and respondentia bonds, seamen's wages, seizure under laws of imposts, navigation, or trade, cases of prize or ransom, contracts of affreightment between different states or foreign ports, charter-parties, contracts for material, maritime contributions and averages, pilotage, surveys of ship and cargo, and, generally, to all damages and trespasses in maritime affairs; its criminal jurisdiction to all crimes and offenses committed on the high seas, or beyond jurisdiction of any country. In England, maritime courts were divided formerly into the *Instance Court* and the *Prize Court*—separate tribunals, though usually presided over by the same judge; the Prize Court existed only during time of war. Jurisdiction in questions of booty of war, and distribution thereof, was in 1865 conferred on the Admiralty Court; and that relating to attack and capture of pirates was vested therein, and also in vice-admiralty courts in the colonies and foreign possessions. *British A. Court* functions are now exercised by the *Probate, Divorce, and Admiralty Division of the High Court of Justice,* constituted in 1873–1875. Civil, and particularly criminal, jurisdiction of *British A. Courts* is much narrower in scope than that exercised in their American counterparts.

Civil jurisdiction is shared with county courts, extending to disputes between part owners of a ship, suits for waivers, pilotage, and those relating to salvage, wrecks, collisions, etc. In criminal matters, the *A. Court* formerly took cognizance of piracy and certain other offenses, but this jurisdiction came to be regulated by the Criminal Law Consolidation Acts generally, and criminal jurisdiction of *A. Courts* may be regarded as obsolete. In war time, questions of prizes, captures, condemnations, and the like, remain vested exclusively in the *A. Division* of the High Court in England. Proceedings *in admiralty* were originally based on civil law, but it is merely as the basis of earlier mercantile codes, and by no means exclusively, that civil law is of authority in these courts. *Courts of admiralty* generally, within their jurisdictional limits resemble courts of equity in practice and modes of procedure, but are even more free of technical rules. **A. droits,** formerly a portion of hereditary revenues of the crown, arising from enemies' ships detained in prospect of a declaration of war, or coming into port in ignorance of commencement of hostilities, or from such ships as were taken by non-commissioned captors, proceeds of wrecks, goods of pirates, and the like. In Britain, proceeds of this nature are now paid into the Exchequer for public use. **A. knot,** measure of speed corresponding to a nautical mile of 6080 feet; *see* KNOT *and* MILE. **A. territorial jurisdiction,** in U.S., that which extends to all matters arising out of navigation of the high seas and public waters, including navigable lakes and rivers of the country.

ADRIFT. State of a vessel or any floating object unmoored and at the mercy of wind and tide.

AD VALOREM. Latin phrase meaning *according to value;* used in levying customs duties when such are fixed at rates proportioned to estimated value of goods concerned; opposed to duties designated as *specific,* or fixed at a specified amount.

ADVANCE. Distance a vessel moves in the line of her original course after putting down her helm, as for a tack, and until she has turned through 90°. A payment of money before it is due: as, that paid to a seaman at an intermediate port in a voyage and charged to his account; or that paid upon signing articles for a voyage, usually amounting to a month's pay. **A. note,** a draft on owner or agent of a vessel, generally for one month's pay, given by the master to a seaman on signing articles of agreement for a voyage or period. In U.S., this practice was outlawed by Congress in 1884. Known also as an *advance bill.*

ADVENTURE. In commerce, a pecuniary risk or speculation. The term applied to small consignments of merchandise exported for sale or barter

at a foreign port by a vessel's master personally. It was general practice in former days to give a shipmaster use of "the square of the main hatch" as hold space for his own interests or "ventures." *See* **B. of Adventure** *in* BILL; **G. Adventure** *in* GROSS.

ADVICE-BOAT. *See* BOAT.

ADZ or **ADZE.** A hand cutting-tool, having an arched blade at right angles with its handle. Since the time of Noah's Ark, the tool most intimately identified with wooden shipbuilding. Three types are in universal shipyard use: *Plain, lipped,* and *scarfing* or *strap adzes.* Cutting edges of these range from 2 to 6 inches in width, and the blade is always ground from a base on its inside to its outer edge, to razor sharpness. A plain adze is oldest of shipyard tools, but largely has been displaced by the lipped tool which has its blade's sides turned up, or *lipped,* this form giving a cleaner cut and preventing raising of splinters. As used by ship carpenters, the adze is a finishing tool, used to shape heavy parts that are too much for chisel or plane. For converting large material when machinery is unavailable, roughing is done with a *broad-axe;* the adze is next used to close in to finished dimensions, finally smoothing off with a plane. To shape a timber is to *dub,* and one thus engaged is known as a *dubber.* Those who fair or "line" sawn timbers use an adze having a hollow blade like a gouge. With this, a series of grooves are cut crosswise before dubbing. A dubber's adze is lipped, with width of blade 5 to 5½ inches; a heavier tool having a lipped blade of 6 inches is used in *squaring* timbers. Smallest is the *scarfing* or *strap* adze with a 2 to 4-inch blade and no lips, used to cut up to a shoulder in a scarf. Adzes of all types are used almost always to cut *athwart* the grain of a timber.

AERIAL. *See* ANTENNA.

AEROPLANE-CARRIER or **AIRPLANE CAR-RIER.** *See* AIRCRAFT CARRIER.

AFFIRMATIVE. Signal flag by which assent or an affirmative reply is expressed; International Code flag *"C."*

AFFREIGHT. To charter or hire a vessel for carrying goods.

AFFREIGHTMENT. Contract by which a vessel is hired for transportation of freight; a charter-party; act of chartering or hiring as above, or shipping goods by *bill of lading* contract.

AFLOAT. Borne by, or floating in, any body of water, as opposed to *aground, ashore,* or *stranded.*

AFORE. Farther forward than; as, *afore the windlass.* **Afore the mast,** before the mast, as referring to men berthed in the forecastle, or forward of the foremast; also, indicating rating or service of an able or an ordinary seaman on a sailing-vessel.

AFOUL. Entanglement; foul; in a state of collision, as two ships. To **run afoul of,** to strike against so as to make extrication difficult or to cause damage.

AFT. At, near, or toward the stern. **Aftcastle,** an elevated structure at the after end of early war-vessels to aid in fighting at close quarters. **Aft-draft,** draft or depth of a vessel below the water-line, measured at the stern. **Both sheets a.,** said of a vessel sailing dead before the wind; running. **Dead a.,** directly toward the stern or astern of. **Flat a.,** said of a fore-and-aft sail's sheet when hauled in as far as possible, as when going to windward or pointing. **Fore-and-a.,** lying in the direction of a ship's length; lengthwise. **Fore-and-a. rig,** see RIG. **Right a.,** directly toward the stern, or astern of. To **haul a.,** see HAUL. To **lay a.,** to go aft.

AFTER. Farther aft; toward the stern. **A.-body,** that part of a ship's hull abaft her midship section. **A. deck,** a weather deck abaft a vessel's midship portion. **A.-ebb,** ebb tidal flow continuing for some time after low water, as occurs at or near a river's mouth. **A.-frames,** radiating cant frames forming a vessel's upper stern structure. **A. hatchway,** opening into an after hold; last large hatch toward the stern. **A. hold,** part of a ship's hold toward the stern. **A.-hood,** a plank next, and fastened to, the stern-post in any strake. **A.-leech,** after edge of a fore-and-aft sail. **A. peak,** compartment at extreme after end of a vessel. **A. peak bulkhead,** partition forming the forward side of an after peak or compartment nearest the stern-post. **A. perpendicular,** see PERPENDICULAR. **A.-rake,** that part of the hull abaft the stern-post. **A. run,** narrowing part of a hold toward the stern. **A.-strain,** distortion or damage remaining after a stress that caused it. **A. yards,** those abaft the foremast in a three-masted ship; those abaft the mainmast, where more than three masts are square-rigged. **After-guard,** men who handle after sails. Originally, the after-guard was comprised of apprentices or unskilled sailors; now, as used in yachting, the term applies to an owner and his guests, or to officers who have their quarters aft. **Aftermost,** nearest the stern; *aftmost.* **A.-piece,** heel of a rudder.

AFTERNOON WATCH. *See* WATCH.

AFTWARD. Toward the after end; after; archaism for opposite to forward.

AGAINST THE SUN. A counter-clockwise rotary motion; contrary to diurnal motion of the sun, as viewed from a latitude higher than that body's northerly declination.

AGE OF THE TIDE. Time elapsing since the moon's transit that originated a tide and occurrence of that tide. Such interval varies from 0 to 7 days; generally from 1 to 2, average for the world being nearly 1½ days. *See* TIDE.

AGETON'S METHOD. Named for its originator, a labor-saving system of determining altitudes and azimuths of heavenly bodies for use in plotting lines of position in navigational work.

AGULHAS CURRENT. A branch of the Indian Ocean Equatorial Current which flows southward through Mozambique Channel and along the south-east African coast. Possessing many of the Gulf and Japan streams' characteristics, this current attains considerable velocity at about 100 miles off shore in the latitude of Durban until it arrives off *Cape Agulhas,* where in being diverted southward by the *Agulhas Bank,* its bulk starts a gradual swing east-ward in the great counter-clockwise circulation of the Indian Ocean, within the expanse bounded by 5 to 35 degrees south latitude and 25 to 90 of east longitude. It is also called the *Mozambique Current.*

AHEAD. Lying in the direction of a ship's course; a distance before a vessel, as, *five miles ahead;* opposed to *astern.* To **forge a.,** to move forward slowly and steadily, as a ship slowly passing another, or continuing to move due to momentum. To **run a. of one's reckoning,** to sail beyond a position calculated to be that in which one's ship is located.

AHOLD. An old term for sailing close to the wind and holding or keeping a vessel on one tack; as, to *lay a ship ahold.*

AHOY! Call used in hailing a ship or attracting attention of persons at a distance; as, *"Ship ahoy!"; "On the dock, ahoy!";* see HAIL.

AHULL. Archaic term for position of a ship in which all her sails are furled and helm lashed a-lee, as in heavy weather, so that she lies nearly broad-side to wind and sea; also, position of an abandoned vessel with decks awash. *A-hull; at hull.*

AIDS TO NAVIGATION. Buoys, beacons, fog signals, lights, radio-beacons, range marks, and, generally, any charted or published information serving the interests of safe navigation.

AIGUILLETTE. (Fr. dim. of *aguille,* needle or tagged point.) Tagged cord or braid worn on shoulder and breast of a military uniform, signifying its wearer is a personal aide to a high official. U.S. navy aiguillettes are blue and gold; those of the Marine Corps and Army, red and gold. Aides to royalty, viceroys, and President of the United States wear the cords on the right shoulder; those to all other dignitaries, on the left.

AIR. (Gr. *aer,* air or mist.) The atmosphere, which consists chiefly of oxygen and nitrogen in the ratio of 1 to 3, its pressure at sea level being very nearly 14.7 lbs. per square inch, or equal to a barometer reading of 30.00 inches. A very light wind; as, *a light air.* **A.-barometer,** an instrument for indicating slight oscillations, as of a water level in a tank, by effect of changes in air-pressure. **A.-bottle,** a portable steel cylinder containing compressed air, used for discharging torpedoes, starting Diesel engines, etc.; less correctly, but commonly, a similar tank containing compressed oxygen, used for oxyacetylene cutting and welding. **A.-bound,** prevented from functioning by presence of air; common to pumps and to circulatory piping systems. **A.-casing,** outer covering made from steel plate, surrounding a smoke-stack and separated therefrom by an air space. Protection from radiating heat and ventilation of fire-room are its uses. **A.-chamber,** enclosed space containing air, as a sealed compartment in a life-boat, for buoyancy purposes, or as a cushion in a force-pump. **A.-cock,** a small valve or pet-cock, used to control passage of air; as, the *bleeder-cock* for relieving an air-bound pump. **A.-cooled cargo,** fruits, vegetables, and other perishables kept at a required low temperature by a mechanical system of forcing cooled air around and through such cargo. **A.-courses,** openings in the ceiling and between beam ends of wooden vessels for circulation of air, necessary for prevention of decay; also, *air-funnels.* **A.-course boards,** planks used for closing or blocking off air-courses. **A.-cylinder,** a nearly air-tight cylinder containing a piston which checks recoil of a gun. **A.-duct,** tube or pipe carrying ventilating air. **A.-funnel,** a ventilating-flue formed by leaving out a timber from a vessel's frame or upper works above her water-line, so as to aid in prevention of decay in frames, ceiling, and planking; same as *air-course.* **A.-hammer,** one driven by compressed air for riveting, or for driving long drift-bolts, etc.; called *pneumatic hammer* by its makers, but commonly referred to as an *air-gun,* or simply *gun.* **A.-jacket,** an inflatable garment used as a life-preserver. **A.-lift,** a pump in which the lifting power consists of air driven down an inner pipe to force water up an outer casing. **A.-line,** shortest distance between two points on the earth's surface. **A.-lock,** an air-tight antechamber of a submarine caisson. Also, stoppage or "binding" of water-flow in a pump, caused by presence of air. **A.-logged,** impeded by air, as a piston-head in a cylinder; *air-bound.* **A.-pipes,** in a ship, those leading from a tank or double-bottom to a weather deck, so that air may be admitted or discharged in accordance with changes of oil or water volume therein; also called *air-vents* or *vents.* **A.-plate,** a bored plate, as a perforated baffle-plate, which permits passage of only a given quantity of air. **A.-plug,** a vent-plug, as fitted in a water-tight man-hole plate or scuttle-cover. **A.-port,** an opening in a vessel's side or a deck house, usually round in shape and fitted with a hinged frame in which a thick glass is secured. Its purpose is to provide light, ventilation, and vision. An air-port also is usually fitted with a solid metal hinged cover, called a *dead-light,* for protection against heavy weather. **A.-pressure,** atmospheric pressure. **A.-propeller,** one of the type

used on aircraft, fitted on certain ice-boats and hydroplanes, and also small Japanese landing-craft during World War II. **A.-strainer,** a filtering device roughly T-shaped or Y-shaped in outline, fitted into a ship's system of air-piping; it contains a small and removable "basket" made from finely perforated metal or wire gauze, through which compressed air passes on its way to Diesel engines, etc. Also, *air-line strainer* or *air-separator.* **A.-strake,** an opening left for ventilation purposes between two planks of a ship's ceiling. **A.-streams,** artificially produced air currents, charged with smoke, used in the study of aero-dynamics; as, in designing so-called stream-lined structures and tracing of wind-currents across variously shaped sails. **A.-tap,** an air-cock. **A.-trap,** small funnel in a barometer-tube for intercepting air-bubbles. **A.-trunk,** a ventilating conduit; air-duct. **A.-wood,** naturally dried or air-dried wood, i.e., not kiln-dried. **A.-meter,** an instrument for measuring flow of air, as circulation of cooled air in refrigerating, forced ventilation, etc.

AIRCRAFT CATAPULT. *See* CATAPULT.

AIRPLANE.   In cargo handling, a large flat wooden tray slung at each end by a bridle; goods thus transferred being protected from crushing injury by sling spreaders.

ALARM. A.-valve, *see* VALVE. **Tidal-a.,** *see* TIDAL. *See* THERMOSTATIC ALARM.

ALBACORE. (Port., from Ar. *al bukr,* young camel or cow.)   A large edible fish of the mackerel family, commonly known as *tunny,* found in warmer Atlantic and Pacific waters and western Mediterranean; especially, the *great albacore,* called also *tuna* and *horse mackerel.* Several related smaller fishes in tropical seas are also called *albacore.*

ALBATROSS. (Port. & Span. *alcatraz,* pelican.)   A web-footed bird of the petrel family (genus *Diomedea*), largest of sea birds and capable of long sustained flight. The great **wandering a.,** well-known to sailors in the southern "roaring forties," is found at great distances from shore and has been observed to follow a vessel for weeks on end. Specimens of this bird have shown a wing-spread of more than 20 feet. **Black-footed a.** and **short-tailed a.** are common in the North Pacific.

ALCAZAR. (Sp., = *palace*)   An old classic word for the *quarter-deck.*

ALDEBARAN. (Ar. *al-debaran,* the following one.) A first magnitude reddish star, often called the *Bull's Eye* (also *Cor Tauri*) in the group *Taurus* (the Bull). *Aldebaran* or *α Tauri* lies about 20° northwest of *Orion's Belt* and about midway between that constellation and the *Pleiades.* It was probably named from its following the last-named group in *ascension,* or rising. Ancient Greeks gave the name *Hyades* to the V-shaped group of five stars in *Taurus* of which *Aldebaran* is chief.

ALEE. At or to the lee, or sheltered, side; away from the wind; opposed to *aweather.* Generally refers to position or motion of the helm. With tiller *alee,* a rudder is moved in the opposite direction, thus causing a vessel's head to swing toward the wind. **Hard a.,** sometimes **luff a.,** an order for *hard down* helm, *i.e.,* with tiller moved hard to leeward. **Helm's a.,** a call that helm is put *alee,* or *put down,* and that head-sheets should be eased off for coming about.

ALEWIFE. (Pl., *alewives.*) A small deep-bellied fish of the herring family, abundant in North American Atlantic waters north of Florida. Of poor food value, it is used extensively for bait.

ALGA. (Pl., *algae.*) Any of several different classes of marine plants, usually termed seaweeds, including dulse, kelp, and sea lettuce.

ALIST. Listed or canted to one side; inclined; heeling; not on an even keel.

ALL. Completely; entirely; as in, *all clear for running.* Altogether, in addressing persons; as in, *All hands aft! Stern all!* Often used to add force to, or enlarge a following word's meaning; as in *cable is all slack; decks are all awash.* **A.-ataunto,** *see* ATAUNT. **A. aback forward!,** *see* ABACK. **A. clear,** no obstruction to hinder a maneuver, working of gear, etc.; as, *vessel is all clear of the wharf; cables are all clear.* **A. hands,** entire crew; ship's whole company. **A. hands high!,** boatswain's old cry for calling *all hands* to assemble on deck; also, *a. hands hoay!; a. hands hoy!* **A. hard,** with greatest exertion, as an order to oarsmen in a boat; also, *Hard all!* **A. in the wind,** too close to the wind, sails all shaking; hence, said of a person in a confused or undecided state. **A. night in,** a full night's sleep, with no watch to stand. **A. water,** a qualifying term indicating carriage or freighting entirely by water transportation. **All's well,** cry or phrase used as, or in, a routine report to an officer by a lookout or deck patrol.

ALLEYWAY. Corridor in crew or passenger accommodation; also, *alley* and *passageway.*

ALLOTMENT. Part of a seaman's wages made payable by an *allotment note,* usually monthly, to a relative or to a bank for his account.

ALMANAC, NAUTICAL. (Ar. *al-manakh,* sun-dial or calendar) Publication containing computed places of celestial bodies at successive regular intervals throughout the current year, their changes in apparent motion, parallaxes, semi-diameters, Greenwich hour angles, and other numerical data required for navigational purposes. Seniority among nautical almanacs belongs, probably, to the French *Connoissance des Temps,* commenced in 1679 by astronomer Jean Picard. A similar work is the *Berliner Astronomisches Jahrbuch,* begun in 1776, and under direction of Johann Franz Encke, noted astronomer, from 1830 to 1862. England's first important work was that of Nevil Maskelyne, astronomer royal, also remembered as inventor of the prismatic micrometer. In 1763, while making tests of Harrison's newly-invented chronometer, Maskelyne published his *British Mariner's Guide,* a noted milestone in navigational science, and in 1767 his government authorized him to publish a *Nautical Almanac.* This book prospered while its brilliant author went on to issue his *Tables for Computing Places of the Fixed Stars,* published by the Royal Society in 1774. Two years later he produced the first volume of *Astronomical Observations made at the Royal Observatory, Greenwich, from 1665,* an invaluable work continued to this day. Following his death in 1811, however, the *Nautical Almanac* gradually lost its character until, in 1830, because of numerous complaints against it, the government requested the Astronomical Society to pronounce on the subject. Suggestions of the Society were adopted, and in 1834 a new number appeared with such additions and improvements as advancing astronomical science rendered necessary. Issue of the *Almanac* four years in advance of each current year was then established. The *American Nautical Almanac* has been issued since 1855 by the U.S. Naval Observatory and may be obtained for the current or coming year from U.S. Government Printing Office, Washington, D.C. In recent years it has run to over 300 pages of necessary astronomical data for any computation in celestial navigation.

ALMUCANTAR. (From an Arabic word meaning a *bend* or *arch.*) A small circle of the celestial sphere parallel to the horizon; a circle of equal altitude. An instrument for determining apparent places of heavenly bodies by observing the time they cross a given almucantar. The word is also written *almucanter, almicantara,* and *almacantar.* **Almucantar-staff,** or **astronomer's staff,** a now obsolete instrument once used on board ship for finding the sun's amplitude (its bearing at rising or setting) in order to determine variation of the compass.

ALOFT. (Of Scandinavian origin, meaning *at a height.*) Any place in the rigging, on the yards, or on the masts; opposite of *alow.* **Aloft there!,** a hail to men working in the rigging aloft.

ALONG. To **leg a.,** to lead out a rope that is ready for manning. To **lie a.,** to lie over, to careen with the wind abeam; to *heel.* To **lie a. the shore;** to **lie a. the land,** to sail parallel to the coast keeping it in sight. To **light a.,** to move ahead by lifting or carrying; said of a hawser or sail. To **moor a.,** to anchor a vessel in a river, steadying her by means of a hawser attached to a point on shore.

ALONGSHIPS. An old term meaning in line with the length of a vessel; in the fore-and-aft line.

ALONGSHORE. Along the shore, either on water or on land.

ALONGSHOREMAN. *See* LONGSHOREMAN.

ALONGSIDE. Along or close to the side of a vessel or pier; as, *a tug came alongside the car-float*. **Delivered a.**, said of goods intended for shipment, as indicating beginning of the carrier's responsibility for safe custody and conveyance of a consignment; also, of stores or other material for a vessel's use; *alongside* here means in close proximity to a vessel, whether on a pier or in a lighter or other vessel. To **range a.**, to lay a vessel parallel to, and close beside, another. To **sheer a.**, to cause a vessel to move sidewise toward the side of a wharf or another vessel by action of the current into which she is heading; to steer a boat or vessel close to an object.

ALONGST. Old term used to designate state of being moored head and stern in mid-stream.

ALOOF. Obsolete term for *windward, seaward,* or *in direction of the sea.*

ALOW. Opposite of *aloft,* meaning low down or near the deck; also, an archaic term for *below decks.*

ALPACA. An old name for the black neckerchief worn by enlisted men of U.S. navy, made from alpaca-wool, a very light cotton-and-wool fabric with a hard shiny surface.

ALPHABET FLAGS. *See* FLAG.

ALPHACCA. (Ar. *al fakkah,* the bright one.) *a Coronae Borealis,* principal star in the *Northern Crown (Corona Borealis)* having a declination of 26° 53′ N. and right ascension 15 hrs. 32½ min. With the *Big Dipper's* tail star and *Arcturus, Alphacca* occupies the right-angled corner of a triangle. Also written *Alphecca.*

ALPHARD. (Ar. *al fard,* the solitary one.) *a Hydrae,* chief star in *Hydra* located in 8° 26′ S. declination and 9 hrs. 25 min. right ascension. It lies at the southern extremity of an almost equilateral triangle formed with *Procyon* and *Regulus.*

ALTAIR. (Ar. *al tair,* the flying.) *a Aquilae,* a first magnitude star in the group *Aquila* (Eagle) near the equator. It completes as southern apex, a right-angled triangle outlined through *Deneb* and *Vega.* A line from the *Great Bear* through *Vega* will pass close to *Altair.* Declination 8° 44′ N.; R.A. 19 hrs. 48 min.

ALTAR. One of the steps forming a graving-dock's sides. An old name for the constellation *Ara; see* ARA.

ALTAZIMUTH. (Contraction of *altitude* and *azimuth.*) An instrument for determining apparent places of heavenly bodies. It consists of a telescope free to revolve upon a horizontal and a vertical axis, the arc through which it turns being, in each case, measured by a divided circle. These arcs give the azimuth and altitude, respectively, of an observed body at instant of observation, and so indicate its place. Small instruments of this kind, called *transits* and *theodolites,* are used in land surveying.

ALTERNATING CURRENT. Electric current whose direction of flow reverses at regularly recurring intervals. Unless otherwise specified, refers to a periodic current alternately of positive and negative values. Hence, a flow whose instantaneous values at any point in its circuit vary from zero to positive maximum, back to zero, then to negative maximum, and back to zero. In generating alternating current, when any given armature coil has passed a pair of poles, current is regarded as having gone through 360 electrical degrees, or one cycle. A cycle is one complete set of positive and negative values, half a cycle being known as an *alternation.* *Periodicity* or *frequency* of an alternating current is its number of complete cycles passed through in one second. In ships having **a.c.**, a frequency of 60 cycles is now almost universally used.

ALTERNATING LIGHT. *See* LIGHT.

ALTERNATOR. A device for generating alternating current; an electrical generator; dynamo.

ALTITUDE. Height or extent upward; angle of elevation of a heavenly body above the horizon, measured as an arc of a vertical circle intercepted by the body and horizon. **True altitude** of a celestial body is that of its *center,* as it would be measured at the earth's center, above a plane lying perpendicular to direction of an observer's zenith, *i.e.,* the plane of the *celestial* or *rational horizon.* At sea, an *a.* is measured by a sextant as a certain value above the *visible horizon,* known as the *observed,* or *sextant, a.,* which, when corrected for *index error, dip,* and (for sun or moon only) *semi-diameter,* is termed the *apparent a.* of an observed body's center. After corrections for refraction and parallax, this is finally reduced to the *true a. See* DIP; INDEX ERROR; HORIZON; PARALLAX; REFRACTION; SEMI-DIAMETER; SEXTANT. In practice, concise tables supply a single value, equal to algebraic sum of all corrections, as that to be applied, in the respective cases of sun, moon, and planets or stars, to an *observed a.* to obtain the *true.* **A. and azimuth circle** or **instrument,** an altazimuth. **A. difference,** in determining a line of position by any calculated altitude method, amount a *computed a.* differs from a *true a.,* expressed in minutes of arc, or nautical miles. If the *true a.* is greater, such difference is measured from ship's assumed place toward, and in the direction of, the body observed; otherwise, away from it. *See* LINE for *line of position.* **A.-gauge,** see GAUGE. **A. (or elevation) of the pole,** arc of the meridian between pole and rational horizon, which value is equal to the *latitude.* **Correction of double a's,** see CORRECTION. **Double a's,** method of finding a ship's position by observing two altitudes of a heavenly body, separated by an appropriate interval in time or azimuth. **Equal a's,** method of determining longitude by observing an altitude of a celestial body usually about a half hour *before* its transit and noting elapsed time by chronometer when such altitude reaches its same value *after* the body's transit; with a correction applied for change of position during the elapsed time, half the latter subtracted from time of second observation gives the chronometer reading at instant of transit. **Ex-meridian (or circum-meridian) a.,** *see* **reduction to meridian** in REDUCTION. **Mean of a's** average or arithmetical mean of a series or set of altitudes. **Meridian a.,** *see* MERIDIAN.

ALTO-CUMULUS. (L. *altus,* high; *cumulus,* heap.) A fleecy cloud formation averaging about two miles in altitude; *see* CLOUD.

ALTO-STRATUS. (L. *altus,* high; *stratum,* to spread.) A cloud formation appearing as a thick sheet of gray or bluish color, averaging about 3 miles high; *see* CLOUD.

A.M. As used in expressing clock time, abbreviation of Latin phrase *ante meridiem,* meaning *before noon.*

AMAIN. With full force or great speed; at once; suddenly. To **let go a.,** to let a line go by the run, let a sail drop, etc.; an emergency measure. To **strike a.,** to suddenly lower a topsail yard, or to strike or lower the flag, as formerly said of a vessel when yielding in a sea-battle. (The word is now seldom heard and may be regarded as obsolete on board ship.)

AMBARY. An East Indian plant (*Hibiscus cannibinus*) yielding a valuable fiber known as *ambary hemp* and *brown Indian hemp* which is much used for making cordage, canvas, and sackcloth.

AMBERGRIS. (Fr. *ambre gris,* gray amber.) A waxy substance ejected from the sperm whale's stomach or intestines, where it gathers as a morbid secretion, found floating in tropical seas or washed ashore in a mass varying from 75 to 200 pounds. It is highly valued in perfume manufacture.

AMBER JACK. An amber fish of the genus *Seriola* found in West Indies and Mediterranean waters, a strong and fast swimmer, and a large excellent food fish.

AMERICAN BUREAU OF SHIPPING. *See* BUREAU and CLASSIFICATION.

AMIDSHIPS. In or toward a ship's middle part; in the fore-and-aft line vertically above the keel; as, to put the helm *amidships.* Approximately midway between bow and stern; as, she parted *amidships.* Often shortened to *midships.*

AMMUNITION. Formerly all military stores, as guns, muskets, swords, arrows, bayonets, spears, etc., or munitions of war generally; now usually limited to those materials employed in charging fire-arms, as shots, shell, gunpowder, cartridges, fuses, and wads. In U.S. navy, *ammunition* means all component parts and substances which, when assembled, form a charge for any type of weapon. Included, therefore, are warheads, mines, bombs, depth-charges, demolition-charges, rockets, fuses, detonators, projectiles, explosives, signaling and illuminating pyrotechnic materiel, and chemical warfare materials. **A. cooling** and **ventilating** is a problem which has never been fully solved. The Cromwellian axiom of keeping one's powder dry long has been of vital concern on all war-craft. Wooden ships made more or less water and, in those of iron and steel there were still the matters of condensation and heat to meet. Various air-conditioning systems, therefore, have been tried in ships' *magazines* and experiments continue. Modern vessels have had cork, and more recently fiber-glass, as insulation around their magazines, and installation of refrigeration-piping carrying freon or a similar gas is usual. Also, the air is changed by a system of duct-work and blowers. **A. details,** component parts of assembled ammunition. U.S. navy designates, as such, primers, fuses, detonators, boosters, adapters, tracers, projectiles, cartridge-cases, ammunition tanks and boxes, powder-bags, mouth-plugs, distance-pieces and wads, powder-tanks, and explosives. **A. stowage,** since gunpowder was first used, war-craft have had specially constructed stowage spaces or rooms for *a.* With the development of ships and increase in number, size, and type of guns, location and detail of these compartments, or magazines, have been a major problem for designers. Safety is, of course, the prime consideration, with accessibility a second factor. In ships, both medieval and modern, magazines have always been located deep within the vessel, as remote from shot and shell as possible. They have been sealed, water-tight rooms, like vaults, and usually beneath the water-line so as to be readily flooded, and in modern vessels, have loops of sprinkler-piping, connected to ship's fire-main. In early armor-clads, magazines were placed in groups, fore-and-aft, connected by wing passages, so that *a.* could be transported from one group to another in case a turret should become disabled. To-day, the arrangement is more complicated and there is no direct communication. They are located on the upper and lower platform decks which, in a large vessel, places them below two protective armored decks, as well as below water-line, and, in battleships may be separated from the vessel's skin by as many as six longitudinally bulkheaded spaces. In combat, effort is naturally made to keep *a.* sheltered in a magazine as long as practicable, and then to keep it under protective cover on its way to the guns. A century ago, boys known as *powder monkeys* used to race back and forth from magazine to gun bearing the charges of powder. This practice now is displaced by a variety of pneumatic, electric, and other mechanical chutes, tubes, and hoists, carried on in special handling-rooms and passageways. This applies particularly to separate-loading or "bag" *a.* used for big guns of battleships and cruisers. Projectiles for these guns are stowed in bins near the broadside-hoists, or in the barbettes. *A.* used on small naval craft is usually of a fixed nature and stowage is relatively simple. There is a magazine forward, below the main deck, and often another aft. Special compartments may be arranged for stowage of depth-charges, torpedo-warheads, saluting charges, and small arms *a.* On all armed craft limited quantities of *a.* are stowed near guns for emergency use; it is kept in metal boxes called *ready service lockers.* **Bag a.,** bags of powder such as used in larger guns where projectile and charge are separately loaded. **Bomb-type a.,** a collective term for aircraft bombs, submarine mines, depth-charges, torpedo-warheads, and wrecking mines; the bursting charge is usually case TNT. **Case a.,** a former name for *fixed ammunition.* **Chemical a.** includes projectiles, projectors, bombs, grenades, and candles containing gas, incendiary, and smoke-making materials; also, gas, smoke, and incendiary materials employed from aircraft supply-tanks, projectors, and sprayers. **Fixed a.,** formerly called *case a.,* that in which projectile and primer are firmly secured in a cartridge-case containing the impelling charge, so that a gun is loaded in one operation. Use of *fixed a.* is limited, generally, by weight of cartridge that can be handled by one man. In U.S. navy, it is supplied for guns of 5-inch caliber or less. **Impulse a.,** contained in cartridge-cases fitted with primers and assembled as blank cartridges, are used for launching depth-charges, torpedoes, line-throwing projectiles, and for catapulting aircraft. **Pyrotechnic a.,** comprises fireworks adapted to military use, as distress signals, position and recognition lights, smoke-bombs and boxes, signaling and illuminating rockets with or without parachutes, Very-pistol cartridges, tracers, illuminating elements of projectiles, hand lights, aircraft wing-tip flares, and rifle-grenade lights and smokes. Difference in pyrotechnic and chemical ammunitions is not always distinct, and hence classification may depend upon usage. **Semi-fixed a.,** that in which primer and driving charge are firmly secured in a cartridge-case, but in which the projectile is separate or fixed loosely in its case. Case and projectile are loaded separately. Formerly known as *separate case a.* **Separate loading a.,** that in which primer, propelling charge, and projectile are loaded into large guns in two or more parts. **Small arms a.,** cartridges for weapons of small bore. U.S. navy thus classifies all cartridges of less than one inch caliber and divides it according to *use* (as for rifles, machine-guns, aircraft); *projectile* (as ball, armor-piercing tracer, blank, dummy); and *quality* (as grade 1, grade 2). **Trench warfare a.,** consists of rifle, hand grenades, and trench-mortar ammunition. **Types of a.,** U.S. navy divides it into separate loading, semi-fixed, and fixed, for guns; small arms; trench-warfare; chemical; pyrotechnic; bomb; impulse; blank; and dummy drill. The material is further divided into three classes, viz., *service,* for use in battle; *special,* for gunnery exercises; and *drill,* usually of dummy type.

AMPLITUDE. Intercepted horizon arc between a heavenly body at rising or setting and true east or west point; or angle at an observer's zenith between the prime vertical and one passing through a body at rising or setting. Use of amplitudes appears the first departure from the use of *Polaris* (*North Star*) and *sun* (at noon) for determining magnetic compass variation from true north. Early compasses were marked to show East and West as zero, an observed *a.* being referred to as W 20° N, E 15° S, etc. Subsequent growing popularity of azimuths in altitude, with ready computed tables at hand, provided means for more frequent compass observation, as required in safe navigation, due to the advent of iron in ship construction. In ordinary latitudes, *a.* is approximately equal to declination times secant of latitude; precisely, it may be computed from the formula, $sin\ amp. = sin\ dec. \times sec\ lat.$ The term is falling into obsolescence, however, and navigators to-day refer to *a.,* which is 90°—azimuth, as simply an azimuth, or, where the sun is observed, a *sunrise* or *sunset bearing.*

ANCHOR. (A.S. *ancor;* L. *ancora;* Gr. *agkura;* a hook.) A weighty hooked instrument which, when lowered to the sea floor, holds a vessel in place by its connecting cable; any weight, such as a stone or piece of metal, used for such purpose. An *old-fashioned* or *common a.* comprises the *shank,* or vertical main part; *ring* or *shackle,* often called *jew's harp* from its shape, to which the cable is bent; *stock,* or transverse piece just below the ring; *crown,* at lower extremity, from which branch two *arms* in a plane right-angled to the stock, each spreading into a broad *palm* or *fluke* and terminating in a sharp *bill* or *pea.* When this *a.* is dropped, it strikes bottom crown first, then falls over so that one end of its stock rests on ground, its arms lying horizontally. From this position any pull to one side capsizes or cants it, turning its stock flat on the bottom and pointing one of its flukes fair for *biting*. Subsequent stress on the cable tends to force such fluke into the ground, sufficient length of cable, of course, being payed out to give an approximately horizontal pull. An *a.* of this type is, unquestionably, most efficient in holding power; however, it has been displaced in all large modern vessels by various forms of a *stockless a.*, which are far more convenient to handle and stow, absence of a stock permitting the shank to be drawn into a hawse-pipe. These were introduced about 1850, and from 1875 have rapidly increased in common use, especially in powered vessels. Anchors of merchant and navy vessels vary in weight and size with tonnage of vessel and character of service intended. A battleship usually carries two *bowers*, one *center-bower*, one *stream*, one *stern*, and two *kedges*. Merchant powered vessels of average size have 2 bowers, 1 spare bower, 1 stream, and 1 kedge, while sailing-ships of any tonnage are equipped with all five noted. Number and weight of *a's* to be carried by commercial craft, as well as size and length of cables, hawsers, and warps, are detailed at length in Lloyd's Rules, those of American Bureau of Shipping, and other classification societies. Anchors, their cables, capstans, and/or windlasses are termed, collectively, *ground tackle*. **A. balancing-band,** steel band fastened round an anchor's shank at its center of gravity, to which a tackle may be hooked for ease in handling. **A.-ball,** a pyrotechnic device attached to a grapnel, fired in former days to catch in a ship's rigging, with the object of setting fire to an enemy. A shot with a small grapnel attached to catch in a ship's rigging for use in life-saving. A spherical-shaped signal about two feet in diameter hoisted forward to indicate the vessel is *at anchor*. **A.-bed,** a platform for supporting anchors on the fore deck of older warships, generally at a lower level than the gun-deck; a *bill-board*. **A.-bolt,** a holding-down bolt; one used to fasten down an engine or other piece of machinery. **A.-bracket,** a heavy iron bracket formerly fitted on a large vessel at the forward end of the bill-board recess; when stowing anchor, its crown and arms rested on the bill-board, while its shank's upper end was supported on the anchor-bracket, a hinged strap on which gripped the anchor's shank just below its stock. **A.-buoy,** a buoy attached to, and serving to indicate position of, a dropped anchor. **A.-cable,** *see* CABLE; GROUND-TACKLE. **A.-chain,** *see* CABLE; GROUND-TACKLE. **A.-chock,** an angular, iron-sheathed timber bolted abaft a cathead in old wooden ships, upon which a bower anchor's inner fluke was hung when secured by shank-painter. One of several blocks of wood, or a special cradle, on which an *a.* rests when stowed

on deck. **A.-davit,** often called a *fish-davit*, a small crane or davit used in taking an anchor aboard; a necessity in yachts and smaller craft where an *a.* is too heavy to handle entirely by hand, is also used in larger vessels stowing *a's* on a bill-board or on deck. Formerly, some large ships employed two anchor-davits for *catting* and *fishing*, respectively. **A.-deck,** called also *monkey-forecastle*, a very short top-gallant forecastle on old ships, chiefly used for stowing their bower *a's*. **A.-drag,** same as draganchor; *see* **sea-anchor** and DRAG. **A.-fluke chock,** same as *anchor-chock*. **A.-flukes,** triangular or spearhead-shaped ends of arms of an *a.*; also, *palms*. In an old-fashioned *a.*, four types of fluke were well known, viz., the *spade, Herreshoff, sand,* and *ship's* flukes. A *spade-fluke* is nearly triangular, with outermost point (*bill* or *pea*) square and blunt; it is good for general service, except in rock; *Herreshoff*, a general service type of diamond shape; a *sand-fluke* is slim, pointed, and much like a spear-head; and a *ship-fluke* is largest, as wide as it is long, having a prominent square bill, and intended for general holding. **A.-ground,** an anchorage. **A.-hold,** strength with which an *a.* holds; in a figurative sense, security, fixedness, immovability. **A.-hoops,** iron bands round an old-fashioned anchor's wooden stock. **A.-hoy,** derrick-lighter for conveying chains, *a's*, and heavy mooring-gear about a harbor; also, *chain-boat*. **A.-ice,** ice formed at bottom of a stream or other body of water. **A.-key,** L-shaped cottar-pin securing a metal stock in position; same as *a.-pin*. **A.-knot,** a fisherman's bend. **A.-light,** also called a *riding-light*, a white light shown by a vessel at *a.*; *see* **Rule 11** *in* REGULATIONS FOR PREVENTING COLLISIONS. **A.-lining,** sheathing of planks or plates fastened to a vessel's bows to prevent injury to the hull by *a's*. **A.-money,** "pieces of eight," or those one-eighth, one-fourth, and one-half value of the Spanish dollar, marked on reverse with an *a.*; coined 1816 to 1825 by British government for circulation in Mauritius and West Indies. **A.-pin,** same as *a.-key*. **A.-pocket,** recess at lower end of a hawse-pipe into which flukes of a bower *a.* are hove in stowing. **A.-ring,** iron or steel ring of an *a.* to which the cable is attached; it is replaced by a heavy shackle in large *a's*. **A.-rocket,** life-saving device consisting of a rocket having an anchor-shaped head for carrying and attaching a life-line fired to a stranded vessel. **A.-rode,** line attached to *a.* of a boat, yacht, or other small vessel. Latest type of such line is of stainless steel wire. **A.-stock,** transverse member or cross-piece at upper end of a common *a.* A *fast stock* is one fixed or immovable, making stowage of the *a.* difficult; a *loose stock* is held by a key or pin to the anchor-shank, which key can be withdrawn and stock turned down alongside of shank when stowing the *a.* Stocks are now made of iron or steel, but in older days were always built of wood. A century ago, a large anchor's stock was as long as its shank, plus one-half diameter of its ring. In cross section, usually it was square with chamfered corners, heaviest material at its middle, thence tapering toward its ends, while keeping its upper face a straight line. It was always made in two full-length halves, notched to take the iron shank, and fashioned to leave a small space between; then, by driving on the iron bands or hoops, its two parts squeezed the shank in a firm grip. **A.-stock fashion,** refers to fitting a hull with planks that are widest in their middle and tapering toward their ends, somewhat like a wooden anchor-stock; *see* PLANKING. **A.-stock tackle,** a small purchase once used to cant an anchor-stock when securing a bower. **A.-trip,** line bent to an anchor's crown and led to a buoy; used, if necessary, to break out the *a.* by a direct pull. A line attached to outer end of a cone *sea-a.*, or *drag,* to facilitate hauling it aboard. *A.-tripper; a. trip-line.* **A.-warp,** *see* CABLE; GROUND-TACKLE. **A.-warp leader,** a fitting having a sheave to take the warp on an open boat's bow, so that a fisherman or other occupant can raise or lower *a.* without going forward. **A.-watch,** one or more men detailed as a deck watch while at *a.* or in port; a *harbor-watch.* **A.-well,** a recess in forward part of early monitor-type warships, where anchors and cables were housed from an enemy's fire. **Admiral a.,** one of a stockless double-fluked pattern, similar to *Dunn* and *Baldt* forms; British equivalent of American navy-type *a.* **Angler's a.,** *see* FISHERMAN'S ANCHOR. **Baldt a.,** stockless, double-fluked type, favored by U.S. navy. Similar to *Dunn a.,* excepting in method of connecting arms and shank. **Boat a.,** commonly of the old-fashioned type, with metal stock, but may be almost any form from a simple stone to a collapsible and stainless steel patented "hook." **Bower a.,** one carried at a vessel's bow. Since early times, ships have carried two *bowers,* often of unequal size, the heavier called *best bower,* the other, *small bower.* To-day, all vessels are equipped with a pair of bowers with cables attached and a *spare bower,* of equal size and weight, usually of stockless type and hence capable of being stowed in the hawse-pipes; one is used as a *working a.,* two when mooring, or riding heavily. **Cone a.,** *see* DRAG; *Sea-anchor.* **Danforth a.,** one of patent design formerly popular on yachts, but used on many U.S. minesweepers, subchasers, etc. in World War II; has long and pointed flukes lying close to its shank; also has a kind of stock at its crown where the flukes are hinged. It is usually made in galvanized cast steel. **Dory-a.,** *see* **Sand-anchor. Double-fluked a.,** one of "patent" type, having its arms hinged or pivoted at its crown permitting the flukes to swing from 30° to 45° on either side of its shank. Its flukes are in the plane of, instead of at right angles to, its arms, as in the old-fashioned *a.* Both flukes of an *a.* of this type, in theory, should *bite* if either one does; to insure

this, its arms usually carry a projecting shoulder which catches bottom and throws the flukes downward. **Drag-a.,** one dropped with a slack chain to indicate drift of a vessel, or drag of her usual *a.;* also, a *sea-anchor,* or *drag,* and *drift-anchor.* **Driving-a.,** a *sea-anchor;* a *drag.* **Dunn's a.,** stockless, double-fluked type, common on U.S. warships; its shank engages the arms by an enlarged head, so that its holding strength is independent of its pivoting pin. **Eell's a.,** patented, stockless type, advertised as available in sizes from 10 lbs. to 10 tons. Its long flukes and wide opened crown render it most effective for "digging in," and is considered an excellent instrument for salvage work. **Fisherman's a.,** made of cast iron, 8 to 16 lbs. weight, used in small boats; resembles a *mushroom anchor,* but squatty and cast in one piece; an *angler's a.* Also, one of long-shanked old-fashioned type, 20 to 30 lbs. in weight, used in holding gear to bottom when fishing with *ground lines,* as for halibut, haddock, and cod. **Floating-a.,** a *sea-anchor* or *drag.* **Folding a.,** one that can be collapsed or folded to facilitate stowing. Commonly, an anchor of old-fashioned type whose stock, and sometimes flukes, may be folded against its shank; a *portable-anchor.* **Grapnel-a.,** one having more than two flukes; a *boat-a.* consisting of a shank terminating in five upturned prongs or flukes, from 4 to 20 lbs. in weight. A *grapnel a.* is also used as a retrieving-hook, being dragged on a short warp to recover lost cables, sunken boats, anchors, etc. It is generally confused with *grappling-irons,* which are of similar appearance. **Herreshoff a.,** an improved form of old-fashioned *a.,* have a movable stock for snug stowage. **Honibal's a.,** *see* Rodgers' *a.* **Ice-a.,** an S-shaped bar of round iron, sharpened at its longer curved end, its other end terminating in an eye to which a hawser may be attached. Its point is thrust into a hole cut in the ice, or into a crevice. **Inglefield a.,** stockless, double-fluked type whose arms are individual pieces separated by crown end of its shank, and joined by a pin through the latter. Its flukes move through an arc of 45° from the shank in either direction. **Jury a.,** a makeshift or temporary *a.* **Kedge-a.,** one used for *kedging,* or hauling a ship by taking an anchor out in a boat, dropping it, and then heaving on its hawser. (If used to change a vessel's heading by heaving her stern around, such operation is termed *warping*). Any ship's *a.* may be used as a kedge, but one carried as specified equipment is usually of old-fashioned type, 400 to 800 lbs. in weight. In event of grounding, a ship may pull herself off by kedging, and this operation may require several large anchors. Those carried at landing-craft's sterns in World War II, with which they hauled themselves off a beach, might be considered as *kedge-anchors.* **Laughlin plow a.,** an American patented *a.* of unusual type, suited to small craft, weighing from 13 to 60 lbs. Its appearance is much like that of a farmer's plow, having its long shank extending horizontally like a tongue. **Lenox's a.,** an early British patent stockless type. **Martin's a.,** an important one of many patented in latter half of 19th. century, and first double-fluked *a.* to receive wide attention. Its arms are in one piece and fitted through its shank's crown end, which is increased in area for this purpose, and are free to turn through a range of 30° from the shank. Its flat broad stock was fitted across its shank parallel to the arms. *Martin's* obtained British Admiralty favor in place of anchors of *Admiralty* or *Rodgers'* design weighing 25 per cent more. **Mooring-a.,** a heavy weight or special *a.* placed as required on a harbor or roadstead bottom, as a more or less permanent mooring for a warping-buoy, lightship, etc. Specifically, one of old-fashioned type having a single arm, commonly known as a *one-armed anchor; a mushroom-anchor (q.v.); see* **mooring-buoy** in BUOY. Old engines, castings, and other heavy scrap, in addition to regular anchors, are used as mooring-anchors by owners of small craft, and larger vessels may use stone or concrete masses known as *mooring-clumps* or *mooring-blocks.* **Mushroom-a.,** has a sauce -shaped head on a central shank, hence resembling a mushroom. Not regularly carried on board vessels, or used as a service *a.,* except in boats, is widely used as a *mooring-a.,* being suited to all softer bottoms. It is usually the type employed in placing channel buoys. Some are made with a swelling or ball on the shank to aid in capsizing. **Navy-type a.,** one of stockless, double-fluked form, especially the *Dunn* or *Baldt* pattern. This type is used generally on large merchant and navy craft; also is widely used on small craft and has found favor in U.S. navy through a considerable range of sizes. **Northill folding a.,** used by yachts, small naval vessels, and aircraft; its parts may be folded up against the shank for convenience in stowing, and strength with lightness is gained by its fabrication from plate, instead of its parts being of cast metal. It is claimed an 80 lb. anchor of this type has a holding power of 3600 lbs. and is suited to a 30-ton craft. **Northill utility a.,** similar to maker's folding type, but with stock only folding against its shank. **One-armed a.,** one having a single arm or blade. Most primitive *a's* were weighted sticks or logs from which extended a hook-like branch or arm, and those of iron in their earliest form were hook-shaped, or one-armed. It is now a single-armed *a.* of old-fashioned type intended for use as a *mooring-a.,* and usually has a crown ring or shackle for attaching a tripping-line. Many of this sort have been made by sawing an arm off an old ship's *a.* **Patent a.,** properly one granted a patent, but commonly a stockless and, especially, a double-fluked one. Nearly all anchors carried by medium and large ships, and particularly those housed partially or entirely

within hawse-pipes, are so-called patent type. Best known patterns include *Baldt, Dunn, Hall, Inglefield, Lenox, Martin,* and *Tyzack (q.v.).* Those of unusual design, such as *Danforth, Northill,* and *Loughlin Plow (q.v.),* are forms covered by letters patent, but are not "patent anchors" in common meaning of the term. **Portable a.,** one for small craft, its arms and stock hinged to fold against the shank for stowing; commonly ranges from 10 to 75 lbs. weight; also, *folding anchor.* **Porter's a.,** an early patent *a.* having hinged arms, preceding and similar to *Trotman's (q.v.).* **Rodgers' a.,** early form of *patent a.,* featuring a hollow shank, first made in 1838; also known as *Honibal's a.* **Sand-a.,** old-fashioned type, characterized by its slender material, compared with its over-all size, particularly adapted to holding in a sandy bottom; often called a *trawl-* or *dory-anchor,* as used by fishing boats and other small craft; made in sizes from 5 to 75 lbs. weight. **Sea-a.,** often called a *drag* or *drogue,* and less frequently a *floating-a., fly-a.,* or *driving-a.,* usually in the form of a funnel-shaped canvas bag, by which, bridled to a connecting hawser, a small vessel may be kept head to wind in riding out a gale. Sea-anchors, in cases of emergency, have been made from sails, doors, spars, small boats, hatchcovers, etc.; *see* DRAG. **Sea-claw a.,** patent type for small craft, similar in form to a *Danforth (q.v.).* **Sheet-a.,** formerly largest one in a ship used only in case of emergency. To-day the term is no longer in use, being replaced by a *spare bower* which larger vessels are required to carry in an easily accessible place,—usually on the fore deck. *Sheet-anchor* is a common figure of speech for anything to be depended upon in danger or emergency, as a chief stay, a refuge, a last resort. **Shoot-a.,** *see* **sheet-a.** **Short-shank stockless a.,** patent double-fluked type, with unusually short shank, especially suited to short hawse-pipes. **Smith's a.,** one of stockless, double-fluked form, distinguished by two tilting-shoulders, one at base of each arm. **Stern-a.,** one carried at the stern. **Stockless-a.,** one without a stock; a *patent anchor (q.v.).* **Stream-a.,** in weight about one-fourth that of a bower, used for special warping purposes, or when necessary, in a stream or restricted space, used as a *stern anchor.* **Trawl-a.,** *see* **Sand-a.** **Trotman's a.,** early patent form developed from *Porter* and *Rodgers* types, in which the arms, as only departure from the old-fashioned type, pivoted about a bolt passing through its shank; differed from *Porter's* mainly in its shape of flukes. In 1852, British Admiralty appointed a committee to try out a large number of *a's* and *Trotman's* was given highest rating. **Tyzack's a.,** stockless patent type which, in place of a shoulder at its crown for throwing the arms downward, has a third fluke which tilts and assists the others in holding. **Waist a.,** formerly a *sheet anchor* stowed in the waist.

ANCHOR PHRASEOLOGY. At a., in a legal sense, means that a vessel is attached to the ground by anchor and cable, by being fixed to a buoy made fast to the ground, or by being moored to a dock. To **back an a.**, to supplement it with another; to lay down a small anchor ahead of, and made fast to a larger one. To **break out an a.**, to heave it from its bed, when it is said to *break ground*. To **bring home an a.**, to heave the ship up to it. To **carry out an a.**, to carry one some distance away by means of one or more boats before dropping it, as done in *kedging*. Depending upon its weight, a small *a.* may be carried out in, or hanging over the stern of, a boat; a heavier one may be slung beneath a boat; and a still heavier one may be slung from a spar or spars laid across two boats lashed together catamaran fashion. To **cast a.**, to drop one on bottom. To **cat an a.**, in older days, to hoist a bower and secure its ring to the *cathead* (*q.v.*). To **cockbill an a.**, to suspend it from the cathead only, preparatory to letting go; or, to have an *a.* hanging from its chain ready for dropping. To **come to a.**, to bring a ship to a desired location and to drop anchor; or, to bring her to a *mooring-anchor*, as indicated by a buoy, and make fast. To **drag a.**, to draw or trail it over the bottom after it has broken its hold; an anchor *comes home* when it begins to *drag*. To **drop a.**, to let go or release it for mooring purposes. **Ebb-a.**, one used to hold a ship against an ebbing tide; *upstream anchor*. To **fish an a.**, to bring a bower to the gunwale, rail, or bill-board for securing, after having catted it or hove it to the hawse-pipe. To *"cat and fish"* appears in English literature as early as 1626. **Flood-a.**, down-stream one when moored in a tideway, ship holding by that *a.* during flood tide. **Foul a.**, having part of its cable turned around the stock or one of its flukes. An old popular symbol used on American and British naval cap-badges, midshipmen's collars, uniform buttons, etc., and in various Admiralty and U.S. navy crests. First used as a seal in 1601 by Lord Howard of Effingham, then Lord High Admiral, but its use as a badge is of earlier and unknown date. To **gimlet an a.**, to turn it around after it has been hove to a hawse-pipe, or when it is swinging from a cathead. To **house an a.**, to heave a stockless one into a hawse-pipe and secure it. **Lee a.**, that one on the lee bow; in a vessel riding at single *a.*, that one which has not been dropped; or, if both are down, that one to which she is not riding. To **lie at a.**, to ride secured to an *a.;* often, but incorrectly, to **lay at a. Nuts of an a.**, projections or shoulders forged on an old-time anchor's shank above and below its stock, to keep the latter in place. To **part from an a.**, to carry away or break its cable. To **ring up an a.**, to heave it up, or *cat* it, with its ring colse up to the cathead. **Shaft of an a.**, its main part, or *shank*. To **shoe an a.**, to bolt planks on its flukes, enlarging their area, so that they may take better hold in unusually soft ground. To **sight an a.**, to bring it into view when heaving in. **Small of an a.**, that part of its shank just below the stock. In the old days, a shank was square in section with rounded corners, and was about one-third smaller below the stock than at the crown. **Square of an a.**, upper part of shank in old-time *a.* To **swallow the a.**, to go ashore and stay ashore; retire from a sea career. To **sweep for an a.**, to search for a lost *a.* by *"sweeping"* bottom with a bight of a rope towed by two boats; same as to *drag for an a.* **Throat of an a.**, inner curved part of an arm where it joins the shank. To **trip an a.**, to break it out, or free it when fouled, by means of a tripping-line previously bent to its crown; *see* **anchor-trip. Tripping-palms**, on stockless *a's*, projections on each arm which drag on bottom and cant flukes downward to their work. To **weigh a.**, to heave in or raise anchor or anchors preparatory to sailing, or getting *under way*. To **weigh a. by a boat**, when it can not be hauled home and no outside assistance is available, a tripping-line is brought in over the stern of a ship's boat and secured to a tackle or improvised windlass; or, the line is made fast while boat's stern is kept down by filling her stern-sheets with men, following which the men sally forward, thus *jumping out* the *a.* To **weigh an a. by the hair**, an old expression covering a similar procedure to above, except that the *cable* instead of a *trip-line* is brought into a boat. **Weather a.**, one lying to windward; if both have been dropped, that one to which ship is riding.

ANCHORABLE. Fit for anchorage or anchoring.

ANCHORAGE. A place where a vessel is anchored; a place where it is suitable to anchor, or where vessels are accustomed to anchor, as an area set apart by harbor authorities. Act of coming to anchor; state of being or lying at anchor. That to which some object is anchored. Equipment for anchoring; ground-tackle. Fee charged for anchoring. Formerly, *ankerage*.

ANCHORATE. Held by an anchor. Something anchor-shaped.

ANCHORED. Fastened to an anchor; held by, or, as if by, an anchor; fixed; *see* **At anchor** *in* ANCHOR PHRASEOLOGY.

ANCHOVY. A small fish of the herring family, usually four to five inches in length, noted for its peculiar flavor and food value; caught in enormous schools in Mediterranean waters and much used for pickling and making an appetizing sauce.

ANDROMEDA. (Gr. myth., *daughter of Cepheus and Cassiopeia.*) A constellation directly south of *Cassiopeia*, containing navigational stars *Alpheratz, Mirach,* and *Almach,* and located in 28 to 42 degrees north declination and 0 to 2 hours right ascension.

ANEMOMETER. (Gr. *anemos,* wind; *metron,* measure.) An instrument for measuring wind pressure or velocity fixed on a yard-arm, atop a mast, or in a similarly unobstructed place on many large vessels, especially navy ships, and at any meteorological station.

AN-END. On end; in an upright position. Topmasts are said to be *an-end* when hoisted into their usual places, or *fidded.*

ANEROID BAROMETER. *See* BAROMETER.

ANGARIA. In maritime law, forcible seizure of a ship for public use; in international law, use or destruction by a belligerent, subject to a claim for compensation, of neutral property within its territory in time of war, a privilege claimed by belligerents under title of *jus angaria,* or *right of angary.*

ANGEL-FISH. Voracious shark of 6 to 8 feet in length, having broad wing-like pectoral fins, found on European and North American coasts. Any of several bright-colored food fishes caught in Caribbean and Central American waters.

ANGEL-SHOT. In early naval gunnery, a kind of *chain-shot* made up of two half-balls connected to a central disc, used to cut the rigging of an enemy vessel.

ANGLE. (L. *angulus,* angle or corner.) Inclination of two lines or planes to each other, or difference in direction of two lines. A common term for an *angle-bar* or an *angle-iron.* **Angle-bar,** iron or steel bar of angle-shaped section used for frames, beams, keelsons, stiffeners, and many other parts of a modern vessel's structure. If its flanges are spread more than its conventional cross-section, the bar is said to have an *open bevel;* if more closed, a *closed bevel.* **A.-beam,** a deck-beam, or other supporting member, having a cross-sectional appearance similar to an angle-bar. **A.-block,** a pulley used to change direction or lead of a hoisting-rope. **A.-bracket,** structural brace or support of right-angled form. **A.-bulb,** the swelling, bulb-shaped in section, along one edge of an angle-bar. **A.-clip,** short piece of angle-bar or bulb-angle, used to connect two parts of a ship's structure. **A.-cock,** one having its outlet at right angles to its inlet, thus combining in itself a cock and an elbow. **A.-collar,** ring formed from a piece of angle-iron, and fitted about a pipe, column, tank, or stack for making an oil-tight or water-tight joint; as where a pipe pierces a deck, bulkhead, etc. **A.-diameter,** *see* PITCH DIAMETER. **A.-iron,** *see* a.-bar. **A.-meter,** device for determining differences in angular velocity of an engine crankshaft; also, a *clinometer.* **A. of depression,** angular distance of a point or object below the visible horizon. **A. of dip,** same as *a. of inclination.* **A. of elevation,** vertical angle between summit of an object and its base or the visible horizon;

angle between axis of a gun and line of aim. **A. of heel,** angular measurement of heel or list of a vessel, *i.e.,* her inclination from upright. **A. of incidence,** one which a line meeting a surface makes with a perpendicular to that surface. In aerodynamics, angle at which moving air strikes a surface, as that of a sail, measured between the surface and chord of the aero-curve. **A. of inclination,** that which a magnetic needle makes with the horizontal; same as *a. of dip.* **A. of repose,** greatest angle with the horizontal at which a bulk heap of coal, grain, gravel, etc. will rest without sliding movement or shifting taking place. **A. of the vertical,** difference between *astronomical* and *geocentric latitudes,* or that which a plumb-line makes with the radius-vector from the earth's center at a given place. At the poles and equator it is zero but gradually attains a maximum north or south of those locations until latitude 45 degrees is reached, where its value is nearly 11½ minutes of arc. *Geographical,* or astronomical latitude, which is that used by a navigator, is greater than geocentric latitude up to the value above noted. **A.-punch,** a heavy machine used in shipyards for punching bolt- or rivet-holes in angle-bars. Also, *angle punch-press.* **A.-shears,** a machine similar to a punch-press, fitted with blades for cutting angle-bars. **A.-smith,** a shipyard mechanic who specializes in bending and shaping angle-bars; a blacksmith who works near the furnace and bending-slab, skilled in forming angle-collars, staples, etc. **A.-staples,** collars forged from angle-bars, fitted around continuous members at their entry through decks or bulkheads for oil- or water-tightness. **A.-steel,** angle-bars of steel, collectively. **Auxiliary a.,** one introduced to facilitate an operation in algebraic or trigonometrical computation. **Back a.,** in coastal survey, a calculated angle at an unvisited point which serves to check a triangulation. **Bearding-a.,** an angle-bar which connects stem and shell-plating. **Bevel-a.,** shipyard term for an angle greater or less than 90°. **Bulb a.-bar,** commonly known as a bulb-angle, has a swelling, bulb-shaped in section, along one of its edges for reinforcement or stiffening; used for frames, longitudinals, deck-beams, stiffeners, etc. **Danger a.,** *see* DANGER. **Frame-a.,** *see* FRAME. **Gunwale-a.,** *see* GUNWALE. **Gutter-a.,** *see* GUTTER. **Hitch-a.,** short piece of angle-bar, or bent plate, used to connect girders with beams or columns; a *clip.* **Hour a.,** *see* HOUR. **Inter-stringer a.,** one on an inside edge of a stringer-plate. **Inter-coastal-girder-a.,** *see* INTERCOASTAL. **Keelson-a.,** *see* KEELSON. **Local hour a.,** *see* HOUR. **Margin-a.,** *see* MARGIN. **Masthead a.,** angle of elevation of a ship's masthead above her water-line; used in determining distance from another vessel, as in station-keeping. **Nautical a.,** archaic instrument for indicating a vessel's departure, meridional distance, etc. **Orlop-stringer-a.,** *see* ORLOP. **Parallactic a.,** that at a heavenly body described by the hour circle and vertical circle passing through such body. **Polar a.,** *see* POLAR. **Position a.,** that which an arc of a great circle intercepted by two points in the heavens (as between two stars) makes with an hour circle passing through one of such points. **Presentment-a.,** or **angle of presentment,** bearing of an enemy, usually with reference to the beam. **Round of a's,** *see* ROUND. **Rudder a.,** *see* RUDDER. **Safety a.,** *see* SAFETY. **Shaft a.,** *see* SHAFT. **Spherical a.,** that formed by two great circles at their intersection; it is measured by angle of inclination of their planes, or angle of meeting of their tangents at intersection point. **Tanchord a.,** any angle at a circle's circumference between a chord and a tangent at point of tangency. **Vertical danger a.,** *see* DANGER.

ANGLER'S ANCHOR. *See* ANCHOR.

ANGULAR DISTANCE. *See* DISTANCE.

ANNAPOLIS MAN. A graduate of, or student at, U.S. Naval Academy at Annapolis, Maryland. Often used in every-day speech to differentiate between a regular, full-fledged, or professional naval officer and one of the Naval Reserve.

ANNEALING. (A.S. *anælan,* to burn.) A heating and cooling treatment, usually implying a relatively slow cooling, given to glass and certain metals in order to equalize stresses of any kind in such material; to induce softness; to alter ductility, toughness, electrical, magnetic, or other physical properties; to refine crystalline structure; to remove gases; or to produce a definite microstructure. Temperature to which heated, and rate of cooling, depend upon nature of material and purpose for which it is being treated. Annealing is of greatest importance in manufacturing many—probably most—materials and parts entering into construction of a modern vessel; especially so with glass, steel, and cast iron; and is of particular interest in present widespread and increasing use of welding in shipbuilding.

ANNIE OAKLEY. *See* SAIL.

ANNUAL. A. aberration; *see* ABERRATION. **A. parallax;** *see* PARALLAX.

ANNULAR ECLIPSE. *See* ECLIPSE.

ANNUNCIATOR. Electrical device for giving an audible and visual signal from a centrally located call-board, so that stewards, for example, may receive announcement from a particular stateroom that a passenger requires attention. Usually the sound of a buzzer is accompanied by flashing, or dropping into view, of a letter or numeral.

ANOA. (*Native name.*) A dug-out canoe found on the Atlantic coast of Colombia in South America.

ANODE. *See* ZINCS.

ANSWER THE HELM. Respond to action of a rudder.

ANSWERING PENNANT. *See* PENNANT.

ANTARCTIC. Of, pertaining to, or designating South Pole regions; opposed to *Arctic.* **A. Circle,** an imaginary circle parallel to the equator, distant from South Pole 23° 28′. **A. continent,** land surrounding South Pole and within *A. Circle.* **A. Ocean,** seas within *A. Circle.* **A. Zone,** area surrounding South Pole, and within *A. Circle;* also, *South Frigid Zone.*

ANTARCTICA. Name given to the great continent lying near the South Pole, for which *Magellanica* was at one time proposed. Others have suggested *Victorialand,* as now given to a part of it, be extended to the whole.

ANTARCTOGEA. In zoögeography, realm or region embracing that portion of the earth which includes *Antarctica* with its islands and *New Zealand.*

ANTARES. *a Scorpii,* principal star in the group *Scorpio,* its name in Greek meaning *similar to Mars,* because of its reddish color; called also *Cor Scorpii* (*Scorpion's Heart*). Located in 26° 19′ S. with a right ascension of 16 hrs. 26 min., it forms with *Arcturus* and *Spica* a conspicuous triangle, nearly right-angled at *Spica.* **Antarian stars** are those whose spectra are fluted and more distinct at the blue than at the red ends, like that of *Antares.*

ANTE MERIDIEM. Usually abbreviated *A.M.,* Latin for *before noon;* as, *6.45 A.M.* **Antemeridian,** pertaining to the forenoon.

ANTENNA. (L. *antenna,* sail yard; pl. *antennæ.*) A wire or set of wires, upheld by a mast or other lofty structure, used in receiving and sending out radio waves whereby wireless telegraph and telephone messages are transmitted; wires, poles, rods, masts, etc., used in transmission and reception of radar, television, and other radio wave signals; essential element in *Marconi* system of wireless telegraphy. Same as *aerial.*

ANTI-CORROSIVE PAINT. *See* PAINT.

ANTICYCLONE. Atmospheric expanse of comparatively high central pressure, conditions in which are opposite to those of a *cyclone,* with respect to height of barometer and wind direction; *cf.* CYCLONE. Also, region subject to that condition, termed a *high pressure area* or a *high; see* AREA. **Anticyclonic storm;—wind;** *see* STORM *and* WIND.

ANTI-FOULING PAINT. *See* PAINT.

ANTIPODES. (Gr. *anti,* against, opposed; *podos,* foot) Any place or region at an opposite side of the earth; any two places so opposed; as, *Australia is the antipodes* (or *at the antipodes*) *of England.* Also, persons living on opposite sides of the globe; as, *our antipodes work while we sleep.* Australia and New Zealand are often referred to as "the antipodes." **Antipodal,** of, pertaining to, or situated at the *antipodes;* state of being at opposite sides of the earth. **Antipodean day,** originally day gained by Australian wool clippers and other Far East traders when homeward bound via Cape Horn on their usual round-the-world voyages. Now denotes day required to be added or dropped on crossing the International Date Line either eastward or westward bound. Since at exactly noon, Greenwich civil time, same day exists at all places on earth, beginning at that instant as 0 hours and ending as 24 hours at longitude 180°, half way round the globe, it follows that at any subsequent hour the date differs at either side of the International Date Line by one day; *i.e.,* Sunday in west longitude is Monday in east longitude. *See* DATE LINE.

ANTI-ROLLING TANKS. A means of reducing a ship's angle of roll by a contra-flow of water between two tanks, or sets of tanks, built in each wing of a lower deck. Volume and flow are regulated by appropriate valves according to vessel's rolling period, chief feature of the system being timing of flow to become effective as ship begins her return roll. First experimented with in 1874, only the *Frahm* system, introduced in early 1900's, appears to have met success, its latest pattern having been installed in the large North German Lloyd liners *"Bremen"* and *"Europa"* (1922).

ANTI-TRADES. Upper tropical winds blowing in opposite directions to those of the *trade winds.* Formerly, the name referred to prevailing winds from S.W. to N.W. in latitudes between 40° and 60° N. and S.; but is now nearly obsolete in that sense.

APEAK. In a vertical, or nearly vertical, position; pointing upward, or in an up-and-down direction; said of an anchor, oars, yards, etc. An anchor is *apeak* when its cable is as nearly vertical as is possible without lifting anchor from bottom. In older usage, a ship with her cable so shortened was said to be *apeak,* or *hove apeak;* sometimes, *apeek.*

APHELION. (Gr. *apo,* from; *helios,* the sun.) Point in a planet's (or comet's) orbit farthest away from the sun; opposed to *perihelion. See* APSIS.

APHLASTON. (*Gr.*) *See* APLUSTRE.

APLUSTRE. (*L.*) Ornament rising above the stern of an ancient vessel, such as a Roman galley, often resembling a plume; same as *aphlaston.* Sometimes, incorrectly, a carved and gilded bow-ornament, or *acrostolium.*

APOGEE. (Gr. *apo,* from; *gē,* the earth.) Point in the moon's orbit farthest from Earth; *see* APSIS. In ancient astronomy, position of a planet or the sun when farthest from Earth.

APORT. On or toward the left or *port* side, formerly called the *larboard side;* as, *hard aport,* or

larboard hard, old order to a helmsman to put his tiller to port, thus turning a vessel to starboard. *See* HELM.

APOSTLE. At a ship's bow, a knighthead or bollard-timber where hawsers and heavy ropes were made fast. (*Old usage*)

APPAREL. Equipment, as masts, sails, rigging, etc.; to equip, as a ship for sea.

APPARENT. Obvious; manifest to the eye; appearing as actual, as distinguished from *true,* as in *moon's apparent distance.* **A. altitude,** *see* ALTITUDE. **A. noon,** actual moment at which the *apparent* or *visible* sun's center crosses a given meridian; *see* NOON. **A. sun,** *see* SUN. **A. time,** *see* TIME.

APPENDAGES. Collective term for relatively small portions of a vessel projecting beyond her main outline. It may include stern and stern-post, bar keel, bilge-keels, propeller-shaft struts or bossing, skeg, etc.

APPRENTICE. In British merchant ships, a youth bound by legal agreement, or *indentures,* to serve for a period of four years at sea, in order to qualify for his *certificate of competency* as 2nd. mate or 2nd. class engineer; a similar rating in fishing vessels. **A. seaman,** rating of a recruit in U.S. navy, who, after two months, is eligible, subject to his commanding officer's approval, for promotion to *Seaman 2nd. class.*

APPROACH, RIGHT OF. Privilege claimed by a naval vessel to approach a private craft for ostensible purpose of verifying flag and character of such craft.

APRON. Piece of curved timber inside a vessel or boat above the forward end of her keel, for strengthening and joining the several parts of her stem; also known as a *stemson,* or *stomach-piece.* A plate made of lead which covered the vent of an old muzzle-loading cannon. **A.-plate,** a continuation of shell-plating above a forecastle at a vessel's stem, in which both towing and warping chocks are fitted in larger craft; also termed *spirketting-plate.* A thwartship plate forming a protective bulwark or rail at an end of a deck.

APSIDAL. In astronomy, of or pertaining to *apsides.* **A. distance,** that from the center of a *line of apsides* to either *apsis.*

APSIS. (Gr., = a connection, hoop, or arch; pl. *apsides.*) Point of an eccentric orbit that is nearest to, or farthest from, the center of attraction, *i.e.,* either extremity of the major axis or *line of apsides* of an elliptic orbit. *Apsides* of a planet are its *aphelion* and *perihelion;* those of the moon, its *apogee* and *perigee;* and those of a satellite of Jupiter, *apojove* and *perijove.* **Higher a.,** same as aphelion or apogee. **Lower a.,** same as perihelion or perigee.

AQUARIUS. (*L.*, = relating to water.) Constellation close to the equinoctial through which the sun passes in February. Located in 21½ to 23 hours right ascension, it contains no navigational stars, *α*, *β*, and *δ Aquarii* being of only magnitude 3.2; 3.1; and 3.5; respectively.

AQUARTER. On the quarter; in or from a direction approximately 45° abaft the beam; said of wind or sea.

AQUILA. (*L.*, = an eagle.) A northern constellation in the *Milky Way*, close to the equinoctial in about 19 to 20 hours of right ascension, containing the bright star *Altair* (*α Aquilæ*) of magnitude 0.9.

ARA. A southern constellation adjacent to, and south of, the tail in *Scorpio*, containing navigational stars *α Aræ* and *β Aræ*. Also called *the Altar*.

ARC. (L. *arcus*, a bow.) Anything shaped like an arch; a curve; a part of a circle, as an *arc* of a sextant. **A. cosecant, cosine, cotangent, secant, sine, tangent,** etc., arc or angle corresponding to a given *cosecant, cosine*, etc. **A. of visibility,** arc of the horizon, observed from sea, through which a light, as that of a beacon or lighthouse, may be seen. Such information is shown on coastal charts and given in Light Lists. **A. welding,** electric welding; *see* WELDING. **Contact a.,** meteorological phenomenon of a luminous arc tangent to a solar or lunar halo; also, *tangent arc*. **Longitude in a.,** *see* LONGITUDE. **Nocturnal a.,** that described by the sun or other celestial body in its apparent diurnal motion between sunset and sunrise. **Zenith-star a.,** 90° — altitude; *see* ZENITH.

ARC-FORM SHIP. *See* SHIP.

ARCH. Descriptive term for a particular structural member or form of construction having the appearance of an inverted bow. **A.-board,** plank curving downwards at its ends, placed across a vessel's counter as an ornamental or prominent base on which her name and port of registry were gilded or painted in former days. **A.-construction,** a system of shipbuilding featuring very heavy deckbeams and web frames, thereby eliminating lower beams and stanchions, and providing a clear hold for bulk cargoes. **A.-knees,** those of wood, iron, or steel, fastened to stern filling-pieces and upper parts of stern and rudder posts, shaped and fitted to form an arch over a *propeller-race*. **A.-piece,** curved portion of a stern frame over the *screw aperture*, or propeller-race, joining stern and rudder posts; also called a *bridge-piece*.

ARCHED SQUALL. *See* SQUALL.

ARCHER FISH. A small deep-bellied fish of the East Indies (*Toxotes jaculator*) about five inches in length, which is said to capture insects flying near the water's surface by ejecting small spurts of water at them from its mouth.

ARCHING. Same as *hogging; see* HOGGED.

ARCHIPELAGO. (Gr. *archi*, chief; *pelagos*, sea.) Any large body of water studded with islands, or such islands themselves, in a collective sense. Originally, the *Ægean Sea*.

ARCTALIA. As defined in zoögeography, northern marine realm which extends southward as far as floating ice is found.

ARCTIC. Of, pertaining to, or designating North Polar regions within the Arctic Circle; opposed to *Antarctic*. Also, pertaining to constellations *Great Bear* and *Little Bear; see* ARCTOS. **A. circle,** imaginary circle or parallel of latitude 66° 32' N., or southern limit of the North Frigid Zone. **A. constellations,** those near the north pole, or of high northerly declination. **A. Current,** a variable current flowing from Davis Strait along the Labrador and Newfoundland coasts toward the Grand Bank, where part of it usually turns to the south and west along the Nova Scotia coast and another part appears to join the northern side of the Gulf Stream drift to the eastward. This current brings ice down to southward and eastward of Newfoundland, and often large bergs thus drive into the trans-Atlantic lanes during April, May, and June. **A. Ocean,** body of water which surrounds the North Pole, north of *Arctic Circle*.

ARCTOS. (Gr. *arktos*, bear.) *Ursa Major* and *Ursa Minor*, or Big Bear and Little Bear, a collective name sometimes given these constellations.

ARCTURUS. (Gr. *arktouros*, bearward.) Brightest star in the northern sky and principal one in the group *Boötes;* easily located by following a curve started by the *Dipper* handle, or tail of *Ursa Major*, the name is sometimes applied, incorrectly, to that constellation itself. In declination about 19° 27' N. and right ascension 14 hrs. 13 min.

ARDENT. Tending to come into the wind in sailing. Vessels having this property, which may be by accident or design, are said to carry *weather helm*, in order to counteract "luffing" when wind is nearly abeam, or opposite of *lee helm*, given a vessel prone to "fall off." *Ardency* is due to effective wind pressure being too weighty abaft a vessel's center of lateral hull resistance. It may be corrected by proper setting or re-arrangement of sails (or ballast, if a boat) as a temporary measure; or, permanently, by re-stepping a mast or masts, or moving keel or centerboard area, farther forward.

ARDOIS SYSTEM. Night signalling at sea by Morse code, in which a series of double electric lamps, arranged vertically, and showing alternate red and white lights, are operated from a keyboard on deck; now believed obsolete.

AREA. Superficial extent; region or tract of the earth's surface. **A's of sections,** in ship calculations, a number of hull cross-section areas, taken at regular intervals in the fore-and-aft line, are required in determining vessel's buoyancy per unit of length, her weight, or displacement, at various drafts, and in locating her centers of buoyancy and gravity; *see* CURVES OF SHIP CALCULATIONS. **High and low pressure a's** commonly are understood to be those of relatively high and low barometric pressure, but, more correctly, are used with reference to the direction of wind circulation about an *area*. Distinction between a *high* and a *low,* as these areas are called, depends upon whether characteristic pressure results from, respectively, descending or ascending air currents, regardless of actual barometer readings.

ARGO. In Greek mythology, Jason's 50-oared galley in which he sailed in search of the Golden Fleece. A large southern constellation extending west and northwest of the *Southern Cross (Crux)* to *Canis Major* and containing several navigational stars; also called *Argo Navis.* Astronomers divide *Argo* into four groups: *Carina* (keel); *Malus* (mast); *Vela* (sails); *Puppis* (poop or stern). *Canopus,* brightest star in this constellation, is designated both as α *Argus* and α *Carinae;* π *Argus* as π *Puppis; Al Suhail* as λ *Argus* and λ *Velorum;* etc.

ARGOSY. A large, richly laden merchant ship of medieval times; especially those galleons built at Venice and at Ragusa (Dalmatia); sometimes used figuratively. The name is thought to be a corruption of *Ragusa,* which was spelled *Aragouse* and *Arragosa* in 16th. century English.

ARIES. (*L., = ram*) The Ram, a sign of the Zodiac. A star group lying west of, and next to, *Leo,* containing *Hamal* (α *Arietis*) and *Sheratan* (β *Arietis*), about 4° apart and, respectively, of magnitudes 2.2 and 2.7. *Hamal* (*Ar. = lamb*) lies in R.A. 2 hrs. 4 min. and Dec. 23° N. **First point of Aries,** *vernal equinoctial point,* or origin of *right ascension* and *celestial longitude* as measured eastward in indicating a heavenly body's place. Early astronomers noted this point, at which the sun's path intersects the equinoctial, or celestial equator, as located in *Aries.* However, due to the phenomenon known as *precession*—a slow circular tilting motion of Earth's axis—the point has become displaced westward by some 30 degrees, in about 2200 years, to its present place in *Pisces.* To-day we say our sun *enters Aries* on or about March 21; *Gemini* about June 22; *Libra,* September 22; and *Capricornus* about December 22; when actually the constellations immediately *west* of those named are visited by "Old Sol" on the dates noted. Hence, out of step with a precessional change of 50½ seconds of arc per year, our usage of an ancient astronomical term has failed to deviate in more than two millennia; *cf.* ZODIAC.

ARK. Vessel built by Noah for preservation of his family and animal life during the Deluge (*circa 2350 B.C.*), in obedience to JEHOVAH, as recorded in *Genesis, 6th chapter.* From the dimensions given, it is most likely she was the only vessel of her kind in history, her triangular-shaped cross-section showing the craft to have possessed ideal stability qualities, considering the purpose for which she was constructed. Accepting the ancient Hebrew *cubit* as 17.6 inches, the vessel had a length of 440 feet; was 73 in width (measured across bottom); and 44 feet in depth.

ARM. To supply with weapons or instruments of warfare. To cover with armor-plate, as a vessel. To furnish with some useful addition, as grease or soap for a sounding-lead. Anything branching out from a main body, considered as a distinct part of such body; an *arm of the sea; arm of an anchor.* Flange or half-section of angle-iron. **A. of the sea,** legally, a body of water in which, by connection with a sea, the tide ebbs and flows. **Beam-a.,** *see* BEAM. **Righting-a.,** horizontal distance of line of total buoyancy force, acting upward, from that of total gravity, acting downward, at any angle of heel. In this couple, a vessel's *righting moment* is equal to her displacement times righting-arm. To **a. a lead,** to set tallow, soap, or grease in a hollow in the lower end of a sounding-lead, so that a bottom specimen may be brought up; such soap, etc. is called *lead-arming.* **Yard-a.,** either end of a yard; specifically, that part of either end outside the sheave-hole (in which sheet of sail next above is rove). **Yard-a. and yard-a.,** said of two vessels close alongside each other, as in old-time combat, when yard-arms touched, crossed, or interlocked. **Yard-a. cleat, yard-a. hoop,** etc.; *see* YARD.

ARMAMENT. All-guns, torpedoes, rockets, bombs, rifles, and other fighting equipment, including ammunition, belonging to a vessel; often used with reference to combined number and weight of a ship's guns; as, *our armament is double the enemy's.* In a large vessel, guns may be divided into several armaments. *Main a.* includes ship's largest guns, generally mounted in turrets; *secondary a.* includes guns of medium caliber; and *tertiary,* or *auxiliary a.,* those of smaller bore.

ARMATURE. A piece of soft iron placed across, or joining, the extremities or poles of a horse-shoe magnet, to preserve its magnetic power; a *keeper.* Formerly, body armor, or personal equipment for battle. A protective cable-covering.

ARMED. Equipped with, wearing, or using arms or weapons. **A. merchantman,** a privately owned vessel provided with defensive armament. Such may be commissioned for naval purposes, in which case is usually termed a *merchant cruiser* or *auxiliary cruiser,* and is also offensively equipped.

ARMOR. A defensive covering, such as metallic plates fitted around and about a warship's water-line; protective sheath of an electric cable. A coat or suit of mail; a diver's suit. **A.-belt,** width or girth of heavy steel plating on a warship's sides extending some feet above and below her water-line. Protective iron plates were used in some degree on war-galleys of the Middle Ages, and an ironclad war-vessel is said to have been built for a Korean admiral in 1594. Floating batteries used at the siege of Gibraltar in 1782 had bomb-proof roofs and sides, strengthened by leather and bars of iron. However, armored vessels appear to have had their real birth about 1850, France having taken a lead in their development, and in America first of such vessels, then termed *ironclads,* were the "*Merrimac*" and "*Monitor*," whose memorable battle at Hampton Roads, March 9, 1862, appears as first in history between armored warships. Production of naval *a.* was first begun in United States about 1889, a new hardening process known as the *Harvey method,* so named after its originator, having improved greatly on protective plate then existing. To-day *a.*-making has been influenced to a great degree by *Krupp's* production of 1893, which apparently superseded all others in that the plate for about one-third its thickness possessed a degree of hardness, together with a toughness, equal to or surpassing all others. U.S. navy now terms as *Class A a.* all face-hardened plate of whatever process forged, and under this heading comes all heavy girding of battleships. *Class B a.,* of a lighter type, is referred to as deck armor, horizontal armor, special treatment steel, etc. A third class known as *light a.* has recently been used in protection of personnel and instruments against rifle and aircraft fire, and in World War II an *a.* of most advanced type was used in helmets, shields, and other special protection requirements in small vessels and aircraft. **A.-bolts,** heavy bolts of a special design, made of high quality nickel steel, used to fasten *a.* to a ship's sides. **A.-clad,** having a protective covering; an armored vessel. **A.-grating,** a heavy steel plate, usually a slab of armor pierced by many holes, which protects a warship's boilers and uptakes during an engagement. **A.-keys,** long bars of steel machined with deep grooves which fit to corresponding grooves in abutting edges of *a.* plates. Upon being driven into place, the keys lock adjoining or abutting plates together. **A.-piercing,** capable of piercing *a.;* designating shot or shell intended for that purpose. During early years of armoring, there was much controversy regarding the respective merits of *racking* and *punching,* the former being produced by very large solid ball-shot at low velocity, which knocked *a.* from a ship's side and exposed her vitals; while *punching* was produced by elongated projectiles at high velocity, resulting in perforation and possible immediate

telling effect on an enemy's hull. To date, most evidence derived from actual combat has favored the punching or piercing process. **A.-plate,** *see* A.-belt. **A.-shelf,** shelf-like structure below water-line which sustains an armor-belt and its backing. **Submarine-a.,** a diver's complete body outfit, including water-tight suit, helmet, breast-plates, weights, and air-hose.

ARMORER. Formerly an armor-smith or maker of arms; to-day a skilled gunsmith; a custodian of arms or armor, as a *ship's armorer.*

ARMORY. An arsenal; place where small arms are stored and repaired; special room in a warship. Also, *armoury.*

ARMS. (Fr. *armes;* L. *arma.*) Weapons or instruments for attack or defense, collectively or in particular, as swords, guns, grenades, etc., especially as used in warfare. Heraldic bearings or devices; a coat of arms. **A.-chest,** box once placed on an upper deck, or in a top, to hold a ready supply of rifles, pistols, cutlasses, etc. **A.-curtains,** cloths of canvas used in boats for shielding arms from weather or spray; called *covers* when protecting small arms on board ship. **A.-locker,** cabinet or locker for ready stowage of small arms on board ship. **A.-rack,** frame or stand, as around a mast, for rifles. **Master-at-a.,** *see* MASTER. **Side-a.,** properly swords or cutlasses, but commonly any weapon that may be carried at one's side, such as a pistol or a bayonet. **Stand of a.,** complete outfit of arms and ammunition for one man.

ARRIS-PIECE. In a built lowermast, small triangular prism-shaped piece of wood under each band or hoop, filling cavities formed by chamfered faces of timber comprising such mast.

ARTEMON MAST. *See* MAST.

ARTICLES. Clauses in a contract; code or system of regulations. **A's of war,** code of regulations governing a navy; especially conduct of personnel thereof; called *A's of the Navy* in Great Britain and, in U.S., *A's for the government of the Navy.* To **sign a's,** to affix one's name to a legal agreement with a vessel's master or owner, binding oneself to perform certain duties throughout a proposed voyage or a stipulated period of time for a stated remuneration and subsistence necessities; usually termed to *sign on* or *sign up.* Such agreement is called the *shipping articles.*

ARTIFICER'S KNOT. *See* KNOT.

ARTIFICIAL HORIZON. *See* HORIZON.

A/S. Abbreviation for *alongside,* as generally used in bills of lading, charter-parties, and other freight documents.

ASCENDING NODE. *See* NODES OF MOON.

ASCENSION. Rising or elevation of a point or star above the celestial horizon. **Right a.,** arc of celestial equator measured eastward from the vernal equinox to an hour circle passing through a heavenly body; one of the coordinates locating a celestial point, or that relative to the vernal equinox, the other being declination. In astronomers' usage, denoted by Greek letter α (*alpha*). **Right a. of mean sun,** abbrev. *R.A.M.S.,* expressed in sidereal time, is the arc of the equinoctial, measured eastward, intercepted by the hour circles passing through the vernal equinox and mean sun, respectively. *Cf.* M. solar day *in* MEAN. **Right a. of meridian,** or **local sidereal time,** (*R.A.M.* or *L.S.T.*), westerly hour angle of the vernal equinox. When vernal equinox, also termed First Point of Aries, is in transit, a sidereal clock shows 0 hrs. 0 min. 0 secs., or *sidereal noon,* thereafter indicating *R.A.M.* or *L.S.T.* of meridian concerned, through the sidereal day of 24 hours. (In accordance with recent methods employed in navigation, the present *Nautical Almanac* replaces *right a.* of the sun, moon, and planets with the *Greenwich hour angle* (G.H.A.) of these, and each listed star's *right a.* is replaced by its *sidereal hour angle* (S.H.A.), all values being expressed in degrees, etc., of arc. The S.H.A. being the easterly hour angle of the vernal equinox and consequently the explement of body's *right a.,* 360° less star's S.H.A. is thus star's *right a.* in arc, which may be converted into time, as the value usually is expressed, at the rate of 15° = 1 hour. To obtain *right a.* of sun, moon, or a planet: G.H.A. of vernal equinox (also given in the *Almanac*) *plus* 360° if necessary, *minus* G.H.A. of body.)

ASH. Any tree of genus *Fraxinus* of the olive family. Ash of nautical interest is a hard, tough, close-grained, elastic wood, light in color, and from 40 to 50 lbs. per cubic foot in weight. Used for thwarts, side-benches, gratings, and other fittings in boats; for oars, accommodation-ladders, mess-tables, and built-in tables of galleys or sculleries, where bare wood is preferred; and for ship's furniture and cabinet work. It has a tendency, however, to become dry and brittle with age. **A. breeze,** or **white a. breeze,** old salts' term for progress made with oars in a calm. **A.-can,** depth-charge or depth-bomb, so called from its resemblance to an ordinary receptacle for ashes. **A.-cocks,** faucets or valves serving to supply water for cooling hot ashes; also, *firemen's cock.* **A.-ejector,** apparatus for discharging ashes overboard by water pressure. **A.-hoist,** gear, including winch, bucket, rope or chain, etc., by which ashes are hoisted from a fire-room. **A.-pit,** space underneath grate-bars in a furnace. **A.-shoot,** portable trough-shaped conduit by which ashes are thrown clear of a ship's side; also, *ash-chute.* **A.-whip,** fall used to hoist ashes.

ASHCROFT PLANKING SYSTEM. *See* PLANK-ING.

ASHORE. To, or on the shore; as, *a ship was driven ashore.* On land; not at sea; not on board a ship; as, *he was left ashore.*

ASLEEP. But slightly filled or distended by wind; said of sails.

ASSISTANT KEELSON. *See* KEELSON.

ASTARBOARD. On or toward the right, or starboard, side; formerly, in helm orders, position of tiller (*helm*) when turned to that side, thus throwing rudder to *port,* or left, as *hard astarboard.* Since 1931, in British ships this order is meant to indicate that a *rudder,* by whatever means controlled, is turned to the right, or starboard, side, thus directing a vessel's head *right,* or toward one's *starboard hand* when facing forward. In U.S. vessels, *right rudder* is used in the same sense. Mandatory since August 21, 1935, "All orders to helmsmen shall be given as follows: *Right rudder* to mean *direct vessel's head to starboard; Left rudder* to mean *direct vessel's head to port.*" *See* HELM.

ASTAY. Old descriptive term for angle at which a cable leads when heaving anchor; as, at a *long stay,* indicating cable was leading roughly parallel with the main stay; at a *short stay,* or simply *astay,* when about parallel with the fore stay.

ASTERN. At any point behind a vessel; away from any craft in a direction opposite her course; opposite to *ahead,* always indicates direction outside and beyond a vessel's stern. **A.-motion,** backward motion; contrary to *headway.* To **go a.** or to **back a.,** to move a vessel stern foremost or backwards. To **be a. of one's reckoning,** to be behind, or actually having not reached, a position indicated by the reckoning. To **drop a.,** to **fall a.,** to pass toward or behind the stern; to fall behind; to be left in the distance.

ASTEROIDS. (From a Greek word meaning *star-like.*) Small planets, or *planetoids,* about 1100 in number and their largest 480 miles in diameter, which revolve around the sun between Mars and Jupiter.

A STRAKE. Line of shell-plating lying next to and on either side of a *flat-plate keel,* or that row next the *garboard strake* (strake riveted to keel) in a ship having a *bar keel.* Next successive rows are named *B, C, D,* etc., omitting *J,* and plates of each strake are named and numbered, usually beginning aft, as A-1, A-2, etc.; B-1, B-2, etc.

ASTRAND. An archaic poetical term for aground or stranded; as, *a tall ship amid the breakers lies astrand.*

ASTROLABE. (Gr. *astron,* star; *labein,* to take.) An ancient astronomical instrument of various forms, used for observing altitudes and for solution of problems involving celestial angular distances. Some astrolabes were armillary spheres of complicated construction; others were planispheres intended to measure altitudes only. One well-known form consisted of a graduated circle suspended in a vertical plane from a ring; a horizontal sighting-bar was pivoted at its center, and this was directed toward a heavenly body observed; altitude reading was noted on the vertical scale. Elaborate forms of the instrument were specially popular in the 16th. century and palmy days of astrology. Chaucer published a learned treatise on the *a.* in 1391. As a nautical instrument it was used well into the 18th. century, when its was superseded by *Hadley's quadrant,* principles of which are now embodied in our present-day *sextant.*

ASTRONOMER'S STAFF. *See* ALMUCANTAR.

ASTRONOMICAL. Pertaining to, or in accordance with, methods or principles of astronomy. **A. time,** formerly mean solar time, as reckoned from noon to noon. Beginning with 1925 nautical almanacs, it now is identical with *civil time,* or that commencing and ending each day at midnight. Thus, until 1924, an *astronomical date,* as, July 4, 14 hrs. meant July 5, 2 hrs., or 2 a.m., *civil time.* The term now refers to hours of *sidereal time,* or interval elapsing since last transit of the vernal equinoctial point (first point of Aries), as indicated on a sidereal clock. **A. triangle,** basic spherical triangle commonly used in navigation for computation of altitudes, azimuths, and hour angles of heavenly bodies; usually designated as $Z\ P\ X$, in which $P =$ hour angle; $Z =$ azimuth; side $P\ Z =$ co-latitude; $P\ X =$ polar distance; and $Z\ X =$ zenith distance; point P being the elevated pole.

AT THE MAST. *See* MAST.

ATAUNT. (Fr. *autant,* as much as possible.) Old descriptive term indicating a fully rigged condition, or synonymous with *all right* or *shipshape.* **All-ataunt-o,** signifying that rigging was set up in good order and generally shipshape.

ATHWART. Across; from side to side; transverse; at right angles to the fore-and-aft line; across a vessel's course. **A. hawse of** (another vessel), referring to lead of an anchor-cable or towing-hawser in its likelihood to foul a neighboring craft's stem. **A. the fore-foot,** across and close to a ship's bows; an old-time expression indicating flight of a cannon-ball fired across a vessel's head as a command to *heave to.* **A. the tide,** lying across a tidal current. To **lie a.,** to float at right angles with: to moor a ship across a stream. To **ride a.,** to lie at anchor across both wind and current, when wind is contrary to, and too strong to allow heading into, the current.

ATHWARTSHIPS. Crosswise of a ship; transversely; athwartwise.

ATKA FISH or **ATKA MACKEREL.** A valuable food fish of the North Pacific coasts, called also *greenling* and *rock trout.*

ATMOSPHERIC PRESSURE. That of the air at sea level, under standard condition in which a mercury barometer reads 29.94 inches or 760 millimeters. *See* BAROMETER; PRESSURE.

ATOLL. (*Malay name.*) A ring-shaped island, or a belt of islands, consisting of a *reef* formed from petrified skeletons of coral polyps and enclosing a central lagoon, common in the Pacific. Though small in width, an atoll may form a ring of nearly 100 miles in length. Larger of these islands are often inhabited and support considerable vegetation. One or more openings in the ring afford passage for boats and, in several instances, good anchorage is provided for large vessels in the lagoon.

ATRIP. An old seamanship term indicating *readiness for completed action;* said of an *anchor* just hove clear of bottom; of *sails* sheeted home and hoisted ready for trimming; of *yards* swayed up ready for crossing; of a *topmast* or *top-gallant-mast* freed from its fid and ready for lowering.

ATRY. Formerly said of a ship in a gale, *hove to* under trysails.

ATTACHED. Connected with something; to be joined with in an official capacity; as, *the officer is attached to a ship of the line.*

ATWAIN. Obsolete term for *asunder;* in two; as, *our mainsail was split atwain.*

AUGMENTATION OF MOON'S SEMI-DIAMETER. Increase of moon's angular semi-diameter with increase in altitude of that body, being at a maximum when she is in the zenith and zero when in the horizon. This is due to an observer being nearer the moon by approximately the length of the earth's radius (about 4000 miles) when she is overhead, as compared with an altitude of zero. Used in correcting moon's observed altitude, augmentation is applied to her *horizontal semi-diameter* as given in the *Nautical Almanac* for each day. Its value attains a maximum of 18 seconds, which is considered, generally, as negligible in practical navigation. *See* SEMI-DIAMETER.

AUK. (Ice. *alka.*) Any sea bird of the family *Alcidæ,* having short wings and tail, webbed feet, thick dense plumage, and usually large head and heavy body; lives in colder northern latitudes and includes the *great auk* (extinct since about 1850), *razor-billed auk, puffin,* and *guillemot.* Expert swimmers and divers, they nest in rocky cliffs chiefly on the northwestern Atlantic shores.

AUKLET. A kind of small auk found on the North Pacific coasts, including the *crested auklet* and *least auklet.* The latter is smallest of the auks.

AULOSTOMA. (Gr. *aulos,* tube; *stoma,* mouth.) A genus of sea fishes found in tropical waters; about 20 inches in length, of elongated form, and having a long tubular snout; generally called *flutemouths.*

AURIGA. (*L.,* = *charioteer.*) A northern constellation lying about half way between *Orion* and the *Pole Star,* containing the bright star *Capella* (α *Aurigæ*).

AURORA. Rising light or roseate glow of early morning in the eastern sky. A form of high voltage electric discharge, which assumes an *aurora borealis* appearance. **A. polaris,** a luminous phenomenon frequently seen at night in a general polar direction in high latitudes. It usually displays streamers of light ascending toward the zenith, may appear like a broad arch with its ends on the horizon, or may be a combination of both. Sometimes it appears in flashes or detached pieces; at other times covers the whole sky. The phenomenon undoubtedly is of electrical origin, but actually little is known about it. Its frequency and its coincidence with appearance of sun spots have received much study; its peculiar effects upon terrestrial magnetism have long been known; and its interference with radio and other electronic apparatus is now under investigation. *Aurora's* colorful streamers were called "Merry Dancers" by old seamen, because of their undulatory or tremulous movements; the French named them "Chevres Dansantes," or *dancing goats.* However, aurora long has been familiarly known in the northern hemisphere as *northern lights,* and *southern lights* in opposite latitudes, or *aurora borealis* and *aurora australis,* respectively, and is sometimes seen in much lessened intensity in lower latitudes. It has been observed by New England fishermen that unusual brightness of northern lights presages easterly wind of some duration. A particularly brilliant display occurred over England on February 24, 1716, on which date James, Earl of Derwentwater, was beheaded, and, in consequence, for generations later the *a.* was known as *Lord Derwentwater's Lights.*

AURORAL CLOUDS. *See* CLOUD.

AUSTRAL. (L. *australis,* southern.) Of, pertaining to, or in the south; southern; hence, *torrid.*

AUTUMNAL EQUINOX. *See* EQUINOX.

AUXILIARY. A sailing-vessel equipped with mechanical means of propulsion for additional power as required, such as when extra speed is necessary, when in light winds or calms, or for better maneuverability in entering port and docking. Many modern sailing yachts are auxiliaries, as were early steam-vessels. A small sail-boat having an outboard motor, however, is not referred to as an auxiliary. **A. machinery,** all units functioning as subordinates to a main propulsion plant, such as air-pumps, ashejectors, blowers, bilge-pumps, circulating-pumps, filters, condensers, distillers, evaporators, fans, feedheaters, feed-pumps, injectors, oil-pumps, and transfer-pumps. **A. screw,** propeller of an auxiliary sailing-vessel; also, such a vessel herself.

AVAST. (Corr. of Du. *houd vast,* hold fast.) Cease; stop; hold; stay; as in the order, *Avast heaving!*

AVERAGE. To calculate arithmetical mean of; divide proportionately; as, to *average insurance losses among underwriters.* Financial loss arising by damage to a ship or cargo; also, proportion of such loss being equitably borne by each party interested, viz., ship, cargo, and freight, considered as entities concerned. An **a. bond** is sometimes entered into by contributories in order to aid an arbiter in adjusting an average; known also as an **a. agreement.** An **a. clause** in a marine policy exempts from particular average or from all averages; in the former, clause and policy are termed *F.P.A.,* and in the latter, *F.A.A.* Also a clause in a policy providing that in event of loss sum payable shall not exceed the proportion that policy's face value bears to covered property's actual value. **General a.** or **gross a.** is a contribution made by the various interests associated in a maritime adventure to restore value of any sacrifice or extraordinary expense voluntarily incurred for the common safety. This equitable rule has been adopted with certain modifications and differences by all maritime nations. Requisites to this contribution are that sacrifice of part of cargo, ship, or rigging has been advisedly made to procure the safety of what remains. Such loss must not be caused by fault of a master or improper stowage; thus, throwing overboard or *jettisoning* deck cargo will not give rise to *a.* unless stowage on deck is customary or agreed to by contributing parties. Value of cargo thrown overboard is, usually, computed at market price at port of delivery, less freight and charges saved. Among other losses covered by *general a.* are those arising from discharge of cargo to lighten a ship, from damage to ship or cargo in order to extinguish fire, or from cutting away masts or slipping anchors and cables to save a ship. Expenses incurred in floating a stranded ship or entering a port of refuge are also included, but no loss or expense falling under a shipowner's contract to keep his ship fit for service will be included. Contributing parties are, respectively, owners of ship, cargo, and freight, or, in modern times, insurers of these, and they are assessed in proportion to their value. Cargo owners pay on net market value at port of destination, or where a voyage is broken up, and goods jettisoned contribute as well as those saved, as otherwise owners of lost goods would enjoy a comparatively favorable position. Seamen's wages, and personal effects of crew and passengers are exempt from contribution. If ship reaches her destination, *a.* must there be adjusted in accordance with legal custom at such port; otherwise, procedure according to law at loading port is followed. *Adjustment* of averages is usually a complicated task, and is left to experts known as *a.-adjusters;* less commonly known as *averagers* or *a.-staters.* Want of a uniform system of *general a.* in different countries in the past has led to much inconvenience, and hence an international congress at Antwerp in 1877 revised and established as a *general a. code* certain rules which were drawn up in York, England, in 1864. Known as *York-Antwerp rules,* their further revision took place in 1890 and to-day they universally govern adjustment of marine insurance *a's.* Bills of lading and insurance policies usually contain a clause indicating adherence to the code in event of losses. York-Antwerp rules define conditions under which a voluntary loss shall be "averaged":—"There is a *general average* act when, and only when, any extraordinary sacrifice or expenditure is intentionally and reasonably made or incurred for the common safety for the purpose of preserving from peril the property involved in a common maritime adventure." **Particular a.** is partial loss of ship or cargo, or damage thereto from accidental causes. Here the common safety is not in question, consequently there is no contribution, loss remaining where it falls. To such cases, the term *average* seems unfitting to apply, but has become the name for all losses at sea when not total, and its use perhaps may be explained by considering such losses under marine policies are usually made good by contribution from various underwriters or joint-insurers; known also as *common a.* **Petty** or **petit a.** is allowance for incidental expenses of a voyage, as pilotage, anchorage, extra wages, etc., shared by ship and cargo.

AWAFT. Afloat; adrift.

AWAKE. Old seamanship term for state of readiness; as, *the anchor is awake, i.e.,* ready to be dropped.

AWASH. Level with, or emerging from, the water's surface; as a reef, wreckage. Tossed or washed about by waves. Overflowed with water; as, *decks are awash.*

AWAVE. In a waving manner; moving like a wave or waves.

AWAY. From a place, or off; as, to *cast a.* Remote or at a distance; as, to *keep a.* In another direction; as, to *square a.* Combining word indicating departure; as, to *sail a.,* to *run a.;* or continuous action; as, to *heave a.;* also, as an imperative; as, *come away! keep away!* **Where away?** call to a lookout aloft to indicate bearing of an object sighted; as in "Sail ho!" . . . "Where away?"

AWEATHER. At, to, or toward the weather side, or side from which the wind blows; as, *her helm is aweather,* meaning tiller has been put to windward. Formerly used in indicating direction as, *aweather of the island.*

AWEIGH. Atrip; said of an anchor when its flukes are just clear of bottom; as, *the anchor's aweigh.*

AWNING. Sheet of canvas spread over a vessel's deck, bridge, etc., for protection against sun and rain, and named according to its location; as, *forecastle a., bridge a.,* etc. That part of a poop deck forward of a cabin bulkhead and projecting over the main deck, common to sailing-ship construction. **A.-deck,** light deck without hatches; deck above a spar-deck; upper deck of an *awning-deck type* vessel. **A.-deck vessel,** a type having a continuous deck above her main deck and whose construction is lighter above that deck than below it. Providing space for light cargo and/or passengers above her main deck, she is not considered a heavy weather-decked craft, such vessels being allotted an unusually large freeboard.

AXIS. (L. *axis,* axle.) Line around which something is more or less symmetrically arranged, or on which something rotates. In astronomy, a line joining the poles of a heavenly body, about which its mass rotates; as, *axis of the earth.* **A. of a storm,** or **storm a.,** *see* STORM. **A. of the ecliptic, equator, horizon** (or other circle of the celestial sphere), diameter which is perpendicular to the plane of such circle. **Magnetic a.,** straight line passing through the poles of a magnetic needle; line joining the earth's magnetic poles. **Neutral a.,** line indicating locus of zero stress in a beam or other structural member, or hull of a ship, subjected to a bending force. Material on one side of neutral axis suffers compression, the other side being under tension while neutral axis is neither under compression nor tension.

AYE. Yes; yea; expression of assent or affirmation. **Aye, aye, sir,** the classical response to a superior in acknowledging an order.

AZIMETER. A now obsolete term for an instrument used in observing *azimuths* or *bearings.*

AZIMUTH. (Ar. *as-summut,* direction.) Commonly known among seamen as a *bearing of a heavenly body,* a. is an arc of the horizon intercepted by either north or south point and a vertical circle passing through the body observed; or, it may be defined as angle at the zenith between the meridian and a vertical circle passing through the body. Formerly, azimuth was indicated as number of degrees from the meridian in each quadrant, as *N. 43° E., S. 25° E.;* later, its value usually was referred to as being in the eastern or the western half of the compass, as *N. 150° E., S. 95° W.;* while present custom of reckoning it from *North* or *0°,* clockwise through 360 degrees apparently has displaced the other two. Thus, *true bearing* or *azimuth* now is expressed and labeled as, for example, Z_n *235°,* and mariner's compass graduated accordingly.

Chief uses of *a.* are in plotting a line of position corresponding to an altitude of a celestial body and in determining *compass error.* It may be found by direct observation, as with an *a. circle;* from published tables; by spherical trigonometrical formula, with or without sextant observation; by an *a.* diagram; from the *Nautical Almanac,* in the case of star *Polaris.* **A.-circle,** graduated ring made to fit flat on a compass-bowl and equipped with sighting-vanes for observing azimuths of celestial bodies or bearings of terrestrial objects. Also, an astronomical term for a vertical great circle passing through the *zenith* and *nadir,* and consequently intercepting an observer's horizon at a right angle. **A.-compass,** a ship's compass specially located and fitted for observing *a's.* **A. error,** that caused by an imperfection in an observing instrument for which allowance must be made in taking an *a.* **A.-prism,** an optical fitting in an azimuth circle, or other instrument for observing bearings, in which the refracted beam of light brings into coincidence the graduated edge of the compass-card and object observed, thus facilitating correct *a. readings.* **Compass a.,** bearing of a heavenly body as observed by compass, as opposed to *true a.,* which latter is found by proper allowance for compass error. A *compass a.,* when taken for determining *compass error* is compared with the *true a.;* difference between the two is the *error.* **Magnetic a.,** angle that a horizontal line makes with the magnetic meridian; a compass *a.* corrected for deviation, when a *magnetic* compass is used. **Time-a.,** *see* TIME. **True a.,** or true bearing of a celestial body, *a.* observed by a compass and corrected for any existing error in that instrument; or, that obtained by tables, graphical methods, or calculation; term used to distinguish an *a.* observed by compass and a true or *astronomical a.*

B

B. In the International Code of Signals, denoted by a *red burgee,* which, flown by itself, indicates *"I am taking in or discharging explosives."* In ships' log-books, *"b"* is often used for *"blue sky"* and *"B"* for *"broken sea."* b corresponds to Greek letter *beta (β),* used from ancient times in designating the second brightest star in a particular constellation, as *β Orionis,* or *Rigel* of *Orion.*

BABBIT METAL. (Named for *Isaac Babbitt,* its inventor.) A soft light-colored anti-friction metal alloy of various proportions of antimony, lead, and tin, with lesser parts of copper and zinc, used as bearing surface material in shafting, cranks, guides, etc. To **babbitt,** to line or furnish with babbitt metal.

BACK. To cause to move backward; to propel backward; as, to *back engines.* Opposite of *veer,* or changing in direction toward the left; *see* BACKING; said of the wind. Keel and keelson of a ship. A broad flat-bottomed *ferry-boat,* hauled by a chain or rope. A shipwright's *punt* for tar and pitch. Timber bolted on the after end of a rudder to complete its form or required area. **Back-angle,** in coast surveying, calculated angle at an unvisited point, which serves to check a triangulation. **B.-bar,** bar used for same purpose as a *bosom-bar,* but placed on the opposite side of members it connects. **B.-chain,** one attached to after part of a ship's rudder and leading to opposite sides of her counter, formerly used on steam-vessels to support or stay a rudder when going astern, especially in or among ice. **B.-cloth,** in old-time sailing-ships, triangular piece of canvas fastened to middle of a topsail-yard, used to facilitate stowing the sail's bunt. **B.-laid rope,** left-handed rope; *see* ROPE. **B. observation,** *see* OBSERVATION. **B.-piece of a rudder,** *see* RUDDER. **B.-rabbet,** innermost angle or line of rabbet in which a garboard strake is set in a wooden vessel's keel; any rabbet cut to receive planking or other structural timber at any angle other than a right angle. **B.-ropes,** stays leading from lower end of a martingale or dolphin-striker, to each bow; also called *martingale back-ropes.* A small line fastened to the back of a *cat-block hook* or *fish-hook* to aid in hooking either to an anchor. **B.-sight,** *see* SIGHT. **B.-splice,** *see* SPLICE. **B.-strapped,** said of a vessel having a fair wind, but not strong enough for stemming a current. **B.-stream,** a current running contrariwise to a regular stream; an eddy current. **B.-sweep,** a shipbuilding term indicating curvature, for example, which forms bowing in a frame. **Cat-b.,** *see* CAT. To **b. an anchor,** to supplement it by another; *see* ANCHOR PHRASEOLOGY. To **b. astern,** *see* ASTERN. To **b. a chain** or **rope,** to relieve it of part of its tension by a preventer. To **b. a sail,** to brace yards so that the wind will press against a sail's forward surface; same as to *back a yard.* To **b. and fill,** to work a vessel to windward in a narrow channel, when wind is against the tide and there is insufficient room for tacking, by drifting broadside to current and filling or backing sails as necessary in order to keep in the channel. To **b. the oars,** *see* OAR. To **b. off,** to lay sails aback in order to make sternway; to go astern and away from some position or danger. To **put b.,** *see* PUT.

BACKBOARD. A board forming a back support for occupants of a boat's stern sheets.

BACKBONE. Of a ship, main longitudinal strength assemblage of keel, keelson, stem, and stern-post; of an awning, rope sewed across the cloths in its middle for additional strength and to which a supporting bridle may be attached.

BACKER. Strop of rope or sennit, fitted with a thimble, used for securing the head earings of a sail against a yard.

BACKHANDED. Said of a rope having its strands laid in the same direction as its yarns, usually left-handed, as strands laid opposite to those in a right-handed rope. Cordage of this type is said to be *soft laid* and is very pliable compared with a *hard lay* in which yarns are laid opposite to the strand lay. Under similar conditions, however, it is much less durable than rope of ordinary lay.

BACKING. Layer of heavy planking, usually of a hard durable wood, such as teak or oak, against which a warship's armor-belt is laid and secured. Act of going backwards or astern. **B.-angle,** a backbar; *see* BACK. **B. of the wind;** in the northern hemisphere outside the trade-wind belt and in usual sea route latitudes, the common circuit of changes in wind direction is clockwise or right-handed, *i.e.,* from north through east, south, and west, round to north, reverse of this being true in the southern hemisphere. A shift of wind in a contrary direction to that indicated in either hemisphere was formerly known as *backing,* which, incidentally, was considered indicative of unsettled or bad weather. However, *backing of the wind,* as agreed by the International Meteorological Conference in 1905, is now understood to mean shifting in a *counter-clockwise direction,* or from north, through west, south, and east, returning to north, usually termed by seamen, *left-handed.* **B.-out pin,** one used for knocking out short or broken tree-nails or bolts.

BACKROPES, MARTINGALE. *See* BACK *and* MARTINGALE.

BACKSTAFF. Forerunner of our present sextant and successor to the *cross-staff;* so-called because an observer stood with his back to a celestial body whose altitude was measured; called also, *Davy's quadrant.*

BACKSTAY. A rope or stay, or one of a set of stays, leading from the upper part of any mast above a lowermast to a ship's side abaft her lower rigging. Backstays serve as lateral support to top-masts, top-gallant-masts, royal-masts, and skysail-poles, prevent the mast ensemble from swaying forward, and securely stiffen all, in unison with an arrangement of fore-and-aft stays leading forward. **B.-stools,** in older wooden ships, detached channels to which backstays are secured at their lower ends. **Breast b.,** *see* BREAST. **Cap b.,** one secured to cap of a lowermast or a topmast. **Shifting-b.,** *see* SHIFTING. **Traveling-b.'s,** in single topsail days, those fitted with a traveler which slid up and down a topmast with its topsail-yard and so placed to advantage, when set up, as a support to the topmast just above the yard.

BACKWASH. Wash of a receding wave; surface agitation or wash driven forward from a propeller or paddle turning in astern motion; *backwater.*

BACKWATER. An eddy. A body of water fed by a side-channel off a river, bay, etc. and relatively still or void of current. Water reserved at high tide for flushing out a channel at low tide. A creek or connected lagoons running approximately parallel to and near a coast and having one or more shallow outlets.

BADGE. Carved ornament formerly placed on a ship's stern, often containing a window or a representation of one.

BAFFLE. (O.F., *beffler,* to mock.) To struggle ineffectually, or strive in vain as, *a vessel baffles with a current.* To fluctuate, as light varying winds. **B.-plate,** one of the plates fitted in a surface condenser opposite the stream entrance for distributing steam equally over the tubes; also, one used in boilers to prevent water from entering a steam-pipe; a plate or board set to divert a current of air in a cooling system.

BAG. Sails are said to *bag* when their leeches are taut and canvas slack. **B.-knot,** one used to hold a cork in a bottle; also used to make a masthead strop. **B.-reef,** lowest reef in a fore-and-aft sail. **Duffle-b.,** *see* DUFFLE. **Hawse-b.,** *see* HAWSE. **Lull-b.,** *see* LULL. **Monkey-b.,** *see* MONKEY. **Oil-b.,** *see* OIL.

BAG AMMUNITION. See AMMUNITION.

BAGGAGE LIEN. See LIEN.

BAGGALA. A two-masted vessel of about 200 to 250 tons burden as usually found trading on the Arabian Sea coasts.

BAGGY. Like a bag in appearance; as a poorly made and *baggy* sail.

BAGGY WRINKLE. Kind of chafing-mat made by hitching a great many short manila rope-yarns around two lengths of small stuff, such as marline. The long bushy product is closely wound around a stay or piece of standing rigging and serves to reduce wear on a sail which chafes against such obstruction.

BAGPIPE. An old term for hauling a fore-and-aft sail's sheet to windward, thus bringing the sail aback; as, to *bagpipe a jib.*

BAGUIO. (Sp.; from Tagal, *bag-yo.*) Native name for a hurricane or typhoon in the China Sea and Philippine Islands.

BAIDAR. (Russ., *baidara.*) Large canoe used in Aleutian and Kurile Islands, usually made of walrus-hide stretched over a stout frame, and propelled by six or eight paddles.

BAIDARKA. (*Russ.*) Portable boat made of stretched skins, used by Alaskan natives.

BAIL. To dip out, as water; free a boat of water. A scoop for bailing. To provide with supporting pieces of metal or wood shaped like bows, as in an awning of a boat or over a gangway ladder. One of the supports by which a life-car is attached to its hawser. A spreader for holding ropes of a bridle apart.

BAILIFF, WATER. *See* WATER.

BALANCE. To reef a standing spanker by taking it in at its peak. To set, reef, or take in any sail which will improve a vessel's steering; to effect same on small vessels or boats with a *balance-reef*. **B.-band,** a strap or band forged with rings or lugs and fitted at an anchor's center of gravity for keeping such anchor in a horizontal position when hoisting it on deck for stowing. **B.-dock,** *see* DOCK. **B.-fish,** same as *hammer-headed shark*. **B.-frame,** one of two frames of a ship, which are of equal weight and at an equal distance from a vessel's center of gravity. **B.-lug,** a lug-sail having a long boom which may reach from a boat's stem to her stern, or one having no boom with its tack made fast at the stem; *see* LUG. **B.-reef,** a reef-band diagonally across a fore-and-aft sail, particularly on a trysail or spanker. **B.-ring,** same as *b.-band*. **B.-rudder,** one having its turning axis nearly half way between its forward and after edges; an *equipoise rudder; see* RUDDER. **Compensation-b.,** balance-wheel of a chronometer compensated for changes in air temperature, in order that the instrument's rate of gain or loss may be as nearly uniform as possible at any temperature met with at sea.

BALANCING-BAND. Same as *balance-band; see* BALANCE.

BALANDRA. (*Sp. or Port.*) Local name for a sloop-rigged trading-vessel of Chile and Peru; also, a one-masted fore-and-aft rigged dug-out with outriggers, peculiar to the Philippine Islands.

BALCONY. A gallery formerly built outside and across a warship's stern for private use of the flag officer. Projecting open gallery of an old-style line-of-battle ship.

BALDHEAD SCHOONER. See SCHOONER.

BALDT ANCHOR. See ANCHOR.

BALE. (G. *balle*, ball or round pack.) A package of goods, often machine-compressed, prepared for transportation by securely binding with cords, wire, bands, etc., as a *bale of cotton*. **B.-band,** a crotch-shaped piece of bar-iron fastened to a topmast-cap for securing a jib stay; also, *bail-band*. **B.-hook,** *see* HOOK.

BALE CUBIC. Space in a ship's hold available for cargo, as measured inside the frame cargo-battens and to under side of beams. In a general cargo of mixed commodities bale cubic applies, since stowage of such cargo usually is confined to the limits indicated. From data taken from an actual case, bale cubic amounts to 470,000 feet, while *grain cubic*, which includes spaces between frames and deck-beams, measures 641,000. (Cf. *grain cubic*: GRAIN).

BALEEN. (L. *balœna*, a whale.) A stiff springy substance, commonly called *whalebone*, growing like a heavy fringe from the upper jaw-bone of certain whales, especially that of a *right whale*. It is a sieve by which food is collected from the water entering a whale's mouth.

BALINGER. A *war-sloop* of the 15th. and 16th. centuries of about 100 tons, of small freeboard, lengthy, and adapted for sail and oars. Its type originated a century or so earlier on the Bay of Biscay. Also, a *trading-boat* of the Philippines and Molukka Islands.

BALL. A spherical body of any dimension for any purpose; as a *ball of spunyarn;* a *signal-ball*. **Anchor-b.,** *see* ANCHOR. **B.-signal,** *see* SIGNALS. **Black b.,** a spherical collapsible shape, usually made of canvas, and black in color. A *black ball* of two feet diameter is required to be displayed forward in a vessel, where it can best be seen, when such vessel, being of more than 300 gross tons and propelled by machinery, is moored or anchored in a fairway or channel, according to U.S. Pilot Rules; also, a steam-vessel proceeding under sail only and having her funnel up is required to carry in daytime forward where it can best be seen, a *black ball* or *shape* not less than two feet in diameter, by International Rules of the Road. **Soft rubber b.,** used as a plug in the draining arrangement in a boat's bottom which allows water to run out upon lifting the boat in her tackles. **Tide-b.,** *see* TIDE. **Time-b.,** *see* TIME.

BALLAHOU. (Sp. *balahu*.) A West Indian schooner with foremast raking forward and mainmast raking aft. Although fast-sailing, they were not trim in appearance; hence the term has been used to describe a slovenly ship. The type is now growing extinct. Also, *ballahoo* and *bullahoo*.

BALLAST. Weight carried in a ship or boat either for effecting a proper stability condition or to secure greatest possible economy of propelling power. In modern steam-vessels or other power-propelled craft, and later large sailing-ships, ballast used is sea-water carried in double-bottom tanks, deep tanks, wing tanks, or other compartments fitted to such use. Lead is much used in sailing-yachts and is often run in a molten state into a space between plates of the keel, or cast into plates of appropriate form and belted to outside of a keel. Gravel, sand, stones, pig-iron, and other weighty materials are commonly used as ballast in cases where requisite weight is not found in cargo itself. **Bag-water-b.,** water stowed in bags as ballast. **B.-boat,** or *b.-lighter,* a vessel used to convey ballast to another. **B.-boat,** *see* BOAT. **B.-fever,** an illness arising among persons on board ship caused by bacterial condition existing in ballast of soil, sand, etc. **B.-fin,** a device used by sailing-vessels to reduce leeway; also, *leeboard*. **B.-heavers,** workmen employed on ballast-boats to handle ballast. **B.-hammer,** *see* HAMMER. **B.-line,** water-line of a vessel in ballast. **B.-master,** formerly, a port officer appointed to enforce ballast regulations, particularly those governing disposal of ballast. **B.-passage,** passage made by a cargo-vessel while carrying ballast only. **B.-plant,** a plant springing from seed brought from one country to another in a ship's ballast. **B.-port,** or **b.-hole,** a side port in a merchant ship for reception and discharge of ballast. **B.-pump,** *see* PUMP. **Bottom water-b.,** water carried as ballast in double-bottom tanks. **Hold water-b.,** water carried in tanks or other hold compartments. **In b.,** said of a vessel when carrying only ballast for her own stability or trimming use, *i.e.,* without cargo. **Sand-b.,** sand carried in bags or in bulk as ballast. **Shifting-b.,** such that may be moved about as required for trimming purposes. **Shingle-b.,** coarse gravel. **Sinking-b.,** *see* SINKING. **Tank water-b.,** water carried in tanks as ballast. To **freshen b.,** *see* FRESHEN.

BALLASTAGE. A fee levied for the privilege of taking ballast at a port.

BALLATOON. A heavy boat used for carrying timber on Russian rivers.

BALLINGER. See BALINGER.

BALLOON. To swell out like a balloon, as a sail distended by pressure of wind. **B.-jib,** *see* JIB. **B. sail,** lighter canvas used in yachts, taken collectively, which includes a balloon-jib, spinnaker, balloon-topsail, balloon-foresail, shadow-sail, and water-sail; also termed *ballooners.*

BALLOW. An archaic term for area of deeper water inside a bar or shoal.

BALSA. (Sp. *balsa,* a raft.) A tropical American tree of the *mallow* family, timber of which is porous and lighter than cork, and is much used for floats, life-rafts, etc. A raft or float on the Pacific coast of South America and the Philippines; also, in southern U.S.A., a raft made of inflated skins or casks of metal or wood (more recently, two cylinders) joined by a framework and used as a lifesaving float or for crossing heavy surf. A catamaran.

BANCA. (*Native name.*) A Philippine Island canoe or dug-out, with or without an outrigger, hewn from a single log 16 to 25 feet long, carrying three or four passengers. Also, *banka.*

BAND. Strip of canvas sewn across a sail to strengthen a vulnerable part. An iron hoop around a spar. See the term combined with caption words: BALANCE; BALE; BELLY; BREAST; EYE; FUTTOCK; GOOSENECK; ROPE; REEF; RUDDER; SLING; SPIDER.

BANGLE. A hoop or band on a spar.

BANIAN DAY. *See* DAY. (Also written *banyan day.*)

BANJO-FRAME. In early auxiliary screw steam-vessels, a frame used in hoisting or lowering the propeller into or from the *screw-well.* (Screw was lifted into a well or trunkway when vessel was under sail only.)

BANK. A number of oars operated from, or rowers seated on, one bench; a thwart; a rowers' bench on a galley. A tier of oars, as in ancient galleys having one or more of such, described as *double-banked, triple-banked,* etc. To bring to a shore; to shelter beneath a bank; to fish on the Newfoundland Banks. A raised part of a river-bed, or bottom of any body of water; a sand-bar; a fishing bank. **B.-fish,** the cod, so named because caught on Newfoundland Banks. **B.-fishing,** cod-fishing; fishing on Newfoundland Banks. **B.-sided,** built with inward sloping sides, as *tumble-home* of a ship's hull. See the word combined with captions DOUBLE; FOG; LEFT; RIGHT; SAND; SEA; SWASH.

BANKER. Vessel employed in fishing on the Newfoundland Banks. In Australia, a river full to its banks. In California, one who picks up flotsam along a shore.

BAR. Bank of sand or silt generally across the mouth of a river or harbor. A hatch-bar; a capstan-bar; a piece of wood, iron, or other solid material, longer than it is wide; a part of a rail fitted to temporarily halt traffic on a stairway. **Air-course b's,** *see* AIR. **Anchor-b.,** *see* ANCHOR. **Angle-b.,** *see* ANGLE. **Back-b.,** one fitted on opposite side of a bosom-bar. **B-bound,** said of a vessel hindered from sailing by a heavy sea on a bar. **B.-pilot,** *see* PILOT. **Batten-b.,** *see* BATTEN. **Bosom-b.,** *see* BOSOM. **Bounding-b.,** angle-bar joining extreme edges of a bulkhead to a tank top, shell-plating, decks, or to another bulkhead, as a strengthening and water-tight connection. **Bulkhead bounding-b.,** *see* BULKHEAD. **Capstan-b.,** *see* CAPSTAN. **Channel-b.,** *see* CHANNEL. **Cross-b.,** *see* CROSS. **Fender-b.,** *see* FENDER. **Fish-b.,** *see* FISH. **Flinders b.,** a piece of soft iron placed vertically on the fore or after side of a compass to counteract deviation caused by induced magnetism in vertical iron. **Guide-b.,** *see* GUIDE. **H-b.,** bar-iron similar in cross-sectional shape to a broadened *H:* same as *I-bar.* **Half-round b.,** one having a half-round cross section. **Hatch-b.,** either a flat iron bar closely fitted over, and to secure, hatch-covers, or a batten-bar for wedging and securing a tarpaulin on a hatch-coaming after covering the hatch. **Helm-b.,** *see* HELM. **I-b.,** a bar similar in cross section to an H-bar, used for bulkhead stiffeners, panting-beams, stanchions, and where local stiffening is required. **Index b.,** moving arm of a sextant to which is fixed at its upper end the index glass (or mirror) and at its lower end a vernier or micrometer for reading an angle observed. **Ledge-b.'s,** *see* LEDGE. **Locking-b.'s,** flat iron bars placed across hatch tarpaulins for securely holding down both tarpaulins and hatch-covers; *hatch-bars.* **Port-b.,** *see* PORT. **Rack-b.,** *see* RACK. **Reverse-b.,** inboard angle-bar of a built frame. **Sand-b.,** *see* SAND. **Set-b.,** *see* SET. **T-b.** or **Tee-b.,** used as a stiffener in various shipbuilding work. bar-iron having a cross section like the letter *T* in shape. **Trigger-b.,** a short rod used to release an anchor's securing chains, when letting go from a bill-board. **Water-way-b.,** *see* WATERWAY. **Z-b.** or **Zee-b.,** structural steel or iron having a cross section like the letter Z, used for light frames, beams, bulkhead stiffeners, etc.

BARBER. A cold weather gale in the Gulf of St. Lawrence which is characterized by driving ice spicules of such cutting violence as to cause bleeding from one's exposed skin. Vapor or low fog rising from the water in freezing weather.

BARBETTE. On warships, an armored cylinder for protection of a revolving turret containing one or more guns. An armor-plated platform with guns pointing over it. **B.-gun,** one mounted upon a barbette. **B.-ship,** a warship, usually the early ironclad, on which its heavier guns were mounted to fire over an armored bulwark.

BARCA. (It. *barca,* bark or barge.) A boat skiff, or barge. **Barca longa,** a long-boat; a fishing-boat having a lateen sail, common in the Mediterranean. **Barco, barca,** characteristic combining term for various local types of fishing and trading craft on coasts of Italy, Spain, and Portugal.

BARDEN'S METHOD. An arrangement of shifting-boards for grain cargoes approved by the New York Board of Underwriters and British Board of Trade. Consists essentially of a row of iron stanchions six to eight feet apart, depending upon thickness of boards used, placed so as to form uprights in a partition along a hold's midship fore-and-aft line. The stanchions are built to receive the boards with a minimum of trouble, while their main objective is to withstand pressure on either side of the partition, *i.e.,* from the bulk of grain as it tends to shift during heavy rolling.

BARE BOAT—; BARE HULL—; BARE POLE CHARTER. *See* CHARTER.

BARE POLES, UNDER. Said of a sailing-vessel when all sail is taken in during a heavy gale.

BARE WIND. Wind too light to fill a vessel's sails.

BARGE. Heavy freight-boat or lighter. A freight or excursion boat, generally double-decked, with no motive power, and intended to be towed. Formerly, an elaborately furnished boat or vessel of state; a large double-banked boat of a warship, particularly one used by a flag-officer. A type of work-boat used in Great Britain. A coal-boat common to the River Tyne in England, carrying 424 hundredweight. A receptacle for crew's bread. **Admiral's b.,** *see* ADMIRAL. **Hopper-b.,** one having an opening bottom, used for conveying and dumping mud, sand, etc., from a dredger at work. **Ice-b.,** *see* ICE. **Thames b.,** a bluff-bowed, broad-beamed, freight-vessel rigged like a ketch or yawl, having a large loose-footed mainsail supported at its peak by a sprit and equipped with brails, and usually carry-

ing a topsail; named for the River *Thames,* these vessels were once numerous on that river and nearby coasts of England. **Tide-b.,** *see* TIDE.

BARGEE. A man employed to manage a barge or lighter. (*England*)

BARGE MASTER. Proprietor or skipper of a barge.

BARGEMATE. Officer who steers a state barge on ceremonious occasions.

BARIC LAW of the WIND. *See* LAWS.

BARK or **BARQUE.** (Fr. *barque;* It. *barca;* LL. *barca.*) A three-, four-, or five-masted vessel having her after mast fore-and-aft rigged and the others square-rigged. To *dye* sails or cordage with an infusion of bark; to *tan.* **Four-masted barque,** one having foremast, mainmast, and mizzenmast square-rigged, the jiggermast having a topmast only and fore-and-aft rigged. **Five-masted b.,** few, if any, of this rig are afloat to-day, last of a few owned by German and French interests and almost exclusively engaged in the west coast of South America nitrate trade having disappeared shortly before World War I. **Jackass b.,** *see* JACKASS.

BARKENTINE or **BARQUENTINE.** A three- or four-masted vessel having her foremast square-rigged and other masts fore-and-aft rigged. Also, *barkantine, barquantine.*

BARKER. A sailor's term for a lower deck gun in old navy ships.

BARNACLES. A general term for those small crustaceans which fix themselves to ships' bottoms, floating timber, piles of wharves, etc., below and especially near the water-line. The **acorn b.,** also called *sea-acorn* and *acorn-shell,* may be found in multitudes on shore rocks, piles of piers, and iron ships' bottoms. The **goose barnacle,** with its leathery stalk, is commonly observed on wooden vessels' bottoms, floating logs, piles, etc. and has a greater affinity for wood than the *acorn.*

BAROGRAPH. A self-recording aneroid barometer.

BAROMETER. (Gr. *baros,* weight; *metron,* measure.) Instrument for measuring changes in atmospheric pressure, which information, coupled with observation of changes in wind direction, temperature, cloud formation, etc., provides basic data required in weather prediction. Barometers used at sea are the *mercury* and the *aneroid.* **Aneroid b.,** a circular box of thin elastic metal, or *vacuum-chamber,* the varying atmospheric pressure upon which causes its surface to rise or fall. These movements are transmitted to a spring and thence by an arrangement of levers to an index pointer. Aneroids are compensated to offset effect of temperature changes in their readings. **Mercury b.,** a glass tube 33 to 34 inches in length, closed at one end and filled with mercury. The tube is inverted with its open end dipping into a cup or cistern of mercury and the column sinks leaving a vacuum in the tube's upper end. Atmospheric pressure on each unit of the mercury's surface in the cup equals weight of mercury in the tube, so that weight or pressure of the mercury column just balances that of the atmosphere. The barometer reading is thus shown by height of the column as measured on an attached graduated scale. Barometers of this type are called *cistern barometers*. **Marine b.,** one of mercury type hung to remain perpendicular and having a narrow neck in its tube for suppressing oscillations of the mercury caused by a vessel's motion at sea. **Pumping of the b.,** an unsteadiness in height of the mercury column due to fluctuations of pressure in gusty winds. **True height of the b.,** mercury reading corrected to its standard density (at 32° F.), for capillarity effect, index error, and height above sea level; also, for scientific purposes, a correction for latitude is made, standard gravity being considered as that of 45° latitude. **Wind-b. table,** *see* WIND.

BAROMETRIC DEPRESSION. See DEPRESSION.

BAROMETRIC PRESSURE. Air or atmospheric pressure.

BARQUE. *See* BARK.

BARRA-BOAT. *See* BOAT.

BARRACUDA. Any of several pike-like fishes of the genus *Sphyræna*. The **great b.** of West Indies and Florida is often six or more feet in length and as voracious and dangerous as any shark. Those of the Pacific and European coasts are smaller and used for food. **Northern b.,** *Sphyræna borealis,* a small one of U.S. Atlantic coast from North Carolina to Massachusetts.

BARRATOR. One who, being master of a ship or crew member thereof, commits any fraud or fraudulent act in management of ship or cargo by which owners, freighters, or insurers are injured, as by running away with the ship, sinking or deserting her, willful deviation from a fixed course, or embezzlement of cargo.

BARRATRY. Fraud or offence committed by a *barrator.*

BARRE. *See* BORE.

BARREL. Quantity constituting a full barrel, depending upon size, shape, and trade use of such measure. Usually 36 gallons (*43 U.S. gallons*) in England; 31½ gallons in U.S., but standard in bulk petroleum use is 42 gallons at 60° *Fahr.* A barrel of flour weighs 196 lbs.; one of beef, pork, or fish usually 300 lbs., one of sugar 350 lbs. In a vessel's steering apparatus, a cylinder on which the

tiller-ropes or chains are wound. Tube **of a gun** which carries the projectile. Rotating portion of a capstan or windlass. Drum or roller of a crane about which a rope or chain winds. A kind of *crow's nest* shaped like, or actually, a barrel, placed at an upper masthead, especially in sealing-vessels, from which the *barrel-man* keeps lookout for field ice and expected herd of seals thereon. **B.-bottom,** descriptive term for a vessel having a round bottom. **B.-bulk,** a measure of capacity for freight, equal to 5 cubic feet; one-eighth of a ton weight. **B.-fish,** the rudder-fish, *lirus perciformis.* **B.-hooks,** *see* **can hooks** *in* HOOK. **B.-man,** an experienced seaman who occupies the *barrel* of a sealing-vessel in directing or conning his ship toward an appropriate berth in the ice upon sighting a herd of seals. **Boss-b.,** *see* BOSS.

BARRICADE. On old sailing-ships, **a** strong wooden rail supported by several small pillars **or** stanchions, extending across the forward end **of** a quarter-deck or poop.

BARRIER BEACH. *See* BEACH.

BARRIER REEF. *See* REEF.

BARU. A fine woolly substance used for caulking, stuffing cushions, etc., obtained from the East Indies sago palm.

BASE. Place from which supplies and reinforcements may be drawn, constituting a basis in operations. Lowest or supporting member of a structure. In ordnance, rounded rear part of a cannon. **B. line,** *see* LINE. **B.-plate,** same as *bed-plate; see* PLATE. **Log-b.,** *see* LOGARITHM.

BASIN. A comparatively circular and shallow part of the sea. In a sea-port tidal dock system, water area between the dock-gates and lock-gates. A dock in which vessels float at any stage of tide. **Model b.,** a lengthy artificial lake or pool, usually wholly enclosed, in which ship models are towed at different speeds in determining proper hull form for a given speed, or power required to obtain **a** certain speed for a particular form of hull. **Swinging b.,** swinging berth; *see* SWINGING. **Tidal b.,** *see* TIDAL.

BASKET. Displayed in the rigging, or where **it** can best be seen, by vessels or boats fishing with lines, trawls, or nets during daytime. If at anchor, this signal is shown on the side on which other vessels can pass. (*Art. 9, International Rules for Prevention of Collisions.*) **Wash-b.,** *see* WASH.

BASKING-SHARK. *See* SHARK.

BASS. Same as *bast.* Basswood. **B.-rope,** cord or rope made from *bast.* **Sea-b.,** a fish of the *Serranidæ* family, distinguished by its peculiar caudal fin and conspicuous colors, its body being brown or black and more or less mottled, with pale longitudinal stripes. One of the most common fishes in the New

York market, it is locally known as *black sea-bass, black perch, blue-fish,* and *blue-bass.*

BAST. Rope, cord, or matting made of inner bark of trees. Strong inner fibrous bark of various trees (originally the *lime*), especially that of a species of *linden,* of which the Russian matting of commerce is made. **B. fiber, b. cells,** essential constituents of all textile fibers derived from bark of plants such as flax, hemp, jute, and ramie. **B. palm,** two species of Brazilian palms that yield *piassaba fiber,* a coarse type used for cordage, brooms, etc.

BATEAU. A flat-bottomed double-ended river boat, such as a *mackinaw,* used especially on Canadian rivers and in Louisiana. A pontoon for a bridge.

BATH-BRICK. See BRICK-DUST.

BATHOMETER. (Gr. *bathos,* depth; *metron,* measure.) An instrument for measuring ocean depths; also, one which determines depth of water on the basis of gravitational force.

BATHYCURRENT. An ocean current flowing at a considerable depth below, and unaffecting, the surface water.

BATHYGRAPHIC CHART. See CHART.

BATHYMETER. Same as *bathometer.*

BATHYMETRIC. Pertaining to measurement of marine depths. **B. zone,** one of the oceans' horizontal divisions.

BATHYMETRY. Science of deep-sea sounding.

BATTEN. Narrow strip of wood for "fairing in" lines. Strip of wood or steel used in securing tarpaulins in place; for fastening objects together; for protecting a spar or mast from chafing; or from which to sling a hammock. To secure by means of battens. **B. bar,** one for securing a hatch-tarpaulin; a *hatch-batten.* **B.-cleats,** see CLEAT. **B.-hook,** see HOOK. **B. seam construction,** see CONSTRUCTION. **Cargo b's,** planks fitted inside of frames in a ship's hold to keep cargo from contact with the shell-plating; also, *spar ceiling.* Strips of wood or steel used to prevent cargo from shifting. **Chafing-b.,** same as *chafing-board.* **Louvered b's,** those fitted in partitions, doors, etc., at such an angle as to admit air while excluding dust, rain, etc. **Rubbing-b.,** see RUBBING. **Sheer b.,** see SHEER. **Spider b.,** see SPIDER. To **b. down the hatches,** to secure hatch tarpaulins by wedging battens over their edges along the hatch-coaming sides, in order to prevent ingress of water.

BATTER. Referred to a vessel's form, indicating topsides of hull having less breadth than that measured at water-line. Inward slope of a ship's side above her water-line; more commonly known as *tumble home.*

BATTERY. Armament of a warship, or a special part thereof, as *the starboard battery.* A position taken awaiting the order to fire. Arrangement of pipe coils used in cooling or heating a compartment. **Main b.,** see MAIN.

BATTLE. A hostile encounter or engagement between opposing forces on land or sea. (*Actions* and *affairs* are engagements of less magnitude). **B. cruiser,** see CRUISER. **B. lantern,** a lamp or portable electric light once placed between decks and near guns during a night engagement. **B. ports,** same as *dead lights.* **B. ship,** see BATTLESHIP. **B.-wagon,** a battleship. **Line of b.,** see LINE. **Order of b.,** see ORDER. To **give b.,** to provoke battle; attack.

BATTLESHIP. Heavily armored vessel carrying batteries of high calibre and rapid-firing guns, with anti-aircraft armament; distinguished from a cruiser by her heavy armor-plating and lesser speed, and from a gun-boat by greater size and heavier armament. She is normally manned by about 80 officers and 1000 men which numbers may be considerably increased in war time. Battleships usually are capable of steaming over 21 knots and their equipment includes from 8 to 12 guns of 12 to 16-inch bore. Those of the U.S. are named after states of the union. **Line of b.,** see SHIP. **Pocket b.,** see POCKET.

BAUMÉ GAUGE. See GAUGE.

BAWLEY. Bawley boat; a Thames fishing smack, broad and of light draft, sloop-rigged with no boom on her mainsail, which sail brails to the mast. *Bawly.*

BAY. Space between an anchor-windlass and the stem. A sick-bay, or hospital, on a man-of-war, see SICK. Area of water between two coastal headlands; sometimes an arm of the sea. Space between adjacent frames in hold bilges. **B. fishery,** see FISHERY. **Lock-b.,** see LOCK. **Tail-b.,** see TAIL.

BAYAMO. A violent blast of wind, accompanied by vivid lightning and heavy rain, from the Bight of Bayamo, in Cuba, and its neighborhood.

BAYMAN. One who serves as attendant in a sick-bay; a loblolly boy.

BAYOU. A sluggish inlet to a lake or bay, or one connecting two small bodies of inland waters, especially in southern U.S.

BAYS. An old navy term for "amidships."

B.C. Official abbreviation for the classification society, *British Corporation.*

B.D. *Bank draft. Bar draft,* or such draft as will carry a ship over a certain bar.

BEACH. To run or haul a vessel up on a beach. Shore of a sea, lake, or large river. Land between high and low water limits. Pebbly or sandy margin of a body of water. **Barr'er b.,** one separated from a main shore by a lagoon, or formed across the mouth of a bay or inlet. **B.-comber,** long wave rolling up on a shore. A vagrant about wharves and beaches. One who gathers flotsam and jetsam. **Pocket b.,** one at the head of a bay or cove between two headlands. **Raised b.,** shelf or terrace of wave-worn matter, located above a present wave-line, caused either by recession of the water or increased elevation of the land.

BEACHMAN. One who conveys passengers and cargo through a surf.

BEACHMASTER. An officer appointed to command a landing party.

BEACON. Pole, tripod, or other conspicuous object bearing a characteristic mark such as a ball, diamond, cone, cage, or broom, and set on a buoy, shoal, reef, or on shore as a guide or warning for mariners.

BEACONAGE. A tax for maintenance of beacons. Beacons collectively. **Beaconage and buoyage,** see BUOYAGE.

BEAD-STRAKE. *See* STRAKE.

BEAK. Rostrum of an ancient war galley; entire prow; ram of a warship; *beak-head.* **Beak-head,** old term for upper part of the hull at the stem. **Fore-b.,** *see* FORE.

BEAM. Extreme width of a ship. One of the athwartship structural units that support decks and stay ship's sides. Straight main part, or shank of an anchor. **Angle-b.,** *see* ANGLE. **Abaft the b.,** *see* ABAFT. **B. angle-bar,** angle-iron used in the construction of a beam. **B.-arm,** same as fork-beam; also, end of a deck-beam which has been split and bent to fasten to a frame. **B.-brackets,** triangular steel plates used to fasten beams to side frames. **B.-carlings,** pieces of timber, bulb-plates, etc., fitted longitudinally or diagonally between deck-beams as stiffeners. **B. clamp,** *see* CLAMP. **B. engine,** *see* ENGINE. **B. filling,** cargo convenient for filling spaces between beams, such as small packages. **B.-knee,** one supporting an end of a deck-beam; a *beam-arm.* **B. line,** *see* **deck-line** *in* LINE. **B. mold,** a pattern showing curvature, commonly called *camber,* of beams for a deck. **B.-net,** a beam-trawl. **B. plate angle,** a beam made from a flat plate, having its flange bent at right angles by an angle-bending machine. **B. stringer,** plate riveted to beams and shell plating, laid fore-and-aft as a deck-plate. **B.-trawl,** *see* TRAWL. **B.-trawler,** *see* TRAWLER. **B. wind,** a wind blowing at right angles to a vessel's course. **Before the b.,** in a direction forward of a line drawn at right angles to the keel. **Bent b.,** same as *camber beam.* **Breast b.,** *see* BREAST. **Built b.,** one built by bolting two or more timbers together. **Bow and b. bearing,** a four-point bearing; *see* TWO BEARINGS WITH RUN BETWEEN. **Camber-b.,** a bent beam; *see* CAMBER. **Cant b.,** one of the beams supporting deck plating or planking in an overhanging stern. These

radiate in fan-shaped formation from the transom-beam to the cant frames. **Deck-b., -clamp; -dimensions; -stringer-plate;** *see* DECK. **Deck molding of b.,** its vertical dimension, or thickness. **Deck siding of b.,** its horizontal dimension fore-and-aft, indicating deck bearing surface. **Fork b.,** a *b. arm* or *crow-foot; see* CROWFOOT. **Forward of the b.,** same as *before the b.* **I-b.,** an iron beam of cross section similar to the letter *I;* also, an *H-beam.* **Intermediate b.,** one of lighter construction than, and fitted between, ordinary beams, where additional support or structural strength is required. **Kerfed b.,** one with slits sawn in one side to facilitate its bending by easing compression on such side. **Off the b.,** same as *on the b.;* abeam. **On her b. ends,** said of a vessel which has heeled to such an angle that her decks approach the vertical. **On the b.,** descriptive of a relative bearing when object noted is at right angles to fore-and-aft line, or *abeam.* **On the weather b.,** indicating a direction at right angles to vessel's course on that side from which the wind is blowing. **Round of b.,** vertical dimension of departure from horizontal attained by curvature or arch in a *b.; see* CAMBER. **Semi-box b.,** one of box-like construction, as made by a horizontal plate and two channel bars or bulb angles. Such beams are located in lower holds as lateral stiffeners to frames. **Spacing of b's,** in small vessels deck beams are about 40 inches apart; in larger ships, 48 to 52 inches. **Trolley b.,** one carrying a traveling hoist; usually laid fore-and-aft directly above main engines for lifting cylinder-covers, etc.; also, *strong b.* (Other designations of *beams* may be found combined with and under captions CAT; FENDER; HALF; HATCH; HOLD; MAIN; MIDSHIP; ORLOP; PANTING; SHIFTING; SKID; SPONSON; SPRING; SPUR; TRANSOM; TRAWL; WALKING.)

BEAMINESS. Term expressing degree of breadth proportional to a vessel's length.

BEAMY. Having much beam or breadth, considering length-breadth ratio of an average vessel, which is approximately 8 to 1.

BEAN-COD. A small fishing-vessel or pilot-boat, common to the seacoast and rivers of Portugal. Usually rigged with one large lateen sail, they are fine-lined and speedy craft.

BEAR. To be directed to any end or purpose; to be inclined to. A hydraulic portable machine used to punch rivet-holes in plating or structural members of a ship. A heavy block of wood, or a coarse mat weighted by a stone, used to scour a ship's decks in the same manner as with a *holystone.* To **bear a hand,** to lend a hand quickly; to take hold. give aid or assistance. To **bear away,** to alter a ship's course farther from the wind. To **bear down,** to approach a vessel, port, or any object from its windward side. To **bear in with,** to run or tend toward; as, a ship bears in with the land. To **b. off,** to keep at a greater distance from. To push a boat away from a ship's side or a landing. To **b. up,** to luff, or steer closer to the wind. To **b. up for,** to sail or proceed toward. To **bring to b.,** to press upon; to cause to carry or endure. **Sea-b.,** *see* SEA. **Water-b.,** *see* WATER.

BEARDING. Bearding-line; line of intersection of a vessel's timber surfaces with her stem, keel, and stern-post; outside planking bearing surface was fashioned according to the *bearding-line,* or *stepping-line,* as a varying angled rabbet cut along the structural members indicated. Diminishing thickness of a stem, rudder, etc., toward its outer edge. **B.-angle,** an angle-bar connecting shell plating and stem. **Rudder-b.,** *see* RUDDER.

BEARER. Term applied to a foundation, particularly one having vertical web plates as its principal members; vertical plates of boiler foundations are called *bearers.* **Rudder-b.,** *see* RUDDER.

BEARING. Direction in which an object is observed; direction of one object from another as indicated by a point of the compass. (See AZIMUTH) A block on, or in which, a journal rotates; a bearing-block; also, that part of an axle or shaft-journal in contact with a journal proper. Widest part of a vessel below her upper deck line or sheer strake. **B. and sounding,** bearing of an object taken simultaneously with a sounding as a means of fixing a ship's position. **B.-binnacle,** one placed in a convenient position for taking bearings. **B.-plate,** a *pelorus.* **Bow and beam b.,** a 4-point bearing; *see* TWO OR MORE BEARINGS *with run between.* **Compass b.,** direction of bearing as shown by a compass. **Danger b.,** that of an object indicating a limit of approach to a known danger. **Line of b.,** *see* LINE. **Magnetic b.,** that of an object with with relation to magnetic north, as indicated by a compass free of deviation. **Main b.; -brasses; -journals;** *see* MAIN. **Outer b.,** in a sponson, that upon which a paddle-shaft's outer end revolves. **One-point b.,** estimate of a vessel's distance off a fixed object by observing distance run required to change its bearing one point to or from abeam, and multiplying this distance by 5. **Propeller-shaft b.,** blocks of *lignum vitae,* a very hard and oily wood, which are set in a stern tube as bearing surface for a tail-end shaft; water filling the tube supplies necessary lubrication. **Radio b.,** compass direction of a radio transmitting station as indicated by signals received in a navigational direction-finder. **Reciprocal b's,** in swinging a vessel for ascertaining deviations of her standard compass, bearings of the latter are taken by a compass set up on shore and free of local magnetic influence simultaneously with bearings of the shore compass taken from ship, by pre-arranged signal. Reciprocals of shore compass bearings, which are correct magnetic, compared with those taken by ship's compass, give deviations for

different selected headings of the vessel. **Relative b.,** direction of an object with relation to a ship's fore-and-aft line; thus, relative bearing 50° is synonymous with "50° on the starboard bow," and relative bearing 270° is exactly "on the port beam." **Roller b.,** substituting sliding friction of a plain bearing in a *dummy* or common block sheave, true rolling motion is obtained by fitting rollers to directly bear upon the block pin. *Roller b's* are used in "patent" sheaves of blocks in halyards, braces, and other purchases chiefly to facilitate quick rendering or overhauling of the running parts. It is claimed that power consumed in overcoming friction is reduced by from 60 to 75 per cent. where roller bearings are fitted. **Rudder b.,** *see* RUDDER. **Shaft b.,** *see* SHAFT. **Spring b's,** *see* SPRING. To **take b's,** to ascertain in what direction by compass an object lies. **Thrust b.,** one or more *b's* fitted in a propeller-shaft arrangement for receiving thrust or axial drive of the screw. **True b.,** direction of an object with relation to that of the meridian; a compass *b.* corrected for deviation and variation; a *b.* taken with an accurate gyroscope compass.

BEARING FINDER. An azimuth circle; *see* AZIMUTH.

BEAT. In sailing, to work to windward by alternate tacks, as in *beating to windward.* A **beating wind,** a contrary breeze which makes tacking necessary. To **b. about,** to hold up against a breeze by tacking. To **b. the booby,** to stimulate warmth by beating the arms across one's chest. To **b. to quarters,** to summon a warship's crew by beat of drum to battle-stations.

BEATEN, WEATHER-. *See* WEATHER.

Beaufort's Wind Scale.

Force	Wind	Velocity per hour	
		Statute miles.	Nautical miles.
0. Calm.			
1. Light airs. Just sufficient to give steerage way.		8	7
2. Light breeze. Speed of 1 or 2 knots, "full and by."		13	11
3. Gentle breeze. Speed 3 or 4 knots, "full and by."		18	16
4. Moderate breeze. Speed 5 or 6 knots, "full and by."		23	20
5. Fresh breeze. All plain sail, "full and by."		28	24
6. Strong breeze. Top-gallant-sails.		34	30
7. Moderate gale. Single-reefed topsails.		40	35
8. Fresh gale. Double-reefed topsails.		48	42
9. Strong gale. Lower topsails.		56	49
10. Whole gale. Lower main-topsail and reefed foresail.		65	56
11. Storm. Storm staysails.		75	65
12. Hurricane. Under bare poles.		90+	78+

BEAUFORT SCALE. Numerical symbols for wind velocities, 0 to 12, with nautical term for each and customary sail spread in a well-found ship of the line, as instituted by Admiral Beaufort of the British Navy; also a scale of sea conditions, 0 to 10, corresponding to any force of wind.

State of Sea.

0. Calm.—Sea mirror-like; smooth.
1. Light airs.—Small wavelets without crests forming.
2. Light breeze.—Short waves with crests.
3. Gentle breeze.—Waves short and more pronounced; their crests begin to break; foam of glassy appearance.
4. Moderate breeze.—Waves become longer; many "white horses" are formed; breaking sea produces a short, continuous rustling sound.
5. Fresh breeze.—Waves take a more pronounced lengthy form with white foam crests. Sea breaks with noise like perpetual murmur.
6. Strong breeze.—Larger waves begin to form; white foam crests more extensive; sea breaks with duller rolling noise.
7. Moderate gale.—Sea heaps up and spindrift begins to be blown in streaks with direction of the wind; noise of breaking sea is heard at a greater distance.
8. Fresh gale.
9. Strong gale.—Height of waves and their crests greatly increase; spindrift appears in dense streaks; sea begins to "roll."
10. Whole gale.—High waves develop with long overhanging crests; spindrift more abundant and whole sea surface takes on a white appearance. Rolling of the sea becomes heavy and shock-like.

BECALMED. Deprived of wind; delayed by, or subjected to a calm.

BECKET. A short piece of small rope, having a toggle at one end and an eye at the other for temporarily confining coils of running gear, small spars, etc. A handle, as a rope grommet. A wood cleat or hook fastened outside of lower rigging for holding tacks and sheets when idle. A grommet in which to hock a block; or one at the breech or base of a block for securing a tackle fall's standing end. A grommet used as a rowlock. Usually in plural, one's trousers' pockets. **B. bend, b. hitch,** a sheet bend; see BEND. **B.-line,** short piece of line used to form a bight on a longer or larger rope, such as is employed in rigging a trawl. **Hand b's,** grommets 6 to 8 inches in diameter made fast at convenient distances apart on the jackstay of a yard, used as safety grips or arm-holds for men when taking in sail, reefing, etc.

BECUEING. Method of securing a hawser to a small anchor by a light seizing to the ring, its end being made fast to the crown. Upon the anchor's flukes being caught among rocks, its release is effected by a sharp upward jerk, which carries away the seizing.

BED. To rest on for support. Cradle of a ship on the stocks. **Anchor-b.,** see ANCHOR. **B.-plate,** see PLATE. **Bowsprit b.,** see BOWSPRIT.

BEDLAMER. A harp seal; see SEAL.

BEE. A rounded block of iron or hard wood through which a stay's lower end is rove before it is set up and secured.

BEECH. A large tree whose timber is found suitable for piling if kept constantly wet. The wood is rarely used in shipbuilding on account of its tendency to rot in damp places, while its toughness and close texture makes it adaptable for tool and furniture manufacture. It is, however, too brittle for delicate work requiring strength. *Beech-wood* weighs about 42 lbs. per cubic foot.

BEESWAX. For waxing twine or thread used in sewing or stitching canvas, leather, etc.; it is usually melted together with one-third part rosin and termed *wax*.

BEEF. Brawn, weight, and strength of a man; as *beef* required to haul on a line. A complaint, usually of a petty nature. **B.-boats,** supply ships of U.S. navy.

BEETLE. Heavy wooden mallet used in driving wedges, pegs, treenails, etc. **Hawsing-b.,** large caulking mallet for "hawsing down" seams. **Reaming-b.,** see REAMING.

BEFORE. Forward of; formerly more commonly expressed as *afore*. **B. and after pump,** see PUMP. **B. the beam,** see BEAM. **B. the mast,** see AFORE. **B. the wind,** see WIND.

BEFORE HAND. To hold on to a line while it is being made fast or belayed, as when completing a pull on a halyard; also, *fore hand.*

BEHIND, UP. *See* UP.

BELAY. To make fast; to fasten a rope by winding it *figure-8 fashion* over a belaying-pin, cleat, kevel, bitt, etc. **Belaying-bitt,** a bitt to which a rope is made fast. **Belaying-pin,** a wooden, brass, or iron pin on which a rope or other running line is belayed. **B. there!,** stop there; halt!

BELFRY. Term for a former ornamental frame in which a ship's bell was hung.

BELL. Unit used on shipboard to announce each half hour of a watch. The day is divided into 6 watches of 4 hours each, first half hours of which are, respectively, indicated on ship's bell by one *stroke,* or *one bell;* next half hour by *two bells;* and so on, *eight bells* corresponding to 4, 8, and 12 o'clock a.m. and p.m., thus:

1 bell at	12.30; 4.30; and 8.30 o'clock.
2 bells at	1.00; 5.00; and 9.00 o'clock.
3 bells at	1.30; 5.30; and 9.30 o'clock.
4 bells at	2.00; 6.00; and 10.00 o'clock.
5 bells at	2.30; 6.30; and 10.30 o'clock.
6 bells at	3.00; 7.00; and 11.00 o'clock.
7 bells at	3.30; 7.30; and 11.30 o'clock.
8 bells at	4.00; 8.00; and 12.00 o'clock.

British practice modifies the above in *2nd. dog watch* (6 to 8 p.m.) to 1, 2, 3, and 8 bells at 6.30, 7.00, 7.30, and 8.00 o'clock, respectively; *see* **M. at the Nore** *in* MUTINY. A ship's *bell* is *rung, i.e.*, given a series of rapid successive strokes by its tongue, as a signal for calling the crew to fire stations; and as a fog signal when at anchor in thick weather. It is *struck, i.e.*, given certain individual strokes, when sounding half-hourly *bells;* in announcing appearance of a light or other object by a lookout, according to an appropriate pre-arranged system; and to indicate length of chain cable payed out when letting go, or outside the hawse, when heaving anchor (usually the number of 15-fathom shots). **B.-book,** a record of engine-movement orders in which character and time of each signal is entered. Symbols based on ordinary check marks generally are employed therein. **B.-mouthed ventilator,** *see* VENTILATOR. **B.-pull,** a wire connection by which a bell or gong is sounded in an engine-room, such as is used on small steamers and tug-boats for signal orders to an engineer. **B.-rope,** a cord or small rope attached to the tongue of a bell; *bell-cord*. **Dinner b.,** one from 4 to 6 inches in diameter with a handle attached, used on merchant vessels to call crew to mess. **Diving b.,** a weighty hollow chamber, originally bell-shaped, open at its bottom and supplied with air by a tube from above, in which men may descend and work under water. **Fog b.,** one sounded as a warning or landmark to mariners during thick weather; one fixed on a buoy and sounded by action of waves for the same purpose. **Jingle b.,** a bell fitted in an engine-room by which signals are transmitted from a pilot-house for full speed ahead or astern. It is used in connection with a gong on which signals for other movements are given. **Pilot-house b.,** one 6 to 8 inches in diameter, usually hung forward of a pilot-house, struck by a quartermaster or helmsman in announcing the half-hourly *bells*.

BELL PURCHASE. *See* PURCHASE.

BELLY. Broadest part of a ship's hull at and below her water-line, especially in vessels having much *tumble-home*. **B.-band,** a horizontal cloth or broad strip of canvas sewn as a strengthener midway between the close-reef band and foot of a topsail or course; a girth-band. **B. in/of a sail,** bulging of a sail caused by pressure of wind; bellying canvas. **B.-guy,** a tackle or guy attached half way up a sheer-leg or spar needing support at its middle. **B.-strap,** rope around a boat from which an anchor being carried out is suspended; a steadying rope placed around a boat swung out and hanging in its davits.

BELLYROBBER. Chief steward on a merchant vessel; commissary steward on a naval vessel; mess sergeant in the Army and Marine Corps. (*U.S. slang*)

BELOW. Underdeck; off duty, as opposed to *on deck*. To **go b.,** to descend to a lower deck; to retire to one's cabin or quarters. **Look out b.!,** a warning coming from aloft to stand out from under; also, **Under b.!**

BELT. Belting; a broad endless strip of leather, rubber, or other flexible material that passes around wheels, cylinders, pulleys, etc. in transferring mechanical power. **B.-gearing,** belt system used in transmitting power as above indicated. **Armor-b.,** girdle of armor-plating for protection of warships along the water-line. **Calm b.,** *see* CALM. **Fog. b.,** *see* FOGS. **Life-b.,** *see* LIFE. **Marine b.,** the 3-mile limit; *see* MARINE. **Storm b.,** *see* STORM.

BELTED CRUISER. *See* CRUISER.

BELTED SHIP. *See* SHIP.

BELUGA. (Russ. *byeluga*.) A cetacean of the dolphin family, white in color when adult and growing to about 10 feet in length; the *white whale;* found in northern seas and well-known in the Gulf of St. Lawrence. Also, the *huso,* or *great sturgeon,* of southeastern Europe.

BENCH MARK. *See* MARK.

BEND. In older wooden construction, *bends* were thick planks on a ship's sides immediately below the waterways or gun-port sills, and more properly called *wales*. These strakes were named upward as 1st., 2nd., and 3rd. bends; beam-knees and foothooks (*futtocks*) bolted to them, they were the chief strength of a vessel's sides. A rib or frame of a boat. To make fast, or connect, as ends of a rope or hawser, or a sail to a boom, gaff, stay, or yard. A loop or knot by which a rope is fastened to any object; that part of a rope thus fastened. To shackle a chain cable to an anchor; *see* **bending shackle** *in* SHACKLE. **Becket-b.,** *see* BECKET. **Cable-b.,** *see* CABLE. **Carrick b.,** used for joining ends of two heavy ropes or hawsers and named as a *single* or a *double carrick*. **Expansion b.,** a U-shaped bend in a pipe-line for taking up expansion and contraction due to changes in temperature, and also to ease stresses on the line caused by vibration and working of a ship. **Midship-b.,** *see* MIDSHIP. **Mooring-b.,** *see* MOORING. **Reeving-line b.,** *see* REEVING. **Sheet b.,** hitch used in forming meshes in a fishing-net; a weaver's hitch; also used to make fast a tackle's standing end to a becket on a block; *becket-bend*. **Y bend,** *see* Y. To **b. to the oars,** *see* OAR. Various names are given rope *bends,* such as *fisherman's, studding-sail tack, studding-sail halyard, carrick, sheet,* etc., depending upon use to which each is adapted. (*See illustrations*).

BENDER. A drinking-spree or frolic. **Keel b.,** *see* KEEL.

BENDING. See the term combined with captions MOMENT; PRESS; ROLLS; SHACKLE; SLAB.

BENDS. A malady caused by a too sudden change to normal air pressure from higher pressure in a caisson or tunnel, or when, as by divers, emergence from considerable depth of water is too rapid.

BENEAPED. Term indicating detention of a vessel in a dock, or aground, pending her release with advent of higher tides.

BENGAL LIGHT. *See* LIGHT.

BENT IRON. *See* IRON.

BENTINCK. A triangular trysail, now superseded by the *storm staysail,* invented by Capt. Bentinck (*1737–1775*). **B. boom,** *see* BOOM. **B. shrouds,** in old wooden square-rigged vessels, additional lowermast shrouds set up when rolling heavily.

BENZENE. *See* BENZOL.

BENZINE. A mixture, less volatile than *benzene* (benzol), chiefly composed of saturated hydrocarbons; used as a motor fuel, solvent, etc., and in paints and cleaning fluids. It is a higher distillate of petroleum.

BENZOL. Same as benzene; a nearly colorless liquid distilled from coal tar, used as a motor fuel and as a solvent for rubber, resins, etc.

BERLIN. *See* BIRLIN.

BERLINER ASTRONOMISCHES JAHRBUCH. The German nautical almanac; *see* ALMANAC.

BERM. A nearly horizontal formation on a beach caused by deposit of material cast up by the waves.

BERMUDA. A British naval station in about 32° N. latitude and 65° W. longitude, comprising a 20 square-mile group of islands of the same name. *Hamilton* is its capital. **B. rig,** or *'Mudian rig; see* RIG. **B. sails,** foresail and mainsail of Bermuda-rigged schooners, characterized by a comparatively short head, lengthy foot, great hoist, and set with more rake than that of usual schooner rig.

BERTH. Bed or cot on which to rest, commonly termed a *bunk.* Berths usually are fitted permanently in state-rooms and officers' cabins, and often temporarily set up in crew, troop, or steerage accommodation spaces. An officer's room or cabin sometimes is referred to as his *berth,* as also is his position or rank, *e.g.,* a *mate's berth.* Sea room; space for safety or convenience between a vessel under way and other vessels or a coast, rocks, etc.; room or space required for a ship in riding at anchor, or in which to turn around. A place where a ship may lie, at anchor or at a wharf. **B. deck,** that on which berths are located; in the old war-vessels, deck below a lower gun-deck. **Foul b.,** *see* FOUL. To **give a wide b. to** (*good* or *clear b. to*), to keep well clear of, or away from, any object or danger; also, *keep a wide b. off.* **Quay b.,** *see* QUAY. **Railway b.,** *see* RAILWAY. To **shift b.,** *see* SHIFT.

BERTHAGE. Charges for a berth at a dock, pier, or anchorage. Place assigned a vessel in port.

BERTHING. Arrangement of berths on a ship; berths collectively. Placing of a vessel in her berth. In former naval construction, ship's side-planking above the sheer strake, designated as *berthing* of the quarter-deck, of poop, or of forecastle; the *bulwarks.* Displacement of side planking due to laboring of a ship. Distance between frames, in shipbuilding. **B. rail,** bulwark rail. **Hammock b.,** *see* HAMMOCK.

BERTHON BOAT. *See* BOAT.

BETA CENTAURI. (*β Centauri.*) A first magnitude star in the group *Centaurus,* in about R.A. 14 hours and declination 60° south; one of the *pointers* to *Crux (Southern Cross).*

BETELGEUSE or **BETELGEUX.** Star *a Orionis,* or first in *Orion;* reddish in color and of magnitude varying from .1 to 1.2; about 5 hrs. 52 min. in R.A. and Dec. 7° 24′ N.

BETHEL. (*Hebrew, house of God.*) Place of worship or a hostel for seamen at a sea-port.

BETWEEN DECKS. Same as *'tween decks; see* DECK.

BETWEEN WIND AND WATER. Outside hull surface in vicinity of the water-line; *awash.*

BEVEL. A tool much used by shipwrights and ship joiners where panel-work, doors, etc., are fashioned to conform to "run of the ship," instead of "square" lines, due to varying departures from the square resulting from sheer lines and camber of decks. Term for a plane forming an angle other than 90° with a plane of reference. To give a bevel angle or sloping edge to, as to *bevel a flange.* To bevel an edge of a beam, flange, plate, etc., preparatory to vee welding. To tilt a girder in conformity with sheer bevel. To open or close an angle-bar of a ship's frame in order to make a faying surface for the plating. **B.-angle,** one other than a right angle. **B. board,** in ship-building, a board on which lines of each frame are marked out, as necessary data for proper bevel at which frames must be set in process of forging. Each frame, excepting those amidships which meet the shell-plating squarely,. is given its own *bevel board.* **B.-faced hammer,** a riveting hammer having a sloping face. **B.-gage,** a bevel-square. **B.-pinion,** a small *b.*-wheel, **B.-square,** a tool which may be adjusted to measure or lay out any angle. **B.-wheels,** those working on each other in different planes, their cogs being set at an angle with their shafts; *mitre-wheels.* **Closed b.,** said of an angle-bar when one of its flanges is bent at an acute angle with the other. **Open b.,** as opposed to a closed *b.,* form of an angle-bar when one flange makes an obtuse angle with the other.

Standing b., an obtuse bevel. **Under b.,** an acute bevel.

BEWITCHED, WATER. *See* WATER.

B/H. Bill of Health; *see* BILL.

B.H.P. Brake horse-power; *see* **Brake hp** *in* HORSE-POWER.

BIB-COCK. Same as bibb-cock; *see* COCK.

BIBB. Cleat or bracket bolted to the hounds of a lowermast as a support to the trestle-trees. A *bibb-cock.*

BIDAR. BIDARRA. *See* BAIDAR.

BIDARKA. *See* BAIDARKA. Also, *bidarkee.*

BID-HOOK. A kind of small boat-hook.

BIG-EYED HERRING. *See* ELOPS.

BIG POND. *See* POND.

BIGHT. A small bay in a seacoast; bend in a coast-line. Loop or turn in a rope, as distinct from its ends. To fold or double so as to make one or more *bights,* as a bighted sail or hawser. *Biglet.* **Bight-seam,** *see* SEAM. **B.-splice,** ends of two ropes respectively spliced into each other's standing part, thus forming an eye or collar in a single rope; used to place over a boom end for guying purposes, over a mast as in light shrouds, etc.; *cont-splice, cut-splice.*

BIGLET. Part of a rope sling through which its hooking-on part is passed when slinging a draft. *Bight.*

BILALO. Two-masted passenger-boat about 65 feet in length, fitted with an outrigger and having a cabin abaft her mainmast; peculiar to Manila Bay.

BILANDER. (Du. *bijlander.*) Former type of hoy peculiar to Holland coast and canals, having two masts, square-rigged with a mainsail shaped similarly to a lateen. *Bylander.*

BILBO. A long bar or bolt of iron with sliding shackles, once used as a fetter on board ship. A rapier or sword, originally of Bilbao, Spain.

BILGE. Part of a ship's hull extending outward from her keel to a point where her sides rise vertically. Lowest portion of a vessel inside her hull; spaces at sides of double-bottom tanks next to the shell, commonly called the *bilges.* To seriously damage a vessel's bottom; to cause to leak in a bilge. *Bulge.* **B.-and-contline;** *see* CONTLINE. **Bilged,** to be stove in or holed in a bilge or bottom. **Bilging,** said of white paint which has turned to a yellowish tint; *non-bilging* paint refers to white paint guaranteed to withstand bilging. **B.-blocks,** supporting blocks under a ship's bilges during construction or dry-docking. **B.-boards,** movable planks covering bilges or *limbers* where bilge-water collects. **B.-**

bracket, same as *wing bracket; see* BRACKET. **B.-chest,** iron box enclosing valves and manifold of a bilge-pumping system. **B.-diagonal,** in shipbuilding drawings, a longitudinal plane extending from the midship center line at load-line level to turn of bilge, shown as a straight line on body plan and as a curve on half-breadth plan. **B.-discharge pipe,** line for conveying bilge-water overboard from a bilge-pump. **B.-ejector,** apparatus for forcing bilge-water overboard, usually on steam-siphon principle. **B. free,** said of a cask stowed clear of adjacent objects and resting only on beds or quoins at its quarters. **B.-injection,** arrangement whereby, in cases of emergency, a ship may be freed of water by taking it through her main condenser circulating system. **B.-inlet,** an aperture in bottom plating, controlled by a sea-cock, through which a ballast tank, boiler, etc., may be filled with sea water. **B. intercostal keelson,** line of plates fitted on edge in a fore-and-aft direction and between floors for greater part of a ship's length immediately below the turn of her bilge. **B. intercostal plates,** those which form a bilge intercostal keelson. **B. intercostal stringer,** a longitudinal fitted across and between frames, and secured to the shell-plating just above the bilge. **B. keel,** a fin or line of timbers or plating set perpendicular to a vessel's shell, along her bilges for about two-thirds her length, as a brake against rolling; fitted on each side and usually called *rolling-chocks.* **B.-keelson,** in older construction, a heavy timber or I-beam laid over floors in each wing parallel with keel, as a longitudinal strength unit; *bilge-piece.* **B.-log,** one of several timbers forming a launching-cradle which is built to support the finer lined ends of a ship during her launching. **B.-plank,** a strengthening plank laid round inside or outside of a ship at the turn of her bilge. **B.-plate,** one of the curved shell-plates at turn of bilge. **B.-pump,** one used to remove water from bilges. **B.-shores,** stout timbers placed in way of a vessel's bilges as supports in dry-dock. **B.-strake,** line of outside plating at turn of bilge; in large ships somewhat heavier than ordinary shell-plating. **B.-suction pipe,** pipe through which bilge-water is drawn to a bilge-pump. **B. tank,** *see* TANK. **B.-water,** that collected in bilges; it may be traced to leakage in a ship's shell or piping, condensation, drainage from liquid cargo, or rain. **B.-well,** lowest part of a compartment into which bilge-water naturally drains; in large vessels, sometimes occupies entire space between two adjacent floors; a *strum* or strainer is fitted therein to cover the end of a bilge-suction pipe. **B. and ballast system,** arrangement of piping and pumps located in a vessel's hold and used for pumping overboard accumulations of water in holds and compartments and for filling or emptying ballast and peak tanks. **Turn of the b.,** curved portion of ship's bottom where it turns from horizontal to the vertical, or nearly so.

BILGEWAYS. Lengthwise members of a cradle which slide on the stepways in launching a ship. Paths over which bilge-blocks may be hauled in placing them for dry-docking a vessel.

BILL. Point of an anchor's fluke, also called the *pea.* End of a curved timber or knee. Any written statement of particulars. **B. of adventure,** a writing made by a shipper of goods or common carrier showing that shipment is a venture of another person and that shipper or carrier is responsible for nothing but delivery of goods as consigned. **B. of entry,** a detailed report of goods for importation or for export as required by a customs collector. **B. of health,** certificate signed by a consul of country to which a vessel belongs, or other competent authority at a foreign port, stating certain health conditions existed at the port at time of ship's departure. The bill is referred to as *clean, suspected,* or *foul.* A *clean bill* signifies that no infectious disorder was known to exist; a *suspected bill,* that there were rumors of such a disorder, but, it had not appeared; a *foul bill,* or absence of a clean bill, that such place of departure was infected. **B. of lading,** customarily abbreviated *B/L,* a document issued by a shipping company, shipowner, or agent of either, to a shipper stating that certain goods received for shipment are promised to be delivered at a specified port either to the carrier's agent or to a particular consignee. Usually 3 or 4 copies are signed, one each being kept by carrier and shipper, and a third forwarded to consignee. As with all other types of B/L, legal importance of this maritime document lies in its being a receipt for goods, a contract for carriage, and a title to property, by which last-named quality it also becomes a negotiable instrument. *Order B/L,* with shipper's endorsement, is required by a carrier upon delivery of goods in accordance with terms specified. *Order-Notify B/L,* enables a shipper to collect for his shipment before its destination is reached. This is done by forwarding original bill with a draft payable by consignee through a bank. The drawee, or party to whom delivery is made, receives the B/L upon payment of draft and surrenders same to carrier's agent as evidence of title to goods concerned. When forwarding goods on this form of lading, it is customary for a shipper to consign his shipment to be delivered only upon his order, naming a firm or person to be notified upon its arrival. *Straight B/L,* a non-negotiable bill, prescribing delivery direct to a specified consignee. A carrier does not require its surrender upon delivery of goods unless identification of consignee be necessary. *Through B/L,* an order and ocean bill combined; a contract of carriage by rail and ocean carrier, subject to similar negotiable features as a *port* or *ocean B/L,* as the usual bill is termed in ocean freighting. *Uniform B/L,* states a carrier has received certain goods which he agrees to transport and to deliver to a designated person or his assigns for such compensation and upon such conditions as are indicated. For *bills* designated by captioned word see PORTAGE; STATION; VICTUALLING.

BILLBOARD. Same as *anchor-lining.* Also, a support upon which an anchor's flukes rest when stowed on deck.

BILLET. Space allotted a navy seaman for his hammock; assignment of quarters. A bar of metal in the rough. **B.-head,** a round upright piece of hard wood fixed in a whale-boat's bow or stern for controlling a harpoon-line; also termed *bollard, loggerhead,* and *snubbing-post.*

BILL-FISH. Any of those pelagic fishes having long slender jaws, as the *saury* and *gar;* a sail-fish; a spear-fish.

BILLYBOY. A flat-bottomed, bluff-bowed barge having a mast hinged to her deck to facilitate lowering when about to pass under a bridge; peculiar to the *Humber River* on east coast of England. Former sea-going billyboys were usually clinker-built and schooner-rigged, many carrying a square topsail and lee-boards.

BILOXI MEAN GULF LEVEL. A tidal datum at Biloxi, Mississippi, of 0.78 foot above *mean level* of the Mississippi River at its mouths.

BINDING. Old term for beams, transoms, knees, wales, keelson, and other chief timbers connecting and strengthening various parts of a vessel's structure. Iron link enclosing a dead-eye. **B.-strake,** a thick strake of side or deck planking; one of the *wales* or *bends; see* BENDS; STRAKE.

BINNACLE. A stand or case for housing, lighting, facilitating steering use of a compass, and/or for taking bearings or azimuths. *B's* differ in shape and size, depending upon size and type of compass accommodated and where it is used. One for a *navigating compass* essentially consists of a pedestal at whose upper end is a bowl-shaped receptacle having a removable cover. Such receptacle contains a set of gimbals in which the compass is fixed and suspended. A **compensating-b.** is provided with a soft iron cylinder or sphere on each side of the compass space for correcting *quadrantal deviation,* a receptacle for a Flinders bar on its fore side, and necessary means of setting fore-and-aft and athwartship magnets directly below the compass for correcting its *semi-circular deviation.* (Since an iron or steel vessel receives magnetic induction from the earth according to well-known laws, consequent errors in her compasses must be corrected by appropriate means for counteracting causes of such errors) This type of b. may be used for a *steering-compass,* or may be fixed as a *standard compass,* by which courses are set at sea, and is usually so placed that a clearest possible all-round view is available in order to facilitate taking bearings and observations for determining compass error. A compensating-*b.* is always placed in the vertical plane of a vessel's fore-and-aft line. **B.-list,** daily sick list on a naval vessel, formerly placed in the *b.* for information of officer of the deck. **B.-light,** *see* LIGHT.

BINOCULARS.   Marine glasses; a pair of small telescopes joined so as to be adaptable to use of both eyes.

BIORLINN.   *See* BIRLIN.

BIRCH.   Any tree of the species *Betula,* which produces a valuable timber extensively used in shipbuilding, especially for finished exterior parts such as rails, coamings, margin-strakes, bitts, and housesills. It is hard, tough, close-grained, and takes a fine polish; weight about 47 lbs. per cubic foot. Also, a *birch-bark canoe.*

BIRD'S NEST.   Same as *crow's nest.* Distended strands in a wire rope caused by a kink.

BIREME.   *See* GALLEY.

BIRLIN.   A historic chief's barge or galley used in the Hebrides and Scottish Isles, rowed with four to eight long oars and seldom furnished with sails. *Berlin, berling, birlinn, biorlinn. (Gaelic)*

BIRNEY GEAR.   Otter gear. *See* PARAVANE.

BIRTH.   *See* BERTH.

BIRTH-MARKS.   Same as *Plimsoll marks.*

BISCUIT.   Flat cakes, unfermented, and baked hard so as to keep sound for a long time; used on long voyages by seamen. *Hard tack. Liverpool pantile; sea-biscuit.* **B. tin,** an airtight galvanized iron container for life-boats' emergency rations. **Captain's b.,** *see* CAPTAIN.

BISHOP'S RING.   *See* RING.

BIT or **BITTEN.**   *See* WEATHER.

BITE.   To take hold of, *e.g.,* an anchor *bites* the ground.

BITT.   Strong short post of wood or iron, usually fastened to a deck in pairs and named according to their use, as, *riding-bitts, towing-bitts, mooring-bitts,* etc. To fasten round bitts. To **bitt the cable,** *see* CABLE. **Belaying-b.,** *see* BELAY. **B.-head,** upper part of a bitt. **B.-pin,** a pin through the head of a bitt or bollard to prevent a line from slipping off. **B.-stopper,** short piece of rope or chain for holding a hawser while bitting or unbitting. **Double-b.,** *see* DOUBLE. **Pawl-b.,** stout upright timber to which windlass pawls are fixed. **Quarter-b's,** same as *towing-b's.* **Rouse and b.,** *see* ROUSE. **Sheet-b's,** *see* SHEET. **Side b.,** (of a windlass), *see* SIDE. **Weather b.,** *see* WEATHER. **Windlass-b.,** one of two bitts between which an old-fashioned windlass was framed; also used singly for securing hawsers, etc.

BITTER.   Turn of a hawser round a pair of bitts. **B. end,** last part to hand of a length of rope; last link in a chain.

BITUMASTIC. (L. *bitumen.*)   Black tarlike composition largely of bitumen or asphalt, with ingredients as resin, portland cement, slaked lime, petroleum, or pine tar; used as a protective coating in ballast-tanks, chain-lockers, shaft-tunnels, bilges, etc. As an adjective, pertaining to any bituminous cement or paint. *See* ASPHALT.

BIVALVE.   Any mollusk having its shell in two valves or parts, as the *oyster, clam,* and *mussel.*

B/L.   Bill of lading; *see* BILL.

BLACK.   To blacken; as to *black down* or *tar down* a ship's rigging. **Black asphaltum,** same as *b. japan* or *japan b.* **B.-backed gull,** *see* GULL. **B. book,** *see* BOOK. **B. bottle,** in U.S. navy, a bottle containing any dark-colored meat sauce. **B. Current,** *see* KUROSHIWO. **B. flag,** *see* FLAG. **B. gang,** *see* GANG. **B. jack,** a pirate's ensign. **B. japan,** *see* JAPAN. **B. lead,** graphite or plumbago, a dark-colored mineral used to lubricate sheaves in blocks. **B. list,** on naval vessels, names of delinquents to whom extra duty is assigned as punishment. **B. Sea mooring,** *see* MOORING. **B. squall,** a blast of wind accompanied by heavy dark clouds. **B. strake,** strake of planking just above the *wales,* in former naval construction. **B. Stream,** same as *Black Current.* **B. whale,** *see* BLACKFISH. To **fly the b. flag,** *see* FLY.

BLACK BALL.   Distinguishing mark of a line of sailing packets (*circa 1850–1880*) in the North Atlantic trade, which was a large black disc painted on the fore-topsail's fore side.

BLACKFISH.   *Globicephala melas,* or *caaing-* or *pilot-whale* of the North Atlantic, a toothed cetacean of about 20 feet in length; usually found in large schools and often confused with the *grampus,* a smaller member of same family. Any of several *fishes* so called from their color.

BLANK BOLT.   *See* BOLT.

BLANK FLANGE.   *See* FLANGE.

BLANKET.   In sailing, to take the wind out of another's sails by passing close on her weather side on an overtaking course. **B. boat,** *see* BOAT. **B. lee,** a snug berth. **B.-piece,** section of blubber cut from a whale in a spiral direction; blubber unwound or stripped from the carcase before sub-dividing for oil-extracting process.

BLARE.   A paste of hair and tar used for calking material in boat seams.

BLASH.   A sudden fall of rain. Watery.

BLAST.   Strong squall or sudden wind. Discharge of an explosive. Sound made by a wind instrument or a steam whistle; *see* SIGNAL. **B.-cock,** a cock fitted to a blast-pipe. **Short b.,** *see* SHORT.

BLAZE AWAY, To. To fire away; keep on firing, as from guns or artillery. **Like blazes,** furiously.

BLEED. To drain off water or other liquid from tanks, pipes, etc. To **b. a buoy,** to drain water from a leaking buoy.

BLEEDER. Small cock or valve for draining a range of piping. A bleeder-pipe. **B.-plug,** screw-plug in a ship's bottom for draining a double-bottom tank or bilges while in dry-dock; also, *bleeder.*

BLIND. In former naval usage, a strong plank shutter placed across a gun-port immediately after a gun was discharged. **B.-buckler,** *see* BUCKLER. **B. holes,** term for rivet holes when they are unfair or misfits. **B. lead,** a break in an ice field indicating a channel but through which no passage is found. **B. pulley,** a deadeye. **B. rollers,** *see* ROLLERS. **B. stitch,** one taken in under side of a fabric and thus hidden from its fair side.

BLINK. Light reflected from ice at sea; *ice-blink. Land-blink* appears over distant snow or ice-covered land.

BLINKER. Flashing lamp or lamps usually fixed on a bridge or mast, by which communication with other ships or shore is made by Morse code signals. *Blinker signal.*

BLIRT. Gust of wind and rain.

BLISTER. A flaw in iron found in plates and flat bars. An outer skin built on a vessel's hull to increase beam or provide tank space. An air or water chamber built to the lower outside part of a warship's hull for protection from torpedo attack; may be constructed over entire underbody, or may extend only a few feet below her water-line.

BLIZZARD. Gale or hurricane accompanied by intense cold and driving snow. General discharge of guns; a rattling volley; a general *blazing away.*

BLOCK. A mechanical device for moving an object by means of a rope or chain leading over its contained sheave or sheaves; made up of the following primary parts: A frame (*shell*) of wood or steel fitted with one or more *sheaves* (pulleys) made of wood or metal; a *pin* on which the sheaves rotate; and a *strap* (strop) of fiber rope, wire, or steel. Its secondary parts are *swallow, becket, cringle,* and *hook* or *shackle.* Blocks receive different names depending upon their shape, purpose, or place on board ship and are termed *single, double, treble,* or *4-fold,* according to number of sheaves contained. In the early 1800's, to fit out a full-rigged ship of the line about 800 blocks were required which ranged in size from 8-inch (*length of shell*) to those of 30 inches weighing 100 lbs. or more. At that time, the block-making craft was an important one, since fighting-ships and merchantmen being sail-driven, blocks controlled their source of power and amounted to considerable cost. With the later ad-

vent of clipper-ships and their tall delicate rig, weight of blocks aloft became of greater concern and steps to reduce their bulk without sacrificing strength were necessary. Results undoubtedly produced our present lighter wooden-shelled block with its enclosed steel strop. The term *block* also is given a temporary support or shore; and a solid piece of wood, metal, or other material. **Angle-b.,** *see* ANGLE. **Bee-b.,** or **bee,** a grooved solid piece of hardwood or iron through which a stay's lower end is rove for setting up. **Bilge-b.,** *see* BILGE. **B. and b.,** two blocks of a tackle drawn together so that no further movement is possible. **B. and tackle,** two blocks with necessary rope rove through them ready for use. **B. coefficient,** ratio which underwater body volume bears to a rectangular solid having its length, breadth, and depth respectively equal to a vessel's length, greatest breadth at her water-line, and her mean draft. **B.-model,** *see* MODEL. **B.-ship,** a ship blocking a harbor entrance. An old hulk used as a store or receiving-ship in a navy yard. **B.-stopper,** short piece of rope made fast on a block for temporarily taking the stress on its *fall* (rope rove through block) while its working-end is transferred to a winch, belaying-pin, etc. **B.-truck,** a 3 or 4-wheeled hand truck used for moving heavy objects. **Bollock b.,** *see* BOLLOCK. **Breech-b.,** *see* BREECH. **Building-b.,** one of many supports on which a ship's keel and lower structure rests while building; any heavy block of wood used under a ship as a support. **Cargo-hoist b.,** usually a heavy single-sheave block having a swivel-hook or swivel-shackle securing it aloft, which permits it to adjust itself to leading direction of the fall. **Cat-b.,** used to hoist an anchor to a cathead. **Chain-hoist b.,** one in an endless chain hoist, usually confined to engine-room work, such as raising cylinder-heads, pumps, turbine casings, etc.; principal types are the *spur-geared, screw-geared,* and *differential.* **Cheek-b.,** one fitted against a spar, davit, rail, etc., having a half shell, part of the objects mentioned in way of the block acting as its other *cheek* or half shell. **Clewline b.,** one at a masthead for leading a clewline of a square sail from a yard. **Clump-b.,** a strongly made hoisting-block with extra heavy sheaves. **Dasher-b.,** one at a gaff end for the ensign halyard. **Dead-b.,** *see* DEAD. **Deck-b.,** *see* DECK. **Differential b.,** one having two or more sheaves of different diameters. **Differential chain b.,** *see* CHAIN-HOIST B. **Dock b.,** one secured to a dock as a lead for a cargo-fall when power is supplied from such dock. **Fall-b.,** *see* FALL. **Fiddle-b.,** one having two sheaves of different diameters above each other in a common plane. **Fish-b.,** *see* FISH. **Fly-b.,** the moving block in which the hauling part of a fall works in a purchase of Spanish burton type. **Gin b.,** a skeleton iron frame fitted with a metal sheave, used as a cargo hoisting or lead block. **Guide b.,** *see* GUIDE. **Halyard b.,** one through which a halyard (*halliard*) is rove; such are named from duty they serve, as *signal-halyard b., topsail halyard b.,* etc. **Hawse-b.,** *see* HAWSE. **Head b.,** cargo-hoisting block at a boom head. **Heart-b.,** *see* HEART. **Heel b.,** one acting as a fair-lead to a winch, placed at a cargo-boom's lower end. **Hoisting-b.,** lower one of a tackle used for hoisting. **Horse-b.,** *see* HORSE. **Jack b.,** formerly one kept aloft for hoisting and lowering top-gallant yards. **Jeer-b.,** *see* JEER. **Jewel-b.,** small single block at a yard-arm through which studding-sail halyards were led; any small single block in which signal halyards are rove, as at end of a signal yard or a gaff. **Jigger-b.,** *see* TAIL-BLOCK. **Keel-b.,** *see* KEEL. **Leading-b.,** a lead block, or one guiding a rope in a direction required. **Link-b.,** a piece of metal, usually of a high grade steel, used to transmit motion from links to valve-stems in a reciprocating engine. **Long tackle-b.,** one having two sheaves in the same plane and above each other. **Monkey b.,** one used to guide running rigging. **Mooring-b.,** a mooring clump; *see* MOORING. **Mortise-b.,** one fashioned from a solid piece of wood. **Nib-b.,** one of iron having a fixed hook which keeps it from turning. **Ninepin b.,** one made like a ninepin, used as a fair-lead on a narrow rail or stanchion. **Non-toppling b.,** a running block in a tackle, so designed as to remain upright, or nearly so, when fall is hanging slack. Those of boat-tackles usually are of this type. **Notch b.,** same as *snatch-b.* **Patent b.,** one in which its sheave or sheaves turn on roller bearings. **Plummer-b's,** wooden structural blocks which support a propeller-shaft. **Purchase b.,** one having two or more sheaves, used in a tackle for lifting or moving heavy weights. **Purse-b.,** *see* PURSE. **Quarter-b's,** those fixed at or near the quarters of yards on a square-rigged vessel as leads for clewlines or leechlines when taking in sail. Blocks acting as fair-leads for tiller-ropes or chains in steering-gear. **Rack-b.,** *see* RACK. **Return-b.,** same as *snatch-b.* **Rouse-about b.,** large all-round duty *snatch-b.* **Running b.,** one which moves in a tackle, or which moves with an object to which it is attached while hoisting or shifting same. **Secret-b.,** one in which the sheave is hidden, its rope being led through holes in its base; made to prevent other ropes or gear from fouling the sheave. **Shoe b.,** one of those in old square-riggers fitted under a top's fore side as buntline-blocks for a course; its sheaves were set at right angles to each other; a *sole-block.* **Shoulder b.,** one having a projection on its shell as a guide to the rope rove in it. **Sister-b.,** *see* SISTER. **Slide b.,** *see* SLIDE. **Snatch-b.,** one in which an opening in its shell permits placing a rope directly over its sheave without reeving; used as a temporary lead to a winch or capstan for warping-lines, halyards, etc. **Sole-b.,** a heavy flat piece of wood placed under the heel of a gin, a sheer-leg, or a scaffolding pole, as a shoe to prevent such spar from sinking into the ground, or to increase its bearing surface; also termed a *shole* or *shoe.* **Span-b.,** *see* SPAN. **Speck-b.,** in whaling, a block in which a speck-fall is rove. (*Speck* refers to whale-fat or blubber) **Spring b.,** on sailing yachts, an inboard sheet-block connected to an elastic fitting such as a spiral spring. **Standing b.,** a *fixed,* as opposed to a *running,* block. **Swage-b.,** a heavy cast iron block having holes and grooves of various sizes and shapes, used in forging; a *swage.* **Swivel-b.,** *see* SWIVEL. **Tack-b.,** one used for securing the tack of a square or lateen sail. **Tackle b.,** one in a purchase tackle. **Tail-b.,** one having its strop elongated and forming a *tail* which may be used to make fast such block in any required position. **Telegraph-b.,** one through which several signal halyards are rove, its shell being long and narrow with sheaves vertically above each other. **Thick-and-thin b.,** one having two sheaves of different thickness to accommodate two sizes of rope. **Threefold-b.,** one having three sheaves; a *treble* block. **Thrust-b.,** a solid metal support having several grooves in which a thrust-shaft's collars revolve, and which bears the *thrust* of a screw propeller. **Top-b's** of main bearings, those holding a shaft down in its bearings. **Treble b.,** a three-fold *b.* **Two b's,** same as *b. and b.* **Tye-b.,** tie-b., one fixed at the middle of a yard and in which the *tye* is rove as part of the hoisting-gear for such yard. **Viol-b.,** *see* VIOL. **Warping-b.,** one used by rope-makers in twisting rope-yarns. **Wrecking b's,** heavy duty blocks such as are used in salvage work for heaving on anchors, heavy lifting, etc.

BLOCKADE. Investment of a port by a hostile naval force debarring it from communication by sea. To **raise a b.,** to end such a situation by either withdrawing blockading ships or by driving off the enemy. To **run a b.,** to pass through a *b'ing* squadron by force or by stealth in entering or leaving a *b'd* port.

BLOOMERS. Canvas cover for a large gun.

BLOW. A violent blowing or blast of wind; a gale, as a *northeast blow.* To exhaust or expel, as steam or water under pressure. **B.-cock,** a cock in a blow-off pipe; also, *b.-down, b.-off,* or *b.-out cock;* a surface *b.-off cock,* or *scum cock.* To **b. great guns,** to *b.* furiously, as a strong gale. To **b. heads and points,** to run in all directions, spouting and blowing in great confusion; said of a gam of whales when attacked. **B.-hole,** one of a pair or a single nostril of a cetacean, opening from highest part of its head. In baleen whales, *b.-holes* are two longitudinal slits side by side; in the dolphin, grampuses, porpoises, and their larger toothed cousins, there is a single crescent-shaped opening. Also, an *ice-hole* to which seals, walrus, etc., come to breathe; a *breathing-hole.* To **b. in,** to spend foolishly, as one's wages. **B.-off valve,** *see* VALVE. To **b. the gaff,** to blab; to disclose a secret. **B.-through pipe,** that through which steam enters a condenser in expelling the air previous to starting engine. To **b. up,**

to increase in force, as a rising gale. **Side-b.,** strong wind on the beam.

BLOWER. A power-driven, encased fan that supplies a current of air to machinery or other enclosed spaces and, also, forced draft to boiler furnaces.

BLOWN UP. An old stevedore term referring to a cargo so stowed as to raise its center of gravity above that of ordinary stowage.

BLUBBER. Layer of oil-yielding fat beneath the skin of whales and other cetaceans, which amounts to from 40 to 50 hundredweight in a large whale. A large jelly-fish. **B.-guy,** in old sailing whalers, rope stretched between masts and to which was attached a purchase for turning a whale's carcase during process of *flensing,* or stripping off blubber. Various self-explanatory terms were used for articles of equipment employed in procuring and preparing *b.* for the boiling stage on board, such as *b.-chain, b.-fork, b.-gaff, b.-hook, b.-knife, b.-spade, b.-tackle,* etc. Modern whalers are constructed and equipped to heave a carcase aboard, where formerly *b.* was cut from whale as it lay alongside ship. **B.-room,** compartment in old-time whaler's hold for temporarily stowing *b.; cf.* ROOM. To **fill the b.-room;** *see* ROOM. **B.-toggle, b.-fid,** *see* FID.

BLUE. Color of clear sky, or a hue resembling it; as, *deep blue sea.* An admiral's rank in British 17th. century use, akin to that of our present rear-admiral; as *admiral of the blue.* **B. Book,** articles for government of U.S. navy; familiarly known as *Rocks and Shoals.* **B. crab,** popular food crab of U.S. Atlantic coast. The *soft-shelled* variety of the species is so called because of having recently begun growing its new shell. **B. ensign,** *see* ENSIGN. **B'fish,** name of many different kinds of fishes from their bluish color. That of the U.S. Atlantic coast, so important as a food fish in America, is found in many other waters of the globe; it is 4 to 5 lbs. in weight and grows to about 20 inches in length. **B'jacket,** a navy seaman as distinguished from a marine. **B. light,** *see* LIGHT. **B. magnetism,** property of south-seeking in *south pole* of magnet; *cf.* MAGNETISM. **B.-nose,** a Nova Scotia vessel; a native of Nova Scotia, so named from the *bluenose* potato which flourishes in that province. **B. ointment,** greasy preparation containing about 30% mercury, used on Diesel engine bearings as a lubricant. An unguent included in a ship's medicine chest for exterminating crab lice. **B. peter,** *see* P. **B. pigeon,** traditional term for the hand *sounding-lead.* **B. ribbon,** in trans-Atlantic shipping circles, a liner making fastest passages is said to hold the *blue ribbon.* **B. shark,** *see* SHARK. **B. water man,** a deep-water, or ocean, sailor, as distinguished from a *coaster* or *mud-walloper.* **B. whale,** the fin-back, or sulphur-bottom whale; also called *rorqual,* from Norwegian *rörhval,* or red

whale, so named from reddish streaks in its skin; *see* WHALE.

BLUFF. Precipitous lofty headland on a sea-coast. **B.-bowed,** said of a vessel having a broad and full form at her bows. **B.-headed,** in ship form descriptive, having an upright stem, or one with little or no rake forward.

BOARD. To go into or on board a vessel; to embark. To hail and enter a ship officially, as in the course of a customs officer's duties. To come alongside, fall aboard of, or enter a vessel by force or in a hostile manner. The vessel herself, as in the phrase *on board.* Course on which a ship sails between each time of coming about, or tacking. In older usage, to tack. **Air-course b.,** *see* AIR. **B. and b.,** or **b. on b.,** situation of two vessels sailing close to each other on parallel courses. **B'ing book,** in navy usage, a note-book in which an officer records data from a vessel boarded. **B. measure,** commercial unit is a *board foot,* which is 1 foot square, 1 inch in thickness; thus, product of width in inches by thickness in inches by length in feet, divided by 12, gives total *board feet* in a piece of square sawn lumber. Also, since 1 cubic foot contains 12 *board feet,* a block of lumber containing a given number of cubic feet, when multiplied by 12, gives total *board feet* in the pile. To **b. the tack,** in a square-rigged vessel, to heave down and secure the tack of a course (lowest square sail) after bringing ship close to the wind. **Float-b.,** one of the fins or *boards* in a paddle-wheel. **General B. of Navy,** *see* NAVY. **Go by the b.,** to be completely destroyed or carried away; act of a mast breaking off at, or a short distance above, the deck. To **make a b.,** to sail a stretch on a tack when head-reaching, or working to windward. To **make a good b.,** to get well on in a stretch to windward, sailing close-hauled. To **make a half b.,** to luff into the wind until headway is nearly lost and then fill away on same tack; a *pilot's luff.* **make short b's,** to tack frequently. To **make stern-b.,** to force a ship astern by her sails, as in the initial stage of *box-hauling.* **Mitch-b.,** fork or crutch for supporting a boom in stowed position. **Name-b.,** place or board on which ship's name is painted or carved. **Paddle-b.,** float of a water-wheel or a paddle-wheel; a *float-b.* **Race-b.,** a gang-plank. **Retiring b.,** a body of army or navy officers reporting on incapacity of personnel for active service. **Scrive b.,** in shipbuilding, large section of mold-loft floor on which lines of the body are laid out for making various patterns or templates for beams, frames, floor-plates, etc.; also, *scrieve b.* (The following caption-words also are combined with *board* in various terms: ARCH; BEVEL; BILGE; BOTTOM; BREAST; CHAFING; HEAD; LAND; LEE; LIMBER; QUARTER; SENTRY; SERVING; SHIFTING; SPRAY; STERN; SURF; TACKLE; TALLY; THOLE; TRADE; TRAIL; TRANSOM; TRAVERSE; WAIST; WASH; WEATHER; WING.)

BOARD OF ADMIRALTY. *See* ADMIRALTY.

BOARDAGE. Planking on a ship's side; area of same above water.

BOARDER. Member of an armed unit detailed to board an enemy.

BOARDING. Act of going on board a vessel or boat. **B.-knife,** a blubber-knife; *see* KNIFE. **B.-netting,** a strong wire or rope net which once was raised above and along the bulwarks as a safeguard against boarders. **B.-pike,** a wooden spear-like weapon having a sharp point usually of iron, formerly used in boarding or repelling boarders during hostilities.

BOAT. Term usually given to small craft, although lake, river, and excursion vessels, also ferries, regardless of build or means of propulsion, are generally called *boats*. As distinguished from a *vessel*, a boat has no continuous deck, while an old wooden construction distinction states that a boat is built with *bent* frames and a ship or vessel with *sawn* or *hewn* frames. To transport in a *b*. To place in a *b.*, as *boat the oars*. To traverse in a *b.*, as a lake. To go in a *b.*; row, sail, navigate. **Advice-b.,** a small vessel employed to carry orders or messages with all possible speed. **Ballast-b.,** *see* BALLAST. **Barra b.,** one of V-shaped cross section and extremely sharp at each end, peculiar to the Hebrides and Scottish Isles. **Berthon b.,** a collapsible lifeboat formerly carried on naval and passenger vessels. **Blanket-b.,** an improvised *b*. made by stretching a soldier's rubber blanket over a wooden frame. **B.-anchor,** *see* ANCHOR. To **b. a seine,** *see* SEINE. **B.-boom,** *see* BOOM. **B.-car,** a carriage used in a lifesaving service to facilitate launching and transporting a life-boat. **B.-chock,** one of the two beds in which a *b*. rests when stowed on deck. **B.-cloak,** formerly used with full dress by naval officers when being conveyed by *b*. **B.-cloth,** a dark blue covering on the stern sheets of a naval vessel's *b*. used by officers on an official occasion; a lap-robe sometimes used in a *b*. as a protection against spray. **B. compass,** *see* COMPASS. **B. deck,** *see* DECK. **B.-drill,** exercise of a ship's crew in lowering, rowing, sailing, and securing life-boats. **B.-fall,** *see* FALL. **B. gear,** equipment of a *b*. **B.-gripes,** lashings for securing a *b*. when stowed in the chocks. **B. harbor, b. haven,** a protected water area equipped with mooring floats, buoys, etc., for mooring small boats, yachts, etc.; also termed *marina*. **B.-hook,** a staff having at its end a sharp point and a hook, used in holding a *b*. alongside or for fending off, etc.; a *gaff-setter*. **B.-knife,** *see* KNIFE. **B.-load,** a boat's capacity; a load carried in a *b*. To **b. oars,** *see* OAR. **B. rivets,** copper or galvanized iron fastenings, principally used in securing planking to the frames; made in sizes from three-sixteenths inch to three-eighths inch in diameter with heads similar to those of carriage-bolts; inboard ends are burred over appropriate

sized washers of same metal. **B.-skids,** *see* SKID. **B.-tackles,** purchases by which boats are hoisted or lowered. **B. stowage,** arrangement provided on board ship for stowing life-boats and facilitating their launching. **B.-thwarts,** thwartship boards which are used as seats for oarsmen and which act as stiffeners for the *b.'s* sides. **B.-tiller,** piece of wood or metal bar attached to a rudder-head, by which rudder is turned in steering a *b*. **B.-yoke,** a crosspiece of wood set on the rudder-head to which two steering-ropes (*yoke-lines*) are attached for steering a *b.*; used where a tiller may be unhandy. **Bowser b.,** vessel equipped with tanks in which to carry gasoline for refueling seaplanes. **Bunder-b.,** in the Far East, a vessel plying between a *bunder* or trading center and other vessels lying off shore. A Bombay *surf-b*. fitted with a cabin and a lateen sail. **Chebacco-b.,** formerly a New England full-bowed, decked, two-masted craft employed in cod and mackerel fishing; the square-sterned type was called a *dogbody* and that having a sharp stern, a *pinkstern*. **Diving-b.,** one fitted with necessary equipment for carrying on diving or submarine work. **Fast b.,** old whaling term for a boat attached by harpoon line to a whale, as opposed to a *loose b*. **Foy b.,** in England, a Tyneside name for a small boat engaged in assisting vessels, as in mooring, piloting, provisioning, etc. **Inland b.,** a vessel suitably constructed for inland navigation, *i.e.*, on canals, rivers, and small lakes. **Loose b.,** whaleboat unattached to a whale, as opposed to a *fast b*. (*q.v.*) **Paddy b.,** craft used in Ceylon and India for carrying rice and other commodities. **Picket b.,** a scouting or guard boat. **Pratique b.,** one used by a port quarantine officer for boarding vessels. **Pulling b.,** one propelled by oars only, as distinguished from any other which is not limited to such means of propulsion. **Shell b.,** a very light, long, narrow *pulling-b*. for racing; a *shell*. **Smug b.,** a contraband craft on the China coast; an *opium b*. **Sneak-b.,** a small punt or flat-bottomed *b*. propelled by oars or hand paddle-wheels and suitably camouflaged so that hunters may steal upon wild fowl unobserved; also, *sneak-box*. **Surf b.,** one built with necessary strength and buoyancy for passing through surf. **Tag b.,** a *rowing-b*. customarily made fast to the stern of, and towed by, a small vessel. (Other names for *boats* may be found under, and used as combining terms with, following captions: BULL; DREDGE; FERRY; FIRE; GUARD; HAAF; HANG; HATCH; HORSE; HOUSE; ICE; JOLLY; KEEL; LIFE; LIGHT; LONG; MACKINAW; MARK; MASOOLA; MAT; MONKEY; PACKET; PADDLE; PILOT; PITCH; POST; POWER; QUARTER; RUNNING; SEA; SEINE; SINKER; SKIN; SNAG; STRIKER; TRACK; TRAWL; TUG; TWIN; WATER; WHALE; WHEEL.)

BOATAGE. Charge for carriage by boat. Transportation by boat.

BOATER, WAIST. *See* WAIST.

BOATING. Pastime of sailing, paddling, or rowing a boat. The business of transporting goods or passengers by boat. In ancient Persia, a former punishment whereby a prisoner was bound face downward and set adrift in a boat.

BOATMAN. One who works on, manages, sails, or rows a boat. Also, *boatsman*.

BOATSTEERER. In former whaling days, a leading seaman whose duty was to harpoon a whale attacked, after which he exchanged places with the officer who left his steering-oar and went forward to lance the whale at the opportune moment.

BOATSWAIN. A warrant officer in the U.S. and British navies, or a subordinate officer in a merchantman, who is in general charge of ship's deck force, rigging, boats, cargo gear, deck gear, deck stores, and deck maintenance work. A *boatswain-bird*. (*Pron. "bō-sun"*) **B.-bird,** a tropical sea bird of the *phaeton* family, so called by sailors because of its tail feathers' marline-spike form. **B.'s call,** same as *boatswain's pipe*. **B.'s chair,** a standard piece of gear on all ships, consisting of a short board slung by a four-legged bridle and used for sitting in while working aloft, or on the ship's side, lowering a man into a hold, etc. **B.'s chest,** a locker in which are kept boatswain's small stores, such as marline, spun-yarn, needles, palms, splicing gear, etc.; also, *b.'s locker*. **B.'s mate,** a petty officer who is a *b.'s* assistant. In former days it was his duty to administer corporal punishment by flogging as required in certain cases of disciplinary infractions by seamen in the U.S. navy. **B.'s pipe,** or **whistle,** a kind of shrill whistle used by a navy boatswain or his mate in signaling attention to a verbal order about to be given; certain orders are also indicated by particular blasts or toots. Also, *b.'s call*.

BOATWOMAN. A woman who sails or otherwise handles a boat.

BOATWRIGHT. One who builds or repairs boats.

BOB. A cork or float on a fishing-line; also, a small bunch of rags, worms, or feathers concealing a fish-hook or hooks; bait. **Plumb-b.,** a small conical-shaped metal weight suspended by a cord to indicate true perpendicular; also used to measure *ullage* in a ship's oil tank.

BOBSTAY. Rope, chain, or bar from a bowsprit end to the stem for counteracting stress on the head stays due, principally, to pitching motion in a seaway. Frequently two or three are fitted, in which case they are designated *cap* and *inner bobstays,* or *cap, middle,* and *inner*. **B.-holes,** in former wooden ships, holes in upper part of stem by which the head stays were secured. **B.-piece,** a timber fastened to the stem to which a *b.* is secured. **B.-plates,** iron straps by which lower ends of *b.'s* are secured to a ship's stem. **Preventer b.,** *see* PREVENTER.

BODKIN. (M.E. *boydekyn,* a dagger.) A sailmaker's tool for piercing holes in canvas; a *pricker*.

BODY. Hull of a vessel; section of a hull as viewed from any particular angle. **After-b.,** *see* AFTER. **B.-post,** same as *stern-post*. **B. plan,** drawing of a vessel's hull as viewed end on, showing curvature and height of frames at a number of cross-sectional "stations" in the ship's length, which stations are indicated on an accompanying *sheer plan,* or side view of the structure. **Cant-b.,** *see* CANT. **Main b.,** *see* MAIN. **Middle b.,** *see* MIDDLE. **Midship b.,** *see* MIDSHIP.

BOGGIN LINES. *See* LINE.

BOGGLE. To make a bungle or botch of a piece of work. **Boggle-de-botch,** a complete botch or bungle.

BOGUE. To fall off from the wind, or drop off to leeward, as said of some vessels of inferior sailing qualities. To **b. in,** to heartily lend a hand or engage in a work. (*Dial., New England*)

BOILER. A strong metallic tank or vessel in which steam is generated for motive power. Marine boilers are identified as *fire-tube, water-tube,* and *special* types, are further grouped according to design, and may be known either by some special arrangement of their component parts, by an inventor's or a maker's name, or by a combination of both. A circular coral reef has been referred to as a *boiler* because of agitation of its inside water when heavy surf is running. (*Bermudas and West Indies*) **Donkey b.,** a small one used for operating auxiliary and deck machinery, heating plant, etc., independently, as necessary, of main *b's*. **Express b.,** water-tube *b.* designed to get up steam rapidly; largely used on destroyers and other smaller naval craft. **Fire-tube b.,** one in which hot gases from its furnace or combustion-chamber are led to the uptake through tubes around which the water circulates. They have advantage over water-tube types in that: Less damage is done if it becomes necessary to use sea-water; regulation of feed water supply requires less attention; tubular elements give less trouble; are better adapted to handling by transient or below-average firemen. **Haystack b.,** water-tube type having four furnaces and two circulating pockets. **High pressure b.,** usually one designed for a working pressure greater than 150 lbs. per square inch. **Low pressure b.,** one designed for pressures of 50 lbs. or less. **Medium pressure b.,** designed for pressures of 50 to 150 lbs. **Scotch b.,** marine fire-tube type, having a cylindrical shell with internal circular-walled furnaces which are usually corrugated to withstand outside pressure. Hot gases pass to a combustion-chamber at its back end and from there return through tubes to its front end and uptake. Water is kept to a level above tubes and combustion-chamber and occupies all space not taken up by furnaces, tubes, combustion-chamber, stay rods and bolts, and steam space. Large Scotch *b's* may have as many as four furnaces; sometimes are made double-ended, in which case there may be a common, or two separate, combustion-chambers. **Water-tube b.,** in this type flames and hot gases act on outside of tubes through which its water circulates. In connection with the tube system, horizontal drums or headers are installed, in ordinary water-tube boilers, at top and at bottom. Feed water enters the top drum or drums and flows down through tubes to lower drum or drums. It then returns through tubes about which hot gases pass to upper drum where steam accumulates. Water level may be below upper drum or at about half its depth. Tubes may be straight, curved, or bent, but in any case fire is below them, so that flames and hot gases may pass around them in rising. Compared with fire-tube *b's,* the water-tube type has advantage in that: Weight of *b.* and its contained water is less; steam may be generated more quickly; danger of a bad explosion is less; higher steam pressures are easily obtained; arrangement is usually more accessible for cleaning; and less space is occupied in a vessel. **Waste heat b.,** one which generates steam for auxiliary purposes by means of exhaust gases from an internal combustion engine. **Yarrow b.,** named for its inventor, one of water-tube type in which two cylindrical headers are connected by small tubes to a steam dome or cylinder, the whole taking a form like an inverted "V." Water is turned to steam by heat applied about cylinders and tubes. **B. back end plate,** plate at opposite end of a boiler to that at which it is fired. **B. bracing,** installed system of stay-rods, stay-bolts, and stay-tubes for strengthening or supporting a boiler's various surfaces. **B. brackets,** those fitted to a *b.-shell* for holding the *b.* in position. **B.-casing,** a protecting wall or trunk leading from a *b.-room* to *b.-hatch* to keep heat from surrounding deck spaces. **B. chocks,** vertical steel plates fitted at each end of a *b.* to prevent it from moving ahead or astern. **B. clamp,** one used to hold *b.* plates in place while riveting. **B. deck,** *see* DECK. **B. efficiency,** depends principally upon a proper firing system and arrangement of heating surfaces, combined with correct combustion space, to ensure greatest possible economy in use of gases before they enter the stack. Good draft, circulation of water, and clean heating surfaces are also important items. **B. electrolysis,** corrosion or pitting caused by "galvanic action." **B. evaporation,** measure of amount of water evaporated, usually expressed per pound of fuel used or per square foot of heating surface per hour. **B. feedwater,** *see* FEED. **B. firing,** *coal,* no general rule for firing may be stated, since desirable thickness of fire and methods employed vary with quality of fuel, draft, and other conditions. With bituminous coal there are two common methods, *spreading* and

coking. In spreading, fuel is distributed evenly in thin layers over each fire, which necessitates frequent firing. In coking, coal is thrown in the furnace front end, allowed to coke, and is then spread out over entire fire. Ashes, in either case, are usually removed by pulling good coal from the furnace back and clearing fire-bars there; front end good coal is then pushed back and ashes in turn taken from that end. Steam jets are sometimes used in ash-pits to soften clinkers. *Oil firing,* important point is to observe that proper combustion is taking place, which requirement is governed by pressure of the fuel and its proper pre-heating, state of cleanliness of atomizers or *burner tips,* and correct supply of air. Depending somewhat on quality and source of fuel used, satisfactory combustion is indicated by color of flame produced, which varies little from an orange red. Also, color of smoke given off is an indication of combustion quality; little or no smoke being satisfactory; *black smoke,* too little air, carbon deposits, dirty burners, and/or improper atomization; *white smoke,* usually caused by too much air for a proper admixture. **B. foaming,** due to a scum of suspended particles on the water's surface, steam has difficulty in freeing itself and a condition of effervescence or foaming takes place. If not due to organic matter, an excess of boiler compound for water-treating may be its cause. **B. forced draft,** artificial means for producing a desired air pressure through the furnace, or a suction above it, in accordance with rate of combustion required. Blowers and fans are employed to accomplish this. **B. front,** end of a *b.* in which are fitted its furnace doors, gages showing water level and steam pressure, fuel regulating valves, etc. **B. fuel,** *see* FUEL. **B. fuel consumption,** rate is expressed in pounds per square foot of grate surface, heating surface, or indicated horse-power per hour; or in pounds or gallons per mile of distance steamed. **B. funnel,** *see* SMOKESTACK. **B. furnace front,** front end of combustion section of a furnace, usually made of cast iron. The access door or doors are fitted in the "front." **B. hand-hole,** a small elliptical-shaped opening in a *b.* shell providing access for cleaning. Its cover is fitted against and inside the shell and held in position by clamps or a strongback on its outer side. **B. hatch, b. hatchway,** space through which a smokestack passes and which is designed for installation or removal of boilers. Iron gratings are usually fitted around a stack for ventilation purposes, and steel covers which may be closed during bad weather are also fitted. **B. head,** end of a *b.* **B. heating-surface,** sum of internal surface areas of a *b.* which are designed to receive heating action of flames and hot gases from burning fuel. For each indicated horse-power required, due to numerous factors in both engine and boiler design, heating-surface area varies, as, for example, two to five square feet may be necessary in a fire-tube *b.* **B.**

horse-power, *see* HORSE. **B. iron,** rolled iron sheets used in making steam *b's;* from ¼ to ½ inch in thickness with minimum tensile strength of 40,000 lbs. per sq. inch. Thicknesses of shell plates for different steam pressures, in American merchant vessels, are determined according to U.S. Coast Guard rules. **B. keelson,** *see* KEELSON. **B. lagging,** covering of insulating material, such as asbestos or magnesium, fitted over a *b.* to prevent heat radiation. **B. manhole,** hole in a *b.* large enough to admit a man for an examination, cleaning, or repair purposes. Manhole covers and their fittings are of various designs consistent with pressure to which subjected and their easy manipulation. **B. mud-drum,** a cylindrical or rectangular container, located at bottom of a *b.* as remote as possible from its fire, for catching impure water deposit. It is provided with access holes for cleaning out. **B. opening,** same as *b. hatch.* **B. pitting,** corrosion of isolated spots in a *b.* **B. plate,** one of a *b.'s* separate metal sheets. Iron or steel plate for making *b's.* **B. priming,** action which causes water to be carried over into steam lines. Similar to *foaming,* this may be caused by water impurities, too much water, or poor firing generally. **B.-room,** compartment in which *b's* are placed and which accommodates all stoking facilities; located in lowest part of the hull, it may be amidships or in an after section, depending on type of vessel. **B.-room bulkhead,** *see* BULKHEAD. **B. saddles,** structure consisting of appropriately shaped plate girders as a foundation for securing and supporting a cylindrical-shaped *b.;* often referred to as *b. seating.* **B. shell,** plates forming body of a *b.,* exclusive of its end or *head* plates. **B.-stays,** various metal rods, bolts, and braces fitted to support and reinforce shells and heads of *b's* and pressure vessels. These are built inside a *b.* **B. stools,** *see* BEARERS. **B. tubes,** generally, lengths of hollow cylindrical iron or steel, as distinct from ordinary pipe, which form the principal heating surface in, and extend almost entire length of, a *b.* In a fire-tube *b.* smoke and hot gases from the combustion-chamber pass through them to the uptake; in the water-tube type, water circulates in tubes, furnace heat acting directly upon them. Often referred to as *fire-tubes* or *water-tubes.* **B.-water testing apparatus,** a set of beakers, graduated tubes, and chemicals used in analyzing *b.* feed water. **Dry-bottom b.,** *see* DRY.

BOLD. Deep, as water close to a shore; said of waters navigable very near to land, as, "soundings showed *bold water* to the Cape."

BOLLARD. A strong post, usually of iron or steel, to which a mooring-line or hawser may be attached, as in securing or hauling vessels alongside a wharf; any small post or bitt used to slack away or secure a rope, such as a boat-fall; an upright piece of wood or metal in either end of a boat for securing or towing purposes. **B.-timber,** in older wooden

construction, a *knighthead;* one of two timbers rising just within the stem, one on each side of the bowsprit, to which the heel, or inner end, of that spar is secured; *see* APOSTLE.

BOLLOCK. Either of two heavy-shelled blocks formerly fitted at topmasthead, through which a topsail-yard tye was rove; a *bollock-block.*

BOLSTER. Piece of wood, a mat, or canvas placed at a point where a rope rests, to prevent chafing. Pieces of rounded wood placed over the trestle-trees to prevent eyes of standing rigging from chafing; they are said to *bolster* rigging from contact with the trestle-trees' edges. A piece of timber laid across an end of a shore or post to provide greater bearing surface; a temporary foundation. **B.-plate,** piece of plate fitted to a ship's bows adjacent to hawse-pipes to take up chafing of anchor cables. A plate for support in the manner of a pillow or cushion. **Hawse-b's,** *see* HAWSE.

BOLT. A rod of metal employed as a fastening. With few exceptions, such as *drift bolts,* a head or shoulder is made on one end and a screw thread is cut at the other. Bolts are named according to their use, as a *fender-b.;* from their construction, as *double ended b's;* and from method of adjustment, as a *flush b.* To fasten together or make secure as with a bolt. A *bolt-rope.* **Ballast b.,** one used in securing lead or iron ballast to a yacht's keel or bottom. **Barrel-b.,** *see* **Door-b. Blank b.,** an unthreaded *b.* **Carriage-b.,** one having a crowned head and a portion of its shank thereunder squared to hold itself in wood against turning when its nut is set up. Greatly used in building boats of heavier type, *carriage-b's* are made of galvanized iron or steel, or of bronze, and are specially adapted to scarf-fastening in keel timber, gunwales, etc. **Chain-b., chain-plate b.,** *see* CHAIN. **Channel-b's,** *see* CHANNEL. **Check-b.,** *see* CHECK. **Clevis-b.,** one having a forked end; a *Lewis-b.* **Clinched b.,** one having either or both ends turned over and hammered flat against a timber after it is in its place. **Coupling-b.,** a heavy hexagonal or square-headed *b.* used in joining sections of propeller-shafting; usually has a large diameter in proportion to its length; its shank is "machined." **Deck-b.,** one with a flat round head and a square neck used to fasten deck-planking to an iron or steel deck or to a deck-beam. Countersunk in such planking, its head is covered by a *deck-plug.* **Devil-b.,** *see* DEVIL. **Door-b.,** a door lock, consisting of an iron frame with a round sliding-*b.* or "barrel." **Double-armed b.,** long headless *b.* having both ends threaded; also called a *double-ended b.* **Drift b.,** a corrosion-resisting rod, such as one of galvanized iron, bronze, or copper, commonly used in fastening heavier timbers in shipbuilding. Its point is tapered, cold, by blows on an anvil and is driven through a clench-ring into a prepared hole which is slightly less in diameter than that of such bolt. A head is formed on it by hammer blows in driving it home, the clench-ring supplying a required bearing surface against the timber. **Dump-b.,** *see* DUMP. **Eye-b.,** one having an open or loop-shaped end to which a hook, shackle, or rope may be secured, its shank end being threaded to receive a nut, or left smooth for clenching or riveting over. A ring-shaped headed *b.* with a threaded shank for screwing into a cylinder head, turbine casing, etc. as a means for attaching a lifting tackle. **Fender-b.,** one driven into a boat's planking for supporting a fender. **Foot-b.,** one attached to a door and operated by pressure of the foot; used to secure a door when ajar or open. **Forelock b.,** *see* FORELOCK. **Furnace-door b's,** special *b's* used in fastening a door-liner on a furnace door. **Garnish-b.,** one having a chamfered or ornamented head. **Holding-down b.,** a heavy *b.* used to secure an engine or a boiler to its bed. **Hook-b.,** one having a screw-thread and nut at one end and a hook at the other. **In-and-out b.'s,** *see* IN-AND-OUT. **Lag-b.,** a heavy wood-screw having a square head by which it is screwed home by a spanner. Used as a fastener in lighter parts of wood ship construction, it requires a properly bored hole in order to take satisfactory hold of the wood, and is made of corrosion-resisting metal. **Lift-b.,** eye-bolt at a boom end or yard-arm for securing a topping-lift. **Mortise-b.,** *see* MORTISE. **Lock-b.,** *see* LOCK. **Port-light dog-b.,** hinged *b.* provided with a large hand or butterfly nut for securing a port-light against the sea or bad weather. **Preventer-b.'s,** *see* PREVENTER. **Rag-b.,** one having ragged or barbed sides as a means of taking hold in the wood. **Ring-b.,** eye-bolt fitted with a ring in its eye, used for hooking on tackles, passing lashings, etc. **Rod-b.,** a rod threaded at both ends; a nut forms its head and, when driven in place, its point is secured by another nut and a washer. This type fills a need when a length required can not be obtained from standard sizes. **Rudder-pintle b.,** *see* RUDDER. **Set-b.,** *see* SET. **Staple-b.,** *see* U-bolt. **Stopper-b.,** *see* STOPPER. **Stove-b.,** small *b.* and nut, with either round or countersunk head. **Stud-b.,** *see* STUD. **Tap-b.,** one having a square or hexagonal head and usually threaded its entire length of shank, used for joining metal without employing a nut. Its receiving hole is bored with a drill and then *tapped* (threaded). **Throat-b.,** *see* THROAT. **Toggle-b.,** *see* T.-pin *in* TOGGLE. **U-bolt,** a piece of rod-iron shaped like the letter *U* and threaded to receive a nut at each leg end; a *staple-b.*

BOLT-AUGER. A shipwright's tool used for boring holes for bolts.

BOLT-BOAT. A strong boat that will stand up to rough sea duty.

BOLT OF CANVAS. Roll or bale of canvas as supplied by a manufacturer. In the U.S. navy, a bolt is usually 80 yards of 20-inch width flax material;

U.S. cotton canvas of 22-inch width is about 100 yards length per bolt; British made 24-inch flax usually runs 42 yards. Generally, length of canvas in similar-sized bolts depends upon weight or thickness of goods.

BOLT-ROPE. *See* ROPE.

BOLT-STRAKE. *See* STRAKE.

BOLTING UP. In shipbuilding, forcing plates and various shaped parts in place by means of bolts and nuts.

BOLTSPRIT. An obsolete name for *bowsprit*.

BOMB. (Gr. thru L., *bompus,* a humming or buzzing noise.) A hollow metal projectile, either cylindrical- or spherical-shaped, containing an explosive fired by a time-fuse or by concussion; a bombshell; a shell. **B-harpoon, b.-lance,** a lance or harpoon having a charge of explosives in its head which is detonated upon being thrust into the body of a whale or other animal. **B.-ketch,** formerly a war-vessel carrying mortars for throwing *b's;* a bomb-vessel. **B.-proof,** so constructed as to resist penetration by, and shattering force of, *b's* or shells. **Depth-b.,** *see* DEPTH. **Rocket-b.,** *see* ROCKET.

BOMBARD. To attack with *bombards,* or earliest form of cannon; or, as in modern times, to attack with bombs or shells by artillery. A *bomb-ketch.* An obsolete name for a large leather bottle or drinking-vessel. (*As a verb, accented on second syllable; as a noun, on the first.*)

BOMBARDMENT. A sustained attack with shot and shell upon a town, fort, or other objective.

BOMB-TYPE AMMUNITION. *See* AMMUNITION.

BONAVENTURE. After mast of a caravel of the middle ages. A 15th. century type of merchant vessel, named from the French or Italian term "good luck." **Bonaventure mizzen,** *see* SAIL.

BONE-BREAKER. The *giant fulmar,* a species of petrel found in far northern latitudes, valuable for its down, feathers, and oil. *Cf.* FULMAR.

BONE IN HER TEETH, To *carry a.* To throw up a foam or spray under the bows; said of a ship turning up a curl of water and foam at her stem when sailing fast. Also, to "carry a bone in the mouth."

BONE-SHARK. *See* BASKING-SHARK.

BON-GRACE. *See* **B.-grace** *in* BOW.

BONITO. (Sp. and Port.) Any of several robust active fishes of the mackerel family; length from two to three feet and bluish with black oblique stripes; found in Pacific and Atlantic and known also as *skipjack* and *frigate mackerel.*

BONNET. A supplementary sail attached to a jib's foot during moderate winds. Any metal hood, canopy, or cowl.

BONNET-SHARK. The shovel-head, or *Sphryna tiburo,* of the hammer-head family of sharks found in warmer parts of Atlantic and Pacific Oceans; length about six feet with a head narrower and less hammer-shaped than the so-named *hammer-head.*

BOOBY. (Sp. *bobo,* dunce, idiot.) A kind of *gannet* native to Central and Southern North American coasts, so named on account of its apparent stupidity. A species of *penguin* of the Antarctic.

BOOBY, To beat the; *see* BEAT.

BOOBY-HATCH. *See* HATCH.

BOOHOO. Sailors' name for a *sail-fish.*

BOOK. In older whaling use, a small piece of blubber cut from the larger *blanket-piece* for processing. **Bell-b.,** *see* BELL. **Black b.,** Lloyd's record of maritime losses, including identities of shipmasters under whose command ship losses have been sustained; also, an important book of admiralty laws published in 1871. *Cf.* OLERON. **Cargo-b.,** *see* CARGO. **Code-b.,** *see* CODE. **Commercial code b.,** International Code of Signals now in use by all maritime nations' vessels. **Day-b.,** a log-book. **Liberty-b.,** *see* LIBERTY. **Log-b.,** *see* LOG. **Loss-b.,** *see* LOSS. **Muster-b.,** *see* MUSTER. **Night order b.,** *see* ORDER. **Slop-b.,** *see* SLOP. **Strake-b.,** *see* STRAKE. **Trip-b.,** one in which are kept accounts and records of a fishing-vessel.

BOOM. Spar used to spread a fore-and-aft sail, especially its foot; one attached to a yard or to another boom as an extension, like a *studding-sail boom.* Formerly a space in a vessel's waist used for stowing boats and spare spars. To roar, as a heavy surf; or as a ship when *roaring* along under a fair wind and a press of sail. To push away with a *boom;* as, to *b. off* a ship from a pier. **Bar-lattice b.,** one constructed of lattice-work steel and serving as a crane or derrick. **Bentinck b.,** a spar once used to stretch the foot of a foresail in small square-rigged vessels. (Named after an English sailor.) **Boat-b.,** spar extending outward for mooring and holding boats off from a ship's side. **B.-boat,** one stowed in the *boom* (formerly so-called). **B.-cover,** large tarpaulin used to cover the *boom,* or space where *b. boats* and *booms* formerly were stowed. **B.-crutch,** a support-bed for a *b.* when it is lowered and not in use (*Cf.* CRUTCH). **B.-ended,** situated at a *b.'s* end; said of a studding-sail or spinnaker when sail is hauled out as far as possible. **B. foresail,** *see* SAIL. **B.-jigger,** a tackle for rigging or running out a topmast-studding-sail *b.;* also, *in-and-out jigger.* **B. mainsail,** *see* SAIL. **B.-mounting,** all metal bands, collars, and other gear secured to a *b.* for connecting it to a mast, its sail, and its sheets and guys. **B.-stowage,** provision for stowing *b's* when not in use, and consisting essentially of crutches, chocks, and clamps. **B.-table,** an outrigger attached to a mast, or a structure around a mast a few feet above the deck as a support on which *b's* are stepped;

fitted where a number of *b's* are installed on a mast, in order to provide working clearance. **B.-tackle,** *see* TACKLE. **B. topping-lifts,** halyards or ropes leading from a boom's outer end through a masthead block and thence to deck. Usually pendants with tackles at their deck ends, they are used for *topping* or lifting a boom end, and, when used with a sail, relieve stress on peak halyards. **Cargo-b.,** one extending from a mast and used as a derrick arm in loading and discharging cargo. **Dolphin-b.,** same as *martingale* or *dolphin-striker.* (*Cf. Martingale-b.*) **Down b's,** *see* DOWN. **Fore-b.,** one spreading the foot of a fore-and-aft foresail. **Fire-b.,** *see* FIRE. **Fish-b.,** *see* FISH. **Guess-warp b.,** spar rigged out from ship's side with a long rope (*guess-warp*) attached to its outer end for securing or moving boats alongside; a *boat-b.* **Hatch-b.,** a *cargo-b.* guyed over a hatchway, as distinguished from the "yard arm," or *b.* guyed to lift or land cargo alongside. **Heavy lift b.,** a *jumbo b.* **Head-b.,** a *jib-b.* **Jib-b.,** *see* JIB. **Jigger-b.,** *see* JIGGER. **Jumbo b.,** one specially made and rigged for lifting heavy weights. Modern cargo vessels usually are equipped with at least one *jumbo* capable of handling 30 to 50-ton lifts. **Lattice b.,** a *cargo-b.* made of two parallel lengths of structural steel connected and stiffened by steel lattice-work on its lower and upper sides. To **lower the b. on; to let the b. down on;** to obtain a loan from a person; to make a party answer for his actions. **Lower b.,** in navy usage, a *guess-warp b.* **Main-b.,** *see* MAIN. **Martingale b.,** a short spar or heavy iron bar fitted perpendicular to and below a bowsprit's outer end and stayed to each bow and the jib-boom. Its purpose is to act as a strengthening bridge for a jib-boom, the jib-stays being extended downward to pass over cleats on its sides and thence close to the vessel's stem where they are set up. **Pudding-b.,** one having a large pudding or pad about its middle and lashed in a horizontal position between two davits, for steadying a boat against it while swung out ready for lowering, as used for a sea-boat. **Propeller-b.,** *see* PROPELLER. **Riding-b.,** *see* RIDING. To **rig in a b.; to rig out a b.;** *see* RIG. **Ringtail-b.,** spar extending beyond a spanker-b. or main-b. end for spreading the foot of a *ringtail,* a sail now obsolete in merchant vessels. **Sounding-b.,** *see* SOUNDING. **Stiffening b.,** *see* STIFFENING. **Studdingsail-b.,** one rigged out on a yard arm to spread foot and/or head of a *"st'uns'l";* now seldom used. **Swinging b.,** in old navy sailing-ships, a *b.* having one end fastened to ship's side in way of her fore rigging and used at sea to spread a lower studding-sail, or when at anchor, as a guesswarp b.; also called *lower b.* A *cargo-b.* free to swing with its load to and from a vessel's hatchway. **Yard b.,** *see* YARD.

BOOMAGE. Additional charge levied as harbor or anchorage dues where vessels are protected by floating booms, or *boomed off* wharves or piers.

BOOMKIN. *See* BUMPKIN. **Brace b.,** *see* BRACE.

BOOSTER. A small tackle attached to the standing end of a heavy fore-and-aft sail's peak or throat halyards for a final setting up in hoisting; also termed a *jig.*

BOOT. A newly enlisted man either at a naval training station or on board ship, easily distinguished by the new appearance of his boots and clothes. **B.-hook,** a long-handled caulking tool. **Sea-b's,** *see* SEA.

BOÖTES. (*Gr. and L.,* a herdman.) A northern constellation whose brightest star is *Arcturus,* a Latin word meaning *bear guard,* which star and its group being considered, in ancient times, as guard or ward of the constellation *Ursa Major* or *Great Bear.* Boötes is located about 30° southward of *Alkaid* (or *Benetnasch*), tail star in Ursa Major.

BOOT-TOPPING. Process of cleaning a vessel's hull about her water-line and coating such area with anti-fouling paint, or, as in old wood-built navy ships, with a mixture of resin, sulphur, and tallow. That portion of a vessel's plating between light and load water-lines. *Paint* used on this part of a hull.

BORA. (It. var. of *Borea,* north wind.) A violent dry wind from the Alps, prevalent over the Adriatic from October to April. Its approach usually is indicated only by a barometer drop about a quarter hour before its arrival. *Cf.* TRAMONTANA.

BORE. (Ice. *bāra,* wave.) Abrupt rise of wall of water caused by heaping of the ocean flood tide wave as its depth and lateral extent is suddenly restricted to narrowing limits through which it must pass. It is said that the Amazon bore, locally termed *prororoca,* reaches a height of 12 to 15 feet; other remarkable bores are those of the Ganges, Indus, and Brahmaputra Rivers, while of lesser importance are those of the Bay of Fundy, Bristol Channel in England, Seine, Garonne, and Dordogne Rivers of France, and Tagus River in Portugal. In England it is called *eagre;* on the Seine, *barre;* and on the Garonne and Dordogne, *mascaret.* **Sand bores,** *see* SAND.

BORE OUT. To, To rime; to cut a cylindrical hole by rotary motion of a boring tool.

BORROW. To approach closely to a coast; to bring a vessel closer to the wind, or to *luff.*

BORNE, WATER. *See* WATER.

BOSOM. A supporting surface; an inner recess. **B.-bar,** an angle-bar fitted inside of another. **B.-knee,** *same as* **Lodging-k.** *in* KNEE. **B.-plate,** a plate bar or piece of angle-iron fitted to fish or join two angle-bars' ends or similar material; a *b.-piece.*

BOSS. Any protuberance made for a purpose on a shaft; a raised rim about a hole; or a projecting portion of a structural member. The projecting part of a stern frame in way of the propeller-shaft tube. The part of a propeller to which its blades are attached; *see* PROPELLER. Cap or central point of a magnetic compass-card, containing a jewel as a ruby or beryl, which bears upon a pivot in the compass-bowl. **B.-barrel,** rounded section of shell-plating in way of a stern tube. **B.-frame,** one of several frames bent outward to allow room for a stern tube, or for tail-end shafts in twin screw vessels. **B. of a propeller-post; b. of a stern-post;** enlarged part of a stern-post through which the propeller-shaft passes. **Screw b.,** *see* SCREW.

B.O.T. Official abbreviation for Board of Trade; *see* TRADE.

BOTH SHEETS AFT. *See* AFT.

BOTTLE-NOSE WHALE. *See* WHALE.

BOTTLE PAPERS. Blanks furnished by U.S. Hydrographic Office or other interested authority to shipmasters which are filled in with requested data prior to throwing overboard in sealed bottles. This is done at sea for determining set and drift of surface currents, subject to subsequent reports of recovery of bottles at places and dates indicated. (*Cf.* TRACK.)

BOTTOM. That part of a ship or other floating craft below her light load-line. Cargo space in a vessel and hence the ship itself, as in *"goods shipped in American bottoms."* Lower portion of the shell from turn of the bilge to keel. **B.-boards,** fore-and-aft planks forming a floor in a boat; gratings are often used for this purpose and usually any kind of floor or *b.-boards* are movable. **B. longitudinals,** fore-and-aft members in bottom structure. **B.-plating,** shell plating which is below a light water-line. **B.-planks,** those of a vessel or boat from turn of the bilge to the garboard; in old naval usage, *b.-plank*ing comprised that area of a hull bounded by the *wales* and *garboard,* bottom being considered as that part below the lower gun deck. **B.-strake,** any strake of plating or planking between the garboard and light water-line. **B.-line,** *see* LINE. **Double-b.,** *see* DOUBLE. **Flat of b.,** *see* FLAT. **Inner b.,** *see* INNER. **Kettle-b.,** descriptive term for a vessel's *b.* having little deadrise, or a flat floor. **Neutral b.,** vessel belonging to a neutral country in time of war. **Outer b.,** bottom shell-plating, as opposed to an inner *b.* or double-*b.* tank-top. **Sailing on her own b.,** *see* SAILING. **Smelling the b.,** said of a ship when she steers badly at ordinary speed in shallow water. *Feeling b.* as with a sounding-lead. **Single b.,** shell-plating constituting a single or only *b.,* as that of cargo space in an oil-tank vessel. In older usage, refers to a wooden vessel without copper sheathing on her *b.* **V-b.,** a fast sea-going type of boat, built extremely sharp forward, her *b.* becoming flat aft and having a sharp turning bilge. (*Cf.* SKIPJACK)

BOTTOMRY. A marine contract whereby an owner or master of a vessel borrows money at an agreed rate of interest solely for meeting expenses necessary to complete a voyage. Vessel and any freight she earns are pledged as security in such a contract and, if ship is lost, a lender loses his money. If more than one *b.* is involved, last lender must be repaid first. A similar contract pledging laden cargo as security is called a *respondentia* and must be repaid only upon safe arrival of some part of such cargo. When both ship and cargo are pledged, bond is termed *bottomry and respondentia.*

BOUND. Destined. Confined. *Cf.* **outward b.**; **homeward b.**; **tide-b.**; **wind-b.**; **water-b.**; **weather-b.**; *under captions indicated.*

BOUNDARY PLANK. *See* PLANK.

BOUNDING BAR. *See* BAR.

BOUNTY, NAVIGATION. *See* NAVIGATION.

BOUSE. To haul vigorously on a tackle; to tauten standing rigging, or parts of a lashing, by frapping or drawing such parts together by turns of a rope employed for the purpose. To **b. up the jib,** *see* JIB.

BOW.[1] (*Pron. bō.*) A rainbow. A rude quadrant; *see Godfrey's Bow in* QUADRANT. A bend in a plank, scantling, etc. To bend. **B.-head,** the Arctic right whale. **B.-net,** a lobster-net. **B. of a rudder,** curved after edge of a rudder; curved metal forming after edge of certain types of built rudders. **Fog-b.,** *see* FOG. **Sea-b.,** *see* SEA.

BOW.[2] (*Pron. with* **ow** *as in* **how.**) Forward end of a vessel; part where a vessel's sides trend inward to her stem, each side in proximity to the stem being termed, respectively, from right to left looking forward, *starboard bow* and *port bow.* Outside forward end of a ship is usually termed *the bows.* Forward oarsman in a boat; bowman. **Bluff b.,** *see* BLUFF. **Bold b.,** bluff-bowed. **B. and beam bearing,** four points and abeam; *see* TWO OR MORE BEARINGS WITH RUN BETWEEN. **B.-and-quarter line,** line of ships in a column where one is four points forward or abaft another's beam. **Bow on; bows on;** same as *head on.* **B.-chaser,** a gun mounted in a vessel's bows, formerly for action during a *chase.* **B.-chock,** one fitted on either bow as a lead for a mooring or towing line. **B.-chock plate,** *see* PLATE. **B.-fast,** a bow-line; a forward mooring rope or hawser. **B.-grace,** fender made of old rope or canvas to protect a ship's bows from floating ice; also, *bon-grace.* **B.-light,** a white light carried at fore end of a vessel; a forward anchor light. **B.-lighthouses,** small towers formerly placed on each side of a forecastle deck for exhibiting and protecting a vessel's side lights; also known as *side light castles* or *side light towers.* **B.-line,** a bow-fast. A curve representing a vertical section of a ship's fore end. *Bowline.* **B. oar,** forward oar of a boat, or person pulling that oar; sometimes in a whaleboat, forward oar but one. **B.-piece,** a gun mounted in the bows. **B.-plate,** *see* PLATE. **B.-plating,** bow shell-plating. **B.-port,** *see* PORT. **B.-rope,** line or hawser leading from a bow to another vessel or to a wharf for mooring or hauling purposes; also, *b.-line* or *b.-fast.* **B.-rudder,** auxiliary rudder fitted at a ship's stem to facilitate turning in narrow waters. **B.-sheave bracket,** on a cable ship's bows, one supporting a heavy sheave over which a cable is hauled in. **B.-wave,** *see* WAVE. **Bulb b.,** a bulbous fore-foot; a *bull-nosed b.* **Bull-nosed b.,** one with a large rounded fore end below water-line. **Clipper b.,** one with an extreme forward rake; a long overhanging *b.,* having a flat or concave entrance, as opposed to a full *b.* or one with a swelling or convex appearance; a cutwater *b.* **Cutwater b.,** a clipper *b.* **Doubling of the b.,** thick bow-planking as protection against injury by an anchor; *b. doubling-plates.* **Flared b.,** one rising with extreme flare or overhang. **Full b.,** having a bluff or convex entrance. **In bows,** a command to *b.* oarsmen to "boat," or take in, their oars in readiness for coming alongside. **Lean b.,** narrow or slender *b.* **Lee b.,** *see* LEE. **On the b.,** indicating relative bearing of an object, within 45° of the fore-and-aft line extended ahead. **Ram b.,** having a stem protruding forward at and below the water-line, as in older types of warships. **Spoon b.,** one having an overhang in which its under side resembles the bowl of a spoon. **Weather b.,** *see* WEATHER.

BOWDITCH, Nathaniel. (*1773–1838.*) American mathematician and author of "Bowditch," seamen's popular name for the *American Practical Navigator.*

BOWER. Either working anchor, usually termed *starboard b.* and *port b.,* respectively, from their permanent positions when stowed; *b. anchor.* Formerly called *best b.* and *small b.,* both are now required to be of equal weight and efficiency. **B. cable,** chain cable attached to a *b.* **Stockless b.,** same as stockless anchor; *see* ANCHOR.

BOWLINE. (*Pron. bōlin.*) A single rope leading forward from a bridle made fast to a square sail's weather leech, used when sailing close-hauled to flatten out the sail as much as possible. A *bowline knot,* made to form a non-slip loop on a rope's end; handy for slipping over a bollard, mooring-post, etc., or for slinging a man aloft or over ship's side. **B. bridle,** span near middle of a square sail's leech to which the *b.* is attached. In single topsail days both topsails and courses were fitted for bowlines; since double topsails were introduced, on courses only. **B. cringles,** those in a leech to which a *b. bridle* was made fast. To **check the b.,** to slacken it when wind becomes favorable, after sailing close-hauled. **Fore-b.,** *see* FORE. **French b.,** a *b.* knot with two bights, used as a safety sling or "chair" for a man; one bight forming a seat while the other encircles the man's body below his arms; *see* KNOT. **Haul-b.,** *see* HAUL. **Main-top-b.,** long single rope usually temporarily made fast in the main top, in single topsail days, ready for making fast to the topsail weather leech as required when sailing close-hauled. *Figuratively* used in referring to a lengthy "yarn" or a serious facial expression, as in "as long as the *main-t'-bowline.*" **On a b.,** once said of a vessel when sailing close-hauled. **Running-b.,** a *b.* knot made at a rope's end and around its standing part, slip-noose fashion. To **sharp the main b.;** to **hale the main b.;** old phrasing for taking a pull on *b.* leading to weather leech of mainsail.

BOWMAN. Man pulling a boat's forward oar.

BOWSE. *See* BOUSE.

BOWSER BOAT. *See* BOAT.

BOWSPRIT. Large boom or spar projecting forward and slanting upward from a sailing-vessel's stem. Its purpose is to meet stress on the fore-topmast stay, or chief staying member for a square-rigged vessel's upper masts (corresponding to a schooner's inner jib-stay), and to form a stiffening support for her jib-boom. (Old English, *boltsprit, boltspreet*) **B.-bed,** seat of a *b.* in a vessel's stem. **B.-cap,** iron band forming a cap on a *b.'s* outer end and shaped to fit around and hold a jib-boom in place. The *bobstays* are usually secured to its under side. **B.-hounding,** that portion of a *b.* outside the stem. **B. ladder,** *see* LADDER. **B. shrouds,** stay-ropes or chains running from outer end of a *b.* to each bow for securing against sidewise stresses. **Head of the b.,** its extreme outer end. **Horn b.,** single spar acting as *b.* and jib-boom combined; also, *spike b.* To **reef a b.,** *see* REEF. **Running-b.,** in small craft, one that may be run out or in like a jib-boom, as opposed to a *standing b.,* or one permanently fitted. **Spike b.,** both jib-boom and bowsprit in one, as in more recent iron sailing-ships and smaller wooden craft.

BOX. Casing about a boat's centerboard. Space between a backboard and stern-post of a boat. To boxhaul. To box off. **B.-chronometer,** *see* CHRONOMETER. **B.-coupling,** a strong cylindrical forging into which ends of shafting are inserted and kept together in line. **B.-girder,** *see* GIRDER. **B.-hook,** *see* HOOK. **B.-keel.** *see* KEEL. **B.-keelson,** one built of two horizontal and two vertical plates, the former overhanging the latter and connected externally by a stout continuous angle-bar at each corner. **B. the compass,** *see* COMPASS. To **b. off,** to turn a ship's head from the wind by hauling her head yards *aback* as in boxhauling. **B.-rowlock,** *see* ROWLOCK. **Carling-b.,** *see* CARLING. **Hawse-b.,** *see* HAWSE. **Light-b.,** *see* LIGHT. **Oil-b.,** *see* OIL. **Paddle-b.; paddle-b. bridge; paddle-b. framing; paddle-b. stays;** *see* PADDLE. **Rose-b.,** a strum-b.; *see* ROSE. **Smoke-b.,** *see* SMOKE. **Stuffing-b.,** the packing arrangement for

maintaining fluid-tight an opening in a bulkhead or cylinder through which a rotating shaft or a piston operates. **Watch-b.,** *see* WATCH.

BOXHAUL. To put a square-rigged vessel on the other tack when turning into the wind is impracticable. Effected by putting helm *hard-alee* and bringing ship into the wind; when she loses way, head yards are braced flat aback, after yards squared, head sheets hauled to windward, and all after fore-and-aft sail taken in. Ship now falls off and gathers *sternway* until wind draws abeam and begins to fill her after sails. As she gathers *headway* helm is shifted and sails trimmed accordingly as she lays up to her new tack.

BOXING. In wooden construction, a scarfed joint uniting a vessel's stem with her keel. Piece of wood, square in cross-section, used in scarfing futtocks or frame-timbers together; a *cog.* **B. in,** old shipyard term for securing or notching cant frame heels in building a ship's counter.

BRACE. (O.F. *brace,* the arm, power.) In square-rigged vessels, a rope or tackle from each yard arm by which the yards are trimmed from the deck as required. A rudder-gudgeon. An arm of the sea. To swing horizontally or "trim" yards by means of their braces. To **b. about,** to haul yards around in a contrary direction, as in tacking. **B.-boomkin; b.-bumpkin;** a small outrigger to which *b's* are led from lower yards and thence inboard; usually stowed flat against ship's side when in port. To **b. in,** to haul in on weather braces. **B.-pendant,** a length of rope or chain forming part of a brace and to which a block is attached. To **b. the feet,** of similar meaning as the phrase *to learn* or *know the ropes,* apparently from a beginner's need of bracing his feet against his vessel's motion in a seaway. To **b. up,** to lay yards more fore-and-aft, as in sailing closer to the wind. To **b. up sharp,** to trim yards at as small angle with fore-and-aft line as possible in order to sail close to the wind. To **splice the main b.,** *see* SPLICE. (For *brace* in terms combined with caption words see COUNTER; HEEL; MAIN; RUDDER; WEATHER.)

BRACED ABACK. Said of yards when swung to lay their sails *aback; see* ABACK.

BRACING, BOILER. *See* BOILER.

BRACKET. A steel plate, commonly of triangular shape with a reinforcing flange, used to connect structural parts, such as a deck-beam to a frame-girder, a frame to a margin-plate, etc.; a *bracket-knee.* **B. end,** a beam end forged in shape of a *b.* **Bilge b.,** same as *wing b.; see* WING. (Also see *bracket* as a combining term with caption words in ANCHOR; ANGLE; BEAM; BOILER; **Bow-sheave** *in* BOW; FLOOR; KEEL; MARGIN; SHAFT; TRIPPING; WING.)

BRACKISH. (Du. *brak,* salt) Salty in a moderate degree, as fresh water adulterated by sea-water.

BRAIL. (M.E. *brayle,* a furling-rope) A rope used as a leechline or buntline for hauling a sail in against a mast, preparatory to or instead of stowing. *B's* are fitted to fore-and-aft and lateen sails, particularly the former of *standing-gaff* rig, where they are named for their positions, as *peak b., throat b., foot b., middle b.,* etc. (In 17th. century usage, sails were said to be *embrayled* when hauled in to any spar from which they were set; *see* EMBRAIL.) **B. up,** or **b. in,** to take in a sail by means of brails; to *embrail.*

BRAKE. Handle or lever of a pump. Any device for stopping or retarding motion in a machine by friction. **B. horse-power,** *see* HORSEPOWER. **Friction-b.,** a device for controlling speed of a shaft, drum, or wheel, which usually includes a lever and a block or band for making frictional contact with an appropriate part of the rotating machine. A friction-*b.* is generally installed in larger vessels for securing control of a rudder-trunk or a quadrant in event of steering-gear failure, until hand or emergency gear can be brought into operation. **Press-b.,** *see* PRESS. **Rudder-b.,** *see* RUDDER. **Solenoid-b.,** *see* SOLENOID.

BRANCH. A certificate of competency issued to a pilot by the *Trinity House* (England) which authorizes him to pilot ships in certain specified waters; a *full branch* is one without limiting restrictions. **B.-pilot,** in England, one holding a branch or special commission. **Navigation-b.,** *see* NAVIGATION. **Y b.,** *see* Y; a wye.

BRASS. Alloy of copper and zinc, of good ductile and malleable properties. Formerly consisting of copper and tin only; now is essentially one of copper and zinc, with sometimes a small proportion of tin or other metal; *see* BRASSES. Also, an old spelling of *brace.* **B. bounder,** a British apprentice bound for four years to serve at sea and given certain privileges stipulated in his *indentures* or agreement with a shipowner, usually in return for a premium paid by his parents. The boy's four years of sea service provide his eligibility for examination for his first *certificate of competency* as an officer, *viz.,* a *second mate* or a *second class engineer,* depending in which department such service was performed. **B. hat,** a commanding officer or high official. Officers of the U.S. navy above lieutenant-commander wear gold markings on their cap visors, which metal has been familiarly dubbed *brass.* Hence the term *brass hats* for such caps and their wearers. **Naval b.,** *see* NAVAL.

BRASSES. Pieces of brass, bronze, gun-metal, or other anti-frictional metal, provided with oil-grooves and fitted in shaft supports as bearing surfaces for the *journals.* **Main bearing b's,** *see* MAIN.

BRAVE WEST WINDS. *See* WIND.

BRAZILIAN CURRENT. A branch of the *Atlantic Equatorial Current* turning southward along the South American coast from Cape San Roque as far as Trinidad Island and Martin Vas Rocks, in $20\frac{1}{2}°$ south latitude and 29° west longtitude, where it bifurcates into south-easterly and south-westerly directions. Its strength is greatly affected by prevailing winds, flowing off Cape San Roque at from 1 to $2\frac{1}{2}$ knots, while $\frac{1}{2}$ to 1 knot is its average at its bifurcation point indicated.

BREACH. Breaking of water, as waves or a surf; a surge. Leap of a whale out of water. Infraction of a law or violation of any obligation or agreement, as a *breach* of contract. Rupture or break as in a vessel's side. Break in continuance of friendly relations; a quarrel. To cause a rupture in a ship's side or dock wall. To leap out of water as a whale. (*From the same root as* **break.**) **B. of arrest,** an offense committed by a naval officer in arrest who leaves his quarters or assigned limits without authority from his superior. It is punishable by *cashiering,* or dismissal in disgrace. **Clean b.,** effect of a shipped sea which sweeps almost everything overboard. **Clear b.,** said of a sea shipped and rolling over a deck without breaking. **Sea-b.,** *see* SEA.

BREACHING. *See* BREECHING.

BREAD-ROOM. A water-tight and rat-proof space or compartment on larger vessels for stowing bread; bread-store.

BREADTH. Side to side measurement of a vessel or boat, taken at right angles to the fore-and-aft line. It is usually taken as *greatest molded breadth,* which, according to *A.B.S.* rules, is that measured between faying surfaces of opposite frames, in feet. **Extreme b.,** maximum *b.* measured over plating or planking, or over beading or fenders, if fitted. **Half-b.; half-b. plan; half-b. staff** or **rod;** *see* HALF. **Main b.,** *see* MAIN. **Main b. line,** *see* LINE. **Molded b,** greatest width of a vessel as measured between outside edges of her frames. **Molded half-b.,** *see* HALF. **Registered b.,** greatest *b.* measured between outside surfaces of shell-plating or planking. **Straight of b.,** that portion of a ship's hull having vertical sides. **Tonnage b.,** *see* TONNAGE.

BREAK. To hog or sag. A starting or breaking away, forth, or out. Point where a vessel's deck terminates and ascent or descent to a next deck begins. To curl over and fall as surf, or as heavy waves on a shoal or sunken rocks. **B.-bulkhead,** *see* BULK-HEAD. **To b. the back of,** a vessel's "back" is said to be *broken* when her lower longitudinal strength members, as keel and keelson, have been fractured or very severely strained. **B. of forecastle,** extreme after end of a *forecastle deck.* **B. of poop,** extreme forward end of a *poop deck.* **B. off the end,** *see* END. To **b. bulk;** to **b.** out a cargo; to begin unloading a cargo. To **b. ground,** to free an anchor from its hold; to *b. out,* in the same sense. To **b. a gun,** to open a pistol or gun at its breech. To **b. leave or liberty,** to remain away from one's ship after time specified for return on board. To **b. in,** to teach a new hand a particular job. To spring in a plate back of a seam by too heavy caulking. To **b. out,** to open or unfurl: said of a flag or a sail. To bring a new article into use. To free an anchor from its hold when heaving it in. To **b. sheer,** to be forced, as a vessel at anchor, to lie in an improper direction by a sudden change in wind or current conditions. To **b. step,** to cease marching in cadence; march at will. To **b.,** or **split, tacks with,** *see* TACK.

BREAKAGE. Empty space left after stowing cargo in a hold; broken stowage. Goods broken in transportation. Allowance for packaged cargo damaged by being crushed or broken during carriage.

BREAKDOWN LIGHTS. "Not-under-control" lights; *see* **Rule 4** *in* REGULATIONS FOR PREVENTING COLLISIONS.

BREAKER. A small water-cask. A wave breaking on a beach, rocks, etc. **Bread-b.,** a substantial water-tight container for hard bread or biscuit required to be carried in life-boats of a merchant vessel, each boat's person-capacity governing amount of bread required. (U.S. Coast Guard requires 2 lbs. per person.) **Ice-b.,** *see* ICE. **Ship-b.,** *see* SHIP. **Water-b.,** keg or small cask used as a container for drinking-water required in a ship's lifeboat. (U.S. regulations require one quart for each person.)

BREAKHEAD. The strengthened bows of an ice-breaking vessel.

BREAKING OF THE MONSOON. *See* MONSOON.

BREAKWATER. A massive structure, such as a sea-wall, mole, or deep-water pier, for breaking the force of waves. Plates or timbers fitted in a flush-decked vessel's forward end to form a V-shaped wall for diverting overboard any water shipped over the bows. **Floating b.,** barrier of floating timbers placed to protect an anchorage from the force of waves.

BREAM. (D. *brem,* broom.) To clear a ship's bottom of barnacles, sea-weed, ooze, etc., by burning, scraping, and brooming off. **Sea-b.,** a fish of the widely distributed *Sparidæ* family, closely related to the *snappers* and *grunts;* valuable as food.

BREAST. To *breast the sea* is to meet a swell or waves head on. To *breast in* is to heave a vessel sideways toward a wharf or quay. **B.-backstay,** in old sailing men-of-war, a stay rigged to support a mast when sailing on a wind or close-hauled: it extended from the topmasthead to ship's side forward of weather standing rigging. **B.-band,** a safety belt or band of canvas or rope appropriately secured to allow a leadsman free use of his arms while taking soundings. A parrel-rope, or one used to hold a light yard to its mast. **B.-beam,** a transverse beam at

the break of a forecastle or poop. **B.-board,** a weighted sled formerly used in rope-walks for maintaining required tension in the yarns while twisting them into strands. **B.-fast,** a mooring-rope leading approximately at right angles to a wharf from a vessel lying alongside. **B.-gasket,** old name for a bunt-gasket; *see* GASKET. **B.-hook,** one of several horizontal crooked timbers or triangular plates fitted inside and across a vessel's stem for tying fore-peak frames and generally uniting and stiffening the bow structure; also, *b.-knee.* **B.-knot,** a knot or ribbon worn on one's breast. **B.-rail,** *see* RAIL. **B.-work,** in older wooden ships, especially those of armed type, a heavy and often ornately fashioned rail across the break of a poop and/or quarter-deck and a top-gallant forecastle.

BREAKING OFF. Shoving and holding a vessel broadside off a quay or wharf by means of long heavy spars in order to permit lighters, bunkering equipment, floating cranes, etc., to work between ship and quayside; also termed *booming off.*

BREATHER, AIR. *See* AIR.

BREATHING-HOLE. *See* BLOW-HOLE.

BREECH. Outer angle of a knee-timber, the inner turn of which is called its *throat.* A tackle-block's becket end to which the fall's standing end is attached. To make fast by breeching; *see* BREECHING. A gun-breech. **B.-block,** movable piece which closes the inner end of a *b.*-loading firearm, and which is withdrawn to insert a cartridge before firing.

BREECHES-BUOY. *See* BUOY.

BREECHES, CLEAR-HAWSE. *See* CLEAR.

BREECHING. In old navy usage, ropes securing a gun to eye-bolts on each side of a gun-port for taking up the recoil when firing and also to hold a gun in place at sea. Sheet-iron pipe or casing which conveys smoke and exhaust gases from a boiler to the smokestack or funnel. **Rudder-b.,** *see* RUDDER.

BREEZE. (It. *brezza,* breeze; Sp. *briza,* north-west breeze.) A wind described as *light, gentle, moderate,* or *strong,* according to its force; *see* BEAUFORT'S SCALE. **Ash b.; white ash b.;** *see* ASH. To **b. up,** said of increasing or freshening wind. **Land and sea b's,** local winds met with on many coast-lines in tropical and sub-tropical latitudes, caused by daily change of temperature over the land. A *sea b.* begins in mid forenoon, as warming air over the land rises, and continues until after sunset. About two hours after sunset a breeze from land springs up and blows seaward displacing the now comparatively warmer and rising air over the water. **Mackerel b.,** *see* MACKEREL. To **shoot the b.,** to gab; to engage in idle conversation. **Spanking b.,** a fresh or strong *b.* favorable for sailing. **Tidal b.,** *see* TIDAL. **Top-gallant b.,** one in which top-gallant-sails, as loftiest canvas, can be carried; usually rated as a *strong b.* **Whiffling b.,** light, changeable or baffling wind.

BREWING. Said of apparent approach of bad weather as indicated by ominous dark clouds gathering on the horizon; as, *a south-easter is b.*

BRICK-DUST. Dust of pounded *Bath-brick* used for many years in polishing brass fittings on board ship. The brick was first made of siliceous silt near Bath in Somersetshire, England.

BRICKFIELDER. In southern and south-eastern parts of Australia, a suddenly rising violent cold wind from south or south-west, regularly preceded by a hot breeze from the northward; also called *southerly buster.* It may be expected during the summer months.

BRICKLAYER'S CLERK. Old sailor's term for one who goes to sea but is dissatisfied with his occupation.

BRIDGE. A high transverse platform, often an extension of a deck-house top, running from side to side of a vessel and from which a complete all-round view is least interfered with. A powered vessel being navigated from her *b.,* an enclosed space called a *pilot-house,* included in the *b.* arrangement, contains and protects such navigating instruments as compass, steering-wheel, radio-direction-finder, telephones, engine-room telegraph, signal flags, and binoculars. A pilot-house is usually extended to include a chart-room, in which are kept charts, chronometers, sailing-directions and other books, sextants, etc. Where there are two *b.'s,* one above the other, the higher may be termed a *navigating b.,* the other, *lower b.* or *captain's b.* (Ger. *brücke;* Ice. *bryggja.*) **B. deck,** see DECK. **B. gunwale,** junction line of a *b. deck stringer-plate* with shell-plating (*b. sheer strake*). **B. house,** superstructure built about amidships on the upper deck, its sides being an upward continuation of the shell-plating, and over which is a *b. deck.* Officers' quarters, staterooms, and accommodations are usually located in a *b.* house; also referred to as *b. space.* **B. islet,** a peninsula that becomes an islet at high water. **B.-piece,** see ARCH. **B.-plate,** support for fire-bars or grates at back end of a fire-box. **B.-rail,** see RAIL. **B. sheer-strake,** line of shell-plating immediately below a *b. deck.* **B. sign,** portable sign set on a pier at a position abreast of a ship's *b.* as a guide in docking and expressly for placing vessel in her proper berth. **Captain's b.,** a lower *b.* adjacent to the captain's quarters. **Closed-in b.,** one of which a pilot-house forms its midship part, its fore side being a shelter common to both; also, with or without such an arrangement, a *b.* fitted with shelters or *cabs* at each extreme end. **Connecting b.,** a fore-and-aft walk-way common to oil-tank vessels for avoiding an often slippery condition of decks and, in bad weather, enabling persons to pass clear of water

shipped when ship is in the loaded condition; also called *catwalk.* **Ferry-b.,** see FERRY. **Fire-b.,** see FIRE. **Floating b.,** one supported by anchored boats, pontoons, rafts, etc. A ferry driven by flow of a current and controlled by a fixed cable to which are attached necessary running sheaves and tackles for placing the craft at an advantageous angle across the stream. A platform affording a landing for boats at all stages of tide and bridged to a pier. Any floating objects or material over which impeding water may be crossed. **Flying b.,** an upper *b.,* often termed *navigating b.* **Fore-and-aft b.,** a catwalk or *connecting b.* (*q.v.*). **King-b.,** truss connecting the heads of, and acting as a stiffener to, a pair of *king-posts* or masts for supporting cargo-booms. **Lift-b.,** see LIFT. **Low b.!,** a warning to lower ones' heads, as to persons on a canal-boat, when about to pass under a *b.* **Monkey-b.,** generally, deck above a pilot-house or chart-room when used for navigating purposes; frequently, a fore-and-aft *b.* on a sailing-ship. **Navigating-b.,** upper or flying *b.,* where two are provided, equipped with a duplicate set of controls for use during good weather; also called *pilot-b.* **Sunk b.,** a structure amidships, partly above and partly below upper deck level. **Warping b.,** a platform or *b.* near a vessel's after end for a deck officer's use when docking or warping.

BRIDLE. Two or more parts of rope or chain rigged to distribute stress on a single part of another rope or chain to which they are connected at a common point; often used in slinging cargo-trays, vehicles, and heavy cases where such articles must be steadied in trim during hoisting. In hoisting such bulky and easily damaged objects as automobiles, engines, large crates, and the like, a stout piece of wood called a *spreader* is placed to separate the parts of a bridle in order to avoid crushing, or chafing against, objects thus slung. **Bowline-b.,** see BOWLINE. **B.-cable,** one attached to the middle of a ground cable. **B.-port,** in old wooden navy vessels, a port-hole in the bows through which *b.*-cable gear, hawsers, etc., were passed in mooring. **Mooring-b.,** both chain cables attached to a permanent chain mooring, end of which is usually supported by a buoy and provided with a swivel. **Towing-b.,** see TOWING.

BRIG. A two-masted square-rigged vessel, her mainmast having a fore-and-aft mainsail or *spanker* in addition to, or without, a square mainsail. A place of confinement for offenders aboard ship. **Gun-b.,** see GUN. **Hermaphrodite b.,** two-masted vessel square-rigged on her foremast and schooner-rigged on her mainmast. Also called a *brig-schooner,* this rig appears to have originated in England where square topsails were used on the mainmast, and was called a *brigantine;* however, upon removing square rig from her mainmast and replacing it with a gaff-topsail, as seems to have been done first in América, the name *hermaphrodite b.* was adopted, but of late years *brigantine* has become the designation on both sides of the Atlantic. **Jackass b.,** *see* JACKASS.

BRIGANTINE. Originally a name for a piratical ship. *See* BRIG.

BRIGHT. Sharp; alert; watchful; as in *keep a bright lookout.* **B. decks,** those of wood, oiled or varnished.

BRIGHTWORK. Those metal objects or fittings on a vessel which are kept bright by polishing. Also, scraped and cleaned woodwork which may, or may not, be varnished, but never painted.

BRIMMING. An old term for the glow exhibited at night by a school of fish, such as herring or mackerel. Phosphorescence of the sea. Also, *briming.*

BRINE. (A.S. *bryne;* Du. *brijn.*) The ocean. Water strongly saturated or impregnated with salt; pickle; any strong saline solution. In a cargo or provision cooling system, fresh water impregnated by calcium chloride which is cooled and then circulated in coils provided in refrigerated spaces. **B.-cock,** a scum-cock; *see* COCK.

BRING. Combining word indicating action or effect of some action. To **b. about,** to put a vessel on the other tack. To **b. by the lee,** to have the wind come suddenly on what should be the lee side due to heavy yawing, sudden change in wind direction, or bad steering; opposite of *broaching to.* To **b. down by the stern,** *see* STERN. To **b. a hawser to,** to take necessary turns with it round a capstan or winch-end ready for heaving. To **b. home,** to return to its place, or drag, as an anchor, by heaving on its cable; to heave a ship up to her anchor. To **b. to,** to heave to; force another ship to *heave to* or stop. Bend a sail to its yard or gaff, after hoisting or placing it for that purpose. **B. to bear,** to bear upon or *b.* into range of: as, to *b.* a gun to *bear* upon a target. To **b. up; to b. up all standing;** to stop a ship's headway by letting go an anchor, or by running her ashore; *fetch up all standing.* (In original sense of such action taking place with no time to take in sail; hence, "all standing.") To **b. up with a round turn,** to stop a rope from running by taking a round (*complete*) turn on a bitt, belaying-pin, etc.; to cause to stop suddenly; to stop effectually. *Fetch up with a round turn.*

BRINK. (Dan. *brink,* edge or verge.) Margin of land bordering on water.

BRISINGA. Deep-sea starfish of the family *Brisingidæ.*

BRISTOL FASHION. In seamanlike style; shipshape; in good order.

BRIT or **BRITT.** Young of herring, or fry of other fishes. The millions of minute organisms called *plankton,* which includes *copepods, pteropods, entomostracans,* and others of the lower crustacean order, found on or near the sea surface and which serve as an apparently inexhaustible food supply for whales and many kinds of fish.

BRITISH CORPORATION. (*Abbr. B.C.*) A society for survey and registry of shipping, founded in England in 1890.

BRITISH SEAS. The four seas by which Great Britain is encompassed.

BRITISH THERMAL UNIT. (*Abbr. B.T.U.*) Amount of heat required to raise the temperature of one pound of fresh water one degree *Fahrenheit,* which energy thus expressed is equal to 778 footpounds of mechanical power.

BRIXHAM TRAWLER. *See* TRAWLER.

BROACH. To tap; to pierce, as a cask; to open for the first time. A gimlet or tapering tool used to sample contents of casks. To **b. cargo,** to break open or into cargo or ship's stores with intent to steal. To **b. to,** when running with a high quarterly sea, to turn toward it broadside on by accident, force of elements, or fault of a helmsman, thus exposing a vessel to danger of capsizing or shipping heavy water.

BROAD AXE. A broad-faced, chisel-edged axe largely used in hewing timber in shipyard work and wharf building; also, in shaping spars. *Cf.* ADZE.

BROAD OFF, BROAD ON. At a considerable angle from a bearing indicated as a basic direction. **B. off the bow,** said of an object whose bearing is four points or more from the fore-and-aft line, looking ahead.

BROAD PENNANT. *See* PENNANT.

BROAD REACH. *See* REACH.

BROADSIDE. Side of a ship from bow approach to quarter. Simultaneous discharge of all guns that can be trained to fire from one side of a ship.

BROKEN STOWAGE. Stowage of unusually bulky units of cargo which leaves broken up and unoccupied space in a hold, as, for example, that of locomotives, boilers, or irregularly shaped pieces of machinery.

BROKEN-BACKED. Said of a ship when so weakened as to be *hogged,* or drooping at each end; having keel or lower longitudinal members fractured or badly strained.

BRONZE WIRE ROPE. *See* WIRE.

BROOM. Same as BREAM, *q.v.* A long prevailing custom in American ports is display of a broom in the rigging, as far aloft as possible, when the vessel is offered for sale.

BROTHERS OF THE COAST. An organization of buccaneers whose activities were confined to the

Spanish Main and shipping to and from that area in the 16th. and 17th. centuries. Operating under a rigid disciplinary code, marooning appears to have been a common penalty awarded offending "brothers," while accident benefits were provided for those wounded in action.

BROW. A gang-plank (U.S.); *see* GANGWAY.

B.S. Official abbreviation for *Boiler Survey*, as in records of, and certificates issued by, a classification society.

B.T.U. British thermal unit, *q.v.*

BUCCANEER. (Fr. *boucanier*, hunter of wild meat.) A pirate or freebooter; especially those sea-rovers of various European nations who, in the 17th. and 18th. centuries, infested the Spanish coasts of America in their generally nefarious pursuits, including plunder of houses and property, and seizure of treasure.

BUCENTAUR. (It. *bucentoro*.) State barge of Venice used each year (*1177–1797*) by the *Doge* at a ceremony known as *Marriage of the Adriatic*, signifying subjection of that sea to her husband, the Venetian Republic.

BUCKEYE. A flat-bottomed centerboard schooner with jib-headed foresail and mainsail, 3 to 15 tons, decked over, usually with a cabin aft; peculiar to Chesapeake Bay, generally used in oyster-fishing. Also, *bug-eye*.

BUCKLE. (Fr. *boucler*, to bulge.) To bend or become distorted permanently; *see* BUCKLING. **Buckled plate,** one that has warped from its original shape; also, one that is wider at its middle than at its ends.

BUCKLER. Block or shutter used to close a hawse-pipe or other opening against ingress of water; a hawse-plug. **Blind b.,** solid *b.*, as compared with a *riding b.* **Riding b.,** one pierced for passage of a cable.

BUCKLING. Dangerous bending or bowing of a spar under stress; warping or distortion under stress of any member of a structure.

BUDGEROW. (Hind. *bajara*.) A heavy barge used by passengers on the Ganges River, India. Also, *budgero*.

BUFFALO. An anchor-fluke chock. The buffalo-rail. **B.-rail,** low rail extending above a forecastle deck on each bow. **B. spray-board,** in older sailing-vessels, a timber rail fayed upon a main or upper rail forward. Also, *false rail.*

BUFFER. (O. Fr. *buffe*, a blow.) Any device for deadening or absorbing force of a shock, such as a heavy *pad* or a strong *spring*. Examples of *spring b's* are those set in steering-chains or on a steering quadrant, and one attached to a fore-and-aft sail

sheet to relieve sudden stress when jibing. A **heavy** *fender* on a tug-boat's stem.

BUG-EYE. Same as *buckeye.*

BUGLER. On U.S. war-vessels, seaman assigned to convey commands by calls sounded on a bugle. On large passenger vessels, usually a member of the stewards' department who announces by *bugle* readiness of luncheon and dinner.

BUILDER'S MEASUREMENT. *See* MEASURE-MENT.

BUILDING-BLOCK. *See* BLOCK.

BUILDING-SLIP. *See* SLIP.

BUILT. Constructed of several pieces appropriately joined so as to strengthen or reinforce each other in a complete whole, as a *built mast*, a *built rib;* formed, shaped, or made, as indicated in compound terms like *clinker-b., clipper-b.,* etc. **B.-up mast,** same as *b. mast.*

BULB, ANGLE. Bulb-angle; *see* ANGLE.

BULB BAR, -BEAM, -IRON. Rolled bar, beam, or other structural iron or steel, thickened on one edge and having a bulbous appearance in cross-sectional area. **T-bulb iron,** *see* T.

BULB BOW. *See* BOW.

BULB-PLATE. *See* PLATE.

BULGE. (Var. of M.E. *bilge*, to swell out.) A protuberance or swelling out; to be bent outward, as a bulkhead under pressure. Same as *bilge.* **B.-water,** same as *bilge-water.* See BILGE.

BULK. (M.E. *bolke*, heap.) Hull or hold space in a ship: hence the cargo. **B. cargo,** *see* CARGO. **B. measurement,** cubic contents of a consignment of cargo, usually expressed in cubic feet. Generally, freight is calculated according to such measure where cargo exceeds 42 cubic feet per long ton weight; heavier goods according to gross weight. **In b.,** said of certain cargoes not packaged or divided into parts, such as grain, coal, or petroleum.

BULKER. A person who determines bulk measurement of goods in freight assessment, or that for dock or warehouse charges.

BULKHEAD. One of several upright partitions separating various compartments in a vessel; a water-tight hull partition for preventing passage of oil, water, or fire from one part of a ship to another. Main bulkheads serve as important strength and stiffening members in a vessel's structure. **After peak b.,** nearest transverse *b.* forward of the stern-post. In steel construction, this partition forms an *after peak tank's* forward limit and is made watertight. **Boiler-room b.,** one enclosing the boiler space. **Break b.,** vertical partition at end of any raised or sunken discontinuity of an upper deck. **B. bounding-bar,** continuous angle-bar connecting edges of a *b*. to a tank top, shell-plating, or another *b*. **B. coaming,** *see* COAMING. **B. deck,** *see* DECK. **B. door,** a watertight door in a *b*. **B. lantern,** *see* LANTERN. **B. line,** extreme limit to which piers or wharves may extend along a water-front; also, *harbor line.* **B.-liner,** doubling-plate fitted on inside of shell-plating in way of a transverse *b's* edges for compensating weakening caused by line of extra riveting of angle-bar connection in shell-plating. **B. sluice,** opening or drain in lower extremity of a *b*., fitted with a valve which can be operated from a deck above. **B. stiffeners,** members fitted to *b*. plating for reinforcing it against structural stresses and water or cargo pressure. Stiffeners are usually fitted vertically, but often horizontally or bridging the former, in which case they are bracketed to a side girder or to a longitudinal *b*. **Cargo-hold b.,** one bounding a cargo compartment or hold. **Center-line b.,** longitudinal *b*. erected in a vessel's center line. **Collision b.,** strong watertight transverse partition near the bows, extending from ship's bottom to upper or freeboard deck, as protection against further influx of water in event of holing damage to bows. In most classification rules, it is required to be located at not less than one-twentieth of vessel's length from her stem, measured at load water-line. **Corrugated b.,** one made of corrugated metal plates, or made of flate plates alternately attached to opposite flanges of stiffeners. The former are often built in state-rooms and crew's quarters; the latter in cargo-holds. **Engine-room b.,** one bounding machinery space. **Fore peak b.,** one nearest the stem, forming a fore peak tank's after wall. When extending from ship's bottom to her *b*. or upper deck, it is also the *collision b.* **Front b.,** same as *break b. (q.v.)* **Joiner b.,** a wood or light metal partition serving to bound state-rooms, offices, etc., and not contributing to structural strength. Included in this category are aluminum, corrugated steel, and pressed panel. **Longitudinal b.,** partition of planking or plating built in a fore-and-aft direction. Oil-tank vessels are required to have at least one of watertight construction in their cargo spaces, and if the only one, it must be built in the ship's center line. This requirement also applies to a *deep tank* in any vessel. **Oil-tight b.,** partition of plating capable of resisting passage of oil from one compartment to another. Where riveted, the work must be closer spaced than in watertight seams and extra care must be taken with caulking. **Partial b.,** one that does not extend upward to the *b*. deck, or completely from side to side. It is usually built as a local strength member. **Peak b.,** *see* PEAK. **Poop b.,** partition forming the forward limit of a poop space. **Recess b.,** a wall bounding a space recessed off from a main compartment. **Screen-b.,** *see* SCREEN. **Splinter b.,** steel partition or shield between or around guns as protection against flying splinters from shell explosions. **Stokehold b.,** *see* STOKEHOLD.

Stuffing-box b., *see* STUFFING-BOX. **Swash b.,** a low fore-and-aft vertical plate or partition for restricting transverse flow of water or oil due to rolling of a vessel; *see* SWASH. **Temporary b.,** one erected for a temporary purpose, such as a cargo separation wall, or a removable bunker partition. **Transverse b.,** wall of planking or plating built in an athwartship direction from side to side; *see* **Watertight b.** **Trunk b.,** casing or partition forming a wall around a hatchway, extending from deck to deck; a casing around any trunkway, such as that of an escape-hatch or an elevator. **Wash b.,** *see* WASH. **Watertight b.,** term for transverse *b's* (also *center-line b's.* in large vessels) which are required for structural strength and for safety reasons in event of serious hull damage. Number of such *b's* required is governed by a vessel's length and whether or not she is a passenger-carrying vessel, but at least four are required in a ship having her propelling machinery amidships, *viz.*, one at least one-twentieth her length from the stem (*collision b.*), one at each end of engine and boiler space, and one at fore end of her propeller-shaft stern tube. **Wire-mesh b.,** partition built of wire netting around store-rooms, special cargo lockers, etc. **Zig-zag b.,** one not in a continuous plane.

BULKY. Referred to cargo, indicates that goods occupy an unusually large space, considering their weight.

BULL. (Gr. *tauros*.) The northern constellation *Taurus,* the *Bull,* in which are located the group *Pleiades* and bright reddish star *Aldebaran (dec.* 16½° n.; *r.a.* 4½ hrs.). A male whale, sea-lion, sea-bear, or fur-seal. To **b. a barrel,** to pour water into a cask when it is emptied to prevent drying and shrinking of its staves and consequent leakage. **B.-boat,** a rude canoe made by stretching a bull elk's hide over a wood frame; said to have been in use among the Mandan tribe of Sioux Indians. Also, an old sailors' term for a cattle-carrying ship. **B.-dance,** a dance performed by men only. **B.-dog,** old navy term for a main deck gun. **B.-earing,** *see* EARING. **B. pine,** *see* PINE. **B.-rail,** a heavy timber set on a wharf's outer edge; also, *guard-rail.* **B. ring,** one for holding piston-rings in position. **B. riveting,** *see* RIVETING. **B.-rope,** any rope used to steady or temporarily secure a moving object; in older sailing-ship usage, a rope rove through a bull's-eye on a forward shroud to control an upper yard when lowered to, or hoisted from, the deck. A line leading from a bowsprit or jib-boom, made fast to, and holding, a mooring-buoy from striking against the bows. A rope serving as a forward guy for, and leading to the outer end of, a boat-boom.

BULLION. Silk cords covered with fine gold or silver threads used as fringing on officers' epaulets; also, *bullion fringe.*

BULLDOZER. In shipbuilding yards, a press whose ram head is supplied with different fullers or heads for pressing metal into special shapes, such as brackets, ladder-steps, and other small material; also used as a straightening press.

BULLHEAD SHARK. A fish of Pacific tropical waters about five feet in length, having two dorsal fins and teeth adapted to crushing shell-fish. Called *Port Jackson shark* in Australia (genus *Heterodontus*), the species now appears to be growing extinct.

BULL'S-EYE. A small ring-shaped piece of hard wood with a groove around its outer surface, chiefly used on a square sail to which it is fastened, for properly leading a buntline or a leechline rove through it. A small thick piece of glass in a deck or a vessel's side for admitting light. One of several bored wooden balls or rollers through which a gaff jaw-rope is rove. A distant isolated cloud seen at approach of a *bull's-eye squall,* marking the top of an otherwise invisible central spout of a whirlwind. Name for a lantern, particularly its lens, which is shaped to intensify rays for spotlight purposes. Center of a target. **B.-cringle,** a wooden ring or thimble used as a cringle in a sail's leech. **B.-squall,** *see* SQUALL. **Deck b.,** a dead-light, or thick piece of glass fitted in a deck.

BULL'S EYE. *Cor Tauri,* or star *Aldebaran* (*q.v.*).

BULL TROUT. In England, any of several kinds of sea trout; the *Dolly Varden* trout of the Pacific coast of North America from Oregon to Alaska.

BULWARK. BULWARKS. (Dan. *bolvärk,* a rampart.) Strake of plating or planking forming an extension of a vessel's side above her weather deck. Strengthened by *b. stanchions,* it serves as a protection against a rough sea when freeboard is small and consequently is a safeguard against loss of deck cargo or fittings. Openings in *b.,* called *freeing ports,* are required to be provided as a means of allowing any water shipped to quickly flow overboard, total area of ports depending upon deck area protected. **B.-netting,** a net-work of ratline stuff secured to an open rail and its stanchions as a skeleton *b.* **B.-port,** a freeing port; *see* PORT. **B. stay,** in steel vessels, braces extending from the deck to upper ends of *b.* stanchions. They are often displaced by a bracket-knee at foot of each stanchion. **Main b.,** *see* MAIN. **Top-gallant b.,** an old term for quarterboards, or timber forming a vertical extension of bulwarks at and near a vessel's stern; any upward extension of a bulwark.

BUMBOAT. A boat used to peddle provisions and small wares among vessels lying in a harbor or roadstead. A scavenger's boat on the Thames River, England. (Said to be a corruption of *bombard,* a barrel once used to carry beer to soldiers on duty.)

BUMPER. A buffer; a fender. The *pompano* or *amber-fish* of the West Indies and southern United States.

BUMPKIN. In a full-rigged ship or barque, a short boom projecting from each bow to which the fore tack was hove down, though in many vessels each *cathead* was used for this purpose; also, one of wood or iron on each quarter to which the lower blocks in main and main-topsail *braces* were fastened, and often the *vangs* of a spanker gaff. A small outrigger over a boat's stern, as in a yawl, to which a mizzen sheet is attached. **Jigger-b.,** *see* JIGGER. **Tack-b.,** *see* TACK.

BUNCH-WHALE. The humpback whale; *see* HUMPBACK.

BUND. (Hind. *band,* a dam or dike.) In the Orient, a pier; landing-place; harbor.

BUNG. Plug fitted to a cask's bung-hole; the bung-hole itself. When fitted with metal hoops, a cask has its bung located in line with the hoop rivets and at its middle or widest part. A close-fitting plug set over a countersunk bolt securing deck or side planking, scarfs, rails, and various items in wood ship-building; a *deck-plug,* as used over a deck-bolt in this manner. **B.-starter,** a kind of mallet used for loosening a bung of a cask; used by striking the cask a few smart blows on each side of its *b.-hole.* **B. up and bilge free,** referred to stowage of casks, indicates position of *b.* and freedom of bilge from outside pressure; a bottom tier is borne by quoins at quarters of each cask.

BUNK. A small compartment, shelf, or recess, used as a bed; a cot. To sleep in a *b.*

BUNKER. A compartment or tank usually situated in vicinity of a ship's boilers or machinery space, specially constructed for stowage of fuel, as coal or petroleum, and usually designated according to location, as *side, wing, reserve, cross,* or *thwartship b.* A large receptacle, such as a coal-bin, sandbox, etc. To replenish *b's* with fuel. **B. frame,** *see* FRAME. **B.-plate,** an iron cover over a hole in a ship's deck leading to a coal-*b.* **Hold-b.,** *see* HOLD. **Pocket-b.,** one of less space than an ordinary *b.* in which coal is kept for handy and immediate use. **Reserve-b.,** *see* RESERVE. **Side-b.,** *see* SIDE. **Trimming-in b.,** *see* TRIMMING.

BUNKERING. A rate per ton or sum of money charged for placing fuel on board; the operation itself.

BUNT. (Sw. *bunt,* a bundle.) Bulky middle part of those square sails which are clewed up to the middle of a yard before being furled; bunchy part of a rolled-up fishing-net. To haul up the middle of a square sail in furling. **B.-glut,** becket at mid-point in a square sail's head-rope to which a bunt-whip is hooked in hauling up a heavy sail for furling. **B.-gasket,** broad piece of canvas, matting, or sennit-work used to secure the bunt of a sail to its yard; a *breast-gasket*. **B.-jigger; b.-whip;** a temporary buntline round the middle of a heavy square sail hauled on by a small purchase to lift up a *b.* for furling.

BUNTING. Light, woollen, loosely-woven material of which flags are usually made, or a cotton imitation of such. A display of flags or *b.* as on festive occasions; flags collectively.

BUNTLINE. One of several ropes attached to a square sail's foot led to a masthead, thence to deck, and used to spill and gather a sail up to its yard when taking it in. **B. bull's-eye,** *see* BULL'S-EYE. **B.-cloth,** a chafing-piece of canvas sewed on a square sail's fore side in way of a buntline.

BUOY. (Du. *boei;* Fr. *bouee;* buoy.) A floating marker moored near dangerous rocks, shoals, wrecks, cables, or other submerged objects to indicate the presence of such; to show limits of special anchorages, or submarine construction work on tunnels and bridges; to indicate breadth and direction of a navigational channel or channels in a bay, harbor, lake, or river; or to provide a means to sustain an anchor cable to which vessels may be moored or temporarily made fast for warping or swinging purposes. *B's* are named from their appearance or construction, as *can b., nun b., spar b., wooden b.,* etc.; by manner in which their presence is indicated, as, *alarm-b., bell-b., electric-b., gas-b., luminous-b., whistling-b.,* etc.; and by their use, such as *anchor-b., beacon-b., cable-b., fairway-b., mooring-b., wreck-b.,* etc. Any device for keeping a person or object afloat, as a *life-b.,* a *fish-net b.* To **b. a cable,** *see* CABLE. To **bleed a b.,** *see* BLEED. **Breeches-b.,** a ring-shaped *life-b.* which forms the waist-line of a pair of short-legged canvas breeches, employed in rescue of persons from a stranded vessel where sea conditions render boat work impracticable. It is slung horizontally from a running-block on a hawser rigged as a span from ship to shore, and by means of an endless fall is hauled to and from the vessel by a life-saving crew. The breeches have proved most satisfactory as a means of securely holding persons during such transportation, and should it be found impossible to rig a span, rescue may be effected by hauling the buoy through the water. **B.-rope,** one for securing a *b.,* as to an anchor. **B.-safe,** a metal cork-armored vessel or boat having watertight compartments and equipped for keeping persons and merchandise safe and dry when landing or putting off through a heavy surf. **Can b.,** cylindrical-shaped *b.* marking the port side of a channel, entering from sea, in the U.S. system; it is given an odd number and painted black. **Channel-b's,** in the U.S. system, are marked as follows: Those on starboard hand, entering from sea, with even numbers and painted red; those on port hand with odd numbers and painted black. (They are numbered consecutively from seaward

end of a channel.) Those with red and black horizontal stripes mark obstructions or channel junctions, a *can b.* with black band or stripe uppermost indicating a main or preferred channel lies to the right, and a *nun b.* with red stripe uppermost, to the left; those with red and white vertical stripes are in mid-fairway and may be passed close-to. First class starboard and port hand *b's* are respectively conical and cylindrical in shape. This system generally is followed by most maritime countries. **Dan-b.,** *see* DAN. **Fog-b.,** a towed marker; *see* SPAR. **Franklin life-b.,** a large ring-*b.* made of copper carried on navy ships at each wing of a bridge and on each quarter, equipped with an automatic release. When dropped overboard, a small store of calcium carbide ignites and thus indicates its presence to a person in the water and to a rescuing boat. **Hong Kong mooring-b.,** a cylindrical one with flat end uppermost having a hawse-pipe through its middle and through which a mooring-chain-cable leads and terminates with a ring, the latter acting as a toggle in securing the buoy. When a vessel makes fast to such ring, chain cable becomes independent of buoy while still holding it in position. **Kedge-b.,** a floating marker for a kedge anchor. **Leading-b.,** *see* LEADING. **Light-b.,** *see* LIGHT. **Mark-b.,** *see* MARK. **Middle ground b.,** one which marks shoaling water with channels on either side. In U.S. waters it is painted in red and black horizontal bands or stripes; *see* **Channel-b's;** when lighted, shows continuous quick flashes. **Nun b.,** one of conical shape or like a truncated cone, placed on starboard hand of a channel, entering from sea; marked with an even number and red in color. **Quarantine b.,** one indicating limits of a quarantine anchorage and usually painted yellow. **Station-b.,** *see* STATION. **Swinging-b's,** a set or number of *b's* placed in harbor for swinging a vessel by her warping lines, as in fairing for entering a dry-dock, or adjusting compasses. **Towing-b.,** a towing-spar, or *fog-b.; see* SPAR. **Whistling-b.,** one equipped with a whistle which is operated by compressed air produced by its rise and fall on waves. Used in fairways and to mark outlying dangers, such *b's* may or may not be lighted, the whistle serving as a warning, or to indicate its presence, in darkness or thick weather. **Wreck-b.,** *see* WRECK.

BUOYAGE. Buoys collectively; a system or series of buoys for marking channels or navigable fairways frequented by shipping. **B. and Beaconage,** dues payable to Trinity House by vessels entering the port of London, England.

BUOYANCY. Total upward pressure of a fluid sustaining a floating body, or that equal to the weight of such body; property of rising or floating in a liquid. **Center of b.,** center of immersion; center of gravity of water volume (or other liquid) displaced by a floating object. **Center of b. curve, or table,** a curve or tabulated values indicating height above the keel, at various drafts, of a vessel's *center of b.* **Curve of b.,** *see* CURVE. **Reserve b.,** *see* RESERVE. **Utilized b.,** *see* FLOATING. **Working b.,** amount of *b.* available for carrying cargo, *i.e.,* difference between a vessel's light displacement and her load displacement, expressed in long tons *(2240 lbs.).*

BUOYANT MINE. *See* MINE.

BURDEN. BURTHEN. (A.S. *byrthen,* to bear.) A term dating from the Middle Ages for cargo-carrying capacity of a vessel, at one time expressed as a number of *tuns* of wine (measuring about 250 gallons each, and, in weight, approximately equal to our present *long ton* of 2240 lbs.); deadweight capacity, as a ship of 600 tons *burden.*

BURDENED VESSEL. *See* VESSEL.

BURDENS. Bottom-boards in a boat for protecting the planking and serving as a floor.

BUREAU. (Fr. *bureau,* desk, office.) A government department or office for transaction of public business; in U.S. and England, subordinate department or division of a principal department. **American Bureau of Shipping,** recognized as official classification society of the United States, controls specifications of construction and other factors concerned with appropriate qualities of vessels built for a particular trade, either as cargo or passenger carriers, or both; its main objective being establishment of classifying standards in construction of vessels and in equipment required for their efficient propulsion and operation. **B. of Fisheries,** a former division in U.S. Dept. of the Interior, now termed *Fish and Wild Life Service,* charged with the propagation of useful food fishes and investigation of matters concerning national fishing grounds, including supervision of the Alaskan salmon fisheries and seal rookeries on Pribilof Islands. **B. of Foreign and Domestic Commerce,** a division in U.S. Department of Commerce which tabulates and publishes reports of foreign and domestic trade. **B. of Lighthouses,** a division in U.S. Treasury Department, now extinct as a *b.* but embodied in the Coast Guard, charged with establishment and maintenance of aids to navigation in territorial waters, excepting those of the Panama Canal Zone. **B. of Marine Inspection and Navigation,** formerly in U.S. Department of Commerce, a division whose functions in supervision of all merchant marine safety requirements, including licensing and certificating of personnel, and vessel inspection, now are included in Coast Guard activities under the Treasury Department *(1942).* **B. Veritas,** a shipping classification society founded in 1828 and officially recognized as the French national society of its kind. **U.S. Navy B's,** *see* **N. Department** *in* NAVY.

BURGEE. A swallow-tailed flag used as a distinguishing pennant and bearing a vessel's name or insignia of her owners or her charterers. Flags *A* and *B* of the International Code of Signals are *burgees.*

BURGOMASTER. The burgomaster *gull* of the Arctic seas, white in color, with gray back and upper side of wings; so named from its tyrannical disposition.

BURGOO. BURGOUT. Oatmeal porridge; a stiff gruel also known as *loblolly.*

BURNER OIL. *See* OIL.

BURNISH. To polish or make lustrous, as by friction.

BURR. In shipbuilding, rough uneven edge of a sheared or burnt plate, or around a punched or burnt hole; also, a washer-shaped piece of metal through which a rivet or bolt is inserted and against which the point of such rivet or bolt is hammered over or *burred.* **B.-pump,** a pump having an inverted cone of leather serving as a valved piston-head.

BURST. A rupture in a pipe, tank, cylinder, etc., caused by internal pressure. **B. of the monsoon,** or **breaking of the monsoon;** *see* MONSOON.

BURTHEN. *See* BURDEN.

BURTON. A handy tackle used for various purposes. **B.-pendant,** the first piece of rigging which goes over a topmasthead, to which is hooked a block and gantline for sending aloft jib-stays, topmast shrouds, and back-stays in rigging a square-rigged vessel. **Sail-b.,** *see* SAIL. **Single b.,** or **single Spanish b.,** a handy purchase used on small vessels for cargo-hoisting, catting an anchor, or as a boom topping-lift. Consists of one standing block aloft through which a runner is rove and attached to a cargo or lifting-hook, the runner's other end being connected to another single block in which the fall is rove, its standing end also being made fast to the hook; also called a *garnet.* Power ratio of this *b.* is 1 to 3, neglecting friction loss. **Spanish b.,** or **double Spanish b.,** similar in principle to the single *b.,* excepting that either a tackle of one double and one single block (luff tackle), or one of two single blocks (gun tackle), is made fast to the runner's hauling part. Lower end of runner and hauling tackle's lower block are both attached to the cargo-hook. Power ratio, with luff tackle, 1 to 7; with gun tackle, 1 to 5; friction not considered. **Top-b.,** small tackle formerly kept in each top on sailing war-vessels; rove as a luff tackle, its double block usually was a tandem or fiddle, *i.e.,* having one sheave above, and in line with, the other; used aloft for setting up rigging, etc.

BURY OF A MAST. *See* MAST.

BUSH. To provide with, or install, a *bushing.*

BUSHING. A bearing of suitable friction-resisting material or metal on which a shaft, rod, or other working part of machinery is supported. A threaded fitting used as a connecting-piece for two pipes of different sizes. Also *see* ABRID. **Rudder-b's,** *see* RUDDER. **Stern b.,** *see* STERN.

BUSINESS, SHIP'S. *See* SHIP.

BUSK. A now almost obsolete term meaning to *tack* or *beat about* in holding one's own to windward, while seeking or waiting for some objective, as a pilot-boat cruising off and on; to cruise as a *pirate*.

BUSS. (Du. *buis*.) A two-masted schooner-rigged Dutch vessel of from 50 to 70 tons burden, once commonly used in herring and mackerel fisheries, characterized by two small deck houses,—one at each end of the hull.

BUTT. End of a plank, plate, bar, timber, etc.; joint made by two ends of such in meeting, as a *b.* in a strake of plating. A flounder or flat-fish; the *halibut*. To place an end of a plank, timber, plate, etc., against some other structural part; to butt against. A large cask, usually for wine or beer; a measure of capacity equal to two hogsheads or 130 U.S. gallons; also called a *pipe*. **B. and b.,** placed with both ends together. **B.-chock,** a short piece of wood used in scarfing futtocks or different parts of a ship's transverse framing. **B.-iron,** *see* IRON. **B.-joint,** *see* JOINT. **B.-plates,** in older shipbuilding, plates connecting ends of outside planking in a composite-built vessel. **B.-riveting,** *see* RIVETING. **B.-seams,** those at butts of planking or plating. **B.-strap,** piece of iron or steel plate riveted to adjoining ends of plates, stringers, etc., as a means of connecting them; to weld two pieces of metal so as to form a butting joint; also, *b.-strip*. **B.-tool,** steel tool for caulking *b.*-joints of metal plating. **B. weld,** joining of abutting ends of metal by welding; *see* WELDING. **Caulking-b.,** open *b.* in deck or side planking, as prepared for caulking; also, *calking-b*. **Close-b.,** close-fitting *b.* made by grinding as necessary and welding. **Hook and b.,** *see* HOOK. **Scuttle-b.,** *see* SCUTTLE. **Shift of b's,** *see* SHIFT. To **spring a b.,** or **start a b.,** to become displaced or loosened; to work open or loose; said of a plank, due to mishap or laboring of ship. **Top and b.,** *see* TOP. **Water-b.,** *see* WATER.

BUTTER-FISH. Any of several fishes so called from their slippery coating, including the *dollar-fish* of U.S. Atlantic coast, the *gunnel* of the North Atlantic, *nigger-fish* of West Indies waters, and *kelp-fish* of New Zealand.

BUTTER-RIGGED. Sailors' distinguishing term for a type of English coasting vessel of topsail-schooner rig in which a top-gallant-sail was sent aloft from her deck each time it was set.

BUTTERWORTH SYSTEM. A method of cleaning oil tanks by two water-nozzles rotating in right-angled planes. By cutting steam into the line, hot water at high pressure is forced against every part of a tank. Now extensively used on tank vessels.

BUTTOCK. That part of a vessel's stern above her water-line which overhangs or lies abreast of the stern-post; the *counter*.

BUTTOCK LINES. In shipbuilding, curved lines described on the *sheer plan* as intersections with outer surface of the hull of planes parallel to the vertical fore-and-aft midship plane. Laid off at convenient intervals from midship vertical plane in *half-breadth plan* and *body plan*, are used in conjunction with lines shown on all three plans to *fair up*, or reconcile, each to each in shaping a required design of hull form.

BUTTON. Leather boss or ring fitted on an oar to prevent it from slipping outboard in a rowlock.

BUYS-BALLOT'S LAW. *See* LAW.

BUZZO. A Sicilian fishing-boat, 20 to 30 feet in length and rigged with one lateen sail. A capacious cargo-carrier of the Venetians in the 17th. century, propelled by both sail and oars; also *bucca*.

B.V. Official abbreviation for *Bureau Veritas; see* BUREAU.

BY. Denoting near to, according to, toward, or in position. **By and large,** *see* LARGE. **By north, by south, by east, by west,** indicating proximity to a principal compass point, as *N.E. by N.,* meaning one point to northward of North-east; *see* COMPASS. **By the board,** *see* BOARD. **By the head,** said of a vessel when she is floating deeper forward than aft. **By the lee,** *see* LEE. **By the run,** rapid motion on being loosed from control or restraint, as, to let a rope *go by the run*. Seamen are said to be engaged *by the run* when shipped to take a vessel from one port to another only. **By the stern,** reverse of *by the head*. **By the wind,** *see* WIND. **Lay by,** *see* LAY. To **lie by,** *see* LIE.

BYLANDER. Same as *bilander, q.v.*

C

C. Square flag denoting the letter *C* in International Code of Signals, when flown singly, indicates *Yes* or *Affirmative;* in semaphore signalling, letter *C*, indicated by the right arm stretched upward at a 45° angle from vertical, is given by receiver at end of each word in message as acknowledgment of its receipt. *C* stands for *centigrade thermometer* reading; also is common abbreviation in ships' log-books for *cloudy,* or for *choppy* or *cross sea.*

C and S. In older navy usage, indicates that a seaman has returned *clean and sober,* as recorded in the liberty-book.

C-FRAME SYSTEM. *See* SYSTEM.

CAAING-WHALE. *Pilot-whale* or *blackfish* of the North Atlantic, resembling the *grampus* but greater in size, reportedly numerous in vicinity of Iceland, the Orkney, Shetland, and Faroe Islands. Also called *rorqual,* it is closely related to the *Orca,* or killer-whale, but has a timid disposition. *See* BLACK-FISH.

CABIN. A room on board ship for use of one or more officers or passengers; space in which the accommodation for officers and/or passengers is located. **C.-boy,** or **ship-boy,** *see* SHIP. **C. compass,** see COMPASS. **C. passenger,** one occupying the best accommodation ship affords. **Fore-c.,** *see* FORE. **Poop-c.,** *see* POOP. **Through the c. windows,** *see same.* **Trunk-c.,** *see* TRUNK.

CABLE. (Ger. *kabel;* L.L. *caplum,* a rope.) A heavy rope or chain used to hold a vessel at anchor. Ropes of hemp, jute, or coir were the cables of former times, but to-day, except in small vessels and fishing-craft, are displaced by the stronger and more durable *chain cable.* The modern term for an extra heavy fiber or wire hawser, one used in towing, or heaving off a stranded vessel. **Anchor-c.,** *see* ANCHOR. To **bitt the c.,** to make it fast round the bitts. To **bring a c. to,** to turn it round the capstan or a mooring-winch, preparatory to heaving away. To **buoy a c.,** to mark the place where the end of a *c.* lies by a buoy; to support a *c.* by floats in order

to keep it off a rocky bottom, coral, etc. **C. bend,** knot or clinch by which a *c.* is bent to an anchor or mooring-post; formerly, the small rope used to secure end of a *c.* after it has been attached to the anchor-ring. **C.-box,** in small vessels, a receptacle in which cable is stowed. **C.-buoy,** an anchor-buoy. **C. clench-bracket,** a reinforced bracket in a chain-locker to which cable is secured. **C.-hook,** a long-shanked hook used to stow chain cable by hand. **C.-laid,** said of a hawser composed of three plain-laid ropes, laid as strands. Though considerably weaker than a rope of same diameter plain-laid, a cable-laid hawser is much more suitable for handling and stowing, due to its comparative flexibility, and line is more readily dried than plain-laid rope. **C.-lifter,** drum or gipsy on a windlass so designed as to grip chain cable links individually when heaving in or slacking out cable; a *cable-wheel.* **C.-molding,** molding made or carved in the form of rope formerly often found on a vessel's stern as an ornamentation. **C.-nipper,** a device for temporarily securing a chain cable, or for relieving stress on its inboard end; a *devil's claw.* **C.'s length,** formerly the length of a ship's anchor-cable, 120 fathoms; now usually taken as 100 fathoms, or approximately the tenth part of a nautical mile, also termed a *cable. Cable's length* is to-day used as a measure of distance, particularly in ship-maneuvering, and no longer may be considered the length of a ship's mooring-hawser or cable, since length of cable required on each bower anchor varies from 60 fathoms in a small vessel to 165 fathoms in one of 27000 gross tons. **C.-stopper,** a devil's claw; *see* **C.-nipper. C.-tier,** a place in the hold where rope cables are stowed. **C.-wheel,** *see* **C.-lifter. Chain c. compressor,** *see* CHAIN. **Ground c.,** *see* GROUND. To **heave a c. short,** to heave it in until it leads nearly *up-and-down,* or nearly vertically from hawse-pipe; *see* HEAVE. **Insurance-c.,** *see* **Insurance-hawser,** *under* HAWSER. **Length of chain c.,** *see* LENGTH. **Mooring-c.,** a cable fixed to a pier or supported by a buoy for mooring purposes. To **nip the c.,** to stop off, or temporarily relieve the stress on inboard part of a cable. **To pay out,** or **veer, the c.,** to let out more cable. **Range of c.,** see RANGE. **Range the c.,** see RANGE. **To serve a c.,** to wind small rope about it as a protection against chafing. **Ship's c.,** same as *anchor-cable.* **To slip a c.,** to disconnect it inboard and let it run out, thus freeing ship from the anchor, as may be required in cases of emergency. **Shot of a c.,** see SHOT. **To snub a c.,** see SNUB. **Stream-c.,** see STREAM. **Sheet-c.,** see SHEET. **Towing-c.,** a cable or hawser used in towing. **Wrecking-c.,** a heavy hawser or chain used in salvage work, such as heaving a vessel off ground or heavy towing.

CABLET. A diminutive of cable; a small cable; specifically, a cable-laid rope less than 9 or 10 inches in circumference.

CABLE-SHIP. A vessel used for laying or picking up submarine telegraph or telephone cables.

CABOOSE. (Du. *cabuis,* a little hut.) A small deckhouse used as a galley on a merchant vessel; also, *camboose.* A cooking-stove used on canal-boats and small coasting vessels, usually on the open deck.

CABOTAGE. (Fr. *caboter,* to sail along the coast.) Coasting trade; navigation along a coast; coast pilotage.

CABRILLA. In West Indies and Spanish America, the *red hind* or any of the *groupers;* any of various edible fishes of genus *Serranus,* found in Mediterranean and in warmer parts of the Pacific.

CABURN. An obsolete name for a kind of spunyarn.

CACHALOT. The sperm whale; see WHALE.

CADET. A youth in training for military or naval service as an officer; especially one in a military or naval college, such as West Point or Annapolis. (Students at Annapolis were officially called *midshipmen* in 1902.) Cadets are nominated for admission to the institutions named, after examination, by President of the United States or a member of Congress. Also, an apprentice officer in the merchant marine. **C. engineer,** see ENGINEER. **C. midshipman,** see MIDSHIPMAN.

CAGE. A framework or grate of metal containing combustibles and elevated on a pole, which formerly was used as a beacon to show the entrance to a harbor or a navigable channel.

CAGEWORK. An old term for the upper works of a ship.

CAIQUE. (Turk. *quaiq,* boat.) A long narrow boat used on the Bosporus, pointed at each end and propelled by oars; also, a small Levantine sailing-vessel.

CAIR. See COIR.

CAISSON. (Fr. *caisse,* a case or chest.) A watertight structure or heavy tank used for raising sunken vessels. It is submerged alongside by filling it with water and made fast to ship's hull; then emptied either by pumping or by forcing out the water by compressed air, buoyancy of caisson or caissons produces the lifting power required; also called a *camel.* A structure around a badly damaged part of a sunken vessel's hull for purpose of effecting repairs preparatory to refloating her. Heavy floating *gate* used to close entrance to a graving dock, often containing the pumping arrangement for emptying dock. A floating or pontoon *dry-dock.* **C. disease,** a malady to which divers are subject due to repeatedly passing from an atmosphere of high pressure into outside air, under unfavorable conditions; also called *the bends.*

CALAMARY. (L.L. *calamarium,* ink-stand.) One of ten-armed cephalopods having a pen-shaped internal skeleton or cuttle-bone. Its body is about a foot long, tapering to a point flanked by two caudal triangular fins, soft, and fleshy and contains two sacs from which a black fluid is discharged, if it is disturbed. It is found in most seas and is more commonly called a *squid;* also termed *sea-sleeve, preke, ink-fish, pen-fish,* and, improperly, *cuttle-fish.* As the *squid,* it is numerous on Atlantic coast of North America, where it is extensively used for fishing-bait.

CALCIUM CARBIDE. See ACETYLENE.

CALCULATED ALTITUDE METHOD. See SAINT HILAIRE METHOD.

CALDERETA. A local name for a warm suddenly arising *wind* from the mountain gorges of northern Venezuelan coast.

CALENDAR, LLOYD'S. See LLOYD'S.

CALENDAR YEAR. See YEAR.

CALF. The young of marine mammals, as that of seals and cetaceans, adults of which are called bulls and cows. See CALVING.

CALIBRATE. To correct errors of scale readings of any graduated instrument, as to calibrate a radio direction-finder.

CALK or **CAULK.** To drive oakum or other fiber into seams of planking of a vessel or boat to prevent leakage, which operation is completed by paying seams with pitch or some such water-resisting preparation. In shipbuilding and boilermaking, to drive down the faying edges of plating or other overlapping metal in order to make the work water or steamtight.

CALKAGE or **CAULKAGE.** Material used in calking; generally, teased out fiber of old hemp or flax ropes, called *oakum,* in ship work; in boat-building, strands of cotton are commonly used in the planking-seams.

CALKER or **CAULKER.** One employed at calking seams on a vessel. An old term for one who sleeps on deck in his usual clothing.

CALKING. Process of making tight seams of planking, plating, etc. *See* CALK. **C.-box,** a chest in which calking-tools are kept, serving also as a seat for the calker. **C.-butt,** an open end-joint between planks in a vessel's side. **C.-cotton,** loose or loosely-woven cotton, often laid in loose strands, used in calking seams of boats or decks of yachts. **C.-iron, calking-chisel,** *see* IRON; also, one of the chisels or punches used in tightening joints in metal. **C.-mallet,** a wooden mallet having a long head which may be used in striking the calking-tool at either end; usually made of live oak, slit through at each side of handle, the head is fitted with a steel band at each end.

CALL. A peculiar silver whistle or *pipe* used by the boatswain and his mates in navy ships to attract attention to orders about to be given and to direct performance of duties by various strains and signals. In former times a gold *call* and chain was the badge of an admiral. A *call* may also be sounded on a bugle, a drum, or a bell, for boat-calls, fire-alarm, etc. To make a brief stop at a port. **C. away,** a preliminary order given when a whaler's boat is about to leave ship. **C.-boy,** formerly a boy whose duty it was to transmit captain's orders on board ship. To **c. the watch,** to awaken watch below, or summon those off duty when and as necessary. **Port of c.,** *see* PORT. **Roll-c.,** *see* ROLL.

CALLAO ROPE. *See* ROPE.

CALM. Quiet state of the elements, especially absence of wind; *see* BEAUFORT'S SCALE. **C.-belt,** a zone embracing from four to six degrees of latitude in vicinity of the equator, characterized by the prevalence of calms during greater part of the year; the calm latitudes; the doldrums. **Calms of Cancer,** belt of high atmospheric pressure, in the vicinity of 30° north latitude, noted for its light baffling winds and calms; *horse latitudes*. **Calms of Capricorn,** region of light, baffling winds and calms in vicinity of 30° south latitude between the south-east trade-winds and the variables. **Dead c., flat c.,** a complete lack of wind.

CALVING. A separating or breaking off so that a *calf* or *calves* become detached, as from a *glacier* or an *iceberg*. Act of bringing forth a calf: said of *whales* or *seals*.

CAMBER. (O.F. *cambre,* bent or curved.) Having a slight upward convexity, as transverse rounding of a deck, sometimes called the *crown*. This arching or rounding is the *camber* or *round of beam* and is expressed in inches as departure from horizontal at midship fore-and-aft line. *Curve* in a ship's plank or timber. In England, a small dock in a navy yard where timber is loaded and discharged, or a pro-

tected area for small craft. **C.-beam,** a beam bent or shaped so as to give a camber to a deck. **C.-keeled,** having the keel slightly arched upward, but not so much as to be termed *hogged*.

CAMBOOSE. *See* CABOOSE.

CAMEL. A buoyant watertight structure placed alongside a vessel to assist in clearing a shoal or bar, or to enable her to float in shallow water; *see* CAISSON. A *float* or *raft* placed between a ship and a pier, against which vessel lies in her berth.

CAMOUFLAGE. (Fr. *camoufler,* to disguise.) Disguising of a ship by painting hull and upper works in deceptive coloration with, also, the object of distorting preconceived lines of the vessel by, and her apparent distance from, the enemy. *Smoke-screen* provided by destroyers for battleships. To *disguise* by camouflage.

CAN. In the U.S. navy vernacular, a term for a destroyer, probably because of light construction of such craft. **Ash-c.,** *see* ASH. **C. buoy,** *see* BUOY.

CANAL. (L. *canalis,* canal or channel.) An excavated water-course; an artificial channel designed for navigation; a long, narrow arm of the sea, nearly uniform in width. **C.-boat,** a long heavy-decked vessel having bluff vertical bows and stern, once always towed by a horse or mule walking along a *tow-path* on the canal bank, but now usually by a towing-boat, or it may be self-powered. **C. Zone,** territory on either side of Panama Canal belonging to the United States. **C.-lock,** *see* LOCK. **C.-lift,** a cradle used to haul canal-boats up an incline or on a railway; a hydraulic elevator for lifting boats from one level of a canal to another.

CANCER. (L. *cancer,* crab.) A northern constellation between *Leo* and *Gemini;* fourth sign of the zodiac. Cancer has no stars of sufficient brightness for navigational purposes. **Calms of C.,** *see* CALM.

CANDLE-FISH. A fish of northern Pacific coasts of America allied to the smelt, excellent for food, and 8 to 10 inches in length. It is said that the fish contains so much oil that, when dried, it may be used as a candle by drawing a wick through it.

CANDY STOWAGE. A stevedore's term for stowage of goods that are perishable or adversely affected by heat.

CAN-HOOKS. A special sling for use in hoisting casks or barrels, consisting of two flat hooks which grip chime of cask by stress on a short bridle connecting them to the cargo fall.

CANIS MAJOR. (L. = *larger dog.*) A constellation lying southeast of *Orion* and containing the brightest fixed star in the heavens, *Sirius* (declination 16½° South; R.A. 6 hrs. 43 min.), the *Dog Star*.

CANIS MINOR. (L. = *lesser dog.*) A constellation located to the east of *Orion* and north of *Canis Ma-*

jor, containing the bright star *Procyon* (magnitude .5; declination 5½° North; R.A. 7 hrs. 37 min.)

CANISTER-SHOT. *See* CASE-SHOT.

CANNED WILLIE. A sailor's term for canned corned beef.

CANNON. (Fr. *canon;* L. *canna,* a reed, pipe, or tube.) A piece of ordnance or artillery; any of heavier projectile-throwing artillery pieces made of brass, bronze, iron, or steel, to-day generally termed a *gun.* Cannon have been classified under various names usually depending on their weight and use; for example, in 16th. and 17th. century usage were the *demi-cannon, saker,* and *culverin,* and in more modern times, the *carronade, howitzer,* and *mortar.* On war-vessels, cannon may be termed as main, intermediate, or secondary battery guns, according to their caliber or position. Power or caliber of cannon may be expressed by weight of projectile fired, as a 32-pounder; by gun's weight, as a 20-ton gun; or by diameter of bore, as a 12-inch gun. **C.-ball,** a missile made to be fired from a cannon, originally spherical-shaped and of solid stone or metal; also, *cannon-bullet.* **C.-lock,** a device for firing a cannon by a percussion primer. **C. royal,** an obsolete gun of 8 to 8½ inches caliber which threw a ball of from 48 to 60 pounds weight; also called a *cannon of eight.* **C.-shot,** the range of a cannon; a *cannon-ball.*

CANNONADE. Act of discharging cannon or heavy guns; an attack by artillery of continued duration.

CANOE. (Sp. *canoa.*) A light boat propelled by hand-paddles; any of the boats made by primitive peoples, such as those fashioned from trunks of trees, or those of frame construction having a shell of animal hides or bark of trees. Probably the most graceful and useful were the birch-bark-covered canoes of Algonquin tribes of North America, while crudest types, usually of the *dug-out* order, are found in Africa. Most elaborate form of canoe or dug-out is the craft used by natives of South Pacific islands, which is fitted with outriggers and remarkably fast under sail. Size of canoes varies from the modern 12-foot pleasure craft to one capable of holding 50 to 60 men like those of the Indians of north-western America. **C.-birch,** bark of the white or paper birch tree used by North American Indians for canoe-making. **C.-gum,** substance made of boiled bread-fruit-tree juice and cocoa-nut oil, used in West Indies for tightening planking-seams of boats. **Chesapeake c.,** a small open boat used on Chesapeake Bay, having two masts and a sharp stern. A larger size of such craft is called a *pungey.* **Ice-c.,** *see* ICE. **Log-c.,** a dug-out.

CANOPUS. Second brightest star in the heavens, of magnitude −0.9, situated in *Argus,* and having a declination of 52° 40′ S. and right ascension 6 hrs.

23 min. It lies about 36° south of the bright star *Sirius.*

CANOPY. A light awning spread over the stern of a boat, or over an open launch.

CANT. A piece of wood laid on a vessel's deck for various purposes, as to prop up some part of a construction. A cant-frame. To place in a position oblique to any definite course or line. To give an inclination to one side, as in preparing a vessel for careening. **C.-beams,** *see* BEAMS. **C.-body,** in plans of a ship, that which shows arrangement lines of cant-frames and bevel-lines. **C.-dog,** a sling by which a cask is raised at one end; a *cant-hook.* **C.-fall,** fall rove through the cant-blocks constituting the purchase rig for turning a whale over during operation of *flensing,* or stripping blubber from, carcase alongside ship; *cant-tackle* was led to the masthead. **C.-floor,** *see* FLOOR. **C.-frames,** ribs or frames whose plane of support to the structure is not perpendicular to fore-and-aft line, such as framing in ship's counter. **C.-hook,** a bar having a curved movable hook at one end, used for turning over heavy logs, etc. **C.-purchase,** *see* **cant-fall. C.-quoin, can-tick-quoin, canting-coin,** a triangular wooden chock for preventing a cask from rolling. **C.-spar,** a piece of timber suitable for converting into a boom, mast, or yard. **C.-timbers,** same as *cant-frames.*

CANTILEVER-FRAMED SHIP. *See* VESSEL.

CANTILEVER TANKS. *See* TANK.

CANTLINE. *See* GUNTLINE.

CANTON. An old term for small rectangular part next to the hoist in an ensign or flag containing the *union,* or other device.

CANVAS. (Fr. *canevas,* hempen cloth; Gr. *kannabis,* hemp.) Strong closely-woven cloth made of hemp, flax, or cotton, used for sails, awnings, tarpaulins, tents, etc. That which is made of canvas, as sails, tents, etc. A ship's sails collectively. *See* SAIL. **C.-climber,** a sailor who goes aloft to handle sails. **C. sling,** *see* **Flour-sling** *under* SLING. **Leviathan c.,** *see* LEVIATHAN. **To live under c.,** to be under canvas, to live or be in tents ashore. **Press of c.,** *see* PRESS. **Under a cloud of c.,** said of a ship carrying a large spread of sail. **Under c.,** under sail, or being propelled by sail.

CAP. (ME. *cappe,* cap or hood.) A band or collar, usually of iron, fitted round end of a spar and extended to receive another spar to which the latter is joined, as *lower-mast cap* or *bowsprit cap,* in which are set the topmast and jib-boom, respectively. A piece of leather or tarred canvas over end of a rope. A metal band round end of a spar. **Bowsprit-c.,** *see* BOWSPRIT. **C.-jib,** *see* JIB. **C.-log,** a heavy timber forming upper edge of a wharf. A **capful of wind,** *see* WIND. **C. of a cannon,** in old ordnance, a piece of lead laid over the vent to keep priming dry; also called *apron*. **C.-scuttle,** a small hatch fitted with a cover which extends over outside of coaming. **C.-shore,** in larger and older sailing-ships, a small spar or shore supporting lower-mast cap on fore side of topmast between the top and cap. Since the advent of lower topsails, lower-topsail-yard crane, which is the bearing pivot for that yard, swings in an extension neck to lower-mast cap; hence the heavy iron shore supporting cap found in vessels of double topsail rig. **Flat c.,** or **hat,** blue cloth cap formerly worn by seamen in U.S. navy. **Hammer-c.,** *see* HAMMER. **South-west c.,** *see* SOU'-WESTER. **Thrum-c.,** *see* THRUM. **Watch-c.,** *see* WATCH.

CAPACITY, CARGO-CARRYING. *See* CARGO. **Capacity plan,** *see* PLAN. **Deadweight capacity,** *see* DEAD.

CAPBALK. *See* KAPPBAULK.

CAPE. A point or extension of land on the coast, as Cape of Good Hope; a promontory. To bear up, as in counteracting a current in steering; to keep a course or head in an obvious direction, as "*How does she cape?*" **C. Ann oars,** *see* OAR. **C.-cloud,** *see* CLOUD. **C. Flyaway,** a name given the fancied or fictitious appearance of land. **C. Horn fever,** an old sailor-term for feigned illness of those who wish to shirk their work. It derives the name from generally disagreeable weather and sea conditions in vicinity of Cape Horn. **C. pigeon,** a black and white petrel commonly found off Cape of Good Hope.

CAPELIN. A small fish of the smelt family, about 8 inches in length, abundant on the coasts of Greenland, Iceland, Newfoundland, and Alaska; used for food and as bait for codfishing.

CAPE SHEEP. Old sailor's slang for the *albatross.*

CAPELLA. The brightest star in the constellation Auriga (*alpha Aurigæ*), magnitude 0.2; declination 46° north; R.A. 5 hrs. 13 min. It lies nearly half way between the belt in Orion and Pole Star (*Polaris*).

CAPER. (Du. *Kaper.*) A light-armed 17th. century vessel used by the Dutch in privateering; also, captain of a privateer; a *corsair.*

CAPPING. Fore-and-aft finishing piece along the top sides of an open boat, often improperly termed *gunwale;* called a *covering-board, margin-plank,* or *plank-sheer,* in a decked boat or vessel. **Keelson-c.,** *see* KEELSON.

CAPRICORNUS. CAPRICORN. (L. *caper,* goat; *cornu,* horn.) A southern constellation of the zodiac, located in about 15° south declination and 21 hrs. right ascension. It contains no stars brighter than those of magnitude 3.0. Called *tenth sign of the zodiac,* it is represented from ancient times by a goat-like figure. **Calms of C.,** *see* CALM.

CAPSIZE. To overturn, or upset, as a boat or other object.

CAPSTAN. (Fr. *cabestan;* L. *capistrum,* a halter.) A vertical drum revolving on a spindle, used for exerting power required in heaving on a rope or on an anchor-cable. Its drum or barrel may be smooth or provided with several upright ribs, or *whelps,* and is turned and supplied with necessary leverage by means of *capstan bars,* which are inserted in holes around the *capstan-head,* or by steam or electric power connected to the drum from a deck below. Some capstans operated by hand are now fitted with a so-called *double-purchase gear* which is brought into effect by heaving capstan-head in reverse direction to that of direct pull. c. is generally placed so as to be convenient for warping, or for hoisting heavier sails and heaving in sheets, etc. **Chinese c.,** one whose barrel has two parts of different diameters and used for obtaining a heaving purchase on a *whip,* rope winding in on one part while winding out on the other. To **come up with the c.,** to turn it reverse way, so as to slacken rope turned on the drum. **Electric-c.,** one run by an electric motor. To **heave on the c.,** to push the bars as in warping in, or to turn on mechanical power, if so fitted. **Jeer-c.,** *see* JEER. To **man the c.,** to place men and ship bars ready for heaving away. To **pawl the c.,** to fix the pawls, which are fitted at outside circumference of lower end of drum, so as to prevent capstan from moving against the heave, or to *hold its own.* To **rig the c.,** *see* RIG. **Steam-c.,** one operated by a steam-engine. To **surge the c.,** to ease or slacken a rope turned on the capstan. To **swifter the c. bars,** in old sailing-vessels, such as frigates and ships of the line, when anchors were hove in by capstan, the bars, numbering as many as twenty, were hitched together all round by the *capstan-swifter,* a small-sized rope spanning their outside ends, in order to prevent them being accidentally unshipped and also to afford a hold for extra men.

CAPSTERN. Same as *capstan.*

CAPTAIN. (O.F. *capitain;* L. *caput,* the head.) In U.S. navy, an officer next in rank above a commander, and equal in rank to a colonel in the army; a title extended by courtesy to any officer commanding a vessel; leader or chief of a group of men assigned to a special duty, as *Captain of the hold, Captain of after guard,* etc. Master of a merchant vessel, yacht, or other kind of vessel. **C.'s biscuit,** a fine quality ship's biscuit. **C.'s bridge,** *see* BRIDGE. **C. of the hold,** *see* HOLD. **C. of the port,** *see* PORT. **C.'s walk,** a balcony constructed on or near the roof of an old shipmaster's residence to provide a view of shipping, with the desirable nautical setting of a place for the seaman to "pace the deck." **C.'s watch,** *see* WATCH. **Fleet-c.,** an officer temporarily appointed to act as chief of staff to commander-in-chief of a fleet or squadron; also, *Flag-Captain.* **Gun-c.,** *see* GUN. **Port-c.,** *see* PORT. **Post-c.,** *see* POST. **Sea-c.,** *see* SEA. **Staff-c.,** *see* STAFF.

CAPTURE. Act of seizing an enemy's vessel, by force or otherwise.

CAPTURE, PRIZE. A vessel taken from an enemy in time of war.

CAR. In U.S., a perforated floating box or crate for keeping fish, lobsters, etc. alive. An old name for the constellation *Ursa Major;* also called *Charlie's Wain* or *Wagon,* the *Dipper,* and the *Plough.* **C.-ferry,** a vessel specially constructed for carrying railroad cars in exposed waters with object of avoiding otherwise necessary transfer of freight or passengers at a terminal port. **C.-float,** a large decked scow fitted with necessary tracks for transporting trains or freight-cars from one wharf to another in sheltered waters. **Life-c.,** *see* LIFE.

CARACK. (Sp. & Port. *caraca.*) A Spanish or Portuguese armed merchant ship of larger type used in American and East Indian trade from 15th. to 17th. century; a *galleon.* Also, *carac, carrack, carryk.*

CARAVAN. A fleet of Russian or Turkish vessels sailing in convoy. (*Now probably obsolete.*)

CARAVEL. (Sp. *carabela.*) A small Spanish or Portuguese vessel of 15th. to 17th. century, of the type used by Columbus, having a long narrow poop and usually three masts with lateen sails. A comparatively recent Portuguese vessel of 100 to 150 tons with two masts and lateen sails. A fishing-boat on the French coast. Term for an old Turkish frigate. Also written *caraval, caravela, caravella,* and *carvel.*

CARBON DIOXIDE. CO_2 gas, popularly known as *carbonic-acid gas;* an incombustible and irrespirable gas used as a refrigerant and as a fire-extinguishing agent on board ship. The CO_2 refrigerating machine, of which there are several types, is largely used in the care of perishable cargo and provisions as a means of safely and efficiently cooling the *brine* which is circulated through batteries of coils appropriately placed in cargo and store-room spaces. In extinguishing fires, supply of gas is opened to compartment containing the fire, which is tightly closed against ventilation, so that fire or combustion process is blanketed or smothered.

CARBURETED ENGINE. *See* ENGINE.

CARCASS. CARCASE. Decaying remains of a bulky object, as a stranded ship; the dead body of a whale; a vessel in the skeleton-like stage of construction, i.e., with frames raised but shell-plating not in place.

CARCHARODON. A man-eating shark found in all tropical and sub-tropical seas. It has triangular serrate-edged teeth, is a voracious fish, and grows to over 30 feet in length.

CARD. **Compass-c.,** circular face of the mariner's compass on which are marked points and/or de-grees indicating local direction relative to *magnetic* north, in the magnetic compass, or to *true* north, in the gyroscope compass. **Forecastle c.,** a copy of the shipping articles, or contract between a master and his crew, stipulating conditions under which each crew member has been engaged for the current voyage. It is required by law to be posted in a place always accessible to the crew. **Indicator-c.,** used in connection with an engine indicator for registering mean effective pressure in a cylinder and, consequently, valve performance and indicated horsepower developed. **Rhumb c.,** a compass-card. **Sea-c.,** *see* SEA. **Shipman's c.,** an ancient name for a chart.

CARDEL. A cask or hogshead, formerly used by Dutch whalers, of 64 gallons.

CARDINAL. Chief; fundamental; of prime importance. **C. points,** four principal points of the compass: North, South, East, and West. **C. points of the Ecliptic,** vernal equinox, summer solstice, autumnal equinox, and winter solstice. **C. winds,** those which blow from cardinal points of the compass.

CAREEN. (Fr. *carène;* L. *carina;* the keel, the bottom of a ship.) To lay, heel, or heave down a vessel on one side, whether afloat or aground, in order to make other side of hull below water-line accessible for cleaning, calking, or effecting repairs. Careening for purposes indicated was the common method prior to advent of the dry-dock. To heel or list, as a vessel sailing with wind abeam. Also written *carene, carine,* and *carreen.*

CAREENAGE. A place where a ship is careened. Fee or amount charged for careening.

CAREENING-WHARF. *See* WHARF.

CARGO. (Sp. *cargo, carga;* burden or load.) Freight or lading of a vessel; goods, merchandise, or whatever is conveyed on a vessel or boat; load. In a legal sense, the term usually refers to goods only, excluding live animals or persons. **To break out a c.,** *see* BREAK. **Bulk c.,** a homogeneous mass of unpackaged goods, such as coal, ore, grain, oil, or sand. **C.-battens,** *see* BATTEN. **C.-block,** *see* BLOCK. **C.-book,** a book kept by ship's officers containing notes on the stowage, damage, or tally of cargo; a book containing the amounts, marks, numbers, measurement, weight, etc. of a cargo. **C.-boom,** *see* BOOM. **C.-carrying capacity,** weight of cargo, usually expressed in long tons (2240 lbs.), which a vessel may carry after allowing for weight and space occupied by her fuel and stores; hold space, in cubic feet, which may be occupied by a light-weight or bulky cargo. **C.-cluster,** a group of electric lights fitted in a reflector for lighting purposes during handling of cargo. **C. deadweight tonnage,** *see* TONNAGE. **C.-door,** *see* DOOR. **C.-gin,** *see* GIN. **C.-hatch, c.-hatchway,** a hatch or opening in a vessel's deck for passage of cargo loaded in, or discharged from, a hold or other compartment. **C.-hoisting block,** *see* BLOCK. **C.-hold bulkhead,** *see* BULKHEAD. **C.-hook,** *see* HOOK. **C.-jack,** a screw-jack used to force baled goods into compact tiers in process of economical stowage. **C.-lashing chain,** *see* CHAIN. **C.-mat,** a large mat, or several small mats together, usually made of manila rope-strands, used as a protection to, and a cushioned landing on, the deck, when taking stores and ammunition aboard; a mat made of cane or bamboo used in the hold to protect cargo from contact with beams, frames, etc., extensively used in loading rice or other bagged goods in the Far East. **C.-net,** a large square net usually made of small hemp rope or wire, used as a sling for small packages of cargo, or as a *save-all* to recover packages accidentally falling from a sling between ship and wharf. **C. plan,** same as *stowage plan,* see STOWAGE. **C.-port,** a door or port in a ship's side for passage of cargo in loading or discharging. **C. stowage factor,** *see* STOWAGE. **C. ton,** *see* TON. **C. vessel,** *see* VESSEL. **C.-worthy,** quality or state of a ship with regard to her fitness to carry a cargo. **Chow-chow c.,** *see* CHOW-CHOW. **Deadweight c.,** *see* DEAD *and* STOWAGE. **Frozen c.,** meat, fish, or other perishables carried at 10 to 15 degrees Fahrenheit. **General c.,** a lading of various kinds of goods; a miscellaneous cargo. **Inflammable c.,** such goods as may easily be set on fire, including materials liable to spontaneous combustion and liquids giving off inflammable vapors; *see* DANGEROUS GOODS. **Jumping c.,** term for an old method of discharging bulk cargoes, such as coal and grain, by hand-hoisting in baskets. Three or four *tails,* or short ropes, were attached to the cargo-fall so that as many men were provided with space to hand the fall. The men stood on a stage close to cargo-hatch and hoisted each basket with a rhythmic hand-over-hand swing, final impetus to the hoist being completed with a *jump* to the deck. The custom appears to have ended either at Rotterdam or Antwerp about 1900. **Measurement c.,** *see* MEASUREMENT. **Shifting of c.,** *see* SHIFTING. **Special c.,** *see* SPECIAL.

CARIBE. (Sp. *caribe,* cannibal) A remarkably voracious freshwater fish native to the Amazon and other South American waters. It will attack men and animals, inflicting dangerous wounds with its unusually sharp teeth. Though rarely more than one foot in length, it will tear another fish to pieces when latter is hooked and before the fisherman can haul it from the water.

CARINATED. (L. *carina,* keel) Shaped like the keel or fore-foot of a ship; or as the *carinate sternum* of a bird.

CARLING. Formerly a piece of timber or heavy plating running fore-and-aft between the two deck-beams at ends of a hatch or other deck opening and to which intervening beams were butted; now replaced by side coamings of a hatch themselves, which before were additional to carlings. Where a carling supports interrupted beams in way of a mast, it becomes a *mast partner,* or a *header.* Carlings are also fitted between deck-beams as stiffeners, where necessary in the structure. Also, *carlin, carline.* **C.-knee,** in wood construction, a knee fitted at junction of a carling and a frame or a deck-beam. **C.-box,** a box built or fastened between carlings for purpose of stowing gear.

CARPENTER. In U.S. navy, a warrant officer who assists executive officer in maintenance of ship's hull, boats, spars, and, generally, all deck fittings; also, is entrusted with certain responsibilities in construction and repair of vessels at a navy yard. In the merchant marine, he assists the chief mate, who is usually the executive, in upkeep of decks, hatch-covers, boats, wood fittings in holds and about the decks; assists in handling anchors and keeps windlass and steering-chains in good working order; takes and records bilge and tank soundings; and is responsible for filling of domestic and ballast tanks. **C.'s certificate,** *see* CERTIFICATE. **C.'s crew or gang,** in the navy, seamen detailed to assist the carpenter. **C.'s mate,** *see* MATE. **Jack-knife c.,** *see* JACK.

CARRACK. *See* CARACK.

CARRICK. A variant of *carack.* **C. bend,** a knot used for connecting ends of a heavy rope or hawser; a single or double *c. bend;* see BEND. **C.-bitts,** in wooden ships the heavy wood pieces supporting each end of the windlass. **C.-heads,** top ends of *c.-bitts,* used for making fast a hawser.

CARRIER. A vessel in which the catch of a fishing-fleet is taken to market. **Aircraft c., airplane c.,** a naval vessel specially designed for carrying, launching from, and landing aircraft on a single weather deck. **Common c.,** vessel carrying goods or passengers for hire as offered, and which, by law, is bound to carry any freight or passengers requiring shipment, while responsible for safe conduct of such.

CARRONADE. (*From Carron, a town in Scotland where it was first made*) A short cannon of howitzer type formerly used to throw heavy shot in naval engagements at close quarters.

CARRY. To bear or cause to be borne, as to *c. sail.* To **c. a bone in her teeth,—in her mouth,** *see* BONE. To **c. away,** to break off; to lose by being damaged or broken off, as, *ship carried away her jib-boom;* also said of a rope or chain parting due to strain. To **c. on,** to continue on a course steered, or with a present occupation. **Carrying on,** keeping an excessive press of sail set; continuing with as much canvas spread as possible. To **c. lee helm,** said of position of the helm when vessel is sailing close-hauled or on the wind, indicating she requires a constant pressure of *lee helm, i.e.,* the tiller drawn to *lee* side of fore-and-aft line, thus turning rudder toward weather side, in order to offset vessel's tendency to "fall off," or head away from the wind. To **c. out an anchor,** *see* ANCHOR PHRASEOLOGY. To **c. weather helm,** to keep tiller toward *weather* side in order to hold vessel from heading into or toward the wind; reverse of carrying *lee helm.* **Lash and c.,** *see* LASH.

CARTEL SHIP.   *See* SHIP.

CARVEL.   A variant of *caravel.* **C.-built,** having planking laid flush at seams, as distinguished from *clinker-built* in which planks overlap, as in boat-building. **C.-joint,** a flush joint, as in a *c.-built* boat's planking. **C.-work,** putting on of planks or plates meeting flush at seams.

CASCABEL.   (*Sp.*)   Old term for that part of a muzzle-loading cannon in rear of the base-ring, or widest part of gun; once applied only to the base knob, or breech end.

CASE.   Cavity in upper front of the head of a *cachalot,* or *sperm whale,* which contains spermaceti and a fine quality of oil. **C.-shot,** a collection of small projectiles enclosed in a case, as a shrapnel shell or canister-shot.

CASEMATE.   In war-vessels, an armored inclosure provided with openings through which guns may be run out and fired.

CASHIER.   (L. *cassare,* to annul)   To dismiss in disgrace from an office or place of trust, as that of a naval officer.

CASING.   Covering or wall around or about any object or space for protection or isolation. **Air-c.,** *see* AIR. **Boiler-room c.,** bulkhead arrangement partitioning space above boilers up to weather deck from holds or other spaces in immediate vicinity. The casing forms a large trunkway capable of allowing removal or installation of any of the boilers and accommodates smoke-stack and ventilator shafts leading to *boiler-room space.* **Boiler-c.,** *see* BOILER. **Engine-room c.,** spacious trunkway extending upward from engine-room and terminating in a skylight fitted with hinged covers for opening to air. Within the space are one or more heavy beams on which a traveling hoist may be used in operation of removing heavier engine parts. Also, *machinery c.* **Funnel-c.,** outer sheet-metal fitted several inches from and around a smoke-stack or funnel; insulating material and paneling built around the funnel on a passenger deck through which it passes. **Jacket-c.,** *see* JACKET. **Keelson-c.,** *see* KEELSON. **Rudder-c., rudder-case;** *see* RUDDER.

CASK.   (Sp. *casco.*)   A barrel-shaped wooden vessel, usually liquid-tight, having a stave-built body and flat heads or ends, its staves being held tightly together by two or more hoops of iron or wood at each quarter. The term is often applied to any such vessel holding liquids, as a barrel, hogshead, pipe, butt, tun, or a keg. **Splayed c.,** one having an unusually deep bilge.

CASSIOPEIA.   (Named after mother of *Andromeda* in Greek mythology.)   A constellation consisting of five stars, three of which are of 2nd. magnitude, in approximately 60° north declination and 0 to 2 hours in right ascension. It may be recognized as a distorted *W,* lying on nearly the opposite side of the *Pole star,* and at about same distance from that star, as the *Great Bear.* Also called *Cassiopeia's Chair* and *The Lady's Chair.*

CAST.   To throw; to cause to fall; to let down; to toss. To turn from the wind or cause a vessel to fall off, especially in getting under way from an anchorage; to tack; to put about. Act of throwing, as a *cast of the lead.* To **c. about,** to tack, put about, or wear ship. To **cast anchor,** to let go an anchor; *see* ANCHOR. To **c. a traverse,** to **c. a point of traverse,** an old expression meaning to determine, or lay down on the chart, the bearing of a point of land. To **c. away,** to wreck, usually in the sense of a willful act, as "the ship was *cast away* on the Cuban coast." To **c. loose,** *see* LOOSE. To **c. off,** to throw off, put off, or let go a rope, boat, etc., as, to *cast off* from ship's side; to *cast off* the jib-sheet; or to *cast off* a vessel in tow. To **c. the lead, take a c. of the lead,** to ascertain depth of water by a sounding with the lead. To **c. up,** to throw or turn up, as an object washed ashore by surf; to calculate or compute. **Land-c.,** *see* LAND. **Weather-c.,** *see* WEATHER.

CASTAWAY.   A person set adrift or put ashore from a vessel against his will; one derelict or shipwrecked, especially on a sparsely inhabited coast.

CASTING.   Motion of turning a vessel's head away from the wind in getting underway, so as to bring it on side desired. Design or drawing of a sail, indicating its shape and dimensions, position of reef-points, bull's-eyes, etc.

CASTLE.   (A.S. *castel;* L. *castellum,* a small fortified place.)   A fighting tower erected on ancient war-galleys near the bows or the stern. These developed into *fore castel* and *æfter castel* of the Middle Ages. Our present *forecastle* still is the raised forward part of a vessel.

CASTOR and **POLLUX.**   Two brightest stars of the group known as *Gemini,* Latin name for *twins,* located in the zodiacal belt between *Taurus* and *Leo* and having a declination of about 30° north and 7½ hours right ascension. In ancient sailor's lore, a twin flame appearance of *St. Elmo's fire* in the rigging, believed to portend the near end of a storm; *see* CORPORSANT.

CAT.   A purchase by which an anchor is hoisted to the *cathead;* to hoist an anchor up to, and secure it at, a cathead. A *catboat.* A *catfish.* A strongly built vessel used in coal and timber trade of western Europe. A former type of Deal lugger having three masts, used in fishing on south and east coasts of England. A catamaran. The *cat-o'-nine-tails*, or any such flogging instrument. **C.-and-fish tackle,** a purchase fitted to an anchor-crane, or suspended from the masthead, for hoisting anchor into its stowing position; also, *fish-tackle.* This tackle is used with the old-fashioned stock anchor. In using the anchor-crane, an innovation in steam-vessels some 50 years ago, the tackle for lifting such anchors, termed *anchor-purchase,* is hooked to the *balancing-ring* on anchor's shank and hoisted inboard to its bed on deck, thus doing away with operations of *catting* and *fishing* anchor to its position on the bow. **C.-back,** a handy line fastened to the lower cat-block hook to facilitate hooking tackle in the anchor-ring. **C.-beam,** in older wooden ships, beam to which cat-heads were secured. **C.-block,** *see* BLOCK. **C.-chain,** a chain fall rove in the cat-tackle. **C.-crane,** an anchor-crane, usually fixed near the stem, for hoisting bower anchors inboard or outboard. **C.-davit,** an iron davit replacing the wooden cathead of old. **C.-fall,** rope or chain rove in the *cat-tackle,* or purchase used to heave anchor from water's edge to cathead. **C.-harpin, c.-harping,** one of the short ropes or iron cramps once used in sailing-ships to bowse in lower shrouds in way of the yard, so that yards could be braced up as sharply as possible. **Cathead, c.-head,** a piece of timber or heavy iron projecting from each bow at forecastle deck and fitted with sheaves which formed upper part of cat-tackle; used as a crane for *catting,* or hoisting anchor from water to bow, and as a means of supporting it in the stowed position. The old-fashioned anchor was always first *catted,* then *fished* by hoisting its flukes to the rail, and finally secured with its flukes abaft the cathead and shank lying horizontally. Before *letting go* (anchoring) its flukes were lowered and cast off, so that it hung vertically by its ring to the cathead. On the order *"Let go," ring-stopper* or *cat-stopper,* was knocked free and anchor dropped clear of bow to water and cable veered as necessary. **Cathead-stopper, cat-stopper,** a short piece of chain in which anchor is hung at the cat-head, its standing end being so secured as to be knocked free with a blow from a heavy hammer at order *"Let go."* **C.-hole,** in old frigates and ships of the line, one of two holes through the stern, above gunroom ports, for passage of hawsers for heaving astern or making fast to a quáy. **C.-hook,** hook on a cat-block for engaging the anchor-ring when catting an anchor. **C.-o'-nine-tails,** a kind of whip, formerly used for flogging offenders in British and United States navies, consisting of several tails of knotted cord attached to a handle of stout rope. A seaman so punished was usually lashed to a gun; hence the pertinent phrase, "introduced to the gunner's daughter." **C.-rigged,** rigged like a catboat; *see* CATBOAT. **C.-rope,** same as *cat-back, q.v.* **C.-tackle,** purchase for raising anchor to the cathead. **C.-tackle fall,** the *cat-fall,* or rope rove in a *cat-tackle.* **C.-tail,** inner end of the cathead which is fastened to a beam or frame.

CATABATIC WIND. *See* WIND.

CATADROME. A catadromous fish.

CATADROMOUS. (Gr. *kata,* down; and *dromos,* a running.) Living in fresh water, but going out to sea to spawn, as the eel; opposite of *anadromous.*

CATAMARAN. (A corruption of a *Tamil* word meaning *tied wood.*) A kind of raft consisting of several pieces of timber or logs laid parallel and lashed to spreading pieces which stiffen the structure and hold logs a few feet apart; it may have two or three single, or two pairs of logs spaced equally apart; used by natives on coast of Brazil and coasts of India, and also, to some extent, in West Indies, it is usually equipped with a sail and under paddles makes a first class surf-boat. Any craft having two hulls side by side, whether propelled by machinery, sails, or oars. A life-saving raft carried on ships, made of two parallel cylindrical tanks with a rectangular slatted floor between them. A raft fitted with a windlass and grapples for recovering sunken logs.

CATANADROMOUS. CATANDROMOUS. Ascending and descending streams from the sea, as the salmon, shad, and other fishes.

CATAPULT. In naval aeronautics, a mechanical device, as a truck moved on a track by powerful springs, for launching airplanes from a ship's deck.

CATBOAT. A sail-boat carrying a single fore-and-aft sail spread by a gaff and boom, mast being stepped well forward.

CATCH. In fishing, number or quantity of fish taken at or in a certain time. To meet pressure of wind, as, "the jib *catches.*" An old English form of the word *ketch.* **C.-fake,** an unsightly doubling or kinking in a coiled rope. To **c. a crab,** *see* CRAB. **C.-ratline,** same as *sheer-ratline; see* RATLINE.

CATCHER, WIND. *See* WIND.

CATENARY. (L. *catena,* a chain.) Parabolic curve described by a rope or chain freely suspended between two supporting points, as that of, or in, a towing hawser, properly termed *common catenary.* The horizontal component of total tension is constant throughout hawser and maximum tension is found at higher point of suspension. At any point in the hawser, total tension is equal to weight of the line between that point and lowest point in catenary, multiplied by the cosecant of angle which hawser makes with the horizontal.

CATFISH. Any of various sized fishes apparently so named from their long whiskerlike barbels about their mouths; in particular, the family *Siluridæ,* most of which inhabit fresh water, as the *bullhead, channel-cat,* and *mud-cat* of America, considered of little value as food fish.

CATHARPIN or **CATHARPING.** Also *cat-harpin* or *cat-harping; see* CAT.

CATHEAD. Also *cat-head; see* CAT.

CATOPTRIC LIGHTHOUSE. *See* LIGHTHOUSE.

CATSKIN. Ruffled surface of a smooth sea caused by light airs or *cat's-paw* breezes.

CAT'S-PAW. Light airs or light baffling winds which temporarily ruffle surface of the water in calm weather. A hitch made in the bight of a rope, forming two small bights into which a tackle-hook may be inserted; hitch will not jam under stress.

CAT THE ANCHOR, To. *See* ANCHOR; CAT.

CATTLESHIP. A vessel used for the transportation of horses, mules, asses, sheep, goats, or swine. Carriage of such live stock is usually subject to regulations of country from which the animals are exported. In this respect, the Bureau of Animal Industry of U.S. Department of Agriculture has issued a comprehensive booklet entitled *"Regulations Governing Inspection, Humane Handling, and Safe Transport of Export Animals,"* which covers details of requirements for space, fittings, feeding, ventilation, attendance, etc.

CATWALK. An elevated bridge running fore-and-aft between midship superstructure and forward or after part of ship for purpose of providing a safe passage-way in rough weather; a fore-and-aft bridge. A walkway over a deck cargo.

CAUDAL. (L. *cauda,* tail.) The tail or tail fins of a fish; short term for *caudal fin.*

CAULK. Same as CALK.

CAVALLA. A food fish found on the coasts of tropical America and on U.S. east coast as far north as Nantucket; 10 to 12 inches in length, a fast swimmer and beautifully colored, has a slender well-defined forked tail, and a deep body with back from mouth to tail forming in profile an almost perfect 90-degree arc of a circle. The *cero,* of like habitat but of the mackerel family, is often improperly called a *cavalla.*

CAVEL or **CAVIL.** Variants of *kevel; see* KEVEL.

CAVITATION. (L. *cavus,* hollow.) In marine engineering, partial vacuum around propeller blades caused by shaft speed exceeding that in which screw attains its maximum effective driving effort. A source of loss in propulsion efficiency, its reduction to a minimum is procured by proper number of blades consistent in pitch and surface area with normal depth of immersion and proposed revolution speed.

CAVITY. A now rarely used term in shipbuilding for volume or space occupied by immersed part of the hull, *i.e.,* vessel's displacement.

CAY. (Sp.-Am. *cayo.*) A low islet of sand or coral, or a ledge of rock; often called a *key* on the Florida coast and in Central American waters.

CAYAR. *See* COIR.

CAYUCA. (*Native name.*) A dugout canoe used by Indians of Panama and adjoining Colombian coasts.

CEILING. The planking fastened to inner surfaces of frames, forming an inner skin and providing additional structural strength in a wooden vessel. In steel ships, planking fitted as a flooring for cargo in lower holds. **C.-hatch,** an opening in the ceiling provided by a portable section of the planking, for access to sides or bottom for cleaning, etc. **Floor-c.,** *see* FLOOR. **Grain-c.,** thin boards placed over ceiling where necessary to prevent a grain cargo from flowing into bilges or pump-well. **Hold-c.,** ceiling below lowermost deck. **Loose c.,** planking laid unfastened to, and covering, the double-bottom tank tops. The sheet-metal or wood sheathing usually found in crews' quarters and store-rooms is also called *ceiling.*

CELESTIAL. (L. *cælestis,* heavenly.) Of, or pertaining to, the heavens. **C. equator,** the equinoctial; *see* EQUATOR. **C. horizon,** *see* HORIZON. **C. latitude,** position of a heavenly body as expressed by its angular distance from the ecliptic, measured on the ecliptic meridian passing through the body. **C. longitude,** *see* LONGITUDE. **C. meridian,** *see* MERIDIAN. **C. navigation,** *see* NAVIGATION. **C. sphere,** *see* SPHERE.

CELLULAR DOUBLE BOTTOM. *See* DOUBLE.

CEMENT. For preservation of shell-plating of steel vessels inside of double-bottom tanks, bottoms of bilges, fresh water tanks, sometimes in waterways on deck, and, generally, in those parts of the hull where a continuous wet or moist condition exists, a mortar consisting of water and one part of Portland cement with two parts of sand is usually laid. In recent years, however, certain patented compositions generally termed *bitumastics,* because of their principal bituminous or gummy ingredients, have largely displaced the cement mixture. **C.-wash,** a mixture of Portland cement and water, often with addition of fire-clay, which is applied by brush to internal sides of water-tanks, bilges, chain-lockers, boiler-stools, etc., as a protection against corrosion.

CENTAURUS. (Gr. *kentauros,* centaur.) A southern constellation lying east, north, and west of *Crux* (the Southern Cross). A line joining its two brightest stars, α^2 *Centauri* (*Rigil Kentaurus*) and β *Centauri,*—called the "pointers," and extended westward about 12 degrees, enters its neighboring group close to β *Crucis. Rigil Kentaurus* (named from the Arabic *al rijil al Kentauros,* the Centaur's foot), of magnitude 0.3, is said to be nearest to the earth of all so-called fixed stars.

CENTER. In a fleet, division or column between van and rear, or between weather and lee divisions, in order of sailing. Also *centre.* **C.-bearer,** in a furnace, support for ends of fire-bars at half length of the furnace. **C. girder,** in vessels having a double bottom, continuous plate lying in the midship fore-and-aft vertical plane between keel and tank top, forming a watertight partition in the tanks; constituting vessel's backbone in conjunction with the flat-plate keel to which it is strongly attached by double angle-bars, it is often called a *vertical-plate keel* or a *c.-line keel;* its rigidity is greatly increased by the floor-plates which are butted to it on each side throughout vessel's length. The term is sometimes used synonymously with *c.-line keelson,* although latter generally is applied to a vertical plate stiffener fitted along upper edges of floors in the midship fore-and-aft line in vessels without, or having only a partial, double-bottom arrangement. **C. keel,** *see* CENTERBOARD. **C.-line,** line indicating the vertical midship fore-and-aft plane in plans of vessel; *see* LINE. **C.-line bulkhead,** *see* BULKHEAD. **C.-line keelson,** *see* KEELSON. **C. of buoyancy,** the center of immersion; *see* BUOYANCY. **C. of buoyancy curve,** *see* CURVE. **C. of effort,** point in sail area on a vessel at which total propelling force of the wind, if applied, would produce same effect as when distributed over the sails as spread. **C. of flotation,** center of gravity of water-plane of a floating body. **C. of gravity,** point at which entire weight of a body, or system of bodies, may be considered as concentrated; also, the geometric center of a plane. **C. of lateral resistance,** in sailing, center of gravity of immersed vertical plane in line with keel, which, as vessel heels, becomes that of vertical plane bounded by the water-line and contour of part of hull most deeply immersed. **C. of pressure,** point at which total pressure on a surface may be considered as concentrated; as *c.* of wind pressure on a sail, or *c.* of water pressure on a bulkhead; sometimes called *c. of gravity of a pressure area,* it is interesting to note that such point on the surface of a rectangular-shaped compartment bulkhead or tank side subjected to water pressure is situated at *one-third* height of the liquid. **C.-through-plate,** another name for the *center-girder.* **C.-velic,** or **velic-point;** *see* **C. of effort;** (*velic* means pertaining to a sail, from Latin *velum,* sail). **C. vertical keel,** same as *center-girder.* **Dead c.,** *see* DEAD. **Height of c. of buoyancy,—of gravity,** *see* HEIGHT. **Neutral c.,** considering a bending stress on a beam or other structural material, is center of gravity of cross-sectional area, at which point in the member the fibres are neither under tension nor compression.

CENTERBOARD. A movable plate of metal or broad board of wood enclosed within the well or slot of a watertight casing in bottom of a vessel or boat and which may be lowered or raised according to sailing requirements in reducing leeway to a minimum. It is usually lowered when sailing close-hauled or on the wind and raised when wind is aft or on the quarter. Also termed *center-keel, drop-keel,* and *sliding-keel.* **C.-casing, c. trunk,** the watertight box in which centerboard is fitted and housed.

CENTER-PLATE RUDDER. A common type of rudder fitted to vessels of moderate speed, consisting of a single heavy plate shaped as required at its after edge and riveted to several stout arms extending at right angles to, and shrunk on to alternate sides of, the rudder-stock. Also called *single-plate rudder* and *flat-plate rudder.*

CENTIGRADE. (L. *centum,* a hundred; *gradus,* degree.) Abbreviated *C,* reading on a thermometer whose scale is graduated in 100 equal parts between freezing point and boiling point of fresh water at a barometric pressure of 760 mm. or 29.92 inches. To convert a *Centigrade* to a *Fahrenheit* reading, multiply by 9/5 and add 32.

CENTIPEDE. A series of short pieces of sennit or small rope attached at intervals of 3 to 4 feet to a rope stretched along topside of jib-boom or bowsprit, or to battens fastened on each side of those spars, for handy use as gaskets in stowing head sails.

CENTRAL STRINGER. *See* STRINGER.

CENTRE. *See* CENTER.

CENTRIFUGAL. (L. *centrum,* center; *fugere,* to flee.) **C. force,** the force opposite in direction and equal to that termed *centripetal.* Since any body constrained to follow a curved path must be acted upon by a force exactly counteracting that force or tendency of the mass to travel in a straight line, the latter is termed *centrifugal, i.e.,* directed outward or "from the center" and its counteracting force, *centripetal, i.e.,* directed inward or "toward the center." **C. pump,** a pump which consists essentially of an impeller mounted on a rotating shaft within a casing. Impeller blades throw the liquid to outer part of pump-casing called the *volute,* where high velocity builds itself up to a static pressure, so forcing liquid on to its destination. This type of pump is commonly used on board ship for such purposes as boiler feed, feed booster, circulating, bilge discharge, sanitary or fresh water supply, and discharging or transferring oil.

CEPHEUS. (Gr. *Kepheus,* father of Andromeda.) A constellation located between the group *Cygnus* and the star *Polaris.* A gentle curve from *Deneb* (α *Cygni*) to *Polaris* passes at nearly halfway mark through α *Cephei* (*Alderamin*) and β *Cephei* (*Alphirk*).

CERES. The first discovered (*1801*) of the many small planets called *asteroids* or *planetoids* which now are known to exceed 1100 in number. *See* ASTEROID.

CERO. A food and game fish of the mackerel family, in length from 2 to 3 feet; found in West Indies and on Atlantic coast of United States.

CERTIFICATE. (L. *certus,* certain; *facere,* to make.) A written declaration of the truth of some fact or facts. **Carpenter's c.,** "in order to the registry of any vessel built within the United States, it shall be necessary to produce a certificate, under the hand of the principal or master carpenter, by whom or under whose direction the vessel has been built, testifying that she was built by him or under his direction, and specifying the place where, the time when, and the person for whom, and describing her build, number of decks and masts, length, breadth, depth, tonnage, and such other circumstances as are usually descriptive of the identity of a vessel; which certificate shall be sufficient to authorize the removal of a new vessel from the district where she may be built to another district in the same or an adjoining state, where the owner actually resides, provided it be with ballast only." (*Revised Statute 4147*) **C. of discharge,** a document required by law to be issued to a seaman upon his discharge or release from his shipping agreement, certifying the period during which man was engaged, identity of vessel, description of voyage, name and capacity in which engaged, character of man, and port and date of his discharge. **C. of disinfection,** a paper required by a vessel leaving United States for a foreign port certifying, for information of sanitary authorities at ports visited, port and date of last disinfection of a specified part of the vessel, type of disinfectant used, and sometimes number of rats exterminated in the process; also termed a *fumigation c.* and a *deratization c.* **C. of identification,** a document issued by the U.S. Coast Guard to a merchant seaman indicating personal description, age, and nationality, and having attached the man's photograph, thumbprint, and home address. **C. of inspection,** a document certifying that annual inspection of hull, machinery, and equipment of a United States merchant vessel has been executed at a certain port and date. The certificate indicates minimum number of licensed officers and certificated seamen required in manning the vessel, various items required in her life-saving and fire-fighting equipment, and, in general, is a declaration by U.S. Coast Guard that vessel has complied with the laws governing safety of vessels of her class. The document must be framed under glass and exhibited in a prominent place on board. **C. of license and enrollment,** issued a vessel by collector of customs, certifies her enrollment in U.S. domestic trade or fisheries. It contains full particulars of vessel, including ownership, dimensions, tonnage, rig, and business in which employed. **C. of origin,** a written declaration by a shipper and authenticated by consul of a foreign country indicating place of manufacture or original shipment of certain goods, for purpose of complying with import laws of some countries and, in some cases, to the business advantage of consignee. Any certificate issued by competent authority showing origin of certain goods or cargo being transported. **C. of registry,** *see* REGISTER. Also, a document issued by U.S. Coast Guard indicating registration of a staff officer, such as a surgeon or a purser, and authorizing him to serve on U.S. merchant vessels; *see* STAFF OFFICER. **C. of sea stores,** a certificate issued by custom-house at a U.S. port, listing stores for use at sea which have been placed under seal on arrival of a vessel from a foreign port. **C. of seaworthiness,** issued by a classification society's appointed surveyor, authorizes a vessel, insofar as her insurances interests are concerned, to proceed to sea subsequent to an accident met with, in order that repairs may be effected or completed at another port. **C. of service,** issued by U.S. Coast Guard to a U.S. merchant seaman other than a *licensed* or a *staff officer,* certifying that such seaman is qualified to perform the duties of rating named thereon on any U.S. merchant vessel of 100 tons (gross) or upward, except those employed exclusively on rivers of U.S. **C. of valuation,** appraisal duly authenticated in writing by a surveyor or ship valuer stating value of a vessel, or that of a damaged cargo, or both. **Certified crew list,** a list of names, places of birth, and residences of persons employed on a merchant vessel bound from a U.S. port on a foreign voyage or a whaling cruise. It is prepared by master of such vessel and certified, upon approval, by collector of customs. The certified document is produced by the master as required when entering or clearing his vessel at ports called at during the voyage. **Classification c.,** issued by classification society in which a vessel is registered, indicating that vessel is classified upon completion of building as specified, or, consequent to certain periodical survey or surveys, or major structural or machinery repairs and/or alterations, retains her original class or is re-classed accordingly. **Custom-house c.,** *see* CUSTOM. **Freeboard c.,** assigns minimum freeboard allowed a vessel at certain seasons in certain geographical zones, according to rules of classification society interested. The certificate indicates markings required on each side of vessel at half-distance between stem and stern posts; *see* LOAD. **Fuel oil c.,** issued by Commandant of U.S. Coast Guard, certifying that vessel is permitted to use petroleum fuel for boiler purposes. **Lifeboat c.,** *see* LIFE. **Load-line c.,** *see* LOAD. **Marine insurance c.,** *see* INSURANCE. **Tonnage c.,** for purpose of registering a vessel, supplied by surveyor appointed to measure her tonnage. It states full measurement particulars of vessel and how her total inclosed space at 100 cubic feet per ton, or her *gross tonnage,* is arrived at. From this total certain deductions are authorized to obtain *net tonnage,* or *net registered tonnage,* which is the basis on which assessments such as anchorage dues, tonnage taxes, harbor dues, etc. are payable, except in the special cases of Panama and Suez Canal tolls. In accordance with regulations of waterways noted, a vessel's measurement is checked and a net tonnage for canals' respective toll purposes is shown in resulting *Panama Canal Tonnage C.* and/or *Suez Canal Tonnage C.* issued to the master.

CERTIFIED MANIFEST. *See* MANIFEST.

CERTIFIED VESSEL. *See* VESSEL.

CESSER CLAUSE. (Fr. *cesser,* to cede or withdraw.) A clause usually inserted in a charter party indicating that charterer's liability ends upon completion of loading of his cargo, shipowner then taking a lien on cargo for freight, dead freight, and demurrage.

CETACEA. (L. *cetus;* Gr. *ketos,* whale.) The zoölogical order of marine mammals which includes whales, porpoises, grampuses, etc. These are divided into toothless baleen whales (*Mystacoceti*) and toothed whales (*Odontoceti*); *see* WHALE.

CETACEAN. Of, or pertaining to, the *Cetacea;* a whale.

CETE. An obsolete name for whale or cetacean.

CETUS. (*L. = whale.*) A constellation lying near the equator, its greater part in the southern sky, extending through right ascension 0 to 3 hours and declination 5° N. to 20° S. Its only two navigational stars, *Menkar* (α *Ceti*) and *Deneb Kaitos* or *Diphda* (β *Ceti*), with *Algenib* (γ *Pegasi*), present a nearly equilateral triangle with sides of about 30°, β *Ceti* occupying the south corner. β *Ceti* is almost on the line joining *Alpheratz* (α *Andromedae*) and *Algenib* (γ *Pegasi*)—the east side of "Square of Pegasus"—extended to twice the distance these are apart in a direction a little east of south from *Algenib.*

CHADBURN. On the Great Lakes, a common term for the engine-room telegraph; probably so-named from Chadburn and Company in England, early manufacturers of present usual type instrument.

CHAFING. Friction or rubbing causing wear or injury to part or parts of objects in contact, as a rope against a spar, a block against a sail, etc. **C.-batten** or **c.-board,** a wooden batten fastened to standing rigging to minimize chafing injury to sails or running gear, or nailed to the deck in way of a block, such as that of a sheet for a fore-and-aft sail. **C.-cheek,** smooth protection, or shell, covering a sheave fastened to an upper yard-arm, gaff, or other light spar, through which is rove a royal sheet, gaff-topsail sheet, boom-topping-lift fall, etc. **C.-gear,** mats, baggy-wrinkle, battens, canvas, etc., fastened on rigging or spars to prevent injury by chafing. **C.-plate,** a plate fitted in way of a hawse-pipe to prevent injury to shell-plating or planking by anchor or chain-cable. A plate around lower edges of a hatch-coaming, usually rounded to prevent excessive wear on a hoisting-fall when working cargo. Any plate fitted to prevent wear or chafing by moving objects.

CHAIN. (Fr. *chaine;* L. *catena,* chain.) A string of connected metal rings or links, as, a *mooring-chain.* A series of things following or related to each other, as, a *chain of soundings.* Metal chain on board ship is usually described as *close-link* or *stud-link,* latter being almost exclusively used as anchor cable. Next to the anchor chain (*chain cable*) in size, largest close-link chain is usually that found in steering arrangement of *quadrant-chains, quarter-chains,* and *barrel-chains* in the case of steering-engines placed amidships or near engine-room. Size of a chain is described as diameter of metal forming the link, as, a *¾-inch short-link* or *close-link c.,* or *1½-inch stud-link c.* **Anchor-c.,** heavy chain or chain cable which is attached to an anchor. **Back-c.,** *see* BACK. **Cargo-lashing c.,** lengths of chain of appropriate sizes used for securing a deck cargo. **Cat-c.,** *see* CAT. **C.-boat,** a lighter or other suitable craft fitted for carrying, raising, and/or laying anchors and chain cable; also called *anchor-hoy* and *mooring-lighter.* **C.-bolt,** in wooden vessels, one of the bolts securing chain-plates (formerly pieces of chain) to the hull; *cf. c.-plate.* **C. cable,** chain used to hold a vessel at anchor. Except in small vessels where close-link chain is commonly used, chain cable is of stud-link type, made of wrought iron, cast steel, or die-forged steel, which will withstand a tensile stress of about one-seventh more than close- or short-link chain of same material. **C. cable compressor** or **c. cable controller,** also called *riding-chock* and *c.-stopper,* a heavy iron block secured to the deck just abaft each hawse-pipe, so devised that it may be raised to hold against forward end of one of the cable links, thus taking stress on chain from windlass or capstan, or preventing chain from running out, independently of windlass. **C.-drum,** on a steering-engine, heavy cylindrical-shaped drum or barrel about which steering-chains are secured and hove in or backed out as required. The drum is supplied with spiral grooves which receive the vertical links so that each second link lies flat as it is hove in. **C. gang,** *see* GANG. **C.-grab,** that part of a windlass or capstan shaped to engage or "grip" the links of a chain cable. Whelps at each end of the nests for each flat-lying link provide necessary grip on the chain in order to hold it to its work. Also called a *wildcat.* **C. hoist,** *see* BLOCK. **C.-hook,** a long-shafted hook used to handle chain cable in stowing it or hauling it along the deck. Also, the constellation *Scorpio* (the Scorpion) so named from its shape. **C.-locker,** compartment used for stowage of chain cable; usually located directly below windlass immediately forward of collision bulkhead in merchant vessels; also termed a *chain-bin* in the U.S. navy and, in the old sailing war-vessels, *the chain well.* **C.-locker pipe,** iron tubular casting through which chain cable leads from windlass or wildcat to chain-locker; also called *chain-pipe, deck-pipe, monkey-pipe, navel-pipe, spurling-pipe.* **C.-plate,** in wooden vessels, one of the flat pieces of iron fastened vertically to the hull for securing lower dead-eyes or ends of shrouds and backstays. Formerly this lower member of standing rigging was a piece of stout chain; hence, *the chains.* See CHAINS. **C.-plate bolt,** same as *chain-bolt.* **C.-pulley,** a sheave or pulley having a chain-grab periphery, *i.e.,* one in which the links fit into grooves shaped to grip chain during rotation. **C. riveting,** see RIVETING. **C.-shot,** two cannon-balls or half-balls joined by a short chain which formerly were fired to cut a ship's rigging. **C. sling,** a short length of chain, usually provided with a hook at one end and a ring at the other, for slinging iron bars, railroad iron, piping, structural steel, etc.; sometimes made in two legs joined to a common ring to which the hoisting-fall is hooked, as used in slinging such cargo horizontally. **C.-splice,** a splice by which a wire or fiber rope is attached to end link of a chain. **C.-stopper,** a *chain cable compressor (q.v.);* a piece of small chain used to relieve stress on a wire from a capstan, bitts, etc., while shifting position of wire. **C.-swivel,** a device in a chain which permits relative rotation of the connected parts, end of one link being shaped as a headed bolt freely turning in an appropriately forged adjoining link. **C.-takerpipe,** same as *chain-locker pipe.* **C.-tierer,** in older navy usage, one of seamen detailed to stow chain cable in chain-locker as anchor was hove in. **C.-towing,** a system whereby canal-boats are pulled along by heaving on a chain laid on bottom or on side of a canal. **C.-wale,** see CHANNEL. **C.-well,** see **Chain-locker. Close-link c.,** chain made of short links as distinguished from that made of longer studded links, or *stud-link chain;* also known as *short-link chain.* **Decking-c.,** a long chain once used in stowing or breaking out a cargo of heavy timber; also called *loading-c.* **Drag-chains,** see DRAG. **Fin-c.,** see FIN. **Fluke-c.,** see FLUKE. **Futtock c.-plates,** see FUTTOCK. **Ground-c.,** in older wooden sailing-ship usage, a length of small chain stopped along first 15-fathom shot of chain cable, for the purpose of swinging anchor clear of the stem preparatory to catting or hoisting it aboard. **Heel-c.,** in earlier sailing-ships of the line, a chain leading from one side of the lowermast-cap to heel of the topmast and up the other side to the cap, as support for the topmast when spar was hoisted into place. It was

later displaced by the *fid,* or bar laid across trestle-trees and under heel of topmast, although for some years both chain and fid were in use, the chain being considered a preventer. Before introduction of the fid, topmast was "gammoned," or lashed, to lowermast just above heel of the former. A heel-chain was also formerly used to hold the jib-boom in position in a similar manner to securing topmast. **Limber-c.,** see LIMBER. **Loading-c.,** same as *decking-c.* **Measuring-c.,** a small-linked chain used for sounding tanks, measuring timber, etc. **Pintle-c.,** see PINTLE. **Pitch-c.,** see PITCH. **Riding-c.,** see RIDING. **Rudder-c.,** see RUDDER. **Stream-c.,** see STREAM. **Stud-link c.,** that in which links are longer than those of short- or close-link chain, and fitted with a *stud,* or distance-piece, between inner sides of the links. The stud-link is thus fortified against deformity due to strain and it is claimed that its tensile strength is increased by about one-seventh on that account. Stud-link chain runs clear when open links of same size are likely to *kink* or lie *athwart hawse* on being broken out of disorderly stowage, as from a chain-locker in the case of chain cable. Stud-links of chain cable type are usually made 6 times diameter of the metal in outside length and 3.6 times, in outside breadth. **Telegraph-c.,** sprocket-chain used in an engine-soom telegraph. **Top-c.,** in the old fighting-ships, a chain used to sling a yard in time of battle, to secure yard in event of halyards being shot away. **Wheel-c.,** see WHEEL.

CHAINS. Iron links, flat or round bars, or the earlier and original pieces of stout chain, bolted to ships' sides and forming lower extremities of rigging supporting the masts, *i.e.,* the shrouds and backstays. In the old frigates and ships of the line, the chains were kept well clear of bulwarks by the *chain-wales* (later corrupted to *channels*) at which they terminated and were secured to lower dead-eyes of rigging. Hence, the chain-wales or channels, which were pieces of stout timber laid fore-and-aft against the side-planking or wales, forming an excellent observation post or position from which the sounding-lead was swung conveniently, give us the phrase *"in the chains"* as referring to a leadsman's station even to-day.

CHAIR. One of the iron supports fitted to hold and raise various steam-pipes leading to the winches, windlass, steering-engine, etc., required height clear of deck. **Boatswain's c.,** see BOATSWAIN. **Steamer c.,** a chair having a semi-reclining back, with leg and foot rests, for deck use by passengers. **The Lady's C.,** see CASSIOPEIA.

CHALOUPE. (*Fr.*) A large two-masted lugger once commonly used in fishing on Bay of Biscay coast.

CHALDER. An old term for a *gudgeon,*—one of the protruding sockets which receive the rudder pintles. **Dumb c.,** see DUMB.

CHAMBER, LOCK. See LOCK.

CHAMFER. The surface formed by cutting away a corner or angle formed by two faces of a piece of timber; beveled edge of a steel plate. To make a chamfer on, or bevel, whole or part of an edge of a plank, plate, etc.

CHANGE OF THE MOON. Beginning of a new synodic month (29 days, 12 hours, and 44 minutes), as measured from the time of new moon; the new moon.

CHANGE OF THE TIDE. Reversal of tidal flow from ebb to flood, or vice versa; change from a rise to a fall in height of water surface, as referred to a tidal datum mark.

CHANGE OF TRIM. *See* TRIM.

CHANNEL. (L. *canalis,* canal or channel.) Part of a harbor, river, strait, etc. used as a fairway for vessels, or through which the tidal stream principally flows; any fairway of sufficient depth for safe passage of shipping. The later corruption of *chain-wale,*—one of the fore-and-aft pieces of timber which served to spread chains outward, thus increasing slant of shrouds and keeping latter clear of bulwarks; also *channel-board; see* CHAINS. **C. bars,** structural iron having a cross-section of the form ⌐⌐. **C.-bolts,** long bolts by which chain-wales or channels are secured to vessel's sides. **C.-buoy,** *see* BUOY. **C.-iron,** same as *channel-bar.* **C.-knee,** in old sailing-warships of heavier type, one of the knees fitted below the chain-wales for support and stiffening. **C.-plate,** same as *chain-plate.* **C.-rail,** a batten or moulding fitted along outer edge of a chain-wale or channel and covering chain-plates or chains. **C.-wale,** in the wooden navy ships, one of the strakes of heavy outside planking (*wales*) between spar deck and gun-ports of deck next below. **Mid-c.,** *see* MID. **Spill-c.,** *see* SPILL. **Swash-c.,** *see* SWASH.

CHANTEY. (Fr. *chanter,* to sing.) A song used by sailors in chorus during the work of heaving anchor, hoisting a yard, or any operation requiring united effort of a number of men. Chanteys were termed "capstan," "topsail-halyard," "topgallant-halyard," "warping," etc., according to their adaptability to the rhythmic swing of work concerned. For example, the monotonous tramp around the capstan when heaving in a scope of anchor-cable was accompanied by a tune of lively tempo; when mastheading a topsail-yard, the *chanteyman* or leader opened the air with a plaintive bar or two, followed by concerted pull and chorus of all, as, in illustration, a familiar *c.* in this operation which began with "Blow the man down, bullies, blow the man down," then two swaying pulls to the chorus, "Yo-ho, blow the man down," and so on, words being changed to suit chanteyman's taste in rhyme and story. This was a "long-pull" chantey; top-gallant and royal halyards were manned to the tune

of a "short-pull" *c.,* a wide range of tune and verse providing fitting song for any pulling, swaying, or hauling required. This morale-lifting custom probably originated in the British navy 200 years ago with the flute-player who took his place on the capstan-head and supplied music for a perhaps 30-man job of heaving anchor. Also spelled *chantie, chanty,* and *shanty.*

CHAPEL. To lay a ship on same tack by action of helm alone, after having been caught aback in a light breeze. Vessel is allowed to make sternway until the wind draws abaft the beam, then she moves ahead with the now fair wind, and is brought round to her original tack. To **build a c.,** an old term for the maneuver of *chapeling.*

CHARACTERS, LLOYD'S. *See* LLOYD'S.

CHARGE. The quantity of explosive material, electricity, fuel, etc. which a gun, battery, furnace, etc. holds, or is fitted to receive or hold. Fee, or amount payable, for a particular service. **Demolition c.,** a quantity of explosive material used to break up a sunken wreck or other obstacle, as in a navigable channel. **Depth-c.,** *see* DEPTH. **Landing c's,** *see* LANDING. **Ocean c's,** freight charges due a vessel as distinguished from railroad charges, where cargo is transported via rail and ship on a through bill of lading. **Outward c's,** pilotage, tug-boat, or other charges incurred by a vessel when leaving a port. **Particular c's,** marine insurance term for expenses incurred by or for the assured for protection or preservation of insured subject matter, other than expense under general average and/or salvage. **Port c's,** harbor dues; *see* HARBOR. **Trimming c.,** *see* TRIMMING.

CHARGES CLAUSE. A clause in a charter party stipulating which of contracting parties agrees to pay wharfage, harbor dues, pilotage, towage, customs duties and fees, etc., incident to the chartered employment of vessel.

CHARIOTEER. The constellation *Auriga; see* AURIGA.

CHARLES'S WAIN or **CHARLIE'S WAGON.** (*Said to be named for Charles the Great—Charlemagne—A.D. 742–814*). The seven bright stars of the group *Ursa Major,* commonly called the *Dipper: see* URSA MAJOR.

CHARLEY NOBLE. (*Of uncertain origin.*) Term commonly used in the U.S. navy for a galley smoke-pipe.

CHART. (L. *carte,* card or map.) A map; especially a draft or projection on paper of the whole or a portion of an ocean, sea, lake, river, or coastal waters, showing with details such as land elevations, lighthouses, signal stations, towns, and conspicuous marks on contiguous land, depth of water, nature of bottom, outlying rocks, shoals, sunken wrecks,

CHART   82

tidal information, set of currents, variation of compass, and other data for use of mariners. The nautical chart is primarily intended to facilitate safe navigation and in its present form may generally be regarded as a compilation of a vast amount of practical survey research undertaken by various maritime nations over the past 200 years. Perhaps the earliest geographer to produce a satisfactory map or chart for navigational purposes was *Gerhard Kremer,* or *Mercator (1512–1594)*, and to-day the Mercator projection with slight modification is the most widely used in making of accurate and most convenient charts for mariners' use in latitudes up to 70 degrees. However, it was not until introduction of the quadrant (*John Hadley, 1682–1744*) and chronometer (*John Harrison, 1693–1776*) that practical accuracy developed in charting of coastlines and outlying dangers. **Bathygraphic c.,** a graphic representation of depth of the ocean floor, either by a system of colors or by curved lines joining all points of equal depth. **Bottle-c.,** a chart of ocean surface currents based upon records obtained by drift of floating bottles in a known period of time. **C.-house** or **c.-room,** space provided for stowage of a ship's charts, nautical books, chronometers, and other navigational equipment; usually furnished with a large table for chart use and often contains the radio direction-finder. **C.-work,** act of shaping the course, laying off bearings, measuring distances, and/or plotting positions on chart. **Dip-c.,** *see* DIP. **Great Circle c.,** a gnomonic chart on which a great circle track is represented by a straight line; used in great circle sailing; *see* **gnomonic projection:** PROJECTION. **Hydrographic c.,** one especially made for navigators; usually applied to charts published by U.S. Hydrographic Office. **Mercator's c.,** one based upon original projection of *Mercator,* a Flemish geographer of the 16th. century in which parallels of latitude and meridians are shown as straight lines, meridians being drawn equi-distant and parallel while latitude parallels are placed at distances apart which vary as length of the degree of longitude times secant of the latitude. Thus, as distance from the equator increases, the earth's surface as represented becomes more and more distorted yet always retaining its true relative form, since both meridians and parallels of latitude are expanded in same ratio. All bearings and courses are laid down on a Mercator chart as straight lines. **Meteorological c.,** *see* **weather-chart:** WEATHER. **Pilot-c.,** *see* PILOT. **Plotting-c.,** used for plotting positions, is a blank chart having meridians and latitude parallels drawn to correspond with particular latitude for which it is used. **Polar c.,** one of the polar regions drawn on the gnomonic projection, usually with point of tangency coinciding with the pole; *see* PROJECTION. **Sea-c.,** *see* SEA. **Star-c.,** *see* STAR. **Synoptic c.,** one giving weather conditions at different points of observation at a certain given time. **Tidal Current c.,** a map or series of maps or small charts, usually in book form, showing direction and velocity of the *tidal stream* in much frequented coastal waters, such as English Channel, New York Bay and Harbor, Chesapeake Bay, and Bay of Fundy. The information covers behavior of the current for each hour before and after predicted time of high water at a port of reference, as, for example, the currents in waters surrounding the British Isles which are given on separate charts for each hour before and after high water at Dover, England, showing normal direction and velocity at both springs and neaps throughout a complete cycle of tidal ebb and flow. **Track c.,** *see* TRACK. **Variation c.,** one showing curves or *isogonic lines* joining all places in a certain area, or on the whole of earth's surface, at which variation of the magnetic needle from geographical or true meridian has same value; it also usually indicates observed annual rate of change of variation. **Weather c.,** *see* WEATHER. **Wind c.,** *see* WIND. **Wreck c.,** *see* WRECK.

CHARTER. To hire or lease a vessel according to conditions agreed upon in a document known as the *charter party.* The leasing or hire of a vessel, usually indicated as a *time, voyage,* or *bare-boat charter,* depending upon agreement between charterer and owner. **Bare boat c.,** as the name implies, is an agreement by which charterer takes over vessel and supplies crew, stores, fuel, and all incidentals, including dry-docking and repairs, and, in effect, practically becomes vessel's owner for sum or rate stipulated; also termed **bare hull, bare pole,** and **demise** charter. **C. party,** specific contract by which a vessel's owner leases entire vessel, or some principal part of her cargo or passenger space, to another person for latter's use in transportation for his own account, either under his own or shipowner's charge. The term is from the French *charte partie,* meaning a divided charter, the legal instrument in its original form being written in duplicate and then divided through a title or rubric, half being given to each party to the transaction. **Lump sum c.,** an agreement to hire a vessel for a given sum under conditions stipulated in charter party. **Open c.,** a charter party which stipulates port of discharge to be at charterer's option. **Time c.,** chartering of a vessel for a certain period of time for a given sum, or at a stipulated rate per month (based on vessel's tonnage), owner usually agreeing to furnish crew, provisions, and working stores. **Voyage c.,** hiring of a vessel for a voyage, *i.e.,* from a home port to an outside port and return; also termed a *round charter.*

CHARTERABLE. Capable of being, or in a condition to be, chartered or hired, as a ship.

CHARTERING, AFFREIGHTMENT. *See* AFFREIGHTMENT.

CHARYBDIS. (*Gr.*) Ancient name for a whirlpool on Sicilian side and near northern entrance of Strait of Messina; now called *Garofaro.* Greek mythological lore has it that *Charybdis,* a lady gifted with an unsatiable appetite, was changed by Jupiter into this dangerous swirl. Mariners were threatened with both the six-headed monster that lived on Scylla, a headland on the Italian shore opposite, and the voracious Charybdis, when making passage through the strait; hence the equivalent of "between the devil and the deep sea" in "*between Scylla and Charybdis.*"

CHASE. A vessel pursued by another. In old navy usage, the *chase-guns* or place where they are mounted. **C.-gun,** a cannon mounted at forward or after end of an armed vessel for use when pursuing an enemy or defense when being pursued; formerly termed, respectively, *bow* and *stern chase.* **C.-joint,** a kind of joint by which an overlapping plate or plank is changed to a flush setting, as at stem of a clinker-built boat. **C.-port,** in old navy sailing-ships, a port in the bows or in the stern for use of a *chase-gun.* To **have a good c.,** said of a war-vessel able to bring to bear several guns in the right ahead or right astern direction. **Stern-c.,** *see* STERN.

CHASSE-MARÉE. (Fr. *chasser,* to chase; *maree,* tide.) A three-masted lugger employed on west coast of France, probably now extinct. Also called a *lougre.*

CHAUNTEY. *See* CHANTEY.

CHASER, SUBMARINE. *See* SUBMARINE.

CHEAT THE GLASS, To. To shorten duration of one's watch, as, in former days, by turning over the hour-glass too soon; hence, to too readily perform a duty requiring timely action.

CHEBACCO BOAT. A schooner-rigged, bluff-bowed, narrow-sterned, beamy vessel used in bank-fishing in early part of last century, so named from Chebacco, the present Essex of Massachusetts, where such vessels were built. *See* BOAT.

CHEBEC. *See* XEBEC.

CHECK. To slack or ease away a rope under tension; to reduce by braking or otherwise the speed of a cable or rope in running out; to haul in on weather braces when sailing close-hauled, as wind draws abeam. A hawser used to control motion of a vessel during process of warping. A longitudinal split in a timber caused by unequal shrinkage during seasoning. **Chafing-c.,** *see* CHAFING. **C.-bolt,** a bolt fitted to prevent motion of an object beyond a certain limit. **C.-line,** *see* LINE. **C.-nut,** a jam-nut or lock-nut; *see* JAM. **C.-pin,** a short iron or steel pin fitted to a crank-pin and projecting into the crank-web, to keep the former from turning. **C.-rope,** in former ship gunnery, a rope used to diminish recoil of a cannon; *see* ROPE. **C.-stopper,** a length of

heavy chain, a wire attached to an anchor, or similar means, used to retard a ship's way upon leaving the ways during launching; a light stop or rope made fast to a cable when running out, stop breaking but controlling cable as required. To **c. the helm,** to meet or turn the rudder against swinging of the vessel toward a certain direction, as when too rapidly nearing required course. **C.-valve,** *see* VALVE. **Running c.,** *see* RUNNING.

CHECKERED PLATES. *See* PLATE.

CHEEK. One of the projections on a lowermast which support trestle-trees and framing of the top; also termed *mast-cheek,* and, in steel construction, *cheek-plate;* the cheeks are called *hounds* on upper masts. One of the sides of a block. **C.-block,** *see* BLOCK. **C.-knee,** one of the knees on either side of stem for securing the cutwater in position. **C.-piece,** a strengthening piece on forward upper end of a boat's rudder.

CHEEKS. The bilgeways; curve or "turn" of the bilges. **Chafing-c.,** *see* CHAFING.

CHELINGA or **CHELINGO.** (Tamil, *shalangu.*) *See* MASOOLA-BOAT.

CHEMICAL AMMUNITION. *See* AMMUNITION.

CHEQUERED PLATE. *See* PLATE.

CHESAPEAKE CANOE. *See* CANOE.

CHESS-TREE. In ships of the 17th. and 18th. centuries, a timber bolted to ship's side at after end of the fore chains, to which the main tack was hove down, and often used to secure the fore sheet.

CHEST. **Arms-c.,** *see* ARMS. **Bilge-c.,** *see* BILGE. **Boatswain's c.,** *see* BOATSWAIN. **C.-rope,** an old term for an extra painter or boat-rope for making fast a boat astern of ship. **Chronometer-c.,** coffer or box in which ship's chronometers are stowed. **Mess-c.,** *see* MESS. **Powder-c.,** *see* POWDER. **Sailor's c.,** a strong wooden box or trunk in which a seaman keeps his belongings. **Sea-c.,** a sailor's chest; also, *see* SEA. **Slop-c.,** *see* SLOP. **Steam-c.,** *see* STEAM.

CHEVRON. Distinguishing mark worn on the coat-sleeve by non-commissioned officers (army) and petty officers (navy) to indicate rating or service, consisting of a pair or pairs of bars meeting at an angle, as a broadened *V.*

CHIEF. Popular short title for the chief engineer on a merchant vessel or a chief petty officer in U.S. navy. **C. constructor,** in U.S. navy, officer (usually a rear-admiral) heading Bureau of Construction and Repairs, a former division of Navy Department now incorporated with *Bureau of Ships.* **C. engineer,** *see* ENGINEER. **C. mate,** *see* MATE. **C. officer,** officer next in rank below the master in a merchant vessel, except in large passenger-ships carrying an assistant master, or *staff-captain,* in which case he ranks next below the latter; chief mate. **C. quarter-**

master, see QUARTERMASTER. **C. steward,** see STEWARD.

CHILEAN CURRENT. *See* CURRENT.

CHIMÆRA. (Gr., *a mythological monster.*) An odd-looking fish of the ray family, or group *Holocephali*, about two feet in length, having a large head and body tapering to a pointed tail; found on the coasts of Europe, the north Pacific, and South Africa.

CHIME. Rim around heads of a cask formed by projecting ends of the staves; also written *chimb*. In wooden vessels, heavy part of the waterway which is next to ship's side. Line of intersection of sides and bottom of a flat-bottomed vessel or boat.

CHINE. A variant of *chime*. **Chine and chine,** said of casks stowed end to end.

CHINESE CAPSTAN. *See* CAPSTAN.

CHINESE, or **DIFFERENTIAL, WINDLASS.** *See* WINDLASS.

CHINSE. To calk temporarily; to force oakum or cotton in seams of a boat with a knife-blade or a chinsing-iron; to calk lightly where heavy blows would injure planking. **C.-iron,** a tool for chinsing planking-seams; any caulking-iron used for chinsing.

CHINTZE. A variant of *chinse*.

CHIP. The *log-chip,* or triangular piece of wood at outer end of the old-fashioned log-line; *see* LOG.

CHIPPING. Act of removing thick scale from iron or steel surfaces, or dressing edges of metal plates, etc. **C.-hammer,** a small sharp-faced hammer commonly used on board ship for removing rust-scale from iron or steel; a pneumatic hammer used for trimming, gouging, rounding, etc. in the modern shipyard.

CHIPS. The colloquial name on board ship for the *carpenter.*

CHIRO. A fish of the tarpon family (*Elops saurus*), growing to about five feet in length and found in all tropical seas under many different names; like the tarpon, it is a fine game fish, but of poor edible quality.

CHOCK. A block or wedge used to prevent a movable object from rolling or shifting; a piece of wood inserted to make up any deficiency in a timber, frame, etc.; a heavy block or casting fitted at side of a weather deck and shaped to act as a fair-lead for a hawser. To secure a cargo against shifting with dunnage-wood, or by jamming cargo tightly in its allotted space; to press hard against, as, to *chock up,* to *chock aft,* etc. **Anchor-c.,** see ANCHOR. **Boat-c.,** see BOAT. **Boom-c.,** a bed shaped to receive the head of a boom, usually fitted with a clamp or means of securing boom when stowed. **Bowsprit-c's,** blocks or chocking arrangement securing a bowsprit in its bed; the *bowsprit bed*. **Bow-c.,** see BOW. **Butt-c.,** see BUTT. **C.-a-block,** said of a tackle when blocks are drawn close together; hence, any object in a position which precludes further motion. **C. full,** filled to capacity. **C. home,** said of square sails when sheeted home as close as possible to the yard-arm. **Cross-c's,** pieces of timber in *deadwood* to fill deficiency where it is impracticable to continue futtocks downward. **Dousing-c.,** in older wooden construction, one of the pieces of timber uniting knightheads and apron, fitted near the stem head immediately under the bowsprit. **Filling-c.,** one of the pieces used to build up a projecting ornamental curve at stem of wooden ships, between stem and cutwater. **Hawse-c.,** see HAWSE. **Mast-partner c.,** see MAST. **Mooring-c's,** see MOORING. **Riding-c's,** see RIDING. **Roller-c's,** see ROLLER. **Rolling-c's,** see ROLLING. **Rouser-c.,** a mooring-chock closed up across the top; also, called a *mooring-pipe* when set in a bulwark-plate, apron-plate, etc., or in bulwark-planking; this type of chock is required for towing-hawsers used by electric mules at locks of Panama Canal. **Rudder-c.,** a wedge or similar piece of wood jammed between rudder-stock and rudder-trunk to hold rudder stationary when not in use; also *rudder-stop*, see RUDDER. **Shell-c.,** the concrete material filling spaces between frames where lower-deck stringer-plates join the shell-plating. **Warping-c.,** same as *mooring-chock,* see MOORING.

CHOCOLATERO. A brisk north-west wind in the Gulf of Mexico, so called from resemblance of the sea during the breeze to a variety of chocolate confection; also, *chocolate gale*.

CHOKE. To foul: said of a rope in a block. **To c. the luff,** to jam hauling part of a tackle between the adjoining part and its sheave, thus preventing tackle from slackening up or rendering, as a temporary measure. **To c. up,** to block, fill, or clog; as a channel by silt; or a scupper-pipe with waste matter.

CHOP. (Hind. *chhap,* seal or brand.) An official stamp on a clearance, passport, permit, etc. in India and China; also, document itself. Brand or quality; as, *of the first chop*. A hulk of a vessel used as a store-house or residence on the China coast, formerly often used as a customs office. **C.-boat,** a lighter used to carry freight and passengers in China; also, *chow-chow chop; see* CHOW-CHOW. **C.-dollar,** in China, Malacca, Burma, and Siam, a dollar or other currency note bearing an impressed private mark as a guarantee of genuineness. It formerly was the custom for each business house to stamp in this way all paper money passing through its hands. **The grand chop** or **the red chop,** a port clearance certificate granted in Chinese ports.

CHOP CHOP. In *Pidgin English,* to make haste or hurry up a job. In semaphore signalling, end of a message indicated by both arms on one side moved rapidly up and down past each other.

CHOPPY. Descriptive term for a short rough sea caused by meeting currents, or a breeze blowing against a current; also said of the wind when changeable and baffling.

CHOPS. Shores or headlands forming entrance to a harbor or channel; mouth or entrance of a channel or strait; as, *chops of the English Channel.*

CHORD METHOD. In navigation, determination of a line of position according to the principles first used by *Sumner.* The altitude of a heavenly body is observed and two values of latitude are assumed in calculation of the longitude, or two values of longitude in calculating the latitude. Line joining the two resulting positions, being a *chord* of an arc of the circle of equal altitude, is required Sumner line, or line of position, on which vessel was located at some point at time of observation, displacement of such chord from the intercepted arc being considered negligible.

CHOW-CHOW. Mixed; broken; miscellaneous. **C.-c. cargo,** an assorted cargo. **C.-c. chop,** on the China coast, the lot of smaller miscellaneous packages sent off in last lighter or cargo-boat to a ship loading in a roadstead or harbor. In China, a provision-boat or lighter. **C.-c. water,** short, irregular waves, or agitation of the water, such as made by propeller or paddles of a steam-vessel, meeting of currents, etc.

CHRISTEN. To give a vessel a name, as in ceremony observed when she is started down the ways in launching. The christening rite appears to have had a religious significance in its practice over some 3900 years, ceremony being thought essential to future blessing of craft concerned. To-day a ship is christened by having a bottle of wine or champagne broken against her bow as she begins to move down the ways. Failure to thus name or baptize the vessel, according to popular belief, invites disaster, or, at least a career of ill fortune is certain to follow.

C.C. or **C.E.** Common abbreviation for *chronometer correction* or *chronometer error*, which is applied to time shown on chronometer to obtain Greenwich mean time (*G.M.T.*) It is additive if chronometer is slow and subtractive if fast.

CHRONOMETER. (Gr. *chronos*, time; *metron*, a measure.) A clock or time-piece specially made to keep accurate time, or maintain a constant losing or gaining rate, under shipboard conditions. Known as the *marine chronometer*, instrument is used principally to obtain correct Greenwich mean time (usually abbreviated *G.M.T.*) in connection with altitude observations of heavenly bodies for determination of a vessel's geographical position at

sea. It is hung face upward in gimbals like the mariner's compass and is fitted in a special glass-topped box. A special compensation balance is provided in the mechanism for purpose of counter-acting effect of contraction or expansion of metals caused by changes of temperature which otherwise would interfere with the instrument's steady performance. Our present chronometer differs little from the original production of *John Harrison (1693-1776)*, who was awarded the prize of 50,000 pounds sterling offered by British government in 1763 for a time-piece of a certain stipulated degree of accuracy under sea-going conditions. Harrison's clock more than fulfilled the requirements, and with subsequent use of the chronometer came much-desired accuracy in charted coastlines and determination of longitude at sea. **C. error,** difference between time indicated on chronometer and Greenwich mean time. *Radio time signals* now furnish the most convenient and accurate means of finding chronometer error. Prior to present systematic broadcasts by principal astronomical observatories, time signals, such as dropping of a signal ball or firing of a gun, were established at principal seaports for the benefit of navigators, and often the practice of checking chronometer error by direct observation was resorted to when position of the ship was accurately known. In addition to determination of the error, rate at which chronometer is losing or gaining is arrived at by comparison with a previously observed error; instrument's behavior is thus expressed as having a certain *daily rate,* and number of days elapsing from date of latest error observed, multiplied by daily rate, must be applied to that error in order to obtain *accumulated* or *current error* required to be added to or subtracted from face reading of chronometer. **C.-chest,** see CHEST. **C. time,** actual time indicated by chronometer. *Original error certificate,* a statement furnished by dealer or maker of a chronometer, or an authority in whose hands the instrument has been placed for rating, stating that on a certain date chronometer was so many minutes and seconds *fast* or *slow* of Greenwich mean time, and that it is gaining or losing (*daily rate*) a certain amount each day. **Sidereal c.,** one that shows sidereal time; *see* SIDEREAL.

CHUBASCO. A violent thunder-squall on west coast of Central America.

CHUB MACKEREL. Small mackerel occasionally found in large schools off Atlantic coast of America, but generally widely distributed. The species is termed *Scomber japonicus.*

CHURCH PENNANT. See PENNANT.

CHUTE. (Fr. *chute,* a fall) A channel or river having a quick descent; narrow passage through which water flows to a lower level; a rapid or *shoot.* **Ash-c.,** see ASH. **Garbage c.,** a conduit for disposing of refuse,—especially that from ship's galley. It is either built into ship through the side or hung overside and sometimes extended downward by canvas for protection of vessel's side. **Head-c.,** *see* HEAD.

C.I.F. *"Cost, insurance, and freight."* As used in quoting price of a shipment of goods, indicates insurance and freight charges incidental to delivery of goods are included in price quoted.

C.I.F.C.I. *"Cost, insurance, freight, commission, and interest,"* means that, in addition to cost, insurance, and freight, shipper includes in his quoted price charges for commission and interest due on consignee's draft in payment for goods.

CIGAR-FISH. A carangoid fish (*Decapterus punctatus*) found in Caribbean Sea and south-east U.S. waters, about one foot in length; so called from its cigar-shaped or fusiform appearance. Also called *round robin*.

CINQUE PORTS. Five ports in Kent and Sussex on the English coast,—Dover, Sandwich, Romney, Hastings, and Hythe, with later detached "members,"—which were incorporated as a sea-coast defense measure in A.D. 1278. They were given special rights and jurisdictional privileges in return for sea service in protecting the coast, their strategic position with relation to the continental shore of the English Channel being considered of much importance. The *"Lord Warden of the Cinque Ports"* was given jurisdiction as admiral of the ports and as *"Governor of Dover Castle."*

CIPHERED. Referred to planking, a method of maintaining tightness of seams in event of shrinkage of the wood, by rabbeting edges of the planks to half thickness of the material. It is used in hold-ceiling, bulwark-planking, sides of deck-houses, etc.

CIRCLE. (L. *circus,* circle.) A plane figure bounded by a curved line, all points of which are equidistant from a point within called the *center.* **Antarctic c.,** *see* ANTARCTIC. **Arctic c.,** *see* ARCTIC. **Azimuth-c.,** *see* AZIMUTH. **C. of altitude,** an imaginary circle in the heavens, parallel to the horizon, all points through which it passes being therefore of equal altitude; *see* ALMUCANTAR. **C. of declination,** *see* DECLINATION. **C. of equal altitude,** a circle whose circumference passes through all points on the earth's surface at which altitude of a heavenly body has same numerical value. In navigational theory, a small arc of this circle is identical with the *line of position* obtained from a sextant observation of sun, moon, a planet, or a star at a given instant of solar or sidereal time. **C. of illumination,** great circle forming boundary between illuminated and unilluminated parts of surface of a planet or a satellite. **C. of latitude,** a great circle perpendicular to the ecliptic, on which celestial latitude of a heavenly body is measured. Any meridian of the terrestrial sphere on which latitude is measured; rarely, also a **parallel of latitude. C. of longitude,** any circle of the celestial sphere parallel to the ecliptic. A parallel of latitude on the terrestrial sphere. **C. of position,** same as *circle of equal altitude.* **C. of right ascension,** a great circle passing through poles of the celestial sphere. The declination of a heavenly body is measured on this circle and angle at the poles formed by zero circle of right ascension passing through First Point of Aries (*vernal equinox*) and that passing through body measures right ascension of the latter, expressed in hours, minutes, and seconds of sidereal time. **Dip-c.,** *see* DIP. **Diurnal c.,** circle or parallel of declination described by apparent daily course of a heavenly body in consequence of the earth's rotation. **Galactic c.,** *see* GALACTIC. **Great c.,** one described upon the surface of a sphere and whose plane divides the sphere into two equal parts called *hemispheres;* center of any great circle coincides with center of the sphere. **Hour c.,** a circle of right ascension; *also see* HOUR. **Meridian c.,** *see* MERIDIAN. **Polar c's,** Arctic and Antarctic circles; parallels of latitude 66° 33′ north and south, respectively. **Reflecting-c.,** an astronomical instrument for measuring large angles, similar in principle to the sextant. **Rolling c.,** *see* ROLLING. **Small c.,** one described upon the surface of a sphere, whose plane divides sphere into two unequal parts; center of a small circle *never* coincides with center of sphere. **Transit c.,** same as *meridian c.; see* MERIDIAN. **Traverse-c.,** *see* TRAVERSE. **Turning-c.,** *see* TURNING. **Vertical c.,** any great circle of the celestial sphere perpendicular to the horizon; an instrument for measuring altitudes; a transit or meridian circle.

CIRCULATING PUMP. A pump used to circulate sea-water through a condenser in process of reconverting exhaust steam to water. **Circulating-discharge pipe,** large pipe or tube through which condenser circulating-water is discharged overboard.

CIRCUM-MERIDIAN ALTITUDE. Old term for an ex-meridian altitude, or one observed for determination of latitude when heavenly body is close to transit.

CIRCUMNAVIGATE. (L. *circum,* round about; *navigare,* to navigate.) To sail round; as, *to c. the earth.* **Circumnavigable,** that can be sailed round.

CIRCUMPOLAR. (L. *circum,* round about; *polus,* a pivot.) In nautical astronomy, descriptive term for a heavenly body which remains above the horizon throughout its apparent diurnal revolution about the elevated pole; a circumpolar star necessarily has a polar distance (*90° — declination*) of a lesser value than latitude of an observer.

CIRCUMSAIL. To circumnavigate.

CIRRO. A combining form from Latin *cirrus,* a lock, curl, ringlet. **C.-cumulus; c.-pallium; c.-stratus;** *see* CLOUD.

CIRRUS. *See* CLOUD. **Cirrus veil,** *see* CLOUD.

CLACK-VALVE. Arrangement at outer end of a scupper or waste-pipe whereby a suspended swinging check or clapper prevents ingress of sea-water, but allows free flow of waste, bilge-water, etc., overboard; also called a *clapper-valve* and a *storm-valve*. **Clack-box,** the containing body of a clack-valve. **Clack-door,** plate or removable cover giving access to a clack-valve.

CLAM. (Formerly *clamp;* from same root as clamp.) An edible bivalve mollusc; especially, the *quahog* or *hard-shell clam* and the *long* or *soft-shell clam* found on Atlantic coast of North America. Both are about three inches in length, shell of the quahog being heavy and rounded and the soft-shell thin and oval-shaped. The quahog is found submerged on both sandy and rocky bottoms; soft-shell species lies embedded in sand where beach is dry at low water, its location being easily recognized by a small vent-hole in the sand through which it occasionally discharges a spurt of water. Both clams are of excellent food value.

CLAMP. (Du. *klampen,* to clasp or fasten.) In wooden construction, a strake of heavy planking laid fore-and-aft and secured to frames as a support for ends of deck-beams of a poop, forecastle, or raised quarter-deck: strake immediately below and re-enforcing the *shelf,* in the case of continuous decks, on which timber the beams rest; in smaller vessels, clamp only supports beams as indicated. A curved piece of flat iron hinged to fit over and secure a boom in its bed, heel of a jib-boom to bowsprit, a mast to a thwart in a boat, etc. A *cap-square,* or one of the metal pieces securing trunnions of a gun to its carriage. A block having one cheek, the part of a spar or other object to which it is fitted forming the other cheek; a *cheek-block*. The screw used to tighten the index bar of a sextant against the arc; also, *clamp-screw*. **Beam-c.,** a device temporarily fitted to grip the edge of an iron deck-beam and providing a means whereby a tackle or lead-block may be secured. **Horseshoe-c.,** in wooden vessels, one of the metal straps fitted to secure the fore-foot arrangement by uniting the *gripe* to *stem* and *keel;* it is laid round the gripe so that its two legs are bolted together through the timber. **Hawser-c.,** *see* HAWSER. **Rudder-c.,** *see* RUDDER.

CLAM-SHELL. A form of grab-bucket used in dredging, excavating, loading coal, gravel, etc. Its two hinged parts are drawn together like valves of a hard-shell clam in operation of scooping up a load. Also, *clam-shell bucket*.

CLAMM, DEEP-SEA. A small grab used to bring up bottom specimens in taking deep-sea soundings, contrived in 1818 by Sir John Ross, British arctic navigator *(1777–1856)*. Also, *clammer*.

CLAP ABOARD. In nautical usage of 16th. and 17th. centuries, to approach, lay alongside of, or board another vessel. To *clap on a wind* meant to haul close to the wind.

CLAP ON, To. CLAP HOLD OF, To. To take hold of a rope with object of hauling upon it. To **clap on** a stopper, strop, tackle, etc., is to attach such instrument to a hawser, lanyard, or other object indicated. To **clap on canvas,** to spread additional sail, especially in sense of carrying an extra press of canvas in a stiff breeze.

CLAPPER. The tongue of a bell. A clack-valve in a pump, scupper-pipe, etc. A piece of wood fitted between jaws of a gaff to bear against, and hold gaff a constant distance from, the mast; also termed *saddle, tongue,* and *tumbler*.

CLASP HOOK. A pair of twin hooks which meet as one and are secured in position by a slip-ring, clasp, or mousing on their shanks. A *spring-hook* used as a hank, as for securing the luff of a jib to its stay in a sail-boat. *See* **sister-hooks** *in* HOOK.

CLASS. A division or grouping of vessels according to their size, strength, and/or common characteristics; as, *destroyer class, collier class*. Rating given a vessel by a classification society according to her degree of conformity with prescribed standards of structural strength, machinery, equipment, and periodical surveys; the expression *"A1 at Lloyd's"* signifies a vessel is assigned highest class in the society's records.

CLASSIFICATION. Act of placing a vessel in a certain class as prescribed in requirements of classification society concerned. **C. certificate,** *see* CERTIFICATE. **C. society,** a corporation or society founded with the aim of establishing certain standards in construction, propelling plant, and equipment of vessels, providing for seaworthiness and safety in connection with marine insurance. interests. Such societies maintain watchful concern over all craft registered in their lists; their surveyors supervise construction; test building material as necessary; inspect and control execution of required or recommended repair-work; and determine schedule for periodic inspections or surveys in connection with prescribed procedure in upholding a vessel's "class." While a shipowner is not compelled to build his vessel according to any classification society's requirements, established practice in marine underwriting of quoting a premium based upon the certified classification of a vessel would render the position of an "unclassed" vessel a difficult one in the question of securing a satisfactory rate of insurance. Names of principal societies active at beginning of World War II are:—*American Bureau of Shipping; British Corporation; Bureau Veritas; Germanischer Lloyd; Imperial Japanese Maritime Corporation; Lloyd's Register of British* *and Foreign Shipping; Nederlandsche Vereeniging van Assuradeuren; Norske Veritas; Registro Navale Italiano; Veritas Austro-Ungarico.*

CLASS-RACING. In yachting, any race in which boats are judged according to their class, certain allowances in time covering the course being given, considering type, length, displacement, etc.; also, *handicap-racing.*

CLAW OFF, To. In sailing, to lay to windward in working off a lee shore. **Devil's claw,** a heavy bifurcated iron hook shaped to fit over the anchor cable and, attached to a small chain, to act as a stopper.

CLEAN. Well shaped; neat; trim; as, *clean lines of a ship.* Free of danger or obstruction; as, *a clean anchorage.* Free of any qualifying or restricting clause; as, a *clean* bill of health, a *clean* bill of lading; *see* BILL. **C. breach,** *see* BREACH. **C. sleeve,** *see* SLEEVE. **C. full,** said of sails when steadily drawing, as on a wind, or nearly close-hauled.

CLEAR. To free from legal detention, as imported goods or a ship, by paying duties or dues and presenting the requisite documents: as, to *clear a cargo;* to *clear a ship* at customhouse. To remove an obstruction. **C. breach,** *see* BREACH. **C. hawse,** *see* HAWSE. **C.-hawse breeches,** a sling in the form of short breeches, formerly used in the navy to lower a seaman over the bows in operation of clearing hawse, *i.e.,* taking turns out of anchor cables. **C.-hawse pendant,** in navy ships, a special pendant consisting, usually, of five or six fathoms of handy chain fitted with a pelican-hook and a tail of flexible wire rope; used to take weight of lee chain cable preparatory to dipping disconnected end of same round the riding cable, when clearing hawse. **C. lead,** said of a rope or cable when leading or running free of obstruction. **C. view screen,** *see* SCREEN. To **c. for action,** or **c. decks for action,** in navy usage, to remove all encumbrances from decks preparatory to engaging in battle. To **c. inward,** or **outward** to conform to customs and port regulations upon arriving in, or prior to leaving, port. To **c. the land,** to make such a distance from shore. as to have the sea-room desirable. To **make c.,** *see* MAKE. To **swing c.,** *see* SWING.

CLEARANCE. In general, any written authority showing that a vessel has conformed to existing customs, naval, or port regulations or laws. **C. inward,** a certificate issued by customs indicating that, cargo having been discharged or accounted for, there remains on board certain stores or dutiable goods which were in vessel upon her arrival. Usually, at a final port of discharge, before issuance of such clearance the master is required to produce a certificate stating that ship's official log and articles of agreement have been deposited at the shipping office and that entire crew has been accounted for. **C. outward,** a certificate issued by customs authorities indicating that the master has complied with regulations of the port and paid all assessed dues and charges on his vessel's account; and therefore authorizes him to depart.

CLEARER. A tool on which the hemp for making twines used by sailmakers is prepared.

CLEARING. **C.-bearing,** bearing of a shore object which indicates a certain local danger is "*cleared.*" **C.-marks,** two conspicuous shore objects which are to be kept in line, as range-marks, in steering to pass clear of some danger or through a channel; also, *c.-line.* **C.-port,** a freeing-port; *see* PORT.

CLEAT. A strip of wood or metal fastened to other material to strengthen, keep in place, prevent slipping, etc. A piece of wood, iron, or other metal, shaped as a short stout bar with projecting ends, on which ropes are belayed; a heavy cleat of this sort being usually termed a *cavil:* see KEVEL. **Batten-c's,** right-angled shaped brackets fixed to hatch coamings for holding and wedging tarpaulin-battens in position; also, *hatch-cleats.* **Comb-c.,** *see* COMB. **Mooring-c.,** a kevel; a mooring-staple: *see* MOORING. **Parrel-c.,** *see* PARREL. **Peak-c.,** *see* PEAK. **Reefing-c's, reef-pendant c's,** *see* REEFING. **Shore-c.,** *see* SHORE. **Snatch-c.,** *see* SNATCH. **Thumb-c.,** a one-armed cleat fixed in the rigging or elsewhere to hold a rope in place or lead it as required. **Yard-arm c.,** *see* YARD.

CLENCH. *See* CLINCH. **Clench-nails,** *see* NAIL.

CLERK OF THE CHECK. In Great Britain, formerly an officer in a royal dockyard who kept a register of men employed aboard His Majesty's ships and others in navy service at port concerned.

CLEW. Either of lower corners of a square sail or lower aftermost extremity of a fore-and-aft sail. Strop, cringle, ring, or spectacle-iron to which sheet of a sail is made fast. A ball of yarn or cord. (Also spelled *clue.*) **C.-cringle,** rope strop or eye worked in bolt-rope at clew of a sail; a ring of thin metal of concave cross section secured to clew by a cringle-strop; on heavier sails, a metal ring or spectacle-iron to which thimbles for splicing in the foot and leech ropes are fitted. To **c. down,** to slack away on halyards and haul away on clew-lines in order to force a yard down, as when caught in a squall. **C.-garnet,** a purchase for hoisting clews of courses to yard: usually a *gun-tackle purchase,* or one of two single blocks. Formerly courses (foresail, mainsail, and crossjack of a full-rigged ship) were clewed up to "*the bunt*" or middle of yard, but in merchantmen of later years hoisting clews to yard-arms appears to have been favored practice. **C.-iron,** a ring, spectacle-iron, or kind of double-bowed shackle, in clew of a heavy sail, to which the sheet, bolt-rope, and (in the case of a square sail) clew-garnet, or clew-line, are attached. **C.-jigger,** a small tackle or whip formerly used to lift clews of a topsail or course over the yard. **C.-ring,** a galvanized iron ring fitted as a clew-iron, *q.v.* **C.-line,** a purchase or single rope leading to deck for hauling up to yards the clews of topsails, top-gallant-sails, and royals. **C.-rope,** a line leading from a mast or a gaff for tricing up the clew of a fore-and-aft sail; also, for lifting the clew of a staysail over a stay next below. To **c. up,** to haul up to a yard the clews of a square sail. **From c. to earing,** from bottom to top of a square sail; hence, *figuratively,* in a thorough manner. **Hammock-c's,** small lines by which a hammock is suspended. **Spectacle-c.,** a clew-iron made in form of spectacles, commonly consisting of three circular shapes in the same plane, fashioned in galvanized iron. To **spread a large (or small) c.,** a descriptive phrase indicating amount of sail carried; hence, *figuratively,* the degree of importance manifested.

CLICK. A detent or pawl, as on a capstan; *see* PAWL.

CLINCH. A fastening in which a bolt or nail is clinched, as in a boat's planking. A kind of knot used to make fast a rope to a cringle, ring, etc., as a buntline on a sail or a warp to a kedge anchor; made by turning end of rope once or twice around its standing part and seizing it so as to form a bull's-eye in which standing part is free to slide; *clinch* thus snugly and effectively takes hold, has no parts to jam, and does no injury to line. To spread or burr the end of a bolt upon a washer or ring by hammering; to turn over the end of a nail, with or without a clinch-ring, as in planking a boat. Also, *clench.* **C.-bolt** or **clinched bolt,** *see* BOLT. **C.-ring,** an open ring or washer laid over a nail or bolt, or rivet, against which such fastening is burred or riveted. **Inside,** or **outside, c.,** on a rope, distinguishing a clinch according to whether seized end is inside or outside the turn or turns of line round object to which it is attached. (Also *clench,* which would seem more consistent with its *M.E.* form *clencher,* to hold fast)

CLINCHER-BUILT. *See* CLINKER-BUILT.

CLINKER-BUILT. Referred to small craft construction, means that each strake of planking overlaps upper edge of strake next below. Width of landing surface depends upon size of planking, a six-inch plank requiring ¾ to 1 inch, and plank edge fastenings 3½ to 5 inches apart. Toward stem and stern planks gradually merge to present a terminating flush surface by rabbeting their faying parts accordingly. This light and strong form of construction is specially suited to rough handling, hoisting, etc., met with in beach work and shipboard use. Planking on *clinker-built* ships' boats is usually five-eighths inch in thickness and may be of cypress, red cedar, white or yellow pine, larch, wych elm, teak, mahogany, or woods of similar texture. **C.-laid,** said of plating laid as in a clinker-

built boat; as steel deck plates of a ship, for purpose of shedding all water toward the sides. **C.-strake,** one having its edges over and under its adjoining strakes, respectively. **C.-work,** lap-jointed planking or plating.

CLINOMETER. (Gr. *klinein,* to incline; *metron,* a measure.) An instrument for measuring angle of a vessel's roll. It usually consists of a suspended metal pointer which indicates direction of the plumb line, as vessel rolls, on a graduated arc of a circle in the athwartship plane; often is a graduated tube of glass containing a liquid in which a bubble marks the degree of roll.

CLIONE. (*N.L.*) A genus of tiny *pteropods* inhabiting Arctic and northern waters in abundance and forming principal food of the Greenland or Arctic right whale.

CLIP. A short piece of angle-bar or plate used to connect various parts of the structure in shipbuilding, such as a floor-plate to a keelson or other longitudinal member, a hold stanchion to a floor, etc.; and frequently as a temporary fitting by which to draw parts together preparatory to welding or riveting. Also termed *lug, lug-piece, angle-clip, angle-lug.* **Angle-c.,** *see* ANGLE. **Beam-c.,** *see* BEAM. To **c. along,** to **clip it,** to move swiftly as in sailing. **Sheet-clips,** *see* SHEET. **C.-hooks, clove-hooks,** same as *sister-hooks: see* HOOK. **Launching-c's,** lugs or short pieces of stout angle-bar temporarily riveted to a ship's side for the purpose of securing ends of *launching-drags,* or means of checking vessel's way as she leaves the launch-ways.

CLIPPER. (From colloquial word *clip,* to move swiftly.) A vessel characterized by fine lines and an unusually large sail area, built and rigged for fast sailing, the term originating in the *"Baltimore clippers,"* speedy brigs and schooners of early American privateering days. What is known as the *clipper ship era* appears to have covered period 1840 to 1870, in which the wood-built full-rigged ship attained her highest development in construction and sailing qualities. Chiefly American and British owned, such vessels were employed in China, Australian, trans-Atlantic, and Californian trades and some remarkably fast passages are recorded of the craft. American-built vessels proved fastest ocean sailers, their peculiarity of hull form apparently allowing greater sail-carrying power in strong winds and rough seas than their British contemporaries, and it is generally accepted that the speediest, and at least equal to the sturdiest, were turned out at Boston by Donald McKay in the 1850's, though a few other New England yards deserve a close second place. As an example of "Yankee clipper" performance, the *Flying Cloud,* built by Donald McKay in 1851, made passage from New York to San Francisco (via Cape Horn), pilot to pilot, in 88 days 22½ hours, in 1854; the *Andrew*

Jackson, Connecticut-built, occupied 89 days 4 hours on same run in 1860;—established records for the 14,900-mile lap indicated. American-built *Sovereign of the Seas, James Baines, Donald McKay,* and *Lightning (1853–1856)* are credited with days' runs of 420 to 440 miles, with spurts of 19 to 21 knots frequently attained. With opening of the Suez Canal in 1869, the clipper gradually gave way to fast-growing steam-vessel tonnage in the far eastern trade, though for some years later they continued to give a good account of themselves in the New York–San Francisco run and Australian wool trade. Cargo-carrying capacity of the clipper varied from 750 to 3000 tons. **C. bow,** see BOW. **C.-built,** said of a vessel having the fine lines of a clipper ship. **Medium c.,** a type of sailing-ship brought out in American yards about 1860, so named for its departure from the original or "extreme" clipper in a lesser spread of canvas, lighter spars, and "fuller" body lines, thus requiring a smaller crew, while capable of carrying a greater cargo. **Opium-c.,** a fast sailing-vessel formerly used in smuggling opium into Chinese ports from India. **Steam c.,** term used in advertising sailing of the first iron-built sailing-ships having auxiliary steam power, which appeared in the England-Australian trade about 1855. **Tea c.,** a clipper ship engaged in the China or India trade *(1840–1870)* whose cargo largely consisted of tea on homeward run to western Europe or east coast of America. **Wool c.,** one of the clippers carrying wool from Australia and New Zealand to England *(1840–1870)*.

CLOCK. (Of Celtic origin; Ir. *clog;* W. *cloch;* a bell.) **Ship's c.,** standard time-piece used to indicate the hour on board ship; a clock which strikes *bells* or divisions of the watches kept on board ship. **C.-calm,** a dead calm, *i.e.,* a smooth, glassy sea and no wind present. **C.-setter,** one who tampers with the clock in order to shorten his watch; hence, a busy-body or mischief-maker among the crew; *sea-lawyer.* **C.-star,** a star used by an astronomer for determining or checking his clock time, by observing its meridian transit. **Tidal c.,** see TIDAL.

CLOSE. In immediate proximity. To come near to; to come together, as, to *close* another vessel. **C. butt,** see BUTT. **C. ceiling,** see CEILING. **C. harbor,** see HARBOR. **C.-hauled,** said of trim of sails when steering as near as possible in direction from which the wind blows, or *"by the wind,"* as termed in merchant vessels. A fine-lined sloop will sail about 3½ points off the wind when close-hauled; a schooner about 5; and a square-rigger not less than 6. Also termed *sailing close to the wind.* **C.-link chain,** see CHAIN. **C. order,** see ORDER. **C. port,** see PORT. **C.-quarters** or **c.-fights,** in merchantmen of the 18th. century, temporary wooden barriers advantageously placed on deck as retreats from which to fire on a boarding enemy or pirates. To

come to c. quarters, to engage in close or hand-to-hand conflict with an enemy. **C.-reefed,** said of a sail when reduced to its smallest possible area, or when all reefs are taken in. **C. reach,** see REACH. **C. up,** referred to a hoist of flags, indicating they are exhibited as high as halyards will allow; when referred to a single flag or answering pennant, hoisted as far as possible, as distinguished from flying it about two-thirds that height, or *"at the dip."* To **c. with,** to draw near to, as, to *close with* the shore. **C.-winded,** descriptive term for being capable of sailing very close to the wind. **Closing-machine,** in rope-making, machine for laying or twisting finished strands into rope. **Closing-strake,** bilge-strake of shell-plating which is last strake fitted in welded construction. To **lay c.,** see LAY.

CLOSED. **Closed chain,** close or short-link chain. **C. chock,** a rouser-chock; *see* CHOCK. **C.-in spaces,** in laws governing measurement for tonnage, those spaces in a vessel above the upper deck which can be permanently closed in protection from weather and which, therefore, must be included in *gross tonnage.* **C. port,** a harbor or seaport closed to entry or departure of shipping. **C. sea,** the legal phrase *mare clausum; see* MARE. **C. stokehold** or **fireroom,** closed-in space used in firing a ship's boilers and in which atmospheric pressure is increased by mechanical blowers for purpose of maintaining an efficient draft through the furnaces; as opposed to an *open* stokehold where natural draft, or forced draft in a closed furnace is employed.

CLOTH. One of the lengths of canvas or duck sewed together to make a sail, tarpaulin, awning, boat-cover, etc., especially so termed in sailmaking, the word being used to denote width measurement of head or foot of a square or a gaff-headed sail for trading and fishing vessels, as, *an 18-cloth mainsail.* American standard sail-cloth is of cotton canvas or duck 22 inches in width, while British choice is 24-inch flax, though lighter sails of yachts and other small craft are often made of 14, 16, 18, and 20-inch duck (cotton or linen). Cloths of square sails run perpendicular to yards; those of gaff-headed sails run parallel to the leech; jibs and triangular staysails, parallel to leech and foot, joined or mitered between clew and luff (or across middle of sail); storm staysails or trysails, or those having a roughly horizontal foot, parallel to leech. Sails of yachts and small craft vary from above according to local custom or preference. *See* CANVAS and SAIL. **Back-c.,** in single topsail days, a triangular-shaped sheet of canvas secured to a topsail or lower yard jack-stay, used for snugly furling the bunt of a heavy sail, as, and in effect, a *bunt gasket.* **Buntline-c.,** a piece of canvas sewed to a square sail in way of a buntline to avoid chafing injury to sail. **Goring-c.,** a triangular cloth added to width of a square sail toward its foot for purpose of distributing stress at the clews and effectively spreading the sail; any cloth forming the *gore* in a sail. **Hammock-c.**, a tarpaulin or canvas covering placed over, or used to protect stowed hammocks from the weather. **Lining-c.**, *see* LINING. **Mast-c.**, same as *mast-lining; see* MAST. **Mess-c.**, mess-tarpaulin; *see* MESS. **Separation c.**, a tarpaulin or other large sheet of canvas, burlap, etc. used to prevent mixture of different grades or consignments of cargo, such as grain, seeds, etc.; to segregate valuable goods; or to protect cargo from condensation of moisture, dust, or contamination. **Slack c.**, in sailmaking, amount of canvas sewed to new bolt-rope which is allowed for "gathering in," to avoid undue stress on the cloth as rope stretches with wear and tear; a bagging cloth in a sail. **Square c.**, as opposed to one cut to conform to the *roach* in a sail, a cloth cut square across at each end. **Waist-c.**, old term for a *hammock-cloth*. **Weather-c.**, a tarpaulin or canvas shelter placed in weather rigging of a sailing-vessel or on a navigating-bridge as a protection against wind, rain, spray, etc.; a *dodger;* any canvas shelter; an old navy term for a *hammock-cloth* or *waist-cloth*.

CLOTHE. To rig and fit sails on a new vessel; to bend the sails. **Clothed,** an archaism indicating a mast hidden almost to the deck by its lower sail. **Clothing,** a quaint term for sail spread on a ship, especially head sails.

CLOUD. (A.S. *clud,* a rock or small hill; from resemblance of clouds to rocks or hillocks.) A visible collection or mass of vapor, or water or ice particles formed by condensation of vapor, in the atmosphere; fog, mist, or haze suspended in the air. To become obscured by clouds, as, *the sun is clouded over.* Greatest in altitude is *cirrus* cloud which may reach 18 miles in tropical latitudes, while lowest, *stratus,* may rest on the earth's surface as a fog. Similar cloud formations lie at greater altitudes in the tropics than in high latitudes. Following are the ten principal clouds as internationally classified:

Upper clouds.

1. *Cirrus (ci.)* Detached; delicate, fibrous appearance; of featherlike structure; generally white, without shading; the sailors' *"mares' tails."* Average height 31,000 feet.

2. *Cirro-stratus (ci. st.)* Thin whitish veil often completely covering sky and giving it a milky appearance; often produces halos round sun and moon. Average height, 29,000 feet.

3. *Cirro-cumulus (ci. cu.)* The *"mackerel sky";* small globular masses, without shadows, or white ripple-like flakes arranged in groups and often in lines showing light shadows. Average height, 23,000 feet.

Middle clouds.

4. *Alto-stratus (a. st.)* Sheet of gray or bluish color, often appearing as thick cirro-stratus; causes sun and moon to appear as blurred light-spots; sometimes thin and gives rise to solar or lunar coronæ; may also form parallel bands as a fibrous veil. Average height, 15,000 feet; thickness, 1,700 feet.

5. *Alto-cumulus (a. cu.)* Groups or lines of globular masses, white or grayish and partly shaded; the *"wool-pack"* of sailors' lore. Average height, 12,000 feet; thickness, 600 feet.

Low clouds.

6. *Strato-cumulus (st. cu.)* Heavy globular masses or rolls of soft, gray appearance; may be compact or small openings may disclose blue sky; often wholly compact, dark gray, and covering the whole sky, especially in winter. Average height, 5,000 feet; thickness, 1,200 feet.

7. *Stratus (st.)* Uniform layer, resembling fog, but not resting on the ground. When close to, or on the surface, termed *fog.* If broken up by wind or summits of mountains, termed *fracto-stratus (fr. st.)*,—the *"scud"* often observed in a strong wind below the *nimbo-stratus.* Average height, 2,000 feet, thickness, 1,000 feet.

8. *Nimbo-stratus (nb. st.)* A low, shapeless layer of dark gray color and nearly uniform, from which rain or snow continuously falls. When broken up in stormy weather, also becomes the *"scud"* of sailors and then termed *fracto-nimbus.* Average height, about 3,000 feet; thickness, about 2,000 feet. Common to the front of cyclone areas.

9. *Cumulus (cu.)* Heavy white cloud with vertical development; base appears horizontal and upper surface dome-shaped with outlying protuberances; the *"big woolpack."* Ragged, detached parts carried along in a breeze are termed *fracto-cumulus.* Cumulus is strictly a fine-weather cloud. May be 1,000 to 12,000 feet in altitude and 300 to 8,000 feet in thickness.

10. *Cumulo-nimbus (cu. nb.)* The thunder-cloud. Heavy masses of great vertical extent; summits rise in form of towers and mountains, often with highest point anvil-shaped; common in rear of cyclones; associated with most summer showers and all thunder-storms. Average height of base, 5,000 feet; varies in vertical thickness from 7,000 to 30,000 feet. **Acoustic c.**, a part of the atmosphere in which sound waves are impeded, deflected, or stopped and which accounts for erratic projections and silencing of fog signals occasionally observed. **Auroral c.**, an indistinct, nebulous area often seen over a blue sky background. **Banner-c.**, one resembling a streamer or banner floating horizontally from a mountain top. **Cape-c.**, one that hangs stationary over a high cape or promontory due to upward deflected course of the wind. **Cirro-pallium,**

thin veil of cirro-stratus which slowly covers the sky as a forerunner of a cyclone; also, *cirro-nebula* and *cirrus veil.* **C. belt,** a region near the equator, approximately coincident with the doldrums, characterized by much cloudiness. **C.-berg,** a mass of white clouds on the horizon resembling an iceberg. **C.-capped, c.-kissed,** having its top in clouds, as a mountain. **C. scale,** in weather observation, a scale ranging from 0, indicating a clear sky, to 10, a completely overcast one. **C.-wreath,** an arched roll of dark cloud often seen advancing broadside on in front of a thunder-squall. **Cotton-c's,** low driving squall-clouds of fracto-nimbus type which appear beneath the cirrus veil, noted as fore-runners of a tropical cyclone. **Cotton-ball c's,** a small variety of cumuli, alto-cumuli, or cirro-cumuli. **Fall c.,** strato-cumulus, stratus, or dark gray clouds frequently noted in the fall season; a low cloud. **Hail-tower,** *see* HAIL. **Mackerel-scales,** small distinct rippled appearance of cirro-cumulus. **Magellan c's,** two conspicuous nebulous patches near south pole of the heavens, named after Fernando Magellan, Portuguese navigator (circa 1500); the larger is called *nubecula major,* the smaller *nubecula minor.* Also a third, but black, space near the Southern Cross, named *Black Magellan c.,* or the *Coalsack.* **Pallio-cirrus,** cirro-stratus cloud. **Pallio-cumulus,** nimbus cloud. **Pallio-stratus,** a general covering of stratus cloud. **Roll-cumulus,** strato-cumulus in its pronounced roll-like form. **Sonder-cloud,** the cirro-cumulus. **Wane-cloud,** the cirro-stratus.

CLOUDBURST. A violent downpour of rain over a small area.

CLOVE-HOOKS. Clip-hooks; same as *sister-hooks: see* HOOK.

CLOVE HITCH. *See* HITCH.

CLOW. A floodgate for a canal lock; a sluice for draining river water from diked land, after flooding to obtain silt.

CLUB. To drift with a current while controlling vessel by helm and an anchor with a short drift of cable, as, to *club down stream;* also termed *dredging.* A light spar used to spread the foot of a gaff-topsail beyond the gaff end; also called a *jack-yard.* A short stout spar across after corner (clew) of a small vessel's jib or fore-staysail to which the sheet is attached; sometimes loosely applied to *boom* of a jumbo or any staysail-boom as sometimes found in small trading or fishing vessels. **C. burgee,** a flag bearing the insignia of a yacht club, flown according to accepted rules in yachting etiquette as follows:—On single-masted vessels, at masthead when at anchor or under way, and not under sail; on vessels having more than one mast, whether under way or at anchor, at fore-masthead. **C. foot,** in shipbuilding, descriptive of a form of construction characterized by unusually full lines of the under-

water body at fore foot; also termed *bulbous bow.* The greater displacement volume thus located appears to result in an increase of speed for vessels of ordinary form having a speed-length ratio of .9 to 1.0. Thus, with no change in waterline coefficient, the club foot apparently reduces residuary resistance. However, where the desired latitude is present in choice of water-line coefficient, it is probable a suitable change in that figure would accomplish equal results in speed. It is claimed for the bulbous bow that extra buoyancy thus provided considerably lessens pitching motion,—necessarily, in itself a contributing factor in speed economy. In view of possible damage by anchors or chain cable, rugged construction is demanded in the *club foot bow.* **C.-foot** is also the term for lower part of stem where it is gradually broadened and flattened in curving to meet and join forward end of a flat-plate keel. **C.-link,** a heavy shackle-shaped link on the pin of which is fitted a strong sleeve having an eye for securing it to the anchor-ring; formerly used to bend two cables to a stock anchor. **C.-top-sail,** *see* TOPSAIL.

CLUBHAUL. To put a vessel on the other tack when in a position fraught with danger in event of missing stays. A hawser is bent beforehand to an anchor on the lee bow, led to lee quarter, and made fast. When vessel loses way on being brought head to wind, anchor is let go; then, as she drops astern hawser holds up the quarter and her head falls off on the new tack. When sufficiently off the wind, sail is trimmed accordingly, and hawser is cut.

CLUE. A variant of *clew; see* CLEW.

CLUMP-BLOCK. A strong egg-shaped block chiefly used on jib and staysail sheet-pendants; *see* BLOCK.

CLUMP, MOORING. A mooring-block; *see* MOORING.

CLUSTER, CARGO. *See* CARGO.

CLUTCH. A forked stanchion; *see* CRUTCH. Throat of an anchor. A mechanism used to connect two shafts and arranged so that one may be stopped or started while the other continues in motion. The two types most in use are called *disc* clutch and *cone* clutch. **C.-pinion,** a wheel brought into connection with another wheel or shaft, or disconnected from same, by means of a clutch. Ship winches are usually fitted with *claw clutches,* or those which engage or mesh on their shafts by protruding parts or claws.

COACH. In older navy use, a cabin under the poop; usually the captain's quarters. Upper jaw-bone of the sperm whale. Also, *couch.* **C.-house,** in more recent American sailing-vessels, a raised companion entrance at fore end of cabin. **C.-whip, a**

long narrow pennant formerly flown at the mast-head by a commissioned war-vessel; also called *long pennant, narrow pennant,* and *whip.* **C.-whipping,** a kind of fancy whipping laid with small cord or twine on the pointed end of a man-rope. **C.-work,** matting or ornamental covering made of cotton cord, plaited or laid as in cross-pointing.

COAK. An old term for metal bushing arrangement in a wooden sheave. A piece of hard wood set crosswise in faying faces of a scarf to resist shearing stress on bolts, as in ships' timbers, futtocks, keel, keelsons, etc.; also *calk, cauk, cog,* and *key.* A projection or tenon made in a timber as part of a scarf.

COAL. Universally used in steam-vessels' boilers until generally displaced by petroleum during the past 25 years. *Bituminous* and *anthracite* coal stow at an average of 44 cubic feet per long ton, which usually loads a cargo-vessel to nine-tenths capacity at load-line draft. Coal may be spontaneously ignited when lying for some weeks in a hold and, it has been observed, particularly liable to this danger is such cargo shipped from Virginia, New South Wales, Calcutta, and River Clyde. Coal subjected to much breakage during loading emits *marsh gas,* an explosive if mixed with required proportion of air. Absorption of oxygen causes generation of gas by coal, especially in warmer temperatures than 80° F., and an accumulation of gas readily lends itself to the spontaneous combustion condition. Thorough surface ventilation is the only effective means of removing gas from a coal cargo. **C.-bunker,** *see* BUNKER. **C.-door,** a sliding-door in a bunker bulkhead through which coal is trimmed or removed; also, *bunker-door.* **C.-firing,** process of burning coal as required in a boiler furnace for production of a certain pressure of steam, as opposed to *oil-firing* in which petroleum is fuel used. **Coaling-hatch,** *see* HATCH. **C.-hoist,** small hoisting-winch used in supplying a ship with bunker coal. **C.-hulk, coaling-hulk,** a dismantled vessel, usually an old sailing-vessel, anchored in harbor as a storage depot from which bunker coal is supplied. (Until recent years at Gibraltar several hulks of former East Indiamen and others from 100 to 150 years old were used for this purpose) **C.-passer,** a member of a steam-vessel's crew who provides coal from bunkers to convenient access of the firemen; trims or shifts coal as required; cleans out furnace pits and disposes of ashes; also called *coal-trimmer.* To **c. ship,** old navy term for replenishing the bunkers. **Coaling station,** a port at which vessels may take on bunker coal; formerly, a port where a supply of coal is kept available for navy vessels only.

COALSACK. A conspicuous dark space in the *Milky Way* caused by an almost complete absence of stars; "Hole in the Sky"; *see* **Magellan Clouds** *in* CLOUD.

CO-ALTITUDE. Complement of the altitude; zenith distance of a heavenly body.

COAMING. The raised wood or iron around a hatchway or other deck opening for strengthening deck in way of such opening and protecting against ingress of water; especially, fore-and-aft sections of such fittings as distinguished from those lying athwartships at each end of a hatchway, called *head-ledges.* **Bulkhead c.,** a term for uppermost or bottom strake of plating in superstructural bulkheads, such as that of poop, bridge, or forecastle. The strake is of greater thickness than remaining plating, being considered important members of the structure. **Hatch-c.,** coaming of a hatchway. **House-c.,** strake of plating bounding top or bottom of a deck-house; timber forming the foundation or sill of a wood-built deck-house. **Manhole-c.,** frame fitted around a manhole to provide necessary stiffening and to compensate for loss of continuity of strength, as in a boiler, pressure-tank, etc. **Skylight-c.,** wood-work or plating forming the base of a skylight.

COAST. (L. *costa,* a rib, side.) The seashore; land bordering on the sea; littoral or coastal region. An archaic term for a ship's timber or rib. To sail along a shore; to navigate in coastal waters. **Coast-guard** (Br. *Coastguard;* U.S. *Coast Guard*), an organized body of men, usually naval in character, whose duties comprise safe-guarding and rescue of life and property on coasts, prevention of smuggling or wrecking, and in some countries, maintenance of lighthouses, buoys, and other navigational aids. In U.S., the Coast Guard is under the Treasury Department in time of peace and operates as part of Navy in time of war, "as the President shall so direct." Specific enforcement agency for many laws concerning navigation and merchant shipping, it originated with authorization by Congress in 1790 of Secretary of the Treasury Hamilton to institute a small fleet of cutters for enforcing custom laws of the new nation. To-day its activities include enforcement of laws applying to documentation and inspection of vessels and merchant seamen, rules of the road, anchorage and movements of vessels, motor-boat regulations, and transfer of dangerous cargoes, with similar though auxiliary interest in laws relating to customs and revenue, immigration, quarantine, fish and game protection, and other matters with which various federal agencies are concerned. In addition to its regular patrol vessels, the service maintains life-saving stations with rescue vessels and aircraft at strategic points on coasts and inland waters, holding its facilities in constant readiness to provide emergency aid, such as medical treatment of merchant seamen and relief operations in flood or hurricane disaster, regardless of locations; it administers the country's system of aids to navigation, which includes installation and maintenance of lighthouses, lightships, buoys, fog signals, radio stations, and beacons; provides administration of International Ice Patrol in the North Atlantic; ice-breaking in inland waterways, lakes, and Atlantic coast harbors; and assists Weather Bureau in collecting and disseminating flood, hurricane and storm information, and other meteorological data. **C. fishery,** *see* FISHERY. **C.-line,** boundary, contour line, or outline of a coast. **C.-liner,** a vessel which is regularly engaged in coastwise trade. **C.-pilot,** *see* COASTING; a book showing in detail the peculiarities of, and necessary information for navigating, certain coastal waters. **C. station,** a radio-telegraph station on a coast for communicating with ships at sea; a signal station for exhibiting storm warnings, tidal or ice information, and often for receiving from, and sending to, passing vessels messages by visual signals. **C. survey,** procurement of topographic and hydrographic information by direct observation of a coast or part thereof, usually for purpose of charting such locality. **C.-waiter,** in Great Britain, a customs officer who superintends shipping or discharge of cargoes of vessels in coastwise trade. **Grain C.,** part of Guinea coast of Africa; *see* GRAIN.

COAST AND GEODETIC SURVEY. In *U.S. Department of Commerce,* a bureau responsible for topographic and hydrographic survey of the country's Atlantic, Pacific, and Gulf of Mexico coasts and establishing primary triangulation data and precise leveling lines in the interior. It publishes charts, coast-pilots, tidal and magnetic information, and currently issues notices to mariners concerning dangers, new charts, changes in water depths, and other information of navigational importance in the coastal field referred to.

COASTER. A coasting vessel; a person or vessel engaged in the coasting trade.

COASTING. Act of navigating along a sea coast; in *U.S. law,* a vessel is coasting when she is navigated in "coastal navigable waters of the United States," or "all portions of the sea within the territorial jurisdiction of the United States and all inland waters navigable in fact in which the tide ebbs and flows." Configuration of a coast; coastline. **C. lead,** *see* LEAD. **C. pilot,** one who is familiar with, and capable of navigating along, a coast. **C. trade,** commerce by sea between ports on a certain coast, usually within limits defined by statute; thus, coasting or "home" trade limits in Great Britain are described as coasts of the British Isles and continent between the Elbe River and Brest. In U.S., the term in its legal sense indicates trade between only U.S. ports and/or those of its possessions, Alaska, Hawaii, and Puerto Rico; it is called inter-coastal when between ports separated by foreign waters or territory, as between Atlantic and Pacific ports. **C. vessel,** a coaster; *see* VESSEL.

COAST-LINING. Surveying of a coast-line.

COASTWISE. By way of, or along, the coast; coastways. **C. vessel,** *see* VESSEL. **C. voyage,** in the U.S., a voyage in the *coasting trade (q.v.).*

COAT. Tarred or painted canvas, sometimes leather, fitted snugly about a mast, rudder-casing, pump, bowsprit, etc. where such pass through a weather deck, to prevent ingress of water. **C.-tack,** a type of nail or tack used in securing a mast-coat, etc. to the deck. **Oil-c.,** *see* OILSKIN. **Pea-c.,** same as *pea-jacket; see* PEA. **Rudder-c.,** *see* RUDDER. **Watch-c.,** a heavy cloth coat worn by seamen; a reefer; a bridge-coat; *see* WATCH.

COB. A sea-gull; especially the black-backed gull (*Larus marinus*). Also *cobb*. A beating or flogging administered in former days to seamen guilty of dereliction of duty; a *cobbing.*

COBBLER-FISH. A carangoid fish (*Alectis ciliaris*) found generally in warmer seas, but common in West Indies waters; of the family including the *cavalla, pompano,* and *amber fishes,* it is characterized by filaments extending from some of its fin-rays.

COBIA. A mackerel-like fish from 4 to 5 feet in length, of dusky appearance and having a long horizontal black stripe on its sides; found in warmer American waters and East Indies; the *sergeant-fish;* sometimes confused with the *robalo.*

COBLE. (W. *ceubal,* a hollow trunk, a ferry-boat.) A stout clinker-built fishing-boat 25 to 30 feet in length formerly common on east coast of Britain. Adapted to beaching, its bottom was flat-floored, rising toward the stern, its rudder, when shipped extending below midship draft; rigged with a single lug sail. Also, a small rowing-boat used in Scottish inland waters. **Salmon-c.,** a flat-bottomed fishing-boat, propelled by oars, used in netting salmon on the west coast of Scotland. (Also written *cobble.*)

COBOOSE. *See* CABOOSE.

COCINERO. (*Sp.* for *little cook.*) A local term for the fish *cavalla (Carangus caballus)* on the U.S. Pacific coast.

COCK. A faucet, tap, or valve used for starting, stopping, or controlling flow of a liquid or gas, usually named according to service performed, as, air-cock, sea-cock, etc. Degree of opening produced in manipulating a cock, as, *half-cock, full-cock.* Old term for a ship's boat; also, *cock-boat, cog;* a viking; a sea-rover; an auk-like bird. **Angle-c.,** a cock whose outlet is at right angles with its inlet. **Ash-c.,** a valve serving to supply water for cooling ashes in a fire-room. **Bibb-c.,** one having a bent outlet; strictly the outlet, only. **Cylinder-c.,** one carrying off condensed steam from a cylinder; a drain-cock. **Drain-c.,** one fitted for draining liquid from a tank, recess in a hold, etc. **Flood-c.,** *see* FLOOD. **Indicator-c.,** *see* INDICATOR. **Oil-c.,** *see* OIL. **Pet-c.,** a small tap fitted on a pump, steam-line, etc. for testing the pressure developing; a drain-cock. **Sea-c.,** *see* SEA. **Sluice-c.,** *see* SLUICE. **Steam-c.,** *see* STEAM. **Test-c.,** one fitted to ascertain height of water in a boiler.

COCKBILL. To have an anchor hanging at a cat-head, secured by ring-stopper only, ready for letting go; to top yards as near the vertical as possible. The spelling *cock-bell* was used in the 17th. century. In old navy days, yards were topped *acockbill* as a symbol of mourning for a sovereign, an admiral, or other high official, yards on fore and mizzen being layed with their opposite ends aloft to those on the main. Up to about 1860, it was customary in vessels of countries predominantly Catholic to cockbill yards on Good Friday.

COCKBOAT. Formerly a ship's boat, especially, one acting as a tender to an anchored vessel. A small fishing-boat; a rowing-boat. Also, *cog, cocket, cockle-boat.*

COCKED HAT. The hat of triangular-shaped profile worn with full dress uniform by commissioned officers in most navies.

COCKET. A customs certificate formerly given to a shipper, stating that his goods have been declared and duty paid. In England, a customs branch office or office of entry. A *cockboat.* **C. card,** *see* **Clearance outward** *in* CLEARANCE.

COCKLE-SHELL. Any dangerously light craft; a frail boat; a cock-boat.

COCKLER. A sailing-boat of light draft formerly used for cockle-fishing in the Thames Estuary, England.

COCKPIT. In the old sailing war-vessels, space located aft on the orlop deck, ordinarily used as quarters of junior officers, occupied by the surgeon, his staff, and wounded men during an engagement. In small craft, a well or sunken space in the deck, which accommodates helmsman and crew, and affords easy access to cabin.

COCKSCOMB. *See* COXCOMB.

COCKSWAIN. *See* COXSWAIN.

COCONUT MATTING. *See* MATTING.

COD. One of the most important and most plentiful food fishes in existence, especially the species *Gadus callarias* found in colder parts of North Atlantic and its close relation, the Alaska cod (*Gadus macrocephalus*), in North Pacific waters. Caught chiefly on Banks of Newfoundland, New England and Nova Scotian banks, Norwegian, and Icelandic coasts; its length averages 2½ feet and weight about 15 pounds, though often attaining 4 feet and 60 to 70 pounds. Depending upon habitat and fishermen's usage, the fish is given different names, such

as *bank* and *shore,* or *native cod* to distinguish those caught on Newfoundland Banks from those off New England; *rock cod* found on rocky bottom, *clam-worm cod, blue cod,* etc. Cod live in depths of 20 to 100 fathoms, and it is commonly accepted that the fish improves in quality with decrease in water temperature, probably best obtainable being caught off Labrador and Newfoundland in temperatures of 28 to 32 degrees. Of the family *Gadidæ,* which includes *haddock, tomcod,* and *pollack,* true cod is often confused with these smaller fishes, especially the *haddock,* which, while having three similar dorsal and two ventral fins, should be easily distinguished by its long lateral black stripe from cod's lateral stripe of white. The name is also given to some fishes of the South Pacific, as *Murray cod; red rock, black rock, blue,* and *red cod* of Australia and New Zealand. **C.-bank,** a comparatively shallow area or submarine bank where cod is caught. **C.-end,** extreme after end of a fishing-trawl (net) into which the fish are gathered as trawl is towed. **C.-line,** small three-strand cotton or flax cord, or "white line," weighing about three pounds per 20 fathoms, so named from its use in catching cod and similar fish; also used for hammock-clews in navy vessels.

CODE. A system of signals or characters used by ships as a means of communicating with each other or with shore. (*See* SIGNAL) **C. book,** a signal code; a book containing many applicable phrases and appropriate answers under various subjects for brevity or secrecy in communicating by telegraph or other signaling device. **C. flag,** a flag flown to show a certain code is to be referred to; *answering pennant* of the International Code (red and white vertical stripes); a flag indicating a letter, phrase, or number in a code of flag signals. **International C.,** system of signals adopted by principal maritime nations to facilitate communication between vessels and shore stations of different nationalities. The code book gives full instructions for using 40 flags in various combinations or "hoists" making up phraseology of messages, and, 26 of the flags representing letters of the alphabet, signal by semaphore, Morse code flashing, or radiotelegraph is made possible. Though several nations used their own systems prior to 1855, first international code was drafted by the British Board of Trade at that time and was adopted by most seafaring countries by 1857. In 1887 the British began revising the signal book and consequent discussions led to a new code brought into effect in 1897; and again a revision was begun at the International Radiotelegraph Conference held at Washington in 1927. Editorial committee concerned with compilation of our present code assembled at London, October, 1928 to correlate the work as written in English, French, German, Italian, Japanese, Norwegian, and Spanish. Compilation was completed in December, 1930.

See SIGNAL. **Morse c.,** as used at sea, a modification of the telegraphic alphabetical code invented by Samuel F. B. Morse (*1791–1872*), or *International Morse C.,* in which letters and numbers are signaled according to a system of "dots" and "dashes," short and long flashes, sounds, or sweeps of a waved flag, respectively. The code may be used in signaling by flashlight, whistle, or foghorn, either in plain language or according to *International C. of Signals.*

CODLING. A young cod. *See* COD.

COEFFICIENT. A numerical constant, empirical or otherwise, used as a comparative value, as in determining resistance and necessary powering of steam-vessels, considering immersed body dimensions and speed required; a ratio or constant used as a multiplier to determine an area, volume, or a change in volume due to a physical change, as a *coefficient of expansion;* the ratio of an irregular-shaped area to that of a circumscribed rectangle, or of a volume to a bounding rectangular parallelepipedon, as a *coefficient of fineness.* **Admiralty c.,** a constant used by the British Admiralty as an index of comparison in early steam power days for determining engine power required in a vessel to produce a certain speed. It is numerically equal to displacement to the two-thirds power, multiplied by speed (knots per hour) cubed, and divided by indicated horsepower. Experience subsequently showed that this value, reasonably satisfactory for generally similar ships within their normal speed ranges, materially failed for vessels differing appreciably in hull form, primarily due to the faulty assumption that a constant propulsive efficiency and total resistance are proportional to the dividend stated in the equation. **Block c.,** *see* BLOCK. **C. of fineness,** referred to ship form, ratio of water-plane area to a circumscribed rectangular area; or, ratio of immersed hull volume to that of a rectangular parallelepipedon of same length, greatest breadth, and draft; *block c.* **C. of performance,** a comparison value for a vessel's speed performance in different weather conditions, indicated by ratio of shaft horsepower to the two-thirds power of displacement times speed cubed. **Displacement c.,** *see* **Admiralty c. Midship section c.,** ratio of vertical immersed midship section area of a vessel to that of a circumscribed rectangular figure equal to water-line breadth by the draft. **Propulsive c.,** ratio of effective horsepower to indicated horsepower. **Prismatic c.,** ratio of displacement volume to that of a prism equal in length to the water-line and having a cross section area equal to immersed midship area; also, *longitudinal c.*

COELHO. (*Port.*) A large mackerel-like fish found in tropical latitudes of the Atlantic. (Pron. *ko-ail'-yo.*)

COFFERDAM. (Lit., *box-dam.*) In ship construction, a space between two bulkheads primarily designed as a safeguard against leakage of oil from one compartment to another. Virtually double oil-tight bulkheads about $3\frac{1}{2}$ feet apart and common to tank vessels, cofferdams are required to isolate cargo space from fire-room or bunker space and from a forward hold; also, one or two are sometimes included to separate groups of tanks in which different grades of cargo may be carried. In war-vessels, the term chiefly denotes protective water-tight compartments in vicinity of water-line along and against ship's sides (also called the *armor-box*) for the greater and more vital part of her length. A *caisson,* or water-tight inclosure erected about a bridge pier, a sunken vessel, etc. from which water is pumped in order to effect construction or repairs. **C.-bulkhead,** one of the bulkheads forming a cofferdam; especially, one on a war-vessel near a collision bulkhead for greater safety. In the compartment thus formed, a water-excluding material was formerly packed, which usually was "cellulose," the ground pith of cornstalks.

COFFIN-PLATE. A plate forming lower side of the housing of after ends of twin propeller-shafts; so named for its shape.

COG. Archaic term for a *cock-boat;* a small rowing-boat or fishing-vessel; a kind of early Dutch ship having a broad beam and bluff bows and stern. A piece of hard wood set in a scarf; *see* COAK. To *calk* a planking seam.

COIL. (O.F. *coillir,* to collect.) A length of cordage stowed or gathered in rings or spirals so as to form a compact mass; a single ring or spiral of such mass. To stow or gather a rope or cable to form a *coil.* Standard length of coil for American rope is 200 fathoms, for sizes greater than 15-thread (about $1\frac{1}{4}$ inches circumference) of manila or hemp, a "*half coil*" being 100 fathoms, while coils of smaller-sized rope, or *small stuff,* are usually manufactured in lengths varying from 270 to 500 fathoms. British standard coil is 120 fathoms for ordinary rope sizes. **Flemish c.,** *see* FLEMISH.

COILS. A series of pipes or tubing laid together in condensers, superheaters, cargo spaces, living rooms, etc. through which cooled or heated water, brine, or steam is passed in order to produce a required change in their surrounding temperature. **Compensation coils,** a group of electric wire coils suitably placed around a ship's magnetic compass for purpose of correcting any error arising while *degaussing* system is operating.

COIR. (Malay, *kayar,* cord.) Fiber obtained from outer husks of coconuts, used for making cordage, matting, brooms, etc. **C. rope,** made of coconut fiber, has advantage of greater elasticity than hemp or manila, though about half tensile strength of these, and consequently is a favorite in larger sizes for withstanding surging in the case of vessels moored therewith in a swell; also, will float while a hemp or manila hawser becomes water-logged and sinks; extensively used for lighter-ropes and in the Far East for running rigging on sailing-vessels, where, also, the yarns are used as *oakum* in calking.

COL. (Fr., from L. *collum*, neck.) A trough of relatively low barometric pressure between two areas of high pressure; usually marked by uncertain weather conditions, often with light variable winds and thunder showers.

CO-LATITUDE. Complement of the latitude; or, 90 degrees less latitude.

COLD. C. shut, a split link or ring used to repair or fasten chains, and which can be closed and sometimes riveted, without heating. **C.-riveting,** *see* RIVETING. **C. wall,** *see* WALL. **C. water test,** *see* HYDRAULIC TEST.

COLLA. A south-westerly monsoon-like wind in the Philippines. A stationary or moderate cyclone.

COLLAPSIBLE BOAT. A boat made of rubber or other material which can be inflated for use and deflated, rolled up, and stowed. A kind of folding boat formerly included in life-saving equipment on merchant ships and carried also with view of economizing stowage space. Though included in this category, certain boats having a pontoon body and whose sides only were made to fold flatwise, as *Engelhardt* and *Lundin* types, perhaps best known as a wholly collapsible craft was the *Berthon*. This boat was made to fold together in concertina fashion, both its flat bottom and thwarts hinging along the center line, and its frames at the bilges. It had a skin of heavy waterproofed canvas. Use of the type was discontinued some years ago chiefly on account of its vulnerability to attack by rodents.

COLLAR. (Fr. *collier*, necklace or collar; from L. *collum*, neck.) An eye or bight on upper end of a stay or shroud to fit over a masthead. A piece of plate or angle-bar fitted around structural members at their entrance through a bulkhead or a tank top for ensuring stiffness and providing means for efficient calking. In mechanics, a ring-like raised portion on a shaft or axle to prevent endwise motion; any ring or flange fitted to restrain motion within required limits. **Angle-c.,** *see* ANGLE. **C.-heart,** a heart-block that is open on side opposite the lanyard; *see* **heart-block** *in* HEART. **Mast-c.,** *see* MAST. **Plate-c.,** a piece of plate, usually shaped like a ring or a horseshoe, as that bolted round a rudder-trunk at its outer entrance; also termed *apron-plate* and *horseshoe-plate*. **Safety-c.,** *see* SAFETY. **Thrust-c.,** *see* THRUST.

COLLIER. (A.S. *col;* Ice. *kol;* Ger. *kohle;* coal.) A vessel used in, or specially designed for, carrying coal; a naval vessel used for coaling ships or delivering bunker-coal to a coaling station. A member of a collier's crew. **Collier's patch,** a smear of thick tar on a worn part of an old sail, or around a tear, as a preventive against further damage. **Collier's purchase,** *see* PURCHASE.

COLLIMATION ERROR. An error in the sight-line of a telescope or transit due to faulty adjustment of its parallelism with a plane of reference, as plane of the meridian. An error in a sextant observation caused by line of collimation, or sight-line of telescope, not being parallel to plane of the instrument. *See* TELESCOPE.

COLLISION. The striking together, with damage usually resulting, of two vessels, or of one vessel with any fixed structure. In maritime law, it is defined as impact of ship against ship, although usage is increasing scope of the term to include striking of a vessel against any floating body or object. **C.-bulkhead,** *see* BULKHEAD. **C. damages,** in U.S. jurisprudence in admiralty, where both vessels are at fault, each bears one half of total loss incurred; in a court of common law neither will be given an award, since contributory negligence bars recovery; thus a suit in admiralty is favorable to a vessel suffering the greater damage, while under common law she alone must bear her loss. Where loss is sustained solely through the other vessel's fault, an owner may recover damages sufficient to place him in same financial position as if collision had not occurred. Where total loss takes place, recovery usually amounts to vessel's value plus net freight lost on voyage concerned; and if it is shown that costs of raising and repairing a vessel sunk will exceed her value at time of collision, her owner may claim for total loss. If collision occurs without fault of either vessel, each bears her own loss. Marine insurance usually provides for collision costs in a special clause in which underwriters agree to pay for damage done to another vessel up to a certain part (three-fourths) of such damage, providing the amount lies within insured value indicated in policy; *see* INSURANCE. **C.-mat,** a square sheet of heavy canvas roped like a sail for placing over a damaged part of a ship's shell-plating in order to stop or reduce ingress of water until repairs may be effected. Carried on U.S. war-vessels other than capital ships and formerly obligatory as part of a steel merchant vessel's equipment, the ready-for-use mat is about 10 feet square and "thrummed," or matted by short rope-yarns sewn on the side which contacts the plating. It is placed in position diamond-fashion by a *hogging-line* attached to its lower corner, passed under the ship's bottom and led to the deck; lowered by a *distance-line* from its upper corner; and laid fore-and-aft as required by *guys* leading from its forward and after corners.

COLORS. Ensign or flag flown to indicate a vessel's nationality. In U.S. navy, a salute to the flag when it is hoisted at 8 a.m. and lowered at sunset. Also, *colours.*

COLT. In the old navy sailing-ships, a rope knotted at one end used by boatswain's mates as a "starter" on those slow in carrying out orders.

COLUMBA. (*L.* = *dove.*) A southern constellation adjacent to, and south-west of *Canis Major*, containing as its brightest star *Phact* (*α Columbæ*) in 34° 6′ S. declination and 5 hrs. 38 min. right ascension, and of magnitude 2.75; called also *Columba Noachi, Columba Noæ,* or *Noah's Dove.*

COLUMN. A formation of a fleet in which ships are placed or proceed one behind another; also termed *line ahead.* A heavy pillar or stanchion supporting a number of deck-beams in a hold. Heavy cast-iron or steel frames supporting cylinders of an engine.

COLURE. Either of two great circles intersecting at right angles in the celestial poles and passing, respectively, through the equinoxes (*equinoctial c.*) and solstices (*solstitial c.*).

COMB. Breaking or curling crest of a wave; a white-cap. A heavy sea or breaker is said to *comb* as its crest rolls over and foams. **C.-cleat,** in sailing-vessels, a piece of hard wood secured fore-and-aft in lower rigging and through which a series of holes is bored to properly lead and place the various clewlines, buntlines, leechlines, or other running gear; a coxcomb. **Tiller-c.,** see TILLER.

COMBAT. An engagement; a fight. **Single c.,** a fight between two ships.

COMBER. A heavy curling wave; a breaker. A beach-comber.

COMBINATION. **C.-buoy,** a buoy showing a light in addition to sounding a whistle or bell. **C. drive,** a now obsolete system of propulsion powering in which exhaust steam from twin screw reciprocating engines was utilized to drive a third and midship screw by a turbine. **C.-framing,** see FRAMING. **C. light,** see LIGHT. **C. vessel,** see VESSEL.

COMBING. A variant of coaming; see COAMING.

COMBUSTION-CHAMBER. *Fire-box,* or space over, or in front of, a boiler furnace where gases from fire become mixed and economically burnt. Clearance space in an internal combustion engine cylinder where compression and ignition of fuel charge takes place.

COMBUSTION, INTERNAL. *See* INTERNAL COMBUSTION *and* ENGINE.

COME. Word employed in various phrases denoting some current action or maneuver and always with a significant preposition, adverb, or objective phrase; as, to *come away*, to *come in sight*. To **c. about,** to turn, change, come round, tack; as, *the wind came about; a ship came about.* To **c. away,** to begin to move or yield; said of an anchor or other object hauled upon. To **c. home,** to drag over or through ground, as an anchor when failing to hold a vessel, or when heaving on its cable; also, to reach place intended, as a sail when hoisted or sheeted in. To **c. in through the hawse-pipe;** *see* HAWSE. To **c. to close quarters,** to engage in hand-to-hand fighting. To **C. off,** to leave shore and approach one's ship; to re-float, as, *a stranded vessel came off.* To **c. to anchor,** to bring a ship to her anchoring berth and drop an anchor; to anchor; also, to **come to an anchor.** To **c. up, c. to,** to steer closer to the wind in sailing; to luff; to bring to an anchor; to ease up and let go a taut rope, hawser, etc. To **c. up behind,** to ease away and slacken a rope stretched out and being hauled upon in order to allow foremost man to belay or make it fast. To **c. up the capstan,** *see* CAPSTAN.

COMING. A variant of *coaming.*

COMMANDER. In U.S. navy, a commissioned officer ranking next below a captain, whose insignia worn on uniform shoulder-straps and sleeves is a group of three parallel ½-inch gold stripes, and, on tropical or undress uniform shirt-collar points, a silver oak-leaf pin. A heavy wooden mallet used by riggers and sailmakers in shaping or beating eyes, grommets, splices, etc., into place. **Staff-c.,** see STAFF. **C.-in-chief,** a naval officer in command of a particular squadron or fleet of vessels. President of the United States, who is in supreme command of armed forces of the country.

COMMERCE. (*L. com,* with; *mercis,* merchandise.) Intercourse in buying and selling of merchandise or exchange of commodities between nations or communities; trade or traffic generally. **Active c.,** imports and exports transported to and from a nation in its own vessels, as opposed to **passive c.,** transportation of goods to and from a country by foreign vessels. **C.-destroyer,** a vessel which destroys or captures merchant shipping of an enemy; usually an armed merchantman, or a war-vessel of light armament, of high speed. **Foreign and Domestic C. Bureau,** see BUREAU. **Water-borne c.,** see WATER.

COMMERCIAL. Of, pertaining to, or occupied with commerce or engagement in trade. **C. blockade,** in naval operations, closing of enemy ports to commerce by sea; particularly, stoppage of entry to such ports by foreign vessels. Provision is made whereby neutral vessels may depart from a blockaded port under certain conditions. **C. code,** an archaic term for *International Code of Signals.* **C. marine,** a merchant marine or combined merchant ship tonnage of a nation; also, *mercantile marine.*

COMMISSION. A certificate conferring rank and authority on a naval officer of the rank of ensign or above. The fee or percentage allowed a broker or agent for transacting a ship's business, chartering, etc. To empower or authorize to perform a certain service; to man, equip, and place a vessel in service after she has been laid up. **C. pennant,** *see* PENNANT. To **put** (a ship) **in c.,** as used in the U.S. navy, means to transfer a ship in charge of a navy yard authority to command of an officer ordered to put her in active service. To **put** (a ship) **out of c.,** to detach officers and crew and retire the vessel, temporarily or permanently, from active service.

COMMODORE. In U.S. navy, an officer ranking next above a captain and equal with a brigadier-general in the army. The rank was abolished in 1899, except for certain retired captains, and was temporarily restored in 1943. In Great Britain, commanding officer of a squadron or fleet of war-vessels. By courtesy, title given the senior master in a line of passenger ships. The president of a yacht club; also, his vessel. Officer in command of a merchant convoy when sailing in a merchant vessel; also, his vessel.

COMMON CARRIER. A person or organization undertaking carriage by land or water of goods or persons for hire and for all persons without discriminative treatment of localities, classes of traffic, or imposition of unequal tariff for similar services. By *common law,* such carrier is bound to transport all goods or persons which he is equipped to carry as and when he has space or accommodation, and is liable for all losses and damage thereto, excepting such as are caused by acts or forces beyond his control, as provided for in bill of lading.

COMMON LAW LIEN. See LIEN.

COMPANION. An old term for a raised upper deck skylight, variously shaped, its structure sometimes including commodious seats on its sides and means for opening some or all of its windows. It now denotes a covering or hooded entrance to a companionway; also, a *companionway* itself. In astronomy, a faint star seen in a telescope very close to a bright one; as, *the companion of Castor;* also termed a *comes* (plural, *comites*). **C.-hatch, c.-hatchway,** a raised hood often fitted with a sliding hatch, over a ladder or stairway leading to a cabin. **C.-ladder,** a ladder leading from a companion-hatchway to a cabin below deck. **Companionway,** a stairway leading from a vessel's deck to a cabin or other accommodation below; general space occupied by such stairway; also, *companion.*

COMPANY. In early days of long sea voyages, ships often sailed *in company* with one or more others; hence, the word was used for a merchant fleet. **Ship's c.,** entire personnel comprising a vessel's crew; also, *ship's complement.*

COMPARTMENT. Any separate space or room in a vessel; especially, one of the subdivisions or sections into which a ship's hull is partitioned by water-tight bulkheads. **Water-tight c.,** a space within a ship having its top, bottom, and sides constructed to prevent ingress or egress of water; specifically, one of those subdivisions required in a steel vessel's hull by law and classification rules for structural strength and safety reasons. *Water-tight subdivision* has for its object protection against foundering by confining locally an uncontrollable entry of water caused by damage to a vessel's hull. **Wing c.,** one of an arrangement of watertight spaces along the sides of a war-vessel: *see* COFFERDAM. A tank or other water-tight space built in either side of a 'tween deck for carrying water-ballast or cargo as required; also, *wing tank.*

COMPARTMENTATION. Partitioning of a vessel's hull by transverse, and, in some cases, longitudinal bulkheads according to rules formulated at International Conference for Safety of Life at Sea, London, 1929. Depending upon number of water-tight bulkheads, compartmentation is designed to ensure a vessel remaining afloat while any one, two, or three compartments are open to sea; *see* LENGTH *for* **floodable length.**

COMPASS.[1] (Fr. *compas,* circle.) The well-known instrument for indicating direction on the earth's surface and, consequently, indispensable in deep-sea navigational practice; in which connection it is usually distinguished as *mariner's compass* from a *surveyor's compass* or other portable instrument of its kind used on land. Essentially a means of determining direction in which the plane of an observer's meridian lies, whether magnetic or true, its circular horizontal card or ring is graduated into 32 points of $11\frac{1}{4}$ degrees each, or 360 degrees, or both, thus providing a distinguishing name or number for any line of direction in question. Until the advent of gyroscopic (or gyrostatic) compasses, present magnetic instrument held a monopoly on our trackless oceans, and its development from the *lode-stone* of viking days occupies a lengthy scroll in history. Mariners of 11th. century record appear to have been familiar with the compass and its earliest form was a narrow piece of magnetite, or magnetic iron ore, floated on cork in a bowl of water, which carries us back to probably A.D. 900 amongst the daring Norsemen, though Chinese ingenuity is said to have antedated the discovery by some centuries. Columbus is credited with being first to observe a variation in direction of magnetic north and, incidentally, in addition to such different values at different localities, a gradual change in polarity of earth's magnetic field is shown in records of *compass variation* (or declination from the true meridian) observed at London, where, in 1580, magnetic north was 11° *east* of true, or geographical, north; in 1812, it had arrived at 24° *west;* and in 1948 it is given as 10° *west.*

Compasses are named from their construction, their position, their use, or from some special characteristic; as, *dry-card c., pole-c., declination-c., standard c.* **Azimuth c.,** *see* AZIMUTH. **Boat c.,** one of small size and usually of the spirit type for use in boats. To **box the c.,** among seamen, ability to name the 32 points of the compass in their regular sequence; thus: *north, north by east, nor'-north-east, north-east by north, etc.; see* **Table of Points of the Compass. Cabin-c.,** one conveniently placed in a cabin or a part of master's accommodation, usually inverted on the deckhead, for noting vessel's heading. **C. adjustment,** practice of reducing to a minimum the deviation of a magnetic compass on all possible headings or courses steered. This is done by appropriately placing bar magnets or soft iron masses about the compass in order to neutralize any existing interference of ship's magnetism in general, or that of her fittings near the compass, as vessel is swung to head on each point or as many points as possible. **C. bearing,** an azimuth or bearing observed by a compass; one to which no correction for variation or deviation has been applied. **C.-bowl,** receptacle in which a *compass-card,* with its attached magnet or magnets, is mounted on a central pivot; usually made of cast bronze and fitted with a glass cover tightly secured to prevent leakage in the case of a liquid compass and to exclude dust from a dry card compass. **C.-card,** horizontal graduated face of a compass borne either by a central iridium-pointed pivot fixed in the bowl, or by a floating device whereby its weight is for the most part borne by a liquid, its pivot merely acting as a means of holding card in a properly centered position. Cards of all magnetic marine compasses are secured directly to, and have their north and south line exactly parallel with, the magnets. In a dry compass, a jeweled cap is fitted at card's center to bear on the fixed pivot. *Spirit* or *liquid compasses* are characterized by a floating unit consisting of an air-tight chamber, encased magnets, and card, in castor oil, a mixture of alcohol and distilled water, or other special fluid, designed to reduce friction on pivot to a minimum and to dampen any possible oscillatory motion such as is caused by a vessel rolling or yawing in a seaway, or heavy gun-fire. **C. corrections,** deviation and variation which must be applied to a compass course or bearing in order to obtain the true course or bearing, in the case of a magnetic compass; algebraic sum of *deviation* for particular course on which a vessel is heading and *magnetic variation* in her locality is termed *compass error.* A gyroscope compass, designed to indicate true courses and bearings, is corrected for any observed error usually due to inaccurate mechanical adjustment, and not more than two degrees. **C. corrector,** a bar magnet, a soft iron sphere, verti-

cal soft iron bar, or other appropriately placed iron for reducing deviation of a magnetic compass to a minimum; also, a professional *compass adjuster.* **C. course,** point or degree-mark indicating a course steered; a course determined to be steered by compass in "shaping the course." **C.-dial,** a compass-card. **C. error,** *see* **C. corrections** above. **C.-needle,** in a marine compass, one of a number of small steel bar magnets attached, and supplying directive power to, the card. The term originated with early use of a single needle-shaped piece of magnetized iron centrally pivoted over a graduated car which was oriented to set its north point (usually distinguished by an ornate design, such as a *fleur-de-lis*) in coincidence with needle's north-seeking end. *C.-needles* may be two, four, or six small bar magnets, usually cylindrical-shaped, as in many dry card instruments; or, as in U.S. navy 7½-inch standard liquid type, they consist of four cylindrical bundles of steel wires which have been laid side by side and magnetized as a bundle between a powerful electro-magnet's poles. Needles of this pattern were adopted because bundles of steel wires are more homogeneous, can be satisfactorily tempered, and for similar weight give greater directive power than a solid bar magnet. **C. reading-glass,** *see* GLASS. **C.-rose,** a circle graduated in degrees and/or quarter-points, printed on a chart for use as a protractor in laying off bearings, courses, and position-lines. On coastal charts a compass-rose usually consists of an outer circle showing true direction in degrees and an inner one showing magnetic direction in quarter-points. Value of magnetic variation is given at place occupied by compass-diagram, together with year of reference and annual rate of change. On small scale charts, such as those covering large areas, track charts, etc. used for general information, a true compass-rose only is generally found. **C. signal,** a signal denoting a course or a bearing, given either in points or degrees; especially, such signal indicated in International Code. **Compensated c.,** one corrected for deviation by means of permanent magnets or soft iron bars, spheres, etc. Of several methods in compass compensation advocated since advent of iron, and later, steel shipbuilding, that known as the *rectangular method* has long been considered most practical; *see* DEVIATION. **Declination c.,** *see* DECLINATION. **Declination of the c.-needle;** same as *c. variation: see* DECLINATION. **Dipping-c.,** used to measure *dip,* or angle of inclination from horizontal of a magnetic needle, upon latter being placed by experiment in direction of the earth's total magnetic force. It consists of a delicately balanced magnetized needle mounted to freely rotate on a horizontal axis and over a graduated vertical circle, and usually is equipped with a graduated horizontal circle for orientation purposes. Also called *dip-circle* and *inclinometer.* **Dry**

or dry card c., one in which no liquid is used, as opposed to a *spirit* or *liquid c.* **Dumb c., dummy c.,** a circular metal disc graduated at its edge to represent a compass card and made to be turned and clamped to correspond with ship's course. It is used to observe bearings when to do so from the compass is impossible or inconvenient, and is generally placed on either wing of a bridge as required; *see* PELORUS. **To fetch a c.,** an archaic term meaning to make a circuit or detour; to sail round a mark or locality. **Fluid, liquid,** or **oil c.,** one having its card floating in a liquid. In U.S. navy standard type, the liquid is a solution of 45 per cent. grain alcohol and 55 per cent. distilled water which will remain in its liquid state below −10° *Fahrenheit.* Castor oil and other special oils chiefly of large glycerin content have been used, but in very low temperatures liquid compasses are considered useless. **Gyro, gyroscope,** or **gyroscopic c.,** unlike the time-honored magnetic instrument, is entirely independent of earth's magnetic force in that its purely mechanical features have embodied the properties of gyroscopic inertia and its attending phenomonon, precession. Dr. Anschütze-Kämpfe of Germany appears to have designed such a compass in 1911 and further scientific research has developed a most reliable instrument in undoubtedly the most popular *Sperry Gyro,* now used on many steam-vessels both of U.S. navy and merchant fleets and those of other nationalities. Consisting essentially of a rotor spinning at high speed and freely suspended to allow its axis to automatically take up a position parallel with earth's axis in accordance with gyrostatic laws, compass thus lines up with *true* or *geographical north* in its arrangement whereby the card always orients itself with the rotor axis. Since rigidity in space, or *gyroscopic inertia,* must be overcome in order to restrain rotor axis in the horizontal plane, advantage is taken of the phenomenon known as *precession,* or tendency of a spinning body to swing round so as to place its axis parallel to that of any impressed force and with its direction of rotation same as that of such impressed force. This is usually done by a ballistic consisting of mercury in a pair of small iron receptacles joined by a steel tube, fixed in same horizontal plane as rotor axis. As earth rotates under the rigid spinning rotor, displacement of rotor's axis from horizontal is at once corrected by the balancing flow of mercury which provides the necessary impressed force to bring precession into action. Means for adjustments for speed and change of latitude are also provided. From the *"master gyro,"* which is usually placed in a suitably arranged compartment, electrical connections are made to repeating compasses, or *repeaters,* conveniently placed on navigating bridge, conning tower, etc. These are mounted and protected in gimbal-suspended bowls, similar in arrangement to magnetic compasses, and are made to receive an *azimuth-mirror* or *sight-vanes* with which to observe bearings. Also usually provided is a special *steering-repeater* which may be inclined from the horizontal to suit helmsman's vision. Directive force of the gyro is much greater than that of the magnetic compass. Both, however, fail at or near earth's geographical and magnetic poles, respectively. **Hanging-c.,** an overhead compass. **Lifeboat c.,** a liquid one, usually having a 4-inch diameter card, required in a lifeboat's equipment. **Magnetic, marine,** or **mariner's c.,** consists essentially of a bowl of non-magnetic metal suspended on two-way gimbals so as to maintain a horizontal position during heeling or motion of vessel in a seaway; a card (*see* C.-card); and magnet or group of magnets (*see* C. needle). It may be either a *dry-card* or *liquid* type. **Points of the c.,** see introduction to COMPASS and TABLE OF POINTS. **Pole-c.,** one raised on a pole, tripod, mast, etc. to lessen effect of an iron or steel ship's magnetism or that of a cargo of iron, iron ore, or steel. In early days of iron vessels, when causes of compass deviation were little understood, it was commonly thought necessary to place a compass at a masthead in order to escape possible disastrous results arising from the then large and changing deviations usually observed. **Radio c.,** *see* RADIO. **Repeater c.,** *see* gyro compass. **Sea c.,** *see* **Magnetic, marine,** or **mariner's c.** **To set by the c.,** *see* SET. **Spirit c.,** *see* **Fluid, liquid,** or **oil c.** **Standard c.,** magnetic compass by which courses are set and steering compass and any others are checked. It is fixed in a position as far from magnetic influence of metal fittings, etc. as possible and from which best possible unobstructed view may be obtained to facilitate taking of bearings and observations for finding deviation. **Steering c.,** one by which helmsman steers the course. **Telltale c.,** *see* TELLTALE. **Variation c.,** a declination compass; *see* DECLINATION.

Table of Points of the Compass

North	0°	East	90°	South	180°	West	270°
N by E	11¼	E by S	101¼	S by W	191¼	W by N	281¼
NNE	22½	ESE	112½	SSW	202½	WNW	292½
NE by N	33¾	SE by E	123¾	SW by S	213¾	NW by W	303¾
NE	45	SE	135	SW	225	NW	315
NE by E	56¼	SE by S	146¼	SW by W	236¼	NW by N	326¼
ENE	67½	SSE	157½	WSW	247½	NNW	337½
E by N	78¾	S by E	168¾	W by S	258¾	N by W	348¾
(E)	90	(S)	180	(W)	270	(N)	360

Further division of the card into half and quarter points is made according to two systems, viz., (*a*) that formerly in use in U.S. navy in which fractional points are named from *N* and *S* toward *E* and *W,* excepting that divisions adjacent to a cardinal or intercardinal point always are referred to that point; and (*b*) that in which fractional points are named *from* each cardinal and intercardinal point *toward* a 22½°-point (*ENE, SSW, etc.*) A comparison of the two systems is indicated in following *half-* and *quarter-point* divisions of the NE quadrant:

(*a*)	(*b*)
N ¼ E	N ¼ E
N ½ E	N ½ E
N ¾ E	N ¾ E
N by E	N by E
N by E ¼ E	N by E ¼ E
N by E ½ E	N by E ½ E
N by E ¾ E	N by E ¾ E
N N E	N N E
N N E ¼ E	N E by N ¾ N
N N E ½ E	N E by N ½ N
N N E ¾ E	N E by N ¼ N
N E by N	N E by N
N E ¾ N	N E ¾ N
N E ½ N	N E ½ N
N E ¼ N	N E ¼ N
N E	N E
N E ¼ E	N E ¼ E
N E ½ E	N E ½ E
N E ¾ E	N E ¾ E
N E by E	N E by E
N E by E ¼ E	N E by E ¼ E
N E by E ½ E	N E by E ½ E
N E by E ¾ E	N E by E ¾ E
E N E	E N E
E N E ¼ E	E by N ¾ N
E N E ½ E	E by N ½ N
E N E ¾ E	E by N ¼ N
E by N	E by N
E ¾ N	E ¾ N
E ½ N	E ½ N
E ¼ N	E ¼ N
East	East

COMPASS.² An archaic term meaning to encircle; to make a circuit; to sail around a point, island, etc. (*Cf.* **fetch a compass**) To bend into a curved form, as to *compass* timber for a ship. **C.-timber,** in older wooden shipbuilding, any curved or arched members in the structure; especially such as are so shaped in their natural growth.

COMPENSATE. (L. *compensatus,* to balance with one another.) **Compensated compass,** *see* COMPASS. **Compensation-balance,** *see* BALANCE. **Compensating-binnacle,** *see* BINNACLE. **Compensating-coils,** *see* COILS. **Compensating-magnet,** *see* MAGNET. **Compensation,** in shipbuilding, strengthening by additional plates, web-frames, stringers, stiffeners, etc. to offset any weakening of structure consequent to a break in continuity, such as hatchways or other deck openings, change or break in line of deck, en-gine-room space, side-ports, etc. **Compensator,** a bar magnet or mass of soft iron, such as a sphere or iron bar, placed in a binnacle or in vicinity of a compass for purpose of neutralizing a ship's magnetic influence on directive power or correct position of the compass-needle; a compass corrector.

COMPLEMENT. (L. *complementum,* filling up together.) Complete allowance; as, *the ship has its complement of men; see* COMPANY. **C. of an angle or arc,** amount it lacks of 90 degrees; complementary angle.

COMPOSITE. (L. *compositus,* made up of parts.) **C. boiler,** in a vessel powered by internal combustion engines, a boiler used for auxiliary purposes heated by exhaust gases from such engines, or by oil-burners when engines are not operating. **C.-built,** indicating hull construction in which frames, beams, keelsons, and all important strength members are of iron or steel, while entirely planked outside and usually having under-water body copper-sheathed. Such construction was common in English yards between 1860 and 1880 and, though costly, was deemed a suitable answer to lack of hold space in the bulky all-wood-built vessel, while providing a clean bottom for satisfactory sailing or steaming, which the notorious barnacle-gathering iron shell-plating failed to supply, more especially on lengthy tropical voyages. **C. sailing,** combination of *great circle sailing* and *parallel sailing,* resorted to when a limiting parallel is decided upon, as on account of ice, storm-infested regions, intervening land, etc. Course is shaped to follow the great circle whose vertex lies on limiting parallel; thence along the latter until reaching the great circle passing through destination and also having its vertex on limiting parallel; thence on such great circle arc to destination.

COMPOUND. C. course, *see* COURSE. **C. engine,** *see* ENGINE.

COMPRADOR. (*Port.,* meaning a *buyer.*) Common term for a store-keeper or ship-chandler throughout the Orient and often in Mediterranean ports.

COMPRESSOR. An obsolete means of checking or holding a chain cable from running out; also called a controller. It was a heavy curved lever worked across lower end of a deck-pipe so as to jam the chain against edge or lip of pipe and so act as a stopper. A tackle was used to apply force to its end. Also, a brakeband on a windlass, fitted with a screw-purchase for checking or securing an anchor-cable. In former *ship ordnance,* a mechanical device for checking recoil of a gun-carriage.

COMPTROLLER. *See* CONTROLLER.

COMPULSORY PILOTAGE. Under law or port regulation in many countries and localities employment of pilots on vessels of certain tonnage and class in specified waters is made compulsory, while in some localities a vessel may elect to proceed without accepting an authorized pilot's services, she nevertheless must pay pilotage, in whole or in part, according to established rate or fee. In U.S. waters, all registered vessels, or, generally, those sailing on foreign voyages, are subject to compulsory pilotage as may be required by state law, while those enrolled or licensed (coasting-vessels, war-vessels, fishing-vessels, yachts, tugs, and other craft) are exempted by federal statute.

CON. To superintend the steering of a vessel, especially through a channel or narrow waters; to direct the helmsman. Also, *conn.*

CONCH. (Pron. *konk.*) A large spiral univalve shell found in sandy bottoms of shallow tropical waters; especially, the *pink conch* of West Indies shores, meat of which is valued as a food. Conchs have for centuries been converted into horns or trumpets and certain African tribes are known to have recently used them to promote fear in their enemies during battle. **C.-harpoon,** see HARPOON.

CONCLUDING-LINE. Seè LINE.

CONDEMNED. Said of a vessel when pronounced unfit for further service; or of a vessel and her cargo adjudged to be forfeited for cause, or as decreed by a prize court.

CONDENSER. (L. *condensare,* to make dense or thick.) A tank or box into which is received exhaust steam from a reciprocating or turbine engine for purpose of converting such steam to liquid state and so recovering in large measure otherwise totally lost boiler feed-water supply. The type used with marine engines is called a *surface condenser,* although common in early low pressure plants were the *jet* and *barometric* types which were characterized by a spray of fresh water mixed directly with the steam. In surface condensers, steam is exposed to aggregate surface of a larger number of small tubes through which, as the cooling medium, sea-water is circulated during operation of engines. **C. discharge-pipe,** that which conveys condenser circulating water overboard. **C. eduction-pipe,** one conducting exhaust steam from engine to condenser. **C.-engines,** those equipped with a condenser system. **C.-feed,** sea-water circulated through a condenser. **C.-head,** one of a surface condenser's ends in which are the *tube-sheet* for supporting, and providing a means to make water-tight, the tube ends; the *water-box,* fitted with a dividing wall which causes the circulating water to pass through half the tubes and return through other half; and water-tight access-door. **C.-tubes,** made of some alloy of copper, more recently one of copper-nickel or aluminum-brass having proved satisfactory resistants to corrosion and erosion; they are approxi-

mately one-sixteenth inch in thickness and usually five-eighths to three-fourths inch outside diameter. **C.-tube support-plates,** vertical cast iron or steel plates about 24 inches apart perforated to receive and support condenser-tubes. **C. vacuum-gauge, a** gauge for showing amount of vacuum in a condenser.

CONDUCT-BOOK. *See* BOOK.

CONE. A signal shape usually made of canvas and like a right cone having a height not less than two feet and equal to its base diameter, used at various coastal stations in different countries in a system of storm or ice warnings, canal right-of-way or docking signals, or as a fleet signal indicating speed or maneuvering by war-vessels. Sometimes a double cone or two cones placed base to base, is used, and, in certain U.S. pilot rules, the two frustra of a pair of cones are displayed in that manner on vessels towing, or moored over or alongside of a submerged object. **C.-anchor,** a sea-anchor or drag; *see* ANCHOR. **Speed-c.,** *see* SPEED.

CONGER EEL. The sea eel (*Leptocephalus*), growing to eight feet in length and about 80 pounds in weight; its back is a pale brown color and lower part grayish white; common in rocky places on European coasts where it is an important food fish, and sometimes found on American Atlantic coast. The name is locally given to the north-east American coast *eel-pout* and the California *moray.*

CONJUNCTION. Apparent close approach or meeting of two heavenly bodies having same right ascension or longitude. When either Mercury or Venus are in that position with the sun, they are said to be in *inferior conjunction,* if between sun and earth, and when on opposite side of the sun, in *superior conjunction;* the other planets, being farther from the sun than Mercury, Venus, or Earth, can be in conjunction with the sun only when in latter position.

CONN. *See* CON.

CONNECTING BRIDGE. A bridge joining two decks of about same height, as a *fore-and-aft bridge* on a tank-vessel; a *cat-walk.*

CONNECTING-ROD. A rod or bar joining two or more parts; especially in a reciprocating engine, rod connecting a crank-pin and a crosshead, beam, or piston-rod.

CONNECTING-SHACKLE. *See* SHACKLE.

CONNING. Directing a helmsman in steering or piloting a vessel, especially in narrow waters or in heavy traffic. Also, *cunning.* **C.-tower,** a low shot-proof pilot-house on a war-vessel, especially that on a submarine. **C.-tower shield,** *see* SHIELD.

CONNOISSANCE DES TEMPS. The French nautical almanac; *see* ALMANAC.

CONSIGNEE. One to whom certain goods are shipped, as indicated in bill of lading, by the *consignor*.

CONSORT. A vessel sailing in company with another. To **keep c.**, an archaic term meaning to keep company; *see* COMPANY.

CONSTANT. A magnitude or value having the quality of remaining unchanged, as a quantity, error, force, or a law, as opposed to a *variable*. **C. of aberration,** *see* ABERRATION. **Meridian altitude** or **latitude c.,** a combination of the several values used in determining latitude by a meridian altitude of a heavenly body in order to obtain a constant to which simple addition or subtraction of observed altitude gives the latitude. **Tidal c.,** *see* TIDAL.

CONSTELLATION. One of the many groups or assemblages of stars, or a portion of the heavens occupied by such a group. *See* STAR. Many constellations, especially those of northern skies, were named by the early ancients, some mythological hero, goddess, animal, or even inanimate object being so honored, probably because of a fancied resemblance in the groups to the original. In the book of Job, whose life-time was 1500 B.C. or earlier, we find a remarkable reference to three celestial names in use to-day. Approximately 90 groups are distinguished by astronomers and, usually beginning with the brightest, with few exceptions each star is designated by a Greek letter, as *α Leonis* (Regulus), first star in *Leo; β Orionis* (Rigel), second one in *Orion*. (Note the *genitive* form when thus expressed) Familiar names are also given many constellations or parts of them, as "Dipper," "Plough," and "Charlie's Wagon" applied to *Ursa Major* or the *Great Bear;* "Lady's Chair" for *Cassiopeia;* the "Sickle" as easily recognized in western end of *Leo;* "Seven Sisters" for a small compact group in *Taurus* called by the ancients *Pleiades;* the "Chain-hook," so named by sailors as more appropriate than the classic *Scorpio;* "Cutter's Mainsail" for *Corvus;* etc. Navigators become acquainted with star groups by observing certain triangles, curves, and figures outlined by various bright stars and thus grow capable of recognizing any particular star while many others are obscured in cloudy weather.

CONSTRUCTION. Form or manner of putting together, or arrangement of, structural parts so as to completely build anything; as, a ship. Determination of a vessel's position by lines and measurements laid off on a chart in accordance with any geometrical principles involved. **Arch c.,** *see* ARCH. **Batten seam c.,** a system in early wood-built steamvessels and other smaller sailing-craft in which battens were secured over all inside bottom and topside planking seams between each frame member. Its objective was to withstand any working of the calking, as well as additionally stiffening the planking, having in view possible damage due to excessive vibration or frequent tidal groundings at some ports. **Deep frame c.,** in a transverse frame system, heavy or deep frames erected 8 to 10 ordinary frame spaces apart chiefly for the purpose of doing away with a large number of the hold stanchions required in ordinary transverse framing classification rules. Later the deep frame system practically has been displaced by *web frame* construction, which is simply a heavier form of deep frame in the transverse system and a kind of bridging frame in *longitudinal-framed* vessels. **Longitudinal c.,** a system characterized by an almost total departure from transverse framing in that deck and shell plating are fastened to, and their stiffening depends upon, fore-and-aft or longitudinal frames, with exception of heavy web frames in transverse form bridging the longitudinals and spaced 10 to 12 feet apart. Variations of this system are the *Isherwood* and *Gatewood*, named for their original designers, and for these it is claimed that greater longitudinal strength and considerable reduction in weight of material, with resulting increase of cargo space, is obtained. **Transverse c.,** that used from earliest times in shipbuilding history is so named from its thwartship rib-like framing. Each frame unit essentially consists of ribs or side-frames proper, both joined by a floor at the bottom and a deck-beam at the top, the whole supplying a transverse stiffening bridge and means of fastening deck and shell plating. Compared with longitudinal construction, this tried and rugged system provides adequate longitudinal strength in part by keel and keelsons, deck stringer-plates, and sheer strakes, greater stiffness in this respect being ensured by sum total of rigidity obtainable in the many local lateral fastenings supplied by frames, and consequent backing of shell-plating's work as chief strength-supplier in the structure.

CONSTRUCTIVE TOTAL LOSS. *See* LOSS.

CONSTRUCTOR, NAVAL. *See* NAVAL.

CONSUL. (*L.*) An agent commissioned by a sovereign state to reside in a foreign port or city for purpose of caring for, and protecting commercial interests of, its citizens, and its seamen's rights and welfare. Such consul usually is not authorized to represent his government in a diplomatic sense. Consuls rank according to following titles and sequence: *Consul general, consul, vice-consul, consular agent*. **Consular agent,** one stationed at a foreign port of small commercial importance and charged with duties similar to those of a consul or vice-consul. **C. general,** a diplomatic service official having supervision of all consulates of his government in a foreign country. He is directly subordinate to an ambassador where such office is provided by his country.

CONSULAR. Pertaining to, or having the nature of, a consul. **C. invoice,** an itemized statement of goods and their values or cost prices presented to a consul for certification and authorization of their shipment to his country. Its chief purpose is to supply necessary information to customs officials at port to which goods are shipped. **C. passenger,** a citizen of a country, usually a destitute or convalescent seaman, for whom a consular official engages transportation and authorizes payment by his government for person's repatriation. **C. salute,** *see* SALUTE.

CONSULATE. Office or jurisdiction of a consul; premises occupied officially by a consul.

CONTACT-MINE. *See* MINE.

CONTINENTAL SHELF. *See* SHELF.

CONTINUATION. A term referring to classification status of wood vessels. A ship is *continued* if, on expiration of period for which she was classed, another number of years in same character has been granted. The term also refers to a clause in a marine insurance policy which provides for *continuation* of policy's force beyond period of time covered, should vessel be at sea on such expiration date, until she arrives at some agreed-upon port, subject to reasonable notice being supplied the underwriters by her insurers.

CONTINUOUS DISCHARGE BOOK. A continuous record in book form issued to, and becoming property of, a seaman, by authority of U.S. Coast Guard, or similar body in other countries, showing each vessel on which he has successively served, description of voyage, etc. It is in effect a combined certificate of identification and certificate of discharge; *see* CERTIFICATE.

CONTINUOUS FLOOR. *See* FLOOR.

CONTLINE. Line of space between strands of a rope. Also, space between bilges of casks stowed side by side; casks or barrels are said to be stowed *bilge-and-contline* when successive tiers are laid *in the contlines* of a tier next below. Also written *cantline.*

CONTRABAND. (L. *contra,* against; L.L. *bandum,* ban.) Goods or merchandise, including live stock, forbidden to be exported or imported; smuggled goods; prohibited traffic. **C. of war,** certain goods prohibited from being supplied a belligerent under penalty of seizure and confiscation of both vessel and goods. Formerly, such traffic was distinguished as *absolute* and *occasional* in so-called international law, the former indicating goods manifestly intended solely for warring purposes; the latter, goods made contraband by reason of being capable of adaptation for warlike purposes. Of late years these distinctions have melted with the apparently arbitrary practice of prohibition by a belligerent of any traffic whatever with an enemy, wherever possible.

CONTRACTED HORIZON. *See* HORIZON.

CONTRACT OF AFFREIGHTMENT. Provisions of a *bill of lading.* Chartering of a vessel or part of her cargo space while such vessel remains in charge of her owners.

CONTRA-PROPELLER. *See* PROPELLER.

CONTRIBUTION, AVERAGE. *See* AVERAGE.

CONTROL. To check, restrain, or influence; as, *the steering is controlled by a rudder.* Power or authority to govern or direct; as, *a vessel under a pilot's control.* **C.-gauge,** an instrument, as an indicator, used as a means of enabling an operator to intelligently control performance of an engine, machine, etc. **Fire-c.,** *see* FIRE. **Zigzag c.,** *see* ZIGZAG.

CONTROLLER. A device for checking or holding an anchor cable; *see* COMPRESSOR. In U.S. naval affairs, formerly a principal officer of the General Board, at which he usually presided, who, directly under the Secretary, was charged with distribution control of expenditures appropriated by Congress; now officially termed *fiscal director.* In the British office of Lord High Admiral, one of the Lords Commissioners who is mainly responsible for construction and equipment of navy ships. Also spelled *comptroller.*

CONTROLLING DEPTH. *See* DEPTH.

CONT-SPLICE. *See* BIGHT.

CONVERGENCY. Referred to bearings taken by a *radio-compass,* difference between a *great circle bearing,* which is that observed by such compass, and the *rhumb* or *mercator bearing;* also termed *conversion angle.* For laying off on the commonly used Mercator chart, a radio direction-finder (*radio-compass*) bearing is corrected for this difference or *convergency* by applying value thereof *toward the equator.* Thus, in *North latitude* given a radio bearing of 250° and convergency 3°, the corresponding rhumb is 247°; with radio bearing 150° we get 153° as the rhumb or Mercator bearing. Radio and Mercator bearings coincide on north and south and, in consequence, no convergency exists on these points, while its greatest values obtain in cases of high and similar latitudes of both ship and station observed. **C. values** are usually found from nautical tables; however, such may be determined by a graphical method in which the hypotenuse of a right-angled triangle is laid off to represent, in degrees, half the difference of longitude between ship and station observed, base angle to represent the middle latitude; length of perpendicular is then *convergency* required, according to scale adopted, in degrees.

CONVERSION ANGLE. Difference in direction at a given point between a great circle and a rhumb line as indicated under CONVERGENCY. *Angle of conversion* or *convergency* may refer also to difference in directions of a great circle tangent and its chord. Since direction of a great circle laid off as a rhumb line at an observer's position is tangential to such great circle, the rhumb representing a chord intersecting that track at a given distance necessarily will be arrived at by a *lesser* 'conversion angle. A practical use of the conversion angle in this respect is to apply half its value to rhumb course to obtain great circle sailing course for say a distance of 300 miles. A rhumb or Mercator course is easily determined by parallel rules or protractor, while azimuth tables provide the great circle course, which is the *tangential course* found by application of conversion angle.

CONVOY. One or more vessels accompanied by an armed vessel as an escort. To accompany for protection or escort; as, *the corvette convoyed a merchant ship (or ships).* **C. pennant,** *see* PENNANT.

CONY. *See* NIGGER-FISH.

COOK-HOUSE. *See* HOUSE.

COOLING, Ammunition. *See* AMMUNITION. **Cargo c.,** generally refers to refrigeration of perishables by the air-cooled system. This consists of a forced circulation through the holds of air blown by fans over batteries of pipe-coils through which a low temperature brine is kept flowing. Fruits, eggs, vegetables, cheese, wines, and commodities requiring 35 to 55 degrees (Fahr.) carriage are usually styled *cooled* cargo; *frozen* and *chilled* cargoes are those kept at from 10° to 30°, as meats, fish, and butter.

COOM. An old term for a wave-crest *comb;* curling top of a *comber* or breaker.

COOPERAGE. Charges payable by a consignee for repairs made by carrier to damaged casks, cases, packages, etc. which are claimed to be too fragile or improperly packed to withstand reasonable and ordinary stowage and handling.

COPING. In shipbuilding, turned up ends of iron deck-beam-knees (*lodging-knees*) so that they hook into the wood beams and thus assist in resisting shearing stresses in the knee-bolts.

COPPER. (Gr. *kupros*, Cyprus, famous in ancient times for its copper mines.) The reddish ductile, malleable, and tough metal (specific gravity 8.8) once extensively used in wooden shipbuilding as preferred material for bolts, washers, and any fastening media; also much used as principal alloy in bottom sheathing, such as *Muntz metal.* **Coppers,** kettles, pots, etc. used in a ship's galley, whether made of copper or other metal. **C.-bottomed,** having the bottom sheathed with copper or some copper alloy, as a protection from fouling marine growth, barnacles, and the *teredo* or *ship-worm.* **C.-fastened,** in wooden boat and ship construction, having the structural parts, especially those below load-line, fastened with copper bolts, etc., or a copper alloy, as bronze. Where copper sheathing is considered a requisite, fastenings of steel or iron are not used in bottom planking, because of resulting galvanic erosion of the sheathing. **C. paint,** *see* PAINT. **C.-worm,** a ship-worm; the *teredo* or wood-borer.

COPPERING. Act of sheathing with copper, as a ship's bottom; the sheathing itself. **C.-hammer,** *see* HAMMER.

CORACLE. (W. *corwgl;* Gael. *curach.*) A small light oval-shaped boat, usually about six feet in length by four in width, covered with oiled or tarred cloth, canvas, etc. In construction, the craft is simply a wicker basket and is a relic of ancient Briton workmanship still rowed or paddled on inland waters in Wales and Ireland. Its original skin consisted of hides or leather.

CORAL. Hard calcareous substance formed by myriads of skeletons of zoöphytes and comprising the sea-fans, red coral, and reef coral. The last-named, generally white in color, has grown through centuries into many reefs and those peculiar islands of the Pacific called *atolls.* Excepting the red coral of the Mediterranean, substance is native generally to tropical seas and, for example, forms the *Great Barrier Reef* of Australia's east coast which extends 1200 miles in length and from a few to 60 miles in breadth. Coral of red and pink variety found in the Mediterranean provides an industry in ornaments, jewelry, etc. **C. mud,** sediment consisting of decomposed coral. **C. reef,** *see above.* Generally, it is made up of fragments of corals and coral sands ground up by action of waves and limestone formed by consolidation of such; called a *fringing reef* when bordering the shore, and a *barrier reef* when roughly parallel with a coast at some distance from it. *See* ATOLL. **C. sand,** a whitish sand formed of debris of coral and shells. **C. zone,** depth of sea in a geographical area where coral flourishes.

CORALLINA. A decked sailing-boat peculiar to coral fishing on west coast of Italy and coasts of Tunis, Sicily, and Sardinia.

CORD. Any small rope made by laying several strands twisted together; specifically, small hard-laid cotton, silk, or nylon line, such as is used in fishing or net-making. **Indicator c.,** one used to transmit motion of an engine part to an indicator. **Whistle-c.,** a lanyard for opening valve to a steam or air whistle, horn, or siren, from the navigating bridge; a lanyard on the boatswain's pipe.

CORDAGE. Ropes, lines, wires, etc. in a collective sense; ropes constituting hawsers and running rigging of a ship.

CORDELIER. (*Fr.*) Earliest form of machine used in combining the operations of twisting and laying strands in rope-making.

CORE. In a wire rope or a shroud-laid fiber rope, *i.e.*, one of more than three strands, heart or center strand around which the others are laid. **C.-yarns,** heart or center yarns of a fiber rope strand; also, fiber yarns in center of wire strands, often found in flexible wire rope.

CORINTHIAN. In yachting parlance, an amateur. The word generally denotes a sportsmanlike gentleman of means who drives his own horses, sails his own yacht, etc., usually in the sense of extravagant show. **C. sailing,** that conducted by amateurs.

CORK. (Sp. *corcho;* L. *cortex;* bark.) A bark of various trees; specifically, that of the cork oak (*Quercus suber*) which grows to an unusually heavy thickness and whose qualities of lightness (specific gravity .24), elasticity, toughness, and imperviousness, render it most satisfactory for life-belts, life-buoys, fish-net floats, cask-bungs, bottle-stoppers, cold storage insulation, handles for implements, etc. Chief sources of best cork are Spain, Portugal, North Africa, and Southern Europè generally, where it is cut from the trees in large slabs every 12 to 15 years. A stopper for a bottle; a cask-bung; one of the floats buoying a fishing-net; a fishing-line float. **C.-buoy,** a life-buoy. **C. fender,** a nearly spherical-shaped canvas bag 12 to 15 inches in diameter, tightly filled with granulated cork and protected by a covering of needle-hitched ratline-stuff or other small line. A lanyard is attached for placing it as necessary to act as a buffer between vessel and dock or other object. **C.-jacket,** a life-jacket, or one having cork enclosed in it for sustaining a person in the water. **C. light,** said of a vessel entirely without cargo. **C. mat,** *see.* MAT. **C. paint,** that containing granulated cork and used as an insulation coating on metal surfaces in living quarters, storerooms, etc., which are exposed to the weather. Its purpose is to minimize condensation during extreme differences in outside and inside temperatures. **C.-rope,** line forming the top or head of a seine or other fishing-net to which cork floats are attached; the *head-line.* Velvet c., best quality cork; that free of woody or porous defects.

COR LEONIS. (*L.,* = *lion's heart.*) The star Regulus (*Alpha Leonis*) (a *Leonis*); *see* REGULUS *and* STAR.

CORMORANT. (L. *corvus marinus,* the marine crow.) Widely distributed genus (*Phalacrocorax*) of expert diving and fishing birds; of dark color, having a heavy body two to three feet in length, long hooked beak, stout neck about as long as head and bill combined, strong wings, and stiff rounded tail. Noted for gluttony, their voracious desire for fish has been turned to profitable account by Chinese and Japanese fishermen who have trained cormorants to retrieve the fish, after making it impossible to swallow the catch by placing a snugly fitting ring around the birds' necks. Of a number of species, the *common cormorant* of N.E. America, Europe, and Asia is best known; others are termed *double-crested, green, red-faced,* etc.

CORNET. A pennant or flag used in navy signalling; a general message from a flagship to a squadron; a signal for every ship to prepare for a forthcoming message.

CORNUCOPIA DRAG. *See* DRAG.

COROCORE. A boat used until recent years by the Malays for warring or piratical purposes. That of the Celebes was propelled by two banks of oars, upper tier from a raised platform projecting beyond the gunwale and over the stern, and often manned by over 60 men. Other craft of same name in East Indian waters are masted vessels, broad with narrow extremities, from 50 to 60 feet in length, and covered throughout about four-fifths their length with a roof of matting.

CORONA. (*L.,* = *crown.*) One or more colored circles sometimes seen close to and around the sun or moon. The phenomenon is produced by diffraction through suspended particles of ice or water droplets at high altitude and often is seen in an intervening *cirro-stratus* cloud.

CORONA AUSTRALIS. (*L.,* = *southern crown.*) A southern constellation, also called *Corolla,* or *The Wreath,* adjoining and north of *Sagittarius.* It contains no navigational stars.

CORONA BOREALIS. (*L.,* = *northern crown.*) A northern constellation adjoining and east of *Bootes.* It contains the bright star *Alphacca* (a *Coronæ Borealis*), magnitude 2.3; declination 27° n.; right ascension 15 hrs. 32 min.

CORPORAL, Ship's. In U.S. navy vessels, formerly a petty officer in charge of instruction in small arms and setting and relieving the watch; later, an assistant to a master-at-arms. The term is now synonymous with *master-at-arms.*

CORPS, MARINE. *See* MARINE.

CORPOSANT. (It. *corpo santo,* holy body.) Ball of light of flamelike appearance sometimes seen running along stays and intermittently flashing or moving about prominent parts of a ship, particularly at the trucks, yard-arms, and jib-boom end, under certain atmospheric conditions immediately before or during a storm; called also *corpse-light, St. Elmo's fire* or *light, dead fire, jack o' lantern,* and *Castor and Pollux.*

CORRECTED ESTABLISHMENT. *See* ESTABLISHMENT.

CORRECTED TIME. *See* TIME.

CORRECTING-PLATE. *See* COMPENSATOR.

CORRECTION. A quantity applied to a given magnitude in order to obtain its exact value, as a *sextant index-error;* a reduction allowance to convert a changing value to that required at a given time, as *an hourly variation in declination of the sun.* Also, procedure involved in application of such errors or allowances, as *correction of an altitude.* **Compass c's,** *see* COMPASS. **C. of altitudes,** *see* ALTITUDE. **C. of double altitude,** as observed in an *artificial horizon* by a sextant, is effected by applying any index error before deviding by two; then corrections for refraction, parallax, and semi-diameter, in the case of sun or moon; if a star or a planet, that for refraction only. Result is termed the *true altitude,* now usually abbreviated H_o. **C. for run,** allowance applied to a plotted chart position, or to an observed line of position, in bringing it forward in accordance with vessel's course and speed to any time required. **Index c.,** usually referred to that of a sextant, is an error which shows itself upon placing the *index-glass* and *horizon-glass* exactly parallel to each other. Difference between zero and angle indicated on the arc is then *index error* or *index c.*

CORRECTOR, COMPASS. *See* COMPASS *and* QUADRANTAL.

CORRESPONDING SPEEDS. In naval architectural design experiments, speeds at which a model of a proposed hull is towed in observing hull resistance, wave-making, steering, etc. expected in vessel's performance, as considered with questions of requisite economical powering to be installed. Such speeds are proportional to the square roots of linear dimensions of ship and model; thus, a 400-foot vessel moving at 12 knots is represented by her 25-foot model at a speed of 3 knots, since $\sqrt{400} : \sqrt{25} = 12 : 3.$

CORRUGATED BULKHEAD. *See* BULKHEAD.

CORRUGATED VESSEL. *See* VESSEL.

CORSAIR. A privateer or pirate; a piratical armed vessel. The name appears to have first denoted a Turk or Saracen on African side of the Mediterranean, or Barbary coast, who was authorized by his government to prey upon Christian commerce from late Middle Ages to 18th. century.

CORVETTE. In old sailing navies, a flush-decked vessel similar in rig to a frigate but next below in armament; called a *sloop-of-war* in U.S. navy. Recently, especially in British navy, a type of small armed vessel used in scouting and convoy work, submarine defense, etc.

CORVUS. (*L. = the raven.*) A small constellation south of *Virgo* in about 20° south declination and 12¼ hrs. right ascension, often called the *Cutter's Mainsail* from its outline; also called the *Crow* and the *Raven.* A line joining its two northern stars and forming the gaff or head of the "Mainsail" extended outward meets, at 10° distance, bright star *Spica* (α Virginis).

CORYPHÆNA. A genus of large fast-swimming acanthopterygian fishes found in tropical and temperate seas, commonly known as *dolphins.* (Not to be confused with a *cetacean* of same name.) *See* DOLPHIN.

COSINE-HAVERSINE FORMULA. In spherical trigonometry, used to find value of a third side when two sides and included angle are known, as in calculating an *altitude* of a heavenly body at a given instant, or a *great circle distance* between two geographical points. The formula may be stated thus: Given sides *a* and *b*, with angle *C*, in triangle *ABC;* to find *c;* then, *hav c = hav (a ⌐ b) + hav θ.*

[*hav θ = sin a . sin b . hav C*],

θ being an auxiliary arc, and, where *a* and *b* are complements of latitudes or declinations, as in navigational use, *sin a . sin b* becomes *cos(90°-a). cos(90°-b).*

COST, INSURANCE, and **FREIGHT.**   *See* C.I.F. *and* C.I.F.C.I.

COSTON LIGHT, or **SIGNAL.** *See* LIGHT.

COT. An kind of hammock made of canvas and stiffened by a wood frame; a bed-frame suspended from a ship's beams. Also, a small rudely built rowing-boat used in Ireland.

COTHON. (Gr. *Kothon.*) In ancient times, an artificial harbor inside an outer anchorage that is protected by a sea-wall or mole. The harbor of *Carthage* was so constructed and a few ports in the eastern Mediterranean to-day are similarly sheltered, as, for example, the port of *Girgenti (ancient Agrigentum, circa 400 B.C.)* in Sicily.

COTIA. A fast sailing-vessel of the Malabar coast of India having two masts and lateen-rigged.

COTIDAL. Pertaining to coincidence in time of high water at various places in a coastal area. **C. hour,** interval between time of the moon's transit and that of high water at a given locality; *lunitidal interval.* **C. lines,** curved lines joining all places, as shown on a chart, at which high water occurs at same time.

COTTER. A flat tapered piece of wood or metal used as a pin to tighten and secure parts of a machine or structure by being driven through a hole in one of the parts; as, the pin used to secure the stock of a stowed anchor. It is often split at the point so that it may be opened to prevent working loose. Also called a *key* and also written *cottar.*

COTTON. Cotton, cotton-ball clouds, *see* CLOUD. **C. canvas,** *see* CANVAS. **C.-hook,** *see* HOOK. **C. rope,** small cordage chiefly used on yachts for lacings.

lanyards, reef-points, sheets, etc.; has less tensile strength than manila, stretches more, and considerably more flexible when dry, but becomes hard and kinky when wet. **C. wicking,** light strands of cotton used for calking boats, for wicks of candles, and for making joints water-tight, such as that of man-hole covers, tank lids, etc.

COUCH. *See* COACH.

COUGNAR. A now probably obsolete Malay trading-vessel; three-masted, square-rigged, and a good sailer; broad of beam and either partly or wholly decked over, and considered a paying carrier.

COUNTER. Rounded surface of a ship's hull between stern-post and rail; outside overhang at the stern. Also, a combining term indicating a contrary or adverse quality or action. **C.-brace,** an archaic term meaning to brace head yards and main yards sharp up on opposite cants; to brace the yards *a-box.* In single topsail days, a brace leading forward from the lee fore-topsail yard-arm to share the stress on the weather brace when sailing close-hauled or on a wind and carrying a press of canvas. **C.-current,** a current running approximately in an opposite direction to an adjacent or neighboring one. **C.-drain,** a ditch running parallel to an embanked watercourse or canal to catch and carry off any water soaking through the bank. **C.-keel,** old term for that part of a wood keel extending above the garboard strake; also, *keel-rising.* **C.-plate,** any unit of shell-plating forming the counter. **C.-rail,** in wooden ships, ornamental rounded wood fitted as a molding and marking termination, or knuckle, of a ship's counter, or fitted on margin of a square stern. **C.-sea,** waves or swell running against the wind. **C.-timbers,** cant or transom frames forming structure of a ship's counter.

COUNTERBORE. In wood shipbuilding or ship joiner work, where it is required to sink a fastening bolt having a flat head, a hole equal in diameter to that of the bolt head and deep enough to take its covering plug, is first bored; then the through hole for bolt itself is bored. This is called *counterboring.* A special auger or drill, called a *counterbore,* is also used to effect the same end *after* a through hole is bored.

COUNTERSINK. To chamfer outer edge of a hole made to receive a rivet, bolt, screw, etc. whose more or less conical-shaped head is to be set down flush with surface of material joined. A reamer or such tool for countersinking. **Countersinker,** one engaged in countersinking rivet-holes in ship-yard work. **Countersunk work,** rivets, screws, bolts, etc. shaped for, and driven in, holes prepared by countersinking.

COUNTRY. In the sense of being the province of a certain group; in older U.S. navy usage, space in and about the ward-room, other than officers' berths, was called *ward-room country;* also, steerage passenger space was often referred to as *steerage country.*

COUPLE, RIGHTING. Referred to ship stability, the equal and opposing forces of gravity and buoyancy acting, respectively, through extremities of the *righting arm,* or horizontal separation of center of buoyancy from center of gravity, due to a vessel's heel. The moment of force in such couple, tending to restore a vessel to the upright, is equal to her displacement times length of righting arm, expressed in foot-tons.

COUPON. (Fr. *couper,* to cut off.) In U.S. shipbuilding parlance, a specimen piece for official testing cut from ship plating, angle-bar, boiler-plate, steel castings, high-pressure tubing, etc. to determine conformity of such material to requirements of a classification society or government regulations as to tensile strength, ductility, bending, etc.

COURSE. (L. *cursum,* to run.) Point of the compass to which a vessel's path is directed; direction in which a ship is steered. When referred to the true, or geographical, meridian, it is called a *true course;* when referred to the magnetic meridian, or a direction differing from true north by the value of local magnetic variation (declination of needle), it is called a *magnetic course,* or that shown by a compass free of deviation or local attraction; and, as indicated by compass, whether free of error or otherwise, a *compass course.* In early days of deep-sea voyaging and up to the 18th. century, points of the compass were referred to as *courses,* as in "lay her *two courses* to the wind." Also, the *sail* bent to lowest yard on each mast of a square-rigged vessel, synonymous terms in a 3-masted ship being *fore-c.,* foresail; *main-c.,* mainsail; *mizzen-c.,* crossjack. **Air-c's, air-c. bars, air-c. boards,** *see* AIR. **Compound c.,** old term for resultant of several different courses steered during a given interval of time; now called a *course made good.* **C.-protractor,** an instrument for laying off bearings or courses, or determining such, on a chart. **C.-corrector,** a trade name for a pelorus; *see* PELORUS. **C.-recorder,** an instrument consisting of a rolling graph, run by clockwork, on which a continuous record of courses steered and time run on each is indicated by a pen electrically and automatically controlled from the master gyro compass. The graph movement is synchronized with ship's time so as to show exact intervals between changes of course. **Direct c.,** a single course or straight track between two points, as compared with various courses steered due to wind, or other conditions, between such points; a course made good. **To lay a c.,** to determine from a chart a required course by parallel rules or protractor; also, a vessel is said to *lay her c.* when sailing close enough to the wind to steer a required course without being obliged to fall off on a tack.

To **set a c.** or **shape a c.,** *see* SHAPING. **Steered c.,** a compass course; one that is not corrected for error or deviation. **Lower staysails** were once also called *courses.*

COURSE SIGNAL. In International Code procedure, a course is expressed in three figures denoting degrees from 000 to 359 measured clockwise, and is always considered *true,* unless expressly stated to be otherwise; thus, hoist *E B X,* meaning *"My present course is,"* followed by the numeral hoist *0 1 7,* indicates *"My present course is seventeen degrees true."*

COURT, ADMIRALTY. *See* ADMIRALTY.

COURT-MARTIAL. A court consisting of military or naval officers for trial of members of the armed forces charged with offenses against military or naval law. In U.S. navy, courts-martial are either general or summary, and in certain cases a number of enlisted men are included in the "court." **General c.-m.,** for major offenses only, consists of five to thirteen officers. If offender is an officer, he must be tried by this court; petty officers and all lesser ratings may be tried by *"general courts"* for major offenses. **Summary c.-m.,** for middle bracket offenses, consists of three officers not below rank of ensign, and has jurisdiction in offenses by petty officers and all ratings below. *Deck court,* for minor offenses, is held by one officer. Certain punishments may be *"awarded"* directly by the captain at *"the mast"* in lieu of a court-martial, and this is generally done. In British navy, similar procedure obtains.

COVE. A very small inlet or sheltered recess in a coast-line affording anchorage for small craft. In 18th. century use, a concave-faced piece of timber forming base of a poop balustrade or taff-rail.

COVER. In yacht-racing, to sail close enough to weather side of an opponent in order to deprive him of as much wind as possible; to "take the wind out of the other fellow's sails." **Bitt-c.,** an ornamental wood cover once fitted as a portable seat over the poop mooring-bitts. **Open coverage,** *see* OPEN. **Sail-c.,** as a weather and dust protection while in port, a snug-fitting covering of light canvas laced on a furled sail. **Skylight-c.,** a protection of canvas made to cover a skylight.

COVERING-BOARD. *See* PLANK. (Same as *planksheer.*)

COW-FISH. Any of various trunkfishes, characterized by hornlike projections above the eyes. A name improperly denoting smaller *cetaceans,* as grampuses, porpoises, dolphins; and *sirenians,* as manatees and dugongs.

COW-HITCH. A clumsily made or any unsuitable hitch or knot; also *see* HITCH.

COWL VENTILATOR. *See* VENTILATOR.

COW-PILOT. A small banded and brilliantly colored coral-reef fish found in West Indian waters; also, *cock-eye pilot.*

COWRIE or **COWRY.** (Hind., *kauri.*) A small colored gastropod seashell, tortoise-backed, and having its mouth in the middle and full length of its ventral side. Smaller species of cowries were formerly used as money in many parts of Africa and southern Asia.

COW-SHARK. A large shark of the family *Hexanchidæ* found in West Indian and European waters; usually 8 to 10 feet in length.

COW'S TAIL. The frayed-out end of a fiber rope.

COXCOMB. In older sailing-ships, a cleat or piece of wood fastened to a yard-arm, suitably notched on its upper side to hold the reef-earing turns in position; it usually was fitted on single topsail yards only; a *comb-cleat.* A method of covering a grommet, ring, chest-handle, etc. with small cord in which, beginning with a clove hitch, each end is alternately half-hitched round such ring, etc., thus producing a fancy plaited ridge around outer edge of such ring, etc.; *cockscombing.*

COXSWAIN. (M.E. *cock,* boat: *swain,* servant.) Steersman of a boat; especially, one who has charge of a ship's boat in absence of an officer or a superior; a former U.S. navy rating now designated *boatswain's mate, 3rd. class.* **Cowswain's box,** space occupied by *c.* in steering a boat. An older form is *cockswain* and the word is abbreviated *coxen, cox'n,* and sometimes *coxon.*

CRAB. A winch or capstan on a dock for hauling vessels; a small hand-winch appropriately placed for heaving on running gear on a sailing-ship. The constellation *Cancer,* the crab: *see* CANCER. To drift sideways, as, to *crab to leeward* in sailing. To **catch a c.,** in rowing, to miss catching the water and thus fall backward in attempting the stroke, or to fail to raise one's oar on completing a stroke. **C.-winch,** *see* WINCH. **Hoisting-c.,** *see* HOISTING.

CRABBER. One engaged in fishing crabs, lobsters, shrimps, etc.; a boat so employed; also, *crab boat.* **Crabber's eye,** *see* KNOT.

CRACK. **Crack-boat, c.-steamer,** an archaic descriptive term for a vessel of averred outstanding qualities, as used in advertising a speedy liner, excursion-boat, etc. To **c. on,** to maintain a spread of sail, which ordinarily would be reduced, in a strong wind or heavy sea; to carry a continued press of canvas. Also sometimes referred to a powered vessel running full speed in adverse sea or weather conditions. **Tidal c.,** *see* TIDAL.

CRACKER HASH. Baked broken sea-biscuit and salt pork, once commonly served to crews of deep-water sailing-ships.

CRADLE. A *frame* of timber or iron moving upon rollers or ways to support and carry a vessel while docking on a marine railway. A pair of *chocks*, or *bed*, supporting and securing a boat, or any specially fitted support for a tank, cask, or other object on board ship. In old navy usage, a special *bed* used for a sick or wounded seaman. A kind of boat-shaped *box* used by a life-saving crew in hauling persons ashore from a stranded vessel; also called a *car*. **Launching-c.,** *see* LAUNCHING. **Yard-c.,** *see* TRUSS.

CRAFT. A vessel or boat; vessels of any kind, especially smaller types, in a collective sense. Gear or tackle used in catching fish or whaling, especially the latter, collectively. **Lifting c.,** *see* LIFTING. **Sea-c.,** *see* SEA.

CRAMPONS. (G. *krampf*, cramp.) An endless chain sling rove through the eyes of a pair of sharp-pointed hooks, used for lifting balks of timber, stones, baled hay, etc. Objects are gripped by *crampons* with a force varying directly as their weight, since stress on hoisting-fall produces such gripping power. Another form of this sling is used for lifting heavy metal plates, hooks or *cramps* being stout pieces of steel, each provided with a slot to fit over the plate edges; cramping effect of upward and inward stress on chain thus securely gripping the plate.

CRANAGE. Charges for use of dock or floating cranes in loading or discharging cargo, repair work, and removing stores or equipment. Rates may be according to weight handled, hourly work, extra gear provided, and type of cargo transferred. At some ports, particularly in western Europe, cranage is included in berthing or dock charges, in which cases a vessel's cargo gear generally is not used.

CRANCE. (Du. *krans*, wreath.) Old name for an iron band or ring fitted to steady or secure a spar, such as was provided on a yard for a studding-sail boom; but, particularly, the *bowsprit cap*, which, in later years, was forged with an extended circular band to hold down the jib-boom and, also, with eyes for attaching bob-stay and bowsprit shrouds. In larger vessels the latter fittings were placed on a *crance-iron* or band round bowsprit only, close abaft cap.

CRANE. A machine built and powered to lift, lower, and horizontally transfer a load; usually either a *jib crane*, in which jib or boom and hoisting-gear are constructed to move horizontally as one body; or a *derrick crane*, whose boom and operating machinery are separate units. Any arm made to turn on a vertical axis at one of its ends; as a *lower-topsail-yard crane*; an *anchor-crane*. **Cat-c.,** *see* CAT. **C.-line,** *see* LINE. **C.-post,** vertical post or shaft on which a crane or its jib pivots; also, *c.-shaft, c.-stalk*. **Lifting-c.,** *see* LIFTING. **Locomotive-c.,** one that is mounted and powered to move along

rails; a traveling-crane. **The Crane,** a constellation; *see* GRUS. **Tower c.,** one having a tower-like structure as its base; it is a *revolving* tower crane when it can swing through a complete circle; a *traveling* tower crane, when constructed to move on tracks. **Walking-c.,** a locomotive crane; *see above.* **Yard-c.,** that on which a lower-topsail or a lower-top-gallant-sail yard is pivoted to swing horizontally; fitted at lowermast and topmast caps, respectively.

CRANK. In general, a part of a machine which changes reciprocal to circular motion, or vice versa, essentially consisting of an axle or shaft suitably bent, or an arm fastened at right angles to an end of a shaft, by which its turning motion is controlled or received from it; as, a *hand-winch c.*; a *stern-wheel c.* **C.-bearing,** a bed in which a crankshaft journal rests or revolves. **C.-disk,** in an engine, projecting disk-shaped end of a shaft in which the crank-pin is fitted. **C.-pin,** a cylindrical pin of steel projecting from a *crank-web*, or fitted between two parallel webs, of a *crankshaft*. **C.-pit,** a trough or recess in which a crank or cranks revolve. **Crankshaft,** the main shaft in a *reciprocating engine* containing cranks that convert up-and-down motion of pistons into rotary motion of shaft; any shaft driven by, or turning, a crank. **C.-web,** a flat plate or arm at end of a shaft in which the crank-pin is fitted; *cf.* **C.-disk.**

CRANKY. CRANK. Quality of being easily inclined; top-heavy; referred to a vessel having small initial stability, or indicating a comparatively high center of gravity and consequent inability to carry sail, or withstand other external lateral pressure, without heeling to unusually large angles; opposed to *stiff*. Due to her longer rolling period, a *crank* vessel is characterized by slow easy motion in a sea-way, while a stiff one, in her tendency to remain perpendicular to the wave-slope, will act with a quick, jerky motion. The *crank* vessel is thus a comfortable "sea-boat," compared with the *stiff* one.

CRARE. (O.F. *craier*, war-vessel.) A small English trading-vessel of the Middle Ages. Also spelled *crayer*.

CRATER. A southern constellation lying to southwest of *Virgo*; also called *the Cup*. It contains no navigational stars.

CRAVAT. A sloping ring-shaped plate around the edge of a smoke-stack forming a cover for space between smoke-stack and casing.

CRAWL. An enclosure in the water for confining live fish, crabs, turtles, and the like. To **crawl off**, to work a vessel off a lee shore in heavy weather, as in sailing.

CREASING-STICK. A piece of hard wood or metal having a slit at one end, used for creasing canvas in sailmaking; also, *creasing-iron*.

CREEK. (Fr. *crique;* Ice. *kriki;* a nook.) A small, narrow bay, inlet, or rivulet on a sea-coast or shore of a lake or river. In inland U.S. and Canada, a small stream, rivulet, or run.

CREEL. A large basket for carrying fish. A trap for catching lobsters, crabs, etc.

CREEPER. An instrument similar to a grapple used in creeping, or dragging the bottom, to recover a cable or other sunken object; a *grapnel* or *drag.* Also written *creepers.*

CRESSET. (O.F. *crasset, cresset;* torch.) A torch or lamp for centuries displayed above the stern before side-lights came into use.

CREST. Curling top of a wave; especially, that of a heavy sea. A ridge on the sea bottom, as indicated on a chart by a narrow and lengthy area of lesser depths than found elsewhere in the vicinity.

CREW. A company of seamen who man a vessel or boat; all persons belonging to a vessel. In common ship parlance, the term denotes all persons below officer rank signed on vessel's articles, while, officially, a ship's company is said to consist of *master and crew;* the master, officers, and crew; or all persons constituting the company engaged in manning a vessel. A gang or body of men assigned to particular duty; as, *a carpenter's c.; a gunner's c.* Prize c., see PRIZE. Skeleton c., see SKELETON.

CREW LIST, CERTIFIED. *See* CERTIFICATE.

CREW'S ACCOMMODATION. Most maritime countries have prescribed by law a minimum deck area and cubic space to be allotted to each seaman in a merchant vessel. In U.S. navigation laws (*Title 46 U.S. Code, Section 80*) all merchant vessels constructed since 4 March, 1915, except yachts, pilot boats, or vessels of less than 100 tons register, must provide properly protected living space for each crew member of not less than 16 square feet of deck area and 120 cubic feet of space; each man to have a separate berth and not more than one built above it. Appropriate hospital and wash-room space, depending upon number of crew, are also prescribed. A similar pattern is followed by other nations.

CREW'S CUSTOMS DECLARATION. An itemized list of all goods brought into a country from a foreign port, or if none, so declared, by each crew member of a merchant vessel. For customs use, the document is essentially a manifest, and any duties on goods thus declared must be paid. Such articles as are prohibited being landed are placed under seal.

CRIB. A heavy box-shaped cellular frame of logs or heavy timber filled with concrete, stones, rubble, etc. and sunk to form a foundation for a revetment, pier, dam, or dock. A raft of timber; to make up such raft; to tow several logs in raft form. The

cluster *Præsepe* (*L.,* = *a stall or fold*) in the constellation *Cancer.*

CRIBBING. Keel-blocks, bilge-blocks, shores, and their accessories collectively, on which a vessel is supported in dry-dock or when building. **C.-ram,** a piece of timber used as a battering-ram and swung by 6 to 10 men in knocking out cribbing before launching a vessel.

CRIMP. One engaged in the past practice of "shanghaiing," or luring or forcing men, by various nefarious means, into shipping as seamen; one who extorts money from, or swindles, seamen. To "shanghai" or illegally procure seamen for a vessel. In shipbuilding, to *joggle,* or *set in,* part of a plate for purpose of obtaining a faying surface for overlapping parts; as, to *crimp* 'or joggle an edge of overlapping shell-plating, which allows the latter to fay against frames and thus dispense with liners, or filling-pieces, between plate and frames.

CRINGLE. An iron or rope strop or grommet on bolt-rope of a sail to which a sheet, tack, earing, leech-line, reef-tackle, etc., is secured. It usually takes the form of a circular galvanized iron ring of concave cross section around which a strand of hemp rope is worked, called a *cringle-strop,* to hold it close and tight-fitting to the bolt-rope. Formerly, strop itself was termed a cringle, but metal ring only now takes the name; however, in light sails, such as carried in boats, the term often denotes an eyelet worked in the canvas, as at clew, tack, throat, or peak, in a gaff sail. **Bowline-c.,** see BOWLINE. **Bull's-eye c.,** see BULL'S EYE. The particular cringle is indicated in such terms as *clew c., head c., leech-line c., luff c., peak c., reef c., spilling-line c., tack c., throat c.* **C.-fid,** a large cone-shaped piece of hard wood, about 6 inches base diameter and some 30 inches in length, used in sail-making for stretching a cringle-strop to receive the metal cringle; also used for splicing large fiber hawsers.

CRINOLINE. A frame-work fitted in a tank of a cable-ship to keep each coil sufficiently spread so that kinking of cable will be prevented as it is payed out.

CRITICAL SPEED. That of reciprocating engines at which abnormal vibration in a vessel's hull takes place. It is usually attributed to synchronization of vibrational period of a vessel's mass with that of a harmonic vibrational cycle resulting from a certain propeller resistance, combined with vertical and circular motion of engine parts.

CROJIK. A sailor's phonetic spelling of *crossjack* as commonly pronounced. *See* CROSSJACK.

CROOK. Any one of various naturally formed crooked or curved pieces cut from a hard wood tree (usually oak), which are made into such angled members as breasthooks, beam knees, thwart knees, aprons, or stern knees, in boat-building.

CROPPING. In *rope-making,* process of combing out short fibers of flax, hemp, etc., to render the yarns suitable for finer and better class rope. In *ship repair work,* cutting away a damaged part of structure which is to be rebuilt or replaced.

CROSS. A descriptive combining term indicating across, athwart, from side to side, contrarily, unfavorably. The southern constellation *Crux;* also, sometimes, the four stars forming a cross in *Cygnus.* To send aloft and secure a yard in proper position or, as formerly, a square sail. **C.-beam,** in older sailing-ship usage, a heavy rounded piece of hard wood supported by, and connecting, the knight-heads or windlass bitts on which the hemp anchor cable was made fast; also, *c.-piece.* A hatch beam; *see* HATCH. **C.-bearings,** *see* BEARING. **C.-bunker,** in coal-burning steam-vessels, a bunker adjoining the fire-room and extending athwartships entire breadth of ship. **C.-channel boat,** a popular name for one of those small liners or packets, chiefly owned by railway companies, running between ports in Great Britain and those on the continent, Ireland, Channel Islands, etc. Many are capable of maintaining schedules, in connection with regular passenger train services, requiring a speed of 25 knots. **C.-chock,** *see* CHOCK. **C.-cut sail,** one in which its cloths run at right angles to its leech, as sometimes found in smaller yachts. **C. hawse, c. in hawse,** said of two anchor cables when crossed due to swinging of a vessel through 180°, as when moored, or having one anchor laid upstream and other downstream. Thus, after riding to starboard anchor, on change of tide vessel swings stern to port, a *c. hawse* will result; whereas, a swing stern to starboard will keep cables clear, or she will have a *clear hawse.* **C.-keelson,** *see* KEELSON. **C.-leech,** one of two bolt-ropes sewn to a main course or cross-jack, extending on sail's forward side from each head cringle diagonally to middle of the foot, where they were spliced to a ring. A *midship tack* was attached to this ring and made fast to a kevel when, in a quartering wind, weather clew of sail was hauled up. Hence, cross-leeches served to take the stress in a similar manner to regular leech-ropes, while giving sail a proper set under conditions referred to. This arrangement is said to have first appeared in American clipper ships and was used in many larger vessels of more recent type. **C.-lining,** *see* LINING. **C.-piece,** same as *cross-beam, q.v.* **C.-planking,** as distinguished from fore-and-aft planking in boat-building, that forming a flat bottom and laid at right angles to the fore-and-aft line, or in V-bottomed craft usually laid canting slightly aft and meeting at the keel. **C.-pointing,** originally, a method of tapering a rope's end by cutting away the inner yarns and braiding or weaving the part with some of its outer yarns; later, a covering of interwoven strips of canvas worked on a stanchion,

ring, man-rope, ladder-rail, etc. **C.-riveting,** *see* RIVETING. **C. sea,** a choppy and often confused sea in which waves are running in different directions; caused by either a sudden shift of wind or a current running against the wind. **C.-seizing,** *see* SEIZING. **C. set,** said of current effect in a direction at or about right angles to a vessel's course. **C.-spale,** in wood construction, a brace used to temporarily hold a frame in position until deck-beams are fitted and secured; also, *c.-spall, c.-pall, c.-pawl.* **C.-staff,** a 13th. to 16th.-century instrument for measuring altitudes of heavenly bodies (usually that of the sun). It was a graduated staff on which a sliding cross arm was mounted as a sighting vane. An observer directed staff toward the sun so that lower end of its arm was in line with the horizon and his eye, while adjusting upper end of arm to line up with sun's center. Thus the cross staff or arm was moved outward for low altitudes and nearer the observer's eye when high altitudes were measured. **C. swell,** one swell running in a different direction to another, causing a confused surface without breaking or chopping as in a *cross sea.* **C.-tackle,** in old hemp-rigging days, a tackle for bowsing lower shrouds together below the top, in order to quickly tauten them as a temporary measure in heavy weather or during extraordinary motion in a seaway. **C. whistles,** referred to U.S. inland rules for prevention of collision, blowing of a one-blast whistle signal in answer to one of two blasts, or vice versa, indicating a steam-vessel desires to reverse the proposal of another. Where such differences occur, onus of keeping clear rests equally on each vessel, and both must reduce speed, stop, or reverse engines, and arrive at a clear understanding as to action to be taken in avoiding risk of collision.

CROSSBAR SHOT. *See* SHOT.

CROSSHEAD. Connecting part between a piston and a main rod on a pump or a reciprocating engine. **C. guide,** piece of hard smooth-faced metal fitted on inside of a cylinder column or engine frame on which the *shoe* of a crosshead slides. **C. links,** connecting links between a crosshead and a pump lever. **C. nut,** that which secures a piston-rod to a crosshead. **C. pin,** a pin connecting the main rod (connecting-rod) of an engine to the crosshead.

CROSSING THE LINE. *See* LINE.

CROSSJACK. (Pron. *krojek*) Square sail spread by the yard of same name, or lowest yard on the *mizzenmast,* of a 3- or 4-masted ship or a 4-masted barque; a mizzen course.

CROSSPIECE. *See* **c.-piece** *under* CROSS.

CROSSTREES. Two pieces of wood or metal laid athwartship on the trestletrees and forming a foundation for the top, or platform at lowermasthead, and also a means of spreading and securing topmast shrouds. They also are fitted at a topmasthead to spread top-gallant shrouds; similarly, at a schooner's lowermasthead.

CROTCH. *See* CRUTCH. **C.-rope,** a rope or tackle for steadying a boom as it lies in a crotch or crutch, as one leading to each quarter in a schooner.

CROW. A crowbar; a handspike. In popular navy usage, the eagle worn on a petty officer's sleeve as a rating-badge. *The Crow,* a constellation; *see* CORVUS. **C.-nest, crow's nest,** originally, a barrel lashed at fore or main topmast crosstrees or at top-gallant masthead in whaling ships, in which a man was stationed to keep a lookout for whales or floating ice; also called *the barrel* and *bird's nest.* The term now embraces any kind of protected station fitted aloft to accommodate a lookout man; especially, the rounded tub-shaped structure fixed to the foremast on large steam-vessels. **C.'s foot,** *see* CROWFOOT.

CROWD. To press, as, to *crowd sail,* or spread an unusual amount of canvas to effect increase in speed. To **c. off,** to work a vessel off from a lee shore under a heavy press of sail.

CROWFOOT. A split end of an iron deck-beam bent to form a knee. A double knee or fork bolted to adjacent deck-beams and forming a carling or side of a deck opening. An old term for a stand on which cooking or mess utensils were hung. A fancy stitch on a corner of a wall-pocket, bunk-curtain, etc. The several small ropes or cords rove through an *euphroe,* or tailed on a single rope, for supporting an awning from above by its backbone; in older square-rig days, a similar arrangement attached to foot-rope of a single topsail and leading forward to hold sail from battering against the top and rigging in light winds and calms. **C. halyard,** a lift or hoisting rope attached to an awning crowfoot.

CROWN. (*L. corona.*) Camber of a deck, tank top, hatch, etc.; *see* CAMBER. Lower or outer end of an old-fashioned anchor's shank, at which both arms meet; in stockless anchors, part at which the arms pivot; *see* ANCHOR. A knot formed on a rope's end by interweaving the strands as beginning of a *back-splice,* in which strands are tucked back into rope, or as a base for several different knots, as a *wall and crown,* a *double wall and crown, man-rope knot, star knot,* etc.; *see* KNOT. Top end, or *throat,* as opposed to the *breech,* of a block, at which end a rope is rove. **C. of a double bottom, c. of a tank,** *plating* forming a tank top; *camber* of such tank top. **C.-plate,** that forming a crown or top of any structure, as, a top plate on a shaft-tunnel. **C.-sheet,** plate forming a fire-box top in certain types of boilers.

CROWNING. *See* BECUEING.

CRUISE. (Du. *kruiser,* to zigzag or cruise.) A sea voyage. To sail in different directions, as for pleas-

ure or exploration, generally with reference to war-vessels and yachts. **Shakedown c.,** a short voyage for the purpose of "breaking in" a new vessel, her engines, and/or her crew to sea-going conditions and requirements.

CRUISER. A cruising vessel. The term appears originally applied to an 18th.-century *privateer,* thence to a *frigate,* and to-day covers several types of naval vessels of lesser armament and armor, but of greater speed than, a battleship. Also, a *motor yacht* fitted with living accommodation. **Armored c.,** one of high speed and large radius of action, having side armor and an armored deck. **Auxiliary c.,** a speedy armed merchant vessel used by a country's naval forces in time of war. **Battle c.,** a warship of equal armament to that of a battleship, but having less protective armor; a fast battleship. **Belted c.,** one with a belt of metal around her water-line and a protected deck. **Protected c.,** one having an armored deck and no side armor. **Scout c.,** one of light armament and high speed, used for reconnoitering; a *scout.*

CRUISER STERN. *See* STERN.

CRUISING RADIUS. Expressed in miles, distance a vessel is capable of covering at normal speed without re-fueling or re-storing; also termed *steaming range.*

CRUSTACEAN. (L. *crusta,* shell, rind.) Pertaining to the *Crustacea;* one of that large and widely distributed class of aquatic horny-shelled animals which includes the lobster, crab, crawfish, shrimp, prawn, barnacle, water-flea, etc.

CRUPPER-CHAIN. A heel-chain; *see* CHAIN.

CRUSHING-STRIPS. In launching a vessel, pieces of soft wood placed under the *fore poppet* on the sliding ways. As after body is water-borne, extra weight supported by poppet is locally cushioned in crushing the strips, thereby effecting a better distribution of load and consequent ease of local stress on hull.

CRUTCH. A forked support or bed, as a semi-circular piece of flat iron mounted on a stanchion, for securing a boom, spare yard, derrick, etc., when such are not in use; any forked, two-legged, scissors-like rest for a fore-and-aft sail boom. A breast-hook; a knee timber fitted horizontally over frames in a vessel's stern. A metal rowlock. Also, *crotch.* **C.-hole,** in a boat's rail, a hole for receiving a crutch stanchion to hold a boom; or a steering-oar crutch or rowlock. **Steering-c.,** a support for the steering-oar at after end of a lifeboat.

CRUX. (L. *crux,* cross, torture, trouble.) A constellation commonly known as the *Southern Cross,* located in about 60° S. declination and about 40° due south of *Corvus.* Four of its five stars, suitable for navigational use, mark the extremities of a well-defined cruciform figure, and, together with two brightest stars of *Centaurus* lying west of, and pointing toward, the Cross at 9½° distance, present an imposing sight. *Alpha* (α) *Crucis,* a double star of magnitude 1.05, is brightest in group and marks Cross's foot, or southernmost limit.

C.T. An abbreviation for *Chronometer Time,* as commonly used in navigation text-books.

CUBIC CAPACITY. As applied to cargo stowage, total space representing a vessel's accommodation for bulky goods; also referred to as *measurement capacity;* and usually expressed in cubic feet. *Bale capacity* is taken as limited by the inward surfaces of cargo-battens, or, in absence of these by inward edges of frames; lower edges of deck-beams; and, usually, inward edges of bulkhead stiffeners. *Grain capacity* is given as total space within a compartment's bounds.

CUBIC MEASUREMENT. *See* MEASUREMENT.

CUBIC NUMBER. For comparative purposes in naval architectural design of similar type vessels, a numeral equal to one-hundredth the product of length, breadth, and depth.

CUCKOLD'S KNOT. The two parts of a bight of a rope simply crossed and seized together at their crossing point; also, *cuckold's neck.*

CUDDY. Formerly, a room or cabin below the poop, in which officers and cabin passengers took their meals. A galley or pantry in a small vessel; also, a small deck-house. A locker in a boat: hence, any cupboard for odds and ends. A wooden tray in after end of a boat for coiling down a drift net.

CULLING. Act of sorting fish, oysters, crabs, clams, etc., according to size and quality, or marketable value.

CULMINATION. (L. *culmen,* top or ridge.) Act of culminating or crossing the meridian; said of a heavenly body at *transit* or *meridian passage.* When a body's apparent diurnal path is circumpolar, *i.e.,* its polar distance less than an observer's latitude, both upper and lower culminations take place in the visible heavens. These are separated by an interval of 12 apparent solar hours, if the sun; and 12 sidereal hours in the case of a star (equal to 11 hrs. 58 min. 02 sec. of mean solar time). At upper culmination body attains its greatest altitude; at lower culmination, its least; and at either point its measured altitude provides the basis for determining latitude by simplest means possible. **Moon culminations,** *see* MOON.

CULVERIN. (Fr. *coulevrine,* serpent-like.) Originally, a kind of musket; later, in 16th. and 17th. century ship ordnance, longest and heaviest gun in ordinary use, corresponding to an 18-pounder of later times. The gun's weight was about 50 cwt. A smaller one of similar form, called a *demi-culverin,* fired a 9-lb. shot and weighed 30 cwt. Such weapons were highly ornamented and those of French make were often cast with handles of serpent design.

CUMSHAW. (Phonetic spelling of an *Amoy* word meaning "grateful thanks.") Originally, a gratuity paid to ships entering the port of Canton; hence, a present, gift, tip, bakshish, Also, *kumshaw.*

CUMULUS. *See* CLOUD.

CUMULO-NIMBUS. *See* CLOUD.

CUNARDER. One of a famous fleet of trans-Atlantic passenger vessels owned by Cunard S.S. Co. of Liverpool, England, and founded by Sir Samuel Cunard (*1787–1865*). First to cross the Atlantic was the *Britannia* in 1840, Liverpool to Halifax, Nova Scotia, and Boston; and first to enter the New York service, the *Hibernia,* in 1847. Other noted vessels of the line were *Persia, Etruria, Umbria, Campania, Lucania, Lusitania* (sunk by enemy action May 7, 1915, with a loss of 1198 lives), *Mauretania* (launched 1906 and holder of speed record for 22 years), *Aquitania;* and present *Queen Mary* and *Queen Elizabeth.* The two last-named, each over 1000 feet in length, of over 80,000 gross tons, and capable of speeds in excess of 30 knots, are largest liners afloat. Although maintaining their individualities as *Cunarders,* the ships now operate with those of White Star Line as Cunard-White Star fleet.

CUNNINGHAM PATENT REEF. A method devised in the mid-clipper era and named for its inventor, for reefing a single topsail by rolling it upon its yard. As yard was lowered, it revolved by its own weight, due to the tye being rigged as a parbuckle, thus rolling up or reefing as required. Owing to necessity of splitting the sail in way of the tye, and requirement of a flat full sail, before an even rolling of canvas was assured; also, due to contemporary advent of the promising double-topsail rig (*1853*), the device appears to have found little favor.

CUPRO NICKEL. An alloy of 70% copper and 30% nickel used in making condenser tubes and sea-water lines on board ship.

CURRACH or CURRAGH. (Gael. *currach;* Ir. *curachan.*) A larger and more boat-like form of a *coracle,* peculiar to Ireland and west coast of Scotland.

CURRENT. A progressive horizontal motion of the water caused by advance or recession of a tide wave in comparatively shallow or restricted waters, or by action of a prevailing wind upon the sea surface; although, to some extent, differences of sea-water density and atmospheric pressure are known to influence, if they are not a source of, certain surface motion observed on the oceans. Direction toward which a current flows is termed its *set,* and its velocity, *drift.* Other than *tidal currents,* or those directly caused by the tide wave in any locality, ocean currents are divided into two general classes, viz., *drift* or *surface,* and *stream currents. Drift c's* are produced by surface wind action, their velocity, depth, extent, and permanence depending upon steadiness in direction and force of the wind. A *stream c.* is a development of a drift current which, in its course, becomes confined to comparatively narrow waters, or is forced to deviate from its original direction of flow by a coast-line or decreasing depth of the sea floor. Other currents of variable or intermittent flow are difficult to account for and generally are considered as resultants of natural flow, generated by displaced levels in the ocean's surface, complicated by obstructing land configurations, variation in sea-depth, and changeable winds. General current circulation in oceanic waters takes a clockwise path over the North Atlantic and North Pacific, and Indian bodies. The beginning of these huge circular sweeps may be placed, respectively, with the great *North* and *South Equatorial* drift currents of the Atlantic and Pacific, and *Indian Ocean Equatorial c.,* which continuously are spurred on by the trade winds in their westward flow along the equator. Important units in these circulations are the *Kuroshiwo* or *Japan Stream (see* KUROSHIWO); *Gulf Stream (see* GULF STREAM); and *Agulhas* or *Mozambique C. (see* AGULHAS CURRENT). **Arctic C.,** *see* ARCTIC. **Black C.,** *see* KUROSHIWO. **Chilean C.,** a continuation of a north-easterly drift from Antarctic regions setting along coasts of Chile and Peru; called also, *Chilean, Humboldt,* and *Peruvian.* **Counter-c.,** *see* COUNTER. **Determination of c.** set and drift is effected by (*a*) direct observation from a vessel at anchor; (*b*) a comparison of positions of a vessel at sea, as, respectively, determined by astronomical observation or bearings of fixed shore objects and by careful reckoning of position by account (dead reckoning); and (*c*) by drift of floating objects carried by a current from a given location to another. **Guinea C.,** a counter stream which is a continuation of the *Equatorial Counter-c.* setting eastward between the *North* and *South Equatorial c's;* it flows close to and along the African Guinea Coast. **Gulf Stream,** an important *stream c.; see* GULF STREAM. **Humboldt C.,** *see* **Chilean C. Kamchatka C.,** a branch of the *Kuroshiwo,* or *Japan Stream,* beginning in 40½° N. Lat. and 146½° E. Long. and flowing toward the Aleutians. **Labrador C.,** same as *Arctic C.; see* ARCTIC. **Littoral c's,** those flowing generally parallel to, and near a coast. **Non-tidal c.,** one not directly caused by ebb or flow of tide; a *drift* or *stream c.* **Rennel's C.,** one setting north-westward across mouth of English Channel, only after continuous westerly gales have forced a rise in water in Bay of Biscay. **Screw-c.,** *see* SCREW. **Storm-c.,** one that is set up by winds of gale force from same general direction; also, one caused by a combination of wind force and tendency of flow toward the low barometric pressure area of a cyclonic storm. **Submarine c's,** those flowing at considerable depths below surface. **Tidal c.,** that directly caused by periodic advance and recession of the tide wave at a local coastal area, or what is commonly termed *tidal flow* and *ebb.* **Tidal c. chart,** *see* CHART. **Wake-c.,** *see* WAKE.

CURTAIN, ARMS'. *See* ARMS.

CURTAIN-PLATE. A vertical fore-and-aft plate to which ends of deck-beams of a superstructure are butted, where such deck is supported by stanchions or open frames.

CURTAL-AX; CURTLE-AX; CURTELASSE; CURTLAX. Archaic corruptions of *cutlass.*

CURVE. (L. *curvare,* to curve.) A line joining a succession of graphically plotted values and that is straight in no part; a bending without angles, as an *arch.* **C's of area,** *see* **C's of cross-sectional areas and waterplane areas** below. **Fair c's,** those in which all points show harmony with respect to their sweep as a whole, as opposed to those containing irregular departures from, or interferences with, an obviously proper delineation. **Loxodromic c., line,** or **spiral,** a rhumb line; a course, other than true east or west, represented by a straight line on a Mercator chart; *see* LOXODROMIC.

CURVES OF SHIP CALCULATIONS. C. of buoyancy, one in which longitudinal strength requirements, considered jointly with a *curve of weights,* are indicated at all points throughout a ship's length. Ordinates representing buoyancy force are drawn perpendicular to a baseline scaled to vessel's length. Height of center of buoyancy above baseline usually is also given. **C. of centers of gravity of water-planes,** shows location of center of gravity of water-plane (*center of flotation*) at any draft. On a transverse axis through this point, which is also called the *tipping center,* a vessel pivots during a change of trim; *see* TRIM. **C. of cross-sectional areas** gives underwater cross-sectional areas throughout a vessel's length at a given draft. **C. of displacement,** one indicating tons of displacement (*tons of 2240 lbs.*) in fresh or sea water at any draft. (Weight of water a ship displaces is equal to total weight of vessel and everything on board.) **C. of flotation,** a locus of centers of flotation (*centers of gravity of water-planes*) for all water-planes, at a given displacement, through a range of possible angles of heel. **C. of loads,** derived from information shown in a *curve of weights* and a *curve of buoyancy,* used in various calculations and investigation in longitudinal strength requirements. **C. of longitudinal shearing stresses** is drawn from conclusions arrived at in calculations producing *curve of loads.* From this information necessary longitudinal structural strength is determined. **C. of longitudinal**

centers of buoyancy, a locus of centers of buoyancy, as measured forward or aft from half-length point, under various draft conditions. **C. of resistance** indicates hull resistance, usually in tons, at various speeds, as determined by experiments made in towing a model of a particular vessel. **C. of righting arms** (*or levers*), same as *c. of statical stability*. **C. of statical stability** gives all values of righting arm in a vessel's range of possible heel (usually 0° to 60°) at various drafts. Since this information takes no account of changes in height of center of gravity, a correction equal to distance in feet of rise or depression of that value times sine of the heeling angle, multiplied by displacement (*in tons*), must be applied to give righting moment for any condition of loading other than that for which curve is calculated. (A rise of center of gravity decreases, and its lowering increases, the righting arm.) **C. of tons per inch immersion** gives number of tons (2240 lbs.) which must be loaded to increase a ship's mean draft one inch at a particular water-line. **C. of transverse metacenters,** one showing height above base-line of metacenter at any displacement or mean draft. (*Base-line* is lowest point of the floor-plates in the midship line.) **C. of vertical centers of buoyancy,** a locus of centers of buoyancy at any angle of heel, as referred to base and vertical midship lines in the cross-sectional area. **C. of water-plane areas,** one giving area (usually in square feet) of water-plane corresponding to any draft. **C. of weights** represents weight of a ship with her cargo, as locally borne throughout each unit of structure's length. The *curve of buoyancy* indicates buoyant force acting contrariwise to weight (or *gravity*) and, consequently discloses presence of any abnormal bending or shearing stress in the structure.

CUSK. An edible fish, 2½ to 3 feet in length, allied to the cod; found on northern coasts of America and Europe; also called *tusk* or *torsk,* and, in some north-east U.S. and Canadian localities, *burbot* or *ling.*

CUSP. (L. *cuspis,* point.) One of the points or horns of a crescent moon; an angular projection of a beach, often near a point, formed by sand or silt deposit from conflicting currents.

CUSTOM OF THE PORT. Established usage or practice at a particular port, generally with reference to stevedoring costs, mooring, docking, towage, etc. Adherence in fact to an uncommon, but prevailing, custom of a port often carries much weight in cases at law arising from cargo expense claims, charterers' redress, and other maritime contentions.

CUSTOM. Customs duties, imposts, or tolls, levied by a country on goods or merchandise imported or exported therefrom. **C's duty,** *see* DUTY. **C.-free,** duty-free; said of goods on which no duty is charged.

C's-house, local headquarters of the customs service. **C's service,** that branch of a government service engaged in collection of duties, enforcing customs laws, including prevention and suppression of smuggling and other practices designed to defraud the government; assisting in enforcement of certain navigation laws; registering, entering, and clearing merchant vessels. **C's surveyor,** an officer who checks contents of casks, quantities of dutiable liquors, etc.; a gauger. In U.S. ports, an officer under Collector of customs charged, among other duties, with execution of measures for determining condition, quantities, and values of imported goods. **C's waters,** term for such areas in which a customs service exercises its lawful right to board and examine a vessel or compel, by force or seizure, obedience of any vessel to customs laws of a country.

CUT. Style, shape, appearance; as, the *cut of a sail.* A combining verb, indicating performance; as, to *cut up a splash,* to *cut across the bow.* **To c. a feather,** an archaic form of *to have a bone in her teeth;* said of a vessel turning up a wave of white foam at her stem. **To c. away the rigging,** to relieve a ship of her top hamper by cutting shrouds, stays, etc., to allow masts to go by the board, as when the vessel has been thrown on her beam ends, or driven ashore. **To c. down a ship,** to reduce her size and class by taking away an upper deck. An old navy term for this procedure was *to razee;* any ship so reduced was called a *razee.* A **c. of oil,** a whaler's term for quantity of oil produced by a whale. **C. of one's jib,** *see* JIB. **To c. out,** in old navy usage, to capture and carry off, as a vessel from a harbor, or from under the guns of an enemy. **To c. and run,** to cut or slip the anchor cable when there is not time to make sail; hence, to suddenly and quickly depart. **To c. one's painter,** to set one adrift; hence, to be on one's way. **To c. the sail,** to cast off its gaskets and let a furled sail fall away from its yard. **C.-splice,** *see* BIGHT. **C.-up,** upward curving of a boat's keel toward either of its ends.

CUTCH. (Malay, *kachu.*) A resin-like extract from several kinds of Asiatic plants, especially, that from wood of the *Acacia catechu* or the *Acacia suma,* used in solution as a preservative for sails and fishing-nets; also called *Bengal catechu.*

CUTLASS. (Fr. *coutelas.*) A short, heavy sword, slightly curved toward its point, and having one cutting edge, formerly used by sailors in hand to hand fighting and in some navies still carried by boarding and landing parties; also, *cutlas.*

CUTLASS-FISH. One of a family of long, thin, eel-like fishes (*Trichiuridæ*), having a sharp-nosed head, tail extending to a slender point, continuous dorsal web-like fringe, and three to four feet in length; found in West Indies and southern U.S. waters, but generally widely distributed.

CUTTER. A single-masted fore-and-aft rigged vessel, usually with two to three head sails and a gaff-topsail. Though similar in rig, her essential difference to the *sloop,* in modern usage, lies in her deeper draft and narrower body lines, often, as in the *cutter yacht,* terminating in a large fin keel. A large general service boat carried by a man-o'-war, square-sterned, fitted for double-banked oars, and usually sailed with two lugs. A small steam-vessel in the revenue service; a U.S. Coast Guard vessel; any small powered or sailed vessel employed in a special service, as, a *pilot-c.;* a *mail-cutter.* **Pilot-c.,** *see* PILOT. **Steam c.,** a steam powered boat or launch carried by a warship or, in some trades, by a merchant-vessel.

CUTTING-DOWN LINE. *See* LINE.

CUTTING-FALL; CUTTING-PENDANT; CUTTING-TACKLE. Gear used in stripping blubber from a whale as, in older whaling days, carcass lay alongside. The *cutting-in-* or *flensing-tackle* led from the main-masthead, was hooked to the blubber, and hauled upon in operation of *flensing, i.e.,* removing blubber in long strips. *Cutting-spade,* a long-handled, flat chisel-shaped implement for cutting blubber from a whale's carcass, as used in sailing whalers from the *cutting-stage,* which was suspended over vessel's side above the floating mass.

CUTTLEFISH. *See* CALAMARY.

CUTWATER. A strengthening and protecting timber bolted to fore side of a vessel's stem. Often applied to the upper ornamental curve in a clipper bow. **C. bow,** *see* BOW.

C — W. (*C minus W*) Abbreviation for difference between time indicated on a chronometer and a navigator's watch time, as used in some navigation text-books and, especially, in standard U.S. navy practice.

CYCLONE. A violent storm originating in a tropical area and characterized by high velocity winds rotating about a calm center of unusually low barometric pressure, with almost continuous blinding rain. The whole circulating mass, from 50 to 200 miles in extent, moves onward at a rate varying from a few miles per hour to as high as 30. In general, storm begins its travel in a westerly direction, then slowly curves to higher latitudes and to eastward, finally dissipating after broadening out in a wide sea area. It revolves left-handed, or counterclockwise, in the northern hemisphere, and in southern hemisphere, right-handed, or clockwise. Cyclone wind velocity has been observed to reach 100 to 130 miles per hour. In *meteorology,* the term also denotes an atmospheric movement of any velocity in which winds blow spirally around and toward a center of relatively low barometric pressure. **C.-infested regions:** Western part of North Atlantic from 10° N. and 30° W. toward and through West Indies, Gulf of Mexico, and southeast U.S. coast, where they are called *hurricanes;* China Sea, Philippines, and Japan, where they are *typhoons* or *baguios;* Arabian Sea and Bay of Bengal, *cyclones;* South Indian Ocean, *cyclones;* South Pacific Ocean, western part, where called both *hurricanes* and *cyclones.*

C. seasons.—*West Indies,* July to October; *China Sea,* have occurred in every month, most prevalent July to October, inclusive; *Arabian Sea* and *Bay of Bengal,* April, May, June, October, and November; *South Indian Ocean,* December to April, inclusive; *South Pacific,* December to March, inclusive; *North Pacific,* July to October.

CYCLONIC. Similar in appearance or movement to a cyclone; situated where cyclones occur; as, a *cyclonic storm.* **Anti-c. wind,** *see* WIND. **C. wind,** *see* CYCLONE *and* WIND. **Secondary c.,** pertaining to a small cyclone sometimes immediately following an important cyclonic storm or disturbance. *See also* AREAS, **High and Low Pressure.**

CYCLONOGRAPH or **CYCLONOSCOPE.** A storm-card, or means of graphically determining bearing of a cyclone's center and consequent probable direction of its path of progression, given direction and shift, if any, of wind, and barometric pressure change. *See* **Buys-Ballot's Law** *and* **Law of Storms** *in* LAW.

CYGNUS. (*L. = a swan.*) A northern constellation in the *Milky Way,* adjoining and east of *Lyra,* in 19½ to 21 hours right ascension and 28 to 45 degrees declination. Its five principal stars form a well-defined Latin cross 22° in length, with *Deneb* (*a Cygni*), the brightest, of magnitude 1.3, marking the head or north-eastern extremity.

CYLINDER. (Gr. *kylindros,* to roll.) A chamber in an engine in which a piston is impelled by pressure of a fluid or gas, as in a reciprocating steam engine or an internal combustion engine. In a marine steam reciprocating engine, its usual three cylinders are named, respectively, *high pressure* (H.P.), *intermediate* (I.P.), and *low pressure* (L.P.). (Exhaust steam flows from H.P. to I.P. and in turn exhausts to L.P.; thence to condenser.) **Balance-c.,** a small one in which piston of a balance-valve works in a steam chest. **C.-columns,** vertical cast steel supports for cylinders and other elevated parts of a marine engine. **C. cover** or **head,** movable lid or end fastened as a marine engine cylinder-top by studs and nuts. Holes are bored in cover to fair with studs in the cylinder-flange. **C.-drains,** valves or cocks at cylinder ends for drawing off condensed steam. **C.-lagging,** covering of asbestos, or similar insulating material, around a steam *c.* encased by wood or metal sheathing. **C.-valve chest** or **receiver,** chamber containing the slide-valve for controlling delivery and exhaust of impelling agent in a *c.* **C.-valve face,** seat on which a *c.* slide-valve travels.

CYLINDRICAL BUOY. One of the can type, appearing above water as round-shaped and having a flat top. *See* **Can b.** *in* BUOY.

CYNOSURE. (Gr. *kynosoura,* dog's tail.) Anything that strongly attracts attention or admiration; that which serves as a guide; hence, an ancient name for the constellation *Ursa Minor,* or *Little Bear,* containing *Polaris,* the "North Star," which marks its tail end and to which the mariner's eyes customarily were directed; star *Polaris* itself.

CYPRESS. An excellent wood for planking material in boat-building, joiner work, and exposed surfaces in house-building. From a pinaceous tree native to southern and western U.S. and some parts of Europe and the Orient, its flexible and durable qualities for centuries have rendered it also adaptable for various curved members in ship construction. It is said that *gopher wood,* of which Noah's ark was built (*Genesis VI, 14*), is probably the *cypress.* The wood, when seasoned, weighs 40 pounds per cubic foot.

D

D. International Code signal flag, "dog," consisting of three horizontal stripes of yellow, blue, and yellow, respectively; hoisted singly, indicates "Keep clear of me—I am maneuvering with difficulty." "*d*" is often written as an abbreviation for *drizzling* in ships' log-books; also corresponds to Greek δ (delta), denoting the fourth star of a constellation in order of magnitude, usually as observed by ancient astronomers, *e.g.*, δ *Leonis*, fourth star (Zosma) in *Leo* (The L: n).

D. A. Abbreviation used in chartering and freighting documents, denoting vessel is to be *discharged afloat;* probably condensed from an old qualifying clause referring to destination of a chartered vessel, "or as near thereto as she can safely get, being at all times afloat."

DAB. An old term for any of the marks indicating unnamed points on a compass-card.

DADO. Area of dark-colored paint around lower part of engine-room and fire-room bulkheads.

DAGGER. Timber or steel plate built diagonally as fore-and-aft bracing in a launching-poppet; generally, any structural unit laid diagonally. **D.-board,** in small boats, a portable center-board, or one which may be lifted from its box into the boat. **D.-knee,** a beam-knee fitted diagonally inclined. **D.-planks,** those uniting heads of timbers in a launching-poppet; also, *d.-wood.*

DAHABIYEH. A large passenger-boat peculiar to the River Nile, of considerable breadth aft and narrowing forward to a gracefully curved cutwater; provided with a raised cabin containing a saloon and sleeping apartments, above which is an awning-shaded deck; formerly propelled by two lateen sails and/or oars, now usually engine-powered. Also, *dahabeah, dahabeyah, dahabieh.*

DAILY RATE. Referred to a chronometer, denotes amount of gain or loss in 24 hours, which change in error of a good instrument is nearly constant within ordinary ranges of temperature, and, generally is not more than 2 or 3 seconds.

DAK-BOAT. In India, a fast boat for carrying mail or passengers.

DALE. A trough or spout to carry off water; as, a *pump-dale.*

DAM. A watertight barrier or wall built to confine or hold back water during such operations as digging a graving-dock or repairing a quay wall. **Wing-d.,** *see* WING.

DAMAGE. **D. certificate,** issued by dock authorities or by a surveyor, stating certain goods in damaged condition are landed, with the apparent cause and extent of such damage. **D. protest,** *see* PROTEST. **D. repairs,** those repairs or replacements required by reason of heavy weather, stranding, collision, or other perils of the sea, as distinguished from those covering ordinary wear and tear. **D. survey,** that held by owners and/or underwriters in order to determine extent of damage to cargo or vessel and steps toward making adjustments or repairs. *See* COLLISION. **Detention d.'s,** charges claimed by a shipowner against a charterer, or by an owner or charterer against a shipper or consignee, for delay of a vessel beyond a specified period allowed for cargo operations. Expenses allowed a vessel for detention in port following settlement of, or repairs due to, a general average act. **Small D. Club,** *see* SMALL.

DAMPER. A movable iron plate, usually regulated by a chain, fitted in an uptake or smokestack, or in air-ducts leading to a boiler furnace, for controlling the draft.

DAN. A *dan-buoy,* or small float for marking position of fishing-gear; also used to indicate limits of mine-sweeping operational areas and usually carrying a flag on a light staff. (*England*)

DANCERS, MERRY. *See* AURORA.

DANDY. A British type of vessel having a large loose-footed mainsail, a jib, and a small mizzen or jigger, similar to the yawl rig; loosely, a *ketch or yawl*. The small sail, or mizzen, set at the stern of a yawl. A Ganges River boatman. An English term for a small capstan or winch fitted on fishing-vessels for hauling in a trawl. **D.-rig,** having the rig of a dandy or yawl.

DANDYFUNK. In American and British sailing-ships of old deep-water type, a dish consisting of broken sea-biscuits soaked in water and baked with salt pork or beef fat and molasses; a kind of *cracker hash*. Also, *dunderfunk*.

DANFORTH ANCHOR. *See* ANCHOR.

DANGER. D. angle, in coastwise navigation, angle between two known points determined by chart as that which would be observed at a safe passing distance from an out-lying shoal, sunken rock, etc.; called a *horizontal d. a.* when the known points are separated in azimuth, and a *vertical d. a.* when such points, as base and lantern of a lighthouse, are separated vertically. In employing a *horizontal d. a.*, advantage is taken of the geometrical theorem that "all angles subtended by a chord of a circle at its circumference are equal in the same segment." Consequently, at a chosen safe position or positions off such danger, angle observed between the two charted (*and recognized*) objects will be the same at all points on a circle whose circumference passes through ship and both shore objects or marks selected. Such marks preferably should be situated at approximately equal distances from ship at her closest approach to danger to be avoided. Nearing the danger, observation by sextant will determine whether ship is inside or outside the circle as laid down on chart: a greater angle indicating the former, and a smaller one, the latter condition. Ship's course is altered accordingly until danger is passed. Similarly, in using the *vertical d. a.*, an angle of elevation of a well-defined object, such as a lighthouse, of known height may be determined upon as that which would be observed at a safe distance off an out-lying danger; a lesser angle observed indicating a greater distance off, and a greater, that ship is closer to such danger than predetermined. Of the two, a *horizontal d. a.* is to be preferred, owing to its greater size and consequent sensitiveness to changes with departures from the *danger circle* drawn on the chart. *Double d. a's* may sometimes be used as checks against each other, when ship's course leads between two dangers. Angle protecting ship from an inshore danger then must not be allowed to increase, while that protecting from an outer one must not be allowed to decrease. **D. bearing,** *see* BEARING. **D. sector,** *see* SECTOR. **D. signal,** in U.S. Pilot Rules for Inland Waters, whistle signal consisting of several short blasts, not less than four, in rapid succession, required to be given by either of two approaching steam vessels (or powered vessels) which fails to understand the course or intention of the other. **D. zone,** an area defined as dangerous to navigation because of mines, sunken rocks, wrecks, etc.; *see* ZONE. **D's of the sea,** *see* **Perils of the sea** *in* SEA.

DANGEROUS GOODS. As a cargo term, includes explosives and all substances of an inflammable nature which are liable to spontaneous combustion, either in themselves or when stowed adjacent to certain other substances, and which, when mixed with air, are liable to generate explosive gases and so produce tainting of food-stuffs, contamination of other cargo, and poisoning or suffocation of persons. Most maritime countries control stowage of such goods by law, and, in general, passenger vessels are forbidden them, excepting under certain conditions as deck cargo, where they may be thrown overboard at a moment's notice.

DANGEROUS SEMICIRCLE. That part or half of a cyclone's nearly circular area in which the wind tends to carry a vessel toward the *line of progression,* or storm's line of advance. In northern hemisphere cyclones, it is half the storm area lying to right of its direction of advance; conversely, that lying to left in southern cyclones.

DANUBE RUDDER. *See* RUDDER; SALMON-TAIL. Cf. *Suez Canal Rudder.*

DANUBE RULE. A rule for calculating *net tonnage; see* RULE.

DAP. A shallow groove cut in a timber to receive a flat metal strap or other fitting.

DARK-LIGHT. A dead-light; *see* LIGHT.

DASHBOARD. A screening board at a boat's bow to throw off spray; a *spray-board*. A paddle-wheel float.

DASHER-BLOCK. *See* BLOCK.

DASH-PLATE. *See* PLATE.

DATE LINE. Usually termed *International Date Line,* fixed by international agreement as joining all places at which each calendar day *first begins.* It roughly follows the 180th. meridian, being laid out so that all Asia, with Chatham Island and Tonga Islands of the South Pacific, lie west of it, and all America, including Aleutian Islands, east of it. In order to reconcile both calendar and ship's log with change of date on crossing the *date line,* navigators adhere to the old practical rule: "*When eastward bound, add a day; when westward bound, drop a day.*" Thus, if crossing is made, sailing eastward, on a Sunday, the following day also is called Sunday; conversely, if sailing westward, next day is called Tuesday.

DATUM. A level or plane of reference from which the height of tide is reckoned. Where small diurnal inequalities in tidal rise or fall exists, such datum is usually level of low water at ordinary springs. At certain localities, mean level of lower low water is taken; at others, mean low water. The tidal *datum* is given on charts of coastal waters published by almost all maritime nations.

DAVID. A small boat, submerged until nearly awash and carrying a torpedo, constructed by Confederates during U.S. Civil War, 1861–1865. **David's staff,** corruption of *Davys's staff* or *quadrant.*

DAVIS'S QUADRANT. See DAVYS'S QUADRANT.

DAVIT. A light curved or straight-armed crane for lifting and lowering boats, anchors, accommodation-ladders, or other permanent equipment; usually in pairs, when fitted for boats. Small single davits are sometimes called *goosenecks.* **Anchor-d.,** see ANCHOR. **Cat-d.,** a cathead, or iron *d.* replacing it. **D.-guys,** ropes leading from davit heads for turning them into a desired position. **D.-socket,** casting or fitting in which the heel of a *d.* of horizontal turning type is supported. **D.-span,** length of chain or rope extending between *d.*-heads as a continuation of guys to prevent rotating *d's* from spreading apart. **Fish-d.,** one used for *fishing* or hoisting an anchor from the water to its place on the bow. **Gravity-d's,** those controlling a boat which is cradled on rollers for carrying it sideways down an inclined skidway to the vessel's side. Upon easing away each boat-fall, both davit and boat move by gravity until boat hangs clear of ship's side ready for lowering. When hoisting boat aboard, as it draws hard up to *d.*-heads, lifting is continued until *d's,* in their vertical planes, are hove inboard with boat rolling up along its skids until finally cradled as before. This *d.* arrangement has the advantage of stowing boats clear of a deck and, also, that a heavy boat may be launched at a moment's notice by simply easing away its wire-rope falls by means of a brake-controlled winch specially provided for the purpose. **Hatch-d.,** a small *d.* fitted at a hatchway for loading or unloading light weights, provisions, stores, etc. **Hose-d.,** one used on oil tank vessels for lifting or supporting cargo-hose. **Mechanical-d.,** one which is swung or turned outboard and inboard by any type of mechanical gearing, as distinguished from one turned directly by hand. **Quadrant-d.,** one having a straight arm at base of which is attached a toothed arc set in a horizontal rack on deck. By means of a crank and threaded spindle it is turned in or out in a thwartship plane. It has the advantage of an ordinary hand-rotated *d.* in that it may easily be moved outward to the high side of a listing vessel, and also that it is entirely independent of guys. Also called *quadrantal-d.* and *Welin d.* **Rotating-d.,** one which turns or may be swung round in its support; common round-bar type. **Swan-neck d.,** one of gravity type, or any one having a curved upper end.

DAVY JONES. Spirit of the sea; the devil; "Jimmy Square-foot." **D.J.'s locker,** bottom of the sea;

grave of those lost at sea; great common receptacle for useless articles or material—overboard.

DAVYS'S QUADRANT or **STAFF.** Named for John Davys (or *Davis*), an English navigator (*1550–1605*), for whom Davis Strait is also named; *see* BACKSTAFF.

DAWN. First appearance of daylight in the eastern sky. **High d.,** that first showing above a cloudbank; an indication of breezy weather. **Low d.,** that first appearing on the horizon; usually presages light winds and fine weather.

DAY. Time interval between two successive meridian transits of a heavenly body, as a *solar,* a *sidereal,* or a *lunar day.* Recurring period of sunlight, as opposed to that of night or darkness. **Antipodean d.,** a calendar day added or dropped on crossing the 180th. meridian or International Date Line; *see* ANTIPODEAN DAY. **Astronomical d.,** period of 24 mean solar hours from midnight to the following midnight, corresponding to the *civil d.* Prior to 1925, it was reckoned from mean noon, since and including which date nautical almanacs conform to the change. **Banian d.,** formerly, among sailors, a day on which no meat was served; probably named for an Indian caste of traders who will eat no flesh; also, *banyan d.* **Civil d.,** same as *astronomical d.* **D.-book,** old term for a *log-book.* **D. gained or lost,** see ANTIPODEAN DAY. **D's of grace,** period during which neutral vessels are allowed by a belligerent to leave a blockaded port; period following outbreak of war in which a vessel is granted permission to depart from an enemy's port or coasts. Number of days (usually three) allowed for payment of a bill of exchange after it becomes due. **D.-shape,** see **black ball** *in* BALL. **Lay-d's,** *see* LAY. **Lunar d.,** *see* LUNAR. **Mean solar d.,** *see* MEAN. **Nautical d.,** period beginning at noon and ending at noon of following day, in accordance with custom of reckoning ship's run, fuel and water consumption, etc., as from noon to noon, Formerly, apparent noon, or instant of true sun's meridian passage, terminated the ship's day, but, of late years, *zone* or *standard mean time* corresponding to each 15th. degree of longitude, and area included between 7½ degrees on either side of such longitude, generally has been adopted; *see* **zone time** *in* TIME. **Overlap d's,** number of days, or "overlap time," in which a charterer holds a vessel beyond date of her re-delivery as stipulated in the charter party. **Reversible d's,** *see* **time reversible** *in* TIME. **Running d's,** *see* RUNNING. **Ship's d's,** those allowed a vessel to load or discharge, as referred to in a charter party. **Sidereal d.,** *see* SIDEREAL. **Solar d.,** *see* SOLAR. **Tide** or **tidal d.,** *see* TIDE.

DAY'S WORK. Account or reckoning of courses and distances run from noon to noon of the nautical day.

DAZZLE PAINTING. Scheme of coloring or camouflaging a ship's outside surfaces with various contrasting tints in order to confuse an enemy as to type of vessel and her estimated course, speed, or distance off; any camouflage pattern followed with the objectives indicated. *Camouflage.*

D.D. Abbreviation used in U.S. navy for *dishonorable discharge.*

DEAD. Inert; inactive; as, a *d. sheave.* Absolute; entire; complete; as, *d. calm; d. low water; d. stop.* Exactly; directly; as, *d. ahead.* **D.-door,** in older sailing war-vessels, a heavy shutter fitted to a stern door for use in heavy weather. **D.-fire,** *see* CORPOSANT. **D.-flat,** part of a ship's side or bottom where planking or plating has no curvature; midship transverse section of a hull. **D.-freight,** money paid by a charterer or shipper for cargo space engaged but not occupied. **D.-head,** *see* DEADHEAD. **D. end of a pipe,** closed end of a line or system of piping. **D. horse,** in British deep water sailing-ships, indebtedness or work performed for the usual *month's advance* which seamen were paid upon signing articles for a voyage. On completion of the first month, or period of "working up the dead horse," at which time wages were considered as really beginning to be earned, an effigy of a *horse* was made of old canvas stuffed with shavings, junk rope, oakum, etc. Ceremoniously and to the tune of an appropriate long-drawn chantey, such as "Poor old man, your horse is dead; hang him, boys, hang him," the *horse* was hoisted by the neck to the weather fore yardarm, there temporarily poised during three lusty cheers from all hands, then cut adrift and overboard. The occasion thereupon was consummated in a serving of rum at the order "All hands—grog-O!" **D. lift,** a direct raising of a weighty object without any mechanical advantage. **D. load,** weight of cargo and stores carried by a vessel; a load steadily applied, as weight of merchandise stored in a warehouse. **D. low,** lowest level reached by a falling tide. **D. man's eye,** *see* DEADEYE. **D. men,** ends of reef-points or gaskets improperly exposed upon furling a sail; empty bottles. **D. men's lines,** long string-like sea-weed; *sea-lace.* **D. muzzler,** a strong head wind. **D.-peg,** to work directly to windward. **D.-plate,** cast-iron piece supporting front ends of furnace fire-bars. **D.-point,** position in which a crank axle, crankpin, and connecting-rod are in a straight line; *d. center.* **D. reckoning,** practice of finding a vessel's position at sea from courses steered and distance run on each course at any time subsequent to determination of the position by shore bearings or celestial observations; originally termed *deduced reckoning,* abbreviation *ded.* was corrupted to *dead.* **D. rope,** a line which is used without being rove in a block or running over a sheave. **D. sheave,** a non-turning half sheave fixed in any position as a lead for a rope; a score in the heel of an upper mast through which the mast-rope runs when lowering or sending the spar aloft. **D. water,** eddying water along a moving vessel's sides, especially under her counter; still water, as that during interval between last of an ebb and beginning of a flood tidal stream. **D.-wood,** *see* DEADWOOD. **D.-works,** *see* WORK.

DEADEN. To retard; hinder; lessen momentum of; as, to *d.* a ship's way; to *d.* a shock.

DEADEYE. A stout flat and rounded block of hard wood, usually lignum vitae, pierced with smooth leading holes, through which a lanyard is rove; fitted at ends of shrouds, stays, etc. for setting up purposes. Now greatly displaced by the *turnbuckle* or *rigging-screw.* Also, *dead man's eye.*

DEADHEAD. Heavy post on a wharf or quay to which hawsers are made fast; a bollard; a block of wood used as an anchor-buoy.

DEAD HORSE. *See* DEAD.

DEADLIGHT. An iron shutter fitted to clamp against the inside of a port-light in heavy weather; a heavy piece of glass inserted in a deck for lighting purposes. In older usage, a wood shutter for a cabin window, side-port, etc. A corposant.

DEADMAN. A log, timber, anchor, etc., placed to advantage on shore as a temporary mooring-post. Also *d.-man,* *see* DEAD.

DEADRISE. Height to which a vessel's frame rises from the horizontal, as measured to intersection of a vertical, tangent to molded breadth distance point, with line of frame extended from vessel's keel; also termed *rise of floor, rise of bottom. See* SKIPJACK. **Deadrising,** a curved line on sheer plan showing sweep of floors throughout vessel's length.

DEADWEIGHT. Total weight a vessel carries when immersed to her authorized load draft, including cargo, mail, fuel, water, stores, crew, passengers, baggage, and personal effects. **D. capacity; d. carrying-capacity;** usually taken as difference between light displacement and load displacement or that when floating at summer load draft, expressed in *long tons (2240 lbs.)* or *metric tons (2204.6 lbs.),* according to use in country concerned. (Each ton weight loaded increases displacement by one ton.) Also termed *d. tonnage.* **D. cargo,** goods stowing at 40 cubic feet or less per ton weight, as distinguished from *measurement cargo,* or that of greater bulk than 40 cu. ft. per ton. Generally, freight is charged for *d.* cargo according to weight; for measurement cargo according to space occupied. **D. cargo capacity,** vessel's *d.* capacity, less weight of fuel, stores, water, and all else not included in her equipment; also termed *cargo d. tonnage.* **D. cargo factor,** for similar type ships, a constant multiplied by the net tonnage to obtain a close approximation to *d. cargo capacity.* **D. efficiency,** ratio of *d.* capacity to designed load displacement. **D. ratio** or *d. — dis-*

placement coefficient, ratio of *d.* cargo capacity or weight of paying load to displacement at load draft; varies from about .25 for an express passenger vessel to about .75 for a cargo vessel. **D. scale,** one indicating *d.* carried at all drafts between light and load lines.

DEADWOOD. In wooden ships, mass of timber built up vertically from the keel at fore foot and stern-post on which the cant frames are stepped; the term has been extended to plating thus built up near the stern-post of a steel ship. In boat-building, knees or inner strengthening pieces joining keel to stem and stern posts.

DEAL GALLEY. (Named for *Deal,* a town on the Kentish coast of England.) A fast-sailing, single-masted boat, 25 to 30 feet in length, having a standing lug, with the remarkable feature of spreading one of her two identical sails at each time of coming about on a new tack. Peculiar to the English southeast coast, the type was for many years extensively used in attendance on the almost continuous fleet of merchant ships arriving in the Downs, as landing and supplying pilots, bringing off provisions, carrying dispatches, etc. With the decline of sail tonnage and advent of motor power, the old Deal galley soon passed into history.

DEC. Abbreviation commonly used in nautical astronomy for *declination,* as *dec. 15° N.*

DECCA. *See* LORAN.

DECK. (Du. *dekken,* to cover.) Plating or planking secured to, and covering all or part of, any tier of beams; the floor of any compartment. Decks laid in the main body of a ship's hull form an important component in her structural strength, both transversely and longitudinally. They are named for their location, as a *weather d.;* for their purpose, as a *promenade d.;* may be specially designated as a *trunk d.;* or, in large passenger vessels as *A* deck; *B* deck; *C* deck; etc., downward. To furnish with a deck. **After d.,** general term for a *d.* or portion of *d.* area abaft the midship part of a vessel. **Anchor d.,** see same in ANCHOR. **Awning d.,** *see* AWNING. **Berth d.,** *see* BERTH. **Boat d.,** superstructural *d.* on which is located the arrangement for stowage of life-boats. Usually so designated only on passenger vessels, may be either part of a *d.* on which housing for state-rooms, etc. is located or an entire *d.* above same. **Boiler d.,** that on which ship's boilers are situated; almost always is an inner bottom tank-top. **Bridge d.,** that above a partial superstructure about amidships, or first *d.* amidships above an upper continuous *d.* **Bright d's,** those of wood, well cleaned and oiled or varnished. **Bulkhead d.,** uppermost continuous *d.* forming limit of watertight subdivision arrangement in the hull. Bulkheads separating watertight compartments required by law extend from ship's bottom to this *d.* To **clear the d's,** to clear for action, as, to remove

gear or other obstacles preparatory to a naval engagement. **D.-beam,** one of the many transverse structural members which support a vessel's *d's,* stiffen her frames, withstand racking stresses, and generally supply the chief requirement for lateral strength. **D.-beam clamp,** *see* CLAMP. **D.-beam dimensions,** *molding* of a *d.*-beam is its form indicated by vertical dimensions, i.e., depth of material and camber; *siding* is its horizontal thickness. **D.-beam stringer-plate,** *see* **D.-stringer. D.-block,** a leadblock secured to the deck. **D.-bolts,** *see* BOLT. **D. bull's eye,** a deadlight; *see* **D.-light. D. camber,** *see* CAMBER. **D. cargo,** goods carried in any exposed or uncovered space; usually termed *deck-load* in the case of considerable bulk, such as timber, barrels, machinery, and structural steel. Certain goods are required by law to be stowed on deck because of their highly inflammable, corrosive, or otherwise dangerous properties. **D.-carling; d.-carlin;** *see* CARLING. **D. department,** that division of a merchant vessel's crew charged with safe conduct of the ship and whose duties include navigation, mooring and unmooring, care and handling of cargo, and maintenance of deck equipment, boats, and life-saving appliances. **D.-dowel,** common incorrect name for *d.-plug; see* PLUG. **D.-ends,** those of planking forming a deck. **D.-erection,** any fixed structure on a weather deck. **D.-flat,** *see* FLAT. **D.-gang,** seamen of the deck department; *see* GANG. **D.-girder,** a continuous longitudinal usually supported by stanchions or pillars and secured to *d.*-beams; sometimes fitted to beams intercostally as *d.-carlings.* **D.-hand,** a seaman of the *d.* department, especially in coastwise powered vessels; on British fishing-vessels, a seaman is called a *hand.* **D.-height,** vertical distance between two adjacent decks. **D.-hook,** *see* HOOK. **D.-horse,** a stout bar of round iron fitted athwartships for securing the lower block of a fore-and-aft sail's sheet and allowing it to move from side to side as required in tacking. **D.-house,** a structure on a weather *d.,* as a galley, crew's quarters, etc., not extending from side to side of the vessel. **D.-iron,** *see* caulking-iron in IRON. **D.-light,** piece of thick glass, having a flat upper surface and lower part as an angular ridge, inserted in a wood deck for lighting; a *bull's-eye* or *dead-light.* **D.-line,** *see* LINE. **D.-load,** *see* **D.-cargo. D.-machinery,** collectively, capstans, windlass, warping and cargo winches, and any other power-driven devices located on deck. **D.-nail,** a cut nail or spike, rectangular in section, usually of galvanized iron, having a raised head and tapering to a chiseled point, used in wood construction for securing deck and ceiling planking. **D.-pillar,** a heavy built hold-stanchion supporting a deck. **D.-pipe,** heavy cast iron tubular passage for chain cable from windlass to chain locker; also called *monkey-pipe, spurling-pipe, spill-pipe.* **D. plan,** *see* PLAN. **D. planking,** wood forming a deck; planks laid as a deck, taken collectively.

Usual material for ship's *d's* are Oregon pine, yellow pine, and teak. Wood *d's* laid over those of steel (*sheathed deck*) generally are of 3 inches thickness, with strakes 4 to 5 inches in width; single *d's*, such as those over houses or superstructure and shelter decks, about 4 by 4 inch; and where a light weather *d.* is to be covered with canvas, 2½ to 3 inches by 4- to 5-inch planking is laid. Width to the weather of planking is slightly less than that of its under side—3/16 to ¼ inch—so that, when laid, a seam opening by that amount is provided for calking. **D.-plate,** small flat brass fitting round an opening in a *d.*, such as a tank vent or a sounding-pipe; name or number of tank to which such pipe leads is indicated on the plate. Also, one laid over a *deck-expansion joint* on a long superstructure *d.* on large vessels; *see* EXPANSION JOINT. Any metal plate set in a wood *d.* **D.-plating,** iron or steel plates forming a deck, collectively. **D.-plug,** *see* PLUG. **D.-pond,** one of several bins in which fish are sorted on a trawler's *d.*; also, *d.-pound.* **D.-pump,** a hand pump for washing *d's.* **D.-scow,** one on which its load is carried above deck only. **D.-spade,** a short-handled spade used for cutting blubber on a whaler. **D.-strongback,** in a *d.* having a midship king-plank, a plank about an inch wider than the latter laid flush with surface of beams along center line of deck and to which the king-plank is securely bolted. **D.-stringer,** outer plate of a deck, laid along the ends of beams and having its outer edge secured to the shell. **D.-stringer inner angle-bar,** that riveted to a d.-stringer and forming inner boundary of waterway. **D.-stringer outer angle-bar,** one of the short angles fitted between frames in transverse framing system, or continuous bar in longitudinal system, which connects outer edge of a *d.*-stringer to shell-plating. **D.-tackle,** a handy purchase, usually twofold, used for various work on deck. **D.-transom,** *see* TRANSOM. **D.-watch,** a timepiece suitable as a substitute for a chronometer in taking observations. It is compared with the chronometer when in use and difference indicated applied to obtain correct chronometer reading at time of observation. Also, *hack-watch, stop-watch, hack chronometer.* **Fidley-d.,** *see* FIDLEY. **Flush d.,** one continuous weather deck having no part of the ship's sides extending above it. **Fore d.,** *see* FORE. **Forecastle d.,** a partial *d.* at the fore end, raised above a weather *d.; a top-gallant forecastle.* **Freeboard d.,** uppermost continuous *d.* of the hull proper having means of permanently closing all openings thereon. It is the *d.* at which the *statutory deckline* is marked on the shell at amidships; *see* FREEBOARD. **Gun d.,** in old-time warships, one next below the weather *d.* on which guns were carried. On a 3-decker, this was called *main* or *middle gun d.* and that next below, *lower gun d.* To-day, a *d.* below a weather or upper *d.* from which guns are fired. **Half d.,** in older sailing-ships, part of *d.* next below the upper or spar

d., extending from mainmast to cabin. Midshipmen or apprentice officers, and sometimes passengers, were berthed in the *half d.*; and, though in later years displaced by a midship deck-house, apprentices' quarters in British ships continued to be called the *half d.* **Harbor d.,** on now practically obsolete turret steam-vessels, flat surface of whaleback portion of hull, or that formed by ship's sides curving or rounding inward and then upward as sides of a trunk or turret, which extended 7 to 10 feet to the upper or *turret d.* Harbor *d.* was about one-fourth the vessel's breadth, thus leaving the turret *d.* half her breadth and in the fore-and-aft center line. **Hatch d.,** *see* HATCH. **Hurricane d.,** term for a light uppermost superstructural *d.* on coastwise and lake passenger-vessels, used as a promenade or shade and sometimes as a *boat d.* To **lipper off the d.,** *see* LIPPER. **Lower d.,** generally, first *d.* above an *orlop d.* in vessels having four or more full *d's*; lowest in those with two or three *d's.* In British naval usage, designates personnel below officer rank, as in the phrase, "popular with *the lower deck.*" **Main d.,** principal continuous or strength *d.*, located in merchant vessels of average type at termination of full framing (transverse). In large ships having four or more full *d's*, principal strength *d's* are both *main* and *upper d's.* Generally, a *main d.* is the upper one in two-decked vessels; that next below an uppermost strength *d.* (*upper d.*), where more than two full *d's* are present. A *main d.*, in U.S. navy is defined as "highest *d.* extending from stem to stern." **Mate of the d.,** officer of the watch. **Middle d.,** chiefly in old navy usage, *main d.* or that next below the *spar, weather,* or *upper d.* in a 3-decker or ship of the line. **Officer of the d.,** *see* OFFICER. **On d.,** indicating state of readiness for duty as opposed to *below*, as, *the watch is on d.*; signifying position on a *weather d.*, as, *cargo stowed on d.* **Orlop d.,** usually lowest of more than four hull *d's*, or, as sometimes defined in such case, lowest continuous *d.* In old 3-deckers it was that next below the lower *d.* or just below the water-line, lowest of all being a *platform d.*, or a partial *d.* over widely spaced hold beams. Originally *orlop* denoted a single *d.* covering a vessel. In U.S. navy nomenclature it apparently has disappeared, continuous *d's* below a main *d.* now being termed *2nd., 3rd., 4th.*, etc. **Panting d.,** platform laid on panting beams in a fore peak. **Partial d.,** a non-continuous *d.*; a partial steel *d.* may be laid for strength purposes under a continuous wood *d.*, such as is found on smaller vessels amidships in way of engine space, or near the stern. **Poop d.,** that covering a poop space or superstructure at extreme after end of a weather *d.* **Promenade d.,** one for use of passengers, usually a *shade d.* area on each wing of a large *d.*-house containing staterooms, etc. **Protective d.,** in a war-vessel, a continuous *d.* of extra strength and thickness for protective purposes, usually at or near the water-line. **Quarter-d.,** originally, that raised part of a weather *d.* abaft the mainmast,—later, that area between mainmast and poop,—considered domain of officers and passengers. In naval vessels, that part of weather *d.* designated by a commanding officer as reserved for officers. **Raised quarter-d.,** *see* RAISED. **Shade d.,** one of light construction not enclosed at sides and supported by stanchions, above a superstructure as protection from sun and rain. **Sheathed d.,** one temporarily covered by planking to withstand rough wear and tear, as when cattle are carried; formerly, a wood deck over an iron one was called *sheathing,* the whole being termed a *sheathed d.* **Shelter d.,** *see* SHELTER. **Single-decked vessel,** *see* SINGLE. **Spar d.,** originally, main or weather *d.* of a sailing-ship; now a weather *d.* of comparatively light construction above a main *d.* **Sponson d.,** *see* SPONSON. To **sweep the d.,** indicating action of a shipped sea carrying away everything movable before it, or a broadside of gunfire over a vessel's *d.* **Texas d.,** *see* TEXAS. **Tonnage d.,** *see* TONNAGE. **Trunk d.,** *see* TRUNK. **Turtle** or **turtleback d.,** in early ocean steam-vessels, a hood-like or rounded top-gallant forecastle for shedding off water in a head sea; also, *whaleback.* The rounded-over sides of a poop or a forecastle as found in older construction were known as the *turtle-back.* **Tween d.,** any hull *d.* below an upper *d.* and above a lowermost or orlop *d.* **Upper d.,** in merchant ships, uppermost strength *d.* of a hull, defined in tonnage rules as uppermost continuous watertight *d.*; in U.S. navy usage, partial *d.* amidships and *above* the *main d.* The term appears to have originated with that given the uppermost (or *weather d.*) of three first installed with increase in size of old sailing war-vessels. To-day it applies to either the uppermost of three or more continuous hull *d's,* or one next below it, depending upon type of vessel; thus, in a full-scantling vessel of three continuous *d's,* an *upper d.* is synonymous with a *main* or *weather d.,* while in the shelter deck type having 4 continuous *d's,* the *upper d.* is next below the weather or *shelter d.* **Weather d.,** *see* WEATHER. **Well d.,** open or weather *d.* lying between a raised forecastle or a poop and a bridge superstructure. **Whale d.,** a turtle-back, *q.v.* **Wing d.,** part of *d.* on older paddle-steamers projecting forward of and abaft the sponsons.

DECKING. Material from which a deck is laid; *d.*-planking; any of several patent cement-like compositions of an insulating, non-absorbent, noncombustible nature and not slippery when wet, smoothly spread to ½ or ¾-inch thickness over a steel *d.* as a substitute for planking.

DECK LOG. *See* LOG.

DECK LONGITUDINAL. *See* LONGITUDINAL.

DECLARATION OF PARIS. Statement of an international agreement concerning rules to be applied in case of war, made at *Paris* and signed by plenipotentiaries of Austria, France, Great Britain, Prussia, Russia, Sardinia, and Turkey, 16 April 1856, and since acceded to by practically all maritime states. It declared: (*1*) Privateering is and remains abolished. (*2*) The neutral flag covers enemy's goods except contraband of war. (*3*) Neutral goods, except contraband of war, are not liable to capture under enemy's flag. (*4*) Blockades to be binding must be effective.

DECLINATION. A sloping, deviation, or inclination from a certain standard or plane of reference; as, *d.* of compass needle; *d.* of a star. **D. of a heavenly body,** angular distance of the body's center north or south of the equinoctial or celestial equator, as measured on an hour circle passing through such body. Corresponding to geographical latitude, numerical values of *d.* and latitude are identical when a body, in its apparent diurnal path, passes through the zenith. *D.* of any body used in celestial navigation (*sun, moon, planets, and fixed stars*) may be obtained from the current nautical almanac. **D. circle,** a great circle passing through both poles of the celestial sphere along which *d.* is measured; an *hour circle.* **D. compass,** a special compass for determining magnetic *d.* or *variation* at any locality. **D. of compass needle,** more often referred to as *variation of the compass,* is angular departure of the magnetic meridian from the true, as indicated at any locality by a *declination-compass* or *declinometer.* Its value is expressed in angular measurement as *easterly* when to the right of *true,* or *geographical, north*; and westerly when to left; and varies over the world's usual trade routes by as much as 60 degrees. In addition to a minor diurnal fluctuation and a generally small but constant increase or decrease each year in any locality, great secular changes have been noted in its value over the past 300 years, indicating cyclic periods of several centuries from maximum easterly to maximum westerly declination. *Compass d.* or variation, with its annual change, is given on all navigation charts. *Also see* COMPASS *and* MERIDIAN. **Magnetic d.,** same as *compass variation.*

DECLINOMETER. An instrument for scientifically measuring the declination of a magnetic needle.

DECLIVITY OF WAYS. Slope or downward inclination of launching ways, which is, generally, five-eighths to three-fourths inch per foot.

DEDUCTED SPACE. In rules for determining *net tonnage,* total, or any single, enclosed space which is deducted from *gross tonnage.*

DEEP. An ocean bottom depression having a depth, as measured from the surface, of more than

3000 fathoms; as, *Nero Deep,* near Guam in the Pacific, named for a cable-ship which found depths therein of over 5260 fathoms. Greatest depth recorded is that of *Mindanao Deep,* near the Philippines, 5900 fathoms (35,400 feet). Estimated depth shown on a hand lead-line between "marks," indicated in a leadsman's cry when reporting a sounding, as, "By the *deep,* six!"—half way between the line marks at 5 and 7 fathoms. **Abysmal d.,** *see* ABYSM. **D. floors,** *see* FLOOR. **D. frames,** those having extra depth for compensating strength loss due to omission of beams, stringers, etc. **D. framing,** in vessels specially built for carrying certain bulk cargoes, system of heavy framing which admits of omission of one or more tiers of hold beams. **D.-sea,** of or pertaining to, deeper waters of the sea; as *d.-sea fish; d.-sea soundings.* **D.-sea leadline,** used in older days for sounding by hand in depths up to 150 fathoms. Lead was 30 to 50 lbs. weight, and line was marked at 20 fathoms by 2 knots on a cord laid in the strands; at 30 fathoms by 3 knots, etc., with a single knot at each intervening 5 fathoms; and at 100 fathoms by a piece of rag, etc. Also called by sailors *dipsey-line.* **D.-sea thermometer,** one made specially for temperature observations taken at great sea depths. **D. six,** an old term for the *big locker;* to give an object the "deep six" means to throw it overboard. **D. stowage,** *see* STOWAGE. **D. tank,** portion of a hold constructed to carry water ballast or cargo as required. Its purpose is to increase a vessel's light draft and also raise her center of gravity on expected rough weather passages. **D.-waisted,** said of a vessel having a poop or forecastle unusually elevated above her weather or upper deck. **D. water,** off shore; opposed to coasting, as in *a d. water voyage;* a *d. sea sailor.* **D. water-line,** a load-line, or that to which submerged with a full cargo.

DEFECT, NATURAL. Term used in marine insurance indicating such damage to a ship or her cargo that can not be attributed to bad weather or to any accident.

DEFLECTOR. An instrument invented by *Lord Kelvin (1824–1907)* for measuring magnetic force acting on a compass, thence rendering possible correction of deviation when bearings of celestial objects or landmarks can not be obtained. Such correction by deflector method is based on the fact that, if directive force is equal on all courses, no compass deviation exists on any course. Accordingly, any required manipulation or fixing of correctors is done to render a given directive force shown by deflector as nearly constant as possible on all courses on which ship is headed.

DEGAUSSING. (From *gauss,* electrical unit of magnetic flux density, named for *Karl F. Gauss, German physicist (1777–1855).* System of protection against magnetic mines by means of electric cables placed around and inside a steel ship above her waterline, and through which a requisite direct current flows from ship's generator. It essentially prevents ship from disturbing direction and intensity of the earth's magnetic flux, upon which depends successful avoidance of detonating so-called *magnetic mines* in question. *Also see* COILS.

DEGRADE. *See* DISRATE.

DEGREE. Unit of angular measure equal to that angle at center of any circle subtended by an arc of 1/360 the circumference; such arc itself. It is divided into 60 *minutes,* each of which contain 60 *seconds;* thus, latitude, longitude, altitude, azimuth, declination, and other values, which may be regarded as either angles or arcs of circles, are written, *e.g.,* 50° 22′ 45″, or fifty degrees, twenty-two minutes, forty-five seconds. Also, unit or division marked on an instrument, as a thermometer, clinometer, galvanometer, etc. **D. of latitude,** due to spheroidal shape of the earth, length varies from 59.66 nautical miles *(68.70 statute miles)* at equator to 60.27 at the poles. **D. of longitude,** length is approximately equal to 60 times cosine of latitude. At equator is 60.07 nautical miles *(69.17 statute miles)* in length; at Lat. 45°, 42.55; and at the poles, *zero.*

DE HORSEY RIG. A British two-mast boat rig spreading a jib-headed foresail and a brailing-in, loose-footed, gaff mainsail.

DELIVERY. Forced flow of water, etc., as *outboard delivery,* indicating water or oil pumped overboard, into a shore line, or vessel alongside; flow of air from fans or blowers, as in a cooling, furnace-draft, or ventilating system. **D.-pipe,** one through which water or oil is led or delivered, as into a boiler or ballast tank. **D.-valve,** *see* VALVE.

DELIVERY ORDER. Written request by an owner of goods, or his assignee, addressed to a custodian of a dock, warehouse, etc. for delivery of his property to a certain specified person or persons.

DELIVERY, PORT OF. Specified port at which certain cargo is to be discharged.

DELPHINUS. (Gr. *delphis,* dolphin.) A small constellation west of *Pegasus* and about 10° northeast of the bright star *Altair,* containing no navigational stars; the *Dolphin;* also known as *Job's Coffin.* A genus of *Cetacea* including the typical *dolphins* and the *beluga* or white whale.

DELTA. Alluvial deposit at a river's mouth forming a considerable fan-shaped area to which the Greek capital letter △ *(delta)* was likened by the ancients. Typical deltas are those of the Nile, Mississippi, and Niger.

DEMERSAL FISH. In zoölogy, a fish that deposits its eggs on the sea bottom. In British usage, "wet fish," or those taken by trawlers and liners, as cod, haddock, halibut, sole, and turbot; opposed to herring, mackerel, and shellfish.

DEMISE CHARTER. See CHARTER.

DEMURRAGE. Detention of a vessel by a charterer or his interests beyond a period known as *lay days* stipulated in the charter party for loading or discharging. Rate, allowance, or sum payable to a shipowner in compensation for such detention of his vessel. Unless otherwise agreed upon, demurrage is counted in running days, regardless of Sundays and holidays, upon expiration of lay days, when vessel is said to be *on demurrage.* **D. lien,** generally, a ship has a lien on cargo on board for *d.,* if so stipulated in charter agreement. However, it has been held in U.S. courts that such lien is enforceable whether agreed upon or otherwise in chartering. Hence, the customary protection afforded a ship in claiming *d.* "daily and on Saturday for Sunday."

DENEB. (Ar. *al danab al dajajah,* the tail of the hen.) *Alpha* (α) *Cygni,* a navigational star, brightest in the group *Cygnus* (the Swan); *see* CYGNUS.

DENEBOLA. (Ar. *al danab al asad,* the tail of the lion.) *Beta* (β) *Leonis,* second brightest star in *Leo* (the Lion); located in R.A. 11 hrs. 46 min., Dec. 14° 52' N., about 39° due south of the Big Dipper bowl, at the eastern corner of a conspicuous right-angled triangle, and a little less than half way between bright stars *Regulus* and *Arcturus.*

DENSITY. Properly, ratio of mass of volume of a substance to that of an equal volume of a standard substance; but commonly confused with *relative density* or specific gravity, *i.e.,* ratio of weight of a given volume of a gas, liquid, or solid to that of an equal volume of standard substance; and, also, expressed as *weight* per cubic unit. For liquids and solids, distilled water at 39° F. (4° C.) is taken as the standard substance and relative *d., e.g.,* of sea water is indicated as 1.025 and that of cast iron 7.2, giving weights of these substances as 64 lbs. and 449 lbs. per cubic foot, respectively, 62.4 lbs. per cubic foot being, very nearly, weight of fresh water.

DEPARTMENT OF ADMIRALTY. See ADMIRALTY.

DEPARTMENT OF THE NAVY. See NAVY.

DEPARTURE. Distance in nautical miles by which a vessel changes her longitude on a particular course or courses; called *easting* when made toward east, *westing* when toward west. Point or time at which a sea passage begins on leaving a port. To **take a d.,** to determine a ship's place in starting a voyage, or at any point thereafter, from which a course may be set, and also, to note the time of such event. **Point of d.,** place or position, as usually determined by bearings of points on shore, from

which the course is set for a point of destination.

DEPRESS THE POLE, To. An archaic phrase, indicating its modern equivalent, to *decrease the latitude;* to sail toward the equator and thus decrease altitude of elevated pole, *i.e.,* latitude. (When pole is in the horizon, latitude is zero.)

DEPRESSED POLE. See POLE.

DEPRESSION. Vertical angular distance of a heavenly body *below* the horizon. Altitude of a circumpolar heavenly body at its lower culmination. **Barometric d.,** relatively diminished atmospheric pressure; area over which such condition is present. **Angle of d.,** *see* ANGLE.

DEPTH. Downward perpendicular measurement from a surface, as *d. of a tank;* quality of deepness from point of view, as, *d. of clouds;* extent or "drop" of a square sail measured from head-rope to foot-rope, as a lower topsail or course, or "hoist" of one on a hoisting yard, as that of a single top-gallant sail or a royal; also, extent of a fore-and-aft sail as measured by length of its after leech. **Controlling d.,** that indicating least *d.* of water in an area, thus limiting draft of vessels intending to navigate such area. **D. bomb; d. charge;** a high explosive bomb dropped from a vessel's stern in engaging an enemy submarine which is below the surface. It may be set to detonate at a particular depth and/or upon striking a submerged object. **D. of vessel** (*A.B.S. rules*), measured at middle of length of load waterline from top of keel to top of upper deck beams. **D.-gage,** *see* GAUGE. **D. of a boat,** distance from inside the planking at keel to top of gunwale at midlength. **Depths of the sea,** deeper parts of the oceans. **Freeboard d.,** same as molded *d.* **Molded d.,** that of the *molded* or main hull form; in 1-, 2-, or 3-decked vessels is measured at mid-length from top of keel to top of upper deck beams at side; in awning or shelter-decked vessels, measured from top of keel to top of main deck beams at side of vessel. **Registered d.,** distance at mid-length from top of double bottom or top of floors, or from a point 2½ inches above these where a wood ceiling is fitted, no matter of what thickness, to top of upper deck beams, or second deck beams in awning- or shelter-deck vessels, as measured in the midship fore-and-aft line; also termed *d. of hold.* **Tonnage d.,** as measured in calculating tonnage, distance from top of double bottom, or top of ceiling where fitted, to a point one-third of round of beam (camber) below the deck, in the fore-and-aft center line.

DERATIZATION. Operation of ridding a vessel of *rats,* which pests are considered the most obnoxious, due to their destructive habits and reputation as plague-carriers. Poisons, such as strychnine and arsenic are used, and also cyanide and sulphur dioxide gases as fumigants in the process. **D. certifi-**

cate, required by U.S. law, and that of most maritime nations, to be carried by all vessels, excepting certain coasting craft, certificate given by port quarantine or health authority stating that vessel has been fumigated or *"deratized,"* or in lieu thereof, a *d. exemption* certificate. Either document is valid for a period of six months.

DERELICT. Property permanently and voluntarily abandoned, or willfully cast away by its owner, as a vessel abandoned at sea. Thereafter, such property belongs to first person taking possession of it, excepting that, in the case of a vessel improperly abandoned by her master and not relinquished by her owner, salvage services alone, as determined by a court in admiralty, may be claimed by the finder and salvor. An abandoned or forsaken vessel.

DERRICK. (Named for *Thomas Derrick,* a hangman in Queen Elizabeth's time who devised an improvement on the gibbet in that the condemned were suspended from the hoisting end of a spar.) Essentially an arm or spar extended to support a tackle or other rig for hoisting. On shipboard, *d's* are fitted to hoist and lower cargo through hatchways or to and from the deck, and are rigged with topping-lifts attached to a mast in order to vary the "lead" of hoisting gear from their heads, or upper ends, as required. Usually two *booms,* as they are often named, are placed in transferring cargo so that one is used for hatchway work while its mate lands or picks up the load alongside, each being guyed in position accordingly. Average outboard reach of a *d.* in cargo ships is from 10 to 20 feet; length varies with size of vessel, those at center line hatchways never less than vessel's half breadth; ordinary working load 3 to 5 tons; usually constructed of tubular steel, often steel lattice-girder type, and, in older ships, of pitch pine. **D.-crane,** *see* CRANE. **D.-guy,** rope or tackle leading from deck to a *d.*-head for placing or steadying the boom as required. **D.-head,** upper end of a *d.* or boom at which guys, hoisting-block, and topping-lift are attached. **D.-table,** steel platform built around and stiffened by a mast, 6 to 8 feet above the deck, for purpose of stepping cargo-booms clear of winches, thus providing additional available length of derrick and deck working space. Such table is often supported by plating erected to form the sides of a handy deck locker. Also called *boom-table* and *mast-table.* **Floating-d.,** one for special use in ship repair yards, or for transferring extra heavy lifts, mounted on deck of a broad-beamed scow, barge, or specially built powered vessel.

DERWENTWATER'S LIGHTS, LORD. *See* AURORA.

DESCENDING NODE. *See* MOON'S NODES.

DESERTION. In merchant vessels, willful act of a seaman in absenting himself from, and without intention to return on board, a ship in which he is bound by legal agreement to serve for a current period or voyage. The offense is punishable by forfeiture of wages and blacklisting, or revocation or suspension of documents authorizing his engagement. In naval forces of most countries it is punishable by death in time of war and by imprisonment in time of peace.

DESTINATION, PORT OF. *See* PORT.

DESTROYER. Originally, *torpedo-boat destroyer,* from the craft's earlier use. A light speedy war-vessel designed for attacking submarines, for convoy escort duty, torpedo attack in protecting a squadron of heavier ships, scouting, etc.

DESPATCH MONEY. *See* MONEY.

DESUPERHEATER. Arrangement whereby saturated or slightly super-heated steam required for operation of auxiliaries is supplied from a main boiler's superheating system.

DETACHING-HOOK. Releasing-hook; *see* HOOK.

DEVELOPER. A skilled draftsman who lays out drawings to full size on a shipyard mold-loft floor, from prepared plans, of all curved structural parts of a proposed hull and makes templates therefrom for purposes of preparing frames, floor-, beams, plates, etc. He must be particularly skilled in development of curved surfaces, in order that each part may be correctly represented preparatory to cutting or shaping the straight or flat material. Also termed *loftsman* and *linesman.*

DEVIASCOPE. An instrument used in navigation schools to explain the causes of, and principles employed in correcting, deviations of a ship's magnetic compass. It is a representation of a vessel's deck about four feet in length on which a compass is mounted and which may be horizontally swung in any direction or given any desired angle of heel. Bar magnets may be placed at any of several positions above or below the "deck" to illustrate changing effects of a steel vessel's magnetic properties on the compass on various headings or "courses" through which the instrument may be swung. The compass is supplied with correcting magnets, soft iron spheres, Flinders bar, etc., for demonstrating procedure in adjusting or compensating for the disturbing influences caused by conditions imitated, as in placing pieces of soft iron or magnets at appropriate positions relative to the compass.

DEVIATION. Error in a magnetic compass caused by a ship's magnetism; or, angle at which *compass north* deviates from *magnetic north,* described as +, plus, or easterly, when north point of compass is drawn toward east of magnetic north, and as — (*minus*), or westerly, when toward west of magnetic north. Due to varying positions from which magnetic properties of a vessel's iron disturb the instrument's correct north-seeking quality, compass deviation changes in value with changes in ship's course, usually attaining maximum values and of different name on two nearly opposite points steered. Analysis of deviation values as found by observation on 8 or more equi-distant compass headings when swinging a vessel, indicates that total deviation on a particular heading is the resultant of several components conveniently designated as $A, B, C, D,$ and $E.$ Excepting $A,$ a constant error on all headings usually attributed to a faulty compass-card or misplaced lubber-line, values of these components or *coefficients,* as popularly termed, are found to consistently wax and wane through equal arcs of the compass. Coefficient B attains a maximum on E. and W. *by compass* and is zero on N. and S.; C is greatest on N. and S. points, with zero on E. and W.; $D,$ greatest on opposite quadrantal points, usually N.E. and S.W. giving $+$ and N.W. and S.E. giving $-,$ and zero on cardinal points; and $E,$ greatest on N.E.S.W. and zero on quadrantal points. Such analysis has for its objective the correction by proper means of each component of total deviation, as opposed to any method which attempts to eliminate or materially reduce the deviation on a general trial and error basis, and which, of necessity, is but a temporary provision and wholly undependable in an all-steel vessel. The analytical method referred to is termed the *rectangular* and appears to be more precise and suitable to requirements of efficient compass adjustment than any other yet devised. Theory and practice of correcting the magnetic compasses installed in a new vessel may be followed in any good work on the subject. *Deviation* is determined by comparing a known magnetic or true bearing of a heavenly body or other object with that observed by compass, which procedure is considered necessary routine in navigation, since, despite initial success in compass compensation, errors may develop, especially in a new ship, due to lengthy continuance on one course, large changes of latitude, or presence of considerable iron in a cargo. Material changes in deviation have been observed to occur in a new vessel when steering for some days in a direction opposite to that in which she lay while being built. **D. table,** list of *d's* observed on each point, or several consecutive points, of a compass, as supplied by a compass adjuster or determined by ship's officers.

DEVIATION CLAUSE. That embodied in a charter party stating that ship is permitted to call at other ports beside place at which cargo is to be discharged. In marine insurance, that indicating penalty for unjustifiable departure from voyage covered in the policy.

DEVIL. Any planking seam difficult of access in caulking. Formerly, when vessels were careened on a beach for bottom repairs, seam between garboard strake and keel. Completing caulking work on this difficult seam was limited in time to a short period during lowest water; hence the phrase indicating unprepared-for serious trouble, "*the devil to pay and no pitch hot.*" **D.-bolt,** an unclinched, sham, or faulty bolt dishonestly placed in shipbuilding. **D.-fish,** a giant ray of the genus *Mobula,* found chiefly in Gulf of Mexico and Caribbean waters, often attaining a width of 20 feet; any of the larger rays. *Cf.* MANTA. **D.'s claw,** *see* CLAW. **Pull-d.,** *see* PULL.

DEW VALVE. *See* VALVE.

DGHAISA. A gondola-like rowing-boat peculiar to harbor of Valetta, Malta. (Native name, pronounced *disa.*) Also, *draissa.*

DHOW. General term for a lateen-rigged, fast-sailing vessel of the Indian and Arabian coasts, characterized by a long overhanging stem, high sheering poop, raking stern, and low waist; described as a vessel at one time notoriously active in East African slave trade. Also, *dau, dow.*

DIAGONAL. A timber, knee, plank, iron strapping, plate, or other structural member fitted slantwise across, and connecting a series of, frames, beams, etc.; a brace or stay obliquely fitted to connect horizontal and vertical members of a truss or frame; a diagonal-line in a ship's body plan. **Bilge-d.,** *see* BILGE. **D.-braces,** in more recent wooden construction, iron straps or trusses secured obliquely across inner surfaces of frames from bilges to first continuous deck. **D.-built,** referred to planking on heavier boats, system in which an inner layer is laid at about a 45° angle with keel, and an outer layer at approximately right angles with the former. Tarred or painted canvas, or similar fabric, is laid between each planking layer. **D. and longitudinal built,** double-layer planking system on longitudinally framed boats in which inner skin is laid diagonally, and outer laid fore-and-aft in carvel-built fashion. **D. ceiling,** a system of laying planking constituting hold ceiling in wood-built vessels; similar to that of **d.-braces,** its purpose was to increase longitudinal structural strength. **D.-cut sail,** any triangular sail, principally in yachting, such as a jib, staysail, or jib-headed mainsail, whose cloths are cut at right angles to both leech and foot, "mitering" in a line from clew perpendicular to the luff; opposed to usual cut of such sails in which cloths run parallel to foot and leech. **D. lines,** in shipbuilding drawings, longitudinal planes represented by oblique lines drawn on the body plan from midship center line at designed load-line level to intersect the molded surface in turn of bilges amidships and throughout vessel's length. Line of diagonal plane's intersection with molded surface is shown on half-breadth plan as a curved line. **D. stanchion,** in smaller vessels, a hold-pillar or stanchion in way of a hatch-coaming so fitted that its lower end is stepped farther toward ship's side than its head, in order to give a clearer space at bottom of hatchway. **D. strapping,** same as *d. bracing.* **D. tie-plate,** principally in iron and steel sailing-vessels, a strake of plating laid diagonally from side to side over main deck beams and under a wood deck, to provide stiffening against racking stresses from ship's rigging in a seaway.

DIAMETER. (Gr. *dia,* through; *metron,* measure.) Length of a line through center of an object from side to side, as, *d.* of a *spar, boiler, barrel, etc.;* often expressed as size, as in ½-*inch bolt,* ¾-*inch wire-rope,* 1½-*inch anchor-cable.* Referred to circle described by a ship's track in turning at constant speed, **final d.** is distance perpendicular to original course between points where 180° and 360° of the turn have been completed; **tactical d.** is distance made to right or left of original course when a turn of 180° has been completed with rudder at a constant angle.

DIAMOND.   A diamond-shaped beacon or day-mark surmounting a buoy. In the buoyage system of Great Britain, placed at outer or seaward ends of middle grounds which may be passed on either side; similarly used in the French system, also marks a point of bifurcation, or where a main fairway completely breaks off into two channels. **D.-knot,** useful and ornamental knot made in the strands of a fiber rope to act as a stopper, hand-grip, or foot-grip, as on a man-rope and foot-rope; made by un-laying the strands as necessary and turning their bights around each other in similar fashion as in forming a *wall knot; see* KNOT. Also an old-time variety of the *carrick bend* or that in which a *double carrick* was supplemented by passing each hawser end round its standing part and up through middle of the bend, instead of directly stopping the ends to their respective standing parts. **D.-plate,** a diamond-shaped plate fitted over intersection of two crossing structural members as a uniting and bracing connection. **D.-rig,** so named for an elongated *d.-shaped* appearance of standing rigging found in some sailing yachts, in which top-mast shrouds are carried outward over long cross-tree spreaders from a point on lowermast some feet above deck.

DIAPHONE FOG-SIGNAL.   *See* FOG-SIGNAL.

DIAPHRAGM-PLATE.   *See* PLATE.

DICE.   *See* DYCE.

DIESEL ENGINE.   *See* ENGINE. **D.-electric drive,** *see* DRIVE.

DIFFERENCE of LATITUDE. (*Usual abbrev., D. Lat.*) *See* LATITUDE.

DIFFERENCE of LONGITUDE. (*Usual abbrev., D. Long.*) *See* LONGITUDE.

DIMINISHING-PLANKING.   In larger wooden ship construction, several strakes of planking gradually lessening in thickness below the *wales,* or outward from the *garboard.* Also **D.-strakes** and **D.-stuff.**

DINGHY. (Bengali, *dingi,* a boat.)   Originally, a row-boat on the River Hugli; any rowing or sailing boat used for passengers or cargo on the Indian coasts, especially those in sheltered waters, usually carrying their load on a whole or partial deck. Any small handy boat; specifically, one for light duty carried by a war-vessel, or as a tender for a yacht, and which may be rowed or sailed. An old type of rowing-boat, clinker-built and broad of beam, once familiar on the River Thames, England. Also, *dingey, dingy, dinky, cock-boat.*

DIOPTRIC LIGHTING.   As used in light-houses, system in which rays from the light are concentrated and directed horizontally by means of refractory prisms and lenses.

DIP.   Depth of immersion of a paddle-wheel or propeller. Downward inclination of the magnetic needle. Depression of the visible horizon. In launching, downward movement of fore end of a vessel as she becomes water-borne on leaving the ways. To pass a rope, tackle, spar, etc., under another object or obstruction; to lower and re-hoist a lug-sail yard on the new lee side when coming about in tacking; to temporarily lower a flag to about half full extent of halyards. **Angle of d.,** angle of inclination; *see* ANGLE. **At the d.,** in flag-hoist signalling, position at which the answering pennant is flown to indicate a signal is seen and being interpreted, or, at half-halyard hoist; opposed to *close up,* or hoisted to full extent of halyards, as in answering, acknowledging, or indicating completion of sending, a message. **D.-chart,** a map or chart of the earth's surface, or part thereof, showing values of *magnetic dip;* usually indicates such values by curved isoclinic lines. **D.-circle,** that on which value of magnetic *d.* is indicated on an inclinometer; *see* **dipping compass** *in* COMPASS. **D.-rope,** *see* ROPE. **D. of the horizon,** vertical angular distance of the *visible horizon* below the *sensible horizon* or horizontal plane centered at an observer's eye. Due to convexity of the earth's surface, its value varies with height above sea level at which considered, being, at ordinary elevations, as on board ship, very nearly numerically equal to the square root of height of an observer's eye; thus at 49 feet it is 6′ 52″, and at 64 feet, 7′ 50″. **D. of the needle** or **magnetic d.,** angle which direction of the earth's total magnetic force makes with the horizontal; or, angle of downward inclination from horizontal at which a magnetic needle freely poised to move vertically in the magnetic meridian comes to rest. Its value increases from zero at the magnetic equator to 90° at the magnetic poles, and, as with variation or declination of the needle, is subject to short periodical and secular changes. To **d. the flag**, *see* FLAG.

DIPHDA. (Ar. *al difdi*, the second.) Also called *Deneb Kaitos, Beta (β) Ceti*, brighter of two navigational stars in *Cetus* (the Whale), of magnitude 2.2; Dec. 18¼° S., S.H.A. 349° 40'; located nearly on a line joining the two eastern stars of the Square of Pegasus (*Alpheratz* and *Algenib*), projected southward about 33°; also written *Difda*. See CETUS.

DIPPER. Popular name for the constellation *Ursa Major*, or *Great Bear*, so called from arrangement of its seven stars forming the outline of a dipper; also called *Charlie's Wain* or *Wagon* and *Plough*. A line joining the two stars at outer side of its bowl, produced for about 28°, will pass very close to *Polaris*, or the North Star. **Little D.**, *Ursa Minor*, or *Little Bear*, a similar arrangement of lesser magnitude stars, the end of its handle being marked by *Polaris*.

DIPPING COMPASS. *See* COMPASS.

DIPPING LUG SAIL. *See* LUG.

DIPSEY. A sinker used on a fishing-line; a line having several branches, each with a sinker, in offshore fishing. Also, *dipsie, dipsy*. **D.-lead**, a deep-sea lead; *see* LEAD. **D.-line**, in the old single-topsail days, sailors' term for the main t'bowline (*maintopsail-bowline*), or longest-leading rope in the ship.

DIRECT COURSE. *See* COURSE.

DIRECT DRIVE. Any propulsion system in which no shaft-gearing is present, engines directly turning propeller-shafting, as with steam reciprocating and direct Diesel engines.

DIRECTION AND REVOLUTION INDICATOR. *See* INDICATOR.

DIRECTIONAL RADIO BEACON. One which sends out radio waves in a beam along a fixed bearing or bearings, or *radio ranges*, and used to guide aircraft. Present progressive development of short wave directional transmission apparently should soon result in its application to surface navigation.

DIRECTION-FINDER. *See* RADIO COMPASS.

DIRECTIONS, SAILING. *See* SAILING.

DIRTY. Colloquialism indicating disagreeable weather. **D. money**, extra wages paid to stevedores for handling offensive-smelling, verminous, badly damaged, or dirty cargo; also called *stink money*. **D. ship**, descriptive term for an oil tank vessel carrying cargoes such as crude, fuel, or gas oils, as distinguished from a "clean ship," or one carrying gasoline, kerosene, naphtha, lubricating oil, etc.

DISABLED. A vessel's condition when, by reason of serious injury or damage to her hull, masts and sails, or propelling machinery, temporarily is incapable of continuing her voyage.

DISBURSEMENTS. Traditional term in shipping affairs for moneys paid for current voyage necessities by a shipowner's agent or a shipmaster. Principal items are costs of loading and discharging cargo at ports of call; cash advances to crew; necessary repairs; fueling costs; provisions. Also, in marine insurance usage, a summary term for expense incurred by ship, cargo, and/or freight, directly consequent to a general average act which are allowed and included in the loss in adjustment of the average.

DISCHARGE. Certificate given a seaman upon completing a voyage or leaving a vessel; certificate of discharge; *see* CERTIFICATE. Operation of transferring cargo from ship to shore or another vessel; usually is ship's responsibility which ceases upon "goods being taken from the vessel's tackles." Any opening or pipe through which a fluid is expelled. **Overboard d.**, *see* OVERBOARD. **Port of d.**, *see* PORT.

DISCHARGING, OVERSIDE. *See* OVERSIDE.

DISEMBARK. To put ashore from a vessel; to land from, or leave, a vessel, as passengers, troops, or cattle, especially in the sense of going on foot.

DISENGAGING HOOKS. Arrangement in which lifting-tackle hooks attached to a life-boat may be disconnected simultaneously in lowering, whether boat is waterborne or not; also, and more commonly, *releasing-gear*.

DISHED. Concave or depressed in its middle like a dish, as a *d*, end of a cylinder or drum. **D. plate**, one trough-shaped or bowed in cross-section, as in a propeller-bossing, or in connecting a stem or a stern post to a flat-plate keel; any round-shaped plate pressed or forged into concave form.

DISMANTLE. To strip a vessel of guns, furniture, or equipment; to unrig; to remove the principal parts of a ship's rigging.

DISMASTED. State of having one or more masts carried away; especially that of a sailing-vessel, as may occur by force of wind, heavy rolling or pitching, stranding, or collision.

DISPATCH. To expedite execution of ship's business, cargo operations, etc., with objective of prompt and timely departure on, or continuance of, a voyage; as, to *dispatch* the vessel. **D.-boat**, a vessel or boat, usually of speedy type, for carrying dispatches. **D. money**, *see* MONEY. Also, *despatch*.

DISPLACEMENT. Volume or weight of fluid displaced by a body floating therein and is exactly equal in weight to that of such body. A vessel's *d.*, customarily expressed in long tons (2240 lbs.), may be determined by taking the aggregate weight of material constituting her structure, fittings, equipment, stores, and all else on board. However, it is considered more practical and less susceptible of error to calculate volume of water displaced by ship's hull, expressed in cubic feet, and dividing such result by 35, or the number of cubic feet in a long ton of sea-water of average density (1.025). **Calculation of d.,** areas of several equi-distant vertical cross-sections of the immersed body at a given draft are taken as ordinates and volume is determined by Simpson's Rules. Result given in cubic feet divided by 35 gives *d. tonnage* at draft in question. **Curve of d.,** *see* CURVE. **D. coefficient,** also termed *Admiralty coefficient; see* COEFFICIENT. **D. scale,** tabulated values of *d. tonnage* or *volume* at all working drafts of a ship. **D. ton,** unit generally adopted in expressing value of *d.;* equal to 2240 lbs. or, in maritime countries using the metric system, 1016.06 kilograms. **D. tonnage,** actual weight of a vessel and everything on board, or weight of water she displaces, at a given draft. War-vessels are usually described in point of size as being of a certain *d.,* such value being approximately constant, while merchant vessels, due to loading or discharging considerable weights of cargo, etc., are subject to wide changes in this respect, and consequently, for purposes of size comparison, such values must be stated as *load d.* or *light d.,* as the case demands. **Light d.,** weight in long tons of a merchant vessel without anything whatsoever, other than her equipment, on board. In steam-vessels, usually taken as the light condition with water in boilers at working level, no stores, no fuel, and no crew aboard. **Load d.,** weight in long tons of ship, cargo, stores, and all else on board, when floating at *summer draft* in sea-water.

DISPUTE THE WEATHER GAGE. *See* WEATHER.

DISRATE. To reduce to a lower rating, rank, or class; said of a seaman or a vessel of a certain qualified group.

DISTANCE. When steaming in formation or convoy, space between centers of ships next each other in line or in column. *D.* between two points at sea may be that measured on a *rhumb line,* as in comparatively short expanses; or on an arc of the *great circle* passing through both points, as usually taken in transoceanic tracks. **Angular d.,** angle at an observer's eye subtended by a line joining two objects; as that between two stars, indicated in degrees, minutes, and seconds of angular measure. **D. made good,** referred to a vessel's progress toward her destination, number of miles between a point of departure and a subsequently determined position. **Lunar d.,** angular *d.* between center of moon and that of another celestial body; *see* LUNAR. **Meridional d.,** archaic term for *difference of latitude.* **Meridian d.,** *see* MERIDIAN. **Moon in d.,** *see* MOON.

Polar d., angular *d.* of a celestial body from the elevated pole. Measured as arc of the hour circle intercepted by pole and body, it is the complement of body's declination. **Radio d.-finding,** *see* RADIO. **Zenith d.,** angular *d.* between center of a heavenly body and observer's zenith; or complement of *true* altitude of body.

DISTANT SIGNAL. *See* SIGNAL.

DISTILLER. A chamber in which steam vapor from an evaporator is condensed, forming fresh water for drinking or other purposes. Essentially consists of a chamber into which vapor enters and is condensed by cooling action of sea-water circulated through a pipe coil.

DISTINGUISHING PENNANT. *See* PENNANT.

DISTRESS. Referred to a state of danger or necessity, a vessel is said to be *in distress* when in circumstances seriously hindering her continuance of a voyage, as due to fire, stranding, heavy weather damage, machinery failure, or provision shortage. **D. signals,** *see* SIGNAL. **Port of d.,** *see* PORT.

DITTY BAG. Small canvas bag used to hold twine, marline, sewing-palm, needles, and marline-spike, such as is required to be carried in ships' lifeboats; any small bag used by seamen for sewing gear, personal trinkets, etc.

DITTY BOX. A small box for similar use to that of a *ditty bag.*

DIURNAL. (L. *diurnalis,* daily.) Recurring every day; happening each day. **D. aberration,** *see* ABERRATION. **D. acceleration of stars,** excess of their apparent *d.* motion to that of the sun, by which their meridian transit occurs 3 min. 55.91 secs. of mean solar time earlier than on a preceding day. **D. circle,** *see* CIRCLE. **D. inequality,** difference in height or time interval between two consecutive tides each day; generally attains a maximum with high declination of moon. **D. motion of heavenly bodies,** their apparent westerly motion due to the earth's rotation. **D. parallax,** *see* PARALLAX. **D. tide,** a single high water and a single low water occurring in one day.

DIVER. One skilled in "diving," or working in considerable depth of water, as in salvage operations, recovering anchors, cables, and other lost equipment, valuable cargo, etc., examination of ship's hull, bridge abutments, etc. Water pressure necessarily limits depth to which a *d.* may submerge, being equal to atmospheric pressure plus 4/9 depth in feet. Thus, divers known to have worked for short periods at 300 feet were subjected to a pressure of 133 lbs. per square inch above that of surface atmosphere. Any of several species of loons and other diving-birds, such as the grebe, sea-duck, penguin, auk, booby, etc.

DIVING BOAT. *See* BOAT.

DIVING-DRESS. Suit and equipment worn by divers in their work, consisting of a heavy water-proof fabric one-piece garment or "overall," topped by a light metal shoulder-piece or corselet to which a metal helmet is secured upon diver entering dress. Feet and waist-line are weighted to keep body erect while submerged; air is supplied at required pressure from an airpump in attendance; and diver himself regulates pressure in suit by outlet valve control. He is lowered by a rope secured to shoulder-piece of dress, which rope he also uses in signalling his requirements to crew attending by a system of sharp jerks. Of recent note is installation of a telephone in the equipment. Also, *diving-suit; submarine armor.*

DIVISION. One of a group of vessels into which a naval fleet or large squadron is divided. Part of a war-vessel's crew assigned certain duty. In U.S. war-vessels, divisions are "Above decks": gunnery, communications, medical or supply, main battery (*turrets*), secondary battery (*broadside guns*), radio, fire control (*gunnery control*), navigation, anti-aircraft battery, repair; "Below decks": engineering department—boilers, main engines, electrical, auxiliary machinery.

DOCK. (Du. *dok;* LL. *doga,* ditch; Gr. *docke,* receptacle.) Artificial basin or inclosure (sometimes called a *wet dock*) connected with a harbor or river of considerable range of tide, provided with lock gates in order to retain a depth of water undisturbed by entering or departing vessels; space between adjacent piers or wharves in which vessels are berthed; also, a pier or dock wall itself. To place a vessel in an inclosed dock or alongside a wharf or pier. **Basin d.,** a comparatively large water area in a dock arrangement, or in a canal system, in which vessels are turned around or otherwise maneuvered for entering or leaving a particular dock or slip. Also, an older term for a *graving dock.* **Box d.,** earliest and simplest form of floating *dry-d.,* in which the hull or main body is a single tank-like vessel, instead of a series of pontoons or tanks as in the larger modern type. **D. rent,** charges for storage of goods on a dock; also, *d. charges; d. dues.* **D. sill,** timber, stone, or concrete supporting lower ends of, or immediately beneath, gates of a *graving d.* or a *wet d.* entrance. Controlling depth for entering usually is indicated as a certain "depth on sill" at high water ordinary spring tides. **D. warrant,** a certificate given to an owner of goods warehoused on a dock, and which must be shown properly endorsed as an order for removal of goods. **Draw-d.,** *see* DRAW. **Dry-d.,** any dock in or on which a vessel may lie entirely out of water for repairs or painting purposes; as, a *floating d.,* or a *graving d.* **Floating d.,** a structure or vessel of L- or U-shaped cross-section, having a series of heavy pontoons or rectangular tanks forming its hull or bottom, so designed that it may be submerged for a vessel to float above it, then pumped out to produce the necessary buoyancy for floating the vessel. All necessary keel and bilge blocks for receiving ship's bottom are set as required as she is carefully placed before dock takes her weight. Pumping and flooding arrangements occupy the dock's raised side or sides. "Dry-docks" of this type are capable of raising average-sized ocean vessels in from one to two hours, and have the advantage of being suited for removal by towing to any site desired, however distant. Also, *floating dry-dock.* **Graving d.,** named for the old-time operation of breaming, scraping, etc., bottoms of wooden vessels, an artificial basin of elongated form opening off a harbor or waterway, fitted to receive vessels, especially those of heavier tonnage, for hull or bottom repairs. Keel and bilge blocks are laid according to ship's bottom plan and one or more series of shores are made ready for placing against ship's sides. Dock is closed and pumped dry as vessel is placed carefully over blocks and finally shored as water level decreases. The sides of such docks are sloped outward and form an array of steps, or "altars," on which the shores are butted, and usually a sinkable caisson containing the flooding arrangement is used to close the entrance instead of gates once commonly fitted. **Half-tide d.,** a small basin connected with a wet dock system to which ships are admitted subsequent to high water, preparatory to shifting into regular dock area upon next sufficient rise of tide, or as water is available to raise its level to that of docks. **Hydraulic d.,** one which has a platform or bed for raising small vessels above water by hydraulic power. **Ice-d.,** basin in a field of ice, where a boat may lie to escape being crushed. **Salvage-d.,** *see* SALVAGE. **Sectional d.,** any floating dock whose bottom structure is made of several separate compartments. **Shipbuilding d.,** any dry-dock on which a vessel may be built and from which she may be floated without aid of a cradle. **Slip d.,** one having a floor slanting from deep water to above high water mark and supporting a cradle on which a small vessel may be drawn from the water by means of purchases and rollers or wheels. Also called a *marine railway.* **Wet d.,** basin into which vessels are admitted at or about high water and in which depth of water is maintained at an approximately constant level, passage at other stages of tide being effected by means of a locking system.

DOCKAGE. Charges or fee for use of a dock, which may be based on gross or net tonnage, or length of vessel, for a specified period. Act of, or provision for, docking a vessel. **D. period,** interval at and about time of high water during which entrance gates to a wet dock may be kept open for passage of vessels.

DOCK DUES. Same as *dockage*.

DOCKER. One who is employed in loading or discharging vessels lying at a dock; a *longshoreman*.

DOCKING. Operation of placing a ship in dock, or charge for piloting or otherwise assisting in berthing a vessel. **D.-keel,** *see* KEEL. **D.-plan,** *see* PLAN. **D.-telegraph,** *see* TELEGRAPH. **D.-telephone,** *see* TELEPHONE.

DOCKMASTER. Chiefly in Great Britain, a harbormaster's assistant who supervises passage of vessels through the entrance locking system of a wet dock and berthing or other shipping movements within his area of control. Person responsible for dry-docking of vessels, including preparation and correct setting of blocks, shores, etc., and emptying or flooding of dock.

DOCKYARD. A yard having facilities for repairing vessels or boats and storage space for shipbuilding material, naval stores, etc. In the U.K., a *navy yard*.

DOCTOR. An auxiliary engine; an auxiliary feed-pump. The cook, or steward, if one is carried, in a sailing-vessel. In West Australia and in several tropical countries, a cooling sea-breeze prevailing in daytime.

DOCUMENT. To register, enroll, or license a vessel as required by law; to furnish with necessary documents; to attach cargo shipment papers to a bill of exchange. *See* REGISTER.

DODGER. A weather-cloth or canvas wind-shield fitted on a bridge or elsewhere for protection against wind, driving rain, etc.

DOG. Any of various simple mechanical devices for clamping, gripping, holding, screwing down, or otherwise securing some object; as, a *bulkhead-door clamp;* a *timber-dog,* a short iron bar bent at right angles near each of its pointed ends; a short bent piece of steel used on a shipyard bending-slab for holding forgings in position; a screw-nut having a short handle; etc. **Cant-d.,** *see* CANT. **D.-curtain,** flap on a canvas binnacle-cover to admit viewing the compass. **Dog's ear,** bight of the leech of a reefed sail; corner of a "shark's mouth," or opening made in an awning in way of a mast, stay, etc. **Dogs running before their master,** old term for the swell running from, and preceding, a hurricane. **D.-fish,** *dog-shark,* or smallest of the shark family, never exceeding four feet in length, native to North Atlantic waters, and regarded as a pest by fishermen because exceedingly destructive to food fishes. Also, the *bowfin, burbot,* and *Alaska blackfish.* **D. star,** brightest star in *Canis Major* and also called *Canicula* (L. dim. of *canis,* dog); sometimes applied also to

Procyon, chief in the group *Canis Minor;* so called by the ancients because of its close proximity to the sun during the uncomfortably sultry part of the summer, or which was termed *canicular* or *dog days.* **D.-stopper,** archaic term for an extra stopper put on a cable to take the stress when cable was transferred from a capstan to bitts; a cable-stopper of any sort in small vessels. **D.-strop,** a strop for suspending a block from a yard. **D.-vane,** in sailing craft, a small feathered arrow or similar device placed on a weather rail, or other position near the helmsman, to show direction of wind. **D. watch,** one of the two-hour watches between 4.00 and 8.00 p.m.; *see* WATCH. **Sea-d.,** *see* SEA. **Spider d.,** *see* SPIDER. **Wind-d.,** *see* WIND.

DOGBODY. A chebacco-boat having a square or "transom" stern. It is now extinct. *See* CHEBACCO-BOAT.

DOGGER. (*Du.*) A broad-nosed, two-masted Dutch fishing-vessel, in rig resembling a ketch, formerly used in the North Sea cod and herring industry. **D'man,** crew member of a *dogger.*

DOGGING THE WATCH. See WATCH.

DOGSHORE. Preparatory to launching, one of several shores placed to hold a medium-weight vessel from moving on the ways while keel-blocks and other shores are removed. Dogshores are knocked down simultaneously and vessel is free to move down the ways.

DOLDRUMS. That equatorial region or belt of low barometric pressure lying between the N.E. and S.E. trade winds in the Atlantic and Pacific Oceans, characterized by light baffling winds, calms, and frequent rain-squalls. Depending on season of the year, its latitude limits are approximately the equator and 12° N., being widest toward the eastern shores of both oceans. In February its average extent is from Lat. 0° to 7° N., and in July 5° N. to 12° N. at its greatest breadth. A sailing-vessel on the usual equator-crossing routes, especially in the northern winter months, may pass through the region with a N.E. squall and immediately pick up the S.E. trades; as a rule, however, she must take advantage of every squall and light fitful breeze to make the passage in two to three weeks.

DOLLAR-FISH. A silvery, deep-bodied fish, laterally compressed, and round in profile, seldom exceeding six inches in length, plentiful on the U.S. Atlantic coast, and of excellent food value; also called *butter-fish, harvest-fish,* and *pumpkin seed.* The smaller similarly-shaped *lookdown* or *moon-fish* of Atlantic and Pacific coasts of America is sometimes called a *dollar-fish.*

DOLLOP. Portion of a sea which leaps over the rail and breaks with its fall on deck.

DOLLY. Small bollard set on the edge of a dock wall or pier for mooring-lines of barges or other smaller craft; also, one fitted inside a vessel's bulwarks for making fast a sheet, tack, bowline, etc. A special hand-bar used in shipyards for turning or holding angle iron, T-iron, etc. **D.-bar,** a holding-on tool for riveting; a short heavy bar with a bevel-faced end used to hold against rivet-heads where obstructions make use of a holding-on hammer impracticable in riveting. **D.-winch,** a small geared hand winch set on a sailing-ship's pin-rail, or otherwise inside her bulwarks, for setting up on halyards, hauling in a sheet, etc.

DOLPHIN. A cluster of piling at the entrance to, or alongside, a dock or wharf for service as a fender; one of a number of groups of piles alongside of which boats may be moored. A heavy mooring-post on a dock. A fixed fender along a boat's sides close below her gunwale; a heavy pudding-fender fixed across a tug-boat's stem. In former days, a kind of wreath made of matted hemp used as a parrel for an upper yard; also, a matted pudding set round a mast as a bolster for hempen standing rigging. A small northern constellation; *see* DELPHINUS. **D.-boom,** a martingale-boom; also *d.-striker; see* BOOM. The *dolphin* is a small-toothed cetacean of the family *Delphinidæ* of which the *common d.* of Mediterranean and Atlantic waters and *bottle-nosed d.* of the Atlantic American coasts, both from 5 to 7 feet in length, are best known. Though differing somewhat, especially in its sharper beak-like snout, from the *porpoise,* to sailors a common *d.* and that similarly playful, gregarious mammal are synonomous. Also, the name given a swift-swimming fish of tropical and semi-tropical seas of the genus *Coryphæna,* 5 to 6 feet in length, of remarkably good food value, and noted for its display of bright variegated skin when taken from the water; also called *dorado (Sp., gilded).*

DOMESTIC TRADE. Carriage of merchandise or passengers between ports on the frontiers or coasts of the United States and ports in the Territories of Alaska and Hawaii. Such vessels as are engaged therein are required to be owned and documented in the United States or in the territories referred to.

DONI. *(Native name.)* A trading vessel of 30 to 50 tons burden on the Ceylon and Coromandel coasts *(India),* having one or two masts and usually lateen-rigged with one or two jibs. Also, *dhoney, dhony, doney.*

DONKEY. Short for donkey-engine, donkey-boiler, donkey-pump, etc. **D.-boiler,** *see* BOILER. **D.-engine,** a small steam or internal combustion engine used on larger sailing-vessels and barges for heaving anchor, pumping water, handling cargo, setting sail, etc.; also, one used with a crane on a dock or scow for cargo work, ship repair operations, etc.

D.-pump, an auxiliary steam pump, usually of the type in which the steam piston directly connects with the pump plunger, used for feeding a *d.-*boiler, pumping bilges, washing decks, etc. **D. topsail,** a gaff-topsail having a small yard at its head; set above a gaff- or lug-sail.

DONKEY'S BREAKFAST. Traditional nautical term for a sailor's straw mattress.

DOOR. As applied on board ship, denotes, in addition to its usual meaning, a removable plate or cover permitting access to some space or protected object; as, a *man-hole d.; a condenser d.* **Boiler-furnace d.,** consists of a steel plate with a cast iron inner plate perforated with small holes, so fitted that there is an air space between the plates. In addition to hinges and opening-bar, usually has a peep-hole through which, in coal firing, a bar may be used in stirring up the fire. **Cargo d.,** usually composed of two half doors meeting laterally or superimposed, fitted in ship's side or in an upper bulkhead as a means through which cargo may be trucked or otherwise carried. **Dead-d.,** *see* DEAD. **Gangway d.,** *see* GANGWAY. **Power-d.,** a mechanically operated sliding *d.* for closing a water-tight compartment; a *long-armed d.* **Watertight d.,** one constructed to prevent passage of water through a bulkhead when closed; usually fitted with a fixed strip of rubber which is compressed against flange of door-frame by wedge-dogs or clamps. Larger passenger vessels are equipped with a bridge-control system by which all or some of *watertight doors* may be closed automatically, either by an electrical trip arrangement or hydraulic power; in the latter case *d.* is usually of sliding type and in the former, *d.* is let fall into closed position. **Weathertight d.,** one on a ship's upper decks designed to keep out rain and spray.

DORADO. A name for the fish *dolphin; see* DOLPHIN. A small star group about 20° east of *Canopus* (*a Argus*), also called the *Goldfish* and the *Swordfish.*

DORMANT MINE. *See* MINE.

DORY. A flat-bottomed boat having comparatively high flaring sides, sloping stem and stern, with counter tapering downward almost to a point; much used by fishermen on banks off New England, Nova Scotia, and Newfoundland in hand-lining for cod, varies from 15 to 20 feet in length, is handled by two men, and its thwarts are removable to allow stowage by "nesting" on deck when parent vessel is under way. Fishing-vessels may carry 15 to 20 dories, depending on number of crew carried. The boat is noted for its stable and maneuvering qualities in rough weather or in a surf. **D.-anchor,** a sand-anchor; *see* ANCHOR.

DOUBLE. To sail round a point of land in following a particular route. To cover an old wooden vessel with an additional layer of planking, either over old ceiling or outside the hull. **Cellular d. bottom,** in larger steel construction, space between inner and outer bottoms divided into a number of "cells" or small compartments as a result of intersecting of center-line keelson and bottom longitudinals with the floor-plates. In general, excepting center-line keelson, longitudinals (*vertical plate girders*) may be either continuous or intercostal. **D.-acting,** operating in two directions, as in both inward and outward actions of a pump or engine piston; *see* ENGINE. **D. altitudes,** *see* ALTITUDE. **D. and single fastening,** system in outside planking fastening in which two bolts are used in alternate timbers and one in the others, usually in addition to same routine with treenail (*wood*) fastening. **D.-armed bolt,** *see* BOLT. **D.-bank,** to man a rope on both sides; to place two men on each oar; to double the number of hands at a capstan, etc. **D.-banked,** said of heavier boats in which two opposite oars are pulled by men on the same thwart; also, *see* BANK. **D.-banked frigate,** *see* FRIGATE. **D.-bitt,** to back up or further secure a hawser by taking additional turns on another pair of bitts. **D. blackwall hitch,** used to attach a rope to a hook by taking a round turn on the hook's shank and crossing rope's end under its standing part across hook itself; *see* HITCH. **D. block,** a tackle-block having two sheaves. **D. bottom,** general term for water-tight space between a ship's bottom shell-plating and her inner bottom plating, or *tank tops,* extending from bilge to bilge and, excepting in tank vessels, longitudinally from fore peak to after peak tanks. A second inner bottom, giving two superimposed bottom spaces, is often built in larger war-vessels. *D. bottom* space is divided into a number of tanks which are used for water-ballast, domestic or boiler-feed water, and oil fuel, as required. Usually each tank is limited in fore-and-aft extent by the water-tight bulkhead arrangement, and is divided laterally by the center-line vertical plate longitudinal. **D. bottom test,** *see* HEAD. **D. danger angle,** *see* DANGER. **D.-decker,** a vessel having two decks above her water-line; a ship of war having two gun decks. **D.-expansion engine,** a compound engine; *see* ENGINE. **D.-ender,** a vessel built for propulsion with either end foremost. **D.-ended bolt,** *see* BOLT. **D. fastening,** referred to outside planking, indicates that each strake has two fastenings driven into each frame. **D. futtock,** *see* FUTTOCK. **D.-gaffed spanker,** formerly on barque-rigged vessels, a divided standing spanker in which the lower gaff acted as a boom for an upper extension of the sail, also supplied with a gaff. Either part could be brailed in or set independently of the other. **D. keel,** *see* KEEL. **D. luff tackle,** purchase consisting of a treble and a double block, its hauling part leading from the treble, or moving, block. **D. light,** *see* LIGHT. **D.-plate rudder,** a built rudder having plates on either side, space between being filled with wood, pitch, or other suitable material. **D. purchase,** *see* PURCHASE. **D. riveting,** *see* RIVETING. **D. roll,** *see* PERIOD. **D. sheet bend,** a round turn of the making end taken on the standing bight, instead of a single turn as in a common *sheet* or *becket bend; see* BEND. **D. Spanish burton,** *see* BURTON. **D. spanker,** same as **double-gaffed spanker. D. tide,** *see* **Tide and half-tide** *in* TIDE. **D. topsails,** *see* SAIL. **To d. upon,** to maneuver a number of ships so as to fire upon an enemy from two sides; to elude pursuers by turning back in running, under cover of night-fall, islands, etc. **D. wall,** a wall knot having the strands followed round a second time; a *stopper-knot; see* KNOT. **D. wall and crown,** a single wall and crown with strands doubled; a *man-rope knot; see* KNOT. **D. whip,** a purchase of two single blocks, its hauling part leading from the moving block; power 1 to 3, neglecting friction; a *gun-tackle.*

DOUBLING. That part of each of two masts which overlap each other, as parts of a lowermast and topmast between lowermast trestle-trees and lowermast cap. A second thickness of plating or planking, outside of hull or elsewhere. Turned in edge of a sail, as at its leech or its foot. **D. angle on bow,** *see* TWO OR MORE BEARINGS WITH RUN BETWEEN. **D.-nails,** clench-nails, such as are used to fasten edges of boats' planking; usually made of copper. **D.-plate,** *see* PLATE.

DOUBLE-FLUKED ANCHOR. *See* ANCHOR.

DOUGLAS SPRUCE. A tough, elastic, durable wood extensively used in America for masts, ship timbers, planking, and joiner-work; weight about 34 lbs. per cubic foot; also called *Douglas fir, Douglas pine, red pine, Oregon pine.*

DOUSE. To suddenly let go, strike, haul down, lower, or take in, as a sail; to quickly stow or close anything; to cease or quit an activity. To plunge into, or drench with, water. To screen or extinguish, as a light.

DOUSING-CHOCK. In older wood construction, a curved timber laid across the apron and secured to the knightheads at the upper deck; a *deck-hook* or *breast-hook.* Also, *dowsing-chock.*

DOVETAIL PLATES. Pieces of non-corrosive plate, usually gun-metal, set in each side of, and binding, a wooden keel and stern-post or a stem and gripe.

DOW. *See* DHOW.

DOWEL. (*Ger. döbel,* plug.) A piece of hard wood or metal, usually cylindrical-shaped, fitted in holes perpendicular to faying wood surfaces for holding the parts in position and resisting shearing stresses. **Butt-d.,** one joining butts of futtocks, frames, etc. **D.-joint,** a connection or joint made with dowels. **D.-plate,** a hard steel plate with gauging holes in which dowels are driven and shaped to size. **Deck-d.,** a common, but incorrect, name for a *deck-plug,* or the wood plug set in a deck over a *deck-bolt; see* PLUG.

DOWN. In the direction of a sailing-vessel's lee, or lower, side; toward a position to leeward; with the course of a current. Often used elliptically, as in *pull d., snug d.;* or intensively, as in *loaded d., tommed d.* To clew **d.,** *see* CLEW. To **drop d.,** to move or drift down a river or with a current. **D. booms,** in the old navy sailing days, command to lower studding-sail booms to deck after taking in the sails. **D. helm,** *see* HELM. **D.-stream,** along with the current; in direction of mouth of a river. **D.-wind,** with the wind; in a direction to leeward; *down the wind.* **Full and d.,** *see* FULL. **Hard d.,** an order to a helmsman, meaning to put helm or tiller toward lee side, thus bringing vessel into the wind as in coming about. To **heave d.,** *see* HEAVE. **Hull d.,** *see* HULL. **Knocked d.,** said of a sailing-vessel when heavily heeled, or "laid down," as in a gale or a heavy squall. **Lay d.,** *see* LAY. To **let d.,** *see* LET. To **round d.,** *see* ROUND. To **run d.,** *see* RUN. To **run d. a coast,** *see* RUN. To **snug d.,** *see* SNUG. To **spar d.,** *see* SPAR. To **tom d.,** *see* TOM.

DOWN-EASTER. Type of wood-built sailing-ship turned out in the New England, New Brunswick, and Nova Scotia yards from 1870 to 1900, well known for first rate sailing qualities combined with a satisfactory carrying capacity, and probably a good all-round second to the clippers. Earlier of these vessels were full-rigged ships, but latterly the barque rig was favored. They were chiefly active in the California–East Coast trade and finally ended in that between South America and Atlantic ports.

DOWNHAUL. A single rope or tackle used to haul down a sail. Fitted as a single line leading from the head cringle of a jib or staysail; as a gun tackle on upper topsail yard-arms; and usually as a single whip on a fore-and-aft sail's gaff end. When a single top-gallant sail or a royal is lowered, its clew-lines act as *downhauls* until yard is down "in the lifts," or in the lowered position; similarly, a gaff topsail clew-line becomes a *downhaul* until the sheet is slacked away. **Peak-d.,** one at outer end or peak of a gaff. **Throat-d.,** one by which the throat of a gaff sail is hauled down.

DOWNTON PUMP. A widely used double-acting hand bilge and force pump operated by a flywheel crank or cranks which lift and lower the piston or plunger. Its suction arrangement admits of pumping from any of several compartments and, also, direct from sea for delivery into a fire main or wash-deck hose.

DOWSE. *See* DOUSE.

DOZY. In a state of decay, as planking or timbers in an old ship.

D. R. Customary abbreviation for *dead reckoning,* as in *position by D.R.,* distinguished from *position by Obs.* (observation).

DRABBLER. Now obsolete in trading-vessels, a small additional sail laced to a jib bonnet (itself an additional fine-weather sail), or to a square sail to give it a greater depth or drop.

DRACO. *(L., =* dragon.) A northern constellation between *Cygnus* and *Ursa Minor,* containing the navigational star *Eltanin* (γ *Draconis*), magnitude 2.4, S.H.A. 91° 07' and Dec. 51° 30' N., which may be located at about 20° north and west of, and nearly in line with, the transept outlined in the cross of *Cygnus.*

DRAFT. (Also, *draught.*) Depth a vessel sinks when afloat, as measured from water-line to lowest immersed part of hull or bottom of keel; depth required to float a vessel. Draft in sea-water is approximately $\frac{1}{4}$ inch per foot less than in fresh water, due to difference in density. A sling or unit quantity of cargo hoisted in loading or discharging. A selection of men sent from one naval ship or station to another; a transfer of ships to a different fleet or squadron. A design or plan of a sail, particularly showing roach or gore, reef-bands, belly-bands, chafing-cloths, etc. Upward current of air in a chimney or stack, carrying off smoke, gases, or exhaust steam. **Aft d.,** as usually measured by draft marks on stern- or rudder-post, depth to which vessel is immersed at her after end. **D.-gauge,** a pressure-gauge; *see* MANOMETER. A ship's draft-indicator based on principle of a hydrostatic gauge. **D. marks,** required by law in U.S. registered vessels to be "marked on stem and stern posts in English feet or decimeters in either Arabic or Roman numerals. The bottom of each numeral shall indicate the draught to that line." British law requires the numerals to be "not less than 6 inches in height" when showing draft in feet. It is customary, however, in all vessels where English feet is indicated, to paint numerals exactly 6 inches in height, such arrangement being conducive toward a close estimate by eye of any draft other than that of an even foot; thus, water level half-way up 15-foot mark = 15 ft. 3 ins.; half-way between 15- and 16-foot marks = 15 ft. 9 ins.; etc. **Extreme d.,** deepest *d.,* or that measured to lowest projecting part of ship. **Forced d.,** *see* B. forced draft *in* BOILER. **Forward d.,** depth to which vessel is immersed at her stem. **Increased d.,** augmentation of draft due to taking cargo or fuel aboard. **Light d.,** depth a vessel is immersed when in the light condition, *i.e.,* ready for sea with no cargo aboard. **Load d.,** extent of immersion allowed a vessel when loading; *d.* in the loaded condition. **Mean d.,** numerical mean of drafts measured at stem and stern. Displacement curve or scale values correspond to *mean drafts.* **Natural d.,** that in a furnace induced only by tendency to rise of heated air and combustion gases; opposed to *forced d.*, or that artificially induced. **Profile d.,** *see* PROFILE.

DRAG. (*Ice. draga,* draw.)   Amount by which draft at stern exceeds that at a vessel's stem. Excess amount of speed of an auxiliary vessel under sail to that indicated by revolutions of her screw; also, retarding effect of screw when making way under sail only. A *drogue, sea-anchor, floating-anchor,* or *driving-anchor,* usually in the form of a conical canvas bag, formerly required to be carried on sea-going steam-vessels for riding out a gale at sea if disabled; now required as part of a life-boat's equipment; any type of improvised sea-anchor or *drag-sail,* such as a *kite-drag,* made by a pair of crossed spars over which heavy canvas is stretched and the whole weighted to float vertically and thus *drag* in the water. One of several heavy weights, such as coils or lengths of chain-cable, used to retard a ship's way upon launching. In former whaling use, a square of several planks joined to present a resisting surface when bridled to a harpoon-line in order to check progress of a wounded whale. Any type of *drag-net* or *trawl* drawn along the sea-bottom in fishing. **Cornucopia d.,** a cone-shaped sea-anchor. **D.-anchor,** *see* ANCHOR. To **d. anchor,** *see* ANCHOR PHRASEOLOGY. **D.-iron,** one of several spare hand harpoons carried in old-time whaling boats. **D.-irons,** a set of hook-shaped irons curving outward from a common shaft used in dragging the bottom for lost cable or other objects; also, *grappling-irons* or *grapnel.* **D.-link,** a bar connecting two cranks or other moving mechanisms; link or bar by which the slotted link is moved or set in Stephenson's link system on a reciprocating engine. **D.-net,** any net used for fishing by dragging along the sea-bottom; a trawl; also, *ground net.* **D.-sail,** a canvas sea-anchor. **D.-surface,** that area of a propeller next to the ship; also, *back of propeller.* **Kite d.,** *see above re* DRAG. **Mud-d.,** a mud-dredge used to deepen a harbor or river. **Wire d.,** a wire hawser used in sweeping a sea-bottom area for ascertaining existence of pinnacle rocks, etc., more efficaciously than may be done with a sounding-lead.

DRAGGER.   General term for Atlantic U.S. coast powered vessels engaged in trawling.

DRAIN.   Hole, pipe, or any means by which anything is drained; act of draining or drawing off. **D.-cock,** a small cock for draining out a steam cylinder, line of steam or water pipes, etc.; a *petcock.* **D.-hole,** one of small draining apertures at lower edges of floor-plates and vertical members in a double bottom; a *limber-hole;* also, a 1- to 2-inch hole opening from each double-bottom tank through vessel's bottom plating for draining tanks dry while in dry-dock; fitted with a brass screw-

plug; a *bleeder-hole.* **D.-plug,** in a boat's bottom, for draining out water when boat is hoisted clear of water. **D.-pot,** small basin-like receptacle fitted in a tank top or 'tween deck corner for taking off condensation, rain, or cargo leakage, sometimes fitted with a steam ejector or, in smaller vessels where tank top is carried straight across to ship's sides, a suction-pipe, for discharging drainage overboard. **D. well,** *see* WELL.

DRAISSA.   See DGHAISA.

DRAUGHT.   See DRAFT.

DRAW.   To occupy a certain depth of water in floating; as, *ship draws 15 feet.* To pull as a sail trimmed to the wind. That portion of a bridge which may be raised or swung to allow passage of vessels. **D.-dock,** an inlet in a river bank used as a dock. **D.-knife,** *see* KNIFE. To **d. on,** to gain on; as, *a ship drew on the flying frigate.* To **d. out,** to move out or away; as, *a vessel drew out from her berth.* **D.-rope,** line by which a trawl-net is hoisted aboard and its open end closed in draw-string fashion. **D.-splice,** *see* SPLICE.

DRAWBRIDGE.   A bridge having a *draw* or section which may be lifted, lowered, swung, or horizontally rolled, to provide a passage for vessels.

DRAWING-STRING.   A workable leech-rope in addition to the usual rope sewn on a fore-and-aft sail of yachts and small craft. It is enclosed in the leech tabling and arranged to be hauled taut or slackened at the sail's clew. Used to stiffen leech or take the stress when sail is shrunk due to wetness and leech-rope does not correspondingly tauten.

DREADNAUGHT.   A type of warship first appearing in British navy in 1907, so named because of departure in armament from that of previous types in that only guns of heaviest caliber were carried and armor protection greatly increased. Later, the term grew to signify a modern battleship of any type, and the name *Super-Dreadnaught* was given any such vessel assumed to be more powerful than any previously built. These ships to-day carry batteries of light guns for defense against torpedo craft, submarines, and aircraft, in addition to the heaviest guns afloat.

DREDGE.   Also termed *dredger,* a vessel equipped with machinery for excavating ditches or canals, deepening channels and harbors, removing sunken rocks, shoals, etc. Three digging methods principally are used: by a series of scoop-buckets operated on an endless chain; by a single clam-shell or scoop-bucket lifted by an arm or crane; and by a suction tube or tubes; the last-named for mud and sand only; a *dredging-machine.* Any apparatus used to gather oysters, mussels, etc. from the water; a *drag-net.* To deepen by dredging, as a river channel; to gather by a dredge or drag-net, as mud or oysters. To drag an anchor in controlling a vessel carried by a stream, as in *clubbing; see* CLUB. **D.-boat,** one carrying a dredging-machine.

DREISONSTOK METHOD. A short method for calculating altitudes and azimuths of heavenly bodies in connection with plotting of position lines, and great circle courses and distances. Explanation of the system and its necessary working tables are embodied in "H.O. 208," published by U.S. Hydrographic Office, Navy Department, Washington, D.C.

DRESS SHIP, To. To array or rig out a vessel with flags and pennants in honor of a person or event. Formerly, such display often was carried to the extreme "rainbow fashion" of running a line of bunting from water's edge to jib-boom end, thence to fore, main, and mizzen trucks, down to spanker-boom, and over the stern to water; also, on special gala occasions flags were displayed in vertical line between each yard-arm, in addition to the *rainbow dress.* To-day, a single vertical line of International Code flags at each mast, with national colors aft, house flag at maintruck, and jack at the fore commonly constitutes *dressing ship* in the merchant service; rainbow dress, however, often is seen, especially in naval vessels, and now amounts to a display above deck on a line from stem to stern via the mastheads. **D. uniform,** that worn by naval officers as prescribed by regulation for certain ceremonial occasions. (At time of writing, it is announced that important changes in present dress uniform for U.S.N. officers will become effective at an early date.)

DRESSING-PLATE. A bending-slab; *see* PLATE.

DRIED FISH. Those that are cleaned and split, dry salted or soaked in brine, then laid out in the sun to dry, as *cod;* often thereafter smoked, as *salmon.*

DRIFT. Distance covered in a given time by, or rate of flow of, a sea surface-current; distance or angle from a set course caused by wind and/or current; leeway. Difference in diameter of two related or fitting parts, as that of a mast and its encircling hoops for a sail; of a treenail and hole into which driven; of a block-pin and sheave-bushing, etc. Length of rope from its part in use to its end; distance between blocks of a tackle, especially limit to which they may be separated. Displacement of rivet-holes intended to fair to each other; a punch for backing out rivets or bolts. An old-fashioned curled or scrolled termination of the main bulwark rail at the break of a poop or top-gallant forecastle. **D.-anchor,** *see* ANCHOR. **D. angle,** that between a tangent to a circular path on which a ship is turning and her fore-and-aft line. **D.-boat,** *see* DRIFTER. **D.-bolt,** a tapered bolt usually driven obliquely in fastening timber; *see* BOLT. **D. bottle,** small water-tight receptacle or bottle thrown overboard for pur-

pose of ascertaining drift of current; *see* BOTTLE PAPERS. **D. current,** *see* CURRENT. **D.-ice,** masses of broken ice driven by curents or strong winds. **D.-lead,** a heavy sounding-lead dropped to bottom for purpose of indicating a possible dragging of, or parting from, an anchor in a current, strong wind, or rough sea. Trend of lead-line will be toward the anchor if ship is moving from her berth. Also, a lead used in shallow water instead of the *log-chip,* when heaving the old-fashioned *log;* direction in which line lies in paying out indicates vessel's course *over the ground* or that she is *making good.* **D.-line,** a fishing-line with one or more hooks paid out and allowed to "drift," its depth being controlled by sinkers or floats. **D.-map,** chart or map showing location of glacial deposits or those by running water from glaciers, ordinarily called *drifts,* as *glacier d., fluvio-glacial d.* **D.-net,** any gill net suspended vertically from floats at required depth and free to *drift.* Boat or vessel in attendance, called a *drifter,* rides to one end of net, or line of nets,—always the *lee end* in a breeze. Used principally in mackerel, herring, sprat, and sardine fishing, such nets may extend for 1½ miles from the drifter. **D.-piece,** old-fashioned scrolled piece of timber joining main bulwark rail with break of poop or top-gallant forecastle; also, *d.-rail.* **D.-pin,** in riveting, a steel tapered pin for opening out rivet-holes that are not fair or in proper alignment. **D.-sail,** a drag-sail; *see* DRAG. **Esker d.,** long ridges of gravel and sand deposited by glacial streams or formed from glacial ice movement itself. **River-d.,** boulders, gravel, sand or other deposit moved from one place to another by a river current.

DRIFTAGE. Archaic term for amount of deviation from a set course due to making leeway or current. Flotsam or litter carried or driven by sea or wind.

DRIFTER. A boat or special type of vessel engaged in drift-net fishing; especially, a vessel much used in United Kingdom waters, about 100 feet in length, having a commodious forward hold space for both nets and fish, and equipped with necessary gear for handling nets. Some of such vessels are used both in trawling and drift-net work and are termed *trawler-drifters.* Formerly, drifters were sturdy ketch-rigged vessels; to-day almost all are steam or motor driven.

DRIFTWEED. Any sea-weed washed up on a shore.

DRIFTWOOD. Wood of any sort, especially timbers and planking of wrecked or broken-up vessels, floating and drifting about; such wood washed up on shore by the sea.

DRILL. Act or exercise of training a ship's crew in a particular duty; as in *boat, fire, collision,* or *rescue drills.* A tool for boring holes in hard substances, as metal or hardwood. A twilled linen or cotton fabric used for white clothes; particularly, as naval seamen's uniforms. **D.-master,** an instructor in military exercises. **D.-ship,** a former term for a moored war-vessel in which men were instructed in use of guns, sails, etc.

DRILLER. One who drills holes in a ship's structural parts in a shipyard, and whose duties also include reaming, tapping, and countersinking.

DRILLING TEST. Operation of drilling small holes in important metal castings in order to determine soundness of material; such as that performed on engine columns or a cast steel stern frame.

DRIVE. Mechanical system or power by which a vessel is propelled. To carry a heavier press of sail than normally is consistent with prudence. To allow a vessel to be impelled by force of wind and/or sea; as, to *let her drive.* To be carried helplessly to leeward by wind and sea; as, *the ship will drive (or be driven) on shore.* **D.-boat,** a striker-boat; *see* STRIKER. **Direct d.,** propulsion system by which propeller-shaft is connected directly to, and turns at same speed as, the driving machinery, as with a *reciprocating engine.* **Electric d.,** system in which propeller is driven by an electric motor or motors, power being supplied by one or more generators operated by steam turbine or internal combustion engines. **Geared d.,** propulsion in which a high speed engine is geared down to turn propeller-shafting at required operating speed.

DRIVER. In 16th. century English vessels, a lateen or square sail set on a short mast at the stern. Later, the *spanker,* or after fore-and-aft sail on a vessel of brig or ship rig; and, more recently, a jib-headed spanker. The sixth mast, or its sail, in a schooner of more than five masts. **D.-boom,** old term for a spanker-boom on a square-rigged vessel.

DRIVING-ANCHOR. A drogue or sea-anchor; *see* DRAG.

DRIVING-SHORE. A heavy timber laid against a small vessel's stem to start her down the ways in launching. It is placed slantwise and wedged for both lifting and pushing effect on the hull.

DROG. *See* DRAG.

DROGHER. A kind of bluff-bowed, sea-going sailing-barge peculiar to the Gulf of Paria (between Venezuela and Trinidad); usually has one mast and a lug or lateen sail split at the mast. Any clumsy cargo-vessel of coasting type. Also, *droger, drogh.*

DROGHING. An old term for the coastwise cargo trade of West Indies.

DROGUE. A sea-anchor; a drag made of planks, a tub, etc., used in older whaling days to check a wounded whale; *see* DRAG.

DROITS OF ADMIRALTY. *See* ADMIRALTY DROITS.

DROMOND. (O.F., *dromont.*) A large fast-sailing war-vessel of medieval times, having three masts, a high ornamental poop, heavily armed, and in addition to a working crew carried a large company of soldiers. Also a large and swift galley. Sometimes written *dromon.*

DROP. Distance or *depth* of a square sail bent to a standing yard, measured at mid-spread from head-rope to foot, as that of a course or lower topsail; distinguished from *hoist,* or similar measurement of a sail bent to a hoisting yard, as of an upper topsail, a single top-gallant sail, or a royal. To sail away from, or out-distance. To fall back or move toward the stern, as a boat alongside a ship; to allow another vessel to pass going in same direction by slackening speed; as, to *drop astern.* To **d. anchor,** to let go an anchor. To **d. astern,** to fall astern or move to a position astern of another vessel; to slow down so as to allow another vessel to pass. **D.-bolt,** a dog-bolt which may be dropped or knocked aside from its securing position in a slit or opening when slacked off; as in an air-port or a deep tank cover. To **d. down,** to sail or drift with a current, as in a river. To **drop a vessel,** to leave one astern by outsailing her. **D.-keel,** a centerboard; *see* KEEL. **D.-line,** a line without a rod as used in still-fishing. **D.-rudder,** *see* RUDDER. **D.-strake,** a shell-plating strake discontinued near a vessel's ends because of hull's decreasing girth toward bow and stern. Two adjacent strakes are tapered and merged into one by butting their narrower ends to a *stealer* or single tapering plate. Each time a stealer is introduced, number of strakes is reduced by one.

DROPPING MOOR. In mooring with both bower anchors, procedure of first dropping the upstream or weather anchor, paying out cable and coming astern to position required for lee anchor, which is then let go, weather cable hove in and lee cable paid out until ship is berthed midway between anchors.

DRUG. A variant of *drogue; see* DRAG.

DRUM. Part of a capstan, winch, or windlass, around which the turns of a hawser, hoisting-rope, etc., are taken or wound in heaving. A cylindrical-shaped receptacle, such as a tub, kind of barrel, case, box, etc., either of wood or metal. A shape of cylindrical form, usually consisting of a metal frame covered with canvas, about two feet in diameter and in height, formerly used in conjunction with the ball and cone shapes in an international code system of *distance signals,* and, also, in conjunction with a cone in *storm warning signals.* **Chain-d.,** *see* CHAIN. **Circulating d.,** in a water-tube boiler, a cylindrical shaped chamber in which circulation of steam and water essentially is secured by unequal heating. **D.-hooks,** a group of pairs of can-hooks attached to a hoisting-ring for lifting two or more drums or similar cargo units; *see* CAN-HOOK. **D.-wheel,** a large reel mounted on horizontal axis and used for winding in or stowing wire hawsers, ropes, etc. **Friction-d.,** a rotating part of a windlass or winch which is arranged to engage the main working or heaving part by frictional pressure in transferring power from the driving source. A friction block, usually shaped like a frustum of a cone, used as a brake on a windlass by engaging with the rotating part, or *wild-cat,* carrying the cable. **Indicator d.,** rotating cylinder on which is set a registering card or paper, as that of an engine indicator, barograph, thermograph, etc.

DRUMFISH. A food fish of the family *Sciænidæ,* so named from its ability to make a drumming noise, well known on the American Atlantic coasts; usually two or three feet in length, large dorsal fins, broad tail, and almost circular curvature of back from mouth to tail.

DRUMHEAD. Part of a capstan in which the bars are shipped; end of a winch where turns of a rope are taken in heaving. **D. man,** one who operates a cargo whip on drum end of a winch.

DRUXEY. A defect in heartwood of timber, usually appearing as white spots or spongy veins. Also, *druxy.*

DRY. Rainless or comparatively *dry season* in some parts of the tropics, as opposed to the *rainy season;* often referred to as the *Dry.* Said of a vessel which ships remarkably little water in heavy weather. **D.-bottom boiler,** any type of boiler having no water space below its furnace. **D. or D. card compass;** *see* COMPASS. **D.-dock,** floating dock, graving dock, slip dock, etc.; *see* DOCK. **D.-dock dues,** charges for use of a dry-dock, usually based on gross tonnage of vessel. **D. fog,** that prevailing when temperature is several degrees above the dew point; believed to be caused by dust particles adhering to and preventing evaporation of real fog particles. **D. harbor,** one in which berths alongside wharves are dry or partly dry at low water. In order to provide an even resting place for vessels lying aground, as in such harbors bordering the Bay of Fundy, a *mattress,* consisting of heavy softwood timber laid close together, is placed athwart the berths, embedded in the bottom. **D. monsoon,** *see* MONSOON. **D. provisions,** *see* PROVISIONS. **D. rot,** a decay of seasoned timber caused by several species of the fungus *Polyporus.* Damp, unventilated situations are favorable for growth of such fungi. **D. tank,** one of the tanks or subdivisions of a double bottom in which no water is carried; usually such space immediately below ship's boilers is kept free of water in order to circumvent corrosive action brought about by combined dampness and heat. **D. wash,**

bed of a stream or bottom of a canyon that has dried up. **D. weir,** a fish-net set vertically on a line of stakes where the tide leaves the site dry at lowest ebb; fish are caught in the weir at higher stages of the flood. **High and d.,** completely clear of the water, as a vessel lying on a beach at low water.

DUAL VALUATION. In marine insurance, two valuations given a vessel; one for purposes of damage or average claims, the other and lower for claim of total loss. A clause covering such agreed-upon valuation is embodied in the policy.

DUB. In shipbuilding, to smooth off a timber or planking with an adze; *see* ADZE; to dress or smooth a wood surface with a plane or scraper.

DUBHE. (Ar. *al dubbu,* the Bear.) *Alpha* (*α*) *Ursae Majoris,* star nearest *Polaris* (North Star) in the *Great Bear* (Big Dipper); magnitude 2.0; dec. 62° N.; S.H.A. 194¾°.

DUCK. (Du. *doeck,* linen cloth.) Strong cotton or linen smooth-woven fabric, lighter than canvas, used for light sails and men's wear; often improperly called *canvas.* **Russian d.,** a white linen duck of fine quality. To **d. up,** to raise the tack of a fore-and-aft sail or clew of a square sail, when it obstructs a helmsman's view ahead. **Ducks,** light clothes made of duck, often worn by naval seamen as uniform in warm weather.

DUCK, SEAGOING. The DUKW of the U.S. Coast Guard, an amphibious craft built with a scow-like hull and raised cabin. This remarkable land-and-water vessel, a product of World War II, contributed materially in the landing, loading, and unloading of men and munitions in practically every instance of beach-landing attack by the allied forces. As a result of experience in use of the *duck,* the Coast Guard has turned it to advantage, with a few modifications, as a rescue-boat at certain life-boat stations on our coasts. After exhaustive tests of the *duck's* behavior in sorties from the beach through heavy surf, it was concluded that, *esp.* for close inshore work, DUKW greatly surpasses the conventional lifeboat both in maneuverability and security against capsizing.

DUCT KEEL. *See* KEEL.

DUE. Directly; exactly; referred to direction, as, the shoal is *due north* of us; a ship sails *due west.* **For a full due,** said of a job that need not be repeated; as, stays and then shrouds are set up *for a full due.*

DUFF. (English dialectal name for *dough.*) A stiff flour pudding, often containing raisins or currants, boiled in a bag or cloth; the *plum duff* of sailors, once considered a treat on deep-water ships. **D.-day,** sailors' old term for the day on which *duff* was served; usually Sunday.

DUGONG. (Malay, *duyong*.) Aquatic herbivorous mammal allied to the *manatee,* inhabiting coasts of Australia, East Indies, Indian Ocean, and Red Sea; attains a length of eight feet and chiefly differs from the manatee in its bilobate tail, or that similar to the whales. It produces a valuable oil.

DUGOUT. The ages-old boat or canoe fashioned from a tree trunk and hollowed out by burning or hewing. Such boats are found in all countries where large trees are available and represent the earliest attempt in history toward obtaining an easily propelled and commodious craft. Whether driven by paddles, as in the rivers of Africa, or shaped and rigged to sail with astonishing speed, as in the East Indies, Oceania, and northern shores of South America, their size, rig, and body form varies with the many peoples amongst whom they are made, sailed, and named. Larger dugouts are often given additional siding by an upper strake or two of planking.

DUKE OF YORK.. In English ships, a sailor's term for the *fore spencer,* a gaff sail formerly set abaft a lowermast; *see* SPENCER.

DULL. To die away, as a breeze; as in *the wind dulled down at noon.*

DUMB. Having no sails or other means of self-propulsion; as a *dumb barge.* **D. chalder,** metal block fitted on lower end of a wooden stern-post for receiving the rudder's convex-ended *bearing-pintle* and thus the whole weight of rudder. **D. compass,** *see* COMPASS and PELORUS. **D. craft,** any vessel or floating structure having no means of self-propulsion, steering, or signalling, but generally considered as *vessels* in maritime law. **D. iron,** in caulking, an iron used to open close seams; *see* **caulking-irons** *in* IRON. **D. sheave,** groove in a spar, bulwark, etc., for a rope to slide in; a block-sheave having no roller-bushing. **D. snatch,** a notch- or snatch-block having no sheave. **D. pintle,** *see* PINTLE.

DUMMY. As a qualifying word, indicating an imitation or copy of something, in the sense of being useful as a substitute. **D.-barge,** a raft, pontoon, or large camel placed between ship and quay for breasting ship off and/or receiving cargo. **D. compass,** same as *dumb compass.* **D. crosshead,** where a steering-engine acts on a rudder crosshead, as in the case of restricted space in extreme after end of ship, the substitute, located forward of rudder-head, from which turning power is transferred by drag-links to rudder-crosshead proper. **D. funnel,** on some larger passenger liners, one not used as a smoke outlet but placed for symmetry of outline, with the suggestive appearance of importance and power. Such "stacks" are used to house forced ventilation machinery, emergency lighting generators, store-rooms, etc. **D. gantline,** a handy old rope kept rove in a single block at a masthead, top of a

smoke-stack, etc., as a means for conveniently reeving a *working-gantline* for a bo'sn's chair, paint-staging, etc.; also, *d. girtline.*

DUMP. A barge for carrying refuse; a place for receiving refuse on a dock. **D.-barge,** vessel used in construction work for placing stones, earth, etc., as required; often constructed to allow load to slide overboard by giving vessel a list. Such barges also may be built to carry material in a hold provided with opening bottom doors, in which case may be used also for disposal of garbage, ashes, excavated mud, etc. Also termed *d.-scow.* **D.-bolt,** a fastening employed similarly to a spike in that it is not driven entirely through both timbers. **D.-fastening,** action or state of being secured by *d.-bolts* or *dumps.* **D.-scow,** *see* **d.-barge.**

DUMPING PLANKS. Planking laid on a tank top, or additional to the wood ceiling of a hold in way of hatch-openings, as protection against wear and tear of falling cargo, such as ore, coal, pig-iron, stone. Also, *d.-boards.*

DUNDERFUNK. *See* DANDYFUNK.

DUNE. A mound, ridge, or hill of loose sand heaped up by the wind on a sea-coast.

DUNGA. (*Hind.*) A large flat-bottomed dugout with long overhanging ends, having one mast and a square sail, used in the marshes and branches of the Ganges delta.

DUNGIYAH. (*Ar.*) Coasting-vessel of the Persian Gulf now growing extinct, but of interest in that their flat bottom, broad beam, long raking stem, and high ornate transom stern differ little from those of the model used to carry the armies of Alexander the Great *(336–323 B.C.)* on his eastern world-conquering expedition. The craft had a single long mast and huge lateen sail, was of about 100 tons burden. For centuries a large fleet of these vessels sailed for India from head of Persian Gulf at the favorable wind season and made a first-stop rendezvous at Muscat (Muskat) in Oman, where their safe arrival was celebrated with prayers, music, flowing banners, and salvos of artillery.

DUNNAGE. Pieces of cordwood, boards, slats, etc. appropriately placed under and around cargo in a ship's hold for protection of goods against contact with bilge-water, leakage from other cargo, contact with ship's sides or structural parts and condensation therefrom; to chock off and secure cargo from moving, thus preventing chafing; to separate different kinds or consignments of goods; and to provide air passage through certain otherwise closely packed commodities, such as bagged rice, onions, and others requiring ventilation. Collective term for working material, such as tools, equipment, and extra building parts found on board ship at a repair yard. Baggage of a seaman. Equipment carried in a boat or canoe for shore camping, etc. Also, *duffle, duffel*. **D.-gratings,** wooden floor gratings upon which cargoes requiring complete through ventilation are stowed. **D.-mat,** a texture of straw, cane, sedge-grass, etc., used to protect goods from chafing against structural parts of ship, for separation of valuable goods, and for protection against damage by contact with sweating or wet surfaces (condensation).

DUNN'S ANCHOR. *See* ANCHOR.

DUPLICATING PIPE. In shipyard work, the piece of brass tubing used to transfer rivet-hole layout from template to frame, plate, or other structural part. End of pipe is dipped in paint and pushed through each template hole against the plate, etc., thus plainly and accurately marking positions of required holes.

DURAMEN. (*L., = hardened.*) Central or *heart-wood* in a trunk of a tree, called the *spine* by shipbuilding carpenters.

DUTCH DOOR. A door having an upper and lower section, either of which may be swung independently of the other; often fitted on a main deck where lower section prevents ingress of water ordinarily shipped in rough weather.

DUTCHIFY. A quaint English term indicating to change a square stern into a round one; as, to *dutchify* a vessel's hull.

DUTCHMAN. Wooden block or wedge used to fill the void in a badly made butt or joint; a *graving-piece,* or repairing patch set in a deck plank. A filling-piece used in riveting where faying surfaces can not be drawn close enough together; also, *filler, shim*. **D.'s land,** an illusory appearance of land, as a distant fog-bank, or cloud on the horizon; "Cape Flyaway." **D.'s log,** *see* LOG. **Flying D.,** the Dutch mariner who is said to have been con-demned to sail his ship till the day of judgment; also, his 17th.-century vessel which repeatedly has been reported as sighted in the vicinity of Cape of Good Hope during bad weather, with consequent misfortune to the observing vessel.

DUTY. Tax upon imported or exported goods. Under the United States constitution no duty may be laid on goods exported from any state. In Great Britain, the term applies to all personal or indirect taxes, such as those on checks, legal documents, licenses, and excise taxes on home manufactured commodities. *See* CUSTOMS. **Ad valorem d.,** *see* AD VALOREM. **D.-free,** that which is free from customs or excise taxes; *custom-free*. **D.-proof,** that which carries a mark used in Chinese customs indicating goods have already paid duty and are not subject to further impost. **Specific d.,** tax on imported merchandise according to quantity, weight, or number, rather than value; opposed to *ad valorem d.* **Tonnage-d.,** tax levied on vessels, usually on net registered tonnage; *see* TONNAGE. **Transit-d.,** that levied on goods passing through a country to destination in another.

D.W.T. Common abbreviation for *dead-weight tonnage.*

DYCE. "Hold her!" "Keep her so!" Order to a helmsman to hold his course, usually in sailing close-hauled, when vessel is lying to wind as required; or, in its fuller form, "Dyce; no higher." (*Archaic*)

DYGOGRAM. An early term for a curve showing magnitude and direction of the horizontal component of earth's total magnetic force, as measured by compass-needle on board ship, and consequent effect of magnetic properties of vessel's iron on her compass, for several or all headings through which vessel is swung.

DYNAMICAL STABILITY. *See* STABILITY.

E

E. Corresponds to Greek letter *epsilon* (ε), designating the fifth star (originally in point of brilliancy or magnitude) of a particular group; as, ε *Orionis,* fifth in the constellation *Orion.* Abbreviation for *East* in compass-points, as in E by S (*East by South*); E N E (*East-north-east*). In International Code of Signals, flag *E,* hoisted singly, indicates "*I am directing my course to starboard.*" In Lloyd's classification system, stands for lowest class; in that of American Bureau of Shipping, an encircled *E* annexed to classification symbols signifies vessel's *equipment* complies with requirements of the Society's rules. **Navy E,** *see* NAVY.

EAGER. (Preferred spelling, *eagre*) *See* BORE.

EAGLE GULL. The black-backed gull; *see* GULL.

EAGLE RAY. One of the larger fishes of the *ray* family; *see* RAY.

EARING. Short piece of handy rope used to secure a corner of a sail in position on a yard, gaff, or boom and for hauling out and making fast a reef-cringle in reefing; also for bending each corner of an awning to a spar, stanchion, etc. **Bull-e.,** a reef-earing formerly made fast at each topsail yard-arm for readiness in reefing. **E.-cringle,** grommet or metal ring in each corner of a sail for receiving turns of the *e.* **From clew to e.,** from bottom to top; hence, figuratively, in a thorough manner; entirely. **Head-e.,** rope for securing either upper corner of a square sail to its yard, or peak of a fore-and-aft sail to its gaff. **Nock-e.,** rope for securing upper forward corner of a fore-and-aft sail having a gaff; also, *throat-e.* **Reef-e.,** that used to lash a reef-cringle to a yard-arm or boom in reefing a sail. **Tack-e.,** rope securing lower forward corner of a gaff sail; a tack lashing.

EARTH. Third planet in order from the sun, is of oblate spheroidal shape having a polar diameter of 7900 and an equatorial diameter of 7927 statute miles. Its mean density is about 5.6 or approximately twice that of granite. Its daily rotation about its polar axis, as measured between two successive transits of a fixed star at a given meridian, occupies 23 hrs., 56 min., 4.09 sec. of mean solar time, or one sidereal day; and its yearly revolution around the sun, as measured by the sidereal year, 365 days, 6 hrs., 9 min., 8.97 sec., of mean solar time. The plane of Earth's orbit or path through the heavens is inclined to that of the equator 23° 27'. Mean distance from sun is 92,897,416 statute miles.

EASE. To lessen stress by any means; to mitigate an aggravated or burdened condition; as, to *ease the windlass brake;* to *ease off a hawser.* **E. her,** an order to reduce speed of engines. **E. the helm; e. the rudder,** command to lessen angle of rudder after giving a hard-over helm; often used as *ease her 10°, 15°, etc.* To **e. away,** to gradually slacken off, as a rope.

EAST. (Gr. *eos,* dawn) That one of the four cardinal points of the compass lying on one's right hand when facing north; point of the horizon at which the sun rises at the equinoxes; general direction in which sun rises. *The East* connotes Asiatic lands in general; *Near East* comprising Arabia, Asia Minor, Iran, Iraq, Turkey, etc.; *Far East,* China, Indo-China, Japan, Korea, etc. From the east; as, *an east wind.* **E. by N.,** one point or $11\frac{1}{4}$° north of *e.* **E. by S.,** one point or $11\frac{1}{4}$° south of *e.* **E.N.E.,** two points or $22\frac{1}{2}$° north of *e.* **E.S.E.,** two points or $22\frac{1}{2}$° south of *e.* **Magnetic E.,** the east point as indicated by a correct magnetic compass. **True E.,** *magnetic E.* corrected for compass variation; geographical east; point in celestial horizon diametrically opposite the west, at which points the *prime vertical* and *equinoctial* intersect each other.

EAST INDIA COMPANY. A shipping organization first granted a charter by *Elizabeth* of England, 31 Dec., 1600, as "The Governor and Company of merchants of London trading with the East Indies." It was given, in 1765, joint territorial sovereignty with the crown in India. In 1698, a competitor named "The English Company trading to the East Indies" was chartered, and in 1702 both combined under the title of "The United Company of merchants of England trading to the East Indies." Stripped of its governing powers in 1858, the company finally was dissolved by act of Parliament in 1874. A similar Dutch company existed 1602 to 1795; a French one, 1664 to 1770; and a Danish, 1729 to 1801.

EAST-INDIAMAN. A sailing-ship that makes voyages to India or East Indies; especially, one of those East Indian traders of English, Dutch, French, and Danish chartered companies which flourished in the 17th and 18th centuries.

EASTING. Distance made good to *eastward;* departure in miles toward the *east* from a given meridian, as, in steering N.E. for 10 miles, vessel should make an *easting* of 7.1 miles; miles traveled on a true *east* course. **Running the e. down,** in sailing-ship usage, expression referring to covering the long eastward stretch in the "roaring forties" from off Cape of Good Hope to Australia, or to the point at which vessel was hauled to N.E., if bound to East Indies; also, from Australia to Cape Horn.

EASY. Not pressing or straining; moderate; as *a ship under easy sail.* A command to slacken effort as in heaving, pulling, lowering, etc. **E. bilge,** descriptive term for a long-curving bilge, or that of a vessel having comparatively great rise of floor (*deadrise*). To ride e., *see* RIDE.

EAT. To gnaw into; wear away; consume; as action of rust or galvanic erosion. To **e. to windward,** to work up to every puff of wind in sailing close-hauled. To **e. to windward of,** to **e. the wind out of,** another vessel, to sail close on her weather side when close-hauled in order to "blanket" her and gain distance to windward.

EBB. Return or fall of the tide-wave seaward; fall of tide; seaward flow of a tidal current; opposed to *flood;* ebb-current; ebb-stream; ebb-tide. Direction of local ebb-current is shown on American and British charts by an unfeathered arrow. **After-e.,** *see* AFTER. **E.-anchor,** where a vessel is moored in a tideway, that anchor to which she rides during the ebb. **E. and flow,** alternate incoming and outgoing stream attributed to tidal effect; properly, *ebb and flood.* **Windward e.,** an ebb-stream running in opposite direction to the wind, or into "the wind's eye."

ECCENTRIC. (Gr. *ekkentros,* out of center) One of two disks or sheaves keyed eccentrically to the driving-shaft of a reciprocating engine, free to revolve inside of rings or straps. *Eccentric* rotation of the disks thus placed provides, by means of a rod attached to each strap, the in-and-out motion required to alternately open and close steam admission valves in the engine cylinders. In order to regulate travel of valves and to reverse engine motion, the rods are interrupted by a curved sliding link on each, lateral position of which is controlled by an appropriate lever mechanism, as in the Stephenson link system. **E. error,** that in sextant

readings caused by a small displacement of the instrument's index-bar pivotal point, which may be due to faulty manufacture, unequal metal expansion or contraction, or injury to frame.

ECHELON. (Fr. *echelle,* ladder) A fleet line formation in which each vessel, proceeding on the set course, lies forward or abaft the beam of her next in line.

ECHO SOUNDING. Determination of depths based upon speed of sound through water (4800 feet per second, nearly), essentially consisting of a means of sending out a sound of sufficient intensity from ship's bottom, receiving the echo from sea floor, and accurately indicating depths obtained; also called *sonic* and *acoustic* sounding. **E. sounding apparatus,** *see* FATHOMETER.

ECLIPSE. (Gr. *ekleipsis,* a failing or leaving out) Whole or partial obscuration of a heavenly body by interposition of another, either between it and the observer, or between it and the sun. **Annular e.,** when moon's angular diameter is less than that of sun, as at apogee, a *solar e.* appearing as a ring of light outlining the moon's periphery. **Lunar e.,** occurring only at *full moon,* interposition of Earth between Sun and Moon; may be *partial* or *total,* depending on relative positions in declination of the bodies, and, as with any *e.* of either luminary, also depending on geographical position from which observed. **Partial e.,** one in which the body is partly obscured by the interposed body's shadow. **Solar e.,** occurring only at *new moon,* caused by interposition of Moon between an observer and Sun; may be *partial, annular,* or *total.* **Total e.,** one in which the body observed is covered entirely by shadow of the body interposed between it and the sun, as in a *lunar e.;* in which the sun is obscured by the moon, as in a *solar e.;* in which a planet *occults* one of its satellites; or in which the moon occults a planet or star. The two last-noted usually are termed *occultations* in astronomer's usage. Probably the phenomenon of a *total e.* of the *sun* occurs as rarely as once in 400 years at any particular place, the average interval being about 360 years; one of the moon takes place with comparative frequency.

ECLIPTIC. (Probably named from the fact that *eclipses* of sun and moon take place on this circle) Apparent path or great circle described in the heavens by the sun, or great circle yearly described by the earth in her orbit, as viewed from the sun; plane of Earth's orbit extended to the celestial sphere and which lies at an angle of 23° 27′ with that of the *equinoctial* or *celestial equator,* termed *obliquity of the e.* The two points of intersection of the *e.* with the equinoctial are called, respectively, *vernal equinox* and *autumnal equinox,* the sun passing through the former March 20–23 and through the latter September 20–23. **Cardinal points of the e.,** *see* CARDINAL.

ECONOMICAL SPEED. *See* SPEED.

ECONOMIZER. Any apparatus for utilizing heat that would otherwise be wasted, as a system of tubing in a boiler uptake for pre-heating feed-water.

ECTROPOMETER. Archaic name for a bearing-plate or pelorus; also, *ektropometer. See* PELORUS.

E.D. Abbreviation in American and British hydrography for *existence doubtful,* placed near a charted rock, shoal, wreck, or other obstruction, indicating that neither actual presence nor reported non-existence of such was verified at time of publishing chart.

EDDY. Current of air or water running contrariwise to a main current; *e.g.,* that found in a river near a point which the main stream has rounded; a whirlpool, such as the sometimes dangerous *Charybdis* on the Sicilian side of the Messina Strait, much exaggerated and fabled in ancient lore as a female monster seeking destruction of the galleys. **E. resistance,** that given to, and thus increasing thrust of, a propeller by return eddies, or eddy-water at the stern, when vessel is going ahead. **E.-water,** same as *dead-water; see* DEAD. **E.-wind,** breeze eddying in lee of a headland, bluff, sail, etc. **Tidal e.,** *see* TIDAL.

EDGE. Margin or sharp terminating border of anything; cutting face of a tool. Combined with *away, down, in,* expresses motion from, toward, etc., as in sailing. **Burr e.,** ridgy roughness along edge of a plate after cutting, around a rivet-hole, etc. **Caulking e.,** accessible or exposed edge to be caulked; as, that of a strake of outside or deck plating. **To e. away,** or **off,** to gradually increase distance from, as from another vessel, a coast, etc. To **e. down,** in sailing, to approach obliquely toward an object lying to leeward. To **e. in,** to move sidewise by degrees toward an objective; to close in with. To **e. in with,** to approach gradually and obliquely a coast, vessel, etc. **Flanged e.,** that formed by bending at a sharp angle a narrow section along edge of a plate; for sidewise stiffening or faying purposes. **Following e.,** that of a propeller-blade opposite the leading or cutting edge when engines are turning ahead; opposed to *leading e.* **Landing e.,** that of a plate faying on a beam, frame, etc., and over which another plate is lapped; opposed to *sight edge,* or that of a lapping plate. **Leading e.,** *see* **following e. Molding e.,** that of a ship's bulkhead, frame, or floor-plate directly in contact with the shell-plating. **Sight e.,** visible or exposed edge of any plate; usually the *caulking e.* in shell-plating, double-bottoms, decks, and sides of deck-houses.

EDGING. Amount required to be cut away from an edge of a plank or plate in fitting or lining up outsides strakes, those of a deck, etc.

EDUCTION. Archaic term for *exhaust,* as in *eduction-pipe, -port, -valve* of a steam engine.

EEL. Any of the elongated snake-like fishes having no ventral fins, a smooth slimy skin, and often without scales. The *common eel* of Europe and North America, which has minute skin-embedded scales, is considered an excellent food fish. It is remarkable that, although preferring fresh-water life, these eels breed only in a warm deep-sea locality, the larvae having been found on coral bottom off Bermuda and the young discovered to have taken up the parents' original habitat. **Electric e.,** an eel-like fish constituting the only genus (*Electrophorus*) of a separate family; able to produce a strong electric shock as a means of attack or defense, being credited with power in this respect to stun a large animal; attains a length of six feet and is native to Amazon and Orinoco River-basins. **Pug-nosed e.,** a shorter and stouter species, compared with the common eel, having a short blunt nose; found in deep-sea fishing grounds, is said to often burrow into the bodies of other fishes and appears to prey particularly on the halibut of the Newfoundland Banks.

EELL'S ANCHOR. *See* ANCHOR.

EELPOUT. The *mutton-fish* of N.E. American waters; about 20 inches in length, having pectoral fins only, laterally compressed body tapering to tail, and blunt whale-like head. Any fish of the family *Zoarcidæ.*

EFFECT. Consequence; result. **Land e.,** deviation of a radio bearing approximately tangent to, or over, land between ship and shore beacon or radio compass, caused by influence of the land upon direction of rado waves. **Night e.,** erratic and unaccountable changing of direction, intensity, and broadening in azimuth of radio bearings observed in some localities just before sunrise and after sunset.

EFFECTIVE HORSE-POWER. Measure of actual power exerted in driving a vessel, less mechanical and hull resistance losses. It is equal to the tension on a tow-line, if vessel were towed, at the speed considered. For a given speed, it necessarily must be increased with increase of displacement; sometimes called *tow-rope horse-power. See* HORSE-POWER.

EFFORT, CENTER OF. *See* CENTER.

E.H.P. Abbreviation for *effective horse-power.*

EIDER. (*Ice.*) The *eider duck* of higher northern latitudes of which probably the best known (*Somateria mollissima*) is found on northern European coasts. The female bird of this species lines her nest with soft down (*eider-down*) plucked from her body, for many years a source of considerable income to coast dwellers of Iceland and Norway. The birds are protected by law during breeding season with the view of maintaining supply of the product.

EJECTOR. A means of discharging or expelling a liquid through a pipe or duct by a jet of steam; a *jet-pump*. **Ash-e.,** *see* ASH. **Bilge-e.,** *see* BILGE. **Sand-e.,** *see* SAND.

EKING. Act, process of, or timber used in, lengthening or building up, in order to supply a deficiency in length, etc., of a knee, deck-hook, or other combining structural member; also, *eking*. Term for carved work supporting the quarter-parts of a stern gallery in old-fashioned ships.

ELBOW. A sudden turn in a river or coast-line. A short pipe-fitting or pipe turning at a sharp angle (usually 90°); an *ell*. **E.-grease,** energetic hand-labor; as in rubbing, scouring. **E. in the hawse,** *see* HAWSE.

ELECTRIC. (Gr. *elektron,* amber, in which electricity was first observed) Electrical; operated or produced by, or pertaining to electricity. **E. drive,** *see* DRIVE. **E. harpoon,** *see* HARPOON. **E. log,** *see* LOG. **E. steering-gear,** *see* STEERING. **E. storm,** *see* STORM. **E. telegraph,** an electrically operated device for transmitting order signals from the navigating-bridge to engine-room or to an after docking bridge. **E. welding,** *see* WELDING.

ELECTRO-HYDRAULIC. Descriptive of machinery in which an electric motor pumps or impels a special oil in order to produce pressure in a cylinder or direct rotary motion. **E.-h. steering-gear,** system in which rudder is turned as required by hydraulic rams acting on each side of the tiller. Pressure of oil is directed into either ram cylinder by a variable delivery pump driven by electric motor, according to desired amount of helm as controlled by tele-motor from the pilot-house. Also called *hydro-electric* steering-gear. **E.-h. winch,** consists of an electric motor running at constant one-way speed which drives an impeller-pump connected to the main shaft by worm or spur gearing. A hand-wheel or lever controls amount of oil and direction of delivery as required. Also called *hydro-electric winch.*

ELECTROLYSIS. Act or process of chemical decomposition by an electric current; *e.g.,* that seen in wastage of iron or steel in vicinity of a bronze-bladed propeller, commonly attributed to "galvanic action," or voltaic current, set up through sea-water between the bronze and steel. As a means of protection against such action, plates of zinc usually are fitted to both rudder- and stern-posts. The zinc only then is attacked and is from time to time renewed as required. Also, *electrolytic action. Cf.* ZINCS. **Boiler e.,** *see* BOILER.

ELEPHANTA. A south to south-east gale, accompanied by rain, prevalent in September and October, or with ending of the South-west monsoon, on the south-west coast of Bay of Bengal.

ELEPHANT-FISH. A chimeroid fish of about two feet in length found in the South Pacific and vicinity of Cape of Good Hope; so-called from **its** snout of remarkable proboscis-like appearance.

ELEVATED. Raised in altitude from some plane of reference. **E. compass,** *see* **Pole-c.** *in* COMPASS. **E. pole,** that of the heavens in either hemisphere. (Altitude of pole is equal to latitude of an observer)

ELEVATION. Side view or *sheer plan* of a vessel's hull. The vertical angle between a celestial body and observer's horizon; altitude. Height above sea-level; expressed on American and British charts in *feet.* **Angle of e.,** *see* ANGLE. **E. of the pole,** *see* ELEVATED.

ELLIOT EYE. A kind of eye-splice used on the former hemp anchor-cable at its outer end. Similar to a grommet-splice, the strands (or *parts,* in the usual cable-laid hawser employed) were divided and worked together so as to reform the rope in the eye of required size and then tucked distributively, according to choice of two or three methods, into standing part of hawser. The whole was then served and, after seating the thimble, a heavy round-seizing was laid across throat of eye.

ELLIPTICAL STERN. *See* STERN.

ELLIPTICAL LIFE-RAFT. A cylindrical float of elliptical form, usually made of water-proofed balsa wood covered with canvas and provided with a strong net which often supports a slatted floor for a foothold or platform for its passengers. The raft is made in sizes varying from 5- to 15-person capacity and weight from 50 to 150 lbs.

ELM. A durable, hard, tough wood rating considerable importance in vessel and heavy boat construction for strength members, as keel, keelson, stem, stern-post, or wales; also, for shells of tackle-blocks. Weight, 34 to 38 lbs. per cubic foot.

ELONGATION. Angular distance between a satellite and its primary, or between the sun and planets *Mercury* or *Venus;* greatest distance in azimuth, east or west, of a circumpolar star from the pole.

ELOPS. A genus of fishes of the tarpon family which contains the *ten-pounder* or *big-eyed herring* found in warmer waters of the Atlantic and Pacific.

EMBARGO. (Sp. *embargar,* to impede or restrain) Order of a government prohibiting entry or departure of merchant ships at any of its ports; termed a *hostile e.* where enemy ships are concerned, and a *civil e.* in the case of domestic vessels. Any law prohibiting carriage of certain goods, or for purpose of controlling a certain trade engaged in, by domestic tonnage.

EMBARKATION. That which is embarked or placed aboard a ship; act of embarking or going on board a vessel or boat. **E. deck,** any deck, usually the *upper,* from which passengers and crew are directed to enter ship's lifeboats in event of abandoning the vessel. **E. notice,** written instructions given by a shipping company's agent to a prospective passenger regarding time and place of going on board and procedure covering proper labeling, delivery to pier, etc., of personal baggage.

EMBAYED. To be sheltered or shut in, as in a bay. Descriptive of a coast-line containing a series of bays or inlets. A ship is said to be *embayed* when unable to work seaward against a strong wind or current because shut in or land-locked in a bay.

EMBOLON. (Gr. *embolon;* L. *embolum*) The pointed prow, beak, or ram built on ancient warvessels.

EMBRAIL. To *brail up* or *brail in,* as a fore-and-aft gaff sail. This archaic form of *to brail* formerly meant to take in any sail fitted with buntlines, leechlines, spilling-lines, or clewlines, as hinted in the following Middle English verse: "He who strives ye tempeste to disarme must alway furst *embrayle* ye lee yerd-arme." *See* BRAIL.

EMERGED WEDGE. *See* WEDGE.

EMERGENCY. A pressing necessity; unforeseen occurrence or conditions necessitating immediate action or remedy; exigency. **E. lighting,** electric lighting system, independent of ship's main power as required by law on passenger-vessels for illuminating passage-ways, decks, and lifeboats in event of failure of regular lighting; usually consists of a single generator driven by an internal-combustion engine, with or without use of the ordinary circuit. **E. steering-gear,** that operated by hand or engine-power independent of usual steering system. In large vessels, a duplicate of, or auxiliary to, the main system is kept in readiness as a stand-by. Generally, provision is made for emergency steering by tackles operated by a deck-winch, or a hand wheel connected to tackles or a screw gear directly controlling the tiller. Often an *emergency tiller* is fitted to facilitate use of stand-by gear.

EMIGRANT SHIP. Term used in British law for a vessel carrying emigrants from the United Kingdom to ports outside of Europe or those within the Mediterranean. It is applied to any vessel carrying more than 50 steerage passengers or to a mechanically propelled vessel carrying a greater number in the ratio of one adult to every 20 tons of net registered tonnage. Perhaps the earliest emigrant ships were the so-called *Western Ocean packets* which yearly carried thousands of settlers to the New World throughout the greater span of the 1800's. A long period of constant emigration to Australia and New Zealand later kept the wool clippers busy on the outward run; and with the advent of steam propulsion increasing numbers were carried to America and the colonies. As late as beginning of World War I, it was customary to use the accommodation space for America-bound steerage passengers for carriage of cattle and sheep on the passage east!

EMPLOYMENT CLAUSE. A charter-party clause stipulating that the vessel's master must follow all instructions given by charterer in matters relating to operation of the vessel.

EMPLOYER, MARITIME. *See* MARITIME.

ENCOMPASS. (*Archaic*) To sail around or encircle, in the sense of performing some major or important maneuver; as, *Drake did e. the globe; our fleet encompassed the enemy.*

END. Last or extreme part or point of any material object; as, *a cable's end.* Conclusion or termination in point of time; as, *end of a voyage.* **Better e.,** less used part, as of a rope not subjected to wear and tear near one of its ends. **Bitter e.,** *see* BITTER. **Break off the e.,** an order to men hauling on a stretched-out rope to let go their holds and return for another drag closer to the lead-block or chock. **Deck-ends,** termination of planking forming a deck. **Dead on e.,** exactly pointing to or from the eye or an object indicated; also, said of the wind when blowing from direction steered. **E. launching,** *see* LAUNCHING. **E. for e.,** in reverse order, as in replacing one end of a rope by the other. **E. link,** first or last link in a length (*shot*) of chain cable and is an open link of heavier material than that of the studded links otherwise composing the cable. Its purpose is to accommodate the *joiner-shackle* which connects each shot (usually 15 fathoms) making up the cable. **E. on,** said of a vessel when heading directly toward, or in line with, an object; opposed to *broadside on.* **E.-seizing,** a round seizing securing a rope's end to its standing part; often incorrectly, a *whipping.* To **give one a rope's e.** (or **ending**), to administer a flogging with an end of a rope. **On e.,** said of masts when stepped or sent aloft in place; also, of any lengthy object placed in a nearly vertical position.

ENDLESS FALL. *See* FALL.

ENGAGE. To enter or join in conflict or hostile encounter, as two fleets in battle. To ship or "sign on" a crew for a voyage, run, or stipulated period of time.

ENGAGEMENT. Hostile combat, as between vessels or between a number of warships and batteries on shore. Act of hiring or engaging a crew.

ENGINE. (L. *ingenium,* skill, invention) Machine by which physical power produces a desired physical effect; especially, one for changing a natural force, as heat, into mechanical power, as in a steam-engine, a gas-engine. Principal types used for ship propulsion are *steam reciprocating, steam turbine, internal combustion,* and *electric motor* (powered from generators operated by steam turbine or internal combustion engines). **Beam e.,** former standard type on paddle-steamers consisting of a centrally pivoted, "up-and-down," fore-and-aft beam which transfers the piston effort of a reciprocating engine to the crank-shaft and thence directly to the paddles. **Carburetor e.,** *see* **gasoline e. Compound e.,** as used for propulsion of smaller vessels, a reciprocating type having two cylinders, steam from one of which exhausts into the other. **Diesel e.,** named for *Rudolf Diesel,* German engineer *(1858–1913),* by whom invented in 1900, internal combustion type in which air drawn into cylinder by the suction stroke is so highly compressed during compression stroke that heat thus generated (about 1000° F.) ignites fuel sprayed into cylinder at a high pressure (usually 400 to 450 lbs. per in.^{2}). Larger Diesels generally are started by compressed air produced by a small gasoline engine; those up to about 150 H.P. usually are started electrically. Also called *Diesel motor.* **Double-acting internal combustion e.,** one in which combustion takes place at each end of the piston-stroke. Although generating excessive heat, about twice the power is developed as in the same-sized cylinder of the single-acting type. **E. department,** division of ship's company charged, under the Chief Engineer, with operation and maintenance of all machinery, including electric and refrigeration installations, in a vessel. **E. efficiency,** ratio of mechanical energy produced by an engine to heat energy put into it. **E. hatch,** *see* HATCH. **E. foundation,** structural strength arrangement constituting desired support of, and means of distributing vibrational stresses to vessel's framing from, a main engine; essentially consists of extra heavy floors, keelsons, and intercostals, topped by a heavy *bed-plate* directly beneath and for securing thereto the engine frame-work or columns; also called *engine seating, engine bed,* and frame structure often termed, in shipyards, *engine sleepers.* **E. keelson,** a fore-and-aft strength member included in an engine foundation arrangement. **E. maintenance-man,** in U.S. vessels, an experienced fireman or oiler engaged to assist engineers in repairing and maintaining all machinery and equipment in the engine department. **E.-room,** space in which a vessel's main engine or engines is located. **E.-room auxiliaries,** all machinery units adjunctive to main engines, including feed-pumps, feed-water-heaters, fan-engines, ash-ejectors, evaporators, and lubricating-system pumps. **E. telegraph; e.-room telegraph;** *see* TELEGRAPH. **E. bell signals,** *see* SIGNAL. **Gas e.,** internal combustion type used ashore, the term being often erroneously applied to the *gasoline e.* found in small craft. Fuel used is a fixed gas mixed with air, the charge being ignited during compression in cylinder by a sparking-plug. **Gasoline e.,** internal combustion type popular in boats and small craft, which uses any relatively light petroleum fuel that may be conveniently carbureted. Ignition of carbureted mixture (fuel and air)

is effected by spark during compression in cylinder. **Geared e.,** one in which a system of reduction gearing is installed to turn a propeller-shaft at a desired velocity, as in a high speed *turbine e.* **Hoisting-e.,** *see* HOISTING. **Horizontal e.,** any engine in which the piston line of stroke is horizontal; as in a stern-wheel river steamer. **Hydro-electric steering-e.,** *see* ELECTRO-HYDRAULIC. **Injection e.,** any internal combustion type in which fuel or fuel and air mixture is sprayed or injected into its cylinders at high pressure. **Internal combustion e.,** one in which pressure energy is developed by explosion of a gas within its cylinders or in an external chamber; as gas, gasoline, or oil engines. In marine use it may be of the carburetor type *(gasoline)* or injection type *(Diesel* or *semi-Diesel),* and also may be of two-stroke cycle (power stroke every two revolutions of crank-shaft), single stroke (one power stroke each revolution), or double-acting (two power strokes each revolution). **Multiple expansion e.,** reciprocating engine in which steam is expanded successively in two, three, or four stages. After expanding in the high pressure cylinder, steam is exhausted into another cylinder, whence it is exhausted into another, etc. Such engine of three cylinders is called a *triple-expansion e.;* one of four cylinders, a *quadruple-expansion e.;* and, other than the *high* (H.P.) and *low* (L.P.) *pressure* cylinders, remaining cylinder or cylinders, *intermediate* (I.P.) *pressure* cylinders. Although to an increasing extent displaced by the Diesel and turbine types, *triple-expansion* engines are still widely used as propelling machinery, especially in cargo vessels. **Non-condensing e.,** one from the cylinders of which exhaust steam passes directly into the atmosphere; used for hoists, pile-driving, etc.; a common type of *donkey e.* **Reciprocating e.,** one in which the piston stroke is converted to rotary motion by appropriate connections to a crank-shaft, as in the marine propulsion type, having its cylinders vertically above the propeller shaft (or that part of which called *crank-shaft),* and of the *multiple-expansion* type, *q.v.* **Semi-Diesel e.,** differs from *Diesel e.* in that vaporization and ignition of the injected charge is effected by contact with a heated plate or other surface instead of heat directly generated from compression in the cylinder. For various reasons, the type appears to have been short-lived as a serious competitor of the Diesel. It now is practically obsolete. **Ship's e.,** same as *main engine.* **Single-acting (internal combustion) e.,** type in which combustion takes place on one and the same side only of the piston; *i.e.,* once at each revolution of crank-shaft. **Steering-e.,** *see* STEERING. **Trunk e.,** any reciprocating *e.* having piston-rods of pipe form *(trunks)* and of sufficient diameter to house the upper ends of its connecting-rods which are secured directly to pistons; chiefly used in internal combustion units. **Turbine e.,** essentially one in which steam at high velocity flows against a series of blades or rotary vanes set on disks fixed at right angles to main shaft. Excessive speed of rotation thus obtained is reduced by gears to desired speed of propeller. Widely used in fast passenger-vessels. **Turning e.,** a small steam *e.* or electric motor arranged to slowly turn main *e.* as necessary during repairs, adjustments, etc. **Vertical e.,** marine type of steam reciprocating or internal combustion propulsion engine or those installed with cylinders vertically above their crank-shafts. Inclined engines were once common on side-paddle steamers and those with oscillating cylinders, walking-beam, and horizontal long-stroke engines have been used on various types of lake and river vessels.

ENGINEER. Officer on a mechanically propelled vessel charged with maintenance and efficient operation of main engines and, usually, all powered machinery on board. In U.S. vessels, engineers are named in order of rank as Chief, First Assistant, Second Assistant, and Third Assistant; in British ships, as Chief, Second, Third, Fourth. In large passenger vessels, these are supplemented by an Extra 1st., Extra 2nd., etc. **Engineer cadet, or cadet e.,** formerly a student of engineering at U.S. Naval Academy, Annapolis, Md.; now officially called *midshipman;* an apprentice *e.* in the merchant service. **Chief e.,** officer in charge or chief of staff in engineering department or division on a powered vessel. **E.'s division,** *see* DIVISION. **E. surveyor,** one who inspects the condition of, or supervises repairs to, boilers and machinery; and, also, checks adherence to classification rules or statutory requirements for machinery being installed in a ship. **Fleet e.,** *see* FLEET.

ENGINEERING. Bureau of E., a division in U.S. Navy Department now included in Bureau of Ships. **Marine e.,** that branch of *mechanical e.* embracing the installation, operation, and maintenance of ships' boilers, engines, and auxiliary machinery; also termed *naval e.*

ENIF. *Epsilon* (ϵ) *Pegasi,* a star of magnitude 2.5 and declination 9° 38′ N., having a S.H.A. of 341½°. A line joining the two stars marking south side of *Square of Pegasus,* extended 20° westward, passes close to *Enif;* also, the transverse of a well-defined cross in *Cygnus,* prolonged south and east for about 25°, will nearly locate the star.

ENLISTMENT. In U.S. Navy, act of being enlisted or enrolled as a seaman. Period of service stipulated in such enrollment, which is six years in regular Navy and two, three, or four in the Reserve.

ENROLLMENT. In U.S., enrolling of a vessel of 20 tons burden or more engaged in domestic commerce or fisheries, including navigation of north, north-west, and north-east frontier waters otherwise than by sea; distinguished from *registry,* for vessels engaged in the foreign trade. **Certificate of enrollment and license,** *see* CERTIFICATE.

ENSIGN. (L. *insignia,* badges, marks)   A flag or banner; the national colors of a country to which a vessel belongs, displayed, especially in naval ships, when in port, at a flag-staff on the stern, and aloft, usually at a gaff on the after mast, when under way; in sailing yachts and merchantmen, usually at peak of an after gaff-sail. An archaic term for a *signal* or watch-word. **Blue e.,** British flag having a blue field with the "union" in upper corner of its hoist; displayed by vessels of certain public offices and may be flown by merchant vessels whose master and a certain quota of officers and men are members of the Royal Naval Reserve. **Red e.,** the "red duster," British colors having a red field with union in upper corner of its hoist; displayed by merchant vessels. **U.S. Revenue e.,** consists of a field of 16 alternately red and white vertical stripes and union of blue spreading eagle under a semi-circle of 13 blue stars, on a white ground; flown by Coast Guard (with C.G. insignia on field), Customs, and Immigration Service. **White e.,** flown by British navy, flag having a white field bearing, at full length, the red cross of St. George, with union of crosses of St. George, St. Andrew, St. David, and St. Patrick in upper corner of hoist; displayed also by vessels of the Royal Yacht Squadron. **Yacht e.** of the U.S., instead of union of stars as arranged in the Stars and Stripes, has a white foul anchor encircled by 13 white stars on a blue ground; flown by yachts at the stern when at anchor or fast in port, and at a gaff peak or other approved point aloft when under way.

ENSIGNCY; ENSIGNSHIP.   Rank or office of an ensign.

ENTER.   To set down in writing; to record; as an entry in a ship's log. To report to, and supply customs authorities at a port with, required information relating to an arriving or soon departing vessel, her cargo, stores, etc.

ENTRANCE.   Part of immersed hull narrowing toward the *stem* from widest part at water-line; opposed to *run,* or the decreasing of beam toward the *stern.* Mouth of, or passage to, a river, harbor, canal, dock, etc. **E.-lock,** arrangement at a dock or canal entrance opening to a tidal area, whereby vessels may be "locked" in or out at any height of tide within ordinary local tidal range, or a certain prescribed range.

ENTRY.   Act of conforming to customs laws relative to information requirements concerning a vessel bound outward or arriving inward. **Bill of e.,** *see* BILL. **E. inward,** report to customs by master of an arriving vessel, usually required before discharge of lading commences. Depending on country visited and sometimes the port in same national jurisdiction, generally includes delivery of certified manifests of cargo and stores, passenger and crew lists, and quarantine clearance (certificate of pratique);

deposit of ship's register and last tonnage tax receipt (light dues, anchorage dues, etc.); and declaration by master concerning derelicts, wreckage, ice, or any dangers to navigation sighted or encountered, and any mishap to ship or crew. **E. outward,** required notification or report by a ship's master or her agent to customs authorities indicating intention to load export cargo. Includes details of vessel, nature of cargo, ports of destination, place and time at which loading begins, agent or broker concerned, and proof of clearance inward. **Port of e.,** see PORT.

EPAULET; EPAULETTE. (Fr. *epaulette,* dim. of *epaule,* shoulder) A shoulder ornament worn on full dress uniforms of commissioned officers in most navies of the world, consisting, generally, of a strap laid on the shoulder and broadened, with a semicircular gold fringe, at its outer end. It usually bears the marks indicating wearer's rank; see SHOULDER-STRAP.

EPHEMERIDES. Plural of *ephemeris;* as, *ephemerides of planets.*

EPHEMERIS. (Gr. *ephemeros,* daily) A tabulation of places of a heavenly body for successive hours or days, with other pertinent data; such as horizontal parallax, semi-diameter, and time of meridian passage, in an *ephemeris of the Moon.* A publication giving computed places and other information concerning the heavenly bodies for each day of the year; an astronomical almanac, as the *American Ephemeris and Nautical Almanac;* see ALMANAC, NAUTICAL.

EQUAL ALTITUDES. See ALTITUDE.

EQUATION. (L. *æquatio,* an equalizing) An additive or subtractive quantity applied to a given value as a reduction to the true value, or to one of a different name; as *equation of time.* A statement of equality of two quantities; as, *11 fathoms = 66 feet.* **E. of equal altitudes,** a now obsolete method of computing a correction to be applied to the mid-chronometer time obtained in an *equal altitudes* observation of the sun in order to compensate for a change of declination of that body during elapsed time between altitudes; see **Equal a's** in ALTITUDE. **E. of time,** see TIME. **E., personal,** see PERSONAL EQUATION.

EQUATOR. (L. *æquator,* one who equalizes) Imaginary great circle on the surface of the earth, sun, planet, or other rotating spherical body, equi-distant at all points from the poles of such body; called, in the case of Earth, *terrestrial equator,* or dividing line between *northern* and *southern hemispheres.* Latitude is reckoned north and south from the *equator,* its own latitude being 0°. **Celestial e.,** great circle of the celestial sphere whose plane coincides with that of the earth extended to infinity. Declinations of heavenly bodies are reckoned north

and south of this circle; also called *equinoctial* and *equinoctial line.* **Magnetic e.,** an imaginary sinuous line encircling the earth in the vicinity of the *geographical e.* and passing through all places at which the earth's vertical magnetic force is zero; *i.e.,* a magnetic needle poised on a horizontal axis and in the plane of the magnetic meridian rests in an exactly horizontal position. From this line *magnetic latitude,* north or south, is measured by the *angle of inclination,* or *dip,* of the needle. *Isoclinic lines,* roughly parallel to it, as shown on a magnetic chart, pass through all points of same magnetic latitude, or, as the term implies, of equal dip or inclination. At places in north magnetic latitude, the north-seeking end of needle "dips"; contrariwise in south magnetic latitudes. Position of the *magnetic equator* constantly undergoes a secular change, with small irregular displacements from year to year, and, generally, only very roughly coincides with the region of the earth's maximum intensity of horizontal magnetic force. **Minute of the e.,** see MINUTE.

EQUATORIAL. Of, or pertaining to, the *equator.* An astronomical telescope mounted so as to maintain its line of sight in the plane of a celestial body's diurnal circle; rotates on a *polaxis,* or axis parallel to that of the earth, and is elevated or depressed according to position in declination of body observed. **E. current,** see CURRENT. **E. tide,** one which occurs during low declination of the moon and which, in consequence, produces a minimum diurnal inequality in the tide; see **D. inequality** in DIURNAL.

EQUINOCTIAL. (L. *æquus,* equal; *noctis,* night) Pertaining to an equinox, the equinoxes, or time or state of equal day and night; also to regions or climate in vicinity of the *equator.* The celestial equator; see EQUATOR. Also called *equinoctial line,* because when the sun's place is on it (*declination zero*) day and night are of equal length all over the world. **E. points,** the equinoxes, or points of intersection of the ecliptic with the *e.* or celestial equator; see EQUINOX. **E. storm,** a heavy gale occurring at or near the equinoxes, or about 21st. March and 21st. September; a term now rarely used, was probably so-called because strong winds and gales often prevail during March in northern latitudes and tropical hurricanes frequently sweep into the North Atlantic near the autumnal equinox (21st. Sept.). **E. tide,** unusual increase of a tidal range occurring at or near one of the equinoxes, when a full or new moon also is in or near the equinoctial, and, especially, if at perigee; caused by joint attraction of sun and moon thus acting in a common direction. **E. year,** period occupied by the sun in making a complete apparent circuit in the ecliptic; or that by the earth in completing one revolution around the sun. Also called *astronomical, natural, solar,* and *tropical year,* it is equal to 365 days, 5 hrs., 48 min., 45.51 sec. of mean solar time.

EQUINOX. Time of passage of sun's center through either equinoctial point, or point at which its apparent path in the heavens (*see* ECLIPTIC) intersects the equinoctial or celestial equator. At the *vernal e.*, or *First Point of Aries,* the meridian passage of which is the zero hour of sidereal time or right ascension of the meridian, and from which right ascension of all heavenly bodies and celestial longitude are measured, the sun crosses the celestial equator in its apparent path northward. This occurs about 21st. March. Six months later, about 21st. September, the *autumnal e.* occurs, the sun having attained a right ascension of 12 hours in re-crossing the equator on his unending course to the eastward. (*See* **E. Points** *in* EQUINOCTIAL.) At the *vernal e.* the sun is said to *"enter Aries"* or first of the 12 constellations through which it completes its yearly round in the Zodiac. However, due to the phenomenon known as *precession,* the anciently established *Aries,* though still named as the sun's location when entering the northern heavens, no longer contains the *vernal e.,* displacement of the original now amounting to some 30°; so that the equinoxes occur during passage of the sun through *Pisces* and *Virgo,* instead of through *Aries* and *Libra* as of old at, respectively, the vernal and autumnal *e's.* Thus, we note, our vernal equinoctial point, the astronomer's *"mean equinox of date,"* or *First Point of Aries,* like the coaster's climbing ivy in the mizzen rigging, simply is out of place. **Precession of the e's,** the slow westward movement of the equinoctial points resulting from a circular motion of the earth's axis, seen in the north and south celestial poles gradually revolving about those of the ecliptic. Similar to the staggering of a spinning top, this great reeling motion completes a cycle in which the equinoctial points will have moved through the ecliptic's 360° in nearly 26,000 years. So called because each successive transit of the equinoctial points on this account occurs earlier than, or *precedes,* the previous one. A small inequality in precession called *nutation* (L. *nutatio,* a nodding) is caused by a wavering or nodding oscillatory motion of the earth's axis in cycles of about 19 years. Present value of *precession* is given as 50.47 seconds of arc, yearly. The phenomenon is attributed to the varying attraction of sun, moon, and planets on the rotating earth's bulging equatorial mass; while *nutation* is said to be a combination of two distinct nutational motions caused by the respective attractions of sun and moon in directions other than at right angles to the earth's axis of rotation.

EQUIP. To provide a vessel or group of vessels with armament, munitions, rigging, stores, etc., particularly in the sense of preparing for an expedition or special cruise; to *fit out.* **Equipped ship,** a vessel having all necessary stores, bunker fuel, feed-water, etc., and crew aboard and ready for sea.

EQUIPPED PORT. *See* PORT.

EQUIPAGE. A now rarely used term, borrowed from the French, meaning the members of a war-vessel's crew, other than her commissioned officers.

EQUIPMENT. Act or state of being equipped. Those necessaries and furnishings required for an expedition, voyage, or other intended service, in addition to, and apart from, all articles or fittings permanently incorporated in a vessel's hull prior to being thus *equipped.* Ordinarily, ship's *e.* includes anchors, cables, ammunition, guns, mooring-lines, boats, life-saving apparatus, signal-lights, radio installation, navigational instruments, cooking utensils, furniture, fuel, provisions, and stores. **E. tonnage,** a number closely approximating gross tonnage, used in tabulated minimum requirements of the American Bureau of Shipping and other classification societies with respect to sizes and lengths of chain cables, steel towing-hawser, spare hawsers, and warping-lines; also, number and respective weights of anchors. Also called *E. numeral.*

EQUIPOISE RUDDER. A balanced rudder; *see* RUDDER.

EQUIVALENT GIRDER. A diagram of the aggregate material contributing longitudinal strength to a ship's hull, showing locus of the neutral axis, in considering the structure as a *girder* subjected to *hogging* and *sagging* stresses. Such a hypothetical beam or girder is used to determine a proposed hull's effective resistance to major hogging and sagging loads set up in a seaway or by extreme mal-distribution of cargo or other weights on board. Principal members contributing strength to the "girder" are keel, keelsons, longitudinal bulkheads, longitudinal framing, shell-plating (especially sheer-strakes), and deck-plating.

ERIDANUS (*Gr. name for Po River*) A long winding constellation extending southward and westward over about 53 degrees of declination and 3½ hours of right ascension from west side of the *Orion* group. The bright star *Achernar* marks its southern end in 57½°S., or about halfway between, and at 40° distance from, *Canopus* and *Fomalhaut.* *See* ACHERNAR.

ERROR. Difference between an observed physical quantity or value and the true value; as, *sextant error; heeling error.* **Azimuth e.,** *see* AZIMUTH. **Chronometer e.,** *see* CHRONOMETER. **Compass e.,** *see* COMPASS. **Gaussin e.,** *see* GAUSSIN ERROR. **Heeling e.,** *see* HEELING. **Index e.,** *see* INDEX ERROR. **Personal e.,** *see* PERSONAL EQUATION.

ESCAPE. Combining word indicating a means of egress under unusual or emergency conditions; as in *escape-ladder; escape-hatch.* **E.-cock,** a drain-cock, or valve for permitting escape of fluid, as from a cylinder. **E.-hatch,** any hatch or scuttle fitted as a means of exit from a compartment when ordinarily used means is unavailable or obstructed; a small hatch opening to a tween deck and providing an exit for men engaged in trimming a bulk cargo, such as grain or coal; also termed *e.-hole, e.-scuttle.* **E.-trunk,** a closed-in ladder-way used as an emergency exit to a weather deck from the propeller-shaft tunnel or other lower compartment. **E.-valve.,** *see* VALVE.

ESCOLAR. (*Sp.*) A mackerel-like food fish attaining a length of 3½ feet, commonly found on the Cuban coast, Canary Islands, Madeira, and occasionally off Nova Scotia, on Grand Banks, and in Mediterranean.

ESCORT. An armed vessel or vessels constituting protection for one or more merchant vessels or troop-ships; a vessel accompanying another one that is partly disabled, or sailing with another in honor of some notable person or persons on board the latter. To convoy; as, to *e. a vessel* or *vessels.*

ESCUTCHEON. Archaic term for the panel or place on a ship's counter where her name and port of registry are painted or set in relief.

ESTABLISHMENT OF THE PORT. Lunitidal interval, or time elapsing from the moon's transit to first high water thereafter at a particular place, at full and new moon; called *common* or *vulgar establishment* and usually indicated on American and British charts as *H.W.F.&C* (High Water, Full and Change). **Corrected e.,** mean of all lunitidal intervals in a lunar month at a particular place.

ESTUARY. (L. *æstuarium;* from *æstus,* swell or tide) Wide entrance to a lake or river where the tide meets the outgoing stream; generally, an arm of the sea at a river's mouth; a firth or frith.

ETAMIN. *Gamma* (γ) *Draconis,* brightest star in the group *Draco;* magnitude 2.4; *see* DRACO.

ETESIAN. (Gr. *etesios,* annual) Periodic; annual. Particularly applied to the yearly recurring northerly winds blowing in summer over the Ægean Sea and eastern Mediterranean; *Etesian winds.*

EUPHROE. A vertically suspended batten of hardwood pierced with a number of holes through which are rove the small lines of a *crowfoot* for suspending an awning; *see* CROWFOOT.

EURIPUS. (*Gr.*) Ancient name for a strait or narrow connecting water through which a strong tidal current flows, as in the channel separating Eubœa and the mainland on east coast of Greece; hence, figuratively, a flux and reflux.

EUROCLYDON. (Gr. *euros,* east wind; *klydon,* wave or billow) Now called *levanter,* ancient name for a strong easterly wind of the eastern Mediterranean, generally occurring in autumn, and described by some authorities as blowing from northeast, by others, as a southeast wind. It appears certain that the *euroclydon* referred to in Acts 27, verse 14, as encountered by Paul the apostle on his voyage to Rome blew from E.N.E., since, following the general law of wind-drift, a course of approximately true West would have resulted in "driving" before an E.N.E. gale.

EUROPE. A former name for Russian or Italian hemp used in manufacture of cordage.

EVAPORATOR. Apparatus for obtaining fresh water by distillation from sea-water; that part of a distilling plant which converts sea-water into vapor. It essentially consists of a chamber in which steam is passed through coils of tubing in order to vaporize admitted sea-water. The vapor or steam thus produced passes thence to a condenser for reconversion to the liquid state. As an auxiliary supply of boiler feed, distilled water thus obtained is added to that condensed from the engine exhaust steam, which latter usually first passes through the evaporator coils.

EVEN KEEL. *See* KEEL.

EVER. A type of ketch-rigged fishing or trading vessel, ranging from 20 to 50 tons burden, peculiar to the Dutch and German coasts.

EVOLUTION. Any maneuver performed by a fleet of ships whereby one arrangement or formation is transformed into another.

EXCEPTIONS CLAUSE. In a charter-party or bill of lading, a stipulation absolving the carrier from responsibility for loss, damage, or delay in delivery or loading of cargo due to, as in the following quotation, "Act of God, perils of the sea, pirates and public enemies, restraint of princes and rulers, fires, strikes, barratry of master or mariners, strandings and navigation accidents, latent defects in, or accidents to hull and/or machinery and/or boilers, even when occasioned by negligence, default, or error in judgment of pilot, master, mariners, or other persons employed by the carrier, or for whose acts he is responsible, not resulting, however, in any case from want of due diligence by owner of ship, or by ship's husband or manager." Also termed *excepted perils clause.*

EXCESS OF HATCHWAYS. In tonnage measurement, British and U.S. rules exempt a vessel's aggregate hatchway space, as measured from top of deck-beam to under side of hatch-covers, from inclusion in gross tonnage to the extent of one-half of one per centum of such gross tonnage, exclusive of tonnage of hatchways. Thus, in a ship of 7000 gross tons whose total hatchway tonnage is 65, *excess of hatchways* is equal to 65 less 35, (.005 × 7000), or 30 tons. The provision apparently was adopted as an encouraging gesture toward supplying ample height of hatch-coamings in the interests of seaworthiness and cargo protection, since tonnage taxation generally is based on net tonnage, or freight-earning space in a vessel. Suez Canal tonnage rules provide for a similar allowance, while those of Panama Canal give little or no exemption.

EXCITER. An auxiliary generator for supplying power in energizing or quickly producing the magnetic field in a main propulsion motor; especially during frequent changes of speed or reversal of motion, as in maneuvering ship. **Pilot-e.,** a generator supplying field excitation power to another *e.*

EXECUTIVE OFFICER. In most navies and public vessels, one usually next in rank to the commanding officer. He is charged with general management of ship, including drills, policing, cleanliness, and shipshape conduct and appearance of both vessel and personnel. Corresponding duties in merchant vessels generally are carried out by the *chief officer.*

EXEMPTED SPACE. In measuring a vessel for *tonnage,* such space, or aggregate of space, ordinarily open to the elements or not provided with ready or permanent means of being closed, and in consequence, not included in the gross tonnage.

EXERCISE. To train, discipline, or drill a crew or part of a crew by practice; as to *exercise crew in gunnery;* to *exercise a sea-boat's crew.* To set an emergency or stand-by apparatus in motion; as, to *e. the hand steering-gear.* Such action itself; as, a *boat drill* or *e.; sailing e.; fire-door e.; bulkhead-door e.;* etc.

EXHAUST. Exit or escape from an engine of steam or gas after it has performed its work; such steam or gas itself; outlet port of an engine cylinder. **E.-line,** pipe conducting steam exhausted from an engine; in marine engines, usually to the condenser. **E.-pipe,** usually applied to a pipe carrying off used steam or gas into the atmosphere. **E.-turbine,** one geared to a propeller-shaft primarily driven by a reciprocating engine. Exhaust steam from low pressure cylinder operates turbine and thence passes to condenser. Turbine is arranged to remain idle during reversal or frequent speed changes as in maneuvering ship. Considered suitable for plants ranging from 500 to 5000 horsepower, it is claimed that its economic advantage of increased engine output is supplemented by a marked lessening in racing of propeller, such as is met with in a heavy head sea. **E.-ventilation,** system in which mechanically driven fans or blowers are used to expel vitiated air from various compartments in a ship, supply of fresh air being admitted as required through ordinary ventilators or ducts.

EX-MERIDIAN ALTITUDE. *See* **R. to meridian** *in* REDUCTION; *also,* CIRCUM-MERIDIAN ALTITUDE.

EXPANSION. The extending, dilating, distending, developing, opening, or spreading apart of any physical condition, object, or substance. **E.-bend,** *see* BEND. **E.-chamber,** in a "spirit" or liquid compass, a compartment made of an elastic corrugated metal, fitted in the bottom of bowl for maintaining full volume of liquid, and thus preventing formation of bubbles, during contraction in lower temperatures. **E.-drawing,** laying out on a shipyard mold-loft floor of frame lines, plating, etc., to full size, as developed mathematically from drawings or models of a proposed hull. **E. engine,** one, especially a steam engine, in which the working fluid expands successively in two or more stages, as in a *compound, triple-e.,* or a *quadruple-e.* engine. **E.-hatch,** *see* **e.-trunk** *in* TRUNK. **E.-joint,** *see* JOINT. **E.-loop,** *see* LOOP. **E.-pipes,** *see* PIPE. **E.-tanks,** *see* TANK. **E.-trunk,** *see* TRUNK. **Shell e.,** *see* SHELL.

EXPLOSIVES. Laws governing carriage of explosives in merchant vessels are in force in most countries and U.S. navigation laws contain such legislation with specific regulations for packaging and stowing this kind of cargo, including provision for magazines specially constructed to accommodate more dangerous types of such goods, as bombs, detonating fuses and primers, dynamite, fire-works, gunpowder, mines, picric acid, torpedoes, etc. *See* AMMUNITION. **Explosive harpoon,** a bomb-harpoon, *see* HARPOON.

EXPORT. (L. *ex,* out; *portare,* to carry) To carry or ship to a foreign country, as goods or commodities, in commercial interests. That which is exported; act of exporting. **E. bill of lading,** as distinguished from one used with domestic shipments, a contract for carriage of goods to a foreign port. **E. duty,** a customs levy on certain goods shipped for export.

EXPRESS LINER. A high-speed first class passenger-vessel engaged on a particular run, carrying mails and a limited amount of only high-grade cargo at special rates. The term is growing into disuse.

EX QUAY. In a contract of sale and shipment, indicates that no charges are payable by consignee for transportation or housing of goods up to the stage of delivery from pier or quay.

EX SHIP. Free of shipment costs to a consignee until goods are discharged from vessel, when his liability begins; also termed *free overside.*

EXTRA MASTER. *See* MASTER.

EXTREME. Utmost edge, limit, or point; farthest; utmost. **E. breadth,** greatest breadth of a vessel, as measured from outside to outside of plating, planking, fenders, sponsons, or any permanently attached fittings on the hull: **E. length,** that of a vessel measured between the forward and after extremities of the hull; also termed *length over all.* **E. draft,** greatest distance from water-line to lowest external point of the hull; also, *keel draft.*

EYE. Loop or bight formed at a rope's end; a projecting ring-shaped part of a metal band, strap, bolt, etc.; hole in an old-fashioned anchor shank in which the ring is secured; the hole in a needle, head of a hammer, adze, etc. **E.-band,** a metal strap or band round a mast or yard having one or more projecting loops or eyes to which tackles or ropes may be attached. **E.-bolt,** a bolt with a looped head, or opening in its head; *see* BOLT. **E.-brow,** a projecting piece of metal above a port-hole to divert water trickling down ship's side or bulkhead; also called a *wriggle*. **Eyes of the rigging,** loops or bights at upper end of shrouds around a masthead. **E.-seizing,** a throat-seizing; *see* SEIZING. **Eyes of the ship,** the bows in vicinity of the hawse-pipes; so called because of eye-like appearance of the latter. Eyes formerly were painted on the bows for life-like effect and the custom still prevails in some eastern countries. **E. of the storm,** center or vortex of a cyclone. **E. of the wind,** in the exact direction from which wind is blowing; *the wind's e.* **E.-splice,** loop or bight made at a rope's end by splicing the unlaid strands into standing part of the line. **Flemish e.,** kind of fancy eye made at a rope's end by first whipping the line at throat of intended eye, teasing out the unlaid strands, dividing fiber equally and meeting it to form eye with tapered ends laid back over the rope; then serving the whole. *Selvagee e.* **Flemish e.-splice,** one in which one strand is unlaid to a greater length than the other two; eye is shaped with the latter and third strand laid in place round eye to make up full rope; strands are then tucked as in a common eye-splice. Used where the parts are spread, as when eye is placed over a mast, etc. **Going e. out,** in whaling parlance, swimming with much of head and body exposed to view, as a whale. **Height of e.,** *see* HEIGHT. To **keep one's weather e. open,** an old sailing-ship expression implying alertness or use of keen eyes,—one on the weather, the other on ship's gear and sails; to keep a good lookout. **Lacing-eyes,** small rings, eyelets, or grommets set in and along the foot of a gaff sail, edge of an awning, boat-cover, etc., to receive a line or lacing for securing such canvas in place. **Lashing-e.,** loop or eye in end of a lashing-strop, boat-gripe, etc., for receiving the lanyard in setting up such lashing. **Patent e.,** a metal link-shaped substitute for an eye, enlarged at one end where it is provided with a hole to receive the end of a wire rope; after passing rope's end into eye, an iron wedge is driven endwise into heart of rope and soldered in place; increased diameter of wire thus effects necessary resistance to a pulling stress through wire being jammed in the eye-hole. **Pad-e.,** a lug-pad; *see* PAD. **Ropemaker's e.,** a double eye formed in an end of a rope when beginning to lay the strands. Two strands are laid to form one eye and the remaining one or two strands to form another. **Weather e.,** *see* **keep one's weather e. open. Wind's e.,** *see* **e. of the wind.**

EYELET. One of the small lacing-eyes in edges of sails, awnings, boat-covers, etc. Depending on strength required, may be a metal ring sewed into the canvas, as in the head of a square sail, luff of a jib, etc.; a hemp grommet sewn in a sail, as for reef-points; or a clenching brass ring or *grommet* set in a cut hole, as commonly fitted in awnings, sail-covers, etc. *See* GROMMET.

F

F. Abbreviation for *fog* in log-books and weather records; for temperature reading by *Fahrenheit* thermometer, as, *50° F.;* and for *forward* in recording draft of ship, as in *25' 10" F.* In International Code of Signals, *flag F*, hoisted singly, or by International Morse Code, as a flashing signal, *F (. . – .)* indicates *"I am disabled. Communicate with me."*

F.A.A. "Free of all average," as abbreviated in marine insurance policies; indicating coverage is for total loss only; *see* AVERAGE.

FABRICATE. (L. *fabricare*, to frame, forge, or build) To build, construct, manufacture; to put together by art and labor, as in shipbuilding. The term *to fabricate*, as applied to vessel construction, appears to have come into use with advent of the so-called *fabricated ship*, especially the standard types of America, turned out during World War I. Instead of former shipyard practice in which all parts of each vessel were made ready for inclusion in the structure at or near site of actual building, standard interchangeable parts were produced at many different places and by many different manufacturers throughout the country. Actual building was reduced thereby to terms of record achievement, both in time and efficient workmanship in the finished product on the ways. Even greater strides in *fabrication* were effected during World War II by a further departure from former methods in that beforehand mass assembly of large sections of the structure became standard practice; whole deck-houses, framed and plated areas of decks, large double-bottom tank sections, and hold bulkheads, for example, undergoing construction before being hoisted into place by specially adapted powerful cranes. "Standard" ships thus became *fabricated* both in the sense of being supplied with their various parts from many widely separated plants, and in that of huge units of the assembled material being pre-fashioned or fastened preparatory to erection of or in the ships on the blocks. Somewhat connected with the *fabricated ship* is the fact that the conventional stern frame of single screw vessels, consisting of a costly single casting of stern- and rudder-post in one, almost from its inception, has been displaced to a considerable extent in many ship-yards on both sides of the Atlantic by one built up of heavy riveted or welded plating, usually termed a *fabricated stern frame.*

FACE. Surface of anything; front, in contrast to back of an object having two or more surfaces; side or surface presented to view or to a co-ordinated object, as, *face of a timber*, or a *valve face*. **F.-bar,** angle-bar stiffener along inner edge of a stringer, web frame, knee, bracket, etc. **F. of a cannon,** plane perpendicular to gun's bore axis, tangent to muzzle. **F. of propeller,** driving surfaces of blades, or those acting against water when engines are working ahead; also, *driving-face; thrust-surface.* **F.-plate,** a covering plate to take wear and tear on an object; a diamond or gusset plate; a stiffening plate riveted or welded to inner edge of a girder, lower edge of a web beam, upper edge of a keelson, etc.

FACILITIES, HARBOR. *See* HARBOR.

FACING. Act or process of, or material used in, building one piece of timber on another for strength or finish purposes.

FACTOR. A constant used as a multiplier or divisor; one of two or more quantities which, when multiplied together, produce a quantity considered. **F. of safety,** *see* SAFETY. **Latitude f.,** *see* LATITUDE. **Permissible f.** or **subdivision f.,** *see* **Floodable l.** *in* LENGTH. **Stowage f.,** *see* STOWAGE.

FACTORY SHIP. "Mother vessel" in attendance on a fishing fleet or her family of whaling craft, equipped with necessary means for preparing, canning, barreling, or otherwise treating the catch with the object of obviating further processing prior to marketing. Largest of such vessels are those in the whaling industry which are capable of heaving whole carcasses on board, extracting and barreling the oil, cleaning and packing baleen, etc. Others of smaller tonnage can or barrel crab, salmon, halibut, herring, mackerel, etc.; extract oil from cod, shark, or the smaller cetaceans; and, also prepare fresh fish for the cold storage market.

FAG-END. Frayed out unlaid end of a rope or unraveled teased end or edge of canvas.

FAHRENHEIT. Thermometer first used by *Gabriel Daniel Fahrenheit,* German physicist *(1686–1736),* and still commonly used in English-speaking countries. Its scale indicates *zero* as that temperature observed in an equal mixture of snow and common salt; 32 degrees as that at which fresh water begins to freeze; and 212 degrees as that at which fresh water begins to boil at sea level; the two last-named being usually termed *freezing-point* and *boiling-point,* respectively. Designating or conforming to the *F.* scale; as, *−10° F.,* "ten degrees below zero"; *15° F.,* "fifteen degrees above zero." *Cf.* CENTIGRADE.

FAIR. To adjust, straighten out, or correct a line or surface, as in a vessel under construction, or in laying out to full size on the mold-loft floor her true lines as indicated in the drawings. To line up a vessel's frames when erected during the building process, as in *fairing the frames; to fair up.* Quality of being favorable in strength and direction; as a *f. current;* a *f. wind.* Rivet-holes are said to be *f.* when exactly lined up in two units to be fastened together. On some domestic aneroid barometers, *"fair"* is written to indicate a fine weather height of the glass. A rope is said to have a *f. lead* when its course is unobstructed by any object, or not subjected to chafing against anything. **F. curves,** *see* CURVES. To **f. in place,** to restore original shape of any damaged part of a vessel's structure without removing or dismantling such parts. **Fairing ribband,** long narrow strip of timber or plate fastened longitudinally to frames to *f.* them or hold them in position while vessel is being built. **F.-lead** or **f.-leader,** any hole, bull's-eye, lizard, suitably placed roller, sheave, etc., serving to guide or *lead* a rope in a desired direction; a stout batten secured horizontally in lower rigging and bored with appropriately sized holes through which buntlines, clewlines, leechlines, etc., are rove, guided to their proper positions for belaying on the pin-rail, and thus prevented from being crossed. To **f. ship,** to "plumb" or set a vessel in correct upright position on the blocks during initial stage of construction. **F.-weather sailor,** figuratively, an inexperienced, timid, or over-cautious seaman; "flying-fish" sailor. **F.-weather vessel,** one fitted for fine weather conditions only.

FAIRWATER. Descriptive for any plating, casting, or other material fitted to the hull for reducing skin resistance or interference with vessel's streamlining; as, filling-pieces between rudder-stock and rudder-post, in rounding out of propeller-strut ends, or in reducing propeller-race area by temporarily fitted plating. **F. cone** or **cap,** cone-shaped metal covering, threaded as a nut and screwed on after end of shaft over the propeller locking-nut.

FAIRWAY. Channel or navigable part of a bay, river, harbor, lake, or strait ordinarily frequented by vessels under way. Besides the limited area of a buoyed channel, a *fairway* includes waters lying outside such area as may be convenient for navigation of light draft vessels proceeding in same general direction of such buoyed channel. **F. buoy,** any buoy marking a fairway or channel; often applied particularly to one marking the *mid-channel.* Other than those entering a river or harbor, coastal *f's* are *buoyed,* according to system adopted in country concerned, as considering their origin at a national coast-line extremity; as, on the U.S. Atlantic and Gulf of Mexico coasts southward or westward from the Canadian boundary, and northward on the Pacific coast; or in the direction of the main flood tidal stream, as in the British Isles. *See* BUOY.

FAKE. One of the circular parts or loops in a coil of rope or wire; also, *flake.* To **fake down,** to coil or lay in *fakes,* either "figure-eight fashion" or with *f's* lying clear of each other and free for running, as required, for example, to avoid kinking or fouling of braces, sheets, rocket-lines, harpoon-lines, etc. **Catch-f.,** a kinked or fouled part of a coil or faked rope. **Figure-eight f.,** one of the parts in a *figure-eight coil,* so called because laid in a series of overlapping 8-shaped *f's,* each of which is placed consecutively toward the running direction, and by the approximate diameter, of the rope. **Flemish f.,** *see* FLEMISH. **French f.,** to lay a rope on deck clear for running by arranging it in a continuous series of serpentine turns, all free of each other and about at right angles to direction of rope's running lead; usually called a *long-flaked coil* when *f's* are laid in same direction as the line of lead. **Tub.-f.,** method of faking small line in a tub; usually *French f.* style, each layer placed crosswise over its next below.

FAKING-BOX. Receptacle for a small line laid in *fakes,* as a life-saving rocket-line. A *faking-tub* is used in fishing-boats for warps; in a whaler's boat for harpoon-lines.

FALBAT. (Sw.) A large clinker-built boat, rigged with a large square or lug sail and sometimes a mizzen as in the ketch or yawl, once commonly used on the Swedish coast of the Gulf of Bothnia, chiefly in the seal-hunting industry.

FALL. The rope rove in one or more blocks as a hoisting rig or tackle, the permanently secured end of which is called the *standing part,* its working end the *hauling part.* Sometimes the last-named is called the *fall;* as in, *take a pull on the fall.* In a crane or other hoisting rig or machine, part of the rope or chain to which power is applied. To befall, occur; or with a combining word, to move, to act; as, to *f. calm;* to *f. astern;* to *f. aboard.* **A fall!,** cry from a whaler's lookout in reporting a sighted whale; equivalent of "Thar she blows!" Also, especially in the old Dundee whalers, exclamation on actual harpooning of the quarry; and term for a chase of a whale by ship's boats. A *loose f.* described a lost or escaping whale. The word is believed to have originated with a northeastern Scottish pronunciation of *whale*, or that resulting from influence of the Scandinavian *hval* (whale). The rope used for hoisting aboard the long strips of blubber (speck) during "flensing" of a carcase lying alongside was called *the f.; see* **Speck-f. Boat-f.**, rope in purchase or tackle used to hoist or lower a boat; generally, in the usual case of boat suspended from two davits, termed *forward f.* and *after f.* according to position as leading to bow or stern of boat. **Cant-f.,** *see* CANT. **Cat-f.,** *see* CAT. **Cutting-f.,** in old-fashioned whaling, heavy rope used to lift a strip of blubber as cut from the carcase while latter was being gradually turned over by the *cant-f.* Depending on custom, generally *cutting-f.* and *cant-f.* were synonymous in flensing smaller whales, in which case *cutting-f.* was sufficient to both cant or turn, and lift blubber away from, the carcase during the process. **Endless f.,** rope or chain rove as a whip, or in a set of purchase blocks, and having no standing end; a continuous fall. **F.-block,** in a purchase, that block to which hauling part of *f.* first leads. To **f. calm,** to cease to blow, as wind; to become calm. **F.-cloud,** a low cloud; low-hanging stratus, as slightly lifted fog-bank. To **f. astern,** to drop astern; *see* DROP. To **f. aboard of,** *see* ABOARD. To **f. foul of,** or **afoul of,** to become entangled or have a collision with; to attack or assault; to have trouble or quarrel with. To **f. down,** to drift or drop down with a wind or current. To **f. home,** to incline inward; to "tumble home" or curve inward from perpendicular, as a vessel's sides. To **f. in with,** to meet, approach, or bring into sight; as, *to f. in with the land.* To **f. off,** to deviate from a course, especially to leeward, or away from one's objective; to run or incline away in direction, as a coast-line from a given point. To **f. out,** to incline outward, as sides of a boat. **F.-tub,** box or tub in which a *boat-f.* is faked or coiled. **F.-wind,** a breeze or gale blowing down a mountainside or down from a headland; any wind having a major downward component. The *bora* of the Adriatic and *mistral* of the northwestern Mediterranean are of this nature. To **let f.,** *see* LET. **Hoisting-f.,** rope or chain used for hoisting; although a hauling part of a halyard, a gantline, mast-rope, etc., may be correctly termed a *hoisting-f.,* it is never thus used on board ship, but generally applied to hoisting ropes of shore cranes, pile-drivers, donkey-hoists, etc. **Overboard f.,** one leading from a boom or yard-arm beyond the ship's side. **Purchase-f.,** rope rove in a purchase or tackle. **Speck-f.,** *see* SPECK.

FALL HERRING. A medium-sized herring which appears in schools during spring along the U.S. Atlantic coast south of Cape Cod.

FALSE. Not according to law or regulation; incorrect; irregular; as, *false papers.* Designating a strengthening or protective fitting or structure over a main part or unit; as, a *false deck.* **F. cirrus,** cirriform extension or overflow on top of a cumulus or cumulo-nimbus cloud; *thunderstorm cirrus.* **F. fire,** ashore or aboard ship, a fire built for purpose of deceiving an enemy; formerly, a fire used for signalling between ships in wartime. A misguiding beacon shown by wreckers, as in former Cornish days, to draw a vessel into disaster on the rocks. **F. horizon,** *see* HORIZON. **F. keel,** *see* KEEL. **F. keelson,** *see* KEELSON. **F. papers,** ship's documents, or licenses and certificates of crew members, designed to deceive. **F. stern-post,** piece of timber bolted to after face of a vessel's stern-post for added strength. **F. rail,** a buffalo or spray-board; *see* BUFFALO. **F. stem,** cutwater or built-up fore part of a vessel's stem. **F. tack,** *see* TACK.

FAN. Revolving, mechanically driven, propeller-like set of blades for producing air-currents, as for ventilation or for assisting combustion in a furnace; screw-fan; fan-blower; fan-wheel. To **f. out,** to slack off the sheets of a fore-and-aft sail when the wind is abeam, in order to ease sail pressure, as customary in small craft in a stiff breeze. To **f. along,** colloquial term meaning to slowly move along with sails alternately filling and flattening in light unsteady winds. Fast ships were said to be *ghosting* when slipping along with upper sails only catching a breeze. or above-surface wind sometimes met with in above-noted conditions, especially in proximity of land.

FANCY-LINE. Small cotton, flax, linen, or nylon cordage used for cover-lacings, man-ropes, lanyards, etc., especially in yachts where good shipshape appearance is considered; also, *see* LINE.

FANTAIL. An American term for that elliptical or round-shaped part of a hull, and space therein, projecting abaft the stern-post. Probably so called because of radial appearance of the transom beams and frames in that part of structure. *Stern* or *counter.*

FANTOD. Old naval seamen's term for a fidgety, nervous, or over-anxious officer.

FARDAGE. Archaic term for all material on board constituting *dunnage,* including loose wood, battens, gratings, and coir or rattan matting.

FARDEL. An old French word meaning a bundle or pack, once adopted in English nautical parlance as to *furl* or to *roll up;* as in "An *fardel* well ye goode main seil." Also, *fardle.*

FARM. Open space adjoining a pier or dock which may be used to receive or temporarily land cargo in event of congested wharf conditions.

F.A.S. Abbreviation in shipping contracts indicating cost of a consignment of goods as delivered to a point within reach of ship's loading tackle, from which point buyer's liability begins: *free alongside ship.*

FASH. A broken, split up, or otherwise irregular condition of a plank seam; such a seam itself, in caulkers' old-time usage.

FASHION. In shipbuilding, to form or give shape to, as a *fashioned plate,* or one which is shaped without heating or forging. **F.-piece,** one of the timbers which design or *fashion* a vessel's counter in the shape desired; also, *f.-timber.* **F.-plate stem,** cold-bent steel plates of U-shaped section united by welding or riveting to form a ship's stem; also termed *fabricated, plated,* and *soft nose stem.*

FAST. Firmly fixed; held tightly. That which holds *fast;* a line holding a vessel to a wharf, dolphin, etc., as a *bow-f., stern-f., quarter-f.;* also named for object to which secured, as *dolphin-f., ring-f., buoy-f.* **F. boat,** in old whaling usage, a boat which is attached to a whale by harpoon and line; opposed to a *loose boat,* or one which has not been as successful. **F. fish,** a whale remaining attached to boat by which harpooned; opposed to a *loose fish,* or one not attacked. **F. ice,** shore-line ice, as distinguished from floating or field ice; also, *bord-ice.* **Land-f.,** any object on shore, as a post, anchor, tree, etc., to which a mooring-line or cable may be fastened. To **make f.,** to secure a working piece of cordage or chain by belaying, bitting, hitching, or knotting; to furl or stow and secure a sail by gaskets.

FASTENING. Anything that binds, secures, or makes fast; as, a bar, bolt, chain, dog, hook, etc. General term for means by which the structural parts of a wooden vessel are connected and secured; as bolts, nails, screws, spikes, treenails. A vessel is sometimes described as *copper-fastened* or *galvanized iron fastened; see* COPPER. In boat-building, *f's* used are bolts, drifts, clinched nails, riveted nails, and screws, usually of copper, a copper alloy, or galvanized iron. **Double-f.; double and single f.,** *see* DOUBLE. **Dump-f.,** *see* DUMP. **Inside f.; outside f.,** those driven, respectively, from inside or outside a vessel's hull. **Single-f.,** system in which one treenail and one metal spike or bolt are driven into each frame timber through outside planking. **Spike-f.,** act of temporarily securing planking by spiking until finally fastened as required. **Through-f.,** a bolt driven completely through two or more joining parts, as outside planking to a frame and beam-knee, and clenched at each end.

FATA MORGANA. (*It.* = *Morgan the fay*) A mirage sometimes observed in the Strait of Messina, so named because once regarded by seamen and local coast dwellers as the work of the fairy *Morgana.*

FATHOM. (O. Sax., *fathmos,* the outstretched arms; Du. *vadem;* Ger. *faden*) Measure of length equal to *six feet,* used in measuring cordage, chain-cable, and depths in taking soundings by lead-line or sonic depth-finder. Excepting certain large-scale coastal, harbor, and river hydrography, in which depths are given in feet, American and British charts indicate soundings in *fathoms* with character of bottom observed. Originally, a *f.* usually varied between 5 and 6 feet in length, depending upon the space that could be covered by a measurer's outstretched arms; and the custom is still in use on board ship, as, *e.g.,* a boatswain's "fathom" in drawing from the manufacturer's coil a well-known length of rope for a boom topping-lift fall. **F.-line,** showing contour of the sea-floor on a chart, a line, usually of sinuous character, joining all positions having the same depth of water, reduced to standard datum given, where necessary, in title of chart; as, the *100-, 10-,* or *5-fathom line.*

FATHOMETER. Instrument for determining sea depths which works on the principle of measuring time elapsed between transmission of a sound directed toward, and return of the echo from, the bottom. It essentially consists of a transmitter, a receiver, and a depth indicator. Type of *f.* installed for ordinary navigational purposes usually is made to obtain depths up to 200 fathoms; special types are used in coastal surveying and for deep-sea work as required in cable-ships. Chief advantages in use of this instrument are that an accurate sounding may be obtained with the mere turning of a control switch and a rapid series and continuous line of soundings instantly are available under the navigator's eye. Also called *echo sounding-machine* and *sonic depth-finder. Cf.* ECHO SOUNDING.

FAT-LEAN. Whaling term for parts of flesh in which fat and lean are mixed; pieces of lean flesh adhering to blubber in the process of flensing.

FAVOR. To make easier; to afford advantage to; to befriend; as, to *favor the ship* by taking in sail when vessel is laboring; to *f. a sprung topmast;* to *f. the old mainsail.* This application of the word, as with many other typical expressions in old-time seamanship usage, apparently has passed into obsolescence.

FAY. To fit or lie closely together, as the meeting surfaces of two joined planks or pieces of plating. Rivet-holes are punched from the *faying side* of plating, in order that no burrs or irregularities arising from the punching process will interfere with close-fitting or *faying* in the intended joint. *Faying surface* is that of either piece of wood or metal *fayed* or closely fitted together.

FEASE. *See* FEAZE.

FEATHERING. In rowing, term indicating turning of the oar-blade in a fore-and-aft direction at completion of each pulling-stroke and through the recovery-stroke (or *feathering-stroke*), in order to minimize wind resistance and to avoid interference of rough water against blade. In *f.,* oar is given a quarter-turn as it is lifted from water by bending wrists downward, bringing hands upward toward the oarsman, which lays oar-blade parallel with water surface. Immediately before again immersing blade, hands are returned to normal position and blade is again brought in vertical position for next pulling-stroke. **F.-float,** paddle or float of a *f. wheel.* **F.-paddle,** same as *f.-float.* **F. screw,** a propeller which may be altered or reversed in pitch while in motion, as used in some one-way motored small craft; also, a propeller of which the blades may be laid edgewise fore-and-aft, in order to offer least resistance when vessel proceeds under sail alone. **F. paddle-wheel,** a ship's paddle in which the floats automatically are turned perpendicular to water-surface during period of immersion, thus presenting maximum driving surface to water.

FEAZE. To unlay strands at a rope's end and "tease out" the yarns; hence, the *feazing,* or ragged end of a hawser.

FEED. To supply material to a machine for processing; material thus supplied. Water supply to a canal for restoring lockage loss. Combining word used in terminology of units in a boiler-water replenishing system. **F.-cock,** control valve for flow of water, fuel, a lubricant, etc. **F.-heater,** an apparatus in which water for a boiler is heated by steam; a boiler *f.-water* heater. **F.-pump,** force-pump for supplying *f.-water* to a boiler. **F.-water,** that for replenishing loss through evaporation, as in a steam boiler. **F.-water filter,** chamber in a *boiler f.* system in which, through an absorption medium such as a loofah sponge, oil, grease, or other foreign matter is removed from feed-water prior to entering boiler. **Drip f.,** arrangement whereby lubricating oil is applied to an engine bearing drop by drop, as from a regulated needle-valve. **Wick f.,** means by which a machine or engine bearing is supplied with a lubricant by capillary attraction in a cotton wick of appropriate size.

FEEDER. In carriage of bulk grain, a trunk or suitable enclosure built around or in a hatchway, as a reservoir from which the loaded grain may flow into, and re-occupy, any space created in a lower compartment due to settling or shifting of the mass. *F's* are required in bulk-grain-laden ocean-going vessels by laws of most maritime countries, enactment of which were prompted by serious marine losses due to shifting of grain cargoes during heavy weather. Provision usually is made for maintaining the supply in *f's* by carrying a supplementary quantity of grain in bags for the purpose. **Center-f.,** one installed in a vessel's center line, as in a cargo-hatch. **Wing-f.,** one of smaller openings or hatchways in which a *f.* is fitted, occupying a position near ship's sides in a 'tween deck.

FEEL. To perceive or observe by touch, as, to *f. bottom* with a sounding-lead; to be affected by an action or condition, as, a vessel *feeling the current;* to observe a state or quality, as, the boat *feels crank.* To **f. the bottom,** *see* BOTTOM. To **f. the helm,** *see*
HELM. **Feeling the way,** proceeding slowly as in making port, or in navigating narrow waters, during thick weather, taking extra precautions, including frequent soundings, radio bearings where possible, and placing additional lookouts.

FEELER. A very thin piece of flat steel used in inspection of riveted work to detect any improper separation of the faying surfaces; for determining clearance between a shaft-journal and bearing, a piston and cylinder-wall, etc. A short round rod of metal, crooked at one end, used, in operating a mechanical sounding-machine, to *feel* contact of lead with the bottom; as the sounding-wire runs out, *f.* is laid against it by the hand and operator detects a sudden slackness as lead strikes bottom. Use of *f.* becomes necessary in depths greater than about 20 fathoms, especially when vessel's speed is upwards of 10 knots, since actual contact as indicated in the wire usually may be observed in comparatively shallow water only; termed *sounding-machine check* and *sounding-machine feeler.* A *f.* also is an old-fashioned term for a gusty breeze immediately followed by a calm with a moderate to light drizzle, which, depending upon previous appearance of the elements, was considered in higher latitudes as forerunner of a gale.

FEESE. *See* FEAZE.

FELT. Matted fibrous material, commonly wool mixed with hair, produced in sheets and impregnated with coal tar, creosote, or similar product, formerly laid between a vessel's outside planking and the copper or Muntz metal sheathing, which extended over vessel's immersed surface to the light water-line. The practice was designed to protect planking, especially that of softer woods as in American ships, from attack by burrowing worm-like mollusks, among which most widely known and destructive is the *Teredo navalis* or ship-worm.

FELUCCA. (It. *feluca*) Class of small vessels once commonly met with in Mediterranean waters and on the Portuguese and western Spanish coasts. Formerly an important, fast-sailing, commercial craft, carrying two large lateen sails, a jib, and a mizzen, partially decked, and sometimes equipped with a bow rudder; in later years, the type discarded jib and mizzen, were built shorter and with broader beam, and carried a proportionately heavier load. Now fast disappearing, last of the *feluccas* are 40 to 50 feet in length and of from 10 to 15 tons burden, used for either fishing or trading purposes.

FENCE. To protect a hole or opening in a sail, awning, cover, or other canvas, by stitching a grommet or piece of small soft line about its periphery. Also *fense.*

FEND OFF. To push or hold off, as in keeping a boat from striking or chafing against a wharf.

FENDER. (Abbrev. from *defender*) Anything acting as a buffer, bumper, or surface protective, placed between a vessel's side and a pier, another vessel, dolphin, etc., as a spar, bundle of old rope, or pudding of matting. A fixed post, pile, or other timber, for protecting the edge of a wharf or house thereon from ice, lighters, moving vessels, etc. See CAMEL. **Bow-f.,** a heavy pudding of old rope, covered by a matting of point line or ratline stuff, and tapered toward each end, fixed as a pushing buffer across the stem of a harbor tug-boat. **Cork f.,** see CORK. **F.-bar,** see F. guard. **F.-beam,** a square timber suspended horizontally between ship's side and a pier, or floating alongside pier, as a *f.* **F.-guard,** a timber often faced with flat iron, horizontally fixed to, and projecting from, a vessel's side for whole or greater part of her length; chiefly fitted to coasting and river power-driven vessels. Also called *f.-bar, guard-rail,* and *permanent f.* **F.-pile,** a post or pile, often one of a group, as in a dolphin, serving as a *f.* between boats or small vessels and a landing; also, *pile-f.* **F.-rail,** see F.-guard. **Grommet-f.,** consists of a handy coil of old rope, suitably covered or served, and fitted with a lanyard; commonly used on small vessels. A good substitute for this type is a discarded automobile tire, of late years in popular use on lighters, fishing-boats, tugs, etc. **Permanent f.,** see **F.-guard. Pile-f.,** see F.-pile. **Pudding-f.,** similar to a *bow-f.,* placed on corners of rectangular-shaped scows, dolphins at pier heads, along sides of large boats, etc. Often called *puddening* where extended along a boat's side or on a transom stern; also, when protecting a corner of a wharf or a boat's stem, sometimes termed a *dolphin.* Various other terms are merely descriptive of the object or material serving as *f's;* as, *cane-f., rod-f., rope-f., spar-f.* Probably no more efficient fender was put to good old-fashioned use on larger wooden vessels than an ordinary pressed bale of hay!

FENLAND PUNT. Small, double-ended, flat-bottomed boat, having straight sides rising direct from bottom planking, commonly used for hunting in the *fens* or marshes of Lincolnshire. The punt's stem and stern posts project below its bottom for the purpose of preventing it from wholly grounding when under way. Also called *fen-boat.*

FENKS. Refuse whale blubber, used as a land fertilizer and also for manufacture of Prussian blue. Also, *finks.*

FENSE. See FENCE.

FERREL'S LAW OF GYRATION. See LAW.

FERRO. (It. *ferro,* iron) The iron prow on a gondola. *Ferro,* now the Spanish *Hierro,* an island in the Canary group, is of interest in that its meridian was once recommended for adoption as the *prime meridian* by several western European nations; its longitude west of Greenwich is 17° 54′.

FERRULE. A wood or copper alloy bushing for making a steam-tight connection at end of a steam, water, or condenser tube, where it enters a tube-plate. Any metal ring round the end of a pipe, chisel-handle, caulking-mallet, etc., to prevent burring or splitting.

FERRY. Provision, as by boat, for transporting goods or passengers across a channel, river, strait, or other narrow body of water at regular intervals; generally by law considered a continuation of a highway, and anyone operating such *f.* as a common carrier. To carry or transport over such waters. A place where boats cross any river or narrow waters. **Car-f.,** see CAR. **F.-boat,** vessel engaged in carrying passengers, vehicles, goods, and/or animals across a narrow body of water; usually double-ended and beamy, with main deck for accommodation of vehicles and an upper deck for passengers. **F.-bridge,** large gangway or landing platform, often supported by a pontoon, capable of being adjusted in height to suit level of ferryboat's main deck. Also, term for a *f.* transporting railroad cars. **F.-flat,** scow-type, flat-bottomed *f.-boat,* either open or decked; local term for such boat in small inland streams. **F.-house,** shelter for passengers and freight, ticket office, etc. at a *f.* landing. **F.-rack,** structure of piles forming sides of a slip or dock, which receive and guide a double-ended *f.-boat* into her berth.

FESTOON CLOUD. The *mammato-cumulus* cloud, or one having a heavy wool-like appearance with low dark protuberances of various shapes; considered a sign of approaching showery weather.

FETCH. To reach by sailing; as, *we fetched the strait.* To make, perform some action, achieve, or accomplish; as, to *f. headway;* to *f. a good offing.* To go or come; to make way; to hold a course; as, to *f. to windward;* to *f. a course.* Archaic term for a tack or reach, or act of tacking or reaching. Stretch or extent of a bay or coast-line indentation. Distance through which sea waves or breakers advance; also, distance off a weather shore at which white-capped waves first appear. To **f. about,** old term meaning to lay ship on a new tack. To **f. away,** to break loose, as an object on a rolling vessel, or something shaken loose from its hold or position. To **f. a compass,** old form of to *f. a course;* set a course. (*Cf. Acts 28:13*). To **f. down,** to bring down, as by gunfire. To **f. headway** or **sternway,** to gain motion ahead or astern. To **f. off,** to carry from shore to ship when at anchor or under way; to rescue, as from a wreck, stranded vessel, etc. To **f. a pump,** to prime, or make a pump work by pouring some of the liquid into it as a starter. To **f. up all standing;** to **f. up with a round turn;** see BRING.

FEVER, BALLAST. See B.-fever *in* BALLAST.

FIBER. Substance composed of stringy tissue of animal, mineral, or vegetable origin, and capable of being spun or woven; as, asbestos, hemp, and wool *f*. **F.-clad rope,** a 4-, 5-, or 6-stranded type of wire rope in which the strands are served individually with marline or other small tarred hemp stuff; used for halyards, boat-falls, cargo-hoists, etc. It is considerably less in weight than manila rope of same strength and its protected strands would appear to be a desirable feature in a wire for ship use. However, it has the disadvantage of being easily opened to the weather by a sharp nip, as in belaying; also, that of allowing moisture to lodge in a strand through an unobserved break in the *f*. covering, its strength thus easily being reduced by resulting corrosion. **F. insulation,** various *f's,* such as mineral wool, fibrous glass, silicate of cotton, and the like, used as insulation material around cold storage compartments, sides and decks of fruit-carrying vessels, etc. **F. rope,** as distinguished from that made of wire, a rope of cotton, flax, manila hemp, coir, sisal, etc. *See* ROPE.

FID. A tapered hardwood pin used to open the strands in splicing rope and shaping or stretching grommets and cringle-strops. A stout square bar of wood or iron at the heel of, and supporting, a topmast or topgallant-mast in the rigged position; it is laid across the trestle-trees through a hole or in a groove at heel of mast. An iron or wooden pin used in anything as a key or temporary support; a toggle. Formerly, a plug of cork or oakum used as a protective measure in stopping a vent in the old-fashioned cannon. **Blubber-f.,** a toggle run through a strip of blubber as a means of attaching a tackle-strop, during flensing of carcase alongside ship, as in older whaling practice. **Hand f.,** round tapered pin of hard wood, from 12 to 24 inches in length and 1 to 3 inches in diameter, used in rope-splicing. Sailors of the old school often carried fids of two or three sizes in their diddy-bags, always companions of a similar set of serving-boards, all fashioned to a polished surface from hardest woods obtainable; sometimes from whale-bone. Also, a *splicing-f.* **F.-hole,** square mortice or hole in a topmast or topgallant-mast heel for receiving the *fid.* **Setting-f.,** one of larger dimensions than those of a hand-fid, sometimes made of metal, conical-shaped, and stood upright when in use; a riggers' and sailmakers' implement for stretching grommets, eyes, and cringle-strops, preparatory to insertion of dead-eyes, bull's-eyes, cringle-irons, etc. In "setting," such hand-fashioned grommets, strops, etc., are placed on the *fid* and stretched by force along its increasing diameter with blows from a wooden mallet. Also termed *standing-fid.*

FIDDED TOPMAST. As distinguished from a *fixed topmast,* or one permanently connected to, or merely an extension of, a lower-mast, one which is supported by a *fid* resting on trestle-trees of lower-mast, or run through lowermast itself, as in the case of a *telescoping topmast.*

FIDDLE. A rack in the form of several compartments, or small cords stretched as a fence, to keep dishes from sliding off a vessel's table in rough weather; also, under same conditions, removable bars fitted across a galley stove or range for securing pots, kettles, etc. **F.-block,** *see* BLOCK. **F. bow,** a clipper bow; *see* BOW.[2] **F.-head,** an ornamental scroll or volute, similar to that on a violin, at upper termination of the cutwater, in lieu of a figurehead.

FIDDLER FISH. A shark-like member of the *ray* family found in tropical waters, so named from its shape. Also *fiddle-fish.*

FIDDLER'S GREEN. Former sailors' name for a place or area on shore providing cheap amusement or recreation; also, in humorous reference to *Jimmy Squarefoot's* domain, general term for an Elysium affording a perpetual round of pleasure.

FIDLEY. Spacious trunkway above and opening into the boiler-room, through which fire-room ventilators, escape-ladders, and, usually, uptakes to smoke-stack, are led; generally has one or more landings or decks, in addition to its weather covering, composed of iron gratings. **F. deck,** partially raised deck in old-fashioned steam-vessels, immediately above the fidley and extending over engine-room. **F.-hatch,** upper entrance to *f.;* usually consists of removable iron gratings, provided with iron covers for weather protection. (Also spelled *fiddley*)

FIELD. Extent; expanse; as, a *field* of sea-weed. Space traversed by lines of force; as, a *magnetic f.* Area in which a device or drawing is pictured or projected; as, a lion on the *f. of a flag; f. covered by a chart or map.* **F. day,** especially in naval use, day for general cleaning up fore-and-aft on board ship. **F.-glass,** *see* GLASS. **F. ice,** *see* ICE. **Magnetic f.,** *see* MAGNETIC.

FIFE-RAIL. *See* RAIL.

FIFIE. (From county of *Fife*) Old type of fast-sailing fishing-vessel of east coast of Scotland; 50 to 70 feet in length and decked fore-and-aft; carried two large lug-sails and a small mizzen; and had stem and stern posts perpendicular to the keel.

FIGHTING. Participial adjective indicating *qualified for fight; warlike.* **F. lantern,** *see* LANTERN. **F.-fish,** the *Betta pugnax,* a small spiny-finned fish of southeastern Asia, so named from its pugnacious warlike qualities. Gambling on results of fights between two of these fishes formerly was a popular sport in Siam (*Thailand*), the combatants being placed in a bottle or glass globe for the purpose. When quiet, its colors are dull compared with a sudden burst into a glow of splendor when irritated by a rival. **F. ship,** a vessel, backed by sufficient capital to withstand losses, placed in a particular trade and offering low freight rates for purpose of crushing competition. Also, a fully-armed naval vessel.

F. stopper, *see* STOPPER. **F.-top,** *see* TOP. **F. trim,** state or condition for entering into an engagement with the enemy, as that required of a naval vessel.

FIGUREHEAD. Ornamental forward-curving termination of the cutwater, immediately below a bowsprit; usually a statue or bust, as of some mythological personage or noted admiral. The custom of displaying a decorative design on a ship's prow dates from Mediterranean antiquity, the *acroterium* of the Greek and Phœnician galleys being, without doubt, originally expressive in a finishing-touch to the craft's expected commercial or fighting prowess. Our comparatively recent *f.* appears as that ornament thrust from its former position by the advent of the bowsprit some 800 years ago.

FIGURE-OF-EIGHT COIL or **FAKE.** *See* FAKE. Also, *figure-eight.*

FIGURE-OF-EIGHT KNOT. Used as a stopper-knot at a rope's end to prevent rope from unreeving through a block, bull's-eye, etc. It is made by laying rope's end over its standing part, thus forming a small bight; then passing end around standing part and through bight. Also, *figure-eight knot.* *See* KNOT.

FILIBUSTER. (*Sp.*) A freebooter or irregular military fortune-seeker; a buccaneer. Originally, a piratical adventurer on the Spanish Main in 17th century; now one who organizes, without authority, a hostile force to attack commerce of any country, or to assist an existing insurgent faction therein.

FILL. To distend, as a sail, by full pressure of wind. To trim a sail or sails so that the wind will press against them as in sailing ahead. To **f. away,** to resume course after sails have been shaking in the wind; to stand on after having brought vessel to the wind. To **f. the yards,** to trim square sail so that wind will press against after side of canvas.

FILLER. In wood ship construction, a piece of timber, plank, etc., set in any part of the structure to build up a deficiency; *see* DUTCHMAN. A composition applied to finished wood for filling the pores before painting or varnishing.

FILLET. Rounded edge or bulb on a rolled-steel angled or flat bar. Small wood strip fitted in rabbets of joining edges of planking, as sometimes used in sides of a deck-house. Strip cut from a fish and free of bone, as *f.* of cod, *f.* of salmon. **F. weld,** joint made between two structural parts meeting at right angles by welding in and along each corner thus formed a triangular strip, or *f.,* of metal.

FILLING. Threads of canvas constituting the *weft* or *woof* of such fabric. A filler, or those parts forming a building-up arrangement, as in the after dead-wood of a wooden vessel. In steel construction, blocks of wood with a cement mixture fitted behind and between frames to provide water-tightness in a 'tween deck. A cement mixture or other plastic substance laid flush with rivet-heads in bilges, waterways, etc., to prevent an accumulation of dirt deposit therein. **Beam-f.,** *see* BEAM. **F.-frames,** *see* **F.-timbers. F.-piece,** a liner or strip of plate inserted between faying surfaces; as, between a frame and a raised strake. **F.-timbers,** extra pieces fitted where additional strength or stiffening is required; as, timbers placed between frames in ship's bottom or additional transoms.

FILTER. A device or apparatus for separating foreign deposits or impurities from a liquid; a strainer. **Feed-water f.,** *see* FEED. **Oil-f.,** *see* OIL.

FIN. Flat spreading appendage on the hull of a submarine forward of her horizontal rudder; a bilge keel; a fin-keel. Membranous winglike member projecting from an aquatic animal used to propel, balance, and guide the body. Fins of a fish are named and located as follows: *dorsal,* on the back; *ventral* or *pelvic,* on deeper part of belly; *pectoral,* at each side near the head; *anal,* below and near the tail; *caudal,* the tail. A cetacean's fin is also called a *flipper* and sometimes *flapper.* **F.-chain,** in older whaling, chain sling made fast to a flipper when commencing to flense, or strip off blubber from, a carcase. Cutting of first strip (*blanket-piece*) began with hauling taut on speck-tackle, thence blubber was lifted clear as cutting progressed. **Fin-keel,** *see* KEEL. To **f. out,** said of a whale when lashing water with its fins and rolling about after being wounded, indicating death agony of the animal. **F.-whale,** a finner or finback; the *fin-fish* of whaler's cant; *see* WHALE. **F.-winged,** having wings like fins or flippers, as a penguin. **Whale-f.,** baleen, or stringy substance in mouth of a whale; *see* BALEEN.

FINAL DIAMETER. *See* DIAMETER.

FINBACK. One of the rorquals or balænopterine whales; *see* WHALE.

FINDS HERSELF. Said of a new vessel, or of one newly rigged or engined, upon having her rigging and/or machinery adjusted to proper working condition; also, of a new iron or steel vessel after divesting herself of a large proportion of magnetism acquired while on the stocks.

FINE. Long and sharp, as the fore body of a vessel. A ship is said to be *fine* when her *block coefficient* is small and hull gradually tapers off toward bow and stern; also, *fine-lined.* To sail **f.,** to sail as close to the wind as possible. **F. on the bow,** said of direction in which an object bears with relation to the fore-and-aft line; at a small angle from the course steered. **F. cordage,** fiber rope of any kind made up from a superior grade of manila, flax, cotton, nylon, etc.

FINENESS, COEFFICIENT OF. *See* COEFFICIENT.

FINGER-PIN. A sounding-wire feeler; *see* FEELER.

FINISHING. Term used in 17th and 18th century shipbuilding for the ornate, often gilded, scroll work, coats-of-arms, and other embellishments on the quarter galleries of naval ships and foreign-going merchantmen.

FINNER. Colloquial term for a *finback whale,* on west coast of U.S.; called an *Oregon f.,* *razorback,* and a young finback, a *sharp-headed f.*

FINNING. *See* To **fin out** *in* FIN.

F.I.O. Free in and out; a chartering term; *see* FREE.

FIORD. (Scand. *fjord,* bay) Narrow inlet or bay on a high or mountainous sea-coast, as in Alaska or Norway.

FIR. A pinaceous tree of any species of *Abies,* growing in temperate regions, and producing timber formerly extensively used in building medium-sized vessels and now providing good boat-building material from its better classes. Best and obtainable in long lengths is *Douglas fir* of western U.S., or *red fir, Oregon pine,* and *Douglas spruce,* as variously named, which particularly is suitable for masts and spars, beams, frames, and heavy planking. *See* DOUGLAS SPRUCE.

FIRE. To discharge firearms. To light and attend a furnace, as that of a boiler. The discharge or firing of arms, as from a ship or body of troops. A **dropping f.,** continuous irregular discharge of small arms. **False f.,** *see* FALSE. **F. alarm signal,** call for crew to muster at fire-fighting stations made by pre-arranged blasts on whistle or ringing of ship's bell. In merchant ships, such signal usually is prescribed by law or regulation, as, in U.S. vessels, a continuous ringing of ship's bell together with continuous sounding of gongs in a general alarm system throughout ship, for a period of 10 seconds or more. **F. area,** that of land or water within range of effective gunfire. To **f. at will,** to shoot at a target or enemy at best opportunity, independently of other guns in same battery or ship. **F.-bar,** one of the iron bars forming a grate in a furnace. **F. and bilge pump,** a service pump intended for discharge of bilge-water and for supplying a force of sea-water to ship's *f. line* system, as required. **F.-bill,** a posted list of stations appointed each crew member and duties assigned each when called to *f.* quarters; a *f. station bill.* **F.-boat,** a harbor vessel equipped with powerful pumps and necessary means for fighting *f.* breaking out in waterfront property or on floating craft. **F.-boom,** one of several long spars extended from a ship's side and connected at outer ends by a rope or chain, in old wooden navy days used as a protection when at anchor against *f.-ships* of an enemy. **F.-box,** that part of a boiler containing the furnace. **F.-bridge,** *see* furnace-bridge *in* FURNACE. **F. bulkhead,** as required in passenger vessels, a *f.-proof* partition extending from side to side of ship in accommodation spaces. The *International Convention for Safety at Sea, London, 1929,* defined a fire-bulkhead as one capable of resisting for one hour a temperature of about 1500° F., and recommended such bulkheads to be installed in passenger ships at intervals of not more than 130 feet; also termed *f.-proof bulkhead.* **F.-control,** a communication system directing *f.* of guns on a war-vessel, as from radar or range-finder to plotting-room and thence to the guns. **F. detector,** a means of locating source of smoke or rising temperatures within ship's compartment arrangement. One or two of the following are usually installed in modern passenger vessels:—*Smoke vent system* in which fire is indicated by smoke drawn by suction fan through a pipe leading from any compartment; *electric system,* where an abnormally high temperature acting on a thermostat closes a circuit, rings an alarm-bell, and indicates location of heat by illuminating a bulb; *expansion of air* in a copper tube exposed to abnormal heat automatically producing a visible signal and sounding an alarm. Desirability of such system as one of these noted was recognized by the *International Convention for Safety at Sea, London, 1929,* and most nations have adhered to rules and recommendations promulgated by that body in making compulsory the installation of fire-detectors in passenger ships of certain capacity and class. **F. door,** one opening through a *fire bulkhead* and which may be closed by mechanical means from a weather deck. **F. drill,** exercise of ship's crew at *f.-quarters* (stations) for instruction in competent use of *f.-fighting* equipment. **F. extinguisher,** as included in a ship's equipment, those of portable type are limited generally to four in number, *viz.,* "*soda and acid*" type, or a container of bicarbonate of soda solution in which pressure is built up by upsetting a vial of sulphuric acid set in container; *carbon tetrachloride,* particularly adapted to fires in electric equipment, because of its non-conductive properties; *foam* type, for oil fires; and *carbon dioxide* type, an effective smotherer, especially in sheltered spaces where the gas is undisturbed by air currents. Also, *see* **F.-smothering system. F.-fishing,** catching of fish with aid of a torch to attract them, as commonly practised in tropical countries. **F. line,** pipe-line through which water is forced by pump primarily for *f.-fighting* purposes, but ordinarily used in washing down decks, etc. At various appropriate locations on the line, hydrants or *f.-plugs* are fitted to receive *f.-hose* of, usually, 2½-inches diameter. Generally, *f. lines* are required to extend full length of weather decks and those of passenger accommodation spaces. **F. point,** temperature to which a combustible liquid must be raised before its surface layers will take fire. **F. quarters,** stations assigned to each crew member and duties required of him, as prescribed by the posted *f. station-bill,* or a *Boat and Fire Station bill.*

F.-raft, as formerly used to harass an enemy vessel or vessels, a float or raft laden with blazing combustibles and allowed to drift with a current setting toward its objective. **F.-roll,** in U.S. Navy, ringing of ship's bell summoning men to *f. quarters.* The term is handed down from former use of the drum on which a certain rhythmic *roll* was sounded for this and other drills or general calls. **F.-room,** the boiler-room or stokehold. **F. slice,** a slice-bar, or long-handled, flat-pointed iron tool for stirring up a furnace *f.,* as in clearing it of clinkers. **F.-ship,** in former days, an old vessel or hulk containing combustibles floated while on fire toward enemy craft, bridges, wharves, etc.; *see* **F.-raft. F.-smothering system,** means installed in a ship for extinguishing inaccessible fires or those against which an ordinary supply of water is ineffectual, as, respectively, in the case of a cargo hold *f.* and a serious oil *f.* Chief of these is *steam smothering,* in which live steam is directed into cargo compartments, store-rooms, engine-room, and other lower hull spaces; *carbon dioxide* (CO_2) system, in which a battery of the gas is discharged into a lower compartment; and *foam* system, which discharges or sprays a foamy liquid in spaces such as boiler-rooms where oil fuel is in use. In all cases, flow of smothering agent is controlled from vessel's deck. **F.-swab,** in old navy days, a swab or mop of cotton or rope-yarns dipped in water and run through a cannon's bore to quickly extinguish any particles of *f.* before reloading. **F.-tube boiler,** as in the popular Scotch boiler, one in which its tubes convey the combustion gases to uptakes and provide heating surface for surrounding water; opposed to *water-tube* boiler, in which water is heated in and circulated through tubes; *see* BOILER. **F.-warp,** a line, preferably a wire, led from ship to end of pier, a buoy, dolphin, etc., as a means whereby the vessel may be hove or pulled clear in event of serious *f.* on pier. **Under f.,** exposed to artillery *f.*

FIREMAN. A member of the engine department of a vessel's crew who regulates boiler fires at proper combustion stage for maintaining a required pressure of steam, keeps oil-burning sprays or tips in clean condition or systematically cleans a coal fire, and generally cares for boilers in the steam-making process. Also, especially in Great Britain, *stoker.*

FIRING. Act or method of supplying fuel to a boiler-furnace and attending to its proper burning; *cf.* FIREMAN. The discharge of firearms. **Boiler f.,** *see* BOILER. **F.-door liner,** *see* LINER. **F. line,** formation of ships actually engaged with an enemy.

FIRST. Foremost in position, rank, or value. **F. dog watch,** *see* WATCH. **F. lieutenant,** *see* LIEUTENANT. **F. magnitude,** in expressing degree of brightness of a celestial body, or *stellar* magnitude, descriptive of brightest stars or planets having a magnitude of 1.0 or less; *see* MAGNITUDE. **F. meridian,** the prime meridian; *see* MERIDIAN. **F. number,** a value used in ship classification; *see* NUMBER. **F. officer,** *see* OFFICER. **F. point of Aries,** *see* ARIES. **F. rate,** old term descriptive of importance of a warship in point of armament and size; such vessel itself. **F. watch,** period from 8.00 p.m. to 12.00 p.m. *Cf.* WATCH.

FIRTH. A long arm of the sea; especially one opening out from a river; also *frith.*

FISH. To strengthen or stiffen a sprung or weakened mast, yard, or other spar by lashing, or otherwise fastening, lengthwise to it another spar, iron bar, plate, etc.; also, such piece of timber or iron thus employed. To hoist and secure an old-fashioned anchor to the bow so that its shank lies about parallel to the rail and upper fluke inboard, as when secured on the *billboard.* To catch, or attempt to capture by any means, any exclusively aquatic animal. In whaling cant, a cetacean is a *fish.* **Bank-f.,** the cod, named from Newfoundland Banks. **Fast f.,** a whaling term; *see* FAST. **F.-back,** a line attached to a *f.-block* hook to facilitate hooking on, as when *fishing* an old-fashioned anchor. **F.-block,** heavy double or treble block to which the *f.-hook* is connected in a *f.-tackle.* **F.-boom,** in former use, a spar rigged as a derrick from the foremast for *fishing* an anchor. To **f. broad,** to *f.* at sea beyond the three-mile limit, or outside the "marine belt" or territorial waters of a state. **F.-carrier,** small vessel engaged as a tender to a fishing-fleet, chiefly in conveying the catch to marketing port; also called *carry-away boat.* **F.-davit,** *see* DAVIT. **F.-fall,** rope rove as a *f.-tackle.* **F.-garth,** a dam or weir in a river or on a sea-shore for holding or catching *f.* **F.-hook,** large iron hook at lower end of *f.-tackle* or pendant for hooking on to an anchor's fluke in *fishing* an old-fashioned anchor. **F.-net,** *see* NET. **F. oil,** that obtained from the bodies of fishes and marine animals, as menhaden, herring, sharks, whales, seals, porpoises; from cods' livers, etc. **F.-pendant,** as sometimes used in a *f.-tackle,* a piece of chain or wire rope extending between the lower block and the *f.-hook.* **F.-plate,** a butt-strap or piece of plate connecting, and fastened to either or both sides of, two butting stringers, rails, keelsons, etc.; also a corruption of *face-plate,* particularly such member to which are secured the ends of beams supporting an open superstructural deck. **F.-tackle,** the purchase and appended gear used in *fishing* an old-fashioned anchor. **F.-tail propeller,** a kind of oscillating blade similar in shape to a fish's tail, used as a hand-paddle over the stern or operated by machinery in driving small craft. **F.-weir,** any garth, pound, trap, dam, etc., arranged to catch *f.* by barring their escape with the falling tide; specifically, a net stretched across a series of driven stakes or posts in which *f.* are caught during higher stages of tide and taken when left clear of water at low tide. **F.-well,**

a compartment in a fishing-vessel in which *f.* are kept alive until brought to port; also, *wet-well.* **Line-f.,** *f.* caught by line, as distinguished from those caught by net, or *net-fish;* to *f.* with a line. **Quarter-f.,** *see* QUARTER. **Ripe f.,** those nearing the spawning stage.

FISH AND WILD LIFE SERVICE. *See* **Bureau of Fisheries** *in* BUREAU.

FISHERMAN. A vessel employed in the business of catching fish. A person engaged in fishing; a fisher. **F.'s anchor,** *see* ANCHOR. **F.'s bend,** as usually employed in making fast a rope to a kedge, spar, buoy, etc., made by taking a round turn about the spar, etc., turning rope's end around and under both standing part and round turn; then completing with a half hitch on standing part. **F.'s grease,** water used as a lubricant. **F.'s log,** *see* LOG. **F.'s luck,** hardship without profit; result of some ineffectual effort. **F.'s staysail,** as chiefly spread on U.S. "Down East" schooners, a kind of leg-of-mutton sail set between masts. A fine weather sail, it is set from the deck with head extending from foremast cap to main topmasthead; its nearly vertical luff from foremast cap to a little below the fore gaff; its foot sloping thence downward to the clew, from which its sheet leads to deck in vicinity of mainmast. A tack leads from its fore lower corner (*tack*), also to the deck. **F.'s weight,** that roughly estimated or guessed at; as, "five quintals by the skipper's eye." To take a **f.'s reef,** to weather a squall by giving a sail plenty length of sheet, as with wind nearly abeam or close-hauled. **Sailor-f.,** *see* SAILOR. **Shack-f.,** a fishing-vessel depending largely on *shack-bait,* or that which may be picked up at sea; one of a fishing-vessel's crew who fishes with several lines from vessel's side, cleans his own catch, and gets credit in *sharing* accordingly.

FISHERY. A fishing-ground or place where fish or other aquatic animals may be taken regularly; activities embraced in a particular field of the fishing industry, as, *cod f., seal f., whale f.;* act or business of catching fish; the right to capture or catch fish within a certain area or in particular waters; fishing-season, as, *during the herring f.* **Bank f.,** industry of fishing on Newfoundland Banks, or other so-called *banks,* which are comparatively shallow sea-bottom areas. **Bay f.,** that carried on in a particular bay; as, on Canadian east coast, *mackerel f.* of Gulf of St. Lawrence. **Coast f.,** the industry conducted within territorial waters or, generally, within three miles of a coast. **Common f.,** common right to fish in public waters, or, generally, those tidal waters extending to three miles off a shore. **Free f.,** an exclusive privilege, granted by royal or public license or letters patent to fish in public waters, independent of tidal limit or shore ownership. **Off-shore f.,** that conducted outside of territorial waters on a sea-coast. **Pelagic f.,** deep-sea fishing, or, generally, that carried on outside the "three-mile limit" of a coast. **Several f.,** exclusive right of a person to fish in an area because of his ownership of the underlying soil. **Strand f.,** that carried on from a coast in open boats only. **Whale f.,** occupation of taking whales; a region in which cetaceans are hunted.

FISHING. The pursuit of capturing or catching fish or any purely aquatic animal. Verbal noun used in many compound words pertaining to *fishing;* as in *f.-crib, f.-smack, reef-f.,* etc. Act of hoisting an old-fashioned anchor from the hawse-pipe to its stowing position on the rail or bill-board; more correctly, especially with a heavy anchor, hoisting the anchor's flukes aboard, after it has been *catted, i.e.,* hove up to the cathead and secured by its ring. **Bank-f.,** act or business of taking fish from Newfoundland Banks or a similar area. **Fire f.,** *see* FIRE. **F.-banks,** undersea plateau at a comparatively shallow depth, much frequented by deeper water ground fish such as cod and halibut. (Such a shelf or shallow usually takes plural form, *banks*) **F.-boat,** any boat or vessel employed in the capture and/or treatment of sea fish and transport of such fish to shore; a boat engaged in *f.* in any waters. **F.-crib,** a partly submerged crate-like enclosure in which captured fish are kept alive for marketing; a small engine used to haul the net in *seine-f.* **F.-smack,** any fore-and-aft rigged vessel engaged in the business of *f.,* but chiefly the small decked schooner of America and the two-masted lugger of Britain. **Great line f.,** as so termed in Great Britain, method of *f.* in which a heavy line extending some miles in length and fitted with snoods and large hooks at about 15-feet intervals is laid out on the sea floor. On such lines the number of hooks varies from one to five thousand and snoods are kept off bottom by attached pieces of cork acting as floats. Included in the catch by this method are cod, dog-fish, halibut, and skate. Also, a term for *hand-line f.* in depths of 50 fathoms or more; *large-line f.* **Ice-f.,** that carried on with lines or nets through holes or other openings in ice. **In-shore f.,** act or occupation of catching fish within a few miles of a coast, or within territorial waters, as distinguished from *off-shore f.* **Reef-f.,** that carried on from a reef, near which deep water is found, as from Florida coast reefs. **Rip-f.,** as pursued in tide-rips or ripplings of surface water over shoals, catching of fish such as pollack (*pollock*). **Small line f.,** similar to *great line f.,* excepting that snoods are shorter and spaced at shorter intervals and smaller hooks are used. Length of line or "trawl" may be ¼ to 2 miles in length; also termed a *spiller. See* **Great line f.** Both *great* and *small* lines of this character are often called *trot-lines.*

FIT. To join, append, shape aright, adjust, or install some appurtenance or unit in a structure; as, to *fit a rudder;* to *fit a plank;* to *fit with topmasts.* Quality or state of being satisfactorily adapted to a purpose or use; appropriateness; as, *boats are in f. condition; ship is f. for sea; sail is a perfect f.* **Drive f.** or **driving f.,** said of a rivet, bolt, or other connecting part when it is a trifle larger than the hole made to receive it. A bolt or treenail securing a ship's timbers, planking, etc., customarily is a *driving f.* To **f. out,** to furnish or supply with necessaries or equipment; as, to *f. out a yacht.* **F.-rod,** piece of small rod-iron, bent at one end in a right angle, for insertion into holes bored in a wooden ship's sides as a gauge for required length of bolts or treenails.

FITMENT. Archaic term for fittings or accessories; as, *a rudder and its fitment.*

FITTER. One who adjusts or secures in place the various parts in machinery. **F. up,** one who prepares and sets up structural parts in shipbuilding; *see* SHIPFITTER.

FITTING. Act of adjusting or securing in place a part or unit in machinery equipment, rigging, planking, etc. An article appended, erected, or supplied to a permanent installation; more commonly used in the plural, in a collective sense; as, *steam f's; boiler f's; cabin f's.* **F. out,** act of completely equipping a naval vessel with crew, stores, guns, ammunition, rigging, and all necessary furniture for an intended cruise or voyage. As applied to a new vessel, act of completing installation of machinery, piping, masts and rigging, cabin furniture, superstructural work, etc.; caulking decks, painting, etc.; subsequent to launching. **F.-out basin,** or **berth,** area or dock in which a newly launched vessel is *fitted out; cf.* **F. out. Grain-f's,** *see* GRAIN. **Tarred f's,** former collective term for tarred hemp cordage, including anchor cables and standing rigging, with which the old sailing-ships were supplied or equipped.

FIVE-BOATER. In older whaling parlance, descriptive of a large vessel in the industry, or one carrying *five boats.*

FIVE-MASTED. Having five masts, as a five-masted schooner. **F.-m. barque,** or **bark,** a sailing-vessel square-rigged on four masts, fore-and-aft rigged on after mast. First of such rig appears in the *"R. C. Rickmers,"* launched by the Germans in 1906 and equipped with auxiliary steam power. Her gross tonnage was 5548 and with a few others, including the *"Preussen"* and *"France,"* were built by German and French interests for the flourishing nitrate trade of west coast of South America in the early 1900's. **F.-m. schooner,** a fore-and-aft rigged, wood-built vessel of American origin employed for a major part of past half-century in the coal trade between U.S. Atlantic ports and lumber trade on Pacific coast. **F.-m. schooner-bark,** an auxiliary-powered trading vessel of German build which appeared about 1920 and is now extinct. Few in number, the vessels were square-rigged on first and third masts and fore-and-aft rigged on 4th. and 5th. Both *foresail* and *mizzen* (lowest square sails) were taken in by brailing to the mast. Of about 6000 gross tonnage, this "jackass" type was considered a most unhandy craft; also called *f.-m. topsail schooner* and *jackass barque.* English-speaking seamen usually named the five-masted vessel's "sticks" as *fore, main, mizzen, jigger,* and *spanker,* although on American schooners in later years *jiggermast* was becoming a discard in favor of *mizzenmast,* with *middlemast* taking the mizzen's former place as third in line. *See also* BARK *and* SCHOONER.

FIX. Charted position of a vessel as determined by observations of celestial or terrestrial objects; establishment of ship's position beyond a reasonable doubt by any of several methods, such as, by a sounding or soundings combined with a bearing of a charted object, by radio cross-bearings, by radar bearing and distance from a charted object, radio bearing and sound travel of a lightship's fog siren, etc. In chartering usage, to secure services of a vessel for carriage of a certain cargo, usually at a specified time; to hire a vessel.

FIXED. Quality of being established, immovable, or unalterable. **F. ammunition,** *see* AMMUNITION. **F. block,** in a tackle purchase, a block which remains stationary during use of purchase. **F. and flashing light; f. and group-flashing light; f. light;** *see* LIGHT. **F. moorings,** *see* MOORING. **F. net,** as distinguished from the usual sea fishing-net, which drifts or is dragged in the water, a stationary or anchored net for catching fish in rivers or sheltered waters. **F. stars,** the millions of celestial bodies which appear as mere points of light, so called from their apparently unvarying positions relative to each other, the small changes or variations in their apparent places, as given in nautical almanacs, being almost entirely due to the earth's motion in precession and nutation. Nearest fixed star is said to be *α Centauri,* some 26 trillions of miles from Earth. *See* STAR.

FLAG. Cloth of light bunting, usually thin woolen stuff, bearing a device to indicate nationality, naval rank, ownership, a reference mark, signal, etc., exhibited from a pole, staff, mast, etc.; an ensign; a standard. The national *f.* or ensign, in most navies, is flown at a flagstaff at ship's stern when moored in port and from an after mast, gaff, or other superior position aloft when under way. In general, merchant ships and yachts follow this practice. A naval officer in command of a fleet or squadron flies a *f.* indicating his rank and such formerly was shown at the fore, main, or mizzen masthead, depending upon whether officer was a vice-admiral, admiral, or rear-admiral. In U.S. Navy, admirals' *f's* have a blue ground with two, three, or four white stars in center, according to rank. The President, as commander-in-chief, on a warship which he boards flies one consisting of an oblong blue ground bearing the official arms of the United States and a white star in each corner. Edge of a *f.* next to the pole or mast is termed the *hoist;* its free end, the *fly;* and a short piece of line attached to lower end of hoist, or an extension thereto, as always provided on signal *f's,* the *tack* or *tack-line.* Flags of rectangular shape are called *square f's;* those of triangular or tapering quadrilateral shape, *pennants;* and those having pointed corners at the fly (swallow-tailed), *burgees.* **Absent f.,** square *f.* flown at a yacht's starboard yard-arm when moored in port to indicate that owner is not aboard. U.S. yachts use one of blue. **Alphabet f's,** those representing letters of the alphabet, as in signalling by *International Code; see* CODE *and* SIGNAL. **Black f.,** formerly code flag *L* (yellow and black squares) which indicated cholera amongst passengers or crew; the *f.* of piracy, often bearing a white skull and cross-bones, prominent in fiction. To **dip a f.,** to lower a national or house *f.* to about half mast and re-hoist it as a salute; *see* DIP. **F. at half mast,** flown at half height of pole or mast as a mourning signal. **F.-captain,** in British navy usage, captain of a flag-ship; may or may not be commanding officer of a squadron, depending usually upon its size or importance in armament; also, *fleet-captain.* **F. clause,** a provision in a bill of lading stating that responsibility and liability of carrier shall be determined by laws of country specified. **F.-drogue or drug,** in whaling, a weighted *drag* attached to a harpoon-line and marked by a flag, serving the double purpose of impeding progress of a wounded whale and "waifing," or temporarily buoying, the body when killed. **F.-lieutenant,** an officer acting as an aide to a *f.-officer* or admiral of a fleet. **F.-officer,** one privileged to display his flag denoting his rank, as an admiral, vice-admiral, or rear-admiral commanding a fleet or squadron. Formerly, in U.S. Navy, an officer next in rank above a captain, commanding a squadron. **F. rank,** that of an officer who may display his flag; rank of a *f.-officer.* **F. salute,** act of courtesy between vessels meeting or passing, or between ship and shore, in which the national *f. (ensign)* is slowly lowered to about two-thirds its above-deck flying height, held in that position until salute is answered, then slowly re-hoisted to normal position. If *f.* is being flown *at half mast,* it is first hoisted *full up* before procedure indicated; upon completion of salute, after a significant pause colors are slowly re-set at half mast. **F. share,** an old navy term for portion of the prize-money due a *f.-officer.* **F.-signal,** one or more *f's* displayed as a signal; a group of *f's* constituting a *hoist* and read downward, as used in the *International Code.* **F'ship,** in a fleet or a squadron of naval vessels, the ship bearing the *f.-officer* or commanding officer of such group; also, vessel bearing the commodore of a convoy of merchant ships. **F'staff,** pole on which a *f.* is displayed; usually that at a vessel's stern on which an ensign is hoisted; a staff at the bow is called a *jackstaff.* To **fly a f.,** to display a *f.;* specifically, to fly a particular nation's colors, as, *she flies the Spanish f.* **Guest f.,** in yachting usage, a blue rectangular *f.* having a diagonal white stripe, flown to show that boat is being used by guests of her owner. It is displayed at starboard yard-arm during daylight and whether under way or at anchor. **Hand f's,** the pair used in signaling by semaphore method. Each usually is a small-sized letter *O* of the *International Code* (square *f.* showing a red and a yellow triangle of equal area) mounted on a short staff; *see* SEMAPHORE. **House f.,** usually flown at the main-truck in merchantmen, showing the emblem or distinguishing mark of her owners or, sometimes, that of her charterers. **Law of the f.,** law of a country to which a ship belongs, or whose *f.* she flies. **Meal f.,** flown from starboard yard-arm or spreader in U.S. yachts, a white rectangular *f.* indicating that vessel's owner is engaged at table. **Pilot f.,** *International Code f. G,* signifying "*I require a pilot*" or the *pilot jack* hoisted at the fore. **Powder f.,** the *explosive f.; see* **Red f. Quarantine f.,** the *International Code f. Q,* displayed by a vessel entering port from a foreign country, indicating "*My vessel is healthy and I request free pratique*"; the *yellow f.; see* QUARANTINE. **Red f.,** *International Code f. B* (red burgee) displayed when taking in or discharging explosives and, as required by some harbor authorities, also at any time explosives are on board during ship's stay in port; the *powder f.* The bloody spout of a dying whale; a piece of red flannel used as a lure on a fish-hook. **Roller f.,** *see* ROLLER. **Signal f.,** *see* SIGNAL. **Storm f.,** *see* STORM. **Weather f.,** *see* WEATHER. **Yellow f.,** *see* **Quarantine f.**

FLAKE. A narrow stage hung over a ship's side for purposes of painting, scaling, caulking, repairs, etc. A *fake,* or one of loops of a rope or chain laid down for clear running. To coil or arrange a rope in long single loops so that it will run free of kinks or snarls.

FLAM. (*Scot.*) An unexpected puff of wind in light weather. Inward turn of a vessel's bows from the deck; *see* FLARE.

FLAME-CUTTING. *See* OXYACETYLENE PROCESS.

FLAME SAFETY LAMP. For testing the oxygen content of atmosphere in tanks or closed-in compartments preparatory to sending persons into such spaces for cleaning purposes, repairs, etc., a lamp designed to burn therein as long as supply of oxygen remains greater than 16%, 21% being content of normal air. Such lamp indicates an explosive atmosphere as well as a deficiency in oxygen, and most maritime countries now require at least two of them as equipment for passenger vessels.

FLANGE. Turned-over edge, bulb, rim, etc., as, *flange of a beam,* plate, bracket, or other structural part; a guide, as, *flange of a roller or wheel;* projecting ring-shaped end of a pipe. **Blank f.,** a *pipe-f.* which is not bored with holes for connecting bolts; a blanking-off disk fitted between *f's* of two connected pipes. **F. joint,** connection made in uniting two *f's,* as at the ends of piping. **Flanged plate,** one that is bent at its edge or edges, as a bracket-knee or a floor-plate, for stiffening or strengthening purposes. **Port-f.,** an eye-brow or wriggle; *see* **Eye-brow** *in* EYE. **Propeller-blade f.,** *see* PROPELLER. **Rudder f.,** *see* RUDDER. **Shell-f.,** bulbous or turned-over edge of shell of a steel block for preventing damage to a rope by cutting or chafing.

FLANGING. Process of cold bending of plate shaped for various units in a vessel under construction; as in shaping flanges by special machine on bracket-plates, bulkhead stiffeners, margin-plates, floors, deck-stringers, etc., for stiffening.

FLAP. A short partial deck or covering over a boat, as for protection for an engine, goods, etc.; a cuddy.

FLARE. Outward spreading or upward curving inclination from the perpendicular of a vessel's bows and side area approaching thereto; opposed to *tumble home.* The final and sharper outward turn near the deck usually is termed *flam.* In older usage, *f.* is referred to as a *flanching* or *flanging,* as in, *her bows have a sharp flanch (flange).* A night signal of short duration given by torch or bright white light, as exhibited at intervals by a pilot boat, or by a vessel requiring a pilot, and by fishing-vessels when engaged in fishing, as a warning to approaching craft. Also called a *flare-up,* often is simply a lighted kerosene-soaked wad of tow or cotton fixed to a metal rod, kept ready at hand in a special receptacle. *F's* in the form of patented *pyrotechnic lights* may be obtained for *pilot signals,* as the *blue light* prescribed for such; for *distress signals,* as the red *f's* required in life-boats; and, though not used as much as formerly, as *recognition lights* for private use, in which the *f.* burns in two or more successive colors, often throwing differently colored stars.

FLASH. Sudden momentary burst of flame or transitory appearance of light; as, *a flash of lightning; a 5-second flash,* or one shown from a lighthouse every 5 seconds. **F.-light,** a lamp capable of showing *f's,* as in signalling; a hand torch that may be flashed or kept lighted at will. **Flashing light,** as exhibited by a lighthouse, lightship, or buoy, shows one or more *f's* at certain intervals; *see* LIGHT.[1] **F. point,** as an index of the safety of an inflammable liquid, is that degree of temperature to which such liquid must be heated to give off vapor in sufficient quantity, when mixed with air, to be ignited by a flame. **F. welding,** *see* WELDING.

FLAT. Having an even surface; without bevel; said of a timber. Having an approximately even horizontal surface, or without camber; as, *a flat tank-top.* A curveless timber in an otherwise curving section; as a *frame,* in shipbuilding. A partial deck in a hold, laid without camber, or nearly so. A scow or barge of broad beam and shallow draft; a flatboat; a railroad-car float, such as is used to transport rolling-stock in sheltered waters. A generally level tract at small depth below a water surface, often dry at low tide; a shoal; also, *flats.* **Dead f.,** *see* DEAD. **Deck-f.,** a partial deck, not necessarily water-tight, or a platform laid over a limited number of beams in a hold. **Ferry-f.,** *see* FERRY. **F. aback,** *see* ABACK. **F. aft,** said of fore-and-aft sails' sheets when hauled in as much as possible, as in sailing close to the wind. **F'fish,** any of a large group of fishes characterized by a compressed body adapted to resting flat on the sea bottom. Of the group many are first order food fishes and include the brill, halibut, flounder, turbot, sole, and plaice. **F. hat** or **f. cap,** *see* CAP. To **haul sheets f. aft,** *see* **F. aft.** To **f. in** or to **flatten in** a sail, to haul in the clew of a fore-and-aft sail as much toward the center line as possible, particularly that of a jib, staysail, or other canvas having no boom. **F'man,** a British term for a man engaged in managing or maneuvering a *f.* or barge; a lighterman. **F. of bottom,** area of a vessel's bottom having no curvature between keel and bilge. **F.-plate keel** or **F. keel,** *see* PLATE. **F.-plate keelson** or **f. keelson plate,** *see* PLATE. **F. scarf,** a scarfed joint formed by cutting from the wider faces of timbers, etc., thus united. **F. seam,** in sail-making, term for ordinary method of joining cloths. Edge of each cloth is sewn to its neighbor along a line 1 to 1½ inches from edge of the latter, thus making two rows of stitching separated by that distance; also called a *lapping seam.* **F. seizing,** in permanently securing two ropes, or parts of same rope, side by side together, a lashing made by taking several turns round both ropes and finishing off with two or three cross turns over the seizing or lashing and between the ropes. Made like a *round seizing,* excepting the riding turns. **F. sennit,** also called *common sennit,* a plaited rope made with any number of rope-yarns or small stuff greater than two; 5-yarn *f. sennit* is often termed *English sennit.* **F.-top,** an aircraft carrier. **Steering-gear f.,** *see* STEERING.

FLATNER. Local term for a boat of similar build and dimensions to those of the American *dory,* once commonly used on the Somerset coast of the Bristol Channel. Used chiefly in fishing, it may be either rowed or sailed; usually fitted with a centerboard and rigged with a sprit-sail and jib.

FLATTER. A flat swage or set-hammer used to hold against a rivet or uneven metal surface while hammering home or *setting* from opposite side of the work. A stevedores' term for a tier of cases or bales stowed on their *flats* or sides of greater surface.

FLAW. Sudden violent gust of wind, often met with during a land breeze when sailing near a mountainous coast; a squall of short duration, with or without precipitation. Break in continuity or cohesion, as in a faulty part of a metal plate; defective metal is said to be *flawy,* when thus reduced in quality.

FLAX. (Ger. *flachs;* Gr. *flekein,* to weave) Plant of the genus *Linum* for centuries cultivated for its long silky bast fiber used in manufacturing linen, canvas, finer cordage used on board ship, fishing-lines, etc. Of all fibers employed in marine requirements, flax undoubtedly is unequaled for strength and durability. As compared with that of cotton or hemp texture, *flax canvas* takes a superior place in wearing qualities and resistance to sea-air or water. The desirable features of this fiber, however, are offset in great measure by its prohibitive cost. **Flax-seed** formerly was used in treating boiler feed-water, its mucilaginous properties having been found effective in collecting and absorbing impurities and foreign deposits in the "softening" process.

FLEET. To change, move, or shift the position of; as, to *fleet* (draw blocks apart) *a purchase;* to *fleet* (lay along a deck) *a hawser;* to *fleet the capstan* (cause turns of a rope to slide down its barrel). To pull in a fresh length or part; as, to *f. in a hawser;* to *take a new f.,* as in hauling up a fresh stretch of canvas when furling a large sail. To skim fresh water from the sea surface, as at a river's mouth. A long fake or flake of a rope stowed clear for running. A group of vessels under a single command, engaged in a common business, or any group in an anchorage; as, a *naval f.;* a *fishing f.;* an *anchored f.* Line of nets (especially in Great Britain) as extending from a *drifter* in herring and mackerel fishing, often extending 3 to 4 miles. **F.-captain,** a flag-captain; *see* CAPTAIN *and* FLAG. **F.-captain; f.-engineer; f.-marine officer; f.-paymaster; f.-surgeon;** senior officers of their respective corps contained in a naval *f.,* who are included in the staff of a commander-in-chief. To **f. a messenger,** to take a new hold on a hawser with a messenger (handy hauling or heaving rope) after hawser has been hauled in as far as possible or convenient by this means. To **f. a stay or shroud,** to shorten it by turning in its end anew, before setting up. **F.-train,** *see* S.-train *in* SEA. **Mosquito f.,** a company or group of small craft; a flotilla. **Round the f.,** *see* ROUND. **Plate f.,** formerly, vessels engaged in carrying precious metal, usually sailing in convoy; especially, as termed by British seamen, the vessels which transported to Spain the product of South American mines in 16th and 17th century days.

FLEETER. One of the vessels constituting a North Sea fishing-fleet of steam trawlers. A fleet usually consists of 50 to 60 vessels, operates under direction of the "admiral," and each *fleeter* regularly delivers her catch to a fast *carrier* during a stay on the fishing grounds of from 6 to 8 weeks.

FLEMISH. Pertaining to Flanders; as used by the Flemings or natives of Flanders. The term appears in English 16th century maritime usage, indicating influence of Flemish custom in good Queen Bess's navy. To *Flemish down;* to lay, as in a *F. coil.* **F. coil,** a rope spirally coiled about its end and all turns lying snug and flat on deck; used as a ship-shape style of snugging down a boat's painter, ends of sheets, or shorter idle ends of various ropes; also, *F. fake; F. mat.* **F. eye,** *see* EYE. **F. horse,** a short foot-rope on a topsail or lower yard-arm, principally for convenience of the man who passes the earing in reefing.

FLENSE. To cut away and remove blubber or skin from the carcase of a whale or other cetacean. Formerly, the operation of *flensing* a whale was performed while carcase lay fast alongside of ship; modern whaling-ships haul carcase on board and *f.* it or otherwise dispose of the whole from the deck. Also, *flench; flinch.* **F.-gut,** in old whaling usage, a strip of blubber cut from the carcase; also, place on board where blubber (*speck*) was stowed before "trying out," or extracting the oil; also, *flench-gut.*

FLETTNER'S SAILLESS SHIP. *See* ROTORSHIP.

FLEXIBLE WIRE ROPE. *See* WIRE.

FLIGHT. A sudden sharp rise in the lines of a hull or principal structural parts; as, *f. of the counter; f. of a rail.* Motion in trajection of a projectile; as, *f. of a shell.* Old term for a fast boat or vessel; *see* FLYBOAT. **Time of f.,** interval between instant a fired projectile leaves a gun's muzzle and that of first impact; trajectory time.

FLINCH. To *snape,* or bevel an end of a timber in order to fit it against an inclined or sloping surface. Also, *see* FLENSE.

FLINDERS BAR. Called after *Matthew Flinders, English navigator (1774-1814),* bar of soft iron placed vertically near a compass for counteracting deviation caused by induced magnetism in surrounding vertical iron; *see* BAR.

FLIPPER. Flat limb adapted for swimming, as those of a seal, walrus, whale, turtle, penguin, etc.; also, *flapper.* **Square f.,** the bearded seal of Arctic waters.

FLITCH. One of several pieces of timber, planking, and/or plates fastened together side by side to form a beam, girder, etc.; a piece of plate secured to a weak part in a girder or beam for strengthening; half of a balk of timber sawn lengthwise. A square piece of whale-blubber. A better piece of the halibut. **F.-timber,** a ship's frame or futtock made up of *flitches* having a natural curvature or bend, set for added strength and stiffness at turn of the bilge.

FLOAT. (M.E. *flote,* boat, ship, fleet; A.S. *flota,* ship; *fleotan,* to float) Cork or light object for buoying a net or fishing-hook; anything used to keep an object or person from sinking; a life-preserver; a life-raft; a buoy. A raft or scow; platform suitably moored for a boat landing. To swim or rest on surface of a liquid; to be buoyed up. To drift with a current; to be held suspended in a body of liquid. To cause to *f.;* as, *a rising tide floated the ship.* To transport on a *f.;* as, *an anchor was floated to shore.* **Car-f.,** *see* CAR. **Feathering-f.,** *see* FEATHERING. **F.-stage,** a raft on which a stage may be set up for repairing, painting, scaling, etc., on ship's side. **F.-line,** rope along upper edge of a fishing-net to which *f's* are attached.

FLOATING. Afloat; free to move about; unattached to moorings; as, *floating wreckage.* State of being buoyed on a liquid's surface; as, a *f. dock.* **F. anchor,** a sea-anchor, drogue, drag, or driving-anchor; *see* DRAG. **F. beacon,** a buoy, as a weighted barrel surmounted by a staff, from which is displayed a flag or other prominent marker, used in hydrographic survey work; a water-marker. **F. breakwater,** an arrangement of heavy timbers, or series of heavy frames of timber, laid out and anchored to protect moored vessels from a heavy sea or swell; *see* **Floating h.** *in* HARBOR. **F. bridge,** *see* BRIDGE. **F. clause,** as stipulated in a charter party, states that vessel will proceed to the port or ports specified, "or as near thereto as she can safely get, being at all times afloat"; also called *berthing clause.* **F. derrick,** *see* DERRICK; a floating crane. **F. dry-dock,** *see* DOCK. **F. harbor,** *see* HARBOR. **F. island,** *see* ISLAND. **F. pier,** *see* PIER. **F. policy,** an open policy, or one in which no special vessel is named. Insurance coverage is therein stated in general terms, particulars being attached by endorsement as "declarations," appropriate to voyage or voyages and ship concerned. **F. power,** sum of utilized buoyancy and reserve buoyancy of a vessel. *Utilized buoyancy* is that upward force or pressure of water which counteracts the weight of a floating vessel and her contents, and is equal to weight of water displaced at a given draft. *Reserve buoyancy* may be considered as measured by that additional weight which a vessel can carry after being loaded to maximum draft as indicated by her load-line marks; or, as sometimes defined, it is the total hold space above load-line water-plane which can be made water-tight; usually expressed as percentage of total water-tight volume of ship's hull.

FLOE. (Ice. *flo,* layer or stratum) Sheet or limited field of floating ice at sea or extending seaward from a coast. Consists of a gathering of broken pieces which freeze together or crack up according to sea conditions. Also called *ice-floe; sea-floe.* **F.-berg,** large mass of *f.-ice* forced together, as by pressure against the shore or bord-ice, and presenting appearance of a small berg. **F.-ice,** that of a *f.* as distinguished from shore-fast or *bord-ice;* it is simply the latter set adrift by strong winds or currents. *See* ICE.

FLOG. To lash or beat with a rod, rope's end, whip, cat-o'-nine-tails, etc., as in administering corporal punishment in former navy days. *Flogging* has been abolished in most navies, that of U.S.A. included; however, with a few exceptions, regulations still empower a commanding officer to thus chastise a seaman in certain specified cases of serious offense. By *Act of Congress, Dec. 21, 1898,* flogging and all other forms of corporal punishment are prohibited on any merchant vessel.

FLOOD. Flowing in, or rise of, the tide; opposed to *ebb.* To cause to be filled with water; as, to *flood a hold.* To inundate; as *a deck flooded by a heavy sea; the engine-room was flooded.* The *F.,* or *Deluge,* (circa *2350 B.C.*) may be noted as the occasion of first authoritative historical mention of persons protected from the elements in a floating structure. It appears, therefrom, that the progenitors of all races made the earliest known voyage under most extraordinary circumstances yet recorded. *See* ARK. **F.-anchor,** *see* ANCHOR PHRASEOLOGY. **F.-cock,** a sea-cock, or similar means for admitting water to a magazine or shell-room of a war-vessel in event of fire. **F. current,** movement of the *f.* tidal stream, as in a river or coastal waters. Direction and rate of *f.* and ebb currents are indicated on coastal charts and, for certain regions, on special tidal maps. **F.-mark,** that indicating level of high water, as on a tidal height-gauge. **F.-pipes,** arrangement of pipes for flooding a magazine with sea-water; flow is controlled by *f.-cocks.* **Main f.,** principal *f. current* where two or more branches of tidal stream occur in same locality. **Windward f.,** a *f.* tidal current running against the wind.

FLOODING, AMMUNITION. *See* AMMUNITION *(stowage of).*

FLOODABLE LENGTH. *See* LENGTH.

FLOOR. That part of a vessel's structure constituting the horizontal, or nearly horizontal, bottom arrangement, considered in a broad sense as the foundation or base of the whole; thus, a *rising floor* or a *flat floor* describes general bottom form. The term *floors* is simply a shortened form of *f.-timbers* or *f.-plates* and denotes those thwartship structural units which connect, or form a continuance of, each pair of the frames or ribs across vessel's bottom. In steel vessels, *f's* are deepened for bottom strength and to provide *double-bottom* tank space, or that between shell and inner-bottom plating. They may be spaced comparatively closely (about 2 feet) as in the transverse framing system, or at intervals of 10 to 15 feet in longitudinal framing; in either case they form the bottom bridging between each pair of thwartship frames. *Molding* of a *f.* is its depth, as measured from bottom to top edge or surface; *siding* of a *f.-timber* is breadth of its faying surface. **Bending f.,** same as bending-slab; *see* SLAB. **Bracket f.,** also called *skeleton f.* and *open f.;* as in smaller steel vessel construction, a *f.* formed of brackets and struts fitted between the continued frame and reverse frame which, respectively, are the lower and upper edges of limiting members of such arrangement. **Cant-f.,** a crooked-grown piece of timber forming both *f.* and cant frame, as at forward end of a small vessel. **Continuous f.,** a *f.-plate* extending in one length from bilge to bilge, as distinguished from one divided by, and butting against, a vertical plate keelson; also called a *through f.* **Deep f.,** so named for its great depth, one of the *f's* at or near a vessel's extreme ends. **Dock f.,** bottom of a dry dock, on which blocks for supporting docked vessels are laid. **Filling-f's,** extra pieces of timber between floors to increase local bottom solidity, especially in larger wooden vessels; also, *filling-frames.* **Flat f.,** quality of having little or no *rise of f.* for a great part of her length; *i.e.,* with bottom flat, or nearly so, and sharply turning bilges; said of a wooden vessel. **F. ceiling,** that area of planking (2 to 3 inches in thickness) laid over *f's* or tank-tops and forming part of a hold ceiling. **F. heads,** in wood shipbuilding, outer ends of *f.-timbers* where they are scarfed to futtocks; also termed *rung-heads.* (*F.,* futtocks, and top-frame timber constitute a ship's "rib," timber, or frame; *see* FRAME.) In steel-built vessels, extreme ends of *f's* (*f.-plates*) where they are pointed or narrowed to meet the separated frame and reverse frame, which, respectively, form the lower and upper stiffening angles along edges of *f's.* **F. plan,** draft of a longitudinal section showing partitioning, etc., of ship at a water-line or on a particular deck. **F.-plate,** a vessel's iron or steel *f.; see* FLOOR *definition.* **F. ribband,** a long strip of wood or metal temporarily fastened longitudinally to ends of *f's* to hold them in position while vessel is building. **Half f.,** a *f.-timber* extending about half-distance of ordinary *f's.* It is butted to second futtock and bolted to keel; also side-bolted to first futtock and another *f.-timber* laid across keel (cross timber). **Intercostal f.,** as built in larger double-bottomed vessels, a *f.* necessarily composed of two or more sections, due to interruption by a vertical plate keelson (*center-line keel*) and two or more continuous longitudinal plate girders, to which the sections are fastened securely by riveting or welding. **Lightened f's,** those having holes cut in them to economize weight, as distinguished from *solid f's,* which form ends of double-bottom tanks. The holes are made large enough to allow a man passage through them. **Long and short f's,** in a wooden vessel, *f.-timbers* so placed that they show long and short arms alternately on same side of keel. **Main f.,** one placed at greatest breadth of ship; usually the *midship f.,* or that fitted at vessel's half length. **Partial f.,** any type of floor which extends only part way across ship's bottom. **Plank f.,** in wood-built vessels a straight-grained sawn *f.-timber,* as distinguished from one made from crooked timber. **Rise of f.,** *see* DEADRISE. **Rising f.,** same as *deep f.,* so called because of its rise above line of ordinary *f's.* **Sea f.,** bottom of the sea. **Shallow f.,** a *f.-plate* of comparatively small depth, as in vessels with no inner bottom. **Skeleton f.,** *see* Bracket f. **Solid f.,** one having no lightening holes and usually forming water-tight end of a double-bottom tank; *cf.* **Lightened f's.** **Transom f.,** aftermost *f.-plate* of the main body; of deep form and secured to stern-post, it serves as an abutment for the cant frames which extend to shape the counter or *fantail.* **Turn of f.,** same as *turn of bilge; see* BILGE. **Water-tight f.,** a *solid f.* forming an end of a double-bottom tank and always fitted below, and as a continuation of, a water-tight bulkhead.

FLOORING OFF. Stevedores' term for leveling surface of a stowed portion of cargo in preparation for stowage of another tier or tiers of the same or a different type of goods. Where a large bulk of cases, boxes, or bales is laid in tier, boards or battens are laid every few tiers in order to give compactness to the mass, thus minimizing chafing damage due to rolling of ship. *Flooring off* is also applied to act of leveling the mass stowed in a narrowing and sloping-sided hold space, as toward a vessel's ends.

FLOTA. (*Sp.*)   A fleet of merchant vessels; especially, the fleet of Spanish ships which, in 16th and 17th centuries, made annual voyages to Vera Cruz, Mexico, from Cadiz, to bring home produce of the colonies.

FLOTATION.   Flotage; act, process, or state of floating; method of causing something to float, or supplying buoyancy. **Line** or **plane of f.,** interrupted area of water surface as bounded by the water-line of a floating vessel. **Stable f.,** condition in which a floating body will resume its original poise after being temporarily disturbed by an outside force. Essentially is conditioned by position of body's center of gravity which always lies vertically below center of displaced mass of liquid.

FLOTILLA. (Dim. of Sp. *flota,* fleet)   A small fleet; a group of small vessels, especially naval craft; as, *a flotilla of mine-sweepers.*

FLOTSAM.   Cargo or wreckage of a lost vessel found floating on the sea. The term often is applied erroneously to goods remaining afloat after having been *jettisoned,* or thrown overboard, for any cause. Older spellings are *flotsan, flotsen,* and *flotson.*

FLOUNDER. (Sw. *flundra*) A typical member of the *flatfish* family, often known locally in North America as simply *flatfish*. The European *f.*, called *plaice;* the American *summer f.*, also called plaice, *southern f.*, and *winter f.* are excellent food fishes. Has an oval-shaped body 6 to 8 inches in width and 12 to 14 inches in length. Known also as *fluke.*

FLOW. Flood or rise of the tide; opposed to *ebb;* as, *the tide flows every 12 hours.* To ease or slack off a fore-and-aft sail's sheet in order to *spill* wind from the sail. With *flowing sheet,* descriptive of sailing with eased off sheets as when wind is abeam or somewhere abaft the beam.

FLOWER OF THE WINDS. As shown on old British charts, figure of the compass-card ornamented with a rose drawn on its center; our present *compass-rose.*

FLUE. Old English name for a fishing-net, whether fixed or dragged; also, *flew.* Barb of a harpoon or an anchor-fluke; a corruption of *fluke.*

FLUID COMPASS. A liquid compass; *see* COMPASS.

FLUKE. The palm, or flat part of an anchor which catches in ground. Barb on head of a harpoon. A flatfish or flounder. One of the lobes of a whale's tail. To attach a sling to the narrow part of a dead whale's tail for towing or securing the body alongside ship, as in older whaling practice. **F.-chain or f.-rope,** chain or rope used to tow or haul and secure tail end of a dead whale alongside a whaler. It was led to forward end of ship and whale was made fast alongside heading aft. **Mushroom f.,** hemispherical-shaped part of a mushroom anchor which digs into ground as a *f.* To **turn f's,** to round out and dive, throwing *f's* in the air, as a whale: hence, the old sailor's phrase, meaning to *turn in,* or go to bed.

FLUKING. Act of securing by, or cutting into (or off), the flukes, as in whaling. **A-fluking or all fluking,** sailing fast with all sail set; running free with a large spread of canvas in a fresh breeze.

FLUKY. Uncertain, unsteady, baffling; said of the wind.

FLURRY. Brief, sudden motion of air; light gust of wind or squall; short, light fall of snow or rain, with or without a breeze. Whaler's term for spasmodic contortions of a dying whale.

FLUSH. Having a flush deck; as, *a flush-built vessel.* Having surfaces in a common plane; as, *f. plating; f. planking.* To run or pump water into an empty tank, well, bilges, or a piping system, for rinsing, cleansing, clearing of deposit, etc. **F. deck,** *see* DECK. **F.-decked vessel,** in nomenclature of types in ship classification, one in which the *freeboard,* or *upper,* deck has no superstructure; *i.e.,* having no part of her sides extending above such deck.

F.-head rivet, *see* RIVET. **F. joint,** junction or butting of planking, plating, etc., presenting a flat surface; opposed to *lap joint,* or one in which joining members overlap each other. **F.-plating,** system or arrangement of plates laid against each other edge to edge, as in shell-plating. Connection between edges and butts is made by *edge-strips* and *butt-straps* which completely bridge the seams on hidden side of plating. This system is now rarely used in merchant or naval vessels.

FLUTE. (Fr. *flûte,* a transport) In old navy usage, a partially armed storeship or transport. A kind of Dutch vessel, or flyboat, having a narrow stern and round-ribbed after part. A kind of ship-rigged vessel of the 17th century. **Armed en flute,** old term applied to a partially armed vessel; *esp.,* to one reduced in armament and fitted for transport duty.

FLUX. Flow or setting in of a rising tide toward shore; rise of the tide. A substance such as borax or lime used to assist fusion in process of welding metals.

FLY. Rotator or part of a mechanical log which is trailed astern. An old term for the compass-card. Length of a flag as measured from its hoist, or edge next the staff, to its outer or free end; also, that end itself. A long conical-shaped bag, piece of bunting, streamer, etc., fixed at a masthead or in rigging for indicating direction of wind. **F.-anchor,** a sea-anchor or drogue; *see* Sea-a. *in* ANCHOR, *also* DRAG. **F.-block,** a tye-block, or one in which a halyard runner works, as in a square-rigger's topsail and top-gallant halyards; *see* BLOCK. **F.-by-night,** a jib used as a studding-sail (*stuns'l*) or a spinnaker; also, a square sail set from the deck of a sloop or small schooner, when running before a breeze. To **f. to, up in,** or **up into, the wind,** to turn quickly toward the wind, all sail shaking, as in averting a collision, or unintentionally, as in losing steering control in heavy weather, or due to accident affecting normal use of helm. To **let f.,** to let go suddenly, as sheets of a sail in an emergency maneuver.

FLYBOAT. Former Dutch flat-bottomed vessel, or *vlieboot,* chiefly employed in coasting trade, ranging in tonnage from 400 to 600 (burden); also, in older usage, any type of fast vessel or boat. To-day, a fast passenger or freight canal-boat used in England. A speedy boat or vessel serving as a tender to an anchored fleet or a number of trawlers engaged in fishing.

FLYING. Combining term connoting a light extension or addition to, as a *flying jib, flying deck;* motion through air, as, a *flying fish;* action extraneous to that implied, as, *flying moor.* **F. bridge,** *see* BRIDGE. **F. deck,** a superstructural platform or deck supported by stanchions; deck over a large accommodation housing or other deck erection. **F. Dutchman,** *see* DUTCHMAN. **F. fish,** any of several species of warm water fishes constituting the family *Exo-cœtidæ*, widely distributed in tropical and sub-tropical seas, characterized by long wing-like pectoral fins and their ability to leave the water and fly for distances of from 20 to 200 yards. Sometimes emerging in schools, they appear to take flight when pursued by larger fish. Natives of tropical coasts often attract and capture them at night by shining a light on a boat's sails; the fish fly against sails and fall into boat. It is usually 10 to 12 inches in length, has brilliant silvery scales, and is considered generally a good food catch. **F.-fish sailor,** one who purposely avoids the "roaring forties" in favor of the more agreeable climatic conditions found in tropical latitudes; a fair-weather sailor. **F. foresail,** a fly-by-night; *see* FLY. **F. gurnard,** a fish of cunard-like appearance, though of a different family (the *Cephalacanthidæ*); about equal in size to the *f. fish* and similarly capable of flight but for shorter distances; has large pectoral and unusually deep spiny dorsal and ventral fins; generally considered of little value for food; also called a *sea-robin.* **F.-jib; f.-jib-boom; f.-jib-boom guys;** *see* JIB. **F. kites,** loftiest and lightest sails formerly set in light winds, chiefly on clipper ships, and variously named according to choice. *Skysail* appears to have been an established term for the square sail set above a *royal;* loftier still was either a square or triangular one capriciously designated as *moonsail, moonraker, cloud-tickler, star-gazer, angel,* etc. Loosely, the term for all light sail, including a *f.* jib, upper staysails, royal and top-gallant studding-sails. In modern yachts, special canvas spreads like spinnakers, balloon jibs, and jib-topsails sometimes are referred to as *kites,* and act of sailing with such often as *flying kites.* **F. light,** said of a vessel in the light condition, *i.e.,* having no cargo aboard and no ballast other than that contained in double-bottom tanks. **F. moor,** *see* MOOR. **F. nightingale,** stay extending from outer end of a *f.-jib-boom* to lower end of martingale, as formerly found in clipper-ship rigs. **F. sail,** *see* SAIL. **F. staysail,** a fore-and-aft sail set between masts by hoisting from deck. Inappropriately named, it has no connection with a stay; *see* **F.'s staysail** *in* FISHERMAN. **F. squadron,** *see* SQUADRON. **F. squid,** one of several kinds of squid having two large lateral fins which assist in enabling it to leap from the water; common in the Gulf Stream. **F. sounder,** *see* SOUNDER. To **set f.,** *see* SET.

FOAM. For combating fires fed by inflammable liquids, a sudsy bubbling compound directed over fire with view of laying a blanket of the mixture as a smothering agent. To foam-making methods commonly are employed aboard ship, *viz., chemical* and *mechanical.* **Chemical f.** basically is produced by interaction of two chemicals, such as a sodium bicarbonate solution and one of aluminum sulphate, with a stabilizing agent added, so held in

readiness that it may be mixed immediately. A heavy mass of carbon dioxide bubbles results from the mixture, a blanket of which is most efficient in fighting fires of highly volatile substances. **Mechanical f.** is produced by a liquid sudsing agent introduced into a water-stream and, while incapable of laying as heavy blanket as compared with the chemical type, it is more readily brought into action and may be used wherever an ordinary hose will reach, foaming agent being introduced at any convenient part of the line; the *chemical f.* requires a stationary plant for its generation.

F.O.B. Abbreviation for *free on board,* indicating seller or shipper of merchandise places goods on board carrier without cost to buyer or consignee. Shipper's responsibility ends with delivery of shipment to carrier.

FODDER. *See* FOTHER.

FOG. (Ice. *fok,* snowdrift, spray) Disturbance of transparency of the atmosphere caused by suspension of fine particles of condensed water vapor; or, simply, a stratus cloud lying on the earth's surface. Dust haze blown off to sea from desert land and smoke from forest fires often thicken into *f.* by retention of tiny moisture droplets which form around the dust particles; indeed, it is established that no *f.* occurs without the presence of some kind of dust particles, since these form the nuclei of moisture droplets. A good example of this combined smoke and water vapor effect is seen in London's "pea-soup" or "arm's length" variety of *f.,* in which visibility being nil, traffic afloat and ashore virtually ceases. In regions where warm air moves over a cold water surface and where cold air contacts warm water, *f.* of some degree of intensity frequently is present, as seen in the remarkable duration of thick weather in summer on the American Atlantic coast from Cape Cod to the Newfoundland Banks, and on the Alaskan, British Columbia, and north-western U.S. Pacific coasts. **F.-bank,** mass of low-lying *f.* observed at sea and often resembling land; sometimes from its appearance called *No Man's Land, Dutchman's land, Cape Flyaway,* etc. **F.-bell,** as a warning, directing, or announcing signal, or aid to navigation, during thick weather, sounded at pier heads, breakwater entrances, certain lighthouses, light-vessels, and other stations. Usually sounded automatically, it commonly is arranged to "strike" a certain number of times at certain short intervals. **F.-belt,** an ocean region noted for frequency of *f.* **F.-bound,** detained by *f.,* as a vessel delayed in port or in narrow waters by very thick weather. **F.-bow,** a yellowish or rosy tinted bow often seen in low fogs. As with the rainbow, it appears opposite in azimuth to the sun. **F.-buoy,** *see* **Towing-s.** *in* SPAR. **F.-eye,** spot of sunlight showing through *f.* **F.-gun,** a *f.* signal made by detonating an explosive, as from a gun, at regular intervals. **F. signal,** any of several means used during low visibility as a navigational aid or a warning of a vessel's presence; as, blasts of a horn or whistle, ringing or sounding of a bell or gong, detonation of an explosive, striking a submarine bell, by submarine oscillator, or radio signal. Such signals given by shore stations, as lighthouses and harbor entrances, consist of distinctive sounds made at regularly recurring intervals by a powerful horn or siren operated by compressed air and sometimes assisted in intensity effect by an electrically oscillated diaphragm, as the *diaphone* and *nautophone*, by a bell, or by an explosive; and ordinary radio-beacon signals having their recurring intervals much shortened. Some light-vessels operate submarine bells or oscillators for such craft as are equipped with receiving apparatus for that type of signal. The following excerpt from the *International Regulations for Preventing Collisions at Sea* currently in force is subject, in the near future, to amendment by legislative act in accordance with a few minor revisions made by the *International Conference on Safety of Life at Sea, London, 1948:—* "*Sound signals for Fog, etc.—Preliminary:* Article 15. All signals prescribed by this article for vessels under way shall be given: 1st.—By "steam vessels" on the whistle or siren. 2nd.—By "sailing vessels" and "vessels towed" on the fog-horn. The words "prolonged blast" used in this article shall mean a blast of from 4 to 6 seconds' duration. A steam vessel shall be provided with an efficient whistle or siren, sounded by steam or by some substitute for steam, so placed that the sound may not be intercepted by any obstruction, and with an efficient fog-horn, to be sounded by mechanical means, and also with an efficient bell. In all cases where the rules require a bell to be used a drum may be substituted on board Turkish vessels, or a gong where such articles are used on board small sea-going vessels. A sailing vessel of 20 tons gross tonnage or upward shall be provided with a similar fog-horn and bell. In fog, mist, falling snow, or heavy rainstorms, whether by day or night, the signals described in this article shall be used as follows, namely: *Steam vessel under way.—(a)* A steam vessel having way upon her shall sound, at intervals of not more than 2 minutes, a prolonged blast. (*b*) A steam vessel under way, but stopped, and having no way upon her, shall sound, at intervals of not more than 2 minutes, 2 prolonged blasts, with an interval of about 1 second between. *Sailing vessel under way.—(c)* A sailing vessel under way shall sound, at intervals of not more than 1 minute, when on the starboard tack, 1 blast; when on the port tack, 2 blasts in succession; and when with the wind abaft the beam, 3 blasts in succession. *Vessels at anchor or not under way.—(d)* A vessel when at anchor shall, at intervals of not more than 1 minute, ring the bell rapidly for about 5 seconds. *Vessels towing or towed.—(e)* A vessel when towing, a ves-

sel employed in laying or in picking up a telegraph cable, and a vessel under way, which is unable to get out of the way of an approaching vessel through being not under command, or unable to maneuver as required by the Rules, shall, instead of the signals prescribed in subdivisions (*a*) and (*c*) of this article, at intervals of not more than 2 minutes, sound 3 blasts in succession, namely: 1 prolonged blast followed by 2 short blasts. A vessel towed may give this signal and she shall not give any other. *Small sailing vessels and boats.—*Sailing vessels and boats of less than 20 tons gross tonnage shall not be obliged to give the above-mentioned signals, but, if they do not, they shall make some other efficient sound signal at intervals of not more than 1 minute." See **Rule 15**, REGULATIONS FOR PREVENTING COLLISIONS AT SEA, which regulations will be effective and in force on January 1, 1954. **Red f.**, a cloud of fine sand dust of reddish brown color blown from the interior on west coast of Africa and often thickening to *f*. **Sea-f.**, *see* SEA.

FOGY.   Colloquialism in U.S. naval circles for longevity pay; *see* PAY.

FOIST.   Old English term for a light barge or galley.

FOLDING-ANCHOR.   *See* ANCHOR.

FOLLOWING.   Succeeding or pursuing. **F. edge,** *see* EDGE. **F. sea; f. swell,** a sea or swell running in same direction as vessel's course. **F. wind,** a breeze blowing from opposite, or nearly opposite, point to that steered.

FOMALHAUT.   (Ar. *fum al-haut,* mouth of the fish) *Alpha* (α) *Piscis Australis,* only navigational star in the group *Piscis Australis* (or *Austrinus*), or *Southern Fish;* is of magnitude 1.3; its S.H.A. is $16\frac{1}{4}°$; and has a declination of 29° 52' S. A line joining *Scheat* and *Markab* (β and α *Pegasi*), two stars marking the western corners of *Square of Pegasus,* will meet *Fomalhaut* if produced 45° southward.

FOOT.   Lower edge of any sail, which, in a jib or staysail, is that side extending from tack (lower forward corner) to clew (after corner). Lower end of a mast, funnel, ladder, or other erection. To sail fast; as, *she foots well.* To make satisfactory progress to windward on a tack; as, *the boat foots best four points from the wind.* **F.-band,** a broad strip of canvas sewn for strengthening purposes along after side of *f*. of a square sail. **F.-boat,** a ferry used to carry foot-passengers only. **F.-board,** piece of wood placed athwartship in a boat for bracing an oarsman's feet. **F.-brail,** *see* BRAIL. **F.-grating,** wood lattice platform in after end of a boat, serving as a floor. **F.-hook,** *see* FUTTOCK. **F.-lining,** same as *f.-band*. **F.-locks,** cleats fitted on a gang-plank as a foothold for persons; also, a similar arrangement in cattle stalls to provide footing for the animals during rolling of vessel. **F.-outhaul,** rope for hauling out the clew in setting a brailing-in boom sail. **F.-rope,** formerly called a *horse,* a stout hemp rope, or a wire-rope heavily served, extending along and suspended from a yard, on which men stand when furling, reefing, bending or unbending sail, etc. It is fitted every few feet with a *stirrup* or short piece of rope which holds up the otherwise sagging bight produced by weight of men. Also rigged on a jib-boom and an overhanging boom, as that of a spanker, they are named for spar to which attached. The *bolt-rope* along lower edge of a sail. **F.-wales,** *see* WALE. **Ice-f.,** *see* ICE. **Stem f.,** lower end of stem where it connects with keel; *fore-foot.* **Under f.,** beneath bottom of a ship or boat; as, *sharp coral heads are under f.*

FOOTING. Boards or strips of wood laid fore-and-aft inside a boat's bottom and secured to the frames; also, *foot-waling.* Lower weighting or anchoring gear on a fishing-net; rope forming lower edge of a net, also called *foot-line.*

FOOTSTOCK. Old shipbuilding term for upright timbers, taken collectively, or material from which these are fashioned.

FORBES DOUBLE TOPSAIL. Named for its originator in 1841, first attempt to reduce the old single topsail to a handier and more manageable area as appeared in the universally adopted double topsail of *Capt. Howes, 1853.* Capt Forbes rigged his small vessel's (topsail schooner) topmast abaft her lower-mast and arranged the *lower topsail-yard* to hoist on the lowermast doubling up to the cap; *upper topsail* similar to Howes' rig. Due to necessity of hoisting two yards instead of one, plus extra gear required, the rig appears to have found little favor, especially in larger vessels.

FORCED DRAFT. *See* B. forced draft *in* BOILER.

FORE. Combining word used to denote a part of the hull, rigging, or equipment located at, near, or toward *forward* end of vessel; also to distinguish various ropes, sails, yards, etc., rigged or connected to the *foremast* from those attached to the main-mast, mizzenmast, etc. Sometimes the *foremast* itself. *Fore* also connotes precedence in time or position; as in *forenoon, forehand.* (As with many instances in combining terms, any rigid adherence to a particular rule for use of the *hyphen* can not be upheld, in view of the many differences of opinion and taste among lexicographers, authors, and printers; *e.g., fore top, fore-top, foretop,* are considered equally proper) **At the f.,** hoisted or displayed on the foremast; said of a flag, usually at the masthead or truck. **F.-and-aft,** from stem to stern; lengthwise, as opposed to *athwartship;* parallel, or nearly so, with vessel's keel. **F.-and-aft bridge,** a catwalk; *see* **Connecting-b.** *in* BRIDGE. **F.-and-after,** longitudinal portable timbers or girders which sup-

port hatch-covers, fitted to bridge hatch-beams where covers are laid athwartship. A fore-and-aft rigged vessel. A boat having a sharp-ending stern. A cocked hat. **F.-and-aft moorings,** hawsers or chain cables securing a ship to anchors or buoys at each end, as in certain harbors where vessels are not permitted, or have insufficient room, to swing at anchor. **F.-and-aft rig,** as opposed to *square rig,* general term for any sailing rig consisting of *fore-and-aft* sails only, or that in which each sail draws by a single sheet and has its forward edge (leech) secured to a mast, stay, or a permanent tack. Sloops, schooners, luggers, lateen and spritsail rigged craft chiefly comprise this rig. That of Chinese junks may be said to conform partly to both square and fore-and-aft categories. **F.-and-aft sail,** any sail that is not set from, or spread by, a yard or horizontal spar fitted with braces for trimming it to the wind, as those trimmed by a sheet only, *viz.,* jibs, staysails, spritsails, lug sails, lateens, boom or gaff sails. **F. body,** forward half of a vessel's hull; especially, as in an end view drawing, or *body plan,* in which are shown the lines of frames from stem to greatest or, usually, midship breadth of vessel. **F.-boom,** spar spreading the foot of a gaff foresail. **F. bowline,** (pronounced *bōlin*) rope used to stretch forward a square foresail's weather leech when sailing close-hauled. In fore-and-aft rigs, a rope fast to a fore staysail's clew or boom of a jumbo for holding sail aback to assist in swinging vessel's head when coming about in tacking; as vessel fills away on the new tack, at command *"Fore bowline!"* the rope is slacked off and sheet takes the stress. **F. brace,** one of the two purchases by which the fore yard is *braced* or trimmed. Each consists of a *f. brace-pendant,* attached to yard-arm at one end and to *f. brace-tackle* at the other, the latter being fast at ship's rail near to, and forward of, the main rigging. **F. cabin,** in British emigrant sailing-ships of last century, a deck house abaft the foremast in which second class passengers were accommodated; until comparatively recently, a second-class passenger was called a "fore-cabin passenger" in England. In later American usage, forward end of master's cabin which contained the respective berths of chief mate, 2nd. mate, and steward, and sometimes also provision store-rooms. **F. course,** old term for the *fore-sail,* or lowest sail on the foremast of square-rigged vessels; *cf.* COURSE. **F. deck,** forward end of a weather deck; especially, deck area between a bridge deck and a forecastle. **F'foot,** upward-curving-timber connecting the keel to the stem; also, area in immediate vicinity of that connection, often called the *gripe* in wooden boats. **F'ganger,** in whaling, strong handy length of line made fast to a harpoon and spliced to the whale-line; it is the working line in operation of attacking a whale; also called *foregoer* and *foreline.* **F'hand,** short form of *beforehand;* to "hang on" or take the stress by hand on a rope while it is being belayed or made fast, or released from its fast position for heaving, etc. **F. hold,** forward part or compartment below decks, other than a passenger or crew accommodation space of a vessel's hull. **F. hoods,** ends of outside planking butted in the rabbet in vessel's stem. **F'hook,** piece of crooked timber across vessel's stem for uniting bow framing; a breasthook; *see* BREAST. Also called *bowpointer.* **F.-leech,** forward edge, or *luff,* of a fore-and-aft sail. (Now seldom used as a term) **F'lock,** iron pin or ring passed through end of a bolt for securing purposes; a cotter-pin, split-pin, or linch-pin; a *f'lock bolt* is one having a hole to receive such pin. Also, in an old-fashioned anchor, that part of its shank through which the ring or shackle passes. **F'mast,** in a vessel with two or more masts, that mast nearest the stem. **F'mast hand,** a sailor on a merchant sailing-ship. **F'mastman,** formerly one who attended to repairs, etc., of gear on the foremast, as in navy sailing-ships. **F'mast-officer,** a former term for a merchant service petty officer, as a boatswain or a sailmaker. **F'noon watch,** *see* WATCH. **F. peak,** extreme forward part of a fore hold. **F. peak bulkhead;** *see* BULKHEAD. **F.-rake,** forward inclination from perpendicular of a vessel's stem or cutwater, or of masts. **F'reach,** to gain upon, or pass, another ship when both are sailing close-hauled or on the wind; also, to forge ahead, or the distance forged ahead, when vessel is *in stays* or coming about, in tacking. To continue to move or hold headway after propelling power is withdrawn, as when sail is taken in or propeller is stopped. **F.-royalmast,** uppermost extension of the foremast in square-rigged vessels, from which the *f.-royal* yard with its sail, the *f. royal,* is suspended; *see* MAST. **F'runner,** on the old-time log-line, piece of colored material attached as a mark indicating end of *stray line; see* LOG. Also, a *f'ganger, q.v.* **F'sail,** *see* SAIL. **F.-sheet,** rope or tackle attached to clew of a triangular, boom, or lug *f'sail,* or to each clew of a square *f'sail,* for trimming sail as required. **F.-sheet horse,** *see* HORSE. **F. sheets,** space in a boat forward of the foremost thwart; also, *head sheets.* **F'ship,** now obsolete term for bows or forward end of a vessel; *cf. Acts 27:30.* **F'shore,** a beach or shore extending to ordinary limit of tidal rise; specifically, that tract of a shore limited by ordinary high water and low water marks. **F.-staff,** as distinguished from the *back-staff,* or later improvement on the *cross-staff,* name given the latter because in measuring altitudes it was directed toward heavenly body observed; in using the *back-staff* observer faced opposite direction; *see* BACKSTAFF *and* CROSS-STAFF. **F.-staysail,** a triangular sail set on the *fore stay,* as in schooner and larger sloop rigs; sometimes fitted with a boom, especially in American vessels, called a *jumbo-boom.* Also, in such vessels, called a *jumbo* or a *stay-foresail.* **F. stay,** heaviest and lowest rope (usually of wire) which stays the *foremast* assembly.

It leads from lower masthead to the stem or knight-heads, and is first of all standing rigging set up when rigging a sailing-vessel. *See* STAY. **F.-topmast-staysail,** in square-rigged vessels, jib-shaped sail set on *f.-topmast stay;* called a *standing* or *inner jib* in fore-and-aft rigs. **F. tack,** weather clew of a square *foresail;* also, tackle used to heave down such clew when sailing close-hauled. **F. top,** platform erected at fore lowermasthead several feet below the cap (upper end of lowermast). Usually confined to square-rig, it is supported by the trestle-trees and forms a spreader for topmast shrouds which are set up to its sides. *See* TOP. **F. top-gallant-mast,** spar or mast in the *foremast* assembly extending above the *fore topmast.* The *f. top-gallant yard* is hoisted on this mast when setting the *f. top-gallant-sail.* Where double top-gallant-sails were set, as in later square rig, the lower-top-gallant yard was fixed just above the topmast cap while upper top-gallant yard was hoisted as with the single rig; the sails are termed *f. upper-top-gallant-sail* and *f. lower-top-gallant-sail.* **F.-topman,** formerly, a man stationed in the *f. top* of a man-o'-war. **F. topmast,** mast next above the *f.* lowermast. As with top-gallant-sails, either a *single* or the more recent *double topsails* were set from this mast. **F. trysail,** a sail of this type bent to after side of foremast; *see* SAIL. **F'wind,** a favoring breeze or one that speeds a vessel on her way. **F. yard,** lowest yard on foremast of a square-rigged vessel, from which the *foresail,* or *fore course,* is spread.

FORECASTLE. The *forwearde castel* on European ships of the Middle Ages, or raised fortified platform at the bows, which gave command of an enemy's decks in battle. In earlier Elizabethan days the structure appears to have been a less prominent feature and termed a *top-gallant fore-castel* on ships of the line, and later became simply a raised deck sheltering crew's quarters. Up to the close of last century it was customary to house the sailors in the space referred to, or the *forecastle,* and to-day a raised deck at the bows in any vessel is called a *top-gallant f.* Also, generally, that part of a vessel's weather deck forward of the foremast, the extreme forward end of which, whether a flush or raised deck, is termed the *f. head.* In more recent sailing-ships, a deck-house used as seamen's quarters was erected immediately abaft the foremast and called the *f.* (Usually shortened to *fo'c's'l;* phonetically, *fokesel*) **Break of f.,** extreme after end of a raised *f. deck.* **Clamp of a f.,** *see* CLAMP. **F. card,** *see* CARD. **F. deck,** *see* DECK. **Monkey f.,** on smaller vessels, a raised *f.* deck serving as a shelter for the windlass and various deck gear. **Sunk f.,** a *f.* space extending above and below the upper or weather deck.

FORECASTLEMAN. One of a number of men stationed on a war-vessel's forecastle.

FOREIGN. As opposed to *domestic* in maritime

affairs, not within jurisdiction of courts in country to which a vessel belongs; related to, or dealing with, other nations; as, *f. trade, f. investments.* **F. general average clause,** stipulation in marine insurance policies that general average losses shall be adjusted according to laws in force at a *f.* port of discharge or destination, or to those of any *f.* port or place at which voyage may terminate through partial loss or shipwreck. **F.-going vessel,** term used in Great Britain for a vessel making a voyage to any place outside Home Trade limits, or that area usually defined as coasts of British Isles and the continent between River Elbe and Brest. **F. trade,** commerce between different countries; business engaged in by a *f.-going vessel,* as opposed to *home trade.* As defined in *Merchant Marine Act* in U.S. law, June 29, 1936, "commerce or trade between the United States, its Territories or possessions, or the District of Columbia, and a foreign country." **F. voyage,** that made by a vessel in the *f. trade;* a voyage which entails entering within territorial limits of a *f.* country. To **go f.,** to ship as a member of a ship's crew for a *f.* voyage; to sail, as a vessel, on such voyage.

FORGE. To force or impel onward; as, to *forge ship through ice.* Usually with *ahead,* to move forward, as a vessel by her own momentum, or as in passing another. To shape or unite metal structural parts by heating and hammering. To **f. over,** to drive, force, or impel a vessel along the bottom, as in crossing a bar, through soft mud, or over a shoal. **F. test,** that made of samples of structural material, as of plates or bars, to prove its required bending strength. **F. welding,** process of uniting structural metal by forging; *see* WELDING.

FORGINGS. In shipbuilding, general term for those masses of iron or steel which have been worked while heated to special shapes by hammering, bending, or pressing, as stern frames, stemposts, rudder-stocks, propeller-struts, tillers, and propeller-shafting. In recent years, improved methods in casting to a large extent have displaced the slower process of forging.

FORK. Junction, or meeting-place, of a branch or tributary with a main river, or dividing-point in a channel; branch of a river or channel. Throat or separation of parts of a double stay where it forms an eye to lay round a mast, or where its ends separate on each side of a bowsprit, as in a fore stay. A two-pronged fixture for holding a masthead lantern in position. **F.-beam,** *see* BEAM.

FORMING. Process of shaping plates, bars, etc., or partially converted timber, into the required curvature or according to special pattern in shipbuilding.

FORTIES. Regions bounded by the 40th and 50th parallels of latitude in both hemispheres, or those

containing the principal East-West ocean trade routes; *see* ROARING FORTIES.

FORTY-NINER. One of the "Argonauts," or gold-seekers who took passage round the Horn to California, following discovery of the precious metal in that region in 1848.

FORWARD. (A.S., *foreweard,* in a leading direction) In, of, or pertaining to, fore part of ship; as, *forward scuttle; forward locker.* In advance of, or leading; as, *f. ship in line; f. shroud; f. funnel.* Fore end and its contiguous area in a vessel; as, *the men are f.* To ship or send goods to a certain destination or consignee. **F. breast,** a hawser or mooring-line leading from fore part of ship to a pier, dolphin, etc., at, or nearly at, right angles to fore-and-aft line. **F. draft,** depth to which vessel is immersed at fore end; *see* DRAFT. **F. leech,** *see* F.-leech *in* FORE. **F. of the beam,** in a direction toward the bow, not exceeding 45° or 4 points, from that at right angles to fore-and-aft line; also, *before the beam.* **F. perpendicular,** *see* PERPENDICULAR. **F. quarter,** obsolete term for turn of the bow from stem to ship's vertical side; now usually *bluff of the bow.* **F. spring,** hawser or mooring-line leading from fore part of ship nearly parallel with fore-and-aft line to a wharf, dolphin, etc. In berthing vessel, used to check her headway; as a mooring-warp, to provide against surging ahead.

FOSFORESCENCE. *See* PHOSPHORESCENCE.

FOTHER. Archaic term meaning to temporarily stop a leak in a vessel's hull while afloat by placing over the faulty part a piece of canvas, as a sail or tarpaulin, heavily thrummed or doubled as a flat bag and filled with oakum, old rope-yarns, or other material to form a padding. To make such a device for use as a collision-mat or leak-stopper from a piece of canvas; as to *fother* a tarpaulin. Also, *fodder.* Formerly, in England, *f.* was a unit of weight used in ballasting ships with pigs of lead or iron. Approximately equal to one ton or to 30 pigs, or *fotmals,* each about 70 lbs. weight.

FOUL. Opposed to *clear* in the sense of being hindered or impeded; as a *foul cable;* or a physical condition; as *f. water, f. bilges.* Not fair, favorable, or advantageous; as, *f. weather,* a *f. anchorage.* Condition of being encrusted with marine growth, etc.; as, a *f. bottom; see* BARNACLES. To become snarled or kinked; as ropes. To collide, or be forced into collision with, as two or more boats. To be impeded or entangled with, as by an obstruction; as, *vessel ran f. of the nets.* **F. anchor,** *see* ANCHOR PHRASEOLOGY. **F. berth,** such a place in which a vessel is anchored or otherwise made fast in a harbor or roadstead while being unable to lie or swing reasonably clear of a neighboring vessel or any obstruction; or, unless customary in the port, becomes grounded at low tide. A vessel making fast or anchoring in proximity to another already berthed, if creating a *f. berth* for the latter, becomes responsible for any subsequent damage to either vessel caused by reason of such condition. **F. bill of health,** *see* BILL. **F. ground,** anchorage providing unsatisfactory holding *ground* or bottom, such as rock or shifting sand. **F. hawse,** condition in which anchor cables are turned round each other; *see* HAWSE. To **get, fall,** or **run f. of,** to collide with; to become entangled with. To **make f. water,** to stir up bottom mud or sand and thus discolor the water, as a ship's paddles, screw, or keel in shallow depths. **F. water,** dangerous area in which to navigate; waters where soundings are uneven and bottom snaggy or rocky with dangerous heads. **F. weather,** squally, rainy, stormy, or otherwise inclement conditions.

FOUND. State of being equipped and supplied with stores and provisions. A vessel is said to be *all found* when fitted with all necessaries for proceeding on a voyage; *well found* when all her equipment, accommodation, decks, and general structure are in first class condition and provisions, stores, fuel, etc., satisfactory in quality and quantity.

FOUNDATION PLATE. Heavy plate or plating to which an engine or pump is bolted down; a bedplate; a sole-plate. Where no double-bottom is built in transverse-framed vessels, a heavy plate laid fore-and-aft in the center line over the floors and forming the base of a *keelson*.

FOUNDER. (O.F. *fondrer,* to fall in; *fond,* bottom; L. *fundus,* bottom) To sink through being overcome by weight of water admitted, as a ship suffering complete loss of her reserve buoyancy; to be engulfed by a heavy sea and lost, as a boat.

FOUR. A boat pulled by four oars; especially, in racing usage. **F.-boater,** said of old whaling-ships, one having four boats in the davits. **F.-cant,** consisting of four strands; a four-stranded rope. **F.-decked ship,** a vessel having four complete decks or their structural equivalent; *see* SHIP. **F'fold block,** a quadruple or four-sheaved purchase block. **F'fold purchase,** a tackle rove in *two fourfold blocks,* standing end of fall being made fast to that block to which hauling part leads; has a power ratio of 1 to 5 when hauling part leads to *moving block;* 1 to 4 when hauling part leads to *standing block;* friction not considered. **F. lowers,** in American fisherman's parlance, lower sails of a schooner; as in, *we set the four lowers,* or mainsail, foresail, jumbo, and jib. **F.-masted barque,** (or bark), *see* BARK. **F.-masted brig,** a U.S. term given a "jack-ass" rig of *f.* masts, forward two of which were square-rigged, the others fore-and-aft rigged; a *jackass barque.* **F.-masted ship,** sailing-vessel having *f.* masts, square-rigged on each; *see* SHIP. **F.-point bearing,** or *f.* points and abeam, also called *bow-and-beam* bearing, method of finding distance off a fixed object; *see* TWO OR MORE

BEARINGS WITH RUN BETWEEN. **F. seas,** as used in a poetic sense, waters surrounding the British Islands; as in *"our fairest isle once by the four seas swathed."*

FOURTH CLASS LIBERTY. See LIBERTY.

FOX. Used as a seizing or roband, in making a paunch mat, or as the warp in weaving a sword mat, an old name for a piece of small cordage which is made by twisting together two or more tarred rope-yarns, or by three lengths of marline, spunyarn, or other small stuff, laid up by means of a spinning-jenny. Process referred to was termed *making foxes.* **Sea-f.,** the *thrasher* or *thresher* shark; *see* **Fox s.** *in* SHARK. To **see a f.,** to sight imaginary land, etc., as result of an optical illusion caused by tired eyes. **Spanish f.,** a single yarn twisted contrary to its original lay, rubbed smooth, and used for small seizing-stuff.

FOXY. Said of timber affected by dry rot; also *foxey, druxy; see* DRUXEY.

FOY. Old British north country dialectal term for a gathering of fishermen in celebration of the end of a voyage or fishing season; a cabin party of whaling masters and officers at sea, especially upon departure of one or more vessels for home port after a successful catch; also termed a *gam.* As formerly much used on British east coast, the word meant to pilot, assist, or render aid to vessels in any way; a **foy-boat** was synonymous with *pilot-boat,* and assisted generally in bringing ships into berth, warping, etc. Like most craft once thus employed, the lug-sailed *foy-boats* no longer are found "seeking" inward-bounders off the Tyne, having discarded mast and sail for harbor duty only.

FRACTO. (L. *fractum,* break) Combining word employed in cloud nomenclature; as in *fracto-cumulus; f.-nimbus; f.-stratus,* indicating a broken condition of *cumulus,* etc. See CLOUD.

F.P.A. Abbreviation for *Free of Particular Average,* connoting, in a marine insurance policy, coverage includes only losses through fire, sinking, stranding, or collision; *see* AVERAGE.

FRAME. Any one of the members constituting the skeleton structure of a vessel, to which the outside planking or plating is secured. From early days the *transverse* frame, rib, timber, or girder extending from side to side and giving the required curvature to the body has been, and still is, that type erected in wooden vessels and in almost all boats. Until about 1908 this system in iron and steel construction remained undisturbed. At that date *Sir Joseph Isherwood* of England introduced his *longitudinal* method which featured narrowly-spaced fore-and-aft framing between widely-spaced transverse heavy *web frames;* and to a great extent this system, especially in tank vessels and certain bulk cargo carriers, gradually has displaced the purely transverse method. For the longitudinal system and its few variations from the original *Isherwood* it is claimed that less weight of metal is required for structural strength equal to that of the older system. In *wooden ships,* excepting a few of the *cant frames* at ends of the body, a frame consists of a pair of timbers laid side by side and united by bolts and/or treenails. Each timber is made up of several lengths so arranged that their scarfed butts lie at or near the middle of the adjoining length; and the lengths or sections usually are named *floors, futtocks,* and *top timbers.* Floor timbers butt to the *1st.* and *2nd. futtocks* respectively; these in turn to *3rd.* and *4th futtocks* (or *foot-hooks,* at upward curve of bilge), which finally butt to the *top timbers. F.* timbers are spaced very closely, usually never exceeding a half-frame faying width apart. In *steel ships, f's* connect to floor-plates which in turn are secured to keel, in keeping with principle of continuous strength from side to side via the keel, as in wooden construction. Ordinary transverse *f's* consist of two angle-bars riveted or welded back to back and fashioned so that the outer flange fays flat against outside plating. At the floor-heads where *f.* turns inward at the bilge, it is forked so that its inner or *reverse bar* forms a stiffener along upper edge of floor-plate, the *shell bar* continuing along lower edge of, and secured to, floor. Heavier type *f's* are bracketed to floors, or floors are simply lapped on and secured to them. In any case, the complete bridging from side to side, with a deck-beam or beams connecting heads of frames (sometimes every 2nd. *f.*), forms an important unit in strength contribution to the hull. **After f.,** *see* AFTER. **Balanced f.,** *see* BALANCE. **Banjo-f.,** *see* BANJO-FRAME. **Boss f.,** *see* BOSS. **Built-up f.,** as distinguished from a solid bar, as channel-iron, bulb-iron, Z-bar, etc., commonly in use to-day, a *f.* made of two angle-bars riveted back to back, thus forming a cross-section similar to that of a Z-bar. Inner bar of this arrangement is termed *reverse bar* or *reverse f.;* outer one, the *f.* or *shell bar,* or simply *f.* **C-f. system,** that in which transverse *f's* are of the *deep* type, or made up of two large angle-bars; the reverse bar being separated from its mate at the bilge to stiffen upper edge of a tankside bracket (at end of floor outside of margin-plate), thence continued a short distance over, and secured to, inner bottom plating in way of floor. **Cant f.,** *see* CANT. **Deep f.,** *see* DEEP. **F.-angle; f. angle-bar; f. bar;** *see* **Built-up f. F. areas,** those of cross-sections of immersed body at particular frames; *see* **A's of sections** *in* AREA. **F.-bevel,** angle faying surface of a *f.* makes with the athwartship line. Since *f's* are set at right angles to fore-and-aft line, their outer faces are shaped to bear against inward-curving plating at and near ends of ship. **F. head,** upper end or section of a *f.,* or that part rising above a weather deck. **F.-liner,**

piece of plate of same width as faying face of a *f.* laid as a filler between *f.* and a raised strake of plating; also, *f.-slip, packing-piece,* and *plating-liner.* **F.-lines,** in the body plan of ship, those showing shape of *f's,* from which each *f.* is fashioned in the forging process. Each *f.*-line is formed by intersection of a vertical transverse plane with hull's molded surface at a specified position in the fore-and-aft line. Shown also in the sheer plan as vertical straight lines, *f's* are numbered consecutively, beginning aft as in common British shipbuilding practice, or from forward, as often found in American yards. **F. mold,** template or pattern of a *f.,* taken from the scrive-board or mold-loft floor (developed to full size from body plan) and used in shaping *f.* to required curvature, etc. **F. set,** thin piece of soft iron bar bent to curvature of a *f.,* as required by template, for transferring the shape to the bending-slab. **F. spacing,** fore-and-aft distance between consecutive *f.-lines.* Governed according to type and size of vessel, classification societies' rules for spacing in steel ships varies from 20 inches in a vessel of about 100 feet in length to 32 inches for one of 600 feet; in wood construction, distance between *f's* varies according to class and size of timber, generally, in sea-going vessels, being not greater than breadth of half-faying surface of *f's.* **F.-timber,** rib or *f.* of a wooden vessel, sometimes called a *bend* or simply *f.* in small vessels and boats; timber for use as *f's.* **In f.,** said of a vessel in process of building when all *f's* have been erected and properly set, preparatory to the outside planking or plating stage. **Intermediate f.,** one for stiffening purposes only and without a continuing floor-plate, and also, not bracketed to a deck-beam. **Joggled f.,** *see* JOGGLE. **Lap f.,** a *f.-bar* joint made by lapping one bar over its neighbor. **Main f.,** one of those at greatest breadth of vessel. **Main body f's,** those below the main or strength deck. In vessels of certain construction having three or more decks, *f.* material is diminished above second deck from below. **Midship f.,** one at mid-length of ship. **Molding of a f.,** depth of material in a wood *f.* as measured from outer to inner surface; its *molding edge* is either one of its outer corners or edges. **Natural f's,** those cut from wood growing in the shape required for *f's,* or nearly so; highly valued for strength. **Panting f.,** *see* PANTING. **Port-f.,** *see* PORT. **Propeller-f.,** stern *f.* of a single-screw vessel, or heavy casting or forging combining stern and rudder posts, between which the propeller turns. **Reverse f.,** *see* **Built-up f. Rider f.,** *see* RIDER. **Rudder-f.,** *see* RUDDER. **Scantling of f's,** dimensions of *f's* to which shipbuilder must adhere in order to obtain class desired for vessel concerned; or minimum cross-section of material prescribed by the classification society's rules. **Scuttle-f.,** *see* SCUTTLE. **Siding of a f.,** fore-and-aft measurement in inches of faying surface of a *f.-timber.* **Solid f.,** as opposed to a *built-up f.,* one made of a single bar, as a bulb angle, channel, or a Z-bar. **Spectacle f.,** a heavy arm in the form of an open casting extending from ship's side, which serves as a support for, and also contains, the stern tube for propeller-shafting in twin- and multiple-screw vessels. **Square f.,** one of those at or near broadest part of ship, which have no bevel, or set square to the planking or plating; a *midship f.* **Square-body f.,** a mid-body *f.* which has sharp curvature at the bilge and lies at greatest breadth of vessel; it is one of longest in the hull. **Stern f.,** *see* STERN; *cf.* **Propeller-f. Transom f.,** *see* TRANSOM. **Transverse f.,** as opposed to a *cant f.* or a *longitudinal f.,* one set at right angles to fore-and-aft line. **Tunnel f.,** *see* TUNNEL. **Web f.,** a very deep transverse *f.* placed to compensate for interrupted continuity of strength, as where beams are absent in an engine-room, or in a specially built hold for bulk cargo. In longitudinal framing system, where ordinary transverse *f's* are displaced by longitudinals, *web f's* are set 12 to 15 feet apart. **Z-f.,** *f.* and *reverse f.,* or *built-up f.,* of Z-shaped cross-section; a *solid f.* of Z cross-section, or *Z-bar.*

FRAMING. Arrangement or system of structural parts constituting framework of a vessel; transverse or longitudinal frames, collectively. **Combination f.,** system in which decks and bottom of ship are principally longitudinally framed and sides transversely. **F. number** or **numeral,** also termed *transverse numeral,* classification society's scantling number governing minimum requirements for *transverse f.; see* **L. numerals** *in* LLOYD'S. **F. plan,** diagram indicating spacing, dimensions, and construction of frames. **F. ribband,** in shipbuilding, long strip of plate or timber extending fore-and-aft across, and secured to, ribs or frames to hold them in position when erected. **Jalousie f.,** slat-work built in sides of a light deck cabin, which admits light and air while preventing ingress of rain. **Longitudinal f.,** fore-and-aft members in the frame structure; Isherwood system; *see* FRAME *and* LONGITUDINAL. **Transverse f. numeral,** *see* **F. number.**

FRANKLIN LIFE-BUOY. *See* BUOY.

FRANCHISE CLAUSE. Immunity or exemption clause in a marine insurance policy releasing insurers of liability for particular average claims (*losses*) amounting to less than a specified percentage of insured value. Such a clause in a *Lloyd's policy* reads: "Corn, Fish, Salt, Fruit, Flour, and Seed are warranted free from Average, unless general, or the Ship be stranded; Sugar, Tobacco, Hemp, Flax, Hides, and Skins are warranted free from Average under Five Pounds per Cent.; and all other Goods, also the Ship and Freight, are warranted free from Average under Three Pounds per Cent., unless general, or the Ship be stranded." *See* AVERAGE.

FRAP. (Fr. *frapper,* to bind) To secure tightly as by lashing two spars together; to increase tension in a lashing by drawing turns around its separated parts; to tauten shrouds by drawing them together by a lashing; to strengthen a ship with chain cables passed around the hull and set taut, as formerly resorted to in old wooden vessels. A **frapping** is the cordage or chain employed to *frap,* lash, or bind objects together; *frapping turns* are the parts drawn around a lashing for increasing its tension.

FRAZIL. A northeastern U.S. and Canadian term for *ground* or *anchor ice; see* ICE. (Pronounced *frazeel'*)

FREE. Loose; adrift; not secured; as, *free end of line.* Invested with a certain right or immunity; as, a *f. port; f. of particular average* (marine insurance policy). A vessel is said to be *running f.* when wind allows her to steer her course with eased sheets or weather braces checked in; or, when wind is from any direction abaft 6 points from ahead in a square-rigger or approximately 5 points in fore-and-aft rigged craft; opposed to *close-hauled.* To clear or release; as, *vessel freed herself from the shoal.* **F. alongside ship,** *see* F.A.S. **F. fishery,** *see* FISHERY. **F. in and out,** term in chartering parlance, meaning that charterer is responsible for costs of loading or discharging cargo only, all port charges and maintenance costs to be borne by vessel's owner. **F. lighterage,** applied to a quoted freight rate, indicates inclusion of lighterage costs to or from ship at port specified. **F. of average** or **f. of all average,** as found in marine insurance policies, indicates insurer is to be exempted from all average claims, the insured being covered for total loss only; often abbrev. *F.A.A.* **F. of particular average,** *see* F.P.A. **F. of turn,** in chartering, stipulation that vessel's allowed *lay days* begin upon arrival in port, regardless of availability of a berth for loading or discharging. **F. on board,** *see* F.O.B. **F. overside,** commercial term meaning goods are *f.* of charges until received from ship's tackles, when buyer's liability begins. **F. pilotage,** condition obtaining in a specified area indicating services of a pilot are optional; opposed to *compulsory pilotage.* **F. port,** a harbor, or certain area within such harbor, where goods may be landed and shipped *f.* of customs duties; also, a port where merchandise may be received from all countries under same conditions with respect to customs duty rates and port charges or privileges. **F. reach,** in boat sailing, a course steered with the wind from a direction between beam and quarter; hence, *f.-reaching* or *on a f. reach.* **F. ship,** vessel of a neutral country in time of war; hence, normally *f.* from liability of seizure. **F. stuff,** ship-building timber *f.* of knots or other imperfections. **F. surface,** the unconfined surface of a liquid, as in a partly filled tank or hold. An aggregate of several *f.* tank surfaces or a half-filled hold may result in a serious lowering of a vessel's metacenter, with consequent loss of stability, by an amount equal to total moment of inertia of such surfaces divided by ship's displacement volume. A water-tight center-line division in a through tank lessens this effect by one-fourth, since value of surfaces' moment of inertia varies as cube of breadth of each surface (transverse dimension). **F. tank,** a partly filled tank; also termed *slack tank*. **F. wind,** a favorable breeze, or one giving advantage of a *f. reach; see* **F. reach. F. zone,** a *f. port,* or segregated area within, or adjacent to, any port, where merchandise for re-export may be landed, stored, converted or processed in manufacture in any way, re-packed, and/or re-shipped without payment of any customs duty. To **sail f.,** to sail with a fair wind. **Wreck f.,** *see* WRECK.

FREEBOARD. Vertical distance from the projected line of top of deck plating or planking of *freeboard deck* at vessel's side to surface of water at mid-length of designed load-line. The minimum *f's* assigned a vessel for different seasons, areas navigated, sea or fresh water flotation, are determined by the classification society's rules which take into consideration details of vessel's length, breadth, depth, structural strength and design, extent of superstructure, sheer, and round of beam, as compared with those of a *standard vessel* to which a definite normal or *summer f.* has been allotted. **F. certificate,** *see* CERTIFICATE. **F. deck,** *see* DECK. **F. depth,** as taken into account in assigning a *f.* value, the *molded depth* plus thickness of freeboard deck stringer-plate or planking, subject to certain modification in ships of unusual bottom or topside construction. *Cf.* **Molded depth** *in* DEPTH. **F. mark,** *see* **Plimsoll mark** *in* MARK. **F. length,** as considered in assigning *f.,* length of vessel measured at *summer load draft* from fore side of stem to after side of rudder-post or, where rudder-post is absent, as in balanced rudder arrangement, to axis of rudder-stock. **F. zones,** ocean regions in which, at certain seasons, a vessel is limited to the minimum indicated in her "birth-marks" (*Plimsoll marks*) and *f.* or *load-line certificate.* Marks are *S* (summer); *W* (winter); and *T* (tropical). *See* LOAD. **Summer f.,** amount of *f.,* expressed in feet and inches, assigned a vessel during *summer* within certain *f. zones,* as defined by *International Load Line Convention, 1930* (effective in U.S. January 1, 1933); *see* **Load-line** *in* LOAD.

FREEBOOTER. (Du. *vrijbuiter,* a plunderer) Member of a predatory band or crew; one engaged in freebooting or pillaging; a pirate or buccaneer.

FREEDOM OF THE SEAS. Recognized law or rule that vessels of all nations are free of any restrictions whatsoever to their right to navigate the high seas; by virtue of which any predatory or unauthorized belligerent acts by persons or vessels against commerce or persons in transportation out-side territorial waters of any country are deemed by all maritime nations as acts of a common enemy.

FREEING. Act or process of ridding, clearing, removing, or releasing from that which hinders, impedes, or interferes with normal conditions or operations; as in, *f. ship of rats; f. pipe-lines of deposit; f. holds of water.* **F.-ports,** *see* PORT.

FREEZER. One in a vessel's engineering staff who is charged with operation and care of the cargo or provision refrigerating plant. (*Chiefly U.S., colloquial*)

FREIGHT. (Old Du. *vrecht,* earnings, reward) The cargo or lading placed in a vessel for transportation. *Cargo,* though synonymous with *freight,* rarely is applied to goods transported by land carrier. Charge made by a carrier for transporting goods or merchandise; sometimes, in a broader sense, total earnings or charter hire of a vessel, including charges for carriage of passengers. **Back f.,** that for which a shipper is liable in event of his goods being barred from landing at port of intended delivery—either by governmental edict or from any physical cause unforeseen by carrier and over which he has no control—and returned, in consequence, to port of shipment. **Chartered f.,** charges as specified in a charter party for part of, or entire, vessel's cargo space. **Dead f.,** *see* DEAD. **Distance f.,** charge for carriage of goods at a rate per unit distance, as legally recognized by some countries, other than U.S. and Great Britain. **F.-ton,** weight or bulk unit on which freight charges are payable; may be either weight of 2240 lbs. (long ton) in case of heavier bulk cargoes, or 40 cubic feet (English-speaking countries) for cargo of 40 or more cubic feet per ton weight. **Fungible f.,** such cargo which permits mixture of different consignments without damage resulting; such as coal, grain, or ores of one kind and grade. **Gross f.,** total earnings or revenue for carriage of cargo, as differentiated from *net f.,* or that resulting when operating expenses are deducted from such earnings. Also, total charges paid by a shipper, including an insurance premium and/or a broker's commission. **Lump f.,** a figure paid as a lump sum for use of a part of, or entire vessel's, cargo space. **Measurement f.,** cargo upon which *f.* is charged according to volume; *see* MEASUREMENT. **Time f.,** payment for hire of a vessel made periodically, as distinguished from *lump f.;* charter hire.

FREIGHTAGE. Lading or cargo. Charge made for carrying cargo. Total space available in vessel for stowing cargo, usually expressed in cubic feet; number of long tons of cargo in question that can be stowed in a vessel. The transportation of goods or merchandise for hire.

FREIGHTER. One who charters and loads a vessel; one who enters into agreement with a vessel's owner to use part or all of her cargo space or passenger accommodation for a specified period or voyage; in a broad sense, a charterer or shipper. A vessel chiefly employed in carrying cargo; especially, a power-driven vessel.

FREIGHTMENT. Act of engaging services of a vessel for carriage of goods or passengers. *Cf.* AF-FREIGHTMENT.

FRENCH. Combining word used in some terms for about 200 years past, originally as a distinguishing name for a method or item in seamanship practice borrowed by English sailors from the French. It may be noted that, in almost all fancy and well-finished rope work, or "marline-spike seamanship," the French seaman far outstripped his English rival in 18th and 19th century days, while for general hard-headed ship maneuvering and all-round mastery of the long-voyage sea-going business, Britain's men of the sea were considered superior to any afloat. **F. bowline,** *see* BOWLINE. **F. coil,** rope laid on deck in *F. fakes;* by some authorities synonymous with *Flemish* coil; *see* FAKE and COIL. **F. fake,** *see* FAKE. **F. lug,** a balanced lug-sail; *see* LUG. **F. reef,** method of reefing square sails in which a rope stretched along, and rove through cringles in, the reef-band was secured to jack-stay on yard by a series of short toggled lanyards. As used in the old single quadruple-reefing topsail, single and double reefs were taken by this means, the remaining treble and close reef by ordinary reef-point system. **F. sennit,** kind of flat braided or plaited cordage made of an odd number of rope-yarns—usually 5 to 7; chiefly used for robands and chafing service. **F. shroud-knot,** another old French wrinkle and improvement on the English knot for uniting ends of a hemp shroud, or other unit of standing rigging, with view of economizing length of rope utilized in the process. Strands are married and a *wall knot* made with each set over the rope, as in the English shroud knot, with the difference that strands of one wall are laid back and secured beneath other wall. The knot was a popular one in old sailing navy ships when clearing up a mess of damaged rigging after an engagement.

FREQUENCY. *See* ALTERNATING CURRENT.

FRESH. Quality of being newly produced, gathered, or supplied; as, a *f.* coat of paint; *f.* fish; *f.* provisions. Not pickled or salted; as, *f.* beef; *f.* water. Comparatively stiff breeze or strong wind; as, *f.* breeze; *f.* gale; *see* BEAUFORT SCALE. **F. run,** said of fish, as a newly arrived school entering a creek, river, etc. **F.-shot,** area or stream of fresh water extending a considerable distance seaward from mouth of a large river, as off the Amazon; also, a *fresh.* **F. water mark,** a load-line indicating limit to which vessel may be submerged in *f.* water below her *summer marks,* or limit of load in sea-water during summer season. *Allowance for f. water is* ¼

inch per foot of summer draft; *see* LOAD-LINE *and* F.W. **F.-water pump,** power-driven pump, usually located in engine-room, for maintaining pressure in the *f.* water supply system. **F.-water sailor,** one not accustomed to the ocean; hence, a green or inexperienced seaman. **F.-water stay,** a triatic stay; *see* STAY. **F. way,** increased headway after a lull or temporary slackening of speed. **F.-water distiller,** *see* DISTILLER.

FRESHEN. To increase in force, as a breeze. To relieve or alter position, as of a rope, in order to avoid undue chafe or stress on one part only, or distribute local wear and tear. To make fresh, or less salt, as by filling and pumping out a salty tank. To renew, as to pump out old ballast water and replace it with clean sea-water; or, to *f.* the ballast. To **f. the hawse,** to slack out or heave in sufficient cable to allow a new portion to receive chafe of the hawse-pipe, as commonly practised in the days of hemp anchor-cables. To **f. the way,** to increase speed. To **f. the nip,** to change belayed turns or bearing-point of a rope to a new portion.

FRESHES. Area of an ebb stream from a river or arm of the sea, increased by effect of heavy rains and often discolored to a considerable distance off shore; as, the *freshes* of the Columbia.

FRESHET. Unusual rise or overflowing of a stream, river, etc., canused by heavy rains or melting snow.

FRET. To wear away or chafe, as by friction. A wasting, wearing, or chafing; *see* CHAFING. **Fretted,** chafed, scored, or worn.

FRICTION. (L. *frictio,* rubbing)   Act of rubbing together; attrition; resistance to motion, or tendency to motion, by two surfaces in contact. **F. brake,** *see* BRAKE. **F. drum,** *see* DRUM. **F. winch** or **f.-geared winch,** a cargo-hoisting engine in which power transmission essentially is effected by *f.* of revolving surfaces instead of meshing of toothed wheels, lowering being controlled by a powerful foot-brake; also termed *cone-f. winch* and *elevator-winch.* **Frictional wake,** a wake-current component attributed to frictional drag of ship's hull through water; *see* WAKE. **Skin f.,** *see* S. resistance *in* SKIN. **Tidal f.,** that caused by the tide wave in its tendency to retard the earth's rotational velocity.

FRIEZING. Richly ornamental, often gilded, designs built on upper part of ship's stern and quarters and sometimes at the bows, once a prominent feature in Spanish, French, and English vessels of importance in the 16th and 17th centuries.

FRIGATE. (It. *fregata,* early type of vessel driven by sails and oars) This originally Mediterranean term was given in about 1750 to western European war-vessels of a class between the corvette and line-of-battle ship. The typical *frigate* was a speedy craft of ship rig carrying a heavy spread of canvas; armed with a full battery on her gun deck and a lighter one on the spar deck, totalling about 40 guns; had a raised quarter-deck and forecastle; and was considered a valuable fighting unit or somewhat analogous to the more recent "cruiser," over a period of 100 years. The *double-banked f., double-banker,* or *two-decker,* of flush deck build appeared in the early 1800's. This type mounted full batteries on both decks, or about 50 guns in all. Later, the larger and more powerful *steam f.* formed the main part of most navies until advent of the "ironclad" about 1870. In World War II the term was given a U.S. naval vessel of 1430 tons displacement and 304 feet length over all, specially designed for patrol and convoy duty. **F.-built,** old descriptive term for a vessel having a quarter-deck and forecastle raised above the main deck. **F.-bird,** of family *Fregatidæ* and genus *Fregata,* the sailor's *man-o'-war bird,* noted for its amazing powers of swift and sustained flight, and also for its habit of robbing other birds of their prey. Said to be fastest feathered flyer, has been clocked at 260 miles per hour. Usually measures 2½ feet in length, has a long deeply forked tail, pointed wings of about 7 feet spread, small feet, long hook-pointed bill, a gular pouch, and generally is whitish on underbody and dark-colored on back. Larger of two known species is *f. aquila,* found on southern U.S. coasts, in West Indies, and throughout the tropics; *f. minor,* or smaller, is native to South Pacific and Indian Oceans. Also called *f.-pelican.* **F. mackerel,** the bonito, or scombroid fish about two feet in length found in all warm seas; *see* BONITO. **Hen f.,** sailor's term for a vessel in which the executive capabilities of the master's wife are amply demonstrated. **Jackass f.,** an old-time sloop-of-war having a light spar deck over the main battery; derisive appellative for any vessel having an extraordinary rig or placement of guns.

FRIGATOON. (It. *fregatone*) A 16th-17th century Venetian war-vessel, lateen-rigged, with a bowsprit, mainmast and a mizzen. Also, a sloop-of-war of ship rig; *see* SLOOP.

FRIGID ZONES. *See* ZONE.

FRITH. *See* FIRTH.

FRITTER. Scraps or residue of whale-blubber after the oil-extracting process; used as fuel.

FRONT. Meteorological term for a surface of discontinuity between two currents of air of different densities, or boundary between two different air masses. **F. bulkhead,** *see* **Break-b.** *in* BULKHEAD. **F.-rail,** a breast-rail; *see* RAIL.

FROZEN CARGO. *See* CARGO.

FRUIT-BOX. Wood or metal box-shaped sling used in loading or discharging fruit, small packages, boxes, etc. Sometimes called an *ambulance* because of often being the means of landing an injured man.

FRUIT-CARRIER. Ships of this class, or *fruiters,* are specially designed for a particular fruit trade, *esp.* for carriage of bananas, and include vessels wholly or in part equipped with, or with no, refrigerated cargo space. Last-noted type are termed "natural draft" ships and are fitted with an elaborate open-to-atmosphere ventilation arrangement. Fruiters are built with more than the usual number of decks found in cargo-vessels, generally, in holds uninterrupted by a shaft-tunnel, having an upper and lower 'tween deck, an orlop deck, and a lower hold, in order to lessen crushing effect in the stowed fruit. Banana stems are stowed on their ends and in portable-sided bins, with view of keeping mass of fruit rigid during seaway motion of vessel. Cooled air system provides a banana-carrying temperature of about 55° F. in refrigerated ships; natural ventilation vessels are employed on short runs or where fruit is consumed at or near port of discharge; cooled cargo admits of long-distance delivery which often includes trans-shipment via railroad. These ships usually are capable of speeds of from 14 to 18 knots; average net tonnage 3500, stowing some 70,000 stems of fruit. **Fruit-clipper,** a small speedy vessel engaged in carrying currants, figs, raisins, and citrus fruits from the Canary Islands, Portugal, and Mediterranean ports to the British Isles and western Europe about middle of last century. Such vessels usually were topsail schooners or brigs. **Fruit fittings,** removable boards and stanchions for separating and securing stems of bananas; also wood deck-gratings giving about 3 inches air space below fruit. Bins average 12 feet square. *Cf.* **Cargo-c.** *in* COOLING.

FRUSTRATION OF THE ADVENTURE. An important *charter party* phrase signifying a condition in which unforeseen circumstances attending execution of an affreightment agreement may result in an embarrassing delay to the venture. A shipowner, charterer, or shipper is entitled to void the contract of affreightment where it can be shown that such delay is, has been, or will be of such period as to render it unreasonable to proceed with such venture. Also, a similar term in *marine insurance* signifying a clause in a policy which provides against claim for loss by a shipper in event of delivery of his goods at destination being rendered impossible due to outbreak of war.

FUDGE. To represent ship's dead reckoning position as that found by observation; hence, to evade effort by some slipshod substitute for a proper job; often with *up,* as, to *fudge up ship's accounts.*

FUEL. (O.F. *fouaille*) Combustible matter used to produce heat by burning; as, coal, gas, peat, petroleum, wood. To supply with, or receive, fuel; as, *ship fueled at Norfolk.* **Boiler f.,** solid type for ships' boilers usually is either anthracite or bituminous coal, sometimes lignite, when obtainable, and wood being in use on river or inland steamers; liquid fuel practically is confined to petroleum in its crude or its processed state; pulverized coal, the use of which involves installation of a special grinding equipment and is similar in the burning process to that of a liquid combustible, has been used with some success. **Diesel f.,** as ordinarily used in internal combustion engines of the type named, a petroleum distillate, often called *gas oil,* of gravity 20 to 30 *Baumé* (.93 to .88 *specific gravity*). Larger plants work with heavier oil, about 15 *Baumé* (.96 *spec. gr.*) **F. conservation,** considering the problem of economic use of fuel supply on hand to cover a given distance, that sufficient to proceed at a certain speed, or rate of consumption at different drafts, in steam-engined vessels the following basic ratios have been found of practical value: Within a few knots' range in vicinity of vessel's normal speed, the *f. consumption* varies (a) as cube of speed; (b) as speed squared times distance covered; (c) and as displacement to the two-thirds power. **F. fever,** fussy anxious attitude of the chief engineer, source of which is traceable to an apprehensive expectancy of a shortage of *f.* **F. oil,** term usually given petroleum used for producing steam. It is the heavy residue after abstracting from crude oil such products as benzine, kerosene, lubricating oils, and many others; varies from .90 to .99 in specific gravity (26 to 11, *Baumé*), depending upon carbon content of basic crude; and has a flash point of 150° to 180° (*Fahr.*). Also called *boiler oil,* for ship use it possesses several advantages over coal, including ease of stowage and transfer, flexibility of combustion control, greater dependable thermal value, ready availability, less fire-room hands required, less bunker space, and cleanliness. **F. oil certificate,** *see* CERTIFICATE. **F.-oil heater,** in an oil-burning system, an apparatus in which *f.* is heated in order to bring its viscosity to proper standard for efficient diffusion or atomizing from the burners and hence with view of obtaining proper combustion. **F. pump,** in oil-firing, means by which constant pressure of *f.* is maintained in line supplying the burners. **F. ship,** vessel supplying *f.* to a naval fleet or station; especially, an *oil-tanker.* **F. tank,** one of the compartments in a double bottom or a deep tank of oil-tight construction used for ship's *f.* supply. **Patent f.,** mixture of coal-dust and coal tar or pitch molded in handy blocks called *briquettes* or *briquets,* used in some high pressure boilers; now rarely found aboard ship.

FULL. Said of sails when drawing under wind pressure. Quality of being complete, attaining height of a characteristic quality, or a maximum; as, *full-rigged; a full ship; full tide.* **At f. sea,** at high water, as observed at a beach or over a shoal. **Clean f.,** *see* **rap f. F. and by,** short for *f. and by the wind,* or term for sailing as close as possible to the wind while keeping all sail *f.* **F. and change,** as chiefly found on charts in connection with tidal data, means times of full and new moon; *see* ESTABLISHMENT OF THE PORT. **F. and down,** state of being fully laden with all cargo space occupied and vessel floating at her load-line marks, which is considered generally as the load condition producing maximum freight return. Considering a full cargo offering, if space were filled with light merchandise, vessel would be *f.,* but not *down;* if weighty goods only be carried, she would sink to her load-line before entire cargo space were occupied and be *down,* but not *f.* **F.-bottomed,** said of a vessel having small rise of floor and of comparatively great capacity below her water-line. **F.-bowed,** "apple-bowed," or having a bluff or swelling entrance on each side of the stem. **F. diameter,** British term for external diameter, as that of a pipe, barrel, etc. **F.-ended,** said of a boat or vessel having *f.* curvature or swelling lines in vicinity of water-line at both ends; *cf. f.-bowed.* **F. gear,** *see* GEAR. **F. head-room,** having a height of more than 6 feet, as in a 'tween deck space. **F.-rigged ship,** vessel with three or more masts, each rigged with its full complement of square sails. The term appears originally to have been adopted in distinguishing a vessel completely square-rigged on all three masts from those departing, about middle of last century, from that traditional arrangement by replacing the after, or mizzen, sails with the fore-and-aft rig, as in what was later called a *barque* (more recently, *bark*). **F. rudder,** maximum angle with the fore-and-aft line at which rudder may be swung; properly, it is the maximum *effective* angle for producing steering effect and is usually 35 degrees. Most vessels are fitted with *stops* or projecting lugs on rudder-stock or rudder-post, which prevent rudder from being turned in excess of *f.* effective angle. **F. poop,** *see* POOP. **F. sail,** vessel is under *f. sail* when spreading "every stitch of canvas to the breeze." **F. scantling ship,** in classification nomenclature, a vessel built to highest standard of structural strength of hull up to her uppermost continuous deck. Such vessels only are assigned the minimum freeboard prescribed. **F. speed,** *see* SPEED. **Keep her f.,** order to helmsman when sailing *close-hauled,* or *by the wind,* to keep sails drawing, or just far enough off the wind to avoid shaking canvas. **Rap f. or clean f.,** said of sails when completely filled with wind, especially when sailing moderately close to wind; also termed *smooth f.* in light winds.

FULMAR. (Ice. *fūll,* foul; *mar,* sea mew) A bird of the Arctic seas, abounding in extreme northern Atlantic waters; of the *petrel* family, similar in size and color to the herring gull, breeds in cliffs of the Orkneys, Shetlands, Iceland, etc., and feeds on fish and floating refuse; said to be particularly fond of whale blubber; much valued for its eggs, feathers, down, and an oil obtained from its stomach which has been a principal product of the lonely isle of St. Kilda off Scotland's west coast. Related species are found in Antarctic and northern Pacific waters and the **giant f.** of southern seas and U.S. Pacific coast, also called a *bone-breaker*, is an outstanding bird in that it attains the proportions of a small albatross.

FUMIGATION. Process of disinfecting ship's various compartments by means of a powerful gaseous agent as potassium cyanide, hydro-cyanic acid, sodium cyanide, etc., with objective of ridding vessel of vermin, especially rats, which are considered particularly noxious because of the plague-bacillus-carrying rat flea; *see* DERATIZATION.

FUNNEL. The smoke-stack of a steam or motor vessel. A metal cylinder fitted round a top-gallant or a royal mast, against which an eye of a stay and eyes of shrouds and backstays are nested. **Air-f.,** *see* AIR. **F.-casing,** *see* CASING. **F. marks,** those painted on ship's smokestacks for identification purposes, as emblems, flags, letters, etc., indicating attachment to a line, shipowner, division of a fleet, special class, etc. **F.-guys,** wire ropes or chains which stay ship's funnel in position; also termed *f.-shrouds, f.-stays.* **F.-paint,** special heat-resisting paint used for coating ship's funnel. **Ventilating-f.,** one into which several ducts are led for expulsion of vitiated air by either natural or forced draft.

FUNNY. Light, long and narrow racing skiff, rowed by one person.

FUR SEAL. *See* SEAL.

FURDEL or **FURDLE.** *See* FARDEL, old word for *furl.*

FURL. To roll up or gather a square sail to its yard and secure it with *gaskets* (small handy ropes kept in readiness on each yard) passed round sail and jack-stay, or round sail and yard in case of upper light canvas. The term was applied by square-rig sailors to taking in a square sail only; all others were *stowed.* A **harbor f.** signifies securing a sail to present a neat symmetrical appearance on its yard by rolling up bulk of canvas at middle of yard and tapering the mass toward each yard-arm, the whole carefully laid along topside of yard. Sometimes canvas covers were placed over the furled sails for keeping them clean and dry. An older term for this snug method, especially referring to a single topsail, was *furling in a body,* as distinguishing from *furling in the bunt,* or usual practice at sea of securing sail as it was handed in, or about evenly along yard. **Furling-line,** a sea-gasket; *see* LINE.

FURNACE. (L. *furnus,* oven) Inclosed part of a boiler in which heat is produced by fuel combustion. Where solid fuel, as coal, is used, that portion of furnace below the fire-grates is termed the *ash-pit.* **F.-bars,** fire-bars, or those making up a grate in a solid fuel *f.* **F. door,** *see* Boiler-furnace d. *in* DOOR. **F.-bridge,** or **fire-bridge,** iron plate supporting a bridge wall, or layers of fire-brick across back end of grate, forming a protection for back end of *f.* space and directing flow of heat and gases upward into combustion-chamber. **F.-crown,** upper portion or roof of a *boiler-f.* **F'd plate,** piece of plate forged to a desired shape, as required where a sharp curvature or special flanging is called for. **F.-man,** a shipyard employee who heats, forges, and fashions frames, plates, and other structural units in a vessel. **F.-slab,** bending-slab or bending-floor; *see* SLAB.

FURNITURE. As distinguished from permanent fixtures, or fittings, sails, rigging, ropes, tackles, stores, navigational instruments, flags, dunnage, tarpaulins awnings, and all reasonably necessary portable equipment for use in proper navigation of vessel and in safe carriage of cargo and/or passengers. Usually, *ship's f.*

FURRING. Strips or pieces of timber secured to inner faces of frames, beams, brackets, etc., to fair or line them up as a foundation for ceiling or sheathing. Act or process of planking a vessel with a double layer of timber; the material so used. Deposit from water on inside of a boiler.

FURROW. Long narrow depression in the sea floor extending in a direction approximately perpendicular to a coast-line. Also termed a *shelf-deep.* Such depressions are useful to a navigator when taking a line of soundings, the sudden increase and decrease of depth serving to indicate passage over the charted *furrow.*

FUR SEAL. *See* SEAL.

FUSIBLE PLUG. A boiler safety-plug; *see* PLUG. An electric wire fuse.

FUSION WELDING. Autogenous fusion welding; *see* WELDING.

FUSS. A boat or small vessel is said to *make a fuss* when laboring, in a seaway, causing much spray to fly over the bows, and generally "throwing her weight about" to an apparently unusual and unnecessary extent. This may be result of carrying too much sail or may indicate the craft has poor model lines for sailing in rough water.

FUTTOCK. (Corruption of *foot-hook*) In wood shipbuilding, curved parts or sections of transverse frames extending from *floor-timbers* at turn of bilge to meet *top-timbers;* a futtock-timber; *see* FRAME. **Double f.,** a cant-frame or port of a transverse frame which in effect forms both a first and second *f.* **F.-band,** iron hoop or band fitted round a lowermast a few feet below the top for securing lower ends of *f.-shrouds,* which, in effect, are extensions of topmast shrouds. Also called *f.-hoop, spider-band, f.-wye,* and, in earlier days when chain strops served same purpose, a *necklace*. **F. chains,** or **chain-plates,** looped irons or pieces of plate secured to each rim of a top and to which the lower dead-eyes of topmast shrouds are attached. Also called *f.-chains,* they usually are three in number, each being connected to a *f.-shroud*. **F.-hoop,** see **f.-band. F.-plank,** strake of plank ceiling next to keelson in a wooden ship; also, *limber-strake; buttock-strake*. **F.-plates,** same as *f.-chains*. **F.-shrouds,** usually of iron rods, are downward extensions of topmast shrouds, leading from rim of top to the *f.-band*. They stiffen the top in addition to taking stress of topmast rigging. Ratlines were fitted on them and their outward slant presented an interesting obstacle to the beginner as he scrambled aloft, if, unlike the earlier large ships, the top had no *lubber's hole,* or opening next the mast, through which he might crawl as a by-passing short cut. **F.-staff,** in old hemp rigging days, bar of wood or iron seized across lower shrouds abreast of the *f.-band* to which were secured the *cat-harpings,* or short ropes for bowsing in shrouds to allow play in swing of a lower yard for bracing sharp up (*see* **C.-harping** *in* CAT). Also, a similar staff sometimes was fitted in topmast shrouds, cat-harpings leading to lowermast cap, for same purpose. Cat-harpings themselves were also termed *f.-staves*. **F.-timbers,** those constituting the *f's* of ship's frames. **Navel f.,** one of the *f's* at greatest breadth of ship, or those of sharpest curvature; a midship *f*.

F.W. Fresh water load-line mark on ship's side at mid-length, indicating minimum freeboard allowed when floating in river or lake water considered as of density 1000 oz. or $62\frac{1}{2}$ lbs. per cubic foot; volume of 1 ton of 2240 lbs. being 35.84 cu. ft., 1 cubic meter or kiloliter (approx.), 269 U.S. gallons, or 1000 liters (approx.). *Fresh water* attains greatest density at temperature of 39° F. or 4° C; freezes at 32° F. or 0° C.; and 1 cu. ft. of solid ice weighs 57 lbs.

FYKE. (Du. *fuik,* a bow-net) Kind of fishing-net toward which fish are directed by a "leader," as a deflecting wall, fence, line of netting, etc.; used in rivers and sheltered waters.

G

G. Abbreviation in ships' log-books and meteorological records for *gloomy* appearance of weather; also for *ground swell*. International Code flag *G*, hoisted singly, signifies "I require a pilot." **G strake,** seventh line or strake of shell-plating from the keel.

GADGET. (*Slang, chiefly U.S.*) Any contrivance, device, or object; often used aboard ship to indicate something novel or not known by its proper name, and extended to such appellatives as *gilguy, gimmick, gilhickey, hootnany, thingumabob, thingimajig,* where specific terms for additional "gadgets" are lacking.

GADIDAE. (NL. *gadus,* cod) The family of fishes which includes several important genera widely used as food, as cod, haddock, pollack, tomcod, and coalfish.

GAGE. Same as *gauge; see* GAUGE.

GAFF. Spar which spreads the head or upper edge of a fore-and-aft sail as that on a mainsail of a schooner or sloop. Its outer end is the *peak;* its forward end, the *jaws, throat,* or *nock.* A *hoisting g.* is usually fitted with jaws, or two pieces of wood forming a crotch that embraces the mast; sometimes is hoisted along a T-bar fixed on after side of mast and fitted with a swinging arrangement obviating necessity of jaws. A *standing g.* such as is found on a square-rigged vessel's spanker, generally is rigged similarly to a derrick, being suspended by a topping-lift or span and hinged at mast in a gooseneck; such gaffs are fitted with *vangs,* or guys leading from deck to *peak.* A *g.* is also a staff having at one end a spear and a hook, used by fishermen in hauling in heavy fish, or as a *boat-hook.* To **bring to g.,** to haul in a large fish by hook and line to within reach of a *g.* **Fore g.,** spar which extends upper edge, or head, of a quadrilateral foresail. **G.-sail,** any four-sided sail the head of which is secured to a gaff and luff, or forward edge, secured to a mast. It may, or may not, be fitted with a *boom* for spreading its foot or lower edge. *Hoisting g.-sails* usually are secured full extent of their footropes (lower edges) to a boom; those of *standing-g.* type, which are brailed in to mast in stowing, are set by being slid or hauled out along g. by their hoops or hanks, in which case sail may be *boomless* and set by simply sheeting it home, or *loose-footed* and set by a *boom-outhaul* leading to boom end from clew of sail. Corners of this sail are named as follows: *tack,* next to mast, lower end; *nock* or *throat,* next to mast, aloft; *peak,* at outer end of *g.;* and *clew* at lower after end. The *luff* is side next to mast; *head,* secured to *g.; leech,* after side; and *foot,* bottom or lower edge. Excepting lighter racing-yachts, cloths run parallel with leech throughout and sail is reefed by taking in canvas along its foot. Narrow cloths running perpendicular to leech appears the favored style in yachts, probably because of a flatter set being obtained, notwithstanding the fact that sail will withstand more pressure of wind when made with cloths parallel to leech. **G.-setter,** a boat-hook. **G.-topsail,** a sail set above a *g.,* its luff being stretched to the topmast. In fore-and-aft rigs, the sail is usually jib-headed, hoisted nearly full height of topmast, is sheeted home to peak of gaff, and has a tack-rope leading to deck from its loose lower forward corner, or tack, always led over weather side of g. On some larger barques, the upper part of a divided spanker (aftermost lower sail) which necessarily was supplied with two *g's,* appropriated this term, and sometimes another and lighter sail was spread above upper *g.,* called a *g. top-gallant-sail.* The **g.-topsail catfish,** a sea catfish of U.S. Atlantic and Gulf of Mexico coasts and the **g.-topsail pompano** of West Indies and southern U.S. are so-called from their high dorsal fins. Both are of little value as food fishes. **G.-travelers,** rings or hanks attached to head of a sail spread by a standing *g.* They slide or travel either on *g.* itself, or along a railway or bar fixed to under side of the spar, when setting and brailing in sail. **G. trysail,** *see* **Spencer** *in* SAIL. **Landing-g.,** a fisherman's hooked staff or *g.* for bringing in a large fish drawn within reach by hook and line. **Mackerel-g.,** long-handled grains or spear having several light barbed prongs for *gaffing* mackerel as the fish pass a vessel or boat in schools. **Main g.**, spar spreading head of a fore-and-aft mainsail. **Monkey g.**, short standing spar, inclined upward as a *g.* fitted at or above the lower masthead for displaying the ensign at its peak while vessel is under way. (A power-driven vessel flies ensign at *stern* when not under way) **Railway g.**, a standing *g.* fitted on its under side with a *rail*, usually of H or I cross section, on which the *hanks* or *travelers* slide as sail is hailed out or brailed in. **Running g.**, a hoisting *g.*, or one to which sail is permanently bent and hoisting of which by its *throat* and *peak halyards* sets the sail, as is customary in the all fore-and-aft rig, excepting some smooth-water craft. **Spanker g.**, spar spreading the head of aftermost lower fore-and-aft sail in a square-rigged vessel or in a 3-masted or 4-masted schooner; may be either a *standing* or *hoisting g.* in the former; always a *hoisting g.* in latter. *See* SAIL. **Wishbone g.**, *see* WISHBONE RIG.

GAG. The *grouper* of southern U.S. coasts, West Indies, and Caribbean waters; considered an excellent food fish.

GAGALI. Former brig-rigged Turkish coasting vessel of about 150 tons burden, having a V-shaped counter and flush-decked.

GAIN. To arrive at, make, or reach in sailing; as, to *gain* the harbor. **Daily g.**, rate at which a chronometer or other time-piece regularly *gains,* or runs faster than normally intended, each 24 hours. To **g. on,** or **upon,** to advance nearer to, or lessen distance separating one vessel from another when both are steering the same, or nearly same, course. To **g. the wind,** to get to windward of another vessel when fore-reaching or tacking, as in racing.

GALACTIC. (Gr. *galaktikos,* milky) Pertaining to the *Galaxy* or *Milky Way,* that faintly luminous belt of nebulous masses and myriads of incomprehensibly distant stars appearing as cloudlike masses of light, interrupted in several places but generally following the trend of a great circle in the celestial sphere, or what is known as the **galactic circle. G. plane,** that of the galactic circle.

GALE. Wind varying in velocity from 35 to 56 nautical miles per hour, or 40 to 65 statute miles per hour, named, according to intensity, as *moderate, fresh, strong* or *whole* gale: *see* BEAUFORT SCALE. **Half a g.**, strong wind, or breeze of about 35 nautical miles per hour; a moderate gale. **Loom g.**, an old term for a breeze developing into a moderate gale. **Mackerel g.**, a breeze sufficient to ripple the water surface and thus render conditions favorable for catching mackerel. **Tail of a g.**, ending or diminution in velocity of a wind of gale force. **Top-gallant g.**, breeze in which a square-rigger can carry no loftier sail than top-gallant-sails; usually one of about 30 nautical miles per hour maximum.

GALEAS. Name for a small ketch- or yawl-rigged vessel of Baltic and Norwegian coasts. Also a variant of *galleass; see* GALLEASS.

GALEON. Old term for any high-sided vessel furnished with three or more batteries of cannon. A two-masted lug-rigged fishing-vessel common to north coast of Spain.

GALIOT. Former trading vessel apparently of Flemish origin used until recently on coasts of Holland, France, and Germany for past three centuries. Typical *g.* was beamy, broad-sterned, and bluff-bowed with kind of clipper stem and long jib-boom; carried lee-boards, was flat-bottomed and low in the waist. Rigged like a brigantine, spread about four-fifths her sail from the forward mast, including three jibs and a large brailing-in gaff sail, with a small mizzen, sometimes topped by a gaff-topsail, on her after mast. The now passed wooden-built *g.* carried a load of about 150 tons; the few recently made of steel about 200 tons, and greatly simplified in sail-rig. A small, swift galley, or *galiote,* driven by both oars and sails, having one mast and pulling about 20 oars; used in Mediterranean waters from 16th to 18th centuries. Also, *galliot.*

GALL. To fret, chafe, or wear away by friction, as a chain in rubbing against a spar, etc. **Weather-gall,** or **gaw; wind-gall** or **gaw;** a secondary or fragmentary rainbow, said to presage windy rainy weather; a sun-dog; also, *water-gall.*

GALLANT. (It. *gala,* ornament) Archaic term for any flag or streamer displayed from the mizzenmast.

GALLEASS. (It. *galeazza*) Large fast Mediterranean galley originally of Venetian 15th-century use, propelled by three lateen sails and 30 to 40 oars; built without sheer, had raised fighting structures at each end, and a straight pointed prow or ram above water. Those of 16th and 17th centuries mounted as many as 20 cannon in broadside. Also, *galeas; gallias.*

GALLEON. (Sp. *galeon*) Heavily built Spanish merchantman or naval ship, or both combined, dating from 15th century to early 1700's. Early vessels of this apparently clumsy type were characterized by a heavy sheer with elaborately fortified forecastle and poop; had three masts with square sails on fore and main and a single lateen sail on the mizzen; also, a small square sail set from a pole mounted on a high-rising bowsprit. Later *galleons* carried three decks of guns, were of increased length with extraordinary extent of quarter-deck, or poop, terminating in a high ornately designed quarter gallery; had four masts, both after ones lateen-rigged; displayed numbers of streamers and banners; painted large crosses and other spectacular emblems on their larger sails; and, as has been said, "did present in general an awe-inspiring, if not a terrifying, appearance." Of note is the fact that jibs or triangular staysails were unknown to these vessels, a single small square sail only being set from the spar corresponding to our present jib-boom. The *g's* were noted for their treasure-carrying role following the Spaniards' subjugation of Central and South America in the 16th century. Also called a *carack* or *carrack*, they formed the backbone of the unfortunate *Invincible Armada*, comprised of some 130 vessels, sent by *Philip II* of Spain against England July, 1588.

GALLERY. Also called *balcony*, a railed platform projecting from each quarter or around the stern of old-time ships, as *quarter g.* and *stern g.* Also, formerly a small structure on each quarter containing lavatory conveniences. Stern *galleries* often partook of the elaborately decorative character of the whole after portion in the Spanish galleon of the 16th and 17th centuries, the French and English ships of the line in 17th and 18th century use, and, though diminished in splendor and reduced to a simple balcony or walk, were found on British warships as recently as 1910.

GALLEY. The *galea* of the ancient Greeks and Romans; still the name given to a large boat propelled by oars, *e.g.*, the *captain's g.* of a warship, or one used by government officials, as customs officers, in visiting ships in harbor; also, a large pleasure or sight-seeing craft. War galleys appear in history as early as 7th century B.C. and were prominent in wars of Medo-Persia, the Greeks, and Romans. Earliest had a single bank of oars and carried one mast with square sail. The Greeks seem to have developed such powerful craft as the *bireme, trireme,* and *quadrireme,* or those of two, three, and four banks of oars, respectively, subsequent to stretching the single *triaconter,* or one pulling 30 oars, to the *penteconter,* or 50-oared vessel. However, it is believed that the number of banks rarely exceeded three, ancient depictions of galleys having more than these obviously being exaggerations with the view of parading the prowess of navy concerned. Phœnician, Greek, and early Roman *g's* developed into formidable fighting units with addition of full decks, towers, rams, and catapults; and the commercial *g.* had been brought to a vessel of great importance at time of decline of the Roman Empire. Subsequently much of the highly fortified upper works disappeared from the craft and we find in the Venetians' *g.* of the Middle Ages a long speedy ship having three masts with lateen sails and a single bank of about 50 oars. This was a typical *g.* of both fighting and commercial pattern which continued in use in the Mediterranean till late in the 17th century and may still be considered as not entirely obsolete, being represented by the *felucca* and boats of similar model. The labor of rowing was from an early date assigned to mercenaries, afterwards to slaves, prisoners of war, and finally to condemned criminals. The types *galleon, galiot, galleass, half-galley, quarter-galley,* and *foist* appear as developments or modifications of the medieval *g.;* a description of an engagement, dated 1544, mentions participating craft as "galleys, foystes, and galyasses." The *g.* is a cook-room or kitchen, of which there may be one or more in modern vessels; also, the range or stove with its appurtenances for cooking is sometimes called by that name. A deck-house used for cooking on small vessels is often called a *caboose.* **G.-dresser,** a cook's work-table. **G. funnel,** metal chimney or stove-pipe for carrying off smoke from a *g.* range or stove; in U.S. ships it is termed the *Charlie Noble.* **G.-gun,** a culverin or similar early cannon; *see* CULVERIN. **G.-man,** one who rows in, or is in charge of, a *g.;* formerly, one who landed merchandise from a *g.* in London. **G.-news,** idle report, such as emanates from the culinary staff. **G.-packet,** imaginary boat which has arrived with latest gossip; hence, source of valuable information regarding ship's destination, length of voyage, change in officers, etc. **G.-pepper,** soot or ash mixed with, or deposited on, food served to the crew. **G. punt,** now obsolete open boat having one mast and lug sail, 20 to 25 feet in length, once peculiar to the Downs (England) where many of the craft were always busy as tenders for the many ships at anchor, or lying-to, in that much frequented area; rated a little inferior to the *Deal galley,* its partner and contemporary; *see* DEAL GALLEY. **G. range,** cooking-stove on board ship; to-day uses coal, petroleum, or electricity as fuel. **G.-slave,** a convict sentenced to labor at a *g.* oar; a slave similarly pressed into service. **G.-stoker,** term of contempt for an idling or shirking crew member. **G.-stroke,** descriptive of a method of rowing with a heavy oar or sweep, as in the *g's,* in which rower rises and steps forward with oar in the recovery stroke, then falls back with his weight in completing the pulling stroke. **G.-yarn,** a far-fetched tale, such as often is "spun" around the *g.* fire. **Mid-g.,** old colloquial term for amidships, or waist of the vessel. **Quarter-g.,** type of *g.* formerly much used on Barbary Coast, of inferior armament to a *half-g., g., galleass,* etc.

GALLEY FOIST. A state barge; *esp.* that officially used by the Lord Mayor of London in 16th and 17th centuries.

GALLIAS. *See* GALLEAS.

GALLIVAT. Former swift East Indian vessel driven by sails and oars; especially one of 50 to 70 tons burden, armed and used by Malay pirates.

GALLOWS. Also termed *gallows bitts,* stout timber frame consisting of two uprights and a surmounting cross-piece (*g's top*), formerly fitted as one of two or more supports for spare yards, topmasts, booms, etc., stowed fore-and-aft on the weather deck. In modern use, a similar arrangement, usually referred to as the "skids," on which boats, spars, and spare gear are stowed. Also a cross timber set on uprights of bar iron used as a rest or support for ends of booms or derricks where such are stowed in a horizontal position; a *g's-frame*.

GALOFARO. *See* CHARYBDIS.

GALTON'S ANTICYCLONIC LAW. *See* LAW.

GALVANIC ACTION. *See* ELECTROLYSIS.

GALVANIZED. Said of iron or steel fittings, such as chains, bolts, shackles, wire rope, ventilators, guard-casings, awning stanchions, and hand-rails, which are covered by a thin coating of zinc as protection against corrosion by one of several processes known as *galvanizing,* including *dipping, sheradizing, electro-plating.* Due to high temperatures to which material is exposed in the coating process—800 to 850 degrees Fahrenheit—tensile strength of wire, shackles, chain, etc., suffers a reduction of about ten per centum. Also, *galvanised.*

GALVANOMETER. Named for *Prof. Galvani (1737–1798),* Italian discoverer of dynamical or current electricity, apparatus or instrument for detecting presence and direction of an electric current, and also its intensity, by the deflections of a magnetic needle. Of several forms of the instrument, that for use on board ship, the *marine g.,* is so constructed as to be unaffected by a vessel's motion and is protected by a magnetic screen, which usually is a soft iron case or box.

GAM. A herd or school of whales. Among whalers, a visit paid by officers of one or more vessels to those of another while at sea; process of communication in a social sense by crew members of meeting ships, or *gamming. Cf.* FOY. *Gamming* in older whalers' usage also referred to the act of two vessels "lying to" for "speaking" or communication, the maneuver involving a point of etiquette in trim of the yards (they usually were barque-rigged), in which the weather vessel braced her main yards aback, while lee vessel backed her fore yards. To pay a visit to; to gather together, as whales. **Gamming-chair,** a kind of box-shaped seat in which a lady included in a *g.*—usually a master's wife—was hoisted from and lowered into a visiting boat. *Cf.* MAMMY-CHAIR.

GAMMON. To permanently fasten the bowsprit in place by a lashing, iron band, or other means of securing it to the stem. The chain or rope lashing for this purpose in former days was called the *gammoning,* and, together with the bobstays and bowsprit shrouds, which, respectively, led from bowsprit end downward to vessel's stem and laterally to each bow formed the necessarily heavy strengthening against stress on head stays set up by pressure of sail or pitching in a seaway. First operation in rigging a ship was that of securing the bowsprit by "passing the gammoning." In later iron ships, the *gammoning* was simplified to a vertical plate which was se-

cured to a pair of forward frames and formed the fore end of top-gallant forecastle. Bowsprit passed through this plate and was collared and riveted thereto. **G'g fashion,** according to method of *gammoning* the bowsprit: forward turn passing over spar, thence through after end of *gammoning-hole;* thence close up to forward turn, etc.; thus working aft on bowsprit and forward in *g'g-hole,* each turn crossing its next in order on either side of bowsprit. In this way, the main strength of lashing is concentrated gradually towards the middle turns. **G'g-fish,** protective batten laid on the bowsprit to take wear and tear of a chain *g'g.* **G'g-hole,** opening in the knee at upper end of stem through which the *g'g* was passed. **G.-iron,** an iron band laid over the bowsprit and bolted down to stem in lieu of the older *g.-lashing.* **G.-knee,** crooked or knee-timber bolted against stem in the fore-and-aft line; the *g'g-hole* was cut in this timber. **G.-lashing,** the old *g'g,* consisting of a number of turns of about 1/2-inch close-link chain or a 4-inch tarred hemp rope. **G.-plate,** in lieu of the *g'g hole,* iron plate fastened to stem for securing *g'g* shackles or bolts for the *g.-iron.*

GANG. Band or group of men engaged in, or detailed to perform, some particular work; as, a *stevedore's gang.* An outfit or full complement of implements or articles; as, a *g. of oars;* a *g. of holystones.* **Black g.,** on a coal-burning vessel, the firemen and coal-passers or trimmers. Generally, entire personnel of engine partment. **Chain g.,** group of laborers in a shipyard whose duties chiefly comprise the heavier manual work, such as moving structural steel and timbers, clearing away waste material, etc. **Deck g.,** seamen constituting the deck department of a vessel's crew; "deckies" of the Navy, as distinguished from the *black g.,* or enlisted men in the engineering force. Also, that section of longshoremen whose duties are confined to deck work or that outside of the holds; includes winchmen, drum-end men, hatch tenders, gangway men, and those slinging or landing cargo on pier, lighter, etc. **Gunner's g.,** *see* GUNNER. **Hold g.,** section of cargo-workers detailed to break out and sling cargo in discharging, or to stow the goods in loading, a vessel's hold cargo. **Press g.,** *see* PRESS.

GANGBOARD. Formerly, a raised wall extending from quarter-deck to forecastle in deep-waisted ships, used as a defence against boarders, as a passage walk, and by sentinels. A gangway or gangplank.

GANG-CASK. As once used to bring off water in ship's boats, a stout cask of about 30 gallons' capacity. A handy fresh-water barrel or cask, such as is kept on a small vessel's deck. *Cf.* CASK.

GANGING. (Pron. *gahnjing*) A snell, or short length of wire or catgut attached to a fishing-hook as an extension to and a protection for the line against being severed by fish's teeth, as in catching sharks. To "gange" (*gahnj*) a hook is to provide it with such protection.

GANGER. Any handy length of chain or rope used to haul a heavy line, cable, anchor, etc., into a required position for making fast. Short length of chain attached to an anchor as a protective extension to a fiber cable. Short wire or chain dropped with a laid-out anchor and buoyed for subsequent connection to a hawser. *Cf.* **F'ganger** *in* FORE. (Pron. *gang'-er*)

GANGSPILL or **GANGSPIEL.** (Ger. *gangspill*, capstan) An old term for an anchor windlass.

GANG-PLANK. Portable platform or passage-way forming a bridge between ship and pier, landing-stage, another vessel, etc., for persons entering or leaving vessel; a *gangway*.

GANGWAY. Opening in the rail or bulwarks or rail for passage of persons or cargo. An alleyway or passage from one part of ship to another. A gang-plank or gangboard. Word of warning or request to make way for a working-party, a senior officer, passengers, etc. Main deck space between bulwarks and sides of a deck-house; area of deck in the waist between hatches and rail or bulwarks. An 18th century definition states that the gangway is "side of the main deck from mainmast to entrance of poop." To **bring to the g.,** in 18th century naval usage, to flog an offender at the g.—the customary site at which such punishment was inflicted. **G. door,** removable or hinged portion of a weather deck bulwark or rail for passage of persons via the g. or to facilitate landing or loading cargo. **G. ladder,** *see* ACCOMMODATION. **G.-man,** a seaman stationed at a g. entrance for safety supervision or preventing unauthorized persons from boarding; a cargo-worker who attends to passage of the slings to and from ship, chiefly in directing winchmen in the operation of hoisting and lowering as required. **G. port,** a door in ship's side leading to a lower deck for same purpose as a g. *door*. To **grease the g.** for a particular crew-member means to slate the man for early discharge.

GANNET. (A.S., *ganot*, sea-fowl) Any of several large web-footed birds constituting the genus *Sula*. Native chiefly to the North Atlantic, particularly around Scotland and in northeastern American waters, the common g. (*Sula bassana*), also called *solan goose,* breeds in colonies on rocky cliffs, is an expert swimmer and diver in following its habit of diligently preying upon almost any sort of fish. It is mostly white in color, similar in appearance to the common goose, excepting its longer tail feathers and bill, and attains a wing-spread of 5 to 6 feet. The birds are said to be diminishing fast in numbers. Allied genera are found in the Southern Hemisphere and a smaller darker species of warmer latitudes is called the *booby-g.*

GANTLINE. Handy-sized rope—usually 2 to 2½-inch manila—rove in a single block aloft, on a bowsprit end, etc., for hoisting or lowering objects, or suspending a man in a boatswain's chair as in painting or tarring down; also termed *girtline*. **Dummy-g.,** length of old or small rope, such as a piece of ratline stuff, kept rove in a *g.-block* as a means of reeving off a working *g.* without sending a man aloft; *cf.* DUMMY. To **strip to a g.,** *see* STRIP.

GANTRY. An overhead cross-girder structure on which a traveling crane is mounted or from which one or more heavy traveling purchases are suspended. Supporting towers at each end of girder rest on wheels and the whole is moved as required on a railway. Such bridge-like hoisting equipment spanning a building-slip commonly is used in important shipyards. Also, *gauntry, gantree.*

GAR. (A.S. *gar*, spear) A widely distributed fish having a much elongated body and long narrow jaws; also known as *gar pike, bill-fish, needle-fish, sea-needle, longnosed gar, shortnosed gar, hornfish,* and *greenbone.* Those of marine habitat, unlike the fresh-water *gars* in general, are good food fishes, *esp.* those of the family *Belonidæ* found in European, Australian, and Central American waters. **Alligator g.,** largest species known, attains length of 10 feet; so-called from its size and shape of head; found in rivers and sheltered waters of southern U.S., Cuba, and Mexico.

GARBAGE. **G.-chute,** *see* CHUTE. **G.-scow,** *see* **D.-barge** *in* DUMP.

GARBLING. Process of separating, in a consignment of cargo, damaged or inferior goods from those in good order, in view of possible non-payment or reduction of customs duty; particularly applies to spices, drugs, tobacco, etc. *Garblings* are residue goods after separation from those in satisfactory condition.

GARBOARD. **G.-plank; g.-plate;** on a vessel's bottom, plank laid next to keel, or, in steel construction, plate secured to a bar-keel or a flat-plate keel, the line of planking or plating thus placed constituting the **garboard strake.** In larger steel ships, thickness of this strake is from one-tenth to one-eighth inch greater than ordinary shell-plating. It is usually named "*A*" *strake,* or first in order of shell-plating strakes; also termed *ground strake.* 17th century forms were *garbord* and *garble.*

GARE. (Fr. *garer,* to shunt) A jetty, pier, or cut-out on side of a canal or narrow river. To **g. ship, a** British navy expression meaning to make fast at an appropriate place on a canal to allow another vessel to pass, as in the Suez Canal.

GARFISH. *See* GAR. A *girrock.*

GARLAND. Old term for a rope grommet laid round a spar, rail, shrouds at a masthead, or elsewhere, as a protection against chafing or wear by running gear. In 17th century usage it appears as a ring or grommet of rope placed over the eyes of shrouds on a mast and, also, as a confining ring of rope, wood, or iron for cannon-shot placed near the guns. Later, the term was used for a bag made of netting in which provisions were carried or hoisted aboard. Generally, in seamanship use, a *g.* is a large selvagee strop or grommet made for a special purpose, and in a **g. lashing,** such strop is secured to a spar by several turns of rope in order to spread surface under stress, as in hoisting and stepping a lowermast when rigging a ship. Of interest is an old naval custom in which a *g.* consisting of three connected hoops or grommets decorated with silks and ribbons was hoisted on the main top-gallant stay in celebration of the captain's wedding-day, while a seaman's nuptials were noted by a similar wreath displayed from the lower masthead nearest his station for duty. **Shot-g.,** receptacle for cannon-shot placed between guns or alongside a hatch-coaming. Originally it was a simple ring or grommet of rope; later, a plank or timber with appropriate cavities for holding the shot.

GARNET. Probably the oldest form of tackle-purchase used on board ship. Consisting of two single blocks, it was used chiefly in halyards, braces, and sheets. As sails were increased in size, the lower main canvas was *"embrayled by fyrst halinge ye clue-garnet,"* lower block of which was attached to clew of such sail—a practice still in vogue on our few square-riggers remaining. The *gun-tackle,* so much in use in the old cannon days, is a good example of the original *g.;* and, as a general handy hoisting purchase, no other rig has been brought into more popular use.

GARNISH-BOLT. *See* BOLT.

GAR PIKE. A garfish; *see* GAR.

GARR. Slimy fungus growth on a ship's bottom.

GARVEY. Open scow-shaped boat propelled by motor, sail, or oars, used by oyster fishermen in Delaware Bay and on New Jersey coast. (*Local U.S. word*)

GARVIE HERRING. British name for the *sprat,* or small herring of the North Sea and Baltic.

GAS. Principal use on board ship is that of CO_2 or *carbon dioxide,* as a refrigerant or a fire-smothering agent; *see* CARBON DIOXIDE and **F.-extinguisher; F.-smothering system** *in* FIRE. Acetylene *g.* was once a fair substitute in deck and hatchway illuminating for the later electric lighting installed in steamers. This was generated as required by adding water to a quantity of calcium carbide confined in a suitable receptacle from which the *g.* was supplied to each jet by small rubber hose or tubing. Under pressure the gas is used in combination with oxygen, or in the oxyacetylene process, in *g.-weld-*

ing; also as an illuminant in *g. buoys* and *lighthouses,* and is the *g.* generated in the canister attached to a so-called *luminous life-buoy.* **Petroleum g.,** or that given off by fuel oil or an oil cargo necessarily must be protected from contact with sparks or flame. This is done by providing vents fitted with flame-arresters and leading to open air from each compartment occupied with fuel or cargo, and approved ventilation of pump-rooms or other spaces where sources of vapor ignition are normally present. This *g.* is particularly dangerous in that its presence may be undetected in places remote from circulation of air. To quote an instance: Subsequent to discharge of a consignment of kerosene in cases, ship's carpenter removed limber-boards to observe condition of bilges, using a common lantern; in the ensuing explosion, the man was blown upward through and with the hatch-covers into the deck next above, minus half his clothing. **G.-check,** an appliance for preventing escape of *g.* at breech of a heavy gun. **G.-devourer,** arrangement whereby cargo-lines and tanks of an oil-carrier are cleared of *g.* after cargo has been discharged. A powerful steam jet is blown from mouth of discharging line (on deck), thus causing a strong current of air to pass through each emptied tank and consequent expulsion of *g.* to open air. Properly carried out, the method also expels all drainage or liquid remaining in the pipe-lines. **G. engine,** *see* ENGINE. **G.-free,** said of an emptied tank, system of tanks, or a pipe-line used for carrying any liquid giving off poisonous or inflammable vapors, when entirely cleared of such danger. Before entry of persons or making repairs to an oil-carrier's tentatively gas-freed tanks, it is universal custom, if not always according to law, to obtain a **gas-free certificate** from an authorized chemist who has determined *g.* content of air in tank or tanks in question, stating that it is safe to enter or carry out repairs, or otherwise. **G.-outlet,** one or more pipes carried to a reasonable height above the weather deck for conveying *g.* from tops of tanks in an oil-carrying vessel; generally a number of tanks are thus serviced by one *g.-line.* **G. storage,** process by which refrigerated cargo is carried in *g.-tight* compartments. Chilled cargo, as meats at 28 to 30 degrees *Fahr.,* is carried satisfactorily therein on lengthy voyages because of control of both composition of the air and temperature, thus obviating necessity of low temperatures for successful carriage, as in frozen cargo of 10 to 15 degrees. **G. welding,** process of joining metals by fusion of faying parts through application of intense heat generated by a *g.* in state of combustion. Most commonly used is *oxyacetylene* flame produced by a mixture of oxygen and acetylene *gases.*

GASKET. Any small line, canvas strapping, sennit, etc., for securing a sail to its yard, boom or gaff in furling or stowing; also *gassit.* Strip of rubber or sennit set in or near the edges of a door or hatch-cover for bearing against the jamb or coaming edge in producing water-tightness. Any packing-piece of rubber, leather, soft metal, sennit, etc., placed between landing surfaces for water-, oil-, or steam-tightness; as between flanges of pipe, a cylinder and its cover, a tank-top and a manhole-cover, etc. **Bunt g.,** *see* BUNT. **Harbor g.,** fancy line, canvas strips, etc., used as a *g.* for neat appearance in port. **Quarter g.,** one that is placed about half-way between the bunt and yard-arm for making a sail fast. **Sea g.,** any ordinary rope used to make fast sail, as opposed to a *harbor g.;* a furling-line. **Yard-arm g.,** one that is fixed at a yard-arm for securing sail.

GASPEREAU. (Fr. *gasparot*) A Canadian name for the alewife, a fish of the herring family; *cf.* ALEWIFE.

G.A.T. Navigators' abbreviation for *Greenwich Apparent Time;* that indicated by the true sun at the Prime Meridian. Reckoned from midnight to midnight, 0 hours to 24 hours of each day, it is equal to 12 hours *minus* the true sun's easterly hour angle or 12 hours *plus* true sun's westerly hour angle (time from noon) from upper transit of that body, *i.e.,* apparent noon; thus, two hours before apparent sun arrives at the meridian of Greenwich, G.A.T. is 10 hrs. 00 min. 00 sec.; while two hours after that event becomes 14 hrs. 00 min. 00 sec. *Cf.* TIME.

GAT. (*Du.*) A channel, narrow passage, or opening in a sea-coast, as between sand dunes, through a reef or bar, etc. Also, *gut, gate.*

GATA. (Sp. fem. form of *gato,* cat) Kind of shark found in West Indies waters; attains a length of 7 feet.

GATE. Entrance to a canal-lock or dock-basin, usually in the form of two heavy doors swung to meet each other when in closed position; a *lock-gate.* A hinged iron band securing in position the heel of a top-gallant mast or a light topmast. A semicircular metal band fitted to a boat's thwart for securing a mast in the stepped position. **Tail-g.,** lower level entrance to a canal-lock. **Tide-g.,** one that permits flow of water into a dock or basin during higher stages of tide.

GATE-VALVE. *See* VALVE.

GATEWAY. Passage for vessels through an opened section of a protective submarine net, a harbor-boom, etc. Any narrow waterway, channel, port entrance, etc., used for navigation.

GATEWOOD SYSTEM. Modification of the *Isherwood,* or longitudinal, method of framing used in shipbuilding; *see* FRAME.

GATHER. To haul or take in, as the slack of a rope or sail; to collect or accumulate, as, *ship is gathering barnacles.* To **g. way,** to begin moving, or to increase motion in an ahead or astern direction. **G'g lines,** those sometimes rigged from a fore-and-aft sail's double topping-lifts to its boom as a means of confining sail to the latter when lowered, as a two-masted schooner's mainsail.

GAUGE. (O.F. *gauge,* measuring rod) Also *gage,* a measure, or standard scale for measuring capacity, dimension, distance, or weight. Any instrument or apparatus used for measuring or *gauging.* To estimate, measure, or compare with a particular standard of reference; as, to *g.* contents of a tank; to *g.* a distance; to *g.* wind velocity. A vessel is said to have the *weather g.* or *lee g.* according to her relative position with respect to wind direction and another vessel, referring, respectively, to windward and lee vessel when sailing together on same course, as in racing or in a chase. In older usage, extreme draft of a ship was referred to as her *g.* in considering passage into a dock, over a bar, or accommodating depth in harbor. **Altitude g.,** any of several instruments that register or indicate height of surface of a liquid in a tank or other receptacle. **Baumé g.,** either of two hydrometers conforming to scales adopted by *Antoine Baumé,* a French chemist (*1728–1804*); one for liquids heavier than water sinks to 0° in pure water and 15° in a 15% salt solution; the other for liquids lighter than water sinks to 0° in a 10% salt solution and to 10° in pure water. Graduations on each are of equal length, as compared with the shortening intervals as density increases by the *Specific Gravity* scale. A close approximation to corresponding value of *Sp. Grav.* for a given *Baumé* reading in liquids heavier than water is found by the formula: $Sp. Gr. = 144 \div (144 - Baumé)$; and for liquids lighter than water: $Sp. Gr. = 144 \div (134 + Baumé)$. Slightly modified by the American Petroleum Institute scale, *Baumé g.* is general standard for measuring density of petroleum products. **Bourdon g.,** named for its inventor, one that indicates pressure of steam, gas, etc., by effect of disturbing curvature of a small tube of oval section; tube is open to the substance at one end and sealed at the other, variations of pressure being registered by a device which moves an indicator by the changing position of tube's blind end. The *g.* is in common use on boilers, pressure lines, etc. **Control g's,** *see* CONTROL. **Depth g.,** general term for an instrument made to indicate depth of water; especially, one in which sea depths are indicated by pressure of water against a spring, or by degree of compression of air in a tube. **Draft g.,** *see* MANOMETER. **G. glass,** tube of glass fitted vertically outside a boiler, tank, etc., to indicate the surface level of contained liquid. **G.-pipe,** tube through which water, steam, etc., is conveyed to a *pressure-g.* **G. pressure,** generally understood as that above atmospheric pressure. Common steam *g's* show such pressure only. **Jacket g.,** *see* JACKET. **Pneumercator g.,** device by which depth or quantity of water, oil, etc., depth of water in a dock, or draft of a vessel is indicated on a graduated scale placed at any convenient location. Essentially it consists of a submerged *balance-chamber* in which air is entrapped by, and in consequence subjected to pressure of, surrounding liquid; a tube leading from chamber allows air thus under pressure to act upon a column of mercury, which in turn rises to a height corresponding to pressure of actual head of liquid present, thus indicating depth or quantity, according to denomination used in calibrating scale. **Rain g.,** instrument for measuring vertical column of rain-fall (usually expressed in inches) during a certain period of time. **Sea-g.,** *see* SEA. **Staff g.,** a rod of wood or metal, appropriately graduated, used for measuring internal depth of barrels, tanks, etc., or depth of liquid contained therein. **Tank g.,** an ullage-rod or line; *see* TANK. **Tide g.,** vertical graduated staff or board conveniently situated for indicating height of tide at any hour; also, an apparatus for continuously recording times and heights of tide or variations in sea level. **Wind g.,** *see* WIND.

GAUSSIN ERROR. (Also *Gaussian e.;* named for *Karl F. Gauss, German scientist, 1777–1855*) As observed on a sharp change of course, a temporary component of deviation caused by magnetism induced by earth's magnetic field in soft iron during a period in which vessel lies in one direction only. *Esp.* in the old iron ships, this error often amounted to 8 or 10 degrees upon a broad change of course after steering in an easterly or westerly direction for some days, as, *e.g.,* in an eastbound trans-Atlantic vessel upon hauling up through Straits of Dover. Its amount and subsiding period normally were constant on such passages in individual ships, found by observation, and allowed for. The rule for *Gaussin error* effect is that it *always carries vessel toward direction of her last course;* the eastbound vessel in example, accordingly, being required to allow for an *easterly* error or deviation.

GAY. Early or bright part of a day; midday or morning; as in *"all sail was set in the gay of the day."* An Annamese prefix in names of different fishing and trading sailing craft on coast of Indo-China; as, *gay-you, gay-diang, gay-bao, gay-ro.*

G.C.T. *Greenwich Civil Time;* mean solar time of the meridian passing through *Greenwich Observatory* (London, England), or *prime meridian,* from which terrestrial longitude is reckoned. Ephemerides of heavenly bodies are given in the *Nautical Almanac* for this time, also known as *Greenwich Mean Time,* and by some astronomers as *Universal Time.* It is reckoned from midnight to midnight, or 0 hours to 24 hours, of each day. *See* TIME.

GEAR. In a collective sense, tackles, various ropes, blocks, etc., constituting working equipment for sailing, working cargo, or other shipboard operation. Any composite piece of mechanism for a specific use; as, *steering-gear; boat-davit gear.* A cog or toothed wheel, as for transferring power in a winch. Personal clothing, tools, and accoutrement, collectively; as, a *sailor's gear.* **Boat g.,** equipment carried in a boat; especially, that required by law for a lifeboat, including bread, drinking-water, compass, distress lights, mast and sail, painter, and spare oars. **Disengaging g.,** means of simultaneously freeing both tackle blocks from a boat immediately before or upon boat being water-borne; also termed *releasing-g.* **Forward g.,** as opposed to *backward g.,* set of valve-motion to drive engine for going ahead; chiefly applied to a reciprocating engine. **Full g.,** affording greatest play in a given direction: *full forward g.; full backward g.* **Geared drive,** *see* DRIVE. **Geared engine,** *see* ENGINE. **Hand g.,** any *g.* operated by hand as a substitute for mechanism normally operating, as in a steam *steering-g.* system. **Head g.,** rigging of bowsprit and jib-boom, jib-sheets, jib-downhauls, and other equipment forward of vessel's foremast. **Herring-bone g.,** cog-wheels having teeth of V-shaped form, instead of straight across face of wheel. **Hoisting-g.,** *see* HOISTING. **Married g.,** *see* MARRY. **Mess g.,** *see* MESS. **Mid-g.,** neutral position, or that in which no valve motion, and hence no engine motion, takes place; said of a reciprocating engine. **Otter g.,** that by which paravanes are towed, taken in, or set; *see* PARAVANE. **Out of g.,** not in working or running order; not in condition for use; short of necessary equipment. **Pneumatic steering-g.,** *see* STEERING. **Pursing-g.,** that by which a purse-seine is closed in capturing fish. **Quick-closing g.,** referred to control of bulkhead doors, apparatus for closing all from ship's bridge at a moment's notice. **Reduction g.,** arrangement whereby suitable rotating speed of propeller is obtained by reduction of a high speed engine's (usually turbine) shaft speed. Reduction may be in a single stage or step, up to 20 to 1 ratio; or, as is usual, in two stages, up to 40 to 1 ratio. **Roller g.,** any of various labor-saving devices for stowing by rolling up a fore-and-aft sail in small craft. Gaff sails are reefed by rolling the boom window-shade fashion to take in canvas as required; *see* CUNNINGHAM PATENT REEF. **Running g.,** as distinguished from *standing rigging, running rigging,* or all ropes and tackle used in handling sail. **Skylight g.,** arrangement by which skylight covers, as those above an engine-room or cabin, may be raised or lowered by a hand-wheel. **Steam steering-g.,** *see* STEAM. **Steam reversing g.,** *see* STEAM. **Steering-g.,** *see* STEERING. **Spar and boom g.,** *see* SPAR. **Wash-deck g.,** hose, scrubbers, buckets, holystones, swabs, etc., used in washing decks.

GEMINI. (L. = *twins*) A northern zodiacal constellation containing the navigational stars Castor (α *Geminorum*) and Pollux (β *Geminorum*), of magnitude 1.6 and 1.2 respectively. Castor lies north of and is nearly 4° distant from its mate; *see* CASTOR *and* POLLUX.

GENERAL. Combining term connoting quality of being common, broadly applicable, or universal. **G. average,** often shortened to G/A in marine insurance field; *see* AVERAGE. **G. average contribution,** proportionate deposit or contribution by ship, cargo, or freight, toward cost of loss incurred for the common safety; abbreviated G/A Cont. or G/A Dep.; *see* AVERAGE. **G. cargo,** *see* CARGO. **G. quarters,** *see* QUARTERS. **G. refrigerated ship,** *see* SHIP. **G. ship,** one carrying cargo for account of any number of shippers, as distinguished from a vessel hired or chartered by a particular party.

GENERATOR. Machine for producing electrical energy. Aboard ship for lighting purposes, auxiliary or propeller drive current, may be either *direct* or *alternating*.

GENOA JIB. *See* JIB.

GENTLE BREEZE. *See* BEAUFORT SCALE.

GEOCENTRIC. In astronomy, relating to, or having the earth as a center; pertaining to, or measured from, earth's center; as, *geocentric ephemerides* of planets. **G. latitude** and **longitude** of a celestial body or point defines such position as would be observed from center of the earth. **G. latitude** of a place; *see* LATITUDE. **G. parallax,** *see* PARALLAX.

GEOGRAPHICAL MILE. *See* MILE.

GEO-NAVIGATION. As distinguished from *celo-navigation,* or determining ship's position and checking course by observations of heavenly bodies, navigation performed by piloting, compass or radio bearings of terrestrial objects, soundings, radar, or dead reckoning.

GEORDIE. In British usage, a collier; *esp.* one of the many engaged in the Tyne-London coal trade. For many years the name was given vessels constituting a fleet of bluff-bowed, capacious brigs engaged in supplying London with "coals" from Newcastle and other east coast ports of Britain until about 1860 when the vessels gave way to their fast-growing steam competitors. A Tyneside native is referred to as a *Geordie*.

GERMANISCHER LLOYD. German classification society established in 1867; *see* CLASSIFICATION.

GET IN, OFF, etc., To. To **get in,** to make, or arrive at, a port or destination. To **get in with,** to draw near to or to join; as, *we got in with the convoy off the Cape.* To **get off,** to draw or work off; to haul off; to depart or be released from; as, *ship got off the sand-bar; we will get off on time.* To **get the wind of,** *see* WIND. To **get aboard,** in maneuvering, to draw close alongside of, or foul, another vessel, boat, etc.; to climb or go on board.

GHOSTING. Sailing with apparently little or no wind; also termed *fanning*. *See* FAN.

GIBE. (Pron. *jibe*) Variant of GYBE.

GIBBOUS. (Pron. with *hard* g) Said of the moon's appearance during period between first and last quarter, or when having a rounded periphery; as in the *gibbous phase;* opposed to the *crescent* phase.

GIBSTAFF. (Pron. with *hard* g) A rod used for sounding or to pole a boat in shallow water.

GIFT-ROPE. Line offered or extended to a boat for assistance by towing; a guest-rope. (*Archaic*)

GIG. (Pron. with *hard* g) Excepting the *dinghy,* where carried, formerly lightest boat on a naval vessel, principally for use of commanding officer; 20 to 28 feet in length, may be either sailed or rowed, but to-day the motor-engine generally has relegated to the past a smart rig and arrangement of oars once typical of the *captain's gig.* Usually propelled with 4 to 8 long oars, each oarsman was seated toward side of his thwart farther from his rowlock and handled his blade in *gig-stroke* fashion, which, with occasional timing variations, generally was performed with a long deliberate sweep and a 2-second pause at end of recovery-stroke, or immediately before re-dipping for next pulling-stroke. Also, a small whale-boat or light boat of almost any type that may be sailed or may be pulled with two oars per man. A *fizgig,* or kind of spear with barbed prongs for capturing fish. *Gig* often is erroneously written for JIG, *q.v.* **Cutter-g.,** naval ship's boat of class between the cutter and *g.;* usually the handy working boat. **G'sman,** member of a gig's crew. **Racing-g.,** long, narrow rowing-boat of light build used for pleasure or racing in smooth water.

GILGUY. Any rope temporarily used as a guy, lanyard, etc.; also, *see* GADGET.

GILHICKEY. *See* GADGET.

GILIGAN HITCH. Any lubberly or slovenly made hitch on a rope; a cow-hitch.

GILL. (Pron. with *hard* g) The *branchia* or respiratory organ of fishes and certain low-order aquatic animals. **G.-cover,** the *operculum* or bony plate at each side of base of the head serving to protect a fish's *g's.* **G.-fishing,** act of catching fish by means of a *g.-net.* **Gill-guy,** *see* GADGET. **G.-net,** any net designed to catch certain fish by having its meshes of such size as to allow of passage of fish's head only. In struggling to extricate itself, its *g.-covers* overlap sides of mesh and fish is thus defeated in efforts to back out.

GILTHEAD. Any of several small food fishes so named from their brilliant colors; the *wrasse* or *cunner* of Britain.

GIMBALS. (Pron. with either *hard* or *soft* g.) Contrivance for suspending an instrument, as a compass, chronometer, barometer, etc., in a constant plumb or level position during motion of ship. In its simplest form consists of a ring which supports the instrument on pivots at extremities of its thwartship diameter, while ring itself pivots at extremities of its fore-and-aft diameter.

GIMLET THE ANCHOR, To. *See* ANCHOR PHRASEOLOGY.

GIN. (Said to be a contraction of *engine*) Movable machine, usually consisting of a tripod with tackle and hand winch, used for lifting heavy weights, as in a shipyard; a light traveling crane. Also a *gin-block*, or *cargo-gin*, formerly consisting of a heavy iron sheave set in a skeleton frame; now any heavy iron block used in hoisting cargo, etc., as that fitted at a boom end. **G.-pole**, an improvised hoisting spar, guyed and set up as a derrick; one of the tripod spars of a *hoisting-g*. **G.-tackle**, old term for a purchase consisting of a standing treble (3-sheave) block and a moving double (2-sheave) block, by which is gained a mechanical advantage of 5 to 1, friction not considered.

GINGERBREAD WORK. An apparently superfluous show of sculptured scrolls, moldings, cordage, or other ornate trappings formerly decorating stern galleries, quarters, break of poop, and stem, found in some 17th and 18th century ships of the line; any additions to a vessel's hull or upper works for ornamental purposes.

GINGER ROLLS. Whalers' term for rolling fat ridges or folds on the breast and neck of a walrus and certain whales as the rorqual and humpback.

GIPSY. *See* GYPSY.

GIRDER. Any large single or compound unit in a vessel's structure serving to supply longitudinal strength and stiffness, as a vertical-plate keel or *center-line girder;* or to bridge and hold frames, floors, or beams to their work, as a *side g., intercostal floor g., deck g.* Often loosely termed a *stri..ger*, general function of a *g.* is to longitudinally bind, stiffen, and/or strengthen the whole structure. *See* EQUIVALENT GIRDER. **Box-g.,** one that is built of plates, having a hollow rectangular cross-section. **Center-g.,** *see* CENTER. **Deck-g.,** *see* DECK. **G.-plate**, any plate used in building or forming a *g.* **H-g.,** one having a cross section shaped like letter H; may be built or rolled in such form. **Intercostal g.,** *see* INTERCOSTAL. **Longitudinal g.,** *see* LONGITUDINAL. **Side g.,** *see* SIDE.

GIRDLE. Band of extra planking build around upper sides of a work-boat chiefly to take wear and tear.

GIRT. Said of a vessel moored with an upstream and a downstream anchor when she lies against her lee cable because of both cables being hove too taut. Vessel is also said to be *girt with her cable* when it leads under her bottom to its anchor.

GIRTH. As used for comparison purposes, classing, etc., in yacht racing, distance measured on outside of frame, from top of upper deck beam end on one side of vessel, around bottom to same point on other side; the *half-girth* is distance from center of keel at a specified station to either point referred to. **G.-band**, strengthening cloth of canvas sewn across jibs or staysails from clew to luff; also, a *belly-band* across a square sail.

GIRTLINE. *See* GANTLINE. **Hammock g.,** line on which hammocks are hung aloft for drying after being scrubbed.

GIVE. Stretch of a new rope, bending of a spar, or other visible effect produced in an object under stress. The weather is said to *give*, or *is giving*, when moderating after a gale. To apply or administer certain action; as, to *give her helm; to give way*. To **g. the keel,** old-time phrase meaning to *careen ship; see* CAREEN. **G. her more rudder,** increase the rudder angle. **G. her sheet,** slack out on sheet of a sail, as that of a boat or small craft. **G. her a spoke,** turn the steering-wheel slightly in a direction indicated. **G. way,** command to a boat's crew to begin or resume rowing (*pulling*).

GLACIER. (L. *glacies,* ice) Body of ice formed from compacted snow slowly moving downward in a valley, or over a sloping area, from a region of perpetual snow until it melts or breaks off in *icebergs* at a sea-coast. Expanse of ice forming source of a *glacier* is termed an *ice-sheet, glacial-sheet,* or *ice-cap*. **G.-bed**, channel, valley, or slope occupied by a *g.*, or site of an extinct one. **G.-berg,** iceberg broken off from a *g.* at the coast, as those from the Greenland fjords which find their way to the trans-Atlantic trade routes. **G.-face,** seaward end of a *g.*, or that from which *bergs* break off and float away. **G.-lake,** body of ice of glacial character in a depression formed by encircling hills; a *glacial lake*. **G.-milk,** water of milky white appearance flowing from beneath a glacier and containing suspended particles of finely pulverized rock produced by the enormous weight of ice crunching the earth in its flow. **G.-mud,** glacial silt, or powdery material produced by glacial erosion that is washed from beneath a *g.* to lower levels by glacial streams. **G.-wind,** air-current flowing from a glacial cavity, due to marked difference of temperature within and without its limits. **Tidewater g., tidal g.,** one flowing into tidal waters, which carry off each berg broken away from the mass.

GLACIS PLATE. Sloping armor plate on a warship's deck, as around base of a turret, hatch opening, etc., to deflect striking projectiles.

GLANCE. Sudden change in direction of motion due to contact with an obstructing object; as, *the glance of the colliding vessels caused both to heel outward*. To polish or give a lustre to; as, to *g.* the brightwork. To move swiftly and elegantly in sailing; as, *the yacht g's along*.

GLAND. Movable part of a stuffing-box, or tube inserted therein, for compressing the packing round a piston, valve-rod entering a tank or through a bulkhead, rudder-stock, etc. **G.-packing,** sennit, asbestos cord, or other fibrous substance compressed by the *g.* in a stuffing-box. **Rudder-g.,** *see* RUDDER.

GLAR. (*Scot. or Eng. dial.*) Muddy deposit in water tanks, bilges, etc.; mire. Also, *glaur.*

GLARE. Brightness appearing in the horizon caused by reflected light from breakers or ice. *See* BLINK.

GLASS. Any of several instruments in which *glass* is an important feature; as, *hour-g., log-g., night-g., weather-g.* **Chart-reading** g., magnifying or reading *g.* used in consulting a chart. **Compass-reading g.,** a semi-circular magnifying *g.* placed on a steering-compass to facilitate reading of card in vicinity of course steered and hence observance of slight changes in ship's heading. **Field g.,** old term for a deck telescope; now applied only by landsmen to the binocular form of telescopic *g*'s. **Gauge g.,** *see* GAUGE. **Hand g.,** a small timing *g.* used in determining ship's speed by the old chip log; a *log-g.* **High g.,** said of a barometer when it indicates an atmospheric pressure above normal, or of a *gauge g.* showing level of boiler water above working requirement. **Index g.,** *see* SEXTANT. **Log g.,** *see* LOG. **Low g.,** converse of *high g., q.v.* **Object g.,** lens at the outer end of telescope or either half of a binocular. **Night g.,** binocular or single telescope having a large field and high light-gathering power, specially made for night vision. **Sand-g.,** instrument for measuring time by flow of sand; as an *hour-g., 3-minute g., 14-second g.* Consists of a sealed glass container having an upper and a lower compartment connected by a small aperture. A quantity of sand flows to the lower compartment in period of time for which instrument is calibrated. On board ship, the number of knots run out in heaving a *hand* or *chip log* was timed by a 14- or a 28-second *sand-g.,* and also elapsed interval between taking a sextant observation and time noted by the chronometer. **Storm g.,** a barometer; especially an *aneroid.* **Spy-g.,** a hand or deck telescope. **Watch-g.,** a half-hour *sand-g.* formerly used to keep time throughout watches at sea. **Weather-g.,** a barometer or baroscope; any instrument that indicates changes in atmospheric pressure and hence means of foretelling approach of changes in weather; a *storm-g.*

GLIM. The old slush-lamp or a glass-protected candle used in crew's quarters of English ships; a lighted lamp. To **douse the g.,** to extinguish the light.

GLIMMER. To shine with a flickering or wavering appearance, as a distant light or twinkling star, due to presence of smoke or haze. A faint intermittent gleam as from a light; as in, *the glimmer of the headland's beacon light.*

GLOBE. Spherical or round-shaped protecting glass on a lantern. Small spheroid or sphere representing the earth, as a *terrestrial globe,* or the surrounding heavens, as a *celestial globe.* One of two soft iron balls or spheres each placed on either side of a compass for correcting quadrantal deviation. **G.-buoy,** a navigational buoy surmounted by a ball or *g.*-shaped mark, usually on a staff; also called *staff and g. buoy.* In U.S. buoyage system, such are placed at turning points in a channel; British usage places them at important points on starboard hand only, entering from sea. **G.-fish,** one of several species of fishes capable of sucking in air or water and distending their bodies into globular form; usually are protected with thorny spines, as the *porcupine-fish.* Called also *balloon-fish* and *puffer,* they are found chiefly in warm seas and generally are considered poisonous. **G.-lantern,** a ship's signal light or lamp having a spherical or *g.*-shaped glass, used to display an all-round red or white light as required by certain of the *International Rules for Prevention of Collisions* and/or similar rules duly made by local authority.

GLOBIGERINA OOZE. *See* OOZE.

GLOBULAR. Globe-shaped; spherical, or nearly so; extending over the earth's surface. **G.-chart,** that of a hemisphere drawn on the *g. projection,* in which point of perspective lies on an extension of axis of sphere beyond opposite hemisphere, at a distance equal to sphere's radius multiplied by sine of 45°. **G. sailing,** practice of navigation, as in *great circle sailing,* in which earth is regarded as a sphere; *see* **Spherical s.** *in* SAILING.

GLOOMY. Descriptive of weather characterized by dark or dismal appearance, as when sky is covered completely, or nearly so, with low-hanging clouds; usually abbrev. *g.* in weather-recording and ships' log-books.

GLORY-HOLE. Opening through which interior of a furnace may be viewed. A lazaret or small storeroom in a poop. Stewards' or firemen's quarters on a passenger vessel. **G.-steward,** one who is detailed to regularly clean and keep in order the stewards' quarters.

GLUE, MARINE. Any of several waterproof adhesive compositions, such as a mixture of shellac and asphaltum, or caoutchouc (rubber) and shellac dissolved in naphtha, used in ship joiner-work. Also, for paying seams in caulked wood decks, a solid substance usually composed of asphaltum, caoutchouc or gutta percha, pine tar, and resin, which, before using, is brought to a liquid state by heating.

GLUT. A becket, sometimes fitted with a thimble, made fast at slings of a yard for attaching a bunt-jigger or whip in furling a heavy sail. In former use with single topsails and courses which were clewed up to the bunt, *gluts* were fixed to jack-stay at middle of yard on after side of sail. *Bunt-whip* or *bunt-jigger,* which led from cross-trees or a top in respective cases of a topsail and course, was passed around fore side of sail in furling, and hooked to glut. Bunt of sail was then hauled up parbuckle fashion and work of securing the bunched-up canvas thereby greatly facilitated; *see* BUNT. Also, an iron connecting-plug temporarily placed in an appropriate hole in adjoining rims of rotating parts, as in uniting a windlass wild-cat with the pawl-ratchet wheel, when heaving in cable.

G M. In ship stability, vertical distance of meta-center from center of gravity; *see* **Metacentric height** *in* METACENTER.

G.M.T. *Greenwich Mean Time.* As used by navigators, time shown by chronometer corrected for error, or that indicating *mean solar time* at Greenwich. See *G.C.T.*

GNOMONIC CHART. Used for navigation in high latitudes or in great circle sailing, chart in which arcs of great circles appear as straight lines; *see* **Gnomonic p.** *in* PROJECTION.

GO. Usually in combination with another word or a phrase, word indicating motion or some action; as, to *go about;* to *go astern.* To break loose, give, or carry away; as in, *if the foremast goes the mainmast will go with it.* To **go aboard,** to enter or go upon a vessel; to embark. To **go about,** *see* ABOUT. To **go below,** to proceed to a lower deck or hold; to leave the deck, as in repairing to one's cabin or quarters. To **go by the board,** *see* BOARD. To **go by the head,** to sink faster forward than aft, as in increasing draft when loading cargo. To **go down,** to sink or founder, as a vessel. To **go foreign,** to ship on a vessel sailing to a foreign port; also said of such vessel herself. To **go free,** to sail free, or with eased sheets as with a fair wind. To **go large,** to sail with wind abaft the beam, all canvas drawing. To **go on the account,** *see* ACCOUNT. To **go to sea,** to proceed on a voyage; to adopt sea-going as one's vocation. To **go through,** to pass through, as a strait or channel. To **let go; to let go and haul;** *see* LET. **Let her go off,** command to a helmsman to steer farther off the wind or away from some obstruction.

GOA. Large Polynesian canoe of plank-built type and some 40 feet in length, peculiar to the Solomon Islands.

GOAL-POST MAST. Pair of masts of stout construction stepped abreast at equal distances from center line of ship and connected at upper ends by a girder, at middle of which is raised the mast proper. By this arrangement, one or two booms, of shorter length than that required by single mast, may be installed on each *"post,"* thus allowing advantageous handling of cargo to or from both sides of vessel at one time.

GOATFISH. A mullet of the family *Mullidæ;* the *red goatfish* or the *yellow goatfish* of West Indies waters. About 15 inches in length, have long barbs from lower jaw, and large scales; are considered good food fishes.

GOB. Colloquial name for an enlisted man in U.S. Navy.

GOB-LINES. Also written *gaub-lines* or *gaub-ropes;* martingale back-ropes; *see* MARTINGALE.

GOB-STICK. A fisherman's handy stick or club used to recover a hook from a fish's mouth, or to stun a large fish in order to successfully haul it aboard. It is commonly employed by Nova Scotian and Newfoundland dorymen. A similar stick among pleasure anglers is known as a *persuader.*

GODOWN. (Malay *gadong,* warehouse) In southeastern Asiatic ports, China coast, Philippines, etc., a store depot or warehouse.

GOD, ACT OF. *See* ACT.

GODFREY'S BOW. *See* QUADRANT.

GOMUTI. (Malay *gumuti*) A strong black fiber obtained from a Malayan palm of that name, valuable in manufacture of ship cordage.

GONDOLA. *(It.)* Long, narrow, flat-bottomed boat, partly decked at each end with rising ornamental beak and stern, used for centuries on the canals of Venice. Usually about 30 feet in length, often has a small cabin amidships for passengers, and is propelled by one rower who stands aft, facing forward. The name often is applied to any pleasure boat of light build driven by oars, or to a ship's dinghy or gig. A *gondoletta* or *gondolet* is a small gondola. *(Pron. gon'-dola)*

GONDOLIER. Man who manages and propels a *gondola.* Venetian gondoliers once were noted for entertaining their passengers with singing of no little merit, particularly in the romantic atmosphere of a summer moon.

GONE. Broken, carried away, parted, or disintegrated; as, *both masts are gone; the braces are gone; see* GO.

GONG BUOY. A modification of the *bell buoy,* in which a *gong,* or two or more gongs differing in tone, are sounded by being struck by suspended hammers during motion of buoy in surface waves.

GONIOMETER. (Gr. *gonia,* angle; *metron,* measure) Instrument for measuring angles; a marine direction-finder; *see* RADIO COMPASS.

GONY. Any of several large sea-birds; especially, the *black-footed albatross* and a young *short-tailed albatross.* See ALBATROSS.

GOOD. Combining word connoting satisfactory quality or condition; as, *the good ship "George"; soundings show 10 fathoms good.* **G. full,** well filled or rounded out; said of sails all drawing when course is moderately close to the wind. **G. shoaling,** gradual lessening of sea depths, as shown in soundings. To **make g.,** actual accomplishment in sailing; as in a course steered or distance covered, expressed as *course made g.; distance made g.*

GOODS. As usually descriptive of a general cargo in marine insurance and affreightment, merchandise of any description carried as cargo only. The *Carriage of Goods by Sea Act, 1936, (46 U.S. Code 1300)* defines g. as including "goods, wares, merchandise, and articles of every kind whatsoever, except live animals and cargo which by contract of carriage is stated as being carried on deck and is so carried." **Bonded g.,** imported merchandise held in a bonded warehouse; g. for payment of customs duties on which an importer or consignee is bonded. Also, *g. in bond.* **Kentledge g.,** old term for heavy cargo given low stowage to contribute stability to a vessel. **Measurement g.,** *see* **M. cargo** *in* MEASUREMENT. **Wet g.,** other than liquids in sealed containers, any cargo containing and giving off considerable moisture, such as salted hides, wood-pulp, or soaked timber.

GOOSE. Any of several species of wild birds included in the family *Anserinæ,* in many respects intermediate between the duck and the swan. Commonly termed *wild-goose* and a popular game bird, it includes the *brant, bernicle-g.,* and *snow-g.* which breed in the far north and migrate long distances southward in winter. The *graylag* of northern Europe is said to be chief ancestor of our common domestic g. **G.-beak,** or **g.-beaked whale,** the dolphin. **G.-gull,** the great black-backed gull; *see* GULL.

GOOSENECK. A return, or 180° bend, having one leg shorter than the other, as in a vent-pipe, metal fitting, etc.; anything curved like a goose's neck, as a bow-headed or swan-neck davit. Any hinged fitting or coupling at swivelling end of a derrick, boom, or gaff, designed to allow such spar free lateral and vertical movement. **G.-band,** metal band fitted on a mast in way of lower end of a boom to secure a g. arrangement; also on a wooden boom for same purpose. **G.-ventilator,** one of swan-neck type; especially one having a 180° bend near its mouth; usually a small deck-vent of such form.

GOOSEWING. To spread one side only of a square sail, especially a topsail or a course, by securing its weather half to the yard and sheeting home the lee clew, as sometimes resorted to during heavy weather. Sail is then said to be *goosewinged.* Also, a once familiar term for a *studding-sail.*

GORCE. Obstruction in a river preventing passage of vessels. Also, a whirlpool.

GORE. Angular cut leech-cloth which widens a square sail downward toward the clew; any diagonally cut or triangular piece in a sail to increase its width or give the desired sweep to its leech, foot, clew, etc.; also, measurement of such *gore,* or *goring* of a sail or awning, expressed in inches of departure from the straight cloth. A tapering piece of plating or planking set in where needed due to curved lines in a ship's side or deck; a *g.-strake.*

GORGE. Concave edge of a block-sheave in which a rope travels. **G.-hook,** or **g.,** a kind of double fishhook designed to be swallowed with the bait in catching certain fish. A heavy deckload or catch of fish is termed a *gorger.* **Ice-g.,** mass of accumulated ice blocking a river bed or channel.

GOUGE. A chisel having a half-round, or nearly half-round, edge. **G.-spade,** round-faced cutting slice or spade formerly used by whalemen for making holes in the blubber when flensing, as required for making fast strops for hoisting tackle, etc.

GOVERNOR. Obsolete term for a shipmaster or pilot, an example of its use being found in James 3:4, of *King James version* of our Bible. It is of interest to note that our present word, with its extensions *government, governess, gubernatorial,* etc., finds its source in the Greek *kubernon,* thence through Latin *gubernare* and Old French *governer,* all meaning to *pilot* or *steer,* in the sense of directing a vessel's course. Similarly, the Latin *gubernaculum* via French *gouvernail,* helm or rudder, gave us the now almost obsolete English word **governail,** meaning a rudder or act of steering. In machinery, a *governor* is a device for automatically controlling engine speed, also flow or pressure of a fluid, as in pumping. **Log g.,** a small fly-wheel, or bar weighted equally at each end, fitted on a patent log line to give a constant rate of rotation in the line.

GRAB. A kind of closing scoop or bucket used in dredging or in lifting coal, sand, etc.; a *grab-bucket; see* CLAM-SHELL. A two-masted, lateen-rigged, broad-beamed, shallow draft coasting vessel common in the East Indies. **Chain-g.,** *see* CHAIN. **G.-hook,** *see* HOOK. **G.-line,** rope hung along ship's side near water-line at a ladder or accommodation gangway to assist in securing or handing a boat alongside; line stretched along a boat-boom or gangplank for persons to lay hold of; any rope used to steady a man, or for a safety precaution, as when at work on a stage, aloft, etc. Also, *g.-rope.* **G.-rod,** one of a number of metal rods or steps secured to a bulkhead, hatch-coaming, etc., and forming a ladder; a *hand-g.* **Hand-g.,** bar or rail along a bulkhead or elsewhere for providing a means for one to steady himself during seaway motion of vessel.

GRACE, DAYS OF. *See* DAY.

GRAFT. To neatly cover a man-rope, strop, ring-bolt, sheer-pole, stanchion, etc., with small stuff, as by cross-pointing or other type of weaving. To **g. a rope,** to taper its end and cover the tapered part either by cross-pointing with some of the outer yarns or by "needle-hitching" (*see* **Needle-h.** *in* HITCH); also termed *pointing a rope.*

GRAIN. Sea carriage of grain wholly or partly in bulk has been regulated for many years, either by law or by rules required to be adhered to by underwriters, because of many serious disasters occurring on ocean voyages as a result of shifting of the grain during heavy weather. Probably earliest of laws prescribing precautions to be observed in grain stowage is that embraced in the *British Merchant Shipping Act of 1894,* which, with subsequent additional recommendations in practical stowage by the Board of Trade, appears to have set the pattern followed or approved by other governments and societies or boards of insurance underwriters. "Grain" is defined generally as including "wheat, oats, barley, maize, rice, paddy, pulse, seed, nuts or nut kernels, or any mixture or combination thereof," and a *grain-laden ship* means a vessel carrying an amount of g. of more than one-third her net registered tonnage, that third being computed, where g. is measured in units of capacity, at rate of 100 cubic feet for each ton of net registered tonnage; and where g. is measured in units of weight, at rate of two tons (2240 lbs. each) for each ton of net registered tonnage. Such g. carriage laws or regulations demand that all reasonable and necessary precautions be taken to prevent cargo from shifting and usually cover minimum requirements for strength and extent of *shifting-boards,* or temporary fore-and-aft bulkheads; arrangement of *feeders,* or bins containing grain for flowing into, and maintaining full volume in, a lower compartment, as bulk settles or is disturbed by ship's motion; and details of required stowage where both bagged and bulk g. are carried. (*See* FEEDER *and* SHIFTING) In U.S. ports, g.-*lading rules* prescribed by *New York Board of Underwriters* usually take precedence, especially where American vessels are concerned. **G. bulkhead,** fore-and-aft g.-*tight* partition in a hold for preventing shifting of cargo; *shifting-boards; see* SHIFTING. **G. cargo certificate,** document issued by a marine insurance surveyor or port warden to master of a g.-laden ship, stating that all precautions prescribed in laws or regulations in force governing g. stowage have been complied with. **G. capacity,** also referred to as g. *cubic,* volume of g. which may be loaded in a vessel, or one or more of her cargo compartments. Usually expressed in cubic feet, is equal to volume of a liquid which would fill such space or spaces to capacity; hence is measured between extreme length, breadth, and height limits of compartments in question. *Cf.* BALE CUBIC. **G. Coast,** that part of the Guinea Coast, west of Ivory Coast and including **part of** Liberia, named for a certain pungent spice

called *melegueta pepper,* also known as *g's of paradise, Guinea g's* and *Guinea pepper,* used in veterinary medicine. **G. ceiling,** *see* CEILING. **G. feeders,** *see* FEEDER. **G. fittings,** arrangement of shifting-boards, stanchions, shores, and feeders set up in loading a g. cargo. **G. measure,** *see* **G. capacity.**

GRAINS. Any of several types of fish-spears, having two or more barbed prongs and a pole handle, for capturing crawfish, eels, and other bottom-living fish.

GRAMPUS. A cetacean of the family *Delphinidæ* found in northern hemisphere seas; attains a length of 15 feet; allied to the *blackfish* (caaing whale or pilot whale), to which the term is often erroneously applied; differs from the latter in having teeth in lower jaw only, its head being distinctly flatter and more uniformly rounded than that of the blackfish. Also called *orc,* not to be confused with the *Orca,* or much larger *killer-whale.*

GRANNY. Also termed *granny's bend, granny-knot, granny's knot.* A beginner's attempted formation of the *reef* or *square knot* in which two ropes' ends are bent together in two successive half-knots, the ends leading *across* the rope thus united, instead of *along* it. Considered anything but sailorlike, the knot will jam in a small rope or come adrift in a larger one when under stress, on which account the novice observed using such a lubberly "giligan" invites the boatswain's quaint corrective, *"Why didn't you take her with you?"*

GRAPE-SHOT. In former ship gunnery, a cluster of small cast-iron balls arranged in an iron frame or enclosed in a canvas bag, used as a projectile charge in a cannon.

GRAPNEL. The *grapenel* dating from medieval times, formerly used by boarders in laying hold of an enemy vessel by throwing it into the rigging, channels, etc.; a small anchor consisting of a shank with four or five claws or curved flukes; a *grapple,* or *grappling-iron,* having pointed claws or hooks for dragging the sea-bottom to recover lost objects. Also, *grapeline, grapnel-hook.* See **Grapnel-a.** *in* ANCHOR.

GRAPPLE. To use a grapple or grapnel, as in dragging for a person drowned, a lost cable, or other sunken object. **G.-shot,** projectile of grapnel form, having hinged claws and attached to a line, as fired by a life-saving crew to catch in a vessel's rigging, or to serve as an anchor by which a boat may be hauled seaward; also called an *anchor-shot.* **G.-ground,** an anchorage; especially, an area in which a small vessel may anchor.

GRASP. Handle or part of an oar grasped by an oarsman in rowing.

GRATE. See **F.-bar** *in* FIRE.

GRATING. Skeleton deck or platform of parallel-laid iron rods or bars, supported at appropriate intervals by cross-bars, as a fiddley-deck, or platforms in an engine-room; a strong wooden cover of lattice-work laid over a hatchway or other deck opening to allow entrance of light and air, while affording protection against persons falling through such opening; any grid or grill arrangement of bars across the mouth of a waste-pipe, scupper, etc.; a wood lattice laid as a protection against wear and tear on a deck, as on a navigating-bridge, at a much-frequented doorway, in an alleyway, etc.; a *deck-grating*. **Dunnage-g.,** *see* DUNNAGE. **Fantail g.,** raised lattice-work platform at after end of a tug-boat for providing drainage, ventilation, and stowage of hawsers and towing-gear. **Foot-g.,** *see* FOOT. **Hatch-g.,** one that is placed over a hatchway in lieu of the ordinary hatch-covers; a *g.-hatch.* **Scupper-g.,** small grid protection on deck end of a scupper to prevent clogging of pipe by waste material, etc. **Skylight g.,** protective metal bars fitted over glass in a skylight. **Top g.,** one fitted in a mast top; the upper *g.-deck* or platform in an engine-room, made of iron bars. **Wood-g.,** any *g.* made of wood; usually consists of a series of crossed slats laid about an inch apart; or, as fruit or cargo *dunnage-g's,* lumber of about 1½ by 2 inches laid fore-and-aft about 1 inch apart on cross-landings about 3 inches deep by 2 in thickness.

GRAVE. Old term meaning to bream, or clean off barnacles, etc., from a vessel's bottom (*see* BREAM), and to apply a protective coating of tar, pitch, resin, or composition of such; also, *greave.* Originally, the *graving-dock* was used solely for, and so named from, the operation referred to; today its principal use is that for extensive repairs to a vessels' underwater body, in addition to routine cleaning and painting of bottom; *see* **Graving-d.** *in* DOCK.

GRAVEL. (Fr. *gravelle,* dim. of *greve,* sandy shore or strand) As chiefly used on coasts of Britain, but now probably obsolete, to run a vessel aground on a gravel or sandy beach, bank, or shoal. In 15th century usage, any craft was said to be *graveled* when grounded on any kind of sea-bottom, other than rock.

GRAVEYARD WATCH. *See* WATCH.

GRAVING-PIECE. Piece of wood fitted to fill a cavity or decayed portion of a plank or timber; *see* DUTCHMAN.

GRAVITY. Terrestrial gravitation; force of attraction downward or toward center of the earth, as measured by *weight.* **Acceleration of g.,** *see* ACCELERATION. **Center of g.,** *see* CENTER. **G. davits,** *see* DAVIT. **G. tank,** for supplying fresh-water or sea-water by *g.* for domestic or waste-flushing purposes, a tank placed above a deck-house, or in some other raised position, and kept pumped up from a low storage tank or from the sea. **Specific g.,** ratio of weight of a given volume of matter to weight of an equal volume of a standard substance, as water or air; for solids or liquids, standard substance is usually distilled water at its maximum density, or at temperature of 4° Centigrade, or 39° Fahrenheit. Distilled water being 62.4 lbs. per cubic foot, any substance of less density, or having a *specific g.* of less than 1.00, will float in water; conversely, substances of greater density, or *specific g.* greater than 1.00, will sink in fresh water. *Specific g.* of sea-water averages 1.025, its weight per cubic foot being very nearly 64 lbs.

GRAY WHALE. A baleen whale of the North Pacific; attains a length of 50 feet; is fiercely active and most difficult to take; also called a *grayback* or *greyback.* **Gray-whaler,** a vessel employed in catching gray whales.

GREASE. To oil or apply any kind of lubricant to bearings in blocks, machinery, etc. **Fisherman's g.,** sea-water. To **g. the gangway,** *see* GANGWAY. To **g. down,** to apply tallow or other *g.* to a mast in way of the travel of a yard-parrel, or hoops of a fore-and-aft sail.

GREASER. Chiefly in British usage, man whose principal duties correspond to those of an *oiler* in U.S. ships, or qualified member of the engine department who attends to proper lubrication of main engines and auxiliary machinery.

GREASY. Said of threatening or dirty appearance of the weather, as seen in oily, heavy, dark cloud formations. **G. luck,** a whaleman's term for a successful catch, inferring a fair load of oil.

GREAT. Distinguishing adjective, now falling into disuse, connoting larger in class or importance; as *g. guns; g. ships; g. lines.* Sometimes, as a noun, meaning the whole or gross quantity or mass; as in, *building of vessels was contracted for by the great.* **G. albacore,** the horse mackerel; *see* ALBACORE. **G. auk,** *see* AUK. **G. barracuda,** *see* BARRACUDA. **G. Bear,** *see* URSA MAJOR and DIPPER. **G. black-backed gull,** *see* GULL. **G. circle,** as described on surface of a sphere, one whose plane passes through the center, thereby dividing sphere into two equal parts; *see* CIRCLE. **G. circle sailing,** practice in navigation of following the track represented by arc of a great circle which passes through points of departure and destination. Such arc is the shortest distance between those points. Excepting where points in question lie in a true north and south direction from each other, *i.e.,* are situated on a common meridian, or lie on the equator, the true course constantly changes due to **g. circle track** intersecting each meridian crossed at a varying angle. In any *g. circle* other than a meridian or the equator, course is true east or west at its *vertex* or point of nearest approach to the pole, and its points of intersection with the equator differ 180° in longitude. **G. Lakes,** the five large bodies of fresh water lying inland on the U.S. northern border, viz., *L. Superior, L. Huron, L. Michigan, L. Erie,* and *L. Ontario.* **G.-line fishing,** *see* FISHING. **G. Sea,** name by which the Mediterranean was known to the ancients. **G. tunny,** *see* TUNNY.

GREAT EASTERN. Steam-vessel launched in 1858 which held the undisturbed record as largest in world's history until advent of White Star liner *"Baltic"* in 1905. Noted as ship employed in laying the Atlantic cable in 1866, was never a commercial success and ended by being broken up in 1887. Had an over-all length of 692 feet, beam of 82, and a gross tonnage of 18,900. She was propelled by paddle-wheels and a single screw, had six masts, and carried eight 3½-ton anchors in her equipment of 10.

GREBE. A fish-eating bird of expert swimming and diving habits, somewhat larger but resembling the loons. Larger species of the family (*Podicipedidæ*) are the *western g.* of America; the *crested g.* of Europe; and *red-necked g.* of both countries. Averaging 10 inches in body length, the birds have little or no tail, but otherwise not unlike the common duck, excepting the feet which, instead of being webbed, have separate lobes extending from each of the three toes. Its young are hatched in a floating nest.

GREEN. **G. fish,** those not pickled or salted, as fresh cod, herring, haddock, etc. **G. sea,** a wave appearing green in the light; especially one boarding a vessel in a solid mass. **G. turtle,** a large greenish or olive-colored smooth-shell turtle widely distributed in warmer latitudes. Its eggs are hatched in the sand of a sunny beach. Turtle-meat from this species and soup made therefrom are highly valued as food.

GREENHEART. A durable, tough, hard wood used in shipbuilding for deck margin and stringer planks, rudder-stocks, stern-posts, towing-bitts, shells of heavy blocks, etc. It is from the *bebeeru* tree of tropical South America, the bark of which yields a valuable substitute for *quinine.* Seasoned wood is greenish in appearance and about 60 lbs. per cubic foot in weight.

GREENLAND. Island of the Arctic regions lying northeastward of North America; has an area of about 840,000 square miles and extends northward from latitude 60°, in longitude 44° W., to latitude 83½°, or some 1400 miles, with greatest east and west breadth of 750 miles. **G. halibut,** *see* HALIBUT. **G. shark,** *see* SHARK.

GREENWICH. A borough of London in which is situated the *Royal Observatory.* By international agreement, geographers and navigators reckon their longitude from the *Greenwich* or *prime meridian,* which passes through the observatory's meridian circle, indicated as longitude 0° 00′ 00″. **G. time,** *see* G.M.T., TIME, *and* ALMANAC.

GREGALE. Local name for a strong dry and cold northeasterly wind occurring in winter in the Ionian Sea, or between Sicily and Greece.

GRENADIER. A peculiar deep-sea fish having a fin-fringed, spear-like, tapering body and tail; about 20 inches in length.

GRETA GARBO. An American innovation in sloop-racing canvas of about 1900. In effect it is a combined jib and flying-jib, is quadrilateral in shape, hence having two clews. Forward sheet leads from lower clew and after sheet well aft from upper one. Also called *double-clewed jib.*

GREYHOUND. A large speedy ocean vessel; especially, a modern trans-Atlantic passenger liner.

GRIBBLE. Small wood-boring crustacean about one-fifth inch in length, smaller, but equally destructive to submerged timber, than the *teredo,* or shipworm. Found both in American and European rivers and lakes, it is zoölogically classified as *Limnoria lignorum.*

GRIDIRON. A floor of parallel timbers laid crosswise on bottom of a dock which dries at low water. Its purpose is to evenly support smaller vessels careened for bottom inspection or repairs, in which connection it is sometimes termed a *careening-grid.* Also called a *grid* or *mattress,* a similar floor or bed is often laid at berths alongside wharves in an area of great tidal range where vessels rest on bottom at low water, as in some Bay of Fundy harbors. A vessel resting on a grid may be kept upright by masthead tackles leading to shore, or by a preponderance of weight, as of cargo, on her inshore side, or may be allowed to list off shore with bilge and keel resting on such floor.

GRILSE. A young salmon at the stage of its first return to its natal stream from sea. The fish at this time has brilliant silver colors and displays remarkable and persistent gameness in overcoming any and all obstacles in its upstream progress.

GRIND. Old term for a curly or kinky shape given to a rope by undue stress when hauled through a short nipping lead. When thus forcibly drawn over an object at a sharp angle, a rope too large for such treatment was said to *grind.*

GRINDHVAL. (Of *Scand.* origin; also, *grind whale;* pron. with short *i*) Same as *blackfish* or *caaing-whale; see* CAAING-WHALE.

GRIP. Grasp or handle of an oar. Hold taken by an anchor in the sea-bottom; as, *the flukes have a good grip.*

GRIPE. (Du. *greep,* grip) In wood construction, the *fore foot,* or area at union of stem and keel; specifically, an upward curved timber connecting forward end of keel to stem, usually forming lower continuation of the cutwater; also, *gripe-piece.* Degree of sharpness or protrusion of the fore foot, as considered influencing vessel's sailing qualities; a 16th century reference reads: *"Ye longer greepe doth seil us closer to ye winde."* Lashing arrangement for securing boats in their stowed position, usually consisting of a quick-releasing clamp fitted over boat's gunwale and secured to deck. A strop or band-brake on a windlass or winch. A vessel is said to g. when tending to luff on a tack or with a beam wind; *see* ARDENT. To bear or rub heavily against; as, *ship g's on her fenders.* **G.-band,** one of two canvas, rope, or sennit bands serving to steady a boat which is swung out in readiness for lowering. Each is secured at a davit head, passed obliquely under boat where it crosses its mate, and set up to hold boat against a pudding on a spar stretched fore-and-aft against both davits; also, *belly-band, belly-strop.* To g. **in,** to secure a boat in her stowed position by use of *g's* or *g.-bands.* **G.-iron** or **g.-plate,** *see* **Horseshoe-c.** *in* CLAMP.

GROG. Any unsweetened drink of spirits and water; especially, that issued as a daily ration in the British navy, which usually is diluted Jamaica rum; named for *"Old Grog," Admiral Edward Vernon (1684-1757),* who first ordered the sailors' good half-gill thinned out with water, about 1740. The admiral's nickname appears to have been derived from his favorite *grogram* foul-weather cloak.

GROIN. A spur or jetty of piling or stones laid at right angles to a river-bank, designed to arrest and deposit flowing silt, shingle, etc., at one side of channel, or to serve as a barrier against erosive action of waves. Also, *groyne.*

GROMMET. Ring or strop of rope made by laying up a single strand round itself to build the usual three strands, as in *stropping a block;* any ring-shaped wire or fiber strand thus fashioned; as, a strop confining an oar to a thole-pin; a hand-becket on a yard. A metal (usually brass) eyelet set in a sail or edge of an awning, canvas cover, bag, etc., to receive a stop or lacing. A ring of oakum or hemp yarn laid with red or white lead round and under head of a deck-bolt for water-tightness; also a fiber ring set under a manhole-cover, between flanges of piping, etc., to ensure tightness of joint. An old ship term for a cabin-boy. Also, *gromet, grummet.* **G.-fender,** *see* FENDER. **G.-ring,** a grommet; a gasket of soft metal set under a cylinder-cover; a washer between moving parts in machinery, etc. **G.-wad,** in older gunnery, a wad of old rope rammed between powder and ball; a *junk-wad.* **Shot-g.,** a ring of rope once used to hold ball shot in place near a gun; a *shot-garland.*

GROSS. Entire; total; whole; opposed to *net;* as, *g. freight; g. weight; g. tonnage.* **G. adventure,** in maritime law, a loan of money on a contract of bottomry, so termed because lender is liable to contribution in *general average* in event of loss; *see*

AVERAGE. **G.,** or **general, average,** *see* AVERAGE. **G. tonnage** *see* TONNAGE.

GROUND. The sea floor; bottom of any area or body of water. To run aground; to place on or touch the ground; to strike bottom and remain fast thereon; as a *grounded vessel.* **G. bait,** any kind of bait thrown into the water to attract fish. **G. cable,** heavy chain cable used with permanent moorings and forming main cable from which short lengths of chain lead, sometimes to buoys, as a means of securing vessels in a limited mooring area. **G.-chain,** as once used with heavy old-fashioned anchors, a length of small chain attached to ship's anchor and stopped along the cable. It was used for hauling anchor clear of stem and bobstays in preparation for again letting go, or in *catting,* anchor. **G. fish,** any fish living at or near the sea-bottom; as, halibut, cod, flounder. **G. hold,** old term for **ground-tackle,** *q.v.* **G. ice,** anchor-ice; *see* **Frazil ice** *in* ICE. **G. line,** *see* **great line f.** *in* FISHING. **G. log,** *see* LOG. **G. mine,** an explosive charge placed at or near the sea-bottom in shallow waters, as at a port entrance, and usually detonated electrically from shore. **G.-net,** an anchored gill-net; a drag-net or trawl-net; a trammel. **G.-rope,** heavy wire or manila rope forming lower edge, or *foot-rope,* of mouth of a drag-net or trawl; protected to withstand wear and tear of dragging on bottom, on rougher g. often fitted with wooden rollers. **G. sea,** heavy rolling swell which, from no apparent cause, appears on a beach, breaking in an enormous surf; sometimes called *rollers,* such undulations occur in regions neighboring great ocean depths, usually at certain seasons, regardless of wind velocity in the area. **G.-shark,** the *Greenland* or *gurry shark;* also called *sleeper; see* SHARK. **G. strake,** same as *garboard strake,* or strake of plating or planking next to keel. **G. swell,** broad, deep swell caused by heavy sea set up by a distant gale, sometimes by a seismic disturbance, and often continuing in spite of a local sea running in another direction. The term has no connection with the sea-bottom, g. simply connoting basic surface of water. On the approach of a cyclone or hurricane in open sea, direction from which a g. *swell* runs indicates approximate bearing of storm center. **G. tackle,** anchors, cables, windlass, capstan, etc., or all gear used in dropping or heaving in anchors and securing ship at anchor. **G. tier,** in stowage of barrels, boxes, etc., in a hold, foundation layer of such upon which the mass of similar goods is laid in successive tiers. Especially toward the ends of smaller vessels, a g. *tier* of casks, cases, or other individually bulky merchandise units, must be so laid that evenness and easy proper stowage will result as work proceeds. **G. timbers,** those constituting bottom frame-work in a wooden vessel. **G. ways,** in launching, tracks on which vessel slides "down the ways." Ordinarily consist of smooth-faced hardwood timber firmly laid in the g. at equal distances from ship's keel or center line. The *sliding ways* which are attached to ship form, as it were, runners of a huge sled and slide along the greased *g. ways,* bearing weight of ship in the launching process. **Holding-g.,** *see* HOLDING. **Middle g.,** in a fairway, a shallow area having a navigable channel at each side of it. **Seine g.,** area over which a seine net is hauled. **Shore g's,** fishing grounds near shore; opposed to *off-shore g's.* **Spoil g.,** sea area in which dredged material is deposited; *dumping-g.*

GROUNDAGE. Chiefly in British usage, a port charge paid by vessels for occupying a berth alongside a pier, moored to buoys, or at anchor; also, *berthage.*

GROUNDING. Act of running aground or coming in contact with the sea-bottom; *see* GROUND. **G. clause,** in a marine insurance policy, provision stating that *g.* of vessel in certain areas specified, as where soft bottom prevails and water depth reaches unpredictable low levels, will be considered as common experience in such localities and, in consequence, excluded from the stranding condition as ordinarily defined. **G. keel,** *see* **Docking-k.** *in* KEEL.

GROUP. Word distinguishing a single-flashing or single-occulting light from one exhibiting two or more flashes or eclipses; as *g. flashing light; g. occulting light; see* LIGHT.

GROUPER. Any of several serranoid fishes of warmer seas, valued as food, more important of which are the **Black g.** (*Epinephelus nigritus*), also called *black jewfish* and *bonaci,* found in the Atlantic from Brazil to the Carolinas, sometimes two to three hundred pounds weight; and **Red g.** (*Epinephelus morio*) of Gulf of Mexico and northward to Virginia, attaining three feet in length and growing a fleshy red color in the adult.

GROW. To lead, tend, lie, or stretch out in a direction indicated; as, *the cable grows to leeward.* To increase, as size of sea or swell; as, *an easterly swell is growing.* Also, *growe.*

GROWLER. Low-lying mass of floating ice; usually a broken-off portion of an iceberg, or a berg approaching final melting decay. It is considered a greater danger to navigation than any form of ice, due to its dark bluish color and its lurking "awash" condition which renders it difficult to discern at night or in hazy weather. *See* ICE.

GROWN. Said of shipbuilding or boatbuilding timbers of curved pattern which roughly conform to required curvature in their natural shape; as, a *g. frame; g. deck-hook; g. knee.* A **grown mast** or **spar** is one made from a tree-trunk of such diameter as to require little or no reduction from its natural size, as distinguished from a *built spar* or from one cut from a balk of timber.

GROYNE. *See* GROIN.

GRUS. (*L. =* a crane) A southern constellation lying immediately southward of *Pisces;* contains the navigational stars *α and β Gruis,* each of magnitude 2.2, east and west of each other about 6° apart. *β Gruis* is located east of its mate and about 17° nearly due south of the bright star *Fomalhaut,* in 47° 08′ south declination and having a S.H.A. of 20°.

GUARANTEE ENGINEER. In a new vessel, or in one with new engines installed, a marine engineer placed on board by engine builders for purpose of observing, and rectifying any fault developing in, performance of the plant for a period agreed upon by builders and owners.

GUARD. A chain, rail, or other protective fitting to keep persons from falling overboard or through a hatchway; coming in contact with moving machinery, hot steam-pipes; etc. Projecting fender-rail or *belting* built fore-and-aft on a vessel's side, or outside a paddle-box or sponson. A sentry or watchman assigned to a specific police duty. The pointers of *Ursa Major* (Big Dipper) and the two outer stars of *Ursa Minor* (Little Dipper) in medieval times were called *The Guards* from their use in measuring time intervals (as in keeping watches) indicated by their progressive change in position relative to *Polaris,* or Pole star. **After g.,** in former days, seamen stationed to attend all after sails and who usually were less experienced than men assigned to more important seamanship duties; more recently, the *officers,* whose quarters were located in the poop. **Coast G.,** *see* COAST. **G.-boat,** a boat assigned to *g. duty,* as a picket or protection against surprise attack; a police-boat, or one detailed to patrol a harbor area. **G.-flag,** in a naval squadron, flag raised on ship performing *g. duty.* **G.-irons,** protective plates or bars over or inside of a wood-built hatch-coaming, on a wood rail, etc.; curved rods protecting a ship's figurehead. **G.-lock,** an entrance lock for passage of vessels to and from a tidal basin, or dock communicating with a tidal area by means of locks. **G.-rail,** "fence" or railing erected in absence of bulwarks at ship's side, at breaks of decks, around deck stairways, etc., height and construction of which usually is prescribed by law. *U.S. Marine Inspection laws* require outboard rails on passenger decks to be at least 3 equi-distant parallel rods, uppermost at least 42 inches above deck; inboard rails and all rails on crew decks to be 2 rods and at least 36 inches in height. Also a timber bolted fore-and-aft and serving as a fender along ship's sides; sometimes called *belting* and *bull-rail; see* **F.-guard** *in* FENDER. **G. ship,** vessel detailed for inspection or control of harbor works in progress or other marine affairs. In British navy, receiving ship for recruits or seamen awaiting transfer to another ship or station; sometimes also a *drill ship.* Ship of a squadron assigned *g. duty.* **Life-g.,** *see* LIFE. **Marine g.,** detachment of marines detailed for service on a naval vessel or at a naval station. **Propeller-g.,** *see* PROPEL-LER. **Rat-g.,** as generally required by port quarantine laws, a disc of sheet metal about two feet in diameter, made to fix on ships' mooring lines as a protective fence against passage of rats to and from vessel. To **row g.,** old term for patrol by ship's boat of an anchorage area occupied by a naval vessel or vessels, chiefly for purpose of intercepting deserters. **Water-g.,** a police or customs patrol in harbor; especially, one detailed to cruise about a dock area by boat.

GUDGEON. (Fr. *goujon*) One of the projecting lugs of a stern-post or rudder-post on which rudder is hinged. They are bored to receive the pintles or vertical pins secured to fore edge of rudder; also, *rudder-lug; rudder-snug.* Notch or bushing-hole in a carrick bitt for receiving the windlass spindle. (In older usage written *goodgeon,* and, indicating *gudgeons,* collectively, *rudder-googing* or *rudder-gooding*)

GUESS-WARP. A hauling-line run out by boat to a buoy, wharf, dolphin, etc., for warping purposes. Rope run along ship's side or to an out-rigged boom as a means by which boats or lighters may make fast or shift as required; a grab-line. A guy-rope or additional tow-line to steady a boat towed astern; sometimes applied to tow-line or painter itself. Also, *guest-rope.* **G. boom,** *see* BOOM.

GUEST FLAG. *See* FLAG.

GUIDE. In a reciprocating engine, track or bars which confine a piston-rod to its vertical motion; a *crosshead guide.* A *guide ship,* or one in a naval squadron which acts as a pivot or leader in fleet evolutions. **G.-bar,** one of the bars on or between which an engine crosshead *g.-shoe* travels. **G.-flag,** that flown by the *g.* in a naval fleet formation or during maneuvers. **G.-rod,** any rod working in a *g.;* a *piston-rod* or *tail-rod.* **G.-rope,** a guying line, or one for directing or controlling lead of a rope used in lifting or hauling. **G.-shoe,** flat piece or block of metal attached to an engine crosshead and forming means of confining latter to the *g.;* also, *g.-block.*

GUILLEMOT. Any of certain small *auks* or *murres* native to northern waters, among which are the *black g.; thick-billed g.* (or *murre*); and common, or *foolish g.* (or *murre*); all of the North Atlantic and Arctic. The birds nest on rocky cliffs and their skins, feathers, and eggs are valuable to natives of the northern coasts. *See* AUK.

GUINEA CURRENT. *See* CURRENT.

GULF. (It. *golfo;* Gr. *kolphos,* bosom, bay, gulf) A large indentation in a sea-coast; as, *G. of Genoa;* also, a partially land-locked sea area, usually of larger extent than a bay; as, *G. of Mexico; G. of Bothnia.*

GULF STREAM. The most remarkable of all ocean currents, is the chief outlet for a considerable part of the combined trade-wind generated North and South Equatorial Currents which continues westward through Caribbean Sea and banks up, as it were, in the Gulf of Mexico, or body giving the Stream its name. Its formative stage as an ocean river begins in Florida Strait midway between Key West and Havana, thence turning northeastward and closing in with Florida coast, where, about 30 miles southeast of Miami, it is joined by a portion of the North Equatorial drift flowing along north coasts of Puerto Rico, Haiti, and Cuba. It continues northward to latitude 31°, thence northeastward, roughly following contour of land to Cape Hatteras, where it begins to widen out and lay to E.N.E., finally diffusing itself in the broad Atlantic some 250 miles southeast of Nova Scotia, The Stream is an indigo-blue color and its edges thus sharply defined against the ordinary sea-water. Its temperature during August reaches 88° F. off Florida and about 82° in mid-winter, and, due to its velocity of flow, suffers little loss of heat up to its arrival off Cape Hatteras. Between Key West and Havana its mean surface velocity is 2¼ knots; off Fowey Rocks, Florida, 3½ knots; off Cape Hatteras, 2 knots; variations in which rates at different hours of the day being accounted for by influences of the lunar tide wave. Maximum velocity is considered generally as occurring about 3 hours after moon's transit. Average width from Florida to Cape Hatteras is 40 miles; off Nova Scotia it has spread to about 250. Influence of the Gulf Stream in raising North Atlantic sea temperatures and the general easterly current driven by prevailing westerly winds toward Europe's northwestern shores account for the comparatively mild climate found from France to the far north of Norway.

GULF WEED. The *Sargassum bacciferum,* or brownish seaweed, bearing air-vessels of berry form, growing in American tropical waters, thence drifting into the *Gulf Stream* where it is often found in large spread-out masses; also, any of several species of *Sargassum,* chiefly comprising the floating masses in the *Sargasso Sea.*

GULGUL. (Hind. *galgal*) A kind of cement coating made of pulverized sea-shells mixed with oil, applied to vessels' bottoms as a protection against wood-boring worms.

GULL. Loosely, any member of a large family (*Laridæ*) of long-winged, web-footed, aquatic birds; strictly, those of a sub-family, *Larinæ,* which excludes the allied *tern* and *jaeger.* Though naturally a sea bird, it also frequents rivers and lakes far inland; spends much of its time on the wing; not a diver, but feeds voraciously on fish offal, etc., and is considered valuable as a scavenger in and about a harbor. The 50 or more species vary in body size from 10 to 20 inches over all and are found in almost all latitudes exclusive of the more frigid areas of polar seas. In color they are usually white with silvery to dark gray upper plumage and sometimes black primaries; have a strong slightly hooked bill; and are noted for their raucous, noisy, squawking when busy at the usual scramble for food. At sea, large numbers follow ships for days on end awaiting and fighting for pickings from the disposed-of garbage. **Black-backed g.**, any of several adult birds having back and upper surface of wings a dark slate color; especially, the *great black-backed g.* (*Larus marinus*) of American Atlantic and European coasts, also called *eagle g.* and *goose g.* **G.-chaser** or **g.-teaser,** any bird which pursues and teases gulls, as the *jaegers* and certain *terns.* **Herring-g.,** the *Larus argentatus,* common large bird of North American Atlantic coasts, Great Lakes, and northern rivers; also widely numerous in Europe and other parts of the world; adult plumage white with bluish gray mantle and black and white specked wings; young, darker colored. **Ice-g.**, any of several Arctic species; especially, the *ivory g.*, a small bird all white when adult, with black feet; migrates to latitude 40° in winter. **Iceland g.**, large white-winged species (*Larus leucopterus*), similar to, but smaller than the burgomaster (*see* BURGOMASTER); breeds in Arctic and migrates to northern U.S. and France. **Kittiwake g.**, so called in imitation of its cry, breeds on rocky cliffs in Arctic, North Pacific, and North Atlantic, migrating south in winter; snow white with pearl blue mantle, primaries crossed with black and tipped with white; has black feet and yellow bill clouded with olive; genus *Rissa.* **Red-legged kittiwake** of North Pacific is a similar species with red legs and bill. **Ring-billed g.**, small American bird (*Larus delawarensis*) similar to *herring-g.* but having, when adult, a dark band on its bill. **Swallow-tailed g.**, a large species having a deeply forked tail; found only in Galapagos Islands and neighboring South American coast. **White g.** or **winter g.**, same as *kittiwake.* **White-headed g.**, properly a *tern,* one of several species having dark sooty plumage, head being white in the adult; chiefly found on Californian coast. **White-winged g.**, one in which a pale pearly mantle fades into white on the primaries without any dark markings. Found in Europe and North America.

GULLERY. A breeding place for gulls or similar birds, usually on rocky cliffs.

GULLETING. The trunk housing a rudder-stock; especially, its lower or outboard end, sometimes widened to give rudder play in shipping or unshipping, as in smaller craft. Also, parts in forward edge of a boat's rudder in way of pintles, which are cut away to allow entry of pintles in gudgeons when shipping the rudder.

GULLY. Trough or lengthy, comparatively narrow, depression in the sea-floor, extending into a continental shelf, or toward a sea-coast. Any channel worn by flow of water, as in a gap or rift in a high coast-line.

GUN. Any piece of ordnance set on a carriage or other mounting; *see* CANNON. Unit term for rounds fired: as, a *21-gun salute;* for a group of similar pieces: as, a *10-gun battery;* for cannon carried as armament: as, a *24-gun frigate.* To shoot a harpoon or toggle-iron; as, *to gun a whale.* **Air-g.,** *see* **A.-hammer** *in* AIR. **Chase-g.,** *see* CHASE. **Fog-g.,** *see* FOG. **G. brig,** handy 18th century two-masted square-rigged naval vessel armed with 8 to 12 guns. **G.-captain,** naval term for a petty officer commanding a gun's crew. **G. deck,** in a warship, deck on which *g's* are mounted, next below the main or weather deck; in old sailing navy days, a complete deck below the spar deck, as in a frigate; if two such decks, as in ships of the line, they were termed *main* and *lower g. deck,* respectively; if three, middle one was called *middle g. deck.* **G. money,** formerly prize-money awarded according to number of *g's* on the captured vessel; also termed *gunnage.* **G.-port,** opening in ship's side through which a *g.'s* muzzle is pointed in firing. **G. room,** in naval vessels, an apartment or mess used by junior officers; formerly by the *chief gunner* and his mates. **G.-tackle,** *see* TACKLE. **Harpoon-g.,** in whaling, a *g.* used for shooting a toggle-iron or harpoon at a whale. In more recent use, head of a special missile is fitted with an explosive which detonates upon entering whale, thus facilitating gripping in the flesh by the barbs or toggles opening from the harpoon's spearhead. **Line-throwing g.,** small mounted cannon, or a shoulder-*g.,* for firing a projectile with a small line attached, as used in getting a hawser to or from a vessel in rough weather, or in rigging the breeches-buoy apparatus for rescuing persons from a stranded vessel; also, *line-carrying g.* and *Lyle g.* **Minute g.,** *see* MINUTE. **Paint-g.,** device for spraying paint on a surface by means of air pressure; a *spray-g.* **Red-lead g.,** tool for forcing red lead between plates to stop leaks that can not conveniently be caulked; consists of a cone-pointed cylinder through which red lead or similar material is forced by screw pressure. **Rocket g.,** a small mortar or *g.* from which rockets are fired; *see* ROCKET. **Top g.,** a quick-firing piece mounted in a fighting-top of a warship. **Whaling g.,** *see* **Harpoon g. Y-gun,** a y-shaped mortar developed in World War I for anti-submarine use; simultaneously discharges two depth-bombs, projected toward each side of vessel from which fired. To **blow great g's,** old descriptive phrase meaning to blow with whole gale or hurricane force: said of the wind. To **house the g's,** in old cannon days, to run *g's* in from firing position and secure them. Breech of each was depressed and muzzle placed against ship's side above *g.*

port; tackles were set up and *g.* further secured by passing the *breeching,* or lashing to ship's side from breech, and *muzzle-lashing;* port was then closed. To **lay a g.,** to direct or aim a *g.* and elevate its muzzle as necessary, preparatory to firing.

GUNBOAT. One of a class next below an unprotected cruiser, having a small number of guns, moderately speedy, and less than 2000 tons displacement; general term for a vessel of light draft armed with one or more guns.

GUNDELOW. (Corruption of *gondola*) A heavy flat-bottomed barge, 50 to 70 feet in length and capable of carrying 60 to 70 tons weight, often rigged with a mast and sail, formerly in use as harbor lighters and in river work in New England. They are said to have been often used as river *gunboats* during the *Revolutionary War (1775–1783).* Also, *gundeloe, gundalow.*

GUNNAGE. Old term connoting number and weight of guns carried as armament on a vessel; *see* **G.-money** *in* GUN.

GUNNER. A person who loads, aims, or operates a gun. A warrant officer in U.S. and British navies who has charge of ordnance and ordnance stores. **G.'s gang,** group of men under a gunner who are detailed to clean and keep guns in good condition, attend to stowage and handling of ordnance stores, and other pertinent duties. To be **introduced to the g.'s daughter,** to be made fast to a gun and flogged, as, in such an event, was customary procedure in older navy days. **G.'s mate,** a petty officer who assists the *g.* He also was called upon to administer a flogging to offenders in "the good old days." **G.'s quadrant,** *see* QUADRANT. **Quarter-g.,** *see* QUARTER. **Seaman-g.,** a naval seaman trained in gunnery.

GUNNING A SEAM. See **Red-lead g.** *in* GUN; *also,* SEAM.

GUNNY. (Hind. *goni,* sacking) Strong coarse sacking or bagging stuff made from fiber of the *jute* or *Corchorus* plant, chiefly grown in India. A bag or sack of *gunny; gunny-sacking.* The material is used extensively for baling goods for shipment and also for cargo separation-cloths in a ship's hold. Same fiber is used in cordage manufacture.

GUNSTOCKING. Deck margin-plank of hardwood, as teak or greenheart, having its outer edge curved, laid at forward or after ends of vessel. It is cut to receive successive terminating butts of deck-planks as narrowing end of deck is approached.

GUNTER. Sliding topmast in the *gunter rig;* the triangular sail spread in such rig; both constituting the usually termed *sliding gunter.* **G. lug,** a small-boat sail having a long yard or gaff setting a high peak because of yard lying nearly parallel with mast. As with a *standing lug,* the tack is fast to mast, sail carries no boom, and yard is held to mast by a

traveler or ring. However, similar to a gaff-sail, lower end of yard is butted to mast by throat-jaws, which, in effect, justifies the term "gaff" in preference to "yard." **G. rig,** in boat-sailing, that in which a triangular-shaped sail is hoisted by sliding a topmast upward along a short lowermast, peak or head of sail being made fast to upper end of topmast and its tack, or lower forward corner, to lowermast. Halyard is rove in a sheave at top of lowermast and topmast is confined to former by two rings, or *g.-irons,* one secured to heel of topmast, the other about two feet farther up. Sail is efficiently spread by this means and, also, may be instantly reduced by letting go its halyard. However, the spars with attached sail make handling awkward in stepping or stowing, and, in boats of navy type, the gear becomes an obstacle to use of oars, when stowed on thwarts after being taken in; for which reasons use of *g's* was discontinued in U.S. Navy. The rig is favored in the French navy and usually is carried on two masts, with a single jib, in boats of the cutter, whaleboat, and gig type.

GUNTER'S SCALE. Invented by *Edwin Gunter, English mathematician and astronomer (1581–1626),* a large rule on which are marked scales of equal parts, chords, and both natural and logarithmic values of trigonometrical ratios. It was once used for solving astronomical and navigational problems; hence the colloquial phrase among seamen, "according to Gunter." *Gunter's sliding scale,* the original of our present *slide rule,* was the term given to his scale for computation of multiplication and division. He also is credited with first use of a *quadrant* bearing his name, by which the sun's hour angle, with its corresponding azimuth and altitude for any latitude, were shown. In addition, *Gunter's chain* is used officially in land surveying by both Americans and British, its value of 22 yards' length being a convenient one in that 10 square chains = 1 acre.

GUNTLINE. Line of depressed surface, or groove between strands on outside of a rope; unused space along bilges of casks laid in tier. Also, *cantline.*

GUNWALE. (Pron. *gunnel,* and thus sometimes written; from *gun* and *wale*) Originally, the uppermost *wale* (also *bend*), or strake of heavy planking on ship's side immediately below the *gun-ports,* or that corresponding to our present *sheer-strake* of plating. Uppermost heavy plank strake on main body of a boat or vessel; hence, loosely, termination of planking at rail of any craft, and often the upper edge of a boat's side (properly *capping*). **Box-g.,** in heavier boat-building, strength arrangement in which a strake of planking, sometimes called an *inwale,* is fastened fore-and-aft to inside of frames at their upper ends, through-bolted to sheer-strake (which, properly, is the *gunwale*), and the whole topped by the *capping* (or *rail*). **G. angle-bar,** or

g.-bar, connects outer edge of a deck-stringer (outer deck-plate) to the sheer-strake (upper strake of side-plating). **G.-plate,** another term for a *deck-stringer,* or outer strake of deck-plating, in any weather deck; as in an upper, spar, awning, shelter, bridge, forecastle, poop, or raised quarter-deck. Also, *g.-stringer.* **G. of poop, forecastle, bridge, etc.,** line of contact of deck-stringers of these decks with upper side-plate, or sheer-strake. **G.-tanks,** ballast tanks built in upper wings of some single-deck cantilever-framed vessels of ore or bulk cargo-carrying type. Usually of triangular section, their inside frames extend obliquely from ship's side to deck, the latter forming tank-top. Their purpose is to raise vessel's center of gravity when filled with water-ballast, in addition to providing immersing weight in absence of cargo. Also called *cantilever, topside,* and *wing tanks.* **Rounded g.,** plating forming a *turtle-back,* or rounded surface between ship's side and a weather deck, such as a forecastle or poop, commonly found in older steam-vessels and iron sailing-ships.

GURDY. A roller fixed on a boat's gunwale, providing a frictionless bearing over which lines or trawls are hauled in fishing.

GURNARD, FLYING. See **F. gurnard** *in* FLYING. Also, *flying-gurnet.*

GURRY. Refuse from operations of cutting in and boiling out whale blubber; fish offal; also, small strips of fish, as from cod or hake, used for bait in catching halibut; *gurry-bait.* **G.-butt,** large cask used by fishermen as a receptacle for cods' livers. **G.-fish,** straggling fish of a school that has left a fishing-ground. **G.-ground,** an area at sea where *g.* or fish offal may be dumped without injury to the fishery. Such places are selected by mutual agreement of fishermen. **G.-shark,** the *Greenland shark, sleeper,* or *ground-shark;* so called from its habit of quietly lying in wait for fish offal thrown overboard.

GUSSET. Also called *gore, gusle,* and *gusset-plate,* a piece of plate, usually triangular in shape, fitted to distribute a strength connection between two structural members; as, at ends of panting-beams, where wide end of gusset is secured to a panting-stringer; at union of a margin-plate bracket with a tank top; or as a knee connection for a light deck-beam with a frame. Also loosely applied to any connecting-plate; as a *diamond-plate,* or one spreading the union of two crossing members. **G.-stays,** triangular plates fitted in a steam boiler for strengthening connection of end plates with sides.

GUST. Sudden blast or squall of short duration, such as is often experienced in vicinity of a mountainous coast-line. Wind is said to be *gusty* when marked by frequent *g's* or *squalls,* as in stormy or "gusty" weather.

GUT. A corruption of *gat; see* GAT.

GUTTER WATERWAY. Channel or gutter along outer sides of a weather deck, formed on the deck-stringer between *gutter angle-bar* (outer edge of deck-planking) and *gunwale angle-bar;* in effect, a gutterway for draining off water from deck, thence through scuppers and overboard.

GUY. (Sp. *guia,* guide) Rope, chain, or tackle rigged to stay, steady, support, or swing a spar; as, *boat-boom g., cargo-boom g., davit g., jib-boom g., main boom g.* Rope leading to a mast and holding in position a hoisting rig suspended from another mast. A steadying or guiding rope attached to an object being hoisted or lowered. To steady or place in a required position by means of a *guy* or *guys;* as, to *g. a boom.* **Belly-g.,** see BELLY. **Blubber-g.,** see BLUBBER. **Boom g.,** rope or tackle for steadying a boom of a fore-and-aft sail. **Davit-g.,** see DAVIT. **Derrick-g.,** usually consists of a luff tackle at lower end of a pendant which is secured to derrick head. **Funnel-g.,** see FUNNEL. **G.-rod,** a metal rod or stay, as for supporting a ventilator shaft, galley funnel, etc. **G.-span,** tackle connecting heads of two adjacent cargo-booms, used, in combination with side guys leading to deck, to set booms in required position for transferring cargo to or from ship; usually rigged on booms of extraordinary length, as in vessels carrying long timber; sometimes called in U.S. *steam schooner g.,* from its early use by craft of that type in the Pacific Coast lumber trade. **Jib-boom g's,** ropes or chains for laterally staying the jib-boom. Depending on length of boom and whether a flying jib-boom was carried, 1 to 3 fitted on each side, leading to bows. In older sailing-ships they were set up to the catheads and, for better staying power, were spread by *whiskers* or booms which projected from, and at right angles to, the bowsprit. These were stayed in an approximately horizontal position by *whisker-g's* leading from their outer ends down to tip of the martingale. Also, *jib-g's.* **Jumper-g.,** another term for a *whisker-g.* **Lazy g.,** a rope or light tackle to steady the boom of a fore-and-aft sail. **Martingale g's,** ropes or chains serving as fore-and-aft stays for the martingale or *dolphin-striker,* leading from tip of latter to end of, and one or more points on, the jib-boom. Combination of these with *martingale back-ropes* and dolphin-striker forms a stiffening bridge against stress in the jib stays due to press of sail or vessel heaving in a seaway. The guys here noted are sometimes termed *martingales* only; as, *flying jib-boom martingale, jib-boom martingale;* and dolphin-striker as *martingale boom.* **Traveling-g.,** short line traveling on a stay, or on a runner in a purchase, for preventing a tackle-block from turning and thus twisting the tackle parts.

GYBE. (Du. *gijben,* to shift) To shift position of a fore-and-aft sail from one side to another; as, when sailing before the wind, or when altering course so that wind is brought on the opposite quarter. Also *gibe; jibe.*

GYPSY.   A drum with raised flanges, projecting from a deck winch or windlass, for heaving on running gear, hawsers, etc.; also termed *drum end, niggerhead, winch end, whipping-drum.* Also, a small hand winch, sometimes called a *crab-winch,* having a similar drum and fitted with a ratchet-wheel and pawl, much used on sailing-vessels; a small capstan operated by steam or electricity; *gipsy, gypsey.*

GYRATION, FERREL'S LAW OF.   *See* LAW.

GYRO.   Short for *gyroscope;* combining term for mechanical instruments the functioning of which is effected basically by applied gyroscopic principles. **G.-compass,** *see* COMPASS. **G. course-recorder,** *see* COURSE. **G.-pilot,** mechanical apparatus for automatically steering a course by *g.-compass.* Power control of rudder is effected electrically and requisite angle of helm is governed by magnitude of ship's deviation from course. Such swing or departure from the steered course, due to rigidity of steering *repeater* card (*see G.-compass*) effects contact for producing necessary amount of helm. In latest *Sperry g.-pilot,* it is claimed that sensitivity of steering control is such that helm action is produced by one-sixth degree alteration in ship's head. **G.-repeater,** *see* Gyro-c. *in* COMPASS. **G.-stabilizer;** advantage of the gyroscope's properties of taking up a rigid position in space, and in that its axis of rotation moves at right angles to direction of an applied external force, has been taken in equipping some vessels with this stabilizer with object of reducing rolling to a minimum. The installation is simply a heavy *gyroscope,* having its spinning axis in the midship vertical plane, fixed in ship's hold. Upon vessel beginning the slightest roll, a *pilot gyro,* or small control, instantly hastens main gyro's axis inclination toward ship's rising side, thus exerting a timely countering force to that causing such roll. Experiments have shown that, with proper *g.* fly-wheel, it is possible to reduce a 30° roll to one of 2° in less than a minute on vessels of the destroyer type. It is claimed that the equipment need not exceed in weight one per centum of ship's displacement. Latest in this field, however, is the *Denny-Brown ship stabilizer* which was tried out with great success in 1936, although the principle on which the apparatus is based was discovered and patented as early as 1898 by a Scotsman named *Andrew Wilson.* The stabilizer consists of two horizontal fins, one on each side of ship, each shaped like an airplane wing with a hinged tail flap. As fins are extended from their housings the required upward or downward pressure, or the ordinary bilge-keel function, is augmented by rudder effect of the flaps, these coming under control of two *gyroscopes.* A recent installation of this British device in a liner 670 feet in length has each fin extending from ship's side 12 feet with a fore-and-aft measurement of 6½ feet. During World War II the British navy fitted 109 of its vessels with this *stabilizer.*

H

H. Hoisted singly, *International Code* flag *H* ("*how*") indicates "*I have a pilot on board.*" As an abbreviation in nautical astronomy, *h* = hour; *h* or *H* = altitude or elevation; *H* = hack watch. In compass magnetism, *H* = horizontal component of earth's total magnetic force. In log-books and weather recording, *H* = heavy sea; *h* = hail. *H-bar*, *H-beam*, *H-girder*, *H-iron* signify structural metal of H-shaped cross-section; also *I-bar*, *I-beam*, etc.

H. A. Abbreviation commonly used in nautical astronomy for *hour angle*. Letter *t* is also employed, *esp.* when angle is noted in degrees, as *westerly*, from 0 up to 360.

HAAF. (Scand. origin; Ice. *haf*, sea) Deep-sea fishing grounds in vicinity of Orkney and Shetland Islands. **H.-boat,** large open boat divided into several compartments, also called *sixern* and *Shetland yawl*, used in *haaf-fishing*, or that carried on by long-lines locally known as *haafures,* for cod, haddock, etc., off the Shetlands.

HACK. A vessel is said to *hack the sea* when sailing close to wind and, with little or no pitching motion, cuts through a prevailing short rough sea. **H.-chronometer** or **h.-watch,** a working timepiece used in taking observations and checking chronometer time by signal, as a protective measure against frequent exposure of the one or more standard chronometers carried. It is compared with the standard immediately before or after use, the difference indicated being termed in U.S. naval practice *C–W,* which is added to *h. time* to obtain standard chronometer reading at instant of observation; *see* **c-w. Under h.,** old naval term for status of an officer confined to his quarters for a minor disciplinary infraction or breach of etiquette; a situation analogous to the merchantman's "*in the dog-house.*"

HACKIA. A heavy wood of hard, tough, oily, irregular-grained texture obtained from a tropical tree (genus *Guaiacum*) about 50 feet in height and over 2 feet in diameter; especially valuable for manufacture of block-sheaves, dead-eyes, bull's-eyes, clump blocks, winch brake-lining and, also, laid in fore-and-aft strips, provides satisfactory material for propeller tail-end shaft bearings. Its weight is about 70 lbs. per cubic foot. With a few other hard woods of Australia and New Zealand, hackia is commonly termed *lignum vitæ* (wood of life).

HACKLE. In rope-making, an instrument for combing, cleaning, sorting, and straightening the fiber, as flax or hemp; also, *hatchel*. To comb, as fiber, in preparation for manufacture.

HACKMATACK. (*Amer. Indian origin*) Also called *tamarack, juniper,* and *American larch,* a tree from which its lower extremity provides natural grained knees, deck-hooks, and other sharply curved timber for shipbuilding use. The wood is resinous, tough, and durable, but not suitable for straight ship timber or planking because of its tendency to warp. Weight of seasoned wood, 38 lbs. per cubic foot.

HACK WATCH. *See* **HACK.**

HADDOCK. Fish allied to the cod, but smaller and having in profile a more arched back, with longer and pointed anterior dorsal fin; has a black line along its upper sides and black spot close behind its gills. Habitat, North Atlantic from Iceland to Cape Hatteras and coast of France; also coasts of Norway to White Sea. The smoked fish is called *Finnan haddie,* from a fishing village of that name (also *Findon*) on northeast Scottish coast. A related species of the same name is found in New Zealand waters. **H.-line,** 3-strand white cotton or flax line used in haddock long-line or trawl-line fishing; usually classed as *2-lb. stuff, i.e.,* its weight is 2 lbs. per 20 fathoms, or 120 feet.

HADLEY'S QUADRANT. Named for *John Hadley, English astronomer (1682–1744),* the original of our present marine sextant and employing the same optical principles therein. Had an arc of 45° and measured angles up to 90°. Though *Hadley* is credited with invention of the instrument, it also is claimed that *Thomas Godfrey, American mathematician (1704–1749)* brought out a similar quadrant subsequently known as *Godfrey's bow,* at about the same time, or circa 1730, independently of Hadley's innovation; also called *Hadley's octant. See* QUADRANT.

HAGDON. Name given to a larger species of *shearwater,* an ally of the petrel or Mother Carey's chicken, by North Atlantic seamen and fishermen; also, *hagden, hagdown, hag. See* SHEARWATER.

HAG'S TOOTH. Sailor's term for a prominent irregularity in a sword or paunch mat, cross-pointing, grafting, etc., detracting from shipshape uniform appearance of the work.

HAGUE CONVENTION. Meeting of delegates of 44 countries at The Hague, 1907, for purpose of agreement in recognition of status, certain rights and immunities, and employment as vessels of war, of merchant ships in time of war, with other pertinent questions of international law. It was the outgrowth of the *Hague Tribunal* established by the *International Peace Conference, 1899,* for the settlement of international disputes. In 1921, what are known as **Hague Rules** were drawn up by a similar meeting for purposes of universal agreement in defining various rights, risks, and liabilities of shipowners, charterers, and shippers in connection with carriage of goods by sea.

HAIL. (Ice. *heill,* sound in health: used in greeting) To *speak* or call out to in salutation or greeting, or in order to attract attention, as from one ship to another. An unidentified vessel customarily is addressed *"Ship ahoy!"; "Steamer ahoy!";* etc.; if known, she is *hailed* by name, as, *"Neptune ahoy!";* or *"Ahoy, on board the Neptune!"* Previous to general use of radio at sea, it was considered the duty of an arriving vessel's master to report any craft *spoken* on the high seas, which, though sometimes done by signal, implied that either vessel was *hailed* by the other. *See* SPEAK. A merchant vessel is said to *h. from,* or belong to, her port of registration, name of which is indicated on her stern or counter. **H.-tower,** an umbrella cloud, or turret-shaped *cumulus* or *cumulo-nimbus,* rising to a great altitude and from which *h.* is falling. To **pass the h.,** to orally report to officer of the deck, as the *"All's well"* of lookouts and sentries in indicating their attention to duty. **Within h.,** at or within such a distance that sound of the voice may be heard distinctly, as passing vessels.

HAIR. A minute measure of time, space, degree, etc. **To a h.,** with utmost exactness or completeness. A comparatively small amount; as in, *heave up just a h.; ease the tackle a h.* To **weigh an anchor by the h.,** *see* ANCHOR PHRASEOLOGY.

HAKE. (Nor. *hake-fisk,* hook-fish) An important food fish of genus *Merluccius,* allied to the cod, found on northeastern American shores and in northern Europe. Smaller than the cod, differs also in having a continuous dorsal fin extending more than half body length to the tail, with similar but slightly shorter ventral fin. Also called *whiting,* a common European species is the *merluce,* while that of America is the *silver h.* (*Merluccius bilinearis*), the flesh of which differs little from that of the true cod. Of lesser importance are the *squirrel h.* or *codling* and *white h.* found on both sides of Atlantic north of 35° latitude. Also, *haak.*

HALCYON SEAS. Poetic reference to a state of peace and tranquility prevailing at sea, occasioned according to the ancients by the presence of the *halcyon* in its floating nest, a bird identified as the kingfisher, during its period of incubation about the winter solstice, or *halcyon days.*

HALE. To drag, pull, draw, or move by dragging; old form of our present word *haul;* as, to *hale an anchor home.* **H.-bowline,** old English contemptuous name for a sailor.

HALF. As used in designating compass direction, marking midway between any two points; as, *N ½ E; NE ½ N; SW by W ½ W; WNW ½ W.* In sounding by hand-lead, indicating an intermediate half-fathom depth, as called out by leadsman; thus, *a half five* (= 5½ fathoms); *a half less ten* (= 9½ fathoms). **H. a gale,** *see* GALE. **H'beak,** small elongated fish resembling the *gar* but having its lower jaw extended to about one-sixth its body length; widely distributed in warmer seas and considered a good food fish. **H.-beam,** a ship's beam interrupted in length by a hatch-coaming, boiler or machinery casing, etc., as distinguished from a whole or through beam, *i.e.,* one extending from side to side of vessel. **H. board,** *see* To **make a h. b.** *in* BOARD. **H.-breadth,** half horizontal distance, usually measured at upper deck, between outer surfaces of planking at each side of a wooden vessel; or, between outside of faying surfaces of frames in steel construction; also termed *h. molded beam.* **H.-breadth plan,** that representing symmetrical longitudinal *h.* of vessel's hull as viewed from above, showing various water-lines, bow and buttock lines, deck lines at side, and frame stations. **H.-breadth staff,** in shipbuilding, a rod or batten on which are marked the *h.*-lengths of beams, as taken from *h.-breadth plan.* **H. crown,** bight of a rope encircling a spar or other object, with both parts crossed and secured together by a seizing; also called *cuckold's neck* and *cuckold's knot.* **H.-davit,** a single davit, as one for fishing an anchor, supporting an accommodation-ladder, oil-hose, etc. **H. deck,** *see* DECK. **H.-decked boat,** designating a sail-boat having a deck covering approximately her forward *h.;* also one having a small *cuddy* in her bows and a broad *washboard* extending along each side as protection against ingress of water when boat heels under sail pressure. **H.-floor,** *see* FLOOR. **H.-floor keelson,** *see* KEELSON. **H. hitch,** a rope's end turned around the standing part and taken through the bight. **H. mast,**

position of a flag at approximately *h.* height to which usually hoisted; as an ensign so displayed in token of mourning, or sometimes as a distress signal. To hoist or fly a flag in such position. **H.-model,** miniature representation of ship's hull as cut in *h.* along its central vertical fore-and-aft plane; principally used in laying lines for proposed shell-plating arrangement. **H.-mile rule,** term for the practice, in observance of pilot rules in U.S. waters, of giving and anwering whistle signals when powered vessels are within sight of, and crossing, meeting, or passing each other at a distance within *h.* a mile of each other. (*Pilot Rules for Inland Waters: Section 312.3*) **H.-poop,** a deck of comparatively small height above after end of weather deck; sometimes applied to a *raised quarter-deck,* as in small vessels. **H.-port,** formerly one of two parts of a gun-port fitted snugly about a gun, one opening upward, the other downward; now, either of *h.*-doors constituting a *side-* or *cargo-port.* **H.-round bar,** iron or steel bar of approximately semi-circular cross-section used for stiffening light bulkheads or casings, edges and inside of hatch-coamings; for molding, as along a bulwark rail or around the counter; and for chafing protection, as outside a mooring-chock or in way of an anchor. **H.-seas over,** halfway across the sea; hence, figuratively, in a semi-intoxicated condition; "*three sheets in the wind.*" **H.-sheave,** a fixed sheave or part of a sheave, grooved hole, or other rounded device providing a lead for, and easing friction in, a rope. **H.-solid floor,** a floor-plate pierced by lightening holes or openings for giving access to either side of it. **H. speed,** referring to rotation velocity of propeller, in U.S. Navy, one-quarter less than standard speed or that set by officer commanding fleet or squadron; in merchant ships, two-thirds to three-fourths of full speed, depending upon practice adopted by operators or arrangement between master and chief engineer. **H. staff,** flown at *h.* height of staff; *see* **H. mast. H. tide,** time, state, or height of tide halfway between ebb and flood or between high and low water. **H.-tide dock** or **basin,** *see* DOCK. **H.-tide rock,** one exposed during fall of tide; also, one partly covered or awash at all times; sometimes applied figuratively to a deeply laden vessel. **H.-timber,** in wooden shipbuilding, one of a pair of timbers bolted together side by side and forming part of a *main body,* or *square, frame;* also, any of shorter timbers constituting the *cant frames.* **H.-top,** *h.* the platform or *top,* on a square-rigged vessel's lowermasthead, when it is divided for sending aloft. **Tack and h. tack,** *see* TACK.

HALIBUT. (M.E. *hali,* holy; *butte,* flounder or plaice; from being much eaten on fast or holy days) Largest species of flatfish (*Hippoglossus*) known, often attaining a weight of two to three hundred pounds, and an excellent food fish; inhabits all northern seas and, like the cod and his allies, prefers colder waters and rarely is caught south of Cape Cod or the English Channel; said to be fast diminishing in Atlantic, found in greater numbers in Pacific waters. With view of preservation of the halibut fishery of northern Pacific waters and Bering Sea, "*North Pacific Halibut Act*" was passed by U.S. Congress, June 28, 1937, following a convention between U.S. and Canada at Ottawa in January of same year (*16 U.S.C. 772*). As a ground fish, it is usually taken in hard bottom areas at depths of from 40 to 60 fathoms. **Arrow-toothed h.,** of the flounder family and intermediate between cod and flounder, a food fish of northern Pacific American coasts. **Greenland h.,** species found in colder North Atlantic waters; remarkable in having both sides colored as opposed to one colored side and other white in other members of flatfish family; weighs 15 to 20 pounds at maturity. **Monterey h.,** also called *bastard h.,* large flounder of inferior food quality found on North American Pacific coasts. **H.-line,** 3-strand white cotton or flax line, about 3 lbs. per 20 fathoms, used in *h.-fishing.*

HALLIARD. *See* HALYARD.

HALMALILLE. A tree of Ceylon, tropical Australia, and Philippines from which is obtained a hard and valuable wood much used in boat-building because of its resistance to attack of marine wood-borer worms and its tendency to preserve iron from corrosion. Halmalille is also known as *Trincomali-wood,* from the sea-port of that name in Ceylon. Also, *halmilla.*

HALO. Luminous ring appearing around sun or moon as result of refracted light passing through suspended ice particles in upper atmosphere; usually of 22° or 46° radius and often reddish in color on its inner side. With gathering cirro-stratus cloud and a falling barometer, regarded as presaging a gale.

HALSE. Also *haulse;* 16th century spelling of hawse, from Norse word *hals,* the neck or extreme bow of a vessel. *See* HAWSE.

HALYARD. (M.E. *hallyer,* a hauler or puller) Usually in plural form as *halyards, halliards,* or *haulyards;* single rope or purchase by which a sail is hoisted or set; as, *jib-halyards; gaff-topsail h's; top-gallant h's.* In a square-rigger, upper topsails, upper top-gallantsails, royals, and skysails are fitted with *h's* which consist of a *tye,* usually a chain. fast to middle of yard and rove through a sheave-hole in the mast, a runner (chain or wire) from one side of ship through a single block fast to tye, thence downward and joined to *halyard-tackle* at other side of ship. Jibs, staysails, and gaff-topsails are hoisted by either a single rope or a double whip; *i.e., h.* works through a single block at head of sail. Gaff sails, excepting those of small craft, have *peak h's* leading to outer part of gaff, and *throat h's* to throat, or end of gaff next to mast. These are in the form of purchases, varying in power with size of sail. The now obsolete studding-sail was hoisted by a single rope *h.* to its boom end. The small line used in hoisting flags is also called *h.* or *h's; as signal-h's; ensign h.;* and sometimes that for hoisting signal-lamps or signal-shapes; as, *lamp-h.* **Crowfoot h.,** see CROW-FOOT. **H. rack,** wooden box or frame in which hauling part of a *h.* is coiled for protection against fouling. **Lazy h.,** old and usually smaller rope rove in place of *h's* during a long stay in port, as a preservative measure. To **settle the h's,** to ease the rope a little, as when sail and gear have shrunk in wet weather. To **slip the h's,** in small craft, to let go the *slip-hitch* with which *h's* should always be made fast; *h's* must be secured in such manner that a simple jerk will release rope in event of a squall or any other occasion demanding instant lowering of sail.

HAMAL. (*Ar. = a lamb*) α *Arietis,* brighter of two navigational stars lying about 4° apart in *Aries;* of magnitude 2.2 and having declination of 23¼° N. and S.H.A. of 329°, may be located about 20° east of the *Square of Pegasus. Sheratan* (β *Arietis*) is his near-by companion.

HAMBROLINE. Three-yarn, tightly laid, left-handed seizing stuff of tarred or untarred hemp. Weight, about 90 feet per pound. Also, *hamber-line; humberline;* originally for River Humber, England.

HAMLET. A grouper of about 2½ feet length, having a large spiny dorsal fin extending more than half body length to tail. A good food fish, caught from Florida southward to Brazil.

HAMMER-HEAD. Any of certain sharks of ugly appearance, so named from the marked lateral expansion of its head. Usually found in warmer seas, are extremely voracious and perhaps most active swimmers among sharks. Of five existing species best known is the widely distributed *Sphyrna zygæna,* also called *balance-fish,* attaining a length of 12 to 15 feet. A "hammer" known as the *shovelhead* with narrower and blunter head, inhabits tropical and sub-tropical parts of Atlantic and Pacific Oceans. Also, *hammer-headed shark; hammer.*

HAMMOCK. (Of Carib origin, referred to by early Spanish traders and explorers as *hamaca,* a native hanging bed made of fiber netting) Hanging bed usually made of a piece of canvas measuring about 3 by 6 feet, slung at each end by several cords, or *clews,* which are connected to a common ring for placing on a hook, or other means of *slinging.* Formerly much used in naval vessels by lower deck personnel, now almost displaced by metal-framed berths set up in tiers of two to three in height, depending on number of men carried and sleeping space allotted. *Hammocks* were slung on the gun deck or decks from *h.-battens* secured to the beams for the purpose, sometimes to *h.-stanchions,* and

when not in use were rolled up neatly with included blanket, etc., and tied up, or *lashed,* before stowing in the *h.-netting,* or *h.-berthing,* which, for many years, was a net or long box-trough in the bulwarks covered by painted canvas called a *h.-cloth,* or *top-cloth.* Later when bulwarks were dispensed with, space was assigned as *h.-berthing* below the weather deck. **H. girtlines,** see GIRT. **H.-shroud,** a regulation hammock used as a covering for a man buried at sea. **H.-stop,** small line for slinging *h.* by its ring, in absence of a hook. To **lash a h.,** to roll it up with its bedding and secure it with a *h.-lashing.* To **sling a h.,** to hang it in position for use.

HAMPER. Necessary gear or equipment which sometimes is in the way or presents an obstacle to certain work. To impede, burden, or encumber; as, *a high deck-load hampered both ship and crew.* **Top h.,** collectively, fittings or equipment constituting ship's upper works or rigging. In a disparaging sense, vessel is said to be *top-hampered* when apparently burdened with too much gear aloft.

HAMSTRING. In older whaling practice, to cut the fluke-tendons of a whale. With objective of rendering the "fish" helpless, this was done from an attacking boat as opportunity afforded by a sharp long-handled *spade* thrown as a harpoon, or used spear fashion.

HAND. To take in and stow or furl, as a sail; to haul on, manipulate, or secure; as, to *hand the fore sheet.* A sailor or other lower-deck crew member. **All h's,** entire ship's crew; total number included in a gang or squad. **Bear a h.,** an order to join and assist in some work being done; *lend a h.* **H.-beckets,** see BECKET. **H.-fid,** see FID. **H. flags,** see FLAG. **H.-glass,** see GLASS. **H.-grab,** see GRAB. **H.-grip,** a handle; grasp or handle of an oar. **H.-hole,** small access opening for admitting the *h.* in cleaning, or for inspection purposes, as in a boiler, casing, covering for machinery, etc. **H.-irons,** manacles or handcuffs connected by a short chain. **H. lead,** sounding-lead used in shoal water; see LEAD. **H. light,** a portable lantern; especially, one used as a signal light in a boat. **H.-line,** in fishing, one attended solely by *h.,* without a pole or rod, as from a vessel's deck or from a boat. **H.-lining,** method of fishing in which a single line is used, as distinguished from *long-lining* in which line is fitted with a large number of snoods and laid out on or near bottom, the work being carried on from boats. See FISHING. **H.-log,** see LOG. **H. over h.,** reaching the *h's* one above or beyond the other, as in hoisting, climbing a rope, or hauling on a line. **H.-pump,** one *h.*-operated by crank or lever, as a galley fresh-water pump, a bilge pump, or force pump. In powered vessels, generally fitted as emergency equipment, as for fire-fighting or freeing bilges. **H.-rail,** see RAIL. **H.-riveting,** as distinguished from that performed by an automatic hammer (usually of the pneumatic, or compressed air operated type) riveting in which *h.* hammers only are used. Automatic hammers for this use practically have displaced *h.-riveting* in shipbuilding to-day, since better and faster work is produced by one riveter who takes the place of two required in *h.*-hammer work. **H. steering-gear,** the tackles or mechanism for steering a vessel by *h.* Source of power is a manually operated steering-wheel of sufficient diameter to provide necessary leverage for controlling rudder by tiller-ropes (or chains) wound on a barrel in the fore-and-aft line, or for turning rudder by right- and left-handed screw arrangement connected directly to rudder-stock. **H.-tally,** *see* TALLY. **H. taut,** *h.* tight, said of a rope when hauled taut by *h.;* moderate tension. **Hold in h.,** keep under control; keep *in h.;* as, to *hold in h. a mutinous crew.* **In h.,** said of initial action promising success in further achievement; a job is *well in h.* when being executed timely and satisfactorily. **Taut h.,** an officer who maintains strict discipline amongst his men. To **lend a h.,** *see* **Bear a h.**

HANDICAP RACING. Yacht racing in which boats are allowed an advantage specified in time or distance, depending upon departure from a standard sail area, size, rig, or type.

HANDINESS. Quality or degree of satisfactory maneuverability exhibited by a vessel under action of propeller or in sailing.

HANDLE. To control or operate, as a vessel, in maneuvering by sail or other power. To load, stow, or discharge, as cargo. **Handling charges** on cargo consignments usually are confined to costs for all necessary care, stowage, and transfer of goods during interval between their delivery to carrier for shipment and reception by ship's tackles, and/or, conversely, from time of landing goods from ship to that of delivery to consignee.

HANDSAW FISH. Large voracious fish of the deeper waters of Pacific; has a long high dorsal fin and long lancet-like teeth from which it gets its name. Also, a small fish having an almost round profile, long dorsal and anal spiny fringes, and lancelike spines on each side of base of tail; chiefly found in East Indian seas; called also *tang, barber-, doctor-,* and *surgeon-fish.*

HANDSOMELY. In ship-shape style; carefully and neatly; skilfully; as, *slack away handsomely.* Sometimes used in a helm order, as, *"Right rudder,— handsomely!"*

HANDSPIKE. A handy bar of wood used as a pry or lever in raising or moving weighty objects, heaving on a windlass, tightening a heavy lashing, etc.; a capstan-bar. **Roller-h.,** as formerly used in moving heavy gun-carriages, a stout lever on handspike fitted at its fulcrum with one or two lignum vitæ or brass rollers by which carriage was lifted clear of deck and shifted or slewed into position desired.

HANDY. Said of a vessel possessing the quality of being easily managed or maneuvered through being obedient to helm or turning action of screw; or adapted to easy handling, as in tacking, shortening or setting sail, etc. **H. billy,** small tackle for general use about the deck, as in setting up on halyards, taking in slack of mooring-lines, etc., where steam or other power is unavailable; usually a *luff-tackle* with tail on double block and hook on single block; a *watch-tackle,* or any such *h.* purchase. Also, a portable *h. pump* for discharging water from bilges or tanks; or, a force pump drawing water from sea for washing decks or as auxiliary fire-fighting equipment.

HANG. Rake or inclination; as, *forward hang of the masts.* Effect of an adverse current or wind on speed; as, *tide gave us a 3-knot hang.* Sny, or upward curve of side-planking conforming to a vessel's sheer. To **h. a boat,** to hold her against wind or current by thrusting an oar or pole in the bottom on her lee side. Boat presses against pole, holder of which regulates position of boat in order to balance her broadside on. To **h. off,** to take stress on a rope while it is transferred from one secured position to another. To lie in vicinity of a port or place without mooring or communicating with shore; as, *ship hangs off the breakwater.* To **h. on,** to hold fast, as men sustaining stress on a rope, etc. To **h. on by the eyelids,** to support oneself by little available means in a hazardous position aloft, as during vessel's motion in a seaway. **H'ing clamp,** a beam-clamp, or such device that may be fixed to a suitable part of ship's structure for attaching a tackle-block, suspending a stage, etc. **H'ing compass,** a magnetic compass suspended from a deckhead, as in the captain's cabin, and which may be read from beneath; an *overhead* or *telltale compass.* **H'ing in the gear,** said of square sails upon being clewed up or hauled in by buntlines and loosely gathered to the yard. **H'ing keel,** a bar keel, or one extending below line of plank or plating surface; opposed to *flat-plate keel.* **H'ing knee,** wooden deck-beam knee one leg of which is secured to ship's side. **H'ing pendant,** *see* PENDANT.

HANK. (Sw. *hank,* band, tie, or clasp) One of the sliding rings, U-shaped fittings, or links securing luff of a jib or staysail to its stay, luff of a gaff sail hoisted on a traveler, or a brailing-in gaff-sail's head sliding on its traveler. Wooden *hanks* are usually fitted in case of a fiber rope stay; otherwise, are of metal, as galvanized iron or gun-metal. A small coil or skein of white line, cord, signal-halyard stuff, or other light cordage. **H. for h.,** in sailing, vessels are said to thus hold their relative positions when tacking or head-reaching and making equal speed; "neck and neck," as in a race.

HANSE. A sudden curved rise or drop in the structure; as, in older vessels, that part of a poop rail (*taff-rail*) turning downward to the main or bulwark rail; also, *hance, haunch.*

HARBOR. (M.E. *herbor*, shelter for soldiers) A navigable area affording safe anchorage and reasonably effectual shelter for vessels; *esp.*, one in which goods may be loaded or discharged and passengers taken in or landed; a haven. Also, as in British usage, *harbour*, an earlier form being *harborough*. **Artificial h.**, one in which principal shelter is provided by a breakwater or mole; also, basin or dock area dredged or excavated to accommodate shipping in a sheltered locality, as at one side of a river. **Close h.**, one lying in a completely sheltered area, as in or off a river, narrow arm of the sea, etc.; opposed to an *open harbor*, or one partly exposed to sea. **Floating h.**, one protected from sea waves by a floating breakwater or system of rafts of heavy timber appropriately moored. **H.-deck**, see DECK. **H. dues**, port charges or fees levied on sea-going vessels for use of a harbor. Usually paid according to vessel's net registered tonnage, such charges are made for maintenance of buoys, breakwaters, lights, navigable depths by dredging, piers, and all administration expenses connected therewith. **H. facilities**, those advantages and conveniences provided vessels making use of a *h.*, in the sense of facilitating successful navigation, as distinguished from *port facilities*, or those provided for transference of cargo and/or passengers. Under this term are included safe anchorage areas, channels, and depths alongside wharves; mooring posts or buoys; tug-boats; dry-docks; and ship repair plants. **H. furl** or **stow**, see FURL. **H.-gasket**, see GASKET. **H. light**, lighthouse marking a *h.* entrance. **H. line**, bounding or water-front line of a port, *h.*, or navigable area to which the land proper extends or may be reclaimed, or buildings abutted, as fixed by law; also, line approximately parallel with that of a water-front, marking projecting limit of piers or wharves. **H. log**, extract from ship's log-book, or section in such book, constituting a journal of happenings during stay in port. **H. manager**, chiefly in British usage, official who is charged with administration of affairs under a governing *h.* authority; a port director. **H.-master**, a government executive responsible for enforcement of regulations governing berthing, loading, and discharging of vessels, disposal of refuse, safety precautions, etc. In some countries called *Captain of the Port*, whose duties also include control of harbor police, quarantine, placing of buoys, dredging operations, etc., and who generally is vested with more extensive authority than that of his American or British equivalent. **H. of refuge**, one providing temporary shelter to vessels in bad weather or contrary winds. Sometimes also, but not necessarily, a commercial port. Also, *port of refuge*. **H.-porpoise**, see PORPOISE. **H.-**

reach, that stretch of a winding stream or river entering or passing a harbor. **H. signals**, see P. signal *in* PORT. **H. survey**, engineering survey of geologic and hydrographic conditions in a *h.* with the view of charting, or correcting an existing chart of, the area. **H.-watch**, an anchor-watch; one or more men detailed for watch duty while in port. **H. works**, see **H. facilities. Open h.**, one protected in part only by the land and open to sea; an open *roadstead*. **Tidal h.**, one in which the tide flows or rises and falls, as distinguished from a dock area in which water is maintained at a required level by a wall.

HARD. To full extent, as in helm order, *"Hard left!"; "Hard alee!"*; extreme in direction or contact, as, *hard aft, hard against the pier;* sharply defined and ominous, as, *hard edge of a cloudbank.* A firm foreshore or beach used as a landing-place. **H. alee**, see ALEE. **H. all!**, in rowing, order to oarsmen to exert their full strength in pulling. **H. and fast**, held firmly to the ground, as a stranded vessel. **H. aport**, see APORT. **H. ashore**, fixed *h. and fast* on a beach, rocks, shoal, etc., as a vessel. **H. astarboard**, see ASTARBOARD. **H. by**, close at hand; close to; as, *vessel is anchored hard by the jetty.* **H. aweather**, order to put boat's tiller full way to *weather* side, thus turning craft away from the wind; also, *h. up.* **H. down**, order to put tiller full way to *lee* side, or opposite to *h.* aweather; also, *h. alee;* descriptive of position of helm in either case. **H. fish**, such as are salted and dried, as cod, haddock, pollack, etc. **H. knot**, one drawn tightly and difficult to loose; hence, a man of unusual physical strength. **H. over**, said of helm when turned as far as possible in either direction. **H. patch**, see PATCH. To **ride h.**, see RIDE. **H.-tack**, thick, hard biscuits, baked without salt and kiln-dried, either round or square in shape, formerly much used as provisions on lengthy voyages; *sea-biscuit; ship-biscuit; Liverpool pan-tiles.* The old-fashioned *tack* required to be softened in one's coffee before attempting the impossible with the teeth; often was prepared in the palatable form of *cracker hash* and customarily included in such dishes as *lobscouse, sea-pie*, and *dog's body.* **H. up**, same as *h. aweather.*

HARMATTAN. An intensely dry breeze from the Sahara Desert prevalent during December, January, and February on the African coast from the equator to neighborhood of Cape Verde Islands. The wind carries an almost continuous charge of fine reddish dust, often obscuring the sun, and current temperatures become unusually high during the day and low at night.

HARMONIC ANALYSIS. As employed in predictions of times and heights of tides, process in which a resultant curve is determined from those representing duration and height of the solar and lunar tide-waves, the periodical inequalities due to changing relative positions of sun and moon, and that due to changing distance of moon from earth between apogee and perigee; originally conceived and successfully applied by *Lord Kelvin, British mathematician* and *physicist (1824–1907)*. **Harmonic constant,** a quantity applied to height or time of a particular tide and indicated in the harmonic curve corresponding to adopted standard constituent values, in order to obtain tidal height or time on a given day under conditions differing from such standard.

HARNESS. Old collective term for rigging, equipment, and furniture of a ship. **H.-cask,** a deck cask or drum, commonly made of teak wood and shaped like the frustum of a cone, in which a few days' supply of salt meat is kept at hand ready for use. The meat was soaked in *sea-water,* usually renewed daily, in order to rid it of brine in which it is preserved in barrels; also, *harness-tub.* **H. hitch,** kind of loop-hitch made with a bowline to secure a man seated and suspended in the latter.

HARP. The *harp seal,* to which various terms are applied, as *hopper-h., jennie-h., turner-h., saddleback; see* SEAL.

HARPINGS. In older wooden construction, planking (wales) of increased thickness on the bows for fortifying resistance to plunging in a seaway and shocks from ice or other floating objects. Also, in shipbuilding, pieces of timber fitted to hold the frames at ends of vessel in position during the plating or planking process. *Harpins.* In older usage, descriptive of a vessel's lines, she was said to have a *full* or *lean harping,* meaning, respectively, bows were of bluff form or were inclined to sharpness. **Cat-h.,** *see* CAT. **Harping-iron,** now rarely used term for a *harpoon.*

HARPONEER, or **HARPONIER.** (Fr. *harponneur*) One whose duty is to harpoon a whale or other sea animal.

HARPOON. (Fr. *harpon;* from *harper,* to clamp or grasp strongly) A spear used in attacking whales, either thrown by hand or fired from a gun, and attached to a line. In its earlier form, the head was pointed in a V-shaped pair of barbs keenly sharpened on outer edges. Later came the *toggle-iron* which had a single sharp-edged pointed barb or fluke fitted to turn crosswise upon stress coming on its line after entering flesh of whale. Prior to present use of the *gun-h.,* object of hand-harpooning a whale was to obtain means of "hanging on" to the animal until attacking boat could be hauled close alongside it in order to dispatch quarry with a *lance,* or long keen-edged spear. Five or six *h's* or "irons" were carried in a whale-boat and each was attached to a *foregoer,* or *foreganger,* a length of strong handy rope, which, upon whale being successfully struck, was quickly made fast to the *whaleline* coiled down ready for running out. The walrus,

porpoise, grampus, dolphin, and seal are sometimes killed or captured by *harpooning.* **Bomb-h.,** *see* BOMB. **Conch-h.,** a fish-spear having a single fixed barb; so called from its original head being made from the conch shell by Central and South American natives. **Electric h.,** one having an explosive charge at its head which is detonated upon entering whale by means of electric contact through small wires in the *foregoer.* **Explosive h.,** *see* B.-harpoon *in* BOMB. **Gun-h.,** *see* Harpoon-g. *in* GUN. **H. log,** a trade name for an early form of speed log in which a rotator, gearing, and indicator dials are contained in a single unit. Instrument is towed astern and must, of course, be hauled in for reading, for which reason it is now undoubtedly wholly displaced by the more serviceable *taffrail log.* **H.-oar,** in older whaling, forward oar in the boat, which was pulled by man selected to *h.* the "fish." **H.-rocket,** another name for a *bomb-harpoon.* **Toggle-h.,** see opening remarks on *Harpoon.*

HARTER ACT. (After *Michael D. Harter, American Congressman, 1846–1896*) U.S. law enacted Feb. 13, 1893, forbidding insertion of any clause in a foreign trade contract of affreightment whereby a vessel's manager, agent, master, or owner shall be relieved from liability for loss arising from negligence, fault, or failure in proper loading, stowage, care, or proper delivery of merchandise committed to such person's charge; and, also, forbidding insertion of any clause in such document whereby obligation of vessel's owner to exercise due diligence to properly man, equip, provision, and make vessel seaworthy and capable of performing her voyage, or whereby the obligation of any of his servants to properly handle, stow, care for, and properly deliver the cargo in any wise shall be lessened, weakened, or avoided. The Act, however, provides for limitation of liability of owners, charterers, agents, or master in the following: "If the owner of any vessel transporting merchandise or property to or from any port in United States of America shall exercise due diligence to make said vessel in all respects seaworthy and properly manned, equipped, and supplied, neither the vessel, her owner or owners, agent, or charterers shall become or be held responsible for damage or loss resulting from faults or errors in navigation or in the management of said vessel, nor shall vessel, her owner or owners, charterers, agent, or master be held liable for losses arising from dangers of the sea or navigable waters, act of God, or public enemies, or inherent defect, quality, or vice of the thing carried, or from insufficiency of package, or seizure under legal process, or for loss resulting from any act or omission of the shipper or owner of goods, his agent or representative, or from saving or attempting to save life or property at sea, or from any deviation in rendering such service."

HASHMARKS. In *U.S. navy*, diagonal red stripes, each representing a period of enlistment (normally 4 years), worn on uniform sleeve of an enlisted man or petty officer; also, similar gold stripe or stripes signifying meritorious conduct throughout length of service thus indicated.

HASP. A hinged piece of metal fitted to pass over a staple or eye before inserting in the latter a padlock, pin, or other securing device, as in fastening a door, chest-cover, etc. **Bowsprit h.,** one fitted at stem of a sailing-boat for holding down the bowsprit heel. It corresponds to the *gammoning* on larger craft. **Mast-h.,** one for securing a boat's mast to a thwart, when in the stepped position; also, *mast-clamp.*

HAT. Also, hat-box; old man's hat; drain hat; *see* **D.-pot** *in* DRAIN.

HAT MONEY or **HATCH MONEY.** *See* MONEY.

HATCH. The covering and protecting arrangement, including *hatch-covers* and *hatch-coamings*, over and around an opening in a deck, or *hatchway,* for passage of cargo, bunker-coal, persons, etc.; a *hatchway* itself; a hatchway cover, or one of several parts composing such, also called *hatch-cover.* Size of *hatches* vary according to type of vessel and their use, generally are rectangular in shape, and range from an opening, or *scuttle,* of a few feet in area to such dimensions as 30 by 50 feet. Large cargo-hatches are provided with movable beams, or *webs,* fitted between the *coamings* for supporting *h.-covers* and stiffening the former. In some passenger-vessels, a house or *booby* is laid over a hatchway as a shelter for a stairway leading to a lower deck accommodation; and special semi-permanent *h'es,* as those above a *boiler* or *engine space,* are made entirely of steel and may be removed for passage of a boiler or bulky machinery parts. **After h.,** the hatchway lying farthest aft. To **batten down h'es,** *see* BATTEN. **Boiler-h.,** *see* BOILER. **Booby h.,** a raised shelter for a ladder entrance on a weather deck, usually curved from its fore side to top, affording passage to a deck below. Also, a movable wood structure laid on an open hatchway, sometimes fitted with a skylight, and having a similar entrance to a lower deck. **Cargo h.,** one for passage of cargo to and from ship's cargo-space; weather deck hatchways may be covered with either wood or steel protective means, or *h.-covers;* usually numbered consecutively from forward and named for deck on which located, as, *No. 1 main deck h., No. 3 lower tween-deck h.,* etc.; *see* CARGO. **Ceiling h'es,** *see* CEILING. **Coaling-h.,** small hatchway in a weather deck for receiving coal in bunker space; sometimes fitted with a trunk casing where coal passes farther than one deck below. **Companion h.** or **h'way,** *see* COMPANION. **Engine h.,** large one over an engine-room, usually having sloping top surfaces in which are fitted several skylight covers often capable of being raised or lowered from below. **Expansion h.,** one in which coamings are extended downward to form an expansion chamber for liquid cargoes; an expansion trunk; *see* TRUNK. **Fidley h.,** *see* FIDLEY. **H.-bar,** *see* BAR. **H.-batten,** one of the flat bars, usually of iron, used for tightly securing tarpaulins to *h.-coamings.* They are clamped against, and near edges of, tarpaulins by wedges driven between them and *cleats,* or *clips,* fixed at short intervals all round the coamings. Also, *batten-bar, h.-bar, side-bars.* **H.-beam,** see opening remarks on HATCH. **H.-boat,** small fishing-vessel having one or more wells for holding live fish, the *h'es* covering same constituting a large deck area; any vessel having her deck largely taken up with *h'ways,* as in those navigating sheltered waters. **H.-boom,** *see* BOOM. **H.-carling,** *see* CARLING. **H.-checker,** person who tallies or records cargo loaded at a particular *h.* and, usually, also records its location when stowed. **H.-cleat,** *see* **Batten-c.** *in* CLEAT; also, *h.-batten clip.* **H.-coaming,** *see* COAMINGS. **H.-cover,** one of a series of removable handy planks, usually 2 to 3 inches in thickness, or one of several metal plates, forming covering of a *h'way.* Also, in tank-vessels and some other bulk cargo types, a single hinged steel cover suitably stiffened and fitted with a *dogging down* arrangement whereby it is tightly borne by a bearing strip of rubber or other packing coming in contact with edge of *h.-coaming.* **H.-davit,** *see* DAVIT. **H.-end beam,** deck-beam adjoining end of a *h'way* and to which forward or after *head-ledge* is secured. It is of heavy construction in compensation for interruption of strength continuity caused by *h'way* opening. **H. foreman,** longshoreman who supervises work of loading or discharging cargo into or from a particular hold. **H.-grating,** or **grating-h.,** *see* GRATING. **H.-ladder,** fixed ladder, usually made of iron, fitted inside a *h'way* for passage of men to or from compartments. **H. locking-bar,** flat iron bar laid across a *h.* in such manner as to prevent covers being removed by unauthorized persons. It is fitted with a padlocking or other security arrangement. **H.-molding,** half-round bar fitted along upper edges of coamings for stiffening purposes and to provide a non-cutting bearing edge for tarpaulins. **H.-money,** or **hat-money;** *see* PRIMAGE. **H. nails,** old name for round-shanked or wire nails made of a corrosive-resisting metal, used in boat-building. **H.-roller,** metal roller about two inches in diameter set on lower edge of a *h.-coaming* to relieve chafe on a cargo-fall, particularly where heavy cargo units must be dragged from a remote end of a compartment. **H. speed,** rate in tons per hour at which cargo is discharged or loaded via a particular *h.* **H. stanchions,** portable uprights supporting a guard-rope or chain stretched round a *h'way* as protection against persons falling below. **H.-tackle,** any running gear used to hoist or lower cargo through a *h'way;* referred to in charter party and cargo insurance usage as the *ship's tackles*. **H. tarpaulin,** water-proofed canvas cover secured over a *h.* for prevention of ingress of water; usually three on each *cargo-h.* on sea-going vessels. *See* TARPAULIN. **H. tender,** a man stationed at a *h.* through which cargo is being loaded or discharged, for purpose of supervising lowering and raising of sling-loads. He gives necessary signals to winchman concerned and attends to loose cargo-falls as required. Also called *h.-man.* **H.-tent,** as a protection during rain, a raised canvas covering or tent spread over a *h'way* while admitting passage of cargo. A complete tent-like covering of canvas over an open *h'way* while vessel is at sea, such as used in natural draft fruit-carrying ships for warm weather ventilation and protection against spray and rain. **H'way tonnage,** *see* EXCESS OF HATCHWAYS. **H.-web,** a hatch-beam, *q.v.* **H.-wedges,** those used for battening down a *h.;* usually of hardwood, 6 inches in length by 2 inches square at butt; *see* **H.-batten. H.-whip,** a single rope used as a hoisting-fall in working cargo through a *h'way;* also, *cargo-fall;* sometimes applied to fall lowering or hoisting through *h'way* only, where two booms are used as a unit, as distinguished from the *yard-arm fall,* or that leading from boom guyed over ship's side. **Insulation h'es** thick tight-fitting *h.-covers,* usually made of wood and containing an insulating material such as granulated cork, laid in a *h'way* leading to a refrigerated compartment or hold. Supplementary to usual covers, they are placed at *lower* edge of weather deck coamings, thus forming a continuation of insulated upper surface of a tween deck space; and usually are fitted to every tween-deck *h'way,* in order that any single or separate compartment may be cooled. *See* REFRIGERATED SHIP. **Main h.,** principal one in a vessel; originally, *h.* between fore and main masts. The *main beam* on which, by law, a vessel's official number and net registered tonnage must be permanently marked, is considered coincident with after coaming, or head-ledge, of the *main h.* **Self-trimming h'way,** one of large dimensions, often more than half vessel's breadth in thwartship extent, as in grain, ore, and other specially constructed bulk-cargo carriers, provided with the view of reducing underdeck wing space, thus partially or wholly obviating need of trimming cargo. **Square of the h.,** space in lower hold immediately below *h'way* above; sometimes applied to deck space on either side of any *cargo-h.* An old English custom allowed a shipmaster privilege of "the square of the main hatch" for stowage of his own goods, in foreign trading ventures. **Trimming-h.,** small *h.* in a tween deck for distributing bulk cargo or bunker coal into wing spaces in a lower compartment. **Trunk h'way,** *see* TRUNK. **Under h's,** kept or confined below deck: said of a crew member in a naval vessel when under arrest or suspended from duty. **Water-tight h.,** one provided with a single *h.-cover* which rests on,

and is secured tightly to, top edge of coamings. It is fitted with a strip of rubber or other cushioning material for a bearing surface. *See* **H.-cover.**

HATCHEL. *See* HACKLE.

HAUL. (Fr. *haler;* Du. *halen;* Dan. *hale;* to draw or haul) To pull, tug, or drag, as on a rope. In sailing, to turn toward the wind; to alter vessel's course, often with *up* or *off;* as, to *haul up for the land;* to *haul off shore.* The wind is said to *haul* in changing direction from which it blows toward one's right hand, as from north to northeast; contra, *see* BACKING. In fishing, a single catch drawn in a net. Distance over which anything is carried; as, a *short h.;* a *long h.;* a *1000-mile h.* In taking in certain sails, used with *up, down,* or *in;* as, to *h. up the mainsail* (or any course); to *h. down a jib;* to *h. in the spanker* (brailing-in type); also, in displaying a flag or signal; as, to *h. down* (or *up) the ensign.* In older and now rare usage, wind is said to *h. forward* and *veer aft,* when changing in direction relative to vessel's course. To **h. aft the main-sheet, jib-sheet,** etc., to pull in on a fore-and-aft sail's sheet in order to draw sail flatter to wind; also, to *flatten aft* the main-sheet, etc. **H. around,** referred to trimming sail in a square-rigger, particular yards being indicated, an order to change from position for one tack to the other; as, *h. around the head yards.* Also, wind is said to *h. around* when changing toward the right, or clockwise. **H.-bowline,** old colloquialism for an able seaman in British navy; originally, *hale-bowline.* To **h. in with,** to steer so as to approach closer to an object. **H'ing line,** a handy manila hawser or warp for heaving ship into her berth, shifting along a dock, etc.; any small line sent down from aloft for pulling up some object, as a piece of gear, tool, etc. **H'ing part,** leading or free part of a tackle-fall, or that part *hauled* upon. **H. of all!,** order to brace, or haul around, all yards for the other tack. To **h. off,** to alter ship's course in order to increase distance from an object; to free a stranded vessel by heaving on anchors, warps, or by towing. To **h. tacks aboard,** *see* ABOARD. To **h. the wind,** or **h. her wind,** in sailing, to steer closer to the wind; also, with a following wind, to alter course so as to bring breeze on the quarter, thus bringing more sail area into action. To **h. up,** to bring up, come to a stop, or heave to; as, to *h. up* at a buoy; to alter vessel's course toward the wind; to beach or heave a small vessel from the water as by a marine railway, by a purchase, etc. **Mainsail h!,** *see* MAINSAIL. To **veer and h.,** *see* VEER.

HAUNCH. Sharper curvature in a vessel's timbers or frames, or rounding of hull in way of such, as at turn of the counter in an overhanging stern.

HAVEN. (A.S. *hæfene;* Ger. *hafen;* Dan. *havn;* originally meaning *holding arm of the sea)* Any harbor, bay, inlet, river's mouth, etc., affording sheltered anchorage for shipping; a port. **Boat-h.,** *see*

BOAT. **H'age,** harbor dues; *see* HARBOR. **H'master,** also *havenor,* a harbor-master.

HAVERSINE FORMULA.   More commonly referred to as *cosine-haversine* formula, or method considered most accurate and convenient in spherical trigonometry for solution of the third side when two sides and included angle are known. In present navigational practice, due to adoption of specially prepared tables for determining the value referred to, the calculation is reduced to comparatively few figures with satisfactorily accurate results. *See* CO-SINE-HAVERSINE FORMULA.

HAWSE. (Appears in M.E. and up to about 1620 as *halse* or *haulse,* neck or extreme fore end of ship; Ice. *hals,* neck, part of ship's bows) A hawse-pipe; that part of vessel's bows containing the *hawse-pipes.* Expanse between an anchored ship's bows and position of her anchor or anchors. Descriptive of lead or situation of cables when two anchors have been dropped: ship has a *clear* or *open h.* when both cables lead directly to their respective anchors; has a *foul h.* when she has swung so that cables are crossed or twisted about each other. **Athwart h.,** across bows of an anchored vessel: said of position of a near-by vessel; *see* ATHWART. **Bold h.,** descriptive of vessel having a projecting stem, as the *clipper bow,* and *h.-pipes* high above waterline. To **clear h.,** when moored with two anchors and cables have become *fouled,* or turned about each other, to unshackle cable to which vessel is not riding (lee cable) and remove turns by dipping end of slack cable round its neighbor; also termed to *open h. Cf.* CLEAR. To **come in through the h.-pipes,** to work one's way up from a low rating to officer's rank, as distinguished from having begun career as an apprentice-officer or midshipman, or having *come through the cabin window.* **Cross in the h.,** or **cross h.,** state of cables crossing each other as a result of vessel moored with two anchors swinging through 180° over her lee cable, or that to which she originally was not riding. **Elbow in h.,** when vessel swings through another 180°, completing a 360° turn, *cross in h.* becomes a half turn, or *elbow; i.e.,* she has completed two 180-degree turns in the wrong direction. **Foul h.,** condition in which cables are turned about each other, or that in which neither anchor can be weighed without fouling cable of the other. To **freshen the h.,** *see* FRESHEN. **H.-bag,** conical shaped canvas bag stuffed with oakum, rope shakings, etc., forced as a plug into a *h.-hole,* or outer end of *h.-pipe,* over the cable, where anchor is not stowed in the pipe. It is a means of preventing entry of sea-water. **H.-block,** where cables are disconnected from anchors and stowed below, as is customary in sailing-vessels on deep-sea voyages, a close-fitting block or plug of wood pulled into a *h.-pipe* and secured by a lanyard at inboard end of pipe; also, *h.-plug.* **H.-bolster,**

thick piece of plate fitted in way of outer lip of a *h.-pipe* for stiffening and wear-and-tear protection. In wooden vessels, block of hard wood, often sheathed with iron, forming outer support of a *h.-pipe* and for receiving chafe of cable. **H.-box,** in older wooden ships, term for the hardwood *h.-hole* or *h.-pipe* which accommodated the hemp anchor cable then in use. **H.-buckler,** iron shutter or plate placed over inboard entrance of a *h.-pipe* leading to a weather deck. It is fitted to lie snugly against the cable for preventing inrush of sea-water and as protection against persons accidentally stepping into pipe. **H.-chock,** stout block or planking of hardwood fitted around deck end of a *h.-pipe* for strength and stiffening purposes. **H. full,** said of a vessel when heavily riding at anchor with seas breaking over the bows; *heavy-weather h.* **H.-hole,** opening or outer entrance to *h.-pipe* through which anchor cable passes; also sometimes applied to a *mooring-pipe* through which a hawser leads to a wharf, etc. **H. hook,** in wooden ships, the breast-hook just above *h.-holes,* or below top-gallant forecastle. (*H.-holes* are located at main deck level, or nearly so) **H. jackass,** a *h.-boy* or *h.-bag; see* **H.-bag. H.-piece,** in wooden vessels, the three or four cant frames fitted close up to each other to form a strength mass through which *h.-holes* are cut; also, *h.-timber.* **H.-pipes,** iron or steel tubular lining in *h.-holes* of a wooden vessel serving as a bearing surface and outboard lead for each anchor-cable; or, heavy tubular steel castings in modern construction, which also are made of sufficient diameter to afford stowage of a stockless anchor's shank. They usually are fitted in the fore-and-aft vertical plane and lead at an angle with deck of about 45°; at inboard ends are flush with deck; and are rounded in a heavy flange at outboard end to resist "wear and tear" by cables. Largest ships to-day are fitted with a *pipe* in, or slightly on one side of, the stem, with nesting arrangement to receive flukes of a third bower anchor. **H.-pipe flange,** rim at either end of *h.-pipe* through which it is bolted or riveted to deck and shell-plating or planking. **H.-plug,** *see* **H.-block. H.-rope,** the *dip-rope* used to *dip* or unwind turns of disconnected cable around cable to which ship rides, as in *clearing h.* It is wound around riding cable with same number and in opposite direction of turns of cable in the *foul;* then secured to disconnected end of slack cable and hove aboard, both cables in meantime being lashed together below location of turns, or slack cable may be thus secured by means of a *clear-h.* pendant. *Cf.* To **clear h. H.-timber,** *see* **H.-piece;** also *h.-wood.* **In the h.,** ahead and close aboard; at or near upper part of stem. To **moor with open h.,** having cables leading in opposite directions and nearly at right angles with prevailing wind. **Open h.,** with cables leading directly to each anchor and widely clear of each other; also, *clear h.*

Riding h.-fallen or **h. full,** pitching and immersing bows up to *h.-pipes; see* **H. full.**

HAWSER. (O.F. *haulser,* to raise, lift; *hausserée,* towpath, towing; 16th and 17th century English spelling appears *haulser, halser*) Any lengthy heavy fiber rope or wire used for warping, mooring, or towing; a mooring-line; a tow-line. The term *cable* for such ropes, or for any other cordage on board, is rarely used in seagoing vessels. Old time hemp anchor-cables which, in larger ships, were made of three *hawsers* (of usual right-handed lay) laid left-handed, or cable-laid, appear as the lone instance of the word's use. From this our present *chain* or *anchor cable* derives its name. **H.-clamp,** a device for checking running-out speed of a hawser, or for taking its stress while rope is shifted to bitts from capstan or winch; *esp.,* one for holding a wire rope, in which rope is nipped bodily for two or three feet of its length, as manipulated by a screw in the manner of a vise. **H.-hole,** a mooring-pipe, or hole in bulwarks through which a line is led. **H.-laid,** plain laid, connoting rope that is laid up with strands leading onward from left to right; right-handed rope; *see* LAID. **H.-port,** opening in a bulwark, side-plating of a forecastle, etc., for passage of a hawser. **H. reel,** horizontally mounted iron drum on which a wire *h.* is reeled for stowage. It is turned by hand-cranks in stowing and is usually fitted with a brake for controlling paying-out speed of rope. **Insurance h.,** as required by classification society's equipment rules, heavy rope for emergency towing or anchor use carried by machinery-propelled vessels. Such vessel of 7850 *equipment tonnage*—a rough approximation to her *gross tonnage*—in order to measure up to class *A1* under *American Bureau of Shipping* rules, must carry a 130-fathom tow-line of either a 16-inch manila or steel wire of one and thirteen-sixteenths inches diameter, having a breaking stress test of approximately 78 long tons. Also called *salvage h.*

HAWSING. (Sometimes corrupted to *horsing*) Act or process of hardening up calked planking seams with blows by the heavy *hawsing-mallet* or *beetle* on the *h.-iron.* In *h. up,* as it is termed, one man holds iron while another uses beetle. Also, practice of using extra force in calking a lapping plate seam where a poor faying fit is present.

HAYSTACK BOILER. *See* BOILER.

HAZY. Visibility conditions characterized by presence of *haze,* or light mist, fog, smoke, or dust particles in atmosphere, rendering distant objects indistinct or completely obscured; not clear, as *a hazy horizon.* Distinguished from the misty or foggy condition proper by a much less vapor content.

HEAD. Foremost or projecting part; uppermost extremity; as, *ship's h.; pier h.; derrick h.; rudder-h.; davit h.; h. of a sail; frame h.* A cape or promontory. Force or pressure; as, *h. of water; h. of steam.* Inland extremity of a bay, fjord, gulf, river, etc. In whaling, end of a strip of blubber hoisted from carcase in flensing. A privy or latrine space for crew use; originally, the *beak-head,* a small platform in fore part of ship containing latrines for crew. To direct vessel's course; as, to *h. Northeast; h. for port; h. into the wind.* Describing location as at or near ship's bows; as, *h. gear; h. sails; h. yards.* Contrary or unfavorable in direction; as, *h. wind; h. sea; h. current.* **Beak-h.,** *see* BEAK. To **blow h's and points,** *see* BLOW. **By the h.,** having a greater draft forward than aft. **Cat-h.** or **Cathead,** *see* CAT. **Cavel h.,** variant of *kevel h.; see* KEVEL. **Floor h.,** *see* FLOOR. **Frame h.,** upper end of a transverse frame; *see* FRAME. To **go by the h.,** *see* GO. **H. and h.,** said of two vessels on opposite courses approaching each other *end on,* or lying in berth, as alongside a quay, heading toward each other. **H.-bay,** portion of a canal at upper entrance to a lock. **H.-block,** cargo block at upper end of a boom. **H'board,** in older construction, either of two heavy ornamented boards acting as braces to peak of cutwater, just abaft and at each side of figurehead; also, *trail board.* A piece of board set in the *h.* of a triangular sail as a stiffener. The *h.-cringle* to which halyards are attached is seized to it, or a hole is substituted for cringle. **H. booms,** jib-boom and flying jib-boom. **H.-chute,** canvas tube, pipe, or box-shaped conduit for refuse matter from crew's *h.* **H.-cringle,** rope strop, grommet, or metal ring in upper corner or corners of a sail; *see* CRINGLE. **H. earing,** at each upper corner of a square sail, piece of small rope for securing *h.-cringle* to, and stretching *h.* of sail along, the yard. **H.-fast,** mooring-rope holding forward end of a boat or small craft to a wharf, alongside a vessel, etc. **H.-gate,** upper-end gate of a canal lock. **H.-knee,** in ornamented bows of older ships, one of the horizontal knee-shaped timbers (usually a pair on each side) leading from above or below hawse-holes and forming lateral support to the *beak,* or upper part of *cutwater;* also, *cheek-knee.* **H'land,** a cape; especially, a promontory or point of land rising more or less precipitously from beach. **H'ledge,** older term for *end coaming,* or coaming forming forward or after end of a hatch. **H'light,** a foremasthead or bow light (white) required to be shown by power-driven vessels. **H.-line,** rope to which upper edge of a fishing-net is secured. It is fitted with appropriate floats, usually of cork, for buoying net in vertical position; also, *cork-line, top-line, float-line,* depending on local usage. A mooring- or warping-rope or a hawser leading ahead from the bow. **H. lining,** chafing-cloth sewn across *h.* of a square sail in way of the yard. **H.-matter,** spermaceti and clear high grade oil found in the *case,* or upper anterior part of the *h.* of a sperm whale. **H. money,** prize money paid by a belligerent to any of its naval personnel taking part in destruction or capture of an enemy vessel. It is calculated at a certain rate per person on board such vessel at opening of engagement concerned. The custom no longer prevails in U.S. navy; *also see* MONEY. **H. netting,** in old-time larger vessels, kind of ornamented network forming a guard-rail round the top-gallant forecastle. In some recent sailing-ships, and required by law in a few countries, a safety net spread under and in way of bowsprit and jib-boom for security of sailors at work on head gear. To **h. off,** to steer away from the wind; to point ship's head away from an object on either bow. **H. of an anchor,** end of its shank at which flukes are spread; *crown of* the old-fashioned anchor. **H. of keel,** forward end of keel; the fore-foot. (*Heel* is its after end) **H. of mast,** the masthead; that part of a mast between the *hounds,* or termination of shrouds, and the *cap,* or upper end; part of mast overlapped by next mast above; uppermost part of mast clear of all standing rigging, as the *royal masthead.* **H.-on,** steering directly for, or pointing toward, an object, the sea, or the wind. **H.-on collision,** impact of ship's stem with another vessel or some object; often applied to act of two meeting vessels striking each other end-on, or nearly so. **H.-outhaul,** *see* OUTHAUL. **H. pump,** a hand pump which draws sea-water through a fore peak inlet; used as a fire pump, for washing decks, or flushing the *h.,* or crew's water-closet. **H.-rails,** in older wooden ships sometimes synonymous with *h.-boards* (*q.v.*) or were additional stout rails above them, leading from each side of figurehead to bows. Any guard-rail or bulwark top at fore end of vessel. **H. reach,** to run for some distance into the wind before filling away on another tack, as in a fast-sailing vessel; the distance so covered. A course sailed when close-hauled; *esp.,* that under circumstances demanding headway to windward by carrying an extraordinary press of sail, as in working off a lee shore; *h.-reaching.* Tacking or working to windward under normal conditions also is often termed *h.-reaching.* **H. room,** deck height, or distance of one deck above another; height of *deck-head.* Varies from 7 to 9 feet in modern cargo-vessels to 10 or more in passenger ships, depending on class of accommodation, public spaces, such as dining-saloon, library, etc. **H.-rope,** boltrope, or rope to which *h.* of a sail is sewn; *h.-line* (*q.v.*) of a fishing-net; rope forming upper edge of a drag-net or trawl. Formerly, a stay or rope leading from stem to foremasthead—our present *fore stay.* **H. sails,** those set forward of the foremast; as, jibs, foretopmast staysail, fore staysail, etc. In vessels of more than two masts, often applied also to all sail set on foremast. **H. sea,** waves running in a contrary direction, or nearly so, to ship's course and usually caused by wind. Not to be confused with its sometimes equally contrary cousin, the **h. swell,** which, in moderate weather, may prevail regardless of direction of sea. **H.-spade,** long-handled chisel-like instrument used by whalers in cutting into *h.* of a whale. **H.-stick,** short stick or piece of wood set in *h.* of a light triangular-shaped sail, such as a yacht's spinnaker or other canvas not confined to a stay, etc., for purpose of preventing peak of sail from twisting when spread. **H. tabling,** *see* TABLING. **H'way,** vessel's motion in a forward direction; opposed to *sternway.* **Liverpool h.,** type of ventilator or galley funnel cowl consisting of a horizontal drum, open at both ends and enclosing a second drum closed at both ends. Exhaust air or smoke enters latter and flows downward into large drum; thence to atmosphere. Its purpose is to supply efficient draft while preventing ingress of spray or rain. **Scroll-h.,** *see* SCROLL. **Test h.,** hydrostatic pressure prescribed as test for tightness and/or strength of a tank, sides of a compartment, boiler, etc. Usual double-bottom tank test consists of completely filling tank with water and pressing it up until showing a *h.* of 8 feet in a vertical pipe fitted to tank top. Such *h.* corresponds to a fresh-water pressure of 500 lbs. per square foot, or 512 lbs. sea-water pressure, on the tank top.

HEALTH OFFICER. *See* OFFICER. **Health guard,** in British ports, an officer or group of officers appointed to enforce quarantine regulations.

HEART. Small strand or line forming core of a 4-strand, or shroud-laid, fiber rope; or, small hemp line in center of a wire rope; purpose is to cushion and maintain proper relative positions of strands; also, in case of wire rope, to provide an absorbent for a lubricant. A wood or metal block acting as a dead-eye at end of a stay; grooved around edge to receive eye of stay, may be round or pear-shaped, and has a single hole for passing the lanyard; a *heart-block.* A weir end shaped like a heart for guiding fish into a pound; *heart-net.* **Collar-h.,** *see* COLLAR. **H.-yarn,** one of the center yarns in a fiber rope strand; core in strands of flexible wire rope, usually hemp; core of a rope.

HEARTH. (Pron. *harth*) Old English term (M.E. *harthe, herthe*) for ship's galley; *esp.,* the once open grate and its cooking appliances.

HEATER. Any heating apparatus; especially, one consisting of a system of coils through which steam flows, such as *heater-coils* at bottom of a fuel oil tank, or those in tank vessels carrying heavy oils, for purpose of reducing viscosity of oil and hence facilitating transfer by pumping. One who heats rivets for a riveting squad in ship construction, repair work, etc. **Feed h.,** a feed-water *h.; see* FEED. **Fuel oil h.,** *see* FUEL.

HEATING SURFACE. In a steam boiler, aggregate of all surfaces exposed to fire or hot combustion gases; *esp.,* such areas in contact with water on their opposite surfaces.

HEAVE. To draw, haul, or pull, as on a rope; to move into a certain position, or in a required direction; as, to *h.* (or lay) *a ship aback; the brig hove alongside;* to *h. ship ahead.* Often with *away;* as, to *h. away the capstan.* To alternately rise and fall, as a vessel in a heavy beam sea. To throw or cast; as, to *h. a line.* Where all heavy *heaving,* as in weighing anchor and warping, formerly was done by the man-powered capstan, such phrases as the following commonly were in use: *h. away; h. in; h. out; h. round; h. taut; h. a pawl; h. and break her; h. away for Rio* (chantey chorus); *h. ho, ye soldiers;* etc. **H. of the sea,** effect on vessel's course or progress by a prevailing sea or swell; *esp.,* leeway caused by sea or swell running approximately athwart the course. To **h. aback,** also to *lay aback,* to alter course so as to bring wind on fore side of square sails, or, to trim head yards aback, as in taking headway off ship. To **h. about,** to put a vessel on the other tack: usually in the sense of a suddenly required maneuver. To **h. apeak,** see APEAK. To **h. astern,** to fall back or be out-distanced, as a vessel overtaken and passed by another; also, to haul vessel into a new berth stern first. To **h. down,** see CAREEN. To **h. in sight,** to come within view, as another vessel at sea. To **h. in stays,** same as to *h. about* or *h. aback.* To **h. out and lash up,** to turn out of a hammock and lash it for stowing. To **h. out a reef,** to shake out or loose a reef taken in a sail. To **h. out a sail,** to loose a heavy square sail from its gaskets preparatory to setting. To **h. the lead,** to determine depth of water by use of the hand lead. To **h. the log,** to ascertain ship's speed by the old-fashioned chip log; *see* LOG[1]. To **h. short,** to *h. in* an anchor-cable until ship is nearly over her anchor, as in getting under way from an anchorage, ready for breaking out upon trimming or setting sail as required; to shorten up the cable. To **h. to,** to stop a sailing-vessel's headway by *lying to,* as in bringing wind a little forward of the beam and bracing after yards aback; to *h. aback;* also, to *lie to* in a gale under shortened sail by holding ship as nearly close-hauled as possible; to lie *atry; see* ATRY. To bring one's vessel to a stop, as required for some special purpose, an emergency, etc.

HEAVER. One of two fore-and-aft arms connected to windlass brakes or levers for transferring each downward stroke of latter to turning motion, as in the slow process of heaving anchor by this means. A small handspike, or round stick 2 to 3 feet in length, for heaving tight a lashing, twisting back the lay in a wire rope when splicing, drawing two parts of cordage together *Spanish-windlass* fashion, etc. A T-shaped metal tool used by sailmakers; about 6 inches in length, has a cupped tip on its conical point for pushing a roping-needle well through the work, as in roping a sail in way of an eye-splice; chiefly used for heaving tight the roping stitches in way of heavy work. A longshoreman or dock-laborer employed in handling cargo to and from vessels; a *freight-h.;* a *coal-h.*

HEAVING-LINE. *See* LINE[1].

HEAVY. Of a weighty nature; as, *h. cargo; h. grain; h. wire.* Having a bulky appearance; as, a *h. main-yard; h. sea; h. counter.* **H. lift,** unit of cargo, such as a locomotive or a large boiler, loading or discharging of which demands extra heavy and special equipment. Usually a lift of one ton or upwards in weight is classed as a *h. lift* and extra freight charges for handling such are billed. **H.-lift boom,** see **Jumbo-b.** *in* BOOM. **H. weather,** conditions characterized by continuous strong winds and high sea running. A vessel is said to be *making h. weather of it* when laboring in a rough sea and shipping an unusual amount of water, as when in the loaded condition. **H.-weather sails, gear,** etc., best available of such for bad weather conditions. On voyages carrying ships through the trade-wind belt and into higher latitudes, it was customary to use fine weather and heavy weather canvas and gear accordingly. **Top-h.,** said of a vessel having a bulky appearance, or actual excessive weight, above her center of gravity. Referred to comparative stability, the term is synonymous with *crank; see* CRANKY.

HECKLE. *See* HACKLE.

HEDGE. A fishing-weir; *esp.* one made of brush; *see* WEIR.

HEDGEHOG. A kind of dredger, consisting of a heavy roller with protruding spikes or spades, dragged on bottom of a river for loosening silt deposit.

HEEL. Lower end of a mast, cargo-boom, stern-post, frame, timber, or other more or less vertical lengthy object; inner end of a bowsprit, jib-boom, sounding-boom, etc.; after end of the keel. Outside corner of an angle-bar. To incline laterally, or list, as a vessel's more or less permanent departure from the upright, due to pressure of wind, greater weight on one side, contact with sea-bottom, or to turning under a large helm angle at high speed. Act of *heeling,* or angle to which *heeled;* as, *ship has a h. of 10 degrees.* A vessel's *roll* partakes of a somewhat rhythmic character, or swing from side to side, and, hence, never is referred to as *h.* or *heeling.* **Angle of h.,** inclination from the upright; as, *an 8-degree h. or list.* To **go round on her h.,** said of turning ship by boxhauling; *see* BOXHAUL. **H.-and-toe watches,** "watch and watch" or division of crew into alternate watch-duty periods, usually of four hours. **H.-block,** *see* BLOCK. **H.-brace,** metal stiffening piece on lower end of a wooden rudder. **H.-chain,** once also known as *crupper-chain,* which supported an upper mast at its *h.* to cap of mast next below; *see* **H.-chain** *in* CHAIN. **H'ing corrector,** a round bar magnet placed vertically below center of a magnetic compass (ship upright) for correcting that part of *heeling error* due to sub-permanent magnetism in ship's hull, or that induced by the earth's magnetic field and rendered permanent to a large extent by the hammering to which vessel's structure is subjected during construction. Value of such component of heeling error to be corrected is determined by indication of a magnetic *dip-needle* placed in position to be occupied by such compass. The soft iron spheres, fixed at each side of a compensating binnacle for correcting quadrantal deviation, also may be considered *heeling correctors* in that the induced magnetism therein to a certain extent counteracts the heeling error component caused by vertical induced magnetism in horizontal iron now assuming a tilted position during heeling of vessel. **H'ing error,** deviation, or angular departure of north-seeking point of a magnetic compass, attributed to heeling of vessel. As indicated under *H'ing corrector,* part of the error is corrected for effect of permanent hull magnetism; thereafter, presence of further error is considerd due to that arising from vertical transient magnetism induced by earth's magnetic field in iron which is tilted from the horizontal as vessel *h's.* It is greatest on *north* and *south* (magnetic) courses; draws north point of compass toward vessel's high side in north latitudes and toward low side in south latitudes; varies directly as angle of heel and as cosine of course. **H'ing magnet,** same as *h'ing corrector.* **H'ing moment,** that of a couple equal, in a listed vessel, to product of upward force of buoyancy times distance between parallel vertical lines passing, respectively, through centers of buoyancy and gravity. **H'ing tanks,** in some ice-breaking vessels fitted amidships at sides for sharply inclining hull to and fro in order to free vessel from wedging effect of heavy ice. **H.-knee,** crooked timber connecting keel to stern-post. **H.-lashing,** rope securing *h.* of a spar; as, in holding in place lower ends of sheer-legs or a temporary derrick. **H.-piece,** short angle-bar connecting ends of butting frames; a *bosom-bar.* Any uniting strap or angle-bar at lower end of a structural part, as on frames footed at a double-bottom margin-plate; a *h.-bar.* The lower end of a mast. **H.-pintle,** lowest, or bearing-pintle on an ordinary type ship's rudder. **H.-post,** term for the stern-post in wooden steamers; *propeller-post.* **H.-rope,** a mast-rope, as one rove through sheave-hole of a topmast near its heel for lowering or heaving aloft, at *h.* of jib-boom for sending out, etc.; a guy-rope for controlling end of a spar suspended in hoisting, etc. **H.-tackle,** handy purchase for securing, shifting, or binding together legs of sheers, as when heaving masts aboard for stepping. **H.-tenon,** tapered or projecting lower end of a wooden mast, shaped to fit into the mast-step. **Parliament-h.,** listing of ship caused by shifting of cargo or ballast; so called because of lively discussions ensuing as to causes, etc., of such occurrence, which eventually

resulted in enactment by *British Parliament* of laws for sea carriage of bulk cargoes (*Merchant Shipping Act, 1894*). **Rudder-h.,** lowest part of a rudder. **Rudder-h. bearing,** the *bearing-pintle,* or that on which weight of ship's rudder rests. Fits in a hole on projecting part of lower end of rudder-post, convex end of pintle resting on convex surface of a replaceable disc at bottom of hole; sides of hole or socket are bushed with lignum vitae. **Stem-h.,** *see* STEM.

HEIGHT. Distance to which anything rises above a surface or plane of reference; as, *h. of tide; h. of eye.* One of the vertical measurements, or ordinates, from base-line to a water-line, deckline, etc., in drawings of a vessel. On coast charts, *h's* of focal planes of lights, rocks showing above water, and prominent land elevations are indicated as *above high water.* Former English usage sanctioned the term as also denoting *latitude;* as, *h. of Cape Horn is 56°;* and *altitude;* as, *h. of the sun is 42°.* **Deck h's,** those indicating vertical distances between decks, or ordinates from base-line to line of a deck or decks. **H. of center of buoyancy,** vertical distance of vessel's geometrical center of displacement (ship upright) above top of keel or lowest faying surface of floors; or above outer surface of garboard strake in wooden vessels. In vessels of ordinary form it is coincident with from .55 to .6 of ship's load draft above base indicated. In stability diagrams it is usually indicated by length of line K B, K being point of origin at base-line. **H. of center of gravity,** vertical distance of center of weight, both of ship and anything carried on board, above base-line or keel; usually indicated by length of line K G. **H. of eye,** elevation of one's eye above sea surface. A correction, termed *dip of the horizon (see* DIP), is applied to an observed altitude of a heavenly body or a distant peak above sea horizon in order that such measurement may be reduced to that which would have been observed with eye at sea level. **H. of high water,** that above chart datum to which water rises at high water. **H. of low water,** difference between height of surface at low water and that of datum from which tidal height is measured; usually expressed with reference to datum as *plus* or *minus.* **Metacentric h.,** *see* METACENTER.

HELENA. (L., from Gr. *Elena,* sister of *Castor* and *Pollux*) A single corposant, or *St. Elmo's light,* appearing at a yard-arm, truck, or elsewhere in ship's rigging; *see* CORPOSANT. Also, name given by ancient mariners to a single star appearing in an otherwise overcast sky and regarded as an unfavorable omen.

HELIACAL. (Gr. *eliakos,* of the sun) Of, pertaining to, or near the sun; said of a star first visible before sunrise after having been in conjunction with the sun, or of one just visible after sunset before conjunction. (Sun advances to eastward in its apparent path in the heavens, the *ecliptic*) **H. year,** Sothic, or canicular year; period between two successive first appearances before sunrise of *Sirius*, the Dog-star (*a Canis Majoris*), or of *Procyon*, "before the Dog" (*a Canis Minoris*), after conjunction with the sun. Its duration was determined by the ancient Egyptians as 365 days, 6 hours.

HELIOCENTRIC. (Gr. *elios*, sun; *kentron*, center) Relating to, or having, the sun as a center. **H. latitude,** angular distance of a heavenly body, *esp.* a planet, north or south of the plane of the ecliptic, as would appear from the sun's center. Greatest *h. latitude* of any planet is that of Mercury—nearly 7° N. or S.; Venus attains a little less than $3\frac{1}{2}°$; Mars and Saturn about 2°; the others smaller; thus indicating little deviation by the family of planets in our solar system from a common orbital plane. **H. longitude,** angular distance of a celestial body, as measured at sun's center, along the ecliptic between the planes vertical to ecliptic passing through the sun and, respectively, through such body and vernal equinoctial point. To visualize a planet's **h. place,** one may imagine himself standing on the "upper" or north pole of the sun and thus approximately perpendicular to the earth's orbital plane. From this fancied position he might follow the various planets' hourly increase in their respective longitudes as they swing through 360° paths in a glorious array of concentric circles (properly, *ellipses* of small eccentricity), all traveling *eastward*, or counter-clockwise, around their resplendent master. Looking toward our Earth, the date being about March 21, he might note the point at which her orbit's plane intersects her body-belt, or *equator*, since, as we know, she leans awry to the tune of $23\frac{1}{2}°$. The point in question is the *vernal equinox* (*see* ARIES, *also* EQUINOX). If now our observer measures the angular distance from this point to Venus, seen over his left shoulder with her fellows of the Uranian concave, and finds it 95°, he has noted the *h. longitude* of that planet. Mars over there on the right, similarly observed, is found to have a longitude of 275°; the angle always measured *eastward* from the vernal equinoctial point, or *First Point of Aries*, as it has been termed from far-gone days.

HELIOTROPE. (Gr. *elios*, sun; *tropos*, a turn) Instrument used in geodetic surveying for making long-distance observations; consists of a mirror adjusted by clock-work so that, at a pre-arranged hour, sun's rays may be reflected directly to a particular station; *heliograph*; also the term for a similar instrument employed in signalling by flashes, as by *Morse Code. U.S. Coast Guard* regulations require ocean vessels' lifeboats to include in their equipment two *signalling-mirrors* of approved type. During World War II many instances of timely rescues were recorded through aircraft being attracted to men adrift at sea by this simple means of throwing sun's rays in a direction desired.

HELM. (A.S. *helma*, Ice. *hjalm*, rudder; Gr. *helm*, handle) The instrument or entire apparatus by which a vessel is steered; usually, steering-wheel or tiller alone. Angle through which rudder is turned from amidship position; as *20-degree helm*. From early English usage, position of the bar or lever, called the *tiller*, attached to head of rudder-stock for turning rudder as required is indicated in *h. orders*, and not that of rudder itself; and, since tiller originally always extended forward of rudder, reference to *h.* being *astarboard, aweather, up, down*, etc., connoted the *opposite* to position of *rudder*. Due to more recent varied arrangements in steering-gear, reversal of the tiller's time-honored position or replacing it altogether with a crosshead, and individual notions as to just which should be proper direction to turn a steering-wheel upon, say, a *hard aport* order to *helmsman*, some 25 years ago it became evident that some universal agreement should be reached in the matter of a common understanding of terms "starboard" and "port" as used in *h.* orders. Accordingly, at the *International Convention for Safety at Sea, London, 1929*, it was recommended that a uniform practice of indicating direction in which vessel is to turn should be adopted in *h.* orders; *i.e.*, whether *rudder* is to be turned to starboard (*right*) or to port (*left*). In 1931, Great Britain apparently took the lead in ordering that "helm or steering commands to steersman shall be given in the direct sense; *e.g.*, when ship is going ahead an order containing the word *starboard* or *right* or any equivalent of *starboard or right* shall only be used when it is intended, on ships as at present generally constructed and arranged, that wheel, rudder-blade, and head of ship shall all move to the right." France enacted a similar law in 1934; and U.S., on August 21, 1935, that "All orders to helmsmen shall be given as follows: *Right Rudder* to mean '*Direct vessel's head to starboard*'; *Left Rudder* to mean '*Direct vessel's head to port*'." (*33 U.S.C. 142*) At *International Conference on Safety of Life at Sea, 23 April–10 June, 1948*, it was recommended that *Article 32* of *International Rules for Preventing Collisions at Sea* read as follows: "All orders to helmsman shall be given in the following sense: 'right rudder' or 'starboard' to mean *put vessel's rudder to starboard;* 'left rudder' or 'port' to mean *put vessel's rudder to port*." **Answers the h.,** said of a vessel responding to steering action of rudder. To **carry a lee** (or **a weather**) **h.,** a necessary more or less constant angle given rudder to counteract vessel's tendency to turn away from or toward direction of wind, particularly when sailing with wind abeam or when close-hauled. With a well-balanced sail area, an increasing wind pressure, resulting in vessel heeling, will always necessitate carrying *weather helm*, due to increased resistance on the more deeply immersed lee bow. Carrying a *lee helm* usually accompanies an uneven balance of sail; *i.e.*, wind pressure either is excessive toward vessel's forward end or insufficient toward after end, or, properly, with relation to her *center of lateral resistance* in either case (*see* CENTER). In powered vessels having superstructural area predominating forward or aft, similar effect often is observed in the steering. It is to be remembered that by *lee* and *weather h.* is meant the respective positions of a *tiller extending forward from rudder-stock*, tiller being put to *lee* side, thus bringing rudder-blade and ship's head *toward the wind*, or to *weather* side, thus steering *away from* the wind. Notwithstanding use of a steering-wheel geared to a tiller extending abaft rudder-stock, the terms *lee* and *weather* have retained their centuries-old significance, and, regardless of steering arrangement or rig, vessel carries a *lee h.* when her *rudder* must be kept more or less turned toward her windward, or weather side; conversely, in the case of *weather h.* **Check the h.,** to stop or slow down swinging of ship due to a previous application of rudder by either placing rudder in midship position or turning it a little against the swing, as in bringing ship's head to a desired course. **Ease the h.,** *see* EASE. **To feel the h.,** to come under influence of rudder: said of ship when beginning to gather steerage-way. **Hard over h.,** with rudder turned to greatest possible angle. **Helm's alee,** *see* ALEE. **H. amidships,** order to put rudder in line with keel, or neutral position; also, *midship the h.* **H. indicator,** device showing movement and position of rudder at all times. **H.-kick,** sharp jerky movement of rudder caused by impact of a sea. **H.-port,** same as rudder-port; *see* RUDDER. **Lee h.,** *see* To **carry a lee h. Mind your h.,** an order to helmsman to exercise care in steering or swinging ship through a particular angle. **Port the h.,** old order indicating tiller is to be moved to *port,* thus turning ship's head to starboard; now superseded by *right rudder* or *starboard.* To **put the h. down,** to apply *lee h.,* as in tacking; to put tiller to *lee* or *down* side in order to bring vessel to the wind. To **right the h.,** obsolete order to put tiller amidships. **Shift the h.,** order to change position of tiller or rudder from hard over on one side to hard over on other, as sometimes required in maneuvering. **Starboard the h.,** old order indicating tiller is to be moved to *starboard,* thus turning ship's head to port; now superseded by *left rudder* or *port.* **Up h.,** to **put the h. up,** to apply *weather h.;* to move ordinary tiller to *weather* or *up* side, as in turning vessel away from wind direction. **Weather h.,** *see* To **carry lee** (or **weather) h.**

HELMSMAN. Person who steers a boat or vessel; steersman; wheelsman. In British and American vessels of the liner type 3 to 6 seamen rated as quartermasters usually perform duties of *helmsmen.*

HEMISPHERE. Half of a sphere or globe; usually referred to half the earth's surface limited by the equator, as Northern and Southern Hemispheres; or limited by antipodal meridians, usually 20° W. and 160° E., and termed Western and Eastern Hemispheres, the former containing North and South America.

HEMP. Tough bast fiber of an Asiatic herb, the *Cannabis sativa,* widely cultivated for manufacture of cloth and cordage, and also, especially in India, for its yield from the flowers and leaves of strong narcotics known as *bhang* and *hashish* or *ganja,* the pharmacist's *Cannabis indica;* also, fiber of many other plants useful in making cordage, as, American, Italian, Manila, Mauritius, phormium, sisal, and sunn hemps, some of which often are blended for the purpose. **Hemp rope,** generally applied by sailors to the softer fiber product, as that of *Cannabis sativa,* distinguishing it from others of stiff texture, as *manila* and *sisal* hemps. For ship use it is almost always tarred, which greatly lengthens its useful life; is used extensively for roping sails; and is standard material for rigging lanyards and small stuff, such as marline, ratline, roundline, and spunyarn.

HENEQUEN. *See* **Sisal r.** *in* ROPE.

HEN FRIGATE. *See* FRIGATE.

HERMAPHRODITE BRIG. *See* BRIG.

HERRESHOFF ANCHOR. *See* ANCHOR.

HERRING. An important food fish (*Clupea harengus*) abundant in North Atlantic colder waters; also the closely allied California herring (*Clupea pallasii*) of North Pacific; 12 to 15 inches in length, swims in schools sometimes containing hundreds of millions; chiefly caught off north-east American, British, and Norwegian coasts; extensively canned, smoked, and pickled, also yields a fine quality of food oil. The term is often extended to several fishes of families similar in appearance to true herring; as, alewife or branch herring, menhaden, pilchard, sardine, shad, sprat, summer herring, etc. **H.-drifter,** vessel engaged in catching *h.* by drift-nets; she rides nose on at lee end of line of nets which sometimes extend more than two miles; *see* DRIFTER. **H.-gull,** *see* GULL. **H.-pond,** humorous term for the ocean, especially the North Atlantic. **King of the h's,** the chimæra; *see* CHIMÆRA. **Kippered h.,** one that has been split, cleaned, and salted; then smoked over burning oak shavings or sawdust; a *kipper.*

HERRING-BONE. Descriptive term indicating resemblance to spine of a herring. **H. gears,** cogs or gears having V-shaped teeth, as differentiated from spur gears (or gearing), or those having teeth parallel with shaft on which mounted. **H. planking,** in boats of flat or V-shaped bottom construction, bottom-planking laid slantwise and aftward from center line or keel to bilges. **H. stitch,** that used in repairing sails or other canvas in which a tear is sewn together by passing needle up through off edge of cloth, then down through near edge, and crossing twine before repeating; also, *herring-boning*.

HIDE-ROPE.   Strong durable cordage made of twisted strips of cowhide, as once commonly used on coasting craft of South American Atlantic countries; considered excellent material for steering-wheel ropes in that it outranks fiber in withstanding wear and tear. To **hide a rope,** to protect it with leather as often done on boltrope of a sail, especially at and near its clew or clews.

HIGH.   Extended in elevation above a particular plane of reference or a familiar standard; as, *high tide; high spars; high sides*. Lofty; as, a *h. light-house;* a *h. sea*. Connoting extraordinary strength, force, velocity; as, *h.-pressure boiler; h.-tension wire; h.-speed turbines;* or important rank; as, a *h.-rank-ing officer*. Descriptive of sailing unusually close to the wind; as, *vessel points h.* In meteorological us-age; a *h.-pressure area*. **H. and dry,** completely out of water, as a stranded vessel at lowest state of tide. **H. area storm,** one resulting from a steep baro-metric gradient about a *h.-pressure area*. **H. lati-tude,** at a great distance north or south of the equa-tor; generally, a latitude of 45° upward. **H. dawn,** first light of day appearing above a cloudy or hazy eastern horizon; usually presages a breezy day. **H. injection valve,** fitted in a steam vessel's side above main injection for use instead of latter in shallow water as a safeguard against entry of sand or mud into condenser circulating system. **H. noon,** exactly mid-day; time of apparent sun crossing local meridian; apparent noon. To **point h.,** to lie unusually close to the wind when sailing close-hauled; said of a sailing-vessel possessing such qual-ity. **H. pressure,** commonly shortened to *H.P.,* in a reciprocating engine denoting units connected with the *h.-pressure cylinder;* as, *H.P. connecting-rod, H.P. piston; H.P. valve-rod, piston-rod, steam-chest,* etc. **H.-pressure area,** region of relatively *h.* baro-metric pressure; *see* AREA. **H.-pressure boiler,** *see* BOILER. **H.-pressure cylinder,** *see* CYLINDER. **H. sea,** waves in open sea generated by winds of from fresh to whole gale force; depending on duration of wind, may be 15 to 25 feet in height, measured from trough to crest; a heavy sea; indicated in *Douglas sea scale* as 6 in a range of symbols from 0 to 9. **H. seas,** internationally regarded as all navigable re-gions or sea areas lying outside territorial waters of any state or country. U.S. navigation laws define the term as meaning "all waters outside the line di-viding inland waters from high seas"; Admiralty jurisdictional usage in Great Britain defines it as "that part of the sea which lies not within the body of a county." **H. tide,** time or state of greatest height of tide which usually occurs twice daily, or at inter-vals of approximately 12 hours; *h. water,* or maxi-mum height attained by the tide wave. **H. water,**

time of *h. tide;* condition of greatest height of water surface in a tidal area, as measured from a datum level variously given on coast and local charts as that of mean low water, low water at ordinary spring tides, mean of lower low water, etc., depend-ing on peculiarities of tidal range in the vicinity. Also, utmost flow or greatest seasonal elevation of a river surface or that of its connecting waters. **Higher h. water,** where a diurnal inequality, or dif-ference in heights of alternate high waters, pre-vails, the higher of two consecutive high waters. **H. water at full and change,** usually denoted by **H.W.F. & C.;** *see* ESTABLISHMENT. **H.W.,** abbrevia-tion for *high water*. **H.W. mark,** or **line,** line on a shore to which water surface ordinarily reaches at *h. water;* mark or line showing highest level reached by surface of water; level attained by water of a river at times of flood.

HIPPING.   Additional timber laid on outside of a wooden vessel's frames before planking, for the purpose of increasing her waterline breadth and tumble home.

HIP TANK.   A double-bottom tank having a slop-ing top from midship line upward to ship's sides.

HITCH.   One of many different kinds of knots, nooses, or loops by which a rope is made fast to an object and may readily by loosed therefrom. In gen-eral, there appears no marked distinction in the terms *bend, hitch,* and *knot,* which often are ap-plicable to same fastening, although a *bend* or a *h.* usually is employed for a less permanent purpose than is the *knot*. A period of one enlistment in the navy. To **do one's h.,** to take one's turn; as, a trick at the wheel, lookout watch, etc. **H.-angle,** *see* ANGLE.

HITCHER.   A boat-hook or gaff.

H.M.S.   Official abbreviation for His (or Her) Majesty's Ship, or Station, applied to all names of British naval vessels and shore stations; as, *H.M.S. Drake; H.M.S. Excellent* (training station at Ports-mouth, England; also known as *Whale Island*).

H.O.   Letters, followed by a number, by which *U.S. Hydrographic Office* charts and other publications are catalogued; as, *H.O.20*.

HOBBLER.   In England, a boatman or unlicensed pilot who assists vessels at less important ports in towing into or out of dock, warping, etc., or in gen-eral piloting; a *hoveler;* also, a dock-laborer.

HOBBY.   A dolly-bar; *see* DOLLY.

HOE.   Long-handled firing-tool shaped like a hoe, used in hauling fires and removing ashes from ash-pit of furnace. A promontory or cliff; now appear-ing only in place names in England; as, *Plymouth Hoe*. **H.-mother,** *see* **Basking s.** *in* SHARK.

HOG.   A heavy brush made of twigs clamped be-tween two planks, once used for dragging along **a**

floating vessel's bottom to clean off barnacles, etc.; to clean the bottom by such means. To droop at both ends, as a structurally strained vessel. **H.-back,** any fish having a humped back somewhat like that of a *hog.* **H.-boat,** any of several old-time coasting vessels, usually clinker-built and having one mast; also, *hag-boat.* **H.-frame,** a truss-like stiffening frame built fore-and-aft above deck in light draft steamers for increased longitudinal strength; usually found in inland U.S. vessels; also, *h.-truss; hogging-frame.* **H.-fish,** any of several fishes so-named because of resemblance of profile to that of a *h.;* especially, a West Indian food fish about 18 inches in length; also, *hog-molly; pig-fish; sailor's choice.* **Hogged,** said of a ship having each end of her hull drooping, a condition resulting from stranding, improper distribution of heavy cargo, or structural weakness. **H.-piece,** a piece of timber laid fore-and-aft over a clinker-built boat's keel. It is made of sufficient width to provide a landing for the garboard strakes; frames rest on its upper surface; and through bolts from keel to keelson secure it in place. **H.-sheer,** curvature of a ship's deck, rising from each end toward amidships, as seen in large ferry-boats.

HOGGING.   Bending of a beam or other structural part upward into convex form; a rounding upward of a vessel's deck in a fore-and-aft direction. **H.-frame,** see **H.-frame** in HOG. **H.-lines,** ropes attached to lower corner or corners of a collision-mat and led under ship's bottom for hauling mat down over injured part; see **C.-mat** in COLLISION. **H.-moment,** in analyses of ship structural stresses, that expressed in foot-tons represented by predominating downward weight over upward force of buoyancy multiplied by distance from midship section, as shown on a curve of *bending moments,* or those showing both *hogging* and *sagging* stresses for a given loaded, or the light, condition.

HOGSHEAD.   Any large cask or barrel-like receptacle; a measure of 63 U.S. gallons = 52.5 Imperial gallons = 238.5 liters. **H.-hooks,** see CAN-HOOKS.

HOIST. (Orig. *hoise,* to raise by means of a tackle) To elevate; lift; raise; as by a single fall, tackle, or a purchase; as, to *hoist* a sail, flag, sling of cargo, etc. An engine for raising and lowering heavy or bulky weights; as, a *coal-hoist,* a *cargo-hoist.* Vertical midship depth of any square sail set by *hoisting;* length of luff of a fore-and-aft sail. Vertical depth of a flag at end next the pole or gaff; a number of flags displayed in a vertical line as a signal. Extent to which a yard and its sail may be raised. Quantity of cargo lifted in one sling; a draft. **Ash h.,** see ASH. **Chain h.,** see **Chain-hoist b.** in BLOCK. **Screw h.,** see SCREW.

HOISTING.   Act of, or relating to, lifting or raising anything. **H.-block,** lower or moving block in a *h.* purchase; a cargo-gin or block through which a

single whip is rove and sometimes called a *hoister.* **H.-crab,** a crab-winch or small hand windlass used for *h.* **H.-engine,** a hoist, as a steam winch or other machine for *h.* cargo, ashes, etc. **H.-fall,** rope or chain used in *h.;* see FALL. **H.-gear,** lifting-gear, or chain hoists, tackles, screws, strops, etc., used in engine-room work for removing cylinder-covers, crank-shafts, and various heavy parts of an engine. **H.-speed,** velocity or time-rate at which a normal load or sling of cargo can be transferred by ship's deck machinery from hold to dock or vice versa.

HOLCAD. (Gr. *olkados,* a towed cargo ship)   A merchant vessel of early eastern Mediterranean antiquity.

HOLD.[1] (A.S. *hol,* hole or cavern)   Entire cargo space below deck; often applied to space below a lowermost deck only. In U.S. naval usage, space below lowest "platform" (deck below lowest continuous deck). Where ship's hull is divided by several transverse bulkheads, it is customary to number each *hold* from forward, consecutively; thus, *No. 1 h., No. 2 h.,* etc. **Captain of the h.,** petty officer or seaman in charge of a *h.* in a naval vessel. **Depth of h.,** see **Registered d.** in DEPTH. **Fish-h.,** that of a fishing-vessel designed for stowage of fresh fish, especially cod, halibut, haddock, etc. It is usually insulated, metal lined, and divided vertically into a series of shelves on which fish are placed in ice. **H.-battens,** see **Cargo b's** in BATTEN. **H.-beam,** in a deep *h.* below lowest deck, one of a series of widely spaced beams fitted for purpose of supplying local transverse strength and stiffening to vessel's side framing. In steel construction, usually a *stringer-plate* is laid over ends of such beams and secured by continuous angle-bar to frames. **H.-bunker,** stowage space for bunker fuel below lowermost deck. **H. ceiling,** see CEILING. **H.-ladder,** one permanently fitted for access to various compartments below deck; may be either in hatchway itself, or clear of it with passage afforded by a small scuttle in each deck. **H. gang,** group of men detailed to work cargo in a *h.* In general cargo work, usually consists of eight men, four on each side of *h.* **H. pillar,** heavy stanchion, or upright, supporting beams of lowest deck; also, *h.-stanchion.* **H. stringer,** a fore-and-aft girder bridging transverse frames in lower part of *h.* and providing additional longitudinal structural strength. **H. water-ballast,** see BALLAST. **Insulated h.,** compartment for carriage of frozen, chilled, or cooled cargo, such as meats, fish, butter, eggs, vegetables, etc. Insulating material may be charcoal, fibrous glass, mineral wool, granulated cork, balsa, etc. **Lower h.,** lowermost compartment in ship's cargo space other than a 'tween deck space. **Main h.,** largest lower cargo compartment in a powered vessel. **Stoke-h.,** stokehold or fire-room; boiler space, or that in which furnaces are fed and attended by stokers or firemen.

HOLD.[2]   To maintain a connection with, or grasp on, something; to cling, or remain fastened to, anything. Act of *holding;* that which grasps or holds. **Ground h.,** old term for *ground-tackle, q.v. in* GROUND. To **h. a close wind,** or **good wind;** *see* WIND. To **h. a good luff;** *see* LUFF. **H.-fast,** a brace, clamp, or dog, with which to secure an object in place. To **h. a wind, the wind,** or **one's wind;** *see* WIND. To **h. on,** to check or stop a rope that is being slacked away; to cease motion, as in hauling on a line; to continue, as in maintaining a certain course, or in carrying a present spread of sail. To **h. on to the land,** to keep in contact with a coast, though not necessarily in continuous sight of it, by soundings and/or occasional bearings. To **h. tacks with,** to sail on same tack, and come about at same time in a series of tacks, with another vessel, as in a race; figuratively, to keep up with another in competitive activity. **H. water,** command to a pulling-boat's crew to set blades of oars vertically in water and at right angles to boat's keel for purpose of checking craft's headway. **Holder-up,** one who assists a riveter by holding a sledge or *holding-up hammer* against heads of rivets as they are hammered into place. **H'ing ground,** sea-bottom at an anchorage, regarded in its degree of dependability as "biting" ground for anchoring. *Good* holding ground is found in clay, thick mud, or marl; *poor,* in most sandy bottoms or in soft mud; *foul,* in rocky bottom where anchors will drag with moderate stress on cable and may become fast in a fissure, resulting, perhaps, in loss of a "hook." **H'ing-down bolts** *see* BOLT. **H'ing-up hammer,** the sledge or dolly used for holding against head of a rivet; *see* **Holder-up.**

HOLE.   A place where water is comparatively deep. A cove; narrow channel. An opening affording access or passage for a person or object; as, *lubber's hole; hawse hole.* Formerly *hold* and *hole* were synonymous, *esp.* when applied to a small lower compartment in a ship. A vessel is said to be *holed* when her outside planking or plating is ruptured or broken through at any place, as from collision or grounding on rocks. Combined with the specific identifying term, denotes an aperture, cavity, or opening; as, *bobstay h., limber h., sheave h.* **Blind h's,** rivet holes supposed to fair each other, but found unevenly matched, or misfits. **Cat-h.,** a mooring chock in stern of old-time ships; *see* CAT. **H. in the sky,** *see* COAL-SACK. **Sludge-h.,** a mud-hole in a boiler; *see* MUD. **Pigeon h.,** aperture in a top through which running gear passes. One of the sockets in a capstan for receiving the capstan-bars.

HOLIDAY.   As a day of exemption from work, legal holidays are taken into account in *charter party* usage as those in force at port in which vessel is to load or unload cargo; hence, *lay days* are counted inclusive of such, where charter party stipulates these as *running days,* as distinguished from consecutive *working days,* or those other than Sundays and holidays. A neglected portion or spot in a surface being painted, varnished, tarred, etc.

HOLLOW.   Trough or depression between crests of sea-waves. A basin, channel, or valley; a cavity or hole. Concave; not solid; having an internal empty space; depressed. **H.-ended,** said of a boat or vessel having a concave entrance of hull at each end of water-line. **H. keel,** *see* KEEL. **H. mast,** or **spar,** a wooden *built* spar or one of metal in tubular form; *see* MAST. **H. sea,** *see* SEA.

HOLMES LIGHT.   A signal or marker, such as is attached to a life-buoy, consisting of a floating canister containing calcium carbide and calcium phosphide from which a bright flame spontaneously arises as result of hydrogen phosphide generated by contact with sea-water. *Cf.* **Franklin life-b.** *in* BUOY.

HOLYSTONE.   A block of soft sandstone, usually set in a frame with a long handle, for scouring wood decks in combination with sand and water. Origin of the term appears from first use for this purpose in British navy of fragments of tomb-stones and monuments from St. Nicholas Church, Great Yarmouth, England.

HOLY WATER TANK.   *See* TANK.

HOME.   In a direction toward one's ship; as, an anchor *comes home* when failing to hold, or is *brought home* when broken out of its hold by heaving on cable, or, also, when ship is hove up to it. Into, or toward, a customary position; as, to *sheet h.* a topsail; anchor is *chock h.* (as when stowed in a hawse-pipe); a piece of cargo is *stowed h.* when forced into position in tier during loading. **H. port,** *see* **P. of registry** *in* PORT. **H. trade,** in Great Britain, shipping trade within limits of United Kingdom of Great Britain and Northern Ireland, Eire, Channel Islands, and continental ports between River Elbe (Germany) and Brest (France), inclusive. **H. wind,** a fisherman's favorable breeze for making his *h. port* from fishing-grounds. **Sailors' h.,** *see* SAILOR. To **sheet h.,** to haul sheets of a square sail out to yard-arms as far as they will go, as when setting sail. **Tumble h.,** inclination inward, from about load water-line, of a vessel's sides at widest part of hull; sides are referred to also as *falling h.* when thus inclined.

HOMER.   Contraction of *hoe-mother;* *see* BASKING-SHARK.

HOMEWARD.   Toward, or in the direction of, home; as, *homeward passage, route, run, track, voyage; homeward log, cargo, bunker supply,* etc. **H. bound,** sailing or destined for the home port or country: said of a ship returning from a foreign voyage. **H.-bound pennant,** a long, narrow, ribbon-like streamer customarily flown in naval ships when *h. bound* after an extended period of duty on a foreign station. Formerly, its length was a foot for every member of ship's company and eventually was cut up for souvenirs on that basis. To-day, its length is made according to number of days' duration of cruise: 200 feet for 200 days, etc. **H.-bound stitches,** sailor's term for long stitches taken in sewing canvas in order to complete job as quickly as possible.

HOMOCERCAL. (Gr. *omos,* one and the same; *kerkos,* tail) In fishes, having or designating a symmetrically formed caudal fin (tail); *i.e.,* each fork or lobe being of similar size and shape; also termed *diphycercal.* Opposed to *heterocercal,* or having upper lobe larger or longer than the other, as found in sharks.

HONG. (*Cantonese*) A mercantile warehouse on the water-front in Chinese ports.

HONG KONG MOORING-BUOY. *See* BUOY.

HONIBAL'S ANCHOR. *See* **Rodgers' a.** *in* ANCHOR.

HONOR POLICY. *See* WAGER POLICY.

HOOD. A protective cover over a companion entrance or scuttle; a steel top or protecting armor over a gun turret; covering for protection against weather on any fitting or fixture; as, tarred canvas over lower ends and lanyards of standing rigging; a box over steering-gear; a round-topped canopy in a boat; short rounded deck at forward end of smaller vessels. An outside plank or plate ending at and butting to stem and stern posts; as, respectively, one of the *fore hoods* and *after hoods;* also termed *hooding-ends.* **Binnacle-h.,** removable top, usually fitted with a glass, for protection of compass in a binnacle. **H. seal,** a species of large North Atlantic seals, the male of which has an inflatable sac for protecting its head. **Navel h.,** in wooden vessels, heavy wood or extra planking built round and supporting projecting end of hawse-pipes. Formerly, a heavy fender placed at a hawse-pipe or mooring-pipe to ease a short nip on cable or hawser having a cross lead, or leading at a very small angle with ship's side. **Sight-h.,** a sighting-hood; *see* SIGHTING.

HOOK. A curved or bent piece of metal or other hard substance used to catch, hold, sustain, or pull anything; as, a *fish-h., boat-h., block-h., chain-h.* A curving point of land, or spit; a sharp turn in a stream or river. Familiar term for an *anchor.* A *breast-hook* (*q.v.*). To catch, hold, or secure with a *h. Hooks* often are fitted in pairs to form a single eye, by meeting and snugly nesting together, as in *clasp-, clip-, clove-, match-,* or *sister-hooks; see* SISTER. *Eye* of a *h.* is that part by which it is suspended or secured; its *shank* or *back,* the main part; and its terminating tip, the *point.* Under load, an ordinary *h.* sustains greatest fracturing stress at its *back quarter,* or turn at base of shank. *Safe working load* of

steel *h's* having round section is considered, in long tons, as two-thirds its diameter, in inches, at back quarter, *squared;* or, S.W.L. = 2/3 d². **Bale-h.,** one of a pair, each having a sharp point, loosely set in a rope sling for gripping and lifting bales of hay, fiber, etc.; also, a short *hand-h.* for handling bales; a *cotton-h.* **Batten-h.,** end of a hatch-batten cross-bar formed like a *h.,* for securing it to the coaming. **Bench-h.,** a *sail-h.,* or one used to hold canvas in position by sailmakers. **Box-h.,** one having a sharp point and short shank topped by a handle set at right angles to latter, used for obtaining a hand-hold in moving boxes, bales, etc., in cargo handling; a *stevedore's hook.* **Can-h's,** a special sling for use in hoisting casks and barrels, consisting of two flat *h's* which grip the chimes of cask by stress on a short bridle connecting them to the cargo-fall. **Cargo-h.,** for connecting slings of cargo to a hoisting-fall or tackle, a heavy *h.* having an arm projecting from its shank, designed to narrow in the hook's *mouth,* or opening between its *point* and *back.* Some are provided with a protective lip fitted to prevent fouling with hatch-coaming, ladders, etc., during hoisting; also, are often fitted with a swivel link to avoid undue twisting in the fall. **Cotton-h.,** similar to a *box-h.,* excepting provided with a longer shank; used for handling bales of cotton, fiber, etc. **Deck-h.,** triangular-shaped plate fitted in extreme ends of a deck to unite frames, hood-ends, and stem (or stern-post). In wooden ships, crooked timber for same purpose fitted close below deck concerned. **Grab-h.,** bifurcated one designed to hold stress in a chain, as in stopping off an anchor. *H.* grabs end of a link while spanning link next in line. *Cf.* **Devil's c.** *in* CLAW. **H. and butt,** shipbuilding term for a kind of scarf shaped to withstand tensile stress in timber thus united; a *h.-scarf;* so called because parts of scarf *hook* together, or interlock. **H.-block,** one fitted with a fixed, loose, or swiveling *h.;* if fixed, *h.* is said to be a *front h.* when pointing in same plane as the sheave or sheaves; *side h.,* when at right angles to sheaves. **H.-damage,** that suffered by cargo due to careless use of *hand-h's (stevedore's, box,* or *bale h's).* **H.-iron,** a piece of ¾-inch iron, 12 to 15 inches long and having a knob at one end and a claw at other, for killing larger fish when captured and for extracting the *h.* from their mouths. **H.-scarf,** *see* **H. and butt;** one of several locking scarfs designed to resist tension in important structural members, as keel, keelson, stem, futtocks, and other heavy work. **Mud-h.,** slang term for an anchor, commonly used by coastwise sailors. **Rave-h.,** also called *reefing-iron* and *reef-iron;* a tool used by caulkers to remove old oakum from plank seams; has a shaft about 15 inches in length, at lower end of which is a thin straight edge with pointed end. It is pulled or knocked along the seams in order to force oakum upward. A kind of hooked instrument called a *rase-knife* is drawn along a seam for same purpose. **Releasing-h.,** one of several patented devices by which boat-tackles may be simultaneously disconnected by means of a lever, pulling on a line, or on a hand grip; or may be self-detaching when boat is water-borne. **Snap-h.,** so named from a spring snap which closes *h.;* of small size, used to quickly connect signal-flags, as on naval vessels; also employed in lieu of hanks for bending a jib to its stay, as often found on yachts. **Stack-h.,** one made of iron and shaped roughly like letter **S** for placing over edge of smokestack to suspend boatswain's chairs or a stage when washing, painting, scaling, etc. **Swivel-h.,** any *h.* to which a swivel link is attached; attached rope may twist without disturbing *h.* thus fitted. *Other compound terms under this caption may be found in the following:*—CANT, CAT, FORE, GRAPNEL, HAWSE, ICE, JUNK, LIP, LOCK, MOUSING, PELICAN, SAIL, SHEER, SLIP, STERN, STEVEDORE, TOGGLE, TOWING.

HOOKER. (Du. *hoeker,* fishing-vessel; from *hoek,* hook) An old-time fishing-boat with one mast, common to Irish and southern English coasts. Any vessel usually fishing with lines and hooks, also termed *liner.* Sailor's depreciative term for a clumsy, old-fashioned vessel; as, *the h. leaks like a basket;* often applied fondly; as, *we prefer to stay on board the h.*

HOOP. One of the rings, usually made of bent wood, to which luff of a fore-and-aft sail is secured and which encircle and slide up or down mast as sail is set or taken in; also termed *sail-hoop.* A metal band round a built mast; also, one of a usual set of four, uniting halves of a built stock on an old-fashioned anchor. One of several bands of wood or thin metal encircling a cask or barrel. **Futtock-h.,** formerly called a *necklace* when formed by a chain, metal band around a lowermast to which *futtock* shrouds are attached; *see* F.-**band** *in* FUTTOCK. **H.-net,** for taking crabs, crayfish, flatfish, lobsters, prawns, etc., a conical-shaped net or bag, mouth of which is spread by a circular band or hoop. Baited, it is dropped flat on sea-bottom and at intervals suddenly pulled to surface. **Mast-h.,** a *sail-h.;* also, one of several fitted round a built mast for uniting the component parts. **Sling-h.,** *see* SLING. **Spider-h.,** a heavy band round a mast about breast high above upper deck, fitted with eyes to hold belaying-pins. **Truss-h.,** one of iron around a lowermast to which *truss* of the lower yard is secured. **Yard-arm h.,** *see* YARD.

HOORI. (*Native name*) A two-masted Indian coastwise trading vessel, either schooner or brigantine rigged and of 300 to 500 tons deadweight carrying capacity.

HOPPER. A scow or a vessel of barge type, either self-propelled or towed, for carrying mud or other dredged material, garbage, etc., fitted with two or more compartments and a bottom arrangement whereby its load is dumped directly through as many pairs of doors into the sea; also termed *hopper-barge.* **H.-dredge,** one capable of carrying and dumping dredged matter by similar means to that characteristic of the *h.-barge.*

HOPPER-HARP. *See* **Harp** s. *in* SEAL.

HORIZON. (Gr. *orizon,* bounding) Bounding line at which earth and sky appear to meet, at sea called the *visible horizon,* its radius or distance from an observer depending upon his height of eye above sea surface, being very nearly equal to, in nautical miles, eight-sevenths times the square root of height of eye in feet, or $8/7 \sqrt{h}$. With use of a marine sextant, all altitudes, or angular distances above visible *h.,* are measured in the vertical plane passing through observer's zenith and body observed. **Artificial h.,** as used on shore for observing altitudes of heavenly bodies, a level reflecting surface, as that of a small quantity of mercury or a heavy oil in a shallow receptacle. This coincides with plane of the *sensible h.* (*q.v.*) Reflection of observed body, as seen in the sextant, is brought into exact contact with that seen in *artificial h.;* hence *double* the altitude above *sensible h.* is measured. **Celestial h.,** also termed *rational h.,* great circle of the heavens, plane of which is parallel to that of *sensible h.* and passes through earth's center. Upper and lower extremities of its axis respectively are termed an observer's *zenith* and *nadir.* In nautical astronomy, at any place the plane of this great circle is that from which a body's true, or corrected, altitude is measured. **Contracted h.,** *visible h.* reduced in distance due to rain, misty or hazy conditions, etc. **Dip of the h.,** *see* DIP. **False h.,** said of *visible h.* at sea when atmospheric conditions render its continuity imperfect or uncertain, as by sunlight glare combined with cloud shadows or passing showers. **H. glass,** or **mirror,** in a sextant (also in a quadrant and a quintant), glass in line of sight directed toward *visible h.* when observing altitude of a celestial body; *see* SEXTANT. **H. glass shade,** one of a set of colored glasses which may be turned in front of the *h. glass* of a sextant to minimize sunlight glare with the view of obtaining a clearly defined *h.* line. **Rational h.,** same as *celestial h.* (*q.v.*) **Sea h.** = *visible h.* **Sensible h.,** also termed *real* or *true h.,* circle of the celestial sphere parallel to the *celestial* or *rational h.,* its plane tangent to earth's surface at place of observer and hence separated from the *celestial h.* by about 3436 nautical miles, or, approximately the earth's spherical radius. Altitudes of fixed stars referred to either *sensible* or *celestial h.* are the same; however, those of the comparatively near members of our solar system, *esp.* the moon, must be corrected for *parallax,* or difference between her altitude as referred to *sensible h.* and what it would have been if observed at center of the earth; *i.e.,* referred to *celestial h.,* because of this separation of the *h's* named. **Visible h.,** see opening remarks on HORIZON.

HORIZONTAL. Lying flat, as opposed to upright; on a level; parallel to the horizon. **H. bar-keel,** *see* **Slab-k.** *in* KEEL. **H. danger angle,** *see* DANGER. **H. engine,** *see* ENGINE. **H. parallax,** *see* PARALLAX. **H. rudder,** as fitted at stern of a submarine, one for increasing or decreasing depth; *i.e.,* by changing direction vertically, steering away from or toward sea surface.

HORN. One of the crosstrees' ends; arms of a cleat; jaws of a boom or gaff; or other protruding or extended part of anything. A *fog-horn* of any type; *see* **F.-signal** *in* FOG. *Cape Horn,* at southern extremity of South America, referred to by sailors as "the Horn," especially in long-voyage sailing-ship parlance. In shipbuilding, to set transverse frames and/or bulkheads square with keel and perpendicular to fore-and-aft line. To wedge or secure end of a spar, boom, etc., in position, as in a crotch; to *horn in,* as, to set a bowsprit in its place. **H.-beak** or **h.-fish,** any of several fishes having pointed jaws; as, the saury, pipe-fish, and, especially, the *gar* or *needle-fish.* **H.-timber,** one or more timbers forming main support of an overhanging stern in wooden vessels and extending aft from upper end of stern-post, and, if a screw-vessel, also connecting shaft-log and body-post with rudder-post. **Rigger's h.,** portion of a cow's horn for holding grease; slung to a man's belt when working aloft, as a ready means of greasing a marline-spike, shackle-pin, etc.; also often used to hold sail-needles and so keep them from rusting. **Rudder-h.,** see RUDDER.

HORSE. Any rope or bar on which a tackle-block, sail-hanks, or other parts of rigging slide; *esp.,* an iron bar, or *traveler,* on which the sheet of a fore-and-aft sail slides as vessel comes about in tacking. Breast-band or safety belt for a leadsman, or similar protection for a man in an exposed position. Old term for a foot-rope on a yard or boom, preserved in *Flemish-h.* (*see* FLEMISH) A framed mold or pattern of a curved area, as built from mold-loft drawing in shipbuilding. As a verb, a corruption of *to hawse* and found in combining words as *horse-iron, horsing-mallet; see* HAWSING. To unfairly and cruelly force men to work; as, to *h. a crew.* In older usage, to be carried or driven with force, as by a current; or into danger by wind or current, or both; a reference dated 1725 states that "*ship narrowly avoided being horsed by the current on to the rocks.*" **Dead h.,** also **old h.;** *see* DEAD. **Fore-sheet h.,** iron rod or bar fitted transversely on deck for securing lower block of the sheet of a fore-and-aft foresail; also called *traveler,* so named for allowing sheet to slide to either side according to tack for which sail is trimmed. **Hard h.,** an exacting or tyrannical officer; a disciplinarian. **H.-block,** small platform or grating extending outside the rail for use of a leadsman

or convenience of an officer. **H.-boat,** a vessel engaged in carrying cattle or horses; a former type of U.S. river boat, paddles of which were worked by a horse tread-mill. **H.-fish,** one of the so-called moon-fishes; dollar-fish; the sea-horse; king, or horse-shoe, crab. **H.-iron,** in square-riggers, stout rod, supported by fife-rail stanchions, for securing lead-blocks for running gear; a *traveler,* such as a *fore sheet h., q.v.;* a hawse- or hawsing-iron. **H. latitudes,** regions of comparatively high atmospheric pressure at northern and southern edges of the trade-wind belt, or in vicinity of 30° latitude, north and south, characterized by baffling light winds and calms, particularly during summer months; also called *Calms of Cancer* and *Capricorn,* respectively. The term is more commonly referred to the North Atlantic region indicated and an 18th-century authority states the name *horse* was given the area because its prevailing calm warm weather proved fatal to many *h's* and other animals en voyage to America; also, a salt-water tradition has it that, on board British ships, the *dead h.* (one month's advance pay) was worked up about time of an outward-bounder's arrival in latitudes in question: hence the term; *see* **D. horse** *in* DEAD. **H's leg,** facetious term for a sextant or quadrant that has seen better days. **H'man,** member of a drifter's crew who places or removes buoys from the line of nets in laying out or hauling in the gear. **Horses' manes,** whitecaps or foaming crests of waves. **H. mackerel,** common tunny; often locally applied to several other fishes, including bluefish, bonito, amberjack, and the chiro. **H.-market,** eddy created by swift tidal streams, rendered dangerous to smaller craft during a breeze because of resulting steep confused sea. **H.-piece,** handy portion of whale-blubber cut from a *blanket-piece; see* BLANKET. **Sea-h.,** a small fish of genus *Hippocampus,* having a head and fore-body suggestive of a horse, a covering of rough bony plates, and a prehensile tail; widely found in warmer seas. The *walrus.*

HORSEPOWER. Usually abbreviated *HP* or *hp,* unit of power equal to that required to lift 33,000 lbs. one foot in one minute, or work = 33,000 foot-pounds per minute (= 550 ft.-lbs. per second). The corresponding metric equivalent is 75 kilogram-meters per second, or 32,500 ft.-lbs. per minute. It is universally understood as work of which average horse is capable on a *short pull,* the animal being credited with ability to *constantly* work at rate of 22,000 ft.-lbs. per minute. Power output of marine engines usually is expressed in *HP,* reciprocating steam engines being conveniently rated in terms of *indicated hp,* internal combustion engines in either *indicated* or *brake hp,* and steam turbines in *shaft hp.* **Boiler hp,** an arbitrary comparison unit for steam boilers equal to evaporation of 30 lbs. water per hour, temperature of feed being 100° F. and steam gage indicating 70 lbs. pressure per inch.[2]

Brake hp, that measured at crank-shaft coupling by means of an electric, hydraulic, or mechanical brake. **Effective hp,** hull resistance of ship in pounds times ship's speed in feet per second divided by 550. Sometimes termed the *tow-rope power,* it represents work performed each second in a rope that would tow vessel's bare hull at a given speed. **Indicated hp,** that measured in an engine's cylinders by means of an instrument which shows the steam or gas pressure throughout length of piston stroke. Product of mean effective pressure thus obtained, times length of stroke in feet, times piston area in square inches, times number of strokes per second, divided by $550 = indicated\ hp$. **Propeller hp,** that actually delivered to propeller, exclusive of all frictional losses. **Nominal hp,** for comparison purposes in engine building, a measure of power output an engine may be expected to develop, using its cylinder dimensions as principal criteria. Classification societies employ their own particular formulæ for determining this value, which is used in registration data and a basis for survey fees. **Shaft hp,** that transmitted through shaft to screw; usually measured as close to propeller as possible by means of a torsionmeter, which instrument determines angle of torsion or "twist" along two sections of shaft, that angle being directly proportional to torque transmitted. *Shaft hp* is then calculated by a formula which takes into account torsion angle, length of shaft in which torsion is observed, diameter of shaft material, shear modulus of elasticity of material, and revolving rate of shaft. It may also be defined as actual *twisting work* done in the shaft under a given load. **Thrust hp,** propeller thrust in pounds measured at thrust-block, multiplied by speed of ship through water in feet per second, divided by 550. Noting the interrelation in foregoing *hp's* in screw propulsion, we have *indicated hp* as gross power. From this subtracting friction losses in engine parts, *brake hp* is obtained; thence, deducting friction losses in reduction gears, shaft bearings, and thrust-block, remainder is *shaft hp.* Further, when friction losses abaft site of torsionmeter measurement, or those in stern tube bearings, are subtracted, we get *propeller hp;* finally, deducting losses in propeller itself from this, we have measure of power required to drive ship at speed considered, or *effective hp.* What is termed the *propulsive coefficient* usually has been taken as ratio of *effective hp* to *indicated hp;* however, in case of turbine-driven ships, it now is frequently applied also to the ratio *effective hp/shaft hp,* and with internal combustion power, as *effective hp/ brake hp.*

HORSESHOE. Metal U-shaped strap fitted over a scarf at a wooden vessel's fore-foot; also called *horseshoe clamp; see* CLAMP, a similar strap connecting stern or rudder post to keel. Anything

shaped like a *h.;* as, *h.-plate, -splice, -channel, -life-buoy,* etc. **H. plate,** light collar-plate fitted to ship's counter around rudder-stock to prevent wash of sea up into rudder-trunk; often made in two pieces, is secured with bolts to facilitate removal in event of repairs or adjustments to rudder; also termed *apron-plate* and *plate collar.* **H. splice,** also called *D-splice,* short piece of rope spliced at each end to main body of another, thus forming a loop attached to latter; a *span-splice.* **H. thrust-bearing,** *see* THRUST.

HORSING.   *See* HAWSING.

HOSE.   Flexible pipe made of canvas or other fabric, leather, or rubber for conveying a fluid, as water from a fire hydrant or petroleum from ship to shore; also, such piping as material, as in *20 feet of fire hose.* **H.-davit,** as used to support *cargo-h.* during discharging or loading tank vessels, or in taking aboard bunker fuel, usually a round bar swanneck davit from which a suitable tackle is suspended. **H. test,** in shipyard work, method of testing watertightness of riveted work by applying a jet of water at about 30 lbs. per inch² pressure to seams or joints. If no water is forced through the work, it is passed as watertight. **Scupper-h.,** *see* SCUPPER. To **underrun a h.,** *see* UNDERRUN.

HOSPITAL. In merchant vessels, a compartment separated from, and in addition to, ordinary crew or passenger accommodation for care and treatment of sick or injured persons, as required by law in most maritime countries. In naval and troop-carrying ships, such space, including dispensary, operating-room, isolation ward, etc., is usually termed the *sick bay.* By U.S. law *(46 U.S.C. 80),* in addition to specified space allotment for living quarters for crew, "on all merchant vessels of the United States which in the ordinary course of their trade make voyages of more than three days' duration between ports, and which carry a crew of 12 or more seamen, there shall be constructed a compartment, suitably separated from other spaces, for *hospital* purposes, and such compartment shall have at least one bunk for every 12 seamen constituting her crew, provided that not more than 6 bunks shall be required in any case." A similar enactment is in force in the British mercantile marine. *H.* space for steerage passengers is provided for in the *Passenger Act of 1882 (46 U.S.C. 155).* **H. ship,** vessel equipped for, and assigned to care and transportation of sick, shipwrecked, and/or wounded persons. In accordance with international agreement by signatory powers at the *Hague Convention, 1899,* all such ships are exempt from capture and must be respected by each belligerent. Generally, they are exempt, also, from dues, taxes, and pilotage. In time of war, their identity must be made known to an enemy by each belligerent and they must provide relief to wounded, sick, and shipwrecked of both sides. *H. ships* in military service must be painted white with horizontal green band about 1½ meters in width (59 inches); private and neutral ships, a similar horizontal band of red; and this distinctive painting must be clearly discernible at night. A belligerent's vessel must fly a flag having a red Greek cross on a white ground; a neutral, also the national flag of her controlling belligerent at the mainmast. **Marine h. service,** *see* MARINE.

HOSTILE EMBARGO. *See* EMBARGO. **Act of hostility,** *see* ACT.

HOTCHPOT. In U.S. and British admiralty law, term sometimes used to signify collective sum of all items of damage costs incurred by vessels found equally culpable in a collision case. Total losses are then borne equally by vessels concerned.

HOTWELL. Casing or trough to receive hot water condensed from steam by the condenser; also *hot-well*.

HOUNDS. (Ice. *hunn,* knob on a mast) Projections at each side of masthead which support trestle-trees and so a topmast or top-gallant mast; or, on small vessels, for nesting or supporting the eyes of shrouds; also, *mast-shoulders*. **Hound-band,** on a single mast, a hoop or band fitted with eyes to secure upper ends of shrouds or back-stays. **H's of the rigging,** eyes or bights of shrouds where they pass over trestle-trees and thence around masthead; often improperly referred to top-gallant shrouds where these set round a *funnel* on mast; *see* FUNNEL.

HOUNDING. That portion of a lowermast between the deck and the *hounds;* or, that of a topmast between lowermast cap and hounds next above. **H. of a bowsprit,** that portion projecting beyond vessel's stem.

HOUND-SHARK. The dogfish or hound-fish, a small shark common on North Atlantic coasts; also, *dog-shark; see* **D.-fish** *in* DOG.

HOUR. (Gr. *ora,* a season; time of day; hour) Sixty minutes, or one twenty-fourth of a *mean solar day* (common clock-time, as referred to a standard meridian) or of a *sidereal day* (interval between two successive transits of a fixed star). Angular unit of 15 degrees used in indicating *right ascension* of an observer's meridian (or sidereal time) or of a heavenly body. One hour of *mean time* (mean solar time) = 60 min. and 9.856 sec. of *sidereal time;* one hour of *sidereal time* = 59 min. and 50.170 sec. of *mean time*. **H. angle** of a heavenly body is that arc of the equinoctial (celestial equator) intercepted by an observer's meridian and the *h. circle* passing through such body. Unless otherwise indicated, is expressed as *westward,* either in arc measure, or 0° to 360°; or in time, 0 to 24 hours; thus, an *h. angle* of 18 hours or 270° may be referred to as one of 6 hours, or 90°, *easterly*. **H. circle,** any great circle passing through the celestial poles; *esp.,* **one** which also passes through a heavenly body observed for determination of its local *h.-angle,* as in nautical practice; also, meridians shown on a terrestrial globe indicating longitudes at 15° intervals, or differences in *h's* of time from a prime meridian, usually that of Greenwich, England. **Local h. angle,** that expressed as East or West of observer's meridian; *see* **H. angle. Lunar h.,** *see* LUNAR.

HOURLY DIFFERENCE. Nautical Almanac term indicating hourly change in tabulated ephemerides of sun, moon, and planets.

HOUSE. An isolated deck erection, as a cabin or caboose in a small vessel; a companion entrance, wheel-house, etc. To stow, secure, or protect, as against bad weather (in this verbal sense, pron. *houz*); to send down and secure an upper spar, as a topmast or a top-gallant yard; to heave a stockless anchor hard home in a hawse-pipe; to stow flukes of an old-fashioned anchor inboard over forecastle rail. *Housed* is state of being protected by a covering or casing, as a *housed gun;* or lowered, taken in, lashed, etc., for security, as a *housed topmast. Housing* of a mast is that portion below deck; of a bowsprit, that portion abaft fore edge of vessel's stem; also termed *bury* of a mast or bowsprit. *Housing* of a topmast or a top-gallant-mast is the *doubling,* or that part between *heel* of such mast and *cap* of mast next below. **Chart-h.,** also chart-room; *see* CHART. **Cook-h.,** ship's galley, or place where food is prepared and cooked; *esp.,* a *deck-h.* for this purpose. **Custom h.,** *see* CUSTOM. **Deck-h.,** *see* DECK. **H.-boat,** a floating dwelling; shallow-draft boat or scow without power propulsion, having a comparatively large *deck-h.* for use as living quarters; often used for pleasure in sheltered waters and towed as required. **H.-coaming,** *see* COAMING. **H.-flag,** distinguishing colors or emblem of a shipping firm or line. Displayed at main masthead; also sometimes painted on each side of ship's funnel or funnels. To **h. a mast,** to send down and secure an upper mast; to lower a mast, as in passing under a bridge. **H'wife,** sailor's canvas bag containing needles, thread, scissors, buttons, etc. **H'ing anchor,** patent or stockless anchor which stows in the hawse-pipe. **H'ing stopper,** means of securing a patent or *housing* anchor in a hawse-pipe whereby stress on cable is relieved, and so on windlass or capstan. Usually consists of a chain and turnbuckle attached to a pad-eye, with a slip-hook to a link of cable close to anchor. **Mast-h.,** *see* MAST. **Pilot-h.,** *see* PILOT. **Scow-h.,** a *h.-boat* or scow sheltering machinery, etc. **Wheel-h.,** a *pilot-h.; see* WHEEL.

HOUSELINE. (Originally, *ouse-line,* from *River Ouse* in Yorkshire, England) Seizing stuff made of tarred hemp, having 3 yarns laid left-handed; somewhat larger than marline, which is of similar material but having 2 yarns (or *threads*); runs about 160 feet per pound. Also has been termed *housing*.

HOVE. Preterit and past participle form of verb *to heave;* as in *anchor is h. apeak; ship h. in her cable; rigging is h. taut; yard had been h. aloft. Cf.* HEAVE.

HOVERING. Said of vessels roving or ostensibly aimlessly hanging about off a coast and suspected, on that account, of attempting violation of customs laws or other illegal act. In 1736, England enacted provision for security of commerce and other interests by prohibiting or regulating *hovering* of both domestic and foreign vessels within certain limits of her coasts. As termed in U.S. law, a *h. vessel* means "any vessel which is found or kept off the coast of the United States within or without the customs waters, if, from the history, conduct, character, or location of the vessel, it is reasonable to believe that such vessel is being used or may be used to introduce or promote or facilitate the introduction or attempted introduction of merchandise into the United States in violation of the laws respecting the revenue." (*19 U.S.C. 1401*).

HOY. (Du. *heu;* Flem. *hui*) Formerly, a decked sloop-rigged vessel on the English and near-by continental coasts used as a packet boat or a tender to large vessels; now, a lighter or barge for carrying bulky or weighty cargo. **Anchor-h.,** *see* ANCHOR. Lighters or heavy service boats attached to a navy yard usually are named according to their use; as, *anchor-h., gun-h., powder-h., provision-h.*

HUER. (M.E. *hue;* O.F. *hu,* from *huer,* to shout, as an outcry in the chase) Old English term for a lookout-man posted at an elevation on a bold shore for purpose of informing fishermen by signal of position of an approaching shoal of fish.

HUFFLER. (Prob. a dialectal variant of *hobbler* or *hoveler*) In British usage, formerly a bargeman or boatman who carried fresh provisions, stores, etc., to ships; now a river pilot on barges and smaller craft.

HUG. In sailing, to keep close to the shore, edge of a channel, a buoy, rock, etc.; as, *ship hugged the point;* also, to keep vessel as close to wind as possible; as, *those yachts can hug a breeze within four points.*

HULK. (M.E. *hulke,* a heavy ship; Du. *hulk,* cargo-vessel; Gr. *olkas,* a towed ship) Body or hull of a dismantled, disabled, or old vessel unfit for further sea service but used as a depot, store, or training ship; also, a vessel built for special use other than for sea-going, as, formerly in Europe, a prison. In a disparaging sense, a heavy vessel of clumsy appearance. **Sheer-h.,** one fitted with sheer-legs and hoisting gear for lifting masts in or out of vessels.

HULL. (Du. *hol,* ship's hold; prob. modification of *hulk*) Body of a vessel exclusive of deck-houses, all spars and rigging, boilers, machinery, and equipment. In shipyard usage, a vessel under construction; as, *Hull 21.* To pierce or rupture a ship's side; *esp.,* below her water-line; as, *the craft was hulled by a 4-inch shell.* To drift with, or be driven by, wind or current, as a ship without power or with all sail taken in; as, *vessel hulled downstream at about 3 knots; she hulled in the gale some 30 miles.* The *hulling* often is the term used for material, collectively, comprising ship's frames and shell-plating or outside planking. **H. auxiliaries,** all auxiliary machinery exclusive of that pertaining to propelling engines; as, windlass, winches, lighting and refrigeration installation, cargo-pumps, ballast-pumps, steering-engine, etc. **H. balance,** referred to sailing qualities of a yacht, vessel is said to have a satisfactory *h. balance* when little or no effect is shown in the steering upon being heeled to normal angles under sail pressure. This condition is made possible by a *h.* design in which no appreciable change in a fore-and-aft direction takes place in boat's *center of buoyancy* and, consequently, also in her *center of lateral resistance,* within ordinary heeling limits experienced in sailing. In order to maintain such balance, the *center of effort,* or geometrical center of total sail area as spread to a beam wind, should lie nearly in same thwartship vertical plane with centers of buoyancy and lateral resistance; if abaft that plane boat will carry *weather helm,* or tend to turn *toward* the wind; if forward of it, she will tend to *fall off* from wind and thus carry *lee helm.* Resulting brake action of the rudder in either case, may greatly add to hull resistance and so retard boat's speed. **H. down,** said of a distant vessel when her masts and upper works only are visible due to convexity of earth's surface, her hull being "over the hill." **H. efficiency,** in considering design of propellers, expressed as a coefficient or the ratio of effective horsepower, or work done in towing a vessel at a given speed, to that horsepower developed by a propeller which would drive ship at same speed. **H. girder,** longitudinal strength components in a *h.* considered as a whole in a representative theoretical girder; *see* EQUIVALENT GIRDER. **H. policy,** in marine insurance, one covering ship's *h.* with all fittings, furniture, machinery, stores, and fuel on board, with any special gear or fittings required for an unusual or particular trade. Person or firm issuing such policy is termed the *h. underwriter.* **H.-strained,** said of a vessel having her plating and frame structure buckled or warped, timbers and planking similarly injured, etc., as from unusually bad weather, improper loading of a heavy cargo, or both, or stranding. **H.-sunk,** having hull entirely submerged, or nearly so. **H. up,** opposed to *h. down;* said of a vessel in sight and showing her *h.* above, or on near side of, the horizon.

Maier form h., named for its German inventor and patentee, one characterized by lines designed to offer least possible water resistance, while possessing comparatively excellent sea-going qualities under all conditions. Outstanding feature is that vessel has a long sweeping fore-foot and a nearly corresponding *run* toward after end, with parallel slope of transverse frame in the under-water body throughout, which latter characteristic naturally departs from full, or nearly rectangular-shaped, midship section found in usual hull form. Of V-shaped section toward each end, both fore and after bodies below water-line have practically the same lines. Consequent curtailment of carrying capacity through sacrifice of body fullness evidently offsets claim for this *h.* of having best possible streamline flow and resulting increase in effective horsepower. To **strike h.,** in older usage, to take in all sail and lash helm hard alee when in a heavy gale; ship is then said to *lie a-hull.*

HULLOCK. A now probably obsolete term for any small heavy weather trysail set in after part of vessel, or a tarpaulin spread against weather mizzen, or aftermost, rigging for purpose of holding ship's head up to wind and sea in a gale.

HUMBOLDT CURRENT. Also called *Chilean* or *Peruvian* Current; see **Chilean C.** *in* CURRENT.

HUMMOCK. Ridge or heap in an ice field or floe, such as is caused by pressure of current or strong winds. As shown on local charts, a small well-defined hill, hillock, or sharp elevation on a flat or low-lying shore, often used as a landmark in piloting; also called a *hump.*

HUMPBACK. The *humpbacked whale;* see WHALE. Also, the *humpbacked salmon,* a small fish of that species found on both sides of North Pacific waters; so called because the male has a swelling or hump anterior to his dorsal fin during breeding season.

HUNDRED. As used in fish-marketing in Great Britain, a unit comprising 28 to 31 *warps* of 4 fish, depending upon local custom and kind of fish. On east coast of England herring are sold from the catch by *long h.,* or 33 *warps* (= 132 fish); mackerel in most localities by 31 warps or *h.* (=124 fish); 120 fish constitute a *h.* of pilchards in S.W. England; etc.

HURDY-GURDY. A kind of hand windlass used by fishermen for hauling in trawl-lines when working in deeper water, as in taking halibut. It is fixed to topside of boat or dory at the bows and one man turns crank while another hands in and stows trawl.

HURRICANE. (Sp. *huracan,* a Carib word meaning *strong wind*) Usual term for a tropical cyclone in West Indies and western Atlantic; see CYCLONE. Any wind of 65 nautical miles or over in velocity. **H.-bird,** the frigate-pelican; see **F.-bird** *in* FRIGATE. **H.**

deck, *see* DECK. **H.-house,** a caboose or temporary protective structure on deck of a small vessel; old term for a canvas or wooden inclosure for protecting a lookout man aloft; original of our present *crow's nest.* **H.-lantern,** portable lamp designed to remain lighted in strong winds. **H. track,** has its origin in the *Doldrums,* or region of calms, heavy showers, and baffling light winds, in about 10° north latitude and 30° to 50° west longitude, birthplace of the Atlantic tropical cyclone; thence in a West-northwest direction toward West Indies where it turns more to Northwest, gradually curving to North and Northeast in about 30° latitude, finally with expansion of its area dissipates in the broad Atlantic about region of 45° latitude and 50° longitude. Earliest *h's* in season of their occurrence (July to October) usually turn N.W. and N. before those of later date, general rule being that, as season advances, track continues longer in W.N.W. direction. Thus, August storms appear to favor a path across Bahamas or more northern of West Indies Islands, while those of September and October drive through Caribbean Sea and curve to northward in Gulf of Mexico or in vicinity of Cuba. *See* CYCLONE. **H. warning,** as displayed at storm signal stations under authority of *U.S. Weather Bureau,* on the Atlantic, Pacific, and Gulf coasts of United States; also at Belize (British Honduras), Bermudas, Cuba, Jamaica, Haiti, Puerto Rico, Turk's Island, Virgin Islands, Dominica, Martinique, St. Lucia, Barbados, St. Vincent, Trinidad, Grenada, Curacao, and Swan Island; *two red flags,* each 8 feet square *with black square center* (3' x 3'), one above the other. By night, on Atlantic, Pacific, and Gulf coasts, *two red lights with a white light between,* hoisted in a vertical line. Both day and night signals also are used to announce approach of those extremely severe storms which occasionally move across Great Lakes and northern Atlantic coast.

HURROK. (Prob. of western Scottish origin) Old north country British term for an oar; *esp.,* aftermost, or stroke, oar in a large pulling boat; the *hurrack* oar, or that at the *hurrack* (also spelled *hurrok*) or *stern sheets* of boat.

HUSBAND, SHIP'S. Person responsible for management of vessels on behalf of owners and having authority as a managing owner at port or ports visited by ships concerned, other than at the home port. Generally, he is empowered to appoint agents in chartering or freight contracting, in addition to engaging crews, contracting for dry-docking, repairs, supplies, towing, etc. *Husbandage* is term used for commissions and other payments made to a *ship's husband* for services rendered.

HUTCH. A fisherman's shanty; shelter for a helmsman on a small vessel.

HVALERBAAT. (*Nor. = whale-boat*) A strongly-built decked boat common to southern Norwegian coast; has one mast, spritsail rigged, is 30 to 35 feet in length, both ends rounded; used in fishing, often as a pilot-boat.

H. W. *Abbrev.* for high water; *see* **H. water** *in* HIGH.

H. W. F. & C. *Abbrev.* for high water at full and change of moon; *see* ESTABLISHMENT.

HYADES. Also, *Hyads,* a V-shaped group of stars in *Taurus,* in which is included *Aldebaran* (α Tauri).

HYDRA. (*L. = sea-serpent*) A long winding constellation extending S.E. and N.W. roughly parallel to sun's path in *ecliptic,* next to and south of *Leo, Virgo,* and *Libra.* Its only navigational star is *Alphard* (*q.v.*). Should not be confused with *Hydrus* (the water-serpent) in about 70° south declination and containing no stars ordinarily used in navigation, brightest being of magnitude 2.90.

HYDRAULIC. (Gr. *üdor,* water; *aulos,* pipe) Of, or pertaining to, fluids in motion or that branch of engineering known as *hydraulics;* designating a device or machine operated by pressure of water or other liquid; as, a *h. jack; h. derrick.* Also, having the quality of hardening or setting under water; as, a *h. cement.* **H. crane** or **H. derrick,** hoisting apparatus in which a tackle is powered by controlled stroke of a *h.* ram. In effect, it is operated as a purchase in reverse, sheaves or pulleys being pushed apart by ram, leaving speediest moving part of chain or wire as the working end, or fall. It is widely used on docksides in British ports and in a few instances the system has been installed aboard ship for cargo work. **H. dock,** *see* DOCK. **H. dredge,** one in which material excavated is mixed with water and pumped through a pipe-line to depositing ground. **H. propeller,** *see* PROPELLER. **H. ram,** heavy solid piston driven from a cylinder by pressure supplied by forcing a liquid therein, such as is used to start a vessel down the ways in launching, or those in a *hydro-electric steering* installation. **H. riveter,** as used in ship construction, usually for heavy work, device by which rivets are forced into place by *h.* pressure; work performed by this means is claimed to be superior to hand-riveting. **H. steering-gear,** *see* ELECTRO-HYDRAULIC. **H. test,** as applied to steam boilers, a test made by filling boiler with water and augmenting pressure as required by a hand *h.* pump. Also, determination of water-tightness of double-bottom tanks, peaks, etc., by filling such with water; an 8-foot head, corresponding to 3½ lbs. per inch,^{2} is usually given double-bottom tanks in surveyor's test in shipyard work; *cf.* **Test h.** *in* HEAD. Also, *hydrostatic test.*

HYDROCHLORIC ACID. Used in solution for spraying or pickling newly rolled steel plates before painting, an acid made from action of sulphuric acid on common salt; used in shipyards, also called *marine acid.*

HYDRO-ELECTRIC STEERING-GEAR. *See* ELECTRO-HYDRAULIC.

HYDROFOIL RUDDER. *See* **Streamlined r.** *in* RUDDER.

HYDROGRAPHIC. (Gr. *üdor,* water; *graphos,* to write) Of, or pertaining to, *hydrography,* or that branch of surveying in which contour of sea-bottom, depths of water, position of channels, shoals, rocks, details of coast-lines, etc., are determined and shown on charts drawn to appropriate scale, together with other data of interest to navigators, including magnetic variation, tide and current information, description of lights, signal stations, etc. An expert in this work is called a *hydrographer.* **H. bulletin,** a publication issued weekly, or oftener if urgency demands, by *Hydrographic Office* of U.S. navy, giving recent information of interest to navigators, including positions of floating wrecks, mines, icebergs, etc., discovery of shallow depths or errors in position of shoals, rocks, etc., changes in character and positions of lights, buoys, or beacons, time signal information, and locations of dredging operations. **H. chart,** *see* CHART. **H. Office,** of *U.S. Navy Department,* collects and publishes information for use of mariners and aviators, such as charts, sailing directions or "pilots," aerial and surface navigational books and tables, light lists (excepting U.S. lists issued by *Coast Guard*), Notices to Mariners and Aviators, and the *H. Bulletin* (*q.v.*). **H. surveyor,** a hydrographer: *esp.* one on active field-duty, as attached to a surveying vessel.

HYDROMETER. Instrument for determining relative density, or specific gravity, of liquids. Consists of a weighted bulb of glass or metal to which is attached a vertical graduated scale, the instrument, as used aboard ship, being designed to float upright with scale showing 0, meaning a density of 1000 ounces per cubic foot, at surface of *fresh water.* As density increases, instrument rises, and *sea-water* will now expose scale with 25 at surface, indicating density of 1025 ounces per cubic foot. In connection with *load draft* allowed (or minimum *freeboard*), a vessel therefore may be likened to a great *h.* registering density of her surrounding water by her draft or loadline marks. Thus, when floating in fresh water, an allowed sea-water draft of 24′ 05″ becomes one of 25′ 00″, very nearly, drafts in each case being in the closely approximate inverse ratio of densities in question—exactly, if ship were rectangular-shaped. *See* FREEBOARD. The term is also applied to an instrument for measuring flow of water in rivers, conduits, etc., and one for registering current velocity combined with rise and fall of tide, as a *tide-gage.*

HYDROPHONE. Instrument for listening to sounds transmitted through water, as those from an oscillator or other submarine signalling device, or for detecting undersea craft from noise made by their propellers.

HYDROPLANE. A fast, powered, flat-bottomed boat designed to glide on, rather than to part, the water. As speed increases, forward end of boat rises clear of water in "planing" effect desired, for which reason some boats are made with two or more "steps" or breaks in their bottom surface continuity corresponding to different speeds. Upper, or forward, step gives initial gliding effect at a lower speed; next step, at a higher speed, etc., that part of boat forward of step indicated rising clear of water. A horizontal *rudder* of a submarine is sometimes also termed a *h.*

HYDROSTATIC TEST. *See* **H. test** *in* HYDRAULIC.

HYMENÆA. A tropical American tree known in West Indies as the *locust* or *varnish* tree (*Hymenæa courbaril*) from which a valuable wood for boat-building is obtained, and which also yields a good quality of balsamic resin called *courbaril copal.*

HYSTERESIS (*N.L. = a lagging or falling behind*) Retardation or lag in the effect of changing forces, as in ship's magnetism induced by the earth's magnetic field. Such lag is observed in that component of compass deviation effected by change of ship's heading after steering some time on easterly or westerly courses, as referred to in GAUSSIN ERROR.

I

I. In International Code of Signals, flag *I* hoisted singly indicates "*I am directing my course to port.*" In mechanics, a symbol for *moment of inertia.* Descriptive of structural steel, iron, or other metal having cross-sectional shape resembling letter *I*, such as is used in ship construction; as, *I-bar; I-beam; I-iron; I-rail;* sometimes, also, when flanges are deeper, called *H-iron,* etc.

I.C. *Index correction;* that quantity required to be applied to readings of a gauge, scale, or other measuring indicator, to determine true reading; *esp.,* to angles as read off on arc of a sextant; *see* **Index c.,** *in* CORRECTION. Also termed *index error.*

ICE. Water frozen or turned to the solid state by cold. Fresh water congeals at a temperature of 32° F. (0° Centigrade); sea-water at 27° F. (−3° C.); and sea-water ice is *fresh.* Specific gravity of ordinary ice being .92 and that of sea-water 1.025, 89.7% of a mass of floating ice is submerged, 10.3% showing above water. Submerged part of an *iceberg* is, therefore, nine times (nearly) greater than its emerged volume. **Anchor i.,** same as *frazil i.* (*q.v.*) **Field i.,** extensive area of floating *i.* which breaks away from bays and rivers in high latitudes on arrival of warmer weather; distinguished from *floe i.* in that it covers a greater area, a *floe* usually being considered a portion separated from an *i.-field.* Good example of *field i.* is that appearing south and east of Newfoundland in April, driven by the Labrador Current, and sometimes covering hundreds of square miles in extent, within limits of 43° and 53° latitude, and 44° to 60° west longitude. Within this area the Newfoundland sealing-ships take their annual catch from the *i.* **Floe-i.,** *see* FLOE. **Frazil i.,** also called *anchor i.* and *ground i.,* a name of French-Canadian origin given to that forming at bottom of fresh water streams or underneath surface *i.* under exceptionally cold water conditions. In the latter case it is usually spongy in character, but in shallower water will accumulate downward 10 feet or more, thereby raising level of *i.,* often irregularly, and causing dangerous fissures to appear. The term is also given to *i.* forming on metal piling, structural frames, sides of ship, etc., to which it adheres in severely cold weather with considerable tenacity. **Ground i.,** same as *Frazil i.* **I. anchor,** *see* ANCHOR. **I.-barge,** scow or lighter, housed over and insulated, used for preserving and transporting *i.* **Iceberg** (*berg* = Scand. for *mountain*), large mass of floating *i.* which has been "calved" by a glacier in the Arctic or by the great ice-barrier of the Antarctic. *Bergs* of Northern Hemispheres are confined to northwestern Atlantic regions and are the offspring of many huge glaciers on west coast of Greenland. Of the thousands set adrift each year, a few find their way into the Labrador Current and are carried toward Newfoundland Banks, becoming in months of April, May, and June, dangerous obstacles on trans-Atlantic trade routes in many instances. Point of southernmost drift averages Lat. 40° N. and Long. 50° W., although they have been known to reach 37° 50′ N., in same longitude, before disintegrating. Region in which bergs appear during season named extends roughly 600 miles NE and SW along SE edge of Newfoundland Banks to about same distance from Newfoundland coast. In Southern Seas, greatest northern limit of bergs occurs during November, December, and January. Have been sighted in 35° S. off Rio de la Plata and in 36° S. in longitude of Cape of Good Hope; elsewhere they are rarely seen north of Lat. 45° S. Arctic bergs are of great variety in shape; the Antarctic product generally larger and regularly formed. Though considerably reduced in bulk due to sea-water action and melting by sun's rays and, also, "calving" or process of shedding large split-off portions thereafter called *growlers,* a berg measuring 500′ x 200′ x 50′ above water, disregarding height of pinnacles, etc., may be considered as of average size. This indicates a weight of some 1,244,000 tons in the entire mass. **I.-beam,** one of a series of additional thwartship strengthening timbers fitted below water-line in wooden sealing or whaling ships for withstanding ice-pressure. **I.-blink,** a whitish glow seen in the horizon over a field of *i.;* appears either by day or on a clear night. **I.-bound,** enclosed or obstructed by *i.*; frozen in; as, an *i.-bound ship;* an *i.-bound harbor.* **I.-boat,** skeleton frame fitted with runners and propelled by sails on surface of *i.*; usually sloop-rigged; also, *i.-yacht.* An *i.-breaking* vessel. Any boat used for transporting *i.* **I.-box,** in ice-breaking steam-vessels, small enclosure over an aperture in ship's bottom through which circulating water for condenser is drawn; usually fitted with a heating coil to prevent freezing. A small refrigerated box or chamber for preservation of provisions, as in ship's pantry or stores space. **I.-breaker,** powered vessel specially built for keeping open an area or harbor for navigation, or for a special run involving passage through fields of *i.* Structure of heavy masonry or timber placed to break up floating *i.*, as in a river, in order to prevent possible damage to a bridge, piers, shipping, etc. The *bowhead,* or Arctic right whale. **I.-canoe,** small boat shod with runners and used either on *i.* or in open water. **I. clause,** in charter party usage, stipulates vessel is at liberty to discharge cargo at a port as close as possible to her destination, subject to agreement with consignees or their agents, in event presence of *i.* hinders delivery of goods. **I. code,** system of signals displayed at certain stations for purpose of informing vessels of *i.* conditions in a particular area, as at entrance to Baltic Sea. **I.-dock,** see DOCK. **I.-doubling,** extra plating or planking on a vessel's bows as protection against injury by *i.*; also, *i.-lining.* **I.-drift,** loose floating ice. **I. field,** see **Field i.** **I.-fishing,** see FISHING. **I.-foot,** belt or wall of *i.* formed by freezing snow and water along the shore in high northern latitudes; usually falls or melts away in summer. **I.-free,** said of a harbor or other navigable area which never freezes over; also, condition of being clear of *i.* at a certain time. **I.-gull,** see GULL. **I.-hook,** an ice-anchor. **I.-knee,** one of several additional elongated breast-hooks built inside the bows of a wooden ship for fortifying against *i.*, as once fitted in whalers. **I.-lead,** temporary channel that *leads* through an ice-field and offering a means of making progress through the pack. **I.-ledge,** same as *ice-foot.* **I.-master,** an ice-pilot, or one skilled in piloting vessels among ice-floes, or in freeing ice-bound ships. **I.-nip,** pressure exerted by two meeting ice-packs; especially, that borne by a vessel caught between such. **I.-pack,** any area of *field i.*; especially that which is closely *packed;* a compact floe. **I.-pan,** area of loosely floating cakes or sheets of *i.*; usually presents little difficulty in navigation. **I.-pilot,** same as *i.-master.* **I. patrol,** vessels and/or aircraft detailed by U.S. Government, in accordance with international agreement, to guard, during the ice season, SE, S, and SW limits of iceberg regions in vicinity of Grand Bank of Newfoundland, for purpose of informing passing ships of extent of this dangerous region, for study of *i.* conditions in general, and for affording assistance to ships and crews as required within limits

of patrol's operation. Under terms of *International Convention for Safety at Sea, 1929,* contracting governments agreed to contribute to expense of maintenance and operation of patrol in proportion to total gross tonnage of vessels of each. **I.-petrel, the** *shearwater* of Antarctic latitudes. **I.-pound,** compartment in a fishing-vessel's hold for storing *i.* used in preservation of catch; also, *i.-room.* **I.-sky,** ice-blink extending above horizon to sky, as appears under certain atmospheric conditions, as on an unusually clear night or during day in clear weather with alto-stratus cloud over *i.* from which *blink* emanates; see **I.-blink.** **I.-river,** a glacier. **I.-rock,** an iceberg; especially, one grounded or held fast in a heavy floe. **I.-sheet,** see GLACIER. **I.-stream,** a glacier; also, field- or floe-ice drifting in a certain direction, as with a current. **I.-yacht,** see **I.-boat.** **Land-i.,** that forming between headlands on a coast; also, *bord i.* **Pack-i.,** see **I.-pack.** **Pancake i.,** flat round cakes that make their appearance on approach of winter in Arctic. It is new *i.* detached from a main sheet and is characterized by built-up edges. **Rafted i.,** floating cakes, one or more above each other. **Sailing-i.,** scattered part of a floe driven by a strong wind. **Sheet-i.,** that formed on smooth water, usually remaining undisturbed throughout winter, as in sheltered areas. **Slob i.,** broken up and an obstacle to navigation of smaller vessels, that drifting on to a coast from an off-shore floe, as to shores of Newfoundland and Labrador by the Arctic Current, or by NE and E winds. **Sludge i.,** soft type first formed on sea-surface by cold; also, broken up *drift-i.* which has become slushy through action and increasing temperature of sea. **Trash i.,** broken up *i.* along Arctic shores. **Winter i.,** that perennially present in polar regions. **Young i.,** as distinguished from that formed in an earlier season, *i.* of current season; so termed in frigid latitudes.

IDENTIFICATION, CERTIFICATE OF. *See* CERTIFICATE.

IDLER. Member of ship's crew having constant day duty and hence keeps no night watch; a day-man or day-worker. (Now rarely used)

I.H.P. Indicated horsepower; *see* HORSEPOWER.

ILLUMINATION, CIRCLE OF. *See* CIRCLE.

IMMERSE. (L. *im,* in; *mergere,* to dip or plunge) To dip, sink, bury, or plunge into a fluid; to immerge. *Immersed* part of a hull is that below water-line. **Immersed wedge,** see WEDGE. In astronomy, *immersion* is disappearance of one body behind another, or of one body into shadow of another, as in occultations and eclipses.

IMMIGRATION OFFICER. Government official whose duty is to enforce laws governing admission of aliens into country concerned. His activities include investigation of persons intending to land upon a vessel's arrival from a foreign port and checking of ships' crews for verification of official crew lists.

IMPORT. To bring goods or merchandise, as a commercial transaction, from a foreign country into one's own country. That which is imported; as, *imports* from China. **I. duty,** customs charges on certain imported goods; *see* DUTY.

IMPULSE AMMUNITION. *See* AMMUNITION.

IMPROPER NAVIGATION. *See* NAVIGATION.

IN. Combining word used in various terms and expressions connoting position in maneuvering: as, *in stays, in the wind, in irons;* placement or location with respect to surroundings: as, *in the hawse, in frame, in shore, in soundings, in the wind's eye;* placing or moving to an inner position: as, *in bows* (oars), to *lay in* (from a yard-arm), to *put in* (to a port), to *haul* or *run in with* (the land or another ship), *in spanker* (take in sail); toward or to a position or place understood: as, to *round in* (a tackle), to *heave in* (a rope), to *take in* (cargo, etc.); and state or form: as, *in bags, in bulk* (cargo), *in liquid measure.*

IN-AND-OUT. Alternately in and out; designating backward and forward movement or adjustment of a working part; extending completely through, as a bolt in a wooden vessel's side. **In-and-out bolt,** a through-bolt, or one uniting and passing through an inner timber, as a knee, and a frame timber; often through an inner timber, ceiling, frame, and outside planking. **In-and-out jigger,** a boom-jigger, as the small tackle formerly used to run out studding-sail booms. **In-and-out strakes,** also termed *raised and sunken,* ship's side- or shell-plating in which alternate strakes fay against frames and are overlapped at their edges by the outer or raised strakes. A filler or liner is set between each of latter and faying surface of frames.

INBOARD. As opposed to *outboard,* within the sides of a vessel; toward center line of ship; as, an *inboard guy.* **I. cargo,** that stowed within ship's hold, as opposed to deck cargo of any description. **I. profile,** plan of center-line longitudinal section of ship, showing disposition of decks, bulkheads, hatches, machinery space, and all other internal arrangement, together with measurements, included between center line and far side of hull. It gives more detail than ordinarily shown on the *sheer plan.*

INCH-TRIM MOMENT. Usually abbreviated I.T.M., moment to change a vessel's trim, *i.e.,* to increase or decrease difference in draft at stem from that at stern by 1 inch; *see* TRIM.

INCIDENCE, ANGLE OF. *See* ANGLE.

INCLINATION. A leaning; degree of slant or slope; departure from a line or plane of reference;

obliquity. *I. of a planet's orbit* is angle at which plane of such orbit lies with that of the ecliptic (earth's orbit). In magnetism, *angle of i.,* or *angle of dip,* is that in which a freely suspended magnetized needle lies with reference to the horizontal, as indicated by means of an *inclinometer,* or *dip-circle.*

INCLINING TEST. That carried out to determine a vessel's *metacentric height* in a test of her initial stability; *see* **S. test** *in* STABILITY. Also termed *inclining experiment.*

INCONNU. *(Fr. = unknown)* The Mackenzie River salmon *(Stenodus mackenziei);* food fish resembling both whitefish and salmon, native to northwestern Canada and Alaska.

INCRUSTATION. In a steam boiler, hard stony-like coating or accumulation of lime or other deposit which sets on surfaces in contact with water.

INDEPENDENT PIECE. A timber in the stem of wooden vessels; *see* PIECE.

INDEX BAR. Part of a sextant, also termed *index arm; see* BAR.

INDEX CORRECTION. Also termed *index error; see* I.C.; also **Index c.** *in* CORRECTION. *Cf.* SEXTANT.

INDIAMAN. A vessel making voyages to India or the East Indies; *esp.* one belonging to any of the early East India Companies formed by British, Dutch, French, and Danish merchants in 17th and 18th centuries. *See* EAST INDIA COMPANY; also EAST-INDIAMAN.

INDIAN TIDE-PLANE. Also termed *harmonic tide-plane,* reference level used on British charts for soundings in coastal areas where diurnal inequality is considerable. It corresponds, very closely, to level of lowest possible low water, or the mean of lower low waters. Thus, charted soundings in such localities indicate, in ordinary conditions, absolute minimum depths of water. *See* **T. planes of reference** *in* TIDAL.

INDIAN SUMMER. Fine weather season in the Indian seas, between limits of Suez and Singapore; defined officially by Indian Government as prevailing east of Tuticorin (near Cape Comorin, or southern extremity of India) from 15th November to 25th May, and west of that point from 1st September to 25th May. Prior to *International Load Line Convention, 1930* (ratified by U.S., 27 February, 1931; effective 1 January, 1933) the term was used in load-line marks *(abbrev. I.S.)* for region and season referred to. Now replaced by the more comprehensive word *Tropical (abbrev. T). See* **L.-line** *in* LOAD.

INDICATED HORSEPOWER. *See* HORSEPOWER.

INDICATOR. Device or apparatus for showing or recording position or motion of anything, flow or pressure of a gas or fluid, etc.; a pointer; a gauge; a recording graph. Usual term for the automatically recording apparatus for testing pressure of working fluid in a cylinder at all points throughout piston stroke. Record thus produced is termed an *indicator card* which, in addition to showing mean effective pressure in cylinder, conveys to engineer certain points of information bearing upon efficiency of the plant. **Direction and revolution i.,** device fitted on navigation bridge designed to show, by direct connection with engine-room, direction and speed of engines. Its object is to minimize possible serious results from misunderstanding of orders given to engineer. **I.-pipe,** connects top and bottom of an engine cylinder with *indicator* when latter is mounted for taking diagram cards. **Navigation lights i.,** *see* N. lights *in* NAVIGATION. **Range i.,** one indicating range at a gun station, as transmitted from range-finding or fire-control station. **Rudder i.,** also *helm indicator,* one showing, as by a pointer, position and movements of rudder; *see* RUDDER. **Salinity i.,** *see* SALINITY. **Tide i.,** *see* TIDE. **Water i.,** gauge-glass, or other device, for showing height of water in a boiler; sometimes fitted with an automatic alarm which gives warning of water approaching dangerously low level.

INDUCED MAGNETISM. The magnetic properties induced in hull of an iron or steel ship as a result, in accordance with well-known laws, of contact with earth's magnetic field. During process of ship's building, a component of this induction is rendered more or less permanent by the hammering hull is subjected to, while upon vessel being floated and headed in another direction, its counterpart is found to be of a transient character. Subsequent compass adjustment, to be reasonably successful, must deal separately with each component. *See* MAGNETISM.

INDUS. (*L. = the Indian*) A small southern constellation between *Grus* and *Pavo.* Its brightest star, *a Indi,* of magnitude 3.21, is located in Dec. 47½° S. and S.H.A. 51½°.

INEQUALITY, DIURNAL. *See* DIURNAL.

INFERIOR. Descriptive of a planet less distant from the sun than is the earth; as, *inferior planets Mercury* and *Venus.* Also, of *conjunction* of such when either is on same side of sun as the earth; *see* CONJUNCTION. **I. passage** of a circum-polar body is its transit below the pole, or, as sometimes expressed, its *meridian passage sub polo,* when its minimum altitude is reached; *see* CIRCUMPOLAR.

INFLAMMABLE CARGO. *See* CARGO.

INFORMATION SIGNAL. As displayed at U.S. coastal stations, a red pennant indicating station has information of strong winds either approaching or in nearby vicinity; chiefly for benefit of small craft or tows.

INFORMING GUN. Blank shot fired across a merchantman's bows by a belligerent naval vessel as a command to stop or bring to, as in exercising *right of search* or in warning of dangerous approach to a mined or prohibited area. Firing of gun is usually accompanied with an appropriate International Code flag signal and display of naval vessel's national colors.

INGLEFIELD ANCHOR. *See* ANCHOR.

INHAUL. Rope used to haul in the head of a standing spanker, or that of any standing gaff-sail, toward the mast; also sometimes applied to a *jib downhaul* and a *brail.* Any rope for hauling an object inboard; as, a line attached to apex of a cone-shaped sea-anchor, a running bowsprit, a tripping-line, etc.

INHERENT VICE. In cargo stowage parlance denotes an innate tendency of certain goods to self-damage through spontaneous heating, wasting, rotting, fermentation, etc., with sequential injury to other merchandise stowed in same compartment. Copra, certain nuts and seeds, dye-stuffs, onions, molasses, green hemp, and some kinds of bituminous coal are included in goods known to possess this fault. It is the shipper's lawful duty to inform carrier of any knowledge he may possess regarding a particular cargo's *inherent vice* and the treatment such cargo requires, in order to lessen or prevent any damage arising from this source.

INITIAL STABILITY. *See* STABILITY.

INJECTION. Opening in ship's side and valve arrangement connected therewith through which seawater is drawn; *specif.,* that leading to a steam condenser circulating-pump in the engine-room. **Bilge-i.,** *see* BILGE. **I. engine,** *see* ENGINE. **I. water,** seawater injected into a condenser; may be drawn through either *main* or *high injection-valve; see* **H. injection-valve** *in* HIGH. **Sea-i.,** system in which *i.-water* is supplied to a condenser direct from sea.

INJECTOR. Apparatus designed to force feed-water into, and against ordinary steam pressure in, a boiler. Essentially consists of a steam nozzle surrounded by water; steam is blown through nozzle, water rushes into vacuum, is impelled by steam, and mixture of steam and water with steam pressure behind it enters boiler via feed-pipe. *Giffard's i.,* named for its inventor, is usual type; may be used also for hosing down engine and fire-rooms in cleaning up.

INK-FISH. *See* CALAMARY.

INLAND. Of, or pertaining to, interior of a country; or within limits of jurisdiction of such country, as pertaining to marine affairs. **I. boat,** *see* BOAT. **I. duty,** that levied on inland commerce, industries, trade, etc., as, excise or stamp duties. **I. navigation,** that carried on in canals, lakes, rivers, etc., as opposed to that on the high seas. **I. rules,** in U.S., those made mandatory by Act of Congress, 1897, and subsequent amendments thereto, referred to as "an act to adopt regulations for preventing collisions upon certain harbors, rivers, and inland waters of the United States." The act also provides for adoption of additions to, or modification of, the rules by the *Bureau of Marine Inspection and Navigation* (now embodied in *U.S. Coast Guard*) to suit conditions existing on certain of these waters. In consequence, the *Inland Rules* now comprize three sets of so-called *Pilot Rules*, viz., (a) those for certain *i.* waters of Atlantic and Pacific Coasts and of Gulf of Mexico; (b) those for Great Lakes and their connecting and tributary waters as far east as Montreal; (c) those for rivers whose waters flow into Gulf of Mexico, their tributaries, and Red River of the North. **I. sea,** properly, a large lake, but, *esp.* if of salt water, a body so-called because almost or wholly surrounded by land; as, *Baltic, Black, Caspian, Dead, Mediterranean, Red,* and *Aegean* Seas. **I. waters,** generally, lakes, rivers, and all other waters within the bordering sea-coasts of a country. As defining limits of *i. waters* in distinguishing such areas from the *high seas* in U.S. regulations for prevention of collisions, certain lines of bearing are drawn from or between outer navigational aids and headlands on Atlantic, Pacific, and Gulf coasts. (*33 U.S.C. 151*)

INLET. A bay or recess in a sea-shore, bank of a river, etc.; a narrow channel connecting an inner body of water, as a lagoon, with the sea; a small passage between islands. **Bilge-inlet,** *see* BILGE.

INNER. Combining word in ship terms signifying interior or internal in position; farther in; opposed to *outer.* **I. bottom,** top part of a double-bottom tank; plating, collectively, forming top of such tank. **I. harbor,** a more sheltered area within a port; often a *basin* for smaller craft. **I. jib,** one set next forward of a fore-topmast-staysail or a fore-staysail; *see* JIB. **I. keel,** upper plate of a double flat-plate keel; old term for a *keelson* in wooden vessels; sometimes applied to a *vertical-plate keel.* **I. peak-brail,** in larger brailing-in gaff-sails, brail for hauling in that half of sail next to mast. **I. post,** an inside stern-post: *see* POST. **I. skin,** ceiling or plating covering inside of frames; inside sheathing laid on frames. **I. waterway,** *see* WATERWAY.

INSHORE. Directed or moving toward, near, or along a shore; as, an *inshore* current; to keep vessel *inshore.* Near or close in to shore with relation to a vessel or other object; as, the *i.* buoy; an *i.* fishing-boat. **I. fishery,** *see* Coast f. *in* FISHERY. **I. fishing,** as opposed to *offshore fishing,* that carried on within comparatively short distances from shore. **I. navigation,** art of sailing or piloting vessels along, and generally at short distances from, a coast-line; act of trading or navigating within such limits.

INSIDE. Internal; inner; as, an *inside* room; *inside* planking. Interior; within; as, *i.* a boat; *i.* the reef. **I. passage,** a coastal navigable channel, bounded or sheltered on its seaward side by an island, rocks, a reef, shoals, etc. An inner alley or corridor in passenger accommodation space. **I. planking,** ceiling or planking laid over inner surfaces of ship's frames. **I. strake,** inner or sunken strake in the in-and-out system of shell-plating; *see* **In-and-out strakes** *in* IN.

INSPECTION, CERTIFICATE OF. *See* CERTIFICATE.

INSTANCE COURT. *See* ADMIRALTY COURT.

IN STAYS. Heading into wind with fore-and-aft sails shaking (if a square-rigger with head yards aback) as in *coming about,* or putting ship on a new tack.

INSTRUMENTS. Those on board ship, commonly termed *nautical instruments,* usually are confined in name to such as are used for navigational purposes and include *azimuth-circle, chronometer, barometer, engine-room telegraph, compass, depth-finder, log,* and *sextant.*

INSULATE. (L. *insulatus,* insulated; from *insula,* an island) To isolate or protect from contact with a conducting medium, as in sheathing or covering a cargo space or an electric cable with a non-conducting material in order to prevent transfer of heat or electricity. **Insulated hold,** *see* HOLD.

INSULATION. Material used as a protective non-conductor; *esp.* that covering deckheads, bulkheads, inner bottoms and sides of a refrigerated cargo hold or other space, which usually consists of blocks or slabs of granulated cork or balsa wood, silicate of cotton, any of several so-called mineral wools, or fibrous glass; also cow-hair and loose granulated cork in older ships. It is protected and kept in place by a double thickness of tongue-and-groove sheathing, which often is again covered, in meat-carrying ships, with thin galvanized iron sheathing. In modern refrigerated fruit-carrying vessels, further *i.* is provided in the air corridor or passage between ship's sides and an inner ceiling of wood, through which cooled air is driven and distributed over fruit. **I. hatches,** *see* HATCH.

INSURANCE, MARINE. Act of insuring, assuring, or securing against damage or loss to a vessel and/or her cargo and/or freight from causes usually fully specified for a stipulated sum called the *premium;* written contract in which one party called the *insurer, assurer,* or *underwriter,* agrees to indemnify another called the *insured,* or *assured* against loss to subject matter insured in a sum of money agreed upon, if such loss is caused by peril or perils, called the *risk,* enumerated and set forth in such document, known as the *policy.* In laws governing insurance, a person having an *insurable interest* in a marine venture usually is defined as one who would suffer damage, detriment, or prejudice in event of loss insured against. *See also* AVERAGE. **I. hawser,** also termed *salvage hawser, see* HAWSER. **M.I. certificate,** a transferable document certifying that a certain shipment of goods is insured under an open or floating policy for protection of consignee. **Mutual i.,** provided for by a group of persons who agree to insure each other against certain marine losses not ordinarily covered in the usual policy, including pilferage of cargo, ordinary stowage damage, breakage, minor accidents or damage to hull and fittings, and compensation for injury to stevedores. Usually takes the form of a protection and indemnity club or association of shipowners, each member contributing to premium fund in proportion to size or value of his tonnage. **M.I. policy,** form of present standard policy is substantially the same as that dated Feb. 15, 1613, a copy of which is now in the Bodleian Library, Oxford, England. Present form was adopted at *Lloyd's,* Jan. 12, 1779, and only changes since made have been substitution, in 1850, of "Be it known that," for "In the name of God, Amen"; and inclusion, in 1874, of *Waiver Clause:* "And it is especially declared and agreed that no acts of the Insurer or Insured in recovering, saving, or preserving the property insured shall be considered as a waiver or acceptance of abandonment." Since basic wording of this generally standard document cannot include all different agreements which vary with numerous adventures, such as route taken, season of year, and other differing causes, extra matters are arranged for by clauses either printed in the policy form, written or stamped upon it, or printed on slips of paper attached thereto. Such included clauses are worded as agreed to by underwriters and assured (usually through brokers) and may be very far-reaching, since they over-ride or take precedence of wording in body of policy. Following is basic form of *Lloyd's* policy to-day:

"BE IT KNOWN THAT ...... as well in ...... own Name, as for and in the Name and Names of all and every other Person or Persons to whom the same doth, may, or shall appertain, in part or in all, doth make assurance and cause .... and them and every of them to be insured, lost, or not lost at and from .... upon any kind of Goods and Merchandises, and also upon the Body, Tackle, Apparel, Ordnance, Munition, Artillery, Boat and other Furniture, of and in the good Ship or Vessel called the .... whereof is Master, under God, for this present Voyage .... or whosoever else shall go for Master in the said Ship, or by whatsoever other Name or Names the same Ship, or the Master thereof, is or shall be named or called, beginning the Adventure upon the said Goods and Merchandises from the loading thereof aboard the said Ship .... upon the said Ship, &c., ... and shall so continue and endure, during her Abode there, upon the said Ship, &c.; and further, until the said Ship, with all her Ordnance, Tackle, Apparel, &c., and Goods and Merchandises whatsoever, shall be arrived at .... upon the said Ship, &c., until she hath moored at Anchor Twenty-four Hours in good Safety, and upon the Goods and Merchandises until the same be there discharged and safely landed; and it shall be lawful for the said Ship, &c., in this Voyage to proceed and sail to and touch and stay at any Ports or Places whatsoever .... without Prejudice to this Insurance. The said Ship, &c., Goods and Merchandises, &c., for so much as concerns the Assured by Agreement between the Assured and Assurers in this Policy, are and shall be valued at .... Touching the Adventures and Perils which we the Assurers are contented to bear and do take upon us in this Voyage, they are, of the Seas, Men-of-War, Fire, Enemies, Pirates, Rovers, Thieves, Jettisons, Letters of Mart and Countermart, Surprisals, Takings at Sea, Arrest, Restraints and Detainments of all Kings, Princes, and People of what Nation, Condition, or Quality soever, Barratry of the Master and Mariners, and of all other Perils, Losses, and Misfortunes that have or shall come to the Hurt, Detriment, or Damage of the said Goods and Merchandises and Ship, &c., or any Part thereof; and in case of any Loss or Misfortune, it shall be lawful to the Assured, their Factors, Servants, and Assigns, to sue, labour, and travel for, in and about the Defence, Safeguard and Recovery of the said Goods and Merchandises and Ship, &c., or any Part thereof, without Prejudice to this Insurance; to the Changes whereof we, the Assurers, will contribute, each one according to the Rate and Quantity of his sum herein assured. And it is especially declared and agreed that no acts of the Insurer or Insured in recovering, saving, or preserving the property insured, shall be considered as a waiver or acceptance of abandonment. And it is agreed by us, the Insurers, that this Writing or Policy of Assurance shall be of as much Force and Effect as the surest Writing or Policy of Assurance heretofore made in Lombard Street, or in the Royal Exchange, or elsewhere in London. And so we the Assurers are contented and do hereby promise and bind ourselves, each one for his own Part, our Heirs, Executors, and Goods, to the Assured, their Executors, Administrators, and Assigns, for the true Performance of the Premises, confessing ourselves paid the Consideration due unto us for this Assurance by the Assured .... at and after the Rate of ....

In witness whereof, we the Assurers have subscribed our Names and Sums assured in ....

N.B.—Corn, Fish, Salt, Fruit, Flour, and Seed are warranted free from Average, unless general, or the ship be stranded; Sugar, Tobacco, Hemp, Flax, Hides, and Skins are warranted free from Average under Five Pounds per Cent.; and all other Goods, also the Ship and Freight, are warranted free from Average under Three Pounds per Cent., unless general, or the Ship be stranded."

Depending upon provisions of coverage embodied in a policy, various names have been given the document; as, *builders', hull, open, port risk, time, voyage,* and *wager policies.*

INTERACTION. The so-termed effect produced in shallow areas by motion of water displaced by moving vessels in close proximity, in which vessels either are drawn toward or repelled from each other. That phase of the phenomenon, or, properly, resultant of forces causing such, which has been rendered more noticeable because of actual collisions attributed thereto, has been called *suction* and may be defined as return of displaced water toward a vessel's stern, both laterally and following her wake. Danger of collision from this cause is present in case of a vessel overtaking another in a narrow channel, because of the indraft which may carry overtaking ship's bows against the quarter of her slower neighbor; and this, generally, is the one real peril that may be assigned to *suction effect.* Where, as vessels meeting in a canal, the laterally displaced water from bows of each tend to throw ships away from each other, combined forces thus brought into action are of but momentary duration and hence seldom have serious results; similarly, the temporary indraft on passing of vessels' sterns usually is effectively countered by the helm.

INTERCARDINAL POINTS. The four compass-points, *Northeast, Northwest, Southeast,* and *Southwest;* also called *quadrantal* or *semi-cardinal* points, each being half-way between two cardinals; as, Northeast between North and East, etc. Abbreviated *NE, NW, SE, SW.*

INTERCEPT. In nautical astronomy, difference between true altitude of a heavenly body, as obtained by sextant observation, and that determined by calculation as occurring at same instant in an assumed position, as by dead reckoning, given the ship. Value of the intercept gives location of point through which may be drawn a *line of position,* at some point on which vessel is located at time of observation. *Cf.* **Line of p.** *in* POSITION.

INTERCOASTAL. As used chiefly in U.S. shipping parlance, of, or pertaining to, trade or traffic between domestic ports located in different coastal regions, as that between Atlantic and Pacific ports.

INTERCOSTAL. (L. *inter,* between, among; *costa,* a rib) Occurring between ribs, frames, etc.; of, or pertaining to, arrangement of ship's structural parts in which short lengths of plate or bar forming a girder, keelson, etc., are butted to crossing continuous floor-plates, frames, etc. Any girder or other structural unit composed of short members running between and secured to continuous members. **Bilge i. keelson, Bilge i. stringer,** *see* BILGE. **I. floor,** a floor-plate interrupted in continuity by, and secured in sections to, a vertical center-plate keelson and two or more parallel keelsons or plate girders, as in bottom construction of larger vessels. **I. girder,** range of short plates fitted vertically and forming a longitudinal member between continuous floors in a cellular double bottom; also termed *i. keelson.* **I.**

plate, any longitudinal plate extending between two transverse units, as one forming an intercostal girder or keelson. **I. stringer,** continuous plate stiffened by angles at its inner edge and bridging ship's transverse frames, its outer edge being secured to shell-plating *intercostally,* or between frames.

INTERMEDIATE. Situated or being in a middle place or degree; interposed; intervening; between extremes or limits; as, an *intermediate* timber, port, class, ship, etc. **I. beam,** *see* BEAM. **I. cylinder,** *see* CYLINDER; the *i. pressure* cylinder of a reciprocating engine. Appurtenances thereto usually are designated by *I.P.;* as, *I.P. piston-rod, I.P. connecting-rod, I.P. crosshead,* etc. **I. frame,** in lighter construction, one situated between ordinary frames, as between those in the transverse system which connect to floor-plates and beams; *see* FRAME. **I. pinion,** in a two-stage reduction gear, the second pinion, as in a turbine shaft arrangement for reducing engine speed to propeller speed. **I. port,** a scheduled port of call between original port of departure on a voyage and final destination. **I. shaft,** any length of a propeller shaft between the thrust-bearing and tail-end, combined lengths being also termed *line-shaft* or *tunnel-shaft.* Lengths are provided with heavy flanged ends which bolt to next in line. **I. ship,** as usually termed in lines catering in part to first class passenger traffic, a slower vessel of limited passenger accommodation but of much greater cargo-carrying capacity than the express liner; any vessel carrying both passengers and cargo, as distinguished from the first class passenger-liner and the cargo-liner.

INTERMITTENT LIGHT. Former term for an occulting light, *q.v. in* LIGHT.

INTERNAL. Inward; interior; within a certain limit. **I. combustion engine;** *see* ENGINE. **I. feed-pipe; i. steam-pipe;** *see* PIPE. **I. navigation,** inside or inland navigation; *see* INLAND.

INTERNATIONAL. Between, among, or participated in by, two or more nations or their citizens; pertaining to intercourse of nations, or their acceptance of certain standards. **I. code,** *see* CODE. **I. Convention for Safety of Life at Sea,** title of a convention or conference of representatives of various maritime nations with objective of lessening risks to lives of persons at sea. First of its kind was held at London in 1914, as a result of world-wide demand for prevention of a recurrence of such disaster as sinking of s.s. "*Titanic,*" April 14, 1912, with loss of 1513 lives. This conference was known officially as *International Convention for Safety of Life at Sea, 1914,* and was participated in by 13 maritime nations. It provided for minimum standards of hull subdivision in passenger ships, minimum boat capacity and life-saving appliances; required use of radio; established the International Ice Patrol;

and recommended use of fixed trans-Atlantic routes. Outbreak of first world war prevented the 1914 convention's work from coming into force as intended, and a second convention was held at London, April 16, 1929. In this, 18 nations were represented in carrying on the work begun in 1914, and, in general, it served its purpose well, a total of 43 countries having accepted its provisions and recommendations. Due to scientific and technical advances brought forth during World War II, before close of hostilities plans were laid for a third convention which was realized in the *International Conference on Safety of Life at Sea, London, April 23 to June 10, 1948*, representatives of 30 countries convening. Included in the subjects covered were: limitation of number of passengers; provisions relating to construction; standards of water-tight subdivision; stability; openings in bulkheads and shell-plating; hatchway covers; fire-fighting apparatus; use of radio-telegraphy in cyclone warnings, distress calls, frequencies, etc.; radio navigational aids; depth-sounding apparatus; lights and uniform buoyage; carriage of dangerous goods; rules of the road; navigation of radar-equipped vessels; coordination of safety at sea and in air; and issuance of international safety certificates to vessels. **I. Hydrographic Bureau,** founded in 1921, institution for coordinating hydrographic activities of interested governments, chiefly in adoption of uniform chart symbols, arrangement of light lists, sailing directions, navigational regulations, etc. Publishes the *Hydrographic Review;* 22 nations were represented in 1939. **I. Load-line Certificate,** document issued by a government or a classification society to merchant vessels of 150 gross tonnage or upwards engaged in *i.* trade, in accordance with provisions of *International Load Line Convention, 1930* (effective in U.S. Jan. 1, 1933). It is valid for five years, subject to certain periodical inspections of vessel, duly certified as having been made by a responsible surveyor. See **Freeboard c.** *in* CERTIFICATE. **I. Maritime Committee,** body of lawyers representing various maritime countries' interests with view of promoting uniformity of procedure, etc., in matters of maritime law; *e.g.,* collision cases, liens, shipowner's liability, salvage, insurance, chartering, etc. **I. maritime law,** that code of rules, mutually acknowledged by civilzed states, relating to commerce and navigation on the high seas and other navigable waters. Based upon traditional usage, rather than the written letter, may be likened to, and indeed is of similar force with, *common law;* and custom and usage in the early days of Mediterranean commerce have formed, in reality, the foundation of present-day law of the sea. **I. rules for prevention of collisions,** commonly termed *rules of the road,* those adopted and made mandatory by maritime nations in interests of safety at sea; *see* REGULATIONS FOR PREVENT-

ING COLLISIONS. **I. salute,** that given by a naval vessel upon arrival at a foreign port where such may be returned. It is the firing of 21 guns, usually with a 5-second interval between each. **I. voyage,** one in which a vessel calls at any port or ports of two or more different countries. As defined by General Provisions of *International Convention on Safety at Sea, 1948,* "a voyage from a country to which present Convention applies to a port outside such country, or conversely; and for this purpose every territory for the international relations of which a Contracting Government is responsible, or for which United Nations are the administering authority, is regarded as a separate country." **I. waterway,** any navigable area or channel ordinarily used by shipping and which is included within the limits of, or separates, different countries.

INTERPOLATE. To determine an intermediate value, as in use of navigational tables, according to rate or variation indicated in a series; *e.g.,* sine of 40° 10′ being .64501 and that of 40° 11′, .64524; by interpolation, value of sine of 40° 10′ 20″ = .64501 + 20/60 (.64524 − .64501) = .64509.

INTERVAL. In naval maneuvering usage, distance between two ships in line or between two tactical units of vessels. **Lunitidal i.,** elapsed time between moon's transit, at or about full or new moon, and high water following; *see* ESTABLISHMENT OF PORT. **Tidal i.,** *see* TIDAL.

IN THE WIND. Said of a vessel when heading into, or so close to, the wind that sails are aback or shaking; in stays; also, chiefly in yacht-racing parlance, a vessel is *in the wind* of another when so close to windward as to more or less obstruct the breeze and thus hamper her rival's sailing capabilities.

INVERTING TELESCOPE. As used with a marine sextant, a glass of higher power than the ordinary *direct telescope.* Arrangement of its lenses has for its object sacrifice of a minimum of light, but thus causes objects to appear *inverted.* Although requiring much practice to become proficient in its use, some navigators prefer an inverting glass for all celestial work.

INVOICE. Itemized list or statement of goods shipped to a consignee or purchaser, with description, marks, prices, and any extra charges payable. **Consular i.,** list or manifest of cargo, giving marks, numbers, value, insurance, name of ship, destination, etc. Required at loading port by consul of country to which goods are being shipped.

INWALE. Finishing piece or strip of wood secured along inside of upper ends of a boat's frames in way of gunwale and also secured to the *topping* (top edge of sides).

INWARD. Toward the inside; interior; as, an *inward passage*. Going in, or to, an inside position; arriving in port; as, *inward bound;* an *inward vessel*. **I. charges,** those incurred by, or levied on, a vessel or her cargo when entering a port. **I. clearance,** custom-house term for formal authorization of a vessel to proceed with her business of discharging or loading cargo upon entry at a port. Generally includes payment of light or anchorage dues, depositing manifest of cargo and stores, crew list, ship's register, and clearance or bills of health issued at a foreign port. *See* **C. inward** *in* CLEARANCE. **I. manifest,** list of cargo, stores, and any dutiable goods in possession of crew required by customs authorities from master of an arriving vessel.

IRISH. Of, pertaining to, or characteristic of, Ireland or its people; often applied humorously, as in **Irish hurricane,** or "up-and-down wind" indicated in slapping of sails and gear caused by ship's motion when in light winds and calms; or *Paddy's gale*. **I. moss,** dried and bleached form of *carrageen* (or *carragheen,* from a village in Ireland of that name), an edible dark purple cartilaginous seaweed found on Atlantic shores of northern America and Europe, especially on west coasts of Ireland and Scotland; also, a kind of *blanc mange* made from the weed. **I. pennant,** *see* PENNANT. **I. Sea stern,** type of stern commonly found on coasting vessels built in northwest of England. In appearance it fans directly outward from rudder-post to rail, forming almost the vertical half of an inverted cone. **I. splice,** method of shortening a rope to a required fit, as a ratline, lashing-strop, crane-line, or other short length, by twisting it *against the lay.*

IRON. Made of iron. Any of several tools used in certain work: as, chinsing-iron; hawsing-iron; whale-iron; toggle-iron; or structural metal: as, Z-iron; T-iron; bar-iron; sheet-iron. The metal, collectively, as that used in shipbuilding: plates, bar material, rod-iron, various castings, etc.; often regardless of whether steel or iron. **Angle-i.,** *see* **A.-bar** *in* ANGLE. **Boiler i.,** *see* BOILER. **Branding-i.,** ship's name in metal on an iron shaft, used for branding wooden equipment, such as lifeboat gear, as required by law. **Calking-i's,** broad flat chisels for driving oakum into planking seams; also, various chisels or punches for tightening riveted seams and rivets in metal work. Those for planking-seams are: the *making* or *creasing i.* for ordinary work; *bent i.* for partly obstructed seams, as between garboard strake and keel; a *sharp* or *butt i.,* having a long sharp blade, for short narrow seams and corners; *deck* or *dumb i.,* used to widen narrow seams; *spike i.* for fine corners and around fastenings, etc.; *clearing i.* or *reefer* for removing old oakum from seams; *reaming i.* used in heavy planking to force narrow seams apart, preparatory to calking; *hawsing i.,* heaviest of all, for driving home finished work, in readiness for paying seams with pitch. **Chinsing-i.,** *see* CHINSE. **Clew-i.,** *see* CLEW. **Crance-i.,** *see* CRANCE. **Crooked i.,** the *bent iron,* one of above-named *calking-i's.* **Drag-i.,** a spare harpoon carried in old-style whaling-boats. **First i.,** in former whaling practice, first harpoon thrown at an attacked whale; *see* HARPOON. **Galvanized i.,** *see* GALVANIZED. **Grommet-i.,** any metal ring used as a grommet; *esp.,* one of those sewn in the head of a heavy sail, as a course or topsail, for securing it to the jack-stay. **Guard-i.,** *see* GUARD. **Gunter-i.,** *see* **G. rig** *in* GUNTER. **H-i.,** iron or steel structural material having an H-shaped cross-section. **Hand-i's,** manacles or hand-cuffs connected by a short chain. **Harping-i.,** old term for a harpoon. **Horsing-i.,** *see* HORSE. **In irons,** position in which a vessel is rendered temporarily incapable of maneuvering; as in missing stays and unable to fill away on either tack; when caught aback, as in a square-rigged vessel during light baffling winds. A towing-vessel is also said to be *in irons* when hampered in steering by stress on tow-line made fast at her stern. **I.-bark,** an Australian hardwood tree of genus *Eucalyptus,* heavy timber of which makes very satisfactory material for principal members in smaller vessels, as keel, stem, and stern posts. The wood is a natural repellent of the ship-worm and also yields a gum called *kino* which is used in medicine as an astringent and for dyeing and tanning. Also called *Australian blue gum tree.* **I.-bound,** said of a rugged, rocky coast which affords no anchorage. **I.-bound block,** a wooden block stropped by an iron band outside the shell. **I'clad,** an early armored vessel; *see* ARMOR. **I-i.,** structural or bar steel or iron having an *I-shaped* cross-section. **I. mike,** the gyro-pilot; "metal mike"; *see* GYRO. **I. rope,** the early type of wire rope used on board ship; now displaced by steel wire rope which has greater tensile strength and wearing capacity, although more susceptible to rust deterioration. More pliable than steel rope, its use for foot-ropes was preferred in later square-rigged vessels; *see* WIRE. **I.-sick,** old term for condition of a wooden vessel or boat characterized by corroded state of *i.* fastenings, as bolts, spikes, etc., and deterioration of wood in contact with such; also, *nail-sick.* **Jib-i.,** a traveler or *tack-ring* around the bowsprit for sliding tack of a jib in or out, as in some small craft in which jib is not spread on a stay. **Leg-i's,** fetters made to fit above a prisoner's ankles and usually connected by a short span of chain. **Lily-i.,** small harpoon with a sharp toggle-barb for capturing sword-fish, porpoises, etc. In throwing the *i.,* a detachable shaft 4 to 5 feet in length is used and thereafter recovered by a separate line attached. Also, in former whaling, the detachable barbed head of a harpoon. **Live i.,** old-time whaler's term for a harpoon being used or ready for use upon nearing a whale. **Lumber-i.,** one of a pair of forked stanchions formerly set inside the bulwarks for holding extra spars, etc. **Pacific i.**, metal band or fixture on a lower or topsail yard-arm to which the studding-sail boom and outer end of the Flemish horse (yard-arm foot-rope) were secured. **Packing-i.**, a tool for forcing packing into a stuffing-box; usually about 14 inches long with flat offset blade. **Pig-i.**, cast crude *i.* in form of *pigs*, or ingots, sometimes carried as permanent ballast or to alter vessel's natural trim (difference between forward and after drafts). **Quarter-i.**, hinged band at quarter of a topsail or lower yard for securing inner end of studding-sail boom. (Older sailing-ship days) **Ripping-i.**, calker's *clearing-i.* or *reefer;* cf. **Calking-i's. Rudder-i.**, a pintle, brace, or other *i.* fitting on a wooden rudder. **Second i.**, in older whaling, second harpoon thrown at whale, as considered by an individual boat. **Slip-i.**, a filler or piece of *i.* inserted between plates or other parts which can not be drawn together in riveting. **Spectacle-i.**, a *clew-i.* of spectacle-like form to which foot and leech roping of a course are spliced and sheet is secured; sometimes fitted with a raised eye for hooking in a clew-garnet block; *see* **Spectacle-c.** *in* CLEW. **T-i.**, bar or structural *i.* or steel of T-shaped cross-section; T-bar. **Toggle-i.**, a whaling harpoon; *see* TOGGLE. **Tow-i.**, harpoon fast in whale, so named from boat being towed by animal in the attack; *see* HARPOON. **Traveler-i.**, a deck-horse or *i.* bar on which the sheet of a fore-and-aft sail may slide when changing from one tack to another; any rail or means by which a sail or other object may be slid into place. **Whale-i.**, a *toggle-i.; see* TOGGLE. **Z-i.**, bar-iron having Z-shaped cross-section; Z-bar.

ISABELITA. An angel-fish of good food value found in Caribbean Sea and adjoining waters; about 12 inches in length, brightly colored in orange, blue, and golden; has deep compressed body with wide rear dorsal and ventral fins, in profile appearing as pointed spreading wings above and below the tail.

ISHERWOOD SYSTEM. Longitudinal framing system extensively used to-day in shipbuilding; *esp.* in bulk carrier and oil-tank hulls; *see* FRAME.

ISLAND. (M.E. *iland, yland*) Area of land surrounded by water and smaller than a continent; usually classed as *continental*, when near and geologically related to a continent; and *oceanic,* when far from a continental shore or shelf, as those in mid-Pacific. **Floating i.**, mass of matted vegetation and earth which has broken away from bank of a river, lake, etc.; often seen at sea, sometimes supporting trees, as off mouth of the Amazon River. **Lagoon-i.**, an atoll; *see* ATOLL. **Three-i. ship**, one, usually of cargo-carrying type, having a raised forecastle, bridge, and poop. Intervening deck space

forward of bridge is termed *forward well*, or *fore, deck;* that abaft bridge, *after well*, or *after, deck.*

ISLE. Chiefly in poetic usage, an island; usually one of small area. **Islet** (diminutive of *isle*), a little island. **Bridge-islet**, a peninsula which becomes an islet at high water.

ISOBAR. (Gr. *isos*, equal; *baros*, weight) Curved line drawn on a chart or map through all places at which barometric pressure, reduced to sea-level, is the same at a given time, or indicating mean pressure for a certain period, such as is shown on weather charts. **Isobaric chart,** in physical geography, map of an extensive region, as a continent, showing by *isobars* average distribution of barometric pressure for a certain period or season.

ISOBATHYMETRIC. (Gr. *isos*, equal; *bathys*, deep; *metron*, measure) Pertaining to equal depths; especially, deep-sea soundings. **I. lines,** or **isobaths,** lines on chart joining places having equal depths of water; *see* **F.-line** *in* FATHOM.

ISOCLINIC. (Gr. *isos*, equal; *klinein*, to incline) Pertaining to or indicating equal *dip* or *inclination* of the magnetic needle from the horizontal; isoclinal. **I. lines,** those indicating on a magnetic chart the value of *dip* for a given year. Roughly east and west in direction, they pass through all places having same inclination of needle, usually for every 5°. *Cf.* **D.-chart** *in* DIP. At magnetic equator, inclination, or value of dip, is *zero.*

ISOGONIC. (Gr. *isos*, equal; *gonia*, angle) Pertaining to, or having equal angles. **I. lines,** those indicated on a magnetic variation chart and on some general charts for purpose of showing value for period concerned of declination or variation of the compass needle from direction of geographical, or *true, north.* They are given for an even degree and join all places at which declination is the same. *See* COMPASS; *also,* **D. of compass needle** *in* DECLINATION.

ISODYNAMIC. (Gr. *isos,* equal; *dynamics,* power) Pertaining to, or denoting equal force. **I. lines,** on a magnetic chart, those joining all places at which the earth's horizontal magnetic force, and consequent directive power of compass, is of same value. The line indicating maximum horizontal force lies nearly parallel with magnetic equator.

ISOTHERM. Line on a weather map or seasonal chart passing through all places having same temperature, either actual value at a given time, or a mean value covering a given period.

ISTHMUS. (Gr. *isthmos*, neck of land between two seas; *esp.,* the *Isthmus of Corinth*) A neck or comparatively narrow strip of land connecting two larger areas, as continents, or a peninsula to the mainland; as, the *Isthmus of Suez.* **Isthmian canal,** name sometimes applied to *Panama Canal.*

ITAKA WOOD. (*Native name*) Also called *tiger-wood,* a beautiful cabinet wood obtained from a tree of that name grown in British Guiana. Richly streaked in black and brown, it was formerly much used in panel-work of ship's cabins.

ITALIAN HEMP. One of the best quality hemps in commercial use, grown in northern Italy; *see* HEMP.

IXTLE or **IXTLI.** (*Native name*) Fine soft fiber of the Central American plant, ixtle grass (*Bromelia sylvestris*), used for making baskets and in blending with certain hemps in manufacture of cordage. What is called *Tampico fiber* sometimes is claimed to be *ixtle,* but usually is a mixture of ixtle with less valuable agave products and often also termed *false sisal.*

J

J. In International Code is called the *semaphore flag* which, hoisted either singly or inferior to a group of signal letters, signifies "*I am going to send a message by semaphore.*" It is kept flying while message is being made and hauled down on completion of message. **J-bolt,** similar to a *U-bolt,* one having legs of different lengths and shaped somewhat like letter *J.*

JACK. The union jack (flag). A sailor. Device for raising heavy weights, as by turning or pumping a lever by hand; a screw-jack or hydraulic-jack. A Newfoundland fishing-schooner of 15 to 20 tons and full body build; of simple rig, rarely carries more than one head sail, sometimes a main-topmast staysail; now nearly obsolete, was once called a *jackass.* One of a pair of bars, usually of iron, at topgallant masthead for spreading royalmast shrouds; also, *jack cross-trees.* One of various sea fishes; as amber-jack, cavalla, jurel, pompano, California rockfish; also several fresh-water fishes, locally so named. **Black j.,** *see* **Black f.** *in* FLAG. **Cargo j.,** *see* CARGO. **Every man j.,** everyone without exception; all hands. **J.-block,** *see* BLOCK. **J. cross-trees,** folding or hinged cross-trees so made for convenience in lowering and sending up a topmast, as in fore-and-aft rigged barges, etc., on River Thames, England. (*Also see above notes on* JACK) **J.-in-a-basket,** a cylindrical-shaped marker made of vertical slats, surmounting a pole; placed as a beacon for indicating a shoal, edge of a channel, etc. **J.-in-office,** an insolent, overbearing official or officer; a beggaron-horseback. **J.-in-the-box,** the hermit crab, which occupies an empty shell of a gastropod; common on U.S. Atlantic shores south of Cape Cod. **J.-knife carpenter,** one skilled in making objects from wood with a jack-knife, as in ship-modeling. **J.-line,** rope stretched along a reef-band of a square sail in French-reefing system; *see* **F. reef** *in* FRENCH. Any small handy line or lanyard; a lacing-line. **J.-mate,** a partner or shipmate. **J.-o'-the-dust,** in U.S. navy, enlisted man who assists a store-room keeper or paymaster's yeoman; so named from sawdust sprinkled on lower store-room deck to keep it dry. **J.-o'-lantern,** *see* CORPOSANT. **J.-pin,** a belaying-pin; *esp.* one of those set in a fife-rail, in a heavy sheer-pole, or in a rail or heavy batten across lower ends of shrouds. **J.-rod,** small metal rod or piping fixed to part of structure, as along the side of a deck-house, to which a screen, weather-cloth, awning, etc., may be secured by a lacing or seizings; also, *jack-stay.* **J.-rope,** wire rope fitted as a *j.-rod* or *j.-stay;* in smaller craft, a lacing of small rope which secures foot of a sail to its boom; in the French-reef, line rove in grommets along reef-band of a square sail; a *j.-line, q.v.* **J.'s land,** a distant fog-bank; part of ship not under care of any particular watch or person; no man's land: hence, nobody's business. **J.-staff,** small pole or staff on which the *jack* is flown; *see* **Union j. J.-stay,** iron rod or wooden batten fitted along a yard, gaff, or boom as a means of bending sail to such spar; a *j.-line;* a *j.-rod,* or any extended rope or batten to which an awning, weather-cloth, etc., may be secured; a rail along which hanks of a sail travel, as on a gaff or after side of a mast; kind of lateral stiffening stay on a sailing-yacht's mast, leading from masthead, over a spreader at about height of throat of sail, thence to lower part of mast where it is set up, usually by a turnbuckle. **J.-tar fashion,** according to method or style of a sailor; *esp.* in knotting, splicing, or otherwise handing a rope. **J. topsail,** British term for a *club topsail; see* TOPSAIL. **J.-yard,** the small spar, like that of a lug sail, at head of a gaff-topsail in some sloop and cutter yachts; called a *jenny-yard* where the *j.-yard* is a spar extending foot of such sail beyond gaff of mainsail. **J.-yarder** or **J.-yard topsail,** lug-headed gaff-topsail, head of which is extended by a *j.-yard* or *jenny-yard; cf.* **J.-yard.** Also called *lug-topsail.* **J'ing engine,** *see* **Turning-e.** *in* ENGINE. **Lazy-j.,** also, sometimes, *lazy-line,* one of several small lines or parts of a single line, leading at intervals from double boom-topping-lifts to the boom, as that of a two-masted schooner's mainsail, for keeping sail, when lowered, from falling on deck, thus placing canvas on boom for easy stowing. **Sand-j.,** as used in shipyards for lowering a hull from blocks to cradle prior to launching, essentially consists of a steel or cast-iron box which is nearly filled with sand, supporting in turn a snugly fitting block of wood or iron. Each *sand-j.* is wedged up against hull to relieve weight of vessel from bilge and keel blocks, and, when the latter are knocked away, an outlet in box is opened to allow sand to escape; thus, in hydraulic fashion, slowly easing down supported hull to the *cradle* with its *sliding ways.* **Union j.,** flag bearing the union or canton of a national ensign, flown at the *j.-staff* placed at bowsprit cap, or, where no bowsprit is present, a stemhead, only when vessel is at anchor or made fast in port. As a signal denoting vessel requires services of a pilot, one, usually of larger size, is hoisted at the fore truck and then termed a *pilot-jack.* In Great Britain, *p.-jack* is the *union j.* with a white border one-fifth breadth of flag. Generally termed *the jack,* that of countries having no canton in national colors is simply a small-sized ensign. **Yellow j.,** sailor's name for the quarantine flag (*Q*); yellow fever.

JACKASS. A plug for a mooring- or hawse-pipe; *see* **H.-bag** *in* HAWSE. Kind of fishing-schooner; *see* JACK. Combining term connoting, often derisively, an extraordinary departure from a particular class or rig; as, *jackass brig; jackass rig.* **J. brig,** two-masted vessel square-rigged on foremast, with a fore-and-aft mainsail, no main-course, and square topsails; vessel of any rig which lacks conformity, in the brig class, to either a true brig or a brigantine; *see* **Hermaphrodite b.** *in* BRIG. **J. bark or barque, 3-** or 4-masted vessel characterized in her departure from true barque rig by spreading a gaff sail on mainmast in place of a square mainsail (*course*). In one or two cases of this rarity, main-mast carried topsail schooner rig, or that having lowermast and topmast only, with lower and upper square topsails set above a fore-and-aft mainsail. Any vessel of barque type having a combination of gaff and square sails in addition to complete square rig on her foremast. **J.-fish,** a spiny-finned fish of the family *Cirrhitidæ,* inhabiting Australian seas. Also called a *morwong* (native name), it is about two feet in length and considered an excellent food-fish. **J. frigate,** old-time sloop-of-war, inferior in size and deck arrangement to ordinary frigate of the day; *see* FRIGATE. **J.-penguin,** medium-sized penguin of genus *Spheniscus demersus* found on southern coast of Africa and that of southwestern South America; so named from its cry being suggestive of braying of an ass.

JACKET. Covering on sides of a steam cylinder, as of asbestos, or lagging on a pipe, to arrest radiation of heat; an outer casing on a cylinder of an engine for confining a current of water or steam around such cylinder; as, a *water-jacket.* Newfoundlander's name for a young seal. **Life-j.,** a life-belt, life-preserver, or other sleeveless coat or body-belt of light material worn to keep one afloat in water; *see* LIFE. **Magellan j.,** hooded coat made of warm material used in cold weather. **Monkey-j.,** *see* MONKEY. **Pea-j.,** coarse, closely-woven, blue coat or *reefer* worn in navy by enlisted men during cold weather; also, *pilot-j.; reefing-j.* **Ragged j.,** a young harp seal. **Steam-j.,** casing, or steam space enclosed by such casing or *j.,* around a steam cylinder. **Water-j.,** casing around internal combustion engine cylinders which contains circulated water for cooling purposes.

JACKMARIDDLE. The chiro or ten-pounder; or any closely allied fish; *see* CHIRO.

JACOB'S LADDER. A handy rope-sided ladder having wood rungs which are set between strands of, and seized to, the rope; used for passage to or from an overside stage, boat-boom, etc.; also called *jack-ladder.* Any ladder rigged aloft, other than the ratlined shrouds, such as that on after side of a royalmast.

JACOB'S STAFF. Old term for the cross-staff, formerly used in measuring altitudes; *see* **C.-staff** *in* CROSS.

JAEGER. (G. *jäger,* a hunter) Pron. *yay'-gar.* Also called *skua* and *gull-chaser,* a rapacious gull-like bird noted for its propensity for attacking or harassing lesser spirited birds to deprive them of their prey. Has dark back and lighter underbody; usually about 16 inches in length; and a strong flyer.

JAEGT. Former type of Norwegian coasting-vessel of small tonnage, having the remarkable rig of a single mast with square sails and a single fore stay-sail. Of very full and bluff lines, had square stern, and was clinker-built with treenail fastenings.

JAG. To lay out a rope or chain in long fakes or bights and secure with stops. To jump or hold unsteadily, as an anchor coming home over rocky bottom. To calk a leaky rivet or any small leak in a plate seam. With *on,* to be in a mild state of intoxication; as, to have a *jag on.* A short pull, heave, or other temporary exertion; as, to take a *jag* at the pump. **J.-bolt,** a rag-bolt; *see* **Rag-b.** *in* BOLT.

JAGGER. In North Sea sailing trawler days, a fast tender or carrier which supplied provisions and stores to a fishing fleet and brought catch to marketing-port.

JAGT. Successor to the *jaegt* (*see above*), vessel of slightly finer lines but fore-and-aft rigged, carrying a single lower yard for spreading a fair wind mainsail, with three or more head sails (*jibs*); also has a raking stern and usually carvel planked. Now also probably obsolete.

JALOUSIE FRAMING. *See* FRAMING.

JAM or JAMB. To become wedged or stuck fast; as a kink in a rope *jammed* in the swallow of a block. To secure by squeezing or wedging into place; as to *jam* a bale of cargo in tier. To be hampered in movement by ice, other vessels, etc.; as, ship is *jammed* in the floe; often with *in*, as *jammed in* by ice, by a fleet of barges, etc. In sailing, to *jam* a vessel in, or into, the wind is to point her as close to wind as possible without actually coming in stays or being wholly aback, as for purpose of taking way off vessel or for avoiding collision. To *jam*, or *choke, a tackle* is to hold it against stress by placing its hauling part across block from which it leads so as to nip it between one or more parts of the rope and sheave or sheaves in same block; *jamming* of hauling part thus renders tackle incapable of *coming up* or *overhauling*. **J.-cleat,** heavy lug or cleat secured to ship's side for purpose of butting a shore against it to secure vessel on the ways immediately prior to launching. **J.-hammer,** type of holding-on hammer used in heavy riveting and in cramped spaces; also called *j.-back* and *j.-riveter*, may be of pneumatic pattern for riveting from holding-on end of work, as in double-riveting, or hammering both ends of rivet. **J.-nut,** second nut screwed to a bolt over first nut to prevent latter from slackening; also termed *check-nut* and *lock-nut*.

JAMIE GREEN or JIMMY GREEN. Apparently named for a shipmaster in the clipper ship era, a sail spread below bowsprit and jib-boom for use chiefly in a breeze nearly on the beam. Made of light canvas, its shape varied according to choice, simplest form being that of an inverted jib sheeted to lower end of martingale-boom, the stay to which it was hanked being the outer jib-boom guy, or that running from jib-boom end to cathead. The term also has been applied to a *water-sail,* or one spread below a schooner's after boom when wind is steady and well on quarter or aft, as on a passage through the trade-wind belt.

JAMOKE. Colloquial term in U.S. navy for *coffee,* where the good stimulant, strong and hot, stands endlessly in demand, *esp.* by men on watch during severe weather.

JANGADA. (*Sp. or Port. = raft*) Kind of catamaran raft made of light logs, usually balsa wood, used in fishing off Brazilian and Peruvian coasts. Raft is sailed by 2 to 4 men, has a single mast and triangular sail, and may be seen as far as 40 miles off shore. Said to be fast sailers, these craft take advantage of land and sea breezes to carry them direct to and from fishing-grounds. They are always hauled high ashore at end of every trip in order that wood may dry out and prevent waterlogging. Also, *jangage*.

JANGAR. (*Tamil word*) A raft of two or more boats joined as one and used to carry a heavy weight, as in transporting a boiler, bulky machinery, etc.; found in East Indian sheltered waters.

JANSEN CLAUSE. In a marine insurance policy, stipulates agreement is "free of particular average on ship under 3 per centum, whether stranded, sunk, or burned"; *i.e.,* shipowner must bear first 3 per centum of loss claimed.

JAPAN STREAM or JAPAN CURRENT. *See* KUROSHIWO.

JAQUETA. (*Sp.*) The cow-pilot, or cock-eye pilot-fish; *see* COW-PILOT.

JARRAH. Wood of an Australian tree resembling mahogany and possessing the durable and ship-worm resistance qualities of the *iron-bark* of same family; *see* **I.-bark** *in* IRON.

JASON CLAUSE. Named from a U.S. court case involving general average on S.S. *Jason,* a bill of lading or contract of carriage clause intended to protect shipowners in event of cargo interests claiming damage or loss due to unseaworthiness, latent defect, or other causes not discoverable by diligent effort on part of vessel's owner. In effect, its aim is to relieve shipowner of any liability for cargo losses for which he is not responsible, and requires that cargo, with ship and freight, contribute in general average following loss laid to fault of vessel but caused by no lack of diligence by shipowner to provide a vessel seaworthy in all respects. (*Cf. Carriage of Goods by Sea Act, April 16, 1936; 46 U.S.C. 1304.*)

JAWS. Projecting parts of inner end of a gaff or a boom for loosely gripping the mast, thus holding spar in position; also, *throat* of a gaff or boom. Similar projections fitted on after side of middle of an upper yard (top-gallant or royal) and partly embracing mast, yard being secured to mast by its *parrel,* or rope bearing several wooden rollers or sliding pieces and joining each *jaw* around after side of mast. Separated parts forming a crotch, as for supporting a boom when sail is taken in, a derrick in stowed position, etc. Opening in a tackle-block in which sheave is set. Parts which grip a wire hawser in a clamping-stopper. Horns, or upper curved parts, of a mooring-chock. **J.-rope,** short rope joining extremities of *j's* of a boom or gaff around fore side of, and loosely securing it to, a mast; a parrel. It is usually rove through wooden rollers for easing friction against mast. **J.-strop,** chain sling passed around *j.* of a whale for attaching a tackle when raising head of carcase during flensing process in older whaling practice. **J.-tackle,** slang term for one's gift of prolixity, in the sense of unnecessarily lengthy oral instructions, complaints, or corrective orders; also, *jawing-tackle*.

JEERS. A pair of heavy tackles, or any combination of tackles, for lowering to the deck or sending aloft a topsail or lower yard. **Jeer-capstan,** in older sailing-ships, a capstan placed forward of the main-mast, originally for heaving on *jeers* in crossing lower yards.

JELLY-FISH. Any of various more or less transparent, round, saucer-shaped invertebrates of gelatinous appearance and consistency; a medusa. Many have long stringy tentacles covered with tiny hairs, the stinging effect of which often has been experienced by bathers. Typical jelly-fishes belong to the class *Scyphozoa*, largest being genus *Cyanea* of the order *Discomedusæ*. *Cyanea arctica* is largest found on American coasts, a specimen of which, observed in Massachusetts Bay by *Alexander Agassiz, famous naturalist (1835–1910)*, measured 7½ feet as diameter of disc, with tentacles extending 100 feet.

JENNIE-HARP. A female harp seal; see SEAL.

JENNY-YARD. See **J.-yard** in JACK.

JERQUE. (O.F. *cherquier*, to search) In Great Britain, customhouse term meaning to finally examine accounts of cargoes landed, or to search vessel for any undeclared goods remaining on board after cargo has been landed. A *jerquer* is officer who is engaged in *jerquing* duties. Also, *jerk*. **J.-note**, final inward clearing bill issued to master of ship by collector of customs after vessel has been *jerqued* and therefore free to take outward cargo on board.

JET. (Fr. *jeter*, to throw) To spout out or spurt, as water from a small opening in a pipe. A nozzle or spout through which a stream or *jet* is emitted, as for a gas or fluid. **J. propulsion**, act or method of propelling a boat or vessel by forcing water astern, as by a powerful pump, from an immersed *j.* or *j's*; also called *water-jet*, or *hydraulic*, propulsion. Compared with screw propeller system, experiments with such installation to date have met with little success in speed-producing with reasonable economy.

JETSAM. Goods or cargo thrown overboard, or jettisoned, to lighten a vessel in distress, or otherwise for safety of ship and cargo; often applied specifically to such goods when washed ashore. *Cf.* JETTISON. Also written *jetsom*.

JETTAGE. Chiefly in England, dues levied on vessels in some ports for use of a pier or jetty.

JETTISON. (O.F. *getaison*, a throwing) To throw, or act of throwing, cargo overboard to lighten vessel in danger of sinking, or being otherwise lost or wrecked. Such loss or sacrifice for the common safety, under rules of *general average*, is borne proportionately by ship, cargo, and freight, according to value of each, except in case of deck cargo "carried at shipper's risk." Where it is shown, however, that deck cargo thus lost was carried according to recognized custom of a particular trade, loss therefore must be contributed to in general average. *Cf.* AVERAGE.

JETTY. Structure of wood, earth, stone, or any combination thereof, projecting from shore, as a mole or pier, for purpose of diverting or confining a current with view of maintaining a channel depth; for protecting a harbor from sea waves, as a breakwater; or for protecting a bridge pier from ice or shipping, as a starling; a wharf. **J.-head**, outer end of a jetty or small extension of a wharf or pier. **Training-j.**, one specially built to direct a tidal flow or river current with purpose of confining movement of silt to a channel, thus maintaining a certain depth therein.

JEWEL-BLOCK. Small single block aloft at a yard-arm; see BLOCK.

JEW-FISH. Large, rough-scaled, dark-colored, serranoid fish, having a thick body, oval-shaped in profile; found in warm seas; often weighs more than 500 lbs. and varies in length from 5 to 10 feet, a species native to South Pacific being said to reach 12 feet; those of Central American waters and Californian coast usually 5 to 6 feet. The *black grouper* of American coasts from Gulf Stream off Carolinas to Brazil is also called a *jew-fish* and several other large fishes have been given same name. True *jew-fish* is not highly valued for food.

JEW'S HARP. Ring or shackle at shank head of an old-fashioned anchor; *anchor-shackle* to which cable is attached, and which formerly connected to the anchor-ring. To-day the term denotes a cable shackle of lyre or bow shape, *i.e.*, bowing outward from its pin end, whether doing duty as an anchor-ring or joining-shackle on end of cable next anchor.

J. G. Abbreviation, usually in lower case type, for *junior grade*, as, *lieutenant* (*j.g.*), indicating U.S. naval rank next below a full lieutenant or next above ensign.

JIB. Triangular-shaped sail set on a stay leading from jib-boom or bowsprit to fore-topmasthead or above. Properly, in fore-and-aft rigged vessels, any such sail set forward of fore-stay; or, in square rig, set forward of fore-topmast-stay, *i.e.*, where both bowsprit and jib-boom are present, as in older rigs, above jib-boom only; in former case a jib-shaped sail set on fore stay being termed *fore-staysail*, while in square rig that set on fore-topmast stay is called *fore-topmast-staysail*. Jibs may be two to four in number, depending on vessel's size and rig, and, excepting fancy yachting arrangements and names for such canvas, are usually called, where four are spread, *inner, middle, outer*, and *flying jibs*; in case of three, *inner, outer*, and *flying jibs*; and two only, *j.* and *flying j.* In small craft, a *j.* is often set by its halyard only; otherwise, its forward or longest side termed the *luff*, is secured at short intervals to its stay by *hanks*, is hoisted by a *halyard* leading from masthead, and, from its after corner, or *clew*, the *sheet* or rope by which sail is trimmed leads inboard. Excepting again some departures from generally accepted best arrangement of canvas in a *j.* by the yachting world, cloths are laid out in *Scottish* *cut* fashion, or that in which they run parallel to after sides (*foot* and *leech*) of sail and meet, or are *mitered*, in a line termed the *last*, perpendicular to stay and extending to the *clew*. A *j.* is also the projecting arm of a crane, as commonly found on a dockside. **Balloon j.,** used in racing yachts and so named from its large bellying area, one set on an outer stay, hoisting well aloft and sheeting well aft, and spread when boat is running freee. **Cap-j.,** as usually termed in small vessels of fore-and-aft rig, a jib spread on a stay leading to bowsprit cap. **Cut of one's j.,** shape and general appearance; as, "*He is a Norseman by the cut of his jib*"; also applied to distinguishing features of a vessel. **Flying-j.,** in older square rig, outermost one which was set on fore topgallant stay, usually having a tack-rope allowing sail to be hoisted well above jib-boom (or flying jibboom in larger vessels). Any *j.* set well aloft from outer end of a *j.-boom*. **Flying jib-boom guys,** stays which gave lateral support to the spar indicated, in older square-rigged ships. Flying *j.-boom* was fitted as a light extension to *j.-boom*. Usually one on each side, guys were set up to the catheads. **Genoa j.,** in yacht-sailing, one of large area set on the topmast stay. Usually carried with sloop rig, it is set to a beam wind or when close-hauled and extends well aft in lee of mainsail. **Greta Garbo,** or **double-clewed j.,** *see* GRETA GARBO. **Inner j.,** in fore-and-aft rig, where two or more jibs are present, first one forward of fore staysail; in square rig, first one forward of fore topmast staysail. **J.-boom,** spar extending forward from, and secured to, a bowsprit. Its purpose is that of an out-rigger for receiving and spreading the *j.* stays which, in addition to supplying means for setting *j's*, stay top-gallant and royal masts or assist topmast stay in its work of supporting the topmast. It may be taken inboard by slacking up its gear, raising its heel, and sliding it through the bowsprit cap ring, which holds it down to bowsprit. In later ships, with reduction in number of crew, head sail, with studding-sails and a few upper staysails, was lessened considerably and, *esp.* in iron vessels, bowsprit and jib-boom were made in one piece, usually of plate. *Cf.* BOWSPRIT. **J.-foresail,** another name for a fore stay-sail, stay foresail, or jumbo: triangular sail set on the fore stay in fore-and-aft rig. **J.-boom guys,** ropes or chains for laterally staying *j.-boom*. Usually two on each side, they were set up to the catheads, and, in older ships, passed over spreaders extending from each side of bowsprit cap, called *whiskers,* which, in still older use, formed a *spritsail yard* for spreading a square sail of that name below bowsprit end. Also called *jib-guys*. **J.-boom saddle,** or **chock,** heavy block or piece of wood in which heel of *j.-boom* was set when spar was rigged in place. **J.-head,** fitting of wood or metal forming head of a *j.* instead of canvas being carried to an extreme point. **J.-headed,** said of any sail that extends in a point at its head (upper corner), as jibs,

staysails, gaff-topsails, etc.; a *jib-header.* **J.-iron,** *see* **j.-traveler. J.-netting,** rope net under *j.-boom* or bowsprit, extending from side to side and secured to *j.-boom guys* or bowsprit shrouds. Its purpose is to save a man from falling into water, as once required by law in German ships, and also to temporarily hold head sails when hauled down in breezy weather; also, *j.-boom netting.* **J.-topsail,** light *j.* set well aloft outside of all head sail, in either fore-and-aft or square-rigged vessels. Also called *jib-o-jib* and *jibber-j.* **J. stay,** any stay on which a *j.* is set; properly, in fore-and-aft rig, any such stay outside of fore stay, and, in square rig, outside of fore topmast stay, the term for sails set on latter being *staysails.* **J.-traveler,** a tack-ring; *see* **jib-i.** *in* IRON. **J. tricing-line,** kind of buntline for gathering in broader part of *j.* when taking it in, as sometimes found in smaller vessels. It leads from clew to a small block on luff of sail, thence down to a block at tack, and inboard. Sometimes rigged as spilling-lines, either extending completely around middle of sail, or two separate tricing-lines hauled on together. **Outer j.,** where two or more are carried, outermost *j.* proper, or foremost one having its tack fast down at boom. (A *flying-j.* sets with tack well above boom) **Quadrilateral j.,** a double-clewed *j.; see* GRETA GARBO. **Spitfire j.,** small *j.* or storm staysail made of strong canvas, such as is used in small vessels for lying to in heavy weather; also, *storm-j.*

JIBBER THE KIBBER, To. Phrase of unknown origin meaning to lure a vessel into running aground by displaying a rising and falling light from shore, in order to convey the impression that sea-room extends beyond light thus exhibited. This was a favorite trick of wreckers on more rugged coasts of the British Isles, and even on U.S. shores, up until as recently as barely a century ago.

JIBE. Variant of *gybe; see* GYBE.

JIG. Device for capturing fish without bait; *esp.* that in which one or more hooks are attached to a piece of bright metal, white bone, etc., designated to attract certain fish by revolving rapidly when towed from a boat. Purchase of small-sized rope, either having two double blocks (*two-fold*) or one double and one single block (*luff*), rigged to standing end of a larger purchase, such as peak halyards of a schooner's mainsail, for purpose of further setting it up, after hoisting as much as practicable by the hauling part; also, *jigger;* in the case indicated, termed a *peak jig.* To fish with one or more hooks, using no bait, as by jerking on line hit or miss fashion, when let down in a school. **J.-tackle,** a *j.* or *jigger* (purchase); also, a handy working purchase, as a watch-tackle or handy billy. **Reef-j.,** a reef tackle; *see* REEF.

JIGGER. Sail set on a jigger-mast. A former yawl-rigged fishing-boat on New England coast. A jig-tackle, or handy billy. A set of hooks fastened to a sinker for *jigging* fish; *see* JIG. Aftermost sail, or *mizzen*, in the yawl or ketch rig. Small purchase, usually of gun-tackle type, formerly used aloft in older square-rigged ships, as *boom-j., bunt-j., clew-j.,* etc., *q.v. in* BOOM, BUNT, CLEW, IN-AND-OUT, LIFT, REEF, *etc.* **J.-block,** a tail-block; *see* BLOCK. **J.-boom,** spar which spreads foot of a fore-and-aft sail on a *j.-mast.* **J.-bumkin,** or **j.-bumpkin,** spar or out-rigger laid horizontally in the fore-and-aft line over stern, at end of which is sheet-block for the mizzen, as in *yawl rig;* also, in small craft parlance, *jigger-boom.* **J.-mast,** in square rig, ships and barques having *more than three masts,* fourth mast from forward; in schooners having *more than four masts,* fourth mast from forward. Four-masted schooners and barquentines, at least in America, appear to have adopted *spanker* as term for fourth mast and its lower sail. **J.-topsail, j.-topgallant-sail, j.-royal,** sails spread on a *j.-mast* in square rig; *see* SAIL. **J.-staysail,** sail of jib or triangular shape set on the *j. stay,* or that stay leading from foot of mizzenmast in square-rigged vessels to *j.-lowermasthead.* **Reef-j.,** a reef-jig; *see* REEF. **Split j.,** in larger four-masted barques, sail similar to *double-gaffed spanker* in three-masters; *see* DOUBLE. **Tail-j.,** handy billy having its hauling-block stropped with a tapered tail for making fast to any object hauled upon.

JIGGING. Act of taking fish with a *jig* or *jigger;* also, of taking short pulls or *swaying up* on a rope or tackle-fall.

JIMMY LEGS. Sailor's name for a master-at-arms, or petty officer charged with maintaining discipline, custody of prisoners, etc.

JIMMY GREEN. *See* JAMIE GREEN.

JIMMY SQUAREFOOT. Davy Jones; "Old Nick, the Devil, or Old Clootie, in stokers' duds and twice as sooty; ne'er a friend o' honest Jack."

JINGLE-BELL. *See* BELL.

JINNY-YARD. Small spar or stick attached to after end of foot of a jigger or mizzen in luggers of southwestern England. It is for stiffening the sail in way of its sheet.

JOB-WATCH. A hack chronometer or watch; *see* HACK.

JOG. Thin end of that part of a timber forming a scarf; also, *lip* or *nib,* and sometimes, *point.* **Jogging,** in boat-building, is to notch a clinker-planked boat's frames in such fashion that they may present a full faying surface to planking, thus giving more rigidity to each plank than in ordinary system in which overlapping parts only lie hard against frames; also termed *joggling. Jogging* is also an American fisherman's term for a state or period of inactivity due to bad weather.

JOGGLE. In shipbuilding, to *crimp,* or sharply bend a plate or bar to fit snugly upon or around a projecting part. Transverse frames at one time were *joggled* at some English yards in order to *set in* each sunken strake, in the usual system of *raised-and-sunken* shell plating, so that raised strakes would also fay hard against frame. This costly experiment soon gave way to *joggled plating,* in which raised plate is crimped at both edges to overlap its neighbors, while faying to the ordinary frame as well. *Joggling,* then, was introduced to obviate use of *liners,* as required in *raised-and-sunken* plating (a point worth considering in matter of economy of weight in cargo deadweight carriers) where such filling-pieces must otherwise be fitted between frame and raised strake. Plates and bars are *joggled* by a special power-driven machine called a *joggler.* **J.-post,** early name for a *king-post.*

JOHN DOREE. (Fr. *dorée,* gilded) Food fish of European coasts, *Zeus faber* of the family Zeidæ, usually called *John Dory* in England, of bright yellow or golden color with silvery reflections, having a dark spot on each side; oval in profile, its compressed body about 10 inches in length, has long spiny appendages on dorsal fin and an extended ventral fin, with upper and lower fringing anterior to tail.

JOHNSON'S METHOD. (Named for a chaplain in British navy) A condensed form of Sumner's method, or that of determining ship's place by two successive altitudes of the sun, or by simultaneous altitudes of two heavenly bodies, with difference in azimuth of at least two points, independently of use of a chart. A small book containing a concise set of 4-figure logarithms and other tables, with explanation of procedure, was published under this title at close of last century and proved popular with navigators prior to advent of the *New Navigation,* or *Marq Saint-Hilaire* method, simplifications of which are found in the *Ageton, Dreisonstok, Ogura,* and *Weems* methods of today.

JOINER. Generally, one skilled in joining wood. In a shipyard, a ship-joiner, or mechanic who fits and installs all finer woodwork in vessels; a high-grade carpenter skilled in making doors, paneling, stairs, skylights, etc., from finer kinds of wood. **J.-bulkhead,** *see* Joiner b. *in* BULKHEAD; a **j. door,** in shipyard usage, is one set in such bulkhead. **J.-shackle** or **connecting-shackle;** *see* SHACKLE.

JOINT. Junction or place at which two or more parts of anything connect; as, a *pipe j.;* a *mitered j.* Any means used to form a connection between parts; as, a *T-joint* on a pipe; a *sleeve-j.* on a rod. Having connected or common interests; as, *j. ownership; j. action.* **Butt j.,** connecting surfaces of two timbers, planks, plates, etc., especially where fitted end to end, as in shell-plating strakes, a butt-strap being fitted to form joint; *see* B.-strap *in* BUTT. **Ex-**

pansion j., device or arrangement in a long pipe-line, steering-rod, or upper superstructural deck and rail in a large vessel (also, sometimes, in sides and top of a deck-house in such case) for allowing linear expansion and contraction during ship's motion in a seaway, or for that due to considerable change in air temperature. **Flange j.,** one in which flanged ends are united, as in piping, or in which flange or flanges of any structural part or parts, fittings, etc., is means of connecting to another part. **J. owner,** one of two or more persons to whom a vessel or number of vessels belong; usually, such an owner who takes an active part in management of ownership interests. **Lap j.,** connection of any two parts, as ends or sides of deck or shell plating, in which one overlaps the other. **Scarf j.,** *see* SCARF. **Universal j.,** union of two lengths of a shaft, steer-ing-rod, etc., lying at an angle, one of which con-veys turning motion to the other within certain limits.

JOLLY. (Dan. *jolle;* Du. *jol;* a yawl) Short for **jolly-boat,** a small sail-boat of any rig used for pleas-ure in inside waters; also, for a small vessel's boat usually carried in davits at the stern. Purely Eng-lish word denoting jovial, pleasantly exciting, or mirth-inspiring; as, she is a *j.* craft with that bull nose! What a *j.* lot of sails she spreads! **J. jumpers,** general term for lofty light sails, or *flying kites,* car-ried in clipper ships; *see* **F. kites** *in* FLYING. **J. Roger,** pirate's flag, bearing a white skull and cross-bones on a black ground,—so described in fiction rather than observed in fact.

JONAH. Person on board ship to whose presence cause of arising misfortune is attributed; *i.e.,* be-cause of his "ill luck" or past misdeeds; a name-sake of *Jonah* of old. (*Cf.* Book of *Jonah* in Old Testament)

JOURNAL. Part of a shaft, axle, etc., which works in its supporting bearing. Older term for ship's log, or daily account of all important happenings, navigational data, weather, tank soundings, drills, men on sick list, etc.; *see* LOG.

JUBILEE RIG. So named in England for its ap-pearance in 1897, year in which 60th anniversary of Queen Victoria's ascension to the throne, or *Diamond Jubilee,* was celebrated, a square rig characterized by unusually lengthy yards, with cor-responding increased breadth of all square sails, and no other loftier canvas than double top-gallant sails. Upper masts, naturally shorter than were royals carried, were termed *stump top-gallant masts.* A few ships—usually 4-masted barque type—of this rig were fitted with a steel lowermast and topmast combined in one spar, and also departed from con-ventional rig in that top-gallant masts were secured on *after side* of topmasthead.

JUG-FISH. A globe-fish or puffer; *see* **G.-fish** *in* GLOBE.

JUG-FISHING. Colloquial U.S. term for fishing with hooks and lines buoyed by corked jugs or bot-tles; also, *jugging.*

JUMBO. Chiefly on American schooners, a *fore staysail,* or triangular sail set on the fore stay, nearly right-angled in shape at its clew and provided with a boom, termed *jumbo boom,* along its foot. Also, a sail of isosceles-triangular shape, set apex down from a lower yard, such as was used in earlier days of combined sail and steam powered liners, with view of giving a clearer view ahead, and in old sailing whalers as a labor-saver when lying-to or cruising. **J. derrick,** boom or derrick for transfer-ring heavy lifts; in ordinary cargo vessels, usually installed on after side of foremast. Also called *j. boom,* it is stepped on the deck in one of several ar-rangements essentially allowing freedom of swing in any direction, among which is the *ball-and-socket step* consisting of a large solid ball-like projection at boom's foot, which fits into a hole or socket in a steel block. Respective falls of its powerful hoist-ing and topping-lift purchases are worked on sepa-rate winches, while another winch is used to heave on either of its guy-tackles as required.

JUMP. Two planks or plates, in older shipbuild-ing usage, were said to *jump with* each other when laid side by side and presenting a smooth surface; also, when necessary adjustment was effected to this end, were said to be *jumped.* To **j. the masts,** to lose masts, or become dismasted, as by heavy weather and sea conditions. To **j. ship,** to desert one's vessel after agreeing to serve on board.

JUMPING CARGO. See CARGO.

JUMPER. Any preventer, as a rope, which secures a yard, boom, awning-spar, or, generally, any ob-ject, against being lifted out of position. The loose jacket with open throat and flap collar worn as uni-form by seamen; *esp.* that worn by enlisted men in naval service. **J.-lashing,** such lashing as holds an object from being lifted, as by boarding seas or ship's motion in a seaway. **J. stay,** temporary pre-venter stay leading from masthead to weather rail and set up with a tackle or turnbuckle, as some-times used in racing yachts and small vessels. A stay leading from top of ship's funnel forward to nearest masthead, often used as means of securing signal halyard blocks aloft. In smaller vessels, a chain or wire leading from lower end of dolphin-striker to end of jib-boom, as a *martingale.* **J.-stay compass,** one placed aloft by hoisting to the *j. stay,* for reasons noted under **Pole-c.** in COMPASS; an arrangement was provided whereby its card was locked during necessary lowering to deck for observing course in-dicated. **Whiskers-j's,** *see* WHISKERS.

JUNCTION. Place of meeting or joining, as that of a tributary with a main river, or of forking channels in a waterway. **J. buoy,** one marking limit of a channel at point formed by two meeting streams or bifurcating channels; one marking bifurcation point of a channel, as at ends of a middle ground. In U.S. buoyage system it is characterized by red and black horizontal stripes; in British system, by white horizontal stripes. **J.-plate,** a butt-strap; *esp.* one of large area, as where extra strength is required in plating.

JUNK. Vessel of ancient build and rig common to Chinese and neighboring waters, characterized by above-water bluff lines, high sheering poop, and large sails of balanced lug type on two to five pole masts. Sails, usually of bamboo, rattan, or grass matting, are spread by a series of bamboo poles extending, radial fashion, from luff to leech; foremast rakes forward, other masts more or less perpendicular, after one of more than two being stepped at stern for spreading a mizzen. Underwater body is well rounded with little or no keel in evidence; a large rudder capable of being raised or lowered according to water depth provides exceptionally good steering qualities. Carrying from 50 to 800 tons weight of cargo, vessel's sailing and sea-going capabilities are comparable to those of any commercial craft afloat. *Junk* is also the term for old cordage which may be used in making chafing-mats, gaskets, oakum, seizings, etc., or for any discarded gear or material whether or not fit for further use on board; substance consisting of a mixture of *oil* and *spermaceti* lying below the *case* in head of a *sperm whale;* and, in a disparaging sense, *salt beef or pork* carried as provisions on long voyages. **J.-hook,** one used for handling whale-blubber. **J.-wind,** southwesterly monsoon in southern part of China Sea. **Salt j.,** slang term for salt beef or pork; also, *salt horse.*

JUPITER. (L. *Jovis,* the god *Jove*) Largest planet and fifth of major planets in order from the sun and next to Venus in brightness. Its mean distance from sun is 483,327,000 statute miles and completes one revolution in its orbit in 11.86 years; has an equatorial diameter of 88,698 miles and polar diameter of 82,789 miles, angular diameter attaining a maximum of 45″ at its closest approach to the earth; and inclination of its orbit to ecliptic is 1° 18′ 21″, showing its range of declination closely approximates that of the sun. The planet is attended by at least 8 moons or satellites and, for four of these, their eclipses by the parent body are timed to the nearest tenth of a minute in the Nautical Almanac, thus often presenting a handy means, with a good ship's telescope, of obtaining a check on chronometer time. **J. whale,** old term for a finback; also, *gibbar. See* WHALE.

JURY. Combining term connoting characteristics of makeshift, temporary, or emergency use, usually in the sense of temporarily replacing damaged or lost object indicated; as, *j. anchor, j.-mast, j. rudder.* **J.-leg,** sailors' familiar term for an artificial leg. **J.-rigged,** said of a vessel having, either wholly or in part, a temporary or makeshift rig of sails, masts, yards, etc., to enable her to proceed after damage or loss of original equipment.

JUS ANGARIA. Term in maritime and international law; *see* ANGARIA.

JUTE. (Bengali *jût,* matted hair) Glossy fiber of an Indian plant resembling *hemp,* of genus *Corchorus,* chiefly used for sacking, burlap, and light cordage; also for making wrapping-paper and often mixed with silk or wool in manufacture of fabrics. In itself of small tensile strength and adversely affected by moisture, is satisfactory material, however, for blending with hemp in manufacture of *tarred cordage.*

JUTTY. Structure projecting from a shore, river bank, breast-work, etc.; as, a mole, small wharf, or revetment; a jetty. *Cf.* JETTY.

K

K. Denotes, as a single-letter flag hoist or Morse code flashing signal, in International Code: "*You should stop your vessel instantly.*" In lower case letter, abbreviation for *knots* in expressing speed of vessel; as, *14 k.*

KAHN. Ketch or sloop-rigged coasting barge of western German coasts, of 20 to 150 tons deadweight capacity. Had a leeboard, or vertical fin lowered from deck on lee side to minimize leeway, and deck-planking laid clinker fashion, *i.e.*, each strake lapping its next outer neighbor. Now probably obsolete, in appearance later craft of this type resembled Dutch *galiots* and were usually indiscriminately so named by British seamen. *Cf.* GALIOT.

KAIAK. Variant of KAYAK, *q.v.*

KAICK. Obsolete spelling of CAIQUE, *q.v.* Now sometimes *kaik*.

KAMCHATKA CURRENT. See CURRENT.

KAMBOU. (*Native name in Kurile Islands*) An edible brown seaweed gathered and used extensively on Japanese and northern neighboring coasts and islands.

KANAE. (*Maori name*) The New Zealand mullet, found in large schools off the coasts and in tidal rivers of that country.

KAPOK. (*Javanese = tree cotton*) Silky fiber gathered from seed pods of a large genus of tree family *Bombacaceæ* known as *Ceiba pentandra*. Earlier called *Java cotton* and *Bombay cotton*, is now extensively cultivated in the tropics, *esp.* West Africa, and commercially used for filling mattresses, pillows, cushions, and upholstery work. Also, on account of its light weight and continued buoyancy (said to be 4 times that of cork in this respect) is largely employed on board ship in life-belts, life-vests, life-buoys, and seat cushions as life-saving appliances.

KAPPBAULK. In Baltic and White Sea timber trade, tree trunks about 18 feet in length by not less than 11 inches diameter at top end. 12 kappbaulks, or capbaulks, or "*bredder*," of 18 feet (or 216 running feet) and 11" top measure make one *Groningen tult*, or about 195 cubic feet. Also, *capbalk; kapbalk;* freight generally is based on number of *tults* loaded, which, also, takes into account longer lengths of *kapbalks* having less diameter, in accordance with what is known as *old Amsterdam* measure.

KAROJAL. Huge dip-net operated by a machine, or by means of a complicated system of bamboo supports and levers, either from a platform on a boat or from shore, as employed by natives of Indo-China and India.

KATABATIC. (Gr. *katabatikos*, downward) Pertaining to downward motion of air; *see* **Catabatic w.** *in* WIND.

KAURI. (*Native name*) A New Zealand pinaceous tree of great size (*Dammara australis*), producing a durable, straight-grained wood which is easily worked and capable of taking a high polish; used in shipbuilding for masts, deck and side planking, etc., and is naturally resistant to the teredo-worm. Weight, about 35 lbs. per cubic foot. The tree attains a height of 180 feet and usually takes the name *kauri pine;* also yields at its base a valuable resin known as *kauri gum* or *copal* used in making varnish. Also, *kaori, kowrie, cowrie,* with a few other variants.

KAUS AUSTRALIS,—BOREALIS,—MERIDIONALIS. (Ar. *qaus*, bow) The three stars in *Sagittarius* (the Archer) forming the *bow*, lying in a north and south direction and nearly equi-distant in declination, or about 5° apart. *Kaus Meridionalis,* or *Kaus Media,* is middle star, or that in bend of bow a little west of his fellows, having a sidereal hour angle of 85½° and declination 30° S. Brightest and southernmost is *Kaus Australis* (ε Sagittarii) of magnitude 1.9; *Kaus Borealis* (λ Sagittarii) and *Kaus Media* (δ Sagittarii) are of magnitude 2.9 and 2.8 respectively. As a means of identifying the *bow*, *Kaus Australis* may be located at about 11° E. by N. from λ Scorpii (Shaula), a star of approximately same magnitude and which, with a close companion of much less brilliancy (*v* Scorpii, mag. 2.8), marks the tail of the *Scorpion,* or point of the *Chain-hook.*

KAWAKA. (*Maori name*) A New Zealand pinaceous timber tree of the cedar family (*Libocedrus doniana*), also named *kaikawaka* and *arborvitæ.* Its fragrant wood is reddish, hard, fine-grained, of remarkable durability, and makes excellent material for spars, boat-planking, and finishing work.

KAYAK. (*Eskimo name*) Canoe used for fishing by Eskimos, chiefly by those inhabiting more remote coasts of the far north included in the region extending from eastern Greenland through Arctic America to western shores of Bering Sea and Arctic northeast shore of Asia. Consists of a light frame, ribs of which are often whalebone, covered completely by seal-skins sewn together in water-tight seaming, excepting the hole in which the usual lone paddler sits wrapped in a seal-skin flap laced to the "deck" for preventing ingress of water. About 16 feet in length, breadth 18 inches, and weight about 40 lbs., is propelled by a double-ended paddle. With this narrow canoe amazing feats of boatmanship which apparently defy every rudimentary principle of stability often are exhibited by the Eskimo. Expert use of paddle enables him to turn his *kayak* bottom up, change his course, and recover upright position in a few seconds; and, as has been noted by observers, laced to the skin decking and in his own water-tight garb, both Eskimo and kayak of necessity thus become one, almost living, unit. Also, *kaiak; kayack; kajak; kayac.* Any canoe of this type.

KECKLE. To serve, as with rope, an eye-splice and its strand-ends wormed into the lay, in a heavy fiber hawser; or, *esp.* and originally, to wind chain round the old hemp anchor-cable to preserve it against chafe on rocky bottom, or, at or near the surface, against floating ice; to place turns of old rope, canvas, matting, etc., on a hawser, rigging, rail, or other fitting, for preventing damage by chafing. **Keckling** is material so used; also termed *rounding.* The term is now rarely used.

KEDGE. To move a vessel by means of a line attached to a handy anchor laid out in direction required; a *kedge-anchor.* Act of so maneuvering ship is termed *kedging.* **K.-anchor,** smallest anchor carried on board ship, in weight usually about one-seventh that of *bower anchor* and of old-fashioned portable stock type; used in *kedging,* or to temporarily hold ship in required position, as, when anchored, to control direction of vessel's swing at change of tide. **K.-buoy,** floating marker attached by a line to a kedge.

KEEL. (Of Scand. origin; Sw. *köl;* Dan. *kjöl*) Main structural member or "backbone" of a vessel, running longitudinally along center line of bottom. May consist of a series of hardwood timbers scarfed together, as in wooden construction; series of heavy together, as in wooden construction; series of heavy bar-iron scarfed or welded together; a vertical plate with garboard strakes flanged upon it; or a heavy flat plate stiffened by a vertical plate on its center line inside the shell, as in steel vessels. Present keel construction is of last-named type, except in some smaller craft. Referring to *keel* of early iron ships, Sir E. Reed in 1869 states: "*It was originally external and not infrequently made of wood.*" Function of a keel also includes, in sailing craft, that of providing lateral resistance, or means of minimizing leeway, and often connotes such purpose alone, as in *sliding k., center-k., drop-k.,* and *fin-k.,* first three named being synonymous with *centerboard.* As early as 15th century, *keel* meant a ship or vessel in a poetic sense; as, in a 1697 line: "*No keel shall cut the Waves for Foreign Ware.*" It was also the term for a former clinker-built barge employed on River Tyne in carrying coal; hence, the present *keel of coals,* or weight carried by such barge, equal to 21 tons 4 cwt. On River Humber, a former square-rigged single-masted barge which carried about 100 tons coal; said to have been only rig of its kind in Britain. The term in both instances apparently stems from the early Anglo-Saxon *keel,* a vessel of long low proportions driven by a square sail and/or oars. A former broad flat vessel on coast of Maine, U.S.A., was called a *keel;* and, in older use, a yacht of cutter design, as distinguished from one having a centerboard, sometimes was dubbed a *keel,* or short for *keel-yacht.* **Bar k.,** as built in small vessels, continuous stout bar, oblong in section, extending below bottom center line and with flanges of garboard strakes riveted to its sides; also, *hanging k.* **Bilge k.,** *see* BILGE. **Box k.,** so named from its cross-section and position, consists of two longitudinal vertical plate girders secured to edges of a broad *flat-plate k.,* its upper or fourth side common with double-bottom plating, or, if no inner bottom, simply plated over. Also called *duct k.,* is for purpose of housing ship's piping (which otherwise would pass through the holds) and is made large enough for effecting normal repairs to pipes therein. In smaller vessels sometimes used as a receptacle for permanent ballast, as pigs of lead, rocks, etc. **Center-k.,** a centerboard; also, *drop-k.; sliding k.* **Center-plate k.,** in older steel construction, similar to a *bar k.* in appearance, but built up by extending a center vertical through-plate below ship's bottom and stiffening it by continuous narrow plates on each side; garboard strakes are flanged to the whole, as in *bar k.* Also termed *side-bar k.* **Center vertical k.,** *see* C. girder *in* CENTER. **Docking k.,** doubling strips of plate, internally stiffened by longitudinal vertical plates connected to floors, built on ship's bottom parallel to *k.* about half way between center line and turn of bilge at broader part of vessel for aiding main *k.* in supporting ship on blocks when in dry-dock. Excepting some broadbeamed vessels of light construction, such provision for dry-docking generally is dispensed with in favor of double-bottom construction sufficiently rugged to withstand docking stresses. **Double k.,** *flat-plate k.* of two plates, one above the other with staggered butts. Upper plate is termed *inner k.;* the lower, *outer k.* **Drop-k.,** *see* **Center-k. Duct k.,** *see* **Box k. False k.,** in wooden vessels, the *shoe,* or facing of heavy planking lightly secured to lower side of main *k.,* designed to bear chafing and rough usage otherwise sustained by main *k.* in dry-docking or event of grounding; also, an added extension, as a vertical plate or plank, to a boat's *k.* for increasing her resistance to leeway; sometimes, a centerboard. **Fin k.,** deep, short *k.,* tapering in fore-and-aft dimension and of weighty material, built on racing yachts to increase lateral resistance in sailing and to supply ballasting in lowest possible position. Boat's rudder is hung upon and extends to bottom of such *k.* **Flat-plate k.,** now generally superseding the *bar* type, heavy plate forming central strake in ship's bottom and to which the center girder, or vertical keel-plate, is secured; usually of less breadth, but about one-third greater in thickness than, garboard strakes which it crowns or overlaps. To **give the k.,** in old days of careening ships for bottom repairs, calking, tarring, etc., to heave vessel down by tackles leading from the mastheads until *k.* was accessible; *cf.* CAREEN. **Hanging k.,** *see* **Bar k. Hollow k.,** also called *hump k.,* a plate *k.* of convex or nearly rectangular cross-section, forming a channel under the floors. **Horizontal bar k.,** *see* **Slab k. K.-blocks,** series of heavy blocks spaced about 4 feet apart, laid athwartships in a shipyard slipway or in a dry-dock, for a bed on which a vessel's *k.* rests. Called *middle blocks* where, for larger vessels, a similar series is laid near turn of bilges on each side. Usually of wood, hard pine being commonly favored, but sometimes cast iron and, in later years, of concrete, capped by a soft wood in either case. They are built 3 to 4 feet above ground. **K.-boat,** small inshore fishing-vessel on northeast coast of England; motor-propelled with small wheel-house aft and single collapsible mast at forward end. **K.-bracket,** as fitted in ships having widely spaced floors, triangular plate erected in thwartship plane and connecting a center girder with a flat-plate keel for stiffening purposes. **K.-bully,** a Tyneside lighterman; one employed in handling *keels* (lighters). **K.-line,** in ship drawings, fore-and-aft center line at lowest part of vessel; center-line of *k.* **K.-piece,** one of the timbers, plates, or bars, of which *k.* is fashioned or built. Lowest projecting part of a stern frame which is scarfed or otherwise joined to *k.,* as in steel-built vessels. **K.-plate,** one of sections constituting a flat-plate keel; in the old composite ships, line of plating connecting floors and forming foundation to which wooden keel was secured; *cf.* **C.-built** *in* COMPOSITE. **K.-rabbet,** groove in *k.* towards ends of vessel

for receiving lower edges of each garboard strake of planking. **K.-rider,** strengthening plate running along inner edge of a vertical-plate *k.* or center girder and on top of floors. **K.-rope,** in old wooden ships, a line, sometimes a small-sized chain, rove through *limber-holes* for loosening dirt, as from ballast, coal, etc., and so allowing bilge-water to flow to pump-well. **K.-staple,** fastening, usually of copper or other non-corrosive metal, which secures a false *k.,* or *shoe,* to a main *k.; cf. False-k.* **K.-track ram,** balk of heavy timber swung as a battering-ram in knocking out *k.* or bilge blocks supporting a vessel in dry-dock or slipway. It is fitted with pieces of rope which serve to lift and swing it on end by manpower. To **lay the k.,** to place a ship's *k.,* as first stage of construction of the hull, on the *k.-blocks.* **Molding of a k.,** depth measurement, especially of a *bar k.,* from lower surface to bottom edge of floor-plates. **On an even k.,** said of a vessel when hull is immersed to same depth fore-and-aft; drawing same water forward as aft. **Outer k.,** *see* **Double k. Plate k.,** same as *center-plate k.* or *side-bar k., q.v.* **Rank k.,** one having unusually great depth; *esp.* a *bar k.* or *k.* of a wooden vessel. **Rising wood of k.,** *k.* timber above the *k.-rabbet;* additional timber bolted along upper side of *k.* in narrowing part of hull toward bow and stern for landing floors or frames thereon. **Rocker-k.,** so called from its resemblance to curved base pieces of a rocking-chair, a form of *k.* once commonly found in fast-sailing fishing-boats of New England and Nova Scotia coasts. **Safety k.,** in wooden vessels, two or three strakes of heavy planking forming a *garboard* (range of planking—usually a single heavy strake—next to keel). **Side-bar k.,** *see* **Center-plate k. Slab k.,** plate *shoe,* or additional plate for stiffening and protection of a flat-plate *k.,* as fitted in vessels built to withstand tidal groundings, crossing a shallow bar, etc., in a particular trade. **Sliding-k.,** a centerboard. **Three-plate k.,** *center-plate k.,* so termed from the three thicknesses of material therein; also, *side-bar k.* **Vertical k.,** *see* **C.-girder** *in* CENTER; any *k.* consisting, either wholly or in part, of a longitudinal vertical plate.

KEELAGE. In Great Britain, charge levied at certain ports for anchoring or mooring therein.

KEELER. Small shallow tub for holding tools in use about the deck, washing clothes, etc. A tub or shallow box used as a receptacle for cleaned fish.

KEELHAUL. (Du. *kielhalen*) As a punishment administered in the old days to offenders in Dutch and British navies, to haul a man under ship's bottom, from side to side, usually by ropes leading from each lower yard-arm, or, in smaller vessels, to haul him under ship from bow to stern. Appears to have originated, as a practice, with the Dutch and is referred to in an ordinance of 1560. They abolished the punishment in 1853. Of interest is a *Lon-*

don Gazette note in 1666: *"He caused Blake to be loaded with chains and ordered him to be three times Keel-hauled (as the Dutch call it)."* Also, *keeldrag, keelhale, keelrake.*

KEELMAN. One engaged on board a keel or barge; a *keel-bully.*

KEELSON. Originally, in wooden construction, an "assistant keel," or re-inforcing structural member laid over the floors, parallel with, and through-bolted to keel. In early iron ships, before advent of the inner bottom, same structural function of keelson continued, with the additional duty of keeping the deeper floors (floor-plates) to their work. To-day any important girder giving bottom longitudinal strength often takes the name *keelson;* as, *bilge-k.; engine-k.;* and, also a *vertical through-plate keel,* or *center-line girder.* **Assistant k.,** in larger wooden vessels, additional timbers bolted to floors and main keelson. They are laid about two-thirds of vessel's length in that part of greater breadth to provide fore-and-aft rigidity and increased strength; also termed *sister k's.* **Bilge k.,** *see* BILGE; also, any strengthening timber laid along outer ends of floors at wider part of vessel; *bilge log; bilge plank.* In steel double-bottom construction, the *margin-plate* (forming outer wall of double-bottom tanks) may be considered a *bilge k.* **Boiler k.,** heavy longitudinal vertical plates laid between floors to withstand local stress set up by weight of a boiler or boilers. **Box-k.,** *see* BOX. **Center-line k.,** in double-bottom construction, synonymous with *center girder, inner keel, center vertical keel, center through-plate keel;* in single bottoms, a girder laid fore-and-aft in the center-line on top of floors. **Cross-k.,** any girder or heavy timber laid in a thwartship direction in vessel's bottom structure as support or bearer for engines or boilers; any such members, whether in fore-and-aft or thwartship setting, are often called **engine-k's.** or *engine-bearers.* **Flat-plate k.,** range of longitudinal plates secured by angle-bars to upper edge of a center-line vertical keel and laid horizontally across floors; it forms the middle strake of an inner bottom. **Intercostal k.,** *see* I. girder *in* INTERCOSTAL. **Half-floor k.,** in larger wooden ships, one laid parallel with floors and between middle line and turn of bilge through wider part of vessel. **K.-capping,** flat plate forming upper surface of a *k.;* a *rider-k.* Additional timbers bolted to a *k.* through about two-thirds vessel's length at her widest part. **K.-casing,** formerly in wooden ships, envelope of light wood built on a *k.* for purpose of keeping in place the salt used as a wood preservative. **Rider-k.,** *see* K.-capping. **Side-k.,** a longitudinal stiffener or *half-floor k., q.v.* **Single-plate k.,** one of single plate cross-section. **Sister k.,** *see* Assistant k. **Side intercostal k.,** line of vertical plates connected to bottom shell-plating and butting against floors, thus forming a *k.* between center-line and turn of

bilge in wider part of vessel. In a single bottom, it is capped by a *rider* plate; in double-bottom, by a tank-top strake. In large ships there may be two or three such *k's,* which, with the floors, mark the subdivisions in the so-termed *cellular double bottom.* **Through-plate center k.,** *see* Center-line k.

KEEP. Combining verb usually confined to expressions concerned with sailing or maneuvering, in the sense of to place in, maintain, and/or continue in a position or course of action indicated. Also, a term for a protecting cover, as that fitted for a deck instrument, such as a telegraph, sounding-machine, binnacle, etc. To **k. away,** in sailing, to steer less close to the wind when close-hauled; to continue on a change of course designed to give some object a wide berth in passing. **K. her full,** order to helmsman to avoid steering too high or close to wind; *see* FULL. To **k. her to,** to sail as close to wind as possible and maintain such course. A vessel is said to **k. her way** when continuing to make progress through the water for some time after engines have been stopped or sail taken in. To **k. off,** to point vessel away from direction of wind or any object in sight; same as to *k. away.* To **k. the land aboard,** *see* ABOARD. To **k. the luff,** or to **k. the wind,** to continue in sailing close to wind, chiefly in the sense of maintaining a course which will clear some object on the lee bow.

KEEPER. Any locking or securing device; as, a lock-nut; sliding link on a slip or pelican hook; small lug or plate for securing a compass-bowl in its gimbals; mousing on a hook; key-pin; etc.

KEG. Small cask of about 10 gallons capacity. **K.-buoy,** commonly used by fishermen for marking position of trawl-lines, lobster-traps, etc.; consists of a keg from which a pole bearing a small flag projects upward.

KELP. Any of the *algae,* or seaweeds, of a class known as the *Phæophyceæ,* especially those of family *Laminariaceæ,* characterized by stalks of great length terminating in a broad, fringed, leathery lamina or leaf several feet in length and brown or olive in color. Widely distributed, it abounds in temperate and colder latitudes on rocky coasts and enormous beds of *giant kelp,* rising sometimes from depths of 35 fathoms, in many places serve as natural breakwaters; *e.g.,* on the Patagonian shelf where many a ship, "out of her reckoning," has been saved from being dashed to pieces on the rocks by the kelp-bed's subduing effect on a gale-driven sea. *Kelp* is also the commercial term for ashes of burned *k.* and other weeds of the ocean from which carbonate of soda and iodine are obtained, sources of supply including coasts of Alaska, France, Ireland, Scotland, Norway, and Japan. The weed also is used extensively as a land fertilizer and, *esp.* in more remote coastal areas, as extreme south of South America, is a staple food for both native and his cattle. In the far north, the Eskimo knows little, if anything, of any other vegetable. **K.-fish,** any of certain fishes inhabiting the kelp-growth, so named in English-speaking countries; usually are of ugly appearance and oddly shaped, as the *blenny* and *flat-tongue* of California, the *odax* or *biter* of Tasmania and New Zealand. **K.-goose,** one of littoral habits found in Falkland Islands and near-by South American coasts; male is white, and female dark brown with white markings. **K.-hen,** a swift-running rail, flightless, dark gray in color, and of marine flesh-eating habits; the *weka rail (Ocydromus fuscus),* native to coasts of New Zealand. **K.-pigeon,** the sheathbill, a bird of gull-like appearance, excepting its short beak, found in colder southern latitudes, always in a locality where *k.* abounds. **K.-whaling,** old term for pursuit of the *gray whale,* which formerly appeared in late summer in and about the kelp-growth of California coast.

KENCH. *(U.S.)* A bin, compartment, or other inclosure in which fish or furs are laid and salted in tier. **Kenching** is act of so treating fish in a vessel's hold, or in a *kench.*

KENNING. (M.E. *kennen,* to know or make known) Now probably obsolete term for distance within which land or a ship's sails ordinarily can be discerned, or about 20 miles; as, *the Cape was well inside our kenning.*

KENT. (Variant of *cant)* In former whaling practice, a band of blubber purposely left on fore part of carcase during *flensing* (removing blubber). It provided means for hooking in the *cant-tackle (kent-*tackle or *kent-*purchase) by which carcase was rolled or turned over as required. *See* **C.-fall** *in* CANT.

KENTER SHACKLE. A connecting-link replacing the older U-shaped joiner-shackle used in chain cable. It is made of interlocking halves held in place by insertion of the stud, which again is keyed in position by a pin passing through it from one side of link into the other. Of same size and shape as cable links, it obviates rough usage given the windlass *wildcat* (cable-grip) by the ordinary joiner-shackle "jumping" on the whelps during heaving in cable, or slacking out under stress.

KENTLEDGE. Pig iron, pig lead, or metal scrap used as permanent ballast or for inclining a vessel. **K. goods,** old term for cargo having a low stowage factor, such as bar iron, metal ingots or plates, kegs of nails, etc., selected from a general cargo for low stowage, with view of *stiffening,* or lowering center of gravity of the mass for stability reasons.

KEPLER'S LAWS. Three laws to which the planets adhere in their orbital motion, discovered by *Johannes Kepler, German astronomer (1571–1630),* viz.: *(1)* Orbit of each planet is an ellipse having the sun in one of its foci; *(2)* radius vector of each planet sweeps over equal areas in equal times; *(3)* squares of periodic times of planets vary as cubes of their mean distances from the sun.

KERF. (A.S. *cyrf,* a cutting off or carving) In ship carpentry, a slit or cut made by a saw, as for improving the fit of a joint or in shortening inner or concave surface of timber for bending; also, channel in metal plate burned out by a cutting torch. To *kerf* a timber is to make several shallow saw-cuts across its grain on one side, in order to bend it; cuts lying on concave side. **Kerfed beam,** *see* BEAM.

KETCH. Two-masted fore-and-aft rigged vessel spreading larger sail on a *mainmast,* after and shorter mast being called *mizzen.* Has a short bowsprit and rarely sets more than two head sails. Similar to the *yawl* rig, except that mizzenmast is stepped forward of rudder-post. Formerly carried square topsail on mainmast, that spar being stepped nearly amidships. *Ketch* has long been a favored rig in trading vessels of coastwise type, larger fishing trawlers and drifters, and also in larger yachts. On the British coasts, usually were from 100 to 250 tons burden; now practically displaced by powered craft. **Bomb-k.,** in old sailing navy days, vessel of *k.* rig carrying mortars for throwing bombs; also, *mortar-k.* **K.-yacht,** *k.*-rigged pleasure boat having either jib-headed or gaff sails; carries fore staysail, jib, and sometimes flying-jib. **Press-k.,** *see* PRESS. **Schooner-k.,** three-masted schooner rig having mizzen much smaller than fore and main, usually with no mizzen gaff-topsail. A few yachts having this type of sail plan have been built in America.

KETTLE-BOTTOM. *See* BOTTOM.

KEVEL. (O.F. *keville,* a peg) Stout piece of wood fastened either horizontally or vertically to inside of bulwark stanchions or in a rail for securing or belaying heavier gear, such as topsail halyards, fore sheets, jib-sheets, boom-guys, etc., and warping lines in smaller craft; also, an old term for a heavy wooden or iron pin fitted through the heads of wooden mooring-bitts to hold down in place the turns of a hawser and, at sea, to serve as a belaying cleat. Also, *kevil;* variants of the word are *cavel* and *cavil.* **K'head,** end of a kevel rising above a rail; any projecting end of a timber used as a *k.;* also, *cavel-head.*

KEY.[1] (A.S. *cæg)* Coak or cog in a plain scarf for resisting longitudinal stress; a piece of hard wood driven in the *key-hole* across grain of timbers in a locking-scarf for drawing parts tightly together; *see* COAK. Any wedge-shaped pin or bar used to unite working parts of machinery; a cotter, split-pin, or other device for such purpose. **Anchor-k.,** *see* ANCHOR. **K.-hole,** for receiving a pin or key in a scarf, or in otherwise pinning or connecting timbers; hole to receive a key of any sort. **K.-ring,** piece of bent metal or ring set as a keeper in a hole at end of a cotter or large metal keying-pin, as an *anchor-k.* **K.-scarf,** any locked scarf in which one or more crosswise-driven keys longitudinally stiffen and tighten such timber-joint; also, *k.-scarph.* **Latching-k.,** bight of small line rove through *laskets,* or *latches,*—a series of loops in the head of a bonnet rove through corresponding eyelets in foot of a jib. As *k.* to the whole fastening arrangement, when withdrawn entire bonnet is cast loose. *Cf.* BONNET.

KEY.[2] (Prob. of Celtic origin, as in Breton *kae,* a wall, embankment, quay; Sp. *cayo*) Low islet, reef, or sandbank; *esp.* one of coral formation, as on southern coast of Florida, Bahamas, and western Caribbean coast; also, *cay.* A quay or wharf.

KHAMSIN. (Ar. *khamsīn,* fifty) In Egypt, a hot, dry, southwesterly wind blowing from Sahara Desert and prevailing for about 50 days from March to May. Also, *khamseen.*

KIBBER, To jibber the. *See* JIBBER THE KIBBER.

KIBBLINGS. Newfoundland bankers' term for portions of small fish used for bait.

KICK. First outward sweep or throw of a vessel's stern from her line of advance upon putting helm hard over. As ship settles down to her *turning circle,* angle her keel makes with line of advance decreases to a constant *angle of drift,* or that which keel makes with tangent to turning circle. **Helm-k.,** jerky motion of rudder caused by impact of sea; often experienced by helmsmen in sailing-ships during a calm with heavy swell prevailing. With old hand steering-gear, surge of swell against a rudder thus not protected by the stream-line flow as when making headway, often threw a man over the wheel with a *k.* of no small mulelike severity. **K'ing stops,** on a hand-steering wheel, pair of beckets, or short pieces of small rope securing the spokes to prevent wheel from *kicking* about, as when lying in port; also *wheel-beckets.* **K'ing strop,** short piece of rope confining the lead of a line, as a hawser, to a required position; in older whaling, rope across fore end of boat and over the harpoon-line to prevent latter from sweeping aft as boat was maneuvered.

KID. Small tub or pan in which rations or food are carried. A box-like wooden pen or bin in which fish are thrown as caught, used on deck of fishing-vessels.

KIEL CANAL. Named for city at its northern entrance, artificial waterway in Schleswig-Holstein connecting River Elbe with Baltic Sea. Runs in general northeasterly direction from a point some 15 miles inside mouth of Elbe River to Kiel Bay in southwest corner of Baltic; length 53 nautical miles; breadth 341 feet; depth 37 feet; passing height under bridges 137.8 feet. Greatest dimensions of vessels accommodated: length 1033 feet; breadth 131 feet; draft 31 feet; masts above water 131 feet; speed allowed 15 kilometers per hour, or 8.1 knots. Usual passage occupies 7 to 8 hours.

KIFFA AUSTRALIS; KIFFA BOREALIS. (Ar. *kiffah,* a balance scale; L. *australis,* southern; *borealis,* northern) The two navigational stars in *Libra* (the Balance), respectively catalogued as α²Libræ and β Libræ, of magnitudes 2.9 and 2.7. α²Libræ, or *Kiffa Australis,* a binary star, lies nearly in a line drawn from the bright star *Spica* (α *Virginis*) to northernmost one (β *Scorpii*) in the handle of the "Chain-hook," or *Scorpio,* a little more than halfway toward the latter. β Libræ, or *Kiffa Borealis,* is located about 9° N.N.E. of his companion and a line joining the two forms base of a neat isosceles triangle having its apex at β Scorpii to the S.E.

KILL.[1] (Du. *kil*) In local U.S. proper names, chiefly in New York State and vicinity, originally settled by the Dutch, a channel, creek, river, or stream, as *Kill van Kull;* and appearing in *Catskill, Schuylkill, Peekskill,* etc.

KILL.[2] To suppress, or deprive of an active quality; as, to *kill the sea,* or cause heavy waves to subside as by a heavy rain-fall or by storm-oil slowly poured from ship's waste-pipes, etc. A vessel's way, or speed, is said to be *killed* by presence of thick barnacle-growth on her bottom; by a heavy head sea; by much top hamper, as that in a steamer against a head wind; by steaming through oozy bottom, as in the Rio de la Plata estuary; by heavy cables often attached to drags, as when launching; etc.

KILLER. Large member of the Dolphin family, genus *Orca;* has high dorsal fin, large anterior lower fins; is dark-colored on back with yellowish areas on sides and belly; and has strong, sharp teeth and stout powerful tail. *Killer* of North Atlantic and South Pacific, *Orca gladiator,* attains length of 20 to 25 feet; preys upon seals, sharks, and large fish; often combines forces with a few others of his kind and furiously attacks whales three times his size. Commonly called *killer-whale* or *orca.* **K.-boat,** one of several small powered vessels specially built for taking whales in connection with a "mother ship" on board which carcase is processed for oil, baleen, etc.; *see* WHALING. **K.-club,** *see* GOB-STICK.

KILLICK. Originally, an anchor made of an oblong stone inclosed in pieces of wood with a pair of projecting cross pieces forming four flukes at one end. An anchor fluke; any weighty object, such as a stone, bar or pig of iron, etc., serving as an anchor; loosely, any anchor. Also, *killoch.* **K.-hitch,** as used in making fast a hoisting-rope to lengthy objects on end, a *timber hitch* supplemented by a *half hitch* in direction in which hoisting takes place; also called *timber hitch and half hitch.* **Trawl-k.,**

small anchor at end of a trawl-line, or boulter, in fishing.

KING. Combining term usually connoting prominence or importance in place, position, or appearance. **K.-bridge,** *see* BRIDGE. **K. crab,** the horseshoe crab, an arthropod having six pairs of legs, a convex hard shell back, and body spreading in almost exact form of a horseshoe, often measuring, with its straight pointed tail of two-thirds body length, two feet over all. Best known species is *Limulus polyphemus* found on muddy shores of American Atlantic from Bay of Fundy to Mexico and West Indies. **K.-fish,** local name for several different food fishes; as, the whiting, opah, cero, and pintado of the Atlantic, and several others of the Antipodes. **K.-mullet,** the red goatfish; *see* GOATFISH. **K. of the herrings,** the chimæra; *see* CHIMÆRA. Also, the opah. **K. of the mackerels,** a species of large sunfish of the Atlantic and Pacific. **K. penguin,** largest of the penguins; *see* PENGUIN. **K.-plank,** broad plank of hardwood, as greenheart or teak, laid in center line of a weather deck; *esp.* such plank stepped on its edges to receive deck-planking in the "swept" system, or that in which planks are laid parallel with gunwale, or with "sweep" of vessel's sides—a yachting notion and a costly one. **K.-post,** *see* POST. **K.-spoke,** *see* SPOKE.

KINGSBURY THRUST BEARING. Patent bearing for propeller-shaft thrust-collar in which friction is borne by wedge-shaped films of oil maintained between bearing and collar. Usually a single bearing is required, as against three or more in the common *horseshoe* bearing system. *See* THRUST.

KINGSTON VALVE. Conical-shaped valve, opening base outward and closed in its seat by pressure of sea, such as is fitted on pipes in ship's side below water-line, or sea connections on submarines.

KINK. Sharp curl or doubling in a rope or short link chain caused by excessive twisting. To become *kinky,* or entangled; to cause to *kink,* as a rope. *Kinks* often are formed in rope by improper coiling; thus, right-handed laid cordage should always be coiled down *right-handed,* or clockwise; and that lifted from a new coil, as supplied by the manufacturer, should be removed so that rope is uncoiled *left-handed,* or counter-clockwise, *i.e.,* it progressively leaves coil in that direction. For this requirement, inner end of rope, which usually is that withdrawn for use, sometimes must be passed through center of coil. The converse of this applies to left-handed laid cordage. Any rope, however, will come away from a new coil free of *kinks,* if the mass is mounted on a horizontal spindle, as a stout bar, and *unreeled.* For wire rope, this is imperative where proper care of ship's gear is in view.

KIPPER. A male salmon after the spawning or *kipper,* season; a *kippered* herring or salmon. To cure, as a herring or salmon, by cleaning, salting (sometimes spicing), drying, and lightly smoking; so termed from process originally applied to *kipper salmon.*

KITCHIN REVERSING RUDDER. Patent device in small craft for increasing steering and maneuvering power, featuring control of propeller-steam direction to that end, without reversal of engines. Consists of two diamond-shaped plates, or "blades," bent to semi-circular form and pivoted at upper and lower apexes, so that they miter, or "cup" together, when required to obstruct propeller-stream immediately abaft the screw. In normal position, its tubular form directs propeller flow to either side or astern and so gives vessel extraordinary steering power, with advantage in speed due to initial confinement of the thrust column. But the "rudder" produces astonishing effects when manipulated in going astern. Although engines may be turning *ahead* at a constant rate, by "cupping" the "blades" abaft propeller, astern power is produced by reversal of the propeller-stream due to reaction on the closed rudder; and, by turning blades thus cupped or opened as required, craft is kept under complete maneuvering and speed control. It is claimed that distance in which vessel may be stopped from full speed headway by sudden closing of blades is less than that covered under reversed engines with ordinary rudder.

KITCHEN. Ship's galley or compartment in which food is cooked or prepared; *esp.,* such space in a passenger vessel.

KITE. Any one of light lofty sails spread on former clipper ships; *see* **F.-kites** *in* FLYING. A contrivance towed for warning of arrival in water of a certain depth. Also called *submarine sentry,* it is shaped like an inverted trough which noses forward and downward at constant depth due to canting effect of tow-line stress on its short-and-long-legged bridle secured to its back, or upper side. Upon arriving in water of depth to which kite is set, a hanging trigger at its fore end strikes bottom, releases the forward, or short, leg of bridle, and kite rises to surface. **K.-drag,** *see* DRAG. **K.-fish,** the flying gurnard, or sea-robin; *see* **F. gurnard** *in* FLYING. **Life-k.,** also termed *storm-k.,* one made of a light wood frame and canvas for carrying a line to or from a stranded or sinking vessel.

KITTIWAKE. The kittiwake-gull, or white gull; the red-legged kittiwake; *see* GULL.

KIYI. (Corruption of *coir*) In U.S. navy, scrubbing-brush made of stiff coir fiber.

KLIP-FISH. (Scand. *klip-fisk;* fish dried on rocks or cliffs) Fish, *esp.* cod that is split, salted, and laid out to dry on rocks, wood rails, etc., along the shore; dried cod.

K MONEL. Whitish metal alloy containing 67% nickel, 27% copper, 2.75% aluminum, remainder iron and manganese. Has a tensile strength of about 150,000 lbs. per in.^{2} of cross-section, stands up to heat treatment, and is non-magnetic. Used where corrosion-resistance, hardness, and good mechanical properties are required, as in sea-water pumps, sea-water service ball-bearings, turbine blades, etc., and in instruments and fittings in vicinity of magnetic compasses.

KNECK. A heavy kink or twisted bight in a slack rope caused by undue twisting in the lay. *Cf.* KINK.

KNEE. Triangular plate or crooked timber fitted for connecting, stiffening, and resisting racking stresses in principal structural parts; as, *beam-k., stem-k., transom-k.* Any bracket, crooked, or triangular piece serving as a *knee*. **K. of the head,** in wooden clipper-bow construction, curved timber forming upper part of stem, or cutwater. It terminated in the *lacing,* or *lace-piece,* to which figurehead was secured in older vessels. **K.-piece,** any plate or curved timber fashioned as a *k.* **K.-rider,** in wooden ships, formerly an extra timber, or superimposed timbers, extending from keelson to deck-beam, over the ceiling, and through-bolted to frame timbers. Deck-beam *k.* was fitted over this, and whole arrangement constituted a deep frame corresponding to *web* frame in present steel construction. **K.-timber,** that naturally crooked or artificially bent for use as *knees* or *knee-pieces* in shipbuilding. **Lodging k.,** one placed horizontally for uniting a beam to vessel's side; also, for securing end of a half-beam to a hatchway carling, mast-partner, or other interruption in a full length beam. **Natural k.,** timber of curved form in its natural state, as obtained from the base of trunks of certain trees, suitable for *k's* in shipbuilding.

KNETTLE. Variant of *nettle;* also, sometimes *knittle.*

KNIFE. Metal cutting blade, usually of steel and sharpened on one edge; may be fixed in a handle, as a *sheath-knife;* or may be hinged and closed in a groove in handle, as a *clasp-,* or *jack-knife.* To stab, cut, or kill with a knife. **Boarding-k.,** large two-edged blade with straight handle or hilt used in cutting blubber from a whale. **Boat-k.,** in older whaling, one carried at each end of whale-boat for handy use in event a foul line must be cut as an emergency safety measure; also, *line-k.* **Draw-k.,** one-edged blade with handle at each end; much used in spar-making, user rounds off surplus wood by drawing knife towards himself. **K.-edge liner,** *see* LINER. **K.-lanyard,** *see* LANYARD. **Oyster-k.,** bar of hexagonal steel 18 inches in length and having a bulb-shaped end, used in conjunction with a ripping-chisel in removing boiler-header tubes. **Race k.,** cutting tool with hooked blade, gouge-shaped

at point, used for marking timber-work or laying off ship-lines on a mold loft floor. It is drawn along by the hand in direction required. Also, *rasing-k.* or *scriber.* **Sculping-k.,** *see* SCULP. **Sheath-k.,** single-edged blade with fixed handle, carried in a sheath attached to waist-belt by riggers and sailors.

KNIGHT. Originally, a short vertical timber, as a bitt, in which sheaves were fitted to form the lower block of a topsail or top-gallant halyard purchase. Now, any vertical fitting, as a fife-rail or bulwark stanchion, in which a sheave is set as a lead for the hauling part of an upper brace, halyard, etc.

KNIGHTHEADS. In larger wooden vessels, the *bollard* (or *ballard*) *timbers,* or upper ends of the foremost pair of *square frames* in hull, between which the *bowsprit* was set for lateral security. They formerly extended above top-gallant forecastle for service as *bitts* or *bollards,* often had ornamental carvings, and were called *apostles.* Later, with raking stems, upper ends of a pair of *cant frames* served same purpose. In either case, bowsprit nests between them and sits on top of vessel's stem. In iron and steel vessels, the term has been continued in the vertical plate forming the forward end of top-gallant forecastle and housing a *spike bowsprit* through its center, and sometimes the frames to which such plate is secured are called *knighthead frames.*

KNITTLE. Variant of *nettle; see* NETTLE.

KNOCK. On southeast coasts of Britain, a sand-bank; as *Kentish Knock.* A sharp striking noise in an engine cylinder, usually due to lack of adjustment of parts. To repeatedly strike against a wharf, rocks, etc., as a boat by action of waves; to strike bottom, as a vessel in a swell in shoal water. A vessel when hove to is said to be **knocked off** when sea throws her head off the wind as she is brought up to close-hauled position; and **knocked down** when heavily heeled by a squall or laid nearly on her beam ends in a strong gale or hurricane.

KNOCKABOUT. Schooner or sloop simplified in rig to extent of dispensing with the bowsprit, setting a single head sail on fore stay, and having no topmast. Originally small craft of such rig; later, some 40 years ago, adopted by bank fishermen of New England, Nova Scotia, and Newfoundland.

KNOLL. Submerged top or rising part of an isolated shoal; *esp.* when surrounded by deep or navigable water.

KNOT.[1] One of many forms of tying, fastening, or connecting a rope or its strands either to itself, to another rope, or to some object. Although, among sailors, the term particularly applies to a more or less permanent connection made with smaller ropes or inter-worked strands in various sized cordage, as a *reef k., lanyard k., shroud k.,* in ordinary connotation it loosely covers the many forms in which a rope may be interlaced for any purpose in the entire field of *knots, bends,* and *hitches.* Thus, for a *weaver's* or *netting k.* we have, as synonymous terms, *becket bend, becket hitch, hawser bend, sheet bend, weaver's bend,* and *weaver's hitch.* Generally, the *knot* carries the idea of more permanency than the *bend,* while a *hitch* is a connection capable of being readily formed and quickly released.

KNOT.[2] (*Abbrev.,* both sing. and pl., *k.* or *kn.*) So named from the *knot* marking each division of 47 feet 3 inches in a *chip-log* line; *see* **Chip l.** *in* LOG. Number of such divisions running out in 28 seconds indicates rate at which ship travels. Hence, a unit of speed, as in *ship makes 10 knots,* or at rate of 10 nautical miles per hour. Also applied to current, as, on a chart, *ebb 2 kn., flood stream 3 kn., current sets N.E. 1½ kn.,* etc. (often with an arrow indicating direction of set) thus expressing hourly flow or drift of current in nautical miles. Distance is never expressed in *knots*—always *miles.* **Admiralty k.,** length of mile corresponding to the *k.* established by British Admiralty as 6080 feet. *Cf.* MILE.

KNOTTING. Knot-work; fancy work made with knotted threads, as in canvas covers, pockets, fringes, etc. **K.-needle,** one designed for use in knotting.

KNOW THE ROPES, To. To be conversant with details of ship's rigging; hence, to know one's business as well as a good seaman knows his vessel's gear.

KNUCKLE. In shipbuilding, abrupt local change in direction, or an angle in side plating, planking, or structural arrangement; *esp.* such ridge or angle extending around vessel's counter and sometimes at the bows a few feet below forecastle deck. **K.-line,** that formed by a *k.* or ridge in line of frames or an abrupt flanging or turn in plating. **K.-mast,** *see* MAST. **K.-molding,** rounded strip of wood or metal fitted for ornamental trim over *k.-line* around ship's counter. **K.-run timbers,** those fashioned to form a *k.* in the frame structure; also, *knuckle-timber.* **K'ing,** distortion in way of a welded joint caused by uneven cooling of weld.

KOCHAB. Star β *Ursæ Minoris,* one of the *Guards* (*see* GUARD) in *Ursa Minor* or "Little Dipper." Of magnitude 2.2, is nearest bright star to *Polaris* (North Star), which marks tail end of the group. It lies 16½° from *Polaris.*

KOFF. Former Dutch or Danish coasting vessel of the *galiot* type, of 100 to 150 tons burden, once commonly engaged in North Sea and Baltic trade. Usually was ketch rigged with sprit-sails, or topsail-schooner rig in larger hulls; of shallow draft and full lines; and fitted with leeboards. Also, *kofschip; kuff.*

KOGIA. Genus of sperm whales belonging to subfamily *Physeterinæ;* commonly called *pygmy sperm*

whale or *pygmy cachalot.* Has from 9 to 12 lower teeth and 2 upper teeth, if any; is from 8 to 12 feet in length; has a head of more moderate proportions than his 60-foot cousin; and is found in warmer southern seas.

KOKU. A Japanese unit in shipping measurement, equal to 10 cubic feet.

KOLEK. Malay combining word denoting various planked sailing craft of different rigs, with or without outriggers, ranging from small canoes to the characteristic *prau* or *proa;* as, *kolek pulo; kolek tetap; kolek pukat;* etc. Common to East Indian waters.

KORNEPHORUS. (*Gr.* = *club-bearer*) β *Herculis,* star of magnitude 2.8 in constellation *Hercules.* It may be located at 10° to southeast of *Alphacca,* brightest star in *Corona Borealis,* the Northern Crown.

KORT NOZZLE. Named for its originator, a cylindrical-shaped "shroud" or tunnel built to encase the propeller in shallow-draft vessels, *esp.* those encountering a high slip ratio, as tow-boats and steam trawlers. Has advantage of allowing a larger disc diameter of screw in such vessels, thus generally producing greater efficiency because of confining effect on the thrust column by such means. Experiments have shown average merchant ship would benefit little more than 1% by this sleeve or nozzle, while smaller hard-working craft, principally tugs, have shown increase of propeller efficiency up to 15% when so fitted.

KRENG. (*Du.* = *carcase*) Remains of a whale after baleen, blubber, oil, and all commercial products are removed; also, *crang; krang.* **Krenging-hook,** a large sharp-pointed hook with a long shaft used, in former whaling, to hold blubber while cutting it away from, or *flensing,* the carcase.

KRILL. Minute, reddish-colored, shrimp-like animalcula existing near the surface in huge shoals in Antarctic waters. It is the food of the *blue whale* and appears to furnish sufficient nutriment to that animal's weight of 1 ton for each of his 80 feet of length.

KRUMAN. A member of the *Kru,* or *Kroo,* tribe of the generally tall and wiry *Mandingo* negro stock of West Africa. *Krumen,* or *Kroomen,* of the Liberian coast are noted for their skill in surf-boat handling and, for this reason, their services always are found most valuable to vessels landing cargo and passengers from the many open roadsteads on the Guinea Coast.

KRUPP ARMOR. *See* ARMOR.

KUROSHIWO or **KURO-SIWO.** (*Jap. Kuroshio;* from *kuro,* black; *shio,* tide) Also called *Japan Current, Japan Stream,* and *Black Stream,* last name being from its dark blue color, an ocean current of similar origin and characteristics as the Gulf Stream of North Atlantic. It is a diverted continuation in congested form of major part of North Equatorial Current, which is set up by N.E. trade winds in mid-Pacific and drives in a W.N.W. direction toward Formosa and Ryukyu Islands. Beginning of the stream proper occurs about 200 miles S. of Kyushu Island of the main Japan group, in approximately 27° N. and 131° E., its flow taking a north-easterly course and closing in with the Honshu coast to latitude of Yokohama, where its western edge averages 50 miles off shore. It then turns more eastward, gradually widens and decreases in velocity until, in about 40° N. and 165° E., it diffuses into the general easterly drift of the North Pacific. Average rate of flow is between 2 and 3 knots, attaining a maximum in late summer of 5 knots along the Honshu shore.

KURRAJONG or **Koorajong.** (*Native name*) One of several species of *Sterculia,* a large genus of tropical trees, bark of which is used by aborigines of Australia for making cordage, matting, nets, etc.

KUTTER. Lager type of fishing-boat of North Sea German coast; usually ketch-rigged, decked, 50 to 60 feet in length, and nowadays powered with an auxiliary engine.

KYLE. (Prob. corruption of Gaelic *caol,* strait) On west coast of Scotland, a sound or narrow strait; sometimes in plural form, as, *Kyles of Bute.*

L

L. As an International Code signal, flag *L*, hoisted singly, or flashed by Morse Code (. — . .), denotes *"You should stop. I have something important to communicate."* In log-books and weather recording, capital *L* usually signifies *long, rolling sea* and sometimes *latitude;* a small *l* = lightning. *L.* is also abbreviation on charts for *lake, loch,* or *lough;* on board ship denotes *lower,* as in *L.H.* (lower hold); *L.T.D.* (lower 'tween deck); *L.M.R.* (lower mailroom); and, in load-line marks for timber-carrying ships, as in *L.F.; L.S.; L.T.; L.W.; see* LOAD LINE. **L-bar** or **L-beam,** angle-iron or structural metal of L-shaped cross section. The **Three L's of Navigation,** originally *Latitude, Lead,* and *Lookout,* elements demanding foremost attention in ship's reckoning; particularly applying to deep-sea vessels in proximity to, or approaching, the land. More recently, the coaster's *Lead, Log,* and *Lookout,*—motto of eternal vigilance.

LABEL CLAUSE. Stipulation in a marine insurance cargo policy to the effect that insurer will not be indemnified for destruction or loss of labels on bottles, jars, carboys, etc.

LABOR or **LABOUR.** To pitch and roll heavily in a seaway; said of a vessel. To "make bad weather of it," thus subjecting masts, rigging, hull, and machinery to unusually great stresses.

LABRADOR CURRENT. Same as Arctic Current; *see* ARCTIC.

LABRIDÆ. Large family of spiny-finned fishes comprising the *wrasses,* of which the *cunner* and *tautog* are American species. Usually ranging from 10 to 15 inches in length, often brilliantly colored, and generally a good food fish, many species are found in tropical Pacific and Indian Oceans, but probably best typified in genus *Labrus* comprising the European wrasses. *See* WRASSE.

LACE. To secure, as a canvas cover, awning, sail to a gaff, etc., by passing a small-sized line through eyelets along edge of such canvas. **L.-line,** small rope used to *lace* or lash as above. **L.-piece,** in older wooden ships, timber at outer end of knee-of-the-head to which the figurehead was secured. In some naval ships, and clippers of later date, it was customary when in port to remove the figurehead for safe-keeping until vessel put to sea.

LACERTA. (*L. = a lizard*) A constellation in the *Milky Way,* north of *Pegasus.* It contains no navigational stars, brightest being of 4th magnitude.

LADDER. Appliance or fitting on which a person may step in ascending or descending; any stairs or steps having no *risers, i.e.,* open between each *tread.* Ladders are named from their location, as, *bridge-l., hatch-l., poop-l.;* from their construction, as, *rope l., rung l., step l.;* or from their use, as, *side l., boat l., companion l.* **Accommodation-l.,** flat-tread flight of steps, usually sloping fore-and-aft on ship's side; a gangway ladder; *see* ACCOMMODATION. **Bowsprit l.,** in larger wooden ships, a notched or slatted plankway on top of a high-pointing bowsprit serving as a means to climb out to stow sail, etc. **Companion l.,** *see* COMPANION. **Gangway-l.,** an accommodation-ladder; any *l.,* used as a means to board a vessel from a pier, wharf, etc. **Jack-l.,** *see* JACOB'S LADDER. **L.-dredge,** a dredging machine having a series of buckets fixed to two parallel endless chains. **L.-screen,** canvas forming a protection along sides of a gangway ladder; a rail-screen for such use. **Pillar-l.,** one formed by rungs or rounds fitted as steps between two hold-pillars, near or in a hatchway. **Pilot-l.,** so named from its use in taking a pilot from a boat, rope-sided *l.* with flat wooden steps, usually 18 inches in width, and of suitable length for its purpose. **Sea-l.,** a side-ladder similar in construction to a *pilot-l.,* but adapted to rugged use in boarding or leaving ship at sea; also, range of rungs fitted to ship's side from waterline to weather deck, so forming a *l.* for sea use. Latter is more often found in naval vessels than in others.

LADE. Now almost obsolete word meaning to take in, or place, a cargo, or part of a cargo, on board; as, to *lade,* or to *lade goods on,* a vessel. Also, a ship was said to *lade water* when in a leaky condition. **Laden,** condition of being loaded or burdened; as *laden with grain; laden with a general cargo; deeply* *laden.* Sometimes such condition with respect to ship's trim; as, *laden by the head; laden on an even keel.* **Lading,** the loading or cargo taken on board; that which is carried; as the *cargo* or *lading* of a ship. **Bill of lading,** see BILL.

LADY. The planet *Venus.* In old-time vessels of the British navy, the *gunner's mate* who was custodian of small deck stores (chiefly such pertaining to the guns) kept in the *lady's hole,* or small compartment below decks. **Ladies' sea,** trade-wind region of North Atlantic in which fine weather prevails; so named by the early Spanish navigators. **L.-fish,** a herring-like fish of brilliant silvery colors, found in all warm seas; the *Spanish l.-fish, harpe rufa,* of the West Indies and Florida, member of the *Labridæ* family and noted for its beautiful colors. **Lady's Chair,** also called *Lady of the Chair,* the constellation *Cassiopeia, q.v.* **Lady's wind,** a gentle breeze attended by fine weather; the southwest summer breeze of North Atlantic trade routes.

LAG. To cover with asbestos or other non-conducting coating or substance, as a steam cylinder, boiler, water-pipe, etc.; such *jacketing* or covering being termed *lagging,* sometimes *jack-lagging.* To loiter, delay, or be tardy; hence, *lag* or amount of retardation as in opening or closing of a valve in a steam engine; or delay in magnetization effect, as indicated in HYSTERESIS. **Lag, or lagging, of the tides,** is a retardation of the tide-wave appearing as an increase in *lunitidal interval* (later tides) during 2nd and 4th quarters of the moon, or about time of neap tides. It is a result of sun and moon being in *quadrature,* or in position in which their respective influences in raising waters on the globe act at right angles to each other. The phenomenon attains a maximum from 2 to 3 days after quadrature. Opposed to *priming,* or acceleration (earlier tides), which occurs in 1st and 3rd quarters of moon.

LAG-BOLT. Also, *lag-screw; see* BOLT.

LAGAN. (O.F. *lagand*) Jettisoned goods or cargo sunk at sea and marked by a buoy for subsequent recovery; also *ligan. Cf.* JETTISON.

LAGOON. (Sp. *laguna;* L. *lacuna,* pool, pond) Shallow lake, pond, sound, or expanded part of a river; *esp.* such body near, and opening by a narrow channel to, the sea; as, an *atoll lagoon;* a *salt-lagoon.* **L.-channel,** navigable water through outlet of a *l.* **L.-island, l.-reef,** an atoll; *see* ATOLL. **Salt-l.,** shallow pond from which salt is obtained after evaporation of sea-water.

LAID. (Past tense, past participle, or participial adjective form of *lay*) Generally, a combining word connoting a setting, condition, state, or form, as in *laid* the keel; *was laid* on the other tack; *cable-laid; laid up.* **Back-l.,** having strands, as a rope, laid left-handed; *i.e.,* slope of strands advancing from right

to left; also, *back-handed.* **Cable-l.,** *see* CABLE. **Hard-l.,** descriptive of tightly twisted *lay* of strands in a rope, resulting in a harder and less flexible line, but, while somewhat reducing its tensile strength, providing the qualities of resistance to water-absorption and lesser stretch under tension; as, *e.g.,* hemp lanyards fitted to shrouds. Due to this tight lay, strands lie at a greater angle to rope's axis line than in ordinary types of stranded cordage. *See* LAY. **Hawser-l.,** also called *plain-l.,* said of right-handed fiber rope, 3-stranded, and having no core, or heart-strand; *cf.* HAWSER. **L. aback,** *see* ABACK. **L. deck,** as found in yachts, deck consisting of narrow planking running parallel to vessel's gunwale, or sweep of her side-lines; also termed *swept deck,* as opposed to a *straight deck,* or one in which planks are laid in fore-and-aft line throughout. **L. down,** said of a ship when *knocked down,* or heavily listed by a strong gale, shifting of cargo or ballast, or making water in hold; also, when *careened* for inspection of, or repairs to, bottom. **L. to the mast,** *see* ABACK. **L. up,** state of being securely fast in berth and not in commission or temporarily unemployed: said of a vessel. Loose strands are said to be *laid up* when twisted and set to form a rope. **Plain-l.,** same as *hawser-laid.* **Short-l.,** same as *hard-laid.* **Shroud-l.,** referred to fiber cordage, denotes rope made up of four strands with a soft core, or center strand. Though having a tensile strength of only 85% of that of *hawser-l.* cordage of same size, it is less susceptible to *kinking* under wet conditions, and hence is favored for sheet-tackles or other fast-moving multiple-sheave purchases exposed to weather and sea, as on a vessel's deck. Source of the term lies in the hemp *shrouds* of old sailing-navy days. Made to stand up to weather conditions, they were spun with a hard lay; *cf. Hard-l.* **Strap-l.,** indicates form of rope made of two or more strands or ordinary rope laid side by side and stitched through to each other. Such flat cordage was formerly used for straps (or *strops*) in hoisting heavy spars, guns, and other weighty objects on which bearing surface of rope required to be widened; also for lashing-strops around stowed spars, heavy casks, etc.

LAKAN. (*Native word*) Prefix in local names for a variety of large dugout canoes of Madagascar, as *lakan-drao, lakan-jilo, lakan-fiar,* etc. Ranging from 20 to 35 feet in length and $2\frac{1}{2}$ to $3\frac{1}{2}$ in width, the primitive craft, particularly those used in fishing or trading along the coasts, are fitted with either single or double outriggers and are rigged with a single lateen, a square, or two sprit sails. They are shaped from a large hardwood tree, with the addition of an ornamental beak or prow and a plank along the upper sides for increase of freeboard.

LAKE. Area of water (usually *fresh*) entirely, or nearly so, surrounded by land; an expanded part of a river, other than that widening towards its mouth. **L. type vessel,** a laker, one built for, and navigated chiefly on, a lake or lakes; *esp.* a vessel engaged on the Great Lakes.

LAMBASTE. Sailors' usual term meaning to beat or thrash soundly with a rope's end, cane, bamboo, etc.

LAMINATED TIMBER. Material consisting of any required number of thicknesses, or *laminæ*, of about one inch, laid together under pressure with a special sea-water resisting glue between surfaces. Used for main structural parts in wooden boat building, a single unit combining keel, stem, and stern-post may be turned out by the process and, it is claimed, such fabricated unit in strength greatly exceeds that of the usual scarfed or otherwise connected parts. Its use is an innovation of comparatively recent date.

LAM-NET. A fishing-net into which the catch is driven by thrashing the water, shouting, striking boat with a stick, etc.; a *lam.*

LAMNIDÆ. Family of voracious deep-water sharks of which the *porbeagle* (*Lamna cornubica*) is typical. Commonly known as the *mackerel sharks* from their form, have stout body, high dorsal fin at about mid-length and one of small size just forward of tail, wide mouth, large teeth, and, unlike most sharks, upper lobe of tail differs little, if any, in size from lower one. *Cf.* PORBEAGLE.

LAMP. The familiar instrument for providing light, which, in its early form on board ship, consisted either of one or more candles enclosed in a glass-sided case, or of an open wick connected to a receptacle containing grease, slush, whale-oil, colza oil, etc. To-day, the kerosene lamp is used in smaller vessels and for emergency lighting in certain ships normally using electricity. Generally, a set of oil-burning lights or lamps is required to be kept ready for use as navigation lights, in event of electric generator failure. **Binnacle-l.,** one placed in a binnacle to illuminate the compass-card. **L.-locker,** small compartment used for stowing ship's oil-burning lamps and lanterns, illuminating oil, cotton waste, wicks, globes, and all necessaries for cleaning and trimming deck and navigation lights; also, a similar space in steward's department on some passenger vessels; *lamp-room.* Such compartment or room is required by U.S. law to be entirely lined within by metal and provided with means for smothering fire within by either steam or an inert gas, such as carbon dioxide (CO_2). **L.-screen,** *see* **L.-screen** *in* LIGHT. **L.-trimmer,** in merchant ships, seaman detailed to keep all oil-lamps in working order, especially navigation and other deck lights.

LAMPREY. An eel-like vertebrate of 2 to 3 feet in length, widely distributed in temperate waters, and often esteemed as food. Some species live in fresh water only; those of marine habitat always spawn in fresh water streams. Some larger lampreys take their prey vampire fashion, or by attaching themselves to fish by their large circular suction-powered mouth, while gnawing at the victim with their hard conical teeth. The ugly creature is of the family *Petromyzonidæ* of the *Cyclostomata* class.

L.A.N. Usual abbreviation in nautical astronomy for *local apparent noon,* or instant at which the true, or apparent, sun's center passes the meridian of any place.

LANCE. Long sharp-pointed spear-like instrument having two keen cutting edges and with recovery-line attached, used in former whaling to pierce vital parts of the animal after it was harpooned, tired out, and so approachable by boat. Usually a boat's outfit included three *hand-lances,* which later gave way to the more effective *bomb-lance, q.v. in* BOMB. **Lance** is also term for a pipe serving as a nozzle in a hose through which steam or compressed air is blown to remove soot and dirt from boiler surfaces, tubes, etc. **L.-hooks,** on sides of a whaling-boat, small iron hooks in which to stow the *lances.*

LANCET-FISH. The surgeon-, barber-, or doctor-fish; *see* HANDSAW-FISH.

LANCHA. Spanish and Portuguese word signifying a large open fishing-boat driven either by oars or any of several rigs of lateen or lug sails. The word usually is combined with the phrase *de pesca,* indicating boat's use, as *lancha de pesca* (fishing-boat); or, specifying her type, with a place name, as *Lancha Caminha* (boat of type originating at Caminha, Portugal). The term is similarly applied on coast of Brazil.

LAND. Of the earth's total sea-level area of some 197,000,000 square miles, about 28% is ocupied by *land,* or about 55,000,000 square miles. In lapped strakes, as in plating or clinker-laid planking, the *land,* or landing, is that area of one strake lying, or lapping, over an adjacent one. As a verb, to disembark or transfer to shore in any way; as, to *land troops* or *cargo;* to go ashore. To capture or bring ashore; as, to *land a fish.* To rest, as a sling of cargo, cask, spar, etc., on deck or elsewhere; *esp.* when lowered by a fall or tackle. To **clear the l.,** *see* CLEAR. To **hold,** or **hold on to, the l.,** *see* HOLD. To **keep the l. aboard,** to keep within sight of shore while sailing approximately parallel with a coast-line. **L.-admiral,** *see* ADMIRAL. **L. and sea breezes,** *see* BREEZE. **L.-blink,** glow appearing over snow-covered *l.;* differs from *ice-blink* in being yellowish in color. **L.-boards,** planking laid on deck between a hatch and ship's side for protection of deck against falling or *landed* cargo. **Landed terms,** those in a contract of affreightment stipulating freight charges include all *landing* costs at destination of goods. **L.-effect,** *see* EFFECT. **L'fall,** the sighting of, or "making the land," at sea. A *good landfall* is made when the point or place expected to be sighted heaves in sight on or near the bearing anticipated. **L'fang,** old term for an anchorage or good holding-ground for anchoring. **L.-fast,** a hold on shore, as a post, dolphin, anchor, etc., on a river bank or elsewhere other than a quay or wharf, to which ship's mooring-lines may be attached. **L.-hemisphere,** that half of earth's surface containing the greater portion of land. **L.-ice,** that formed along a shore and fast to it; *bord-ice.* **L.-lane,** opening through an ice-floe leading to shore; also, *land-lead.* **L.-line,** rope leading to shore for hauling in a seine-net. **L'locked,** said of an area inclosed or surrounded by land, or nearly so, as a harbor, loch, or arm of the sea. Also said of a sailing-vessel when unable to maneuver under sail power upon finding herself in close proximity to surrounding rocks, shoals, or *l.* **L'lubber,** one more in his natural element when on shore; hence, a person out of place on board ship; an awkward or *lubberly* crew member; a first-voyager. **L'mark,** a conspicuous object that serves as a guide or marks a locality in piloting or navigating in vicinity of a coast. **L. shark,** a swindler of seamen on shore; a *land pirate.* **L'sick,** hampered or uneasy on account of proximity of land: said of a ship being cautiously "nursed" as when in shallow or narrow waters with much traffic in the vicinity, or approaching harbor during darkness; often used contemptuously in the sense of accompanying nervous tension on board. **L.-stream,** current flowing out to sea from a river, usually marked by discoloration of sea-water. **L.-tied,** said of islands that have become connected to one another or to a coast by accumulating sand-bars. **L.-trash,** broken-up ice along shores in Arctic regions; *trash-ice.* **L.-wash,** line of high water along a shore; wash of the sea on a beach. **L. waiter,** in Great Britain, customs officer who keeps records of imports for taxation purposes and certifies to proper observance of required formalities in recording exports; a *searcher.* **L.-water,** open water along an otherwise ice-bound shore, as a result of tidal currents or a strong offshore wind. **L. wind,** a *l. breeze,* or wind blowing seaward. **Land ho!,** lookout's cry upon sighting land. **To lose the l.,** to lose sight of *l.* due to increasing distance or change in visibility conditions. **To make the l.,** to sight and recognize the *l.* as ship steers toward it; also, to successfully *l.* on a beach, as in a boat; to *make l.* **No man's l.,** see **J.'s land** *in* JACK. **To raise the l.,** to sail toward it and so increase its apparent elevation. **To shut in the l.,** to lose sight of part of a coast-line through intervention of a point or promontory; also, *l.* is said to be *shut in* when obscured by fog, haze, or mist,—sometimes by smoke. **Tide-l.,** area periodically covered by water at high tide; *esp.* such tract, as a marsh or mud-flat, adjoining a river or estuary.

LANDING. Act of going on shore from a vessel, as persons; or of being removed to shore, as cargo. Place where passengers or cargo may be placed on shore. Width of lapped seams in plating or planking; that part of a plate or plank overlapping another, as in clinker-laid plates or planking. Distance from center of a rivet-hole to edge of plate or angle-bar in which it is punched or bored. **Brow l.,** a gangway platform at head of the *brow* (gangway), or entrance to ship's deck. **L. apron,** platform or bridge capable of being adjusted to level of a ferry-boat's deck and so provide an even *l.* passage to and from boat. **L. card,** for purposes of ready identification by officials checking passenger lists or manifests, card containing personal information (name, number on list, citizenship, etc.) issued to each passenger before *l.* at destination, as customarily used on larger ocean ships. Also, a permit issued to individual crew members by port authority in some foreign countries authorizing such persons to go ashore. **L. charges,** general term for costs covering *l.* of cargo at destination port, such as lighterage, warehouse storage, delivery or transfer to trucks or cars, etc. In Great Britain such costs are termed *landing rates.* **L. edge,** that of a plate or plank over which edge of an adjoining plate or plank laps; the *under edge.* **L.-gaff,** see GAFF. **L.-net,** a pole-, or scoop-net, used for taking or landing fish from water; a seine-net drawn to a shore. **L. party,** group or company of persons proceeding to shore from a vessel; *esp.* an armed force from a warship, or a group having a specific purpose in view, as a surveying party. **L.-place,** wharf, stage, or other provision for *l.* persons or light goods; as suitable location on a beach for *l.* a boat. **L.-skid,** see SKID. **L.-stage,** floating platform supported by pontoons anchored alongside a quay wall or pier head for *l.* or embarking passengers, baggage, mails, and light cargo at any stage of the tide. Good example of such *l.* is the noted Liverpool stage on River Mersey, England, where spring tidal range is about 27 feet. The structure is capable of accommodating largest ocean liners and thus provides dispatch otherwise not possible because of limited periods in which ships may enter or leave tidal docks in that area. **L.-strake,** in a boat, next strake of planking to upper one. **L. surveyor,** British customs officer superintending work of, and appointing *landing* (or *land) waiters; cf.* **Land waiter** *in* LAND. **Shell-l's.,** see SHELL.

LANDSMAN. One who lives on the land only; a sailor on his first voyage; a landlubber; former low rating in artificer or special branches in U.S. navy.

LANE. Prescribed track or route on the high seas; a lead or clear passage through an ice-field. **L.-route,** a trans-ocean track followed by vessels of a regular line, or that agreed upon by maritime nations to be adhered to by their merchant shipping. **Land-l.,** *see* LAND. **Trans-Atlantic lanes,** routes agreed upon by the various shipping concerns operating vessels in North Atlantic trade with the view of reducing collision risks while avoiding, as far as practicable, regions of floating ice. Near their western end, or in vicinity of Newfoundland Banks, *l's* are moved north or south according to ice season or unusual ice conditions. They lie at a maximum of 60 miles apart, eastbound traffic in a particular run passing to southward of ships bound west, and, where of necessity tracks cross each other, locations of such crossing occur in regions comparatively free of fog. Principal routes, or those from New York, Boston, and Halifax, terminate off Fastnet Rock at southern extremity of Ireland and off Bishop Rock of the Scilly Isles at mouth of English Channel. Also referred to as *shipping l's, Atlantic tracks,* or *routes.*

LANG LAY ROPE. *See* WIRE.

LANGRAGE. In old-time naval warfare, a missile consisting of a bunch of old bolts, nails, scrap-iron, etc., sometimes confined in a canister, which was fired at an enemy with the aim of cutting or tearing up her rigging and sails. Also, *langrel; langridge.*

LANTERN. A portable lamp; a protective receptacle or inclosure for a light, usually provided with a transparent globe, lens, or pane, as of glass, and either portable or fixed, as a ship's *hold l.*, a *masthead l.*, a *lighthouse l.* The *lanthorn* of older sea parlance appears to have been a reluctant loser to our present *lantern,* its continued use in English works on seamanship and navigation laws being noted up to within past half century; *e.g.:* "Such light shall be carried in a *lanthorn* so fixed and constructed as to throw the light over an arc of the compass of 10 points." **Battle-l.,** *see* BATTLE. **Bulkhead l.,** one fixed on a bulkhead, usually glassed on three sides, and containing an oil lamp. Prior to present requirement in passenger vessels of an emergency lighting system, such lanterns were provided to light passageways, stairways, etc., in accommodation spaces in event of failure of ship's electricity supply. **Fighting l.,** as used on war-vessels, portable or fixed one provided with means for instantly screening light. **Hurricane l.,** one designed to successfully protect its light in any strong wind; also, *storm-light* or *hurricane-lamp.* **L.-keg,** keg or similar receptacle in a ship's boat to protect a lantern; in former use, chiefly in whaling-boats, large keg in which a lantern, candles, flint and steel, biscuits, tobacco, and small necessaries were kept in view of the possible emergency of lengthy separation from ship. **Poop l.,** in old-time vessels, an ornate *l.,* usually hexagonal in form and widening toward its top, mounted on a stout pole at after end of poop. It was the only navigation light exhibited and threw light from all sides. **Signal-l.,** one for signalling purposes; any *l.* containing a light pre-

scribed in *Rules for Prevention of Collisions;* a *signal light,* or *lamp.*

LANTERN FISH. Any of a variety of small deep-sea fishes having a large mouth, unusually distended disc-shaped eyes, and luminous body spots or glands. Many come to surface at night or in rainy stormy weather and groups or schools of the little creatures often present a beautiful display of flashing colors on a dark night. The family name is *Myctophidæ* or *Scopelidæ.*

LANYARD. (Fr. *lanière;* thong, strap) Piece of small rope or cord for fastening or temporarily holding an object, as *knife l., guy l., bucket l., port-l.;* hard-laid hemp rope or served wire rove tackle-fashion through dead-eyes at inner or lower ends of standing rigging (back-stays, bowsprit shrouds, jib-boom guys, mast shrouds, stays, etc.) for setting up such rigging. **Knife-l.,** cord attached to a jack-knife and worn round the neck for security. **L. hitch,** that used to secure the end of a rigging-lanyard. It usually takes the form of a *cow hitch* round the stay or shroud, above outer or upper dead eye. **L. knot,** stopper-knot made with strands of the *l.* at its standing end, as rove in rigging dead-eyes. Indicating right-handed method of reeving the *l.,* knot in a shroud dead-eye must face inboard "opposite the left eye," *i.e.,* must lie in upper dead-eye hole toward observer's left hand as he looks outboard. Knot thus lies on fore side of upper dead-eye in starboard rigging, and after side in port rigging. **L.-stopper,** short piece of rope for temporarily holding a hawser or mooring-line while it is transferred to or from the bitts, as when heaving on such line by a winch. Such *stopper* is equipped with a *l.* of smaller stuff at its free end which also bears a toggle or a knot such as a Matthew Walker, double wall, etc. A half hitch is taken round hawser with stopper, which is then lashed with the *l.* to the hawser next to the knot, thus preventing stopper from sliding on hawser when under stress. **L. stuff,** as used with dead-eyes for setting up rigging, a good class of hard-laid tarred hemp of 2 to 3 inches circumference, depending on requirements for rigging size, etc. **L.-thimble,** metal thimble at inboard ends of davit-guys, ends of permanent lashing-strops, lower ends of standing rigging in small craft, etc., through which a *l.* is passed for *setting up,* or *heaving taut,* such gear.

LAP. Distance one piece of material lies over another, as in strakes of planking or plating in sides of a boat or in a ship's outside plating; a lap-joint. In a reciprocating engine, distance a slide-valve overlaps a steam port, when at piston's half stroke. To place or fit anything to partly lie over another, as in a clinker-built boat's planking system. **L.-frame,** one in which connecting or extending parts overlap at their ends. **L.-joint,** connection made by one part or piece overlapping another; a scarfed joint. **L.-ring,** circular piece of metal, diagonally severed at one point, for fitting over a cylindrical-shaped object, as a pipe. **L.-rivet,** to connect lapping edges of two plates by riveting. **L'strake,** descriptive of planking system as, a *lapstrake* boat (= a *clinker-built* boat). Commonly, in America, *lapstreak.* Also, a strake of plating overlapping edge of another. **L.-weld,** to join lapping edges or ends of metal, as plates or frames, by welding.

LARBOARD. (M.E. *laddeborde*) Formerly, of or pertaining to left side looking forward; now superseded by *port.* Pron. *labbord* by sailors of the day, origin of the term is said to lie in the fact that early merchant ships always loaded from *left* side in which was located their one and only *cargo-port,* its etymology being *lade,* load, and *bord,* side, out of Scandinavian. Apparently with this in mind, British Admiralty ordered *port* in its stead, chiefly owing to confusion with *starboard,* particularly in helm orders. **L.-quarter boat,** in former whaling-ships, the *larboard,* or port, aftermost boat, always assigned to chief mate's charge; the *mate's boat.*

LARBOWLINES. In sailing-navy days, the men of the port, or *larboard,* watch; also, *larbolins.*

LARCH. *See* HACKMATACK.

LARGE. Said of a breeze when favorable in direction, in the sense of allowing all sail to draw "spanking full," as when abeam or one to two points abaft the beam; having the wind in such direction, as, to *sail large;* wide of a bearing, course, or object in sight, as, *ship's course is large of the rocks.* Though now falling into obsolescence, the word appears to have had good standing in square-rigger days and in its verbal form also commonly was used to express a favorable shift of wind from before the beam, as in *the breeze is larging;* and also, in the sense of to get away from, or "claw off" an object, when under sail, as in *ship larged from the rocks, lee shore, etc.; larged off the cape.* **By and l.,** by and off the wind, *i.e.,* close-hauled and sailing free. Range of sailing; as, *she sails well by and large.* Hence, in every way or in all respects; as, *by and large, she is well fitted for the wool trade.* **L.-line fishing,** *see* **Great-line f.** *in* FISHING. **Running l.,** sailing or going *l.; see opening notes above.*

LARK'S HEAD. Hitch made in securing bight of a strop to a ring, spar, hook, etc.; made as a simple *cow,* or both parts of strop passed through its bight, when fastened to a ring; or formed as a *cow hitch* and slipped over end of a spar or a hook.

LASCAR. An Indian seaman; *esp.* a member of a crew of such seamen as often found in British ships engaged in Far East trade.

LASH. To fasten or secure any object by turns of a *lashing,* or piece of rope, chain, etc.; to dash or strike against with force, as waves or wind-driven

rain, or as strokes of a whale's tail on sea-surface. A stroke with a rope's end, cat-o'-nine-tails, etc., **an** older form in this sense being *lasche.* **L. and carry,** in war-vessels, an order to men to pack up hammocks, blankets, etc., and carry them to the *nettings,* or space in which these were stowed; *see* HAMMOCK. To l. **about,** to thrash or fly about as a free rope's end aloft in a gale. **L.-rail,** in wood-built vessels, particularly old-time whalers, a strong batten or railing secured fore-and-aft along bulwark stanchions for purpose of lashing casks, spars, and other bulky gear. **The l.,** punishment by, or the instrument used in, flogging; *see* FLOG.

LASHING. Fastening made by a piece of cordage, chain, or wire in securing a movable object or uniting two or more parts or objects together; the rope, chain, etc., forming such fastening. Use of the *lash;* a flogging. **Gammon-l.,** the old *gammoning,* or means by which a bowsprit was held down to ship's stem; *see* GAMMON. **Hammock-l.,** *see* HAMMOCK. **Heel-l.,** one for temporarily securing lower or inner end of a boom, lower ends of sheer-legs, spars, etc. **L.-eye,** *see* EYE. **L.-ring,** metal ring on a harness-cask, tank, or other object, providing handy means whereby such may be secured or *lashed* in place; a ring in a bulkhead, bulwark stanchion, hatch coaming, or other convenient position, for receiving turns of a *l.* in securing a spare anchor, deck cargo, spars, etc. Also, in old-time ship gun-carriages, a ring to which tarpaulin, sponge, rammer, and worm were secured when not in use. **Parrel-l.,** *see* PARREL. **Pearl-l.,** jaw-rope of a hoisting gaff, or rope between extremities of jaws across fore side of mast to prevent displacement of gaff. With its wooden rollers or *beads,* suggestive of a string of pearls; *see* **J.-rope** *in* JAWS. **Poppet-l.,** *see* POPPET. **Rack-l.,** one which is hove taut by twisting a stick, or rack-bar, inserted in the turns. **Rose-l.,** as used to secure a rope to side of a spar, rail, harpoon-shaft, etc.: an eye is first spliced in rope; then *l.* is passed around spar alternately over and under each part of eye. Upon completion of necessary turns, remaining end is two or three times passed around all parts between spar and eye and hove taut. Also called *rose-seizing.* **Soul and body l.,** one holding intact, or securing, a mass of objects, as cargo, during motion of vessel; piece of handy cordage used as a waist-belt outside of one's oilskins or heavy clothing.

LASK. Term now falling into disuse, meaning to sail with a leading wind; to *sail large,* as with wind abaft the beam; *see* LARGE. A *lasking breeze* or a *lasking course* were descriptive of conditions satisfactory for sailing, or with wind favorable, all sail drawing.

LASKET. Also latch; latching; *see* LATCHING.

LAST. In early English shipping use, originally any quantity constituting a consignment, or in smaller vessels, a full load, of a homogeneous cargo. Later used as a unit in estimating a ship's capacity for carrying certain cargoes, either according to bulk or weight. Now a weight or measure varying with goods or trade concerned; as a *last* of codfish = 12 barrels; of herrings = 10 to 20 thousand, depending on port shipped, but now giving way to a measure of 10 crans (or crannes), or 375 gallons (Imp.); of corn = 80 bushels; of pitch or tar = 14 barrels; of wool, 12 sacks; etc. *Last* is also a sailmaker's term for the seam constituting butting or *mitering* of diagonally cut cloths; as, that from clew to luff of a jib in which cloths run parallel to foot and leech.

LASTAGE.   Old term for ballast or lading of a ship; also, space available for stowing cargo; a former tax for privilege of loading a cargo at certain ports and for landing a catch of fish. Now rarely heard, *tonnage* of a vessel.

L.A.T.   Local apparent time; hour angle of true sun measured at a particular place. It is time shown by a sun dial.

LATCHINGS.   Series of loops or eyes of small stuff along head of a *bonnet,* or extension attached to foot of a sail. Bonnet is fixed by reeving *latchings* in eyelets along sail's foot and *keying* the whole series by a line run through all bights. By withdrawing such line, called the *latching-key,* bonnet is very quickly detached. Also termed *laskets* and *latches,* chiefly used in yachts and small craft. *Cf.* **Latching-k.** *in* KEY.

LATEEN.   (It. and Sp. *vela latina;* Latin sail)   Designates a rig or sail said to have originated with the Arabs and, with the probable exception of that of Chinese junks, the oldest now extant; came into general use in eastern Mediterranean as early as 12th century and to-day is still popular, particularly with fishermen, on almost all southern European and North African shores, Red Sea, Persian Gulf, and Arabian Sea. Shaped nearly like a 45° right-angled triangle, hypotenuse side, or luff, of sail is spread on a long yard hoisted on a stumpy mast. Forward end of yard remaining close to deck, its halyard at about two-fifths its length from the latter, gives sail a lofty peak and the desirable quality of comparatively large spread at moderate height from deck. Although in rough sea conditions, the long weighty yard has its disadvantages in wear and tear, with unhandiness in reefing, a better rig for sailing close-hauled or on a beam wind has not yet been devised. It is of interest to note the *lateen sail* was recognized as more suitable for steering up to the wind than the *square sail,* but less adapted to a following wind, in rigs of the 15th century, as in Spanish caravels and English ships of the day. The compromising spread, therefore, of square sails on one or two forward masts and lateen sails on one

or two after masts had developed in vessels of Columbus's and John Cabot's time and appears to have continued well into 17th century. Present-day performance in speed of the two or three mast all lateen-rigged Arab *dhows* and Italian *feluccas* is well known, as is also that of single-sailed fishermen under various names from coasts of Greece, Italy, Spain, and North Africa. **L.-rigged,** having lateen sails on all masts; a *lateener.*

LATENT DEFECT.   In maritime legal parlance, a fault not apparent or visible, such as a hidden flaw in a machinery part or in a vessel's steering-gear, to which might be attributed cause for loss or damage to ship or cargo, in event of failure of such equipment. One clause of *Carriage of Goods by Sea Act, 1936 (46 U.S.C. 1304)* provides that neither vessel nor carrier shall be responsible for damage or loss arising or resulting from "*latent defects* not discoverable by due diligence."

LATERAL.   Of or pertaining to the side; at, toward, or from the side of anything; sidewise; as, *lateral stresses in a ship's hull.* **L. plane,** as considered in comparison of hulls, chiefly in yacht-building or racing, the immersed profile area, or that of boat's immersed mid-hull vertical fore-and-aft plane, usually expressed as number of times the midship cross-section area below water-line, hull upright. It is the value representing boat's *l. resistance,* or that presented to water for holding her own against sidewise motion, or *leeway,* in sailing. Increase of lateral plane area is obtained by providing a deeper keel, installing a *centerboard,* or fitting a *leeboard* on each side. Sidewise component of total wind pressure on a given sail area is usually termed *l. pressure.*

LATITUDE.   (L. *latitudo,* breadth)   In navigation and cartography, distance of a place north or south of the equator, or arc of the meridian intercepted by equator and place or point considered. *Specif.* termed *astronomical* or *geographical latitude,* with its sister co-ordinate, longitude, it names position of a point on earth's surface; thus Cape Horn is located on a certain meridian (67° 16′ W.) in *Lat. 55° 59′ S.,* or 3359 minutes, or (very nearly) nautical miles, south of equator; and Manila, in *Lat. 14° 35′ N.,* on meridian of 120° 58′ E. For its determination, we depend upon places of the heavenly bodies as given in the *Nautical Almanac,* since its value is equal to declination of the zenith or to angular elevation, or altitude, of the nearer pole of the heavens. Thus, at the equator, altitude of either pole is zero, plane of equator extended to the heavens cutting through observer's zenith and forming the imaginary *celestial* equator, or *equinoctial. Lat.* of equator, therefore, is 0°; of either pole, 90°; and a heavenly body having a declination of, say, 40° N. will pass, at upper transit, exactly through zenith of an observer in *Lat.* 40° N. *Geographical l.,* then, is dependent upon *direction of the plumb-line,* which line, being perpendicular to plane of horizon, if extended downward, will pass through earth's *geometric center only at either pole or at the equator.* This is due to plane of meridians being elliptical in shape, since the earth, being an oblate spheroid (or properly, an *ellipsoid*), departs from the spherical by a slight flattening at poles and a bulging at its equatorial parts; and which accounts for the small difference in length of a degree of *l.* at different distances from equator. At the poles, length of degree is 60.27 nautical miles; at *Lat.* 45°, it is 59.96; and at equator has decreased to 59.66 miles. *Geocentric,* or *true, l.* with which the navigator has no concern, is the angle at earth's *geometric center* subtended by the meridian arc intercepted by a place and the equator. Its value is always less than that of *geographical l.,* difference being zero at equator and poles and attaining a maximum of 11′ 37″ in *Lat.* 45°. Simplest method of determining terrestrial *l.* is by observing the altitude of a heavenly body at upper or lower transit. Declination of body being known (from *Nautical Almanac*), then, at upper transit, its zenith distance, or 90° less its corrected altitude, is arc of meridian to be applied to declination, according to observer's position, whether north or south of body; thus, if altitude is 50° and observer is north of a body whose declination is 15° S., since declination of zenith is equal to *l.,* zenith distance, or 90° less 50° (= 40° north of body), applied to body's declination gives 40° north of 15° S., or 40° less 15° = *Lat.* 25° N. At a body's lower transit, or instant at which its altitude reaches a minimum value, then, since elevation of pole = *l.,* body's polar distance, or 90° less its declination, plus its corrected altitude, also equals *l.* **Celestial l.,** as used by astronomers, angular distance of a heavenly body north or south of plane of the ecliptic. **Difference of l.,** in navigation, distance between, or arc of a meridian intercepted by, the respective parallels of *l.* passing through two places. **High l's,** those at great distances from equator; usually any *l.* greater than 45° N. or S. **Horse l's,** *see* HORSE. **L. by account,** that deduced from course and distance made good since last "fix" or departure was taken; *estimated l.;* in older usage, *l. by dead reckoning.* **L. by observation,** that determined by one or more observations of heavenly bodies, or by bearings of terrestrial objects. **Magnetic l.,** *see* MAGNETIC. **Middle,** or **mean, l.,** that of the parallel lying midway in *l.* between two places; used in connection with *middle latitude sailing; see* SAILING. **Parallel of l.,** small circle of the globe running parallel with equator and passing through all places having same *l.;* rarely, a *circle of l.* **Station error in l.,** difference between what is sometimes termed *geodetic l.,* or that obtained by refined measurement, as in a triangulation survey, and *l.* obtained by astronomical observations. Rare-

ly exceeding 1½ minutes of arc (or miles of distance), it is result of a slight deflection of the plumbline which affects accuracy of observed altitudes of heavenly bodies. (*See opening notes on "astronomical"* or *"geographical" l.*) Such *error* is chiefly found in a mountainous region; *esp.* in vicinity of a nearby area of great ocean depths.

LATTICE-BOOM. *See* BOOM.

LAUGHLIN PLOW-ANCHOR. *See* ANCHOR.

LAUNCH. To cause a vessel or boat to slide from land into water of floating depth; to put out from land, as a boat; to set afloat, as a boat from a ship; to *launch* a ship or boat. To move or slide on end, as a timber or heavy lengthy object; as, to *launch the gangway ashore.* In older usage, to send aloft and place a yard; followed by *ho,* order to cease hoisting, or *"launch-ho!"* In war-vessels, a heavy-duty boat, usually largest aboard, mounting a light gun in bows and equipped with a motor; a *motor-l.;* corresponds to *l.* or *longboat* of former days, which was largest in a man-o'-war, carried sails, and pulled from 16 to 22 oars. Any boat driven by engines; *esp.* one for pleasure or for carrying passengers within sheltered areas. **Towing-l.,** boat of rugged construction and appropriately engined for towing work in harbors or sheltered waters, as in handling lighters and other small craft. In some merchant ships engaged in trades involving considerable surf-boat or lighter work, as on Guinea Coast of Africa, a ship's *l.* is carried for towing such craft, rafted timber, etc., in course of loading or discharging.

LAUNCHING. Act of setting a boat or vessel afloat; *specif.,* the sliding of a new ship from her building berth into water by action of gravity along an inclined track called *launching ways* or *launchways.* General shipyard practice is that of *end-launching,* or sliding vessel stern first at any angle with the shore-line, depending upon area and depth of water available, most convenient position in which ship may be built, or other local conditions. Sometimes *side-launching,* or sliding vessel sidewise, must be resorted to where building berth is restricted to a site lying parallel with water-front. In end-launching, usual procedure is to slide vessel on two "ways" (*launch-ways*), each placed about two-thirds of ship's breadth apart and at equal distances from keel, but hulls up to 7500 tons weight have been handled in *single-way* launching, or that in which one main *way* is used under ship's keel, an auxiliary way along each bilge being provided to steady ship upright. *Side-launching* requires a large number of ways, placed at right angles to keel and spaced according to size of hull. **L. clause,** in a shipbuilder's insurance policy, that defining risks covered in underwriting against possible losses during *l.* of a particular vessel or vessels. **L. cradle,** arrangement of timber and/or steel in which vessel is *cradled* or supported during *l*. In the more usual *end-l.,* may be likened to a giant sled, runners of which, called *sliding ways,* move along the fixed ones, or *ground ways.* Toward each end, or narrowing parts, of hull, *cradle* must be built up by upright timbers, etc., to engage sloping sides, and such erections, called *fore* and *after poppets* respectively, are temporarily wedged up to hull under projecting brackets specially fitted for the launching. The whole cradle (poppets usually made to detach themselves) floats clear as vessel is waterborne. *Cf.* **L.-ways. L. drawings,** those prepared from calculations determining various stresses set up during *l.* operation. Usually take the form of curves showing loci of longitudinal hull stress; hull weight on fore poppets as ship becomes waterborne aft; maximum after draft attained; speed and distance hull travels; etc. **L. drags,** bights, piles, or fakes of heavy chain cable, bridled plates, or other weighty objects attached to hull as towing brakes dragged on bottom for purpose of decreasing *l.* speed and bringing ship to a stop within a desired distance after she leaves ways. **L.-tube,** in a submarine or other warvessel, that from which torpedoes are fired or *launched* against an enemy. **L. ways,** *l.-planks* or *launch-ways,* the inclined tracks, made of smooth-faced hardwood, on which ship slides during *l.* In the more usual end-launching, *standing,* or *ground ways,* are fixed to receive the moving or *sliding ways* on which hull is *cradled.* (*Cf.* **L. cradle**) Prior to transferring support of hull from building blocks to cradle, ground ways are *well greased* for the sliding process. When weight of ship is on ways, a controlling device called a *l.-trigger* prevents hull from moving until moment arrives for the launch, when, trigger being released, by means of a hydraulic ram or other powered arrangement vessel is given a usually necessary start down the ways toward her natural element. Both sliding and ground ways are from 3 to 4 feet in breadth and bearing surface and from 12 to 18 inches in thickness. Along outer edges of ground ways, a heavy strip of hardwood, termed a *l.-ribband,* is secured as a flange to prevent any sidewise movement of sliding ways, or to keep ship "on the track." *Declivity,* or inclination, of ways is from five-eighths to eleven-sixteenths inch per foot; in *side-launching,* it is three-fourths inch or more.

LAW. Rule or principle observed in nature as governing growth, motion, etc.; generalized statement of a natural process; as, *law of storms; law of gyration.* Code of rules or mode of conduct recognized as customary in accordance with established practice, or made obligatory by prescribed sanction enforceable by a controlling authority; as, *maritime law; law of the flag.* **Buys-Ballot's l.,** in meteorology, states that, if observer *faces the wind* in northern hemisphere, region of low barometer lies on his right hand; high barometer on his left. Conversely, in southern hemisphere, barometric pressure increases toward his right hand and decreases on his left. **Ferrel's l. of gyration,** expresses influence of earth's rotation on direction of a moving mass, in that such direction tends to deviate to eastward, if mass is moving poleward; and to westward, if moving toward equator. The law is seen in general circulation of waters on the globe and, also, in directions of trade-winds, monsoons, and paths of cyclones. The birth of tropical storms—hurricanes, typhoons, or cyclones—is attributed to this law. **Froude's l. of speed resistance,** after *William Froude, English naval architect (1810–1879),* who, in correlating model and full-size resistances during experiments aimed at determining necessary powering of ships to obtain a required speed, found that the corresponding speeds of vessels of similar form varied as the square roots of their linear dimensions. From this he deduced his *Law of Comparison: "Total resistance varies as displacement, when speed varies as square root of length."* **Kepler's laws,** *see* KEPLER'S LAWS. **L's of Oleron,** named for an island in Bay of Biscay, site of probably earliest maritime judicial court in western Europe, an important maritime code compiled from all then-known customary laws of the sea in 12th century. The code was introduced into England by Edward I *circa* 1300. **L. of the flag,** *see* FLAG. **L. of storms,** that which states the movement of wind in storms, *esp.* those originating in tropical latitudes, is *cyclonic,* or more or less circular, about a center of small area in which barometric pressure is abnormally low and storm area itself travels in a direction consistent with *Ferrel's law of gyration* (*q.v.*). In Northern Hemisphere storms, wind blows in counter-clockwise direction, or left-handed, around the center; in those of Southern Hemisphere, clockwise, or right-handed; such direction, when plotted, taking in general a spiral form with nearest approach to the circular in area nearest center of storm. **Maritime l.,** that relating to commerce and navigation on the high seas and, generally, other navigable waters. Laws under this caption are chiefly based on those of *Oleron* and *Wisby* (12th century) and *Consolato del Mare* code (14th century), which, in turn, were based on the *Rhodian laws* or customs and usages of Mediterranean powers of early antiquity. (*See* ADMIRALTY COURT) Although properly a branch of Maritime Law, **Navigation** or **Shipping l's** of a nation, distinct from the broader sense of commercial usages and customs of the sea, are concerned with protective measures against encroachment of foreign competitive interests; protection of domestic fisheries; documentation, inspection, manning, equipment, safe operation of vessels; customs regulations with respect to entry and clearance of vessels and cargoes; pilotage;

casualty investigations; quarantine regulations; legislation regarding carriage of goods and passengers; etc. Navigation *l's* of England first appear in regulations governing rights and privileges of her ships and conditions under which foreign vessels were admitted to her coasting trade, in reign of Richard I (*1194*). About 1550, this legislation was extended to exclude all foreign craft from coastwise trading, and the *Navigation Act of 1651* forbade importation of goods into England by foreign ships, unless such were under flag of country from which goods originated. This act was amplified in 1672 by requiring that importing ships not only be English, but be manned by crews in which at least 75% of their numbers were Englishmen. As result of this step, the Dutch merchant marine was all but ruined and, it appears, the American colonies were harshly dealt with in similar vein. In 1826 the act was repealed; in 1854, Britain's coasts were opened to the foreigner. **Naval l.,** rules and regulations governing conduct of ships and personnel of a navy; in U.S. navy, familiarly termed "*Rocks and Shoals.*" **Prize l.,** certain universally recognized regulations governing rights of captors of enemy property during time of war; and sale, condemnation, and distribution of proceeds from such prizes; *see* ADMIRALTY COURT. **Sea l's,** those included in *Maritime l.;* the commercial or maritime codes which grew up with the progress in development of commerce from early Mediterranean days; *see* **Maritime l. Shipping l's,** *see* **Navigation l's.**

LAY. To place or put in position, operation, or action; as, to *lay* a ship alongside; to *lay* a deck; to *lay* head yards aback; sometimes with *out;* as, to *l. out* a kedge; to *l. out* a net; or with *off:* as, to *l. off* ship drawings on mold loft floor; to *l. off* a course or bearing on the chart. To go, come, or place one's self in a position indicated: as, to *l* aft; to *l.* aloft; to *l.* out on a yard. In certain senses, *lay* and *lie* are used synonymously: as in, to *l.* or *lie to;* to *l.* or *lie* her course; to *l.* or *lie* athwart. In rope-making, to twist or *l. up* yarns in a strand, or strands in forming a rope. Cordage is described as having a certain *l.:* as, right-hand *l.;* Lang *l.;* etc. (See ROPE). In fishing, sealing, or whaling, where crews' earnings are partially or wholly according to share in proceeds, a *l.* is a man's share of the catch, rated a *short* or a *l.* as respectively apportioned to officers and men. To **l. aboard,** *see* ABOARD. To **l. a gun,** *see* GUN. To **l. athwart hawse,** *see* ATHWART. **L.-board,** also called *keel-batten,* the hog-piece in a wood-built boat; *see* **H.-piece** *in* HOG. **L.-boat,** a boat lying at anchor for a specific purpose; as one carrying a flag or light for marking position of sub-surface work, a cable, wreck, etc.; a marker-boat; a light-boat. **L.-by,** berth in a widened part of a canal or other narrow channel for temporarily securing a vessel while allowing use of channel by another. To **l. by,** same as *lay to (q.v.).* To **l. by the lee,** same as

to *bring by the lee; see* BRING. To **l. close,** to steer as near as possible to direction from which wind is blowing, as in sailing close-hauled; vessel is said to *lay* or *lie close* in describing her good sailing qualities for "holding a good luff." **L. days,** those stipulated in a charter-party as the period in which cargo is to be loaded or discharged, at expiration of which time charterer is charged *demurrage; see* DEMURRAGE. To **l. down,** in shipbuilding, to place first parts of structure on the blocks; to lay the keel; as in, *last hull was laid down a year ago.* Also, to *lay off,* as lines of a frame on a scrive board or mold-loft floor. To **l. in stores,** to provision or store ship for a certain period or voyage. To **l. in the oars,** to unship and replace oars in boat after pulling; equivalent of *boating oars.* To **l. on** (object indicated), to steer for a certain point or object; as, *orders were to lay on the buoy.* To **l. off,** to stand off or sail away from shore, another vessel, etc.; to lie off or outside a harbor, coast-line, etc., as a ship awaiting a pilot, engaged in signalling to shore, shortening a tow-line, or for quarantine reasons. Also, to *lay down* full-size drawings on a shipyard mold-loft floor for the purpose of making templates, or patterns, of the various structural parts of a vessel being built. Together with certain expansion drawings of curved surfaces and shapes, the process is termed *laying off.* To **l. on the oars,** to give way, or bend to full stroke in rowing; also, to *lay out* on oars. (The expression to *lay,* or *lie, on one's oars,* meaning to adopt a resting or waiting attitude with respect to some activity, has no place in nautical parlance) To **l. out,** in shipbuilding, to indicate necessary instructions on plates, beams, frames, and various-shaped structural parts for bending, bevelling, flanging, punching, etc., as taken from templates made in mold-loft or on board ship. The process is known as *laying out.* To **l. the course,** to steer desired course unhampered by wind direction, as when vessel is just free of being close-hauled; to determine course to steer upon consulting the chart; to draw a line representing the course on a chart. To **l. the land,** or **a ship,** old expression meaning to increase distance from land, a ship, or fleet of ships, so that such disappears below the horizon. To **l. to,** or to **lie to,** *see* **Heave to** *in* HEAVE. To **l. up,** to dismantle and withdraw from employment, as a vessel. To **l. up for,** to steer or shape a course for: as, *we lay up for the cape on this tack.* **L'ing up,** in riveting, term for expanding a rivet by blows from each end in order to completely fill rivet-hole before clenching and finishing off. **On a l.,** on shares, as a crew of a sealing-vessel or a whaler *shipped on a lay,* or by agreement paid according to proceeds of the catch, instead of wages; *see opening notes on* LAY.

LAYOUT. The extent of, or stretch occupied by, a set-line or trawl, as in long-line fishing; area dragged over by a seine. Plan of an area occupied by, or an assembly of, anchors, cables, tugs, etc., in a salvage operation. A *laying-out* or planning.

LAZARET. A store-room space in the after peak, usually immediately below the poop in sailing-vessels; any small store-room below decks; also, *lazarette*. (Often pron. *lazareet*)

LAZARETTO. Special isolation hospital for contagious cases from ships, as required by quarantine service in large ports.

LAZY. Combining term for a temporary or labor-saving line, one or more parts of rope, etc., usually not subjected to stress. *See* **Lazy-g.** *in* GUY; **Lazy-h.** *in* HALYARD; **Lazy-j.** *in* JACK; **Lazy-p.** *in* PAINTER; **Lazy-t.** *in* TACK.

LEACH. Variant of *leech: see* LEECH.

LEAD.[1] The soft heavy metal chiefly obtained from the sulphide *galena,* an ore sometimes producing silver also, in sufficient proportion to merit distinction as *silver ore.* Of specific gravity 11.4 or weighing about 710 lbs. per cubic foot, is much used in alloys such as Babbit metal, solder, and pewter; also in production of litharge, minium or red lead, and white lead,—all valuable pigments in marine paints. Rolled or sheet lead and piping of the metal, being resistant to corrosive action of sea-water, is valuable material in wooden vessels for water-tight work where caulking is impracticable, scupper-pipes, rudder-trunk lining, temporary patching, etc. The *lead,* or short for *sounding-lead,* is a cylindrical or prismatical shaped piece of the metal—though the term is also applied to a piece of cast iron or other heavy substance—which is used as a sinker or plummet in taking soundings, or ascertaining depth of water. Lower end of lead is hollowed to receive the *arming,* or a small amount of soap or tallow to which a sample of sea-bottom will adhere, or which will be marked or dented by rocky bottom, and thus provide information for comparison with the charted character of bottom in ship's vicinity. The *hand lead,* familiarly known as the *blue pigeon,* of 7 to 14 lbs. weight, is an old favorite in approaching harbor and navigating in shallow areas, or in depths under 20 fathoms. *Coasting lead* is 14 to 28 lbs., adapted for soundings of from 20 to 60 fathoms. *Deep-sea* (or *dipsey*) lead, 56 lbs., is for depths of 60 fathoms or more. Two last-named to-day are almost displaced by patent sounding-machines or the echo-sounding device called a *Fathometer* (*q.v.*). **Black-l.,** *see* BLACK. **To cast,** or **take a cast of, the l.,** to ascertain depth of water by sounding with a lead. **Drift-l.,** *see* DRIFT. **To heave the l.,** to take soundings by hand-lead; usually in a continuous sense. **L.-line,** a sounding-line, or length of small cordage or wire attached to the *l.* For use with a *hand l.,* usually is braided cotton stuff about ¼-inch diameter; for *coasting* and *deep-sea* leads, of left-hand, hard-laid, fine hemp or flax

line about three-eighths inch diameter; and, for a sounding-machine, usually 7-thread galvanized steel wire approximately .05 inch in diameter and 300 fathoms in length. Most common in use is the first-named, and U.S. navy standard for *hand l.-lines* is braided cotton ¾-inch in circumference, having a minimum breaking strength of 220 lbs. and a stretch of not more than 1¼ inches in 8, under 200 lbs. tension. *Marking* of the line is one of those traditionally proper customs of the sea which brooks no interference, although its *coasting* and *dipsey* cousins have all but bowed to the mechanical sounding-wire or the electrically operated echo-sounder. It is first well soaked and stretched before marking, its 20-fathom registering part being then laid off as follows:—

At 2 fathoms, 2 tails of leather.

3	do. , 3 do. do.
5	do. , white linen rag.
7	do. , red bunting rag.
10	do. , piece of leather with hole in it.
13	do. , blue flannel or cloth rag; or same as 3-fath.
15	do. , white linen rag.
17	do. , red bunting rag.
20	do. , piece of cord with 2 knots in it.

These constitute the 9 *marks* of the *hand l.-line,* the even 11 unmarked depths being called *deeps.* Excepting a line of 30 fathoms used in reconnoitering work in surveying vessels, similarly marked at 23, 25, and 27 with blue, white, and red, respectively, and cord with 3 knots at 30, *coasting* and *deep-sea* lines continue with a single knot at 25, 35, 45, 55, etc.; 3 knots at 30; 4 knots at 40; 5 at 50; etc., up to 100 or more. The 100-fathom mark is a piece of leather with two holes in it. Following a style of calling out each sounding obtained which dates back to East Indiamen days, the *leadsman,* or man *in the chains,* reports a 5-fathom result as *"By the mark five";* 5¼ as *"And a quarter five";* 5½, *"And a half five";* 5¾, *"A quarter less six";* 6 fathoms, *"By the deep six";* and so on; but usually garnished with such niceties as *"Mark under water 7";* *"Hard floor at 10";* or *"No bottom at 13."* An expert *leadsman* can get an accurate sounding with the *blue pigeon* up to 15 fathoms at a speed of 7 knots, but probably would be severely taxed to show reliable results beyond 7 fathoms at 12 knots; hence, for properly *feeling bottom,* vessel should be slowed down accordingly. Use of the *coasting* and *deep-sea l's* in depths of 30 fathoms or more demands little or no way on vessel, the operation of *taking a cast* in a sailing-ship usually requiring ship to be *hove to* for an "up-and-down" result. Line was passed forward outside all and *l.* was let go from forecastle head, a number of men stationed along the rail each holding a few coils of line which he payed out as he *felt the l.* drawing aft and downward, and sounding taken—usually by one of the mates—from the poop. Interesting here to recall is the traditional shout, *"Watch-ho, watch!"* from the boatswain or his mate as he threw the heavy *l.* overboard from his forward station, repeated by each man in turn after feeling its weight and letting line go to his next in order along the rail. (For use of *sounding-machine, see* SOUNDING) **L.-nail,** a scupper-nail, or nail having a broad flat head, such as is used in wooden vessels to secure opened ends of leaden scupper-pipes to waterways or planking. **Red l.,** red oxide of *l.,* or scarlet-colored powder obtained from *l.* by oxidizing process. Much used on board ship as a pigment in anti-corrosive paints, in putty form for water-tight joints in exposed woodwork or metal, and, mixed with a mastic, as a cement for steam-joints, crack-filling, waterway courses, etc. **Sounding-machine l.,** sinker of cast iron or *l.* about 1½ feet in length, 25 to 40 lbs. in weight, according to speed of ship, which is fixed at end of an iron shaft 2 to 2½ feet in length. Depth-recording apparatus is suspended between end of shaft and lower end of sounding-wire. Total length of sinker and shaft—about 4 feet —prevents recorder from violently striking bottom during sounding operation. *See* **S.-machine** *in* SOUNDING. **White l.,** heavy white substance produced by several different processes and consisting of approximately 75% *l.* carbonate and 25% *hydrated l. oxide.* Extensively used in paint manufacture, also valuable in oil paste form for water-proofing wood joints and seams, bolt-heads, flange joints, etc., in boat and ship construction and, mixed with tallow, as rust-resisting application on wire rigging, chain-cable pins, spare machinery parts, etc.

LEAD.² (Pron. *leed*) To conduct, direct, or guide by any means, as in controlling the trend or path of a rope. Direction or course of a strand in a knot, a stretch of rope, chain cable, etc. A *leader,* as a bull's-eye or a cringle through which a rope is guided or *led.* A navigable passage in an ice field. In sailing-vessels, horizontal distance of center of effort forward of center of lateral resistance; for hull comparison purposes, usually expressed as a fraction of water-line length, or *factor of lead,* which varies from .03 in a large yacht to .07 in large square-rigged vessels. **Blind l.,** *see* Ice-l. Fair-l., *see* F.-lead *in* FAIR. **Ice-l.,** channel or passage through an ice floe or field; when open toward land, called a *land-l.;* when found to be non-continuous, a *blind l.* **L.-block,** any block through which a rope passes to allow of hauling in a direction required; as, a heel-block for fall of a halyard purchase, a cargo-fall block at heel of a boom; a snatch-block. To **l. fair,** as a rope, to have an unobstructed course; to run clear. To **l. out,** to lay out a rope on deck in readiness for manning it; order *"Lead out!"* on naval ships, means to stretch boat-falls, a hawser, etc., along the deck preparatory to hauling on such by detail concerned.

LEADFAIR. (Pron. *leedfare*) Old term for a *fair-lead,* or *fair-leader; esp.* the horizontal batten in lower rigging through which hauling parts of running gear are separately led; *see* **F.-lead** *in* FAIR. Also, a *leader.*

LEADER. A fence or barrier, as of stakes, brush, stones, etc., extending from shore for *leading* fish into a weir or fixed net; *see* FYKE. A snell, or snood, of fine line to which one of the hooks is attached on a long-line or trawl; piece of fine line next to hook on any fishing-line. Foremost vessel in a line-formation of ships, as a naval fleet or a convoy. A *fair-lead.* **L. cable,** in the *Audio-Piloting,* or *Leader Cable,* system experimented with some 30 years ago both by British Admiralty and U.S. Engineers, an electric cable laid along the axis of a harbor entrance channel. Also called *piloting-cable,* continuous signals were transmitted by its means for purpose of guiding vessels through channel in thick weather. Through the necessary equipment of a telephone receiver on each side of vessel, equal intensity of sound in both receivers indicates ship is in mid-channel, or directly above submerged cable. If signals are comparatively weak in starboard side phone, ship is too far toward starboard side of channel; the converse, if weak in port phone. For a number of reasons, the system failed to gain serious attention beyond its experimental stage.

LEADING. Foremost in position; guiding; directing; as, a *leading ship;* a *leading buoy;* a *leading channel.* **L.-block,** a lead-block; *see* **L.-block** *in* LEAD.² **L. edge,** forward edge of propeller-blade, or that edge which cuts water, engines turning ahead. **L. fireman,** in larger British vessels, member of engine department who acts as foreman of stokehold watch; his work corresponds to that of a water-tender in U.S. steam-vessels. **L. lights,** *see* RANGE. **L. marks,** prominent objects on shore, such as painted posts surmounted by triangle or diamond shapes, a church steeple, conspicuous hill or point, etc., serving to guide a pilot in keeping to a channel; *esp.* two such objects or marks which, when in line, indicate direction of channel or bearing of a danger, position line of soundings, an anchor, or place in which to drop anchor, etc. **L. part,** hauling part of a tackle; *esp.* that led through a snatch or *leading* block. **L. seaman,** rating in British navy corresponding to *Seaman, first class,* in U.S.N. **L. wind,** a fair wind; *esp.* a good sailing breeze on beam or quarter, or in which all sail is drawing.

LEADS. (Pron. *leeds*) In a purchase, parts of rope (or chain) other than the hauling part; *i.e.,* parts *leading* from block to block, or, as in a Spanish burton, from block to lifting-hook.

LEADSMAN. (Pron. *ledsman*) Seaman who heaves the *hand lead* in taking soundings; the man "in the chains"; *cf.* CHAINS. **L.'s gripe,** a body girth or breast-band, usually made of canvas and appropriately secured, used by a leadsman as a safeguard against falling overboard. Sometimes takes the form of a canvas apron stretched between two stanchions at outer edge of a special *platform* extending outside the rail at either side of ship.

LEAGUE. An old measure of distance varying from 2½ to 4½ statute miles, depending upon country in which used. In English-speaking countries, a *land league* is 3 statute miles; the *marine league*, 3 nautical miles. Outside its use in certain older American and British statutes, the term is now employed poetically only.

LEAK. Any defect, such as a crack, fissure, or hole, which admits water or other fluid, or allows it to escape; as, a *leak* in a boat's planking, a tank, a pipe, etc. Act of leaking; leakage; point at which leak is located; as, *the leak was found in fore peak*. Loss of electricity, or point at which loss occurs, as by faulty insulation. To let water or other fluid in or out, as through a defect in a cask, tank, pipe, ship's side, etc. **L.-stopper,** any material or device used to arrest influx of water, as in a boat; or its escape, as in a pipe or tank. To **spring a l.,** to begin to make water, as in a vessel's hold, through defect or injury to bottom plating or planking.

LEAKAGE. A leaking; amount or quantity that escapes or enters by a leak or leaks. An allowance for cargo loss caused by escape of contents of containers; sometimes including breakage of empty containers. Such losses usually must exceed 3% of the shipment's value in marine insurance coverage.

LEAN. Quality of having clean cut, fine lines, as a vessel's hull; opposed to flat or *bluff*. Flesh adhering to blubber in flensing a whale; to remove such, as by means of a whaling-knife, in the process known as *leaning*. **L. bow,** sharp-lined approaching the stem; not bluff; said of a vessel.

LEATHER. To protect from chafing wear, as a square sail's foot-rope in way of a stay, a spar in way of a rope, clew of a sail, etc., by covering with raw hide or leather. Such protection is termed *leathering*. **L. jack,** fish of the *Carangidæ* family, or that including the amber jack, cavallo, and pompano; so called from leathery quality of its comparatively small scales combined with the skin in which they are embedded; habitat in West Indies waters and off southern Atlantic and Pacific coasts of U.S. **L'neck,** in U.S. navy, colloquial name for a marine, originating from stiff high collar of his tunic. **L.-back,** largest of sea-turtles, often attaining 1000 lbs. in weight, so called from its leathery flexible carapace (shell). Its back has five parallel equally spaced longitudinal ridges and is composed of a mosaic of small bones embedded in the thick skin. Habitat in all warm seas, *esp.* in tropical Atlantic.

LEAVE. To depart or set out; as, *we leave the pier at six; the fleet has left for China*. Permission to absent one's self from duty: as, to *take l.;* period of such absence: as, *two weeks' l*. As distinguished from *liberty,* or authorized absence of an enlisted man from duty, *l.* is applied only to such privilege granted, or due to, an officer, although *liberty* in excess of 48 hours usually is also termed *l*. **Shore l.,** permission given to naval enlisted man to absent himself from his ship for a period in excess of usual *liberty* of 12 to 48 hours; in merchant service, permission given to any crew member to land from his vessel, with or without stipulated time for return on board.

LEDGE. In shipbuilding, a thwartship timber or girder set between two main beams and forming a *coaming* for a deck opening, as a forward or an after hatchway coaming, which formerly were called *head-ledges*. A ridge or shoal-like area of rock near a coast; an under-water projecting part of a rocky shore. **L.-bars,** old term for strongbacks, or heavy bars laid fore-and-aft between hatch-ledges to support hatch-covers.

LEE. Sheltered side or area, or that protected from wind or sea; as, *under the lee of a cliff; other ship was on our lee*. Referring or pertaining to the sheltered or protected side, or that farthest from direction of wind; opposed to *weather;* as, *lee boat, brace, rail, side, etc.* Unless lying at anchor, becalmed, or having wind nearly aft, in sailing-vessels the word is commonly preferred to *port* or *starboard* in designating outer parts of hull, above-deck equipment, and gear which are duplicated on either side of ship; thus, *port rail* becomes *lee* rail, when wind is on starboard side; *starboard rigging* is *lee rigging,* as opposed to *weather* (or *port*) *rigging,* when breeze is on port side of vessel. **Blanket l.,** a snug berth, or one well protected from wind and sea. To **bring by the l.,** *see* BRING. **L. anchor,** when vessel is under way, anchor on *lee bow;* when two anchors are in use, that one to which ship is not riding. **L.-board,** a wide board, or number of planks fitted edge to edge forming a vertical fin, which is pivoted at its forward end and lowered on a shallow-draft vessel's *l.* side for increasing area of hull's lateral resistance, thus reducing leeway. To **l.-bow a current,** in sailing, to have current setting against the *l.* bow, thus gaining advantage of holding one's own to windward. **L. cable,** that attached to the *l.* anchor, or one on which there is no stress; *cf.* **L. anchor. L. fore brace!,** order to commence hauling in on fore braces as wind draws ahead, or becomes less favorable; also, *brace up fore-and-aft!* **L. gauge,** *see* GAUGE. **L. helm,** *see* HELM. **L. lurch,** heavy roll to leeward made by vessel, as when struck by a sea on her weather beam or quarter. **L'most,** farthest to leeward, or in direction opposite to that from which wind is blowing; as, *leemost vessel of* *the squadron.* **Lee-O!,** in tacking ship, or "coming about," advising cry from the poop indicating helm has been *put down* and head sheets are to be eased off to assist vessel in turning into the wind; also, *hard-a-lee!* **L. port,** harbor or port which provides good shelter from prevailing wind and sea. **L. shore,** a near-by shore on *l.* side of vessel; *esp.* in the sense of being a danger to a sailing-ship when trying to *claw off,* or work to windward, in a gale, the situation being then described as *on a lee shore;* hence, to be in trouble or difficulties. **L. tide,** a tidal current setting in same or nearly same direction to which wind is blowing; a *leeward tide.* **L. wheel,** position of an assistant helmsman where two hands are required to man the *hand steering-wheel,* as in a sailing-ship with heavy quartering sea prevailing. Regular helmsman, whose duty is to steer by compass, stands on *weather* side of wheel; an assistant takes the *l. wheel* in circumstances noted, and, if running before a gale, usually the *port* side of wheel. In any case, an assistant, or *lee helmsman,* is said to *take l. wheel.* **On the l. beam, -bow, -quarter,** descriptive of bearing of an object from a vessel; indicating its relative direction is off ship's *l. beam,* or side; off the *l. bow;* or off the *l. quarter.* To **take care of the l. hitch,** colloquialism meaning to keep ship on her course; to see she does not sag to leeward. **Under the l.,** off the *l.* side; in the shelter of vessel's hull. With *of,* sheltered by something; as, *ship lay under the l. of St. Kilda.*

LEECH. (Of Scand. origin) One of the outer, or vertical, edges of a square sail, or after edge of a fore-and-aft sail; also, chiefly in yachts, sometimes applied to *luff* of a fore-and-aft sail as *fore leech* or as *mast leech* to luff of a gaff sail or one set on and abaft a mast. Properly, the word denotes area of canvas immediately in way of such edge of a sail; particularly, the *tabling,* or doubling, of canvas from 2½ to 6 inches in width, together with sail's strengthening roping, or *leech-rope,* to which it is stitched. In sail-making, *leech-tabling* is laid to *l.-rope* so that latter lies on *after side* of square sails and on *port side* of fore-and-aft sails. *Leech* roping usually is of fine quality tarred hemp, although heavy sails may be fitted with served flexible steel wire. **After l.,** in a fore-and-aft sail, where its *luff* is termed *fore l.,* distinguishing term for *l.* proper, or after edge of sail. **Cross l.,** *see* CROSS. **Lee l.,** of a square sail, that on lee side; opposed to *weather l.,* or that of leading or windward edge of sail. **L.-line,** rope attached to *l.-rope* of a square sail and leading to deck for purpose of gathering in *l.* to the yard when taking in sail.

LEEWARD. Pertaining to, or in direction of, opposite point from which wind is blowing; away from the wind; opposed to *windward;* as, a *leeward course;* the *leeward ship.* Such direction itself, as, vessel drifted fast *to leeward.* **L. squall,** one ap-

parently changing direction and threatening to catch ship aback. **L. tide,** a *lee tide, q.v. in* LEE. (The older nautical pronunciation, *"loo-ard,"* still generally prevails among seamen)

LEEWARDLY. Tending to fall off or make unusual *leeway;* carrying *lee helm,* as opposed to *ardency;* said of a vessel unable to sail close to wind without making great leeway, as opposed to *weatherly;* as, *she sails leewardly courses.* Pertaining to quality of *leewardness,* or tendency to make leeway.

LEEWAY. Difference between course steered and that actually made good through the water; deviation to leeward, or *angle of drift,* due to wind blowing at an angle with vessel's fore-and-aft line; angle at which vessel's wake lies with course steered. Thus, with wind N.E., compass course S.E., and leeway ½ point, compass course made good is ½ point to right, or S.E. ½ S. Sometimes also applied to deviation from course steered caused by both wind and a *lee tide* or *leeward current.* **Allowance for l.,** angle applied to course by compass to *counteract leeway;* thus, in example above, if course to be made good were S.E. ½ S. by compass, leeway allowance of ½ point toward wind (or current) gives S.E. as course to steer by compass. **L. indicator,** a sighting vane, usually fixed at middle point of stern taff-rail, for observing leeway angle, or that which vessel's wake makes with her fore-and-aft line. To **make up for l.,** to increase speed or hasten some activity to compensate for lost time.

LEEFANG. Old term for a rope holding the clew of a jib in midship position while a bonnet is being laced on the sail. Also, an iron traveler or horse on deck for a staysail sheet. Once written *lee-fange* and *lee-fang.* (The word *fang* or *fange* is an obsolete form of present *vang,* a rope or tackle for steadying the peak of a standing gaff)

LEFT. Opposed to *right;* toward one's left hand. **L. bank of a river,** that on one's *left* when facing down stream, or toward mouth of river. **L.-hand propeller,** or **screw,** one in which upper half of its revolution is from right to *l.* when engines are turning ahead, observer facing forward. Such propeller is rarely found in single-screw vessels; usually, in twin or multiple-screw design, port screw or screws are *left-handed,* starboard ones *right-handed.* **L.-hand rope,** cordage in which its strands are laid up *left-handed,* or slantingly advance from right to *l.* **L. rudder!,** order to helmsman to turn rudder to *l.* of midship position; by U.S. law, it means *"Direct vessel's head to port"; see* HELM.

LEG. One of parts of a rope in a bridle, crowfoot, leech-line, lazy-jack, or in any combination of single parts sustaining similar stress. One of a pair of sheers, or sheer-legs; one of a pair or tripod of timbers staying and stiffening a derrick: often termed a *stiff-leg.* A reach or straight stretch in a generally crooked channel. Distance sailed on one of a series of tacks. One of two or more shores propping a boat in upright position when hauled out of water. Flange of an angle-bar or other structural metal. One of projecting ends of a knee; *esp.* the upright one in a *beam-knee.* **A good l.,** in sailing, a tack or reach approximating the desired one. To **l. along,** to lead out a rope along the deck preparatory to manning it. **L.-irons,** *see* IRON. **L.-of-mutton sail,** a fore-and-aft sail of triangular shape set abaft mast in small craft; sometimes applied to a *lateen* sail. Also, *shoulder-of-mutton* sail. To **l. up,** to fix shores about a dry-docked vessel; to prop up. **Show a l.!,** order given by boatswain's mate in a naval vessel directing men to turn out of their bunks or hammocks.

LEGAL. Conforming to, or permitted by, law; lawful; legitimate; valid or sound according to law; as, *legal tender; legal entry.* **L. weight,** in certain questions involving collection of customs duties, that of a shipment of goods exclusive of packing or containers. **L. quay,** chiefly in Great Britain, a pier or wharf licensed and equipped to receive and house bonded goods.

LENGTH. Extent from end to end, as of a ship, spar, rope, etc.; portion of space or a distance considered as a measure; as, a *cable's length;* a *ship's length.* L. of a vessel is measured according to particular use for which such value is intended. In every-day language, this measurement is the *registered l.,* or distance between fore side of stem under the bowsprit (if any) and after side of head of the stern-post, or to center of rudder-stock in vessels of cruiser stern type. **Cab'e's l.,** *see* CABLE. **Floodable l.,** maximum *l.* of hull space which may be flooded without causing ship to sink. Such *l.* differs with location in the fore-and-aft line. What is called the *subdivision factor,* multiplied by the *floodable l.* gives maximum *l.* of each compartment permitted at that location. This is known as the *permissible l.,* or maximum distance allowed between water-tight bulkheads for that locality. *Subdivision,* or *permissible, factor* is determined according to rules prescribed at *International Conferences on Safety of Life at Sea, 1929* and *1948.* As defining the limit to which a vessel may be immersed in event of uncontrolled entry of water throughout her *floodable l.,* the *margin line* is drawn at least 3 inches below upper surface of bulkhead deck (that deck to which water-tight bulkheads extend from ship's bottom) at vessel's side. **L. between perpendiculars,** unless otherwise stated, this is identical with *registered l.* which is measured along line of uppermost continuous deck of hull. It is, however, for calculations of displacement, reserve buoyancy, structural stress values, etc., also measured on line of lower decks or a number of water-planes, and thus may be appreciably affected in case of a sloping or curved stem. Usually short-

ened to *Length B.P.* **L. by American Bureau of Shipping Rules,** also known as *Lloyd's Length,* used for classification purposes in determining sizes and disposition of structural members consistent with other dimensions and type of vessel concerned, is measured from fore side of stem to after side of stern-post, or where there is no stern-post, to axis of rudder-stock, on the *summer load line.* **L. on summer load line,** or *freeboard length,* as established by U.S. law, in conformity with *International Load Line Convention, 1930,* is that measured on *summer load line* from fore side of stem to after side of rudder-post (stern-post). Where there is no rudder-post, from fore side of stem to axis of rudder-stock. In vessels having cruiser sterns, *l.* is taken as 96% of total *l.* of summer load line, or as from fore side of stem to axis of rudder-stock if that be the greater. **L. over all,** distance between forward and after extremities of ship's hull; *L.O.A.* **Tonnage l.,** an inside *l.* used in measuring vessel's tonnage; *see* TONNAGE.

LENGTHENING. Besides a few instances in wooden shipbuilding history, there have been in recent years a number of steel vessels subjected to the process of lengthening, chiefly for the purpose of accommodating a new type of propulsion plant. Ship is placed in a graving dock and cut through amidships or at a desirable point in that vicinity. One portion is hauled on *ways* to exact required distance from the other and intervening space is then built in with necessary structural arrangement to form a new hull.

LENS, FRESNEL. (Named for *Augustin Jean Fresnel, French optician* and *geometer (1788–1827)* A lens originally designed for lighthouses and now also extensively fitted in signal lanterns—particularly in those prescribed in Regulations for Prevention of Collisions. By its means light is sent out in horizontal parallel rays and thus may be seen at comparatively great distance. A lantern thus equipped is often termed a *Fresnel lantern.* **Axis of a l.,** line of central ray, or that passing through the optical center of lens, which suffers no change in direction.

LEO. (*L. = Lion*) A northern zodiacal constellation containing the bright star *Regulus* (α *Leonis*), of magnitude 1.3, which lies very close to the sun's path, or *ecliptic,* in declination $12\frac{1}{4}°$ N. with a S.H.A. of $208\frac{1}{2}°$. The group may be located by extending southward a line joining the "Pointers" in the *Dipper (Ursa Major)* for about 40°. It is readily recognized by the *Sickle,* at end of the handle, or southern extremity, of which *Regulus* lies, with a right-angled triangular formation a few degrees east of it containing at the eastern angle another navigational star, β *Leonis* (*see* DENEBOLA). Also, at back or curve of *Sickle* lies *Algeiba,* or γ *Leonis,* a star of magnitude 2.6.

LESTE. A dry warm easterly wind blowing over Madeira and Canary Islands from the North African deserts.

LET. Combining verb connoting to allow, permit, or cause to initiate some movement or action indicated. To **l. down,** to allow to descend; to lower; as, to *let down the booms; let down your nets.* To **l. fall,** to drop, allow or cause to drop; as, to *l. fall* a square sail at the word, after loosing gaskets, *"Let fall!"*; which is also the order to a pulling-boat's crew having oars *tossed* to lower them horizontally across gunwale. To **l. fly,** to loose quickly and completely, as sheet of a boat's sail in an emergency. To **l. go,** to loosen hold upon; to cast loose; as, to *l. go* anchor; *l. go* the halyard. To **l. go amain,** older expression equivalent to *l. fly; see* AMAIN. **L. go and haul!,** final command in maneuver of tacking in square rig, indicating head yards are to be hauled around and trimmed for the new tack. **L. go by the run!** or **L. her run!,** order to *l. fly,* or allow to freely run, as braces, halyards, or other running gear. To **l. her luff,** to allow vessel to run into the wind; particularly, in an ardent vessel, to ease helm and let her come toward wind until sails shake.

LETTER. A written document addressed to a party therein specified; *esp.* one authorizing a certain action, or activity, to be undertaken by such party; sometimes in plural, as *letters of marque; letters patent.* A certificate of authorization or identification; any written communication. **L. of advice,** a communication from consignor to a consignee informing him that a certain shipment is being forwarded, with details of costs payable, etc.; *esp.* such letter indicating that arrangements have been made with a local bank at port of discharge of goods to deliver bills of lading to consignee upon settling of all moneys due consignor; often simply termed *advice.* **L. board,** ground or board on which vessel's name is carved or painted; a *name-board.* **L. of credit,** written authority given by a banker to a shipmaster (or traveler) to draw upon a certain bank at a port specified any sum of money required for ship's disbursements up to a stipulated figure. **L.** or **l's of marque,** also, **l's of marque and reprisal,** in 17th, 18th, and early 19th century custom, a document issued by a sovereign to a private individual, authorizing him to seize subjects of another country or their goods as a matter of retaliation or reprisal. This appears to have developed into a sovereign's permission to one of his worthy subjects to fit out an armed vessel, or *privateer,* with the object of capturing vessels flying flag of another country, such capture not being considered piracy. Also, *l's of mart.* (The word *marque* appears originally to have meant a seizing as a pledge or a means of retaliation) **Sea l.,** a document issued to a neutral vessel in time of war, certifying her master is entitled to sail under the flag of nation to which she belongs, and specifying cargo on board, names and nationali-

ties of crew members, owners, port of registry, loading port, and destination. In U.S., use of *sea l's* was discontinued by Presidential proclamation, April 10, 1815: last one was issued at New York, Dec. 24, 1806. **Signal l's,** *see* SIGNAL. **Voyage l.,** a summary, in *l.* form, of happenings during a voyage, with details of circumstances attending any unusual events, written by a shipmaster and addressed to owners of his vessel.

LEVANT. (It. *levante,* point of sun-rising; the east; the Levant) Region east of Italy bordering on the Mediterranean Sea and contiguous waters. **L. Company,** an English company of merchants formerly engaged in shipping in the southeastern European and eastern Mediterranean trade. It originated with its first charter by Queen Elizabeth in 1581. A second charter was granted by James I in 1605 and, with supplementary statutes and usages to be observed by the Company in its activities, as confirmed by King Charles II (circa 1670), formed the basis of British consular jurisdiction in the *Levant.* The Company was dissolved in 1825.

LEVANTER. Old term for a ship trading to the *Levant; esp.* one trading for the *Levant Company.* A strong easterly wind peculiar to the Levant; also called *Euroclydon* and *Meltem; see* EUROCLYDON.

LEVECHE. (*Sp.*) A dry warm southwest wind prevailing in summer on southeast coast of Spain; also, *lebeche.* Cf. *Libeccio.* It is one of the many local names given to different winds on the Mediterranean coasts.

LEVEE. (Fr.: from *lever,* to raise) Chiefly in south and southwestern U.S., an embankment or dike along a river's edge to prevent inundation of land; also, a landing-place, as a quay or wharf. Accumulation of silt, in the form of a low ridge at either side of a river channel, deposited during flood or freshet stage of stream.

LEVEL. Property of lying exactly perpendicular to the plumb-line; having no part higher than the other; as, a *level sea-bottom.* A stretch in a canal or river between two locks. A surveying instrument, consisting of a sighting telescope mounted on a tripod and capable of being adjusted to lie exactly parallel to plane of horizon, used to determine differences in elevations of surrounding points. **Sea l.,** that of the sea surface; *specif.,* datum line from which land elevations are measured, or *l.* of midway position between mean of all high waters and that of all low waters, termed *mean sea l.* Strictly, however, this datum may be locally disturbed, as in vicinity of strong currents or where a prevailing wind blows into or out of a partially closed sea area. Also, it has been determined that mass attraction of a mountainous region bordering on a sea-coast raises sea level in its vicinity by a few feet, as, for example, the Chilean coast and head of Bay of Bengal. **Water l.,** position or height of surface of a bay, lake, river, etc., with relation to a fixed datum; sea level; surface of a body of water. Position of water surface in a steam boiler, as indicated in attached gauge-glass.

LEVER. (Fr. *lever,* to raise) Bar of wood or metal used to gain mechanical advantage in lifting, pushing, turning, applying pressure, etc.; as, a prize; a pinch-bar; a capstan bar; a brake-lever. Perpendicular distance between lines of opposing forces, as in a *couple;* or between line of force and a point about which such force acts. **Righting l.,** also termed *righting arm,* in ship stability, horizontal transverse distance between vertical line representing direction of buoyancy force acting upward through ship's center of buoyancy and that acting downward through center of gravity. With ship upright, length of righting lever is zero and, within a certain limit, depending upon vessel's range of stability, increases with angle of heel. **Upsetting l.,** where, as in the case of a shallow draft vessel listing to such an angle that lower side of her deck becomes immersed, center of buoyancy will have moved from its position as a righting force toward the fore-and-aft line, buoyancy force acting upward now is on wrong side of downward acting force of vessel's center of gravity. A capsizing couple results. *See* STABILITY.

LEVIATHAN. (*Heb.*) A huge and formidable aquatic animal referred to in ancient writings; probably the crocodile or the whale. Description of such occupies entire chapter 41 of *Book of Job* in which *Leviathan* is seen to typify *Satan* and his powers of darkness. Figuratively, a large ocean-going vessel, as one of trans-Atlantic greyhounds.

LEWIS-BOLT. A deck eye-bolt enlarged in diameter at its lower end and set in a socket of similar shape. A wedging-piece inserted against its side, or molten lead set around bolt withstands upward pull by jamming against sides of socket. Also called *movable eye-bolt,* used in wood decks of yachts and passenger vessels.

LIBECCIO. The warm southwest wind of western shores of Italy; the *leveche* of southeast coast of Spain. It is the old Italian name for the *S.W.* point of the compass.

LIBERTY. Permission given a seaman to absent himself from duty; *esp.* that usually given a naval enlisted man for a period of 24 to 48 hours. *Cf.* LEAVE. To **break l.,** *see* BREAK. **Fourth class l.,** looking through binoculars at the shore when denied *l.:* said of a naval rating. **L.-book,** record kept on a naval vessel or at a naval station or barracks showing length of *l.* allowed and time of each man's return, and, also, his condition upon returning. **L. man,** an enlisted man granted *l.* **L. ship,** standard EC-2 type of vessel built by *U.S. Maritime Commission* during World War II. Of design embodying minimum cost and simplicity of operation, with first requirement of rapid construction (chiefly welded),

vessel is of full scantling, transverse frame, two continuous deck build; has 5 cargo holds, 8 watertight bulkheads, 1 deep tank abaft machinery space (amidships) and 2 others in No. 1 hold; single screw, reciprocating engine propulsion, giving speed of 11 knots. Length over all, 441½ ft.; breadth, 57 ft.; depth to upper deck, 37½ ft. Carries 10,500 tons deadweight on draft of 27½ feet; load displacement 14,100 tons. Normal complement, 44 men. About 2300 of these vessels were built.

LIBRA. (*L. = a balance*) A southern constellation lying to northwest of *Scorpio* and which the sun passes through in November. It contains two navigational stars: *Kiffa Australis* and *Kiffa Borealis. See* KIFFA BOREALIS.

LICENSE. A legal permit or document issued by recognized authority granting liberty to a person or persons, or to a vessel, to engage in certain activity; as, a *pilot's license; cod fishery license.* In U.S., *licenses,* corresponding to *certificates of competency* in Great Britain and other countries, are issued by the *Coast Guard* to officers who qualify to act as masters, mates, or engineers in certain types of vessels by meeting required minimum of sea service and standards of professional knowledge in written examinations. Licenses to *pilots* operating in principal harbors and waterways, where pilotage is compulsory under laws of state having jurisdiction, are granted by state authority, and a master or mate having his *l.* endorsed to the effect that he is qualified to pilot a vessel within specified harbor limits or other inland waters may act under such Federal authority only in a vessel under U.S. flag, and when such vessel is under *license* and/or *enrollment* in U.S. domestic trade. Licenses are issued to *radio operators* of merchant vessels by the *Federal Communications Bureau.* In conformity to laws for regulation of vessels in domestic commerce, all U.S. trading vessels engaged in coastwise or lake navigation, all fishing vessels, and yachts intended to cruise from port to port in U.S. or to any foreign port, are required to be *licensed;* excepting flatboats, barges, and like craft not propelled by their own power and carrying freight on lakes and rivers. *Cf.* **C. of License and Enrollment** *in* CERTIFICATE; *also,* ENROLLMENT.

LID. A wood or metal covering for an aperture; as, a garbage-chute lid; a hinged top on a chest, gear-box, etc. **Port-l.,** a blind or metal storm-cover fitted to inside of a port-light. **Scuttle-l.,** watertight cover or hatch over a small deck opening, or scuttle. **Tank-l.,** steel hinged cover for hermetically sealing opening to a tank; *esp.* such cover in a tank-vessel.

LIE. Combined with an adverb, preposition, or phrase, almost exclusively connotes a vessel's position with relation to some object, or as being in a certain trim, heading, or condition. While *lay* and *lie* are often used synonymously, as in, to *lay,* or *lie, along the shore,* former is preferable word in that it really signifies to *lay ship along the shore,* or *sail along,* etc. As compared with *lie,* which implies position, *lay* generally is connected with the idea of motion; hence, to *lie up* a vessel is better usage than to *lay up,* although both expressions are commonly employed. The following are used with either *lay* or *lie (see* LAY): To **l. athwart;** to **l. close;** to **l. off;** to **l. the course;** to **l. to;** to **l. up.** To **l. at anchor,** to ride at anchor. To **l. by,** to remain near, as one ship to another. To **l. in berth,** to occupy an allotted space, as alongside a pier, moored at buoys, dolphins, etc., in harbor. To **l. over,** to careen, list, or heel, as a vessel; in older usage, also to *lie along, esp.* applied to a vessel heeling under pressure of sail. *Cf.* **H. to** *in* HEAVE; AHULL; ATRY.

LIEN. (Fr. *lien,* bond or tie) A legal claim; charge against property for satisfaction of a debt; the right to hold property of another person until a claim is satisfied or paid. **Baggage l.,** that by which an owner or master may hold luggage of a passenger for unsettled transportation charges. **Common law l.,** one's right to hold and retain another's property until a claim is paid; as, in shipping, for unpaid construction or repair charges to a vessel. A shipmaster has a *contract lien* on cargo for freight, dead freight, demurrage, general average contribution, and extraordinary expenses incurred in protecting cargo carried while goods are in his ship or temporarily landed in his custody. **Maritime l.,** a distinguishing feature of *Admiralty Law,* is a claim *in rem* against a vessel and may arise where a debt is owing, as for crew's wages, towage, stevedoring, stores supplied, wharfage, etc., or where a *tort* has been committed, as by a vessel at fault in a collision. Such liens follow a vessel anywhere she goes and may be enforced by a *libel in admiralty* at any port by a court having jurisdiction over such vessel. This procedure is called *libeling the ship,* and in an American port the *United States Marshall* is the functionary in such cases. Seamen have a *lien* for wages on both vessel and freight; a master on the freight, or on the cargo, if freight is unpaid, but not on his ship. **Priority of l's,** in the following order: (1) Seamen's wages; (2) salvage; (3) collision and other torts; (4) for services such as repairs, supplies, towage, wharfage; (5) bottomry bonds; (6) non-maritime claims, within which class recent *l's* outrank earlier ones.

LIEUTENANT. (Fr. *lieu,* place or stead; *tenant,* one holding or caring for property of another. Literally, *"in place of a tenant"*: from the early custom of a *tenant*—custodian or holder of an estate in the realm—being represented by another in his duty to serve in the royal forces) A commissioned officer in U.S. navy, U.S. Coast Guard, and in British navy, in rank next below a lieutenant-commander and equal to a captain in the Army. U.S. naval insignia

of rank are two gold sleeve-bands, or bars **on** shoulder-straps, ½-inch in width, with single gold star above. **First l.,** formerly, in naval vessels, officer next in order of command to captain; now, chiefly in British navy, senior executive officer, or senior on staff of executive on a battleship. The term denotes a duty, such officer not necessarily being a *l.* in rank. He is charged with cleanliness, efficiency, and general upkeep of vessel's hull, discipline, general drills, etc. **Flag-l.,** an officer, not below a *l.,* acting as an aide to a flag-officer or admiral. **L.-commander,** naval commissioned officer ranking next below a commander and next above **a** *l.;* he is equal in rank to a major in the Army. Insignia are two ½-inch gold sleeve-bands, or bars **on** shoulder-straps, with ¼-inch band or bar between, and gold star above (U.S. navy). **L. junior grade,** U.S. naval commissioned officer next in rank above that of ensign and next below *l.* Insignia, ½-inch stripe or bar and ¼-inch one above it; gold star above all. (In U.S. Coast Guard, gold star is replaced by C.G. miniature shield) **Sub-l.,** colloquially known as a *snotty,* officer graduated from midshipman class in British navy, holding his first commission, or that next below lieutenant. (The pron. *leftenant* is usual with the British)

LIFE. Combining word used in terms designating articles of ship equipment designed for, or something essential in connection with, preservation, protection, or saving of human life; as, *l.-buoy; l.-rail; l.-line.* **L.-arrow,** heavy arrow-shaped projectile fired from a line-throwing gun, as in sending off **a** life-saving line to a stranded vessel. **L.-belt,** also called *l.-jacket* and *l.-preserver,* broad belt-like jacket of buoyant material, such as flat blocks of cork or kapok suitably covered, easily secured to the body for keeping a person afloat. An approved life-belt, as prescribed by *International Conference on Safety at Sea, 1948,* "shall be constructed with proper workmanship and materials; shall be capable of supporting in fresh water for 24 hours 16½ lbs. of iron; shall be reversible; shall be capable of holding up an unconscious person's head. Life-jackets, buoyancy of which depends on air compartments, are prohibited." **L.-boat,** usually *life-boat,* a ship's boat, specially designed, equipped, and provided with means of quickly launching, for carrying a certain number of persons in event **of** necessity for abandoning ship; a similar boat maintained in readiness on shore for rescue of persons from vessels stranded or in distress. Ship's *l.-boats* are of the open, sharp-ended stern type, are fitted with water-tight air tanks for extra buoyancy, and have *l.-lines* festooned in bights all around their sides. The following is the gist of requirements for construction of such boats as agreed upon at *International Conference on Safety at Sea, 1948:* All life-boats to be properly constructed and of such form and proportions that they shall have ample stability in a seaway and sufficient freeboard when loaded with full complement and equipment; must be open boats with rigid sides and have internal buoyancy only; and shall be not less than 24 feet in length, unless carriage of boats of such length is considered unreasonable or impracticable due to size of vessel or other reasons, but in no ship shall *lifeboats* be less than 16 feet. No *lifeboat* may be approved if weighing more than 20 long tons with full complement and equipment. All boats certified to carry more than 60 persons shall be approved motor-lifeboats or other mechanically propelled type, duly approved, which shall have sufficient power to enable boat to be readily cleared from ship's side when launched and to hold course under adverse weather conditions. If propelling gear is manually operated, it shall be capable of being worked by persons untrained in its use, and of being operated when *lifeboat* is flooded. All *lifeboats* must be of sufficient strength to enable them to be safely lowered into water when fully loaded. They must have a mean sheer at least equal to 4% of their length. Those certified to carry 100 or more persons shall have their buoyancy increased to the satisfaction of governing administration. Buoyancy of a *wooden lifeboat* shall be provided by water-tight air-cases, total volume of which shall be equal to at least one-tenth of boat's cubic capacity; that of a *metal boat* shall not be less than required above for a *wooden lifeboat* of same cubic capacity, volume of water-tight air-cases being increased accordingly. All thwarts and side-seats shall be fitted as low in boat as practicable and bottom-boards fitted so that thwarts shall not be more than 2 feet 9 inches above them. Number of persons which a *lifeboat* can accommodate is greatest whole number obtained by dividing boat's capacity in cubic feet by 10, this being reduced when it is greater than number of persons for which proper seating room is provided without in any way interfering with use of oars. In determining number of persons which boat can accommodate, each person shall be assumed to be an adult wearing a life-jacket. It was resolved at *International Conference on Safety at Sea, 1948,* that the foregoing requirements, among others pertaining to life-saving appliances, would be brought into practice not later than December 31, 1950. For present *lifeboat* requirements, all information pertaining thereto may be obtained from the *Commandant, U.S. Coast Guard, Washington, D.C.* **L.-boat certificate,** issued by U.S. Coast Guard to any seaman who satisfactorily passes examination in handling and taking charge of a ship's lifeboat. Seamen thus certificated are called *lifeboatmen.* In U.S. merchant vessels, a certain complement of lifeboatmen is required among the crew, depending upon boat accommodation and number of persons carried, as noted in each vessel's certificate of annual inspection. (*See* **C. of Inspection** *in* CERTIFI-

CATE). **L.-boat compass,** *see* COMPASS. **L.-buoy,** designed to be thrown to a person in the water for his support, usually ring-shaped, 30 inches outside diameter, covered with painted light canvas; made of cork or equivalent solid buoyant material. An approved *l.-buoy* must be capable of supporting 32 lbs. of iron in fresh water for 24 hours; also must be fitted with a grab-line secured to its outer side so as to present 4 equal hanging bights, according to merchant vessel requirements. (*Cf.* **Franklin life-b.** *in* BUOY.) U.S. regulations provide that at least one of a merchant vessel's buoys on each side shall be fitted with an attached line not less than 15 fathoms in length; minimum number of 30-inch buoys required being according to vessel's length, ranging from 2 for vessels under 100 feet to 30 for those 800 feet or over. Also, a number of *l.-buoys,* from 2 for vessels 100 feet to 200 feet in length to 15 for those of 800 feet or over, must be fitted with self-igniting *water lights.* (*See* LIGHT). **L.-car,** a water-tight boat-shaped chamber suspended from a hawser which is stretched from a stranded ship to shore. By its means persons and valuables may be hauled through the breakers to safety. Also called a *safety-car* and *ark.* **L.-float,** an O-shaped life-saving float made of balsa wood, or a cork-sheathed water-tight metal tube, across which is stretched a net, or a platform suspended by netting, so that float may serve its purpose either side up. It is fitted all around with a grab-line. Such floats usually are about 200 lbs. in weight and are stowed so that they may be launched or let fall overboard direct, or they may float away if ship sinks too quickly for their release by launching. **L. guard,** an expert swimmer employed at a beach resort to rescue persons in danger of drowning. **L.-jacket,** *see* **L.-belt. L.-kite,** *see* KITE. **L.-line,** a rope to which persons may cling for safety; as, a temporary man-rope stretched along a weather deck in bad weather; a grab-line around a lifeboat or life-raft; any line thrown to a person in danger of drowning; one of several ropes, knotted at intervals throughout its length, hung from a span between boat-davit heads for safety of boat's crew during lowering or hoisting of boat; a guard-rope to prevent persons falling from any level, as around a hatchway or opening in ship's rail; a line bent to a man's waist for hauling him to safety, as in descending a side-ladder in bad weather, or in entering a tank or compartment suspected of being foul with gas. **L.-preserver,** *see* **L.-belt. L.-raft,** a decked float or raft made sufficiently buoyant to accommodate persons clear of the water. Usually of catamaran type, having two parallel tubular floats about 15 inches in diameter between which are laid two slatted decks. Space between decks is used to house equipment, including oars, sea-anchor, storm oil, and distress signals; also drinking-water and provisions. Raft is equally serviceable with either deck upward. Such rafts generally are passenger ship equipment covering deficiency, if any, in lifeboat capacity for all persons on board. With other requirements for "buoyant apparatus" (by which is meant buoyant deck-seats, deck-chairs, life-floats, or other articles designed to support persons in the water, other than lifeboats, life-buoys, and life-belts) *International Conference on Safety at Sea, 1948,* prescribes the following for *life-rafts,* effective January 1, 1951: They shall not exceed 400 lbs. in weight, unless suitable means are provided for launching without lifting by hand; shall be of approved material and construction; shall be effective and stable when floating either way up; air-cases or equivalent buoyancy shall not be dependent upon inflation; shall be fitted with a painter and have a line securely becketed round the outside; shall be of such strength that they can be launched or thrown from place where stowed into water without being damaged; shall have not less than 3 cubic feet of air cases or equivalent buoyancy for each person certified to carry; have a deck area of not less than 4 square feet for each person certified to carry; shall effectively support occupants out of water; and shall be equipped with 2 paddles. **L.-rail,** any guard-rail, chain stretched between stanchions, or other safety "fence," to prevent persons being washed overboard, falling through a hatchway, etc. **L.-rocket,** a line-carrying rocket used to establish communication between a stranded vessel and shore. **L.-saving apparatus,** any device for saving life,—particularly from drowning; commonly applied to equipment at a lifeboat station ashore. **L.-saving gun** (or **mortar**), *see* **Line-throwing g.** *in* GUN. **L.-saving Service,** formerly under the Treasury Department, created by Congress June 18, 1878, in connection with *U.S. Revenue Service.* Established stations along sea-coasts and Great Lake shores equipped with *l.-saving* apparatus and manned by crews whose duties included patrol of beaches. First *l.-saving station* was erected in 1872 under supervision of Revenue Service. Both *L.-saving Service* and *Revenue Cutter Service* were consolidated to form *U.S. Coast Guard,* effective by law January 28, 1915. **Lundin l.-boat,** a metal decked boat of broad flat bottom design with rounded bilges and spoon-shaped ends, water-tight compartments, and thick layer of balsa wood encased in sheet metal along each side. Man-hole covers opening to each compartment afford means of stowing provisions and equipment. The type is termed a *pontoon l.-boat.* **Steward l.-boat,** metal boat of flat-bottom open build, pointed ends, slightly rounded at fore-foot and heel and fitted with air-tanks as in standard *l.-boat.* (*Cf.* **L.-boat**). Its almost vertical sides eliminate much of curving form in ordinary boats, thus reducing number of plates and hence lessens danger of leakage from started seams. Also, the sudden upward turn of bilges allows buoyancy tanks a lower position in boat, thus giving the advantage of a more roomy craft.

LIFT. To raise or hoist, as a sling of cargo. To rise in appearance of elevation; as, *the fog lifts; we steered S.W. until we lifted the land.* To shake lightly, as luff of a sail when too close to wind. Rope or chain extending from a mast to each end of a yard, or end of a boom, as a support or means of *lifting* such spar; also called *topping-lift.* A hoisting device used to raise canal-boats to a higher level, or in lieu of a lock; a *canal-lift.* Chiefly in Great Britain, an elevator. Extent to which anything may be raised; as, *lift of canal lock is 20 feet.* **Heavy l.,** *see* HEAVY. **Heavy l. boom,** *see* **Jumbo-b.** *in* BOOM. **L.-bolt,** *see* BOLT. **L. bridge,** kind of drawbridge, part of which is raised to allow passage of vessels. **L.-jigger,** a light tackle attached to standing end of a topping-lift purchase for increasing its power. **L. lock,** entrance lock in a tidal basin or dock system, or one in which vessels are raised for entering such dock proper; a canal lock.

LIFTING. Act of supporting or raising, as by a topping-lift or other tackle. Act of transferring measurements from a drawing, model, or part of ship, by making a full scale pattern or template of structural part considered, for the purpose of preparing material required. Capable or having the property of raising anything; as, a *lifting-tackle.* **L. craft,** barges or other specially constructed vessels which may be partly submerged by flooding, secured to a wreck, then pumped out, in the operation of raising a sunken or stranded hull; *see* CAISSON *and* CAMEL. **L.-crane,** in older steam-vessels, a crane fixed in the bows for hoisting either bower anchor aboard or lowering it to the hawse-pipe ready for letting go; sometimes for hoisting only to a *billboard* from which it is let go direct. **L. gear,** hoisting tackle, strops, etc., as for handling cargo. **L.-magnet** *see* MAGNET. **L.-sail,** any sail, or spread of sail, in which wind pressure has a *l.* component, as jibs, staysails, the dipping-lug, and lateen sails. A square foresail, when running before a gale has a valuable *l.* effect, or property of increasing buoyancy of ship's forward end, and hence assisting bows "on the back of" a heavy following sea.

LIGAN. Variant of LAGAN, *q.v.*

LIGHT.[1] Emanation from a luminous body or apparatus, as that from the sun or moon, or from a lamp; opposite to darkness. A lamp or lantern: *esp.* one exhibited as a signal; as, a *stern light;* a *flashing light.* To illuminate, or cause to be marked by lights; as, *channel is well lighted. Velocity of l.* is 186,324 statute miles per second, that from the sun occupying 8 minutes 19 seconds in its travel to earth over a mean distance of 92,897,416 statute miles. Hence, the sun shows himself in a position in which he actually was located 8 min. 19 secs. ago; and so the reason for designating, in the *Nautical Almanac,* sun's declination and right ascension as *"apparent."* *Cf.* ABERRATION. **Alternating l.,** as shown from a lighthouse or other aid to navigation, one which changes in color at regular intervals; on U.S. charts, abbrev. *Alt.* = a *fixed l.* thus changing; *Alt. Fl.* = *flashing l.* in which different colored flashes are shown; and in all cases where interruption of steady *l.* occurs with change of color *Alt.* is placed before description of a *l.'s* characteristic phase. **Anchor l.,** a riding *l.,* or one carried by a vessel at anchor; *see* **Rule 11,** REGULATIONS FOR PREVENTING COLLISIONS. **Bengal l.,** a pyrotechnic torch or *l.; esp.* the blue fire made by such; a *blue l., q.v.* **Binnacle l.,** one of two small lamps usually carried in binnacle for illuminating the compass-card where an electric bulb is not used or not available for such lighting. **Blue l.,** pyrotechnic torch or *l.* giving off a blue flame; shown every 15 minutes by a vessel wanting a pilot at night, according to *International Code of Signals.* **Bow l.,** white *l.* carried on the stem of some U.S. inland power-driven vessels not having a foremast. In conformity to *U.S. Inland Rules for Preventing Collisions,* such *l.* is shown when vessel is under way. It must be so constructed as to throw the *l.* over an arc of 20 points of the compass, *viz.,* from right ahead to two points abaft the beam on either side, and must be visible at a distance of at least 5 miles. Also, sometimes, a forward *anchor l.* **Breakdown l's,** also called *Not-under-control l's, see* **Rule 4** *in* REGULATIONS FOR PREVENTING COLLISIONS. **Combined l.,** also called *combination lantern,* one having two or three different colored lenses, for use as required by **Rules 7** (a), (b), (c); **8** (a); and **9** (e) OF REGULATIONS FOR PREVENTING COLLISIONS. **Cargo cluster l.,** *see* CARGO. **Coston l.,** or *Coston signal,* named for its inventor and first used about 1840, a hand torch giving a pyrotechnic flame, or one from burning chemicals, of a certain color or sequence of colors and sometimes throwing stars of different colors. Formerly much used as an identification signal by many shipping companies, each of which adopted a certain sequence of colors, with or without shooting stars, to be shown by their vessels when reporting at signal stations, meeting others at sea, etc. Our present *blue l.* and *red distress* signals of this type may be correctly termed *Coston signals.* **Dead-l.,** *see* DEADLIGHT. **Deck-l.,** *see* DECK. **Double l.,** a pair of *l's* shown at different heights from a lighthouse or each from separate towers at a certain station. **Fixed l.,** as shown by a lighthouse, a continuous *l.* of constant brilliancy. It may be green, red, or white in color, or may be *alternating,* or changing color, as from white to red, at regular intervals. On coastal charts, printed near position of such light, abbrev. *Lt. F.* = *fixed white l.,* and *Lt. Alt.* or *Lt. F. Alt.* = *fixed alternating l.,* or one presenting a change of color in its regular phase. The term also is applied to a stationary ship's lantern show-

ing a regulation *l.,* as a masthead, a side, or stern *l.* **Fixed and flashing l.,** one having a characteristic phase in which *l.* is fixed but interrupted at certain intervals by one or more flashes. Chart abbrev., *F.Fl.,* if a white light; *Alt. F.Fl.,* if any change in color occurs. **Flashing l.,** shown from a light-tower or light-buoy suddenly and regularly appearing and disappearing, duration of appearance being less than that of intervening darkness. Formerly termed *revolving,* after movement of lighthouse lenses which causes a beam to revolve and so produce a flash at all points throughout its sweep. Chart abbreviation, *Lt.Fl.* or, if showing different colored flashes, *Lt.Alt.Fl.* **Group flashing l.,** one showing at regular intervals a group of two or more flashes; *cf.* **Flashing l.** Abbrev. *Lt.Gp.Fl.* or *Lt.Alt.Gp.Fl.* Sometimes a *fixed l.* may show interruption by a group of flashes; *cf.* **Fixed and flashing l.;** abbrev. *F.Gp.Fl.* or *Alt.F.Gp.Fl.* **Group occulting l.,** abbrev. *Gp. Occ.,* or, if any change in color, *Alt.Gp.Occ.,* a steady *l.* with two or more successive eclipses at regular intervals, duration of *l.* being equal to, or greater than that of eclipse; sometimes called *intermittent l. Cf.* **Occulting l. Harbor l.,** one marking a harbor's entrance: *esp.* that of a small or unimportant harbor. **Holmes' l.,** *see* **Water l. Intermittent l.,** *see* **Occulting l. L.-board,** a screening board on inboard side of either of a vessel's *side-lights,* for preventing *l's* from being seen across the bow; sometimes made as a box at its after end to secure lantern set therein and to insure light not being seen more than two points abaft the beam, as also required by law. Also a similar board or screen for a fixed *stern l.* Also, *l.-box; l.-screen.* **L.-boat,** a small boat bearing a *l.* as a warning or marker of presence of a sub-surface danger; a *lightship.* **L.-buoy,** one usually made of steel and showing a *l.* from a short tower thereon. Chiefly for marking channels or dangers, *l.* may be fixed, flashing, or occulting. Its illuminant may be acetylene gas, compressed petroleum gas, or a lamp oil. **L.-keeper,** person charged with care and operation of lighting apparatus of a lighthouse or a lightship. **L. money,** also called *light dues* and *light duty,* charges levied on vessels, usually according to net registered tonnage, and payable at the custom-house for upkeep of lighthouses, lightships, and other navigational aids. **L.-port,** as sometimes found in small vessels, small thick glass set in side of hull for lighting purposes only. **L.-room,** formerly a small room next to powder magazine in a war-vessel for lighting magazine through protective glass windows. Space in a lighthouse tower containing the lamp. **L.-screen,** *see* **L.-board. L. tower,** a lighthouse. **L'ship,** vessel anchored for purpose of exhibiting a light or lights as an aid to navigation at a place where erection of a lighthouse is impracticable. Such vessels are often equipped as radio-beacon stations, usually sound powerful fog signals and, as day-marks, are painted a distinctive color with name in large letters on each side. To-day they are, with few exceptions, capable of self propulsion, thus greatly minimizing the possibility of driving on shore in heavy weather. Also called *light-vessel.* **L.-year,** distance *l.* travels in one year; used in astronomy in expressing distances of stars from the earth, one *l.-year* being greater than 63,000 times the sun's distance. **Leading l's,** see **R.-lights** *in* RANGE. **Masthead l.,** one carried at a masthead: *esp.* the one required by law to be exhibited by a power-driven vessel under way, as prescribed in **Rule 2**(a), REGULATIONS FOR PREVENTING COLLISIONS, *q.v.* **Navigation l's,** those required to be shown by Regulations for Preventing Collisions; also called *regulation lights* and *running lights.* In naming such *l's* according to their arcs of visibility, or points of the compass through which they shall be seen, a *32-point l.,* or *all-round l.,* means one visible all round the horizon; a *20-point l.,* one showing over an unbroken arc of 20 points, or 225°, of the horizon, as the *masthead l.* of a sea-going power-driven vessel; a *12-point l.,* over 12 points of horizon, as a fixed *stern l.;* etc. **Navigation-l. indicator,** an electrical device by which a visible or sounding signal indicates failure of power or faulty performance of ship's regulation *l's.* **Northern L's,** *see* AURORA. **Not-under-control l's,** *see* **Breakdown l's.** **Occulting l.,** as shown by a lighthouse, a steady *l.* suddenly eclipsed at regular intervals, duration of *l.* being always equal to, or greater than, period of darkness; abbrev. *Lt. Occ.,* or, if changing color, *Lt.Alt.Occ.* **Period of a l.,** referred to *l's* exhibited from navigational aids, is time occupied by a flashing or occulting *l.* in completing its characteristic change or changes; thus, in the case of a group flashing *l.,* its period is the elapsed time between beginning of first flash in the group and instant of its recurrence. It is usually included in information given near position of *l.* on coastal charts; thus, *Lt. Gp. Fl.* (3) *ev.* 20 *secs.* means *l.* shows a group of 3 flashes *every 20 seconds.* **Polar l's,** *see* AURORA. **Port-l.,** also termed *air-port, side-light,* and *side-scuttle,* small opening for *l.* or air; *see* **A.-port** *in* AIR. **Position l.,** in former days, the single *l.* shown from the poop when sailing in company with other vessels, but seldom exhibited on moonlight nights. To-day a small *l.* showing astern from an after mast, by which ship next astern may be guided in keeping station, distance from next ahead being determined by angle of elevation of such *l.* above a stern *l.*—now usually found by range-finder. To **raise a l.,** to sail toward a *l.* so as to bring it in sight above the horizon; to observe a *l.* as it appears over the horizon. **Range l.,** *see* RANGE. **Regulation l's,** *see* **Navigation l's.** **Revolving l.,** former term for a *flashing l.,* or one showing a single flash; *cf.* **Flashing l. Riding l.,** *see* **Anchor l. Running l's,** *see* **Navigation l's.** **Search-l.,** large electric lamp which projects a powerful beam of approximately parallel rays and may be turned about to throw *l.* in any di-

rection desired. One or more are included in naval vessels' equipment and they are much used by coastwise and inland passenger vessels, salvage craft, Coast Guard patrol vessels, etc. **Side-l.,** one of the *l's* required to be shown at each side of a power-driven or a sailing-vessel under way, to indicate general direction in which such vessels are heading: viz., *green l.* on starboard side and *red l.* on port side, each to show an unbroken *l.* over an arc of 10 points of the horizon, from right ahead to 2 points abaft the beam on their respective sides. Also see **Port-l. Stern l.,** *see* **Rule 10,** REGULATIONS FOR PREVENTING COLLISIONS. **Top-l.,** one fixed on the truck of a naval vessel's mast for signalling by flashing or for station-keeping by next in line of formation; a lantern formerly used in a masthead top of warships. **Towing l's,** those required to be shown by a vessel towed or towing; *see* **Rules 3** *and* **5,** REGULATIONS FOR PREVENTING COLLISIONS. **Water l.,** a floating self-igniting *l.* attached to a life-buoy or a life-float. Consists of a small copper canister in which are separated quantities of calcium carbide and calcium phosphide. A small opening at one end of canister is uncovered upon pulling *l.* away from its secured position for throwing overboard with buoy or float to which it is attached. This admits water required to generate acetylene gas and ignite the calcium phosphide, which, in turn, ignites the acetylene gas. Flame thus produced serves as a marker for rescuers in locating such buoy or float. Also called *Holmes' l.* **Watch-l.,** a handy lantern, usually of the bull's-eye type, for use of the watch on deck.

LIGHT.² Having little weight; not burdened or laden; as, *ship is proceeding light.* Of comparatively little force, strength, or magnitude; as, *a light wind; light gear; light fog.* **L. air,** *see* BEAUFORT'S SCALE. To **l. along,** to lighten effort of sliding or otherwise moving, as a chain cable, spar, or lengthy object, by lifting, carrying, pushing, etc. **L. breeze,** *see* BEAUFORT'S SCALE. **L. displacement,** weight of water ship displaces in the *l.* condition, which is equal to total weight of vessel and everything on board. Referred to a sailing-vessel, it is weight of ship fully equipped and stored, but with no ballast or cargo on board; a steam-vessel, usually when equipped, stored, water in boilers at working level, no fuel, ballast, or cargo; other power-driven vessels, when equipped, stored, no fuel, ballast, or cargo on board. **L.-handed,** short of a full crew, or not sufficiently manned; said of a vessel. **L. line,** *light load line,* or that to which ship is immersed in normal *l.* condition, or that in which no cargo is on board, but carrying necessary fuel and ballast. **L. sails,** those of lighter texture than the principal working sails; those spread during moderate or *l.* winds (clipper-ships and other *crackers-on* excepted), such as royals, skysails, studding-sails, flying-jib, upper staysails, gaff-topsails, Jamie Greens, spinnaker, etc. To **l. up,** to ease or slacken, as a rope under stress; to assist, as in clearing a moving rope from an encumbrance. **L. water-line,** *see* **L. line.**

LIGHTEN. To lessen the displacement, or total weight, of a vessel, as by discharging ballast or cargo: *esp.* to discharge sufficient weight, including removable fittings or equipment, if necessary, in order to refloat a stranded vessel. An instance of relieving a vessel of her lading in anticipation of stranding is found in the apostle Paul's account of his shipwreck, about A.D. 62 in *Acts 27:38*. **Lightening holes,** those cut in structural parts, such as floor-plates, double-bottom girders, web frames, and brackets, with the view of reducing total weight of building material without sacrifice of strength. Size of such holes in double-bottom tanks, or other spaces otherwise inaccessible, is such that a man may pass through an intercostal or floor-plate for cleaning, inspection, or repair purposes.

LIGHTER. A large boat, scow, or barge, usually non-powered, for conveying cargo to and from vessels in harbor, transporting coal, construction material, garbage, etc. The term generally denotes such craft operating in sheltered waters, although *barges* may also carry cargo on coastal or deep-sea voyages. **Ballast-l.,** one engaged in supplying or receiving ballast from vessels—a familiar craft in sailing-ship days. **Derrick-l.,** a decked barge or scow equipped with a derrick for loading or discharging cargo; *cf.* **Floating-d.** *in* DERRICK. **Mooring-l.,** *see* **A.-hoy** *in* ANCHOR. **Steam l.,** broad-beamed, shallow-draft, steam-powered vessel transporting cargo in sheltered waters; usually fitted with large-area hatchways and a steam-driven crane or derrick. The type, much in use in Britain, now often is propelled by internal combustion engines—chiefly Diesel installation.

LIGHTERAGE. Transportation of goods by lighter; charges for such use of a lighter or lighters, which usually includes work of loading or unloading the craft.

LIGHTERMAN. A person employed on a lighter; a manager of one or more lighters, sometimes called a *master lighterman* who, generally, is considered a *common carrier* in commercial law.

LIGHTHOUSE. A special structure, or building usually in the form of a tower, appropriately situated, as on a headland, rock, on or near a shoal, or entrance to a channel, for exhibiting a light of certain distinguishing characteristics as a guide to mariners at night, and also, in many instances, by means of its particular shape or color, or both, as a navigational *day mark*. This most notable aid to navigation appears in history as early as 660 B.C., in the form of a beacon fire on a Grecian headland, and the great Pharos of Alexandria, some 500 feet in height, is known to have exhibited a huge flame by night and a smoke by day about 260 B.C. The "watch-tower light" appears to have advanced only in number through the Middle Ages, and not until about middle of 17th century was any improvement made in the ancient headland bon-fire. Then came the first illuminant, the candle, hundreds of which were consumed in a night in the new protected tower. One of the earliest principal *lighthouses* was that established about 1680 on the Eddystone Rock, south coast of England, and first *lightship*, or floating *l.*, as we may term it, began duty at the *Nore* in the Thames estuary in 1732. In U.S.A., first lighthouse, a masonry tower at entrance to Boston Harbor—the *Boston Light*—was erected in 1716, although it is recorded that pitch and oakum were burned to give light as a *l.* at that sight from 1673. The light at Sandy Hook, New Jersey, appears second in line, with established date of 1764. World's most powerful lights are found on the French coast. That from the Hillsboro Inlet *l.* tops the list of American lights with its 5,500,000 candlepower, although any reason for this extraordinary brilliancy is far from being as clear as the prevailing weather on that bold stretch of Florida's coast-line. Of approximately 85 principal *l's* maintained by *U.S. Coast Guard* (including 7 in Territory of Hawaii), 21 have lights of one million candlepower or above, least powerful of remainder being 200,000. Illuminant chiefly used in important lights now is electricity, petroleum vapor holding close second place. Secondary lights may burn a compressed acetylene or oil gas with flame mantle, or a special kerosene lamp may be in use, among other systems in various parts of the world. Rays of light are magnified and concentrated in a beam by the *catoptric,* or reflecting system; the *dioptric,* or refracting system; or a combination of lenses and reflectors embodying both, termed the *catadioptric* system. Visibility of principal lights, or what is called their *geographic range,* is calculated for an assumed height of an observer's eye as 15 feet. Hence, from a greater elevation aboard ship, light will be sighted, under normal conditions, at a greater distance. In some cases, a secondary light may have sufficient elevation but not brilliant enough to be seen at a distance corresponding to such height. Its distance of visibility is then known as its *luminous range.* (*Cf.* VISIBILITY.) *Lighthouses* may exhibit a steady, or *fixed,* light or certain characteristic phases of color, flashes, or occultations; *see* LIGHT.[1] The light may be limited to a certain arc or arcs of visibility; as, *e.g.,* a red sector may be visible through 45° between the bearings of 200° and 245° (true), as given on the chart, which means that light bears from an observer somewhere between 200° and 245° (true) while showing red. Through remaining arc of the compass, it may show white, green through another sector, or other division or limit of visibility. Often the *red sector* is used to indicate the bearing of a danger or to give warning of proximity of danger. With a given candlepower, respective brilliancies of green and red lights are ¾ and ½ that of white lights. Maintenance of lighthouses in U.S. is under the Coast Guard, having been transferred to that body from *Bureau of Lighthouses* under the Department of Commerce, July 1, 1939; likewise, all maritime nations have a responsible governmental department charged with establishment and maintenance of *l's* and other navigational aids. **Bow l's,** see BOW.² **L. tender,** originally, a special vessel engaged in transporting crews to and from, delivering supplies to, and performing other duties in connection with, *l's* and lightships. Now, duties of such vessels also include placing, removing, and servicing buoys; towing lightships, where necessary; destruction or marking of wrecks; and generally attending to navigational aid requirements.

LIGHTNING. Flashing of light produced by discharge of electricity from one cloud to another, or from a cloud to earth; variously named from its appearance, as, *ball, chain, fork, streak,* and *grounding;* and from its reflected brightening of the sky in the horizon, as, *heat* or *sheet lightning.* The American-built clipper ship *"Lightning"* established world's record day's run of 436 miles while on her maiden voyage from Boston to Liverpool, March 1, 1855; and, in the southern roaring forties, bound for Melbourne, made 430 miles on March 19, 1857. **L.-conductor,** or *l.-rod,* a copper rod or heavy wire extending from truck of a wooden mast to water-line in a wooden ship, or to a lower steel mast or the hull in a steel vessel, as a means of at least partially grounding a lightning charge and so lessen or prevent damage to mast or hull. Many instances of shattered wooden upper masts and unharmed steel or iron lower masts in a metal hull have left the general impression that lightning-conductors on wooden masts are next to useless, in that voltage capable of destroying the spar would also burn up conductor provided for such an event. However, conductors led to water's edge are commonly fitted in oil-tank vessels as a safeguard—in some countries required by law.

LIGHTS, NORTHERN; SOUTHERN. *See* AURORA.

LIGHTSHIP. *See* L'ship *in* LIGHT.¹

LIGNUM VITÆ. (*L. = wood of life*) *See* HACKIA.

LILY. The traditional *fleur-de-lis* commonly marking the North point of a magnetic compass card. **L.-iron,** *see* IRON.

LIMB. Designated part of extreme edge of apparent disc of sun, moon, or a planet; as, *sun's lower limb; moon's eastern limb.* Graduated arc or other indicating part of an angle-measuring instrument; as, *limb of a sextant.* **Sliding l.,** the *vernier,* or graduated end of a sextant's *index,* or movable, *arm* or

bar, by which precise reading of angle indicated on *l.* proper is completed; *see* VERNIER. **Vertical l.,** as distinguished from a horizontal *l.,* that of an astronomical or surveying instrument used in measuring vertical angles, and, usually, lying in the vertical plane, or very nearly so, through which a telescope or other sighting device is designed to move.

LIMBERS. (Combining form, *limber*) Originally, space along each side of keelson, including the *limber-holes* cut in lower edges of floor-timbers, which allows accumulated bilge-water to flow to the *pump-well.* Now, also such gutterway along outer sides, or margin-plates, of double-bottom tanks, usually termed the *bilges,* designed to drain water to nearest *bilge-suction,* or in larger ships, to a *bilge-well; see* BILGE. **L.-board,** one of the short planks constituting the *limber-strake,* or strakes, in ship's inner skin, or *ceiling,* for providing access to *l's.* **L.-chain,** as formerly used in wooden vessels, a chain rove fore-and-aft through *limber-holes* by which they may be cleared of dirt. **L.-holes,** those cut in lower edges of floor-plates, floor-timbers, margin-plate brackets, intercostals, etc., for drainage purposes; *esp.* such holes of 2 to 3 inches diameter which facilitate flow of water in *l's* or bilges, or in a double-bottom tank (also often containing fuel oil), to a bilge or tank discharge-suction. **L.-kentledge,** permanent ballast, such as pig-iron or pig-lead, placed between vessel's floors in way of *l's.* **L.-plate,** a removable plate for same purpose as a *limber-board, q.v.* **L.-rope,** for same use as a *limber-chain, q.v.* **L.-strake,** in wooden vessels, planking strake in ceiling, next to keelson, and in way of *l's; see* **L.-board.** In older usage, often termed *buttock strake.*

LIME-JUICER. As often termed by American seamen, a British ship or sailor: so called from the fact that for generations British crews were served, according to law, a daily ration of *lime-juice*—a well-known anti-scorbutic, rich in vitamin C—after being 10 days on preserved provisions. Also, *limey* or *limy.*

LIMING. Solution of lime and water swabbed on a wood deck and allowed to dry for bleaching purposes.

LIMMER. Old term for a man-rope at side of a ladder; a temporary life-line.

LINCHPIN. A small pin or forelock through a shaft, axle, bar, etc., for securing a wheel, to prevent sliding, etc.; *see* F'lock *in* FORE.

LINE.¹ (A.S. *line,* cable or hawser; from *lin,* flax; *L. linum,* flax, thread, cable) General term for a length of cordage, particular size of which usually being understood by its use as indicated in a combining word; as, *fishing-l., heaving-l., lead-l., gantline, leechline, life-l., mooring-l., tow-l.* Use of a *line* in fishing is indicated in *long-l.* or *great-l. fishing;* often shortened to *lining.* A series of lengths of pipe constituting a *pipe-line;* as, *steam-l., ballast-l., fire-l.* Ship-operating business or firm, or number of vessels managed by such, engaged in regular transportation service between certain ports; as, *Cunard L., American–South African L.* **Becket l.,** handy short rope in which a tackle-block may be hooked; *see* BECKET. **Boggin l's,** as commonly used in older vessels, one or more chains shackled to rudder at upper extremity of blade *(rudder-horn)* and secured to ship's counter as a means of recovering control of rudder in event of steering-gear carrying away. **Bow-l.,** mooring-rope at bow of ship; a *bow-fast.* **Bowline,** *see* BOWLINE; *also* **D.-line** *in* DIPSEY. **Check l.,** hawser used in taking way off ship or snubbing her toward a wharf or pier alongside which she is moving, rope being made fast on dock and *checked* on ship's bitts as required. A small *l.* attached to a fishing-*l.* that is secured to an outrigger, by which means fishing-*l.* may be hauled into the boat without disturbing outrigger. **Clew-l.,** usually *clewline; see* CLEW. **Concluding l.,** small rope running down middle of a side ladder and secured to each step. **Crane-l.,** in early square-rigged ships, the midship backstay leading from spritsail topmast to about middle of fore stay; also, a *l.* for hauling lee backstays inboard to clear topsail and lower yards when braced sharp up. Now, a rope or ratline stretched across backstays for men to stand on when working aloft; also, in a purchase composed of a runner and tackle, as a lower yard brace, a short *l.* attached to moving block and held to the runner by a cringle or bull's-eye to prevent block from twisting and thus hold it to its work. **Dipsey-l.,** *see* DIPSEY. **Fancy-l.,** chiefly an amateur yachtsman's word designating any small rope not directly concerned with "sailing the boat"; as, a downhaul; *l.* for overhauling a lee boom-topping-lift; a *tripping-l.;* a guy-rope; a *crane-l.;* etc. *See* FANCY-LINE. **Furling-l.,** a rope for securing a sail to a yard in furling; a gasket. **Gant-l.,** a gantline or girtline; *see* GANTLINE. **Grab-l.,** also *grab-rope,* a life-line along sides of a boat or life-raft; also *see* GRAB. **Great l.,** long heavy *fishing-l.* laid out on sea-floor for taking cod, haddock, halibut, etc.; *see* **Great-line f.** *in* FISHING. **Hand-l.,** one used in fishing by *hand-lining; see* HAND. **Heaving l.,** length of small rope, usually 20 fathoms of 15- or 18-thread manila or hemp, used in throwing to or from a vessel for hauling a heavier line, as a hawser. **Hogging-l's,** *see* **H.-lines** *in* HOGGING; also, **C.-mat** *in* COLLISION. **Land-l.,** rope for hauling a seine ashore in taking the catch. **Large-l. fishing,** same as **Great-line f.** *in* FISHING. **Lead-l.,** *see* LEAD.[1] **Leech-l.,** *see* LEECH. **Life-l.,** or lifeline, *see* LIFE. **L.-carrying gun,** *see* **Line-throwing g.** *in* GUN. **L.-knife,** in former whaling, a sharp knife kept handy in bows of the boat for cutting harpoon-line in event of fouling. **Log-l.,** that by which a patent log rotator is towed,

or which is payed out when heaving the old-fashioned *chip-log; see* LOG. **Long-l. fishing,** *see* LONG. **Mooring-l.,** rope used for securing a vessel to a wharf, buoy, dolphin, etc. **To part a l.,** to break a *l.* by excessive tensile stress. **Purse-l.,** rope by which mouth of a purse-seine is closed in taking fish. **Ratline,** 18- or 21-thread, 3-strand, tarred-hemp stuff, such as is used to form ladder-steps across shrouds for climbing aloft; also *ratlin.* **Reef-l.,** rope rove through cringles in reef-band of a square sail for taking in a French reef; *see* **F. reef** *in* FRENCH. **Running l.,** hauling or warping line run out by boat to a buoy, pile, wharf, etc., in warping ship; a guess-warp. **Sea-delivery l.,** pipe-line opening to sea for taking in and discharging water ballast. **Slab-l.,** an auxiliary buntline or spilling-line; *see* SLAB. **Slue-l.,** rope for sluing a spar or other suspended or movable object; a *slew-rope.* **Small-l. fishing,** *see* FISHING. **Smiting l.,** rope for breaking out a light sail sent aloft in stops and ready for setting. **Snake-l.,** short piece of small rope fitted at one end with a lizard or bull's-eye through which some working rope is rove; *esp.* such device suspending a gantline by which a man in a bos'n's chair lowers himself, as in tarring down rigging, painting a mast, etc. **Snub l.,** a warping rope used as a *check-line, q.v.* **To sound a l.,** to **sound all l.,** said of a whale when harpooned and submerging, or *sounding,* to such depth as to take part or all of harpoon-line down with him. **Spilling-l.,** a special *buntline* fitted to a square topsail or a course in heavy weather for effectively spilling the sail for taking in or reefing. It is passed down fore side of sail and up to the yard on after side, thus doing duty much like a *brail;* was once termed *brayle* in 17th-century English ships, the operation of taking in a square sail being called *embrayling.* **Spring l.,** a mooring hawser running in a fore-and-aft direction; *see* SPRING. **Spurling l.,** rope stretched athwartships between the two forward shrouds of lower rigging and having round thimbles or bull's-eyes spliced in it as fair-leaders for running gear secured to or near the mast. Also, formerly, a cord connected with the steering-wheel spindle or barrel by which an index-arrow (helm indicator) was operated to show position of the rudder. **Stern l.,** a mooring-rope or hawser made fast at or near the stern; a *stern-fast.* **To stopper a l.,** or **stop off a l.,** to temporarily secure a *l.* with a stopper: *esp.* a rope under stress, as a hawser, until it may be fastened to bitts or taken to a winch or capstan for heaving. **Stray l.,** first 15 or 20 fathoms run out when heaving the old *chip-log,* or that part of *l.* first allowed to run out clear of eddies in ship's wake before count of *knots* began at *stray-line mark.* It was usually 3-strand, hard-laid, 9-thread, untarred hemp. *See* LOG. **Trawl-l.,** *see* TRAWL. **Tow-l.,** or **towing-l.,** rope used to tow a vessel or other floating object. **Trailing-l.,** small rope securing an oar that is temporarily left hanging in its rowlock and *trailed.* **Tricing-l.,** rope used for lifting up, lashing, or securing any object clear of another. **Tripping-l.,** rope for releasing anything, as a hook; for guiding a lengthy object, as a yard or a suspended sling of cargo; for collapsing a sea-anchor; a squilgee (for releasing a studding-sail when being set); an anchor-trip, (*see* ANCHOR). **Twiddling-l.,** small *l.* or becket for holding steady a hand steering-wheel; a cord attached to gimbals of a steering-compass as a means by which the helmsman kept compass "alive" in smooth water, *i.e.,* aroused to its work by a necessary jerk on such cord. **Warping l.,** a mooring-line: *esp.* one used in heaving ship; a hauling line. **Weighing l.,** a rope, usually of wire, by which an anchor is recovered. It is secured to crown of anchor and supported by a buoy, thus being in readiness for use in event of cable parting. **Whale-l.,** rope to which harpoon is attached in attacking a whale; *see* WHALE. **White l.,** small, untarred, cotton, flax, light hemp, or nylon cord or rope, usually laid in strands and generally sized according to weight per 20 fathoms; used for fishing, lacing or stops on boat-sails, fancy lashings and lanyards, etc. **Working l's,** those ordinarily used in towing, mooring, or warping ship. **Yoke l's,** *see* YOKE.

LINE.[2] Length without breadth; as, *fore-and-aft l.* A series of related positions or objects forming a *line,* either curved or straight; as, *a coast-l.; 10-fathom l.; a l. of bearing.* Mark representing direction, division, limit, outline, or contour; as, in ship drawings, *base l., buttock l., center l., diagonal l., frame l's, water l's;* or on charts, as, *course-l., isogonic l., range-l.* The equator; as, *to cross the l.* A row or extended symmetrical arrangement of a number of objects; as, *l. of docks; l.-of-battle formation.* In plural, appearance of a ship's hull to a seaman's eye; as, *she has fast l's, fine l's, full l's;* or *is fast-lined, fine-l'd, full-l'd,* etc. Of, or pertaining to, a foremost position or duty in naval warfare or ship motive power therein; as, *a line officer; line-of-battle ship; line-duty.* **Agonic l.,** curved *l.* joining all places at which the compass needle points to true, or geographical, north; also, as shown on a chart, called *line of no variation.* **Aclinic l.,** same as *magnetic equator, q.v. in* EQUATOR. **Base l.,** as indicated in body and sheer plans in shipbuilding drawings, straight *l.* representing reference plane or *base* from which all vertical distances in setting of structural parts are measured. In modern practice, it is the fore-and-aft *l.* or plane tangent to lower edges of main body floors at keel and at right angles to vertical longitudinal center plane through hull. **Beam l.,** *see* **Deck l. Buttock l.,** in ship plans, *l.* representing one of a number of vertical planes parallel to vertical longitudinal center plane and shown on body and half-breadth plans as a straight *l.,* its loci of intersection with molded hull surface being indicated by a curved *l.* on sheer plan. Also called *bow and buttock l.* Also *see* BUTTOCK LINES. **Center**

l., in hull drawings, *l.* representing vertical longitudinal center plane. Forming reference plane for all transverse measurements, it is indicated on body and half-breadth plans as a straight *l.* and is in the plane of the paper in sheer plan. **Check l.,** an auxiliary reference *l.* in ship plans. **Coast-l.,** outline or contour *l.* of land where it meets the sea: *esp.* that forming, or included in, a country's national boundary. **Co-tidal l's,** *see* COTIDAL. **Crossing the l.,** ceremony in which "polliwogs" are graduated to "shellbacks" upon first crossing the equator. Under supervision of *"Neptune"* himself, who boards ship at the appropriate moment, an exhaustive initiation ritual must be submitted to by all new arrivals at *Latitude Zero.* The ceremony varies according to Neptune's whims—to a great degree upon quality of reception he has enjoyed—but usually includes a good ducking, a few doses of a mysterious medicinal concoction, unexpected electric shocks, and a goodly smearing of tar. **Deck l.,** in ship drawings, *l.* in body and sheer plans showing sweep or fore-and-aft *l.* of upper edges of deck-beams; also, in connection with freeboard measurement, *see* STATUTORY DECK LINE. **Diagonal l.,** *see* **D. lines** *in* DIAGONAL. **Frame l's,** *see* FRAME. **Fathom l.,** depth *l.,* or curve indicating on chart the contour of sea-floor in passing through all positions having same depth of water; as, *10-fathom l.* A sounding-line. **Harbor l.,** *see* HARBOR. **High water l.,** *see* **H. W. mark** *in* HIGH. **International date l.,** *see* DATE LINE. **Isoclinic l.,** *see* ISOCLINIC. **Isodynamic l.,** *see* ISODYNAMIC. **Isogonic l.,** *see* ISOGONIC. **Keel l.,** midship fore-and-aft *l.* over lower edges of floors; *see* KEEL. **Knuckle l.,** *see* KNUCKLE. **Light l.** or **light water-l.,** *see* LIGHT.[2] **L. abreast,** squadron formation in which ships are abeam or abreast of each other, with stems equally advanced. **L. of apsides,** *see* APSIS. **L. of battle,** that formed by a fleet or squadron upon engaging the enemy. **L.-of-battle ship,** *see* SHIP. **L. of bearing,** formation *l.* in which each ship bears a prescribed direction, either by compass or relative to the fore-and-aft *l.,* from the guide or from a particular ship in the fleet or squadron. A *l.* drawn on a chart to represent a bearing of some point such as a lighthouse, cape, buoy, rock, etc. **L. officer,** chiefly in U.S. navy, officer afloat and actively concerned with naval warfare or motive power of a war-vessel; a commissioned officer. In other navies, *line* usually refers to regular forces. **L. of no variation,** *see* Agonic l. **L. of position,** also called *Sumner l.* and *position l.,* one laid on the chart at right angles to the azimuth of a heavenly body whose altitude is observed at a given instant of time. Ship's place is at some point on this *l. See* SUMNER. **L. of squadrons** or **divisions,** vessels in parallel rows in formation by squadrons or divisions. **L. squall,** sudden gust or increase of wind so named from accompanying *l.* of black clouds; *see* SQUALL. **L. storm,** one occurring at or near the equinoxes; *see* **E. storm**

in EQUINOCTIAL. To **l. up,** to put in alignment, as a marine engine, in order to ensure correct adjustment and smooth working of each part. To fair, or correctly set, newly erected frames in early stage of building a vessel; to make true. Also, to evenly set up shrouds and backstays of a mast so that upper and lower masts will be in correct alignment. **Load l.,** that marking a vessel's depth of immersion when in loaded condition; *see* LOAD. **Low water l.,** that indicating lowest stage or point of water's vertical fall, as limit of receding tide on a beach, a tide-gauge mark, *l.* on side of a pier, piles, etc. **Lubber-l.,** on inner fore side of a compass-bowl, vertical *l.,* usually black in color, representing ship's head. Its coincidence with one of compass-card divisions indicates direction in which ship is heading, or course steered by compass. Sometimes similar *l's* are marked to indicate beam bearings of objects (their directions 90° on either side of ship's heading), as in navigating within sight of land. **Main breadth l.,** that representing greatest breadth of vessel as measured at right angles to the vertical longitudinal center plane. **Margin l.,** *see* MARGIN; *also* **Floodable l.** *in* LENGTH. **Molded l's,** those making up the form of ship's hull without plating or planking; as, *molded base-l., frame l., deck-l.* As datum *l's* for various measurements, whether curved or straight, they are necessarily laid out on *mold-loft* floor of the shipyard. **Pass down the l.,** order to repeat a signal received from next ahead (in formation) to vessel next astern. **Pier-head l.,** that prescribed by a harbor authority limiting distance a pier may extend from shore; contour of a port or harbor as formed by *l.* joining outer ends of wharves or piers therein. **Plimsoll l.,** *see* **Plimsoll m.** *in* MARK. The *load line.* **Plumb-l.,** direction assumed by a plumb-bob when freely suspended and at rest; direction perpendicular to a plane tangent to earth's surface at a given place and terminating in the zenith. Determination of ship's position by altitudes of heavenly bodies fundamentally is dependent upon direction of the *plumb-l.* **Quarter l.,** also termed **bow-and-quarter l.,** formation of ships in *l.* oblique to direction of advance, each vessel keeping her next ahead a required angle on the bow. **Rhumb l.,** also called *loxodromic l.,* one described on a globe or chart at a constant angle oblique to all meridians intersected; a bearing or course *l.,* other than one in direction of one of the four cardinal points, as described on a Mercator chart by a straight *l.* Cf. LOXODROME. **Rib-band-l.,** *see* RIBBAND. **Rising l.,** curved *l.* on sheer plan indicating ends of floors throughout length of vessel. **Sea-l.,** visible horizon at sea, or *l.* formed by apparent meeting of sea and sky. **Sheer l.,** that on sheer plan indicating *l.* of upper deck at ship's side. **Stepping-l.,** *see* BEARDING. **Stream-l.,** *see* STREAM. **Tangent l.,** in ship drawings, a straight *l.* touching a curved surface and lying at right angles to the normal or radius of curvature at point of tangency.

Water-l's, as described on shipbuilding plans or models, *l's* representing several planes parallel to *base l.* and to *water surface* at assumed even keel drafts. They are shown as straight *l's* on body and sheer plans and, also, as outward curves on half-breadth plan, their use being chiefly for calculation of displacement at various drafts, thence certain mathematically determined data concerning stability, trim, subdivision of hull into water-tight compartments, bending stresses, etc. Also, a *water-l.* is a dividing *l.* in the painting or a painted mark on the hull indicating vessel's light and loaded limits of immersion when on an even keel; a free-board mark. **Wave-l.,** curvature outline of bow wave against vessel's side as observed in model-towing trials. For a given draft, speed, hull form and size, in normal water depths *l.* assumes a constant curved line, variations from which, under different conditions, closely follow experimentally determined laws of resistance values, hence providing an important criterion in design of propulsion power and strength required in proposed hulls.

LINER. Strip of plate, tapered or otherwise, filling space between a raised plate and a frame or other structural part, to ensure solid riveting work. A person or vessel engaged in line-fishing at sea. Merchant vessel on a regular run or belonging to a line of vessels; as, a *cargo l.; Cunard l.; express l.; passenger l.; trans-Pacific l.* **Bulkhead l.,** *see* BULKHEAD. **Coast-l.,** vessel employed in a steady coastwise run. **Fire-door l.,** a shield plate fitted on inside of a boiler-furnace door. **Frame-l.,** strip of plate between faying surface of a frame and a raised strake of shell-plating. **Knife-edge l.,** thin wedge-shaped piece of plate inserted as a liner in poorly faying work with aim of improving job's appearance rather than its required solidity. **Tapered l.,** any wedge-shaped piece of plate fitted as a *l.*

LINE-THROWING GUN. *See* GUN.

LING. (M.E. *lenge;* lit., long-fish) A North Atlantic gadoid fish in length about 1¼ times that of the true cod and having dorsal and ventral fringe-like fins extending half-body length to tail. An important food fish, it is often salted and dried. The *white* and *squirrel hakes* of U.S. coast south of Cape Hatteras are also called *ling*, and various similarly shaped fishes are locally so named, as the *buffalo cod* of U.S. Pacific coast, the American *burbot*, and the *sergeant fish.*

LINING. Act of fishing by means of lines; as, *hand-lining; long-lining; see* FISHING. Process of marking lines on a plate or other structural part preparatory to fitting, boring holes, cutting, etc.; *lining out.* Interior covering of wood, or *cleading,* as over steel structural parts in a cabin, lockers, store-rooms, etc. Covering as protection from chafing, as an extra piece or cloth of canvas sewed on a sail. Temporary wood sheathing over an unceiled tank-top to prevent contact of cargo with metal, as in carrying bulk grain. Insulating mixture of thick paint and granulated cork covering exposed steel in crew accommodation, cabins, store-rooms, etc., for minimizing condensation during cold weather. **Anchor-l.,** *see* ANCHOR. **Cross-l.,** fishing by dragging a snooded line between two boats. **Foot-l.,** *see* **F.-band** *in* FOOT. **Head-l.,** chafing-cloth along head of a square sail in way of yard. **Ice-l.,** also *ice doubling,* extra plates or planking on bows as protection against floating ice. **L. cloth,** band, strip, or piece of canvas sewed on a sail as a chafing or a strengthening piece. As chafing material, includes *buntline cloths, mast-l., top-l., head-l.;* and for strengthening, *reef-band, leech-l., middle band, foot-l., reef-tackle cloth, clew, throat, peak,* and *tack pieces.* **L.-piece,** a small lining-cloth; a *liner,* or thin piece of metal used as a filler. **L. up,** *see* **to l. up** *in* LINE.² **Mast-l.,** *see* MAST. **Top-l.,** *see* TOP.

LINK. One of the rings or units composing a chain. Any intermediate rod or piece of machinery receiving and transmitting power from one part of an engine to another. **Club l.,** *see* CLUB. **Drag l.,** *see* DRAG. **L. block,** piece of high grade metal at end of extension of a valve-rod for transferring motion to the latter from the slotted link in eccentric reversing arrangement of a reciprocating engine. **L. motion,** general term for action of contrivance controlling sliding motion of a valve-rod in a reciprocating engine; *esp.* in the *Stephenson l.* system commonly found in marine plants; *see* ECCENTRIC. **L. rooming,** or **worming,** practice of laying chain in spiral depressions of the old hemp anchor cable for 10 to 15 fathoms next the anchor. Its purpose was to provide a more uniform cable surface and so protect fiber from abrasion on gravel or rocky bottom. **Open l.,** ordinary chain *l.* as distinguished from the *studded l., q.v.* **Patent l.,** a chain *l.* composed of two parts and designed for insertion in chain, as in replacing a faulty *l.;* when united according to patent method concerned, *l.* is equal in strength to forged unit replaced; also used to connect one chain to another or to some object as a substitute for a shackle. *Cf.* KENTER SHACKLE. **Reversing l.,** in a reciprocating engine, link at upper ends of eccentric-rods, transverse position of which controls motion of valve-rod and hence that of engine in either direction of revolution. **Slot l.,** reversing link in the form of a slotted bar, as in *Stephenson l.* motion. **Stud l.,** or **studded l.,** in larger chains, *esp.* chain cable, one in which is cast or forged a *stud,* or inside cross-piece, at its mid-length. Purpose of stud is to stiffen sides of *l.* against collapse under heavy tension, which provision, it is claimed, strengthens a *stud-l.* chain one-fifth more than one of *open l's;* also serves to avoid kinking when chain is withdrawn from a confused heap or rough coil, as from the chain-locker. Stud *l's* usually measure in out-

side length six times diameter of metal; outside width, 3.6 times.

LINSTOCK. (Du. *lontstok*)   Used for firing old-time cannon in naval engagements, a staff holding a slow-burning match or torch at one end and attached to a flat iron base. It was placed on deck near a gun or guns ready for instant use. Also, *lintstock.*

LINT. English fishermen's term for meshed area of a fishing-net.

LION-FISH. A scorpænoid food fish of West Indies and tropical Pacific waters, characterized by its thick armor of ctenoid scales, large head, and prominent stiff, spiny, anterior dorsal fin.

LIP. Projecting edge, rim, or margin of a vessel or cavity, as that of a bell, a sheave, or a hawse-pipe; cutting edge at end of an auger; turned up end of cutting face of an adze; thin end of a scarf (in timber). **L.-hook,** a grapnel or large hook secured to *l.* of a whale by which the animal is towed to the ship after killing. **Scupper-l.,** protruding piece of leather or metal beneath outer end of a scupper-pipe for throwing waste water, etc., clear of ship's side.

LIPPER. In former whaling, a slitted oblong piece of blubber used to wipe up, or *lipper off,* the refuse, or *lipperings,* after processing a carcase; also, a kind of scoop-ladle for recovering waste oil from the deck. Slight roughness of sea surface or light spray thrown aboard from a "chop"; a *lippering sea.* To wipe with a *l.,* as the deck. To be immersed to the gunwale, as a heavily loaded boat; as in, *the barge was dangerously lippered.* In older usage, descriptive of drizzling or showery weather; as in, *we were caught in the l.*

LIQUID. Any substance in the flowing state; flowing freely, as water; not solid. **L. cargo,** general term for liquids carried in bulk, including petroleum, whale oil, creosote, turpentine, vegetable oils, molasses, and fresh water. **L. compass,** *see* COMPASS.

LIST.¹ A more or less permanent inclination to one side; as, *ship has a 5° list to port.* To lean or incline, as a ship; as, *brig listed heavily to starboard.* Strictly, *listing* of a vessel is to be distinguished from *careening* and *heeling* in that it is caused by an unequal lateral distribution of weights on board or, when in the light condition, she has a neutral stability condition at or near the upright and seeks a positive stable position at either side of that point; whereas *careening* and *heeling* are produced by forces exterior to the hull. *Cf.* CAREEN and HEEL.

LIST.² A roll, manifest, inventory, register, classified record, or schedule; as, *crew l.; passenger l.; sick l.; l. of cargo; l. of ports.* **Active l.,** a roster of naval officers performing, or prepared to perform, active duty. **Binnacle l.,** *see* BINNACLE. **Black l.,**

record of delinquents in a naval vessel's crew who are assigned extra duties as punishment; list of undesirables dismissed from a line of merchant ships; also, said to be kept by marine insurance interests, record of shipmasters under whose command losses have been incurred, as from fire, stranding, or cargo damage. **Lloyd's L.,** see LLOYD'S. **Navy l.,** periodical roster of commissioned officers; see NAVY. **Prize l.,** see PRIZE. **Retired l.,** *l.* of retired officers, especially those from a government service, showing length of service, date of retirement, rank held at termination of service, etc. **Sick l.,** roster of crew members not reporting for duty because of sickness or wounds; see **B. list** in BINNACLE. **Stemming l.,** chiefly in Great Britain, *l.* of vessels drawn up by harbor authorities assigning vessels·berths in turn for loading coal. When vessels are allowed to berth at will, *free stem* is said to exist.

LITHSMAN. (*Scand. origin*) A sailor in the navy of the early Danish and English kings, circa A.D. 1000.

LITOSILO. Trade name for a decking material consisting largely of magnesite in the form of a cement. It is spread on a steel deck as a substitute for wood planking. Also, *magnesil* and *mirum.*

LITTLE. Small in size or extent; diminutive; of small degree or importance. A small amount in distance, degree, or time. **L. Bear,** constellation *Ursa Minor* in which the North Star, or *Polaris,* is located at end of the "tail." **L. brother,** a minor or secondary hurricane following in wake of a major disturbance. **L. Dipper,** same as *Little Bear,* or *Ursa Minor.* **L. guillemot,** a small short-billed auk, habitat in Arctic and extreme northern Atlantic coasts; also called *rotche.* See GUILLEMOT. **L. gull,** *Larus minutus,* smallest of the true gulls, found on coasts of Europe; also called *black-headed gull; cf.* GULL. **L. piked whale,** or *piked whale,* a small finback; see WHALE. **L. tern,** a very small tern, classified as *Sterna minuta; cf.* TERN. **L. tunny,** a small tunny or tuna fish, habitat in North Atlantic and Mediterranean; *cf.* TUNNY. **Right** (or **left**) **a l.,** order to helmsman to steer a few degrees to *right* (or *left*), as in conning ship through a channel or fairway.

LITTORAL. (L. *litoralis*) Pertaining to, near, or living on, a shore, *esp.* a sea-shore. The shore and the country in its vicinity; a coastal region. **L. currents,** those flowing parallel to, and near, a coastline. **L. drift,** mass of matter, either floating, as seaweed, wreckage, drift-wood, ice, etc., or submerged, as loose rocks, shells, sand, or sunken objects, driven or forced on a sea-shore by action of waves or currents. **L. rights,** certain privileges or rights accompanying ownership of property bounding on navigable tidal waters. Generally, actual limit of a privately owned water-front site is the *high water*

line, outside of which erection of a jetty, pier, or other structure, placing of mooring-buoys, fishing-weirs or nets, dredging, etc., are subject to governmental regulation or statute. The term *"riparian"* usually replaces *"littoral"* where non-tidal waters are concerned. **L. zone,** foreshore, or tract limited by ordinary high and low water marks on a shore. In zoögeography, area in which marine life is most abundant, or that near the shore; *also, see* ZONE.

LIVE. (Pron. *līv*) To float, in the sense of surviving a danger; as in: *we thought no boat could live in such a breaking sea.*

LIVE. (Pron. *līv*) Having life; lively; in an active state; opposed to inert. **L. box,** a crate or perforated box in which fishermen immerse the catch for preserving until landed. **L. iron,** in older whaling, a harpoon in use or ready for use. **L. load,** as distinguished from dead weight or load, a varying or springy load, as that of passengers moving on a gangway, cattle on a deck, etc. **L. oak,** see OAK. **L. steam,** that direct from a boiler; opposed to *exhaust steam,* or that which has already passed through expansion stages in an engine. **L. stock,** general term for cattle, horses, mules, hogs, and sheep, and also their feed, as usually distinguished from *cargo* in shipping usage. *Cf.* CATTLESHIP.

LIVELY. In an active or sprightly manner; briskly; vigorously; as to *slack away lively; heave in l.; the men pull a l. stroke.* A vessel or boat is said to be *l.* when riding the sea in a buoyant manner.

LIVERPOOL. On River Mersey, in northwestern part of England, one of the world's most important commercial ports and for many years once the leader in shipping. Several objects and devices found aboard ship have taken the designation *Liverpool,* probably for no other reason than having been first used or adopted by vessels hailing from that port. **L. head,** see HEAD. **L. hook,** a cargo-hoisting hook having a protective upper lip extending downward toward point of hook, thus narrowing its entrance or mouth. It is usually fitted with a swivel to which the fall is attached. **L. house,** in more recent larger steel sailing-ships, a space amidships formed by a superstructural or bridge deck extending from side to side. This addition to usual hull type contributed greatly to vessel's longitudinal strength and to diminished deck area under water in event of heavy seas boarding when in the loaded condition. It contained the sail-room, carpenter shop, deck store-rooms, galley, and quarters of boatswain, carpenter, donkeyman, cook, and sailmaker. However, in a few vessels the space was used by master and officers, fore end of covering deck being used as a navigating bridge from which ship was steered. **L. pantile,** hard-tack or sea biscuit of the original "Liverpudlian" make; see **H.-tack** in HARD. Also written *pan-tyle* and *pan-tile.* **L.**

splice, one of several methods of splicing an eye in wire rope; said to be the simplest and can not be beaten for a straight pull. **L. virus,** a destructive bacillus used for extermination of rats or mice in a ship. Harmless to other animals, it spreads a disease in the pests which is claimed to be most effective, largely due to cannibal habits of the hungrier ones.

LIZARD. A short piece of rope having a small block, bull's-eye, or thimble spliced in one, or each, of its ends and fixed as a guy or leader for a rope or ropes. Also called *crane-line,* or *traveling lizard,* when used to prevent a purchase block from twisting, as when fixed to block and sliding along a backstay; *cf.* **Crane-l.** *in* LINE.[1] A tail-strop. **L. Head,** or **The Lizard,** headland marking extreme southernmost point of England, of historical interest as first landmark for sailing-ships making the coast, and for many years chief signal station receiving arriving messages from vessels entering English Channel.

LLOYD'S. An association of underwriters in London, England, incorporated by Act of Parliament in 1871. As a corporation, does not undertake insurance business, but is conducted solely by its members on their own account, subject to the society's rules. Briefly, it is a great market for every kind of insurance excepting that of human life, and *Lloyd's Committee* may be said to be the umpire body in conduct of insurance activities. The name is derived from a coffee-house in Tower Street, London, kept by *Mr. Edward Lloyd,* where, about 1688, underwriters began meeting for transacting business, chiefly that in the marine field. In 1692, the coffeehouse removed to Lombard Street, and the society, then established for some 80 years as *Lloyd's,* left its old home in 1774 for premises at the Royal Exchange where it has since remained. In 1696, Mr. Lloyd started his *L.'s News* which became, in 1726, the present *L.'s List,* a publication giving all latest information relating to shipping and movements of vessels of every nationality. Objects of the Society, as defined in the Act of its incorporation, are: (a) carrying on of marine insurance business by society members; (b) protection of members' interests in shipping, cargoes, and freights; (c) collection and publication of information with respect to shipping. **L.'s agents,** persons at many different ports and places all over the world appointed by *Committee of L.'s* as representatives of the corporation. Their duties include the reporting of losses, casualties, movements of ships, and any other information of likely interest to insurers or insured; also, are required to give every assistance to masters, owners, shippers, and consignees in event of casualty or loss. **L.'s calendar,** a publication issued yearly by *Committee of L.'s.* It contains valuable information for all persons connected with shipping, including an astronomical ephemeris, tide tables, recent data on ports, pilotage, quarantine, tonnage dues, drydocking facilities, legislation affecting seamen, lists of *L.'s* agents, signal stations, salvage contractors, surveyors of *L.'s Register of Shipping,* with various professional data of interest to merchant marine officers. **L.'s characters,** various marks in classification information concerning each vessel listed in *Lloyd's Register.* **L.'s length,** *see* **L. by A.B.S. rules** *in* LENGTH. **L.'s numerals,** or numbers, certain numerals chosen to regulate sizes of a vessel's framing and plating for purposes of recording classification in *L.'s Register of British and Foreign Shipping: first, framing,* or *transverse,* numeral is for all transverse members of structure; *second,* longitudinal, or *plating,* numeral, for all longitudinal structural parts, as, keel, stem, sheer-strake, deck-stringers, etc. *First numeral* is obtained by adding depth, halfbreadth, and half-girth of vessel, in feet; *second numeral* is product of first numeral by length of vessel, in feet. **L.'s Register of British and Foreign Shipping,** oldest of the classification societies, founded in 1760, and entirely independent of the underwriters' corporation of same name, although affording great assistance to members of the latter with respect to insurance offering on a particular vessel; *see* CLASSIFICATION. The society annually publishes a list of merchant vessels and yachts, with some minor exceptions, of every foreign flag in addition to all those of British registry. It is commonly called **Lloyd's Register,** and includes particulars of each ship as to age, build, dimensions, power, tonnage, ownership, with classification of hull, machinery, and equipment. **L.'s signal stations,** those under control and maintenance of Society of Lloyd's on coasts of Great Britain and Ireland and at many prominent points in all parts of the world for the purpose of receiving reports from, and transmitting information or messages from shipowners to, passing ships. Reports from vessels are immediately forwarded to *Lloyd's,* London, for publication in their *L.'s List.* The stations are always reliable sources from which particulars regarding navigation toward ports in their vicinity may be obtained, such as mined areas, positions of wrecks, pilot-boats, and like information. **L.'s standard marine policy,** *see* **M.I. policy** *in* INSURANCE, MARINE. Other standard documents instituted by *Lloyd's* largely have set the pattern for wording of policies, bonds, and agreements in the marine world, as, its *Average Bond, Bottomry Bond, Salvage Agreement,* and *Respondentia Bond.*

LOAD. That which is borne or carried; complete burden, lading, or weight of cargo; a ship-load. A local measure of quantity that may be carried in a standard vehicle; as, a *load of wheat, coal,* etc. Total force or weight applied; as, to a safety-valve to limit steam pressure in a boiler; work imposed on an engine, dynamo, etc. To take in cargo; as, to *load a ship.* To charge a gun. **Dead l.,** *see* DEAD.

Live l., as opposed to a dead or inert weight or *l.,* one that is moving, as bridge traffic, or cargo in transit from dock to ship; a mass of springy substance, as natural rubber carried as cargo. **L. displacement,** *see* DISPLACEMENT. **L.-line,** that on the sheer and body plans indicating water-plane to which vessel is immersed in the *l.* condition and on an even keel; actual contact line of water's surface with vessel's side; the *Plimsoll marks,* or those painted on each side of ship at mid-length, indicating maximum depth vessel is allowed to be immersed; *freeboard marks; see* FREEBOARD; **Freeboard c.** *in* CERTIFICATE; **I. load-line certificate** *in* INTERNATIONAL. **L.-line certificate,** = freeboard certificate. **L. water-line,** see first definition of **L.-line. L. water-plane,** plane bounded by ship's *l. water-line,* when floating on even keel.

LOADING. Act of placing cargo in, or transferring it to, a vessel, as from a pier or another vessel. Designating that which pertains to, or is used for, loading; as, *l.-time; l.-gear; l. port.* **L. berth,** place occupied by a vessel in *l.,* as alongside a pier; any space in a port allotted to vessels for operation and duration of *l.* **L. broker,** agent appointed by a shipowner to procure cargoes offering at a particular port; one whose business is to engage or find cargo shipments for a vessel or vessels. Such agents usually work on a commission basis, being remunerated by a percentage of freight collected. **L.-chain,** a decking-chain; *see* CHAIN. **L.-chute,** a large inclined trough or spout through which bulk cargoes such as coal, grain, ore, etc., are loaded from a high pier, elevator, or the like. **L. days,** number of days allowed a vessel for taking in a cargo, as specified in a charter-party; usually synonymous with *lay days; cf.* LAY. **L. on the berth,** said of a vessel available for, or receiving, cargo shipments for a certain port or ports as advertised; as, *ship is l. on the berth for West African ports.* **L. turn** (*or discharging turn*), where two or more vessels await berthing space in which cargo may be handled, *turn* or order allotted each for occupying such berth. **L. warranty,** in marine insurance, stipulation that certain goods or cargoes, or no more than a certain quantity of such, may be carried on vessel concerned. **Overside l.,** operation of taking in cargo from a lighter or other vessel alongside.

LOBBY. An apartment or passage-way below the quarter-deck forward of captain's cabin in old-time ships; *specif.,* such room or apartment occupied by ship's surgeon.

LOBLOLLY. A thick gruel; burgoo; oatmeal porridge. Old sea term for medicine. **L.-boy,** a surgeon's attendant or steward.

LOBSCOUSE. (Formerly, *lob's course,* a sailor's term for a stew) A cracker hash consisting of salt meat, baked or stewed with preserved vegetables and hard-tack. A remaining portion of this dish was often fried and eaten with molasses. Such preparations were commonly found in American and British deep-water sailing-ships in the "good old days," on which account a sailor often was humorously, if not contemptuously, referred to on the waterfront as a *lobscouser.*

LOBSTER. One of the several large crustaceans popularly esteemed as food and found chiefly in cooler waters of North Atlantic coasts, *esp.* where rocky bottom exists; particularly, the *American l.* and *European l.* of genus *Homarus,* and the *Norwegian l.* of genus *Nephrops,* the two first named being found on northeastern American coasts. The more widely distributed *spiny lobsters,* or sea crawfish (or crayfish) differ from the *Homarus* in that the large claws are absent. All, however, are more or less valued for eating. **L.-box** or **l.-car,** a submerged box or crate through which water may circulate, moored near shore as a pen for keeping captured *l's* alive until removed for marketing. **L.-claw,** kind of screw-jack having a claw which was secured to the upper dead-eye in setting up lower shrouds in older ships. It simplified operation of setting up a stay or shroud in that the lanyard then was merely hauled taut with a watch-tackle and re-secured. **L.-pot,** or **l.-trap,** a crate-like trap, variously shaped according to local custom, for capturing *l's.* All are made with one or more funnel-shaped entrances of netting, into which lobster crawls upon scenting the bait (usually a piece of fish or meat); he drops to bottom after passing through netting and then is unable to regain mouth of netting. Traps usually are anchored by flat stones placed inside them, are set 4 or 5 fathoms apart, in rows often of 10 to 15, and appropriately buoyed. Also called *l.-basket* and *creel,* the term *l.-pot* is in common use in Britain, while *l.-trap* is favored in America.

LOBTAIL. To beat surface of water with lobes or flukes of its tail, as a whale at play or when attacked.

LOCAL. Occupying, characteristic of, or relating to, a particular place. **L. apparent time,** that indicated on a sun-dial; hour angle of the true sun at a given place. It is *local apparent noon* when center of apparent sun crosses an observer's meridian, or at instant in which sun bears exactly true north or south according to observer's position in latitude. **L. attraction,** deflection of the compass needle from the magnetic meridian due to local disturbance such as that caused by magnetite iron ore deposits in the vicinity, steel-framed buildings, tanks, etc., or a sunken iron vessel. Also, deflection of plumb-line due to a mountain or other irregularity in earth's crust. **L. horizon,** the visible horizon; *see* HORIZON. **L. hour angle,** *see* HOUR. **L. transit** of a heavenly body is its passage over an observer's meridian. Also called *meridian passage* and *culmination,* is designated *upper* or *lower* according to that branch of meridian considered. Body is visible at *lower transit* only when observer's latitude is greater than its polar distance (90° — declination), in which case body is said to be *circumpolar*. Local transit of the mean sun is termed *l. mean noon* (see MEAN); that of vernal equinoctial point is *l. sidereal noon*.

LOCH. (*Gaelic*) In Scotland, a lake or nearly land-locked bay or arm of the sea. The equivalent *lough* is used in Ireland.

LOCK. Enclosed space in a canal, river, or at entrance to a tidal dock, for raising or lowering vessels in passing from one water level to another. Locks are built with heavy gates usually termed *upper* and *lower*, respectively, according to position relative to water levels at which they are opened. A vessel is raised by entering lock and having lower gate closed astern; sluices then are opened to allow entrance of water from high level area; upon water in lock reaching higher level, upper gate is opened and vessel proceeds. Conversely, vessel is lowered by running water out of lock until it reaches lower level. Size of locks usually is governed by that of largest vessel expected to pass through them; *e.g.*, those of the *Panama Canal* are 110 feet in width and can accommodate ships 1000 feet in length. To move a vessel through a lock, or system of locks, as in passing through a canal, etc. To secure a nut, pin, or other mechanical part, as by a locking-nut, fore-lock, key-ring, etc. **Foot-l.**, see FOOT. **Guard-l.**, one situated at entrance to a canal or dock basin opening to a tidal area, for purpose of moving vessels in or out at any stage of tide; also, *tide l.* **Lift-l.**, see LIFT. **L'ing bar**, flat iron bar secured by a *l.*, as across a store-room door or a hatch; *also see* BAR. **L.-bay**, wide area of a canal in vicinity of a *l.* entrance; the body of water in a *l.* itself. **L. chamber**, enclosed area between gates of a *l.*; the *lock* proper. **L.-bolt**, any bolt used to secure some fitting or machinery part. **L.-hook**, as often used on yachts, a small hook having a tongue or spring across its mouth to prevent unhooking, such as for bending sails to stays, securing sheets to light jibs, etc.; also, *snap-hook.* **L.-nut**, see J.-nut *in* JAM. **L'ing pintle**, in a vessel's rudder, one fitted to prevent rudder from lifting; *see* PINTLE. **Locked scarf**, any of several forms of scarfed joints in which timbers are joined and stiffened to withstand a longitudinal, and sometimes a sidewise, shearing stress, independently of the connecting through-bolts. This is effected by driving one or more cogs or keys across the faying parts, by a lengthwise tenon setting, or by both. **L. signal**, a flag or shape hoisted at a *l.* entrance indicating to approaching or waiting vessels that *l.* is, or may be, opened, or is closed, to traffic. **L.-strake**, in wooden vessels, one of the strakes in the waterways "locked" or set down into the deck-beams. It is usually next one to inside line of bulwark stanchions; *cf.* WATERWAYS. **L.-string**, also *fir-ing-string*, a cord connected to *l.* of a cannon for firing. To **l. through** (or **in, down, out, up**), to move, or give passage to, a vessel through a *l.* or series of *l's.* **L. weir**, a dam for retaining water at upper end of a *l.* or system of *l's.* **Rudder-l.**, see RUDDER. **Tide-l.**, see **Guard-l. Water-l.**, a *l.* weir.

LOCKAGE. Toll charged for passing through a lock or series of locks, as in a canal. Process of moving a vessel through a lock. Amount of elevation or descent, or both, covered in a system of locks, as in a canal.

LOCKER. A chest, cupboard, or small compartment for stowing gear, supplies, tools, etc.; as, *boatswain's l., chain l., mess l., sail-l.* **Davy Jones's l.**, see DAVY JONES. **Snack l.**, cupboard or small compartment in a fishing-vessel where night lunches are kept available for crew.

LOCUST-WOOD. Timber of the American *acacia*, or *black locust*, tree; a hard, durable, straight-grained, yellowish wood used for cleats, dowels, and treenails; weighs about 48 lbs. per ft.[3]

LODE. (A.S. *lād*, way or course) A reach of water, as a straight stretch in a canal, river, or stream. A loadstone, or lodestone; hence, anything that leads or attracts. Guidance; pilotage. **Lodeman**, or **lodesman**, Old English term for a pilot. **L.-ship**, a pilot-boat. **L'star**, a guiding star; the pole star (*Polaris*); star that leads; *cf.* CYNOSURE. **L'stone**, preferably *loadstone*, a natural magnet or piece of magnetite having the property of seeking direction of the magnetic meridian when freely suspended; *cf.* COMPASS.

LODGING-KNEE. See KNEE.

LOFT. An upper floor in a warehouse or shipyard building, especially one having a clear floor, or without partitions, as a *rigging loft* or a *sail loft* where, respectively, standing and running rigging are prepared for ships and sailmaking is carried on. **L. paper**, as used in making templates for flat plating or other straight work from the mold-loft drawings of a vessel, a heavy paper made to withstand undue shrinkage, wrinkling, expansion, etc., under severe atmospheric changes. **L. rigger**, one engaged in a *rigging l.* at work of cutting, splicing, and otherwise preparing rigging or gear for vessels. **Mold l.**, see MOLD.

LOFTSMAN. In shipbuilding, person who lays off ship's structural lines, prepares templates therefrom, supplies necessary data for preparing frames, girders, etc.; *see* DEVELOPER.

LOFTY. A sailing-ship is described as *lofty* when rigged with unusually high masts. The clipper ships were of *lofty* rig, with increase of yard-arm spread effected by studding-sails, while in vessels of more recent build, the tendency was to provide greater width of ordinary sail, or longer yards, with corresponding reduction in *loftiness*. *Cf.* JUBILEE RIG.

LOG.[1] (Of Scand. origin; Sw. *logg*, a ship's log, or a floating log; prob. from early log of wood used for same purpose as the later *log-chip*) Any of several different devices for measuring a vessel's speed through the water, as the old-fashioned *chip-l.;* for measuring and registering distance traveled through the water, as the *taffrail l.;* or for both indicating speed and registering distance run, as the *pitometer l.* In referring to vessel's speed, she is said to *l.* a certain number of miles per hour, as indicated by the *l.;* as, *she is logging 12 knots. Cf.* KNOT.[2] **Chip l.,** named from the chip, or *log-chip*, which provides resistance at trailing end of *l.-line* in the operation of *heaving the l.,* earliest known means of accurately measuring speed through the water, consists of the *l.-chip* (also commonly termed the *log*), or quadrant of thin wood 5 or 6 inches in radius weighted on its curved side; *l.-line,* usually of hard-laid hemp ¼-inch in diameter and about 150 fathoms in length; a special easy-turning *l.-line reel;* and a 28-second *time-glass* (later often superseded by a watch with a seconds hand). In *heaving the l.,* the *l.-chip* remaining upright in water carries line with it, and when stray-line (*see* **Stray l.** *in* LINE) of about 15 fathoms has passed astern, as indicated by *stray-line mark,* or piece of colored rag, officer cries "Turn!" to an assistant holding the time-glass. When sand has run out in the glass, its holder cries "Stop!" and officer instantly grabs line and notes length run out, or *knots,* as shown by marks on the line, the sudden stoppage, incidentally, jerking out one of the bridle legs connecting line to *l.*-chip, so that line is easily hauled in. Thus length of line run out in 28 seconds is the basis for calculating that which would run out in 3600 seconds, or one hour, and hence speed of ship. This is taken care of by dividing the line into consecutive divisions (beginning at stray-line mark) of 47 feet 3 inches, or that length which would run out in 28 seconds at a speed of one *knot* (1 mile per hour), each being marked by a number of *knots,* as on a piece of small cord spliced in the line. If, for example, at the word "Stop!" officer catches and holds the running line at its *9-knot* mark, that is vessel's speed (*see* KNOT). Half and quarter knots were marked, and sometimes also *tenths* by a chosen system of knotted pieces of cord or colored rags. Also called *hand l.,* its accuracy compares favorably with any *patent l.* up to speeds of 10 to 12 knots. At greater speeds, required length of line becomes cumbersome and recourse is then had to use of a 14-second glass, number of knots run out being doubled. **Dutchman's l.,** an old method of determining speed on the basis of time occupied by a floating object in passing a measured part of ship's length. Thus, a piece of wood is thrown overboard from the forecastle; as it strikes water abreast of mark on deck, thrower shouts "Watch!"; interval in seconds is then noted between that instant and instant of object passing abreast of an after deck mark; then, according to an easily remembered rule which gives a close approximation to the speed (*knots*), distance multiplied by 3 and divided by 5 times the seconds completes the operation. Also based on same principle, another method used in slow vessels is time taken for floating object to pass 47 feet 3 inches, or length of the *l.*-line knot; if time occupied is 28 seconds, speed is 1 knot; if 14 seconds, 2 knots; if 7 seconds, 4 knots; etc. **Electric l.,** general term for a *patent l.* (*q.v.*) which, by electrical connection with its taffrail mechanism, registers distance run in ship's chart-room or wheel-house. **Ground l.,** as used in determining speed *over the ground* in shallow water, the old-fashioned *l.* in which a *hand-lead* replaces the *l.-chip.* Lead remaining on sea-bottom during operation of *heaving the l.,* vessel's true speed is found, or that with reference to the ground and thus independent of the water, which may or may not be in motion as a current. Also, relative direction in which line trends or leads indicates course vessel is making *over the ground,* thus apprising navigator of local current effect on course steered. **Hand l.,** *see* **Chip l. Harpoon l.,** *see* HARPOON. **L. glass,** as formerly used in American and British vessels, an hour-glass running out in 28 seconds for convenient timing in operation of heaving the *chip l.* The 28-second glass appears to have been of long traditional standing in the British navy and corresponded to 47 feet 3 inches length of knot division in the *l.*-line. Many merchant vessels, however, adopted the 30-second glass, or its convenient equivalent on the second-hand dial of a watch, in which case the corresponding knot length was 50 feet 8 inches. At a speed of 15 knots, working length of *l.*-line with a 28-second glass required to be at least 135 fathoms, and in order to consistently reduce such length to handy limits, a 14-second glass was brought into action when ship was dancing along at greater than 10 knots, the number of knot-divisions on line then being doubled. *Cf.* **Chip l. L. governor,** a small fly-wheel, or pair of metal spheres joined by a bar, fitted as a governor for giving constant rotatory motion to a *taffrail l.*-line. It is secured in the line just abaft the "clock," or register. To **heave the l.,** to determine vessel's speed by means of the *chip l.* In old navy days this was done as matter of routine every hour, usually by a group of four midshipmen. *Cf.* **Chip l. L. indicator,** the registering mechanism of a *taffrail l.;* the clock or register. **L. rotator,** towed at end of a *taffrail l.*-line or at after end of a *harpoon l.* for producing rotary motion in the line and thence to the registering mechanism, or direct to last-named *l.* It is a small metal cylinder from which 4 blades or fins slantingly project; also called a *fly.* **L.-ship,** variant of *l.-chip; see* **Chip l. Patent l.,** general term for any patented device or mechanism which determines vessel's speed; *esp.,* as distinguished from the old-fashioned *chip l.,* such devices as depend upon rotation of a towed *fly* (*cf.* **L. rotator**) for continuously registering, by a system of gears contained in the "clock" fixed at after end of ship, the distance ship travels through the water. **Pitometer l.,** used in larger ships of U.S. navy, a speed-indicating and distance-registering instrument operated by pressure of passing water in a *Pitot tube* which extends vertically below ship's bottom. Its mechanism, which includes electrically controlled repeater-indicators in various parts of ship, is extremely sensitive and the instrument must be calibrated for all speeds before brought into practical use. Other *l's* based on similar working principles have from time to time been used with more or less success, among which the British *Chernikeef l.* perhaps is best known. As with the *Pitometer,* a vertical tube extends below ship's bottom, but contains a small impeller which sets registering mechanism in action, instead of direct hydraulic pressure arranged to control an electrically operated mechanical integrator. **Shaft l.,** *see* SHAFT. **Spring l.,** speed-registering device in which resistance of a towed *chip* is indicated as vessel's velocity in knots on a *spring balance;* now little used, was reasonably accurate in smooth water for speeds up to 7 or 8 knots. **Taffrail l.,** any *patent l.* the registering mechanism of which is set on the taffrail or at any suitable point at vessel's stern, or from a projecting spar with view of keeping rotator to one side of vessel's wake currents; a *patent l.*

LOG.[2] (Originally, the *log* record, or distance made in a day's run according to speed by *log*) The log-book; ship's journal or day by day record of events, observations, courses steered, weather experienced, etc. From a simple journal covering in a single book the principal shipboard happenings for many years in the old sailing days, development of ships' records to meet growing demands of shipping management to-day has reached, for a single voyage, the proportions of a sizable library. We now have the *deck scrap,* or *rough, l.; chief officer's,* or *smooth, l.; abstract of deck l.; official l.; engine rough l.; chief engineer's,* or *smooth, l.;* and *abstract of engine l.;* all covering the same period and which, incidentally, form but a fraction of a merchant vessel's paper-work volume turned out in, say, a 4-week foreign voyage. **Deck l.,** journal kept by officer of the watch, or his junior, where two officers are in each watch. It is a full first-hand record of day to day happenings with which the deck, or navigating, department is concerned. Also termed *scrap,* or *rough, l.,* shows the following: courses steered, speed, compass error, sea and weather conditions, barometer and thermometer readings, noon position, distance made good as day's run, current experienced, correction in ship's time due to change of longitude, times of passing and distances off lighthouses or other shore points, names of lookout

men and helmsmen with their hours of **duty,** times of opening and closing side-doors or ports in cargo spaces, soundings of tanks and wells or bilges, times of engine movements if any, ships signalled, and particulars of any unusual events, such as a death, collision, stranding, fire, cargo damage, etc. The *deck l.* is principal document used in evidence at a court of inquiry, litigation concerning insurance losses, collision, etc. **Engine l.,** *scrap* or *rough engine l.,* in effect, is of similar import to the *deck l.* in that it contains continuous record, written by engineer of the watch, of performance and operation of propulsion plant and auxiliary machinery. Entries therein vary according to type of engines. **L.-fish,** the rudder-fish, *see* RUDDER. **L.-slate,** usually of the folding type, a slate used in some engine-rooms instead of the *rough l.-book.* The data entered is transferred each day to *chief engineer's l.* **Official l.,** record for which master of a merchant vessel is responsible, showing certain entries therein required by law. It may be included with the *deck l.,* but, generally, for convenience of masters, is published in special book form by government concerned and supplied by official superintending engagement of crew a beginning of voyage. U.S. law (*R.S. 4290*) requires every vessel of 75 tons burden and upward making a foreign voyage or one between Atlantic and Pacific ports to keep an *official l.-book,* which book must be delivered to the shipping commissioner, together with ship's articles of agreement, upon completion of voyage and not less than 48 hours before paying off crew (unless special arrangement is made for lesser period). Entries required cover every offense committed by crew members and legal conviction or punishment inflicted, or for which it is intended to prosecute; statement of conduct, ability, and character of each crew member; every case of illness or injury with medical treatment given therefor; every case of birth, death, or marriage taking place on board; name of every seaman who ceases to be a member of the crew, with time, place, manner, and cause thereof; wages due any crew member who dies during voyage, showing lawful deductions therefrom; sale of effects of a crew member who dies, with detailed statement of sums received therefor; every case of collision and circumstances attending same; times of closing and opening water-tight doors or openings below the bulkhead deck; draft and freeboard before departure from every loading port; times of all lifeboat, fire, and bulkhead-door drills and all inspections of life-saving equipment. Each entry must be signed by the master and the mate or other member of crew, and must be made as soon as possible after each event required to be "logged." (*R.S. 4291* or *U.S.C. 46: section 202*) (It is noteworthy that *R.S. 4290* (*U.S.C. 201*) omits any reference to entries regarding *fire* or *stranding* amongst those required) **Radio l.,** required by regulations of *International Conference for Safety at Sea,* as applying to merchant shipping, is kept by the radio operator on watch. He must enter in the *l.* his name, times at which he goes on and off watch, and all incidents occurring during his hours of duty which may appear to be of importance to safety of life at sea. Also required to be "logged" are details of maintenance, including record of charging of batteries and tests of emergency transmitter and power; details of tests of automatic alarm which receives distress signals in vessels having a single operator; and record of tests and maintenance of radio equipment in motor lifeboats where carried. Also called *wireless l.,* it is often officially termed *radio-telegraph l.* to distinguish it from *radiotelephone l.,* in which latter book, also, must be recorded times of battery-charging or renewal and all maintenance details in lifeboats, where such equipment is installed in conformity with International Conference regulations.

LOGARITHM. (Gr. *logos,* word, account, ratio; *arithmos,* number) Abbrev. *log,* usually without the period. In simplifying calculations in navigation and nautical astronomy, *esp.* in trigonometrical work involving products of several values, the *common* or *Briggs* (after *Henry Briggs, English mathematician, 1561–1630,* their first proposer) *logarithm* is used generally by navigators. Since a *l.* is the index (or exponent) of that power of a fixed number (termed the *base*) which equals a given number, simple addition and subtraction of *l's* of numbers involved performs multiplication and division, respectively. Thus, the *base* being 10 in the *Briggs* system, if $100 = 10^2$, *log* of 100 is 2; 1000 being 10^3, *log* of 1000 is 3; and product of 100 and 1000 being $10^{2+3} = 100,000$, sum of *logs,* or exponents of 10, is 5; then *log* of product is also 5, written *log 100,000 = 5.00000* in a table of *l's* given to five decimal places. Conversely, division is effected by subtraction of exponents or *logs,* while roots of numbers are extracted by dividing *log* of number by the root index, resulting *log* being that of root required; or a number may be raised to any power by multiplying *log* of number by power index, product being *log* of result. The *natural* and *Napierian l's,* used by astronomers and in other advanced scientific work, are rarely applied to navigational problems. **Logarithmic trigonometrical functions,** as included in navigational tables, *l's* of sines, cosines, tangents, cotangents, secants, and cosecants of all angles; also, those of haversines of angles usually tabulated apart from the former functions.

LOG CANOE. A dugout or double-ended boat made from a large log, or part of a log with sides built up by one or more strakes of planking. A craft of this designation, but composed of several parts of logs hollowed and shaped as required, then bolted together, formerly was commonly found in oyster dredging and fishing industry on the shores of Chesapeake Bay.

LOGGED. Said of a crew member when note of an offense committed by him is entered in ship's *official log,* with statement of any admonition, fine or forfeiture imposed, or punishment inflicted; as, *Jones was logged for insubordination; logged a day's pay for failure to work;* etc. Also said of any occurrence or phenomenon noted in any log; as, *the after draft was logged* as 24 feet; *we logged the gale as N.W., force 10.*

LOGGER. A former Dutch ketch-rigged decked vessel used in the North Sea fisheries. About 80 feet in length by 16 feet beam, she was the vessel from which the English borrowed the term *lugger* for a smaller craft with *lug sails,* also engaged in fisheries.

LOGGERHEAD A bollard or snubbing-post in fore end of a whaling-boat for holding on or snubbing the line after harpooning a whale; a billethead; a kevel. A very large marine turtle, commonly attaining 800 lbs. weight, found in Pacific and Indian Oceans and warmer western parts of the Atlantic. It is used for food, but not valued as highly as the *green turtle,* its smaller and non-carnivorous cousin.

LOG-RAFT. *See* RAFT.

LOLLEY NEEDLE. Named for its original maker, a roping-needle of short spur type used in sailmaking.

LOLLY. A term used chiefly on northeast U.S. and Canadian coasts for slushy or granulated ice formed by grinding together of floating ice, as in a floe.

LONG. Having relatively great lineal extension; opposed to *short;* as, a *l. poop; l. booms.* Occupying considerable duration; not brief; as, a *l. voyage;* a *l.-foretold gale.* Covering a great length or sweep in space; as, a *l. tack;* a *l. scope* or *drift* (of line or cable); a *l. stretch of breakers.* **As l. as the main t'bowline,** descriptive of a lengthy appearance—often that of one's facial expression when relating a serious experience, or, humorously, when a tall seayarn is being spun. So called from the longest stretch of single line in the old single-topsail days, the *main topsail bowline,* shortened to *main t'bowline.* **At a l. stay,** *see* ASTAY. **L.- and short-armed floors,** *see* **Long and short f's** *in* FLOOR. **L.-armed door,** *see* **Power-d.** *in* DOOR. **L. blast,** as required in *Article 18* of the *U.S. Inland Rules for Prevention of Collisions,* is generally understood to mean one of 4 or 5 seconds' duration given on the steam whistle or siren, although its length is not specified therein. Many seamen hold that the prescribed *prolonged blast* of 4 to 6 seconds required by **Rule 15,** REGULATIONS FOR PREVENTION OF COLLISIONS AT

SEA, is equivalent to the *long blast; see* SIGNALS. **L'boat,** old term for many years applied in merchant vessels to larger of two boats carried, or largest in the ship. Depending upon size of vessel, such boat averaged 30 feet in length, was of rugged construction and full form with square stern. Usually capable of carrying a load of 10 tons, she was used to transport cargo, ballast, guns, stores, etc., and was equipped with one or two lug sails and oars. **L. bridge,** a bridge house or space of considerable length, or of such length (usually greater than 15% of vessel's length) that sheer strake and upper deck stringer of main hull are raised to the bridge deck—a valuable advantage in longitudinal strength; *see* **B. house** *in* BRIDGE. **L. fake,** *see* **French f.** *in* FAKE. **L.-haul seine,** kind of seine which is hauled to shore over a considerable distance when the catch is enclosed or trapped between the net and shore. **L.-jawed,** said of a rope having, through undue or improper use, its lay softened, *i.e.,* rope is untwisted to the extent of greatly decreasing the slope of its strands. **L. lay,** seaman's share of the catch in sealing, whaling, etc.; *see opening notes on* LAY. **L.-legged,** said of a vessel fitted for, or capable of, undertaking a lengthy cruise; having a comparatively great cruising radius. Also, sometimes by merchant seamen, used as descriptive of a deep-draft vessel. **L.-lining,** fishing with *long lines* or trawl-lines, a small edition of *great-lining; see* **Great line f.** *in* FISHING. **L'nose,** a garfish; *see* GAR. **L. scope,** as applied to chain cable, length greater than 5 times depth of water in which vessel is anchored, such as would be payed out in a strong current or wind. **L. sea,** descriptive of a *l.* regular-running sea, having unusually great distance between crests. **L. sheet,** also called *deck sheet,* that leading from a topmast-studding-sail clew to the deck. **L. ship,** *see* SHIP. **L. splice,** *see* SPLICE. **L.-staff,** the shank, or longer part, of the old cross-staff; the staff which was directed toward the horizon and which was graduated to show altitude of body observed, according to position of vertical arm, or *cross-staff; see* **C.-staff** *in* CROSS. **L. stay,** *see* ASTAY. **L. stud link,** *see* STUD. **L. tackle,** the old *top burton,* or tackle chiefly used to hoist or lower a topmast. It was hooked to the lowermast cap and consisted of a two-sheave fiddle-block (*see* BLOCK) and a running single block. **L.-tackle block,** a fiddle-block, such as was used in the *l. tackle.* **L. timber,** one of the longest and least curved cant frame timbers in the fore body, so named because requiring no scarfing. **L. togs,** old navy expression for civilian clothes; as, "Jack soon was at home in his best *long togs.*" **L. tom,** a *l.* pivot or swivel gun mounted on deck; *esp.,* in early days of breech-loading ordnance, one supplied to a merchant ship for protection against pirates in the Far East. **L. ton,** weight of 2240 pounds, the unit employed in calculating a vessel's displacement or burden; *see* TON. **L. top-gallant-mast,** also termed *pole top-gallant-mast,* single spar rigged next above a topmast to serve as a top-gallant-mast, royal-mast, and sometimes a skysail-pole, in one.

LONGER. In old wooden ships on long voyages, the line of water-casks stowed fore-and-aft against the keelson. A deep narrow cask suitable for such stowage. In order to age and mellow certain good wines, it was customary for East Indiamen to take in a *"longer of Madeira"* on the passage outward for discharge in England perhaps 18 months later.

LONGITUDE. (L. *longitudo,* length) Arc of the equator intercepted by the *Prime Meridian,* or that of the meridian circle at the *Greenwich Observatory* near London, England, and meridian of a place; or, angle at the pole formed by meridians of Greenwich and place in question. Geographers and navigators now use Greenwich meridian as *zero,* or *prime meridian,* from which *longitude* is reckoned eastward and westward as an arc of the equator up to 180°, or halfway mark around the globe, *longitude* 180° E. being synonymous with 180° W. *L.* may be expressed both in arc and time; as that of New York, N.Y., 73° 57' 30'' W. or + 4h. 55m. 50s.; that of Wellington, N.Z., 174° 46' E. or −11h. 39m. 04s., time equivalent of arc being at rate of 15° per hour, which is the equatorial velocity of earth's rotation, or, very nearly, 900 nautical miles per hour. Hence, *l.* is determined by comparison of a given instant of local time (mean, apparent, lunar, or sidereal) as found by observation at place considered, with that of Greenwich time of same denomination, as shown by, or obtained from, a chronometer or accurate timepiece indicating Greenwich mean or sidereal time. **Celestial l.,** angular distance measured *eastward* from the vernal equinox (strictly, from *mean equinox* at beginning of year, as so used by astronomers) on the ecliptic to the ecliptic meridian passing through the celestial body or point in question. It is expressed in arc measure up to 360°. **Circle of l.,** *see* CIRCLE. **Difference of l.,** usually abbreviated *D.Long.,* arc of equator intercepted by, or angle at pole between, respective meridians of two places. As used in navigation, numerical difference between *l.* of ship's place and that of a point or place steered for; or that between position left and position arrived at; named East or West according to bearing of destination or progress of vessel; thus *D.Long.* to be covered may be 10° 50' W. and ship may have made a *D.Long.* of 5° 10' W. in past day's run. Value of *D.Long.,* expressed as distance measured on the equator, is the equivalent in nautical miles of number of minutes contained in such difference, very nearly, considering earth as a perfect sphere; while, owing to convergence of meridians toward the poles, *D.Long.* decreases as cosine of the latitude, taken as a distance along a given parallel, or thus converted into *departure* (see DEPARTURE). Accordingly, in determining a course and distance, as in plane sailing, or a distance in parallel sailing, *D.Long.* is converted to *departure* by multiplying number of minutes therein by cosine of latitude in which ship is navigating. Conversely, to find *D. Long.* made in sailing, departure, or distance in nautical miles vessel has made to eastward or westward, is multiplied by secant of latitude, or mean of latitudes traversed. **Heliocentric l.,** *see* HELIO-CENTRIC. **L. by account,** or **L. by dead reckoning,** that *l.* arrived at according to easting or westing made in sailing one or more courses from a previous position that was determined by observation of altitudes of one or more heavenly bodies or by terrestrial bearings. **L. by chronometer,** that determined by comparison of time as found by celestial altitudes at place in question and corresponding time as indicated, with any necessary correction, on a chronometer which keeps Greenwich mean or sidereal time; *see opening remarks on* LONGITUDE. **L. by lunar distances,** former method of finding Greenwich time by measuring distance between the moon and a heavenly body in or near her orbit, and thence the *l.* of place; *see* LUNAR. **L. by eclipses of Jupiter's satellites,** another method of obtaining Greenwich Mean Time for purpose of comparison with local time and thence the *l.* Times of eclipses and occultations of these bodies are given to nearest tenth of a minute in *Nautical Almanac,* so that such phenomena may be observed to about 6 seconds limit of accuracy at best. Present almanac information covers phenomena referred to for 4 of the planet's 7 moons or satellites. **L. by transit** of one of several selected low declination stars, with aid of the telegraph, has been the means of establishing many geographical positions with relation to the Greenwich meridian in various parts of the world. By pre-arranged signal, exact instant of star's transit over local meridian is noted on the chronograph at parent observatory. This time is compared with register of chronograph at same star's transit at latter station and difference is that in longitudes of two stations, expressed, of course, as a time interval. Observatories of importance have established their precise *l's* with reference to Greenwich by similar procedure and, also, in a large trigonometrical survey, or triangulation, various points in the field are checked by this means with a principal station or observatory.

LONGITUDINAL. Of, or pertaining to, longitude, length, or the lengthwise dimension; laid or running fore-and-aft or lengthwise, as distinguished from athwartship or transverse; fore-and-aft. One of the structural members or girders laid parallel with keel in a ship's bottom; a side-keelson. **Bottom l's,** the fore-and-aft strength members in a ship's bottom. **Deck l's,** in a longitudinally framed vessel, those constituting stiffening and support

framing between the widely-spaced web beams. They displace the closely-spaced deck-beams in the transverse framing system. **L. bulkhead,** *see* BULKHEAD. **L. center of buoyancy,** geometrical center of displaced body of water or immersed part of ship's hull, as located in the fore-and-aft vertical center plane. **L. center of gravity,** point at which total weight of ship is considered as concentrated, or mean position of all weights, as located in the fore-and-aft vertical center plane, ship lying upright. **L. framing,** *see remarks in* FRAME. **L. metacenter; L. metacentric height,** *see* METACENTER. **L. numeral,** *see* **L.'s numerals** *in* LLOYD'S. **L. strength** of a vessel is the quality by which she endures hogging or sagging stresses without breaking or yielding, as when partially supported in the fore-and-aft line by a heavy wave or waves. In shipbuilding, minimum sizes of structural parts providing longitudinal strength are prescribed according to value of *l. numeral.* **L. system,** general arrangement of fore-and-aft strength members in a vessel. As distinguished from the transverse system of framing, that in which framing in general is laid lengthwise; *see remarks in* FRAME.

LONGSHOREMAN. Chiefly in North American ports, a laborer about the docks in a sea-port; *esp.* one who works at discharging and loading vessels and often called a *stevedore,* although latter term properly is applied to a contractor or superintendent of such activities. In Great Britain, a *dock laborer.* Cf. STEVEDORING.

LOOF. Variant of *luff.* Old term for fullest and broadest part of ship's bows.

LOOK. Appearance, suggesting a certain quality; as, *the yacht has a speedy look; sky holds a threatening look.* To exhibit zeal, alertness, or alacrity in carrying out a job of work, as when taking in, or setting, sail; as, *Look* lively! *Look* slippy! (slang). To **l. out for squalls,** to maintain an alert attitude toward probable weather changes, as sudden shifts or increase of wind; hence, to watch for some expected change from the normal as the climax of an event: "If the skipper sees her shaking and the breeze is in the making; then O Johnny, O Johnny, —then *look out for squalls!*" To **l. up,** to steer more direct for point of one's destination, as by a favorable change of wind; as, *she is now looking up for the cape.*

LOOKOUT. A seaman stationed on the forecastle or in the crow's nest for purpose of maintaining a watchful eye for any lights, land, or floating objects that may heave in sight, and reporting such to officer of the watch. It is customary, if not compulsory, for vessels above a certain tonnage to place a *lookout man* on duty between hours of sunset and sunrise, at any time approaching land or in vicinity of fishing-vessels, and during low visibility conditions.

Station at which lookout is kept is also called *the lookout.*

LOOM. Appearance of exaggerated elevation or extent, as bold land or a vessel seen in darkness or fog. Reflection in the sky or clouds from a light below the horizon; dark-colored or shadowy appearance of sky over distant land; lightening of the horizon, or *ice-glow,* indicating presence of an ice-field. Round part of an oar between blade and handgrip. Older form of *loon,* a sea-bird; an auk, guillemot, or puffin. To come dimly into view, having a magnified appearance, as through haze, fog, or darkness. In older usage, the raised outline or abnormally elevated shadowy appearance just above the horizon in direction of a shore-line was termed the *looming of the land.* **Loom-gale,** archaic term for a moderate gale.

LOON. (Formerly *loom,* of Scand. origin) A fish-eating diving bird of genus *Gavia,* distributed over colder latitudes of the Northern Hemisphere; also called *diver.* The *common loon (Gavia immer)* averages 30 inches in length, has a short tail, dark white-spotted back and wings with white underparts, and is not unlike the common goose in appearance. It is remarkable for its lengthy plaintive cry during light winds and calm weather. Two other smaller species, the *black-throated l.* and *red-throated l.,* are classified as *G. arctica* and *G. stellata,* respectively.

LOOP. A fake of a coil of small line. A bight in a rope, cord, twine, etc.: *esp.* one in which another piece of cordage is rove or a hook may be fastened; a small eye. Any circular-formed part of a line, pipe, rod, etc. **Expansion l.,** a U-shaped bend or a short spiral coil in a lengthy pipe-line for taking up contraction or expansion in the line. **Tidal l.,** *see* TIDAL.

LOOSE. To free, let go, or slacken off; as, to *loose a sail* for setting. Not fastened or secured; slack or only lightly made fast; as such condition of a door, a sail hanging in the buntlines, or a stay. **Cast l.,** to set adrift, as a boat; to unlash, set free, or clear encumbrances from, as a gun, cask, spar, etc. **L. boat,** *see* BOAT. **L. ceiling,** *see* CEILING. **L. fish,** in whaling, as opposed to a *fast fish,* animal which has not been successfully attacked, and so *loose* in the sense of being free of a harpoon and its line. **L.-footed,** said of a fore-and-aft sail without a boom, or one having a boom but its clew only secured to such spar. **L. ice,** a more or less scattered floe, easily passed through by a vessel. **L. the anchor!,** order used in old-time ships, meaning to *weigh anchor;* hence, to hurriedly shove off, turn-to with a will, etc. **L. water,** that having a free surface in a vessel, as contents of a partly filled tank or water in a hold.

LOP. Condition of sea surface characterized by short choppy or lumpy waves, or such as result from a cross sea. It is caused by a breeze against a current, meeting of currents, or change of wind direction after regular sea has been set up by a former breeze. *Loppy* = choppy.

LORAN. Coined from words *Long Range Aid to Navigation,* term for a radio system developed during World War II for determining ship's position at sea. From a master transmitting station, simultaneous signals are sent out via two "slave" stations situated three to four hundred miles apart. A special receiving instrument on board automatically indicates the small time interval between arrivals of signal from each station. With this time difference, inspection is made of a special chart on which hyperbolic curves or lines of position are drawn. Ship's position will be at intersection of two such lines corresponding to time differences observed in signals arriving from two pairs of stations. The method is one of surprising accuracy at distances up to about 600 miles, and, especially at night, gives satisfactory results at about 1200 miles, from the stations. A similar method developed in England is known as the *Gee* system, and the British also have brought into practical use the *Decca* system in which the *phase difference* is used instead of the *time* difference as in *Loran.* Capt. Gordon C. Steele, V.C., R.N.R., in his *"Electrical Knowledge for the Merchant Navy Officer,"* describes the *Decca* system thus: "An alternative method of determining the difference in time transit of waves from two transmitting stations to a single receiving station is based upon the use of continuous, or modulated-continuous, waves and the use of a known radio or audible frequency to make the time determination. A system based on these principles has already been developed in this country, and is known as *Decca,* using continuous waves. By measuring the phase difference between the waves received from the two transmitting stations maintained in exact synchronism, the difference in time of transmission, and so of the path difference between the receiving and the two transmitting stations can be measured to a very high order of accuracy."

LORCHA. (*Port.*) A vessel of southern China and Gulf of Siam, about 200 tons burden, carrying two or three masts, and characterized by an European-built hull, while rigged like a Chinese junk.

LORD DERWENTWATER'S LIGHTS. See AURORA.

LORD HIGH ADMIRAL. Former British naval officer, appointed by special desire of the crown as supreme administrator of Admiralty affairs; *cf.* ADMIRAL.

LOSE; LOST. To lag or fail to maintain a certain velocity; as, *ship loses her way quickly; chronometer lost 10 seconds.* To stray from, or fail to find; as, *vessel lost the light in thick haze.* To suffer loss of; as, *we lost the mainsail in a gale.* To wreck, sink, or deprive of possession of, said of a vessel; as, *he will lose the ship by such tactics; the brig was lost to the pirates.* To perish or founder; as, *all hands were lost; vessel was lost in mid-Atlantic.* **To lose the land,** to leave it in the distance below the horizon. To **lose the number of one's mess,** colloquial navy phrase, meaning to die, be killed, or drowned.

LOSS.   State or fact of being lost or destroyed; as, *loss* of 5 men; vessel is a total *loss.* That which is lost; as, *loss* of cargo by leakage; ship is written off as a *loss.* In marine insurance usage, a partial *l.* or expense covered is termed *average,* and may be *particular,* as a *l.* to vessel's hull only, or *general,* as one borne by ship, cargo and freight; *see* AVERAGE. A *total l.* may be *actual, constructive,* or *presumed.* It is *actual* where destruction or damage beyond required repair cancels the existence of matter insured; *constructive,* where cost of repairs to vessel is estimated to exceed her value to her owners; and *presumed,* where a vessel is overdue and posted as missing. A *salvage l.* is one in which ship or cargo or both have been retrieved or rescued from a situation of peril and salvage costs paid accordingly. Property salved is termed *the salvage,* and in the situation where such is whole or part of a cargo sold because of further loss necessarily incurred in forwarding to original destination, *salvage l.* is the insured value of goods less proceeds of such sale. **L.-book,** Lloyd's record of all vessels lost, showing identity of master, owners, cargo carried, etc.

LOST OR NOT LOST.   Phrase appearing in marine insurance policies to cover the fact that any loss insured against is not known to either insured or insurer at time of drawing up the policy, thereby entitling insured to claim for such subsequently discovered loss.

LOUGH.   Irish equivalent of the Scottish *loch; see* LOCH.

LOUGRE.   A cousin of the English coasting and fishing *lugger,* the French *chasse-marée,* varying from 50 to 80 feet in length, now, like the former, fast disappearing. *Cf.* CHASSE-MARÉE.

LOUVER.   Small opening in a wood bulkhead, fitted with a sliding cover, for ingress or discharge of cooled air, as found in fruit-carrying vessels; the sliding cover itself, which may be adjusted to form any desired area of opening. **L'ed battens,** *see* BATTEN.

LOW.   Having little altitude or elevation; as, a *l. star;* a *l. coast;* a *l. swell.* Comparatively small in degree, number, or quality; as, *l. pressure; l. latitudes; l. declination; l. sound* of a fog-whistle. **Dead l.,** said of state of tide at its last stage of ebb or its greatest fall. **L. and aloft,** from water-line to truck; as in, *she is shipshape and trim a-low and aloft* (or, *low and aloft*). **L. area; L. pressure area,** *see* AREA.

L.-area storm, a cyclone, or strong winds revolving about, and more or less spirally toward, a surface area of *l.* barometric pressure; *cf.* CYCLONE. **L. bridge!,** *see* BRIDGE. **L. glass,** barometer reading markedly below normal for the locality; usually indicative of approaching rain or, with increasing wind, a cyclonic gale. **L. latitudes,** the tropics generally; those within the belt bounded by about the parallels of 25°, north and south. **L. tide,** waters of a tidal region or locality at its lowest point; *l. water.* **L. water,** *l. tide;* lowest point to which tide normally falls; *l.* stage of water in a river, lake, etc. **L.-water indicator,** *see* **Water-i.** *in* INDICATOR. **L.-water line,** that marking edge of water on a shore, pier, etc., when water has receded to its lowest point; also, *l.-water mark.* **L.-water stand,** duration of no appreciable change in depth of water at its lowest stage; also, duration of no tidal current at or about time of *l.* water. **L. water ordinary springs, Indian springs,** etc., *see* **T. plane of reference** *in* TIDAL. **Secondary l.,** a minor cyclonic or *l.* pressure area following close on the heels of a cyclone and usually found near the southeast quadrant of the larger storm in northern hemisphere and the northeast quadrant in southern hemisphere; often called *little brother* of main disturbance.

LOWER.   To let down or allow to descend by its own weight; as, to *l.* a boat, a sail, or a sling of cargo. To cant or depress; as, to *l.* muzzle of a gun, or a yard-arm. To place at a lesser height; as, to *l.* a lead-block; to *l.* vessel's center of gravity. Indicating secondary importance or less elevated position; as, the *l. deck;* a *l. topsail.* **Four l's,** *see* FOUR. **L. berth,** *l.* of two bunks built one above the other in a cabin, or other living compartment. **L. boom,** formerly, the spar for spreading foot of a lower studding-sail; now a boat-boom, or guess-warp boom; *see* **Boat-b.** *in* BOOM. **L. deck,** *see* DECK. **L. funnel,** below-deck part of smokestack or funnel to which are connected the several boiler uptakes. **L. hold,** in a merchant vessel, lowest cargo compartment, or that next to ship's bottom. **L. keel,** additional timber laid along bottom of keel, as sometimes found in wooden vessels. Old craft have been given more strength by this addition, the *shoe,* or false keel, being fastened below all as before. **L. limb,** lowermost point of the apparent disk of a heavenly body, as the sun, moon, or a planet; thus distinguished from the *upper limb,* or uppermost point of disk, either of which may be brought in contact with visible horizon when measuring altitude of body with a sextant. **L.-mast,** usually written *lowermast,* as distinguished from the topmast, top-gallant mast, or royal-mast, lowest spar making up a square-rigger's complete mast; in any compound mast, the part stepped in the hull. **L. platform,** term used in larger naval vessels for *l.* of two partial decks below lowest continuous deck. **L. rigging,** arrangement of shrouds running from *l.-*masthead to each side of ship. Also called *l. shrouds,* their chief purpose is to give lateral support to the *lowermast,* while, with exception of the forward one (called a *swifter* in square-rigged vessels), assisting more or less, according to degree of aftward lead or slope, in stiffening mast against forward-pulling stresses. *See* SHROUD. To l. **the boom on,** *see* BOOM. To l. **the land,** to increase distance from land so that it appears less elevated or disappears below horizon, wholly or in part. **L. thwart,** one fitted near bottom of a life-boat to seat persons as low as possible for stability reasons when boat is loaded to or near capacity. **L. topsail,** in square rig, sail set on second yard from the deck, thus first named in 1853 upon advent of *double topsails* taking place of the old *single topsail.* In effect it is a permanently close-reefed single topsail and so a heavy weather sail of strongest canvas in the ship. *See* SAIL. **L. transit,** meridian passage, or culmination, of a heavenly body below the pole. Such body is visible at that point only when its polar distance, or angular distance from elevated pole, is less than observer's latitude. **L. yards,** heaviest and lowermost yards; generally, those on which the courses are set and the lower topsail yards.

LOXODOGRAPH. Instrument for registering course or courses steered; a course-recorder. *See* **C.-recorder** *in* COURSE.

LOXODROME. (Gr. *loxos,* oblique; *dromos,* running) A loxodromic curve or line drawn on the globe shown as a spiral, intersecting in its course all meridians at a constant oblique angle and, theoretically, never reaching the pole while closely approaching it. Also called a *rhumb line,* it is a ship's true course as represented by a straight line on a Mercator chart, other than one in direction of the cardinal points. **Loxodromic projection,** map or chart on which a straight line represents part of a *loxodrome,* or is a rhumb line; a Mercator, or Mercator's, chart.

L. R. Abbreviation for *Lloyd's Register of British and Foreign Shipping.* It is marked in 3-inch letters above the horizontal line running through load line disk (*Plimsoll mark*) on each side of a vessel assigned such marks by Lloyd's.

L S; L T; L F; L T F; L W; L W A. Letters designating the various freeboard, or load-line, marks assigned a powered vessel which carries or may carry a *timber deck cargo,* or any vessel carrying a complete timber cargo. The *L* presumably indicating *lumber* and chosen rather than *T,* the letter indicating *Tropical Zone,* above letters read, in order given: Summer, Tropical, Fresh (water), Tropical Fresh, Winter, Winter North Atlantic. *See* FREEBOARD; **L.-line** *in* LOAD; PLIMSOLL MARK.

L.S.T. Usual abbreviation for *local sidereal time; see* TIME.

LUBBER. An awkward or unskilled seaman. **Landlubber,** *see* LAND. **L.'s hole** or **l.-hole,** in larger square-rigged ships, hole in a top-platform next to lower-masthead through which a man may crawl instead of climbing over outer edge of top when going aloft. **L.-line,** *see* LINE[2]; also called *l.'s mark* and *l.'s point.* **Lubberly,** like a lubber; unhandy; slovenly; as, *lubberly steering; jib was bent in lubberly fashion.* **L.'s knot,** a granny, or a *lubber's* attempt at making a square knot.

LUCIDA. (*L.*) Brightest star in a particular group; as, *Polaris* is the *lucida* of *Ursa Minor.*

LUCKY BAG. In a naval vessel, receptacle for enlisted men's personal property items mislaid or out of place. Such articles are auctioned off if owners are not found; otherwise, the men concerned are reprimanded and sometimes punished.

LUFF. Forward edge of a fore-and-aft sail: the fore leech. Old term for weather side of ship; also, broader and fuller part of ship's bows; in both cases once spelled *loof.* Former colloquial name in British navy for a lieutenant, from the older *luftenand: esp.* applied to the *first lieutenant* or ship's executive officer. (Present prevailing pronunciation with the British is "*leftenant*"). To sail closer to, or turn vessel's head toward, the wind; as in the order "*Luff!*" to a helmsman. To **choke the l.,** *see* CHOKE. **Double l.,** *see* **D. luff-tackle** *in* DOUBLE. To **hold a good l.,** to steadily maintain a course as close as possible to the wind; *cf.* **K. the luff** *in* KEEP. To **let her l.,** *see* LET. **L. cringle,** in a fore-and-aft quadrilateral sail, cringle spliced in upper forward corner for lashing or otherwise securing sail to gaff, mast, or yard, as in respective cases of gaff, sprit, and lug sails; also called *throat cringle* in a gaff sail. **L. earing,** short piece of handy rope for securing fore end of reef-band by its cringle when reefing a fore-and-aft sail. **L.-hook,** the common steel hook on a tackle-block. Its point is always sharply curved outward as means for holding a *mousing,* or turns of small stuff or wire across mouth of hook, from slipping off or being knocked out of place. **L. on l.,** a *l.-tackle* made fast to hauling part of another; sometimes called *double rigging-l.* when used to set up lanyards of heavier standing rigging, jib-stays, etc. **L.-rope,** forward leech-rope, or that along fore edge of a fore-and-aft sail. As in all leech-roping on such sails, it is always sewed to *port side* of sail. **L.-tackle,** a handy purchase consisting of a double and a single block; often same tackle as a *handy billy* or a *watch-tackle.* Depending on whether moving block is the double one or the single, neglecting friction, power of this purchase is either 4 or 3 times pull on hauling part, respectively. **Pilot's l.,** to turn into the wind, as in clearing an object when under sail, and then filling away on same tack, or what is termed *making a half-board;* to throw boat into the wind to reduce her way, as in approaching a vessel's side or berth alongside a wharf, etc.; *see* To **make a half-b.** *in* BOARD. **Rigging l.,** tackle used in setting up rigging; usually is made up of two double blocks. To **spring her l.,** former phrase meaning to steer more toward the wind when sailing just free of close-hauled, in the sense of correcting a leewardly course.

LUG. Small piece of angle-iron used in connecting various parts in steel shipbuilding. as in butting a plate against another; a bosom-piece; a lug-piece; *cf.* CLIP. A *pad-eye,* or small plate or casting having a projecting eye in which to hook a tackle-block, to pass a lashing, etc. A lug sail. A projecting part of a sail or awning when roughly furled or stowed. **L.-a-leaf,** southern England name for the *brill,* a flatfish of the turbot family. **L. foresail,** a gaff sail having no boom, such as once commonly found in English vessels of ketch or yawl rig and in the old Thames *wherry.* **L.-pad,** a pad-eye; *see above.* **L. rig,** or **lug-sail rig,** that of a *lugger,* or boat rigged with l. sails. Providing a large and efficient spread of canvas, this simple rig long has been a favorite in fishing and pleasure craft on the coasts of Great Britain and western France, formerly also extending to small trading coasters of 2- and 3-mast types. The sail is quadrilateral in shape, its head stretched on a yard sloping upward from forward, while it may or may not be fitted with a boom. Generally, its halyard and sliding-ring securing it to mast are located about one-third length of yard from forward. The several variations of this rig are *French,* or *balance l., standing l., dipping l.,* and *split l.* Balance l. has portion of its area extending forward of mast; often has a boom; sail may remain on one side of mast, or may be dipped to lee side, when tacking. *Standing l.,* small portion of head of sail extends forward of mast and tapers downward to foot of mast where its tack is fast. Yard remains on same side of mast, as opposed to requirement of *dipping* to lee side when coming about in the case of a *dipping l.* Boats thus rigged often carry a jib, as in sloop rig. Luff of sail is kept taut by leverage of sail's heavier after part on yard—an advantage when sailing close-hauled. *Dipping l.,* best driving sail of all lugs, has about ¼ sail area forward of mast and tack stretched well forward. When coming about, sail is partly lowered and reset on lee side; hence the name *dipping l.* Probably there is no more suitable single sail rig for a ship's life-boat, with its ample spread and minimum of gear. *Split l.,* as with a *dipping l.,* one-fourth to one-third of yard lies forward of mast, but sail is split vertically in way of mast, so that, in effect, forward part functions as a jib. In larger boats, luff of after part of sail is secured to mast by rings or hoops. An excellent spread in a beam wind, it was once a favorite in the British navy and, more recently with north country fishermen, in spite of its drawback of being

harnessed with rather much gear. Both *standing* and *split l's* may have a boom; *dipping l.* is always loose-footed. To **l. sail,** to carry an excessive spread of canvas; as, "she was *lugging* royals with lee scuppers awash"; "we tried to set the topsail, but the critter wouldn't *lug* it."

LUGGER. Lug-rigged boat or vessel carrying 2 or 3 masts, often with one or more jibs. Now practically displaced by motor and steam craft, they were extensively used in fisheries off the British coasts and for both fishing and trading on the channel coast of France. Several varieties of the craft were easily distinguished by their choice of rig; as, *Falmouth l., Deal l., Normandy lougre,* etc. Some of the English boats differed little from a yawl or ketch of gaff-sail type, as we now know them, particularly those formerly engaged in drift-net fishing and trawling, in that they carried a large loose-footed standing lug mainsail and small mizzen of same cut, with running bowsprit and one or more jibs. Others carried the simple rig of two large dipping lugs, forward one usually greater in area than the other. The 3-masted *lougre* was of definite French origin and often was employed as a cargo carrier, while English lug-sailed craft rarely extended beyond the fishing, pleasure, or ship-tender classes. **L. topsail,** as formerly sometimes carried by a *lugger,* a fore-and-aft topsail set above a standing lug-sail.

LUGSAIL. Better *lug-sail; see* LUG.

LULL. (Ger. *lullen,* to sing to sleep)   Temporary subsidence in force of wind, violence of a surf, heavily running sea, firing of guns as in battle, etc. In older whaling, a canvas tube or chute through which blubber was carried from hatchway to tubs in a hold; a *lull-bag.*

LUMBER. Chiefly in America, popular term for *timber, esp.* that sawn, hewn, or split for use as beams, joists, planking, laths, barrel-staves, and such, having comparatively small dimensions. A *cargo of lumber* is, in North American ports, the equivalent of the English term *timber cargo.* Timber, however, rather than *lumber,* was the usual word for wood of any shape or size in American shipbuilding yards; likewise, trees in their natural state, cut into logs, or roughly squared. **L.-iron,** *see* IRON. **L.-port,** a harbor or sheltered area in which shipping of l. is predominating business. A port in a vessel's bows or stern through which l. may be discharged or loaded; more especially, such opening for facilitating transfer of long heavy timber.

LUMINARY. (L. *luminare,* light or lamp)   An object or body giving forth light: *esp.* the sun, moon, and brighter planets; an illustrious or notable person: "that gold-trimmed *luminary,* Admiral of the Blue, Ben Bowline."

LUMINOUS. Emitting or reflecting light; shining; phosphorescent. **L. buoy,** a light-buoy; *see* LIGHT. **L. range,** *see* RANGE.

LUMPER. An unskilled laborer employed at handling cargo about the docks or aboard ship; a dock laborer; one engaged at heavier manual work in a shipyard.

LUMP SUM CHARTER. *See* CHARTER. **L. freight,** *see* FREIGHT.

LUNAR. (L. *luna,* the moon) Of, pertaining to, or measured by, the moon; as, *l. phases; l. eclipse; l. day.* Affected by, or attributed to effect of, the moon; as, *l. tides.* Lunate; resembling the moon: *esp.* in its crescent phase. Short for *l. observation.* **L. cycle,** also called a *Metonic cycle,* after *Meton,* an Athenian astronomer of 5th century B.C., the period of 19 years elapsing between successive occurrences of full and new moon on same days of the year. **L. day,** expressed in solar time, interval between two successive transits of the moon, or that averaging nearly 24h. 50m. **L. distance,** angular distance between moon and sun, star, or a planet, used at sea before advent of reliable time-keepers, or chronometers, for determination of Greenwich mean time in connection with finding ship's longitude. An *observed l. distance* was that measured by sextant between moon's illuminated limb and nearer limb of sun or center of a planet or star. This value was converted to the *true* or *geocentric distance* for comparison with that given in *Nautical Almanac* as occurring at a certain Greenwich mean time, the mathematical process involved being known as "clearing the distance," or what amounted to the sum total of corrections for semidiameter, parallax in altitude, and refraction affecting both bodies applied to the measured distance. *Geocentric l. distances* formerly were given in *Nautical Almanac* for every third hour of mean time at Greenwich in respective cases of the sun, Venus, Mars, Jupiter, and Saturn, and, also, certain selected stars, when favorably situated for *l.* observations. These distances were those of the respective centers of such bodies lying in or near moon's orbit, as viewed from center of the earth, and hence unaffected by refraction or parallax in altitude. The navigator's *observed l. distance,* duly "cleared," was that corresponding to a certain Greenwich mean time, which, if other than an even 3-hour almanac distance, was arrived at by making appropriate allowance according to rate of change in nearest tabulated distance to time in question. **L. hour,** one-twenty-fourth part of the variable lunar day which averages 24h. 50m. of solar time, or about 62 minutes. **L. inequality,** a very small fluctuation of the magnetic needle, not considered in practical navigation, due to attraction of the moon. **L. method,** that of finding ship's longitude by comparison of local time with time at Greenwich (or other standard meridian) as determined by *l. distance.* **L. observation** usually was performed by 3 persons, one measuring the *l.* distance, the others, altitudes of moon and selected body, respectively. Often another assistant noted time or times by chronometer or other time-piece. The observation, however, might be taken by one person only, in which case changes in altitudes due to elapsed intervals between measuring distance and observing each altitude must be allowed for. In any case, *exact local time* of observing the distance, as determined by either or both altitudes, necessarily is required in order to find ship's longitude, by comparison with *Greenwich time,* or that corresponding to, and determined by, measurement of the distance. Incidentally, since rate of change in moon's angular distance from another body in or near its orbit is about ½ minute of arc in 1 minute of time, resulting longitude from this observation is affected to the tune of at least 30 times an error in observed distance. Considering the strong probability of a 2' discrepancy under sea conditions, it would be surprising to find the longitude resulting from a single observation within a degree of the truth. However, the mean of several east and west *l's,* or those measured in both directions from moon, in the old days produced fairly satisfactory longitudes in charting positions of places during, for example, the exploratory voyages of *Capt. Cook,* who met with an untimely end at the hands of Hawaiian natives in 1779. **L. star,** one of a number of stars lying in or near the moon's apparent orbit whose geocentric angular distances from center of that body formerly were tabulated in *Nautical Almanac* for use of navigators in determining longitude; *cf. L. distance.* **L. tables,** those used by navigators in "clearing the distance," or correcting an observed *l. distance* for refraction, parallax, and semi-diameter. **L. tide,** that component of the tide-wave due to moon's attraction, as distinguished from the *solar tide,* or that attributed to attraction of sun. **L. year,** a period of 12 *l.* months, or intervals between successive times of new moon, or 354 days, 8 hours, 48½ minutes of mean solar time.

LUNARIAN. A persistent advocate of determination of longitude by lunar distance observations; one of the old "die-hards" who spurned use of chronometers only as the means of providing navigators with approximate Greenwich time.

LUNATION. A lunar month, or time elapsing between two successive new moons; a synodic month; period averaging 29 days, 12 hours, 44 minutes, 3 seconds, through which moon completes a full cycle of phases, viz., *new moon, first quarter, full moon, last quarter.*

LUNDIN LIFE-BOAT. *See* LIFE.

LUNITIDAL INTERVAL. *See* ESTABLISHMENT OF PORT.

LURCH. Heavy, sudden roll toward either side, as in a high irregular sea. To suddenly heel or roll to one side from any cause. **Lee l.; weather l.;** a *l.* toward side thus specified.

LURE. Something for attracting fish to a hook; as, a colored rag, an artificial fly, bright spoon, etc.; distinguished from *bait,* or that which fish may eat.

LUSITANIA. Quadruple-screw, direct turbine driven, express passenger liner of Cunard S.S. Co., Liverpool; 35000 tons gross; length over all 792 feet; launched 1906; sunk May 7, 1915, by German submarine off Old Head of Kinsale, southeast coast of Ireland, with loss of 1198 lives (including 124 Americans). Noted for record crossing, in October, 1909, from Queenstown to New York in 4 days, 11.7 hours—a shorter passage by 19 hours than previously made by any trans-Atlantic vessel—or at an average speed of 25.8 knots.

LUTCHET. In smaller vessels, a nest or stepping-box, usually of heavy wood, in which heel of mast is secured on deck; also termed a *tabernacle.*

LUTE STERN. *See* STERN.

LUTING. (L. *lutum,* mud) Also called *lute,* thick mixture of white lead and linseed oil, sometimes with whiting added; red lead and pine tar; or similar paste-like cement. It is used in boat-building for preservation and water-tight purposes in all faying joints or surfaces; *esp.* in laps of clinker-laid planking. To **lute her up,** to run a boat or small vessel in mud with object of temporarily stopping her leaking bottom-planking seams; also variously referred to as *choking her, mudding her in, giving her the mud cure,* etc.

L. W. Usual abbreviation for *low water.* L W designates *winter season* line in freeboard, or load-line, marks cut and painted in sides of vessels carrying timber cargoes.

L.W.L. Load water-line, as indicated in sheer plan of a vessel; sometimes L.W.P., or *load water-plane.*

L.W.O.S.T. *Low water ordinary spring tides; see* **T. reference plane** *in* TIDAL.

LYRA. (*L. & Gr. = kind of harp*) Named for the *lyre of Orpheus* in Greek mythology, a small northern constellation on west side of *Cygnus* (the Swan). It contains the navigational star *Vega,* or *α Lyrae,* magnitude 0.1; sidereal hour angle 81° 10' and declination 38¾° N., and which, with *Deneb* (*α Cygni*) and *Altair* (*α Aquilae*), marks out a neat triangle, nearly right-angled at its brightest corner, or that occupied by *Vega* itself.

LYING TO. Act or position of lying under easy canvas, or *hove to;* said of any vessel under way when stopped or brought to the wind, as in awaiting arrival of a pilot, launching a boat, or communicating with shore by flag signals. *See* **H. to** *in* HEAVE.

LYLE GUN. *See* **Line-throwing g.** *in* GUN.

LYTHE. Name on Irish and western Scottish coasts for the gadoid fish *pollack* or *pollock; see* POLLACK.

M

M. In International Code of Signals, *M* flag, hoisted singly, denotes "*I have a doctor on board.*" In form *M* or *m,* signifies *moderate* sea or swell and *misty* in ships' log-books or weather observation records; *main,* as in *m. hatch, m. topmast,* etc.; and *minute* of time, as in "*clocks advanced 17m.*" In navigation, *M* is often used to denote *meridional parts; m* for *meridional difference;* while on charts, *m* also indicates *mud* sea bottom.

MACHINE. (L. *machina;* machine, engine, device, trick) A contrivance or device, usually of a mechanical nature, for performing, or assisting in performance of, specified work; as, *dredging m.* (or dredge); *riveting m.; sounding m.; towing m.; welding m.* (See these various terms)

MACHINIST. One who repairs machines or metal appliances: *esp.* one understanding their design and working principles; one skilled in use or making of machine tools. In U.S. navy, a warrant officer in engineering department. **M.'s mate,** a petty officer in engineer department in U.S. navy. **Outside m.,** as distinguished from one ordinarily engaged in a shipyard's machine shop, *m.* who erects machinery and other metal equipment on board ship and assists in their operation on trial runs or tests.

MACHINERY. General term for ship's main and auxiliary engines, pumps, deck winches, steering-engine, windlass, capstans, special hoists, etc. **M. casing,** *see* **Engine-room c.** *in* CASING. **M. chock,** heavy hardwood floor on bed-plate to which a deck winch, windlass, capstan, or other auxiliary engine is bolted down; sometimes two heavy wood pieces, each under a sill of a deck winch, steam pump, etc. **M. space,** in a powered vessel's hull, that occupied by, or set apart for, propulsion plant and its auxiliaries, boilers, and permanent bunkers. In connection with water-tight subdivision of hulls, *International Conference on Safety at Sea, 1948,* defines *machinery space* as that "extending from the molded base line to margin line and between extreme main transverse water-tight bulkheads bounding the spaces devoted to the main and auxiliary propelling machinery, boilers when installed, and all permanent coal bunkers." *Cf.* **Floodable l.** *in* LENGTH.

MACKEREL. General name for members of a family of fishes known as *Scombridæ* (from Latin *scomber,* mackerel), which includes the *horse m.* or common tunny; *Spanish m.;* and *frigate m.* Best known is the *common m.,* important food fish of North Atlantic, averaging 16 inches in length, having a greenish back with slanting dark blue stripes and silvery under parts; found in enormous schools near European and American coasts during spawning season; said to be carnivorous and predatory in habit. Small *m.* are given many different names by fishermen, including *spikes, blinkers,* and *tinkers,* in order of increasing size. **M.-bob,** a 3- or 4-pointed fish-jig used in *jigging m.* **M. breeze,** one ruffling the water's surface and thus favorable for netting *m.* **M.-gaff,** *see* GAFF. **M. gull,** a sea-swallow or tern, so named from its forked tail suggestive of that of the *m.;* sometimes, a *razor-bill,* because of its sharp beak. **M. pocket,** large bag-shaped net held in position off vessel's side by outriggers for capturing *m.* from a passing school. **M. shark,** one of the family *Lamnidæ; see* LAMNIDÆ. **M. sky,** considerable area of *cirro-cumulus* cloud; *see* CLOUD; also called *mackerel-back sky,* from its appearance suggesting bars or stripes on the back of a common *m.* Small cloudlets of this type are sometimes termed *m. scales.* This cloud formation usually presages rainy or stormy weather, *esp.* the latter when accompanied by *cirrus* streamers, as thus noted in the old rime: "*Mackerel skies and mares' tails make tall ships carry low sails.*"

MACKINAW BOAT. Named for *Mackinac Island* where it probably first was made, a large flat-bottomed square-sterned boat used by early explorers and traders on upper Great Lakes and their tributaries. The craft was propelled by oars or sail, or both.

MacINTYRE TANK. Early and perhaps first form of double-bottom ballast space built in iron ships. *See* TANK.

MACRURA. (Gr. *macro,* large, long; *oura,* tail) A division of decapod (ten-legged) crustaceans including the lobster, crawfish or spiny lobster, prawn, shrimp, and many others of less importance. **Macrurous,** pertaining to the *Macrura;* long-tailed.

MADE. Preterit form of verb *to make,* appearing in certain terms and expressions, as in *course and distance m. good;* we *made sail* at once; she *made a weatherly course; made the land;* etc. Also, as a participial adjective in a **made block,** or one having its component parts built together, as distinguished from a *mortise-block,* or one carved from a single piece of wood; a **m. eye** (= Flemish eye), *see* EYE; a **m. mast** (= built mast), *see* MAST.

MADREPORA. A genus of hard branching corals common to all tropical seas, where its amazing formation of myriads of adhering calcareous skeletons is chiefly responsible for building the nuclei of coral reefs; also termed *Acropora. See* CORAL.

MAELSTROM. (Du. *malen,* to grind or whirl around; *stroom,* stream. Dan. *malström*) Famous tidal whirlpool between Moskenäsö and Moskenö of the Lofoten Islands off northwest coast of Norway. Called by Norwegians *Moskenström,* actually it is far removed from the exaggerated character ascribed to its horrors in fable; particularly, its old-time fanciful capacity for drawing ships to destruction as described by *Edgar Allan Poe.*

MAE WEST. American name for a parachute spinnaker; *see* SPINNAKER.

MAGAZINE. (Ar. *makhzan,* store-house or cellar) Compartment in a warship for storing ammunition; often termed *powder magazine; cf.* AMMUNITION. A temporary specially built room or compartment, usually in a 'tween decks space, for stowage of explosives carried as cargo in a merchant vessel. A special room or locker, protected from fire and heat, in a salvage vessel or dredge for keeping dynamite or other blasting explosives. In armed vessels, *magazines* are located below sea-water level and may be flooded in an emergency through pipes connected directly with sea, either from *m.* itself or from a deck above. Also, larger ships are provided with a sprinkling system extending to, or specially installed for fire protection in and near a *m.* **M. cock,** valve which may be opened to sea for flooding a *m.;* also *flood-cock.* **M. rifle,** or one from which several bullets may be fired without reloading. **M. screen,** a curtain having an aperture through which ammunition is served; used on warships for protection of a *m.*

MAGELLAN, Ferdinand. (Port. *Magalhaes*) Portuguese navigator credited with first circumnavigating the globe. He was, however, killed by natives in Mactan, an island of the Philippines, April 27, 1521, and *Juan Sebastian del Cano* assumed command of the remnant of his original fleet. Out of the 5 small ships which set out under Magellan, Sept. 20, 1519, only one, the *Vittoria,* returned to Portugal 3 years later, after what was perhaps the most ambitious, if not the most unfortunate, voyage in history, with 31 men of an original fleet complement of 280. Sebastian del Cano, therefore, properly must be chronicled as first navigator to sail completely round the world by steering to westward. **M. clouds,** *see* CLOUD. **M. jacket,** a heavy woollen watch-coat fitted with a hood. **Straits of M.,** between largest island of Tierra del Fuego and southern end of mainland of South America, noted for its strong tidal currents; discovered by Magellan in 1520.

MAGGED. Frayed, fretted, and generally badly worn; said of a rope. (Now rarely used)

MAGNESIL. Also *magnasil; see* LITOSILO.

MAGNET. Bar or piece of steel having the well-known property of attracting iron or steel, or of imparting such property—called *magnetism*—into another bar of iron or steel. Of special interest to the navigator is the steel *magnet* of the straight bar type in that it is used in compensating a magnetic compass, and that directive power is given the compass-card by its means (*see* C.-needle *in* COMPASS), remembering that the earth itself is a huge *m.* capable of inducing magnetism into a ship's hull, as well as providing the guiding or attractive force on which the mariner's compass has depended for centuries. It will be found that a bar *m.,* if freely suspended at its mid-length, will rest in the *magnetic meridian,* its *North-seeking, red,* or *positive pole* pointing roughly in direction of earth's North magnetic pole area (*see* M. poles *in* MAGNETIC), such direction being controlled, however, by influence of earth's magnetic field at place in question, rather than direct attraction of the pole itself. Conversely, *South-seeking, blue,* or *negative* pole of magnet roughly indicates direction of earth's South magnetic pole. Hence, practical use of the compass and the knowledge that "like poles repel, unlike poles attract, each other" since red or positive pole of *m.* always is attracted to blue or negative pole of earth (North magnetic pole), converse of this being true of south end of *m.;* and, also, that the induction in iron or steel of a magnetic polarity from earth's magnetic field gives the material the character of a temporary *m.* having poles of *opposite* names to those of the earth. **Artificial m.,** mass or bar of iron or steel to which magnetic properties have been imparted, as opposed to a *natural m.* or piece of *loadstone* (or *lodestone*), a variety of magnetite or iron ore possessing magnetic polarity in its natural state. **Compensating m.,** a permanent *m.,* usually in round bar form 6 to 8 inches in length, used in a compensating binnacle for compass correction. Deviation of a magnetic compass caused by more or less permanent magnetism acquired by vessel's hull during her construction is corrected by such *m's*, respectively termed *fore-and-aft, thwartship,* and *heeling m's. See* COMPASS; *also* DEVIATION. **Heeling m.,** *see* **H'ing corrector** *and* **H'ing error** *in* HEEL. **Lifting m.,** electro-dynamic device for lifting masses of iron or steel without use of slings. Usually takes the form of a shallow inverted bowl containing a series of soft iron blocks set in coils of electric wire. Upon flow of direct current, each iron block by induction, and consequently the whole series, becomes a strong electro-*m.* which attracts and thence lifts scrap-iron, steel plates or bars, etc., in transferring such, as by crane or boom in loading or discharging. Immediate release of *m.* from its load takes place upon turning off current. **Natural m.,** loadstone or magnetite of magnetic polarity in its natural state; *cf.* **Artificial m. Permanent m.,** hard steel bar such as is used as a *compensating m. (q.v.).* Such bar is magnetized permanently either by electrical induction, *i.e.,* by placing it in the field of a direct current, or by the *touch* process in which, by one method, it is magnetized by drawing a strong magnet's pole a number of times along its half length, always in same direction; if red pole of *m.* is applied, blue polarity will be given that end of magnet so charged, and vice versa. **Temporary m.,** piece of soft iron magnetized by induction, but losing its magnetism upon such inductive force being removed or discontinued, or quickly changing its polarity upon being reversed or otherwise turned in position relative to the magnetizing source. The soft iron correctors for transient magnetism induced in fore-and-aft, thwartship, and vertical iron, or the usual spheres and Flinders bar of a compensating binnacle, essentially are temporary *m's,* since they receive their magnetism by induction from earth's magnetic field.

MAGNETIC. Having the properties of a magnet; of or pertaining to magnetism. **Correct m.,** in older navigational usage, designation of a course or bearing relative to the local *magnetic meridian.* Now simply *magnetic.* **M. amplitude,** true or astronomical amplitude converted to that which would be indicated by a *m.* compass; thus, if *true* amplitude were W 10° N and variation of compass 15° W, *m.* amplitude = W 25° N. *See* AMPLITUDE. **M. axis,** straight line joining poles of a magnet; of the earth, line joining north and south magnetic poles. **M. azimuth,** arc of the horizon between *m.* meridian and a vertical circle passing through object observed; a true azimuth converted to that which would be indicated on a *m.* compass having no deviation, by applying variation of compass for locality concerned; an azimuth or bearing observed and corrected for deviation; also, *m. bearing.* **M. brake,** on an electric cargo winch, capstan, windlass, etc., electro-dynamic brake which automatically sets when power is turned off and vice versa. **M. chart,** one of all or part of earth's surface showing *isogonic, isoclinic,* and *isodynamic* lines. (*See these*

terms) A *variation chart* is the usual term for one showing only isogonic lines, or curves passing through all places at which variation or declination of compass needle has same value; also indicates annual change in those values. **M. cirrus,** formation of cirro-stratus cloud appearing as long parallel bands converging in perspective toward the horizon; once supposed to accompany *m.* disturbances; also called *Noah's ark* and *salmon cloud.* **M. co-efficients,** also called *deviation coefficients; see* DEVIATION. **M. compass,** *see* COMPASS. **M. coupling,** in a high speed engine, members which electro-dynamically connect propeller-shafting to engine with view of allowing engine to start without load, torque being brought into action as required by, essentially, application of electro-*m.* principles; also, *m. gearing.* **M. course,** angle from *m. meridian,* as steered by vessel; that indicated on a *m.* compass free of deviation; angle of fore-and-aft line with *m.* meridian; *m.* heading. **M. declination,** angle which *m.* needle makes with geographical meridian; difference in direction of *true north* and *m. north;* also, and more commonly, termed *variation of the compass; see* **D. of compass needle** *in* DECLINATION. **M. deviation,** usually termed *compass deviation; see* DEVIATION. **M. dip,** *see* **D. of the needle** *in* DIP. **M. equator,** *see* EQUATOR. **M. field,** region or space through which *m.* force is exerted. It is the *m.* field about the earth (a huge magnet itself) which holds a freely suspended magnet in the north and south line, or in the *m.* meridian, and hence gives directive power to mariner's compass. **M. gearing,** *see* **M. coupling. M. induction,** *m.* properties imparted to a mass of iron or steel lying within a *m.* field. It is of temporary duration in soft iron when removed from such influence; permanent in case of steel. *See* INDUCED MAGNETISM. **M. latitude,** distance north or south of *m. equator,* or *aclinic* line, as indicated by an *isoclinic line,* or line of equal dip of magnetic needle, passing through place in question; *see* ISOCLINIC. **M. meridian,** vertical circle whose plane lies in same direction as a compass needle undisturbed by deviation or local attraction. **M. moment,** as measured by a magnetometer, a comparative moment of force used as a criterion of a *m.* compass's efficiency in overcoming friction to which compass-card is subjected, as that of its pivot or the liquid sustaining it. It determines the compass's directive power, or, properly, its velocity of recovery when deflected from the meridian. Such comparisons of moments, together with oscillations observed, must be reduced to a standard *m.* latitude, in cases of different locations concerned, since needle's horizontal force or directive power varies as cosine of *m. dip.* **M. needle,** a light bar magnet suspended at its center of gravity so as to admit of free horizontal and vertical movement. Upon coming to rest, needle will lie in the plane of *m.* meridian and, also, in the direction of earth's total magnetic force, which, except at the *m. equator,* inclines from the horizontal at an angle equal to the *dip,* its north-seeking pole being depressed in north *m.* latitudes and south-seeking pole in southern latitudes. It is customary, in illustrating the comparative values of earth's total *m.* force components, to draw a right-angled triangle with hypotenuse representing the needle's length in magnitude equal to total *m.* force, the upper and horizontal side indicating horizontal force, and vertical side, or that opposite *angle of dip,* earth's vertical force. At a given place, then earth's horizontal force is equal to total force times cosine of dip, and vertical force to total force times sine of dip. We note, accordingly, that with increase of distance from *m.* equator and consequent increase of the dip angle a serious diminution of horizontal, or directive, force of needle takes place, while earth's vertical force increases in ratio of tangent of dip. The effect, then, of vertical soft iron unsymmetrically distributed about a ship's, compass in higher latitudes, if not properly compensated for, may be of such magnitude as to render the instrument almost useless, since the *m.* axis of such iron lines up with direction of earth's total force in process of induction by that great magnet until it reaches the vertical at *m.* poles. **M. north,** direction indicated by north-seeking or red pole of *m.* needle; *see remarks on* MAGNET. **M. poles,** the two ends of a magnet. A bar magnet used in compass compensation is colored red at its north or positive pole and blue at its south or negative pole, and these usually are called *red* and *blue* poles, respectively. As a great magnet, the earth's *m. poles* are areas of some extent in which the line of her total *m.* force coincides with the plumb-line, or nearly so, dip of the needle being 90°, and horizontal force *nil.* Due to apparently inexplicable changing of earth's *m.* field, a slow shift of their respective positions to westward has been observed during past half century. Present mid-area of *North magnetic pole,* which covers a region of maximum vertical force intensity of probably 150 miles radius, lies in Lat. 72° N., Long. 95° W., about 1080 nautical miles from geographical pole, or some 1200 miles due north of Winnipeg, Canada; while *South magnetic pole* is in about Lat. 68° S., Long. 145° E., about 1300 miles from geographical pole and 1450 miles due south of Tasmania. From this it is noted that earth's *m. poles* are far from being at opposite ends of a diameter of the globe. **M. Range,** *see* RANGE. **M. storm,** marked disturbance of earth's *m.* conditions as seen in rapid oscillations and sudden displacements of the *m.* needle. That such storms accompany appearance of sun spots and unusual display of auroras has been well established. **M. shoal,** area of *m.* disturbance covered by comparatively shallow depth of water, observed to produce large errors in compasses. Among others are a region in vicinity of Anticosti Island in Gulf of St.

Lawrence and a small area off North West Cape, Western Australia. Probably one of such spots was encountered by *Sindbad the Sailor* who tells of all the nails being drawn out of his vessel's bottom by a "magnetic hill"—and *"down she went, plunk-O!"* **M. survey,** scientific observation and recording of *m.* phenomena, as carried out in a *non-magnetic vessel.* Such data as declination, dip, and directive force of the needle are included in charted results covering all navigable waters of the globe. **M. variation,** usually termed *variation of the compass* by seamen; *see* **D. of compass needle** *in* DECLINATION.

MAGNETISM. Science which treats of properties of the magnet; cause of attraction shown by a magnet; quality or state of being magnetic. This property manifested in the magnet may be illustrated as a continuous invisible flux emanating from the blue or negative pole, spreading or diffusing around magnet and thus creating a "field," but curving toward and re-entering magnet at its red or positive pole. In this sense, earth's North magnetic pole must be considered as having *blue* polarity, and her South pole, *red,* in order to conform to the law that "like poles repel and unlike attract each other" and to be consistent with accepted coloring of bar magnets' poles (*cf.* **M. poles**). In a ship's hull, that acquired by induction from earth's magnetic field takes on a similar polarity to, and lines up with direction of, earth's total magnetic force (*cf.* **M. needle**). *See* INDUCED MAGNETISM.

MAGNITUDE. As met with in the term *stellar magnitude,* degree of brightness of a celestial body, especially a star, as expressed in *first, second, third,* etc., *m., sixth* being faintest to unaided eye. Scale used by astronomers gives a body *m.* numerically *less* by 1 when it is 2.512 times brighter than one with which it is compared; thus star *Capella* of *m.* 0.2 is 1 *m.* brighter than *Pollux* with his 1.2 *m.* Generally, however, stars of *m.* —1.5 to 1.4 are classed of *first m.;* those 1.5 to 2.4 as *second m.;* 2.5 to 3.4 as *third m.;* and so on. Stars of lesser *m.* than third are seldom used in navigation.

MAGNUS HITCH. Similar to a clove hitch, but with an additional turn around spar, etc., on which made fast.

MAHOGANY. The hard, close-grained, reddish brown or brownish yellow wood of any of several large tropical and sub-tropical trees; *esp.* that of the *Swietenia mahagoni* of America, often called *Honduras mahogany* and *baywood.* It is excellent material for joiner and cabinet work, turned patterns, boat-planking, and ship's furniture, endures great temperature changes, and has lasting qualities comparable to teak. Seasoned wood weighs from 40 to 50 lbs. per cubic foot.

MAIDEN OAK. Wood of the British *white oak* tree; the European oak; once extensively used in shipbuilding.

MAIDEN VOYAGE. First voyage of a newly built vessel, exclusive of any trial trip or runs made by her builders.

MAIER FORM. *See* **Maier form h.** *in* HULL.

MAIL. In rope-making, a square mat-like contrivance of interwoven metal rings used for rubbing off loose fibers from manufactured cordage; a similar *piece of mail* formerly employed by naval gunners for burnishing their guns. Matter conveyed by the postal service or the entire service itself. **M. declaration,** in U.S., among other legislation designed to protect postal revenue, *Revised Statute 3988 (18 U.S.C. 327)* reads: "No vessel arriving within a port or collection district of the United States shall be allowed to make entry or break bulk until all letters on board are delivered to the nearest post office, and the master or other person having charge or control thereof has signed and sworn to the following declaration before the collector or other proper customs officer: I, John Doe, master of the ...., arriving from ...., and now lying in the port of ...., do solemnly swear (or affirm) that I have to the best of my knowledge and belief delivered to the post office at .... every letter and every bag, packet, or parcel of letters which were on board the said vessel during her last voyage, or which were in my possession or under my power or control." **M. flag,** the International Code flag *Y* (square flag with red and yellow diagonal stripes), flown at starboard yard-arm, at triatic stay, or on mast inferior to house flag, indicating "*I am carrying the mails*"; a special flag or pennant similarly exhibited by vessels carrying mails under contract, as the U.S. red pennant with upper and lower blue borders, spread eagle in upper corner, and words "*United States Mail*" or white pennant of Great Britain, having a crown in red between words "*Royal Mail.*" U.S. vessels of regular lines not having *m.*-carrying contract but conveying *m's* usually fly a blue square flag with letters "U.S.M." in white. **M.-room,** compartment in a vessel for stowing *m's.* **M. ship,** vessel carrying *m's; esp.* one making regular calls at scheduled ports; also, *m.-boat, m.-packet, m. steamer, m. vessel.* **M. signal,** the flag or pennant exhibited by a vessel indicating she has *m's* on board for port she is entering or has entered. **M. subsidy,** an award or payment made to a shipping line having a government contract for carriage of *m's.* Ostensibly common remuneration for express transportation, actually it is a subvention or bounty paid as an incentive for shipowners in supplying regular and speedy service on certain routes in particular, and to encourage maintenance of a first class merchant marine in general. Payments are made according to requirements in speed of vessels and regularity of scheduled voyages, class of ship and trade importance of voyage, etc.

MAIN. (A.S. *mægen*, power, force; O.F. *magne*, great) Chief or principal in strength, size, or or-

der; as, *m. deck; m. hatch; m. beam; m. bearings; m. engine.* Attached to, or rigged from something connected with, the mainmast; as, *m. rigging; m. yard; m. stay; m.-topgallant braces.* As a noun, chiefly poetical, as in *Spanish Main;* the high seas, as distinguished from coastal waters. A principal conduit or pipe-line; as, *power m.; fire m.* (As indicated in remarks under FORE, no rigid rule seems possible with regard to use or non-use of the *hyphen* in terms in which *main* is first component word. Generally, however, it is considered good usage to insert hyphen in that part of name taking adjectival sense. For example, while we may write *main topsail,* in denoting an accessory to that sail, *main-topsail clewline* seems preferable form. Terms beginning with *main,* whether separated by hyphen or otherwise, if not included in following, should be referred to under appropriate caption; as, for *m. topgallant sail, see* SAIL; for *mainroyal, see* ROYAL; for *main-topmast, see* TOPMAST) **M. battery,** heavy guns or those of largest caliber on a warship. **M. beam,** greatest transverse measurement of a vessel; formerly, beam at greatest breadth of hull, generally corresponding with that beam in way of after end of *m. hatch.* To-day, in conforming to requirement that ship's official number and registered tonnage shall be marked on the *m. beam,* the term is considered synonymous with after coaming of *m.,* or principal, hatch. **M. beam-longitudinal,** formerly a timber supporting ends of beams at sides of *m.* hatch; a carling-piece; *see* CARLINGS. **M. beam-transverse,** formerly the heavy beams forming forward and after ends of *m.* hatch, respectively, and from which the head ledges or coamings extended. **M. bearing,** one of the propeller-shaft bearings, usually with brasses and journals included. **M. body,** hull proper, exclusive of any erection, such as a bridge house, raised forecastle, poop, etc. **M.-body frames,** *see* FRAME. **M. boom,** spar on which foot of a fore-and-aft mainsail is extended. **M. brace,** either of braces or tackles for trimming a square mainsail; *see* BRACE. **M.-breadth line,** that on which greatest breadth of ship is measured. **M. bulwark,** that fitted at sides of a weather deck or upper deck of ship's *m.* body; *see* BULWARK. **M.-deck stringer,** such plate on a *m.* deck; *see* D.-stringer *in* DECK. **M.-discharge pipe,** *see* CIRCULATING PUMP. **M. drain,** *m.* suction line in a bilge-pumping system for either entire hull or for machinery space only. **M. injection,** intake of sea-water to circulating system; *see* CIRCULATING PUMP. **M. keel,** true keel of a wooden vessel as distinguished from the false keel, or shoe. **M. post,** archaic term for ship's stern-post. **M. steam-pipe,** line conveying steam from boilers to *m.* engines. **M.-topman,** in older navy days, seaman stationed aloft for general rigging duty above the *m. top.* **M.-topsail schooner,** *see* SCHOONER. **M.-trysail ketch,** a yacht rig in which mainsail is jib-shaped and its clew is stretched aft to end of a split sprit or wishbone; *see* WISHBONE. **M.-yard man,** in old sailing-navy days, one of a number of men whose special duties were concerned only with the *m.* yard, mainsail, and gear attached thereto. In British navy, a sailor on the surgeon's list for light duty; probably from the fact that limit of the *m.* yard was prescribed for his height of rigging climb.

MAINMAST. Originally, principal and heaviest mast in ship and second in order from forward. Excepting such rigs as ketch and yawl in which after mast is much smaller than forward or *main* one, that traditional order still is followed. **M. man,** in sailing-navy times, one in a division detailed to attend to gear attached to the mainmast.

MAIN-MIZZEN. In a four-masted caravel of 15th or 16th century, which was square-rigged on foremast and mainmast, the forward and larger of two lateen-rigged mizzenmasts; the sail itself. Aftermost sail was called a *bonaventure mizzen* in English ships of that day.

MAINSAIL. (A.S. *mægen segel*, power sail; of Scand. origin) Excepting in more recent square and fore-and-aft rigged vessels having more than three masts, largest sail carried and perhaps earliest so named, evidence in Old Norse history indicating that even the single square sail spread by the Vikings was called *megin segl* (*cf.* derivation). It is always set on the *mainmast*. Also called *main course* in square-rigged ships. See SAIL. **Mainsail haul!,** in a square-rigged vessel of brig, barque, or ship rig, order given when coming about to swing round after yards for the new tack. When *m.* is not set, order becomes *Main tops'l haul!* or simply *Tops'l haul!* Appropriate time for this operation is when ship has come up to about one point off the wind, as sails being aback on weather side and sheltered by forward canvas on lee side, after yards will come round unassisted in even a light breeze. In fresh or strong breezes, order is delayed accordingly, so that yards will not require checking against an otherwise violent swing.

MAKE. To arrive at, or sight, a place or position steered for; as, to *m. the cape; we made the light-ship right ahead.* To work to windward or fall off to leeward; as, *she makes weatherly courses; she makes too much leeway.* To act, move, or produce a certain effect; as, to *m.* a tack; to *m.* sternway; to *m.* bad weather of it. To perform something or accomplish a purpose; as, to *m.* fast; to *m.* sail; to *m.* good a course steered; to *m.* a seam (in calking). To grow or increase in appearance or fact; as, *bad weather is making; ship is making water.* To indicate or observe an occurrence; as, to *m.* sunset (by formally lowering the colors); to *m.* eight bells (by striking ship's bell as so ordered). To **m. a board,** *see* BOARD. To **m. a tack,** to sail close-hauled for a limited time or distance; to come about on a new tack. To **m. bad weather of it,** to labor heavily and

excessively in sense of "overdoing it"; said of a vessel in a rough sea. To **m. colors,** to formally hoist the ensign, as in a war-vessel—usually at 8 a.m. To **m. fast,** to secure by belaying or hitching, as a rope; to fasten in place, as a sail by its gaskets; to secure a ship at a pier, etc., by her hawsers. To **m. foul water,** *see* FOUL. To **m. good weather of it,** to take a heavy sea "easily," as opposed to *making bad weather of it,* or laboring heavily; *cf.* To **m. bad weather of it.** To *m.* **her number,** *see* NUMBER. **M. it so,** as in the old navy custom in which a midshipman reported the hour to officer of watch, order to strike ship's bell accordingly. To **m. land,** *see* LAND. To **m. off,** in sailing, to increase sea-room by standing out to sea, as from a coast; *esp.* with wind blowing on shore; also, to *m. an offing.* An old whaling term meaning to clean or pare off blubber and stow it in barrels. To **m. sail,** to set sail, as in departing for sea; to spread more canvas, as with view of increasing speed; sometimes, to *m. all sail.* To **m. up a sail,** to roll up a sail and secure it with rope-yarn stops every few feet in preparation for stowing it away. Square sails are always made up *on the head, i.e.,* head of sail is stretched along deck, *roping down,* canvas being rolled up from the foot with clews turned in a few feet, so that head-rope is accessible all along finished roll. This is done to avoid re-arranging sail when it is to be bent to its yard. Fore-and-aft sails are made up *on the luff* for same reason; particularly in case of a gaff sail. To **m. the course good,** in steering, to offset a departure from compass course by a similar angle on opposite side; to avoid allowing vessel to deviate from the course more toward one side than the other; also, to allow a full measure of leeway in the sense of avoiding any falling off to leeward or toward a danger. To **m. water,** to leak; *esp.* when taking in an unusual amount of water, as in a hold.

MAKING-IRON. Tool used by calkers in ordinary seam work; *see* IRON.

MALLEMAROKING. (Corruption of an *Eskimo* word of similar meaning) In older whaling days, a carousal or social gathering of sailors of icebound vessels held on board one of the craft. Such party was announced by a bucket hoisted at the fore truck. Also termed a *mollie,* particularly when captains only were in company. *Cf.* GAM.

MALLEMUCK. From the Dutch *mollemoke,* a corruption of an Eskimo word meaning a follower, and so the name given by old Dutch whalers to the *fulmar,* a bird of the *petrel* family (see FULMAR), noted for its selfish interest in operations of harpooning and processing the catch. Said to have been an ardent follower of the harponier and first to land on a captured whale. Also called *molly, mollyhawk,* and *mallymauk,* name was extended to the *giant fulmar* and even to the *albatross* of cold southern seas.

MALLET. A wooden maul or instrument for driving or hammering used on board ship, as in driving hatch wedges. For mallets used in calking and serving, see CALKING; HAWSING; SERVING; SETTING.

MALUS. (*L. = mast*) The *mast* in constellation ARGO, *q.v.*

MAMMATO-CUMULUS. A cumulus cloud having dark nipple-like lower protuberances; *see* FESTOON CLOUD.

MAMMY-CHAIR. An open box-like sling, usually made to seat two persons facing each other, for transferring passengers by hoisting to and from ship in an open roadstead. Used in waters where a heavy swell renders passage to and from boats difficult or dangerous, as, *e.g.*, at anchorages on west coast of Africa.

MAN. To provide or detail a number of men for a certain service or work; as, to *man* a vessel, a gun, a life-boat, etc. To exert strength upon; as, to *man* the capstan, the topsail halyards, the pumps, etc. A vessel, in compound words such as *fisherman, India-man, merchantman, man-o'-war.* **Act of m.,** *see* ACT. **Liberty-man,** *see* LIBERTY. **M.-bound,** said of a vessel when detained by shortage in number of crew-members. **M.-eater,** one of several kinds of voracious sharks; especially, *carcharodon carcharias* of the *Lamnidæ* family, found in all tropical seas and known to attain 30 feet in length. *Cf.* LAMNIDÆ. **M. overboard!,** alarm cry when a person falls into the water. **M.-rope,** a line used as a hand-rail on a gangway, steadying-rope on a yard or boat-boom, etc.; a life-line. **M.-rope knot,** a double wall and double crown, or stopper knot made with strands at end of a man-rope, for neat appearance where rope is rove through eyes at upper ends of stanchions. To **m. the side,** *see* SIDE. To **m. the yards,** as a salute in honor of a sovereign, a high official, or in celebration of a national event in old navy days, to take up formation in which men stood along the yards facing forward, each grasping outstretched hand of his next in line. In ships of the line, the arrayal was often "topped off" by a man standing on each truck. **Ready m.,** one of a number of sailors sent aloft to prepare for execution of a maneuver, such as sending masts or yards down, bending sail, or reefing, as in navy sailing days. **Run m.,** former term for a deserter in British navy parlance.

MANAGING OWNER. See OWNER.

MANATEE. A now almost extinct member of the *Sirenia,* an order of sea mammals which includes the *dugong* and *sea cow.* At least three species are known: *Manatus americanus,* habitat in West Indies, shores of Gulf of Mexico, and western Caribbean; *M. inunguis* of South American shore from Orinoco to Amazon Rivers; and *M. senegalensis* of west coast of Africa. About 10 feet in length, has a heavy rounded body with two large flippers, small bulbous head and lobeless horizontal tail and is dark in color with tough thick skin. The animals feed on sea-grasses and weeds only. Also *manati.*

MANCHE. An East Indian lighter or coasting vessel rigged with one mast and a settee sail. Also known by its native name, *manji.*

MANEUVER. A tactical operation in seamanship; *esp.,* any orderly change made in a formation of naval ships with view of obtaining an advantage at scene of hostilities. In *plural,* exercises of a fleet in operations of changing formation, lines of advance, etc., with view of theoretically obtaining advantage in attack or defense. To perform such naval operational tactics; to sail a vessel with different changes of courses, trimming of sail, use of anchors, etc., in order to arrive at a certain position or point of vantage. **Maneuvering board,** *see* **M. board** *in* MOORING.

MANGANESE BRONZE. A tough corrosion-resisting bronze containing about 2 per centum of manganese. Alloy varies according to required use of metal. Propeller-blades and their bolts, rudder fittings, stern propeller-shaft stuffing-boxes, and sometimes bottom sheathing for wooden hulls made of the metal have given very satisfactory results. That for propeller-blades of larger type recently has been reported as 59% copper, 38% zinc, 1% aluminum, 1% iron, and 1% manganese.

MANGER. Chiefly in older vessels, space on deck in way of the hawse-holes, having a transverse *manger-board* as its after limit, for confining water shipped through hawse-pipes. The *manger*-scuppers carried off water thus entering. Also, perforated elevated bottom with space below in a chain locker. Water from latter drops into *manger* and is thus free to flow into bilges. **M.-plate,** old term for a breakwater on forecastle head; *see* BREAKWATER.

MANHELPER. A long stick or pole used in painting beyond arm's reach, as in working on ship's side in places where rigging a stage is impracticable. The brush is lashed to end of such pole.

MANHOLE. Oval-shaped or round hole of sufficient size for a man to enter, as in a boiler, tank, deck, machinery-casing, etc., for cleaning purposes, examination of parts, or repairs. **M.-cover,** or **m.-door,** lid or plate which covers and/or tightly seals a *manhole;* a *m.-plate.*

MANIFEST. List of shipments contained in a cargo, showing items, amount, or quantities of goods, identifying marks and numbers, names of shippers and consignees, and, sometimes, corresponding number of bills of lading and weight or measurement of goods. The document is of special interest to ship's agents at port or ports of destination, to customs officers at port of departure, and to consular representative of countries to which goods are consigned. **Certified m.,** one that is carried with ship for entry at customs upon arrival at destination port. It is so called because authenticated by consul of country to which ship is bound. **Inward m.,** *see* INWARD. **Outward m.,** one handed to customs office at port of departure before vessel sails. **Passenger m.,** also termed *passenger list*, document showing detailed information concerning each passenger embarking for a foreign country, as required by customs or emigration offices at port of departure and by immigration officials and sometimes also customs authorities at port of arrival. U.S. and Canadian Immigration Services supply passenger vessels with an elaborate manifest form which must be completed on board before arrival. The document is a questionnaire requiring such information as education of each person, his political beliefs or opinions, reasons for entering country, expected length of stay, etc., in addition to usual identification items of age, sex, nationality, race, final destination, etc.

MANIFOLD. A large pipe, valve-chest, or distribution box from which several pipe-lines lead and flow of water or oil may be directed from one to another, or one or more lines may be connected to an adjunctive pump, by manipulation of valves, as in a bilge or ballast pumping system.

MANIGLION. (Pron. *maneel'-yun*) In older ship ordnance, either of two handles cast on the back of a small cannon.

MANILA. The manila hemp, or fiber of a species of banana tree (*Musa textilis*), native to Philippine Islands, where it is known as *abaca*. Its finer grades are used for various native textiles; coarser quality for matting and cordage. The great tensile strength and length of the fiber (5 to 10 feet), with its durable qualities and resistance to sea-water, places manila cordage in the lead for general use on board ship. Excepting the more recent costly *nylon* hawser, towing rope and other heavy cordage of the fiber have been found second to none. *See* HEMP. **M. rope,** cordage made of *abaca* fiber; *specif.*, such cordage of one inch or more in circumference. Strongest form is 3-strand plain-laid, 4-strand rope being made for gear in which it is important to keep free of *kinking*. Due to its qualities of strength, flexibility, lightness, and durability is found more suitable for running gear and hawsers than the other hemps used in cordage manufacture, the softer of which must be treated with tar for protection against ruinous action of sea-water while they also possess lesser elasticity than the *m.* product. Smallest *m. rope* in use on board ship is ¾-inch circumference and is called *6-thread m.* (has 3 strands each made of 2 yarns or threads), and 9-, 12-, 15-, 18-, and 21-thread being, respectively, the usual terms for 3-strand line measuring 1, 1⅛, 1¼, 1⅜, and 1½ inches in circumference. Good hawser-laid rope of this fiber is proportionately stronger in the smaller sizes, its breaking stress being, in pounds, nearly equal to circumference in inches squared times 1000 for ropes up to 4 inches, while a 12-inch hawser will stand up to approximately $circ.^2 \times 750$. Its weight per fathom in pounds $=$ $circ.^2 \times .18$.

MANJUARI. (*Sp.*) The alligator gar; *see* GAR.

MAN-OF-WAR. A war vessel; *esp.* one of larger type, as a battleship, ready for active hostilities; a warship. Also, *man-o'-war*. **M. bird,** also called *m. hawk*, the frigate-bird or frigate-pelican; *see* FRIGATE. **M. fashion,** in an orderly and seamanlike manner: said of execution of any work or maneuver exhibiting good discipline or preparatory training. **M. fish,** the small fish having a deep compressed body of silvery appearance, noted as companion to the *Portuguese man-o'-war* among the tentacles of which it habitually finds shelter. **M's-man,** a seaman serving on a man-o'-war. **Portuguese m.,** one of the so-called siphonophores of the genus *Physalia*, characterized by its bladder-like or dirigible-balloon appearance with its surmounting silvery and bluish tinted *sail*, or vertically projecting crest. Its underwater parts consist of a tangle of short and long tentacles, any of which is said to be capable of giving one a smarting sting. The "hull"—6 to 8 inches in length—with its "sail" is termed in zoology a *pneumatophore*. *P. arethusa* is commonly met with in tropical seas, often in the Gulf Stream carried far into the North Atlantic.

MANROPE. *See* M.-rope *in* MAN.

MANTA. A devil-fish. The genus of rays containing the devil-fish of West Indies and Gulf of Mexico; also, *Mobula*. The *M. birostris*. *See* D.-fish *in* DEVIL. The ugly fellow's tough and leathery skin is valued among the Mexicans for shoe-making and his liver for oil and food.

MANTELET. (*Dim. of Fr. manteau*, cloak) Shield of metal, rope, wood, or other material formerly used to protect men serving guns in casemates, from entry of shot into port-holes, etc.; also, *mantlet*. **M. plate,** for protection of personnel, a sheet of metal fitted over bolt or rivet heads to prevent such from flying about when plating is subjected to impact of shells, as in an engagement.

MANUAL. Done or operated by hand. **M. pump,** one that is worked by hand, as opposed to a steam-pump, windmill pump, etc. **M. weld,** a joining of metal parts by free-hand welding, as distinguished from that done with assistance of any controlling device.

MAP-PROJECTION. *See* PROJECTION.

MAPLE. Wood of several species of trees of genus *Acer*; *esp.*, in shipbuilding, that of the *sugar*, or *rock maple*, a hard, light-colored, close-grained, durable timber suitable for boat and vessel framing. Capable of taking a high polish, is much used in furniture manufacture, flooring, etc., and makes first class material for launching-ways in shipyard work. It is also valued for tool handles, as for chisels, axes, etc. Weight of seasoned wood, 45 lbs. per foot.[3]

MARCH, ADMIRAL'S. Short lively tune played by ship's band when an admiral receives "honors" upon coming aboard or leaving the ship.

MARCONI RIG. That characterized by jib-headed foresail or mainsail of unusually lofty hoist; also, *Bermuda rig; see* RIG.

MARCQ ST. HILAIRE METHOD. First introduced by *Commandant M. St. Hilaire* of French navy, about 1885, an important improvement in determination of the *line of position,* called *New Navigation* for a probationary period of something like 30 years. Its marked departure from prevailing practice lay in a short cut offered by the solution of spherical trigonometrical problem involved for value of a heavenly body's altitude at ship's estimated position at instant corresponding to an altitude of same body observed by sextant; and in using the difference between such calculated and observed altitudes, called the *intercept,* for laying off position line on chart. Thus, if observed altitude exceeded the calculated altitude by 5′, a distance of 5 miles is laid off on chart from ship's estimated or assumed position in direction of azimuth of body observed; conversely, away from body, if observed altitude were less. Position line is drawn through point thus plotted at right angles to, or 90° from, the body's true azimuth. The method has been greatly simplified by comparatively recent tables of *Ageton, Dreisonstock, Weems, H.O. 214,* and others. Those named may be obtained from U.S. Hydrographic Office, Washington, D.C., or its agencies at principal sea-ports of U.S. *Cf.* **Line of p.** *in* POSITION.

MARE. (*L. = sea*) The sea. **M. clausum,** as sometimes used in legal phrasing, is a sea subject only to jurisdiction of a particular nation and, as such nation decrees, may be a *closed sea* in the sense of prohibiting certain or all vessels from sailing in such area; opposed to **M. liberum,** or high seas, on which all vessels have equal rights.

MARES' TAILS. Long, featherlike streamers appearing in *cirrus* cloud formation; accompanied by *cirro-cumulus,* presages bad weather; *cf.* **M. sky** *in* MACKEREL.

MARGIN. Border; edge; verge; limited area near border of a surface; space between edge of a plate and nearest row of rivet-holes. Limiting point or mark; as, *margin-line.* Degree of reserve strength; as, *margin of safety* in boiler-plating, a crane, etc. **M.-angle,** bar of angle-iron connecting lower edge of a double-bottom tank *m.-plate* to vessel's shell

plating; *cf. m.-plate.* **M. bracket,** one of the vertical triangular plates butting to a *m.-plate* of a double-bottom tank and forming a continuation of a floor. In usual construction it connects and stiffens frame and reverse frame where these fork apart at bilges. It is joined to *m.-plate* by the *m.-angle.* Also termed *tank-side bracket* and *wing bracket;* sometimes, *m.-plate bracket.* **M. line,** in a transom stern vessel, that at which after ends of side planking terminate. Also, line indicating limit to which ship may be immersed in connection with safety arrangement in bulkhead spacing; *see* **Floodable l.** *in* LENGTH. **M. plank,** in a deck, plank forming side boundary or butting edge; made of hardwood, such as teak or greenheart, in case of a soft-wood deck. In ordinary straight-laid decks, *m. plank* is joggled or nibbed as necessary at inward curvature toward forward and after extreme ends in order to receive butts of the more outer plank-strakes. Also termed *waterway plank* and, where cut to take butts, *nibbing-plank* or *joggling-plank.* **M. plate,** that forming sides of a double-bottom tank. It is usually fitted normal to shell-plating to which it is attached by the continuous *m.-angle,* and has its top edge flanged inward to make a lap seam connection with inner bottom plating (tank top). Side frames are connected to it by *m. brackets, q.v.* **M. waters,** those immediately bordering on a coastline; *esp.* the area extending three sea miles off and along a coast forming a national boundary.

MARIGRAPH. Instrument by means of which a continuous record of duration of rise and fall and, also, times of high and low water, is graphically indicated at a selected station. Record thus obtained is called a *marigram* or *tidal curve* and is used in connection with predictions of times and heights of high and low water.

MARIMETER. An early name for the sonic depthfinder; *see* ECHO SOUNDING.

MARINA. (*It. = sea-coast*) An area in a harbor devoted to berthing of small boats and yachts at wharves, buoys, etc.; it is usually provided with one or more slipways, repair yards, handy means of obtaining fuel, stores, etc. Also, a seaside promenade or any clear level area on a sea-coast used as a park, for pleasure driving, etc.

MARINE. A sea soldier or member of a military body trained for duty in a navy, as one in *U.S. Marine Corps* (permanently established in 1798) or *Royal Marine* forces of Great Britain. Normally, a detachment of marines is detailed to each battleship and cruiser on board which they act as police, sentries at important posts, and as orderlies for higher ranking officers; man certain guns and battle stations at "general quarters"; and are equipped for active hostilities as a landing force. Their duties are not concerned with the engineering department. The commercial and naval fleets of a country, taken collectively; maritime force or interest as represented by sea-going vessels; shipping tonnage collectively, with respect to class or nationality, as the *merchant m., Danish m.* In France and some other countries, the term corresponds to *U.S. Navy Department* or *British Admiralty.* Of or pertaining to navigation or sea commerce; nautical; naval; maritime; oceanic; as, *m. glass; m. engine; m. insurance; m. life; m. hospital.* Although the word connotes belonging to, produced by, or used at sea, etc., in many instances *maritime,* designating bordering on, connected with the sea, or pertaining to navigation or sea commerce, is similarly used; as in *marine* or *maritime affairs, insurance, law, loan, perils, risk, etc.* **M. adventure,** early legal term denoting the act or process of carrying a shipment of goods to a foreign port and effecting sale of such property at best price obtainable. Now denotes any voyage of a merchant vessel for the account of her owners or charterers. Also *see* ADVENTURE. **M. barometer,** *see* BAROMETER. **M. belt,** also called *territorial waters,* area or belt extending off and along a shore to limit of a state's jurisdiction seaward. Sea boundary of such marginal territorial area usually is considered as three miles off shore, called the *3-mile limit,* and, it is conceded, this is "so far fixed that a state must be supposed to accept it in absence of express notice." **M. board,** in Great Britain, two or more government officials located at principal ports and vested with authority for executing requirements of the *Merchant Shipping Act.* Among other responsibilities, certain members of such board authorize issuance of certificates of competency to masters, mates, and engineers upon candidates passing supervised examination for such documents. **M. boiler,** one used to produce steam for a vessel's propulsion plant; a Scotch or a water-tube boiler; *see* BOILER. **M. borer,** any of several wormlike mollusks which burrow in submerged wood; a shipworm. Best known and most destructive to vessels' bottoms, piling, wharves, etc., is the widely distributed *Teredo navalis.* **M. chair,** a reclining chair, suspended so as to remain still with relation to vessel's motion, from which an observer measured a lunar distance at sea; also, *lunar chair.* (Prior to advent of accurate chronometers, observations for longitude involved measuring distance of moon from sun, planet, or a star, which procedure often required observer to lie on his back in order to successfully manipulate the sextant or quadrant.) **M. chronometer,** time-piece for indicating correct prime meridian time in navigational work; *see* CHRONOMETER. **M. engine, engineer, engineering,** *see* ENGINE, ENGINEER, ENGINEERING. **M. glue,** *see* GLUE, MARINE. **M. guard,** *see* GUARD. **M. Hospital Service,** former hospital and relief service for seamen under direction of Treasury Department of U.S. Now a branch of *U.S. Public Health Service* under the Federal Security Agency. **M. insurance,** or

maritime insurance, *see* INSURANCE. **M. interest,** or **maritime interest,** that payable for a maritime loan, as in cases of bottomry and respondentia bonds. Sometimes called *bottomry premium,* there is no legal rate to which such interest is restricted because of recognized risk involved, lender losing all if loss occurs. *Cf.* BOTTOMRY. **M. league,** a distance of 3 nautical miles; *cf.* LEAGUE. **M. loan,** or **maritime loan,** one secured by a bottomry or a respondentia bond, or both; *cf.* BOTTOMRY. **M. metal,** usually a copper alloy, used for bottom sheathing in wooden vessels; *see* METAL. **M. policy,** *see* INSURANCE. **M. railway,** inclined railway extending into water for purpose of hauling up smaller vessels for bottom cleaning and painting, inspection, repairs, etc. It may be constructed to haul a vessel ashore either on end or sideways. Also, *slipway* or *slip-dock* and, sometimes, a *patent slip; see* **Slip-d.** *in* DOCK. **M. rainbow,** a sea-bow, or arc showing colors of the spectrum, often seen in a spray during sunshine. **M. risk,** chance of loss or any of several perils to which ship and/or cargo are, or may be, exposed. In *Lloyd's* standard policy, list of risks or perils insured against follow "*Touching the Adventures and Perils which we the Assurers are contented to bear and do take upon us in this Voyage, they are,*" (as given in **M.I. Policy** *in* INSURANCE). **M. soap,** also called *salt water soap,* as used at sea in interest of conserving vessel's fresh water supply, a soap containing a small amount of sodium and largely composed of coconut or palm oil, easily soluble in seawater. **M. store,** shop or ship-chandlery at which vessels' supplies may be obtained. Such supplies as are required for equipment or maintenance, as ordage, paints, flags, oakum, and tar, are termed *m. tores. Cf.* STORE. **M. superintendent,** often a former shipmaster, one responsible to owners for care, maintenance, manning, and berthing of vessels, their proper loading and discharging of cargo, drydocking, and general supervision of ship activities at a home port. Also called an *overlooker, port superintendent, port captain.* **M. surveying,** hydrographic surveying; *esp.* that branch which is concerned also with a topographic survey of coast or limits of a harbor, port entrance, or other narrow waters frequented by shipping. Also, *nautical surveying.* **M. surveyor,** one who inspects or examines vessels' structural condition, machinery and equipment, or who supervises building or repairing of vessels in interests of a classification society or insurance company. Also called *ship surveyor* and often also applied to an *engineering surveyor,* or one who is similarly interested in ships' engines and boilers, propeller-shafting, etc. Also, *esp.* in U.S., a representative of an insurance company who inspects condition and stowage of ship cargoes upon arrival or departure of vessels on which carried. **M. telephone,** a ship telephone, or one of the instruments in any of several patented communication systems installed aboard ship; particularly, that used for conveying orders from ship's bridge to engine-room, forecastle head, docking-bridge, etc. **Merchant m.,** the mercantile shipping of a country; total tonnage of vessels currently engaged in commerce of a nation. Also termed *merchant navy* and, *esp.* in Great Britain, *mercantile m.*

MARINER. A seaman or sailor; one whose vocation is that of sailing or navigating vessels, or in any way assisting in such occupation. The word usually is confined to legal use in which it is defined as "every person, male or female, employed in whatever capacity on board ship and whose labor contributes in any way to the accomplishment of ship's voyage." **M.'s compass,** *see* COMPASS. **M.'s lien,** *see* **Maritime l.** *in* LIEN. **M.'s needle,** *see* **C. needle** *in* COMPASS. **M.'s splice,** *see* SPLICE. **Master m.,** a skilled and experienced seaman who is certified as competent to command a merchant vessel. In old-time usage, a shipmaster actively in command; now usually referred to as "the master," "the captain," "the skipper," and, by the lower deck, "the old man."

MARINER'S MEASURE.

6 feet	= 1 fathom[1]
100 fathoms	= 1 cable[2]
10 cables	= 1 mile
6080 feet	= 1 mile[3]
3 miles	= 1 league

([1] *See* SOUNDING. [2] *See* **C.'s length** *in* CABLE. [3] *See* MILE)

MARITIME. Situated or living near, or bordering on the sea; as, a *m.* plant; a *m.* country. Pertaining to or connected with the sea in respect to commerce, navigation, or shipping; as, *m.* law; *m.* belt; *m.* lien. (In many instances synonymous with *marine*) Nautical; seamanlike. **M. belt,** *see* **M. belt** *in* MARINE. **M. Commission,** former U.S. government agency created by Act of Congress, June, 1936, as prescribed in *Chapter L of Merchant Marine Act, 1936 (46 U.S.C. 1101),* to foster development and maintenance of a U.S. merchant marine in interests of national defense and expansion of the nation's foreign and domestic commerce. The agency was absorbed by the *Commerce Department,* June, 1950, and replaced by the *Federal M. Board* consisting of three members headed by a Chairman, who is also chief of the executive body termed the *M. Administration.* Objectives provided for in the Act are: (*a*) to develop a merchant fleet sufficient to carry domestic water-borne commerce and a substantial portion of water-borne import and export commerce of U.S. and to provide shipping service on all routes essential to maintaining flow of such commerce; (*b*) capable of serving as a naval and military auxiliary in time of war or national emergency; (*c*) owned and operated under U.S. flag by U.S. citizens, insofar as practicable; and (*d*) composed of best-equipped, safest, and most suit-

able types of vessels, constructed in U.S. and manned by trained and efficient citizen personnel. **M. declaration,** chiefly in Great Britain, an extract from ship's log attested or sworn to by the master or other authorized officer of ship concerned, as in noting or entering a protest before a notary. **M. employer,** in connection with maritime labor relations in U.S. legislation under *Merchant Marine Act, June 29, 1936, sec. 1003 (46 U.S.C. 1253),* is defined as meaning "any person not included in the term '*carrier*' in Title I of *Railway Labor Act,* approved May 20, 1926, as amended, who (1) is engaged in the transportation by water of passengers or property in water-borne commerce; (2) is engaged in towboat, barge, or lighterage service in connection with transportation of passengers or property in water-borne commerce; (3) operates or manages or controls the operation or management of any wharf, pier, dock, or water space, for accommodation of vessels engaged in transportation of passengers or property in water-borne commerce; (4) is engaged in the business of loading or unloading vessels engaged in the transportation of passengers or property in water-borne commerce; or (5) operates any equipment or facility connected with the services set forth in clauses (1), (2), (3), and (4) hereof, which is necessary for the continuity of flow of passengers and property in such water-borne commerce." **M. exchange,** a port organization for mutual benefit of carriers, shippers, and others interested in water-borne commerce, similar in its purposes to a local chamber of commerce and, in fact, identical with that institution in less important U.S. ports. It fosters generally the shipping trade of port at which established and, in addition to collecting statistics, standardizing charter-party and bill of lading clauses, and arbitrating shipping disputes, establishes rules for local cargo handling, charges for demurrage, delivery, storage, etc. **M. insurance,** more commonly, *marine insurance; see* INSURANCE. **M. interest,** *see* **M. interest** *in* MARINE. **M. law,** *see* LAW. **M. lien,** *see* LIEN. **M. loan,** one secured by a bottomry or respondentia, or both; *see* BOTTOMRY. **M. nation,** a country bordering on, or near, the ocean and having maritime commercial interests. **M. perils,** *see* **M. risk,** *in* MARINE. **M. Service,** a voluntary organization for training of citizens of U.S. for service in licensed and unlicensed capacities in vessels of the nation's merchant marine under direction, supervision, and maintenance by the *Federal M. Board,* in accordance with Merchant Marine Act, 1936, sec. 216 (*46 U.S.C. 1126*). Ranks, grades, and ratings of personnel are same as prescribed in U.S. Coast Guard. Instruction at several shore stations with vessels attached thereto for sea training is maintained. **M. territory,** as understood in international law, waters within a *marine belt* (*see* MARINE) forming an ocean highway, as a strait, subject only to "innocent passage," or through which passage of a belligerent or hostile vessel may be forbidden. The *Dardanelles* and *Strait of Messina* are examples of such waters.

MARK. A line, notch, groove, etc., for indicating a limit, measure, or position of something; as, *freeboard* or *Plimsoll m.; lead-line m.; high-water m.* Indicated depth by hand lead-line when one of its *marks* is at water surface is reported, "*By the mark, 5,*" etc.; *see* **L.-line** *in* LEAD.[1] "*Mark!*" is often the call or order to a helmsman or by an observer to an assistant, as in noting exact heading by compass, time by chronometer, or an azimuth. **Bench m.,** as cut in a stone pier, piling, or other fixed object, a *m.,* usually in form of a horizontal line with an arrow-head showing its mid-point, for indicating a datum level in tidal observations or on a line of survey. **Birth m's,** Plimsoll, load-line, or freeboard marks, so called because placed on a new ship's sides before her first voyage; sometimes also applied to a local oddity in build or faulty feature in design of a new vessel. **Draft m's,** *see* DRAFT. **Flood-m.,** that indicating height to which a flood tide rises; line or *m.* on a riverside indicating limit of water rise during flood or freshet season. **Freeboard m's,** *see* **Plimsoll mark. High-water m.,** also *high water line; see* **H.W. mark** *in* HIGH. **Low-water m.,** *see* **L.-water line** *in* LOW. **Lubber's m.,** same as lubber-line; *see* **Lubber-l.** *in* LINE.[2] **M.-boat,** an anchored boat showing a flag or other distinguishing marker for use in nautical surveying or as a turning point in yacht-racing; also, for marking site or limit of submarine construction, a wreck, cable, etc., and sometimes at seaward end of fishing-nets extending from shore. **M.-buoy,** for similar uses as a *mark-boat.* **Plimsoll m.,** the various lines cut in and painted on each side of a vessel at half load-line length (*cf.* **L. on summer load line** *in* LENGTH), named for *Samuel Plimsoll (1824–1898),* British reformer called *The Sailors' Friend,* who conducted a strong campaign for fixing load-lines on British vessels. Plimsoll held that the many shipping disasters occurring for years were due chiefly to overloading and contended that Parliament should establish a load-line for every vessel. As a result, Parliament passed the *Merchant Shipping Act of 1876,* which provided that a circular disk with a horizontal line through its center must be painted on each side amidships on every British vessel, excepting those under 80 tons register in coastwise trade. *Plimsoll's line,* as it then was called, was to indicate greatest depth to which vessels should be loaded and the exact position of such mark naturally was the subject of many disputes. However, that question appears to have been settled some years later by general acceptance of both the *Board of Trade* and shipowners of fixing the mark according to reserve buoyancy tables of *Lloyd's Register of British and Foreign Shipping* (see LLOYD'S). It later was decided that load-lines should be placed on a more scientific and definite basis and

accordingly, in 1890 the *Load-line Act* was passed providing that marks should conform to Board of Trade regulations and position of disk to tables fixed by the Load-line Committee. Finally, this act was incorporated in the *Merchant Shipping Act of 1894,* provision being made for its modification by Board of Trade without reference to Parliament. Plimsoll's disk now is accompanied by several marks indicating vessels' allowed immersion in fresh water and during certain seasons within defined geographical zones in which vessels are navigated; *see* FREEBOARD. In U.S., assigning of load-lines was established by law March 2, 1929, effective Sept. 2, 1930, in conformity with *International Load Line Convention, 1930,* which was ratified Feb. 27, 1931, becoming effective Jan. 1, 1933. Assigning authorities in Great Britain are *Board of Trade, British Corporation,* and *Lloyd's Register;* in U.S., the law provides that *American Bureau of Shipping* or "*such other American corporation*" shall assign load-lines under regulations established from time to time by Secretary of Commerce (now by Commandant of Coast Guard). **Sea m.,** a lighthouse, beacon, or conspicuous object serving as a guide or marker in pilotage; often termed a *landmark; see* **L. marks** *in* LEADING. **Shoal m.,** a beacon or buoy marking a reef or shoal. **Square m.,** a few turns of spunyarn suitably placed on a brace as an indicator in squaring a yard; usually fixed near belaying-pin for easy reference. **Stray m.,** *see* **Stray-l.** *in* LINE. **Tide-m.,** a tidal height *m.; see* **H.-water mark** *in* HIGH *and* **L.-water mark** *in* LOW. **Top-m.,** shape or object surmounting a beacon or a buoy, as a ball, cage, arrow, cross, or the like. **Watch-m.,** *see* WATCH. **Water-m.,** *see* WATER.

MARKAB. *a Pegasi,* a star of magnitude 2.57 situated at S.W. corner of *Square of Pegasus.* In 1953 its sidereal hour angle is given as 14° 23' and declination 14° 58' N. A line from *Scheat,* or *β Pegasi,* his neighbor at N.W. corner of the Square, drawn through *Markab* and produced 45° southward passes very close to *Fomalhaut* (*a Piscis Australis*). (*Markab* should not be confused with *Markeb,* a 3rd magnitude star in *Argo* and catalogued by astronomers as k *Velorum* or k *Argus,* having a S.H.A. of 219° 50' and declination 54¾° S.)

MARKER. A short-range, local automatic radio-beacon fixed on a dolphin, pier end, buoy, etc., for indicating a channel entrance or turning-point, a pier, mouth of a small harbor, etc. Also, a marking-pin, or piece of small pipe used for marking intended rivet-holes on plates or templates; dipped in light paint and carefully laid on end at each required hole, thus leaving a small circular mark; used by the workman called a *marker-off, liner-off,* or *marking-off plater* in a shipyard.

MARKET. **M.-boat,** an inland water vessel or boat engaged in taking produce to a market. A fishing-boat which brings a fresh catch from a fleet to port for marketing. Colloquial term for a ship's boat detailed to carry provisions off from shore. **M.-fish,** as distinguished from cannery-fish, or such as is used in the canning trade, fresh, cured, or barreled fish, *i.e.*, other than the canned product. Formerly, *esp.* in New England, any fish suitable for marketing; often, *specif.*, a cod over 6 lbs. in weight. **Horsem.,** *see* **H.-market** *in* HORSE.

MARL. To secure with turns of marline, spunyarn, twine, or other small stuff, as canvas parceling to a hawser, each turn being held by the *marl*, or *marling, hitch* which is in effect an overhand knot made so that the worked part comes under the turn and thus substantially jams itself in place. In sailmaking, served flexible wire is secured to heavier sails as boltrope (leech, foot, etc.) in this manner, with 6 or 8 threads of twine or a good grade of marline.

MARLIN. (Short for *marline-spike*, as suggested by its protruding spike-like beak) A large oceanic game fish closely related to the sail-, spear-, and sword-fishes. Classified as genus *Makaira*, one species, *M. ampla*, is found in the Atlantic; three others, called *barred m.*, *black m.*, and *striped m.*, respectively, are taken in Pacific waters. The fish is known to attain a weight of 700 lbs. Commonly, a *spearfish*.

MARLINE. (Du. *marlijn*: from *marren*, to tie or bind; *lijn*, rope) Small stuff made of 2-yarn lefthand lay American or Russian hemp, usually tarred; used for service on smaller wires, small seizings, etc. A fine grade is called *yacht marline*. The untarred product makes a smooth job when used as service on a wire, but will not stand up to weather like the tarred stuff; for this reason not often used in merchant vessels. Weight, about 300 feet to the pound. Also, *marlin* and *marling*. **M.-clad rope,** *see* **F.-clad rope** *in* FIBER. **M. hitch,** or *marling hitch,* that used in securing parceling, lashing a hammock, lacing a sail to a boom or gaff, etc.; *see* MARL. **M. needle,** a pricker, or small pointed spike for piercing canvas, as in marling a leech-rope to a sail. **M.-spike,** the tapering, pointed, steel implement 12 to 24 inches in length, for separating strands of a rope in splicing, heaving taut parts of a seizing, screwing shackle-pins, etc. The boatswain-bird; *see* **B.-bird** *in* BOATSWAIN. **M.-spike hitch,** as used in heaving taut a seizing turn with a *m.-spike,* a lashing turn with a handspike, etc., a small loop made in the line and bight of standing part entered in loop; spike is inserted in bight and hitch jams when stress is brought on spike as latter is used lever-fashion. In practice, hitch is made about end of spike with turn of spike itself forming loop and its point picking up bight through the loop. The hitch is a convenient one, where rope's end is not in hand, for slipping line over a post, stake, etc., as in making fast a boat, stretching a guard-rope on a row of

stanchions, etc. **M.-spike seamanship,** that branch of seamanship concerned with splicing, knotting, seizings, lashings, and general rigging work in which use of the *m.*-spike is prominent; opposed to *deck seamanship,* or the art or practice of handling ship's equipment, as booms, boats, sails, anchors, cargo-gear; or stowage of cargo, mooring, and maneuvering vessel generally.

MARQ ST. HILAIRE METHOD. *See* MARCQ ST. HILAIRE METHOD.

MARRY. To set together the unlaid strands of each rope's end, as first step in putting in a long or a short splice. To stretch out two hauling parts of rope, as boat-falls, side by side so that both parts may be grasped and hauled on as one line by a number of men. To join two ropes end to end for reeving through a block, as in renewing a tackle fall. Two parallel ropes seized together at intervals are said to be *married;* also, a rig in which two cargo whips connect to one cargo-hook sometimes is called *married* gear, or whips thus connected, a *married fall*.

MARS. (Named for ancient Romans' god of war) Fourth planet from the sun and next outside the earth, easily recognized by its steady reddish light; mean distance from sun about 141,000,000 statute miles; its orbit from that of Earth, 35,000,000 miles; has a diameter of 4216 miles which gives an angular measure of 18″ at his nearest approach to earth; completes a revolution around sun in 687 days; has two small satellites; and plane of his orbit is inclined 1° 51′ from that of earth (the ecliptic). For navigators' use, planet's declination, Greenwich hour angle and time of transit are given in the *Nautical Almanac*.

MART or **MARQUE.** *See* **L. of Marque** *in* LETTER.

MARTENSITE. Named for *Prof. A. Martens, German metallurgist,* a condition of hardening and brittling in surfaces of wire rope, caused by alternate heating and cooling during running of wire over sheaves, which greatly reduces bending resistance of the material.

MARTINET. A rigid disciplinarian; officer who requires strictest adherence to detail and routine on the part of personnel under his command. In older square rig, a small leech-line handled from the yard for hauling sail close up to yard in furling; also, *martnet*.

MARTINGALE. (Said to be named from that part of harness which holds a horse's head down and prevents him from rearing) One of two or more chains extending from lower side of a jib-boom to lower end of *dolphin-striker* for sustaining stress on jib stays; also called *m. guy* and *m. stay* where dolphin-striker itself is termed *m. boom* or *martingale*. **M. backropes,** standing rigging from lower end of dolphin-striker (or *m. boom*) leading to each bow. With these holding against stress on *m's,* the whole *i.e., m's,* dolphin-striker, and backropes, forms a stiffening bridge-work against upward pull on jib-boom consequent to pressure of sail or aftward stress of upper masts during pitching of vessel in a seaway. *M. backropes* are also called *gob-lines* and *gaub-ropes.* **M. boom,** *see* BOOM.

MARTIN'S ANCHOR.   *See* ANCHOR.

MARU.   Part of name given each Japanese merchant vessel, as in *"Midori Maru," "Toyo Kuni Maru,"* etc., said to carry the idea of rounded-out perfection or completeness in accord with original symbolic meaning attached to a circle or a sphere.

MASCARET.   A flood tide wave peculiar to the Garonne and Dordogne Rivers on S.W. coast of France; *see* BORE.

MASHWA. *(Pers.)*   Name of a type of fishing and trading boat in the Persian Gulf and adjacent waters; varies from 30 to 50 feet in length. Noted as fast sailers, their one or two masts are stepped with a remarkable forward rake and carry settee sails.

MASK.   A vertical, transverse area of heavy planks braced by timbers attached to after end of a vessel to act as a retarding brake to her speed during launching, as within a limited stretch of water. Also termed a *shield* or *braker.*

MASOOLA.   Large oar- or paddle-propelled boat used on Coromandel coast of India for carriage of cargo and passengers between ships and shore. Averaging 30 feet in length by 10 in breadth and an excellent surf-boat, typical *masoola-boat* has no metal fastenings, all planking and framing being secured by coir yarns. Also called *masulah, chelinga, padagu,* and *salangu* (Tamil names).

MAST. (A.S. *mæst,* trunk of a tree; Scand. *mast*) Pole or spar of wood or tubular metal which supports a vessel's booms, gaffs, yards, and all gear for spreading sail or working cargo; also, as in a war-vessel, for raising a signaling or observation post, radio antenna, etc. Masts may be single wooden poles, as in boats and smaller vessels; single tubular steel spars; or a number of spars in consecutive extension, each of which also takes the name *mast,* as in *lowermast* and *topmast.* As larger ships were built, additional sail was spread farther aloft by fitting a *topmast* to the original single spar, which development appears in 14th-century vessels. A further need for sail spread was satisfied early in 16th century by the *top-gallant m.* and early in 18th century this gay-sounding spar was capped in the even loftier *royal-m.,* which later, except in some larger navy ships, became simply a lengthened topgallant *m.* on which to hoist the *royal,* or highest sail. To this series constituting a square-rigged ship's *m.* was added, in clipper ship days, a *skysail pole,* or further extension of topgallant *m.* This brings us to about 1850 when evolution of the square-rigger's mast had run its course, if we may except the *jubilee rig* that appeared in 1897, charac-

terized by *stump topgallant m's* which, in several instances fidded abaft the topmast, lowermast and topmast being in one steel spar. For centuries the three *m's* of the *ship* rig have been called, beginning forward, *foremast, mainmast,* and *mizzenmast,* respectively. In the 1870's came the 4-masted ship and barque in which the after *m.* was named *jiggermast;* and in the '90's a few 5-masted barques brought the *spankermast* as last in order from forward. Coincident with this multi-mast development in European square-rigged vessels was that of American-built *schooners* and by 1902 the *"Thomas W. Lawson"* appeared with 7 and their topmasts complete! The 4-masted schooner had *foremast, mainmast, mizzenmast,* and *spankermast;* 5-masted: *fore-, main-, mizzen-, jigger-,* and *spankermast* or *fore-, main-, middle-, mizzen-,* and *spankermast;* 6-masted: *fore-, main-, mizzen-, jigger-, spanker-,* and *drivermast;* 7-masted: *fore-, main-, mizzen-, jigger-, spanker-, driver-,* and *pushermast.* However, there appears to have been no fixed rule for the order in which these names were applied to *m's* abaft a mizzen. Craft having two *m's* of same size, or nearly so, have *foremast* and *mainmast.* The ketch and yawl rigs in which taller and larger spar is stepped forward of its mate, name the former *mainmast* and the after one, *mizzen-* or *jiggermast. M's* are held in position by *stays* leading forward and *shrouds* leading to each side of vessel, *backstays* leading from abaft shrouds to upper parts of each spar constituting the *m.* assembly. In modern war-vessels, *m's* have departed far from the spar form to structural towers or heavy tripods, though still adhering to original term *mast.* To *mast* a vessel is to fit her *m's* in place; *esp.* the lowermasts, upper *m's* being usually referred to as "sent aloft," "sent up," or "fidded." **Afore the m.,** or **before the m.,** indicating status of a "foremast hand" or sailor in a sailing-vessel; *cf.* AFORE. **Artemon m.,** kind of forward-raking foremast in ancient Mediterranean vessels, sail on which served same purpose as our present jib or jibs. It was forerunner of the later *bowsprit.* **At the m.,** on spar deck, at or near mainmast, or its regulation equivalent in modern naval vessels, official mustering place where Captain "holds mast" or deck court for investigating infractions of discipline, awarding punishment for offenses, and hearing complaints of lower deck personnel. **Before the m.,** *see* AFORE. **Built m.,** *see* BUILT. **Bury of a m.,** that part of *m.* which is below decks; also, *housing* of a *m.* **Collapsible m.,** *see* **Knuckle m. Dolphin of the m.,** *see last def. of* DOLPHIN. **Fore-m.,** usually written *foremast,* in vessels having two or more *m's,* that one next the bows. Often, in a ketch or a yawl where forward *m.* is much longer than after one, called *mainmast.* **Half m.,** *see* HALF. **Hand m.,** British term for a pole-mast; *specif.,* in mast-making, spar of from 24 to 72 inches (6 to 18 *hands* of 4 inches) in girth at one-third length from butt end.

Depending on wood concerned, number of hands in girth bears a certain proportion to length of *m*. **Head of m.,** *see* **H. of mast** *in* HEAD. To **hold m.,** *see* **At the m.** To **house a m.,** to lower, as a topmast or a topgallantmast, and temporarily secure to *m*. next below, as for passing under a bridge, effecting minor repairs, etc. **Jigger-m.,** usually written *jiggermast,* in square-rigged vessels of more than 3 *m's,* 4th one from forward; same in schooners having more than 4. To **jump the m's,** *see* JUMP. **Jurymast,** a temporary *m.; see* JURY. **Knuckle m.,** one hinged just above deck in small vessels for purpose of lowering the spar clear of bridges, as in a canal or river; also, *collapsible m.* **Lower-m.,** *see* **L.-mast** *in* LOWER. **M.-band,** metal hoop or band on a *m*. for strengthening purposes, as on a built *m.,* or one fitted with eyes for securing various blocks, belaying-pins, stays, etc. **M.-bed,** in wooden boats or small vessels, wedges or blocks around *m*. where it emerges from deck. **M.-cap,** *see* CAP. **M.-carling** or **carline,** one of two fore-and-aft timbers or steel girders between deck-beams in way of a *m*. for purpose of supporting ends of a cut-away beam and/or providing means for attaching and stiffening the *m. partners (q.v.); cf.* CARLING. **M. cheek,** *see* CHEEK. **M.-clamp,** hasp or hinged piece of metal for securing a boat's *m.* to a thwart; usually thwart is cut to receive *m.* behind the clamp or hasp. Also, a stout piece of hardwood fitted between beams in way of *m.* for strengthening deck; *m.* is wedged in a hole in clamp through which it passes. **M. cleat,** piece of wood or lug of metal fastened to a *m.* for holding a part of rigging from slipping in direction of stress, as a stay, eye at end of a lift, etc.; also, a horned piece of wood on a boat's *m.* for securing halyards, etc. **M.-cloth,** extra width or two of canvas sewn on after side of a square sail in way of the *m.* to take chafe against latter, as when sail slaps in light winds, when coming about, when aback, etc.; also termed *mast-lining.* **M.-coat,** heavy canvas fitted round *m.* and secured to deck as a means of preventing ingress of water where *m.* passes through deck; also called *petticoat* in small vessels. **M.-collar,** in steel vessels, angle-bar encircling and secured to a *m.* by its vertical flange, horizontal flange secured to deck, which latter is re-inforced by partner-plate. In some wooden vessels, it is a ring of hardwood fastened to both mast and deck in a similar way, but covered by a *m.-coat.* **M.-cover,** protective canvas laced about a *m.* in way of smoke from a funnel; also, *m.-cloth.* **M.-funnel,** broad metal band fitted on an upper *m.* to receive eyes of standing rigging, with view of sliding it upward as *m.* is lowered through cap of *m.* next below and as readily replaced upon sending *m.* aloft; *cf.* FUNNEL. **M.-head,** usually *masthead; see* **H. of mast** *in* HEAD; *cf.* MASTHEAD. **M.-hinge,** a *m.-clamp* or hasp; *see* **M.-clamp.** **M.-hole,** opening in deck through which a *m.* passes. **M.-hoop,** also termed *m.-ring,* one of the wooden or metal rings

or hoops which hold the luff of a fore-and-aft sail to its *m.* Seized to sail's luff *(fore leech)* at intervals, they slide up or down *m.* as sail is hoisted or lowered. Also, a *m.-band* girding a built *m.* at intervals of a few feet, as in lowermasts of many square-rigged vessels. **M. house,** formerly a high tower-like building at a quayside for hoisting *m's* in or out of vessels. Also called a *masting-house,* a heavy timber protruded from its upper part to serve as a crane, all necessary heavy hoisting-gear and sometimes a capstan being contained in the house. Later, a building in which *m's* are made, as at a shipyard. The term also denotes a small deck-house built around a *m.* serving as a derrick-table, or support for cargo-booms, a locker for cargo gear, etc., and, where required, control equipment for electric winches. **M.-ladder,** iron or steel ladder built to side of a *m.* It replaces older means of going aloft provided by ratlines on the shrouds. **M.-leech,** rarely used term for the *luff* or *fore leech* of a sail secured to after side of a *m.* **M.-lining,** *see* **M.-cloth.** **M.-partners,** stout framing or timbers fitted just below deck through which *m.* passes. Their function is to locally stiffen a deck in way of *m.* and also to distribute *m.* stresses via the *m. carlings* through the deck structure; *cf.* **M.-carling.** **M.-partner-plate,** or chock, one of the pieces of metal or timber fitted about partners as connecting pieces or chocks between partners and carlings. **M. pedestal,** *see* **M.-trunk. M.-plate,** particular type of steel plate used in construction of masts. **M.-prop,** a spar fitted as a support for a *m.* and so for relieving stress on shrouds when vessel was *hove down,* or *careened,* as in older sailing-ship days. (*Cf.* CAREEN) All upper *m's* were sent down and prop was fixed with its lower end on lee waterways, its upper end lashed to or cleated against lowermast. **M.-rope,** line used for sending up or striking an upper *m.* It is rove through sheave-hole at foot of *m.,* its end made fast at one side of cap of *m.* next below, and leads through a block at other side of cap; thence to the deck. In yachts and small craft, the term often is applied to *fore leech* of a sail; *see* **M.-leech. M.-step,** socket or strong box-like cavity that receives *heel,* or lower end, of a *m.* on the keelson, etc. *Mast* is said to be *stepped* when raised in position with its heel secured in *m.-step.* **M.-table,** *see* **D.-table** *in* DERRICK. **M.-tackle,** heavy purchase used for hoisting out or placing lowermasts of a ship; any tackle fitted on a *m.* for handling a heavy weight, sending aloft a heavy yard, etc. **M.-thwart,** in an open boat, thwart to which a *m.* is secured in stepping. **M.-track,** metal rail or track of H-shaped cross-section fixed vertically on fore or after side of a *m.* for confining luff of a sail by its hanks or a hoisting-yard to the *m.* Same arrangement is often found on under side of a standing gaff to take head of the sail. **M. truck,** a rounded flat block of wood fitted on extreme upper end of a single *m.,* or on that of uppermost *m.*

where more than one spar comprise the mast arrangement; usually fitted with a sheave or two, or as a dead-eye, for use of signal halyards in hoisting flags. In old sailing-navy days, "manning the yards" in ships of the line included a sailor standing on this lofty perch. By means of a small iron rod temporarily inserted in a hole between his feet, the man thus detailed steadied himself throughout a sometimes prolonged ceremony. *Cf.* To **m. the yards** *in* MAN. (There is no *"top of the mast"* in sea parlance; upper end of mast is either the *cap* or the *truck,* latter only being applied to upper end of uppermost spar in *m.* **M.-trunk,** a stout supporting structure for heel of a *m.* that is stepped on deck, as in some smaller craft, powered fishing-boats, etc. It is often arranged so that *m.* is pivoted on a thwart-ship bolt for lowering and held in upright position by a cross chock, as a stout pin or bolt. Also called a *tabernacle.* **M.-wedge,** one of the tapering pieces or blocks of wood driven between a *m.* and the partners; *cf.* **M.-partners.** A *m.* is *wedged* in its place immediately after being stepped and before any of its rigging is set up. **M.-whip,** a gantline or single rope rove in a block on a *m.,* as for sending gear aloft or lifting light weights. **M.-winch,** one attached to a *m.* in small vessels for heaving on halyards in setting sail, working cargo, etc. In its simplest form consists of a gipsy, hand-crank, and pawl. **M.-yard plate,** *same as* **M.-plate. M.-yoke,** or *yoke of m.,* that part of a *m.* on which the trestle-trees are laid, or part embraced by the shrouds at masthead. **Middle-m.,** usually written *middlemast,* on American 5-masted schooners, third mast from forward. **Military m.,** stout mast-like structure carrying a turret, an observation-tower, signal-bridge, etc., as on a war-vessel. **Pair m's,** two cargo-masts abreast each other at equal distances from midship center-line and joined by a heavy wire span or steel bridge-work at their upper ends; also called *goalposts.* **Pole m.,** one consisting of a single spar; *esp.* a lowermast and topmast, or a topgallantmast and royalmast, in a continued spar. A *m.* complete as a single spar is often termed a *single tree* or *single spar m.* **Rake of a m.,** inclination of a *m.* either forward or aft from the vertical. To **rake the m's,** to fire a broadside or a succession of shots aimed at an enemy's *m's* and rigging, as in old cannon days. To give *m's* a *rake* or certain inclination forward or aft, as when *masting* a vessel. **Royal-m.,** usually *royalmast,* continuation of a topgallantmast in a square-rigged vessel's *m.* assembly. The royal yard with its sail (*royal*) is hoisted or lowered on this *m.* Excepting a skysail pole which was a further upward extension and carried the *skysail* in clippers and later larger vessels, it is highest spar of all. In more recent frigates and ships of the line, *royalmast* was a spar apart from, and set up to, a topgallantmast. **Sheer m.,** so called from its resemblance to a pair of sheer-legs, two spars, each stepped at opposite sides of boat and meeting aloft, such as is

found in some East Indian and tropical Pacific craft. **Single tree m.,** *see* **Pole m. Skysail-m.,** often called *skysail pole,* extension of royalmast on which the small light-weather sail of that name was set; *cf.* **Royal-m. Sliding gunter m.,** *see* GUNTER. **Snow m.,** a *trysail m., q.v.* **Spare m.,** an extra *m.* kept aboard or ashore for a replacement. It was customary and sometimes required by underwriters for deep-water sailing-vessels to carry at least one spare lowermast and a spar which would make either a topmast or a lower yard; many carried more replacements than this on long voyages. **Spencer m.,** a trysail mast on which a *spencer* or *Duke of York* was set (*cf.* **Spencer** *in* SAIL); *see* **Trysail m. Structural m.,** one of square cross-section having continuous steel members at each corner and obliquely crossing steel bars or steel plates forming each of its sides; also, *lattice m.,* from its open-work form. **Stump m.,** any *m.* that is shorter than conventional spar of its kind; as, a *stump topgallantmast,* or one having no royalmast as an extension of such. **Telescope m.,** a topmast having its heel set in an iron or steel tubular lowermast so that, when struck (lowered), enters the lowermast telescope fashion. (An instance is recalled in which the *m.*-rope carried away and a topmast of this type disappeared into lowermast, apparently beyond recovery. Lowermast was filled with water and enough end of topmast reappeared to sling it for re-hoisting with a lengthened cargo-boom) **Tow m.,** spar for elevating a canal-boat's tow-line to clear bushes, etc., on bank of canal. **Tower m.,** a structural or lattice *m.; see* **Structural m. Trim of m's,** alignment or rake of *m's* with relation to ship and to each other. **Trysail m.,** formerly in square-rigged vessels, an auxiliary *m.* stepped on deck abaft a lowermast to which it was secured at its foot and head. The hoops of a spencer or trysail were set on this spar for securing luff of such sail; *cf.* SPENCER, *also* TRYSAIL *in* SAIL. Also was termed a *snow m.* from its first appearance on a brig having square sails of same size on each mast and called a *snow* in England, the *m.* being used to set vessel's spanker, or aftermost fore-and-aft sail, and sometimes referred to as the *spankermast. Cf.* **Spencer m.**

MASTED. Rigged or furnished with masts; chiefly as descriptive of a rig, as in *four-masted barque,* 5-*masted schooner.*

MASTER. Officer in command of a merchant or a fishing vessel, usually given the courtesy title of *captain;* shipmaster. Generally, a master must be certified as competent to take complete charge of a vessel and, due to his usually isolated position, in this respect is vested with considerable legal authority with regard to control of property in his custody and care. As the owner's representative and manager of his vessel, during a foreign voyage he may bind the ship, or even pledge a cargo in extreme cases, where funds are not immediately available for continuing a voyage; he may enforce a lien on his cargo for payment of freight or demurrage; and, in general, is provided with forceful legal backing in taking active steps to safeguard business interests of his vessel. By laws enacted in favor of the seaman, however, he is strictly accountable for any ill-treatment, real or imaginary, of members of his crew and must have clear-cut grounds for taking disciplinary action against any seaman he has engaged; in which respect his position is far removed from that of half a generation ago when rarely was his word or action questioned. To-day his responsibilities have increased under the more recent ponderous regulations prescribed for safety of life at sea which, particularly in U.S.A., have reached the proportions of an almost insurmountable mass of detail covering fire equipment, life-boats, maintenance and use of life-saving appliances, drilling of crew in use of equipment, precautions against accident to crew, cargo gear, hull, passengers, lading, etc., etc. The *master* formerly was a commissioned officer in U.S. and British navies whose duties corresponded to those of present *navigator* or *navigating officer,* usually of lieutenant rank. As describing a type of schooner, barque, etc., used as in *four-master, i.e.,* having 4 masts. **Ballast m.,** *see* BALLAST. **Extra m.,** in Great Britain, a certificated master (merchantman) who successfully passes a voluntary examination requiring more extensive practical and theoretical professional knowledge than demanded of a candidate for the *certificate of competency* awarded a *master.* **Harbor m.,** *see* HARBOR. **M. and commander,** title of present rank of commander in British navy prior to 1814. **M.-at-arms,** in a war-vessel, petty officer having charge of policing details in disciplinary matters; in a passenger vessel, crew member charged with general patrol and police duties. **M. compass,** in a gyroscope compass system, instrument containing mechanism providing directive power, as distinguished from a *repeater,* or compass-card electrically connected to the *m.* and showing same direction of ship's head by such means; *see* **Gyro c.** *in* COMPASS. **M. mariner,** *see* MARINER. **M.'s mate,** in British and U.S. navies, formerly a petty officer who acted as an assistant to the *master.* **M. of the hold,** chiefly in British cargo liners, a petty officer who supervises handling of cargo and luggage, cleaning and ventilation of holds, separation of consignments, etc. **M. porter,** in principal ports of Great Britain, agent who sorts or separates landed goods as a service to receivers or consignees of cargo and vessel concerned. Such agent or firm is subject to control of the port authority. **M. sh'pbuilder,** formerly, in wooden shipbuilding, the highly skilled directing superintendent who was responsible for proper construction and good workmanship. **M. shipman,** archaic term for a *m. mariner* or sailing-master; appears in Anglo-Saxon literature circa A.D. 500. **M. valve,** *see* VALVE. **Prize m.,** *see* PRIZE. **Ship-m.,** usually written *shipmaster,* person in command of a merchant vessel; a *m. mariner.* **Shipping m.; Sluice-m.; Whaling-m.;** *see* SHIPPING; etc. **Wreck m.,** person in charge of operations in salving a stranded or otherwise disabled vessel; a salvage-master; also, one put in charge of a wreck, wreckage, or cargo washed ashore, by its owner or salvor.

MASTHEAD. Upper part of a mast between a top or crosstrees and the cap, as *lowermasthead* or *topmasthead;* or between uppermost standing rigging and the truck, as *royalmasthead;* highest part of a mast. To display at, or raise to, the truck, as a flag; to raise a yard to full hoist of its sail. **M. angle,** *see* ANGLE. **M. compass,** same as **Pole-c.** *in* COMPASS. **M. knot,** also called *jury-mast knot,* made in bight of a rope and placed over a masthead, as in rigging a *jury mast.* When set on mast it has one small bight on fore side, to which a stay may be made fast; one on each side to which shrouds are secured; and remaining single parts lead abaft the shroud bights to do duty as backstays. Knot tightens up with stress on any of protruding parts noted. **M. light,** *see* LIGHT.[1] **M. lookout,** seaman stationed aloft on lookout duty; position from which such lookout is kept; *see* **C.'s nest** *in* CROW. **M. man,** seaman whose duty is to attend to sails and gear aloft, as in a large sailing-yacht; one who keeps lookout for schools of fish and directs vessel's course with aim of advantageously netting or seining; a *barrel-man* or *barrel's man,* as noted in BARREL. **M. pendant,** *see* PENDANT.

MASTIC. Wood of the *mastic tree* found in Florida and West Indies. It is hard, close-grained, durable, and valued in shipbuilding.

MASTING. Arrangement of masts in a vessel; the masts collectively. Disposition of masts in a sailing-vessel with regard to their function in spreading a balanced sail area and so providing craft with satisfactory steering qualities with particular rig considered. Special attention is given to position of hull's *center of lateral resistance* and, depending upon vessel's underbody lines, *masting* is so planned that center of gravity of ordinary sail area lies slightly forward of center of lateral resistance; *cf.* ARDENT. **M.-house,** same as *mast-house in* MAST. **M. sheers,** hoisting device for lifting masts into position or removing them; *see* SHEERS.

MASTMAN. In sailing-navy days, a seaman whose duty was to keep all gear of a particular mast clear for running and in good order. In British navy, for each mast a leading seaman called *captain of the mast* was charged with supervision of maintenance and working order of rigging, ropes, blocks, etc.

MASULA- or **MASULAH-BOAT.** See MASOOLA.

MAT. Piece of rough fabric made from interwoven rope strands or yarns, used in rigging to protect sails from abrasion against stays; yards against shrouds; ropes against rigging-lanyards, cross-trees, and edge of a top; to withstand wear of a block against a deck or other surface; etc. *Matting* is material for making mats; also, the manufactured webbing of coarse texture commonly laid as a carpet-like protection for part of a deck, a gangway, etc., or to muffle sounds of footsteps; as, *coco-nut, split bamboo, grass matting,* etc. Such material also is extensively used in hold stowage for protection of cargo from chafing or soiling against ship's ceiling, beams, stringers, etc., as in carriage of bales of silks, jute, burlap, etc., chests of tea, bags of rice, and other goods, chiefly from Indian and Far East ports. **Calking-m.,** originally a *m.* or piece of matting used by calkers when sitting or kneeling at their work; later, also a similar convenience for sailors when taking a nap on deck and corrupted, generally, to *corking-mat.* (*Calk* is an old sea term for a short interval of rest or sleep "all standing," *i.e.,* without removing one's clothes) **Cargo-m.,** *see* CARGO. **Chafing-m.,** any *m.* used as indicated in definition of MAT. **Collision m.,** *see* COLLISION. **Cork m.,** one made like a cushion, having a filling of granulated cork; used as a fender, particularly between vessel's side and a boat. **Corking-m.,** *see* **Calking-m. Dunnage m.,** or **matting,** for protection of cargo; *see* DUNNAGE. **Flemish m.,** a Flemish coil; *see* FLEMISH. **M.-boat,** kind of flatboat or scow, or two or more such craft fast together, on which *m's* made of brush are prepared and thence laid along banks of a river, as on submerged side of a levee, for protection against erosive action of current; also, *matting-boat.* **Mooring-m.,** any *chafing-m.* serving as protection for a mooring-line, as at line's bearing point in a chock, edge of a wharf, etc. **Paunch m.,** originally and literally, a *belly-mat,* or one laid around a lower yard as chafing protection where yard bears against shrouds and backstays, as when braced "sharp up" in sailing close-hauled; a *chafing-m.* made of a series of rope strands consecutively turned about each other and like knitted fabric in appearance. Also *panch* and *punch.* **Shag m.,** a *thrum m., q.v.* **Sword m.,** a *chafing-m.* made of rope strands or small stuff in same fashion as in weaving. So called because each time the weft is passed across the warp, former is struck into place by edge of a flat stick termed the *sword.* **Thrum m.,** *chafing-m.* made by sewing on, or thrusting through, a piece of canvas many short pieces of rope-yarn, thus forming a shaggy surface; also *shag m.; thrumb m.*

MATCH. Formerly a bunch of flax, hemp, cotton, cloth, wood, or paper saturated with sulphur for burning in a ship's hold as a fumigating agent; the hold was said to be *matched* by this means. Quality of having equal strength, fitness, etc.; as, *our brig was no match for the cutter.* **M.-hooks,** another name for clip-, clove-, or sister-hooks; *see remarks in* HOOK. **M.-rope,** formerly a small line made of inflammable material and slow-burning, such as was used in firing cannon.

MATE. (Old Du. *maet,* companion or mate) Officer next in command and assistant to the master of a merchant vessel; one of a number of officers in a merchant ship—from 2 to 8 or more, depending on size and type of vessel—who assist in navigation and operation of the ship; usually called *officers,* as, in a 3-mate ship, in order of rank, *chief* or *1st., 2nd.,* and *3rd. officers.* (*Cf.* OFFICER) A petty officer assisting a naval warrant officer; as, *boatswain's m.; gunner's m.; machinist's m.* A former special rating in U.S. navy designating a man placed in charge of small craft, watch officer on a laid-up ship, a receiving ship, etc., or such harbor duty. In legal parlance, "the mate" refers to person second in command, whether styled *chief officer, chief mate, first mate,* or otherwise on board; and ordinarily is also so termed, *esp.* in cargo vessels. Most maritime nations have laws requiring a minimum number of certificated or licensed *m's* to be carried, according to size and type of sea-going merchant vessel concerned. U.S. laws provide that every ocean and coastwise machinery-propelled vessel and every ocean-going vessel carrying passengers shall have in her service and on board a licensed *m.* or *m's* according to following scale: Every such machinery-propelled vessel of 1000 tons gross and over, 3 licensed *m's,* unless vessel is engaged on a run of less than 400 miles to her final destination, in which case, 2 licensed *m's* are required; every such vessel of 200 tons and less than 1000 tons, propelled by machinery, shall have 2 licensed *m's.* Also, a machinery-propelled vessel of 100 tons and less than 200 tons shall have 1 licensed *m.;* but, if engaged in a trade in which more than 24 hours are occupied on passage to port of destination, 2 licensed *m's.* (*46 U.S.C. 223*) From this statute it appears that a sailing-vessel, unless over 100 tons gross and carrying passengers, is required to carry 1 licensed *m.* only if over 700 tons (*46 U.S.C. 224*). A notable difference is seen in the British requirement that no more than 2 certificated *m's* is prescribed for *any* vessel above 700 tons gross. In U.S., *m's* are *licensed* upon passing the Coast Guard examination in professional ability as *chief, 2nd.,* or *3rd. m.,* according to qualification in service, on ocean or coastwise power-driven vessels. In Great Britain, a *m.* is "certificated," or issued a *certificate of competency,* upon successfully meeting the examination requirements, as either a *1st.* or a *2nd. m.* in foreign-going vessels, or a *mate* (formerly *Only Mate*) in those of the Home Trade. **Boatswain's m.,** *see* BOATSWAIN. **Carpenter's m.,** in a merchant vessel, assistant to ship's carpenter, usually rating as able seaman; in U.S. navy, a petty officer under the carpenter, recently changed in rating to *Damage Controlman; see* CARPENTER. **Gunner's m.,** *see* GUNNER. **Machinist's m.,** *see* MACHINIST. **Master's m.,** a former petty officer assisting the master, or navigating officer; *see* MASTER. **M. of the deck,** officer of the watch in a merchant vessel; in former navy days, a junior officer who attended to and reported on condition of weather decks and outside of ship's hull. **M. of the hold,** officer in charge of one or more of ship's holds in connection with loading or discharging of cargo. A naval rating in old sailing ships of the line, often also called *captain of the hold; see* HOLD. **M. of the hull,** synonymous with *m. of the deck (q.v.)* in naval history. **M. of the watch,** officer in charge of the deck in merchant vessels. Also a former naval title for a junior officer in charge of the lower deck in a ship of the line. **M.'s log,** chief officer's log; *see* LOG.[2] **M.'s receipt,** or ship's receipt, that given by the chief mate in acknowledgment of a specific consignment of cargo received on board, as when a vessel loads at a port in which an owner's interests are borne chiefly by the shipmaster. Upon presentation of *m.'s* receipts, master signs bills of lading after checking description of cargo indicated thereon with the receipts, thereafter retaining the latter in exchange for signed B/L's. **Navigating m.,** officer charged with care of navigational equipment and whose duties include special attention to navigation of vessel; *see* OFFICER. **Sailmaker's m.,** former ship rating of petty officer whose duties were chiefly maintenance of ship's sails under the sailmaker of sailing-navy days; in merchant vessels, an able seaman assisting ship's sailmaker.

MATTHEW WALKER. Probably named for some noted sea-dog, a stopper-knot made with the strands unlaid at a rope's end, suitable for securing rope from unreeving through a hole, as in a bulwark stanchion, rail, etc., or at ends of deck-bucket beckets, particularly in past days of sail. More appropriate for use with 3-strand rope than the *lanyard knot,* which was used with 4-strand hard-laid hemp in rigging dead-eyes, the *single M.W.* is practically same knot. The *double M.W.* is more bulky and perhaps not as neat in appearance. Such knots are made by passing each strand around rope *with the lay* and dipping its end up through either its own bight, bights of the other two, or through all bights thus made. In each case, the strands emerge from the knot lying close together; thus may be whipped before ends are cut off.

MATTING. *See* MAT.

MATTRESS. Heavy rough matting made of brush, poles, saplings, etc., for protecting river embankments, dikes, or a shore from erosive action of current. In some ports having a great tidal range, a horizontal surface or bed, usually consisting of a series of closely spaced timbers laid on the bottom at right angles to a wharf or pier, upon which a vessel berthed alongside may rest or ground at low water.

MAUI. (Pron. *mow-ie;—ow* as in *how*) In Polynesian mythology, a personage credited with establishment of general cosmic order and beginning of human culture. Traditional lore among the *Maoris* includes the controlling of the winds and placing of the sun to man's advantage by this hero and, also, his fishing the land from the sea, from which, in the Maori tongue, New Zealand is called *"The Fish of Maui."* **Ropes of Maui,** *see* ROPE.

MAUL. Heavy wooden hammer or mallet variously used aboard ship, as for driving hatch-wedges, hawsing down seams in calking, hammering down a cringle strop on a fid, etc.; a *beetle,* as usually termed by calkers; also written *mall.* The name today is extended to a heavy steel hammer usually having a pointed peen for driving out rivets or cable shackle-pins and other uses.

MAURITIUS FLAX; —HEMP. Made from fiber of the Australian giant lily, or giant fiber lily, and similar in texture to *sisal hemp.* It is cultivated in several countries chiefly for blending with manila hemp in rope-making; *see* HEMP.

MAYDAY. Corresponding to French pronunciation of *"m'aider,"* the spoken word prescribed by International Code of Signals to be used by *radiotelephony* in the case of aircraft in distress and requiring assistance. *International Conference on Safety of Life at Sea, 1948,* revised *Article 31* of International Regulations for Preventing Collision' at Sea to include, as *Rule 31 (e),* the above signal among other distress signals prescribed for *"a vessel or sea-plane on the water."*

MEAGRE. An European food fish of the *Sciænidæ* family (*Sciæna aquila*) similar in appearance to the *red drum-fish (cf.* DRUMFISH) of southeastern U.S. coast and member of same family, which also includes the *croaker, grunt, drum* and others noted for their croaking or grunting habits—a characteristic of the entire tribe. The *meagre* attains a length of 5 to 6 feet, is well-proportioned and has a long dorsal fringe extending almost to the tail from an anterior distinctive dorsal fin.

MEAKING-IRON. Older name for present *clearing-iron* or *reefer,* a tool used by calkers for removing old oakum from planking-seams. Probably the *making-iron* has stolen this original title in addition to corrupting it; *see* **Calking-irons** *in* IRON.

MEAL. **M.-flag,** *see* **Meal-f.** *in* FLAG. **M.-pennant** or **m.-signal,** also *mess-pennant; see* PENNANT.

MEAN. Occupying a middle position between limits or extremes; average; having an average value as of successive values in a complete cycle of a variable quantity. **M. draft,** numerical *m.,* or half the sum of vessel's forward and after drafts, or *draughts.* **M. effective pressure,** in a reciprocating engine, average pressure exerted on piston throughout each stroke in one revolution. It is the pressure used in calculating indicated horse-power of engine. **M. latitude** = middle latitude; *see* LATITUDE. **M. low water,** a plane of reference used on charts of a locality in which range of tides is small and consistently regular throughout a lunar month. It is the average level reached by water's surface in a lunar month, as expressed in distance below *mean sea level.* Depths indicated on such charts are those at *m. low water. Cf.* **T. plane of reference** *in* TIDAL. **M. noon,** *see* NOON. **M. of altitudes,** average value of a set of observed altitudes of a heavenly body. **M. of the tides,** average height to which tides rise at a given place within a certain period of time. **M. range of tide,** difference between levels of *m. high water* and *m. low water* at a given place. **M. refraction,** *see* REFRACTION. **M. sea level,** datum level from which heights of land elevations are measured. It is half tide level as obtained from a lengthy series of observations of tidal range. **M. solar day,** a period of exactly 24 hours as reckoned between successive transits of the *mean sun,* or fictitious point in the equinoctial having a constant increase of right ascension throughout the year. This motion is equal to the *m.* rate of the true sun's travel eastward and, as a consequence, *m. sun* is ahead or behind the *true sun* at different and approximately constant dates (maximum of 16m. 24s. in November) by an interval termed *equation of time* (*see* TIME). *Mean solar time* then may be indicated on a time-piece without the frequent adjustments required to keep it in step with the variable *sun-dial time* given by the true sun and chiefly for that reason was the imaginary *m. sun* introduced. Perhaps the best definition of the *m. solar day* is that it is the average length of all the days in a year. **M. time,** that kept by our clocks and corresponding to that referred to the *m. sun* at a standard meridian; astronomically, westerly hour angle of the *m. sun* reckoned from lower transit (midnight), or 0h. to 24h., *i.e.,* midnight to midnight.

MEASE. In Great Britain, a north country measure of herrings, mackerel, etc., equal to 5 hundreds, the "hundred" being from 100 fish to 124, according to local market custom; also *maze.*

MEASURAGE. Old term for customs duty on a vessel's cargo.

MEASURE. To compute or determine by any means the extent, quantity, dimensions, or capacity of; as, to *m.* the altitude (by sextant), a lot of cargo, a vessel's depth, cubic contents of a hold, etc. A table of measuring standards and their equivalents; a system followed in measuring; as, *board m.* (*see* BOARD); MARINER'S M. (*q.v.*); *Moorsom's m., see* TONNAGE.

MEASURED MILE. *See* MILE.

MEASUREMENT. Act, process, or result of measuring something; *specif.,* determination of number of units in a bulk of cargo; space within a hold;

or capacity of ship herself—also termed *admeasurement.* Present internationally recognized method of measurement for tonnage of vessels, in which 100 cu. ft. (2.8307 cu. meters) equal 1 ton, became law in *Revised Statute 4153* (*46 U.S.C. 77*) in 1895, following enactment of the British *Merchant Shipping Act,* containing similar legislation, in 1894. However, this method, known as the *Moorsom* system (after *George Moorsom,* surveyor-general of shipping in England, 1854) had become general ship *m.* practice 25 to 30 years before its inclusion in either country's statutes. M. by *Moorsom's rules* prescribed a satisfactory method of mathematical procedure and superseded what was termed the *New Measurement* that appeared as law in England in 1835—a rough method falling below Moorsom's in accuracy but giving a tonnage of similar value. It is difficult to discern the point in view, unless it were the fact that a *ton weight* of general merchandise occupies from 60 to 100 cubic feet, in that the old measure of *tons burthen,* or weight a vessel could carry, was so early considered insufficient for shipping requirements. At all events, with the enactment in 1773 of a law, subsequently termed *Builders' Old M.,* governing determination of tonnage came a difference in the meaning of a *ton,* insofar as merchant vessels were concerned, from that used for at least 200 years prior to that date. The *space ton,* or unit of capacity in which *gross* and *net registered tonnage* are expressed had then arrived. See TONNAGE. **Builders' Old M.,** as referred to above, a former customary rule rather than a law for measuring a vessel's tonnage by an empirical formula which considered length and breadth of hull only, depth being taken as equal to the half-breadth. Its use resulted in builders deepening and narrowing their ships with view of economy in tonnage taxes—a practice which also led to increased losses at sea due to lessening of vessels' stability under sail. The rule gave a tonnage of something like 60 cu. ft. to the ton as a fair average. **Cubic m.,** referred to freight charges where these are paid according to bulk or space occupied by cargo, as distinguished from weight of cargo regardless of measurement. **M. cargo** or **goods,** such as occupies generally, more than 40 cu. ft. per ton weight (2240 lbs.) and on which freight is charged according to bulk measure; opposed to *deadweight cargo* on which charges are made according to weight. **M. rate,** freight rate or charges on cargo stowing at more than 40 cu. ft. per long ton, or goods less in weight than 56 lbs. per cubic foot. Sometimes, however, this figure varies according to carrier's requirements and, where affreightment contracts read "freight according to weight or measurement at ship's option," *m. rate* may even be limited to goods more bulky than 50 cu. ft. per ton in general cargo freighting. In Great Britain, the rate usually applies to goods of more than 42 cu. ft. per ton. **M. ton,** generally, in America the *ship-*

ping ton of 40 cu. ft.; in British use, 42 cu. ft.; used as a standard in calculating bulk of cargo to which measurement rate applies. **New M.,** so called because of doing away with *Builders' Old M.* (as noted in opening remarks), was determined by product of mean length, mean breadth, and mean depth of inclosed spaces and dividing sum of products thus found by 92.4. The resulting tonnage gave a greater figure than Moorsom's rules, the system now in use. **Old M.,** = *Builders' Old M.*

MEAT-CARRYING SHIP. One specially built for carriage of *frozen* or *chilled* meats. Frozen beef, mutton, pork, fowl, and fish usually are carried at a temperature between 10 and 15 degrees *Fahrenheit;* chilled meats usually at 29°. For successful turnout the latter demand maintenance of a constant temperature while frozen products are not affected by variations of a few degrees. Each piece or carcase of chilled meat is suspended from a hook which slides along a rail secured to deckhead, thus allowing entire surfaces of the pieces contact with cooled air. Frozen meats require no such particular stowage, but must be kept clear of piping, etc., and raised clear of deck by wood gratings.

MECHANICAL. Of or pertaining to a mechanism; performed by machinery. **M. bilge-block,** in a dry-dock, one of several types of blocks so fashioned and rigged that they may be placed under a vessel by a tackle, hand screw-gear, hydraulic piston, etc., immediately after keel rests on its blocks, for supporting vessel as water leaves dock. Simplest and most usual form is one traveling on a heavy thwartship timber fitted with a pawl-rack, pawl on block holding it to its work as block is hauled into position by a tackle. Also termed *m. side-block* and *sliding bilge-block.* **M. davit,** any davit turned inboard or outboard by means of some mechanism, such as a screw-threaded spindle turned by a hand-crank, as used in launching or taking in ships' life-boats. **M. depth-recorder,** *see* SOUNDING. **M. stoker,** *see* STOKER. **M. ventilation,** system or process whereby various compartments, *esp.* in passenger vessels, are ventilated by forcing or inducing air circulation by means of blower fans usually electrically driven.

MEDICAL SUPPLIES. Ocean-going vessels of most countries are required by law to carry a chest of medicines, commonly referred to as the *medicine chest.* Medical supplies also include anti-scorbutics, as lemon or lime juice, which in American and British vessels must be served to crew within 10 days after diet has consisted mainly of salt provisions and as long as such diet continues. U.S. law in *Revised Statute 4569 (46 U.S.C. 666)* states: "Every vessel belonging to a citizen of the United States, bound from a port in the United States to any foreign port, or being of the burden of 75 tons or upward, and bound from a port on the Atlantic to a port on the Pacific, or vice versa, shall be provided with a chest of medicines; and every sailing-vessel

bound on a voyage across the Atlantic or Pacific Ocean, or around Cape Horn, or Cape of Good Hope, or engaged in the whale or other fisheries, or in sealing, shall also be provided with, and cause to be kept, a sufficient quantity of lime or lemon juice, and also sugar and vinegar, or other anti-scorbutics, to be served out to every seaman as follows: The master of every such vessel shall serve the lime or lemon juice, and sugar and vinegar, to the crew, within 10 days after salt provisions mainly have been served out to the crew, and so long afterward as such consumption of salt provisions continues; the lime or lemon juice and sugar daily at the rate of half an ounce each per day; and the vinegar weekly at the rate of half a pint per week for each member of the crew."

MEDREGAL. An amber-fish of the *Carangidæ* family, classified as *Seriola fasciata,* found in West Indian and other tropical waters; *cf.* AMBER JACK. Also, *madregal.*

MEDRINAQUE. (*Sp.*) Kind of coarse cloth made from fiber of same name obtained from the sago palm in Philippine Islands. It is used in packaging valuable cargo. The old name *medrinacks* for a heavy coarse canvas probably stems from *medrinaque.*

MEET HER! In steering, order to shift the helm to counteract vessel's swing, as toward a new course, or to timely check a tendency to luff or fall off, as on approach of a squall or influence of a current; also *check her! Cf.* **C. the helm** in CHECK.

MEETING VESSELS. Those proceeding on such courses as to involve risk of collision; *esp.* in an end-on situation, or when approaching each other *head to head,* or nearly so.

MEGAPHONE. (Gr. *megas,* great; *phone,* voice, sound)   The *speaking-trumpet* or conical-shaped funnel through which one's voice may be directed in giving orders, hailing, etc. Any instrument for magnifying or directing sound in greater volume, *esp.* in increasing range of the voice.

MELTEM. The *Levanter,* or tempestuous wind of the eastern Mediterranean; *see* EUROCLYDON.

MEND. Old word meaning to re-adjust or set in order, *esp.* in to *mend sail,* or to refurl sails poorly made fast; also, to renew defective robands, lacing, etc., securing sails to their yards, booms, or gaffs.

MENHADEN. (From a Narragansett Indian word meaning *fertilizer,* the fish having been used as such in corn-fields)   Fish of the herring family, resembling the shad but with more compressed body and proportionately larger head; averages about 14 inches in length and has closely set bluish silvery scales. Of North Atlantic habitat, it is found in enormous schools on eastern U.S. coasts. In 1948, the menhaden yielded some $10,000,000 worth of oil, meal, and dry scrap, representing a catch of about 900,000,000 fish; from which it appears the *mossbunker,* as it is sometimes called, is America's most valuable fish. It is, however, of little worth as food. Powered vessels about 150 feet in length, equipped with two or three boats and seine-nets, capture the fish for processing at various factories along the coast from Florida to New Jersey.

MENKALINAN. Star of magnitude 2.07 in *Auriga,* located about 8° east of *Capella,* the second brightest in the northern sky. Usually catalogued as β *Aurigæ,* it has a sidereal hour angle of 271° and declination of nearly 45°, lying 37½° due north of the red *Betelguese* in *Orion's* group, or roughly half way from that star toward *Polaris.*

MENKAR. α *Ceti,* a star of magnitude 2.82 lying somewhat isolated at about 40° W. by N. of *Orion's belt.* Only member of consequence in *Cetus,* it makes a tolerable western corner for an equilateral triangle formed by *Aldebaran* to the N.E. and *Rigel* toward the S.E. Its S.H.A. is about 315°; declination 4° N.

MERAK. One of the *pointers* in *Ursa Major,* the *Great Bear,* or *Big Dipper,* star at lower corner of the *bowl* and farthest from *handle* of *Dipper.* Listed as β *Ursæ Majoris,* has a magnitude of 2.44, S.H.A. of 195¼°, and declination 56½° N.

MERCANTILE MARINE. *See* **Merchant m.** *in* MARINE.

MERCATOR, Gerhard. Flemish geographer (*1512–1594*) credited with introducing a projection of earth's surface subsequently found second to none for mariners' use in latitudes up to about 75°; *see* **Mercator's c.** *in* CHART. **M. sailing,** in navigation, art or practice of following a track laid down on a chart constructed on principles of *Mercator's projection; see* SAILING.

MERCHANT. One who engages in large scale traffic, *esp.* in foreign trade. Old term for a trading-vessel; a merchantman. Pertaining or belonging to the mercantile marine of a country or its ship-borne commerce; as, *m. navy; m. shipping.* **Merchants Adventurers** (or **Venturers**), noted English chartered trading company which carried on an enormous business, chiefly in export of cloths, its important monopoly, with the Netherlands and neighboring continental countries during 14th and 16th centuries. Its successful broadening activities served as a model for the great companies instituted in 16th and 17th centuries for a wider and far-reaching foreign trade. In 1555, a company also under this title was granted the royal charter for discovery of unknown lands, *Sebastian Cabot* (*died 1557*), the famous navigator, being named life-long governor of the "venture." **M. marine,** *see* MARINE. **M. navy,** total fleet or tonnage of all commercial vessels under a nation's flag. **M. seaman,** person qualified for duty on board, or engaged as a member of the crew

of, a *m.* vessel. **M. service,** maritime commerce; *m.* marine as a field of employment, distinguished from naval service, that in yachts, fishing-vessels, harbor craft, etc. **M. shipping laws,** branch of a nation's navigation or maritime legislation concerned with rights and obligations of persons, including masters and mariners, and also vessels considered as entities, engaged in the business of transportation and protection of merchandise or passengers by sea; providing for questions of claims for services to shipping, such as salvage, supplies, pilotage, towage, and wages; and governing practice in freighting contracts, insurance, general average, charter-parties, and other business matters. Notable under this caption is the British *Merchant Shipping Act of 1894,* with subsequent amendments, which in many respects has served as a model for similar legislation by other maritime nations. **M. vessel,** a trading or commercial vessel; a merchantman. The term ordinarily is applied to any vessel employed in carriage of goods or passengers for hire. However, as distinguishing a class of shipping, other than naval or government-owned craft employed in special services, or yachts, a *m. vessel* has been held to mean any commercial vessel or privately owned craft engaged in carrying goods or passengers, fishing, dredging, towing, or other business or occupation.

MERCHANTMAN. A trading-vessel; a ship employed in transportation of merchandise or passengers, as distinguished from a naval vessel, fishing-vessel, yacht, whaler, etc.

MERCURY. Smallest major planet in our solar system and nearest known body to the sun around which at a mean distance of 35,960,000 statute miles he makes a revolution in 88 days. About 1½ times the moon in diameter, when nearest the earth his angular diameter is barely 11″, making clear atmospheric conditions a necessity for observing the planet shortly before sunrise or after sunset during the few days near his W or E elongation, maximum value of which is about 23°.

MERCURIAL BAROMETER. *See* **Mercury b.** *in* BAROMETER.

MERIDIAN. (L. *meridianus,* pertaining to noon) A great circle of the celestial sphere passing through the poles and the zenith of any place. A heavenly body reaches its greatest altitude when passing from east to west each day, as the sun at noon, across the *meridian,* which event is termed *culmination, transit,* or *meridian passage* of such body. The hour circle of a celestial body, therefore, coincides with the *meridian* at that instant, since body's local hour angle is *zero; cf.* **H. circle** *in* HOUR. The opposite halves of an observer's meridian, or those passing through his zenith and nadir respectively, usually are termed *superior* or *upper m.* and *inferior* or *lower m. Cf.* CULMINATION. On the earth's surface, a *meridian* is that half of a great circle included between the geographical poles and passing through a given place; or, as indicated on a chart or map, any part thereof drawn in a true north and south direction, and therefore through all points having same *longitude*. The plane of such great circle coincides with that of the *celestial m.* and sweeps eastward through 360° each day with earth's rotational motion. Thus, position of a given meridian with relation to a celestial point, as the sun or a star, marks solar or sidereal time at place in question. (*See* LONGITUDE) Latitude of a place or point is measured on its *meridian,* or point of intersection of latter with parallel of latitude considered plots geographical position of place; *cf.* LATITUDE. **Astronomical** or **celestial m.,** the great circle passing through an observer's zenith and both celestial poles; *see opening notes,* MERIDIAN. **Magnetic m.,** *see* MAGNETIC. **M. altitude,** angular elevation of a heavenly body above an observer's horizon at instant of body's transit, as used in determination of latitude; *cf.* LATITUDE. **M. circle,** astronomical instrument essentially consisting of a telescope mounted to turn in plane of observer's *m.* and a vertical graduated circle for setting axis of telescope at any desired angle with the horizon or for measuring altitudes (or zenith distances = complements of altitudes) of heavenly bodies at transit. Also called *transit circle* and *m. instrument,* is often employed solely for observing exact time of transit of a body and hence a means of checking clocktime to any desired degree of accuracy. **M. distance,** an obsolete term for arc of a parallel of latitude limited by the respective *m's* of two places, expressed in nautical miles. It corresponds to our present *departure* or a distance equal to the difference of longitude times cosine of latitude considered. **M. passage,** transit or culmination of a celestial body; *see opening notes,* MERIDIAN. **M. sailing,** steering a true north or south course with purpose of maintaining vessel's same longitude. **M. zenith distance,** angular distance or arc of an observer's *m.* between center of a celestial body and the zenith at instant of upper transit. Used in determining latitude, it is equal to *90°* less *corrected meridian altitude.* **Observer's m.,** as often used in nautical astronomy, celestial *m.* of a place at which a person takes an observation, as with a sextant at sea. **Prime** or **first m.,** that from which longitude is reckoned; *see* GREENWICH, *also* LONGITUDE. **Reduction to m.,** *see* REDUCTION. **Secondary m.,** in an extensive survey, a *m.* accurately established with relation to the *prime m.* and located in or near the field for more convenient reference in determining longitude of basic points in the triangulation or hydrographic survey. *Cf.* **L. by transit** *in* LONGITUDE. **Terrestrial m.,** one of the lines running true north and south on a map or chart, usually drawn to indicate an even degree of longitude; *see opening notes,* MERIDIAN. **Tertiary m.,** one established as a sec-

ondary to another previously instituted with reference to a prime *m.; see* **Secondary m.**

MERIDIEM. (*L.* = *midday*)   Usually abbreviated *M.* or *m.* in *A.M.* (or *a.m.*) and *P.M.* (or *p.m.*) in designating hour by clock with respect to midday or noon. **Ante m.** = before noon. **Post m.** = after noon.

MERIDIONAL.   Of, pertaining to, or like a meridian. In older use, also pertaining to the sun's position at noon; as in *meridional reduction,* the later *reduction to the meridian; see* REDUCTION. **M. difference of latitude,** as used in *mercator sailing,* numerical difference between *meridional parts* corresponding to latitudes of points of departure and destination, respectively. **M. distance,** archaic term for *difference of latitude;* also, but incorrectly, for *m. diff. lat.* **M. parts,** in mercator sailing and construction of a Mercator's chart, the numerical value to which latitudes of places considered must be increased in order to maintain their true relation to each other in bearing and distance, when charted according to Mercator's projection. *M. parts* are given in navigation tables for each minute of latitudes, usually up to 80° (practical limit of Mercator's chart), a minute of latitude at the equator being the unit adopted. Based on the assumption that our planet is a perfect sphere, Mercator's projection originally was laid out by increasing the distance between each parallel of latitude according to *secant of latitude,* meridians being equidistant and parallel; present values are those revised to conform to the now known oblate spheroidal shape of the earth. In constructing a Mercator's chart of a few degrees in latitude extent, ample accuracy is obtained in spacing the latitude parallels according to measurement of 1° of longitude times the secant of latitude considered; thus, if 1° of longitude = 2 inches, with base of chart at 50° latitude, then 2″ times *sec* 50½° (half-way between 50° and 51° parallels) = 2 x 1.572 = 3.14 inches, or distance between 50th and 51st parallels of latitude. *Cf.* **Mercator's c.** *in* CHART.

MERRY DANCERS.   *See* **A. polaris** *in* AURORA.

MERLON.   In a raised deck bulwark, *esp.* that of a poop in early gun-armed vessels, that part between openings for guns—similar to each raised part between embrasures in a battlemented wall.

MERMAID. (A.S. *mere,* sea; *mægden,* maiden) The fabled beauty represented as having a graceful form like the tail end of a fish from her waist downward; a sea nymph. She appears to have been handed down from the marine branch of Greek mythology in which is included an important group of such hussies called *Oceanids,* some 3000 in number and constituting the offspring of the god *Oceanus* and *Tethys,* brother and sister in the *Titan* family of original great ones in the earth.

MERO. (*Sp.*) The large members of the grouper family—*black jew-fish, guasa,* and *red grouper*—that are found in warmer seas; *see* GROUPER.

MESH. One of the openings or spaces formed by the threads, cord, wire, etc., of which net-work or meshing is made, as in a fishing-net, wire screen, or a sieve. Size of the usual square *mesh* in a fishing-net is usually its length as fully stretched from two of its opposite corners, but sometimes considered as length of one side; thus a mesh measuring 6″ by former method has a 3″ side. Fishing-nets usually are made *diamond-hanging m.* fashion, *i.e.,* each *m.* being secured at a single corner to head-rope of net, all parts lying at a 45° angle with rope. *Mesh-work,* or *meshing,* as in such nets, is formed by making a *weaver's knot* or *m. knot* (same as *becket* or *sheet bend*), or a square knot in small work, at projecting corner of each successive *m.* in a row, size of opening for new *m.* being gauged by a short stick, oval-shaped in cross section, variously named as *m.-stick, m.-pin, moot, gauge, spool,* etc. For conveniently passing the material in making each knot, line is wound on a kind of wood shuttle termed a *meshing-needle.* In machinery, toothed gear wheels are said to be *in mesh,* or *mesh,* when they engage or are in working contact. **Square-hanging m.,** as describing a fishing-net, each *m.* lying square to the head-rope, or having two sides parallel to it.

MESS. In a ship's complement, group of persons who customarily take their meals together; as, *warrant officers' m.; wardroom m.; steerage m.* Place or room on board in which meals are served; a mess-room. To **lose the number of one's m.,** *see* LOSE. **M. beef,** as included in ship provisions, barreled salt beef chiefly consisting of the lesser marketable cuts. **M.-boy,** one who waits on table and generally serves in a mess; *esp.* in U.S. merchant service, a *messman.* **M.-chest,** chiefly in older naval use, one of the covered chests belonging to each *m.* of the crew for keeping small articles of tableware, etc. **M. gear,** pots, pans, knives, forks, etc., for use in a *m.* **M'mate,** an associate in a *m.;* a member of a *m.* composed of enlisted men. **M. pennant,** *see* **Meal p.** *in* PENNANT. **M. pork,** barreled salt pork, usually consisting of shoulders and sides of light weight hogs, in pieces of 4 to 6 lbs. each. **M. whistle,** boatswain's pipe calling men to meals. **Wine m.,** chiefly in older naval custom, total charges constituting an officer's wine account for a voyage or certain period of time: such account rendered.

MESSENGER. Any handy length of rope bent to a cable, hawser, etc., as a means of hauling or heaving such into a desired position, as in taking end of a heavy line ashore or heaving it aboard. **M. chain,** as used in driving a pump, windlass, capstan, etc., an endless chain connected to and operated by a winch; grab-wheels or gypsies hold the chain in its working bights. An enlisted man, equivalent to an *orderly* in the army, who attends the officer of the deck in a war-vessel, is usually called a *messenger.*

MESSROOM. Dining-room or space in which all or part of ship's crew eat their meals. In a merchantman, *saloon* is general term for an officer's dining-room; in naval use, *wardroom mess.*

METACENTER. (Gr. *meta,* over, about; + *center*) In ship stability, the *transverse m.* is that point of intersection of a vertical line through vessel's center of buoyancy, when she is floating upright, with a vertical line through the new center of buoyancy upon being inclined, no change in displacement taking place. *Positive* initial stability is present when *m.* occurs *above* vessel's center of gravity; *neutral,* if coincident with *m.;* and a *capsizing force* obtains where *m.* is *below* center of gravity. Similarly, the *longitudinal m.* is point of intersection of a vertical through ship's centers of gravity and buoyancy, when she is on an even keel, with a vertical through new center of buoyancy upon vessel being depressed at either end. *Positive* longitudinal stability is always present since that point of intersection always is located at a great height—generally about vessel's length—above the hull. **Metacentric height** is vertical distance of *m.* from center of gravity of vessel and all weights on board, and usually is referred to or indicated in a stability diagram as *G M.* Unless otherwise specified, it is vessel's transverse *G M,* the *L G M* being usual notation for *longitudinal metacentric height* which, ordinarily, is not considered in questions of stability. The *G M,* or *metacentric height* for small angles of heel (up to about 12°) is very nearly constant and, mathematically, is a function of vessel's initial dynamic stability or righting power, expressed as a moment in foot-tons and equal to *G M x sine of angle of heel x displacement,* G M times sine of heel angle being the *righting arm* (or *lever*), or horizontal distance between center of gravity of the mass and a vertical line indicating upward thrust of total buoyancy (considered as concentrated in center of buoyancy). *Cf.* STABILITY. **Curve of m's,** *see* **C. of transverse metacenters** *in* CURVES OF SHIP CALCULATIONS.

METAL. Effective power or caliber of a war-vessel's guns; usually in a comparative sense, as in *more metal in her battery than the cruiser's;* guns, collectively, as carried in a war-vessel's armament. To sheathe a wooden vessel's bottom with sheets of copper or other protective metal, which is sometimes referred to as the *metalling* (or *metaling*). **Composition m.,** also termed *Muntz m.* and *marine m.,* as used in thin sheets for bottom sheathing on wooden vessels, and said to be less expensive and more efficient than the pure copper originally employed for protection against marine growth, teredo worm, etc., a yellow alloy of about 3 parts copper and 2 parts zinc, malleable when hot and more easily welded than copper; generally termed *copper sheathing*. **Heavy m.**, guns or shells of large caliber. **M. mike,** the gyro-pilot or iron mike; *see* GYRO. **M. grommet,** small ring of brass, galvanized iron, or other non-corrosive metal, sewn in a sail, awning, canvas cover, etc., around each hole through which a lacing or stop is passed for securing; an *eyelet* of brass, having opposite sides interlocking, fitted around such hole.

METALLIC. Of the nature, or consisting of, metal. **M. ammunition,** formerly *case ammunition; see* **Fixed a.** *in* AMMUNITION. **M. lifeboat,** one in which entire shell and frame-work are made of metal, to-day usually of a non-corrosive type; *cf.* **L.-boat** *in* LIFE. **M. packing,** *see* P.-ring *in* PACKING.

METEOROLOGICAL. Of or pertaining to *meteorology,* or science treating of the atmosphere and its phenomena, including winds, storms, precipitation, variations of heat and moisture, and predictions of changes in weather conditions over specified areas of land or sea; or, as pertaining to *ocean meteorology,* also including, by extension, wind-drift currents, origin and paths of tropical cyclones, sea temperatures, trade winds, water-spouts, and other hydrographic phenomena. **M. chart,** a weather-chart; *see* WEATHER. **M. tide,** *see* TIDE.

METER. Head-rope or foot-rope forming upper or lower edges of a fishing-net. Also *metre,* unit employed in depths and heights indicated on charts published by most countries using the *metric system* of measurement, including Austria, Chile, Holland, France, Germany, Italy, Norway, Portugal, Spain, and Sweden. It is equal to 3.281 feet or 39.37 inches. *Cf.* METRIC SYSTEM. **Angle-m.,** *see* ANGLE.

METHOD. Mode of procedure; regular style or way of accomplishing an end; ·*specif.,* that concerned with navigational work; as, *Ageton's m.; Todd's m.; rectangular m.* **Ageton's m.,** *see* AGETON. **Rectangular m.,** *see* DEVIATION. **Sumner's m.,** *see* SUMNER. **Todd's m.,** used in calculating correct time interval between observations, considering vessel's change of position in longitude; *see* TODD'S METHOD.

MEW. A gull; esp. *Larus canus,* the common European gull; also called *mew gull* and *sea-mew. Cf.* GULL.

METRIC SYSTEM. The decimal system of measures and weights which originated in France about 1800 and subsequently made law in many countries. It is based on the *meter* (or *metre*), which is one ten-millionth of the distance measured at sea level on a meridian between the equator and either pole, equal to 3.281 feet or 39.37 inches. Primary units are the *are,* = 100 square meters; the cubic meter, or *stere;* the *liter,* = volume of a cube having sides one-tenth meter in depth; and the *gram* (or *gramme*) = weight of a cube of distilled water at 4° *Centigrade* having sides one-hundredth of a meter in depth. Multiples of these are designated in increasing order by Greek prefixes *deca-, hecto-, kilo-, myria-,* as in decameter, hectometer, kilometer, myriameter, or 10, 100, 1000, and 10,000 meters, respectively, in measures of *distance;* decaliter, hectoliter, kiloliter (or *stere*), or 10, 100, and 1000 liters as measures of *capacity;* and decagram, hectogram, kilogram, and myriagram, or 10, 100, 1000, and 10,000 grams, respectively, as measures of *weight.* Parts of the primary units are designated successively by Latin prefixes *deci-, centi-, milli-,* as, in measures of *distance,* decimeter, centimeter, millimeter, or one-tenth, one-hundredth, and one-thousandth of a *meter,* respectively; in *capacity,* as, deciliter, centiliter, milliliter, or one-tenth, etc., of a *liter;* and in *weight,* decigram, centigram, milligram, or one-tenth, one-hundredth, etc., of a *gram.* In surface measure, the *are* is multiplied in the *hectare* to 10,000 square meters, while divided in the *centare* to one square meter. **Decimeter,** unit often used in marking stem and stern drafts on vessels of nations employing the *metric system,* is equivalent to 3.937 inches. For English *feet,* multiply *decimeters* by 23 and divide by 70. **Gram,** weight of a cubic centimeter of distilled water at greatest density, or 15.432 grains *avoirdupois,* or .035 of an ounce. **Kilogram,** usually shortened to *kilo,* 1000 grams or 2.2046 lbs. *avoirdupois.* To convert *kilos* to pounds, very nearly, multiply by 11 and divide by 5. **Kilometer,** a distance of 1000 meters, equivalent to 3280.8 feet or .54 of a nautical mile, very nearly, or about five-eighths of a statute mile. For *nautical miles,* multiply *kilometers* by 41 and divide by 76. **Liter,** capacity measure of 1 cubic decimeter, = 61.02 cubic inches, = 1.0567 U.S. liquid quarts or .908 dry quart. **Meter,** also *esp.* in British use, *metre.* To convert meters to *feet,* multiply by 3.28; to *fathoms,* multiply by 6 and divide by 11; *also see* METER. **Metric ton,** also termed *tonneau* and *millier,* weight of a cubic meter of distilled water at 4° *Centigrade* (39° *Fahrenheit*), or 1000 kilograms (or *kilos*), equivalent to 2204.6 lbs. In converting kilos to tons, as sometimes required in handling heavy cases, machinery, etc., for shipment, a close approximation to the 2240-lb. ton (as used in shipping) is obtained by dividing by 1000; thus, a piece of cargo weighing 4015 kilos is only about a hundredweight less than 4 long tons. An exact result here may be found by multiplying the 4.015 *metric tons* (represented in 4015 kilos) by .984, which gives 3.95 *long tons,* or 112 lbs. short of the former method. **Millimeter,** frequently used in scientific work, refined gauge or instrument readings, etc., one-thousandth of a meter, or .03937 inch; also *millimetre.* **Quintal,** weight of 100 kilos, or 220.46 lbs. Confined to the *metric system,* not to be confused with British and U.S. hundredweight, also called *quintal* in certain trades, or a few other weights of the name in different countries. **Stere,** measure of volume equal to the *cubic meter* or 35.34 cubic feet. It is the space which 1 metric ton (2204.6 lbs.) of distilled water at 4° *Centigrade* would occupy.

MIAPLACIDUS. Star of magnitude 1.8 in *Argo,* catalogued as either *β Argús* or *β Carinæ* (see ARGO), having a S.H.A. of 221° 50′ and declination 69½° S. Southernmost of all stars suitable in magnitude for navigational observation, it may be located S 71° W and distant about 20° from *Acrux,* the star marking lower extremity, or "foot" of the *Southern Cross,* at that group's upper transit.

MICHENER COALING GEAR. A patented system featuring one or more electrically-driven elevators used in bunkering large steam-vessels with coal from lighters lying alongside. Each elevator delivered the coal to ship through two coaling-ports by separate spouts or chutes and included in the system was a series of rotating discs, permanently installed in ship's bunker space, for trimming the coal into remote corners as necessary. Chiefly employed by trans-Atlantic liners, the system greatly shortened both time and labor required in former methods. Since general displacement of coal by petroleum as boiler fuel, *Michener* gear is now but a matter of history.

MID. Shortened form of *middle,* employed as a combining word denoting the middle or middle part; as in *mid-ocean; mid-length; mid-channel.* An abbreviation for *midshipman.* **M.-channel,** middle or line of deepest water of a narrow waterway or channel; especially that followed by vessels, as in a river or a harbor entrance. *M.-Channel* designates middle waters of the English Channel, or roughly half-way between French and English coasts. **M.-galley,** old term for middle part or *amidships* in a small vessel. **M.-gear,** *see* GEAR. **M.-perpendicular,** *see* PERPENDICULAR. **M.-watch,** the middle watch, or that from midnight to 4 a.m.

MIDDIE. Colloquialism for *midshipman;* also, *middy.*

MIDDLE. Occupying a position equi-distant from extremes; mean; intermediate in space, time, or value. To fold in the middle, as a sail or a tarpaulin; to double, as a length of rope, and so determine its middle point. **M. body,** midship portion of vessel's hull, or that having a uniform cross-section. **M. deck,** *see* DECK. **M. ground,** shallow water in a fairway, having a channel on each side. *Cf.* **Middle ground b.** *in* BUOY. **M. jib,** where three jibs of similar size and cut are carried, one set on a stay leading from about mid-length of jib-boom; jib set between an *inner jib* and an *outer jib.* **M. latitude,** as used in plane sailing, that lying midway between any two latitudes; also, *mid-latitude.* **M. latitude sailing,** *see* SAILING. **M. line,** also termed *center*

line, fore-and-aft or longitudinal line lying in the vertical longitudinal plane extending from vessel's keel; situated in *m.* line, as in *m.-line keelson, m.-line pillar,* etc. **M.-mast,** an American name for the third mast from forward of a 5-masted vessel; *cf.* MAST. *Middlesail, m.-topsail, m.-topmast, m.* rigging, *m. sheet, m. throat-halyards, etc.,* were thus named as belonging to the *m.-mast* or *middlemast.* Also a former term for the *mainmast* of a 3-masted ship. **M. passage,** stretch of the Atlantic between West Coast of Africa and West Indies, thus commonly termed in connection with the slave trade. It probably was so called because lying about middle of north and south extent of Atlantic. **M. staysail,** as formerly set on square-rigged vessels having a comparatively lofty topgallantmast, sail spread on a stay leading to topgallant masthead from below the top of a lowermast next forward, or between a topmast staysail and a topgallant staysail. **M. stitching,** also *m. seaming* and *monk seam,* as a strengthening measure in sailmaking, an extra seam sewn along the canvas between edges of a flat seam. **M. timber,** a strengthening timber inside ship's counter in the midship line. In old-fashioned ships, it was outside the planking, extending from rudder-hole to poop rail. **M. watch,** period from midnight to 4 a.m.; members of crew on duty during that period; also, *midwatch.*

MIDNIGHT SUN. The sun above the horizon at midnight, as occurs only within the Arctic and Antarctic circles in summer. When observer's latitude is greater than sun's polar distance (90° − declination), sun is always above the horizon, attaining his lowest altitude at lower transit, or *midnight.*

MIDSHIP. Pertaining to, or situated in, middle part of a vessel, or that portion of the hull at or in vicinity of midway point between stem and stern; as, *m. cargo-port; m. fender; m. hatch; m. house.* **M. beam,** main or upper deck beam at midship section, or dead flat. **M. bend,** vessel's transverse frame at midship section; also, *m. frame.* **M. body,** *see* **M. body** *in* MIDDLE. **M. buntline,** in a square sail—usually a course—one of two buntlines nearest middle of sail; *cf.* BUNTLINE. **M. floor,** one of the floor-plates or timbers in *m.* body; that of *m.* section. *Cf.* FLOOR. **M. frame,** *see* **M. bend. M. oar,** in boats used in former whaling practice, longest oar in a usual complement of five, pulled from the *m.* thwart; also, the man pulling such oar. **M. section,** in ship drawings, a cross-sectional plan of vessel's hull at mid-length, showing details of construction; also, *m. bend; dead flat.* **M. section coefficient,** ratio of area of immersed part of *m. section* (or that of maximum body section, if greatest sectional area is not coincident with midship point) to a circumscribed rectangle, or one having a depth equal to vessel's draft and sides equal to her breadth. It is used in model experimenting for suitable hulls consistent with speed and power requirements, comparisons of hull resistances, etc. **M. spoke,** in a steering-wheel, uppermost spoke when rudder is in *midship* position, or in line with keel. It usually is marked, as with an ornamental brass cap, turk's head, etc. **M. stop,** in head-rope of a square sail, piece of small stuff indicating position of middle of head of sail. In bending sail, it is made fast in proper place before head-earings are hauled out. **M. tack,** as fitted in middle of foot-rope of a course in more recent larger square-rigged vessels, a stout rope used to hold foot of sail from slapping back against mast and rigging in light winds or for stretching foot of sail when its weather clew was hauled up in a quarterly breeze, as in the case of a mainsail or crossjack.

MIDSHIPMAN. In U.S. navy, a youth enrolled for training as an officer at the *Naval Academy, Annapolis, Maryland,* and who, upon successful examination, at end of four years attains officer status as an *ensign.* In British navy, a youth of rank next below a warrant officer completing his training either ashore or afloat subsequent to instruction as a *cadet* for one year at the naval college at Portsmouth, England (*H.M.S. Britannia*). After a total period of five years he becomes eligible for promotion to *sub-lieutenant,* or lowest commissioned officer rank. The term appears to have been in use in 17th-century ships for an apprentice officer who was quartered *amidships* and in the old East Indiamen a cadet was rated as a *m. apprentice* for his first year, a *full m.* in his second year, and at termination of four years' total service became eligible for position as 4th mate. In U.S. navy, the rank was changed from *naval cadet* in 1902; prior to 1882 was called *cadet m.* or *cadet engineer* for some 20 years; and earlier was *midshipman.* Before institution of *Naval Academy* in 1845, the *m.,* or *middy,* received his education and training at sea. *M.* is also a name for a toadfish of the U.S. southwest Pacific coast, so called from its rows of phosphorescent spots on its belly being likened to the array of shiny buttons on the budding officer's jacket. **M.'s hitch,** kind of jamming knot made by passing end of a rope around an object, then twice around rope's standing part (round turn), so that turns jam against object. The rope's end may be either half-hitched or seized to its standing part outside the jammed turns. **M.'s nuts,** an old-time dessert made of broken up sea-biscuit and raisins. **Passed m.,** in former naval usage, a *m.* awaiting promotion after having successfully passed his examinations. (An apprentice officer in merchant marine is sometimes called a *m.; see* APPRENTICE; CADET.)

MIDSHIPS. Loose form of *amidships;* middle part of vessel.

MIK. (*Prob.* an Eskimo word) Old Dundee whalers' term for the crotch in which harpoons lay ready (*live irons*) for use on starboard bow of boat.

MILE. Unit of distance used in navigation is the *geographical* or *nautical mile,* one-sixtieth of a degree of a great circle on a sphere whose surface is equal to that of the earth. This gives 6080.20 feet and corresponds very nearly with the average length of a minute of latitude, actual value of which, due to the oblate spheroidal shape of our globe, is 62 feet shorter at the equator than at the poles, so that in latitude $48\frac{1}{4}°$ only do we find a minute of latitude equal to that average. As a consequence, we note that distance on a navigational chart, as taken from the scale of latitude and which our worthy chart-makers have led us to accept as the truth, is not always in accord with the *nautical mile.* However, for the mariner's purpose, chiefly as a standard basis for speed and distance registering, the *U.S. Coast and Geodetic Survey* mile of 6080.20 feet and the Admiralty knot of 6080 feet have been adopted in America and Britain as practically the equivalent of 1/21600 of a great circle, or an arc of 1′ thereon, the minute or *m.* in any latitude. Austria, France, Germany, and a few other countries take the *m.'s* value as 1852 meters, or 6076 English feet, very nearly, corresponding to the length of a minute of latitude in 45° N. or S. The *American Ephemeris & Nautical Almanac, 1949,* indicates the nautical $m. = 1.151594$ times a statute *m.* (5280 feet), which gives us 6080.416 feet as another value for our slippy quarry; and *Bowditch* tells us "the average length of 1′ of curvature of the meridian is 6076.77 feet." In these niceties of measurement, some faith is required in certain authorities' determination of earth's size and shape, as *Clarke's spheroid* of 1866 or that of *Hayford,* 1909; which reminds us of the skipper's remark regarding taking a pilot for a fog-infested Bay of Fundy port: "It depends on the point of view!" To **convert nautical miles to statute miles:** Their lengths being, respectively, 6080 and 5280 feet, or in the ratio 38:33, multiply by 38 and divide by 33; conversely, for **statute miles to nautical,** multiply by 33 and divide by 38; or, approximately, *stat.* $m. = 8/7$ *naut. m.* and *naut.* $m. = 7/8$ *stat. m.* In a traverse table, under course 41°, *stat. m's* in *d. lat.* column have their equivalents in *naut. m's* in *dep.* column, within a mile of the truth up to 600 miles. **Measured m.,** a length of one nautical *m.* laid off along a shore and marked at its termini by conspicuous ranges at right angles to its line of measurement. Used for speed trials of powered vessels, such a stretch may be augmented to 2 or 3 *m's* and sometimes the course also is appropriately marked by buoys. **Statute m.,** the land *m.* of 5280 feet, so named because made law under an English statute, generally used in lake and river navigation. Also used by American and British astronomers, is equal to 1609.3 meters or 1.6093 kilometers, the latter measure being widely used by other nations.

MILITARY MAST. *See* MAST. A *military top* on such mast is an armored platform for mounting one or more light guns or for a lookout or observation station.

MILITARY SALVAGE. Rescue of floating property from an enemy; *esp.* such rescue which entitles the salvor to a monetary reward in a prize court.

MILKFISH. A silvery fish of the herring family found in tropical Pacific waters. It attains a length of 2½ feet.

MILKY WAY. *See* GALACTIC.

MILL SAIL. One of the four wings or sails spread on a windmill, such as often formerly carried in Scandinavian deep-water sailing-vessels for operating ship's bilge pumps.

MILLIBAR. (L. *mille,* a thousand; Gr. *baros,* weight) Internationally adopted unit of atmospheric pressure in scientific use, equal to .02953 inch of the mercury column. The *bar,* or 1000 *mb.* or *millibars,* is the equivalent of 29.5306 inches (750.076 millimeters) at 32° Fahrenheit (0° Centigrade) at sea level in latitude 45°. A barometric reading of 30.00 inches = one of 1016 *millibars.*

MILL SCALE. The thin black scale or magnetic oxide of iron formed on surface of steel or iron plates in the rolling process during manufacture. Since presence of this scale invites corrosion in the plate due to an electrolytic action in which the iron provides a flux to the *mill scale,* the metal being what is termed *electro-positive* in this combination, it is considered important to rid ship plating of the scale before application of a protective coating against ordinary "rusting" or oxidation caused by contact with air or water. This is done by either *pickling* the plates with a weak acid solution or allowing them to be exposed to the elements for some time so that the loosening scale may be removed by wire-brushing.

MINCING. Process of cutting blubber in pieces; *esp.* that carried on in the old sailing whalers wherein *horse-pieces,* or strips of blubber about 2 feet long and 6 to 8 inches wide were placed on a heavy bench called the *mincing-horse,* skin side up, and cut in slices of about ½-inch in thickness, without actually severing the piece, by the *mincing-knife,* or sharp blade about 24 inches long, fitted with a handle at each end. When thus prepared, blubber was placed in one of the *try-pots* for rendering into oil. **M.-spade,** a sharp spade-like implement for cutting whale-blubber.

MIND. Take heed; regard; pay attention to; as used in a cautionary or admonitory sense. **M. your helm!** (or **rudder**), order to a helmsman to give more of his attention to the steering or to meet an impending condition, as in entering a tideway, in which vessel is likely to be forced off her course. **M.**

your luff!, order to a helmsman to keep sails just full without shaking at the luff, as in sailing close to wind; also, in a boat or small vessel, order to maintain a heading close to wind during, or on approach of, a squall.

MINE. A charge of explosives in a more or less spherical container placed on the sea-bottom or moored to float on or near the surface, as in a "field" of such charges laid out in a fairway for destruction or impairment of an enemy's vessels. Mines have been set adrift with objective of allowing a tidal current to carry them into an enemy port or at sea to cause damage to an approaching fleet. They may be detonated by electricity, as when placed at or near the bottom for protection of a harbor and termed *dormant* or *ground mines;* by direct contact (*contact m.*); or by near contact, as in the case of a German-made *magnetic m.* which is discharged by influence of vessel's magnetic field on an intricate device set within the mine itself. A vessel is said to be *mined* when damaged by explosive effect of a *m.* **M.-field,** area in which fixed or moored *m's* are laid, either for protection against or destruction of vessels of an enemy. Mine-fields were laid in many strategic areas on western coasts of Europe, in Mediterranean and Adriatic waters, and various places in western Pacific during World War II. Subsequent to cessation of hostilities (*VE Day, May 8; VJ Day, Sept. 1, 1945*), losses to shipping through faulty navigation in entering mined areas or the breaking adrift of many mines have been recorded as 116 vessels sunk or totally wrecked out of a total of 251 suffering damage from this cause (*Oct., 1948*). **M.-layer,** vessel equipped for purpose of placing mines. **M.-ship,** another name for the old-time *powder-ship,* or vessel carrying gunpowder; *esp.* one in military service. **M.-sweeper,** vessel equipped for removing submarine or floating *m's;* so termed because operations consist mainly of *sweeping* or towing a long wire hawser extended by *otters,* or by a vessel at each end of such wire; also, *m.-dragger.* **Submarine m.,** one fixed on sea-bottom and usually detonated from shore, as where placed in a harbor channel; a *dormant* or *ground m.*

MINOR PLANETS. *See* PLANET.

MINTAKA. (Ar. *mintaqah,* belt) Westernmost star of the three comprising the belt of *Orion* and catalogued as δ *Orionis.* A double star of magnitude 2.48, has a S.H.A. of 277° 35′ and declination 0° 20′ S.

MINUTE. (L. *minutus,* small; from *minuere,* to lessen) One-sixtieth of a degree of angular measure; 1/21600 of a circle; or 60 seconds (60″). Expressed by the symbol (′), as in 0° 15′, in a circle the radii limiting an arc of 1′ are inclined to each other at an angle of 1′. In a *great circle* described on the earth's surface, 1′ is practically equal to 1 geographical or nautical mile (*cf.* MILE); thus, a place in Lat. 20° N. is 20 x 60, or 1200', or *miles,* north of the equator; and a *great circle* distance of 18° 10', as computed between two points, is 18 x 60 + 10' = 1090', or miles, very nearly. The *minute* of arc in a *small circle,* as 'a parallel of latitude, however, varies in length with distance from the equator, or very nearly as cosine of the latitude, being in Lat. 60° for example, half the length of a minute of the equator, considering our planet a perfect sphere. As a measure of *time,* the *minute* is 1/60 of an hour, and expressed as a difference in longitude of two places, is equal to 15 minutes of arc (15'). *Cf.* LONGI-TUDE. **M. gun,** discharge of a gun at intervals of one *m.* as a token of mourning, usually on occasion of burial of an admiral or other high-ranking officer; an older term for a distress signal made by firing a gun at intervals of about a *m.*

MIRACH. β *Andromedæ,* a star of magnitude 2.37 lying 25° nearly due south of *Cassiopeia's* middle star (γ *Cassiopeiæ*) and easily recognized, when the *Square of Pegasus* is on the meridian, at about 14° E.N.E. of *Alpheratz,* star marking N.E. corner of *Square. Mirach* (or *Mirac*) is central in the group representing, according to ancient Greek mytho-logical lore, the lovely *Andromeda* who was chained to a cliff for no fault of her own and rescued from a devouring monster by brave *Perseus,* hero of the adjoining constellation of that name. The star has a S.H.A. of 343° 12' and declination 35° 23' N.

MIRAGE. (L. *mirari,* to wonder at) An optical ef-fect, due to excessive bending of light-rays in travers-ing layers of the atmosphere differing widely in temperature or humidity, in which objects in or near the horizon assume an abnormal appearance in shape or elevation, or both, often showing a vessel or low-lying land inverted and raised sky-ward, where normally such would not be visible. *Cf.* FATA MORGANA and LOOM.

MIRUM. *See* LITOSILO.

MIRZAM. Star in *Canis Major;* also, MURZIM, *q.v.*

MISSING. A vessel is referred to as *"missing"* when overdue by such period as circumstances in-dicate with no reasonable doubt she is lost at sea. When vessel is "posted as missing" by *Lloyd's,* the *Lutine Bell* (from *H.M.S. Lutine,* lost in 1799) is tolled and insurance becomes payable.

MISS STAYS. To fail in the maneuver of *coming about,* or placing vessel on a new tack, usually be-cause of losing headway in the attempt. A typical situation features vessel hanging in the wind "in irons," eventually falling off on same tack as she gathers sternway. *Cf.* **In i's** *in* IRON.

MIST. Thin fog; precipitation consisting of ex-tremely fine droplets of water, much smaller and more closely aggregated than in rain. It is generally distinguished from *fog* proper in that the droplets are larger and have a perceptible downward mo-tion. Among seamen, usually defined as a condition in which prevailing visibility is not less than 1 mile and thus often termed *light fog.* It differs from *haze* in that much more humidity is present; *cf.* FOG and HAZY. Abbreviated *m* in log-books and weather-records. **M.-bow,** *see* **F.-bow** *in* FOG.

MISTICO. (*Sp.*) A two- or three-masted lateen-rigged Spanish vessel of the Mediterranean; usually carries two jibs.

MISTRAL. (From old Italian name for *N.W.* point of compass) A dry, cold, violent N.W. wind of the Mediterranean; *esp.* such wind of short duration which frequently arises suddenly in the Gulf of Lyons during winter; also, *maestrale, mistrale.*

MITCH-BOARD. *See* BOARD.

MITCHELL THRUST BEARING. A British pat-ent similar to the KINGSBURY, *q.v.*

MITER. A joint made at the angular meeting of two similar pieces of timber, iron, etc., in which the parts connect in a line bisecting their angle of junction. To join, as by *mitering.* **M.-jib,** an im-proper term for a *diagonal-cut* jib, or one in which the cloths run at right angles to both foot and leech, mitering, as in other jibs, in a line perpen-dicular to the luff from the clew. Also *mitered jib* and *patent-cut* jib, it is a yachting notion of a prettier spread of seams than the time-tested Scotch cut presents; *cf.* remarks in JIB. **M.-wheel,** *see* **B.-wheel** *in* BEVEL. (The word is also written *mitre*)

MITTEN MONEY. *See* MONEY.

MIXED. Blended; made up of two or more quanti-ties or kinds; as, a *m. cargo; m. timber;* a *m. crew.* Irregular in occurrence, height, size, etc.; as, a *m. sea;* a *m. tide.* **M. policy,** an insurance coverage for a vessel on a voyage or voyages between ports specified for a certain period of time; a combined *time* and *voyage* policy. **M. steam,** *see* STEAM. **M. tide,** *see* TIDE. **M. timber,** a vessel is said to be built of *mixed timber* when different kinds of wood are included in her structural parts.

MIZAR. (*Ar.*) Second star in tail of the Great Bear (*Ursa Major*), or handle of the Big Dipper, listed by astronomers as ζ¹ *Ursæ Majoris,* S.H.A. 159° 29' and Dec. 55° 11' N. It is a binary star of magnitude 2.40 and lies exactly opposite the pole and about same distance from it as δ *Cassiopeiæ* (*Ruchbah*). The faint close companion of this star is called *Alcor,* from an Arabic word meaning the *weak one.*

MIZZEN. (In older use, also *mizen, misen*) Of or pertaining to the *mizzenmast;* as, *m. rigging; m. stay; m. topmast; m. royal.* Aftermost lower sail, or that set abaft the *mizzenmast,* in a 3-masted barque, barquentine, lugger, schooner, or ship; also often called *spanker.* After sail of a ketch or yawl. To **bagpipe the m.,** to haul its sheet well to windward, as in *lying-to* a square-rigged vessel in light winds.

Bonaventure m., *see* SAIL. **M. crosstrees,** *see* CROSS-TREES. **M. top,** platform at a *m.* lowermasthead; *cf.* TOP. **M.-topmast stay, M.-topgallant stay,** *see* STAY. **Storm m.,** in a square-rigged vessel, as a ship or a barque, a triangular or jib-headed mizzen made of heavy canvas; also, *storm spanker.*

MIZZENMAST. Third mast from forward in a vessel having three or more masts, with the known exception of some 5-masted American schooners in which it was fourth, third in the list being termed *middlemast. See* MAST.

MOCK. Simulation or resemblance of a thing denominated; as in *m. fog; m. moon; m. sun (see* PARHELION); *m. rainbow.* In shipbuilding, a steel model or pattern on which the heated plate is forged to shape in the case of a part of hull plating having short irregular curvature lines; also, *m. mold* and *bed.* **M. fog,** resemblance of low-lying fog due to certain atmospheric refraction conditions. **M'ing up,** process of constructing a pattern of a curved part of hull plating from ship's lines as laid down on the mold loft floor, or from a special drawing, for purpose of making a *m. mold: see above.* **M. moon; m. sun,** similar phenomena termed, respectively, *paraselene* and *parhelion; see* PARHELION. **M. rainbow,** a secondary bow either above or below a well-defined rainbow.

MODEL. An exact miniature representation of a vessel; *specif.,* one of a vessel's hull for experimental use in a *model basin* or *tank* (*cf.* **Model b.** *in* BASIN) or the longitudinal half (*half model*) of such, as prepared in some shipbuilding yards for laying off shell-plating strakes, etc., of a proposed vessel. Our present knowledge of hull resistance, and hence desirable forms of the under-water body for economical powering in attaining required speeds for various types of vessels, has been derived from scientific investigation of behavior of both towed and self-propelled *m's,* which also includes trials of propeller efficiency, shape and area of rudders, and other related data. **Block m.,** one made of a single block of wood or, sometimes, of wax; also called *solid block m.,* as distinguished from a *half-block m.* or *half m.,* a longitudinal half of vessel's represented hull; in shipyard use, called a *builder's m.,* made generally on scale of ¼-inch to 1 foot, of ship concerned. Where the last-named is marked with positions of frames, arrangement of shell-plating butts, seams, etc., and line of each deck, it is usually termed a *plating m.;* and where used to show the various waterlines used in ship drawings, a *waterline m.*

MODERATE. Characterized by mediocre strength or magnitude; limited in degree; as, *m. rain; m. fog.* To become less violent or intense; as, *both wind and sea have moderated.* **M. breeze,** a wind of force 4, or having a speed of about 20 knots, according to BEAUFORT'S SCALE, *q.v.* **M. fog,** that in which

visibility is limited to about half a mile. **M. gale,** wind between a strong breeze and a fresh gale; *see* BEAUFORT'S SCALE. **M. sea,** state of sea in which waves average in height from trough to crest 3 to 5 feet; that produced by a *m. breeze,* or in which light "white caps" are present. **M. speed,** as required by *Rules of the Road* for vessels in thick weather, has been defined by *U.S. Supreme Court* as "that speed at which it is possible to stop the vessel's way within half the distance of visibility"; generally, three-fourths vessel's full speed. **M. swell,** intermediate in height compared with a *low* and a *heavy* swell; according to formation, may be a *short m. swell* or a *long m. swell,* but, generally, 3 to 6 feet from trough to top.

MOHN EFFECT. Aberration in direction or complete damping of *sound* due to differences in atmospheric surface density, more frequently occurring during intermittent fog; *specif.,* such effect on fog signals, as often experienced at sea when passing through scattered fog-banks, *e.g.,* on Newfoundland Banks during summer. Faint echoes of ship's whistle are an indication of this menace and a signal sometimes may be heard at a comparatively remote distance while inaudible near by, in such conditions. Instances occur in which a ship's whistle may be heard by another vessel while both are enveloped in fog but, upon entering a "clear patch," signals of either or both are completely blanked out.

MOKI or **MOKIHI.** (*Native name*) A kind of raft made of dried reeds—chiefly bulrushes, as formerly much used by the Maoris; a *moguey.*

MOLD. (O.F. *mole* or *modle;* from same Latin root as *model*) As used in shipbuilding in preparing frames, plates, etc., from lines on the *mold loft* floor, a pattern made of thin wood with any necessary details marked thereon; a template. A shape of metal or wood over or in which a piece of plate may be hammered or pressed to required shape, as a *mock m.* (*see* MOCK). Also, *mould.* **Beam m.,** *see* BEAM. **Block-out m.,** a template of approximate size and shape of a plate to be forged. **Frame m.,** *see* FRAME. **M. loft,** the large, enclosed, smooth-floored space—usually a loft—in which a vessel's structural lines are laid out to actual size. *M's* or templates are taken from the lines drawn on its floor for fashioning all frames and plating built in a vessel. Also called *molding* (or *moulding*) *loft* and *m. room.* Auxiliary to the *m. loft floor* is the *scrive board* on which full-sized lines of ship's body plan are laid out for ready reference by the smiths in connection with shaping frames and beams on the bending-slab. **Sheer m.,** a long thin plank shaped as a pattern for a vessel's sheer, chiefly in connection with lining up correct height and sheer of the deck beams and rail in wooden ships.

MOLDED. As qualifying certain hull dimensions, word indicating measurement is taken to outside faying surface of frames, floors, or beams, *i.e.*, the *molded* or inside surface of planking or plating. **M. breadth,** *see* BREADTH. **M. depth,** *see* DEPTH. **M. draft,** in connection with assigning *load lines,* vertical distance from lower edge of midship floor at keel, or *m. base line,* to the *summer load line,* or summer freeboard mark, on each side of vessel amidships. In wooden or composite vessels, it is usually taken from lower edge of the keel rabbet, or outer surface of planking next to keel (*garboard strake*). **M. lines,** *see* LINE.[2] (*Esp.* in British use, the word is often spelled *moulded*)

MOLDER. Also *moulder;* one skilled in making molds or patterns for castings or structural parts; a *loftsman* in a shipyard.

MOLDING. Ornamental or trimming-piece of wood or metal, as around upper corners of a deck-house, a hatch-coaming, on ship's counter, etc. A half-round stiffening strip of wood or metal along a boat's sides at her gunwale; also called *nosing, ribband, rubbing-piece.* In wooden shipbuilding, measurement of a plank or timber from inboard to outboard, *i.e.*, parallel to the plane in which a member lies; opposed to *siding,* or thickness dimension at right angles to such plane; thus, *m.* of a frame timber is measured in a thwartship direction, while that of a stem is its cross-section dimension fore-and-aft. **Cable m.,** carved representation of a rope, or the old-time hemp cable, formerly often fitted for ornamental purposes on a vessel's stern. **Hatch m.,** *see* HATCH. **Knuckle m.,** *see* KNUCKLE. **M. edge,** curved line defining the form of a frame in its **m. plane,** or thwartship plane through middle of a frame timber or of the outer angle-bar flange in a metal frame. **Sheer m.,** a half-round strip following the deck line on outside of planking or plating, as often found in small vessels. **Stern m.,** sculptured ornamental wood or metal work across vessel's stern, as frequently fitted on old-time ships.

MOLE. (It. *molo*) A massive jetty or pier, usually of stone, built for protection of a harbor against sea waves while, generally, affording berthing and cargo handling space for shipping; often simply a breakwater. **M.-head,** seaward end of a mole.

MOLLIE. *See* MALLEMAROKING.

MOLLY or **MOLLYHAWK.** *See* MALLEMUCK.

MOMENT. In mechanics, tendency or measure of tendency to produce motion, *esp.* about a point or axis. In general, it is expressed by product of a mass, velocity, or force and perpendicular distance of such from point or axis considered, such distance being usually termed the *arm* or *lever.* **Bending m.,** that tending to bend a beam, girder, or ship herself. It is the algebraic sum of all forces or weights bearing upon either side of longitudinal axis of ma-

terial or thing considered. Also termed *m. of resistance.* **Hogging m.,** *see* HOGGING. **Inch-Trim m.,** also termed *m. to change trim one inch, trim m.,* and *tipping m.,* as used in calculating vessel's change in draft due to shifting, taking aboard, or discharging a given weight, that about ship's transverse axis passing through the geometrical center of immersed body, or center of flotation, which produces a change in trim of *one inch, i.e.,* an increase of draft of one-half inch at either end of ship and a decrease of one-half inch at opposite end. Expressed in *foot-tons,* its value decreases with displacement. *Cf.* **Change of trim** *in* TRIM. **M. of effort,** in stability considerations of vessels under sail, product of distance of *center of effort* (center of gravity of sail area) from *center of lateral resistance* by an assumed total wind pressure; usually expressed in *foot-pounds. Cf.* **C. of effort** *and* **C. of lateral resistance** *in* CENTER. **M. of inertia,** used in ship stability calculations, as in *m. of i. of water-plane,* either longitudinal or transverse axis referred to, which is equal to integral sum of all products of small units of area times squares of their distances from axis considered; or, in *polar m. of i.,* that equal to integral sum of products of weights in all parts of ship times squares of their several distances from a horizontal fore-and-aft axis passing through vessel's center of gravity. **M. of resistance,** *see* **Bending m. Righting m.,** in the couple formed by equal parallel and opposite forces of gravity, acting downward, and buoyancy, acting upward, when a floating vessel is heeled from an external cause, horizontal distance (or *righting arm*) from ship's center of gravity to line of upward force of buoyancy times vessel's displacement, expressed in *foot-tons. Cf.* STABILITY. **Sagging m.,** *see* SAGGING. **Upsetting m.,** converse of *righting m.;* or that in a condition in which gravity acts downward farther toward vessel's side than upward buoyancy force; also, *capsizing m.*

MONEL METAL. A strong, non-corrosive, non-magnetic, whitish alloy of about 67% nickel, 28% copper, and 5% iron and manganese, much used as high grade material for fastenings, propellers, and various fittings in yachts and small craft; also in large vessels for pilot-house instruments, such as barometer and clock cases, direction-finders, gyro compass accessories, and other fittings near magnetic compasses. *Cf.* K MONEL.

MONEY. The common medium of exchange or nominal value in trade; bank notes, coins of gold, silver, copper, etc.; sometimes termed *m. of account* when used as a basis for estimating values. Wages. A toll, tax, fee, or extra charge; as, *bridge m., light m.; commission m.; stink m.* (The older plural *monies* sometimes still appears in legal writings) **Anchor-m.,** *see* ANCHOR. **Dispatch m.,** an allowance made to the charterer by a shipowner when loading or discharging of cargo is completed in a shorter time than lay-days or lay-hours stipulated in charter-party. **Gun-m.,** *see* GUN. **Hat-m.** or **hatch-m.,** *see* PRIMAGE. **Head-m.,** *see* HEAD. **Light-m.,** *see* LIGHT. **Mitten m.,** charge above a pilotage fee during cold weather; *winter-m.* **Passage m.,** that charged for a person's transportation. It is generally limited by law or authorized by government regulation. **Prize m.,** *see* PRIZE. **Ration m.,** allowance paid in lieu of rations, as when a vessel under repairs provides no meals for her crew, or in the case of running short of provisions at sea. **Ship m.,** *see* SHIP. **Smart m.,** *see* SMART. **Stink m.,** equivalent of *dirt* or *dirty m.* in modern stevedore usage, a Bristol Channel dock-laborers' term for an early union demand for extra pay when cargoes giving off offensive odors were worked or handled (about 1910); *see* DIRTY. **Straggling m.,** in British navy, a reward paid for apprehension of deserters or stragglers; also, wages deducted for absence without leave. **Subsistence m.,** per diem allowance to an officer, *esp.* in merchant vessels, when meals and/or quarters are not provided on board; *cf.* **Ration m.**

MONITOR. A now obsolete armor-protected steam-vessel, having a low freeboard and carrying one or more revolving turrets with one or two large guns each, built for coastal defense and designed to combine maximum gun-power with minimum exposure. The type was so called after name of first vessel of this class which was designed by *John Ericsson,* Swedish engineer and inventor in America (*1803–1889*), was completed in 1862 and thus appeared in time to arrest the destructive course of the Confederate ironclad ram *Virginia,* rebuilt from the 40-gun steam frigate *Merrimac.* On March 8, 1862, the *Virginia* destroyed Union frigates *Congress* and *Cumberland* at Hampton Roads, Va., and next day she was engaged, driven off, and disabled by the *Monitor.*

MONKEY. A small English merchant ship of 16th century. Slang term, especially in British navy, for utensil in which allowance of grog was served to a mess. As a combining word, generally implies peculiarity in appearance, arrangement, location, or use. **M.-bag,** small draw-string pouch or bag in which money, trinkets, etc., commonly were carried slung round the neck by sailors of the old school. **M.-block,** a small single swivel-block used as a lead or guide for running gear, as buntlines, signal halyards, etc. **M. boat,** small, usually half-decked, boat formerly used on the River Thames, England. **M. bridge,** *see* BRIDGE. **M. fist,** a ball-like knot made in similar fashion as a turk's head on the throwing end of a heaving-line. It is usually worked over a weight such as a piece of lead or a heavy nut. **M. forecastle,** also once called *anchor-deck; see* ANCHOR *and* FORECASTLE. **M. foresail,** a square sail set on foremast of a schooner or a sloop in a fair wind. **M.-gaff,** *see* GAFF. **M. jacket,** short

white dinner jacket worn by officers in summer temperatures; has shoulder-straps with ranking stripes and buttons; also, a short warm coat or reefer worn by seamen in cold weather; a pea-jacket. **M. pump,** the straw introduced through a gimlet-hole in a cask of liquor in the well-known pastime of "sucking the monkey." **M. rail,** in older wooden vessels, a topgallant rail above the quarter-deck or poop bulwarks (*quarter-boards*). In modern vessels, a small rail above ship's stem enclosing standing-room for an officer supervising handling of mooring-lines in docking. **M. rope,** a life-line secured to a man's waist while he works in a hazardous position, as over ship's side; once a common name in the old whalers for such a line attached to a man sent down on a carcase alongside in connection with work of *flensing.* **M. spar,** a mast or yard of reduced size used in training young seamen on board ship or at a shore station; any light spar used for a temporary purpose. In a disparaging sense, a vessel is referred to as *monkey-sparred* when rigged with unusually light masts, yards, etc.; also *m.-rigged.* **M.-tail,** handy line used in tripping or guiding a heavy hook; piece of small stuff fast to a boat-tackle hook for use as a lanyard and a mousing. A *rudder-horn,* or curved bar fitted to upper after end of rudders in older ships as a means of attaching pendants for use in event of mishap to steering-gear. In old ordnance, a short iron lever for training a carronade. Loose-hanging end of a gasket, etc., in non-shipshape style. **M. wheel,** a skeleton-framed gin-block sheave; such gin itself; a sheave in end of a spar, as a cathead. **M. yard,** *see* **M. spar. Powder m.,** *see* POWDER. **Water m.,** a chatty or water-cooler; *see* WATER.

MONK SEAM. *See* **M. stitching** *in* MIDDLE.

MONOMOY SURF BOAT. Named for the island of Monomoy, its birthplace, on southeast Massachusetts coast, a double-ended pulling boat about 26 feet in length by 7 feet beam, 30 inches depth at middle, and a sheer of 20 inches (height gunwale rises from midship section to each end), full-lined and strongly built. Of excellent rough-water capabilities and good carrying-capacity, used as a lifeboat and for general ship's work by U.S. Coast Guard.

MONSOON. (Ar. *mausim,* a season or time) A seasonal wind chiefly characterized by its reversal in direction about every six months; *specif.,* either of such winds on the southeastern coasts of Asia which are attributed to effect of alternate increase and decrease of barometric pressure over the Asiatic plateau in winter and in summer, respectively. Following the law of atmospheric flow outward and around a high pressure area, from October to April a vast body of air sweeps down the China Sea and across the Bay of Bengal and Arabian Sea with generally fine and clear weather. This is the N.E. trade wind, called in those regions *N.E., dry,* or *winter monsoon.* Conversely, the air flow from over the Indian Ocean, bringing generally wet, sultry, unpleasant conditions, prevails from about May 1st. to September in the *S.W., wet,* or *summer monsoon.* Reversal in direction, or what is called the *breaking* or *bursting of the m.,* takes place in many localities, especially in China Sea at change to S.W., in a series of tempestuous rain-squalls, after which the new *m.* settles down to business for another half year. Greatest force of wind occurs about mid-season in each case, *S.W. m.,* particularly in Arabian Sea, sometimes reaching that of a fresh gale during June and July, with its attending bad weather. In China Sea area, *N.E. m.* usually grows to a moderate gale in December and January with generally clear atmosphere. **Northwest,** or **Middle m.,** a reversal of S.E. trade wind in Indian Ocean between Equator and Lat. 10° S., eastward of Seychelles Islands; generally light with frequent rain-squalls and prevailing from November to March. **M. of the line,** a generally light wind between west and south prevailing along West Coast of Africa from Cape Verde to about Lat. 20° S.

MONSOONAL. Of or pertaining to *monsoons.* Of regular or periodic occurrence; said of winds.

MONTAGU RIG. Much favored for boat-sailing in British navy, two-mast rig consisting of a standing lug, a stay foresail, and a jib-headed mizzen; also, *Montagu yawl.*

MOON. A secondary planet or satellite; as, *Jupiter's moons.* The satellite of the earth. Since our *moon* changes faster in position in the sky than any other celestial body, observations of the luminary for ship's position must be computed with extreme care, particularly in extracting her ephemeral values in declination, correction for altitude and Greenwich hour angle from the *Nautical Almanac.* Declination of this body has a maximum value of about $28\frac{1}{2}°$ N. and S. and in two weeks races through that range of about 56° from her hiding-place nearly in front of the sun at *new moon* to *full moon* position approximately opposite the sun in declination value. This last-named feature provides a wonderful compensation for loss of sunlight in the polar regions during winter. Her mean distance from us is 238,857 statute miles; has a diameter of 2160 miles; and revolves round the earth during a complete *lunation* (*synodical month,* or mean period between two successive *new moons*), occupying 29d. 12h. 44m. 2.8s. of mean time. This latter value, however, is greater than the satellite's true running time occupied in one lap, since a *lunation* is completed while catching up with the sun in his eastward march in the ecliptic. We then have, as *Selene's* real period of revolution, the *sidereal month,* or average time elapsed between two successive conjunctions with the same star, 27d. 7h.

43m. 11.5s., measured in *mean time.* And all through her orbital swing our attentive satellite presents toward us the same surface, if we except the "peeps around the corner" made possible by her slow oscillatory motion called *libration,* as amply supported in the unchanging facial expression of her "man." **M.-dog,** a paraselene; *cf.* PARHELION. **M.-fish,** any of several small brilliantly colored, compressed, deep-bellied, food fishes; *esp.* the genus *Selene,* as the *S. vomer* of Atlantic and Pacific coasts of North America; the opah; a butterfish; *cf.* **Horse-f.** *in* HORSE. **M. in distance,** old phrase indicating suitable position of *moon* for measurement of her angular distance from the sun or a given star in determining longitude by lunar observations. **M.-sheered,** said of a boat or vessel having an unusually pronounced sheer; so called from crescent-shaped appearance in profile of her upper works. **M.'s acceleration,** *see* ACCELERATION. **M.'s age,** time elapsed since last conjunction of moon and sun, or *new moon.* **M.'s nodes,** points at which moon's orbit intersects that of the earth; or, nearly diametrically opposed points at which *m.'s* path intersects plane of the ecliptic. (Plane of *m.'s* orbit is inclined to ecliptic about 5°) That point through which *m.* passes moving northward is termed the *ascending node;* the other, in passing from north to south, the *descending node.* Time elapsed between two successive ascending nodes is called a *nodical month,* and averages 27d. 5h. 5m. 35.8s. of mean time. **M.'s phases,** different appearances or changing shapes through which *m.'s* exposed part of her illuminated surface passes in a *lunation* or *synodical month.* At *new moon* she is in conjunction with the sun and hence presents her darkened half toward the earth (away from the sun); as she advances eastward in her orbit, part of her lightened surface appears as a growing crescent, until in about a week one-half of her light is open to view, or *first quarter* is reached; continuing on her way, she leaves the *crescent phase* and some of the eastern portion now appears in the *gibbous phase* which, at end of about another week, develops into the whole illuminated surface, *full moon,* her position in *opposition* to the sun. Another week sees her light diminish by one-half at *last quarter* when she again enters the now receding crescent phase until once more darkened completely at *new m.* In both crescent and gibbous phases, between times of *new* and *full m.,* the western *limb* is illuminated; from *full* to *new m.,* the eastern one. At *first* and *last quarter, m.* is said to be in *quadrature,* or differing from the sun in right ascension by 6 hours (90°); in *syzygy,* when in conjunction with or in opposition to the sun, as at *new* and *full m.*

MOONRAKER. A lower deck term for a *moonsail,* or light square sail once formerly set above a skysail in a few clipper ships; *cf.* **F. kites** *in* FLYING.

Old name for a night smuggler on south coast of England; also, *moonshiner.*

MOOR. (Ger. *muren;* from Du. *marren,* to make fast or moor a ship) To secure a vessel with two anchors, cables of which lead in opposite directions, or nearly so, with object of reducing space required for ship to swing, as in a tideway; to secure vessel at about right angles to a pier, mole, etc., with one or more anchors laid out ahead and hawsers leading from stern to such pier, etc.; to make fast to one or more mooring-buoys at each end of ship. The term has been extended to mean to secure or make fast by cables or lines, as alongside a pier or dolphins, whether or not one or more anchors are in use. (A ship is *not* moored when riding to one or more anchors leading ahead; she is then *at anchor.*) To secure ship by making fast to the shore or by anchoring as above; as, *we shall moor upon arrival.* **Flying m.,** also called *running m.,* operation of mooring ship, *esp.* in a tideway or river current, by dropping first anchor while vessel has headway, paying out about double the length of cable decided upon, then holding on, dropping second anchor and heaving in on first cable until about same length of cable is given each anchor. Ship's bow is then about mid-distance between anchors. To **m. along,** to anchor in a river and hold ship in position by one or more hawsers leading abeam to shore. To **m. head and stern,** to make fast at each end, as to buoys, or with anchors out ahead and stern secured by hawsers to a pier or to a stern anchor or anchors. In ancient Mediterranean days, it was customary, as to-day, to *m.* the galleys stern to a mole or pier with anchors out ahead. To **m. with an open hawse,** *see* HAWSE.

MOORAGE. Old term for a berth or area in which a vessel may be secured; also, a charge for occupying such berth or place of *mooring.*

MOORING. Act of securing a vessel by means of her anchors or hawsers. Usually in plural form, hawsers, cables, etc., by which vessel is secured; also, berth in which made fast or moored; as, her *moorings* are hanging slack; ship lay at her *moorings* all week. **Fixed m.,** one of several chain cables or hawsers permanently attached to a pier for use of vessels berthed thereat; heavy extra lines, chains, etc., supplied by a pier where a prevailing swell demands use of such, as in some ports open to, or only partly protected from, the sea. **M.-anchor,** *see* ANCHOR. **M.-bitts,** a pair of stout wood or iron posts about which to take turns of a hawser in mooring; *see* BITT. **M.-block,** a weighty mass of concrete or cast-iron block fitted with a heavy eye; used as an anchor for a mooring-buoy, channel-buoy, or a *fixed m.;* also called a *m.-clump, m.-sinker.* **M. board,** also called *maneuvering board,* a chart or plotting sheet, usually mounted on a board, on which is described as its working boundary a graduated

circle representing the compass rose. Equi-distant concentric circles are drawn with radii 10° apart. It is used in men-of-war for solving various problems in tactical maneuvers, including the placing of a vessel in required position with relation to a flagship or guide when coming to anchor. **M.-boat,** an anchor-hoy; *see* ANCHOR; any boat used in connection with *m.* **M.-bridle,** *see* BRIDLE. **M.-chock,** block or casting fitted at side of a deck as a lead for a hawser; distinguished from a *m.-pipe* in that its rounded surface on which hawser bears is not entirely enclosed. *Cf.* CHOCK. **M. cleat,** a heavy kevel on which a mooring-line is belayed; *cf.* CLEAT. **M.-clump,** *see* **M.-block. M.-kit,** as used by yachts and smaller craft, a buoy, often a keg, supporting the end of a *m.-*chain and to which a *m.-*rope is, or may be, attached. **M. line,** any rope or hawser used to secure vessel in berth. **M.-pipe,** heavy block or casting fitted in a bulwark as a circular or oval bearing-surface for a hawser leading from ship; sometimes termed a *bell pipe* where its inside end is expanded like mouth of a bell; *cf.* **M.-chock. M.-post,** also termed *m.-pall, m.-bitt, dock-post,* strong, firmly fixed post on a pier, quay, jetty, etc., for receiving shore ends of hawsers or cables used in making fast. **M.-rack,** row of piles or dolphins, sometimes connected by planking or bridgework, constructed for temporary berthing of vessels, as at a canal entrance, or alongside which vessels may be laid up. **M.-rope,** a *m.* line. **M. shackle,** as used chiefly by large war-vessels, a heavy swivel-shackle inserted in one of the cables and to which the other bower cable is connected outside the hawse-pipes. With one part of cable leading aboard and the others leading to their respective anchors, ship is thus free to swing without putting any turns, or twists, in her cables. It is also called a *m. swivel.* **M.-staple,** usually fitted to warships only, a heavy staple-shaped forging fitted on ship's side to receive a chain cable or hawser in *m.;* also, *m.-dog.* **M.-stump,** a post fixed in a heavy stone for purpose of securing small craft. Post is long enough to appear above surface at high water, while stone anchors it in position. **M. swivel,** *see* **M. shackle. M. telegraph,** instrument similar to an engine-room telegraph used for transmitting orders from ship's bridge to forecastle in connection with *m.* or handling forward lines in making fast, etc.; found only in large vessels. **Screw-m.,** a heavy broad-flanged iron shaft, fashioned like a screw, used as an anchor in yielding bottoms, such as soft mud or clay, for an important buoy in a channel or a *m.-buoy.* **Swinging m.,** any permanent *m.,* as that provided by a *m.-buoy,* to which a single chain cable or hawsers may be attached, vessel being free to swing to wind or tide; also, such *m.* used in swinging a ship for adjustment of magnetic compasses, which operation requires vessel to be placed on various headings. **Three-leg m.; two-leg m.;** permanent *m's* in which 3 or 2 cables leading to as many anchors meet in a *m. swivel* to which the *riding-chain* may be attached. Riding-chain may terminate in a *m.-buoy* or its end may be buoyed for heaving up and aboard, usually being connected to one of ship's cables. Also termed *three-arm m.* and *two-arm m.*

MOORSOM TONNAGE. That determined by Moorsom's rule; *cf.* TONNAGE and MEASUREMENT.

MOOT. In older wooden shipbuilding, a ring gauge used in shaping treenails to a required diameter; the finished diameter, or that to which a treenail is to be *mooted,* or gauged to correct size as by a *moot.* A workman who made or prepared treenails was called a *mooter;* sometimes a treenail itself, or a bolt or a spike driven in the planking also was given same name.

MOP. The conventional bunch of cotton strands, rope-yarns, or absorbent cloth, fast to a handle, for swabbing or wiping the decks.

MORNING. Early part of the day; between dawn and noon. **M. order-book,** *see* ORDER. **M. star,** any of the planets Mercury, Venus, Mars, Jupiter, and Saturn appearing in the heavens shortly before sunrise. **M. watch,** that from four o'clock to eight o'clock in the *m.;* members of ship's company on duty during that period. **Pride of the m.,** a fine fog or mist hanging over a coast, said to indicate a clear day; a light *m.* shower; end of the land-breeze, or interval of calm, before arrival of the sea-breeze; *cf.* **Land and sea b's** *in* BREEZE.

MORSE. To signal by *Morse* code, as by means of a flashing lamp or ship's whistle; *Morse-code* signaling. According to signaling procedure prescribed in the *International Code of Signals,* use of *M. code* now is limited to flashing and sound signals. Formerly its use was extended to signaling by short and long strokes made in waving a flag. *See* CODE. **M. lamp,** a light or lamp arranged to emit flashing signals, as by an electric make-and-break circuit or by sliding shutter which exposes and obscures the light as required. Former requirement that a *M. lamp* must be carried for *night* signaling has been modified under *Regulation 11, Safety of Navigation,* prescribed by *International Conference on Safety at Sea, 1948,* "All ships of over 150 tons gross tonnage, when engaged on international voyages, shall have on board an efficient daylight signaling lamp."

MORTAR-BOAT. *Cf.* **B.-ketch** *in* BOMB.

MORTAR LINE. Life-saving or other small line fired from a *line-throwing gun* or *mortar; see* GUN.

MORTISE-BLOCK. A tackle-block fashioned from a solid piece of wood and *mortised* to receive the sheave. Blocks of this type, having an egg-shaped shell, are used in jib-sheets for easy tumbling over the next inboard stay.

MOSES BOAT. A broad, flat-bottomed, rowing boat formerly used in West Indies for carrying one or two hogsheads of sugar or molasses from shore to ship in operation of loading. Local term for a small keeled sailing-boat.

MOSSBUNKER. (Du. *marsbanker*) Another name for the *menhaden;* also *mossbanker. See* MENHADEN.

MOTHER CAREY. Among sailors, the traditional owner of certain birds of the *Petrel* family; *esp.* of the *stormy petrels* of North Atlantic habitat, noted for their frolicsome flight in and out of the troughs of heavy seas during gales in the *"roaring forties,"* and known as *Mother Carey's chickens; cf.* PETREL. The term is a corruption of the Portuguese and Spanish seamen's *Mater cara* (dear Mother) so often uttered in prayers to the Virgin Mary during those weather conditions of such cheerful interest only to birds. **M. C.'s goose,** the giant fulmar, another member of same family; *see* FULMAR. **M. C.'s hen,** any petrel of medium size or somewhat larger than the *chickens.*

MOTHER-OF-PEARL. *See* PEARL.

MOTHER SHIP. Vessel controlling, escorting, or guarding a fleet of smaller craft, as whale-catchers, fishing-smacks, submarines; a supply-ship; an airplane carrier.

MOTION. A mechanism or power-transfer system; as *geared m.; link m.* Change of position; movement; as, *ahead m.; screw m.* **Diurnal m.,** apparent movement of heavenly bodies from east to west due to earth's daily rotation; also termed *sidereal m.* **Link m.,** *see* LINK. **Retrograde m.,** changing in position of a planet among the stars from east to west; retrogradation. **M. bar,** a slide-bar or *guide* for a crosshead in a reciprocating engine; *cf.* GUIDE. **M. block,** a guide-shoe or guide-block; *see* GUIDE.

MOTOR. (L. *motum,* to move) A machine for producing motive power; as, an *electric m.;* a *gasoline m.* Any small powerful engine for driving a winch, pump, or a boat, or for controlling a ship's rudder in steering. **M'boat,** generally any boat propelled by an internal combustion *m.* or engine. According to the *Motor Boat Act, June 9, 1910 (46 U.S.C. 511),* "the words '*motor boat*' where used in this Act shall include every vessel propelled by machinery and not more than 65 feet in length, except tug boats and tow boats propelled by steam." Also written *motor-boat.* **M. sailer,** as used chiefly in U.S., term for any craft propelled by either a *m.* or sails, or by both, being so dually equipped. **M'ship,** vessel propelled by internal combustion engines, as distinguished from one deriving her propulsion, direct or indirect, from a steam engine or engines; also *m. ship; m.-ship; m. vessel* (usually abbreviated *m.v.*). **M. launch,** in U.S. navy, as distinguished from the large metal-canopied and decked *m. boat,* also known as *admiral's barge* or a commanding officer's *gig,* and also from the *m. whale-boat* of lighter build, a heavy-duty, square-sterned, open boat designed for carrying stores, liberty parties, kedging or mooring work, surveying, etc. (Gasoline-powered boat engines now are being displaced by the Diesel) **M. winch,** a hoisting or warping winch driven by an attached *m.;* also termed *electric winch, gasoline winch,* etc., according to source of power. **Steering m.,** an electric *m.* installed for powering ship's steering-gear, its movements being controlled by the steering-wheel and its connections, as through a *telemotor* system, from the navigating bridge.

MOUILLAGE. (Fr. *mouiller,* to anchor)   Term used in French ports for an anchorage or berth occupied by a vessel at anchor.

MOULD; MOULDED; MOULDING.   *See* MOLD; MOLDED; MOLDING.

MOUNT MISERY.   The disparaging appellative given by older British trans-Atlantic officers to the scene of many a most uncomfortable four-hour watch period—the ship's *bridge.*

MOUSE.   A knob on a rope made of turns of spunyarn, as a Turk's head, to prevent an eye, lizard, etc., from sliding along such rope. As a verb (pronounced *"mowse"*), to span the mouth of a hook across shank and point with a few turns of small stuff or wire to prevent hook from being disengaged; to seize together both shanks of sister-hooks, or clip-hooks, for same purpose; to seize an eye of a rope in place around another rope, as a stirrup to a foot-rope; to provide with a *mousing,* as above.

MOUSING.   Turns of spunyarn, wire, etc., comprising seizing for securing a hook; *see* MOUSE. (Pron. *"mowsing"*) **M.-hook,** kind of hook fitted with a latch or spring contrivance for preventing it from being disengaged; a snap-hook.

MOUTH.   Opening likened to a mouth in affording entrance or exit; as, sea-entrance to a harbor or river, or *harbor's m.; river's m.; m. of a hawse-pipe.* To **carry a bone in her m.,** *see* BONE IN HER TEETH. **In the m. of the breakers,** situation of being at or near an area of breaking seas, as near a coast or bar in bad weather. **M. of a hatch,** entrance to a hatchway. **M. plug,** wad of oakum, rope-yarns, etc., or a fitted block of wood inserted in a hawse-pipe, mooring-pipe, etc., to keep out the sea.

MOVABLE EYE-BOLT.   *See* LEWIS-BOLT.

MOZAMBIQUE CURRENT.   Another name for the *Agulhas Current;* properly, that part of it flowing along the coast of Portuguese East Africa. From thence it is sometimes called *Natal Current* to about latitude of Port Elizabeth. *See* AGULHAS CURRENT.

MUD.   Pasty mixture of earth and water; any slimy deposit; miry sea-bottom. *Abbrev.* on American and British charts as *M.* or *m.,* indicating type of sea-

bottom. **M. box,** a trap, usually box-shaped and having a perforated plate, for straining bilge-water of solid matter before it reaches the pump; a *strum.* **M. drag,** a *m.* dredge of any description for deepening a river channel, harbor entrance, etc. **M. drum,** *see* **B. mud drum** *in* BOILER. **M. hole,** opening in bottom of a boiler for removing *m.* and scale in cleaning; also, *sludge-hole.* **M'fish,** any of many fishes that frequent muddy water or burrow in *m.* **M.-hook,** an anchor; *esp.* a working anchor of a coaster. **M. land,** marshes or muddy beaches left dry by the low tide; reclaimed land consisting of *m.* dredgings. **M. pilot,** a river pilot; *cf.* PILOT. **M.-plug,** *see* PLUG. **M. scow,** flatboat for carrying *m.* to dumping-grounds from a dredge; a *m. boat.*

'MUDIAN RIG.   Among yachtsmen, colloquial name for the *Bermuda* or *Bermudian rig; see* RIG.

MUFFLED OARS.   Those wrapped with canvas or special rope-yarn mats about the looms in way of thole-pins or rowlocks, as in older naval practice in silencing usual noise of oars in rowing, *esp.* in night operations by boats.

MUFFLER.   Device in exhaust pipe of an internal combustion engine designed to deaden noise of exhaust from explosions in cylinders to atmosphere. It usually takes the form of an increase in cross-section area of exhaust line near its end so that gases reach the atmosphere at reduced speed and pressure; generally enclosed in a *dummy funnel,* or casing built like an ordinary smokestack.

MUGGY.   Said of the weather condition of being damp and close or sultry; warm and humid. India's Southwest monsoon has often been referred to as the *muggy monsoon,* because of prevailing damp, sultry conditions. Also said of a moist, unventilated part of a lower hold, *esp.* in wooden vessels; as in *"China tea not half a ton in her muggy after run"* (where hold narrows aft).

MULE.   A fishing-boat of northeast coast of England similar in rig and construction, excepting her sharp pointed stern, to that of the *coble; see* COBLE. An electrically driven carriage used for towing vessels in a canal; *esp.* one of a number of so-called *electric mules* employed in the Panama Canal system for towing vessels through locks, where use of ships' engines normally is forbidden. These are equipped with a towing-wire reeled on a powered drum and are driven on a railway with traction supplied by a pinion working in a rack laid between rails. For each ship at least four *m's*—one on each bow and one on each quarter—are used and towing-wire leads at an angle of about 30° with fore-and-aft line, so that vessel thereby is kept in middle of lock in the process. **Sea m.,** a box-shaped powered vessel designed to push scows, car-floats, lighters, etc., in sheltered waters; usually equipped with a vertically adjustable propeller, or one which may be raised or lowered in its well, according to depth of water in which working.

MULLET. Fish of the *Mugilidæ* family, of which best known are the striped *m.* (*Mugil cephalus*) of North American and European coasts and the Mediterranean *Liza capito.* Generally called *gray m.,* distinguishing it from the *red m.,* or *goatfish,* averages 18 inches in length, has a stout body, blunt nose, and heavy caudal fin; of bluish silvery color, usually with faint dark lengthwise stripes on upper half of body. *Cf.* GOATFISH.

MULTISTEP HYDROPLANE. A fast motor-boat having a series of "steps" in her bottom surface with view of presenting as initial gliding surface that step farthest aft at highest speed. Such steps reduce weight forward in boat and hence allow her to *nose up,* or lift, in the gliding process; *see* HYDROPLANE.

MULTIPLE EXPANSION ENGINE. *See* ENGINE.

MUMSON LUNG. Breathing device used for escaping to surface from a sunken submarine.

MUNTZ METAL. *See* METAL.

MURDERING PIECE. In old-time naval ordnance, a mortar or short cannon charged with slugs, scrap metal, bullets, etc., for firing at close range, as in clearing decks of boarders; also called a *murderer.*

MURSIM. Star of magnitude 2.0 catalogued as β *Canis Majoris.* It is easily recognized as nearest bright star to the brilliant *Sirius,* from which it is distant about 6° toward W.S.W.

MUSCA. (*L. = a fly*) Small constellation located immediately south of the *Southern Cross.* Its brightest star is *α Muscae,* of magnitude 2.94 which lies 6° about S by E from *Acrux* (*α Crucis*), southernmost and brightest of the *Cross.*

MUSHROOM. Descriptive combining term indicating an object of mushroom form; a *m. anchor* (*see* ANCHOR). In ordnance, nose-plate or obturator at forward end of a breech-block; also, *m. head.* **M. fluke,** *see* FLUKE. **M. ventilator,** *see* VENTILATOR.

MUSTANG. In U.S. navy, colloquialism dating from the Civil War for one who enters naval service as an officer direct from the merchant marine; a commissioned officer in U.S. navy or Coast Guard who has not graduated at Naval or Coast Guard Academy.

MUSTER. An assembling of ship's company, passengers, or special detachments thereof. To summon together or assemble whole or part of ship's complement or passengers; as, to *m. all hands;* to *m. sea-boat's crew;* to *m. for quarantine inspection.* **M. list,** also termed *station bill* and *m. roll,* poster showing duties of each crew member at Boat, Fire, Collision, or Watertight door drills, including, where applicable, assignments to duties involving assembling, care, and supervision of passengers on such occasions. *M. lists* are required by law to be posted in appropriate conspicuous places in crew's and passengers' quarters. **M. roll,** in naval vessels, the equivalent of a crew list in a merchantman; *cf.* **Certified crew list** *in* CERTIFICATE. Document showing name, rank or rating, age, and other particulars of each member of ship's company; any list of seamen or passengers, or group of such, indicating individual assignments to stations or duties at *m.* or drill; a *m. list.* To **m. the watch,** to summon together the men comprising a watch to check up for absentees, for instruction regarding duties, or for performance of some special work. To **pass m.,** to be approved upon inspection; said of a seaman regarding his appearance or fitness; also, of an object so considered. **Tarpaulin m.,** a joint contribution by members of a crew, as money for a worthy cause, *e.g.,* a shipmate in distress. Said to have originated among whalemen, the term signifies placing of donations on a hatch tarpaulin for open and above board inspection.

MUTINEER. A seaman guilty of the felony known as *mutiny;* any mutinous person, or one who openly resists lawful authority, *esp.* such authority vested in an officer in charge of a vessel.

MUTINY. A felony which may be described as the usurpation by one or more members of a vessel's crew of the command of such vessel from her master or lawful officer in charge by force, fraud, or intimidation, or unlawfully deprives him of authority and command on board, or resists or prevents him in the free and lawful exercise thereof, or transfers such authority and command to another not lawfully entitled thereto. (*18 U.S.C. 484*) **M. on H.M.S. Bounty,** a notable case in British navy annals. In 1789, the frigate's mate, Fletcher Christian, backed by majority of the crew, took charge of ship and set adrift *Capt. William Bligh* with 18 men in a boat somewhere in vicinity of Tahiti, mid-South Pacific. Christian took the *Bounty* to Tahiti where most of his followers remained; then some months later sailed with eight of them and a group of Polynesians, landed at Pitcairn Island about 1170 miles ESE of Tahiti, and burned the vessel. Capt. Bligh landed at Timor, Dutch East Indies, after a sail of about 4000 miles. **M. at the Nore,** another incident of note which took place in the fleet at the anchorage of that name in the Thames estuary in 1797, curiously enough, is responsible for the change in British ships of the number of *bells* struck in keeping time during the *2nd. dog watch.* The *m.* was scheduled for 6 bells, or 7.00 p.m.; thereafter the sequence of bells in that watch became 1, 2, 3, 8, instead of 5, 6, 7, 8. Whatever benefits were derived from this turn of events, the occasion surely left its mark on the clock dial!

MUTTON. **M. fish,** *see* EELPOUT; also, the *m. snapper,* or *mojarra,* a food fish resembling the sea bass but having a deeper and more compressed body; family name *Gerridæ;* found from Brazil coast to West Indies. **M.-legger,** a boat carrying a *leg-of-mutton* sail or sails (those having a horizontal foot and a jib head); a *m.-sail* or *leg-of-m.* **M. spanker,** a storm spanker or one having a jib head, triangular in shape, with foot laced to, or hauled out along, a boom; carried sometimes by barques and ships; a *leg-of-m. spanker.*

MUTUAL INSURANCE. *See* INSURANCE.

MUZZLE. To control wind-swollen canvas in furling a sail; to secure a piece of canvas over mouth of a ventilator, pipe's end, etc. To **m. an anchor,** in small craft, to secure bight of the anchor cable (rope or chain) to an arm of an old-fashioned anchor, as in light weather conditions, with view of easily lifting anchor clear in getting under way. **M.-bag,** canvas cover shaped like a bag, for covering outer end of a gun. **M.-lashing,** in old-time ships, rope used to lash *m.* of a gun to vessel's side above a port, when housed.

MUZZLER. A stiff head wind; often termed a *dead muzzler.*

MYSTICETE. A sub-order of mammals consisting of the baleen whales; also, *mystacoceti; see* CETACEA. **Mysticetous,** pertaining to such.

N

N. In International Code, denoted by square flag *"Negat,"* having four horizontal rows of alternate blue and white squares. Hoisted singly, signifies "No" (*negative*); as initial letter in radio call signs of civil aircraft indicates nationality as of *United States of America,* which 5-letter call is painted on lower surface of a plane and on each side of its fuselage, the *N,* or *nationality mark* in this case, being separated from rest of the group by a hyphen. As an abbreviation *N = Navy; Nimbus* (cloud); *Noon; North* or *Northern.* It is signified in Morse code by — • (*dash dot*).

N. A. Abbreviation for *Nautical Almanac.*

NABBY. Large fishing-boat of east coast of Scotland, characterized by a pronounced aftward rake of her single mast and stern and also, heavy after draft. Carries a standing lug and large jib. Also, *nabbie.*

NADIR. (Ar.) Point in the celestial sphere directly opposite an observer's *zenith;* inferior pole of the horizon; figuratively, the lowest possible position or point.

NAIL. Any of the various slender pieces of metal usually driven into place by a hammer in fastening wood together or securing something to wood; its distinction as intermediate between a *tack* or a *brad* and a *spike* is chiefly in size; as, *boat n.; scupper n.; sheathing-n.* In old-time usage, to *spike* a cannon, *i.e.,* to render it temporarily useless by driving a nail or similar piece of metal into the touch-hole or vent; also, in modern use, to destroy or carry away a part of the breech mechanism for same purpose. **Clinch n.,** or *clench n.,* as used in boat-building, one of non-corrosive metal which may be bent over or clinched at its protruding point, after hammering into place, chiefly through overlapping planking seams. **Hatch n.,** *see* HATCH. **N.-sick,** said of a boat or vessel when making water through many nail or rivet holes; often simply describing the leaky condition of an old boat. **Ribband n.,** *see* RIBBAND. **Rove-clinch n.,** used in boat-building for securing lapped planking together. Its point end is burred over a *rove,* or washer, rivet fashion, thus drawing planks firmly together. **Rudder n., one** having a stout shank and full head used in fastening iron parts on a wooden rudder. **Scupper n.,** one of brass or Muntz metal, short and broad-headed, for fastening leather or sheet lead to wood, as in a scupper lip or flanged ends of a lead scupper-pipe. **Seam n.,** one of any type for securing seams of lapped planking in building boats. **Sheathing-n.,** short, stout, broad-headed copper or Muntz metal nail for fastening metal sheathing to a wooden vessel's bottom.

NAIR-AL-ZAURAK. (Ar.) α *Phœnicis,* or principal star in *Phœnix,* having a declination of 42½° S. and right ascension 0h. 24m.; magnitude 2.44. Lying about midway between *Achernar* and *Fomalhaut,* it may be located by extending the line representing east side of *Square of Pegasus* 57½° southward. Also called *Ankaa.*

NAKED. Said of a wooden vessel's hull when not sheathed below about light load line; having no bottom *sheathing.*

NAME BOARD. Board or surface on which a vessel displays her name. U.S. law requires that every documented vessel shall have her name marked on each bow and upon the stern and also her home port marked on the stern, in roman letters, smallest of which shall be not less in size than four inches; to be in light color on a dark ground or dark on a light ground and to be distinctly visible; and every machinery-propelled vessel shall, in addition to her name shown on her stern, have same displayed in distinct plain letters not less than six inches in length on each outer side of her pilot-house and, also, if a paddle steamer, on outer sides of her paddle-boxes. (*46 U.S.C. 46, 493*)

NANTUCKET SLEIGH RIDE. Old New England whalers' term for an exciting tow given the attacking boat by a harpooned whale.

NAOS. (Gr.) ʒ *Argus* or ʒ *Puppis,* star of magnitude 2.27 in *Argo,* located in right ascension about 8h. and declination 40° S. Lying 21½° about N.E. by E. of *Canopus,* brightest of that group, it marks the right angle of a right triangle formed by lines drawn to that star and to the brilliant *Sirius* to north and west.

NAPIER'S CIRCULAR PARTS. Used in solution of right-angled and quadrantal spherical triangles according to *Napier's Rules*, as in many computations in navigation and nautical astronomy. Named for their originator, *Lord John Napier (1550–1617)*, a Scottish mathematician, who is also credited with invention of *Napierian logarithms.* (See any good work on spherical trigonometry.)

NAPIER'S DIAGRAM. A device in graphic form for facilitating conversion of magnetic courses to compass courses and vice versa from a deviation curve; also for laying curves of semi-circular and quadrantal components of total deviations obtained by a given set of observations. It consists of a vertical middle line graduated to represent degrees on rim of a compass-card from N. downward through E. Dotted lines sloping downward from left to right are drawn at a 60° angle with compass-rim line and plain lines at same angle upward from left to right, each of which lines cross at their intersection with the compass-rim line, usually at every 15°. Deviations from a set of observations are plotted on the appropriate *dotted lines,* where, as is usual, observations are those for ship's head *by compass;* if for *magnetic headings,* on the *plain lines;* scale used being that of the compass-rim and measured from latter along such line (or one parallel with it). Then a fair curve drawn through all plotted observed deviations indicates such values for any other courses on the compass-rim line. As illustrating use of the diagram in converting a *magnetic* course to a *compass* course, assume any heading on the compass-rim line; then follow *plain* line, or one parallel with it, from assumed heading toward the deviation curve and return to compass-rim line by following *dotted* line, or one parallel with it; point on compass-rim line is then *compass course* required. Since all sides of a 60° triangle are identical (equilateral), we thus simply have allowed deviation as indicated in the curve to the right or to the left, according to its name, with the assurance that it is applied *in the right direction.* Practical use of the diagram is nicely summed up in the old rhyme:

"From compass course, magnetic course to gain,
  Depart by dotted and return by plain.
From magnetic course, to steer a course allotted,
  Depart by plain and then return by dotted."

NARROW. **N. seas,** old term for waters between France and England, and those between Great Britain and Ireland, over which England has claimed certain jurisdictional rights or supremacy outside the three-mile limit, never by the world powers generally agreed to. In *plural,* or *narrows,* denotes a contracted or narrow passage, as part of a river, between rocks, entrance to a bay or harbor, etc.; *e.g., Narrows* at entrance to New York Harbor; also sometimes, a strait.

NARWHAL. (Dan. *narhval; nar* = corpse [from its pallid skin]; *hval* = whale) The *sea unicorn, Monodon monoceros* of the family termed *Delphinidæ,* which includes dolphins, porpoises, grampuses, and blackfish, an arctic cetacean, mottled gray and white in color, attaining a length of 15 to 20 feet. Has two small flippers, no dorsal fin, and bulbous head similar to that of the sea cow. In the male, a single long pointed tusk of twisted rope-like form projects horizontally forward from the upper jaw, is about four feet in length in an adult, and considered valuable ivory. Also written *narwal, narwhale.*

NATATORY. Pertaining to, or characterized by, *natation,* or the act or art of swimming; as, *n. birds; n. reptiles; n. skill.*

NATIONAL. **N. flag,** see ENSIGN. **N. salute,** see SALUTE.

NATIONALITY MARK. In International Code requirements, first one or first two letters of the 4-letter group authorized as a vessel's radio call sign or signal letters; or, first one or first two of the 5-letter radio call sign or signal letters of aircraft. In both cases, radio call sign and signal letters are identical.

NATURAL. In accordance with or governed by law or design occurring in nature; not artificial. **N. draft,** see DRAFT. **N. frame,** see FRAME. **N. harbor,** a haven or sheltered area, as an inlet or small bay, which, in its natural state, provides reasonably sufficient depth of water and shelter from sea waves for vessels. **N. knee,** see KNEE. **N. magnet,** see **Artificial m.** *in* MAGNET. **N. scale,** as usually indicated in title of a chart or plan of a locality, ratio which linear measurements bear to actual measurements on part of earth's surface thereby represented. **N. ventilation,** see VENTILATION. **N. year,** see YEAR.

NAUFRAGE. (Fr.) Now obsolete term for shipwreck; also *naufragie.*

NAUROPOMETER. Archaic name for a clinometer, or instrument for measuring vessel's heel or list; also *nauropemeter.*

NAUSCOPY. Supposed ability or gift of sighting, or being conscious of the presence of, ships or land at great distances. "By some *nauscopic* sense beyond the ken of common mortals, Sir Humphrey scented land in the N.E. quarter." (*Hakluyt*)

NAUSEA. Seasickness; feeling of distress accompanied by vomiting or loathing of food; stomach disorder caused by rolling or pitching of vessel.

NAUTICAL. (Gr. nautikus; *nautes,* seaman; *naus,* ship) Of or pertaining to seamen, ships, or navi-

gation of surface craft; marine; maritime; naval.
N. almanac, *see* ALMANAC. **N. angle,** *see* ANGLE. **N. astronomy,** that branch of navigation which deals with determination of ship's position and compass errors by altitude and azimuth observations of the sun, moon, planets, and stars; also termed *celestial navigation.* **N. Box,** an early subdivision of constellation *Argo,* or group of faint stars called by astronomers *Pyxis,* or the *Mariner's Compass.* Only one of this group listed in American Ephemeris (1949) is *θ Pyxidis,* magnitude 4.93, located in right ascension 9h. 19m. and declination 25° 45' S. *Cf.* ARGO. **N. day,** *see* DAY. **N. instruments,** *see* INSTRUMENTS. **N. mile,** *see* MILE. **N. surveyor,** one whose profession is that of marine or hydrographic surveying; *cf.* **M. surveying** *in* MARINE. **N. tables,** tabulated computed values of various mathematical and astronomical data, usually in book form, for use in navigational practice.

NAUTOPHONE. Electrically operated fog signal sounded from coastal stations and lightships. Sound of great intensity, generally of a deep tone or similar to that emitted by a reed horn, is produced by vibratory action of a metal diaphragm and directed seaward by a cone-shaped horn. The apparatus is controlled by clock-work which makes electro-magnetic contact at regular time intervals, resulting recurring blast or blasts indicating the particular station heard by vessels in vicinity. Also termed a *diaphragm horn; cf.* **F. signal** *in* FOG. (For procedure of finding ship's distance from a station synchronizing such signals with a radio-beacon, *see* **R. distance-finding station** *in* RADIO.)

NAVAL. (L. *navalis;* from *navis,* ship) Pertaining to, connected with, or characteristic of, war-vessels or a navy; as, *n. dock; n. forces; n. discipline.* Former use of the word as pertaining to ships and shipping in general now appears in very few terms; as, *n. architecture; n. stores.* **N. architect,** one who practices the designing of ships, or specializes in **n. architecture,** the art or science of planning size, structural strength, and general arrangement of hull sub-division of vessels, having due regard to their intended service, stability, speed, and power requirements. **N. auxiliary,** vessel attending a fleet as fuel-supply ship, store ship, etc. **N. brass,** Muntz metal; *see* **Composition m.** *in* METAL. **N. cadet,** a young man in training for commission as an officer; *cf.* MIDSHIPMAN. **N. constructor,** in U.S.N., member of a corps of officers having charge of design, construction, and repairing of hulls and fittings, exclusive of armament and main engines. Such officers generally have received supplementary technical education before graduating from Naval Academy. **N. districts,** in U.S., the sixteen areas into which continental United States with Alaska, Hawaiian Islands, Panama Canal Zone, and Puerto Rico (with Virgin Islands) are divided for navy

jurisdictional purposes. **N. dockyard,** waterfront premises owned by a state and provided with facilities for building, repairing, equipping, and provisioning its vessels of war. **N. engineering,** *see* **Marine e.** *in* ENGINEERING. **N. law,** *see* LAW. **N. officer,** an officer in a navy; especially one of commissioned rank. In U.S., a custom house official at larger ports who certifies collector's accounts, authenticates certain documents, and, in co-operation with the collector, estimates duties to be levied on merchandise. **N. rating,** grade or class of an enlisted man; the man himself; as, *seaman 1st class; boatswain's mate;* any grade below warrant officer. **N. reserve,** the body of officers and men, consisting largely of ex-navy and merchant marine personnel, also certain merchant vessels, which may be called upon to augment forces of a navy as required. **N. square,** *see* SQUARE. **N. station,** port where vessels of a navy may take in fuel, supplies, etc., or obtain minor repairs; sometimes applied to a training or receiving station for a navy. **N. stores,** *see* STORE. **N. strategy; n. tactics,** "*strategy* has been curtly described as the art of concentrating an effective fighting force at a given place at a given time; *tactics* as the art of using it when there." (*Encyl. Britt.*)

NAVE or **NAVEL.** (Akin to *hub*) Term designating a central part or point; the middle; especially of a rounded part of anything. **Navel futtock,** also called *navel timber,* a first futtock at broad part of ship's bottom; *see* FUTTOCK. **Navel hood,** *see* HOOD. **Nave-line** or **navel-line,** rope or tackle leading from topmasthead to support after part of a topsail-yard parrel; now an obsolete term. **Navel pipe,** a chain-pipe; *see* **C.-locker pipe** *in* CHAIN.

NAVICERT. (Abbreviation for *Navigation certificate*) As first used in World War I, a document issued in a neutral country by consular service of a belligerent, certifying that a cargo departing for a neutral port is of such nature as not to be subject to seizure or detention by forces of such belligerent.

NAVIGABLE. Having sufficient width and depth to provide passage for vessels; said of a river or other stretch of water. In a technical sense, as determining the right of public use of certain waters as a highway, it is accepted generally that to be *navigable in fact* the body of water, or considered part of such body, must be customarily used, or may be used in its natural state if required, as a highway for commerce or traffic. In Great Britain, however, any river or other body of water is considered navigable only to the limits of ebb and flow of tide, unless otherwise prescribed by law. **N. semicircle,** in a tropical cyclone, area in which wind blows away from the *line of progression,* or path of storm; so named because in that half of storm it generally is possible to run and avoid its center or most violent part adjacent thereto. In Northern

Hemisphere, it is that part of a cyclone lying to *left* of storm's path; in Southern Hemisphere, that part to *right* of it; observer facing direction of storm's advance. *Cf.* CYCLONE.

NAVIGATE. To manage or direct in sailing; as, *the brig is navigated by a blue-water seaman.* To use or traverse a body of water as in sailing; as, *"across the Atlantic the Norsemen navigated in deckless vessels."* To sail over or across; as, to *n.* the Gulf. To steer, manage, sail, or direct a vessel; as, *"among the ice our skippers n. their steamers with unusual care."* **Navigating bridge,** *see* BRIDGE. **Navigating officer,** *see* NAVIGATOR.

NAVIGATION. Act of navigating; art or science of conducting a vessel from one place to another, as by use of a compass and sails or other means of propulsion, embracing, more especially, determination of ship's position by celestial observations or bearings of points or places on shore, shaping the course and checking of compass error by observations, and generally keeping account of vessel's progress along the desired track. Passing of shipping over a waterway or body of water; as, *inland n.; river n.; ocean n.* **Bureau of Marine Inspection and Navigation,** *see* BUREAU. **Bureau of N.,** former title of a division of U.S. Navy Department; now *Bureau of Personnel.* **Celestial n.,** *see* **N. astronomy** *in* NAUTICAL. **Cœlo-n.,** archaic term for *celestial n.* **Geo-n.,** *see* GEO-NAVIGATION. **Improper n.,** marine insurance term connoting departure from reasonably normal conduct by a master or crew in the navigation of, or attention to duty on board, a vessel; also, any misuse of vessel or any part thereof, as, *e.g.,* failure to provide proper ventilation for a cargo where means for such care are at hand; or the uncorrected presence of a structural defect, faulty cargo gear, ship's equipment, or machinery. **Inshore n.,** *see* INSHORE. **N. laws,** *see* **Maritime law** *in* LAW. **N. lights,** *see* LIGHT. **N. school,** institution at which theory and practice of navigation is taught; especially, such school or *nautical college,* as it is sometimes called, attended by merchant marine officers; also, *nautical school.* **N. rules,** *see* REGULATIONS FOR PREVENTING COLLISIONS. **Steam n.,** chiefly in older usage, distinguishing term in shipping, indicating vessels using steam as means of propulsion. **N. subsidy,** a subvention, bounty, or grant of funds by a government to shipowners under its flag in recognition of transportation services considered important to the public weal. Such payment may take the form of supplying capital for new construction, free dry-docking, ordinary repairs and renewals, etc., in the case of vessels designed for possible war-time use as naval auxiliaries; or, depending upon a vessel's age, size, speed, and tonnage, may be an outright cash bounty for maintaining a special service, as in carriage of mails to ports beyond the more commonly used shipping routes; a *n. bounty; mail subsidy.*

NAVIGATIONAL STARS. *See* STARS.

NAVIGATOR. (L.) One who navigates; one skilled in the art of navigation; specifically, an officer of a war-vessel, usually ranking next below the executive officer, or third in order of command, who is charged with navigation of the ship and has under his immediate care all navigational instruments, charts, and matters pertaining to navigation in general. In merchant vessels, particularly those of liner type, the *n.,* or *navigating officer,* usually is a senior watch officer third or fourth in line of command. As a point of interest, the word *navvy,* in England denoting a laborer who digs canals, ditches, etc., or similarly is engaged with pick and shovel, is a shortened form of *navigator,* meaning one employed at digging a canal, or a *navigation,* as an artificial waterway has been called. **Eye-sight n.,** a mud pilot, one who directs vessel's course, as in a river, entirely by eye.

NAVY. (O.F., *navie,* ship or fleet; L. *navis,* ship) War-vessels of a nation, collectively; entire naval system or establishment embracing administrative offices, dock-yards, fueling stations, gun factories, personnel, ships, training stations, etc. In older usage, a *fleet* of warships; the merchant marine as *merchant navy.* **General Board of the N.,** in U.S.N., a board of senior officers who act in an advisory capacity as directed by the *Secretary of the Navy.* **N. agent,** in Great Britain, an attorney who acts in the interests of naval officers in financial matters, including distribution of prize money awards. **N. bean,** common dried white bean, so named for its extensive use for many years as an important long-voyage food in naval ships. **N. board,** a former colloquial term in England for the British Admiralty. **N. Department,** established 30 April, 1798, after being a division of *Department of War* from the nation's birth, one of the executive branches of U.S. Government presided over by a member of the Cabinet, called *Secretary of the Navy.* Its functions in management of the nation's naval establishment are carried on by seven *Bureaus, viz.,* Bureau of Aeronautics,—Medicine and Surgery,—Ordnance,—Personnel,—Ships,—Supplies and Accounts,—Yards and Docks. **N. "E,"** in U.S. navy, the award for first class efficiency in operation, or *excellence.* Gunnery award is an *E* painted beside gun or turret concerned; engineering award, a red *E;* and that for general battle efficiency a white *E* painted on ship's smokestack. Also given, in time of war, for production awards to defense factories. **N. list,** in U.S. and British navies, official list of officers in the service, issued periodically. **N. plug,** a dark, hard-pressed, strong tobacco made in cakes, figs, or *plugs,* once a favorite in the navy,—now largely displaced by the packet of "shag" and papers for hand-made cigarettes; *blackjack.* **N. publications,** following list concerns personnel of U.S.N.: *Naval Regulations; Bureau of Personnel Manual*—regulations governing interior operation and personnel matters aboard ship; *Naval Courts and Boards*—the conduct of naval courts-martial and boards and matters pertinent thereto; *Register of Commissioned and Warrant Officers*—complete lists of all officers, nature of service, dates of birth and entry into service, date of rank, states appointed from, signal numbers, special qualifications, etc., plus officers' pay schedule; *Navy Directory*—lists of all officers on active and retired lists, with present ships, stations or retired addresses; lists of officer personnel on various ships and at different naval stations and establishments; *Bureau Manuals*—each Bureau has its manual for guidance therein; *Bluejacket's Manual* —information valuable for the bluejacket; *Recruit's Handy Book*—same; *Watch Officer's Guide.* **N. Relief Society,** an American organization principally concerned with charitable work for benefit of families of navy personnel. A branch of the Society is established in each Naval District and usually is presided over by the wife of the District Commander. **N. sherry,** British seamen's depreciative term for diluted rum served as *grog* in the navy. **N. yard,** a naval shore station usually equipped with material and appliances for repairing, building, and fitting out vessels of the fleet; a *naval dockyard.* U.S. yards of importance are located at Boston, Brooklyn, Philadelphia, Washington, D.C., Norfolk, Mare Island, Cal., Bremerton, Wash., Pearl Harbor, T.H., and Balboa, C.Z.

N. E. Abbreviation for *northeast* or *northeastern;* compass point or direction halfway between north and east.

NEAP. A neap tide; designating a tide of least rise and fall from mean sea level, or that usually occurring twice in a lunar month, one or two days following first and third quarters of the moon. A tide is said to *neap* when diminishing in range after advent of *spring tide,* and a vessel is said to be *neaped* (older form *beneaped*) after stranding at high water on a spring tide, in the sense that a decreasing tidal rise delays prospect of refloating until recurrence of usual two weekly-springs. *Cf.* TIDE. **Deep n.,** a tide of greater rise than that usually occurring at neaps.

NEAR. Close, as to the wind in sailing *close-hauled.* To approach anything; as, to *n.* the land. **No nearer!,** order to a helmsman to steer vessel no closer to the wind.

NECK. Throat, or forward upper corner, of a gaff sail. Narrow part of an oar next the blade. A small or comparatively narrow isthmus; a long, narrow point extending from a coast. A narrow channel connecting two expanding bodies of water; a strait.

NECKING. In large ornamental taffrail stanchions found on poops of older ships, molding around their upper and lower ends, usually sculptured in the wood itself.

NECKLACE. In older sailing-ships, chain set up around a lowermast for securing lower ends of futtock shrouds; later displaced by the *futtock hoop* or *band.* Also, a heavy strop about a lowermast below the top for securing various leads or lead-blocks through which running gear was rove. *Cf.* **F.-band** *in* FUTTOCK.

NEEDLE. Sharp-pointed steel instrument used in sewing; as, a *sail n.* One of the slender bar magnets giving directive force to a compass-card; *compass n.* A sharp pinnacle of rock on a coast. Short for the *magnetic n.* **Compass-n.,** *see* COMPASS. **Declination of the n.,** *see* **D. of compass-needle** *in* DECLINATION. **Dip of the n.,** *see* DIP. **Lolley n.,** a short spur or *roping n.* used in sailmaking; *Lolley's n.; see* **Sail n. Magnetic n.,** *see* MAGNETIC. **N.-fish,** *see* GAR. **N. hitch,** so called from its use in *pointing* an end of a rope, as a man-rope, boat's painter, etc., by means of a sail-needle and twine. *N.-hitching* is simply a continuous series of half hitches round and round the rope, starting from a few whipping turns and working toward rope's end. Also used in covering cork fenders, bow puddings, or making chafing-mats with any small line, a marline-spike being employed to open the parts for reeving through. **Netting-n.,** slender piece of wood appropriately shaped to act as a hand-shuttle in making each mesh in a net; *cf.* MESH. **Sail n.,** named for its original use, special *n.* for sewing in canvas. It is triangular in section and tapering from the point to about half length, thence round in shape to the eye, its greatest outside diameter being about one-third length from point. *Long spur n.,* or one having a longer triangular section than the *short spur,* is usual kind employed in ordinary seam work, short spur *n.* being the type for roping work, *i.e.,* sewing edge of sail to its roping. Needles are designated by whole numbers 6 to 14; thence 14½, 15, 15½, 16, 16½, 17, 17½, last-named being finest in the scale. In usual sail work on board ship, Nos. 14 to 15½ are employed, these being 3 to 2½ inches in length. In sailmaking practice needles are often named for work in which used; as, *flat-seam, tabling, small bolt-rope, head-rope, large bolt-rope, etc.*

NEF. (Fr., from L. *navis,* ship) A trading vessel of medieval times; as depicted in 11th. century drawings, a ship having a superstructure or *castle* at each end, and one mast and single square sail; such a craft was then also termed a *round ship.* The term appears to have been applied in Middle Ages to a costly coffer made in shape of a ship; such as a cadenas or casket for the tableware of a great personage, or a similar container in a church for keeping the incense; and also was applied to an early clock of elaborate ship form.

NEGATIVE. Opposed to affirmative: as in *a n. signal;* or to positive: as, *n. pole* of a magnet. Of or having an indicated value or condition less than, below, or opposite a definite standard, parity, or mark; as, *n. slip; n. stability; n. angle.* **N. angle,** a depression angle, or that measured vertically downward from the true horizontal or the visible horizon; opposed to angle of elevation. **N. flag,** see N. **N. pole,** blue or south-seeking pole; opposed to positive or north-seeking pole; the *blue pole; cf.* MAGNETISM. **N. slip,** difference in speed of vessel over the ground and that calculated according to revolutions of propeller expressed as a percentage of latter speed, where speed over the ground is *greater;* opposed to *positive slip. Cf.* SLIP. **N. stability,** condition in which a vessel having all weights on board symmetrically distributed with relation to the fore-and-aft line has insufficient righting power to remain at rest in the upright position. Due to position of her center of gravity being a little above the metacenter, vessel naturally assumes a list to regain stable equilibrium, or fulfill the conditions obtaining when floating at rest, *viz.,* that the center of buoyancy and the metacenter must lie in a vertical line intersecting ship's fore-and-aft vertical midship plane *above* her center of gravity. See STABILITY.

NEGLIGENCE CLAUSE. In a marine insurance policy, a clause generally disclaiming the carrier's responsibility in case of loss or damage to cargo for negligence of master, crew, or pilots; latent defects in machinery or hull; damage by accidents to loading or unloading gear; or other hidden causes over which carrier has no control; where it can be shown that he has exercised due diligence in providing a vessel to the best of his knowledge seaworthy in every respect.

NEPTUNE. (L. *Neptunus*) In Roman mythology, god of the waters; identified with *Poseidon* of the Greeks; distinguished for his unfailing attention to initiation of new arrivals at *Latitude Zero; see* **Crossing the l.** *in* LINE.[2] (His somewhat rusty and salt-crusted crown and trident now bear witness to his royal office rather than to that of deity. It has been said that too many gods drove kindly *Neptune* to the humble avocation of ship-visiting and the use of wash-deck tubs and tar-pots). The planet *Neptune* is eighth in order from the sun and distant from that body 2,793,488,000 statute miles; completes an orbital revolution in about 165 years. Although having a diameter of 32,932 miles, presents a maximum of little more than 2½ seconds of arc in angular measurement and thus difficult to recognize in the heavens. *Neptune* has one satellite only which revolves round the planet in 5d. 21h. Figuratively, the ocean; sea.

NERO DEEP. *See* DEEP.

NESS. (A.S. *naes;* Sw. *nas;* Dan. *naes;* Russ. *nos;* all meaning *nose*) A cape, headland, or promontory; as in *Dungeness, Skagness, Orfordness.* The *Naze* at southern extremity of coast of Norway is another *nose* or *ness.*

NEST. To place or stow one within the other, as boats. In fishing-vessels of the Newfoundland Banker type, it is common practice to thus stow their 6 to 10 dories on deck, "spoon fashion," as it is sometimes called. Also, similar stowage is used with lifeboats of the flat-bottomed *Lundin* pattern, which system requires use of only one set of davits and tackles for two or three boats. Fishermen's dories are fitted with removable thwarts to effect the deep snug *nesting* demanded for economy of space.

NET.[1] Remaining after deduction of space, charges, losses, etc.; as, *n. tonnage; n. freight.* Free and clear of tare, waste, or that which is allowed for; as, *n. weight; n. load.* **N. capacity,** usually, total weight of cargo, exclusive of fuel and stores required, which a vessel can carry loaded to her summer salt water load-line; also, *cargo-carrying capacity; deadweight cargo capacity.* The term is sometimes applied to *space* remaining in a hold or in entire ship's cargo compartments after being partly loaded, as when arriving at another loading port. **N. form charter,** that in which a charterer meets all ordinary cargo operating and navigation expenses and pays shipowner net freight proceeds. Such expenses usually exclude only fuel, crew's wages, repairs, and stores. **N. tonnage,** see TONNAGE.

NET[2] An open fabric of thread, twine, cord, etc., woven or worked in meshes (*cf.* MESH), as a *fishing-n.;* net-work or netting, as that between a ship's open rail and the deck or forming the sides of a receptacle for stowage of hammocks, etc.; a *net sling* or *cargo-n.* **Fish nets,** or **fishing-nets,** local names for which are legion, may be divided into two classes: *Gill nets,* as used for example, in catching the herring, in which the meshes are of such size as to allow fish to nose in, but not large enough to pass through; so that in trying to extricate itself its opening gills anchor or hold the unfortunate tike, barb fashion, from going astern; and *inclosing nets,* or those that trap or surround the fish, as various drag-nets, seines, weirs, etc. Nets are named from their designed catch, as *crab-n., tunny-n., herring-n.;* from their construction or form, as *heart-n., purse-n.;* or for their manner of use, as *casting-n., drag-n., drift-n.* **N.-fishing,** that carried on by use of nets, as distinguished from line or drag methods in the industry. For various *nets* used in fishing, see under captions BOW, DRAG, GROUND, HEART, LAM, LANDING, PLOUT, POUND, PURSE, SCAFF, SCOOP, TOWING, TRAMMEL, TRAP, TRAWL, TIDE. To **pass** or **run the n.,** to feel along the cork-line or head-rope of a set net in determining presence of any captured fish. Experienced fishermen can tell by lifting net a little by hand whether enough fish are caught to justify labor of hauling in. However, a disturbance of the cork-line, as observed by eye, usually is sufficient indication of a sizable catch in any *gill-net* lay-out. To **shoot a net,** *see* SHOOT.

NETTING. Act or process of making net-work or nets; or of fishing by use of a net. Any open-work fabric of crossing or meshed cord, rope, wire, etc. **Boarding-n.,** *see* BOARDING. **Bulwark n.,** *see* BULWARK. **Diamond n.,** simple form of net-work in which meshes are diamond-shaped and made by seizing contacting bights together instead of forming mesh-knots. **Hammock-n.,** *see* HAMMOCK. **Head n.,** *see* HEAD. **Jib n.,** *see* JIB. **N.-needle,** a meshing-needle; *see* NEEDLE *and* MESH. **Quarter-n's,** same as **Hammock-n.,** so named for position along quarter bulwarks in old-time naval ships. **Splinter n.,** in old sailing-navy days, rope nets spread to advantage on ships weather deck to prevent injury to men from falling pieces of spars, blocks, etc., during an engagement. **Top n.,** safety "fence" of net-work made of small stuff, fitted around a top in larger old-time sailing war-vessels.

NETTLE. Small line made of twisted rope-yarns; usually made in a short handy length; often in plural, as *nettles* for hammock-clews, robands, etc. Twisted half-yarns in the tapering process of *pointing* a rope's end are also called *nettles,* but original form of term appears as *knittles.* In ropemaking, to join ends of yarns by a twisting process, termed *nettling;* this also designates the joining of two ropes by a method of intertwining the yarns so that no trace of such a "splice" is visible to the inexperienced eye.

NETTLE-FISH. A jelly-fish; so called from the stinging quality of its hair-like tentacles being likened to that of the *nettle plants.* Also, *sea-nettle.*

NEUTRAL AXIS. In considering stresses to which structural material may be subjected, term given in mechanics, especially with regard to longitudinal bending stress, as in a beam, to the center line or plane throughout the material, which is subjected to neither tension nor compression. Calculations for required strength in a vessel's hull are largely governed by distance of structural units from the longitudinal *neutral axis,* since magnitude of bending stresses,—as, for example, when ship is pitching in a heavy head sea,—increases as the squares of distances of the members from axis in question. **N. center,** *see* CENTER. **N. equilibrium,** *see* **N. stability** *in* NEGATIVE.

NEW MEASUREMENT. *See* MEASUREMENT.

NEWEL. In 17th. century ships, ornamented upright timber or post receiving the rail for ladder or stairs leading from main deck to poop. A similar post at foot of a companionway leading to a deck above.

NEW YORK SAILING BARGE. A now extinct sloop-rigged craft for many years extensively used as a cargo-carrier in New York Harbor and contiguous waters. Last few vessels of the type disappeared in 1912. They averaged 55 feet in length; breadth 25 feet; and carried 50 to 75 tons weight on 5 to 6 feet of draft. Rigged with a short bowsprit, single jib, and brailing-in boomless mainsail, were decked fore-and-aft, and with their moderately fine lines were reasonably fast sailers.

NIB. Pointed extremity of an object; specifically, lip or narrow end of a scarf in timber. **N.-block,** *see* BLOCK. **Nibbing-plank,** margin plank in a deck, notched or *nibbed* to receive butting ends of planking where it curves inward in following lines of ship toward forward and after ends; *cf.* **M. plank** *in* MARGIN; also termed *nib strake.*

NIBBLER. A small rocky-bottom food fish of the New England coasts, so named from its habit of *nibbling* bait off fishermen's hooks. Also called *sea-wife,* but more generally the *cunner,* it is a genus of the *wrasses; see* WRASSE.

NICKEY. Typical fishing-boat of Isle of Man for many years. Rig is similar to a yawl, but with lug sails, foresail being a dipping lug, mizzen a standing lug; no jibs but usually an after staysail.

NIGGER. Small steam capstan or winch fitted forward in a river vessel for hauling ship over shallows and snags. **N.-fish,** a serranoid food fish about 12 inches in length, spotted with black or blue on a color ground varying from yellow through scarlet to dark brown, and carrying an extensive spiny dorsal fin. It is found on coasts of Florida and West Indies. **N'head,** American term for a drum, or *drum end,* of a winch around which turns of a hawser, fall, or other rope are taken in heaving. Also, heavy towing-bitts on a tug, usually consisting of a pair of posts abreast each other and connected by a heavy wood or iron cross-piece which projects about two feet beyond each bitt or post. The bitts are suitably braced against stress in a tow-line.

NIGHT. Period between dusk and dawn, or that of darkness in the day of twenty-four hours. At sea, generally, that part of the natural day in which the sun is below the horizon. In connection with *Rules for Preventing Collisions,* although therein not defined specifically, in a technical sense *night* must be taken to mean period between sunset and sunrise, since exhibition of prescribed lights as night signals for vessels is required during that time. **All n. in,** having a full night's rest; no watch duty to perform. **N. effect,** *see* EFFECT. **N.-fish,** a kind of large cod, having a very dark back, taken on some parts of Newfoundland Banks and Gulf of St.

Lawrence; so named because it bites the hook only at night; also *n. cod.* **N. glass,** a telescope or binoculars for night use; *see* GLASS. **N. order book,** special book in which a master or commanding officer writes his orders for the night; *see* ORDER. **N. tide,** a flood tide occurring at night; especially, that distinguished from the day tide by its difference in height, as occurs at some places when sun and moon differ widely in declination and moon is in the gibbous phase. **N. watch,** a guard on night duty; any watch period during the night.

NIMBUS. (L. for rainstorm or cloud) The raincloud; *see* CLOUD.

NINEPIN BLOCK. An old-fashioned block made from a solid piece of wood and shaped like a ninepin. Used as a fair-lead, it was fixed to swivel at each end and so adjust itself to direction of pull in the rope.

NIP. To stop, rack, or seize a taut rope against another, as a part in a tackle; to jam a rope, as in turning hauling part of a tackle under other parts at entrance to block (called *choking* the tackle). To pinch or close in upon; a vessel is said to be *nipped* when caught between moving ice-fields; *cf.* **I.-nip** *in* ICE. A sharp turn in direction of stress due to an improper lead of a rope. That part of a rope or chain in way of a seizing or nipper. To **n. the cable,** to temporarily secure it with a stopper, nipper, or devil's claw in order to relieve the capstan or windlass, or for purpose of fleeting the messenger for a new heave on capstan, as in weighing anchor in old hemp cable days; also, to *nipper off the cable.*

NIPPER. An iron clamp or a selvagee strop used in heaving in ship's cable by messenger led to a capstan; cable-nipper; devil's claw; any strop, short rope, clamp, or other means of *nipping* a hawser, cable, etc. A stuffed mitten worn by New England fishermen to protect the hands in hauling fish-lines. **Cable-n.,** *see* CABLE. **N. men,** in sailing-navy days, seamen detailed to secure the messenger to ship's cable by use of nippers and also to *nipper off* cable each time a new fleet of the messenger was taken; *cf.* MESSENGER.

NOAH'S ARK. A sailor's quasi improvement on the title of *Argo* for that important southern constellation; *see* ARGO.

NOBBY. A variation of the *nickey,* found on west coast of England; usually larger and having lowering masts; *see* NICKEY.

NOCK. Upper fore corner of a gaff sail or a trysail; throat of a gaff sail. In older usage, extreme end or tip of a yard arm; also pointed end or tip of any sail or spar. **N. earing,** *see* EARING.

NODDY. A large tern, dark brown in color with some gray or white on the head; widely distributed in lower latitudes and common on Gulf of Mexico and U.S. southeastern coasts. Due to its stupidly docile nature, said to be easily picked up from its nest by the hand. It hatches in bushes along the shore.

NODE. In astronomy, either of two nearly diametrically opposed points at which a planet's orbit intersects the plane of the ecliptic, or at which the orbit of a satellite intersects plane of its primary's orbit. At time of passing from south to north, planet or satellite is said to be in the *ascending n.;* when passing from north to south, in *descending n.* **Nodes,** or **nodal points of the tides;** *see* **Nodal p.** *in* POINT. **Nodical month,** elapsed period between two successive *ascending nodes* of the moon, averaging 27d. 5h. 5m. 35.8s. of mean time.

NOG. In older shipyard practice, a treenail securing the heel of a shore, a timber in a launching cradle, or other temporary frame-work. To fasten, as shores, by *nogging.*

NOGGIN. Archaic sea term for a small tub made by sawing through middle of a keg; hence, a washing-tub. Also, a small mug or cup; a gill or "dram" of grog.

NO HIGHER! Same as "No nearer!" "No closer!" *See* NEAR.

NO MAN'S LAND. *See* J's land *in* JACK.

NOMINAL HORSEPOWER. *See* HORSEPOWER.

NON-CONDENSING ENGINE. *See* ENGINE.

NON-HARMONIC CONSTANTS. In predictions of times and heights of tides, those derived from a series of actual observations, as distinguished from *harmonic* constants; *cf.* HARMONIC ANALYSIS.

NOON. (A.S. *nōn;* L. *nona,* the ninth hour or 3 o'-clock, p.m., according to Roman and early ecclesiastical reckoning, or time of church services at that hour, called *Nones,* which was later changed to midday, the Anglo-Saxon *nōn-tid,* or noontide) Middle of the day; 12 o'clock in the day by standard local time; time of sun's upper transit. It is customary at sea to reckon the day's run, fuel consumption, and work done by engines from *noon* to *noon.* Astronomical time, prior to 1925, also was thus reckoned; *see* ASTRONOMICAL. **Apparent n.,** instant of meridian passage of sun's center at a given place; 12 o'clock in the day by a sun dial; usually referred to in navigation as an observer's *local apparent n.* **Mean n.,** or **local mean n.,** instant of the mean sun's transit at a given place; *cf.* **M. solar day** *and* **M. time** *in* MEAN. **Sidereal n.,** instant of upper transit of the vernal equinoctial point at a given place; 0h. 0m. 0s. or 24h. 0m. 0s. of sidereal time; *cf.* TIME.

NORDLANDSBAT. (*Northland boat*) Old-fashioned open clinker-built fishing-boat of northwestern coast of Norway, probably nearest recently surviving relative of craft sailed by the vikings. Chiefly used in cod-fishing, ranges from 20 to 40 feet in length with a 5- to 10-foot beam, has a pointed stern and unusually great sheer; rigged with one mast stepped about amidships; spreads a large square sail and, under favorable conditions, often a square topsail. An interesting feature in steering the craft is that her rudder is fitted with a thwartship tiller or "yoke" which her *rormann* moves forward or aft from his seat in either quarter of the boat. Few, if any, of the old-timers here considered now may be sighted in the *Vestfjord,*—once much frequented by this homespun craft.

NORMAN. Also, *norman-pin* or *norman-bolt,* in an old-fashioned windlass, a bolt inserted in a hole on one side of the drum to separate payed-out part of chain cable from the standing turns when veering chain; same pin or bolt was used to support or hang off the slack turns of cable on one of the windlass bitts while the other cable was being hove in. Also, a bitt-pin; *cf.* BITT. In older usage, a *norman* designated a pin of wood or iron inserted in a hole for securing any movable object, such as a gangway rail, a boat's rudder, or a bulwark port.

NORSEL. One of several different names given to a short piece of line attached to a fish-hook or a fish-net; especially, to one of many short lines spaced at regular intervals along top edge of a fish-net for securing net to, and at required depth from, the cork line or top-rope. A snood, or one of short lines securing the hooks of a hand-trawl line; a snell. Also, *nosle, nostle, daffin,* and other generally unfamiliar terms of local choice.

NORSKE VERITAS. Shipping classification society of national importance in Norway, instituted in 1864 and patterned after *Lloyd's. See* CLASSIFICATION *and* LLOYD'S.

NORTES. (*Sp.* = *north winds*) *See* NORTHER.

NORTH. (A.S. word; Ger. and Scand., *nord;* Du. *noord*) One of the four cardinal points of the compass; specifically, that point of a true compass indicating direction of *true,* or *geographical, north,* or direction of the geographical *North Pole;* direction of intersecting point of horizon and meridian, or that point of an observer's horizon vertically below the elevated celestial pole in any northern latitude. The *compass n.,* or *n.* point on a compass card, usually denoted by an ornamental design such as a *fleur de lis.* The *magnetic n.,* or direction indicated by a freely suspended bar magnet's north-seeking, red, or positive pole; or by *n.* point on a compass card where no deviation is present. Northern, or designating something lying toward, relative to, from, or toward, the *n.;* as, *n. coast of Ireland;* a *n. course;* a *n. wind* (from the *n.*); a *n.* (or northerly) *set of current* (toward the *n.*) Usually abbreviated *N.* in designating compass points from *West* through *N.* to *East;* as in *N by E, NNE, NW, WNW, etc.; cf.* **Table of Compass Points** *in* COMPASS. **N. about,** by way of a northern track, as in passing an island; among trans-Atlantic navigators, designates a passage or route rounding north of Scotland, usually via Pentland Firth. **N. Atlantic Drift,** a drift current setting in a general easterly direction between parallels of 35 and 55 degrees of latitude in North Atlantic Ocean. It is caused by prevailing westerly winds of that region. A similar current is set up in the *North Pacific* between 35° and 50° latitude parallels from same cause. **N. magnetic pole,** *see* MAGNETIC. **N. of Hatteras,** U.S. navy expression indicating zone in which it is improper to refer to what was seen or heard *south* of that point (*Cape Hatteras*). Hence, something one must "keep under one's hat," as in "that is all south of Hatteras." **N. polar distance,** angular distance of a celestial body from the north pole of the heavens in the equinoctial system. It is equal to 90° — declination of body, if N.; and 90° + declination, if S. **N. pole:** of the earth; of a magnet; *n.* magnetic pole; *see* POLE. **N. Star,** the Pole Star; *see* POLARIS. **N. temperate zone,** *see* ZONE. **N.-water,** among whalers, space of open sea left by winter pack of ice moving southward.

NORTH ATLANTIC TRACKS. *See* **Trans-Atlantic l.** *in* LANE.

NORTH EQUATORIAL CURRENT. *See* CURRENT.

NORTHEAST. Usually abbreviated *N.E.* or *NE,* point of the compass or the horizon lying midway between *north* and *east;* in a direction toward both *north* and *east.* Pertaining to the northeast; as a *N.E. gale.* **NE monsoon,** *see* MONSOON. **NE passage,** that along the Arctic coasts of Asia discovered and navigated from west to east in 1879 by *Baron Nordenskjöld,* Swedish arctic explorer. The entire route from the Barents to the Bering Sea is navigable in summer months, but risks to vessels of serious damage by ice have left the passage still little frequented by any but regular Russian local traders. **NE trades** or **trade winds,** *see* TRADE. **NE'er** or **northeaster,** a gale from a *NE* direction.

NORTHER. A cold seasonal northerly wind, often of considerable force, in north latitudes; especially, *El Norte* or the *Nortes* of the Mexicans, occurring between October and April over western part of Gulf of Mexico, along the Texan and Mexican coasts and extending sometimes as far as Gulf of Panama. An anti-cyclonic wind, it arises from advance of a high pressure area close in the wake of one of low pressure moving southeastward from the Rockies; often attains gale force and is accompanied with more or less rain and overcast skies. Unusually fair weather precedes its approach. Several hours before its arrival a cloudbank is seen in north or northwest; increasing northerly puffs are felt;

glass begins rising and the *norther* soon makes into its full intensity.

NORTHERN. Of or pertaining to the *north;* lying northward or in the *north.* **N. cross,** constellation *Cygnus; see* CYGNUS. **N. glance,** same as **N. lights,** *q.v.* **N. Hemisphere,** that half of the earth's surface lying north of the equator. **N. lights,** *see* AURORA. **N. whiting,** the kingfish of genus *Menticirrhus saxatilis,* about 16 inches in length, habitat on American Atlantic coast; *see* **K.-fish** *in* KING.

NORTHING. In sailing, difference of latitude made toward *north* from a previously determined position; opposed to *southing.* A breeze is said to *have n.* in it when apparently more northerly than from point indicated; as, "wind must have more *n.* than NE to make an E course."

NORTHILL FOLDING ANCHOR; N. UTILITY ANCHOR. *See* ANCHOR.

NORTHWARD. Toward the *north,* or nearer in direction to N. than to E. or W.; situated, facing, or extended in an approximate northerly direction. Word is usually cut to "*northerd,*" "*no'th'd,*" and often "*nor'rd,*" among seamen.

NORTHWEST. That point of the horizon or the compass lying midway between N. and W.; situated in, directed toward, or coming from, the *northwest* (or *N.W.*); as, the *NW entrance;* a *NW gale;* a *NW set of current.* **NW by N, NW by W,** etc., *see* **Table of Compass Points** *in* COMPASS. **NW monsoon,** *see* MONSOON. **NW passage,** a route from Davis Strait along the northern Canadian shores to those of Alaska, for centuries, beginning with an exploration voyage by *Sir Martin Frobisher,* under Queen Elizabeth in 1576, looked upon as a commercial possibility, but found impracticable after the harrowing experiences of *Sir Robert McClure,* 1850 to 1854, in finally negotiating the route only in part from the westward. The previous experience of *Sir William Parry* in 1819 is remarkable in that he succeeded in getting as far west, after starting from the Atlantic end, as to have nearly reached open water in Beaufort Sea when his ship became jammed and frozen in south of Melville Island. To Norway's *Roald Amundsen,* discoverer of the South Pole, December, 1911, belongs the credit in 1903–1906 of completing a voyage through the passage in his 50-ton sloop after narrowly escaping the usual shipwreck or freezing in of his predecessors. The passage proper, or most difficult stretch of the entire 3500 miles from Atlantic to Pacific, begins at Lancaster Sound in the NW corner of Baffin Bay and leads nearly due west through Barrow Strait, Melville Sound, McClure Strait, and into the generally open Beaufort Sea, a distance of about 730 nautical miles. It is generally shallow and never free of ice, wholly or in part.

NORTHWESTER. A gale blowing from northwest; a *nor'wester.*

NOSE. Stem or extreme forward end of a vessel. A prominent point or seaward-projecting part of a cliff or bold shore. To point, or head, a vessel into a narrow or congested area; as, to *n.* into a berth; she *nosed* through a fleet of trawlers. **N.-plate,** a plate presenting a rounded surface across upper part of a ship's stem for purpose of preventing chafing of mooring-lines; also *see* PLATE. **War-n.,** in a torpedo, a pointed part housing a primer and screwed on head of the missile; also, *war-head.*

NOSING. A projecting half-round molding around a boat's side immediately below the gunwale; a *rubbing-piece* or *rubber.* Protective strip of metal on fore side of a boat's wooden stem.

NOTCH-BLOCK. Same as snatch-block; *see* BLOCK.

NOTE. A brief writing; as a memorandum, directive, order, etc. To take account of by writing; as, to *n.* an item of expense; to *n.* an event or happening in ship's log. **Advance n.,** *see* ADVANCE. **Jerque n.,** *see* JERQUE. To **n. a protest,** *see* PROTEST. **Pricking n.,** *see* PRICKING. **Trans-shipment n.,** *see* TRANS-SHIPMENT.

NOTHING OFF! Cautionary order to a helmsman to keep vessel up to the wind, as in sailing close-hauled; or, in steering a course or directly for an object, to keep vessel from swinging off to leeward.

NOTICE. Information, announcement, or warning of an occurrence, an event pending, or of a cautionary nature in view of some probable happening, especially in a legal sense. **N. of abandonment,** that informing the underwriters of insured's decision to abandon his vessel as a constructive total loss, claiming indemnity accordingly. It is usually given in writing. *Cf.* ABANDONMENT. **N. of readiness,** written advice given by a shipmaster to a charterer, indicating his vessel is ready to take in cargo in accordance with terms of the charter-party. Such a document in connection with coal cargoes at English ports is termed a *stem note.* **N. to Mariners,** any information posted or circulated in interests of safe navigation within a given area. A pamphlet periodically issued for purpose of acquainting mariners with newly acquired information affecting, and so usually necessary corrections to, charts, Light Lists, Sailing Directions, and other publications of maritime importance. The *Hydrographic Office* of U.S. navy issues such information each week and currently supplies the *notice* to all naval vessels in commission, branch Hydrographic Offices, and U.S. consulates at principal world ports. Chief purpose of thus circulating the *notice* is to keep all Hydrographic publications up to date, the booklet being issued to mariners free of charge at offices noted. Additional information is circulated by means of the weekly *Hydrographic Bul-*

letın (*cf.* HYDROGRAPHIC), which is limited principally to co-operating maritime observers.

NOT-UNDER-COMMAND LIGHTS. Also termed
not-under-control lights and *breakdown lights; see*
Rule 4 in REGULATIONS FOR PREVENTING COLLISIONS.

NOVA. (L. *novus,* new) A blaze star, or one observed to glow or to almost suddenly burst into brilliance for a brief period and return to its former
magnitude or into obscurity. Such stars are named
by astronomers according to constellation in which
appearing; as *Nova Andromedæ; Nova Cygni.* Of
the few more recent important phenomena of this
kind was that appearing in *Perseus,* February 22,
1901, which for the night of February 23 became
brightest star in the sky. It then slowly diminished
in lustre until it disappeared in July of same year.
It was called *Nova Persei.*

NUGGAR. (Egyp.) Kind of barge or goods-boat of
the River Nile; about thirty feet in length and
rigged with a single lateen sail. Also, *noggar, nog-*
gur, nugger.

NUMBER. A vessel's identifying four-flag signal,
displayed in accordance with International Code;
it is same as her *radio call signal;* also called *ship's*
numbers, probably because associated with the
official n. allotted each vessel; *cf.* NATIONALITY MARK.
In American shipbuilding, frames or the combined
beam, frame, and floor in the transverse system,
and also all hold stanchions, shell and deck plating, were *numbered* beginning from *aft,* following time-honored British practice. In recent years,
particularly during World War II, this procedure
appears to have been reversed,—at least in majority
of yards. **Cubic n.,** *see* CUBIC. To **lose the n. of one's**
mess, to perish. To **make her n.,** to display the 4-
flag hoist denoting ship's name and *official n.;* to
gain a desirable position in the shipping list or
classification register (said of a ship). To **make one's**
n., to present one's self; especially in sense of having a visit with an important person. **Official n.,**
that assigned a vessel at the time she is documented,
or "registered" by government authority. In U.S.,
such *n.* is assigned by Customs Division of Treasury
Department and appears on vessel's certificate of
registry (or "register"), certificate of enrollment, or
license, according to class of vessel concerned; and
the *n.* must be cut in or otherwise permanently
marked on vessel's "main beam" together with her
registered tonnage; also commonly termed *vessel's*
n. **Racing n.,** identification mark,—usually a *n.,*—
painted or otherwise shown on a yacht's mainsail,
assigned to the boat by the judges or "racing committee." **Watch n.,** in naval vessels especially, that
assigned to each seaman of a watch and so indicated on the *watch bill.*

NUMERAL. A number. A group of digits representing a *number* or value used as a standard. Per-

taining to a *number* or *numbers.* **Equipment n.,**
see **E. tonnage** *in* EQUIPMENT. **Lloyd's n's.,** *see* **L.**
numerals *in* LLOYD'S. **N. pennant,** any one of the
ten in the International Code of Signals used to denote a number. **N. signal,** any signal representing a
number; specifically, in International Code, one
consisting of a hoist of one or more *n. pennants* denoting a *number* thus signalled; *cf.* SIGNAL. **Scant-**
ling n., either of *Lloyd's n's.;* also *scantling number.*
Transverse n., first, or framing, *n.; see* **L. numerals**
in LLOYD'S.

NUNATAK. (*Eskimo*) On Greenland and far
northern American coasts, an isolated hill or peak
rising from an ice sheet.

NUN BUOY. *See* BUOY.

NUNKI. (Babylonian name) A star of magnitude
2.14 in the group *Sagittarius,* listed in Nautical
Almanac as *σ Sagittarii,* having an 18h. 52m. right
ascension and 26° 22′ S. declination (1949). It may
be located $32\frac{1}{2}°$ due east of the well-known reddish-hued *Antares* in the *Scorpion.* A line representing this distance forms the base of an isosceles
triangle having its apex at λ *Scorpii,* bright star at
extreme end of Scorpion's tail.

NURSE SHARK. Also *nuss shark;* the Greenland
shark; the gata; *see* GATA *and* SHARK.

NUT. One of the projections or shoulders forged
in an old-time anchor's shank to secure the wooden
stock; *cf.* **Nuts of an a.** *in* ANCHOR PHRASEOLOGY. The
heavy bulbous or ball-shaped end of the iron stock
in later anchors of that type also has been termed a
nut. **Locking-n.,** *see* **J.-nut** *in* JAM. **Propeller n.,**
also, **propeller-shaft n.,** heavy octagonal-form screw-
nut securing a propeller to tail end of its shaft. It is
considered good practice to arrange that *nut* be
screwed in place in the direction contrary to that
of the revolving propeller in ahead motion; thus,
a left-handed thread is provided for a right-handed
propeller, and vice versa, since pressure of propeller-boss against *nut* takes place only when engines are turning astern. **Propeller-blade n.,** one of
a number of nuts which secure a propeller-blade to
the boss in a screw having removable blades, or, as
it is often termed, a *built propeller.* The *nuts* screw
up on strong studs fitted in the boss, or hub, of the
propeller or *screw.*

NUTATION. (L. *nutatio,* nodding) A slow libra-
tory or oscillatory movement of the earth's axis as
observed in the wavering of our celestial poles in
their gradual sweep around the poles of the ecliptic
in the phenomenon termed *precession.* It may be
likened to the staggering motion of a spinning top
as it slowly swings, axially inclined, about its bearing center. The movement produces a small variation in position among the stars of the equinoctial
points, modifying displacement of these due alone
to westward motion in precession of about 50″ an-

nually. (*Cf.* PRECESSION) This wobbling of our planet is attributed to unequal forces of attraction, chiefly of sun and moon, on the earth's mass due to her departure from spherical form in a "big waistline," or bulging with an excess of equatorial diameter.

NYLON. A coined word for a synthetic protein-like substance of great elasticity and toughness, which, in addition to its uses as a fabric, such as a silk substitute for hosiery and other articles of clothing, boat sails, parachutes, etc., in recent years has been produced in fiber form suitable for manufacture of *rope*. Results of rigorous tests made by U.S. Coast Guard to determine relative advantages of *nylon* and *manilla* hawsers in towing at sea established that an 8-inch nylon line equals a 12-inch (circumference) manilla in tensile strength, besides being lighter in weight, easier to handle, and capable of being stowed in less than half the space required for its competitor. Since a 12-inch manilla hawser withstands a pull of about 55 long tons and an 8-inch line of same type nearly 26 tons, *nylon* is fully double the strength of same sized manilla. Its cost, however, nearly approaches four times that of the Philippine product. *N.* also appears destined to replace our present standard cotton-and-wool bunting in larger flag-making. Recently in Washington, D.C., engineers of the Public Buildings Services completed a series of tests of the fabric with results definitely favoring its general use as flag material. It is claimed a *n.* flag "will last three times as long, is easier to keep clean, tears less, and flies lighter in the breeze," which, if true, at least will bid fair toward reducing annual renewals of some twelve thousand national flags flown by government offices and institutions.

O

O. Square flag, in color diagonally halved in red and yellow, hoisted singly, or Morse flashing signal (— — —), denoting letter *O*, indicates *"Man overboard"* in International Code of Signals. The symbol *ö*, as that occurring in German and Scandinavian alphabets, in visual and sound signaling by use of International Morse Code, is indicated by (— — — •). *Overcast sky*, in ships' log-books and weather records, usually is indicated by *O* or *o*.

OAK. Timber of a tree of the genus *Quercus*, widely distributed in Northern Hemisphere, better classes being native to temperate latitudes. Of some 200 species extant, *Quercus* is best represented in the black, British or English, live, pin, red, and white *oaks*, with their various close cousins, which yield a good quality of hard, tough, close-grained wood especially valuable in shipbuilding, shipyard use, construction work, furniture-making, etc. **British**, or **English, o.,** wood of *Quercus robur*, a centuries-old producer of excellent ship-building timber, once so much valued in construction of Britain's "wooden walls." For strength and durability it has few equals, but its content of gallotannic acid, or *tannin*, as in some other species of the family, bars use of iron fastenings for lasting work, because of serious corrosive effect on the metal. Copper or some copper alloy is therefore preferred for fittings, bolts, nails, etc., in this oak. It is much used for strength members in boats, as, keel, keelson, stem and stern posts, gunwales, and thwarts. In weight, about 52 lbs. per foot.[3] **Cork o.,** *see* CORK. **Live o.,** the American *Quercus virginiana* of southern U.S. or *Q. wislizeni* of Pacific coast, evergreen trees yielding a heavy fine-grained wood free of gallic or tannic acid and especially prized for shipbuilding; weight, about 58 lbs. per foot.[3] **Maul o.,** a close relative of the above and native to California, also called *canyon live oak* and *black live oak*, classified by botanists as *Q. chrysolepis*. This is the live oak preferred by caulkers for their mallets, "the kind that gives that resonant ring, the life of every shipyard." **O. leaves,** as the ornamental device on visors of the caps of naval officers above rank of lieutenant-commander, are said to have originated as a symbol of the excellent *oaken* ships of old sailing days. A point of interest in this connection is that in early U.S.N. yards huge logs of *live oak* were kept under water for years prior to being fashioned into "timbers" in the shipbuilding art. **Red o.,** an American coarse-grained reddish wood from *Q. rubra* and a few related species, all strong and durable, of southern U.S.; weight, about 45 lbs. per foot.[3] **White o.,** another important timber oak similar to the *British o.* in its light color and acid content. It is the English *maiden oak* or *Q. sessiliflora* and about same as the eastern U.S. *Q. alba*. Considered excellent wood for frames and strength members in boatbuilding, but requires more seasoning than *Q. robur*. Weight, about 46 lbs. per foot.[3]

OAKUM. Originally, the coarser part of hemp or flax separated by the *hackle* and called *tow;* loose hemp fiber used as *calking* (or *caulking*) material in planking seams. It is usually made of teased out scrap rope treated with pine tar and often is prepared in "thread" form before pressing into handy bales. *Cf.* CALK *and* HACKLE. (Old forms of the word are *oacombe, ockam,* and *ocum*) **To spew o.,** said of a vessel's planking seams when the material starts working out as a result of unusual straining of hull, *e.g.,* due to grounding. **Thread of o.,** a strip or string of the fiber rolled in preparation for inserting and driving into a seam as in calking. **White o.,** coarse hemp or flax *hacklings* (or *hecklings*) in natural state.

OAR. (A.S. word) Rowing implement of wood consisting of a shaft or *loom* having one end reduced in thickness to afford easy grasp and a broad surface at the other, called the *blade*. Use of oars dates from early antiquity and once were sole means of propulsion in such vessels as Phoenician galleys of 1000 B.C. In rowing, the loom pivots in a *rowlock* or crotch, between two *tholes*, or *thole-pins*, or may be loosely secured to a single thole, in boat's gunwale. Rower or *oarsman* usually sits facing aft, from which comes the term *pulling*, as the actual propelling stroke is called, and hence general use of that word instead of *rowing*. An oar is also used for steering, especially in surf-boat management, where better control of boat may be effected than is possible in rough water by a rudder; and may be used in *sculling* a light boat, *i.e.*, by placing oar over boat's stern and moving it sideways to and from while alternately turning its blade propeller-fashion, much in same manner as a fish uses his tail. Ships' boats carry oars 12 to 14 feet in length, usually made of white ash or white spruce. Size of a pulling boat is often indicated by number of oars that may be shipped; as, a *five-oared gig*. To **back the oars,** to reverse direction of pulling stroke, as in driving boat astern or to hold water against boat's headway; action required at the old-time whaler's order, *"Stern all!"* To **bend to the oars,** to *give way*, or put a lively vigorous swing to each stroke, as in a case of attaining speed. **"Boat oars!",** order to boat's crew to stow oars inboard; also, *"Lay in oars!"* **Bow oar,** *see* BOW. **Cape Ann oar,** New England fishermen's term for a square-loomed oar. **Condemned to the oars,** said of one forced to row in the galleys as penal servitude in the Middle Ages. To **feather an oar,** *see* FEATHERING. **Harpoon oar,** in older whaling, foremost oar of boat; it was pulled by the harponeer when catching up with a sighted whale. **Loom of an oar,** the shaft, or that part between blade and handle. Probably depending upon local usage, the term sometimes designates the *handle,* and that part between handle and blade as above, the *shaft;* also, some authorities define the *loom* as simply *inboard part* of oar. **Midship oar,** *see* MIDSHIP. **Muffled oars,** *see* MUFFLED. **Oar-hole,** opening through which an oar was operated in a war-galley; an *oar-port;* also designates an **oar-lock,** or one of several metal-lined notches or rounded depressions in a large naval boat's gunwale for receiving the oars in rowing; a rowlock. **Oar peg,** a thole or thole-pin. **Oar propeller,** a contrivance for sculling operated by turning a crank. **Oarsmanship,** skill in rowing or handling a boat under oars. **Oar swivel,** a crotch-shaped rowlock which swivels on a vertical shank inserted in a socket. **Oar thole,** an oar peg or thole-pin on which an oar is pivoted in rowing. **Oars!,** order by a boat's coxswain to cease pulling and to rest oars horizontally at right angles to keel, with blades *feathered.* To **put in one's oar,** to intrude in a conversation by others with one's own remarks. **Rigged oar,** one set in a becket, rowlock, etc., at boat's stern ready for use in steering or sculling. **Slope oar,** an oarsman who feigns pulling by making a show and simply dipping his oar; hence one who shirks physical exertion. **Spoon oar,** one having its blade curved longitudinally, concave side facing aft in pulling; used in racing or other light boats. **Steering-oar,** as used in surfboats or lifeboats for better control of steering in rough water, or where turning quickly is a necessary

maneuver, a long oar operated over the stern as a rudder or a sweep. **Straight oar,** as distinguished from a *spoon oar,* one having no curvature. **Stroke oar,** aftermost oar (or oars, where *double-banked* or two oarsmen on each thwart) or man or men pulling such; the *stroke rhythm* is set by this oar or oars. To **take the laboring oar,** to perform the difficult part of any work. To **toss oars,** also to *peak oars,* to raise them to a vertical position with handles resting on bottom of boat. In U.S.N., the command *"Toss!"* is given on approaching ship's side or a landing and boat's crew retain the position until all officers have left boat; if boat is again shoved off (the job of bow and stroke oarsmen with boat-hooks) rowing position is resumed at order *"Let fall!"* To **trail oars,** to allow them to trail alongside boat free of oarsman's hands. **Tub oar,** in the old whaling-boats, usually second oar from aft, or that pulled from position where whaleline was stowed in its tub. **"Up oars!",** order by boat's coxswain to raise oars to same position as at the word *"Toss!",* boat lying ready alongside to shove off on her mission. As in the *toss* or *peak* position, blades of oars are always placed in fore-and-aft line.

OARFISH. Remarkable eel-like fish of genus *Regalecus* which attains a length of 25 feet. It has a narrow body with no ventral fins but surmounted by a dorsal finny fringe from its short blunt head to its pointed tail; about a dozen spiny rays from one to two feet in length extend upward like antennæ from its head; in color, is generally silvery. This near-approach to the sea serpent of fame and fiction has been found in the China Sea and on warmer Pacific coasts of America and is said to have been taken also on European Atlantic coast.

OARWEED. Variant of *oreweed* or seaweed; any of the *algae* growing from the sea bottom. Also *oarsweed.*

OATH. In U.S. navigation laws certain officers of the Customs and other government departments concerned with shipping are authorized to administer *oaths* in connection with registration, manning, and movements of vessels and also cargoes, mails, and passengers carried therein. Included in *oaths* required of shipmasters and others are: *Oath of entry* in which *master* attests to truth of manifest of cargo submitted to Collector of Customs (*46 U.S.C. 94*); that by *master* declaring that all letters and other pieces of mail on board have been delivered to Post Office before entering at Customs (*18 U.S.C. 327*); that in connection with licensing a vessel stating that master is a citizen of United States (*46 U.S.C. 262*); that made by every *master, mate, engineer,* and *pilot,* affirming truth of contents of required written application for license and every such person who receives a license, declaring that he will faithfully perform duties required of him by law (*46 U.S.C. 231*); that of an *owner* who applies for documentation or registry of his vessel, affirming that written particulars as to place and year of building, burden, details of origin and title, are true and that master thereof is a U.S. citizen (*46 U.S.C. 19*); that by which a *staff officer* upon receiving a certificate of registry declares he will perform faithfully all duties required of him by law (*46 U.S.C. 244*).

OBEY.   To execute commands of; to carry out wishes of; as, to *obey* a lawful order. To yield to operation or influence of; as, the vessel promptly *obeys* her helm. To submit, or yield obedience; as, crew refused to *obey*.

OBISPO. (Sp. = bishop; so named for its miter-shaped head)   The eagle ray; *see* RAY.

OBJECT GLASS.   *See* GLASS.

OBLIQUE.   In a slanting direction or position; inclined; neither horizontal nor perpendicular; as, an *oblique line*. **O. angle,** an acute or an obtuse angle; opposed to a *right angle*. **O. sailing,** steering on a rhumb line, or course other than that coinciding with a meridian or a parallel of latitude; navigating on a course in which vessel makes both a difference of latitude and departure or a difference of longitude; traverse sailing.

OBLIQUITY OF THE ECLIPTIC.   *See* ECLIPTIC.

OBSERVATION.   Act of noting some fact, occurrence, or phenomenon, especially where measurement of a magnitude or value is involved; as, a *lunar o.*; a *tidal o.*; an *o. for latitude*. **Back o.,** an altitude of a heavenly body measured by sextant, observer having his *back* toward the body. Resulting altitude is greater than 90°, since body's difference in azimuth from that point of the horizon to which its altitude is ordinarily measured is 180°. Actually, value of such measured angle is *180°—body's true altitude*, assuming it to be corrected for observer's height of eye, refraction, and, if sun or moon, parallax and semi-diameter; but, since tables of altitude corrections are given for angles up to 90° only, simplest method for finding *true altitude* is to subtract *back o.* value from 180° and apply corrections to result as in the case of usual observed altitude, with exception of that for height of eye, or *dip*, which must be applied with sign reversed, *i.e.*, always added. A *back o.* is resorted to only where a faulty horizon, presence of land or fleet of ships, a rain-squall, fog bank, or other obstacle renders indistinct or obscures that part of horizon directly below body observed. **Latitude by o.,** *see* LATITUDE. **Lunar o.,** *see* LUNAR. **Meridian o.,** same as **latitude by o.;** *see remarks in* LATITUDE. **Tidal o.,** a series of measurements of heights of successive high and low waters with times of their occurrences noted, duration of slack water, maximum velocity

of current, and other pertinent data for use in predictions of tidal phenomena in a given locality. **Weather o.,** *see* WEATHER. **To work an o.,** to determine ship's latitude or longitude, a line of position, or a definite *fix* by calculations based on one or more altitudes of a celestial body or bodies measured at given instants of local or Greenwich civil time; also, to determine the compass error by comparison of an observed azimuth with that by calculation or from tables,—more commonly referred to as *working an azimuth*.

OBSERVATORY.   One or more special buildings, an institution, or place equipped with necessary instruments for observing and recording natural phenomena; especially, for astronomical use; as, *Greenwich O.; U.S. Naval O.* Cf. ALMANAC *and* GREENWICH. Among the many functions of an *astronomical o.* is that of regularly indicating exact time by telegraph and radio signals as given by a *transmission clock*. This time-piece is regulated by frequent direct transit observations of heavenly bodies. Hence, with a minimum of effort the navigator today may obtain precise Greenwich civil time for his chronometer by radio in any part of the world at almost any hour. **O. rate,** that at which a chronometer gains or loses per day as checked for precision at an *o*. Since advent of radio time signals that practice largely has been discontinued. *Cf* CHRONOMETER.

OBSERVED ALTITUDE.   *See* ALTITUDE.

OCCIDENT. (L. *occidere*, to go down, as the sun)   The west; that part of the earth lying toward the setting sun; countries lying west of Asia,—usually applied to western Europe and Western Hemisphere; opposed to *Orient*, or the east. **O. æstival; o. equinoctial; o. hibernal;** archaic terms, now only in poetic use, for respective points of horizon at which sun sets at the *summer solstice, equinoxes,* and *winter solstice*.

OCCULTATION.   Disappearance of a heavenly body due to intervention of another; especially, the sudden obscuring of a star or planet by the moon due to her orbital advance, or that of a planet's satellite behind its primary. The term often is applied loosely to an *eclipse*, or phenomenon in which a darkened body obscures a luminary, wholly or in part.

OCCULTING LIGHT.   *See* LIGHT.

OCEAN. (Gr. *okeanos*, the ancient's "great river encircling the earth")   The *great sea*, or vast body of salt water which covers about three-fourths the earth's surface, geographically divided into five great areas, *viz., Arctic, Antarctic, Atlantic, Indian,* and *Pacific Oceans*. Arms and contiguous waters of these, generally regarded as smaller divisions, in order of size are seas, gulfs, bays, sounds, and straits. Mean depth of the great expanse is about 12,500 feet, Pacific showing greatest average of some 14,000 and Arctic least with about 4,000. Deepest water found is 34,440 feet off the Philippines; a hole north of Puerto Rico, called Milwaukee Deep, has 30,246 feet; 31,000 is greatest in South Pacific; 23,000 in Indian Ocean; 26,575 in South Atlantic; 14,275 in Antarctic; and 13,420 in Arctic Ocean. Excepting a few canyon-like formations and "holes," the ocean floor in general is an undulating surface of a wide variety of colors in clay, mud, ooze, and deposits of shells and myriads of tiny dead creatures. Density of ocean water averages 1.026, being least in polar regions and greatest in Atlantic near the equator; its weight, therefore, is taken as 64 lbs. per foot,[3] or one-fortieth greater than fresh water (river). Its mineral content is about 3.5% of which 78% is sodium chloride or common salt, magnesium chloride 11%, and remainder a mixture of perhaps a dozen sulphates, etc. General circulation of the global waters is generated more by prevailing winds than by tidal action, a great right-handed sweep taking place from this cause by the trade-wind drift of lower latitudes and easterly drift in higher latitudes of the Northern Hemisphere; converse of this being true of Southern Hemisphere waters. **O. bill of lading,** that customarily used in ocean freighting; *see* BILL. **O. current,** *see* CURRENT. **O.-going vessel,** in U.S. navigation laws, any vessel which in usual course of her employment navigates seaward of line of demarcation between inland waters and high seas. **O. lanes,** *see* LANE. **O. spring,** fresh water spring issuing from sea bottom, marked by a clearer and lighter patch or limited area on the surface. Examples of such springs are those off Nassau Sound, N.E. Florida, and off Sanibel Island, S.W. Florida, respectively, of which it is said that unusual numbers and varieties of fishes frequent the strange waters for a tasty change. **O. trout,** trade name for the *menhaden; see* MENHADEN. **O. tug,** a sea-going tug of a type designed for long-distance towing; chiefly characterized by her larger size, stouter build, greater power and fuel-carrying capacity than her smooth-water cousin. **O. waters, as** distinguished from bays, harbors, and other coastal waters, those of the high seas.

OCEANIC. Of or pertaining to the ocean; pelagic. **O. island,** *see* ISLAND. **O. meteorology,** science that treats of atmospheric phenomena, including variations of heat and moisture, fog formation, storms, etc., over the oceans. **O. river,** descriptive term for an ocean stream current, suggested by its confinement to definite limits in lateral extent. A good example of such "river" is found in the GULF STREAM, *q.v.; also see* CURRENT.

OCEANID. *See* MERMAID.

OCEANOGRAPHY. That branch of geography which treats of phenomena and characteristics of the several oceans. *Dynamic o.* deals with currents, tides, sea waves, and formation of islands, reefs, and shoals; *static o.*, with depth, topography, and nature of the sea floor, chemical and physical properties of sea water, etc.

OCTANT. Another name for the *quadrant,* or instrument for measuring angular distances up to 90°, so called from length of its limb, or arc, which is *one-eighth* of a circle.

OCTOPUS. (Gr. *oktopous,* eight-footed) Largest of the *cephalopods* having a large rounded head and small sac-like body from which radially project eight arms, each tapering to pointed tentacles and provided with rows of suckers for grasping the prey or holding fast to rocks, etc. Many of the numerous species are small, however, and even those of greatest size fall markedly short of the proportions assigned the monster of fiction. The creatures, some of which are taken for food, generally are timid and inoffensive and prefer to remain on bottom among the rocks. *Octopus vulgaris* of the North African coast attains a spreadout span of eight feet; *O. punctatus,* a North American Pacific coast frequenter, is said to measure up to 18 feet,—with due regard for the often faulty foot-length of that region!

ODOGRAPH. (Gr. *odos,* way; *graphein,* to write) An instrument which records courses steered and distances (or time intervals) run on each course; a course-recorder; *cf.* COURSE.

OFF. Combining word generally denoting *from, away from;* in an adverbial sense, indicating action of *removing* or *separating,* as, to *cast off, keep off, stand off;* adjectively, denoting *removed, distant, apart,* as in the *off ship,* to *steer more off;* or in prepositional form, as in *we are five miles off shore, two points off the wind, off the course, etc.* **Off and on,** to and fro, on alternate tacks, or standing toward shore on one tack and off shore on another, in sense of maintaining position to windward of some point, or to avoid being set down to leeward, as in awaiting arrival of a pilot. To heave to under easy sail and allow vessel to come to and fall off the wind at will is described as *lying off and on.* **Off the wind,** said of a vessel when sailing with wind abaft the beam; having a fair wind. To **sheer off,** to steer clear of an object approached, as away from a ship's side, a landing, etc.; to turn an anchored vessel away from, and so work clear of, the shore, another vessel, etc., by action of current. Uses of **off** with words indicated as captions may be found under following: COME; CAST; HEAD; HAUL; KEEP; KNOCK; LAY; LIE; MAKE; NOTHING; PRICK; SHOVE; SOUNDING; TOPPING.

OFFAL. Small inferior fish or any of an unmarketable kind or quality, as distinguished from *prime* fish of the catch. Fish gurry, or refuse left from cleaning or canning process; whale blubber refuse; *see* GURRY.

OFFICER. One holding a position of authority or command, as in a navy; specifically, a *commissioned*, a *warrant*, or a *petty* officer. The captain or master, or a mate, in a merchant ship, a fishing-vessel, or a yacht. In U.S.N., commissioned ranks in order of seniority are *ensign, lieutenant (junior grade), lieutenant-commander, commander, captain, rear-admiral, vice-admiral,* and *admiral.* Similar designations of rank are used in British navy. *Cf.* ADMIRAL; CAPTAIN; COMMODORE; COMMANDER; LIEUTENANT. *Warrant officers,* or those appointed by "warrant," have risen from enlisted ratings in a special branch of duty, as boatswain, gunner, machinist, pharmacist, etc. *Petty officers,* or those of lowest rank, are drawn from enlisted ratings as leaders and bear titles such as boatswain's mate, machinist's mate, aviation machinist's mate, pharmacist's mate, turret captain, master-at-arms, etc. Officers of the line, or *line officers,* are those afloat and actively engaged with matters concerning warfare or motive power of a war-vessel, as distinguished from *staff officers* as, medical, pay, chaplain, instructor, supply, etc. ranks. In merchant vessels, *mates* usually are called *officers* (*cf.* MATE) although the master is himself an officer, as in naval custom. **Chief o.,** *see* CHIEF. **First o.,** in a merchant ship, usually the *chief mate,* or next in command. In some larger vessels,—particularly passenger liners, however, *first o.* may designate rank next below *chief o.* **Flag o.,** *see* FLAG. **Health o.,** one charged with enforcement of quarantine laws; especially, in connection with medical inspection of arriving vessels' crews and passengers and sanitary conditions on board. **Naval o.,** *see* NAVAL. **Navigating o.,** *see* NAVIGATOR. **O. of the deck,** one temporarily in charge of the deck and supervising work being carried on. As the captain's representative, in that capacity he is senior to all officers but the executive. **O. of the watch,** *see* WATCH. **Ordnance o.,** one in general charge of a warship's guns and training of gunners; *cf.* ORDNANCE. **Torpedo o.,** one charged with care and handling of all torpedoes on board a war-vessel. **Watch o.,** one who regularly stands watch,—not necessarily *o. of the watch, q.v.*

OFFICIAL LOG. *See* LOG.[2]

OFFICIAL NUMBER. *See* NUMBER.

OFFING. (From *off*) At a distance from, but within sight of, the shore; as, *the brig has a 5-mile offing.* Approaches to a harbor entrance; as, *an inward-bound ship in the offing.* To **get a good o.,** to get well clear of the land; to get sea room.

OFFSETS. Those parts of joggled plates turned or bent off from main body of each; joggled edges. In shipbuilding, distances measured horizontally and vertically from certain base-lines or planes of reference for purposes of accurately forming required curvature of the hull. When measured vertically above base-line (keel), they are termed *heights;* when from midship fore-and-aft vertical plane, *half-breadths.* Usual three reference planes are a vertical longitudinal plane, a water plane (one parallel to water's surface at a designed even-keel draft), and a vertical thwartship plane. The measurements are shown in tabular form on *offset sheets,* each of which is devoted to one series referred to same reference plane; as, *half-breadths* on several different water planes; *heights* of decks; etc.

OFFSHORE. Away, or at some distance from, the shore; as, *our boat drifted offshore; she capsized offshore.* Moving or directed from shore; as, *an o. breeze; an o. tack.* Situated, existing, or carried on at a distance from land; as, *o. rocks, birds, fishing, etc.* **O. area,** that extending indefinitely seaward from a low water shore-line. **O. dry dock,** an L-shaped floating dock having its high side secured to piling, dolphins, etc., along a shore or side of a wharf; used for moderate-sized vessels; *see* **Floating-d.** *in* DOCK. **O. fish,** those taken in comparatively deep waters and farther at sea than usual grounds for *inshore* fish. Cod and halibut are examples of such. **O. fishery,** deep-sea or pelagic fishing; *see* FISHERY.

OFF SOUNDINGS. A vessel is said to be *off soundings* when in water of greater depth than one hundred fathoms. In general, depth soundings by present electronic devices have almost thrown this term into discard with the old deep-sea lead. Soundings of much greater depths to-day are commonly observed, although, as a matter of importance in practical navigation, there is little or no need, in most localities, for charted depth detail beyond 100 fathoms.

OFFWARD. Toward the sea; away from the land; leaning or inclined seaward, as a stranded vessel; also, *offwards.*

OIL. (L. *oleum*) Unctuous, usually combustible, liquid substance used for fuel, lighting, lubricating, paint-mixing, etc. It is divided generally into animal, mineral, and vegetable oils; as, *whale o., petroleum,* and *linseed o.* **Cut of o.,** amount of oil yielded by a whale (*whalers' cant*). **Fuel o.,** *see* **F. oil** *and* **Diesel f.** *in* FUEL. **O. bag,** canvas bag stuffed with oakum or cotton waste saturated with *storm oil.* It is made to allow oil to ooze out in its use for keeping down a heavy sea. **O. box,** or **oil cup,** receptacle from which lubricating oil is supplied to a bearing or other working part, as in machinery. **O. burner,** appliance attached to fuel oil supply line at front of a boiler. Its purpose is to "atomize" the oil and supply proper amount of air thereto before final delivery to burner *tip* from which actual firing takes place. The term also denotes a steam vessel which uses oil for fuel, as opposed to a *coal burner*. **O'cloth,** any coarse fabric treated with oil; a tarpaulin. **O.-coat,** an oilskin coat or jacket. **O. compass,** a liquid compass in which a special oil is the agent for floating the card; *see* COMPASS. **O.-fish,** a deep-sea, spiny-finned, mackerel-like fish having remarkably oily flesh, akin to the ESCOLAR, *q.v.* **O. hose,** heavy flexible hose manufactured for ship use in transferring oil cargoes and bunkering; usually in lengths of 25 feet and inside diameters of 4, 6, and 8 inches, fitted at each end with a coupling-flange. It is made of layers of rubber and a strong fabric, reinforced by one or more close-laid servings, or helixes, of flat wire. An 8-inch hose usually is capable of standing up to an internal pressure of 150 lbs. per inch.[2] **O. line,** any pipe-line through which oil is conveyed. **O. permit,** in connection with inspection of U.S. vessels, certificate issued by Coast Guard granting permission to use a process or invention for utilization of petroleum in production of motive power (*46 U.S.C. 467*). Also, special written permission for a passenger vessel to carry refined petroleum as cargo where it is shown that no other practical means of transportation is available. **O. Pollution Act,** enacted in 1924, statute prohibiting discharge of oil in any form into coastal navigable waters of U.S. by any vessel (*33 U.S.C. 433–437*). **O. separator,** as used in some larger ships, mechanical apparatus for separating fuel oil from water, as in case of recovering oil from a leaking double-bottom tank or where water ballast has been carried in such fuel tank. The separator is often installed in a lighter or barge for receiving "slops" pumped from an oil tank vessel during operation of hosing down or cleaning tanks; also may be installed at an oil dock or a refinery for same purpose. **O. service pump,** in a mechanical lubricating system, pump which circulates oil to the various bearings from the *oil service tank*. A straining device for ridding oil of impurities is also part of such system. **O. shark,** any of several sharks yielding oil; especially, the *basking-shark* and the *tope*. **O. shell,** projectile containing oil for allaying a heavy sea. Bursting upon striking water, it thus spreads oil as required (has been used with more or less success but considered impractical in general). **O.-slick,** smooth glossy surface produced by oil spreading over the water. **O. tank,** a tank for storing oil; colloquial term for an *oil tank-vessel; see* **Tank vessel** *in* TANK. **O.-wash,** a light oil used to wash down sides of tanks after they have been steamed, as in operation of cleaning. **Storm o.,** also termed *wave oil,* that used for allaying a rough or heavy sea. It may be distributed by use of *oil bags* trailed overboard or by slow-drip process through waste-pipes,

etc. Most effective oils are *vegetable* products with *animal* oils next. **Straits o.,** that pressed from carcases of *menhaden;* formerly, a pure cod-liver oil from fish caught in Strait of Belle Isle (between Newfoundland and Labrador). **Train o.,** an older name for oil obtained from sea animals; especially from seals and whales. (From Dutch *traan,* blubber) **Whale o.,** that obtained from blubber of seals, whales, and other mammals; epecially, from the *right whale;* train oil; *cf.* WHALE.

OILER. Vessel used for transportation of oil; especially, one built for supplying a naval fleet with fuel oil. A member of engineering department in a merchant vessel; *see* GREASER.

OILSKINS. Jacket and trousers made of cotton, linen, or silk and waterproofed by treating with oil (usually *linseed o.*), worn by seamen in wet or heavy weather. The accompanying hat having a broad rim to protect the neck is termed a *sou'wester.*

OILTIGHT. Quality of being impervious to passage of oil, as effected by packing, calking, or riveting; said of a bulkhead, deck, or shell plating of a vessel. **O. riveting,** where required in a bulkhead, etc., is spaced 3 to $3\frac{1}{2}$ rivet diameters; *see* **Oil-tight b.** *in* BULKHEAD.

OLD. Aged; venerable; out of date; antique. Sometimes used in a disparaging sense; as, the *old crock, old hooker,* etc., in referring to a vessel. **O.-fashioned anchor,** *see* ANCHOR. **O. horse,** same as dead horse; *see* **D. horse** *in* DEAD. **O. Grog,** *see* GROG. **O. Ironsides,** U.S. frigate *Constitution* launched at Boston, Sept. 20, 1797, so popularly named from her engagement successes in War of 1812–14. Vessel was contemporary of frigates *Constellation* and *United States,* launched at Baltimore and Philadelphia, respectively, in same year. All three were designed by Joshua Humphreys, a Philadelphia Quaker. First reconditioned in 1830, public sentiment prevailed against subsequent proposals to break up the old ship. She now lies, tenderly cared for, at the port of her birth. **O. man,** the *skipper;* familiar term for captain of a naval vessel or master of a merchantman. Also, a shipyard worker's or machinist's term for a portable fixture for holding a drill to its work when boring holes in a plate, etc.; its base is bolted to plate while its arm keeps drill in required position. **O. man's hat,** also *hat-box* or *drain hat, see* **D.-pot** *in* DRAIN. **O. measurement,** *see* MEASUREMENT. **O. salt,** landsman's term for an old and experienced sailor; among seamen, a man of long experience in sailing-vessels of *deep water* type; an *old-timer.*

OLÉRON, LAWS OF. *See* LAW.

OMNIBUS BILL OF LADING. For purposes of economy in shipment of a number of small packages of miscellaneous sizes and/or contents, a bill of lading covering entire consignment as a single shipment.

ON. As used in various phrases, has significance of (1) direction toward, as in *head on, end on, on and off, stern on;* (2) direction relative to ship, as in, *on the bow, on the beam, on the quarter;* (3) motion, as in *carry on, draw on, hold on, lay on;* and (4) of position or situation, as in, *on board, on a bowline, on end, on the berth, on a lay, on shore, on soundings, on the wind.* (For meanings of phrases noted, see under captions indicated by principal words therein)

ONE-ARMED ANCHOR. *See* ANCHOR.

ONE-POINT BEARING. *See* BEARING.

ONLY MATE. A former grade of certificate of competency in British mercantile marine, authorizing person to whom issued to act as the *only mate* required by law in Home Trade or Foreign-going vessels not exceeding a certain tonnage. *Cf.* MATE.

ON THE ACCOUNT, To go. *See* ACCOUNT.

OOMIAK. (*Eskimo*) Large open boat used by Alaskan Eskimos in hunting walrus, seals, etc. Has a frame-work in which all parts are secured by seal- or walrus-skin strips or thongs, the whole being completed entirely apart from its outer covering or skin. The latter is a skillfully shaped arrangement of walrus hides sewn together by seal-skin thongs and is drawn over the finished frame-work much like a tight-fitting glove, being secured only along the gunwale. The boat is driven by paddles but often a small square sail is spread forward when wind is fair. Also, *oomiac, umiack, umiak.*

O.O.D. Usual abbreviation for *officer of the deck; see* OFFICER.

OOTRUM. Strong white silky fiber from a climbing plant of India, used as a substitute for flax; also, the plant itself.

OOZE. (M.E. *wose,* dirt, mud) Soft slimy mud or silt at bottom of a river or an estuary. A soft deposit on the ocean floor consisting of accumulation through the ages of dead minute pelagic plants and animalcula. Carpeting the bottom at great depths and far removed from sediment or wastage in *mud* form, or that washed from the continents, *ooze* has been broadly divided into *calcareous* and *silicious* classes. Calcareous, or limy, division comprises infinite myriads of remains of tiny shelled creatures called *pteropods* and *globigerinæ* and disintegrated skeletons of fish and sea mammals; silicious division, of colder waters, consists chiefly of dead minute floating plants called *diatoms* and *radiolarians.* Color of pelagic *ooze* ranges through the lighter tints of red, yellow, blue, green, and sometimes, especially in the globigerina type, attains a deep brownish hue. On American and British charts, ab-

breviation *oz.* or *Oz.* denotes bottom in vicinity indicated is of *ooze.*

OPAH. A brilliantly colored deep-bellied food fish of the Atlantic; length about four feet, its compressed body measures in depth nearly half its length, and, as implied in its ichthyological name, *Lampris guttatus,* is dotted with small silvery spots over beautiful tints of blue, green, golden, and purple.

OPEN. Exposed; free of stipulated limits or conditions; not closed; not connected; uncovered; opposed to *shut.* To make accessible or free of obstacles; as, to *open a hatchway;* to *open a channel.* To *open,* or *open out,* a shore mark or prominent object is to proceed on such course as will bring about a change in its bearing to right or left of a less distant mark or object, as in piloting. A *range,* or two *leading lights* or *beacons,* is said to be *open* when the objects are not in line, thus indicating vessel is on one side of channel or fairway axis so marked. On local charts, or indicated in sailing directions, as a guide in piloting, *open* is used in such information as, "*Gull Point open to westward of Seal Head Lt. leads clear of Oyster Shoal.*" **O. basin,** a dock area or terminal basin in which no provision is made for holding water at constant level, or one in which tidal rise and fall is unrestricted. **O. boat,** one not protected by a continuous deck; an undecked boat. **O. bridge house,** midship structural space not permanently closed at forward or after ends; *cf.* **B. house** *in* BRIDGE. **O. charter,** *see* CHARTER. **O. chock,** a mooring-chock open at top, as distinguished from a *rouser-chock* or *mooring-pipe; cf.* **Rouser-c.** *in* CHOCK. **O. class,** yacht-racing term for a competing group or fleet of boats of various sizes and rigs. Handicaps are established according to trials of each boat's performance as compared with fastest boat in the fleet or in one of its divisions. **O. coast,** a coast-line having no outlying dangers, or one free of rocks or shoals. **O. coverage,** cargo insurance policy in which underwriter contracts to insure, or reinsure at stated intervals, all shipments by certain carriers up to a stipulated limit on each vessel. **O. dock,** see **O. basin. O. gunwale,** as opposed to a *box-gunwale,* that of a boat in which the *capping* and *inwale* are omitted; *cf.* **Box-g.** *in* GUNWALE. **O. hawse,** *see* HAWSE; opposed to *foul hawse.* **O'ing iron,** also termed *reeming-iron,* or *reaming-iron,* a broad-faced tool used by calkers to open seams of heavy planking preparatory to actual calking. It is driven by a heavy mallet called a *reeming-beetle; cf.* **Calking-i.** *in* IRON. **O. link,** *see* LINK. **O. order,** *see* ORDER. To **o. out,** to bring within view, as to sail past an intervening object so as to bring another in sight; *also see remarks above.* **O. pack,** ice floe rendered navigable by its loose condition, or that in which many open patches are visible throughout the field or floe. **O. policy,** one in which value of subject insured is not fixed, but, in event of loss, value thereof must be proved by the insured; also, as opposed to a *valued policy,* one in which property insured and its value vary from time to time and appropriate endorsement on policy is changed accordingly. **O. port,** harbor or terminal open to foreign commerce; a port ·or harbor the use of which is not prohibited by government regulation or health conditions. A port at which ice conditions permit navigation throughout the winter season; an ice-free port. **O. rail,** as fitted around a weather deck in lieu of bulwarks, a "fence" or guard-railing for safety of people on board. Usually on principal passenger decks its upper member is made of *teak* wood about six inches in width, rounded at outer and inner edges; the opposite of a *bulwark rail,* or finishing-piece along tops of bulwark stanchions. **O. rates,** in shipping parlance, cargo-carrying charges arbitrarily fixed by a shipping line where there exists no agreement with other companies as to standard freight rates in particular run or trade concerned. **O. roadstead,** an anchorage area more or less *open* or exposed to the sea. **O. sea,** generally, the *high seas;* that part of the sea outside of a line joining headlands on a coast or outside a strait. **O. space,** in tonnage measurement, any covered space above an upper deck having no permanently fitted means of closing such space against exposure to weather. All such spaces, as deck-houses, certain shelter deck areas, forecastle, bridge, and poop erections, etc., are exempt from inclusion in vessel's *gross tonnage.* **O. stern frame,** in some smaller single screw vessels, one having no rudder-post, or after vertical member to which rudder ordinarily is pintled. With such frame rudder bears on a *skeg,* or stout arm extending aft from keel. **O. water,** any area of water that is free of ice; a passage through an ice floe.

OPERATING DIFFERENTIAL SUBSIDY. In U.S. shipping circles, term for a government subvention awarded a shipowner or ship operator in the public interest of maintaining a national merchant marine. Its direct purpose is to compensate such owner or operator for excessive expense outlay due to higher wages, construction and repair costs, subsistence standards for crew, etc., obtaining under U.S. flag, as compared with less costlier operation of foreign vessels engaged in same given service or trade.

OPHIUCHUS. (*Gr. = serpent-holder*)   An equatorial constellation lying immediately north of *Scorpio. See* RAS-AL-HAGUE.

OPIUM CLIPPER. *See* CLIPPER.

OPPOSITION. Situation of a celestial body when differing from another by 180° in longitude or 12 hours in right ascension; especially, that of a planet with respect to the sun; as expressed in *Mars is now in opposition to the sun.* Our *moon* is in that situation when at the *full.*

OPTION, SHIP'S. An affreightment term used in phrases such as, "freight charges according to weight or measurement, *ship's option."* **Optional cargo** means goods which may be landed at one of two or more ports in a coastal region, according to choice, or *option,* of shipper or consignee. Discharging port is usually determined and vessel instructed accordingly when one or two days from region concerned.

ORBIT. (L. *orbita,* circuit, track made by a wheel) Path described by a planet, satellite, or a comet, in its revolution around its primary. In our solar system, *orbits* of the several planets are ellipses having the sun in one of their respective foci. *Cf.* KEPLER'S LAWS. Point in earth's *orbit* at which she is nearest the sun is termed *perihelion* and occurs about January 3; when farthest from the sun, she is in *aphelion* at about July 3. In moon's orbit, corresponding points are *perigee* and *apogee,* or when she is nearest and farthest from earth, respectively. *Cf.* APSIS.

ORCA. Genus consisting of the killer whales; *see* KILLER.

ORDER. Written rule, regulation, direction; command; as, a *harbor-master's order;* often in plural, as *night orders.* Arrangement or formation of lines of ships in a fleet; as, *open order,* in which each ship's next astern and next abeam are four cables (2400 feet) distant; opposed to *close order,* in which station is set at two cables (1200 feet); however, vessels may be *ordered* to maintain a specified distance apart, according to flagship's *orders.* A merchantman is said to sail for a certain port *for orders,* by which is meant she there will be directed to load or discharge at one or more of a range of ports in coastal region concerned. To give o's = to issue commands. **Lawful o.,** a term brought into prominence in recent years in connection with labor union disputes and disciplinary proceedings involving seamen. To-day a shipmaster and his officers must be careful to issue none but *lawful orders,* since the courts will uphold a seaman's refusal to obey should, for example, a deck officer order an able seaman to perform duty in the fire-room or bring him a cup of coffee! **Morning o. book,** as used in naval and larger merchant vessels, special book in which captain or executive officer writes orders to be carried out by officer of the deck during following morning watch. **Night o. book,** that in which captain writes his orders to officers in charge of each watch throughout the night. Such orders usually cover alterations of course or other special navigational requirements, and are signed by each officer of the watch. **O. bill of lading,** *see* BILL. **O. of battle,** tactical disposition of ships of a fleet when engaging the enemy. **O. of sailing,** departure in succession of ships comprising a fleet or convoy, with view of taking up a certain formation or executing a desired maneuver when clear of port. **Sailing o's,** written instructions given a commanding officer with regard to route, ports of call, arrival and sailing dates, etc., upon departure on a voyage or cruise. **Sealed o's,** instructions under seal given a commanding officer, as in time of war. Such are to be opened and read at a specified date or position arrived at and are highly confidential, chiefly concerning routing; also *secret o's.* **Standing o's,** as usually written in opening pages of the *night order book,* orders of master or commanding officer which are continuously in force; sometimes also outlining responsibilities of each officer, with special points to be observed.

ORDINARY. In former naval usage, group or staff of persons taking care of a laid-up vessel; now applied only to such vessel, which is said to be *in ordinary* when in an inactive status, or out of commission. **O. seaman,** *see* SEAMAN.

ORDINATE. In naval architecture, one of a series of measurements perpendicular to a base-line or plane and extended to meet, and thus delineate, a curved line; as those in a given water-plane projected at certain adopted intervals, called *stations,* from midship fore-and-aft line to vessel's molded surface. *Cf.* STATION.

ORDNANCE. Generally, heavy guns and their mountings or equipment for use in warfare; in U.S. navy, includes all material for fighting use, such as guns, armor, mines, depth charges, range-finders, radar equipment, torpedoes, etc. **O. officer,** on a war vessel, officer in general charge of ship's battery, ammunition, and all ordnance equipment; also, of training of crew in gunnery.

ORE CARRIER. Vessel specially constructed for carriage of heavy ores in bulk. Such ships are sturdily built, usually with engines at after end, deep double bottom, and spacious wing tanks or buoyancy spaces which narrow the holds so as to raise center of gravity of cargo. Some ore ships have been built to carry either crude oil or heavy ores, in which case wing tanks are used to receive oil, when carried, and also midship space primarily built for ore is then used as in a tank vessel.

OREGON PINE. Douglas fir or red fir; *see* FIR.

ORGAN FISH. Another name for the drumfish (*Pogonias chromis*); *see* DRUMFISH.

ORIENT. (L. *orientis,* from *oriri,* to rise; same root of *origin*) The East, or countries eastward of the Mediterranean; especially, the Far East, or China and adjacent lands. In a poetic sense, point at which the sun rises. *Cf.* OCCIDENT. **O. equinoctial, o. æstival, o. hibernal,** points at which celestial equator, tropic of Cancer, and tropic of Capricorn, respectively, intersect the eastern horizon; or, points at which the sun rises at equinoxes, summer solstice, and winter solstice, respectively. (*Now archaic or poetic*)

ORIGIN, CERTIFICATE OF. *See* CERTIFICATE.

ORIGINAL ERROR. *See* CHRONOMETER.

ORION. (Gr.) Bright constellation situated on both sides of the equator, largely between five and six hours in right ascension and thus conspicuous in the northern winter months. Said to represent, in that ancient Greek heathenish humbug we have glorified and sheltered under the cloak of "culture," a certain hunter who was slain by *Artemis,* goddess of this and that with the moon thrown in, for taking unsolicited liberties with *Eos,* goddess of the dawn; but why the character was thus pictured in the heavens is perhaps as clear as his nebulous figure. The fellow's dog is supposed to be outlined in *Canis Major,* which group contains the brilliant *Sirius,* the *Dog Star,* lying south-eastward of three equi-distant luminaries marking *Orion's belt.* The belt lies about midway between reddish-hued *Betelgeuse* (α *Orionis*) to the northward and bright Rigel (β *Orionis*) to southward. The equator passes very close to and northward of *Mintaka* (δ *Orionis*), northwest member of the belt. *Alnilam* (ε *Orionis*) is middle star in belt. The constellation is on the meridian on January 1st. at about 11 p.m.

ORLON. The recently manufactured synthetic textile fiber which is reported to possess strength and durability qualities far exceeding those of its older sisters, *rayon* and *nylon.* Made chiefly of carbon, hydrogen, and nitrogen obtained from such common sources as air, coal, limestone, natural gas, petroleum, and water, experiments have proven the material at least a 25% advance, as compared with nylon (*see* NYLON), in tensile strength, toughness, durability under weather exposure, and resistance to smoke and gas, while it absorbs a remarkably low percentage of its weight in water. Orlon, therefore, has much in its favor toward a successful career in manufacture of sail-cloth, tents, tarpaulins, and marine cordage.

ORLOP. (Du. *overloop,* a covering or upper deck; from *overloopen,* to run over, in sense of running off, *i.e.,* shedding water) Originally, the single deck of a small vessel, gradually has been removed downward as a secondary deck until to-day it appears in merchant vessels as a lowermost partial or continuous deck where four or more decks are present; while in naval ships, especially battleships, the term has been displaced by a *1st.* or *2nd. platform deck. Cf.* **Orlop d.** *in* DECK. **O. beams,** those fitted as strength members in a lower hold; usually have no deck laid thereon, but sometimes a platform or partial deck. Found only in transverse-framed vessels, for continuous lateral stiffening an **o. beam plate** or **stringer-plate** is laid along ends of beams and secured to shell plating by the **o. stringer angle-bar.**

ORTHODROMICS. (Gr. *orthos,* straight; *dromos,* a running)   Art or practice of great circle sailing, or steering a direct straight line for point of destination, *i.e.,* an *orthodrome; also, orthodromy.*

OSCILLATOR.   Instrument which produces sound required in a sonic depth-finder or *fathometer; also* used for sending out submarine fog-signals, as from a lightship. Consists of an electrically vibrated diaphragm emitting a sharp high tone, continuous in fathometer or interrupted to provide distinguishing notes when used as a fog-signal. A submarine *o. signal* is used for determining ship's distance from a station in connection with a radio signal. *O. signal* and that by radio are indicated at same instant and time elapsed between reception of the latter at ship and that of corresponding *o. signal,* multiplied by .8 or divided by 1.25 gives distance off station in nautical miles.

OSCILLATION PERIOD.   *See* PERIOD.

OSPREY.   The fish hawk; a large bird of prey found on shores of most countries; remarkable for its continuous hovering and swift diving in capture of fish; said to be harmless and easily domesticated. Also called *ossifrage, fishing-eagle,* and *fishing-hawk.* The so-called *osprey plumes* are obtained from the *egret* or *aigrette,* of the *heron* family,—the fish hawk has none to give us.

OTARY. (Gr. *otaros,* long-eared)   Any member of the family *Otariidae,* consisting of eared seals, including the so-named *sea elephants,* of S. Hemisphere habitat, *sea lions,* and *sea bears,* found on most northern sea-coasts, excepting those of North Atlantic. The sea bear (*Callorhinus ursinus*), native of North Pacific coasts and islands, is chief source of our material for sealskin garments.

OTTER.   An aquatic fish-eating mammal found throughout northern regions of America, Europe, and Asia, much valued for its fur which resembles that of the beaver; in length averages three feet; has short legs and webbed feet, flattened tail about length of its body, and stubbed nose with many bristly whiskers. The rarer *sea otter* is a different species (*Latax lutris*) and yields the most valuable of furs. It was hunted to near extinction until under protection in recent years of *U.S. Fish and Wild Life Service,* which has brought back the animal to satisfactorily increasing numbers in its Alaskan and Aleutian Islands habitat. *Otter* is also a name given a mine protection device and so termed in merchant ships; *see* PARAVANE. **O. board,** *see* Otter t. *in* TRAWL. **O. torpedo,** a towed explosive for use against submarines, similar to a *paravane.*

OUT.   Away from port, usually in sense of progress on a voyage, cruise, or offshore fishing; as, *five days out.* A combining word connoting expansion, motion, endurance; as, to *open o.,* to *heave o.,* to *ride o.;* in this use see captions DRAW, FIN, HEAVE, LAY, LEAD,[2] LOOK, OPEN, PUT, RECKONING, RIDE, ROUSE, SNAKE. As a prefix, denotes away from, distant, exceeding; as in *outlet, outport, outsail.* **O'bound,** *see* OUTWARD. **O'fall,** place or area where a river discharges; mouth of a stream or river. **O'foot,** to beat another in sailing; to *outsail.* **O'going,** in act of departing, as a vessel leaving port; also, describing the ebb flow, as, *outgoing tide.* **O'let,** mouth of a river or stream; point or orifice at or from which water or other fluid escapes; a vent. **O. oars!,** order to a crew of oarsmen to place oars in ready position, or to ship them in rowlocks direct from their stowed position in boat; same position as indicated in **Oars!;** *see* OAR. **O. of trim,** said of a vessel when not properly balanced in position of masts or area of sail; or when trimmed *by the head* or too much *by the stern, i.e.,* loaded or ballasted so that her draft is excessive at either end. **O'point,** to sail closer to the wind than a competitor, as in a sailing race. **O'port,** a harbor or port outside the limits of a given district or region; any port beyond jurisdictional limits of a central port; any lesser or secondary port. **O'range,** to outsail or pass beyond effective range of an enemy's guns; also said of a ship's guns when superior in effect than those of an enemy; as in, *our guns did far outrange the Frenchman's.* **O'reach,** distance at which end of a cargo-boom, boat-boom, yard, etc., projects beyond vessel's side; horizontal distance from heel of a boom, gaff, or crane, to a plumb-line dropped from end of such. Also, an extended top or heavy built arm projecting athwartships at a masthead for securing cargo-boom topping-lift blocks so that these will plumb a boom stepped one side of midship fore-and-aft line; also termed an *outrigger.* **O'sail,** to exceed speed of another vessel or vessels; to win a race from another, as by superior seamanship.

OUTBOARD.   Toward the outside; exterior to a vessel's hull lines; laterally removed from ship's midship fore-and-aft line; opposed to *inboard.* **O. delivery,** *see* DELIVERY. **O. motor,** portable motor, usually gasoline-powered, which may be attached to stern of a boat for propulsion. It is a combined engine, screw, and rudder; engine driving a vertical shaft bevel-geared to propeller arm, and the whole turned as required by a tiller as in ordinary steering. **O. profile,** plan showing longitudinal exterior, or profile view of entire vessel, including rigging details, deck erections, rails, scuppers, mooring-chocks, sideports, etc. **O. shafting,** that part of propeller shafting in twin screw vessels exposed between hull and propellers in the arrangement where aftermost bearing is in a *strut,* or bracket extending laterally from ship's skin just forward of each screw. Where *shaft-bossing,* or rounded projection in shell plating houses shafting, no *outboard shafting* is present. **O. shot,** short length of chain cable between anchor and beginning of first length or *shot* of those comprising cable proper. It is provided where joiner shackle of a stockless anchor is inaccessible due to its position in a lengthy hawse-pipe, so that cable may be disconnected without disturbing the stowed anchor. Also termed a *swivel-piece* when fitted with a swivel, as in larger war-vessels.

OUTER. On the outside; external; farther or farthest from a given position or chosen starting point; opposed to *inner*; as, *o. jib; o. planking; o. buntline; o. bottom*. **O. casing,** outside wall enclosing the smokestack or funnel proper in larger steam vessels; outside wall of a steam boiler, often termed the *air-casing*, as in some modern boilers. **O. halyard,** a peak halyard on a gaff; a yard-arm signal halyard. **O. harbor,** as opposed to an *inner harbor*, an extension of a port affording anchorage or mooring facilities seaward from a less roomy, protected area; a roadstead. **O. keel,** lower of two plates in a flat-plate keel; the shoe, or false keel, of a wooden vessel. **O. strake,** raised strake of *raised-and-sunken system* of shell plating, *i.e.*, every second strake lapping over both its neighbors. (Where *outer* is descriptive word, see captions BEARING, BOTTOM, JIB, SKIN.)

OUTFIT. All equipment and requisites placed on board for a voyage or expedition and which necessarily are consumed or used for such particular undertaking; to provide a vessel with such, which includes fresh water, fuel, provisions, stores, special instruments, etc. In a broader sense, to completely prepare a vessel for sea by providing all necessaries for navigational purposes, including sails, rigging, spare cordage, provisions, stores, fuel, etc., and in fishing-vessels, all necessary gear, dories, casks, etc. Such provisions and equipment collectively are termed the *outfitting*. **O. insurance,** that in which special equipment or outfitting, as provided for an expedition, whaling voyage, or other activity requiring extraordinary expense outlay, is covered financially in event of, usually, total loss. An **outfitter** is a person or firm that furnishes consumable equipment to vessels or their crews; particularly, uniform clothing, overalls, mattresses, oilskins, tobacco, etc. **Outfitting** is a common term for that phase of shipbuilding work which entails completion of various details, installation of minor fittings, piping, rigging, deck machinery, etc., subsequent to launching vessel.

OUTHAUL. A rope used for hauling out a sail on a spar, as the clew of a loose-footed spanker, tack of a jib in small craft, head of a standing-gaff sail, outer end of a *Jamie Green* or watersail to a jib-boom, etc. Any rope leading to a projecting spar's end for such purpose; as, for hauling a *sounding-wire block* out to end of the *sounding-boom;* or a line temporarily rigged for hauling gear out to a jib-boom, as when rigging a vessel. On a standing-gaff sail, a **head,** or **peak, o.** and a **foot o.** are used to haul out head and foot of sail when setting it.

Also, *outhauler;* especially, when applied to a rope for pulling a fishing-net to the surface.

OUTRIGGER. A projecting frame, usually of iron, fitted to upper side of a narrow boat, such as is used in smooth-water racing, for purpose of extending rowlock outboard and so facilitate pulling an effective stroke in rowing; also, a *racing-boat* so fitted and varying in size according to number of oars, the **eight-oared o.**, or that of *"varsity"* fame, being barely two feet in breadth and 50 feet in length and probably largest of its kind. As chiefly used in boats and canoes of East Indian and Polynesian natives, one or more laterally projecting poles or spars attached to a float or log as a means of stiffening craft against pressure of wind in sailing and so avoid capsizing. Depending on size and local custom, there may be either a single *outrigger* or one on each side, a single one often made capable of being shifted to either side, *i.e.*, to that which happens to be weather side. A spar or bar of iron horizontally fitted at cross-trees of a sloop or schooner for spreading topmast backstays, or, also, serving as a leader for running gear. A *bumpkin* or short boom extending outboard for attaching standing blocks of lower and topsail braces. Any boom or spar projecting outward from vessel's hull; as, a boat-boom; a spar for sheeting home a yawl's mizzen; a sounding-boom.

OUTSIDE. Away from a coast; beyond a harbor; as, *a heavy sea is running outside*. External; exterior; pertaining to outer limits; as, *o. plating; o. turns; o. berth*. **O. cabin,** one located at or close to ship's side. **O. clinch,** as made in a rope, a running or sliding knot or knuckle formed by taking a single or a round turn with the end around standing part and seized to its own part, the end always lying *outside* the bight thus formed around object to be secured. **O. fastenings,** bolts, treenails, or spikes driven from the outside in a wooden ship's hull. **O. machinist,** see MACHINIST. **O. planking, o. plating,** that forming outside skin or surface of vessel's hull. **O. port,** a harbor or port located beyond a usual route on which a vessel or line of vessels is engaged; a secondary port. Also, a port or area within limits of a port in which absence of quays or wharves for cargo handling renders necessary use of lighters or direct transfer to other sea-going vessels. **O. strake,** see **O. strake** in OUTER.

OUTWARD. In a direction away from a port; as, *the fleet passed outward*. Pertaining to departure from port or act of sailing on first leg of a voyage; as, *log abstract for outward voyage;* an *outward store list*. **O. bound,** said of a vessel under way and heading for her first port of a voyage; especially, after leaving a home port for a foreign destination, when such vessel is referred to as an *o. bounder*. **O. clearance certificate,** see **C. outward** in CLEARANCE. **O. manifest,** see MANIFEST.

OVER. As a combining word in prefix form, primary meaning of which is *above* or *from above,* occurs in many terms as an attributive adjunct connoting such qualities as covering, exceeding, extending, outside of, passing, and inverting. **O'age,** chiefly a U.S. term for a quantity of cargo tallied in excess of that indicated in bill of lading or manifest. **O.-all,** covering the entire mass, as in *length over-all,* or length inclusive of projections at either end of ship; *cf.* LENGTH. **O.-all efficiency,** in a propulsion plant, ratio of shaft horsepower developed to that theoretically determined by fuel consumed in given performance of engines. **O'bear,** to outsail another vessel because of ability to *bear* or spread more canvas in a breeze, in sense of being in a stiffer or more stable condition than her rival. **O'blow,** said of the wind, to blow too strong for lighter sails (*archaic*). **O'board,** over the side; from on board into the water; as, *Man o.!* (*see* MAN) Sometimes *outboard,* in sense of pertaining to ship's outside surface or sides; also, *overbord,* the word being of Anglo-Saxon origin in *ofer bord* (off from the deck). **O'board discharge,** any pipe leading through ship's side for conveying waste matter, bilge water, condenser circulating water, etc., overboard. **O'board fall,** hoisting rope leading to a burton suspended from a yard-arm, as used in square-riggers for lifting cargo clear of ship's side during loading or discharging; also, in a two-fall rig for cargo work, the fall leading from head of boom that is guyed to extend beyond ship's side; an outboard fall. **O'carried cargo,** goods not landed at port to which consigned and so carried beyond such port. **O'cast,** uniform covering of cloud formation over entire sky or nearly so. **O'cast staff,** *see* STAFF. **O'due,** said of a vessel failing to arrive at her destination at proper time or within a reasonable time thereafter; as in, *the brig is ten days overdue.* **O'fall,** a basin to hold surplus water from a canal or one of its locks; a sudden increase in depth of sea bottom; also, often in *plural* form, surface turbulence caused by tidal current running over sharp inequalities in sea depths, or submerged ridges, shoals, rocks, etc. **O'hand knot,** simple knot made by turning rope's end around standing part and drawing it through the bight; often used as a temporary measure to prevent unlaying of a rope. **O'hang,** projection or measure of projection of upper sides of vessel at bow and stern beyond the water-line considered. **O'haul,** to examine thoroughly, as a ship's rigging, engines, etc., with view of renewals and repairs; to overtake or gain ground on, as a speedier vessel on same course as a competitor; to thoroughly search a ship, as in quest of contraband goods or stowaways. To *o'haul a rope* is to light or lift it along toward the block through which it is being hauled; to pull it through a block or lead so as to ease or slacken it; or, to clear or straighten out the line to allow it clear passage, as through a block. To *o'haul*

a tackle is to separate its blocks by hauling through all parts of its fall and thus prepare it for further use. **O'hauling weight,** an iron ball, block, or the like attached to the hoisting-fall of a crane for providing weight enough to lower the hook when not engaged. **O'laden,** condition of a vessel when immersed to an excessive draft due to weight of cargo on board; loaded deeper than load-line marks allow. Vessel also may be *o'laden* by reason of having her weather deck so encumbered with goods, cattle, lumber, etc., as to render her navigation difficult and dangerous, entailing, in latter sense, an obvious hazard to lives of persons on board. **O'lap,** in *yacht-racing,* position in which overtaking boat can not pass to other side of boat overtaken without dropping astern, or in which either can not turn toward the other without risk of collision. Termed "establishing an overlap," in such situation overtaking boat must keep out of the way of the other, but latter must allow room for her rival to pass between her and a marker, and if she is weather boat, must not steer off to obstruct course of overtaking one. A *chartered vessel* is said to be on *overlap time* during period she is kept by charterer beyond date of termination of charter; opposed to *underlap,* such period is usually reckoned in *overlap days,* and, depending on terms of charter, sometimes carries a penalty at a higher rate per day than that for charter period indicated in charter-party. **O'lap of plating,** *see* PLATING. **O'lapping strake,** *see* **O. strake** *in* OUTER. **O'launch,** older shipbuilding term meaning to unite timbers, etc., by scarfing or lap-splicing. **O'load,** to load a vessel with an excessive weight of cargo; *cf.* **O'laden. O'looker,** a British name for a marine superintendent; especially, such officer in employ of a Home Trade company or a tramp steamer concern. **O'mast,** to fit a vessel with masts too heavy or too lofty and so out of proportion with dimensions of hull; craft so rigged are said to be *overmasted.* **O'rake,** heavy seas are said to *overrake* a vessel when making a clear sweep over her decks, as in case of a heavily laden ship in bad weather. **O'reach,** to sail on same tack longer than is necessary; to continue on a course for a greater distance than required and so missing a mark or point, as in thick weather; as, *we overreached the buoy.* **O'run,** a vessel is said to *overrun her distance* when she sails past a position originally decided upon as that for altering course, heaving to, or anchoring; she is also said to *overrun her schedule* when completing calls at different ports earlier than anticipated. **O'sea,** abroad; across the sea to foreign lands; as *oversea commerce;* also, *o'seas.* **O'set,** to turn or tip anything over from the upright or proper position; archaic or poetic word meaning to capsize or "turn turtle," as in, "*a landbreeze shook the shrouds and she was overset.*" **O'side,** outside of or over a vessel's side. **O'side delivery,** act of discharging goods from a vessel to a lighter or other vessel alongside, as distinguished from discharging cargo to a dock or quay. Where vessel is berthed at a terminal dock, a consignee requesting *overside delivery* usually provides the lighter or other vessel to receive his goods. **O'side discharging** and **o'side loading,** respective operations of transferring cargo from a vessel *to* a lighter or other craft and *from* such craft to the vessel, directly over ship's side. **O'sparred,** said of a vessel having masts or yards, or both, of excessive length, too heavy, or greater in number than necessary, thus making her top-heavy in appearance, if not in fact; also sometimes termed by old salts *overhatted.* A sailor is humorously referred to as *oversparred* when showing effects of strong drink. **O'stand,** same as *overreach, q.v.* **O'stayed,** condition of a mast when pulled too far forward by its stay or stays; also said of a vessel having stays too heavy or too taut generally. **O'stowage,** error in order of loading cargo destined for two or more ports, or in disposition of cargo in ship's hold, whereby goods which should be landed at a given port are stowed beneath those for port or ports next in order of call. Goods not landed at port to which consigned due to *overstowage* are termed *overstowed cargo.* **O'take,** to catch up with, as a speedier vessel coming up from astern. To be *overtaken* by a squall, bad weather, etc., is to be subjected to its onslaught with little or no warning; also, in sense of being unprepared, due to unwatchfulness, for approach of such event. **O'taking vessel,** as defined by *International Rules for Prevention of Collisions,* means every vessel coming up with another vessel from any direction more than two points abaft her beam. Regardless of her rig, size, or class, an *overtaking vessel* must keep out of the way of such *overtaken vessel.* **O. the side,** situated on vessel's side; as, *sailors are painting o. the side.* Overboard; as, *all ashes are thrown o. the side.*

OWNER. Short for *shipowner.* **At owner's risk,** phrase appearing in a *bill of lading* covering a consignment of deck cargo, as in "stowed on deck *at owner's* (or *shipper's*) *risk,*" indicating owner of shipment assumes risk of loss due to exposure of goods to weather and possible boarding seas.

OX-DRIVER. Another name for the constellation *Boötes; see* BOÖTES.

OXTER PLATE. *See* PLATE.

OXYACETYLENE PROCESS. That now commonly used in ship repair and shipbuilding yards for cutting plates, frames, etc., and in welding together structural parts. Such work is performed by means of a jet of flame produced by igniting a mixture of acetylene and oxygen, both gases being conveyed to the *burner* or *torch* by tubing from separate cylinders or other containers fitted with pressure-regulating valves. Temperature of flame is upwards of 6000° Fahrenheit, which is considerably higher than that produced by the earlier *oxyhydrogen* system, or that in which oxygen and hydrogen were similarly employed.

OYSTER. The well-known bivalve mollusk those species of which found on coasts of North America and Europe are most important as food. Growing on hard bottom, it attaches itself to rocks, old shells, etc., in bays and at or near mouths of rivers, only in water of more or less salty content. Oysters are gathered by means of *tongs* or *rakes,* which may be likened to a pair of long-handled large-sized garden rakes worked scissors-fashion, so that the catch is taken between the rakes' meeting teeth. A more elaborate device for this purpose is a heavy toothed *drag,* hauled over the bottom (*oyster bed*) by an *oyster dredger,* as craft using this method are called. Vessels engaged in taking oysters, or *oyster-fishing,* locally are termed *o. sloops, o. schooners, o. scows,* etc., according to rig. Laws limiting season for oyster-fishing and size of the mollusk captured are in force in U.S. and Canada, both countries including in their programs for maintaining propagation of oyster life the yearly replenishing of beds with seed oysters produced by laboratories devoted to the work. **O. knife,** *see* KNIFE. **O. rock,** among fishermen in the Chesapeake Bay region of the industry, natural *oyster bed,* or hard bottom consisting of a more or less compacted mass of dead and broken shells, on which the oysters grow.

P

P. In International Code, a square blue flag with a white square in its center, popularly known as the *Blue Peter* (a corruption of *blue repeater*, as used in a former British naval code). Hoisted singly at the fore, denotes, "All persons are to repair on board as the vessel is about to proceed to sea." As a Morse Code flashing signal at sea (• — — •), denotes, "Your lights are out or burning bad." Also, as a towing signal, or that between a towing vessel and her tow, flag *P* held in the hand or shown by hoisting to an appropriate position, or Morse *P* at night, by *ship towing*, signifies, "I must get shelter or anchor as soon as possible"; by *ship towed*, "Bring me to shelter or to an anchor as soon as possible." As a symbol in a log-book or weather record, *p* = *passing showers*; also, in nautical astronomy, often denoting *polar distance*, and in navigation, *departure*.

P. A. Abbreviation used on American and British charts for *position approximate*, as indicated with reference to a shoal or rock.

PACIFIC. Largest of the oceans, so named by *Magellan* from fine weather conditions he experienced as first European navigator of that expanse; *see* MAGELLAN. About 70,000,000 miles² in area, extends from Bering Strait to Antarctic Circle, but usually divided in cartography as North and South Pacific, or respective areas north and south of the equator. From America it extends westward to Japan Islands, Philippines, New Guinea, and to longitude of southwest extremity of Australia (about 114° E.). **P. blockade,** that effected by a state against the ports of another without recourse to hostilities, an example of which is blockade by Great Britain and Germany against Venezuela in 1902. **P. cod,** the Alaska cod; *see* COD. **P. iron,** *see* IRON. **P. salmon,** any fish of that name native to North Pacific; *see* SALMON.

PACK. To stow or press closely together; as, to *p.* cases in tier; to *p.* a vessel's stores. To insert *packing,* or appropriate elastic material, in a gland or stuffing-box, so as to prevent escape of air, steam, water, etc., around a working part; as, to *p.* a piston or a valve stem; or between flanges, as in a pipe joint. That which is *packed* or pressed together; as an *ice-p.* **Gland p'ing,** *see* GLAND. **P. ice,** that constituting an ice-pack; especially where more or less permanently confined in polar seas; *see* ICE. **P'ing-box,** a stuffing-box, or receptacle for confining *packing* around a piston rod, etc. **P'ing-iron,** *see* IRON. To **p. on sail,** to spread all possible sail, as with view of increasing speed; also shortened to *pack on.* **P'ing lashing,** shipyard term for one of a number of chains or wire ropes extending between launching-poppets' ribbands thwartships under the hull and set up as lashings for stiffening poppets to their work in supporting ship on the sliding ways; also, *poppet-lashing.* **P'ing piece,** a liner or filling-piece; as a strip of plate between a frame and a raised strake of plating; *cf.* LINER. **P'ing ring,** metal ring in the form of packing; as a piston ring. A metal ring fitted to evenly compress fiber packing, as in a gland or stuffing-box. **P'ing screw,** also termed *packing-worm,* a cork-screw-like tool for withdrawing packing from a gland. **P'ing stick,** piece of hardwood of special shape for pushing or compressing packing into a gland. **P'ing timber,** longitudinal pieces fitted between sliding ways and vessel's bottom at broader part of the hull, as when preparing vessel for launching; also called *making up* and *top-chocking.*

PACKAGE FREIGHT. Cargo or freight consisting of goods put up in barrels, boxes, crates, rolls, etc., and usually excluding liquids in drums or casks; a miscellaneous cargo, as distinguished from a homogeneous or bulk cargo.

PACKET. Once a fast-sailing craft for carrying *packets,*—mails and dispatches, for a government, and originally called a *packet boat.* Now a vessel engaged on a regular run in carriage of mails, passengers, and cargo; also, *p. ship.* **Galley-p.,** *see* G. **packet** *in* GALLEY. **P.-day,** sailing-day of the packet, as formerly often locally so termed. **P. rat,** former term of contempt for the generally undesirable type sailing as crew members in North Atlantic *packets,* particularly in those of the overlapping and highly competitive period embracing beginning of steam navigation and its final displacement of sail in the American-European *packet trade,* when "tough was the going and tougher the men." **Royal p.,** vessel chartered or appointed to carry mails and dispatches for the British government; one of the Royal Main Steam Packet Company's ships.

PAD. Piece of timber laid on a deck beam for purpose of giving beam its necessary camber; *cf.* CAMBER. Small piece of plate secured to the deck, bulwarks, etc., as provision for attaching a removable bolt, hook, screw-eye, or other fitting, or for a base to which an eye, end of a rail, etc., may be welded or forged. **Lifting-p.,** stout piece of plate supporting an eye, or a forging with an eye projecting from its base, permanently secured to ship's counter for attaching tackles used in lifting propeller or rudder; any such fitting for lifting a heavy object, as indicated; a *lug pad.* **P.-eye,** general term for a pad with an eye forged thereto, such as is commonly fitted to deck, side of a deck-house, bulwark, etc., for receiving a tackle-hook, shackles at ends of rigging, deck-lashings, and such uses; *lug p.* **Shroud p.,** one of the *pad-eyes,* or *lug pads,* in a steel vessel, for securing ends of shrouds. Those for lower ends are usually riveted to inside of sheer strake, close to its upper edge and in modern vessels shrouds' upper ends are shackled to *pads* of same name fitted on masts.

PADDLE. Oar-like implement for propelling a boat or canoe, its use differing from that of the oar in that it is drawn through the water clear of boat's side or gunwale. *Paddles* are usually of single-bladed type which an operator manipulates with both arms, his outboard hand grasping the shaft just above the blade, while inboard hand holds top end of shaft. Double-bladed, or double-ended, *paddles* have a long shaft with a blade at each end; operator, holding shaft before him and across boat, draws a stroke at alternate sides of his craft. Latter type is used only in small light boats or canoes and is particularly adapted to smart, single-handed maneuvering of the *kayak,* skillful use of which by the Eskimos is unsurpassed; *cf.* KAYAK. The radially set *blades, boards,* or *floats,* in a paddle-wheel, such as is turned on a thwartship horizontal axis at each side of a *paddle-boat,* are also termed *paddles.* The blade of an oar is sometimes referred to as its *paddle;* also, the term denotes a small sluice-gate or water-door in a lock gate of a canal. Short for *paddle-board, paddle-wheel, paddle-boat,* etc. To use a paddle or something serving as a paddle in propelling a boat, raft, etc.; to use the hands or feet as paddles, when swimming or keeping afloat. **At the p.,** rowing easily or with little or no exertion; hence, at a leisurely pace; "taking it easy." **Feathering-p.,** *see* F. paddle-wheel *in* FEATHERING. **Paddler,** a p.-boat; a p.-vessel. **P.-board,** one of the blades or floats in a *p.-wheel;* a *p.-float.* **P. boat,** any type of craft propelled by a *p.-wheel* on each side; a *side-wheeler.* **P.-box,** protective casing or box enclosing each *p.-wheel* of a vessel. It is built on timbers or structural steel projecting from, and forming an integral part of, the hull. **P.-box annex,** in some river-boats, extension of housing forward and aft of each *p.-box,* so constructed as to contain cabins, lockers, toilets, etc.; a *p.-box cabin* is so named because located in the *annex.* **P.-box bridge,** platform or navigating-bridge extending across vessel from top of one *p.-box* to the other. **P.-box framing, stays,** etc., structural work contained in a *p.-box.* **P.-propeller,** an early device in which a series of paddle-boards attached to a frame at vessel's stern were controlled by a mechanism designed to drive in much the same manner as by hand paddles. Blades were dipped vertically, drawn towards astern in one sweep, then raised vertically, and drawn forward for next dip, and so on. **P. race,** water agitated by working of paddles; especially, that abaft *p.-boxes,* vessel going ahead. **P. shaft,** that carrying rotating paddles and extending from engine-room; depending on type or maneuvering requirements, shaft may be common to both wheels or may be shafts independent of each other. **P. sloop,** in early days of steam, a British *sloop-of-war* fitted with paddles. **P. wheel,** that carrying a series of blades, boards, or floats at its circumference and rotated to give propelling effect. Such wheel is so called only when fitted at each side of a vessel; a single wheel mounted in a frame at vessel's stern, as confined to river-boats, is termed a *stern-wheel* and boat or vessel using such propulsion means, a *stern-wheeler.* The crude side-paddles in wheel form were found to be the only practical method of converting steam power into speed through the water until advent of the screw propeller in 1838. Since then the paddle has been driven from the ocean to rivers and inland waters where it still is preferred for shallow-draft conditions in towing and ferrying. However ill-suited to heavy weather at sea, the fact remains that barely half a century has elapsed since the side-wheeler had become fastest powered vessel afloat, notably in the cross-Channel service between British Isles and the continent. It is recalled that the paddler *Prince Rupert* of the old Dominion Atlantic Railway service between Boston and Digby, N.S., equaled the crack German *Deutschland's* record of 22¼ knots in 1900. **P. wing,** platform-shaped strength structure at forward and after ends of a projecting paddle-box. Also called the *sponson,* it serves as protection for *p.-box* similar to that afforded by a fender when vessel is being docked or moved along a quay, etc. To **reef p's,** *see* REEF.

PADDLEFISH. A remarkably shaped food fish of the Mississippi and its tributaries; has a length of about four feet, one-third of which is occupied with a flat snout much resembling the blade of a canoe paddle.

PADDY'S HURRICANE. Old humorous sailing-ship term for a *calm* during which loose-hanging sails slap about from heaving of vessel in a swell; also, *Irish hurricane* and *wind up-and-down the mast.*

PAINT. In iron and steel construction, it is of first importance to protect the metal from corrosive effects of sea-water and the salt-impregnated sea air. *American Bureau of Shipping* requires that all steel and iron work should receive at least two coats of good oil paint, and no outside surface, particularly the shell plating, should be painted until shortly before ship is launched, in order that removal of *mill scale* may be assisted by full exposure to weather (*cf.* MILL SCALE); all faying surfaces throughout vessel's structure are to be well coated with red lead or other approved composition. **Anticorrosive p.,** any of several compositions applied as first coat or coats to iron or steel surfaces as protection against corrosion. **Anti-fouling p.,** coating applied to steel vessels' under-water surfaces for protection against barnacles or other marine growth. A poisonous ingredient, such as mercuric oxide (or copper oxide for wood bottoms), is included in its pigment, the vehicle being a volatile, such as alcohol, benzine, naphtha, or turpentine. **Copper p.,** as used for wooden vessels' bottoms, an *anti-fouling* composition principal pigment of which is *copper oxide.* **P. gun,** device for spraying paint on a surface by means of air-pressure. **P. locker,** small compartment in which painting material and equipment are stowed. Such locker in U.S. passenger vessels is required to be of internal fire-proof construction and permanently fitted with a fire-extinguishing inlet from steam-smothering or carbon dioxide system installed on board. **Painted ports,** *see* PORT. **War p.,** *see* CAMOUFLAGE *and* DAZZLE PAINTING.

PAINTER. Length of rope permanently secured at bow of a boat for towing or making fast. For lifeboats, U.S. Coast Guard Inspection Regulations require such rope to be not less than 2¾ inches in circumference, of manila, and in length not less than three times the distance between boat deck and light draft line. To **cut one's p.,** to be on one's way; to sever personal contact. **Lazy p.,** short handy makeshift for a painter; a *bowfast.* **Sea-p.,** as used by an *emergency* or *sea boat,* a long painter made fast on board ship well forward and slipped from boat when she is waterborne or when ready to sheer off from vessel's side. It is thrown to the boat when she returns alongside and manipulated by bow oarsman or man stationed in bows of boat according to position desired, as placing boat directly below davits, at a ladder, etc. **Shank p.,** *see* SHANK.

PAIR MASTS. *See* MAST.

PALE. A temporary shore or brace for holding beams or timbers in position during construction of a wooden vessel.

PALINURUS. (From an ancient Greek pilot who is said to have tumbled overboard after falling asleep at the helm in vicinity of *Cape Palinuro,*—also named for the unfortunate fellow,—on west coast of Italy) An obsolete instrument, basically similar to the *pelorus,* for determining ship's true course by bearings of a celestial body. Also the name of typical genus of *spiny lobsters,* or *sea crayfishes.*

PALLET. In old-time war-vessels, a compartment in which ballast was stowed. A platform-sling or tray; *see* TRAY.

PALLETING. A secondary or raised floor of light wood in a powder magazine of older naval ships; its purpose was to provide an air space with view of keeping magazine as dry as possible.

PALM. Flat, or inside, surface of the fluke of an old-fashioned anchor; holding face of the fluke; sometimes loosely applied to entire fluke of any type of anchor. Flattened top end of propeller-post or rudder-post in an iron or steel stern frame; it is thus forged to facilitate riveting to transom floors, etc., in securing and stiffening frame to the hull. A sailmaker's instrument for driving the needle in sewing canvas, whipping ropes, etc.; consists of a stiff rawhide or leather band which fits around the hand, a hole for the thumb being provided, with purpose of holding in proper position a thimble next to the *palm* of sewer's hand; needle is held between thumb and forefinger and its eye end in thimble, and thus is pushed by *palm.* For use with smaller needles, as in sewing ordinary seams, the *seaming p.* is used; a heavier one for large needle use, as in roping sails, is termed a *roping-p.* The flattened end of a stanchion or strut where it fays against a plate, beam, etc., is also termed a *palm.* **Tripping-p's,** *see* ANCHOR PHRASEOLOGY.

PAMPERO. (Sp.) A cold dry south-west windstorm that originates on the Argentine pampas and blows itself out at sea off coasts of that country and Uruguay. Of line-squall type at its outset, may last from an hour to a day or two and is of considerable violence. Generally occurs between July and September, but sometimes up to December.

PAN. The broad inner extremity of a whale's lower jaw-bone,—particularly that of the sperm whale. A sheet of flat ice. **P. ice,** loose sheets of comparatively smooth ice, such as forms in bays or bights of a coast and is broken adrift by tides, winds, or contact with heavier floe ice; *cf.* **I.-pan** *in* ICE.

PANAMA CANAL. The important waterway connecting Atlantic and Pacific Oceans through Isthmus of Panama. Construction of canal was begun by a French company Jan. 20, 1882. U.S. purchased the uncompleted work in 1904 and present water-way was opened to traffic August 15, 1914, although until 1920 passage was hampered somewhat by land-slides in that section known as Culebra cut. Its to-tal length is 44 nautical miles; has a least channel width of 300 feet; and minimum depth of 41 feet. At its Atlantic end, ships are raised approximately 85 feet to level of Gatun Lake in three successive steps by Gatun Locks and a similar lowering to sea level takes place at the Pacific end, at which, how-ever, a tidal spring range amounts to 16 feet as against about 1 foot at Atlantic entrance. The lake mentioned, which was made by damming the Chagres River, provides a navigable stretch of 21 miles from Gatun Locks to the Gaillard cut, or principal excavation of 7 miles through the in-terior hilly divide. At the Pacific end of the cut is Pedro Miguel Lock and farther on, following the old valley of the former Rio Grande, canal proper terminates in the two Miraflores Locks. From Colon, at its Atlantic end, canal follows general di-rection of south-east, so that a vessel enters the Pacific about 24 miles to *eastward* of her Atlantic starting-point; which is explained by the fact that the Panama Isthmus lies in a NE and SW direction at site of canal. In 1947, some 24,000,000 long tons of cargo were carried by vessels through the canal. **P. C. tonnage,** *see* TONNAGE.

PANCAKE ICE. *See* ICE.

PANGA. (*Native name*) Large dugout canoe of Central America used for carrying loads of produce in sheltered waters. Typical craft is about 18 feet in length, 4½ in breadth, sharp-ended, and flat of bottom for greater part of length.

PAN HEAD RIVET. *See* RIVET.

PANIWALLAH. (*Hind.*) Member of an East In-dian crew, or *lascar*, who is detailed to supply drink-ing-water to his fellows; especially, such crew mem-ber attached to the engine department.

PANTILE. Sailors' old familiar term for the sea-biscuit; *see* **H.-tack** *in* HARD.

PANTING. Alternate bulging in and out of ves-sel's plating caused by wave pressure, occurring chiefly at the bows during plunging and rising, or *pitching,* in a head sea. Unless fortified against such effect, *p.* is found more marked in sharp-bowed ves-sels than in those of bluff bow build, since curva-ture of bows in itself is an element of strength against this motion. Forward of the collision bulk-head, steel vessels are stiffened against *p. strains* by **p.-beams, breasthooks, p.-frames,** and **p.-stringers. P.-deck,** *see* DECK.

PAPAGAYO. A strong north-easterly wind occur-ring between October and April along Pacific coast of Central America, from Salvador to Costa Rica. Regarded as an "overflow" of the *norther,* it results from the circulation about an area of high pressure advancing south-eastward in the Gulf of Mexico. The wind is accompanied by generally cool, dry, and clear weather, due to its loss of moisture in passing over the Cordilleras highlands. *Cf.* NORTHER.

PAPERS, SHIP'S. Documents required to be car-ried on board. A merchant vessel's papers include: Articles of agreement between master and crew; bills of health; bills of lading; certificates of classifi-cation, inspection, and registry; cargo manifest; con-sular invoice; customs clearance; charter-party; free-board or load-line certificate; fumigation certificate; log-book; passenger manifest; receipts for tonnage tax; and tonnage certificates for Panama and Suez Canals. **False p's,** *see* FALSE. **Paper nautilus,** female of a species of small cephalopod, also called *argo-naut,* so named from its thin delicate shell.

PARACHUTE FLARE. As a distress or warning signal, a pyrotechnic flare fired upward from a pistol and delayed in its fall by a small attached parachute. *Cf.* FLARE. **P. spinnaker,** *see* SPINNAKER.

PARALLAX. (*Gr.*) Apparent difference in direc-tion of an object as observed from two different points; specifically, in astronomy, angle at center of a body subtended by radius of the earth at an observer's place, or that termed *diurnal,* or *geo-centric, p.;* and angle at center of a body subtended by *radius vector* of earth's orbit, or that called an-nual, or *heliocentric, p.* **Horizontal p.,** maximum geocentric *p.* of a celestial body; so named because body is then in the horizon. Values of this angle are given in Nautical Almanac for sun, moon, and planets. That for the *sun* at mean distance from earth is 8.80″, its value at *aphelion* being 8.66″, and at *perihelion,* 8.95″. That given for the *moon* is the *equatorial horizontal p.,* or its value as observed at the *equator,* and attains a maximum of about 61½′ (at *perigee*), minimum of 54′ (at *apogee*), 57′ 02.7″ being its value at moon's mean distance from earth. Due to our satellite's comparatively short distance away and the lessening of earth's radius with in-crease of latitude, a correction must be subtracted, where great accuracy is required, from the Almanac value for date in question. This amounts to, very nearly, the product of *equatorial horizontal p.* times versed sine of half the latitude. **P. in altitude,** that of a heavenly body (sun, moon, or planet) cor-responding to a given altitude. It is equal to the *horizontal p.* (corrected in case of moon as above) *times the cosine of body's apparent altitude.* In re-ducing a sextant altitude to a true altitude, *p. in altitude* is *additive* and last correction applied.

PARALLEL. (*Gr. para,* beside; *allelon,* of one an-other) Surfaces, planes, or lines lying in same di-rection at equal distances apart, however far ex-tended, are said to be *parallel.* Such *lines,* as those running east and west indicating latitude on a chart, map, or globe, are called *parallels.* **P. of altitude,**

small circle of the celestial sphere, parallel to the horizon. All celestial objects having same altitude, therefore, are located on such *parallel*. **P. body,** that part of a vessel's hull length,—usually extending forward and abaft her mid-length,—throughout which any cross-section is identical in form and area. **P. of declination,** any small circle of the celestial sphere whose plane is parallel to that of the equinoctial. It is, therefore, coincident with the plane of a *p. of latitude* extended heavenward. **P. of latitude,** *see* LATITUDE. **P. rule,** instrument for drawing parallel lines, as in transferring a course or bearing line on a chart. Consists of either two parallel straight-edged rules connected by links in order that they may be spread apart as desired, or a single rule fitted with two identical rollers as means of carrying it exactly parallel with its original position. **P. sailing,** practice of navigating along a given parallel of latitude, or sailing true east or west; miles of easting or westing are converted to *difference of longitude* by multiplying such distance made good by *secant of latitude* concerned.

PARASELENE. (Gr. *para*, beside; *selene*, the moon) A moon-dog; *cf.* PARHELION.

PARAVANE. A water-plane or submarine kite, shaped like a torpedo and fitted with a pair of vanes or wings, towed as a means of warding off anchored mines and cutting their moorings. *P's* are towed in pairs, one leading out from each bow, both towlines being secured to a boom extended below ship's forefoot. Each *p.* is set to tow at a depth exceeding vessel's draft by a few feet, with its wire tow-line leading at an angle of about 45° with ship's fore-and-aft line. A contacted mine-mooring slides along tow-line and into the toothed jaws of a cutter that severs the wire mooring in the resulting snapping jerk. Mine then floats to surface where it may be destroyed by gun-fire. Generally termed *otters* by merchantmen, paravanes were invented and first fitted to vessels by *Lieut. Burney* of British navy, and so, often termed *Burney gear* in referring to tow-lines, hoisting-lines, and all equipment involved in the device.

PARBUCKLE. (Formerly *parbunkel*) To lift or lower by hand a round bulky object, as a cask or a spar, by rolling it in the bights of two or more ropes. For example, in raising a barrel to the deck from a wharf, two ropes (or bight of one rope) are made fast on deck and passed around and under barrel, thence back to deck. Each line is then hauled upon and barrel is rolled in direction of pull. Advantage is thus taken of leverage afforded by diameter of barrel. Such a device is a *parbuckle;* also, the term formerly designated a sling, or end of a hoisting-fall thus formed, secured to a cask or such bulky article in same manner as a *cow hitch, i.e.,* bight passed around object and standing parts rove through bight. **P.-screw,** a turnbuckle screw, such as

is fitted at lower ends of shrouds, used to heave taut the meeting ends of chain or wire lashings placed to secure a deck-load of timber.

PARCEL. Besides designating a bundle or package, *p.* is a shipping term for a specific small consignment in a homogeneous cargo; as, *a p. of 500 bushels for Doe & Son.* **P. receipt,** issued by a shipping company in lieu of a bill of lading for one or a few small packages or parcels; a *p. ticket* is receipt for payment of freight charges on such items.

PARCELING, or **Parcelling.** Strips of burlap or canvas, two to three inches in width and treated with tar, laid round a rope bandage fashion as a protective covering in connection with application of *service* to such rope; strips of canvas of any convenient width laid about a fiber hawser for protection against damage by chafing, as in way of a mooring-chock. *P.* is applied to standing rigging by working upward, thus lapping each turn over its next below, and always *with the lay* of rope's strands. Process of *serving* a rope comprises first, the *worming,* or laying of small stuff in contlines of strands as a filler; then *parceling* with the lay; finally applying the *service,* or turns of spunyarn wound close about rope *against the lay.* "*Worm* and *parcel* with the lay; turn and *serve* the other way" is the old rule. *See* SERVE.

PARHELION. (Gr. *para*, beside; *elios*, the sun) A mock sun or bright light, usually tinged with colors and sometimes having a bright train, appearing near the sun. Generally, two or more *parhelia* are seen at same time. Also called a *sun dog* and often written *parelion.* Sometimes when sun is low in altitude a like phenomenon appears in opposite direction in the sky, in which case it is termed an *anthelion.* A *paraselene* is the term for a similar appearance during moonlight; also, *moon dog.* Both phenomena are considered signs of approaching windy weather.

PARLIAMENT HEEL. *See* HEEL.

PARREL. Fitting which holds a hoisting yard to its mast. It is usually in the form of a sliding collar on a topsail yard and, on upper yards, a piece of wood secured to after side of yard, shaped with a concave part which partly embraces the mast. Also, *parral.* **Jaw p.,** one consisting of a semi-circular shaped *cleat* which bears against fore side of mast, and a *p.-rope* around after side of mast secured to each horn or *jaw* of cleat. **P.-cleat,** semi-circular shaped piece of hardwood termed a *jaw p.,* as fitted to yards above the lower topsail, or those more frequently sent down from aloft. **P. lashing,** that securing together the eyes of a *p.-rope,* where such are fitted to meet at after side of mast. **P.-rope,** piece of rope around after side of mast and connected to each jaw or horn of the *p.-cleat.* **P.-truck,** a *p.-rope* equipped with small wooden rollers for lessening friction against mast as yard is hoisted. **Tub p.,** as fitted on an upper topsail yard, sometimes on an upper topgallant yard, one shaped like a deep collar, usually lined with leather and made of steel plate, which embraces the mast. It is secured to yard by a bolt which allows vertical movement of yard-arms.

PARROT FISH. So named from its bright colors or its parrot-like jaws, any fish of the *Scaridæ* family and, also, several of the *Labridæ,* found in warmer seas. An European *blenny* also known as the *shanny* on coasts of Britain. *See* SCARIDAE.

PART. To break asunder; as, *both chains parted.* To divide, or be divided, into separate sections; as, *the hull parted* (or *was parted*) *in three pieces.* To leave or depart; as, *vessels will part company at dawn.* A piece or section; as, forward *p.* of the hull. *Parts* of rope in a tackle are referred to as *leading p.,* or that in which initial stress is applied, also called *hauling p.; running p.,* or such section as *runs* in blocks; and *standing p.,* or that extending to first moving block from the fixed end. *Standing p.* is also that principal section of a rope about which turns of its end are taken in forming a knot, hitch, etc. To **p. a line, hawser, etc.,** to cause it to break by excessive stress. To **p. from an anchor,** to break loose by carrying away a link or shackle of the cable.

PARTIAL. Combining term denoting *not wholly, incomplete,* or *in part only;* as in *p. double bottom; p. bulkhead; p. floor; see combination of caption word with p. in* DECK; ECLIPSE.

PARTIALLY HANGING RUDDER. One in which the blade extends below vessel's keel or lowermost pintle.

PARTICULAR. See term used with captions AVERAGE; CHARGE; F.P.A.

PARTITION. A lightly constructed bulkhead subdividing a main compartment; any bulkhead or partial bulkhead which is not a strength member in the structure.

PARTNERS. (Originally, knee timbers fitted horizontally as pairs between beams at a mast-hole in the deck) Stiffening or supporting pieces of timber, structural iron, or plate, fitted in way of a mast where it passes through a deck, or under deck machinery, capstans, bitts, etc. *Cf.* **M.-carling** *and* **M.-partners** *in* MAST. **Partner plate,** heavy deck plate which stiffens and unites the partner arrangement in way of a mast. It is either directly riveted to mast through a steel collar angle-bar or hardwood wedges are driven between such collar and mast.

PASS. (Fr. *pas*) A passage from one body of water to another; particularly, a waterway suitable for deeper draft vessels; as, *South Pass* at entrance to Mississippi River; the French *Pas de Calais* (or *Strait of Dover*). A passport or personal identification document. In older usage, a customs clearance, authorizing a vessel's departure and, as at U.S. ports about 1800, bearing such opening words as, "Suffer the brig Mary to *pass.*" To reeve or take a turn or turns through or about an object as in securing by means of a rope; as, to *p. a lashing;* to *p. a reef-earing.* To throw or transfer anything from ship to shore, to another vessel, etc.; as, to *p. a line ashore.* To clear or leave an object on either hand or on the beam; as, *passed Seal Rocks at 4.15 p.m.; we shall p. 5 miles off Cape Cod.* **P. down the line,** supplementary flag signal indicating message is to be repeated to each vessel's next astern, as in the case of a squadron in *line ahead* formation; abbrev. *P D L.* To **p. the hail; muster; the net;** *see* HAIL; MUSTER; NET. **P. the word,** order to repeat a command or instructions to other members of the crew. **Sea-p.,** the former *sea-letter; see* LETTER.

PASSAGE. A navigable channel or region providing a vessel access to one body of water from another. Journey from one port to another; a part of a voyage distinguished as *outward p.* or *homeward p.,* according to progress from or toward a home port in a scheduled round of ports of call. Act of passing or transit over an observer's meridian, as a heavenly body at culmination, termed *inferior p.* or *superior p.,* according to body's position *below* or *above* the pole; *see* MERIDIAN. Transportation; as, to *work one's p.; his p. amounted to $20; we took p. on a schooner.* An alleyway or corridor, as in a passenger accommodation space; a *passageway.* **P. money,** charge for a person's transportation. **P. winds,** prevailing westerly winds of trans-oceanic sailing routes between latitudes of 30° N. or S. and polar regions; "the fair winds of the roaring forties." (For terms in which *p.* is combined with caption word, see: BALLAST; MIDDLE; NORTHEAST; WING)

PASSAREE. As used in the old wool and tea clippers for spreading the foresail to best advantage when running before the wind, a small tackle at each clew leading to lower studding-sail boom end. Clews were hauled out by this means, thus giving sail more effective area. A sail spread in this fashion was said to be *passareed.* Also, *pazaree.*

PASSED. Qualifying word denoting having *passed* an examination or test of proficiency and awaiting promotion, formerly included in official title of naval rank; as, *p. midshipman; p. assistant paymaster.* Also, especially in British colonial usage prior to enforcement of requirement by law for professional examinations of masters and mates, a *p. master* was one who successfully took such examination, as distinguished from one who held a *service certificate.* Latter document certified holder as having performed satisfactory service in the capacity of a shipmaster, based upon testimonial of a shipowner.

PASSENGER. A traveler using a *passenger vessel* as a conveyance; every person carried on such vessel, other than the master and members of crew or other persons employed in any capacity on board in the business of vessel concerned, a child under one year of age, or a stowaway. Generally, persons under this caption when carried in a cargo vessel, are termed *persons in addition to crew,* and may not exceed 12 in number, according to U.S. law, if carried to or from a foreign port, or 16 between domestic ports. **Cabin p.,** originally, one to whom a cabin or part of a cabin was allotted, as distinguished from a *steerage p.,* or one berthed in common with a number of his fellows in a 'tween deck space; now applied to one occupying best accommodation afforded on board, usually where two, or at most three, classes are carried. **Consular p.,** *see* CONSULAR. **Deck p.,** one for whom no private accommodation or quarters is provided other than freedom to occupy any part of an allotted 'tween or weather deck space. Number of such passengers and maximum length of passage they may be carried generally are stipulated by law. Following complaints of excessive crowding of Mecca-bound Mohammedan deck pilgrims from Persia and India, special regulations were formulated by the *International Sanitary Convention, 1926,* which provided for adequate washing and cooking spaces, screened latrines, etc., and a minimum deck space per person of six square feet. **P. accommodation,** minimum space allowed each *p.* is regulated by navigation laws of nation concerned and, generally, for this purpose, *cabin* and *steerage* classes only are considered. U.S. law provides minimum requirements for steerage *p's* in the comprehensive *Passenger Act* of 1882 (*46 U.S.C. 151–155*). The Act requires that lowest deck on which *p's* of any class are carried must be that deck next below the waterline. **P. certificate,** a British document issued by the Ministry of Transport and Shipping authorizing a *p.* vessel to carry a certain number of *p's* of class or classes specified. It is granted annually, subject to compliance of vessel with laws governing equipment and fitness requirements of ships of her class. **P. list,** *see* **Passenger m.** *in* MANIFEST. **P. spaces,** those for accommodation and exclusive use of *p's,* as distinguished from cargo, baggage, mail, store, and provision spaces. **P. ship,** as defined by *International Conference on Safety of Life at Sea, 1948,* is a vesel which carries more than 12 *p's.* This applies only to the status of a vessel engaged in an international voyage, and has no bearing on the statutory requirements of any nation with respect to shipping within its own territorial or inland waters. **Steerage p.,** according to British law and *U.S. Passenger Act of 1882 (46 U.S.C. 151),* the expression means any *p.* other than a *cabin p.* Generally, such *p.* is one given a berth, mess, and general accommodation at the cheapest rate; not to be con-

fused with *deck p., q.v.* **Tourist class p.,** in large trans-Atlantic liners, one of a special class intermediate between 2nd. and 3rd. class rating.

PASSPORT. *See* **Sea l.** *in* LETTER. A formal document issued by a state officer to a citizen of such state granting permission to leave the country, attesting to his citizenship, and requesting that a foreign country grant him protection and unhindered passage while traveling therein. A license or *safe conduct* authorizing passage of goods through a foreign country by a specified route, as in time of war.

PATACHE. In sailing navy days, a small vessel or dispatch-boat used as a tender to a fleet in conveying men, orders, treasure, and official letters to and from shore or between vessels. The term appears to have been stolen from the Spanish, such vessel having been an important adjunct to their 16th. century galleons at a home port.

PATAMAR. (Marathi, *patemar*) An important trading vessel of the Malabar coast of India; rigged with lateen sails, usually two masts; partly decked at each end; averaging 90 feet in length; and some 200 tons burden. Also, *pattamar, pattimar.*

PATCH. A piece of canvas sewed on an awning or a sail for protection against chafing or localized stress; as, a *clew p.; reef-tackle p.;* also, for covering a torn or rent part, or for strengthening purposes. Piece of plate riveted, welded, or bolted over a break, hole, or corroded part in another plate; termed a *hard p.,* when riveted or welded and a *soft p.,* when tap-bolted with a gasket or filler between faying surfaces; also, a piece of sheet lead or canvas, served over with spunyarn, as in temporarily stopping a leak in a pipe, is called a *soft p.* Cakes or pieces of ice detached from a pack are called *patches.* **Collier's p.,** *see* COLLIER. **Standard p.,** as formerly used in naval vessels, a kind of portable *p.* consisting of several pieces of planking joined edge to edge, fitted with one or more eye-bolts at its center, and weighted to sink in a vertical position. In event of vessel being holed by gun-fire or collision, particularly below water-line, *p.* was lowered over side and laid on hole, so that eye-bolts were accessible from inside of ship for lashing contrivance in place. Any necessary additional eye-bolts were then fitted and final lashing, calking, or cementing completed.

PATELA. (*Hind.*) A broad, flat-bottomed boat used for transporting produce on the River Ganges. The craft carries a single square sail and is covered by a flat-topped shed, as a house-boat. Also, *puteli, putellee.*

PATENT. Qualifying term indicating object named therewith originally was protected by *letters patent;* as in *p. anchor; p. log.* (As a combining word in such terms, see under ANCHOR; BLOCK; EYE; FUEL; LINK; LOG; SHEAVE; SLIP; SOUNDER)

PATTERN. Same as MOLD, *q.v.*

PAUL. Variant of *pawl.*

PAULIN. Fabric material for covering purposes, as waterproofed canvas; short for *tarpaulin;* also *paulin stuff. Cf.* TARPAULIN.

PAUNCH. A heavy chafing-mat, or *paunch mat,* made of intertwined rope strands, used chiefly for protection of rigging against chafe of yards, or sails against rigging; see **Chafing-m.** and **Paunch m.** in MAT. Also, *punch* or *wrought mat.* **Rubbing-p.**, in older sailing-ship usage, a shield of thin wood laid on fore side of a lowermast to prevent injury to yards being lowered or sent aloft, in the case of a lowermast of built type, which was encircled by several heavy iron bands.

PAVISADE. (It. *pavesata;* from *pavese,* a shield) In old-time war-vessels, a development of the ancient array of shields set along the rail, as in Norse viking-ships; or that in the form of a temporary extension of bulwarks or shield-like protection from boarders or a rough sea. Later, a canvas screen raised along a ship's weather rail. Also, *pavise, pavisse.*

PAVO. (*L.* = peacock) A small southern constellation containing a single navigational star,—*Peacock,* of magnitude 2.12 and located in declination 57°, right ascension 20 hours, 22 minutes.

PAWL. A short piece or tongue of metal, pivoted at one end to allow it to drop or spring into notches in a toothed wheel, or into a fixed interdented space, to arrest reverse motion, as in a ratchet, a windlass, or a capstan; a *click, catch,* or *detent.* To hold or secure by, or rest against, a *pawl* or *pawls.* Also, *paul.* To heave a p., see HEAVE. **P.-bitt,** in an old-fashioned windlass, heavy post to which the pawls are attached; fitted at fore side of middle of windlass and usually held three *p's* of different lengths to reduce *backslack* to a minimum. **P. head,** projecting lower end of a capstan barrel to which *p's* are attached. **P. rim,** fixed trough-like base of a capstan which contains notches or interdented spaces for receiving the *p's* as *p. head* is revolved. To **p. the capstan,** see CAPSTAN.

PAY.[1] To slack away or allow to run out (usually with *away* or *out*); to pass out; as, to *p. away* a line; to *p. out* cable. A vessel under sail is said to *p. off* when she swings to leeward of her course or original heading, or to *p. round,* as when forced by backing head sail in *casting.* (In above uses of the word, preterit and past participle form is *payed*) To *pay off* a crew is to discharge and settle all payments due each man, as at end of a voyage. Compensation, payment, or salary for one's services; as, *port p.; sea p.; half p.* **Longevity p.**, as awarded officers and men in U.S. Navy, Army, Marine Corps, and Coast Guard, increase of salary at regular periods of continuous service, currently amounting to five percent of base pay for present rank or rating every three years. **P. clerk,** a subordinate in the paymaster's staff who has charge of payment of wages. To **p. with the topsail sheet,** to leave an unpaid debt behind. **Port p.,** salary or wages during stay at a home port, as that paid a person employed on board a merchant vessel but not formally engaged by signing the articles of agreement; often distinguished from *sea p.* in that latter is increased by an allowance for subsistence. **Sea p.,** that earned under sea-going conditions; as where no subsistence or other port allowance is included.

PAY.[2] (O.F. *peier,* from L. *picare,* to pitch) To coat or smear a wood surface with a water-resisting preparation such as hot tar and pitch, resin and tallow, or creosote, as on a vessel's bottom, a deck, or a spar; to run a mixture of melted pitch and resin, marine glue, etc., into planking-seams as the completing operation in calking; as, "we *payed* our decks with Stockholm tar and fish oil, piping hot"; asphalt and gum to *pay* the seams. (Preterit and past participial form is *payed*)

PAYMASTER. Staff officer in charge of payment of personnel in a naval vessel or station; usually as in U.S. navy, also has charge of provisions and issue or sale of clothing to crew. **P.-general,** in U.S. navy, chief of *Bureau of Supplies and Accounts,* executive personnel of which, termed *Pay Corps,* consists of staff officers ranking from captain to ensign, with titles in order of rank, as *pay director, pay inspector, p.,* and *assistant p.* He holds rank as rear-admiral. **Fleet p.,** see FLEET.

PAZAREE. See PASSAREE.

P. D. Abbrev. for *position doubtful,* as printed on American and British charts to denote that the geographical position of a shoal, reef, rock, or other isolated danger, or of a place at which comparatively shallow water is reported to exist, is indicated with uncertainty or has not been satisfactorily established.

P. D. L. See **P. down the line** *in* PASS.

PEA. Point or extreme end of fluke of an anchor; also, *peak, pee, bill.* **P.-soup fog,** humorous term for dense fog; *see* FOG.

PEACOCK. A navigational star in constellation *Pavo.* It lies about 30° SE by E of the *Scorpion's tail; see* PAVO. **P. fish,** a wrasse of the Mediterranean, so named from its beautiful colors, chiefly blue. **P. flounder,** a large West Indian species, characterized by its bright blue spots.

PEA-JACKET. (Du. *pij,* a coat of coarse woollen cloth) See JACKET. Also, *pea-coat.*

PEAK. Upper or outer end of a gaff. Upper after corner of a gaff, a lug, or a lateen sail; upper corner or head of a jib or triangular staysail. Inside space at either end of a vessel in vicinity of her stem or stern-post, termed, respectively, *fore p.* and *after p.* To *top up* or raise vertically to its limit, or nearly so, the end of a boom, gaff, or yard; to *cockbill* a yard. *Cf.* APEAK. **P. brail,** uppermost brail of a standing-gaff sail; formerly in large sails distinguished as *inner* and *outer p.* brails, where the former terminated at middle instead of at leech of sail; *see* BRAIL. **P. bulkhead,** *see* **After peak b.** and **Fore peak b.** *in* BULKHEAD. **P.-cleat,** piece of wood fitted in a boat for resting inner end of an oar when oars are in *a-peak* position, or blades elevated at a common angle and ready for dropping into position for pulling. In the old whaling-boats, oars were set in the cleats of a *fast boat,* or one that was attached to a whale by harpoon line, so that the men might rest while oars were in readiness for instant use. **P. downhaul,** *see* DOWNHAUL. **P. halyard,** rope or tackle by which outer end of a gaff, especially that of a fore-and-aft sail, is hoisted; *see remarks in* HALYARD. To **p. oars,** to rest oars in the position indicated in **P.-cleat. P. of an anchor,** bill, pea, or pee; *see* PEA. **P. pendant,** a chain or wire rope supporting outer end, or *p.,* of a standing gaff, such as that leading to a barque's mizzenmasthead from gaff of a brailing-in spanker; also, *p. span.* **P. tanks,** *see* TANK. **P. purchase,** also termed *p. jig; see* JIG.

PEARL. The well-known gem sometimes found within certain mollusks, as the oyster, clam, mussel, and conch, but especially in the *p. oyster* which is taken chiefly on west coast of America, in Australian waters, Ceylon and East Indies, and Persian Gulf. It is formed by a growth of extremely thin layers of a shiny calcareous concretion about a foreign particle, such as a grain of sand, body of a dead parasite, or other tiny source of disturbance to the mollusk. It may or may not be attached to the shell; is usually more or less globular in shape; in color may be black, blue, gray, pink, purple, white, or yellow; and finest grade is of a silvery or satin-like luster. **Mother-of-p.,** lustrous inner layer of several kinds of shells; especially, that of the abalones, *p.* oyster, and river mussel. Also called *nacre,* the substance is much used in manufacture of buttons, knife-handles, and many other articles. **P. diver,** one who dives for *p.* oysters in the *p.-diving* or *p.-fishing* industry, or that of gathering such mollusks in hunt for *p's*. Also called *p.-winner.* **P. lugger,** a ketch-rigged boat engaged in pearl fisheries of north-west Australian coast. **P. lashing,** *see* LASHING.

PEARLER. A boat engaged in *p.-fishing;* a trader in, or diver for, pearls or pearl-shell.

PEAVEY. A lever like a cant-hook but having a sharp metal spike at its lower end; *see* **C.-hook** *in* CANT. Also, *peavy, peevie.*

PEDESTAL. Any raised base or support, as a pivot-mount for a rapid-fire gun, a foundation for a propeller-shaft bearing, or the like. **Mast p.,** a mast-trunk or tabernacle; *see* **M.-trunk** *in* MAST. **P. rail,** in old-time ships, lower rail of the poop balustrade, or that on which the balusters stood. **P. socket,** that securing the foot of a davit and in which such davit is free to revolve; a *davit stand* or *shoe.*

PEE. Bill, pea, or peak of an anchor; especially, that of an old-fashioned anchor; *see* PEA.

PEEL. Broadest part or blade of an oar or paddle.

PEEN. To use the *peen,* or secondary head of a hammer or sledge, as in bending, straightening, smoothing, etc., a piece of metal; in shipbuilding practice, to round off sharp or ragged edges of plates, or trim a rough beaded weld joint, as with an air hammer and special chisel in *peening.* Also, *pane, pein.*

PEG. A sharp-pointed harpoon having a single barb, such as is used in taking turtles. A wooden pin for fastening or securing anything; a treenail. To *peg,* or pin, a cloth down as with a sailmaker's *pegger,* when laying canvas for cutting to shape desired. To practice *pegging,* or a New England Banks method of catching cod, haddock, etc., by constantly dropping line-sinker to bottom and pulling line with a jerk, while boat drifts over a selected fishing-ground,—preferably a shoal over which current sets strongly. **Dead p.,** a stretch of sailing which entails a continuous beat to windward, as when vessel is directly to leeward of her point of destination; to make frequent tacks as in working to windward; to *dead-p. it.* **Oar-p.,** a thole, or thole-pin. **P.-top form,** shape of a vessel's hull in which a deep rise of floor is in evidence, as appears in her midship cross section lines resembling the outline of a *peg top.*

PEGASUS. (*Gr.;* a winged horse of ancient fable) A northern constellation, three principal stars of which, with a fourth (*Alpheratz*) in the group *Andromeda,* form the *Square of Pegasus.* A line from *Polaris* through the eastern member of Cassiopeia (*Caph*), when latter is above the pole, extended southward for 30° passes through a *Andromedæ* (Alpheratz) and 14° farther on meets γ *Pegasi* (Algenib). The two last named form the eastern side of *Square.* Its western side has *Scheat* (β Pegasi) at the N.W. corner and *Markab* (a Pegasi) at S.W. corner. *Algenib,* at the S.E. angle, is closest navigational star to the *vernal equinoctial point,* being about 15° nearly due north of it.

PELAGIC. (Gr. *pelagos,* sea) Of or pertaining to the ocean; oceanic; especially applied to deep-sea life or something connected therewith; as, *p. animalcule; p. whaling.* **P. fishery,** *see* FISHERY.

PELICAN. Any of certain large web-footed coastal birds of genus *Pelecanus* found in warmer latitudes round the globe. It is characterized by its very large bill, long wings, and capacious gular pouch in which it stores a catch of fish obtained by the dive-and-carry process. Two species are common to America: the *white p.* and *brown p.* **P. hook,** a hinged hook fitted to an end of a lashing, boat gripe, etc., where quick release is required. It connects with a meeting link, is turned back against link to which it is attached, where it is secured at its point by a slip-link. By knocking slip-link clear, hook is released immediately. Also called *slip-hook* and *Senhouse slip.*

PELORUS. A dumb compass card in the form of a metal plate mounted in gimbals to maintain a horizontal position, and fitted with sight-vanes for observing bearings where direct use of the compass for this purpose is impracticable. The instrument is said to have first been used by a Carthaginian pilot for whom it is named about 200 B.C. In its simplest make, the plate, graduated at its rim to degrees, may be clamped in any position corresponding to ship's course and is used (*a*) to determine compass error by bearings of objects whose true or magnetic bearings are known; in which case plate is clamped to correspond with ship's head by compass and bearing is observed as vessel is exactly on her course; (*b*) to place ship's head on a desired true or magnetic course: plate is clamped to indicate course in question as ship's heading and sight-vanes at known bearing of a distant object (celestial or terrestrial), vessel being maneuvered so as to bring object in the sight-vane line; ship's head by compass is then noted as course desired; (*c*) to observe relative bearing, or angle on the bow, of an object, as in determining distance off a lighthouse, etc., by two bearings and distance run between them; plate is clamped to indicate ship's head as 0° and thus becomes a simple dial for measuring angles which bearings make with vessel's fore-and-aft line.

PELT. A spherical buoy about 18 inches in diameter used on east coast of Britain for marking position of fish nets. Usually made of tarred canvas inflated with air, it is mounted on a wooden base to which its mooring-rope is secured. Also, *pellet, pallet.*

PENALTY. Forfeiture, impost, or charge for damage or inconvenience incurred or suffered. **P. cargo,** chiefly in U.S., such goods as are considered, according to opinion of longshoremen's union concerned, hazardous or difficult to handle in loading or discharging, additional remuneration being demanded in consequence. **P. clause,** that in a *charter party* stipulating penalty for non-fulfillment of agreement. Ordinarily, by law such charges may not exceed value of freight on cargo concerned. **P. dock charge,** that against a vessel for occupying a berth for a period in excess of an allotted number of hours or days; also, *p. wharfage.*

PENDANT. Any single rope or chain attached to a yard-arm, sail, masthead, etc., to which at its free end a thimble or a block is secured; as, a *brace p.; jib-sheet p.; reef p.* Also, but improperly, *pennant;* probably through the word *pennant* (a flag) being earlier spelled *pendant.* **Brace p.,** attached to a yard-arm and forming part of a brace to which a tackle or whip block is secured. **Burton p.,** any *p.* secured aloft and to which a burton or lifting tackle may be secured; also see BURTON. **Centerboard p.,** rope or chain for raising a centerboard. **Clearhawse p.,** see CLEAR. **Cutting-p.,** length of rope at lower end of *cutting-tackle* and fitted with a hook for attaching to blubber during *flensing,* or stripping blubber from a whale's carcase in the good old days; see CUTTING-FALL. **Fish p.,** see FISH. **Fish-tackle p.,** one secured to fore-topmasthead in a square-rigger or lowermasthead in a schooner for attaching the *fish tackle;* see FISH. **Hanging p.,** a short wire rope used to hang an anchor under middle of a boat, when carrying out a kedge in this manner. The *p.* is secured to a *belly-rope* which is passed round boat and is fitted with means of being easily released to let go anchor. **Main p.,** a *burton* or *masthead p.* secured to main topmasthead. **Masthead p.,** one leading from main lowermasthead or topmasthead for purpose of attaching a tackle to its lower end, as required for lifting a weighty object, setting up lower rigging, etc. **Mooring p.,** a length of small chain leading from and supported by a buoy at a berth in which permanent moorings are installed. By hauling chain aboard end of chain cable or mooring is brought to surface for securing on board vessel. **Peak p.,** see PEAK. **P. tackle,** a purchase attached to a *p.;* especially, to a *p.* secured at a masthead. **Port-p.,** in older ships, a rope used to lift open the gun-ports. **Reef p.,** see REEF. **Rudder p.,** one of the single chains leading from each quarter to upper end of rudder-blade (*horn* of rudder) in older wooden ships. They were for recovering or controlling rudder in event of it being carried away or of badly damaged steering-gear. **Whip and p.,** a purchase consisting of a whip rove in a single block at one end of a *p.,* the latter being rove in a heavier single block. When other end of *p.* and standing end of whip are made fast at a common point, as a hook, the purchase becomes a *single Spanish burton.* Also termed *whip and runner.* **Winding p.,** as rigged in a square-rigged vessel for lifting a heavy weight, a *p.* leading from a lower-masthead and secured to a lower yard-arm, thence receiving a purchase leading to the deck; such purchase being called a *winding tackle,* an old term for a *three-fold purchase* or one of two blocks and having a total of five or more sheaves; sometimes any *p.* leading aloft and suspending a *winding tackle* was called a *winding p.*

PENFISH. *See* CALAMARY.

PENGUIN. A short-legged flightless aquatic bird of higher southern latitudes, especially about the Antarctic continent. It stands erect on land and walks clumsily, but exhibits great agility in swimming and diving; has feathers of scale-like appearance, short and stiff; generally white on breast and belly with dark-colored back; feeds chiefly on shellfish. Of about a dozen known species, smallest is *Eudyptula minor,* which stands about one foot in height; largest are the *emperor* and *king p's,* standing three to four feet. A small-sized species is the *crested p.,* or "rock hopper," of southern New Zealand, Falkland Islands, and South Shetlands. The *jackass p.* (genus *Spheniscus*), named from its suggestive squawking note, is found on South African shores and along those of South America between Cape Horn and Rio de La Plata.

PENNANT. A special flag, variously shaped, but usually having a greater length or "fly" than its breadth or "hoist." A blue triangular flag flown by a U.S. naval vessel to denote ship carries the senior officer of force or squadron present. Any small flag of peculiar color, design, or shape exhibited by a government vessel to denote a department to which she is attached. Older form *pennon* designated a triangular streamer or swallow-tailed tapering flag. **Answering p.,** that of the *International Code of Signals,* bearing alternate red and white vertical bands, tapering toward its fly end, and in length about three times its hoist; also called the *Code flag.* Hoisted singly and "close up," or to full extent of halyards, signifies *"Your signal is read and understood";* when displayed at the "dip," or about two-thirds up, means *"Your signal is seen but not yet understood."* **Broad p.,** formerly in U.S. navy, a swallow-tailed flag indicating presence on board of a commodore, as distinguished from the *narrow p.,* or that of a captain or commander, and an admiral's flag. **Church p.,** flown on naval ships during church service. In U.S. navy, a tapering *p.* showing a blue Roman cross on a white ground. **Commission p.,** long, narrow, ribbon-like streamer flown from the main truck of a government vessel in commission; also called *long p., narrow p., coach whip, whip,* and other colloquial names. That of U.S. navy shows a single line of seven white stars (formerly 13) on a blue ground of about one-third total length of *p.,* remaining part being horizontally divided into half red and half white. U.S. Coast Guard *p.* differs from navy *p.* in having the red and white in equal alternate vertical bands. In these services, it is flown by a vessel in command of an officer of less than flag rank. **Convoy p.,** special flag hoisted by the guide when vessels are sailing in convoy or by senior officer present in various naval convoy uses. **Homeward bound p.,** *see* HOMEWARD. **Irish p.,** a loose rope-yarn, fag end of a rope, strip of

canvas, etc., untidily hanging in the rigging. **Mail p.,** same as **M. flag** *in* MAIL. **Meal p.,** same as **Meal f.** *in* FLAG; also, **Mess p.,** or *chow rag,* as termed by the lower deck in U.S. navy, a triangular red flag flown at port forward yard-arm, or corresponding position in single-mast vessels, indicating it is mealtime on board. It is displayed only when ship is at anchor or otherwise berthed in port. **Narrow p.,** *see* **Commission p. Night p.,** a streamer, burgee, or small *p.* flown by a yacht or naval vessel after sunset during the period in which no other flags are displayed. **Numeral p.,** one of the ten tapering *p's* used in signalling by International Code. Each digit is denoted in the series. **P. ship,** vessel flying the flag of senior officer in a squadron or convoy; also, ship acting as guide in a fleet formation, as distinguished by a special flag or *p.* **Repeater p.,** one used in flag-hoist signals to indicate repetition of a letter or digit shown in same hoist. International Code has three *repeaters,* as commonly called. **Storm p.,** the red or white *p.* used in coastal *storm signals, q.v. in* STORM.

PENUMBRA. During phases of an eclipse, partial shadow of the intervening body, as distinguished from the *umbra,* or total shadow cast upon body observed. Phenomenon of a *penumbral eclipse,* usually referred to that of the moon only, occurs when our satellite passes through the *p.* without a partial or total eclipse taking place. *Cf.* ECLIPSE.

PENTECONTER. (Gr. *penteconta,* fifty) A galley propelled by 50 oars, as the Greek war-vessels circa 500 B.C. *See* GALLEY.

PERCH. (O. Fr. *perche,* a pole) A pole or staff on which is mounted a distinguishing mark, such as a ball, cylindrical cage, cross, or board bearing a letter or number, and so constituting a beacon indicating a shoal, edge of a channel, rock, or reef; also, a similar mark surmounting a buoy; especially, in U.S. buoyage system, in which it indicates a turning-point in a channel. **Sea p.,** any of several spiny-finned fishes resembling the familiar *p.* of U.S. lakes and rivers; as, *American sea bass; European bass; black p.; white p.; rose-fish;* and *morwong.*

PERCUSSIVE TEST. *See* TEST.

PERFORMANCE, COEFFICIENT OF. *See* COEFFICIENT.

PERIGEAN. Of, or pertaining to, *perigee.* (Pron. *perijée-an*) **P. tide,** *see* TIDE.

PERIGEE. (Gr. *peri,* near; *ge,* the earth) Point in the moon's orbit that is nearest the earth.

PERIHELION. (Gr. *peri,* near; *elios,* the sun) Point in the orbit of a planet or a comet which is nearest the sun; opposed to *aphelion.*

PERILS OF THE SEA. *See* **M. risk** *in* MARINE.

PERIOD. (Gr. *peri,* about; *odos,* a way) Portion or division of time as defined by completion of a recurring phenomenon or successive phases in a cycle; as, *wave p.; p. of a light; p. of oscillation.* Time occupied by a planet or satellite in completing a revolution about its primary; as, *the earth's p. is 365¼ days;* also called *periodic time.* A vessel's *p.* of roll. A portion of time, specified or indefinite; a cycle. **P. of a light,** time interval, usually expressed in seconds, occupied by the characteristic cycle of flashes, occultations, or other changes exhibited in the light of a lighthouse, buoy, or other lighted navigational aid. It is the exact interval between instants of successive corresponding stages in the cycle; thus, in a light showing two flashes every twenty seconds, from completion of the two flashes to their next completion occupies twenty seconds. **Rolling p.,** *p. of roll* or *p. of oscillation* of a vessel, number of seconds of time in which a single roll is completed, as from port to starboard or from upright to starboard and back to upright. The *double rolling p.* is that occupied in making a complete roll, as from port to starboard and back again to port. Value of the *p.* may be stated, very nearly, in the formula $t = .22B \div \sqrt{GM}$, where *t* is *single rolling p.; B* = greatest breadth of ship; and *GM* = metacentric height; so that, as a criterion of vessel's stability, the *p.* varies inversely as the square root of her metacentric height. Thus, a vessel 50 feet in breadth having a metacentric height of one foot has a *p.* of 11 seconds, while for a 4-foot metacentric height (*GM*), *p.* will have decreased to 5.5 seconds; the *stiff* condition corresponding to the quicker roll. **Sidereal p.,** *see* SIDEREAL. **Wave p.,** elapsed time in seconds between passing of two successive wave crests over a fixed point. It is equal to the square root of the quotient of distance between wave crests divided by 5.124. This works out as 11.7 seconds for *p.* of a North Atlantic storm wave of 600 feet length; *see* WAVE.

PERIODIC. Performed in, pertaining or conforming to, a regular period, phase, or cycle; as, *p.* motion of a planet; a *p.* star; *p.* winds. **P. survey,** that of a vessel's structural condition prescribed by a classification society to be carried out at regular intervals. Those conducted every four years are termed *special surveys* and usually are distinguished as No. 1, No. 2, No. 3, their purpose being to satisfy requirements for maintaining vessel's original rating, or for re-classification in event of vessel falling below standards originally met. **P. winds,** those recurring at certain seasons; as the *monsoons* and *trade winds.*

PERISCOPE. (Gr. *peri,* around, about; *skopein,* to view) Optical instrument chiefly used by submarines for observation or lookout purposes when vessel is submerged. It is mounted so as to be vertically raised as required and rotated in azimuth at will. Bearings of objects may be observed by means of a relative azimuth plate or compass card on which is indicated direction of observer's sight. Formerly called an *omniscope.*

PERISHABLE CARGO. Such merchandise or products included in a cargo which are subject to deterioration, damage, or destruction, due to lack of proper ventilation, refrigeration, or particular stowage required; or unusually lengthy duration of confinement on board, inherent vice, or contamination from certain substances in its vicinity.

PERMANENT. Combining term denoting fixed, continuing in a given state, or lasting. **P. ballast,** weighty material or substance, such as concrete, pig iron, rock, scrap metal, sand, or the like, placed in a vessel's hold or bilges to correct an unsatisfactory condition of stability or trim, or both; *cf.* KENTLEDGE. **P. bunker,** fuel space or compartment designed for stowage of fuel only; especially, for sole use of coal for ship's boilers; *cf.* BUNKER. **P. fender,** *see* F.-guard *in* FENDER. **P. magnet,** *see* MAGNET. **P. magnetism,** that remaining in an iron or steel object when the exciting force has been removed; especially, that part of magnetism which is induced by earth's magnetic field into a vessel's hull while being built and which remains greatly fixed due to the hammering vessel is subjected to during construction. *Cf.* MAGNETISM.

PERMEABILITY. In connection with subdivision of ships' hulls into watertight compartments in the interests of safety at sea, calculation of a vessel's *floodable length* involves consideration of total water which may enter compartments in question. What is termed *permeability* of spaces considered is taken into account according to certain mathematical formulæ adopted by *International Conference on Safety of Life at Sea, 1929 and 1948.* Generally, an average of 95% is taken as *p.* of passenger spaces below the margin line (*see* **Floodable l.** *in* LENGTH); that of machinery spaces below same limit as 80%; and cargo and coal spaces as 60%. **Cargo p.,** by this term is understood the percentage of a given block of stowed cargo which will be occupied or permeated by water in event of such goods being wholly submerged, as when a hold compartment containing a given volume of cargo is holed and open to the sea. Extremes under this caption may be seen in the case of sheets of tin or zinc slabs, one ton (2240 lbs.) of which is stowed in 7 cubic feet, as compared with a ton of bales of cork which stow at 187 cubic feet. While 15% of space occupied by the metal may be permeated by water, that entering the cork is 24% of its stowage volume. Hence, as a comparison of the buoyancy element in these respective cases, a resulting weight of about 330 lbs. per cubic foot for the zinc and 27 lbs. for the cork leaves us with little doubt as to which commodity offers less resistance to vessel's sinkage in event of cargo compartment concerned being flooded. As before noted, *p.* of average cargo space is taken as 60%.

PERMISSIBLE FACTOR,—LENGTH. *See* **Floodable l.** *in* LENGTH.

PERMIT. In U.S. customs usage, as provided for in Act of June 17, 1930, document issued by Collector to a shipmaster, granting his vessel permission to unload or load passengers, cargo, or baggage upon complying with certain requirements of customs regulations; as, *e.g., p.* to proceed to different ports with cargo from a foreign port (*19 U.S.C. 1443*); *p.* to unload goods and baggage at a U.S. port other than that which was vessel's original destination (*19 U.S.C. 1449*); *p.* to unload passengers, merchandise, or baggage, after formal entry at Customs has been made; special delivery of goods deemed necessary (*19 U.S.C. 1448*). **P. to Touch and Trade,** written permission issued by the master of a vessel engaged in fishing to trade at any foreign port, provided Customs regulations concerning delivery of manifests and entries of vessel and merchandise, as applying to vessels in the foreign trade, are complied with. (*46 U.S.C. 310*)

PERPENDICULAR. In connection with ship measurements, a line drawn perpendicular to the base line, or keel, for purpose of providing, at its intersection with a deck-line or water-line, a point of reference, as in defining vessel's *registered length* or *length between p's. Cf.* LENGTH. **After p.,** that coinciding with after side of stern-post at designed load water-line. Where there is no rudder-post, as in the case of a balanced or hanging rudder, it is the axis of rudder-stock. **Forward p.,** line vertical to ship's keel and coinciding with fore side of stem at uppermost strength deck, or that in merchant vessels usually termed *upper deck.* **Length between p's,** that of a vessel as measured between *forward* and *after p's; see* **L. between p's** *in* LENGTH. In smaller vessels of one-deck type, however, coinciding point of *forward p.* with fore side of stem at designed load water-line, from which *freeboard length* is measured, sometimes also is taken as reference point for *length between p's.* **Mid-** or **midship p.,** vertical line from keel midway between *forward* and *after p's.*

PERSEUS. (*Gr.*) A northern constellation lying south-east of the *Cassiopeia* group and north-east of *Andromeda.* It contains two navigational stars: *Mirfak* or *Marfak* (α Persei) of magnitude 1.9; and *Algol* (β Persei), remarkable for its periodic changes in brilliance from magnitude 2.2 to 3.5. A line from *Algol* westward to the bright *Capella* forms the base of an isosceles triangle having its apex at reddish *Aldebaran* 30° to SE. *Mirfak* lies 9½° N by E ½ E from *Algol.*

PERSONAL EQUATION. Also termed *personal error,* a consistent error in taking observations, as with a sextant, which is characteristic of an individual observer. Such error is determined and allowed for in astronomical work, such as observing transits of stars, and among navigators takes the form of measuring angles as greater or smaller than their true values, usually by a very small amount. Elimination of effect of such error in sextant observations, especially when an artificial horizon is used and a high degree of accuracy is desired, is effected by taking the mean of altitudes of stars lying nearly opposite each other in azimuth.

PERSONAL SALUTE. *See* SALUTE.

PERUVIAN CURRENT. Also called *Chilean* and *Humboldt; see* **Chilean C.** *in* CURRENT.

PETAL. A metal clip on a rail stanchion for securing a wire rope in use as a guard around a hatchway, sides of ship, etc.

PET-COCK. *See* COCK.

PETER-NET. (Named for the apostle) A local name in England for a fish-net which is made fast to shore at one end and anchored at the other.

PETER'S FISH. The haddock; so called from the dark spot behind each of its gills as being the traditional marks of Peter's thumb and forefinger on the occasion of catching a fish of this species to obtain from its mouth the tribute money referred to in *Matthew* 17:25–27.

PETREL. (Dim. of *Peter*) Sea bird of the family *Procellariidæ,* or that containing the albatrosses, fulmars, and shearwaters, of which several small dark-colored species of the North Atlantic called *stormy p's* or *Mother Carey's chickens* are well-known to sailors. The true *stormy p.* is classified as *Procellaria pelagica,* thus well named from its apparent delight to dodge and gambol about in a heavy raging sea. *Cf.* MOTHER CAREY. Others of the type are *Leach's p.* found in vicinity of American coast and *Wilson's p.,* a native of southern latitudes but often seen in North Atlantic in summer. They are long-winged and fly to great distances from land; feed on refuse from ships and on small surface-living creatures; and breed on rocky coasts, chiefly in temperate latitudes. **Diving p.,** a short-winged and short-tailed expert-diving sea bird resembling the *auk* in appearance, native to higher southern latitudes. It belongs to a sub-family of the group containing the pelicans.

PETTICOAT. *See* **M.-coat** *in* MAST.

PETTY. **P. average,** *see* AVERAGE. **P. officer,** *see* OFFICER.

PEWTER. (Alloy of tin and copper) Old British naval sailors' slang term for *prize-money.*

PHACT. (Also, by some authorities, PHAET) Star of magnitude 2.75 of the small southern group *Columba.* Catalogued as α *Columbæ,* it is located in right ascension 5 hrs. 38 min. and declination 34°

06' S., or 32° nearly due south of *Alnilam,* middle star of the three in *Orion's Belt.*

PHAROLOGY. (Gr. *pharos,* lighthouse; *logos,* discourse) Art or science which treats of directing the course of vessels and warning them of presence of dangers to navigation by means of light-signals, as from lighthouses, lightships, beacons, and buoys.

PHAROS. (*Gr.*) A lighthouse or beacon. One of the small towers resembling lighthouses from which, particularly in steel-built sailing-ships and older steam-vessels, the side lights were displayed; a light-tower. The word appears to have its source in the *Pharos* of Alexandria, Egypt, a white marble lighthouse or watch-tower built on an island of same name in the third century B.C. and often referred to as one of the *Seven Wonders* of the ancient world. *Cf.* LIGHTHOUSE.

PHASES OF THE MOON. *See* **M.'s phases** *in* MOON.

PHECDA. (Also, *Phacd* and *Phad*) Star γ *Ursæ Majoris,* or that marking the lower inner corner of the "bowl" in the *Big Dipper,* or *Plough,*—the group *Ursa Major.* It has a sidereal hour angle of 182° and declination of nearly 54° N., and magnitude 2.54.

PHŒNIX. (Gr. *Phoinix,* Phœnician, or father of the Phœnicians; also, a mythical bird of wondrous capabilities in ancient Egyptian lore) A small constellation in about 45° S. declination, between *Grus* and *Eridanus.* It contains one navigational star, *α Phœnicis,* called by the ancients *Nair-al-Zauraq* (Arabic = star of the boat), located in right ascension 0 hr. 24 min. and declination 42° 35′ S., and of magnitude 2.44. The star is "in range" with east side of the *Square of Pegasus* at 57½° to the southward.

PHOSPHOR BRONZE. An alloy of copper and tin in which is introduced a small amount of *phosphorus.* Its superior qualities of great hardness, elasticity, and toughness, together with its resistance to corrosive action by sea water, renders it specially desirable for use in many fittings aboard ship. Besides producing a satisfactory wire rope for certain special uses, it has been found first class material for propeller-shaft bearing-liners, rudder-gudgeon liners, roller bearings in sheaves, bevel gears in steering-gear, pump pistons, hydraulic rams, etc.

PHOSPHORESCENCE. Appearance of sea surface at night which gives general impression of a glowing light. Often attaining considerable brilliance, particularly in splashing waves or crests of breaking seas, it is said to be caused by oxidation of jellyfish and other animalculæ secretion when disturbed.

PICAROON. (*Sp.* = *rogue, thief, brigand*) A pirate or corsair; a piratical vessel. To prey upon or loot, as a wrecker; to cruise in search of prey, as a pirate.

PICKED PORTS. As designated in connection with chartering of vessels, especially in British use, certain ports selected from a number within a given coastal region as preferred for purpose of discharging a cargo; or, those at which port charges, labor conditions, and facilities admit of economical advantage to charterer, as compared with other destinations within the particular optional range.

PICKET BOAT. A police or naval boat doing duty as a guard or scout; a police-boat.

PICKINGS. Damaged portion of a baled product, especially cotton, which has been removed in order to render the bale or bales salable. Loss incurred by reduced marketable value of such goods. Also, shakings, or pieces of old rope, rope-yarns, oakum, etc.; junk rope or cordage fiber.

PICKLING. Process of removing mill scale from newly rolled plates by spraying with an acid solution or placing them in a bath of hydrochloric, sulphuric, or other acid mixed with water; then, after some hours or days, depending on strength of solution, plates are wire-brushed and washed down with fresh water. *See* MILL SCALE. *Pickling* of fish, chiefly herring and mackerel, is carried on extensively during the netting season off New England and eastern Canadian coasts, British Isles, Norway, and western Europe generally. Fish are split, cleaned, packed in salt, and later barreled with the addition of strong brine or "pickle."

PICUDA. (Sp. *picudo,* sharp) A local name for the *great barracuda; see* BARRACUDA.

PIECE. A part, portion, or section of anything, as specified by a combining term designating a unit in a vessel's structure, in a boat, sail, etc.; as, *hawse p.; rubbing-p.; lining-p.* A deck cannon; as, a *bow p.;* a *saluting p.* A portion of whale-blubber; as, a *blanket p.* **Independent p.,** in older ship construction, the main part of a beak-shaped projection at vessel's stem head, often terminating in the figurehead; also, *stem p.* **Stomach p.,** another name for the apron or stemson; *see* APRON.

PIER. A breakwater, mole, dock wall, or such protective structure in a harbor; a wharf or jetty used as a promenade, for bathing or boating purposes, etc. Especially in U.S., a large wharf or similar structure at which ships are berthed for transferring cargo or passengers. A support, usually of heavy masonry, on which a span of a bridge rests. **Floating p.,** a landing-stage usually consisting of pontoons or barges suitably decked, fitted with a single span bridge which connects it with shore and allows it to rise and fall with the tide. *Cf.* **L. apron** *and* **L.-stage** *in* LANDING. **P. crew,** or **p. men,** chiefly in U.S., longshoremen who transfer cargo to and from vessels berthed at a pier, and do all required handling of goods received at or delivered from such pier or wharf; also, *wharfmen;* in Britain, *quaymen.* **P.**

head, outer or projecting end of a pier, breakwater, dock wall, etc. **P.-head jump,** act of boarding a ship as she leaves a dock; hence, engagement of a crew member at the last minute before sailing, when the seaman is said to have *made a p.-head jump.* **P.-head line,** *see* **Pier-head l.** *in* LINE.[2]

PIERAGE. Charges payable by a vessel for use of a pier; also, *wharfage.*

PIERCER. A sailmaker's pricker, or pointed piece of steel having a bulbous handle, for piercing heavy canvas, as in marling a wire foot- or leech-rope to a sail.

PIG. An ingot or bulky piece of iron about three feet in length, as cast from the molten raw metal obtained from iron ore. The term is often also applied to copper and lead, but corresponding castings of rough metal generally are called *bars, bricks, blocks,* and *cakes,* in the respective cases of gold or silver, copper, tin, and zinc. Iron and lead *pigs* are used in some smaller vessels for *permanent ballast; see* PERMANENT. **P. boat,** naval colloquialism for a submarine; also, slang term for the now obsolete *whaleback* steamboat (*see* WHALEBACK); sometimes, *p. steamer.* **P'fish,** the *sailor's-choice,* a small *porgy* of U.S. coasts south of Cape Cod; any of several sea *grunts,* so named from their grunting noise when taken from the water, at least two of which are food fishes of Atlantic U.S. coast. Also, a local name for several different fishes of pig-like snout profile. **P. yoke,** old slang term for an octant or sextant.

PIGEON HOLE. *See* HOLE.

PIGTAIL. A short piece of thick rope; a rope's end,—especially an end of a lashing or that used in making a hitch or knot dangling or untidily showing.

PIKED WHALE. A small *finback* whale having an elongated snout, found in the North Atlantic; *cf.* WHALE.

PILE. A pointed timber or heavy stake driven into the earth, as in pier, cofferdam, or wharf construction; a mooring-post. *Piles* (or, collectively, *piling*) are made also of cylindrical-shaped or tubular iron and concrete. Also, *spile.* **P.-driver,** a machine for driving piles, commonly consisting of a vertical frame in which is raised and let fall a driving or hammering weight, sometimes called the *monkey.* In more modern use is a heavy automatic hammer operated by steam or compressed air and applied directly to top of pile. **P. fender,** one or more *p's* or a row of *piling* acting as a fender in absorbing shocks of vessels entering a slip, as commonly placed at ferry landings, at a pier end corner, alongside a dock, etc. Such piling is so driven as to provide a certain amount of "give," and so a desirable cushioning effect at point of impact. **P.**

moorings, clumps of piling, dolphins, or any arrangement of piles, alongside of which vessels are berthed; a mooring-rack (*see* MOORING). *Cf.* DOLPHIN. **Sett piling,** driven piles forming a foundation for launching-ways in a shipyard.

PILGRIM SHIP. Vessel engaged in carrying Mohammedan pilgrims from Persian and East Indian ports to *Jidda* (or *Jedda*), nearest port to *Mecca;* especially, one of the regular cargo liners in British Indian trade, which provide 'tween and weather deck space for this purpose. *Cf.* **Deck p.** *in* PASSENGER.

PILLAR. A column or post supporting a deck beam or series of beams, as commonly fitted below decks. It may be built of channel bars, riveted back to back, of riveted plating in tubular form, as a *built p.,* or may be solid or hollow in round bar form, in which last-named case often is loosely termed a *hold stanchion.* Depending upon vessel's size and construction, *p's* may be fitted at intermediate beams in the midship center line; may additionally be placed at each quarter length of beam; or, as in web and longitudinal framing, may be heavily built and widely spaced, particularly where design calls for minimum interference with cargo space in holds. **Diagonal p.,** *see* **D. stanchion** *in* DIAGONAL. **Middle-line p.,** one fitted in center fore-and-aft line of ship. **P. buoy,** chiefly in British usage, a buoy having a tall surmounting mark of cylindrical shape or like a frustum of a cone. It is placed at important points in channels or off coastal dangers. **P.-ladder,** a hold ladder, the rungs of which extend from a *p.* to an adjacent stanchion; a series of iron steps fitted on a built *p.* **Quarter p.,** one fitted midway between center line and ship's side. **Split p.,** a double or divided stanchion or *p.,* between which parts shifting-boards may be fitted.

PILLOW. A block, rest, or support, by which pressure is equalized or distributed; a *pillow-block,* or support for a propeller-shaft bearing; the *bowsprit p.* or bed at vessel's stem in which the spar rests.

PILOT. (Fr. *pilote;* Du. *piloot,* from *pilein,* to sound, and *loot,* a sounding-lead) A helmsman engaged to steer a vessel or boat. A person qualified or licensed, by reason of being familiar with certain navigational routes, channels, and local dangers of region concerned, to conduct or guide vessels into or out of a port, along a coast, or through restricted or narrow waters, as a canal or a strait. Only licensed *p's* may be obtained at all principal sea ports and, generally, only coastwise vessels of a nation are exempt from taking such *p.* In U.S., a licensed master or mate may be authorized to pilot coastwise vessels in specified local waters, his license being appropriately endorsed to that effect, but commercial vessels arriving and departing in the foreign trade must engage a *State p.,* or one duly licensed by state concerned at a principal port. In the former case, a mariner whose license is thus endorsed is often called a *Federal p.*, as distinguished from a *State p.* State *p's* are enrolled in a Pilots' Association which finds the boats, sets pilotage fees (subject to approval of port authority), and generally regulates salaries and requisite staff of *p's* to accommodate current traffic. A book, formerly known only as *Sailing Directions*, devoted to providing detailed navigational information for guidance of mariners in certain waters; as, *North Atlantic P.; Pacific Coast P.* To direct the course of, or guide, a vessel, as through a channel. **Bar p.**, one who conducts vessels over a bar, as at a river entrance, or other comparatively shallow depths at approaches to a harbor; generally a distinguishing term in localities where a *river p.* takes over upon vessel clearing a bar or channel entrance. **Exempt p.**, in Great Britain, one engaged by a vessel which is not compelled by law to take or carry a pilot in waters concerned by reason of being under limiting tonnage or by her master possessing a pilotage certificate. **Gyro-p.**, *see* GYRO. **Hobbler p.**, in England, an unlicensed *p.* whose services are limited to one or more smaller ports; *cf.* HOBBLER. **Ice p.**, *see* I.-master *in* ICE. **Mud p.**, a *river p.*; especially, one who conducts vessels in shallow muddy waters. **P. boat**, or **p. vessel**, any craft from which vessels are supplied with *p's* and which receives *p's* from outgoing vessels, such as is *on station* at a harbor entrance; any vessel cruising off shore for purpose of supplying a *p.* to coastwise or inward-bound vessels. The former nowadays usually are steam or powered craft, while the latter, especially in west European waters, often are small handy sailing-vessels of schooner, ketch, or yawl rig. **P. bread**, ship's biscuit or hard tack. **P. chart**, a track chart giving meteorological and hydrographic information valuable to navigators; specifically, those issued by U.S. Hydrographic Office for the North Atlantic, Central American waters, South Atlantic, North Pacific, South Pacific, and Indian oceans, and supplied to navigators at a small price, or free of charge to vessels co-operating in supplying observational data to publishing office. Excepting those for South Atlantic and South Pacific, which are issued quarterly, the charts cover prevailing weather conditions, storm data, etc., for each month, in addition to latest information on ice, derelicts, mines, expected total duration of fog, currents, and other items of interest to mariners. **P. cloth**, a sturdy sort of woollen cloth, usually blue in color, used as material for outer cold weather garments, as overcoats and reefers, by deck crew members. **P. cutter**, originally a *p. boat* of cutter rig; now also applied to a powered vessel of yacht-like design used in a pilot service. **P. fish**, so named because customarily accompanying or "piloting" a shark, a herring-like fish about 12 inches in length, characterized by its

five transverse colored bands; classified as *Naucrates ductor*. The name is also applied to a transverse-banded amber fish of warmer parts of the Atlantic. **P.-house**, enclosed space or house on ship's bridge sheltering the helmsman, navigational instruments, etc., and from which vessel's course may be directed, as in piloting. Also called *wheel-house*. **P. jack**, *see* **Union j.** *in* JACK. **P. jacket**, *see* **Pea j.** *in* JACKET. **P.'s lien**, claim against a vessel for pilotage fees; *cf.* **Maritime l.** *in* LIEN. **P's luff**, *see* **To make a half b.** *in* BOARD. **P. office**, room or building in which pilotage business of a sea port is conducted; pilots' headquarters. **P. skiff**, a fishing-boat thus locally termed on U.S. Carolinas coast and remarkable for its surf-riding capabilities. **P. waters**, such bodies of water in which the assistance of a *p.* is necessary. **P. whale**, the *blackfish, caaing-whale,* or *social whale,* of the North Atlantic; *see* BLACKFISH. **River p.**, one who steers or conducts vessels in river navigation. **Sea p.**, one who conducts vessels from or to sea; often used as a distinguishing term where *river p's* also are engaged; a *bar p.* (Also see *pilot* as used with caption word in BRANCH; COAST; COASTING; COMPULSORY; EXCITER; FLAG; LADDER; LUFF; SIGNAL)

PILOTING. Chiefly in U.S. usage, that branch of navigation, or practice of such, by which a vessel's position is determined by soundings, shore fog signals, or bearings of visible landmarks. Act of conducting a vessel through a channel, strait, etc., as by direction of a *pilot*.

PILOTAGE. Act or business of piloting; pilotship. Fee or compensation for a pilot's services. **Compulsory p.**, *see* COMPULSORY PILOTAGE. **P. authority**, body having local jurisdiction over appointing pilots, with control and regulation of *pilotage* generally.

PIN. A bar, bolt, peg, or such piece of metal or wood, used for joining or securing parts, as an *anchor p.*, a *cotter p.*; for holding something in position, as a *block p.*, a *thole p.*; or for sighting or other instrumental purposes, as a *shadow p.*; a *vane p.* To secure or fasten with a *p.* **P.-rack**, that part of the *p.-rail* in way of a sailing-vessel's lower rigging for holding the series of belaying-pins used for securing various units of running rigging; any piece of timber, metal band on a mast, etc., fitted to receive belaying-pins. **P.-rail**, in sailing-vessels, a stout hardwood rail fitted along ship's bulwarks parallel to, and about a foot below, the bulwark rail. It is rounded on its projecting edge and fitted with necessary holes to receive belaying-pins for running gear. (For *pins* designated by caption word, see ANCHOR; BLOCK; BELAY; CHECK; JACK; SHACKLE; SHADOW; TACK; THOLE; TOGGLE)

PINCH. To sail as close to the wind as possible, or with weather leech or luff of sails lifting; as in *"Pinch her well!"*, an order to the helmsman to steer to this end, sometimes termed in boat-sailing *pinching the wind*.

PINDJAJAP. (Malay, *penjagap*) A Malayan cargo vessel having two or three masts rigged with lug or lateen sails and projecting upper works over stem and stern. From 50 to 60 feet in length and fine-lined, craft of this type formerly were preferred in the world-famed piratical activities of the Malay archipelago.

PINE. Timber of any tree of the genus *Pinus*, usually very durable and straight-grained, much used in shipbuilding. Included in this family are the *bull*, or *California yellow p.*, used for framing and heavy decking; *Oregon p.*, for masts, beams, frames, and heavy planking (*see* DOUGLAS SPRUCE); *white p.*, for interior finishing, pattern-making, light decking, etc.; and *yellow p.*, also called *hard p., pitch p., Georgia p., long-leaf p.*, for heavy frame timbers, decking, machinery beds, and heavy ship-yard work. Of the *yew* family, or *Taxaceæ*, is a beautiful wavy-grained, light yellow, aromatic wood of Tasmania, called *Huon p.* which is much prized for boat-building. **P. rosin,** *see* ROSIN. **P. tar,** *see* TAR.

PINK. Originally, a small Dutch fishing-vessel characterized by a full fore-body narrowing to an almost pointed stern with an overhanging false counter. Later, any vessel having a narrow over-hanging stern, or *pink-sterned* type. The extinct schooner-rigged *chebacco-boat* of early New England days was a kind of *pink;* also, *pinkie* or *pinkey*. *Cf.* **Chebacco-b.** *in* BOAT.

PINNACE. (Fr., *pinasse*) Formerly, a large boat or light vessel, usually of lug or schooner rig and often propelled by oars, used as a tender to large vessels or men-o'-war. In British navy, a pulling or powered carvel-built boat over 30 feet in length; the *steam p.* In older merchantmen and sailing men-o'-war, the *p.* was next in size to ship's long-boat or galley. A workboat or tender included in complement of boats on a surveying-vessel, yacht, lightship, etc.; a police boat.

PINTLE. A pin, bolt, hook, etc., upon which any-thing pivots; specifically, one of the vertical pins or bolts on forward edge of a rudder, which fits into its corresponding *gudgeon* on the stern or rudder post, thus forming a hinging unit on which rudder is turned; a *rudder-p.* **Bearing-p.,** lowermost *p.* of a rudder, or that usually resting in lowest projecting part, or heel, of rudder-post or stern-post in steel vessels. Ordinarily, it supports entire weight of rudder, its lower end being rounded and borne by a steel hemispherical removable bearing-piece as a means of minimizing friction; also called *bottom, dumb,* and *heel p.* **Fitted p.,** as commonly found in ordinary ships' rudders, a removable *p.* usually tapered and drawn upward, or snugged home in its

socket by a heavy nut. **Locking p.,** an upper *p.* hav-ing a forged or turned head on its lower end to pre-vent rudder from being lifted by force of the sea or by heavy pitching of vessel. **P. boss,** cast or forged projecting sockets on forward edge of a rudder for receiving a *fitted p.;* also called *rudder-snug*. **P. chain,** that usually fitted in a bridge telegraph or in some steering-gears of smaller vessels for working on sprocket wheels. Its links are formed of two side pieces and a crossing *pintle* common to ad-jacent links. **P. score,** in a boat's rudder, the *gullet-ing,* or part cut away below and in way of each *p.* to allow rudder to be readily shipped or unshipped. **Solid p.,** a *rudder-p.* cast or forged as part of a rud-der arm; found only in boats and small vessels.

PINWHEELING. American term for turning a twin screw vessel short around by going ahead on one propeller and astern on the other; half ahead on one screw, full astern on the other, usually turns vessel within smallest possible maneuvering area.

PIPAGE. Pipes collectively, or system of piping; especially, those used for cargo in an oil tank vessel.

PIPE. A tube or hollow body, usually of metal, for conducting a fluid; a conduit. A boatswain's whistle used for "piping" or calling attention to verbal commands; *cf.* **B.'s pipe** *in* BOATSWAIN. To call by means of a *boatswain's p.* To install a *p.* or *p's.;* as, to *p.* the hold for a steam fire-smothering-system. A heavy pipe-like opening in a bulwark or ship's side for passage and seating of a hawser or a cable; as, a *mooring-p.;* a *hawse p.;* a similar fitting for leading chain cable; as, a *chain-locker p.;* a *navel p., spill p.,* or *deck p.* **Bilge-discharge p., bilge-suction p.;** *see* BILGE. **Eduction p.,** exhaust line from low pressure cylinder of a reciprocating en-gine which conducts used steam to condenser; archaic term for *exhaust p.* **Exhaust p.,** any *p.* con-ducting waste or used steam to atmosphere or to a condenser; a *p.* carrying off waste gases from an in-ternal combustion engine. **Expansion p's,** in a re-frigerating system, those in which ammonia or a similar agent changes into a gas upon release of pressure, drawing heat in the process from the sur-rounding atmosphere and erections. **Internal feed-p.,** that leading from the feed valve to interior of boiler. It carries feed water direct into hot water in boiler, so averting contact with steam or heated parts of boiler. **Internal steam-p.,** a perforated *p.,* situated in steam space of boiler and leading to main steam valve, installed for separation of any water raised with, and held in suspension by, the steam. **To p. down,** in navy parlance, to observe silence, as in retiring hour for sleep; to cease talk-ing; to dismiss from muster, as by bos'n's *p.* **To p. the side,** to call by bo's'n's *p.* (or boatswain's *call*) a muster of "side boys" at ship's gangway to formally receive a visiting officer. Two to eight boys, depending on visitor's rank, stand facing each other and, as officer passes between them, at the *p.* note hands are brought smartly to the *salute.* Other navies have a similar custom to above U.S.N. procedure. **P. tunnel,** in larger vessels, usually tubular and in the midship fore-and-aft line, a protective space for bilge, ballast, and other lines extending from engine-room to holds, between inner bottom and shell plating. To **p. up,** to increase in force; said of the wind; to begin a chantey or song. **Steam waste-p.,** or **escape p.,** that carrying off steam escaping from safety valve of a boiler. It usually is fitted to lead up to top of smoke-stack, on after side of latter; also, *blow-off p.*

PIRACY. Depredations on property, pillage, or robbery conducted on the high seas in defiance of all constituted authority or law. Generally, it also includes depredations on land property where base of such felonious acts or operations is on board ship, whether on the high seas or elsewhere.

PIRAGUA. A Spanish word, borrowed from the Caribs, designating a dugout canoe; especially, one which has been longitudinally halved with planks inserted to form a flat bottom and to build up its pointed ends. A two-masted sailing barge fitted with lee boards; also called a *pirogue.* Basically, the word *pirogue,* designating also a dugout canoe or any canoe-like boat, is identical with *piragua.*

PIRATE. One who practices piracy; a vessel armed for the purpose of pursuing piratical adventures; a corsair; a sea-rover. *Cf.* PIRACY. **Land p.,** a swindler who preys upon sailors ashore; also, *land shark.* **P. bird,** the *gull-chaser,* or *shua; see* JAEGER. **P. flag,** the *jolly roger* or banner bearing a skull and cross-bones; the black flag, or "hangman's ribbon," "of frequent fancy in far-fetched fiction told."

PIRAYA. The ferocious water-gangster called by Tupi Indians of the Amazon *piranha* (pron. *pir-aṅ-ya*), but generally better known as *caribe.* The fish has a deep compressed body with a keel-like rudder-fin below and forward of its tail. *See* CARIBE. Also spelled *pirai.*

PISCES. (*L. = Fishes*) A constellation southward and eastward of the *Square of Pegasus,* containing no navigational stars. The so-called *First Point of Aries,* or *vernal equinoctial point,* is located in this group. *Cf.* ARIES.

PISCIS AUSTRALIS. (*L. = Southern Fish*) A southern constellation, also sometimes called *Piscis Austrinus,* containing the navigational star *Fomalhaut* (α *Piscis Australis* or α *Piscis Austrini*) of magnitude 1.29; *see* FOMALHAUT.

PISTOL. As used in throwing parachute flares or signals of colored balls or stars of fire, a firing-piece of similar construction and shape as that of the common single-shot pistol, but having a large caliber barrel; *cf.* PARACHUTE FLARE and VERY'S SIGNALS.

PISTON. The sliding-piece which is moved in a cylinder by fluid pressure, as in a steam engine, or is moved against a fluid pressure, as in a pump. Usually included with a *p.* is the *p. rod,* which is connected to center of *p.* and slides to and fro through center of the cylinder head. *P. rod* joins a *connecting-rod* in producing rotary motion as in an engine, or may act directly through a pump cylinder-head in working a *plunger* or *pump p.* **Clearance of p.,** distance between *p.* and cylinder head at extreme limit of *p. stroke,* or end of its *travel.* **P. eye,** hole in center of *p.* in which *p. rod* is secured. **P. guide,** also called *tail rod,* extension of a *p. rod* through center of cylinder head, or that end of cylinder opposed to working end of piston. **P. pump,** *see* PUMP. **P. ring,** close-fitting metal ring around periphery of *p.* for preventing leakage of fluid between *p.* and cylinder wall. **P.-rod crosshead,** part at which the connecting-rod joins *p. rod.* The connecting-rod delivers cranking motion to crankshaft, being "hinged" to end of *p.* in the *crosshead.* **Travel of p.,** distance *p.* moves between extreme limits of its stroke.

PIT, ASH. In a steam boiler, space below furnace bars for receiving ashes.

PITCH.[1] Dark-colored residue obtained in process of distillation of coal tar, wood tar, petroleum, etc., consisting chiefly of hydrocarbons; or a similar viscous substance found in its natural state and known as *asphalt.* Any bituminous mixture of asphalt, resin, balsam, or vegetable pitches, commonly called *marine glue,* of which several patented kinds are on the market, principally used for paying *deck planking* seams after calking. In wooden vessels, *rosin,* or the residue from distilled turpentine, and *asphalt* in about equal parts commonly were melted together as a securing agent for oakum in calked seams of *outside planking.* The hot mixture was applied to seams, or *payed,* by means of a long stiff brush. To *pay,* or pour, molten *p.* into calked planking seams; to smear or coat a wood surface with a hot preservative, as *p.* or any bituminous mixture, coal tar, etc., which formerly was common treatment for ships' bottoms before copper sheathing was fitted thereon. *Cf.* PAY[2]. **P. boat,** a vessel or boat in which *p.* is heated for melting as a precaution against fire on board vessel concerned with the process. **P.-payer,** a kind of ladle for lifting hot *p.* from a *p. pot* and pouring or *paying* it into deck seams. It usually has a cone-shaped end through a hole in the apex of which *p.* is poured as it is run along each seam. **P. pine,** any pitch-yielding species of pine, generally hardest and heaviest of the family; *cf.* PINE.

PITCH.[2] Distance a propeller would advance in a single revolution if turning in a solid. *P.* varies according to design of screw in meeting conditions of available horsepower, economical speed, build, type, and draft of vessel. As a basis for determining ship's speed by revolutions of propeller, *p.* times revolutions is reduced by a percentage known as *slip; see* SLIP. *P.* of a paddle-wheel is the distance between centers of floats measured on a circle passing through those points. In riveting, *p.* is the spacing between centers of consecutive holes, as usually reckoned in diameters of rivets employed. For watertight work, *p.* is from $3\frac{1}{2}$ to 5 diameters; oiltight seams, $3\frac{1}{2}$ to 4; other work, 6 to 8 diameters. **Adjustable p. propeller,** as distinguished from a screw having fixed blades, one fitted with an arrangement whereby blades may be turned to any *p.* desired while propeller-shaft is revolving. In a recent gas-engine installation, blades may be set to produce astern motion or in neutral position in which thrust is nil, without manipulation of main engine. **P. chain,** same as *p. chain* in PINTLE. **P. ratio,** that of a propeller in which *p.* is expressed as a multiple of propeller's diameter; thus a *p. ratio* of 1.4 means that *p.* of the screw is 1.4 times diameter of a circumscribed circle through tips of blades. Generally, a ratio of 1.2 is considered a value for satisfactory efficiency in merchant vessels; about .3 for highly-loaded tugboat propellers, and the other extreme of 2.0 for those of high-speed motorboats.

PITCH.[3] To plunge or heave, as the alternate lift and fall of each end of a vessel in a head sea. Also, in the sense of loosening or tossing something, or causing it to carry away, by such motion, a vessel is said, *e.g.,* to *p. her topmasts overboard;* to *p. her foremast by the board.* **P'ing period,** as with *rolling,* a vessel's period of making a single "dip and heave" has a constant value for a given distribution of weights on board, with the difference that *rolling period* is affected by a change in vertical arrangement of weight, while *pitching period* varies with that of longitudinal distribution. A vessel comparatively heavily loaded toward her ends will have a lengthened period and a consequent sluggish rise or deeper plunge in head-on sea conditions, with, in a deeply laden hull, attending heavy water shipped over the bows. Conversely, she will act more lively with weights on board concentrated more toward her mid-length and *pitching period* will be lessened, since duration of period varies directly as moment of inertia of the mass about midship transverse axis.

PITCHPOLE. A boat is said to *p.,* or to take a *p. tumble,* in capsizing end over end, as in running before a heavy breaking sea or a surf.

PITOMETER LOG. *.See* LOG.

PITTING. Irregular corrosive effect of electrolytic or galvanic action appearing as small cavities in iron or steel surfaces; more commonly occurring in shell-plating "between wind and water," or, in cargo vessels, between load and light water-lines. It also is often observed in metal in vicinity of storage batteries, electric winches, etc., and, in electrically driven ships, may appear in almost any part of the hull. It is recalled that a certain turbo-electric vessel suffered continuous corrosion of her fore peak shell-plating rivets in an unvarying area at one side of the stem, as a result of this curious form of attack. Another example indicating the presence of a pernicious current was noted in *pitting* of steel engine-room skylight covers. One and the same corner of each cover in a row of four was badly corroded with no appearance of any attack elsewhere on the metal. It was concluded that the source of this mischief lay in the radio operator's storage batteries, about ten feet from nearest skylight cover.

PIVOTING. In shipbuilding parlance, term given that stage in endwise launching of a vessel during which after part of hull is entirely water-borne, while forward end remains supported by the ways. Chief aim in the launching operation is to provide, as far as practicable, a constant burden by the *fore poppet* throughout period in which hull is partly-borne. Also termed *lifting,* called *pivoting* from the fact of vessel vertically "hinging" at bearing-point in the fore poppet. **P. point,** that in the fore-and-aft line about which a vessel turns in swinging under her helm. Its position varies with hull form, draft, and distribution of weights on board, but in vessels of average type may be taken as at one-fourth to one-third ship's length from her stem. **Pivot span,** that in a bridge, mounted to horizontally swing open for passage of vessels.

PLAICE. *See* FLOUNDER.

PLAIN. Ordinary; simple; without embellishment; as, a *p. scarf;* a *p. whipping.* **P. chart,** one laid out on Mercator's projection; chiefly so termed as distinguishing it from the less commonly used *gnomonic, polyconic,* etc. (Not to be confused with *plane chart; see* PLANE) **P.-laid,** designating stranded cordage in which the strand-yarns are laid left-handed and strands laid right-handed, or advance from left to right in the finished rope; usually applied to a rope of three strands, laid as above, and commonly termed *hawser-laid; cf.* **Hawser-l.** *in* LAID. **P. sail,** ordinary working sails, collectively, as distinguished from special canvas spread in light winds, such as upper staysails, studding-sails, skysails, etc.

PLAN. Representation or drawing on a plane, as a map or chart of a harbor. As distinguished from a chart, properly a depiction of a local area without regard to rotundity of the earth, *i.e.,* such area being considered a plane. A diagram or drawing of a structure, a surface, etc., as that of a particular part of, or space in, a vessel; as, *half-breadth p.; floor p.* **Capacity p.,** that showing spaces for cargo in a vessel, giving cubic capacities of each, measurements of hatches, and deadweight corresponding to vessel's draft. **Deck p.,** scale drawing showing layout and arrangement of deck planking or plating, hatchways, partitions, alleyways, ventilators, etc., on a particular deck. **Docking p.,** that showing form of ship's bottom at several cross-sections of hull, location of propellers, sea connections, and all necessary information for use of *dry-dock* operators in preparing bilge and keel blocks for reception of vessel in dock. **Half-breadth p.,** that showing longitudinal half of vessel's hull as viewed from above, with various water-lines, buttock lines, deck lines, and frame stations. **Profile p.,** also termed *sheer p.,* projection of a vessel's lines on a vertical plane representing that longitudinally dividing vessel in halves. It shows frame stations, buttock lines, deck lines, bulkheads, side openings, with various measurement data for use in actual construction of vessel. The term *profile draft,* on same projection as *profile plan,* usually refers to a depiction of interior details, as fittings, hatchways, pillars, ventilators, etc., with dimensions of materials. **Sail p.,** drawing representing a side view of ship's sails, masts, spars, and standing rigging, with details of measurements, particularly of sails. A *rigging p.* usually supplements or accompanies the *sail p.* **Sheer p.,** *see* **Profile p.** (Also see *plan* designated by caption word in BODY; FLOOR; STOWAGE)

PLANE. A surface, imaginary or real, having an uninterrupted zero curvature; as, *p. of the ecliptic.* A line representing a standard level or height; as, a *tidal p. of reference.* Short for *airplane* or *seaplane.* Having the properties of a *p.;* level; even. **P. chart,** one representing a local area without regard for curvature of earth's surface; a plan, as of a bay, harbor, etc. **P. sailing,** *see* SAILING. **P. scale,** a Gunter's scale; a flat scale or graph from which may be taken fractional parts of inches, centimeters, etc., values of chords, tangents, sines, etc. **P. table,** as used in hydrographic surveying, a device essentially consisting of a portable drawing table, oriented by means of a compass, on which coast-line details are laid out on the working chart. **Sea-p.,** an airplane designed to take off from and descend upon the water. **Water p.,** *see* WATER.

PLANET. (Gr. *planetes,* wandering; from its apparent continuous change of position in the heavens) Any celestial body revolving about, and receiving its light from, the sun; *esp.* one of the so-called *primary p's,* named, in order from the sun, *Mercury, Venus, Earth, Mars, Jupiter, Saturn, Uranus, Neptune,* and *Pluto.* Satellites, or moons, as those of *Jupiter, Saturn, Uranus,* and *Neptune,* with our own faithful attendant, are termed *secondary p's. Mercury* and *Venus,* whose orbits lie between Earth and Sun, are called *inferior,* or *inner, p's;* those farther from the sun, *superior,* or *outer, p's.* Periods of revolution about "old Sol" vary with

distance of *p.* from that body, from Mercury's 88 days to Pluto's circuit of 90,470 days. A *p.* shines with a steady light (reflected sunlight) by which it may be distinguished from a fixed star. The latter shows a more or less twinkling light. Four only of the *major p's* are used in nautical astronomy, *viz., Venus, Mars, Jupiter,* and *Saturn,* chiefly for the reason that they are easily recognized by their outstanding brilliance. Incidentally, the recently discovered *Pluto* (1930) can not be seen by the naked eye, its magnitude being about 14. **Minor p's,** a large group of small planets whose orbits lie between those of *Mars* and *Jupiter; see* ASTEROIDS. **Major p's,** the nine *primary p's.*

PLANETARY ABERRATION. *See* ABERRATION.

PLANETARY HOIST. A kind of differential endless-chain hoisting-purchase or tackle having an epicyclic train in its upper block. It is commonly used in ships' engine-rooms and repair yards for lifting heavy machinery parts, propeller-blades, rudders, etc.

PLANISPHERE. Representation on a plane of the circles of a sphere; especially, a polar projection of the heavens for use in locating positions of stars and planets, with adjustable appendages for indicating part of celestial sphere visible in any given latitude, time of meridian passage, rising, and setting of stars, etc.

PLANK. A dressed or sawn piece of timber, usually, in U.S., of 1½ to 4 inches in thickness and at least 6 inches in width, although in boat-building side and bottom *p's* (*planking*) may be as thin as one-half inch, and, in shipbuilding, *deck-p's* may be of such cross-section as 3 by 4 inches, 4 by 5, or 3 by 6 inches; and hold ceiling *p's* of square section 4 to 6 inches. Depending upon size and type of vessel, with consideration of best timber available, planks comprising the outer skin (planking) of wooden ships varies generally from 2½ to 4 inches in thickness with widths of 6″ to 8″. Oak and teak timber used in former days for this purpose, particularly in sides of war-vessels often measured 5 by 10 inches with greater thickness in the *wales,* or *bends; cf.* BEND. **Boundary p.,** a deck margin *p.; see* **M. plank** *in* MARGIN. **P. keel,** in some types of boat construction, keel composed of a narrow *p.* secured to and laid over another of greater width. The rabbet formed by difference in width of *p's* houses lower edge of each garboard strake. **P.-sheer,** in wooden vessels, broad timber or *p.* laid along upper deck beams and covering the frame heads, its outer edge trimmed flush with surface of outside planking. Also called *covering-board,* only those frames which form bulwark stanchions pass through it. The *p. sheer* corresponds to the *deck stringer-plate* in steel-built vessels. To **walk the p.,** to walk outward on a *p.* laid across the bulwark rail until it is over-balanced and one falls into the deep. This was a method of disposing of captives or offenders practised by pirates of old; hence, to be compelled to resign or withdraw from office. (Also see *p.* as designated by and under BILGE; BOTTOM; DAGGER; DUMPING; FUTTOCK; KING; LAUNCHING (*L. ways*); MARGIN; NIB; FLOOR; SPIKE; TIE)

PLANKAGE. (Fr. *plancage*)   A form of port charge, once customary in several western European ports, nominally or actually based on use by merchant vessels of planks, chutes, skids, etc.

PLANKING.   Planks collectively, as forming a deck, outside or inside covering over a vessel's frames, or that forming the shell of a boat. Act of fitting planks, as in building a vessel or boat. **Anchor-stock p.,** consists of planks of equal length, each having one straight edge, the other tapering from mid-length toward each end, or similar in shape to profile view of an old-fashioned anchor's wooden stock. Formerly fitted as heavy outside *p.* in war-vessels, in this system a complete strake is made up of two rows of planks by interfitting the tapered sides, butts occurring at widest part of each plank. The *top-and-butt* system is a variation of this procedure, widest part of planks being at one-third length instead of at mid-length. In both systems, butts of successive strakes are staggered as desired. **Bottom p.,** *see* BOTTOM. **Carvel p.,** *see* CARVEL. **Clinker p.,** *see* CLINKER-BUILT. **Cross p.,** that laid as bottom *p.* at right angles to fore-and-aft line, as in some V-bottom or flat-bottom craft. **Diagonal p.; diagonal and longitudinal p.,** someimes referred to as the *Ashcroft* system, or that used with double-layer *p.* in boat-building; *see* DIAGONAL. **Diminishing p.,** *see* DIMINISHING. **Double fore-and-aft p.,** as fitted to pleasure craft, two layers of thin *p.* laid longitudinally, so that outside seams line up with centers of inside layer. Usually a covering of muslin or cotton duck is laid in thick paint or varnish over inner layer before fitting outside *p.* The system provides great longitudinal strength, calking is eliminated, and lighter transverse framing required than with ordinary single *p.* **Garboard p.,** in a wooden vessel's bottom, strake of *p.* next the keel with several strakes adjoining,—from 2 to 6 or 7,— of greater thickness than ship's side *p.* **Herring-bone p.,** *see* HERRING-BONE. **Inside p.,** that constituting *ceiling,* or inner *p.,* laid on inside of frames in a wooden or composite vessel. **Outside p.,** that forming outer skin or surface of a wooden vessel's hull. **Ribband p.,** method of supplementing *carvel p.* by fastening ribbands or thin battens on inside of *p.* to cover each seam. Ribbands run continuously, frames being notched over them. **Sewn p.,** a British method of "planking" small light craft by securing layers of thin mahogany with copper wire passed through holes made in the frames. A few variations of the system are in use, but all fashion boat's shell

by strips or layers of suitable light wood, approximately square in section, fastened or "sewn" together as noted and/or to the craft's ribs. **Spline p.,** as found in some larger wood-built racing-yachts, a method of obtaining water-tightness and a smooth outside surface by inserting snug-fitting *splines,* or thin strips, of mahogany or teak over the calking in each seam. Splining is glued in place. **Strip p.,** that in which a boat's shell is built up by a succession of narrow wood strips appropriately tapered from amidships toward each end. Paint or marine glue is set in each seam and each strip is nailed to its next below, working upward from keel. When smoothed off, this *planking,*—if it may so be termed, —presents a neater appearance than the ordinary *carvel* system, but is difficult to repair in event of holing. **Swept,** or **sprung, p.,** system in which *deck-p.* is laid to follow sweep of vessel's side fore-and-aft, plank ends being *nibbed* in a center-line plank termed *king-plank;* see **K.-plank** *in* KING. **Top-and-butt p.,** a variation of *outside p.* fitted *anchor-stock fashion; see* **Anchor-stock p. Treble p.,** a three-layer system used in pleasure boats and some larger lifeboats of passenger ships. It consists of two flush-laid layers of thin *p.* running diagonally and approximately at right angles to each other, topped by a layer laid fore-and-aft as in the *carvel* system. In addition to perfect water-tightness, the comparatively great longitudinal strength obtained by this method allows considerable reduction in framing material and consequent weight of boat, as compared with ordinary *single-p.* system.

PLANKSHEER.   Same as *plank-sheer; see* PLANK.

PLANKTON.   Collective term for minute organisms of plant and animal life floating in the sea; especially at or near the surface; but also includes slow-moving life, as jelly-fishes and salpas. Opposed to *benthos,* or fauna and flora of the sea-bottom, *p.* forms the principal and often the sole diet of thousands of fishes and sea-mammals. Countless myriads of dead and dying creatures of this order drop downward each minute and through the ages these have built the "carpet on the ocean floor."

PLAT.   Archaic term for any flat *sennit,* or small cordage made of braided or plaited rope-yarns, chiefly used as chafing material or robands for heavy sails; also *plait. Cf.* SENNIT.

PLATE.   A flat, or nearly flat, piece of solid material relatively thin in measurement; especially, iron or steel sheets of uniform thickness, or a relatively thin casting not necessarily of one thickness throughout. Generally, the mild steel plates used in modern ship construction are from three-eighths to three-fourths inch in thickness, two to five feet in width, and from fifteen to thirty feet in length, depending on size and type of vessel considered. As distinguished from *sheets, plates* of metal are

PLATE   402

greater in thickness, the dividing line usually being taken as one-eighth inch. With few exceptions, the numerous *plates* in a modern vessel are identified by a combining term indicating the location or use of each; as, *armor-p., baffle-p., bracket p., bed p., deck p.* As applied to precious metals, especially silver in coin, the term appears to have its source in *plata,* the Spanish word for silver; hence, also, gold, platinum, and silver in ingot or other form. *Cf.* **Plate f.** *in* FLEET. To overlay with *p's;* as, to *p. a ship's side.* **Anchor-p.,** in wooden vessels, a protective *p.* on each bow to prevent damage to planking by anchors; *p.* on a billboard or forecastle rail for a similar purpose. **Apron-p.,** *see* **A.-plate** *in* APRON. **Bow-p.,** any of the shell plates in bows of a vessel. **Bow-chock p.,** that fitted as a foundation for a mooring-chock on either bow. **Bed-p.,** also **base-p.,** casting in *p.* form constituting the base or foundation of an engine, winch, etc. **Bulb p.,** narrow structural *p.* having a bulb or rounded swelling along one of its edges; used for low hatch coamings, built-up beams, stiffeners, stringers, etc. **Checkered p.,** so named for its small squares forming a roughened surface, that laid for providing a foothold during vessel's motion, as in an engine-room platform, ladder-steps, stair-landings, etc. **Dash p.,** that fitted in a steam boiler to receive impact of feed water. **Diaphragm p.,** as a means of compensating for a break in longitudinal continuity, as in the case of a raised quater-deck in smaller vessels, one of several web or deep *p's.* extending for several feet between, and secured longitudinally to, overlapping ends of main and quarter decks, these decks being considered, for structural strength purposes, a single through member in the hull. By extension, the term also is applied to a *doubling-p.* securing and uniting the overlapping or passing ends of the sheer strake at such interruption in the structure. **Doubling-p.,** an additional *p.* secured to side of another for strengthening or stiffening purposes; sometimes, a heavy *butt-strap.* **Dressing p.,** also called *bending-block, bending-floor, bending-table, bending-platform, furnace-slab, leveling-block.* See **Bending-s.** *in* SLAB. **Furnaced p.,** in shipbuilding, any *p.* which is heated in order to be fashioned into a required shape; as, *propeller-boss p's; oxter p's;* and others in extreme ends of ship which demand such treatment. **Hand-hole p.,** steel cover for a boiler *hand-hole.* It is a round or oval *p.* seated against inside of hole's rim and set up by a bolt and nut in a yoke or bridge-dog, the latter spanning hole on outside. **Manger p.,** vertical *p.* for diverting water overboard from forecastle head; *see* BREAK-WATER. Also, that forming a partition in a bin in which fish are stowed, as in a trawler. **Nose p.,** a protective strip or narrow piece of plating fitted to fore side of the wooden stem of a boat; a *p.* forming an upper continuation of a ship's stem and rounded to present a convex surface as a protection

against severe chafing of mooring-lines leading across the bow. **Oxter p.,** one of sharp curvature covering junction of shell-plating immediately above stern- or rudder-post. It usually is furnaced and molded into shape. **P. collar,** *see* **H. plate** *in* HORSESHOE. **P. hanger,** in ship construction, one who sets plates in their proper position on the frames, so that the *plater,* or *bolter-up,* may secure them in preparation for riveting. **P. keel,** *see* KEEL. **Rubbing-p.,** any *p.* or strip of plating fitted to a vessel's side to take up chafe against a pier, dock-wall, wharf, etc.; strip of *p.* secured along lower surface of a *keel-p.* to afford protection to latter in grounding; any *p.* used as a protection against chafing, such as that on a wood deck in way of heavy blocks or a sheet of iron on a cargo chute or skid. **Spirketting p.,** another name for an **Apron-p.;** *see* APRON. **Stringer p.,** strake of plating which strengthens connections between beams and frames, stiffens shell-plating in way of beams, and forms outside strake in deck-plating. It is an important member in providing longitudinal strength to a vessel. **Zinc p.,** a small slab or *p.* of solid *zinc,* usually one-half to one inch in thickness, appropriately placed in a steam condenser, in vicinity of sea-valves, on a stern-post, rudder-post, etc., to take up corrosion from galvanic action generated by bronze or brass through the sea-water and attacking iron or steel in the vicinity.

PLATER. In shipbuilding, one who sets in place, fairs, and secures plates and other units in the hull preparatory to riveting or welding; also called *bolter-up* and, especially in U.S., a *p. erector.* Outside *p's* are those concerned with shell-plating and vessel's outer surface generally; *inside p's,* those engaged in interior work, as deck and bulkhead plating, etc. **Marking-off p.,** one who marks material as required by drawings, molds, or patterns or various parts of a steel hull. He usually is engaged in a special line of work, such as framing, decks, tank tops, etc. **P.'s squad,** group of *p's* and their helpers who set up and prepare plates and various sections for the riveters; *cf.* PLATER.

PLATFORM. Partial deck composed of detachable plates, usually checkered or otherwise surface-roughened to provide a foothold, as the working deck in a boiler- or an engine-room. Any partial deck or specially situated grating, floor, or walk; as, *gangway p., tunnel p.; winch p.* **Compass p.,** raised stand on which is mounted a standard or special compass (*magnetic*) and which affords foot or walking space about the latter for an observer in taking bearings, etc. Also, topside of a wheel-house, chart-house, etc., for same purpose. **Gangway p.,** a landing surface, usually of grating form, at head or bottom end of an accommodation ladder, or gangway. **Grating p.,** one of a number of steel-rod gratings or walks appropriately placed in an engine-room or stokehold for providing access to various machinery parts, doors, etc., at different heights. **Landing p.,** *see* **Brow l.; L. apron; L.-place; L.-stage;** *in* LANDING. **Leadsman's p.,** small wooden stand fitted to ship's rail for purpose of giving standing-room outside and clear of all obstacles when swinging the *blue pigeon.* **P. deck,** a partial deck laid on a ship's hold beams. In U.S. navy terminology, a partial deck below the lowest complete deck; "where there are two or more partial decks below the lowest complete deck, the one immediately below the lowest complete deck shall be called the *first platform;* the next shall be called the *second platform,* and so on." **P. sling,** *see* SLING.

PLATING. Arrangement of plates, or plates collectively, forming a deck, vessel's outer surface or skin, a bulkhead, etc.; as, *deck p.; shell p.; house p.* Shipbuilding material in plate form; as, *armor p.; checkered p.; galvanized p.* Act or process of laying or fitting plates, as in building a vessel, a boiler, etc. Thickness of *p.* for a vessel's sides and bottom *(shell),* decks, bulkheads, inner bottom, superstructure, and bulwarks is regulated by the classification society's rules, or according to *Lloyd's second, longitudinal,* or *p. numeral; cf.* **L. numerals** *in* LLOYD's. It is general practice to lay *p.* with overlapping seams, *i.e.,* with edges of strakes *(rows of p.)* lapping over their next below or outer neighbor, as in what is termed *clinker-laid p.,* often seen in shell and deck *p.;* or, as now commonly favored for heavier cargo and passenger vessels, in the *raised-and-sunken,* or *in-and-out,* system, in which alternate strakes fay against frames while overlapped by the *raised* strake at both edges, a *liner* or *filler* being inserted between raised strake and each frame to take up the deficiency. *Overlap* of *p.* generally is regulated by diameter of rivets used. If single-riveted, it has a 3½ to 4-diameter *landing* or overlap; if double-riveted, one of 6 to 7 diameters. Welded laps are made according to thickness of *p.* and are of similar proportions. **Armor-p.,** *see* **A.-belt** *in* ARMOR. **Flush p.,** *see* **F.-plating** *in* FLUSH. **Joggled p.,** system in which overlapping edges of *p.* are crimped or *joggled,* so as to allow all *p.* to fay directly against frames, thus obviating use of liners; *see* JOGGLE. Where alternate strakes are *joggled* on both edges, the method is termed *double-joggled p.;* where one edge of each strake is so treated, *single-joggled p.* **Shell p.,** also called *skin p.,* that constituting vessel's outside wall or shell, including bottom, bilge, and side *p.* As the great binder of the hull's frame-work, it greatly contributes to hull's transverse strength and is chief member of the structure in that it provides most longitudinal strength and stiffness to the whole. **Tank-top p.,** that forming vessel's *inner bottom;* topside of a double bottom. Also, sometimes, the *p.* in a *watertight flat,* or part of a deck constituting topside of a *deep tank.*

Thimble p., a method in boiler-making in which a succession of rings of plate with riveted overlapping seams form main body of boiler.

PLATING MODEL. *See* MODEL.

PLAY. Free motion or movement, as that of a sheave in a block, a rudder in its gudgeons, steering-gear, etc.

PLEBE. U.S. Naval Academy name for a midshipman in his first year of college training.

PLEDGET. A length or roll of oakum prepared for use in calking. Also, *pledge.*

PLIMSOLL'S LINE. *See* FREEBOARD; **Plimsoll m.** *in* MARK; **L.-line** *in* LOAD.

PLOC. A mixture of coal tar and hair formerly smeared on ships' bottom planking before the copper sheathing was fitted.

PLOT. To mark or delineate, as ship's position, a course, or a bearing, on a chart. **Plotting chart,** a working sheet or chart usually showing only meridians, latitude parallels, and scales, as used for laying down position lines, courses, etc., in fixing ship's position, indicating positions of special buoys, etc.

PLOW, or **PLOUGH.** The constellation *Ursa Major;* also called *Charlie's Wagon* or *Wain* and *Big Dipper; see* URSA MAJOR. **P. anchor,** *see* **Laughlin plow a.** *in* ANCHOR. **P. steel wire,** *see* WIRE.

PLUG. Any removable piece of wood, metal, or other material fitted to stop or fill a hole; a permanent filling-piece, as in a crack or hole in wood. A connecting piece or fitting; as, an *electric light p.;* a *fire p.* Local name for a bluff-bowed beamy fishing-boat *(New England).* A flat cake of pressed tobacco; *navy p.* **Bleeder p.,** a *bottom p., drain p.,* or *docking p.; see* BLEEDER. **Boat p.,** that used in ships' boats for draining off water when boat is hoisted clear of the surface; sometimes takes the form of a small rubber ball held in an open receptacle at mouth of drain-hole, so arranged that ball is held against hole by water pressure when boat is afloat and drops clear as boat is lifted from water, thus automatically *plugging* or *draining* as required. **Deck p.,** one fitted tightly over a sunken head of a deck bolt in a wooden deck. Sometimes incorrectly termed a *deck dowel.* **Drain p.,** any *p.* fitted to a drain-hole; as, a *bleeder* or a *pipe-line drain; a drain-bolt.* **Fire p.,** hydrant or outlet in a water-supply line to which a fire hose may be connected. **Fusible p.,** a tapering screw *p.,* five-sixteenths to three-fourths inch in diameter, made of an alloy consisting chiefly of tin, fitted in the top of a boiler furnace crown. Should water surface in boiler fall below this *p.,* the metal *fuses* or melts and steam blows into furnace; also called *safety p.* **Hawse p.,** *see* **H.-block** *in* HAWSE. **Mud p.,** a screw for closing a mud-hole in a steam boiler; *cf.* **M.-hole** *in* MUD. **P. cock,** a spigot driven plug fashion into a cask; any spigot having a plug-type valve. **P. hatch,** an insulation hatch-cover, so termed from its beveled or tapered edges for snug fitting; *cf.* **Insulation h's** *in* HATCH. **P. weld,** term for a method in which lapping parts are connected by welded metal fused in a hole that is drilled or punched in one of such parts. **Safety p.,** *see* **Fusible p. Ullage p.,** a small oil-tight cover fitted to the *ullage-hole* in a hatch-cover of an oil tank vessel; *cf.* ULLAGE.

PLUGMAN. U.S. naval word denoting a member of a gun's crew who is charged with opening and closing the breech-block or *plug*.

PLUMBAGO. Graphite; *see* **B. lead** *in* BLACK.

PLUMBING. In shipbuilding, operation of fairing and setting a section of transverse frames with view of erecting each frame so that its molding plane is perpendicular both to vessel's keel-line and longitudinal center vertical plane of hull. Also termed *horning the frames*.

PLUM DUFF. Sailors' once-a-week treat in the good old salt horse and cracker hash era; *see* DUFF.

PLUMMER BLOCK. A wood or metal standard or block supporting the bearing of a shaft; a *pillow-block* for a propeller-shaft; *cf.* PILLOW. The term often designates combined pillow and bearing; and is also referred to as *line-shaft bearing* and *tunnel-shaft bearing*.

PLUM PUDDING. In whalers' cant, a muscular fibrous tissue found throughout the tongues of certain whales, as the sperm and humpback.

PLUMMET. Piece of lead or other weighty metal attached to a line for use in sounding depth of water or oil in a tank. Archaic term for a *sounding-lead*.

PLUNGE. To descend heavily into a head sea, as a vessel in pitching. **P. point,** *see* POINT.

PLUNGER. The bucket of a hand pump. Any reciprocating part driven by or against fluid pressure; a *piston*; especially, that in a force-pump, or in a hydraulic crane or hoist; the *ram* in a hydro-electric steering-gear.

PLY. Thickness or strength of small stuff, as indicated by a combining number meaning that of the threads, yarns, twists, or turns comprising the material; as in, *topsails are roped with 8-ply twine; 3-ply houseline foxes*. To make more or less regular passages between certain ports, as a packet-boat or a ferry. To beat, tack, or work to windward in sailing (*archaic*).

PLYWOOD. Construction material made of two or more thin sheets or laminæ of wood glued together under pressure. Light, strong, and practically free of warping, hard woods prepared in this form are extensively used for inside finishing work, such as cabin sheathing, paneling, and room partitions, and often is faced with asbestos or metal for fireproofing in passenger vessels. It is also excellent material for small craft construction, including boat planking, where adaptable wood so treated is obtainable.

PNEUMATIC. (Gr. *pneuma*, air, wind) Driven or worked by air pressure, as certain tools used in ship construction, including *p. drill; p. hammer* (calking and riveting); *p. holder-up* (in riveting); *p. jack.* **P. steering-gear,** *see* STEERING.

PNEUMERCATOR. Trade name for a gauge which indicates volume of a liquid in a tank, draft of ship, etc.; *see* **Pneumercator g.** *in* GAUGE.

POCKET. Any small more or less secluded space below decks; as, that between a boiler-casing and ship's side; a bay or space between floors in the bilges; one of the spaces between frames at side of a 'tween deck. In a boat sail, a strip of canvas sewn at right angles to the leech and forming a sheath for inserting a light batten, as a means of stiffening or flattening sail when "on a wind" or "close-hauled." A sharp indent in a coast-line. A pound in a fish-weir; part of a trawl-net which prevents escape of fish. A small bag or sack used to pack certain goods for shipment. **Anchor-p.,** *see* ANCHOR. **P. battleship,** vessel of such class built so as to be within limitations of size and armament specified in a treaty; specifically, "a German war-vessel of 10,000 tons (displacement) having six 11-inch guns, Diesel-engined, and capable of making 26 knots." (*Funk & Wagnall*) **P. bunker,** *see* BUNKER.

POD. Group or school of large fishes, seals, whales, etc.; a flock of birds. To gather in groups, as seals, sea-lions, and walruses. To drive such animals into groups or *pods*, as in hunting.

POHUTUKAWA. (*Maori* name) A myrtaceous tree, or one of the myrtle family, native to New Zealand, which yields a tough, durable wood much favored as material for ship framing.

POINT. One of the 32 divisions of the compass; arc of the horizon or compass equal to that between two *p's*, or 11¼ degrees, as customarily used in helm orders, such as "*Luff a p.*"; "*Right two p's*"; and in estimating relative bearings; as, *the light is a p. and a half on our port bow,*—i.e., angle such bearing makes with ship's fore-and-aft line. In astronomy, a starting-place or zero of reference; as, *vernal equinoctial p.; solstitial p.* Short for *reef-p.,* or one of a number of pieces of rope fixed to a sail for reefing. A projection of land on a shore or coast-line; a small tapering cape or promontory. Stage or condition marking a start or occurrence of something; as, *dew p.; fire p.; flash p.; turning-p.* To

taper or graft a rope's end; *see* GRAFT. To furnish a
sail with *reef-p's.* To head more or less close to the
wind in sailing; as, *a schooner p's higher than a
brigantine.* **Cardinal p's,** *see* CARDINAL. **Dew p.,** the
temperature at which water content of the atmosphere condenses, or that of a surface exposed to
surrounding air and beginning to gather condensation *(dew).* It varies in amount less than air
temperature according to *relative humidity;* thus,
if latter is 75% and air temperature 80° F., *dew p.*
is 70°, while with 60° air temperature and same humidity, dew forms at 47° F. **Equinoctial p.,** *see* EQUI-
NOCTIAL. **Four-p. bearing,** *see* TWO OR MORE BEAR-
INGS WITH RUN BETWEEN. **Lubber's p.,** *see* **Lubber-l.**
in LINE.[2] **Nodal p.,** in tidal phenomena, local area
on a coast or line between opposite places on the
shores of a lengthy bay or strait at which tidal current runs with greatest velocity in such area, while
little or no rise and fall takes place. This occurs by
reason of high water arriving at one end of the
strait, etc., while it is low water at the other end,
the *nodal p.* being likened to a tilting or pivoting
point on the surface. **P.-line,** manila rope of 1½″
circumference, or 21-thread (3 strands, each of 7
yarns), so called from its use as *reef-p's* in merchantmen's sails. **P. of tangency,** that at which a plane
is imagined as touching the earth's surface in making a *gnomonic* or *great circle chart.* It is central
point in the projection. **Plunge p.,** that at which
surf waves break before rushing up a beach. **To
p. the yards,** to brace them up as in sailing close-
hauled; also, to lay them at smallest possible angle
with the fore-and-aft line, so as to reduce their resistance to wind force when ship is at anchor.
Stepping-p., that indicated on sheer plan as line of
intersection of frame timbers with keel or their
line of meeting with the deadwood; also, *see* BEARD-
ING. **Sub-solar p.,** that on earth's surface which at
any given instant has the sun in the zenith.

POINTER. That which points or directs attention
to something; an indicator in the form of a rod or
sharp-ended piece of wood or metal; as, a hand on
a gauge; an index at a steering-wheel to show position of rudder; a wind vane. In older whaling, a
horizontal pole at the masthead, conspicuously
marked, as with a black ball at its end, for indicating direction of a whale for benefit of men in the
boats. Member of a gun's crew who lays gun to
proper elevation *(U.S.)* **Plural,** the stars *Dubhe* and
Merak (α and β *Ursæ Majoris*) in the *Great Bear* or
Big Dipper, a line joining which, projected northward, passes close to *Polaris,* or the *Pole Star; cf.*
DIPPER and URSA MAJOR. One of a pair of timbers
laid inside the ceiling at fore and after ends of a
wooden ship. In more recent construction made of
iron, they connect to the stemson or sternson at a
deck and lie about 45° with frames and, like the
breasthook, their function is to stiffen and unite the

structure in vicinity of stern and stem posts. They
are termed *bow p.* and *stern p.* according to location. **Station p.,** *see* STATION.

POKER. An iron or steel tool for driving hoops or
bands on yards or masts. It has a flat foot, sometimes curved, at one end and a round knob at the
other.

POLACCA. *(It. = Polish vessel)* An old type of
Mediterranean vessel having two or three masts and
rigged with a combination of square and lateen
sails, masts commonly being in one piece. An
Italian variety of the craft was one having three
masts and a jib-boom; fore and main masts each
in one piece and mizzenmast having a topmast;
lateen sail on foremast; a square mainsail and
square topsail; and a lateen mizzen with square topsail; also, *polacra.*

POLAR. Of or pertaining to the poles of the
earth, of the celestial sphere, or those of a magnetic field. Proceeding from or found in vicinity of
either of the earth's geographical poles; as, *p. winds;
p. ice.* **P. axis,** that of an astronomical instrument,
as an equatorial, which lies parallel to the earth's
axis, or in the direction of either celestial pole. **P.
angle,** that formed by two meridians at their meet-
ing-point, or pole of the heavens; difference in right
ascensions of two celestial bodies or points. **P.
chart,** a *gnomonic,* or *great circle,* chart the point
of tangency of which coincides with one of the
earth's geographical poles. **P. circles,** parallels of
latitude whose distance from the earth's north and
south geographical poles, respectively, is equal to
the *obliquity of the ecliptic (in 1950, 23° 26′ 45″),*
or those of 66° 33′ 15″, called *Arctic* and *Antarctic*
circles on our maps. Conventionally marking the
outer limits of Arctic and Antarctic regions, on the
polar side of either circle the sun is not visible at
the winter solstice, or when that luminary has its
greatest declination of opposite name to latitude of
observer, while at the summer solstice (six months
later), "old sol" is above the horizon for the full
24 hours. **P. distance,** *see* DISTANCE. **P. lights,** *see* **A.
polaris** *in* AURORA. **P. star,** *see* POLARIS. **P. whale,**
the bowhead, or Greenland right whale; *cf.* WHALE.

POLARIS. The star α *Ursæ Minoris,* or brightest
in *Ursa Minor,* or the *Little Bear,* a constellation
also known as the *Little Dipper,* extremity of the
"handle" of which is marked by this star; also called
Polestar and *North Star,* from its close proximity
to the north pole of the heavens. Due to its slow apparent diurnal motion, *P.* has long been a favorite
with navigators for determining latitude by its altitude; in lower latitudes for compass observations;
and as a ready reference point for showing direction at night. On January 1, 1950, as given in the
Nautical Almanac, declination of the star was 89°
02′ N. and its magnitude, 2.12; *cf.* POINTER.

POLE. Either extremity of the axis of a sphere; north or south extremity of the earth's axis: *north p.* or *south p.* One of two points of apparent flux or concentration of force, as in a magnetic field; distinguished as *positive* and *negative p's* or, respectively, *N.* and *S. p's; cf.* MAGNETISM. Part of a mast above uppermost shrouds or standing rigging. A flag-staff. Portion of lower jaw of a sperm whale which contains the teeth (*Whaling cant*). To **depress the p.,** *see* DEPRESS. **Depressed p.,** *celestial p.* below the horizon; diametrically opposed to *elevated p.* **Elevated p.,** that of the heavens above the horizon; its true altitude is equal to observer's latitude. **Gin-p.,** *see* GIN. **Magnetic p's,** *see* MAGNETIC; north magnetic *p.,* as recently reported by Canada's Dominion Observatory (*1949*), has been located anew, after extensive surveys during past two years, as at a point in the northwestern part of Prince of Wales Island, in approximately 73° north latitude and 100° west longitude. Observations at 18 stations in the Canadian arctic islands determined the fact that the *magnetic p.* travels daily in an irregular circle having a radius of about 30 miles. **P. compass,** as formerly used in iron and steel vessels, a magnetic compass mounted on a mast or pole with the object of locating it beyond the influence of ship's magnetism; hence its use as a standard compass; *also see* **Pole c.** *in* COMPASS. **P. hook,** a boat hook. **P. star,** also written *Polestar; see* POLARIS. **P. trawl,** a beam trawl. **P's of the heavens,** two opposite points in the celestial sphere at which the earth's axis produced is imagined to pierce the heavens; hence, points about which all celestial bodies appear to revolve. **Under bare p's,** said of a sailing-vessel at sea with no canvas spread; especially, during heavy weather; as, *she scudded before the gale under bare p's.* (Also see *pole* as designated by caption word in SHEER; SOUNDING; STEERING; TIDE.)

POLEAX. As used by boarders in naval combat in 17th. and 18th. centuries, a short-handled axe having a hook at back of its blade; primarily intended for cutting away an enemy's rigging.

POLICY. *See* INSURANCE. **Floating p.,** *see* FLOATING. **Open p.,** *see* OPEN. **Time p.,** a marine insurance *p.* under which a risk is covered for a period of time stipulated in the document. **Wager p.,** a marine *p.* characterized by its requirement that possession of the document *per se* is sufficient proof of interest in property insured.

POLLACK. (Gael. *pollog,* a whiting) Food fish of the cod family found on Atlantic coasts of Europe and North America; also called *coalfish,* from its dark back. The name is also applied to the *greenling* or *rock trout* of Alaskan waters.

POLLUX. β *Geminorum,* brighter of two navigational stars in *Gemini* (the Twins). It lies 23° due north of the bright *Procyon* and 4½° SE by S of his younger brother *Castor; see* CASTOR AND POLLUX.

POLLIWOG. In U.S. navy parlance, any member of ship's complement who never has crossed the equator. Also, *polly wog. See* **Crossing the l.** *in* LINE.[2]

POLYCONIC CHART. A sea map or chart constructed on the polyconic projection; *see* PROJECTION.

POMPANO. An excellent food fish (*Trachinotus carolinus*) of U.S. Gulf and southern Atlantic coasts. It attains a length of 18 inches; has a deep compressed body, rounded head, and sharply spreading caudal fins; scales beautifully colored in orange or golden on the belly and bluish silver on its sides. Approaching close to shore in schools, the fish is a favorite "fighter" to surf fishermen on the Florida Atlantic coast, where it appears from January to March. Larger but less valued species are the *great p., round p.,* and *banner p.* of southern North Atlantic and West Indies. (Pron. *pomp-a-no*)

POND. (Etymologically same as *pound*) An artificially or naturally confined body of water usually smaller than a lake; an enclosure for fish in a running stream. **Big p.,** that section or area of a shoalwater weir first entered by fish. Familiar term for the Atlantic Ocean.

PONTOON. (It. *pontone;* L. *pons,* bridge) A flat, rectangular, decked vessel or scow supporting a crane, pile-driver, cargo-conveyor, dredging apparatus, etc. Any such decked scow or combination of tanks used as a ferry landing; an intermediate landing for cargo between a large vessel and a pier; one of the units in a landing-stage (*cf.* **L.-stage** *in* LANDING) or a floating bridge; a caisson for raising sunken vessels. A kind of raft of heavy logs or heavily built tank scow used as a *camel. See* CAISSON and CAMEL. **Careening p.,** formerly much used at chief sea-ports, a *p.* equipped with capstans, purchases, and necessary gear for the operation of careening or heeling vessels. *Cf.* CAREEN. **P. bridge,** passageway or structure spanning a river stream, etc., and supported by *p's.* **P. dry-dock,** *see* **Floating-d.** *in* DOCK. **P. hatch,** a metal hatch-cover fitted to cover an entire hatchway or a substantial cross-section of such. It is provided with means for hooking a sling in removing to or from the hatchway. **P. lifeboat,** one constructed *p.* fashion, or having a watertight double bottom. It may be flush-decked with collapsible sides or may have a well deck with either permanent or collapsible sides, in which latter case often is fitted with non-return scuppervalves. The *Lundin* boat is one of this type: *see* **Lundin l.-boat** *in* LIFE.

POOL. A combination of shipping interests in a certain trade, having as its objective the discouraging of competition in freight or passenger rates. In its common form, traffic is apportioned, as far as possible, according to tonnage and/or passenger accommodation controlled by each line and profits *pooled* for appropriate distribution to the several members concerned; sometimes referred to as a *tonnage p.* or a *passenger p.* according to whether carriage of freight or passengers is involved. Such *combines,* as they have also been termed, are frowned upon in U.S. under anti-trust legislation, yet there prevail more or less open understandings between certain lines, which, however limited in effect, are equivalent to the practice referred to. A small and comparatively deep body of water, as found in a stream; a small pond or collection of stagnant water. **Tide-p.,** water left in a depression on or near a beach after tide has fallen. **Working-p.,** open water area in an ice floe in which a vessel may maneuver.

POON-WOOD. (Native name)   Hard, light, oily timber of a tree of the genus *Calophyllum,* native to India and Burma, much valued for ship planking, masts, and spars.

POOP. (Fr. *poupe;* L. *puppis;* the poop)   Space below an enclosed superstructure at extreme after end of a vessel; also, *deck* extending over such erection. From earliest times, the *p.* in sailing-ships has been considered the place of honor, quarters of the master or captain and his officers being always located within that space. In medieval English vessels of war it had its beginning as "*æfter castel,*" a kind of battlement from which the archers "plied a sturdy bow"; thence it developed, in 16th. and 17th. centuries, into an elaborately sheered housing raised to a height greatly exceeding that of the forecastle; and finally rounded itself out to a mere raised part of the structure, yet holding the same air or reverence which appears to have had its source in obscure antiquity. To *p.* a sea is to ship heavy water over the stern, as in running before a high sea and vessel fails to lift clear of the "comber"; also, in old navy sailing-days, an enemy was said to have been *pooped* when considerable damage was suffered in her *p.* by gun-fire. **Break of p.,** extreme forward end of *p. deck.* **Full p.,** as distinguished from a *half-p.* or *raised quarter-deck,* a *p.* extending from side to side of ship and, usually, having its covering at least six feet above the upper deck. **Half-p.,** *see* **H.-poop** *in* HALF. **P. bulkhead,** that forming forward limit of a *p.* space. **P. cabin,** any room or berth in the *p.;* especially, one used as sleeping quarters for passengers. **P. lantern,** *see* **Poop l.** *in* LANTERN. **P. rail,** bulwark rail or open railing around sides and fore end of a *p. deck.* **P. royal,** in 16th.- and 17th.-century vessels of war, a short deck above the aftermost end of the *p.* **P. staff,** the flag-pole or *ensign staff* at after end of *p.* from which the national colors are shown. **Sunken p.,** a *p.* space set partly below an upper or weather deck and

having a partial deck height above the latter; a *monkey p.*

POPPET. In construction of a *launching-cradle,* upright pieces of timber supporting the narrowing ends of vessel's hull on the sliding ways; arrangement of such timbers as a whole, as *fore p.* and *after p.* P. heads are butted against lugs or brackets riveted to ship's shell-plating; their lower ends rest on the *p.-board* or *sole piece.* The latter usually is made with a groove to receive tenons shaped in *p. timbers,* and wedges are driven between sliding ways and sole piece to solidly jam the whole *p.* in place before keel-blocks, etc., are knocked away to rest entire weight of ship on the launching-cradle. A *p.* is also a common term for a small block of wood in boat construction; as, one supporting or containing the rowlock holes in the topping-piece; a bracket support for a washboard; a chock base; etc. **P.-holes,** one of the holes in a capstan head for receiving the bars; also, *pigeon hole.* **P.-lashing,** *see* **P'ing-lashing** *in* PACK. **P. ribband,** horizontal angle-bar, heavy planking, or plate secured to *p.* timbers for uniting and bracing purposes; also, *p. stringer; dagger-wood.*

PORCUPINE. Wire rope sometimes is referred to as *porcupining,* when having some of its outer threads broken and projecting through wear and tear; also, a *p. end* is the spreading and projecting form of threads in end of a broken wire rope. **P. fish,** a species of globe-fish having long thickly strewn spines on most of its body; *see* **G.-fish** *in* GLOBE.

PORBEAGLE. A small rapacious shark of North Atlantic and North Pacific Oceans, classified as *Lamna cornubica.* It has a pointed nose and both tail-lobes of about equal length; attains a length of about eight feet. *Cf.* LAMNIDAE.

PORGY. A valuable food fish of European and North American coasts of the Atlantic, also known as *paugie* or *paugy, scup,* and *scuppaug.* Not to be confused with the *pogy,* another name for the *menhaden,* it attains a length of twelve inches; has a deep compressed body, appearing hump-like in profile and bearing a spiny dorsal fringe. A small member of the species, habitat in West Indies, is *grass p.,* so named from living in eel-grass; and a larger, the *jolt-head p.* frequents same waters.

PORKFISH. A close cousin of the *porgy,* somewhat larger, but having narrow horizontal black and yellow stripes instead of the silvery appearance of his relative; habitat in West Indies and Central American waters.

PORPOISE. (O.F. *porpeis,* = hog-fish)   Popular name for the common or *bottle-nosed dolphin* of similar appearance and habits, but, properly, any small cetacean of the genus *Phocæna;* especially, the common or *harbor p.* of North Atlantic and North Pacific waters, which grows to 6 or 7 feet in length. There are several allied species of the mammal in Southern Hemisphere seas. *Cf.* DOLPHIN. A speed-boat is said to *porpoise* when jumping clear of water upon encountering larger waves, especially when meeting them head on. **P. oil,** a fine quality of oil obtained from the *p.*; used as a lubricant for delicate machines, such as watches, sewing-machines, and the like. **Skunk p.,** a genus of *p's* identified by their black and white longitudinal stripes.

PORT.[1] (L. *portus,* a harbor) Any harbor, haven, roadstead, inlet, cove, etc., in which vessels may find shelter. A place in which vessels load or discharge their cargoes, which locality may be a harbor itself or comprise two or more harbors or other sheltered areas for shipping. In a commercial sense, generally accepted meaning of the term is a sheltered local area affording facilities for landing and taking on cargo or passengers and regulated by a controlling board or other constituted authority, although a *port* also may be a landing or loading place without a harbor or haven, as one of the "open" type, or one affording anchorage only and unsheltered from the sea. **Captain of the p.,** *see* H.-master *in* HARBOR. **Close p.,** in Great Britain, a *p.* located on a river; opposed to an *outport,* or *p.* opening directly to the coast. **Equipped p.,** harbor or *p.* at which a branch of the customs service is established. **Establishment of the p.,** *see* ESTABLISHMENT. **Free p.,** *see* FREE. **Hailing p.,** a merchant vessel's *home p.,* or that written on her counter indicating her *p. of registry,* as required by law. **Home p.,** generally, a merchantman's *hailing p.;* often, however, that at which her owners are located, which may be far removed from her original *p. of registry.* **Open p.,** *see* OPEN. **P.-Admiral,** commander-in-chief of a British naval *p.* **P. bar,** a protective obstruction laid across an entrance to a *p.,* as, in former days, a chain cable; or, to-day, a floating *boom* or stretch of floating timbers, a submarine net, or series of pontoons, etc. **P.-bound,** said of a vessel detained in harbor because of bad weather. **P. captain,** *see* M. superintendent *in* MARINE. **P. of call,** one at which a vessel usually enters on a regular voyage, as for transferring cargo, taking in bunker fuel, water, provisions, etc. **P. of delivery,** that specified as place where certain cargo, mails, or passengers are to be landed; also, *p.* at which a shipowner turns his vessel over to her charterer. **P. of destination,** any *p.* toward which a vessel is bound during normal course of a voyage; her *final p. of destination* usually is defined as that *p.,* on either an outward or a homeward passage in a voyage, at which all cargo or passengers will have been landed. **P. of entry,** a harbor, port, or place at which a customs service provides facilities for "entry" or clearing inward of merchant vessels. In U.S., in addition to headquarters located at a principal

p. in each customs district, there are several *p's of entry* appropriately situated at or near shipping points of lesser importance. **P. of refuge,** *see* H. of refuge *in* HARBOR. **P. of registry,** that at which a merchant vessel, fishing-vessel, yacht, or any type of craft, excepting naval vessels, subject to a nation's laws governing registration, is documented as to tonnage, ownership, trade or use, etc. In U.S. registry or documentation of vessels is executed by Customs Division of the Treasury Department. As in all transactions involving title to registered property, any document, such as a bill of sale, hypothecation or pledging vessel in a bottomry bond, any form of mortgage, and, generally, any lien or salvage claim, is considered invalid unless reported to and recorded by Collector of customs at vessel's *p. of registry.* **P. pay,** as distinguished from *sea pay,* wages earned by crew members during vessel's stay at a home port. It usually amounts to sea pay plus subsistence per diem, victualling being temporarily suspended on board. **P. rates,** term used in Great Britain for tolls imposed on cargo landed at a port and not billed for transshipment. **P. risk,** in marine insurance parlance, a vessel insured against loss for period of her stay in a particular port. **P. sanitary statement,** document issued by port sanitary authorities to master of a ship for information of foreign quarantine officials. It usually indicates the number of cases of, and deaths from, contagious disease at port in question for a certain period (generally, two weeks) prior to vessel's departure. **P. signals,** a list of urgent and important signals published by a port authority for use between ship and shore at port concerned. **P. warden,** an officer charged with the administration of regulations concerning shipping at a given *p.;* specifically, in British *p's,* an official who inspects and holds surveys as required on cargoes and vessels; checks on the seaworthiness of vessels insofar as proper cargo stowage is concerned; supervises necessary measurement for tonnage of vessels; and generally is charged with carrying out regulations concerning safety of ships and interests of the *p.;* sometimes called a *p. reeve.* In U.S., an officer having general charge of enforcement of regulations concerning anchorage grounds, channels, mooring-buoys, dolphins, dumping-grounds, etc., of a harbor or *p.* What is termed *p. warden's fee* in U.S., is simply a surveyor's compensation for assessing damage to a vessel's cargo, fittings, or hull; current value of a vessel; or admeasurement for tonnage. **Salute to a p.,** *see* SALUTE. **Standard p. of reference,** *see* STANDARD. **Touch at a p.,** *see* TOUCH. **Treaty p.,** that of one country opened to commerce and trade of another according to terms of a treaty; particularly, certain *p's* in China. **Unequipped p.,** one at which there is no custom-house, no collection of duties, and no ships are allowed to enter except by order of a military governor or other competent authority.

PORT.[2] (L. *porta,* a gate)   An opening or door in a vessel's side for admitting light or air, as a *p.-light* or *p.-hole;* for passage of cargo as a *cargo-p.,* side *door,* or *side-p.;* for taking in bunker fuel, as a *coaling-p.* or *bunker p.;* for receiving a rudder-stock, as a *helm p.* or *rudder p.;* for dumping ashes overboard, as an *ash p.* **Battle p.,** older term particularly in naval ships, for a deadlight; *see* DEADLIGHT. **Bow p.,** a small rectangular-shaped opening near the stem in timber-carrying vessels for loading and discharging of lengthy pieces of lumber; a *lumber p.* In wooden vessels, it is opened by removing three or four pieces of the outside planking; iron vessels usually are provided with a watertight door. **Freeing p.,** one of several openings, close to the deck, in ship's bulwarks for *freeing* decks of heavy water. They usually are fitted with hanging doors or flap covers which open outward under pressure of water shipped. **Lumber p.,** one provided in the side for passage of lengthy pieces of timber; especially, a *bow* or *stern p.* which opens direct to ship's hold; *see* **Bow p.** Sometimes called *raft p.,* where timber is loaded from, or discharged into, the water. **Painted p's,** a series of simulated *gun-p's* painted fore-and-aft along a ship's sides; usually white on a black hull, each "port" measured about four feet square and spaced about six feet apart. This impressive scheme was followed by a few British sailing-ship lines in early years of present century and probably was adopted by several owners in the early 1880's. **P. frame,** stiffening and strengthening arrangement fitted around a *cargo p.* to compensate for break in continuity of longitudinal strength due to cutting away of plating and transverse frames to provide such opening in vessel's side. **P.-lid,** a blind, or metal cover, fitted to close against a *p.-hole* or *p.-light;* a flap cover on a *freeing-p.* **P.-light,** also termed *p.-hole, side-light,* and *side-scuttle; see* **A.-port** *in* AIR. **P.-rope,** that used to lift open the lid of a *gun-p.* in older ships; a *p.-pendant;* a *p.-tackle.* **Raft-p.** *see* **Lumber p. Rudder-p.,** also termed *helm-p.,* the *rudder-hole* or lower entrance to a rudder-stock casing, or watertight enclosure in which rudder-stock works or is housed. **Stern p.,** any *p.* in a vessel's stern; especially, one used for passage of long timber; a *lumber p.; cf.* **Bow p. Wash p.,** a *freeing-p.* or *freeing-scuttle;* sometimes also, *bulwark p.; see* **Freeing-p.** (For other *ports* designated by caption word, *see* BALLAST; BRIDLE; CARGO; CHASE; GANGWAY; HALF; HAWSER; LIGHT; PENDANT; SALLY; STEAM)

PORT.[3]   Formerly *larboard,* the left side of a vessel, looking forward; belonging or pertaining to the *p.* side; as, *ship cants to p.;* the *p. anchor; she has a heavy p. list.* As formerly used in helm orders, *p. helm* meant position of rudder when its tiller (leading *forward* of rudder-stock) was moved toward ship's *p.* side; *see* HELM. **P. tack,** in sailing, a vessel's course when wind is anywhere from her *p. beam* forward of that direction; popularly, how-ever, when sailing close-hauled with wind on her *p.* side. *Cf.* LARBOARD.

PORTABLE ANCHOR.   *See* ANCHOR.

PORTER'S ANCHOR.   *See* ANCHOR.

PORTAGE. (Fr.; from *porter,* to carry)   Formerly, goods which a sailor was permitted to carry as his share in a marine adventure, proceeds of his trading being considered as partially or wholly in lieu of wages; also, space assigned such cargo. Hence, crew members' wages or account current concerning such, as in our present *portage bill.* Carriage of goods overland from one waterway to another; place where goods are so transported. **P. bill,** statement made out by a vessel's master at conclusion of a voyage, showing total earnings of each crew member, with all cash payments or advances to each, in the form of a balanced account. Owners are debited with total earnings of crew and credited with all payments against that sum in a final summary.

PORT CHARGES.   *See* **H. dues** *in* HARBOR.

PORT ENGINEER.   A superintendent engineer at a home or principal port of a line of merchant vessels. His responsibilities cover maintenance of ships' machinery, arrangements for surveys of boilers and engines, placing of engineer personnel on the various ships, and general efficiency of engine performance throughout the fleet.

PORTER.   Chiefly in Great Britain, a dock laborer who is engaged at handling a particular kind of cargo; as, a *coal p.;* a *deal p.; fruit p.; grain p.,* etc. **Master p.,** *see* MASTER.

PORTHOLE.   Any opening in a ship's side; especially, a *port-light, side-light,* or *side-scuttle;* also, *port-hole. See* **A.-port** *in* AIR.

PORTLAST.   An old term for a bulwark rail or upper edge of a boat's gunwale; also, *portoise.* Lower yards were said to be *laid a-portlast* when sent down and rested athwartships on each bulwark rail; also, *a-portoise.* To **ride a-portlast,** *see* RIDE.

PORTLET. (Dim. of *port*)   A small harbor affording accommodation for fishing-craft, boats, yachts, etc. (*Chiefly poetic*)

PORTOISE. (Pron. *port-is*)   *See* PORTLAST.

PORTOLANO. (It.; from *porto,* harbor)   An old-time book for use of navigators. It contained sailing directions, charts, and descriptions of harbors, coasts, etc.

PORTREEVE. (A.S. *portgerefa*)   From 15th. to 18th. centuries, the *reeve* (earlier *gerefa* or *gereofa*) or bailiff of an English port who was charged with keeping the peace, enforcement of laws pertaining to ships and mariners, collection of king's revenues, etc.

PORT TACKS ABOARD, With. *See* ABOARD.

PORTUGUESE MAN-o'-WAR. *See* MAN-OF-WAR.

POSEIDON. (*Gr.*) In Greek mythology, god of the seas and all waters, corresponding to *Neptune* of the Romans. *See* NEPTUNE.

POSITION. Location, place, situation, or station of a person or thing; specifically, such point on the earth's surface as defined by its latitude and longitude or its bearing and distance from a known fixed point or object; as, *ship's p. at noon is 45° 10′ N. and 30° 15′ W.; at 1420 our p. was 15 miles 130° from Cape Race;* the latter form often being expressed as *from* the ship, as in *p. was Cape Race bearing 310° 15 miles; p. of St. Paul's Island is Lat. 38° 43′ S., Long. 77° 35′ E.* Place of a heavenly body, as indicated by its celestial latitude and longitude or by its declination and right ascension. **Circle of p.,** of which a **line of p.** is a small arc, *see* **C. of equal altitude** *in* CIRCLE; *also,* **L. of position** *in* LINE.[2] **Maritime p's,** as given in navigational epitomes, *e.g., Bowditch, Norie,* and *Raper,* or included in several different books of nautical tables, latitudes and longitudes of principal capes, harbors, ports, shoals, rocks, etc., of the globe. The lists are arranged as nearly as possible in geographical order, according to country, sea, or coast to which each point belongs. **P. angle,** *see* ANGLE. **P. buoy,** an anchored marker or buoy placed to show position of a sunken or submerged object, such as an anchor, a wreck, a submarine cable, etc. **P. doubtful,** *see* P.D. **P. light,** *see* LIGHT. **P. line tables,** *see* TABLES. **P. sheet,** a *plotting chart; see* CHART. **P. signal,** that denoting a geographical *p.* International Code requires uppermost flag in hoist to be letter *P;* next two, the two numerals denoting *degrees* of *latitude;* followed by two numerals denoting the *minutes;* next hoist similarly indicating the *longitude.* Where *p.* is expressed as a bearing and distance, it must be given as *from* a certain point; thus, a bearing of 130°, 15 miles from Sandy Hook, is signalled as *130—15—Sandy Hook. Cf.* RECKONING.

POSITIVE POLE. *See* POLE.

POST. A pillar, stanchion, mooring-bitt, pawl-bitt, or other upright piece of timber or metal used as a prop, support, to withstand lateral pressure, etc. In old sailing-navy days, rank attained by a captain who was appointed to a vessel of at least 20 guns; to appoint an officer to command such vessel. To list or publish, as at *Lloyd's,* the fact of a mishap to a vessel; as, *the "Waratah" is posted as missing.* **False p.,** *see* **F. stern-post** *in* FALSE. **Inner p.,** in wooden ships, piece of timber bolted to fore side of the stern-post for purpose of seating the main transom frame. **Joggle-p.,** an early name for a **king p.** or short sturdy mast, usually fitted about halfway between midship fore-and-aft line and ship's side, for supporting a cargo-boom; also, *samson p.*

Main p., old term for a ship's *stern-p.* **Pawl p.,** *see* **P.-bitt** *in* PAWL. **P. boat,** older term for a vessel or boat regularly carrying mails; a passenger vessel engaged on a fixed run; a packet boat. **P. captain,** formerly, in British and U.S. navies, an officer of rank of captain appointed to command of a ship, as distinguished from one holding rank of commander in a similar position, the latter being called captain by courtesy only. Also, formerly in British navy, an officer who was promoted, or *posted,* to rank of captain. **P.-entry,** an addition made to ship's manifest of cargo subsequent to time of vessel's entry at custom-house; any correction so required. **P. meridian** or **p. meridiem,** *see* MERIDIEM. **P. rank,** that of post captain; *cf.* **P. captain.** (For *post* in terms combined with following caption words, *see* PROPELLER; RUDDER; SAMSON; SCREW; SIGNAL; SNUB; STERN; STRETCH)

POT. A portable receptacle for various uses on board ship; as, *grease p.; pitch p.; slush p.; tar p.* That part of a pound-net into which fish are directed; also termed *crib, pocket, bowl.* It is provided with a netting bottom. Chiefly so termed in Great Britain, a special trap anchored on bottom and baited for catching crabs, crayfish, eels, and lobsters; a *lobster-trap.* **Drain-p.,** *see* DRAIN. **Lobster-p.,** sometimes called an *English p.* or *creel,* common term for a trap for taking lobsters on coasts of Britain. It is usually hemispherical in shape with a single entrance for the crustacean at top of its convex side. Generally called a *lobster-trap* in America, where its usual form is arched and oblong, four to five feet in length, top, bottom and sides of open slat-work, and a non-return entrance at each end for the catch; *see* LOBSTER. **P'hole,** a more or less circular pit or depression in a rocky-bottomed stream or river. **P.-lead,** a mixture of graphite and oil for smearing on bottoms of racing vessels for purpose of lessening skin resistance. **P.-pike,** in old whalers, a pointed iron rod or pike used to lift pieces of blubber into the *try-pot.* **P.-spade,** a cutting instrument resembling a chisel, having a long handle, used in cutting up blubber in a try-pot during process of *trying out* in old whaling days. **Try-p.,** in older whaling, large metal receptacle in which blubber was *tried out, i.e.,* rendered or melted, on an elaborate brick-built furnace in vessel's hold called the *try-works.* Two or more *try-p's,* each having a capacity of about 150 gallons, were kept going day and night during periods of successful "fishing." To-day, the oil is extracted on board whale *factory-vessels* by steam-heated boilers.

POUCH. A division in a hold made by partitions or bulkheads to separate a particular shipment in a bulk cargo or to prevent such cargo from shifting; also, a *pocket.* **Gular p.,** *cf.* PELICAN.

POUND. The *pot,* or inner enclosure of a *pound-net;* also called bowl, crib, pocket, pouch; *see* POT.

Also, short for *pound-net*. A series of bins or cribs in which fish are sorted or stowed on the deck of a fishing-vessel; a *fish-pound*. (*Chiefly British*) **P.-net**, a fishing-net set on vertical stakes in a sheltered area, as at side of a river or estuary, with objective of ensnaring and impounding the catch. It essentially consists of a *leader* which extends to deeper water (*see* LEADER) for turning the schools toward *wings* of the net which, in turn, direct the fish funnel fashion into the *pot*. (*See* POT) What is termed *lifting the p*. means that the netting bottom of *pot* is raised for purpose of scooping out the catch.

POUND AND PINT. British term for victualling scale, or allowance of food for each seaman *per diem*, as prescribed in the *Merchant Shipping Act* (*1906*). This recalls a line or two of an old *top-gallant-halyard chantey*: "Lime-juice and vinegar according to the Act; what's the use of growling when you're getting all your whack?"

POUNDING. Act of coming down heavily upon sea waves, as bows of a light vessel in a head or cross sea; distinguished from *plunging* in that vessel's bottom strikes the sea with a resounding thud felt throughout the hull.

POWDER. Short for *gunpowder*. **P.-chest**, in former naval warfare, a wooden box filled with a mixture of gunpowder, nails, scrap metal, slugs, etc., which was exploded as a mine in the path of boarders. A series of such chests were placed to advantage along ship's bulwarks, particularly in way of the lower rigging or chains, which was a favorite spot for scaling the side. **P.-flag**, the explosive flag; *see* **Red f.** *in* FLAG. **P. hoy**, a small vessel specially constructed to carry gunpowder or other explosives to naval ships; also, *p. hog*, which term formerly was particularly applied to an anchored *p.-vessel* serving as a magazine for a fleet. **P. magazine**, room or compartment aboard ship for stowing gunpowder; now usually termed *magazine*, such compartment is specially constructed for stowing any kind of explosives and, in naval vessels, is provided with a flooding arrangement by which, in case of danger by fire, a series of sea-valves may be opened; *see* MAGAZINE. **P. monkey**, in former navy days of sail and muzzle-loading cannon, one of a number of boys carried to supply powder to the guns. The lads had a busy time of it in the heat of action. **P. room**, a ship's magazine. **P. scuttle**, a small hatch through which *p*. was passed from magazine to a deck above in the "good old days." **P. tank**, a special wood- or felt-lined metal tank used as a magazine for carrying gunpowder as cargo; a receptacle for temporarily safeguarding charges of powder in vicinity of a heavy gun.

POWDERMAN. Member of a gun's crew responsible for carrying powder from magazine (or magazine-hoist) to gun; one in charge of stowage and delivery of gunpowder.

POWER. Applied force; as that on a lever or tension imparted to a tackle. Rate at which mechanical work is performed or energy is exerted, as expressed in *horsepower* or *watts* in an engine or in an electric motor. Result of multiplying a number by itself a given number of times; as, 9 is the *2nd. p*. of 3 (or its square); 27, its *3rd. p*. (or its cube); 81, its *4th. p*. A country or nation possessing important military or naval strength; a *sea p.; a maritime p*. To *p. a vessel* is to equip her with propulsion engines. **H'power**, *see* HORSEPOWER. **Floating p.**, *see* FLOATING. **P. boat**, any small craft propelled by an engine or motor. **P. capstan**, one operated by an engine or motor; *cf.* CAPSTAN. **P. door**, a mechanically operated door; particularly one used in closing a watertight compartment, often by a hydraulic system. **P. ratio**, in a purchase, that of the tension exerted in hauling part to *lifting p*. of the tackle; or, in the common tackle-purchase consisting of two blocks, ratio of 1 (the hauling part of rope) to number of parts of rope at the *moving block*, neglecting friction of sheaves in the rig considered. Thus, a threefold purchase (two three-sheave blocks), having six parts of rope at moving block, has a *p. ratio* of approximately 1:6. However, it is customary to allow one-tenth the theoretical lifting *p*. for each sheave in purchase, as loss of mechanical advantage due to friction; so that our ratio of 1:6 becomes 16:60 in practice. This means that, friction not considered, a pull of *one* ton on the hauling part theoretically will lift *six* tons, but actually such pull must be increased by .6 ton to do the job in question. Hence, *p. ratio* of tackle noted, with this generous friction allowance, is reduced to 1:3¾. **P. tonnage**, *see* TONNAGE.

P. P. I. Marine insurance abbreviation for *policy proof of interest; see* **Wager p.** *in* POLICY.

PRACTICO. (*Sp.* = experienced or skilled) Spanish-American term for a *pilot*.

PRAM. A flat-bottomed barge or lighter used in the Netherlands and Baltic ports for carrying cargo to and from anchored vessels; also, *prahm, praam*. A kind of boat once usually found on Norwegian vessels as a handy working-craft and an old favorite with fishermen on coasts of Norway. Characterized by an upward rising forward end, its bows are formed by the tapering or narrowing bottom which terminates in a blunt semicircular cross-section well clear of the water. The *p*. has a greatest breadth abaft amidships; a square stern; 15 to 18 feet in length; and is said to be an excellent craft in a heavy sea. **P. bow**, fore end of a boat or vessel having characteristics of the Norwegian *pram*.

PRAO. (Malay *prau; prahu*) Probably a Portuguese rendering of the Malay word,—usually written *proa* in English,—for an Indonesian craft of almost any kind, its particular type or use being designated by a following combining word or words.

PRATIQUE. (Fr. = practice; Gr. *praktikos*, practical) Term in general use by most maritime nations for permission of persons to land from, or to board, any merchant vessel, fishing-vessel, yacht, or other vessel,—usually excepting naval craft,—arriving from a foreign port, upon compliance by such vessel with quarantine regulations or presentation of a clean *bill* (or bills) *of health*. A *certificate of p.* or *quarantine clearance* usually is granted vessel's master where port officials are satisfied no contagious disease exists or is likely to arise amongst crew and/or passengers. Vessel is then said to be *granted p.* or *admitted to p.* If *p.* is not obtainable, vessel is placed in *quarantine;* cf. QUARANTINE. Excepting naval vessels generally, all others arriving from a foreign port are required to display International Code flag *Q*, denoting "*My vessel is healthy and I request free pratique.*" Presence of contagious or infectious cases on board should be announced by appropriate signal indicated in Code Book under QUARANTINE. Also written *pratic* and *pratick*. **P.-boat**, vessel or boat used by a quarantine officer in boarding ships, or preventing persons from landing. **P.-house**, quarters or office at a quarantine station. **Radio p.**, permission granted certain larger passenger liners,—particularly those in the transAtlantic run,—to proceed to dock without stop at quarantine anchorage of specified U.S. ports. Request for such is made by radio from ship, giving necessary information regarding health conditions on board, from 12 to 24 hours before vessel's expected arrival.

PRAWN. Any of a large family of shrimp-like decapod crustaceans found throughout the globe in temperate and tropical regions, both in fresh and salt water, and extensively used for food. Excepting its more or less pointed tail, it greatly resembles the sea crayfish or spiny lobster and one species in the tropics attains a length of nearly two feet. The *common p.* of temperate latitudes, however, is only a few inches in length.

PRAYER-BOOK. In old sailors' slang, from an irreverent reference to the genuflective posture of its user, a small piece of sand-stone used in the hand to scour crevices or corners in a deck where an ordinary *holystone* can not be manipulated. A larger piece, or small holystone, similarly employed was termed a *bible*.

PRE-ASSEMBLING. In shipbuilding, act or process of fitting together large units of the structure before hoisting such aboard for securing in place. Double-bottom sections, whole bulkheads, and deck-houses are examples of parts thus *pre-assembled*.

PRECESSION OF THE EQUINOXES. *See* EQUINOX.

PREDY. A now obsolete expression of British origin formerly used in naval ships for *ready*, in sense of being prepared to execute a certain order or maneuver. Ship was said to be *predy* when decks were cleared, etc., for action; also, as a verb, the word meant to prepare, or make ready, for action or maneuver indicated; as, "*Predy ship for wearing!*" Also, *pready, preedy*.

PRECIOUS CARGO. Term sometimes applied to bullion, precious stones, goods of unusual value, or small packages likely to suffer pilferage, carried at special rates and stowed in a strong-room or otherwise secured from theft or breakage; also, more commonly, *special cargo*.

PRE-EMPTION. Internationally conceded right of a belligerent to seize cargo of a neutral vessel which is contraband or conditional contraband, provided owners of such cargo are justly compensated therefor.

PRE-ERECTION. A shipbuilding term denoting the beforehand construction of various large parts of a hull on the ground. Such units are hoisted into place on the ways or into the hull by heavy cranes for inclusion in the structure; also referred to as *pre-assembling* and *pre-fabrication;* cf. PRE-ASSEMBLING; *also see* FABRICATE.

PREFORMED WIRE ROPE. *See* WIRE.

PRELIMINARY ENTRY. As provided in U.S. navigation laws, that made through the boarding customs officer by an arriving vessel's master, with objective of proceeding with landing of baggage or cargo prior to formal entry made at Customs house. (*19 U.S.C. 1448*)

PRESIDENTIAL SALUTE. *See* SALUTE.

PRESS. Formerly, in England, a commission or order to force men into service in the Royal Navy. To impress or force a person into service, as above. Any powered machine used in shipyard work for flanging, joggling, or otherwise fashioning plates, etc. **P. gang**, a detachment of men under an officer formerly charged with *pressing* men into naval service, as in England's old days of her wooden walls. **P. ketch**, a British naval patrol vessel of the rig indicated which carried a *p.-gang*. Fishermen and merchant vessels appear to have been legitimate prey for the *p. master* who was empowered to board any type of craft for his unwholesome ends. **P. of sail**, or **p. of canvas**, a greater spread of sail than ordinarily is carried in the breeze prevailing. *Cf.* CROWD.

PRESSURE. A squeezing or compression; action of a force against a resisting force; electromotive force. **Absolute p.**, that reckoned from a vacuum, as distinguished from pressure above that exerted by the atmosphere. It is *p.* indicated by a steam gauge plus *atmospheric p.* **Atmospheric p.,** that exerted in all directions by the atmosphere at a given height; normally, at sea level it is 14.7 lbs. per inch^2; at an altitude of 10,000 feet above sea level, about 10.3 lbs.; at 20,000 feet, 7.0 lbs.; and at 30,000 feet, about 4.5 lbs. per inch.^{2} **Barometric p.,** that of the atmosphere as measured by a barometer; *see* BAROMETER. **Center of p.,** *see* CENTER. **Gauge (or gage) p.,** *see* GAUGE. **High and low p. areas,** *see* AREA. **Mean effective p.,** *see* MEAN. **Sea p.,** that exerted in all directions at a given depth. Its value varies directly as the depth and is very nearly equal to depth in feet multiplied by four-ninths, expressed as *lbs. per inch.*²

PRESUMED TOTAL LOSS. *See* LOSS.

PREVENTER. An auxiliary bolt, rope, stay, tackle, or other contrivance for re-inforcement purposes or as a stand-by in case of accident to its primary; as, a *p. guy; p. sheet; p. plate.* **P. backstay,** an additional backstay leading from head of a lowermast or topmast to vessel's rail, well abaft the permanent backstays, and temporarily set up to assist the latter when a press of sail is carried, particularly during a breeze which allows vessel to steer a steady course for considerable time. **P. fid,** an auxiliary fid set in a hole in a topmast or top-gallant mast about two feet above the ordinary fid groove or hole; *cf.* FID. **P. bolts,** in larger wooden or composite vessels, those securing lower ends of *p. plates,* or auxiliaries to the *chain-plates,* which, in effect, were simply short additions to the latter; *see* CHAINS; *also* **C.-plate** *in* CHAIN.

PRICK. In older usage, to sew a false or blind seam through middle of a sail for strengthening or adorning purposes. A tightly wound hank of spun-yarn. A roll of tobacco leaves treated with rum and sometimes sugar or molasses, pressed tightly by serving with marline or spunyarn. To **p. off,** to trace a vessel's course or mark a position on the chart, as that of ship, a wreck, etc. To **p. up,** to freshen or increase in force; said of the wind.

PRICKER. A small marline-spike or pointed steel tool fitted with a wooden knob handle used for splicing small fiber or wire rope, making holes in canvas for eyelets, etc.

PRICKING NOTE. Now seldom used term for an invoice sent by a shipper to a vessel's master or agent authorizing receipt of the goods listed therein for shipment. The name is said to have originated from practice of *pricking* holes in the document as a tally of packages counted into vessel. In Great Britain, a customs document addressed to master or commanding officer of a vessel requesting him to receive on board certain indicated bonded goods for export or for ship's stores.

PRIDE OF THE MORNING. *See* MORNING.

PRIMAGE. Formerly, a sum of money or percentage of freight paid by a shipper to a vessel's master for care and protection of goods placed on board. Excepting, perhaps, the customary *cumshaw* of Far Eastern ports, the master no longer enjoys this *hatch* or *hat money,* as it also was called prior to its surrender to the shipowner in the form of extra freight. The nearest approach to *p.* to-day is a gratuity given by a shipper of live stock to a master or mate in recognition of extra care demanded of his consignment by ship's officers. The term nowadays often is applied to an additional freight charge for use of ship's cargo gear or any unusual expense incurred by ship under certain transportation conditions.

PRIMARY. First in importance; principal; as, *p. planets.* A planet with respect to its satellite; as, *Neptune's moon revolves about its p. in 5 days 21 hours.* The brighter component in a *binary* (double) star. **P. planets,** *see* PLANET.

PRIME. First in rank or importance; chief; primary; original; as, *p. meridian; p. mover.* To start by a preliminary operation; as, to *p. a pump* by pouring some water into its barrel during initial strokes to obtain necessary "suction"; or to *p. a gasoline engine* by introducing a small quantity of fuel into its carburetor or its cylinders. To prepare for firing, as a gun, by providing the necessary *priming,* or *primer.* **P. meridian,** zero meridian from which longitude is reckoned; *see* GREENWICH; *also,* LONGITUDE. **P. mover,** natural agency which puts power in a machine; as steam, electricity produced in a battery, or flow of water; or simply drives, as the wind. Any machine or engine that drives other machinery in a plant. **P. vertical,** in the celestial sphere, a great circle whose plane lies at right angles to that of the observer's meridian, passing through his zenith and true east and west points of the horizon. It intersects the equinoctial (*celestial equator*) at latter points, and a body, at instant of passing through this great circle, lies in azimuth 90° from the meridian, or true east or west. At the equator it coincides with the equinoctial; at the poles it does not exist.

PRIMING. That with which anything is *primed;* as, a combustible used to ignite a charge of gunpowder, explode a mine, etc. First of a series of applications of paint, etc., to a surface; a *p. coat.* **Boiler p.,** undesirable condition in which water is carried with steam from boiler to engine, among the causes of which are: Boiler water too high; poor firing or unequal forcing of different boilers; salted condition of feed-water; scum or froth of impurities on water surface which effervesces into steam line (also termed *foaming*). **P. of the tides,** *see* **L. of the tides** *in* LAG. **P. valve,** a spring safety valve on an engine cylinder for releasing water carried into cylinder through *p.*

PRISM, Azimuth. *See* AZIMUTH. **Water p.,** *see* WA-TER.

PRISMATIC Coefficient. *See* COEFFICIENT. **P. sextant,** *see* SEXTANT.

PRIVATE. Belonging to, or concerning, an individual company or person; personal; not general or public; as, a *p. vessel; p. docks.* **P. armed vessel,** *see* **A. merchantman** *in* ARMED. **P. carrier,** a vessel (or her owner) that carries goods or cargo for hire under particular agreement and not as a more or less public convenience, as distinguished from a *common carrier; cf.* COMMON CARRIER. **P. flag,** distinguishing colors or device of a shipowner or shipping line; *see* **H.-flag** *in* HOUSE. Also, usually a swallow-tail flag, or burgee, containing the chosen device or emblem of an owner of a yacht, duly registered with yacht club concerned, and flown according to flag etiquette in customary use. **P. port,** a harbor or port owned or leased by private interests; such as is used by an industrial concern, a railway system, a mining company, etc. Buoyage, lighting, channel depths, berthing accommodation, port charges, dues, etc., however, generally are controlled by government regulations. **P. signal,** pyrotechnic signal adopted by a shipping line for identification of its vessels, as in meeting other ships at sea and reporting at night to a coast signal station. Now little used since advent of Morse flashing and radio; *see* **Coston l.** *in* LIGHT.

PRIVATEER. Formerly a privately owned vessel authorized by a sovereign state to destroy or capture war-vessels or commerce of an enemy. Owners of such craft usually were allowed to retain a large portion of, if not all, the booty taken on a "cruise"; *see* **L. of marque** *in* LETTER. By the *Declaration of Paris,* April 16, 1856, *privateering,* or act of cruising as a *p.,* "*is and remains abolished by the signatory powers.*" Commanding officer or a member of the crew of a *p.;* an officer or crew member of such vessel also was termed a *privateersman.* To sail in a *p.;* to engage in privateering.

PRIVILEGED VESSEL. *See* VESSEL.

PRIZE. Capture of property, or property captured by a belligerent in accordance with internationally accepted rights of war; especially, property on the high seas or in territorial waters of an enemy, as an enemy vessel or any neutral craft directly aiding and abetting an enemy; as, "*the p. amounted to 20 tuns of good Madeira wine*"; *our p. was a 10-gun brig.* To seize as a *p.;* as, *three ships were prized for unneutral conduct.* To force open, move, lift, or turn with a lever; to *pry;* also written *prise.* **P. court,** a tribunal sitting in time of war to determine the validity or otherwise of captures of enemy vessels and/or their cargoes; *see* **A. court** *in* ADMIRALTY. **P. crew,** a detachment of a warship's crew placed on board a captured vessel to take her to port. **P. flag,** in yacht-racing parlance, a flag displayed by the winners of first, second, and third places. Colors and devices of such flags vary according to local custom. **P. law,** *see* **Prize l.** *in* LAW. **P. master,** officer detailed to take command of a captured vessel; *see* **P. crew. P.-money,** that paid to captors of a vessel taken as a *p.* from an enemy, the money being realized by or from sale of such *p.* Cash awards made by a government to officers and men of its own ships for taking part in destruction of enemy vessels in battle; this was abolished in U.S. in 1899. **Scotch p.,** humorous term for a captured ship subsequently freed by a *p. court.*

PROA. *See* PRAO.

PROCYON. (L.; from Gr. *Prokuon: pro,* before; *kuon,* dog; so named by the ancients because of its rising about an hour before the *Dog Star,* or *Sirius*) Star of magnitude 0.48 in the *Canis Minor* (Little Dog) group situated next to and east of *Orion.* It has a declination of 5° 21½′ N. and right ascension 7 hrs. 36½ min. Lines joining the bright *Sirius,* ruddy *Betelguese* of *Orion,* and *Procyon* form an almost perfect equilateral triangle.

PRODUCER GAS ENGINE. A reciprocating engine operated by gas which is generated by burning a solid, as coal, coke, charcoal, or wood in a *gas producer.* The system has been in use in small vessels, particularly on the canals of Europe, for past 25 years. Principal advantage of the plant is its low fuel cost which apparently offsets its greater weight than that of an internal combustion installation, although it represents a saving in this respect compared with steam boilers and usual reciprocating engine.

PROFILE. Chiefly applied to drawings of vessels, showing the longitudinal structural arrangement, transverse framing, water-lines, bulkheads, decks, houses, etc., as viewed at right angles to fore-and-aft line; side elevation or longitudinal view of a vessel. **Inboard p.,** *see* INBOARD. **Outboard p.,** *see* OUTBOARD. **P. draft** (or **draught**); **p. plan;** *see* **Sheer p.** *in* PLAN.

PROJECTION. In cartography, the representation on a plane of part or whole of the earth's surface so that all points and areas thereon, with their directions of bearing from each other, conform to those existing in nature. Since it obviously is impossible to depict a considerable area of the globe without some degree of distortion taking place, a projection suited to navigators' use must be such that a direction or a course line may be plotted thereon as a straight line. Hence, the necessity that all points and areas, no matter to what degree such depiction may be distorted, must lie in same relative direction to each other as on the earth itself. Of the several projections in use two only are necessary for navigation in any latitude; *viz., Mercator's* *p.,* or that generally used in latitudes up to 75°, and the *gnomonic p.* for polar navigation and for great circle sailing in generally higher latitudes. **Gnomonic p.,** made on a plane tangent to earth's surface at a given point called *point of tangency.* Part of earth's surface concerned is depicted as if viewed from earth's center, all points therefore becoming termini of radials from the latter. All great circles on this *p.* of necessity will appear as straight lines, meridians converge poleward, and parallels of latitude are shown as curves concave toward pole with distances between each increasing with distance from point of tangency. Where point of tangency coincides with the geographical pole, such *p.* for navigational use is termed a *polar chart,* parallels of latitude being represented as concentric circles varying in their distances apart as *cotangent of the latitude.* Also called a *great circle chart,* a *gnomonic* chart is used to show a great circle sailing track,—always a straight line thereon. **Loxodromic p.,** one in which a *loxodrome,* or *rhumb line,* is represented as a straight line; as, *Mercator's p.* and *polyconic p.* Cf. LOXODROME. **Mercator's p.,** see **Mercator's c.** *in* CHART. **Polyconic p.,** that in which several *conic p's* are combined in mapping an area. Part of earth's surface considered is projected on a tangent cone, apex of which meets a prolongation of earth's axis above nearest pole. Thus, at middle latitude of area represented, the cone may be considered as *rolled* over the globe at that line of tangency, receiving the imprint of the surface in the process. A series of *conic p's* at closely spaced latitudes, or a *polyconic p.,* therefore, is capable of developing a considerable area with a high degree of accuracy. Charts of the Great Lakes are made on this *p.*

PROJECTOR.   Device for projecting a beam of light from a lighthouse, searchlight, etc., as a lens, a combination of lenses, or a parabolic mirror.

PROLONGED BLAST.   As prescribed in *International Rules for Preventing Collision* (Rules of the Road), a single blast of from four to six seconds duration to be made by certain vessels on the whistle or foghorn during thick weather.

PROMENADE DECK.   *See* DECK; *also* **Shade d.** *in* DECK.

PROMONTORY. (L. *pro,* forward; *montis,* mountain)   A headland, high point of land, or cape, projecting into the sea.

PROOF.   Test of strength of a material to determine its suitability or conformity to a required standard; specifically, a *p. test* applied to anchors, chain, davits, derricks, steel plating and shafting, wire rope, etc. *P. strength* of materials usually is empirical in character, or is not governed by any rigid rule beyond that of common experience (all due regard to requirements of the classification societies); thus, that of steel chain is twice its working strength and about two-fifths its breaking strength according to some authorities, while others give 2½ times the working stress as a satisfactory value for *p. strength.* This also applies to hooks, rings, shackles, and swivels. Chain used as a hoisting fall in cranes and derricks, as given by some qualified persons, is *proved* by a test of 1½ times its working load; others hold a *p. test* of twice the working load is proper. A *p. load* for a cargo winch with all gear accessory thereto is given as 25% in excess of a safe working load up to 20 tons, according to one authority; 30% by another. *P. test* of anchors and stern frames is made by letting these drop from a certain height to hard ground; *p. strength* of plating, propeller shafting, etc., is expressed in lbs. per inch²; *p. stress* is that actually applied in proving samples of plating, shafting, structural steel, etc.

PROP.   To support or sustain an incumbent weight or pressure; as a bulkhead by a shore or timber. A stay, bolster, timber, etc., used as above. **Mast-p.,** *see* MAST.

PROPELLER.   Anything that propels; especially, the well-known "wheel," also termed *screw-propeller* because of the twist in each of its blades which, if the device were turned in an unyielding substance, would "carve out" helices or spirals as the threads of a *screw.* *P's* have two to four blades and may be a solid casting or blades may be detachable from the *p. boss,* or "hub." Generally, small craft *p's* are 2-bladed; large vessels of moderate speed, 3-bladed; those of fast vessels, 4 blades. Material may be cast iron or steel, a non-corrosive alloy, or, as in large well-found ships, the highly satisfactory manganese bronze is used in the blades (*see* MANGANESE BRONZE). Blades increase in width toward, and are rounded at, their tips or outer ends, their after faces being flat and slightly convex on forward faces, with knife edges. A *p.* is *right-handed* when, with engines turning ahead, its upper half revolves from port to starboard; *left-handed,* when the motion is from starboard to port. Twin and quadruple screw vessels usually carry right-handed *p's* on starboard side and left-handed *p's* on port side, this being the best arrangement for maneuvering ship by means of the engines. Single-screw equipped vessels usually have right-handed *p's.* First *screw p.* was used in England in 1838 and first vessel to cross the Atlantic with the device was the British ship *Great Britain,* 1845. *P.* design in the past half century has been the subject of extensive investigation both in model experiment and advanced mathematical theory. It is by no means a simple task to arrive at the most suitable size and shape of a screw *p.* or *p's,* considering displacement, power, required speed, draft, coefficient of fineness, skin resistance, etc., of vessel concerned. Among the latest developments applied to smaller vessels and with promise of adoption in more important tonnage is a departure from the conventional knife-edged blade to one of *aerofoil* pattern, or having a blunt leading edge, in cross section much like an airplane wing. Thus, it would seem, the final answer to "wheel" design has not yet arrived. **Contra-p.,** term for a contrivance of vertical and sometimes also horizontal pieces of plate attached to the rudder-post in a single-screw vessel or forward of each of twin screws (or others at either side of center line). Purpose of such is to divert, as far as possible, the rotary current set up by *p.* into the fore-and-aft line, or that in which *p.* may attain its maximum thrust. **Controllable pitch p.,** also called *reversible pitch p., variable pitch p.,* and *feathering screw,* one in which the blades may be turned on their respective vertical axes, as, to neutral position, astern position, etc. It is fitted chiefly in smaller vessels whose engines,—usually internal combustion type,—turn *p. shaft* continuously in one direction. *Cf.* **F. screw** *in* FEATHERING. **Fish-tail p.,** *see* FISH. **Hand-operated p.,** as fitted in some lifeboats, one that is turned manually by simply working each of a number of small levers to and fro, this motion being conveyed to *p. shaft* by an appropriate mechanism. Levers usually are placed so that two may be worked at each thwart. Such means of propulsion requiring no knowledge of handling oars or sails, it is specially adaptable for use under emergency conditions in large passenger vessels. **Hydraulic p.** or **jet p.,** *see* **J. propulsion** *in* JET. **Paddle p.,** *see* PADDLE. **Pitch of p.,** *see* PITCH.[2] **P. arch,** also termed *screw aperture, screw race,* and *p. race;* properly, in a single-screw vessel, that part of the stern frame extending between rudder-post and propeller-post above the *p.,* usually termed *arch-piece* and *bridge-piece,* but applied generally to space in which upper half of *p.* turns; *cf.* **A.-piece** *in* ARCH. **P. boom,** one or more floating timbers or logs moored as a protection for *p. blades,*—particularly those of *wing p's,*—against lighters and other harbor craft having business near or alongside a moored vessel. **P. boss,** central part or "hub" of a *screw p.* It is bored to slip over the tapered end, or *tail-end,* of the shaft to which it also is keyed to resist rotating stress. Where detachable blades are fitted, it is appropriately shaped to receive the flanged ends of blades, and often is supplied with an inset rubber ring on its forward face for resisting electrolytic, or galvanic, action. **P. bracket,** also, *p.-shaft stay, shaft bracket; see* **S.-strut** *in* SHAFT. **P. cap** or **cone,** *see* FAIRWATER. **P. frame,** the stern frame of a single-screw vessel, or that structural unit constituting chief strength of hull in way of *p.* Forward part of this frame contains the bearing in

which *p.* shaft's tail-end is confined; *see* **S. frame** *in* STERN. **P.-guard,** as sometimes fitted in smaller twin screw vessels, a protective frame jutting from the hull to prevent contact of boats, lighters, etc., with *p. blades,* or to hold *p.* away from a pier, quay wall, etc. **P. horsepower,** *see* HORSEPOWER. **P. inspector,** old humorous term for a half-waterlogged timber, spar, pile, etc., floating end up in a channel and so presenting a hazard to a vessel's *p.;* also called *tidewalker.* **P. nut,** *see* NUT. **P.-post,** in a stern frame, forward vertical part containing the *p.-shaft bossing,* or that through which shaft passes; sometimes called *body post; cf.* **P. frame. P. shaft,** that section of *line-shafting* which carries a screw *p.* and conveys rotary motion from main engines. Made of heavier material than that in the *main-* or *line-shafting* to withstand shocks and severe stresses immediately received by *p.,* it is further protected by a casing of bronze at its bearing surface in the *stern tube* (or *strut bearing,* in the case of twin screws or those at either side of fore-and-aft line). Also called *tail shaft* and *tail-end shaft.* **P.-shaft bearing,** *see* BEARING. **P.-shaft boss,** also termed *bossing of p.-post,* bulging part of *p.-post* through which *p.* shaft passes and which contains the *tail-end bearing.* **P. thrust,** *see* THRUST. **P. well,** in older auxiliary steam vessels, particularly those navigating among heavy ice, a trunkway extending vertically through the hull directly above *p.* When under sail only or as required, tail-end shaft was drawn inboard and *p.* hoisted clear of water into the *well.* **Shrouded p.,** one that is enclosed in an open cylindrical-shaped "shrouding" for directing water-flow in the fore-and-aft line, thus avoiding losses due to rotary current and turbulence set up by an ordinary naked *p. See* KORT NOZZLE. **Skew-back p.,** *see* SKEW-BACK BLADES. **Solid p.,** one in which blades and boss are contained in a single casting; larger screws being of iron or steel, those of smaller craft often of a non-corrosive alloy, such as manganese bronze. **Tunnel p.,** in some small shallow-draft vessels, one set in a *tunnel-stern,* or that formed in the hull for purpose of housing a screw of sufficient size so that blades do not extend below vessel's deepest draft. As headway increases water fills tunnel and *p.* becomes wholly immersed. **Vane p.,** or vane wheel, a large diameter *p.* used on some shallow-draft river boats. It is almost a replica of the common farm windmill. About 40% of its diameter is immersed, blades are unusually wide at tips, and for noisy operation compares favorably with a Mississippi stern-wheeler. **Voith-Schneider p.,** another shallow-draft wheel, which has proven satisfactory for maneuvering at slow speeds in crowded waters in that vessel also may be steered by its means. It rotates on a vertical shaft with only blades, or floats, extending below vessel's bottom. *P.* itself is a disk with the several floats, of spade-like shape, hooked up to a mechanism similar in character to that for feathering the floats in a paddle-wheel, but which allows the feathering or set of blades to be performed at will, thus providing a means of steering vessel in maneuvering. A similar but less successful *p*. is the *Kirsten-Boeing* invention which has been used on some small craft.

PROPELLING POWER SPACES. That portion of a vessel's gross tonnage, or total internal capacity at 100 cubic feet per ton, occupied with engines, boilers, bunkers, shaft tunnels, escape and skylight trunkways, machine-shops, store-rooms, and other spaces used exclusively in connection with vessel's power plant. In determining *net tonnage*, total of these spaces, or an arbitrary percentage of gross tonnage amply covering such total, is termed *deduction for propelling power. See* **Gross t.** *in* TONNAGE.

PROPULSIVE COEFFICIENT. *See* **Thrust hp** *in* HORSEPOWER. Magnitude of this value varies through a range of from about .50 to .65, which means that actual horsepower represented in a moving vessel is that fraction of the mechanical efficiency of vessel, which figure, in turn, rarely attains .95 of power delivered by engines in any craft under ideal conditions. *Propulsive* coefficient, then, may be termed *propulsive efficiency*, better expressed as a percentage of ship's *mechanical efficiency*.

PROROROCA. *See* BORE.

PROTECTED CRUISER. *See* CRUISER.

PROTECTION AND INDEMNITY CLUB. *See* **Mutual i.** *in* INSURANCE.

PROTECTIVE DECK. *See* DECK.

PROTEST. An affidavit or declaration, formally termed a *writ of protest*, made by a master of a vessel before a magistrate, notary public, or consul of country to which vessel belongs, stating that he *protests* against possible claims on his vessel due to any alleged neglect or failure of her officers and crew in the matter of suspected or actual damage or loss to ship or cargo through stress of bad weather encountered or any other cause; or that he protests against any action jeopardizing rights of his owners, as, *e.g.*, a violation of a charter-party by vessel's charterer. Act of drawing up such document is termed *noting a p*. and, generally, is required by law to be executed within 48 hours—in some countries within 24 hours—of vessel's arrival in port. Information set forth in *p*. must be substantiated by pertinent extracts from ship's log. In the event of litigation or damage claims arising in matters with which the *p*. is concerned, the instrument may be *extended*, or more fully drawn up, as with additional pertinent facts, with objective of contesting damage claims or other court action, within six months of date of *noting*. Truth of particulars indicated in a *p*.

must be attested by master and at least one member of his crew,—usually two. Also termed *sea p*. A sworn statement made by one or more survivors, indicating particulars of or leading to the wreck of a vessel, is sometimes referred to as a *protest*. **P. flag**, in yacht racing, that hoisted by a contestant to advise the judges a violation of the racing sailing rules has been committed by one of the boats. **Shipping p.**, *see* SHIPPER.

PROTRACTOR. Instrument for laying off or measuring angles on paper, as a chart. It consists of a semi-circular disk, often of transparent material, having its arc graduated to degrees and is used in conjunction with a ruler, as to find inclination or angle latter makes with a meridian; hence, a course or bearing expressed in degrees. It is often called a *course p*. **P. rule**, parallel rules graduated as a *p*. and which may be used without it in measuring a course angle, etc. **Three-arm p.**, *see* **S.-pointer** *in* STATION.

PROVIDENCE, Act of. *See* **A. of God** *in* ACT.

PROVISION. Store of needed material for a voyage; especially, a stock of food for use of crew and passengers; usually in *pl*. To supply a vessel with a store or stock of eatables. **Dry p's**, foods containing little or no moisture; as, beans, biscuit, coffee, flour, sugar, tea, etc. **Salt p's**, pickled beef and pork, dried cod, salted herring, etc. **Wet p's**, all pickled foods, syrup, rum, vinegar, and other fluids.

PROVISO. Old-fashioned term for a hawser or line temporarily steadying a vessel or boat in position; as, a quarter-line run to shore from an anchored vessel or a sternfast from a boat.

PROW. (It. *prua;* Gr. *prora;* forward of, or before) Extreme fore end of a vessel's hull which is above water. It is chiefly a poetic word and sometimes written *prore;* also, a variant of *prao*. A large single-masted sailing-barge of Bombay and Poona, in India.

PRY. To lift as with a lever; *see* PRIZE.

P. S. C. *Per standard compass;* indicating a given course or bearing according to ship's standard compass.

PSYCHROMETER. A hygrometer, or instrument for measuring the aqueous content, or humidity, of the atmosphere.

PUBLIC. As opposed to *private*, belonging or relating to a nation, state, or a community; as, a *p. vessel; p. enemies; p. works*. Open to general use of vessels, boats, and persons; as, *p. waters;* a *p. beach*. **P. armed vessel**, any armed craft commissioned by a state for a *p*. purpose and usually manned by a naval crew. **P. enemies**, naval or military forces of a country with which a nation is at war. As employed in maritime law, the term means only enemies of the country to which a vessel belongs; termed *King's enemies* in Great Britain. **P. port,** a harbor or port wholly or principally used by a national government, state, or municipality. **P. room,** in a passenger vessel, a general room included in accommodation for passengers of each class; as, dining-saloon, library, lounge, smoke room, etc. **P. vessel,** any state-owned vessel or one chartered by a state for any purpose of its government; especially, those other than naval ships of the line and auxiliaries, such as lighthouse tenders, revenue vessels, school ships, store ships, surveying-vessels, and transports. It is generally held that a *state-owned* or *public vessel* is one which is not permitted by law of country to which she belongs to engage in any commercial activity. **P. waters,** those open to use of general public; especially, navigable channels, etc.

PUCKER. To gradually gather, or "eat in," the slack of a seam in sewing canvas, as where one cloth is required to be so treated in order to bring ends of both cloths together at end of seam. A wrinkled, or *puckered,* seam, such as occurs in *puckering* and, also, where sewing-twine has been pulled too taut in a flat seam.

PUDDENING. Bunch of soft material, such as teased-out old rope, oakum, canvas, etc., used as a fender, chafer, or buffer; also called *pudding;* a dolphin. Such means of fending, etc., collectively. *See* DOLPHIN; **Pudding-b.** *in* BOOM; **Bow f.** *and* **Pudding-f.** *in* FENDER.

PUDDING CHAIN. Short link chain, usually of galvanized iron, formerly much used in square-rigged vessels for topsail sheets, or in that part of any sheet which works in a sheave or sheaves; for jib-pendants, halyard-pendants and tyes, and other heavy running gear. Flexible steel wire rope to-day has greatly replaced the chain for above-noted uses.

PUFF BALL. An extension to a lower square sail spread in light or steady breezes, as in the old clipper ships. It was attached to foot of sail in same manner as a bonnet on a jib.

PUFFY. Gusty or blowing in *puffs;* but more often describing a variable light wind; as, a *puffy breeze.*

PUFFER. A globe-fish, swell-fish, or balloon-fish; *see* **G.-fish** *in* GLOBE. A porpoise, so called from its *puffing* noise in expelling air at short intervals.

PULL. To operate an oar in rowing; to row; to transport by propelling with oars as in rowing; hence, to *p. a boatload up the river.* To haul, drag, or tug; as, to *p. a rope;* often with *away* or *on,* as in "*P. away* (or *p. on*) *the topsail halyards!*" **P.-devil,** a device for catching fish, made of several hooks seized back to back, grapnel fashion. It is dragged

or jerked through a school to hook the fish on the hit-or-miss plan. To **p. for,** to propel with oars toward; as, to *p. for the shore.*

PULLEY. A sheave or small wheel having a grooved rim over which a rope or chain moves, as in a purchase-block. Excepting its use in engine-room parlance in which, *e.g.,* the wheels in a chain hoist, blocks of a purchase, etc., often are termed *pulleys,* the word *sheave* has long been established as the ship term for this indispensable mechanical aid. *See* SHEAVE. **Chain-p.,** *see* CHAIN.

PULLING-BOAT. *See* BOAT.

PULPIT. A support or platform at the bowsprit end or on bows of a vessel, fitted with a guard rail or rope, used by a harpooner (or *harponeer*) in taking porpoises, sword-fish, blackfish, grampuses, etc.

PULVERIZED FUEL. Anthracite or bituminous coal of any grade ground to a fine powder in an installation included in ship's equipment. It is delivered to boiler furnaces in much the same manner as oil fuel, *i.e.,* sprayed through a nozzle by air pressure, with the advantage that no pre-heating is required and little, if any, difference in steaming qualities is found in the various grades of coal so treated. Against its favorable comparison with oil fuel are installation, operation, and maintenance costs of the *grinder* or *grinders* for converting coal to the pulverized state. A number of British vessels have adopted the pulverized system since its inception some 25 years ago, but continued reasonable petroleum costs in America have resulted generally in a complete departure from the black diamond in any form.

PUMP. Any of several mechanical devices on board ship for circulating, raising, or forcing a flow of oil or water; as, a *brine p.;* a *bilge p.;* a *fuel p.* To manipulate or operate a *p.,* often with *out;* as, *p. feed-water;* to *p. out the bilges, a tank,* etc. Practical value of the *p.* for freeing a vessel of water has been realized from earliest antiquity. Sailing-vessels have long been required by law to install at least two *p's* for this purpose and powered ships in these days must carry an efficient pumping plant "capable of pumping from and draining any watertight compartment under all practicable conditions after a casualty, whether ship is upright or listed." (*From International Conference on Safety at Sea, 1948*) As ships became larger, the advantage of having access to a *fire p.* also was realized and the hand *force p.* with its attached length of hand-made canvas hose for combating fires and washing down decks made its appearance long before steam power attained any importance. To-day, ship's *p's* provide a fire-fighting supply of water to any deck or compartment in accordance with regulations governing equipment of vessels by most, if not all, maritime nations. **Ballast p.,** used for transferring, taking in, or discharging water-ballast. It usually is arranged to work the bilges, fire system, or sanitary circulation as required. Often also called *bilge-and-ballast p.* **Before-and-after p.,** a lubricating-oil *p.* worked by one end of a motor-driven shaft and a fresh water circulating *p.* by the other; used before starting and after stopping main Diesel engines for respective purposes of insuring proper lubrication and sufficient cooling-water, and for removing heat from bearings and water-jacket. **Bilge p.,** *see* BILGE; generally, a *fire p., ballast p.,* or *sanitary p.,* either individually or together, may be brought into service as a bilge-pumping necessity under emergency conditions. **Burr p.,** *see* BURR. **Centrifugal p.,** *see* CENTRIFUGAL; in this family are included *mixed flow, peripheral, propeller,* and *turbine p's,* all of which do their work by rotary motion, whether in building up a pressure flow at sides of a casing, as in the true *centrifugal p.,* or in impelling it directly onward. First-named of these, intermediate between the true *centrifugal* and the *propeller,* or *impeller,* type, is favored as a main **circulating p.;** *see* CIRCULATING PUMP. **Deck p.,** on smaller vessels used for washing decks, etc.; fitted with a suction hose which is led into water; usually worked by hand. **Donkey-p.,** *see* DONKEY. **Downton p.,** named for its inventor, a fixed double-acting force *p.; see* DOWNTON. **Feed-p.,** *see* FEED. **Fire p.,** any *p.* held in readiness to supply sea water to the *fire line* (*see* FIRE). **Fire and bilge p.,** *see* FIRE. **Force p.,** any *p.* adapted to drive or force a flow of liquid; as, a *fire p.* or a *feed p.* **Fuel p.,** *see* FUEL. **Hand-p.,** *see* HAND. **Head-p.,** *see* HEAD. **Monkey p.,** *see* MONKEY. **Oil service-p.,** *see* OIL. **Piston p.,** a double-acting or a single-acting reciprocating *p.;* any *p.* in which both suction and discharge are effected by means of a piston working in a cylinder. **Plunger p.,** a common reciprocating or "up-and-down" *hand p.; see* PLUNGER. To **prime a p.,** to put a *hand p.* in working condition by pouring some water into its barrel in order to prevent downward passage of air and so obtain the necessary vacuum below plunger, or "get the suction." **P.-brake,** handle or lever for operating a *hand p.* **P.-coat,** a canvas or sheet lead covering about a deck *hand p.* where it passes through a wood deck; it is fitted same as a *mast-coat.* **P.-dale,** the discharge spout of a deck *hand p.;* often also denotes a detachable canvas hose for carrying overboard bilge-water from such *p.* **P'ing of the barometer,** vertical oscillatory movement of mercurial column or unsteadiness of the index in an aneroid observed during squalls in bad weather and often during heavy pitching of a vessel; *see* BAROMETER. **P'ing plan,** a drawing of the pumping arrangement in whole or part of a ship. All pipe-lines are indicated together with locations of *p's* and suction ends in the various bilges, cofferdams, deep tanks, double-bottom tanks,

fresh-water tanks, peaks, etc. **P'ing windlass,** *see* WINDLASS. **P.-manifold,** *see* MANIFOLD. **P. room,** hold compartment in a tank vessel, extending from side to side and from upper deck to bottom of hull, in which the *cargo-p's* are located as low as possible, this position being regarded as that most economical in the discharging of liquid cargoes by ship's *p's.* Generally, a *p. room* is situated amidships, but tankers of large size usually are built with two such compartments,—one at each of vessel's cargo space. To **p. ship,** old expression meaning to free ship of bilge-water by *manning the p's.* **P.-strum,** a strainer or *rose-box* at the suction end of a bilge or tank pipe-line; *see* ROSE. **P.-well,** in sailing-ships and other vessels having no double-bottom tanks, a protective casing about the *hand-p's,* extending from main deck to floors at either side of keelson. Properly, in wooden vessels, it is the space between floor-timbers at which *p.-barrel* (or *p.-stock*) terminates or that into which, through the limbers, leakage or bilge-water flows during process of pumping. Order given to ship's carpenter to *sound the p.-well,* in the "good old days" simply meant to determine the rise, if any, of bilge-water in *well;* the familiar back-breaking *p.-brake* or the arm-cracking flywheel crank would do the rest! *Cf.* **B. well** *in* BILGE. **Reciprocating p.,** any *p.* in which a piston or plunger works to and fro in a cylinder or barrel; a *plunger p.* **Rotary p.,** sometimes called a *positive displacement p.,* usually designed for transferring oil, operates in a casing on the principle that a pair of rotating screws, lobes, or gears trap the liquid in suction side of casing and impels it to discharge side. **Sanitary p.,** usually located in engine-room, supplies sea water to toilet-rooms and latrines either by continuous pressure in the *sanitary line* or by maintaining a head in a gravity tank from which overflow is carried to closets, baths, etc. **Stripping p.,** in tank vessels, employed for *stripping,* or more thoroughly removing last of contents in cargo tanks as *cargo-p's* become more or less ineffective due to liquid surface nearing tank bottoms. Much smaller than *cargo-p's,* it is connected to the correspondingly smaller *stripping-line* for its purpose. **Submersible p.,** any *p.* capable of functioning efficiently while entirely submerged. Such a *p.* in larger vessels generally is required to be available for use in all ordinary circumstances in which a vessel may be flooded at sea, its source of power situated above the bulkhead deck. **Variable delivery p.,** one of rotary type moving at constant speed, but delivery from which is automatically controlled, as in a hydraulic steering system. **Water-service p.,** a *general-service p.,* or one used as required on the fire, bilge, or sanitary lines. A *p.* for circulating cooling water, as in supplying the cooling system for engine bearings, crosshead guides, shaft bearings, etc. **Windmill p.,** as formerly carried in larger Scandinavian sailing-vessels, a *bilge p.* operated by a windmill having four *sails* (canvas blades). In three-masted vessels it was set abaft the mainmast and in some of the older wooden craft assuredly commended itself in its labor-saving advantages.

PUMPKIN SEED. Local name for a small pulling or sailing boat, broad of beam and sharp at each end, so called from its shape. It is used in fishing in shallow protected waters of Florida and Gulf states. A butterfish, dollar-fish, or harvest fish; *see* DOLLAR-FISH.

PUNA WIND. A cold dry wind blowing out to sea from the Andes and over the table-land in Peru from which it takes its name.

PUNCH. A mechanical device for making rivet-holes in metal plate, structural iron, etc., by forcibly pushing disks of required diameter out of the metal; a *bear* (*see* BEAR) A hand tool driven by a hammer, as a *drift* or *drift p.*, for enlarging a rivet-hole, backing out a bolt, shackle-pin, etc.; or for making indentations or measurement marks on a metal surface, as a *center p.* or a *prick p.* **Angle-p.,** *see* ANGLE. **Armor p'ing,** *see* A.-piercing *in* ARMOR. **Grommet p.,** a hand *p.* having a circular point for cutting holes in canvas preparatory to fitting brass *grommets* therein, as in sailmaking. **P'ing machine,** a mechanical *p.*; a *p'ing bear* or *bear.*

PUNCHEON. A large cask of varying capacity in the past; now generally accepted in Great Britain and U.S.A. as a measure of 70 Imperial, or 84 U.S., gallons. The term often is loosely applied to a cask of greater capacity than a *hogshead* (63 U.S. or 52.5 Imperial gallons).

PUNGY. A small, fine-lined, fast-sailing fishing or trading schooner formerly turned out by the Baltimore and Chesapeake Bay yards and said to have been modeled on the lines of the *Baltimore clipper; cf.* CLIPPER. Also written *pungey* and *pungie* (*pron. with hard g*), the term later denoted a large canoe of Chesapeake Bay area and probably is of Indian origin.

PUNT. Generally, a flat-bottomed boat of varying dimensions and shape, usually propelled by oars; often square-ended, or the same as a small *scow*, but, more commonly, having a sharp bow and square stern, as a dinghy attached to a small yacht; a fishing-punt, or pleasure rowing-boat. **Falmouth quay-p.,** former straight-stemmed, square-sterned, ketch-rigged vessel used for fishing and taking off stores to ships when *"Falmouth for orders"* was the common destination of homeward bulk-laden sailing-vessels for the final word as to their discharging port or ports. **Galley p.,** *see* GALLEY. **Launching-p.,** also called *sledge p.*, a light oblong *p.* with flaring ends, chiefly used in England in shallow rivers, fens,

etc., for pleasure, fishing, or hunting. It is propelled by a *push-pole,* or pole thrust against bottom in direction contrary to that in which boat is required to advance. **Painting p.,** a rough, square-ended, flat-bottomed boat or small scow used for painting or other work along or near ship's water-line while in port.

PUPPIS. *See* ARGO.

PURCHASE. Any power or advantage gained by means of a mechanical aid in raising or moving a weighty object or applying stress to anything, as by a lever, screw, tackle, windlass, etc.; also, the means or instrument by which such advantage is obtained; especially, a *tackle,* or set of two or more blocks through which a chain or rope is rove for lifting a weight, setting up standing rigging, bracing yards, etc. Also termed *mechanical advantage, p.* obtained in a tackle is governed, in the ordinary rig of two blocks, by *number of parts at the moving block;* thus, in a *luff tackle,* or *p.* consisting of a double and a single block, with standing end of rope secured to the latter, if its double block be suspended aloft and single block attached to a weight, a tension equal to one-third the weight applied to the hauling part of rope will just balance or hold weight in suspension, since there are three parts of rope sharing the burden. In this case, without taking friction in blocks into account, mechanical advantage, or ratio of power applied to weight, is said to be as one is to three, or 1:3. Theoretically, a slight additional tension on hauling part of rope will set tackle in motion and so raise the weight, but actually a substantial increase of power is required to overcome *friction* in blocks, magnitude of which depends upon type and diameter measurement of sheaves, whether ball-bearing, dummy, etc., and in a given tackle progressively increases with decrease of speed of sheave, *i.e.,* sheave taking the hauling part of rope, and so turning faster than next sheave in order, is least affected by friction, next one a little more, and so on. An old seamanship rule, in allowing for this obstacle, gives the generous addition of one-tenth the weight for each sheave in the *p.;* thus, with our simple luff-tackle rig, a lift of 1500 lbs. would be reckoned as $1500 + 3(1500 \div 10)$, or 1950 lbs., in considering adequate strength of gear for the occasion. With first class modern blocks, however, probably half of that allowance would be a just figure; but, based upon the rule referred to, in practice it still is customary to consider the mechanical advantage of a tackle thus conservatively reduced. Our estimated 1950 lbs. in above example now being that supported by the three parts of rope at the moving block, each part is considered to lift 650 lbs., so that mechanical advantage becomes $650:1500 = 1.3:3.0$, or 13:30, instead of the theoretical 500:1500, or 1:3. Similarly, with 4 parts of rope at moving block and 4 sheaves contained, as in a *two-fold p.*, advantage ratio = 14:40. In the case of a *p.* other than one having two blocks of similar pattern and function, as in a single or a double *burton, Bell p., tackle-and-runner* in a *fish-tackle,* or other odd rigs, mechanical advantage of tackle is arrived at by considering relative tension in each part of rope leading from moving block, or blocks, or from the lifting hook. As a simple example, in the *single Spanish burton (see* BURTON) the part leading direct to hook from fixed block obviously is in *double tension,* while one part of the *whip,* also leading to hook, is in *single tension,* or that equal to power applied to fall or whip. Mechanical advantage, then, is 1:1 + 2 = 1:3 or, allowing for friction, 12:30. **Bell's p.**, consists of two fixed and two moving single blocks, hauling part of fall leading from one of the latter; once used in topsail halyards in small vessels; power ratio, 14:70. **Cant p.**, *see* **C.-fall** *in* CANT. **Cat p.**, *see* CAT. **Collier's p.**, so named from its use by the old collier brigs in the Tyne-London trade, was rigged to assist in breaking out the anchor by hooking the *cat-tackle* to cable as far out from *hawse-pipe* as possible and hauling on *cat-fall* with the *fish-tackle.* **Double p.**, a *gun-tackle p., q.v.* **Fourfold p.**, consists of two blocks each of which has four sheaves. As in all tackles of two blocks in which each block has same number of sheaves, the standing end of fall is made fast to same block from which its hauling part leads; *see* **F'fold purchase** *in* FOUR. **Gun-tackle p.**, named for its use in moving the guns in and out of firing position at the *gun-ports* in old naval days, a tackle of two single blocks, with hauling part of rope leading from the *moving block;* practical power ratio, 1.2:3. Where, as in a hoist, a *gun-tackle rig* has its fall leading to the upper, or *fixed,* block, it becomes a *single p.*, or one of theoretical mechanical advantage of *twice* the power applied; in this case practical power ratio is 1.2:2 or 12:20. *Cf.* **Single p. Kent-p.**, a variant of *cant-p.*, or *cant-tackle; see* **C.-fall** *in* CANT. **Peak p.**, often called *peak jig; see* JIG. **P. block**, *see* BLOCK. **P. fall**, the rope or chain rove in blocks of a *p.;* often denotes only its working or *hauling part; i.e.*, part to which initial power is applied. **P. power**, effective power or mechanical advantage obtained by a *p.*, as by a lever or a tackle. It usually is expressed as the ratio of power applied to that gained, as 1:3, or simply as a factor, as in "the mechanical advantage or *p. power* of the *gun-tackle p.* is *three*," and sometimes as a fraction in which the numerator is *power applied* and denominator, *power gained*, as 1/3, in the case of the *gun-tackle.* Generally, however, *p. power* or power ratio of a tackle is given as expressing *theoretical advantage* of the rig, *i.e.*, friction of working parts is not considered. From a practical standpoint, therefore, we may term the *p. power,* in accordance

with our opening remarks regarding an allowance of one-tenth the weight for each sheave in the *p.*, the *practical power ratio,* or theoretical mechanical advantage corrected for friction; thus, our *gun-tackle p.* is regarded as having a *p. power* of 12:30. To **raise a p.**, *see* RAISE. **Single p.**, that obtained in a moving single block, as where a cargo-fall is "doubled up" by making fast its end at the boom head, a single block to which the cargo-hook is attached being suspended in bight of fall; also, a gun-tackle having its fixed block that from which hauling part of rope leads; *see* **Gun-tackle p.** (*2nd. part*) **Threefold p.**, tackle of two blocks, each having three sheaves; if block from which fall leads is the moving one, practical power ratio is 16:70; if that block is fixed, 16:60. Much used in larger vessels for raising and lowering life-boats, where manilla rope is employed. **Topping-lift p.**, tackle attached to a topping-lift pendant for raising a boom, yard, etc. **Treble p.**, term sometimes used for a *threefold p.* (*q.v.*). **Twofold p.**, consists of two blocks, each having two sheaves; power ratio when moving block is that from which fall leads, 14:50; when that block is fixed, 14:40. (Generally, in ship's gear, the terms *purchase* and *tackle* are synonymous. Important rigs, such as those for lifting heavy weights or for special work, usually are granted the former appellative, while *tackle* is applied to those of lesser consequence. Thus, a *topping-lift purchase* seems to *rate* higher than a *life-boat tackle,* though actually the genus indicated in either term is one and the same.)

PURGA. (*Russ.*)   A violent snowstorm or blizzard in the Bering Sea.

PURIFIER, Oil.   Also called a *separator,* a machine that removes water, carbon, metal grindings, dirt, sludge, etc., from *lubricating oil* by centrifugal force or by straining the oil under pressure through a special fiber.

PURL. (Nor. *purla,* to bubble up)   To flow or ripple with a low murmuring sound, as a stream; to eddy or swirl. The murmuring of rippling water, as in a flowing current; a small whirlpool or eddy.

PURSE.   A *purse net,* or fishing-net in the form of a long deep pocket, the mouth of which is provided with *p.-strings* or *draw-strings* for closing it upon trapping a school of fish. To close a *p. net* by such means, or a *p. seine* by means of its *p.-line* and *brail-ropes.* **P. boat**, a rugged, beamy open boat, to-day usually power-driven, used in fishing by *p. seine.* **P. seine**, *see* SEINE. **Sea-p.**, *see* SEA.

PURSER.   In larger merchant vessels, particularly in passenger-liners, a *staff officer* who takes care of ship's papers and accounts, including all documents concerned with cargo, crew, mails, and passengers. He also is charged with general welfare of passengers, and in larger liners his department includes one or more *assistant-p's* and several *p.'s clerks.* Formerly, in U.S. navy, present rank of *paymaster* was called *purser.* **P.'s dip,** kind of small candle once used in navy ships; named for the *p.'s* office where it chiefly was employed. **P.'s name,** old term for a fictitious or assumed name· given by an enlisted seaman.

PURSING-GEAR. Purse-line, brail-lines, etc., by means of which a *purse seine* or any *purse net* is closed in capturing fish.

PURSUIT, Right of. *See* RIGHT.

PUT. To move or impel in any direction; bring to a certain position; place; lay; or take a certain action. Usually with a combining preposition; as, *in, for, out, to, etc.* To **p. about,** to bring vessel on the other tack, or *go about;* to alter course to the opposite direction. To **p. away for,** to make a start toward; as, *we p. away for the coast.* To **p. back,** to return or turn back; as, *the brig p. back to Brest with fire in the hold.* To **p. for,** to start toward, usually in sense of making all possible speed; as, *she p. for harbor with every stitch drawing.* To **p. forth,** to set out or leave a port, anchorage, etc., for sea, as a ship. *(Chiefly poetic)* To **p. in,** to enter a harbor or sheltered area, as on account of bad weather, need of supplies, an accident, or other cause, during course of a voyage; as, *we p. in at Rio to land four stowaways.* To **p. in** (or **out**) **of commission,** *see* COMMISSION. To **p. in one's oar,** *see* OAR. To **p. off,** to leave land, as a boat from a beach; to depart, as in a boat, from alongside a vessel, pier, etc. To **p. out,** to sail or start out, as from a haven; especially, in sense of suddenly departing in an emergency; as, *the lugger p. out from Deal in a southwest gale, but failed to reach the wreck.* Also, to get out or suddenly leave, as by compulsion; as,

we p. out under a hail of shrapnel, in spite of our neutral colors. To **p. the helm down** (or **up**), *see* HELM. To **p. to sea,** to leave a harbor or anchorage for sea; to start on a voyage; to steer away from the land.

PUTELI or **PUTELEE.** *See* PATELA.

PUTTY. The common cement of dough-like consistency, made of boiled linseed oil and whiting, used to fill crevices and holes in wood-work, as a bedding for port-lights, deck-lights, etc. Any of several cements of similar consistency variously employed in metal work, piping, etc. **Manganesite p.,** made of a mixture of oxide of manganese and boiled linseed or other special oil, used in steam-joints, turbine casings, etc. **Red lead p.,** *see* Red l. *in* LEAD. This *p.,* in shipyard work, is forced by pressure between surfaces of metal which do not properly fay against each other, by a *red lead injector,* or *p. gun.* **Rust p.,** also called *iron p.,* made from a mixture of borings or filings of cast iron with sal-ammoniac; pasty in consistency, it is used as a *luting* in joining flanges of iron pipes, etc.

PYROTECHNIC. (Gr. *pyr,* fire; *tekhne,* art) Of or pertaining to *pyrotechnics,* or manufacture and use,—especially display,—of *fireworks.* **P. signals,** blue lights, Coston lights, red distress flares, detonating rockets, parachute flares, etc., usually covered by patent. *Cf.* **Blue l.** *and* **Coston l.** *in* LIGHT. **P. ammunition,** *see* AMMUNITION.

PYX. (Gr. *puxis,* a box) A term, dating from the Middle Ages, for the box or binnacle in which the compass was kept. *(Now rare or obsolete)* **Pyxis,** as recognized by some astronomers to-day, was an early subdivision of the constellation ARGO *(q.v.),* or that representing the *"nautical box or mariner's compass,"* an only star of which is catalogued in the *American Ephemeris* as θ *Pyxidis* of magnitude 4.93.

Q

Q. Denoted in *International Code of Signals* by a square yellow flag or by flashing or sound signal (*International Morse Code*) — — • — (*dash dash dot dash*). Flag *Q,* hoisted singly by a vessel arriving from a foreign port,—in some countries required of a foreign vessel arriving from *any* port,—signifies "*My vessel is healthy and I request free pratique.*" Also, as a towing signal, displayed by vessel towing, denotes "*Shall we anchor at once?*" or by towed vessel, "I wish to anchor at once." Such towing signal may be made at night by flashing (*Morse*). Abbreviation *Q* or *q,* in ships' log-books and weather records, is used for *squalls* or *squally weather.*

Q. M. Abbrev. for *quartermaster; see* QUARTERMASTER.

Q-SHIP or **Q-BOAT.** So called from letter *Q* under which such vessels were classed and often also called *mystery ship,* one of many small merchant and fishing vessels of various rigs, sail and steam, employed by British navy in anti-submarine activities during World War I. The craft were designed to lure an inquisitive U-boat (German submarine) within gunfire range, while affecting the innocent air of a fisherman or trader. At the appropriate moment, the mystery-boat's armament suddenly was uncovered and brought into play, usually with excellent results.

QUADRANT. (L. *quadrans,* a fourth part) Navigational instrument designed to measure angles,—especially altitudes of heavenly bodies,—up to 90°. Also called an *octant* from its arc length being one-eighth of a circle, it was the forerunner of our present *sextant,* having first appeared as a "*reflecting quadrant*" about 1730 and known for many years thereafter as both *Godfrey's bow* and *Hadley's q.* (or *octant*). (*See* HADLEY'S QUADRANT *and* SEXTANT) Radius length, or height, of early *q's* was as much as four feet; by about 1800 their usual size was reduced to a 12-inch radius. Better instruments were made of ebony wood, with graduations marked on inlaid ivory on the arc, or *limb,* and a handle fitted.

An arc of 90 degrees or quarter of a circle; sector equal to one-fourth area of a circular figure. Any direction between two specified cardinal points; as, *prevailing winds are in the N.E. q.* Any casting, forging, or built-up frame in the form of, or suggesting, a quarter of a circle; as, a *steering-q.* fixed to head of a *rudder-stock.* **Dangerous q.,** that area in a cyclonic storm in which wind blows directly, or nearly so, toward the storm's path, or line of progression; so called because a vessel, in addition to danger of being blown into the latter, is subjected to the possibility of recurving of storm's advance, as in a tropical cyclone at or near outer limits of the tropics. *Dangerous q.* in northern hemisphere is right forward *q.,* as viewed from storm's center in direction of its path; conversely, it is left forward *q.* in southern latitudes. *Cf.* CYCLONE. **Davis's q.,** *see* DAVYS'S QUADRANT *or* STAFF; *also* BACKSTAFF. **Gunner's q.,** a graduated sector of about 90°, used to show a gun's angle of inclination with the horizontal. **Q.-block,** piece of wood hollowed to form a rest for a boom; a saddle. Hardwood timber laid on deck in form of an arc as a support or bed for the rack in which a steering-gear pinion works in the case of a steering-engine acting directly on *q. Also see* SADDLE. **Q. davit,** a boat-davit the foot of which is arc-shaped and toothed for working in a rack. Davit is supported in a frame and turned outward or inward in athwartship plane by means of a crank and screw arrangement at top of frame, about four feet above deck. The *Welin Q.-davit* is one of this type. **Q. tiller,** also called *rudder q.* and *steering q.,* a casting or built-up attachment to upper end of a rudder-stock and taking the place of a *tiller.* So named because suggestive of a *q.* of a circle, its purpose is to maintain a constant lead for each steering-chain, both of which are secured to, and bedded along arc of *q.* Thus, regardless of rudder's angle with the fore-and-aft line, the athwartship line of each chain is always tangential to arc of *q.* and hence maintains a constant leverage for turning rudder. **Skylight q.,** arc-shaped bar of metal attached to an opening skylight for a support. It is clamped or pinned to hold skylight open at any desired angle. **Steering-q.,** *see* **Q. tiller. Valve q.,** curved link-bars which regulate travel of valve-piston in a reciprocating engine; *cf.* **Slot l.** *in* LINK.

QUADRANTAL. Of or pertaining to a quadrant; shaped like a quadrant. **Q. correctors,** as accessories to a compensating binnacle for a magnetic compass, are two soft iron globes or spheres (sometimes boxes of soft iron chain), one at each side of binnacle, at equal distances from, and centered to lie in same horizontal plane as, the compass card, when vessel is upright. Their purpose is to compensate for, or *correct,* that component of total deviation, called *q. deviation,* of the compass due to transient magnetism induced by earth's magnetic field in fore-and-aft and athwartship soft iron (or mild steel), that in the last-named,—chiefly deck-beams,—usually predominating. **Q. deviation,** in compass deviation analysis is expressed as *coefficient D* and has a maximum value on the *q. points.* An uncompensated compass, if ship is swung for deviations before the *adjusting,* or *correcting,* procedure, will show the *D* component by taking the algebraic sum of deviations observed on *NE, SW, SE,* and *NW by compass,* after reversing the signs of that observed on last two, and dividing by 4. Thus deviation on *NE* given as $+10°$; on *SW,* $+15°$; on *SE,* $-6°$; and on *NW,* $-7°$; we have $(10 + 15 + 6 + 7) \div 4 = 38 \div 4 = +9\frac{1}{2}°$, or value of the *q. deviation;* coefficient $D = +9\frac{1}{2}°$. In almost all cases D has a *plus,* or *easterly,* value on both *NE* and *SW* points; *minus,* or *westerly,* on *SE* and *NW;* this being due to greater effect of transient magnetism in ship's beams than in her fore-and-aft iron; *see* DEVIATION. **Q. triangle,** a spherical triangle which has one or more of its sides equal to a *quadrant,* or $90°$.

QUADRATURE. Relation of two heavenly bodies appearing $90°$ apart; as, *the sun is in q. with Mars.* Also, either of the halfway points in an orbit between the *syzygies,* or conjunction and opposition; thus, the *q's* of our moon coincide with times of *first* and *last quarters,* when exactly one-half her illuminated surface is visible because of her halfway position between *full* and *new moon.* Loosely, the moon is said to be *in q.* at or about first and last quarter.

QUADRILATERAL SAIL. Any sail having four sides; as, a *square,* a *gaff,* or a *lug* sail.

QUADRIREME. (L. *quattuor,* four; *remus,* an oar) Ancient galley having four banks of oars; *see* GALLEY.

QUADRUPLE. (L. *quadruplum,* four-fold) **Q.-screw,** designating a vessel having four propellers; sometimes seen in *abbrev.* Q.S.S., for *quadruple-screw ship,* as *Q.S.S. Mauretania; see* SCREW. **Q.-expansion engine,** *see* **Multiple-expansion e.** *in* ENGINE.

QUAKER-BIRD. The *sooty albatross* of the South Pacific, so named for its sombre color; *see* ALBATROSS.

QUARANTINE. (Fr. *quarantaine;* from *quarante,* forty) A period of forty days, or formerly that during which a vessel arriving in port with actual or suspected malignant contagious disease amongst persons on board was forbidden to have intercourse with shore. Such vessel then was said to be *quarantined;* now *in quarantine.* The system or measures of enforcement of laws governing medical inspection, fumigation, and *quarantining* of vessels; also, the place, usually at or near a port entrance, at which arriving vessels are isolated, or detained pending determination of health conditions on board. *Cf.* PRATIQUE. **Q. anchorage,** area set apart as an anchorage for arriving vessels requiring, or required to obtain, *pratique.* It usually is located off or near a *q. station,* its extent, particularly in U.S., indicated by yellow-painted buoys. In U.S. waterfront verbiage, a vessel arriving in such area is said to be *at q.* **Q. boat,** also pratique-boat; *see* **P.-boat** *in* PRATIQUE. **Q. declaration,** as required by some countries, including U.S., document signed by master of a merchant vessel and ship's surgeon (if carried) before the *q. officer* who boards vessel, giving particulars of vessel and cargo, ports of call during voyage, number of crew and passengers on board, number of infectious or contagious cases and deaths on voyage, etc. Such document, more generally, is executed at office of captain of the port, port office, or other competent port authority, and, with manifests of cargo, passenger and crew lists, and ship's register, often constitutes entry at Customs. Also termed *entry declaration.* **Q. fee,** a port charge levied on vessels in foreign trade for maintenance of *q. service.* **Q. flag,** *see* Q. **Q. signals,** those of the *International Code* to be shown on arrival by vessels requiring or required to show their state of health: In daytime, *Q flag (see* Q.); *Q flag* over first repeater, or *QQ,* signifying "*My ship is suspect; i.e., I have had cases of infectious diseases more than five days ago, or there has been unusual mortality among the rats on board my ship*"; and *Q flag* over *L flag,* signifying "*My ship is infected; i.e., I have had cases of infectious diseases less than five days ago.*" By night, a red light over a white light, signifying "*I have not received free pratique.*" (Lights should not be more than six feet apart and are to be exhibited only within the precincts of a port) **Q. station,** site of the office of *q. officer* of a port, *q. hospital* for patients removed from vessels because of suffering from or showing symptoms of contagious disease, and sometimes accommodation for crews and passengers landed during necessary fumigation of their ships by staff attached to station. It usually is located within sight or convenient distance of the *q. anchorage.*

QUARTER. (L. *quartus,* fourth)　After part of ship's side, generally in way of the *q.-deck* or the *poop,* but often simply the rounded part or entrance toward vessel's stern. Part of a yard between its *slings* or middle and about half yard-arm length. One-fourth of a fathom; as, in the leadsman's call, *a q. less seven.* Arc of the compass equal to a fourth part of a *point,* or about 2¾°; precisely, 2° 48′ 45″; as expressed in *NE* ¼ *N,* that mark on a compass card graduated to *q. points* indicating one *q. point* to northward of *NE.* A bearing or direction relative to ship's fore-and-aft line, looking astern, often is referred to as number of points *on the q.;* as, *the light is two points on our port q.;* but never more than an arc of four points is so expressed. Thus, the improper *five points on the q.* becomes *three points abaft the beam,*—there being an arc of eight points between *abeam* and *astern.* In approximate usage, *four points on the q.* is termed *broad on the q.* The moon's position in quadrature, or at *first* and *third* (or "*last*") *q.* To *q.* the sea or the wind is to steer on such course as will bring wind or sea *on the q.,* as in sailing. In plural form, *quarters,* denotes stations at which officers and men are posted in action, drills, inspection, etc.; also, living spaces assigned members of the crew. To assign to a berth or living space; as, *the men were quartered in the half-deck.* *Cf.* QUARTERS. **Q. badge,** in old war-vessels, a coat of arms, royal insignia, or other ornate design, usually in gilt, fitted on the counter or *q. gallery,* particularly in French and Spanish ships of the line. **Q. bill,** *see* S. bill *in* STATION. **Q.-bitts,** posts or bollards at after end of ship for securing mooring or towing hawsers; *towing-bitts; cf.* BITT. **Q.-block,** a lead-block on a yard at the slings or *q.* for a sheet of sail next above, or a leech-line or clewline of sail next below. **Q.-boards,** light bulwarks or raised extension of main bulwarks in way of a *q.-deck* or a *poop;* also, *top-gallant bulwarks* in older usage. **Q.-boat,** any boat which is stowed or hung from davits on either *q.* **Q. breast,** a mooring-line holding ship's *q.* alongside a pier, etc.; also, *q.-fast, q.-rope,* and *q.-line,* in smaller vessels. **Q.-cloth,** in the old sailing warships, painted canvas cover, or *hammock-cloth,* protecting the hammock nettings along aftermost part of bulwarks. **Q.-davits,** those for hanging a *q.-boat,* (*q.v.*) **Q.-deck,** *see* DECK. (For *Raised q.-deck, see* RAISED) **Q.-decker,** an officer who is considered a stickler for ceremony and etiquette rather than a good seaman. (*Older naval usage*) **Q.-deckish** = over-punctilious. **Q.-fishes,** bands or hoops around a built mast. They are provided with means of tightening up, such as toed ends with a setting-up bolt, as mast becomes weathered. **Q. gallery,** in larger war-vessels of 17th. and 18th. centuries, an ornate balcony on each *q.; see* GALLERY. **Q. gasket,** *see* GASKET. **Q. gunner,** formerly, in U.S. navy, a gunner's assistant; a petty officer now called

gunner's mate. **Q.-irons,** *see* IRON. **Q.-knee,** in wood-built vessels, a *lodging-knee* fitted at after side of the transom-beam; *cf.* KNEE. **Q. lift,** on heavier topsail and lower yards, a lift, or one of the legs of a lift-bridle, leading to each *q.* of yard; also, one of a pair of *topping-lifts* fitted to a boom of a fore-and-aft sail about one-fourth of boom's length from outer end; weather one takes weight of boom while lee lift is slacked off. *See* LIFT. **Q. line,** position of ships in *column,* in which one is four points forward or abaft another's beam; also called *bow-and-q. line.* A rope leading to a ship's *q.* for any outside purpose; a *q.-fast;* any mooring-hawser secured on the *q.* A line attached to lower side of a seine to assist in dragging net to shore or closing it. *Q. lines,* in ship's drawings, as in the half-breadth plan, indicate longitudinal planes, parallel to midship vertical plane, halfway between latter and vessel's side at her greatest breadth. **Q. mat,** chafing-mat placed on the *q.* of a yard to act as a protective cushion between yard and standing rigging when former is braced sharp up. **Q. mooring,** chain cable or a hawser leading to an anchor, buoy, dolphin, etc., from ship's *q.,* as in the case of holding vessel clear of a pier, or for hauling ship broadside from her berth. Loosely, any hawser leading from a vessel's *q.* **Q. netting,** *see* NETTING. **Q.-piece,** one of the horizontal timbers forming after limit of a *q. gallery* in old-fashioned ships; horizontal timber or heavy iron strap fitted around the *q.* or *knuckle* at junction of ship's side and a "square" counter; a platform on the *q.* forming the base of a projecting cabin, or for mounting a chase-gun. **Q. pillar,** stanchion or pillar supporting a deck-beam or a series of beams between ship's center line and her side; also, *q. stanchion.* **Q. point,** *see opening remarks in* QUARTER. **Q. rail,** any form of guard-rail around a vessel's stern and *q's* in the absence of a bulwark; a top-gallant or monkey rail; *see* M. rail *in* MONKEY. **Q. rudder,** one of a pair of rudders hung at either side of the fore-and-aft line, as in a stern-wheeler; or one hung from a cross timber at boat's stern, as in some larger native craft in South Sea islands. **Q.-sawed,** said of planking cut from the log in such manner that, as nearly as possible, the tree's annual rings are severed at right angles to broad surface of the timber. Planking thus cut is stronger, more wear and weather resisting, and less affected by warping than is the case with common through-sawn lumber; also, *q.-cleft; q.-rift.* **Q. sling,** a temporary lift or sling supporting a lower yard in way of a hoisting-purchase, or *q. tackle,* rigged to *q.* of the yard; also, in larger older ships, one of the supporting chains or *slings* leading from the lowermast cap to each *q.* of a lower yard. **Q. stanchion,** *see* Q. pillar. **Q. strop,** a grommet or iron band for supporting a block, as for a leech-line, at the *q.* of a yard; also, *q. strap.* **Q. tackle,** a purchase rigged to the *q.* of a lower yard for hoisting. **Q. timber,** one of the frames, or framing collectively, abaft the transom frame in a ship's counter. **Q. turn,** change of direction in which a moving vessel or formation of vessels makes a turn of 90°, or through an arc of 90° of the compass. **Q. watch,** as referred to the *two-watch,* or *watch-and-watch,* system, particularly in naval vessels, one-half of either watch, or *one-q.* of number of crew members on watch-duty. **Q. wind,** that blowing toward ship's *q.;* a *quartering,* or *quarterly,* wind; usually so termed when from a direction *broad on q.,* or about 45° from right aft. **Weather q.,** that *q.* on windward side; opposed to *lee q.,* or that on side away from the wind.

QUARTERING. Coming toward the quarter, or from a direction well abaft the beam; said of the sea or wind; as, *a moderate q. sea;* synonymous with *quarterly;* as, *a heavy q.* (or *quarterly*) *gale.* Also, procedure of sailing with wind on alternate *quarters,* as in a fore-and-aft rigged vessel having a breeze from opposite direction to course to be made good. Vessel is thus maneuvered in order to more effectively spread her sail area and so make better speed than if sailed directly before the wind.

QUARTERLY. Of or pertaining to ship's *quarter;* as, *a fresh q. breeze;* off or on the quarter; quartering.

QUARTERMASTER. In merchant vessels, particularly those of liner type, one of a number—from 4 to 8, depending on size and class of ship—of able seamen who steer, keep navigating-bridge and equipment, wheel-house, chart-room, etc., clean and in order, stand gangway watch in port, attend to flags displayed, and generally assist in matters pertaining directly to safe navigation of vessel. In naval ships generally, a petty officer whose duties include care and operation of signals, sounding gear and apparatus, steering ship, receiving and transmitting orders over telephone system, etc., under supervision of officer of the watch.

QUARTERS. Living or other accommodation spaces to which persons on board ship are assigned; as, *firemen's q.; seamen's q.; steerage passengers' q.* Individual stations, collectively, in which each member of crew takes up his assigned post, as at battle stations, inspection, fire drill, etc. Space for an operation or some activity; as in *close q.; see* C. **quarters** *in* CLOSE. **Fire q.,** *see* FIRE. **General q.,** battle stations of ship's company complete. **Winter q.,** chiefly in yachting usage, berth in which a boat or vessel is laid up for winter season.

QUASI DERELICT. Term often used in admiralty courts to denote a vessel in status of more or less implied helplessness, while not definitely "forever abandoned to mercy of wind and sea." Thus, a ship

may be temporarily abandoned because of fire on board, crew intending to return upon explosion of certain dangerous cargo, and hence may be called a *q. d.* until such return takes place. Also, such status is evident in the case of a crew physically incapable of navigating their vessel.

QUAY. (Of Celtic origin, as in Breton *kae,* an enclosure) (Pron. *kee*) A wharf or other waterside construction at which vessels are berthed; especially, a masonry-built breastwork or artificial embankment along a waterfront at which ships may berth for landing or loading cargo and passengers. **Legal q.,** *see* LEGAL. **Q. dues,** charges levied on vessels berthed at a *q.; cf.* DOCKAGE. **Q. pier,** structure extending shoreward from a *q. wall,* or outer limit of an enclosed dock system, sometimes forming a dividing pier between two areas in such system. It usually is constructed and equipped for berthing vessels and transferring their cargoes. **Q. punt,** *see* **Falmouth quay-p.** *in* PUNT. **Q. wall,** outside waterfront limit of a *q.;* especially, that forming the outer boundary of a tidal basin or dock.

QUAYAGE. Charges for use of a quay, as for berthing of a vessel or for deposit of merchandise; quay dues; dockage; wharfage.

QUEEN. In yachting terminology, a triangular sail set on the main-topmast stay in schooner rigs; also, *q. staysail.*

QUERIMAN. The *white mullet,* a small member of the *Mugilidæ* family found in West Indian waters. It is classified as *Mugil curema* or *M. brasiliensis. Cf.* MULLET.

QUICK. (Originally meant *alive, living, lively*) Active; rapid; speedy. **Q.-closing gear,** *see* GEAR. **Q.-flashing light,** that shown by a lighthouse or buoy, so termed when it flashes continuously at rate of not less than 60 times per minute; abbrv. on charts, *Qk. Fl.* An *intermittent q.-flashing light* shows quick flashes for about four seconds followed by a dark period of about four seconds; abbrev. *I. Qk. Fl. Cf.* **Flashing-l.** *in* LIGHT. **Q.-saver,** in 16th. and 17th. century usage, an elaborate bridle fitted to the midship portion of the foot of a lower square sail (*course*). It was connected to a rope or tackle by which it was hauled downward and toward the mast for reducing bellying of the canvas when sailing with a "flowing sheet." The more recent *midship tack* was a quasi-revival of this *life-* or *production-saver,* as we may so express its equivalent. **Q.-water,** ripplings on the surface indicating presence of a local current. **Q.-work,** in older shipbuilding parlance, certain planking in a vessel's upper works so termed because *quickly* put in place; specifically, the short pieces between gun-ports; all parts of inner upper works above the *covering-board;* the spirketting; etc. Also, now rarely used term for planking on immersed part of the hull when vessel is in the laden condition.

QUICKEN. In boat and ship construction, to shorten the radius of, or sharpen, a curved line in the structure; as, to *q. the flare* (of the bows), the *turn of the quarter,* the *sheer,* etc.

QUICKSAND. A deep mass of sand saturated with water, characterized by its yielding quality whereby weighty objects may be rapidly engulfed. Some shifting sands, or mixture of sand and mud, such as those in the *Amazon,* while of solid consistency when emerged at low water, change to the "quick" order as the rising tide covers such areas. A slower-acting variety of this danger is seen in the *Goodwin Sands* in the Strait of Dover; hence its early name, *"Ye Shippe-swallower"*;—its harmless-looking surface at low tide covers the common grave of thousands of vessels.

QUILTING. A layer or series of pieces of sennit sewn as a chafing protective on a canvas drawbucket, rail-cover, etc. Act or process of sewing sennit to canvas, as in making a chafing-mat; sewing a padding on a canvas cover; a chafing-cloth on a sail; etc. Heavy coir or manila matting or wood sheathing nailed to a vessel's planking about her water-line as a protection against injury by floating ice. In the "good old days," *q.* was a colloquialism for a rope's-ending or flogging. **Q. rivet,** for holding together the faying surfaces of a doubling-plate, one of the rivets driven in at about mid-area of such plate; a *tack-rivet,* or rivet securing one plate to another within the line of the ordinary uniting rivets. **Q. weld,** a plug weld used in securing plates together in lieu of rivets as indicated above.

QUINTAL. (Ar. *qintar*) A unit of weight of several different values according to country in which the term is used. In Great Britain and America, a weight of 112 lbs. (*8 stone*) or 100 lbs., according to custom, commonly used in the dried fish trade. A *q.* in the metric system is 100 kilogrammes, equal to 220.46 lbs. avoirdupois; sometimes designated in France as *quintal métrique.*

QUINTANT. (L. *quintus,* fifth) An instrument similar in construction to that of the *sextant,* but capable of measuring angles up to about 140°; so named from its arc of 72°, or *fifth* part of a circle. It is used chiefly in hydrographic surveying for boat work, where measurement of horizontal angles by a theodolite is impracticable.

QUOIN. Also, *coin;* any cantic or angular-shaped piece of wood employed as a wedge, as in chocking a mast in position; in securing a round weighty object, as a cask, spar, boiler, etc., against rolling. A small block of hardwood having one of its sides tapered to a point as a wedge, placed under the breech of an old-fashioned cannon for elevating gun's muzzle as required. **Cant-q.,** as used in *bilge-and-contline* stowage of casks, one of four *q's* placed under the quarters of each cask in the ground tier for purpose of both holding cask in position and raising its bilge clear of deck; *cf.* **C.-quoin** *in* CANT. Also *see* CONTLINE. To **q. a cask,** to place it on *q's* as in stowing the first tier of a consignment of casks.

R

R. As an abbreviation in ships' log-books and weather observation records, *R* or *r* denotes *rain;* also, *rough sea.* In U.S. navy, abbrev. *R,* in records of enlisted men signifies *deserted.* International Code flag *R* (indicated orally as *Roger*) is a yellow Greek cross on a square red ground; International Morse Code *R = dot-dash-dot* (• — •) Flag *R,* hoisted singly, or Morse Code *R,* by flashing, means *"The way is off my ship; you may feel your way past me."* Also, as a towing signal, as above, means, when shown by ship towed, *"Go slower";* by towing ship, *"I will go slower."*

R. A. In nautical astronomy, abbrev. for *right ascension;* in naval records, often used for *Rear Admiral.*

RABBET. A channel or groove cut along the edge or face of a piece of timber or plate to receive the edge of a plank or plate fitted to it; as, the *keel-r.* along a wooden ship's keel, or that on the stem, into which edge of the garboard strake and ends of side planking, respectively, are snugged. Also, *rebate.* **Back-r.,** *see* **B.-rabbet** *in* BACK. **R. line,** the line indicated by the entering of an edge of a plank in a *r.* or that of the butts of a series of planks set in a *r.* Specifically, such line of intersection of the garboard strake with the keel or ends of planking in the stem and stern posts. **R.-plank,** the *hog-piece,* or *keel-batten,* fitted along top of a boat's keel to serve as a landing for garboard strake planks, thus dispensing, wholly or in part, with a *keel-r.; see* **H.-piece** *in* HOG.

RABBIT-FISH. A kind of *globe* or *porcupine fish,* 6 to 7 inches in length, oval-shaped in profile, and of ugly appearance; *see* **G.-fish** *in* GLOBE. A species of *chimæra,* classified as *C. monstrosa; see* CHIMÆRA. Also, a food fish closely related to the *Escolar;* about 3 feet in length; found in tropical seas; *see* ESCOLAR.

RACE. A speed contest, as in yacht-sailing. A tide-rip or surface tidal turbulence caused by meeting or sharply deflected currents, often aggravated by strong winds into a steep breaking sea; a rapid current flow in a channel, or channel characterized by such. In a single-screw vessel, space limited by propeller- and rudder-posts in which the propeller rotates; agitated water in way of a turning screw or paddle-wheel, often referred to as *r. of the screw* (or *screws*) or *r. of the paddle.* Due to ship pitching in a head sea, a screw-propeller is said to *r.* when engines suddenly are relieved of their load, and so their turning velocity increased, as screw becomes partly emerged. **R.-board,** an old name for a gangplank or brow. **R.-knife,** *see* KNIFE. **Tide r.,** a tide-rip; accelerated flow of a tidal current, as when passing over a shoal.

RACEABOUT. Small sloop-rigged racing-yacht having a short bowsprit.

RACER. A swift-sailing boat or vessel; a racing-yacht; a clipper.

RACING. Sudden speeding up of engines due to vessel pitching and bringing propeller partly or wholly out of water; also may occur in lesser degree in a heavy following or confused sea. Either propeller or engine is said to *race* in conditions noted. (Governors for controlling *r.* have been employed in reciprocating engines with more or less success.) Act of sailing vessels or boats in a speed contest. **R. flag,** distinguishing pennant or flag flown at masthead by a vessel engaged in a race. It is displayed throughout period of craft's actual status as a contestant; *i.e.,* must be hauled down upon event of withdrawal from race. **R. number,** that shown on the mainsail of a yacht participating in a race; *see* NUMBER. **R. skiff,** a light, long, narrow boat pulled by one oarsman in speed contests; fitted with out-rigger rowlocks and sliding seat.

RACK.[1] (Du. *rek,* framework) Any frame, appropriately shaped batten, etc., for securing movable objects; as, a *fairleader r.; a pin-r.; a pot-r.; a table-r.* A row or series of piles to which vessels may be secured, as a *mooring-r.;* or for shouldering a vessel into a slip, as a *ferry r.* A *r.-block,* or piece of timber, such as a rail stanchion, in which are set two or more sheaves serving as fairleaders for running-gear like upper yard braces and halyards. Such *r.* in older vessels often consisted of a piece of hardwood secured to the inner face of a bulwark stanchion and forming the *half shell* in which sheaves were set. A sheave set in a bulwark for a fairleader. A toothed rail in which works a *pinion,* or toothed wheel, as in a *r.-and-pinion* steering-gear. To seize two ropes together side by side to secure against movement of either in a lengthwise direction; to put on a *racking-seizing* for such purpose. A vessel is said to *r.* when showing signs of lateral strain, as in the beam knees, due to violent rolling. **Belaying-pin r.,** also *pin-rail r.* and *pin-r.; see* **P.-rack** *in* PIN. **Ferry r.,** *see* FERRY. **Halyard r.,** *see* HALYARD. **R.-bar,** a stick or bar used to twist the parts of a lashing and so tauten the whole; sometimes called a *swifter;* also, *r.-rod; r.-stick.* **R.-lashing,** *see* LASHING. **To r. a tackle,** to seize two parts of a purchase-tackle together in order to hold the stress when hauling part of fall is slackened.

RACK.[2] (Ice. *rek,* drifting wreckage) Thin, broken-up clouds driven by the wind; scud; fracto-stratus cloud; *see* CLOUD. Also, sometimes written *wrack.*

RACKING. Lateral deformation or strain occurring in a vessel's structure due to excessive rolling; usually limited to vessels in the *stiff* condition when subjected to such violent motion in a beam sea. A seizing or piece of small stuff used to *rack* two parts of a rope, as in a tackle; *cf.* **r. a tackle** *in* RACK; a *rack-lashing* or *r.-seizing.* **R.-seizing,** ordinarily, where two fiber ropes are *racked,* simply a piece of small stuff tightly wound around the ropes, as in a *round seizing.* Where two spars or unserved wire rope parts are *racked,* however, in order to prevent seizing or lashing from slipping on such smooth surfaces, *r.* is turned about the pair in *figure-eight* fashion; *i.e.,* turns are taken alternately over and under the parts thus *racked.* **R. stress,** that borne by vessel's structure during sharp heavy rolling; *see remarks above.* **R. turns,** those taken *figure-eight* fashion in a *r.-seizing* or *r.-lashing.* (The terms *racking-lashing* and *rack-lashing* should be distinguished in that the latter is not used in *racking* and, properly, with its *rack-bar* or *rack-stick,* is a landsman's name for a *turnbuckle,* or *swifter, lashing.*) *Also see* **A.-piercing** *in* ARMOR.

RADAR. (Coined from initial letters of *"radio direction and range"*) Electronic device developed in World War II for detecting the presence of objects, as vessels, buoys, a coastline, etc., by means of radio waves sent out on a narrow beam which sweeps the horizon or is otherwise directed as desired. The radio waves rebound as echoes from objects in path of the beam and outline of such objects or coastline is shown instantaneously on the oscilloscope, or *scope,* as it is familiarly called, with *bearing* (relative to ship's fore-and-aft line or true, as required) and *distance* from vessel (or *range*) indicated. With promise of further development and

simplification, the *r.* system appears destined to become an outstanding anti-collision device and means for successfully navigating in narrow waters during thick weather, apart from its use as a detector of surfaced submarines or other enemy craft in the dark hours or other period of shortened visibility for which it primarily was designed. At time of writing (*1950*), a small *r.* equipment is being manufactured for harbor craft, fishing-vessels, ferries, and yachts. The apparatus, according to a press report, operates on a wave of 3.2 centimeters, with power enough to "pick up" ships 20 miles off.

RADEAU. (Fr.) A heavy raft or float; a floating battery.

RADIAL. Radiating; consisting of or pertaining to *radii* or *rays.* **R. davit,** a quadrant davit; also called *luffing davit,* because its head is *luffed,* or raised, as davit is moved into the vertical position (so designed to lift boat clear of its bed); *see* **Q. davit** *in* QUADRANT. **R. paddle wheel,** one having fixed *floats,* or paddles, as distinguished from a *feathering* wheel; *cf.* **F. paddle-wheel** *in* FEATHERING.

RADIO. The radiant energy of electric waves; hence, pertaining to or employing radio waves as in *r.-telegraphy, r.-telephony,* or other system characterized by essential use of radio waves. *Wireless.* A message sent or received by *r.-telegraphy* or *r.-telephony.* A *radio* receiving set. To communicate by *r.* First long-distance use of radio waves is recorded as December 12, 1901, when *Guglielmo Marconi,* Italian electrician, sent signals from England to Newfoundland by his invented radio-telegraph system and a year later first *r.* message across the Atlantic announced the birth of wireless communication at sea. From this memorable event continued development of *r.* possibilities has given us for navigational use the *r.-compass* or *direction-finder,* the *r.-telephone, loran,* and *radar.* **R. alarm signal,** that used at sea in announcing a vessel in distress or a danger message concerning location of ice, derelicts, drifting mines, etc., or particulars of a tropical storm. Signal consists of 12 dashes of 4 seconds' length given in one minute on a frequency of 500 kilocycles (600 meters) with the purpose in view of setting in operation the *automatic r.* alarm which is required in all vessels carrying a single *r. operator.* **R'beacon,** a charted station from which distinctive *r.* signals are emitted at certain scheduled intervals for use of vessels equipped with *r. direction-finders.* In thick weather, intervals between signals are shortened; thus, while in clear weather signal may be operating for 10 minutes of each hour, in foggy weather it may be heard continuously or at very short intervals. Also called *wireless beacon,* it may be located on a lightship, at a lighthouse, or at any appropriate point on a coast. **R. call sign,** or **signal,** *see* NATIONALITY MARK. **R. com-**

pass, a *r.* receiving set designed to indicate direction from an observer, or *bearing,* of the station from which *r. signals* are transmitted. A dumb card or a gyro-repeater is provided and, by manipulation of a small loop-antenna, observer ascertains the minimum or zero point of intensity of signals, or their direction as indicated on the compass-card by a pointer geared to the antenna. Also called *direction-finder,*—usually abbrev. *"D F"; wireless compass;* and, in earlier use, *r.-goniometer; r.-pelorus; r. position-finder.* **R. compass station,** coastal station equipped with a *r. compass* for determining the true bearing of vessels sending out *r. signals.* Ships may obtain their bearings from two or more of such stations at a given instant, according to prescribed procedure, and thence their position by cross-bearing method. **R. direction-finder,** *see* **R. compass. R. distance-finding stations,** those indicated in a coastal Light List as stations at which *r'beacon* and sound signals are synchronized for enabling a vessel to determine her distance off such stations in thick weather. At certain intervals,— usually at end of each three minutes of operation of the *r'beacon,*—a distinctive sound signal (as on the horn or submarine oscillator) is given simultaneously with the same signal by *r'beacon.* Based on time interval elapsing between reception of each signal, vessel's distance off then is easily ascertained. In the case of a synchronized air signal (horn, explosive, etc.), observed interval in seconds multiplied by .18 or divided by 5.5 (or, double the seconds and divide by 11) gives distance in *nautical miles;* and, where submarine signal is synchronized, multiply seconds by .8 or divide by 1.25 (or, 4 times seconds divided by 5). **R. fog-signal,** a regularly recurring distinctive signal sent out by a *r'beacon* during thick weather. **R. operator,** qualified crew member who controls and is responsible for maintenance of vessel's *r.* installation at sea; sends and receives messages to and from shore or other ships; records all weather reports and navigational information broadcast to vessels; and notes in the log, as required by law, all times at which communication with other ships and shore stations takes place. In U.S. merchant ships, he must be licensed by the Federal Communications Commission and hold a service certificate issued to him by U.S. Coast Guard. Number of *r.* operators varies from one to three, depending on class of vessel. Also called *wireless operator, wireless telegraph operator,* and in some merchant lines, *radio officer.* **R. pratique,** *see* PRATIQUE. **R. room,** also termed *wireless cabin, wireless room,* and, colloquially, *r. shack;* house or space containing ship's *r.* installation and office in which messages are sent and received. Generally, it is located as high as possible above ship's water-line and must be provided with means of communication with the navigating-bridge; also, the apparatus must be supplied with

an emergency power generator, independent of vessel's electrical circuit, and, in some cases, an emergency transmitting set, where the ordinary installation is deemed unsuitable, considering the capacity of emergency generator and other statutory requirements. **R. time signal,** broadcast signal indicating exact Greenwich Civil Time according to an observatory transmitting clock. Usually accurate to within a tenth of a second, navigators use such signal, or "time tick," as it is familiarly termed, to check the chronometer error. The various systems of signifying time by *dots* and *dashes* automatically sent out from observatory clocks in different parts of the world is given in Hydrographic Office publication *Radio Aids to Navigation, H.O. 205.* **R. watch,** one of a *r. operator's* daily periods of duty in which he must listen continuously with his receiver adjusted to wave lengths prescribed for marine telegraphic communication, including the 500 kilocycle distress frequency during the internationally agreed-upon *silent period* of three minutes which begins at 15 minutes past, and again at 45 minutes past, each hour of *Universal,* or *Greenwich civil, time.*

RADIOMETER. The old scholarly term for the *forestaff,* also known as the *cross-staff,* an instrument used in Columbus's time for measuring altitudes of the sun; *cf.* BACKSTAFF; **F.-staff** *in* FORE; *and* **C.-staff** *in* CROSS.

RADIUS. Distance of the center from any point in the circumference of a circle or on the surface of a sphere; half the diameter, or semi-diameter, of a circle or of a sphere. Scope; range; as a vessel's *cruising r.* The pivoted *index bar* or *arm* of a quadrant or sextant. **Operating r.,** also termed *steaming r.* and *steaming range; see* CRUISING RADIUS. **R. vector,** line representing the distance at a given instant between the center of a planet or satellite and that of its primary, or body about which the former revolves. **Turning r.,** half the diameter of circle through which a vessel would turn if helm is put hard over, ship going full speed. It usually approximates three ship-lengths. *See* **T. circle** *in* TURNING.

RAFFE or **RAFFEE.** A triangular sail set above the upper yard in a schooner carrying a square foretopsail. Once a favorite in Great Lake vessels of smaller tonnage for augmenting spread of canvas in a fair wind, it was clewed to each yard-arm, with its broad-angled corner hoisted to topmasthead. Also, *raffie.* A sail of similar shape, called a *moonraker,* was set above a skysail in some American clippers.

RAFFLE. A tangle of cordage, blocks, spars, etc.; rubbish; wreckage; especially, a mass of carried away rigging gear.

RAFT. A collection of timber towed, poled, or floated with a current. Any float, pontoon; number of barrels, drums, tanks, logs, squared timber; **or** other buoyant material fastened together for a support or a conveyance. The primitive *r.*, that first used by man to ferry him over obstructing streams, still is with us in a few different forms and kinds of wood, such as the paddled or sailed craft used by fishermen off the sea-coasts of widely scattered lands; *e.g.*, the *caballito* of Peru; *jangada* of Brazil; *tekpal* of Formosa; and the *shasta* of southern Arabia. *See* BALSA *and* CATAMARAN. **Fire-r.,** *see* **F.-raft** *in* FIRE. **Life-r.,** *see* **L.-raft,** *in* LIFE. **Log-r.,** a large bulk of log timber, in form of a hulk held together by chains, such as is towed between Pacific U.S. ports. **R.-ice,** also termed *rafted ice,* cakes or sheets of floating ice piled above each other, such as occurs during *rafting,* i.e., forced buckling and overlapping of edges of colliding floes in meeting currents. **R.-port,** same as lumber-port; *see* **L.-port** *in* LUMBER. **R.-rope,** in seal-hunting, a short piece of handy rope used by each man for hauling his catch over the ice to his vessel; also, in older whaling, a rope for hauling pieces of blubber along the deck or stringing blubber for hoisting from carcase of whale alongside the vessel. **Torpedo-r.,** a low-decked craft or raft used in grappling for and recovering submarine *mines.* (*Torpedo* was the original term for a *mine*)

RAFTER. A supporting spar for an awning; an *awning-spar;* usually, one of the sloping spars butting against the ridge-spar in a large awning; so named from its likeness to the timbers in a sloping roof.

RAG-BOLT. *See* BOLT.

RAGGED JACKET. A young *harp seal;* especially, one during its first molt.

RAIL. The heavy plank, timber, or plate, forming the top of a vessel's bulwarks. Open fence-like structure serving as a guard at sides or break of a superstructural deck; as, *poop r.; promenade deck r.; bridge r.* A bar or timber for supporting belaying-pins around a mast, in way of lower rigging, etc.; as, *fife r.; pin-r.* Any bar, batten, timber, etc., fitted as a stay, support, or guard; as, a *hank-r.; tow r.; ladder r.* A bar of H- or I-section, sometimes called a *railway,* fitted along the after side of a mast, or under side of a gaff of a standing fore-and-aft sail (one which brails to the mast), as a means of confining the hanks in sail's luff or head. **Berthing r.,** old term for *main bulwark r.* **Breast r.,** guard-railing, usually of fence-like appearance, fitted across fore end of a poop, after end of a top-gallant forecastle, around a bridge, etc. **Bridge r.,** that at either side or ends of a bridge deck, or about a navigating-bridge. **False r.,** *see* **B. spray-board** *in* BUFFALO. **Fender r.,** *see* **F.-guard** *in* FENDER. **Front r.,** same as **Breast r. Fife r.,** as commonly fitted in square-rigged vessels, a stout wooden *r.* mounted on stan-

chions near a mast. Sometimes semi-circular in shape, it extends on each side and abaft the mast and serves as a *pin-r.* for making fast braces and sheets of upper yards, clew-garnets, and other running gear. **Hand-r.,** metal or wood bar fitted as a guard along the side or sides of a poop ladder, bridge ladder or stairway, etc.; a balustrade. **I-r.,** an *I-bar,* or structural iron of approximately I-shaped cross-section; a *double-headed r.; railway r.* **Main r.,** timber, plank, or heavy piece of plate running along the top of bulwarks on the main or weather deck, as distinguished from that of a poop, or other raised deck. **Roughtree r.,** old term for a wooden vessel's *main r.* **R's of the head,** in old-time ships stout bars of wood extending from each bow as supports for a figurehead or other ornate device at upper part of the beak or cutwater; *head-r's.* **R. stanchion,** one of the upright metal bars supporting the *r.* in an open railing, or "fence," at sides or break of a deck. **Safety r.,** *see* **L.-rail** *in* LIFE. **Taff-rail,** a *r.* supported by balusters and forming a *guard-r.* around after end and sides of a poop deck. **Towing-r.,** in larger tug-boats, especially those having the towing-hook or bitts amidships, a sturdy iron bar or piece of timber in the form of an arch. It spans the deck at after part of vessel and serves to support the towing hawser clear of decks and stern end. (See *rail* as combined with following caption words in: BUFFALO; BULL; CHANNEL; COUNTER; GUARD; HEAD; LASH; LIFE; PIN; PEDESTAL; POOP; QUARTER; SHEER; TOP; TUCK)

RAILWAY. A jack-stay, rail, or track, on which the hanks of a sail travel, as in a brailing-in gaff-sail; *see remarks in* RAIL. Also, such a track fitted on a mast for confining the heel of a gaff or parrel of a yard to its proper place during hoisting and lowering. **Marine r.,** *see* MARINE. **R. berth,** place at which a vessel may lie and discharge or load cargo to or from *r.* cars, as alongside a quay having one or more *r.* sidings. **R. gaff,** *see* GAFF. **Ship r.,** a *marine r.;* also, a *r.* on which vessels may be transported overland, as at an isthmus.

RAINBOW. The bow or arch of concentric bands of colors of the spectrum, caused by a not-too-well-understood refraction and reflection suffered by rays of light from the sun in shining through rain or mist. The mid-point of the arch differs in azimuth exactly 180° from that of the sun. Lowermost band of the *primary bow* (there may be a *secondary bow,* fainter than and parallel to the *primary*) is *violet,* thence following the spectrum colors in succession outward, the others are *indigo, blue, green, yellow, orange,* and *red.* As seen during moonlight, is then called a *lunar bow;* in misty or foggy conditions, a *fog-bow.* The "bow" often appears in miniature as sun shines through spray about vessel's bows or crests of breaking seas; then called a *marine r.* or *sea-bow. Cf. Genesis 9: verses 13–16.*

RAIN-CLOUD. The *nimbus, cumulo-nimbus,* or *nimbo-stratus cloud; see* CLOUD.

RAISE. (From the same root as *rise* and often of the same meaning) To give rise to; originate; or start; as, *this breeze will r. a choppy sea.* To cause to rise; to lift; or elevate; as, *salvors were sent to r. the wreck; anchor was raised at dawn;* and, as in the order "*R. tacks and sheets!*", preparatory to coming about or wearing ship. To cause the land or other object to appear above the horizon by approaching it; as, *we shall soon r. Boston Light.* To lift or cause to be lifted, in the sense of cessation; as, *a northwest wind will r. this fog; blockade of the port was raised at noon.* To rig or prepare a lifting device, tackle, etc.; as, to *r. a purchase;* to *r. a boom.* To **r. the frames,** in shipbuilding, to place transverse frames in position in the structure.

RAISED. Elevated; lifted above a surrounding surface; superimposed; as, a *r. deck;* a *r.-head rivet;* a *r. strake.* **R.-and-sunken system,** also termed *in-and-out system, see* **In-and-out strakes** (shell plating) *in* IN-AND-OUT. **R. beach,** *see* BEACH. **R. diamond checker-plate,** non-skid tread-plate; also termed *diamond, checker,* and *multigrip plate; see* **Checkered p.** *in* PLATE. **R. face flange,** in high-pressure pipe, *r.* portion of a flange of this type is inside bolt circle in which gasket is fitted. Height of the *face* varies from one-sixteenth to one-quarter inch. **R. fore deck,** forward portion of a weather deck, or that between a bridge deck and vessel's stem or forecastle, which is built above after deck line or level. **R. quarter-deck,** in some smaller type cargo vessels, after portion of vessel's single deck which is elevated a few feet above forward portion. Break of continuity of deck line occurs about two-thirds vessel's length, measured from her stem. Purpose of such construction is to increase depth of hold and so a corresponding cargo capacity in way of a propeller-shaft tunnel. Provision is thus made against a trim *by the head* (draft too great at fore end) when vessel loads a homogeneous cargo of the *full-and-down* type or one in which sufficient weight may be accommodated abaft amidships to counterbalance that stowed in forward hold. Such a vessel is termed a *r. quarter-deck vessel.* **R. tank-top,** inner bottom, or upper surface of double-bottom tank, having a slope from fore-and-aft center line toward the bilges. Found in vessels of smaller type, such form of tank-top usually accompanies a deep center-line girder or keel-plate.

RAKE. Inclination from the perpendicular of a mast, funnel, stem, or a stern-post. Formerly, outward slope of a vessel's bows or counter; now, *flare.* To violently pass over or along; as, *heavy breaking seas raked her fore-and-aft; the decks were raked with shrapnel.* In modern shipbuilding, the stem usually is given a forward *r.* chiefly for the reason that collision damage at that point is more likely to be confined to vessel's above-water structure. *R.* of masts, smokestacks, etc., especially in passenger liners and yachts, is for the sole purpose of appearance, in point of which many cargo vessels possess little to be admired, with their perpendicular, square-cut lines *alow and aloft. R. aft* given to masts of sailing-vessels perhaps found its extreme in the American clippers. This, it was claimed, provided more lifting power in the sails when vessel was sailing free (those "sea-birds" *knew* where to find fair winds!) and, also, within reasonable limits, was the ideal set of masts for their efficient *staying,* while it allowed yards to be *braced up* to a sharper angle because of the more aftward position of shrouds and backstays. For fore-and-aft sails it also is claimed that a better *set* of the sail is provided with a *r. aft* in a mast, which gives the *leech* of a *gaff sail* (after edge of sail) a perpendicular drop instead of a sloping one in absence of such *r.* Masts of larger schooners, however, are given little or no *r.,* chiefly for the reason that lower shrouds must be placed so as to be clear, as far as is possible, of the sails when vessel is sailing free. Hence the problem of *staying* the fore-and-after's masts to equal that sturdy possibility in the square-rigger. **After r.,** that part of a vessel's hull overhanging the stern-post; the counter. **Over-r.,** *see* O'rake *in* OVER.

RAKISH. Having a smart appearance, suggestive of speed in a pronounced *rake* of masts. Formerly, in an apprehensive sense, as describing a strange speedy craft having raking masts and "sneaky" appearance characteristic of Mediterranean piratical vessels of 18th. century.

RALLY. To sharply round in or let run a piece of running gear; as, to *r. in* (or *out*) *the royal braces;* to *r. round* (or *in*) *the capstan.* (*Old-fashioned*) In shipyard use, a drive with a battering-ram; especially, a series of blows given by such means in driving in a section of wedges between a ship's hull and the sliding ways or cradle, in order to relieve the keel blocks of ship's weight prior to launching. Each wedge in the section is given identical treatment in a *r.,* with view of evenly distributing vessel's weight along cradle. This procedure is known as *ramming up* or *wedging up.*

RAM. Strong projecting beak at a vessel's stem above or below water-line, as used in ancient war-galleys for cutting into enemy craft. With advent of the steam ironclad the under-water beak or *r.* was revived and war-vessels up to the turn of present century were thus equipped. Any heavy weight, balk of timber, etc., as a *battering-r.,* used for delivering forceful blows; the heavy block of wood or metal used in a pile-driver. To strike or batter with a *r.* To strike against head on, as a colliding vessel. To force or drive, as with a heavy maul, a *r.,* etc. **Hydraulic r.,** plunger operated in a cylinder by pressure of a liquid. In a hydro-electric steering system, one of such *r*'s at each side of the tiller forces ship's rudder into any position required by the steering control, as from ship's navigating bridge. In launching, a *hydraulic r.* often is used to give a vessel a start down the ways. **Ice-r.**, as built in some early ice-breaking steam-vessels, an underwater *r.* at the stem for attacking ice with a *lifting* force. Later experience showed that present *crushing* or *depressing* force, facilitated by a "sleigh-runner" stem, is more effective in ice navigation. **R.-bow,** *see* BOW.

RAMED. (Fr. *rame*, a branch; Du. *raam*, a frame) In wooden ship-building, having the frames, stem-, and stern-post set on the stocks and adjusted by the *ramline*, or *faired*, to their respective proper positions in the structure. (Pron. *rahmd*)

RAMHEAD. A now obsolete term for a halyard-block at a masthead; so named from the earlier *ramhead*, or hooked arm or crane to which block was secured. Also, *ram's-head*.

RAMLINE. In shipyard work, a cord or small rope stretched to indicate a center line, line of beams, or other fairing-line; *cf.* RAMED. Also, in spar-making, a cord, or chalk-line made by such cord, indicating a longitudinal cutting-line on the timber.

RAMP. A large sloping platform, gangplank, or brow over which cargo or live stock may be transferred to or from a vessel. Usually with *along*, to sail on a tack with all canvas *rap full*, as in boat-sailing; to *r. along*.

RANDAN. In England, a boat having three thwarts and operated by three oarsmen, single oars being pulled from forward and after thwarts while man on midship thwart pulls two oars. This arrangement often is termed *randan fashion*; as, to row *r. fashion*.

RANGE. Scope or radius; as, *r.* of a light; *r.* of stability; steaming *r.* A tier, row, or line of similar objects; as, a *r.* of cable; *r.* of nets. A direction indicated by two objects *in line* or *r.*, as leading lights of a channel. Effective distance of gunfire. A group of ports in a given region, optional use of one of which for loading or discharging a cargo often is agreed to in a charter-party; as, U.K. and Continental *r.* In older usage, a large cleat or kevel fastened to bulwark stanchions for securing tacks and sheets of courses, hawsers, etc. To lay out or set in order; as, to *r. the cable.* Usually with *along*, to sail parallel with and in sight of the shore; as, *we ranged along the Lapland coast.* To steer close to the side of another vessel, a pier, etc., usually with *alongside*; as, *the oiler ranged alongside the cruiser.* To place vessels in tier, as in mooring side by side and to each other; as, *they will r. the destroyers four abreast.* Often with *about*, to sheer to and fro as a light vessel at single anchor in a stiff breeze; as, *"the brig ranged about so wildly, it was deemed needful to drop a second anchor."* With *by*, in older usage, to pass another vessel sailing in same direction; as, *the clipper ranged by under a heavy press of sail.* **Compass r.,** two conspicuous marks which, when in line from an observer's position, indicate a certain *true* or *magnetic* direction. Used for checking errors of, or adjusting, compasses. An elaborate system of *compass r's*, for example, is found in River Mersey, where the large painted numbers on the Liverpool dock walls indicate true bearings of the high Vauxhall chimney as mid-point of each number (degrees) "lines up" with chimney. **Luminous r.,** distance a light may be seen under normal atmospheric conditions. On charts, such *r.* of visibility is given for lights which are of insufficient power to be seen at their full *geographic r.*, or that distance which is limited only by the earth's curvature. (*See* remarks in LIGHT-HOUSE) **R.-finder,** instrument for measuring distance of an object from an observer. Unlike the *stadimeter* by which resulting distance is dependent on accuracy of given height of object observed, the *r.-finder's* use is founded on the solution of a right-angled triangle having its base equal to horizontal distance between the telescope lenses at each end of the instrument. Consisting of a cylindrical tube mounted horizontally on a pedestal to freely swing in azimuth, with binocular pieces at its mid-length, an observer views the "target" via reflecting prisms in and at each end of the tube. Trained toward a very distant object, lines of vision from each telescope are parallel and therefore each makes a 90° angle with axis of tube. As distance from object lessens, a horizontal displacement occurs in appearance of object through the right eye-piece; *i.e.*, upper half of image as seen from right telescope appears to left of that seen from left telescope. By bringing both halves into alignment by a screw arrangement which moves a deflecting prism in right end of tube, range is determined and indicated on a scale appearing in left eye-piece. Thus, the *r.-finding* is done in the right end of the tube, or solution of the triangle is made possible by determination of angle which base (length of tube) makes with the hypotenuse (or angle at object subtended by the base). Accuracy of a properly adjusted instrument obviously depends greatly upon length of its base (tube). It is claimed that a *r.-finder* of 2 feet 6 inches length will give results at about 10 miles with no greater error than $1/4$ mile. Navy pattern instruments are from $4\frac{1}{2}$ to 12 feet in length. They are used chiefly for finding gun-ranges in war-vessels and by some merchant marine masters are rated as invaluable in coastwise navigation. **R. heads,** old term for the *windlass-bitts; see* BITT. **R. light,** either of two lights (often called *leading lights*) placed at appropriate horizontal and vertical distances apart to indicate a line of direction, as for guidance of ships navigating a channel. Also, in powered vessels, a masthead *white light* fixed abaft and at least 15 feet above the head or foremast light when ship is under way. It is so placed that both lights are in line with vessel's keel and vertical distance between them less than the horizontal distance. Purpose of carrying such *r. light* is, generally, to show vessels concerned the approximate direction in which powered vessel is heading and, particularly, to show her exact direction of approach in a *head-on* situation. **R. of stability,** angle through which a vessel may be inclined to reach the vanishing point of her righting power; *see* STABILITY. **R. of tide,** *see* **T. range** *in* TIDAL. To **r. the cable,** to fleet sufficient anchor cable along the deck to allow anchor when dropped to strike bottom before its weight is taken up suddenly by the windlass or cable-bitts, as practised in vessels fitted with the old-fashioned windlass, or, in old-time ships, with capstans and cable bitts only. Modern windlasses and powered capstans for anchor use being controlled by a brake, cable is run out direct from chain-locker when letting go anchor. Also, to run or heave out all chain cable and lay it in long fleets on shore or on bottom of a dry-dock, as for cleaning, inspection, repairs, etc. **Ratio of r's,** *see* TIDAL. **R. transmitter,** an instrument for transmitting the range of a target to one or more indicators for information of gunners in action.

RANK. Official grade or position; especially that of a naval officer; as, *r.* of captain. A line or row of men standing side by side; station; standing; order of precedence. Equivalent *r's* in U.S. Army and Navy are as follows: General and admiral; lieutenant-general and vice-admiral; major-general and rear-admiral; brigadier-general and commodore; lieutenant-colonel and commander; major and lieutenant-commander; captain and lieutenant; first lieutenant and lieutenant (*junior grade*). To take precedence; as, a commander *ranks* a major. *Cf.* OFFICER. Generally, *r.* connotes grade of a commissioned officer, *rating* being that of a non-commissioned or petty officer. **R. keel,** *see* KEEL. **R. sheer,** *see* SHEER. To **take r. with,** to be equal to in official standing or grade; to equal in accordance with *lineal r.* as prescribed in military and naval canons of etiquette and precedence.

RANTIPIKE. Local name for one of the topsail schooners, brigs, and brigantines constituting the Scottish fleet formerly chiefly engaged in carrying pig and scrap iron from the Clyde to the Mersey. They averaged about 300 tons burden.

RANSOM. Payment demanded by a man-o'-war or a privateer for relinquishment of a captured ship or cargo. **R.-bill,** a contract given to a ransomed ship by her captor, guaranteeing her safe conduct to a friendly port; also, *r. bond.*

RAP FULL. *See* FULL.

RAPID. That part of a river in which current flows most swiftly; especially where the surface is rendered turbulent by obstructions. Usually in *pl.,* as *Lachine Rapids.*

RAPIER-FISH. A sword-fish. (*Archaic*)

RAPSON'S SLIDE. Named for its inventor, a steering-gear device designed for effective use of an approximately constant force in turning a tiller. Consists of a straight track laid athwartships, along which tiller slides in a pivoted block and is free to also slide in the latter. As tiller is moved from midship position by a force applied to the block, leverage on rudder-head is equalized by consequent increase of length of arm, or distance from block to rudder-head. It is sometimes called *compensating-gear* of a steering arrangement.

RAS-AL-HAGUE. (Ar. *ras al hawi,* head of the serpent-charmer) *α Ophiuchi,* brightest star (magnitude 2.14) in the group named by the ancients *Ophiuchus* (*Gr.* = serpent-holder), located in 12° 35′ N. declination and 17 hrs. 32½ min. right ascension. A line from this star to *Spica* forms the hypotenuse of an isosceles triangle having its right-angled apex at the ruddy *Antares.* It also lies at the western corner of a nearly isosceles triangle having its apex in *Vega,* with *Altair* at eastern angle.

RASING-IRON. The calker's *clearing-iron, reefer,* or *ripping-iron; see* **Calking-i's** *in* IRON.

RASING-KNIFE. Also *race-knife, q.v. in* KNIFE.

RAT. This almost universally well-known rodent from earliest antiquity has maintained a record for destruction of property and the carrying of disease. Cargo losses from the pest's wanton habits have been enormous and spread of the bubonic plague, particularly in the Orient, has been laid to the rat's account. Fumigation or "*deratization*" of ships according to prescribed quarantine regulations today is carried out by most maritime nations, in contrast to general pest-ridden conditions allowed to exist on board ship of but a quarter century ago. *Cf.* DERATIZATION. It was the common experience of seamen in larger wood-built vessels to have the ever-present rat habitually jump or run over one's person while enjoying a restful watch below,—and that in a vessel trading to foreign ports the normal sanitary status of which often was more than questionable! **R.-guard,** *see* GUARD. **R.-tail,** tapering end of a rope. **R.-tail splice,** union of a small-sized rope with a larger by splicing; so called because strands of larger line are *rat-tailed* or tapered to meet the lay of smaller rope. *R.* also was an Old English term for a *tide-race,* or swift current.

RATCH. To lay on a course with wind forward of the beam in sailing; a variant of *reach; see* REACH.

RATCHET. A device which prevents backward rotation of a wheel, drum, etc., by means of one or more *pawls* or *detents* fitting against and into a *ratched* or *toothed* surface on such wheel, etc. Cf. PAWL. **R. windlass,** as used on small vessels, a hand windlass having a horizontal drum which is turned by a *hand-spike,* appropriate holes for insertion of such bar being provided at either end of drum. It is worked on same principle as the capstan. Also termed a *handspike windlass.*

RATE. (L. *ratus,* reckoned or calculated) Quantity or amount measured or estimated in a given unit of time; as, *loading proceeded at r. of 100 tons per hour.* Class or order to which a war-vessel belongs, according to size, type, armament, etc., as, *first r., second r.,* etc. Formerly found only in descriptive term, *first-rate warship,* meaning a *ship of the line.* Class of a merchant vessel as an insurance risk, considered according to standards required in structural strength and equipment by *classification society* concerned; as, *an A1-at-Lloyd's rate was given the barque.* To fix relative class, position, rank, etc., of a vessel or a seaman; as, *ship is rated 100A1 in A.B.S.; our stowaway was rated as ordinary seaman.* To merit or deserve, as by reason of rank or grade; as, *this officer rates a single-berth cabin.* To determine number of seconds a chronometer gains or loses per day; as, to *r.* the time-piece by radio signals. To arrange for carriage of goods via a certain route or vessel; as, *a shipment was rated to London by the Cunard Line.* **Daily r.,** *see* C. **error** *in* CHRONOMETER. **Freight r.,** *see* FREIGHT. **Management r.,** chiefly in Great Britain, a charge or commission for receiving, handling, storing, and marketing a shipment of merchandise. **Sea r.,** as distinguished from the *maker's r.,* or that determined on shore, actual performance of a *chronometer* at sea, as expressed in seconds of gain or loss per day. **Through r.,** charge for transportation of goods which includes transshipment at one or more points en route; generally, a *through bill of lading* is issued by first carrier who collects total freight charges. Cf. **B. of lading** *in* BILL.

RATING. Position or grade of a member of ship's crew; especially, that of an unlicensed or enlisted man. Classification of naval enlisted men according to relative standing or grade; *r. of boatswain's mate.* The number of *ratings* in, for example, the U.S. navy had increased from the relatively few in sailing-ship days to about 200 in 1948. A drastic change then took place both in nomenclature and reduction of that number to 77, divided into about a dozen branches of the service. The Deck Branch has changed the *r.* of *Coxswain* into *Boatswain's Mate, 3rd. class; Signalman* into that of *Quartermaster; Seaman, 1st. class,* becomes *Seaman; Seaman, 2nd. class* is now *Apprentice Seaman;* last-named is now *Seaman Recruit; Bugler r.* disappears into *Sea-*

man; Carpenter's Mate has been absorbed into Engineering and Hull Branch as *Damage Controlman;* former *Water Tender* is now *Boilerman;* and the old *Ship's Cook* grins and bears it under *Commissary-man.* In keeping with the modern step in aeronautics, in the Aviation Branch we now have such *r's* as *Aviation Machinist's Mate; Aviation Electronics Technician; Aviation Electronicsman; Aviation Structural Mechanic; Parachute Rigger;* and *Aerographer's Mate.* **R.-badge,** mark or insignia worn on the uniform sleeve to indicate *r.* of wearer.

RATIO OF RANGES. *See* TIDAL.

RATION. A daily allowance of provisions for each man; especially, that allotted to enlisted ratings in a navy. In merchant ships generally, while customary to provide meals without strictly adhering to any *r.* system, a victualling or rationing scale, indicating provisions each seaman is entitled to per day or week is included in the articles of agreement (*shipping articles*) which are signed by vessel's master and each crew member at time of engagement of latter. **Emergency r.,** as provided in lifeboats, a condensed food prepared with view of occupying as little room as possible in boat. U.S. regulations prescribe that, in lieu of two pounds of hard bread (*sea biscuit*), there may be provided "its equivalent in any approved *emergency r.* of cereal or vegetable compound packaged in hermetically sealed containers of an approved type and stowed in provision lockers or other compartments providing suitable protection. No meat or other *r.* requiring saline preservative shall be allowed." **R. money,** cash allowance in lieu of *r's.* **Spirit r.,** as customary in British and other navies, an allowance per diem of spirits,—usually rum; grog allowance. *See* GROG.

RATIONAL HORIZON. *See* **Celestial h.** *in* HORIZON.

RATLINE. Small 3-stranded, right-hand laid, tarred hemp line, varying in size from 15-thread to 21-thread (1¼- to 1½-inch circumference). Also, *ratlin,* and older forms, *ratling, rattling.* Named from its original use for *ratlines,* or small ropes across a vessel's shrouds, forming the series of steps or *runs* in a ladder-like arrangement which provided means for climbing aloft. Such rope now is used chiefly for permanent lashings, heaving-lines, heavy service, lanyards for small stays, cargo-nets, and buoy-ropes. In larger square-rigged vessels, *r's* extended between 4 or 5 lowermast shrouds, between all topmast shrouds (3 or 4), and the usual 2 top-gallant shrouds. *Rattling down* was the term for fitting new *r's* in the rigging. Each *r.* was seized through a small eye in each of its ends to forward and after shroud concerned and a *clove hitch* secured it to each intervening shroud. Chief reason for employing *r. stuff,* as the line is called, in this "ladder" set-up was that it presented smallest possible surface to the wind. A *catch r.*, or more commonly, *sheer r.*, was the 5th. or 6th. *r.* extended to span *all* lower shrouds and backstays and was intended, in the hemp rigging days, to hold aloft the ends of these where severed by an enemy's gunfire, but generally served to facilitate sailors' work aloft, as in bowsing rigging, clearing and repairing gear, etc. Since the advent of wire rigging, *r's* often were displaced by hardwood battens seized across at most three shrouds of lower rigging, accompanied by a greatly reduced number of *sheer r's* of the hemp line; but the *batten* still held the term *ratline*, excepting the rare mention of it as *rigging-batten*.

RAT'S-TAIL. Pointed or tapered end of a small-sized rope, as on a lacing or a lashing, to facilitate reeving in small grommets, holes, etc.

RAT-TAIL. Another name for the *chimæra* or the *grenadier*, odd-shaped fishes having a long tapering tail; *see* CHIMÆRA and GRENADIER. In radio-telegraphy, colloquialism for the wire leading from antenna to operating-room.

RATTAN. (Malay *rotan*) The tough fiber, or slender stem itself, of a genus of climbing palms termed *Calamus*, native to the Far East. Source of the *rattan cane* of commerce, cordage made from this fiber, once extensively used in the East, is said to rival *manila* in strength and durability, though of less flexible texture.

RATTLE DOWN, To. *See* RATLINE.

RAVE-HOOK. A calking tool; *see* HOOK.

RAVEN'S-DUCK. A fine quality of hempen sailcloth; often shortened to *ravens*.

RAY. Any member of a large family of thin flatfishes, including the *skates* and also embracing the less typical *saw-fish* and *guitar-fish*, characterized chiefly by their great spreading pectoral fins, eyes on upper side of head, mouth well back from snout on under side of body, and, especially in the typical *ray*, a long slender whip-like tail. Largest is the *manta r.*, or *devil-fish*, which may weigh more than half a ton, the *eagle r.* running a close second with its wing-spread of 12 to 15 feet. Others of some 20 species of the ugly creatures are the *sting r.*, which is armed with a poisonous barb at end of its tail, and the *electric*, or *torpedo, r.*, famous for its shock-producing powers, which equal those displayed in the electric eel. The *rays* generally are bottom fish and feed mostly on mollusks and crustaceans. *See* D.-fish *in* DEVIL; MANTA; OBISPO.

RAZE. To use a *race-knife* (rasing- or razing-knife) as in scribing marks in timber, etc.; *see* Race-k. *in* KNIFE. In older usage, to *r.* a vessel meant to discontinue her classification grade by reason of limiting age or failure to maintain structural and/or equipment standards required by classification society concerned.

RAZEE. To cut down or reduce the number of decks and hence the capacity of a vessel. Archaic term for a ship converted to a lower class by such measures; especially, a naval vessel.

RAZOR. Combining word denoting quality of sharpness, razor-like form, or outstanding ridgelike appearance. **R.-back,** older whalers' familiar term for a *fin-back*, a rorqual of great size; *see* WHALE. **R.-bill,** the *razor-billed auk;* stands about 16 inches; has white front with dark back; so named from its compressed sharp-edged bill; *see* AUK. **R.-bowed,** having a very sharp stem and long forward entrance to the hull. **R.-clam,** a bivalve shell of long, narrow, slightly curved shape suggestive of the handle of an old-fashioned *r.* It is about six inches in length; sits erect in the sand where its sharp protruding end often is responsible for annoying cuts in bathers' feet.

REACH. (A.S. *ræcan*, to stretch out) To sail with wind forward of the beam, but not *close-hauled*, which latter sometimes is termed *head-reaching*. Generally, in yacht-sailing, to steer a course with a free sheet; *i.e.*, having wind anywhere between the quarter and before the beam. *See* **F'reach** *in* FORE; *also*, **H.-reach** *in* HEAD. A leg sailed in beating to windward; tack or board made in sailing close-hauled; also, course steered with wind about abeam or before the beam, but vessel not close-hauled; termed a *close r.* when *nearly* close-hauled and a *broad r.* when breeze is about on the beam. A straight stretch in a river, as between two bends. Portion of a canal between two consecutive locks. Sometimes, a bay or inlet running straight in from a coast; or a tongue of land, as a narrow projecting point or an isthmus. Distance from a given plane through which an object may be raised by a particular tackle or hoist, or extended beyond ship's side. **Free r.,** *see* **F. reach** *in* FREE. **Harbor r.,** *see* HARBOR. **Sea r.,** straight part of a river leading to the sea; outer *r.* of a stream or river, or that widening into the mouth of such stream.

REACHING FORESAIL. A yacht-racing sail set on the fore stay. Also called *Genoa foresail*, it is similar to the *Genoa jib; see* JIB.

READY.[1] Prepared for some action or undertaking. **R. about!,** command to prepare at once for tacking ship, or *coming about;* also, *About ship!* **R. for sea,** said of a vessel when in a state of preparedness for leaving port, outfitted and provisioned for a voyage. **R. man,** *see* MAN.

READY.[2] The prepared strand for making plain-laid cordage. It is formed by laying together *left-handed* the requisite number of *right-hand* twisted yarns according to desired size of rope. The left-hand twisted *readies* are then laid in a *right-hand* or *plain-laid* rope. *See* **Regular-lay r.** *in* ROPE.

REAM. To open a planking seam, as with a *reaming-iron,* preparatory to calking; *cf.* **Calking-i's** *in* IRON. To enlarge, fair, or bevel out the edge of a bored hole in a plate or timber; in British usage, to *rime,* as with a *rimer,* or *reamer,* the fluted-sided and sometimes tapered tool used for the purpose. The shipyard employee who operates a *reamer* (or *rimer*) by an electric or a pneumatic drill and one who *reams* deck or outside planking for calking are called *reamers.* A *reaming-beetle* is the calker's heavy mallet used in driving the *reaming-iron* where required.

REAR. That line or division of an armed fleet which is stationed behind the main body of ships; opposed to the *van.* **R.-admiral,** naval officer holding lowest rank of admiral; *cf.* ADMIRAL. Also, the flagship of a *r.-admiral.*

REBATE. Commonly *rabbet,* but etymologically probably more proper than that word. Pron. *rebait,* with accent on second syllable. *See* RABBET. (Not to be confused with word of same spelling accented on first syllable and meaning a deduction or discount, as a *r.* on freight charges)

REBUILT. A vessel is said to be *rebuilt* when a great or major portion of her hull structure has been replaced with new material.

RECALL. Any pre-arranged signal, as by flag, flashlight, or whistle, denoting that boat addressed is ordered to return to ship. In yacht-racing, a flag showing the number of one of the competitors who must return to the starting-line because of having sailed past it before starting-signal was given. It usually is accompanied by a sound signal, as from a horn or a gun. To call back from a distance, as a vessel on a cruise or voyage.

RECEIPT, MATE'S. *See* MATE.

RECEIVE. To accept, take, or hold that which is given, offered, or delivered; as, *ship will r. cargo at noon; we r. orders from the harbormaster only; the locker is designed to r. the chain as it is hove in.* **R'd for shipment B/L,** a bill of lading issued upon receipt of goods *intended* for shipment, as distinguished from the more desirable *shipped B/L,* or that issued upon actual stowage of goods in vessel concerned. Since the original and principal legal import of a B/L is that it is *prima facie* evidence of title to cargo which already is shipped on board and in the custody of a certain vessel named, issue of a *received-for-shipment* bill is avoided as far as is practicable in modern ocean commercial activities. **R'ing clerk,** person who accepts and issues receipts for cargo delivered for shipment, as at a pier or quay. *Cf.* **M.'s receipt** *in* MATE. **R'ing note,** chiefly in British usage, a document signed by a shipper, listing goods in a consignment and addressed to the mate or officer in charge of a vessel with the request that such goods be received on board. **R'ing ship,**

a naval vessel, usually one laid up or unfit for further service, used as a station for admitting recruits to the service and for certain instruction and drill for these, prior to being placed on regular active duty. **R'ing tank,** in a condenser system in connection with a steam engine, a tank into which water produced from exhaust steam by condenser is stored for further use as boiler feed.

RECEIVER OF WRECK. In Great Britain, an officer of the Coastguard, of the Customs, of Inland Revenue, or any other person appointed by the Ministry of Shipping, to assist in saving life or property in event of a vessel being stranded or in distress within his specified district. Under the *Merchant Shipping Act* he is empowered to call upon masters of other vessels at hand to render assistance with their ships, boats, and men; to requisition use of horses, trucks, or other vehicles locally available; to pass over any private lands or enclosures and to require all gates therein to be opened. Failure of persons to comply with or hinder such measures renders such persons amenable to heavy fines. He also has authority over all goods or wreckage which may be found at sea and brought into port, washed ashore, or otherwise taken from a vessel, the law requiring all such property to be delivered to him at once under serious penalty. Among his broad powers in the salvage of goods and ships' property, he has full authority to put down by force all plundering, destruction, or disorder at a wreck. It is his duty also to take the depositions of any persons belonging to any vessel in distress on the coast or of any person who can give an account of the ship, or her cargo, or the occasion of her distress; and any person called upon who refuses to make a statement to the *Receiver* is liable to a fine of ten pounds. A *Receiver of Wreck,* however, has no power to interfere between the master and crew of a wrecked vessel with respect to the management thereof, unless the master expressly requests him to do so.

RECESS. A step, sharp discontinuity, or indentation in an even surface; as, a *r.* (or *recessed*) bulkhead, or one in which a step or break occurs; also called a *stepped bulkhead.* A niche; as, a *tunnel r.* A recession; as, **R. of the tides,** a daily lessening of the tidal range or height of tide, as during the weekly change from springs to neaps. **Tunnel r.,** enlarged part of a propeller-shaft tunnel (or *shaft-alley*) as that at its forward end in which the *thrust-block* is fixed, or *thrust r.;* and that at its after end which is built roomy enough for the operation of drawing ship's *tail-end shaft* and termed *stuffing-box r.*

RECIPROCAL BEARINGS. Simultaneously observed bearings of a shore compass from a ship's compass and vice versa; *see* **Reciprocal b's** *in* BEARING.

RECIPROCATING. Having a to and fro motion, as that of a *r. pump* and a *r. engine;* opposed to *rotary; see* **Reciprocating e.** *in* ENGINE; *also,* **Reciprocating p.** *in* PUMP.

RECKONING. Calculated or estimated position of a vessel; especially, that arrived at according to course and distance made good from a reliable *fix,* as that obtained from celestial observations or from bearings of shore objects. Cf. **D. reckoning** *in* DEAD. To be **astern of one's r.,** *see* ASTERN. **Out of one's r.,** to be in error with respect to ship's position; hence, to be mistaken in one's calculations or reasoning. To **run ahead of one's r.,** to find ship has sailed farther than was allowed for or calculated in the *r.* (Certain text-books on navigational theory have introduced unnecessarily what they term *estimated position.* In this they distinguish ship's position calculated from courses and distances sailed only, which they call *dead reckoning,* abbrv. *D.R.,* the *estimated position* being that obtained by considering, in addition, the effect on ship's place by a given current or currents, or by unusual leeway due to strong winds, or by both. Since the purpose of the *r.* is to establish ship's most probable position by keeping account of *all* her movements on the earth's surface, whether we call that position *estimated* or *reckoned,* it still is *deduced r.,* or good old established *D.R.,* and no apparent justification for such distinguishing point exists.)

RECOGNITION LIGHTS. Two or more lights, usually red and/or white, displayed aloft, as by a vessel entering or leaving harbor at night during time of war, for identification purposes. *Also see* **Coston l.** *in* LIGHT.

RECONCILE. To smooth or *fair* the lines of a surface, as at a planking butt-joint, in ship construction; to reduce an irregularity in a surface, line of curvature, sheer, etc., so as to present even curvature, etc., according to plan; *see* FAIR.

RECOVER. In pulling an oar, to swing the blade forward for next stroke upon completion of a sweep from the *recovery point,* or that at which oar is lifted from water.

RECORDER. Any instrument or device for enumerating, as a *revolution r.* (*see* REVOLUTION); for depicting on a time-graph, as a *course r.* (*see* COURSE); or for pointing or indicating a value, as a *depth r.* or *depth-gauge* (*see* SOUNDING).

RECTANGULAR METHOD OF COMPASS COMPENSATION. *See* **Compensated c.** *in* COMPASS; *also* DEVIATION.

RED. Characterized by a reddish hue; having the color of red; as, the *red duster* (British ensign); the *red drum* (drumfish). For *r.* as a combining term with the following, *see:* ENSIGN; FOG; LEAD; GUN; OAK; MAGNET (*r. pole of*).

REDELIVERY NOTICE. In accordance with the *redelivery clause* commonly prescribed in a *charter-party,* written notice,—usually not less than ten days in advance,—given by a charterer to vessel's owner, indicating that, on date of expiration of charter, vessel will be returned to owner's custody at a named port or place.

REDUCER. A fitting used for joining two pipes of different sizes; a *pressure-valve,* or valve which automatically opens upon rise of pressure above a certain limit, as in a fire-line or in a cargo-line in an oil-tank vessel; a *relief valve.*

REDUCTION. Act or process of converting a value to its equivalent in a different denomination; as, *r.* of longitude in degrees of arc to longitude in time. Act of correcting a changing value to that corresponding to a given instant; as, *r.* of declination, hour angle, etc., of a heavenly body to a certain *Universal* or *Greenwich Mean Time.* Application of a determined correction to a given quantity, for comparison with a standard value; as, *r.* of soundings. Change of speed, as in a system of gears, in which a given wheel meshes in a larger and thus *reduces* velocity in the latter; thus, *r.* being usually expressed as a ratio of circumferences of such wheels, if one wheel is five times that of the other in circumference, *r.* is said to be 5 to 1, or speed varies inversely as circumference of meshing gears. **R. gear,** *see* GEAR. **R. of soundings,** correction applied to depth found by *sounding* for purpose of *reducing* such depth to that shown on chart of the locality, as in coastal regions having a large *tidal range.* Thus, tidal datum being *low water ordinary springs,* for example, and rise of tide for date in question 16 feet, given observed depth as 50 feet at *high water,* then 50—16, or 34 feet, is the depth for comparison with surveyed depth indicated on chart. At half-tide, correction would be 8 feet; at ¾-tide, 13½ feet; and at ¼-tide, 2½ feet; height of tide usually varying as the sine of hours, expressed in degrees, from time of half-tide, assuming a 6-hour rise at 15° per hour, a 5-hour rise at 18°, etc. **R. to meridian,** in determining latitude by an observed altitude of a celestial body, process of *reducing* such altitude to that value it would have assumed had it been observed with body *on the meridian,* or *in transit,* at instant of observation. Principal factor controlling accuracy of results in application of this method is the *azimuth* of the body observed; *i.e.,* greater the bearing from true north or south, less dependable will be the latitude obtained, as, for example, when declination and latitude are within a few degrees of each other. A good rule to note is that, in using any *r. to meridian* calculation, the number of minutes in the hour angle should not exceed the number of degrees in the body's *meridian zenith distance.* In any case, since *r.* value varies as the square of the interval from time of transit, with increase of that interval greater accuracy in the longitude and hence local time (solar or sidereal) or hour angle of body is required. Primarily intended for use in cloudy weather, when the meridian altitude may not always be observed, *ex-meridian altitudes,* as those so treated are called, to-day are falling into disuse owing to the present popularity of short methods for obtaining a *line of position* corresponding to any observation.

REED HORN. Sound trumpet or horn used as a fog-signal; a fog-horn. Such instrument, as used for navigational aid purposes at a coastal station, consists essentially of a *reed,* or thin metal blade, fixed to produce sound from vibrations which are set up by a jet of compressed air. The blast or blasts are sounded automatically and one or more large-mouthed trumpets throw signal seaward or as directed. It now is superseded at first-class lighthouses and stations by the powerful electrically operated diaphragm "horn"; *see* NAUTOPHONE.

REEDING TOOL. As used in calking seams of plating, a tool for *reeding,* or. smoothing out the turned edges in the finishing process.

REEF.[1] To take in a part of a sail, as a stretch along its head or foot, for purpose of setting a less area of canvas. Usually with *out,* to rip or clear out oakum from planking seams, as with the caulker's *reefing-iron.* To shorten the projecting length of a bowsprit or height of a topmast by partially drawing it inboard or lowering. To move the boards or floats of a paddle-wheel toward center of wheel in order to decrease their depth of immersion, as in a deeply laden paddle steamer. Reduction of a sail's area by *reefing;* as, *a r. in the mainsail.* That part of a sail taken in by *reefing.* Where a sail may be "shortened" by two or more *r's,* these are named 1st., 2nd., etc., or, as in the larger old single topsails, *single-r., double-r., treble-r.,* and *close-r.* Square and lateen sails are *reefed* at the head; fore-and-aft and lug sails at the foot. **Bag-r.,** first or lowest *r.* in a fore-and-aft sail. **Balance r.,** *see* BALANCE. **Barrier r.,** *see* REEF.[2] **Close-r.,** to reduce a sail's area to the minimum possible; especially where means for taking in more than two *r's* are present. In old single-topsail days, that sail was said to be *close-reefed* when its last *r.* (3rd. or 4th. *r.*) had been taken in. **Cunningham r.,** *see* CUNNINGHAM PATENT REEF. **French r.,** *see* FRENCH. To **heave out a r.,** *see* HEAVE. **Lagoon r.,** *see* ATOLL. **R.-band,** the strengthening band or strip of canvas across a sail for taking the stress of the *r.-points.* In effect, this band forms the head or the foot, according to type of sail, of the reefed canvas. **R.-cringle,** as fitted in a sail at each end of a *r.-band,* a cringle through which the *earing,* or rope securing leech of sail to a boom or yard, is passed. **R.-earing,** *see* EARING. **R.-hook,** same as *race-knife, q.v. in* KNIFE. **R.-jig,**

small handy tackle used in reefing to stretch taut the *r.-band* before making fast the *r.-points;* also, *r.-jigger.* **R. knot,** the *square knot,* used in making fast the *r.-points.* Among sailors, opposed to the *granny,* or lubberly bend or knot commonly used by landsmen in joining ends of a line. *R. knot* differs from the *granny* in that each end lies parallel to its own standing part and hence with the rope thus connected. In boats and small vessels and also as sometimes required by the Mate in square-riggers, the *r. knot* is made as a *single slip;* i.e., the riding half-knot is made with a bight in one of the points. By a simple pull on the bighted end, knot is released. **R. line,** also called *jack-line* and *reefing-jackstay,* the rope secured to and along a *r.-band* in the *French r.* system; *see* **F. reef** *in* FRENCH. **R. pendant,** rope leading from a boom end or a yard-arm and hooked to a *r.-cringle* for stretching out the *r.-band* in reefing. A *r.-jig* (or *r.-tackle* in larger fore-and-aft sails) is used to haul on it along boom or yard. In large fore-and-aft sails, a special *cringle* in which to hook the *r.-pendant* is fitted in the leech close to and above the *r.-cringle.* **R. point,** one of the short pieces of *point-line* (usually 21-thread manila or about $1\frac{1}{2}$ inches in circumference) fitted in grommets at each seam of the sail-cloths along the middle line of *r.-band.* This means that a square sail having a head-length of 75 feet and made of 22-inch canvas contains about 45 *r.-points.* Each point, which is 6 to 7 feet in length in large sails, is stitched at its middle to *upper* side of its grommet in a square sail and to *lower* side in a fore-and-aft sail, or in direction of the stress in both cases. In *reefing,* each pair of *r.-point* ends are knotted together over the gathered-in canvas, as soon as the *r.-earings* are passed, or *over the head-rope* of a square sail and *over the foot-rope* of a fore-and-aft sail. **R. tackle,** for facilitating reefing of a heavy sail, a purchase for hauling the canvas up and out, as in square rig, or for stretching out the *r.-band* in a boom sail. Excepting perhaps its use on a large foresail in heavy weather latitudes, since the advent of *double topsails* the *r.-tackle* as a necessary adjunct to a square sail has disappeared. In single-topsail days, when larger ships carried as many as four reefs in topsails and two in the courses, the purchase consisted of a gun-tackle rig from each yard-arm to a point on sail's leech two or three feet below the lowest *r.-band.* Its purpose was to lift and haul up the canvas so that the stretching-out and tucking-in process on that portion of sail taken in by reefing was considerably lightened. Lower block of this tackle was hooked or secured in the *r.-tackle cringle* and a strengthening band or strip of canvas, called a *r.-tackle patch,* was sewn diagonally downward from the cringle to meet the sail's *belly-band.* **Roller r.,** in some small pleasure craft, a portion of a boom sail taken in by rolling the canvas on either the boom itself or a special *roller* fitted above it. **Rolling r.,** *see* CUNNINGHAM PATENT REEF. **To shake out a r.,** to release and spread that portion of a sail which has been *reefed* or one *r.* where two or more have been taken in. **Spanish r.,** that taken in a triangular fore-and-aft sail by making a half-knot in the head part or peak of the canvas. Also, an old term for lowering a top-gallant or a topsail yard the full extent of its hoist and so reducing sail to a *belly.* **Slab r.,** first *r.* in a single topsail. To **take a fisherman's r.,** *see* FISHERMAN.

REEF.[2] A ridge of sand or shelf, ledge, line or range of rocks or coral at or near the sea surface. **Barrier r.,** a reef lying parallel, or nearly so, to an adjacent or near-by coast and separated from the latter by a navigable passage; opposed to a *fringing r.,* or one jutting from or contained in the coast line. An outstanding example of this formation is the *Great Barrier R.* of Australia; *see* CORAL. **Coral r.,** *see* ATOLL *and* CORAL. **R.-fishing,** *see* FISHING.

REEFER. Lower deck colloquial name for a midshipman (*older use*). Any fish usually taken in a surf. A short double-breasted *jacket* of thick material, —usually of pilot cloth; a pea-jacket; a watch-coat. *Cf.* **P. cloth** *in* PILOT. American fisherman's term for an *oyster* growing on a reef; a reef-oyster; so distinguished from the mollusk of mud-banks because of its superior quality. Chiefly in U.S., short or colloquial for *refrigeration*; as, a *r. ship; r. engineer.*

REEFING. Combining word designating that which may be *reefed* or used to *reef* with. Procedure of reducing sail area by taking in a reef; *see* REEF.[1] **R.-batten,** one of several light battens sewn in a sail nearly parallel to the mast, as fitted for reefing in some small pleasure craft. Portion of sail between batten and mast is drawn in to the latter by *brails,* or *hulling-lines,* thus reducing spread of canvas. **R.-becket,** in a French reef, one of a number of short pieces of sennit or small rope, corresponding to *reef-points* in the common reefing system. It is passed around the *jack-line,* or *reefing-jackstay,* which lies across fore side of sail, and its end brought up and made fast to jackstay of the yard. It often was made with an eye which was placed over a toggle fitted to its fixed end on the yard. **R.-bowsprit,** as fitted in some small craft, a bowsprit which may be shortened by sliding it inboard and setting it at any required projecting length; also termed *running-bowsprit* and *sliding-bowsprit.* **R.-cleats,** those fitted on a boom near clew of sail for purpose of taking the hauling-out turns of the *reef-earing.* **R.-iron,** caulker's ripping- or clearing-iron; *see* **Calking-i's** *in* IRON. **R.-jacket,** same as *pea-jacket; see* REEFER. **R.-jackstay,** the rope stretched along a reef-band for use in the French reef; *see* **R.-line** *in* REEF. **R.-plank,** extends across and is secured to stern davits of schooners having a long after boom. While acting as a thwartship stiffener

for davit heads, serves as a platform for access to sail in *reefing.* **R.-topmast,** one that may be lowered and secured at any required height.

REEL. Any revolving contrivance on which a wire hawser, leadline, or other cordage may be stowed by winding. To wind on a *r.,* usually with *in* or *up;* as, to *r. in* (or *up*) a mooring-wire. To roll or stagger about: *chiefly poetic;* as in, "the tall ship *reels* like a drunken man." **R.-holder,** man detailed to hold the *log-r.* in the operation of *heaving the log;* also, *reeler, reel-stand. Cf.* **Chip l.** *in* LOG. **Wire-r.,** a drum-shaped *r.* with raised or framed ends for stowing a wire rope. It is turned by a hand-crank in *winding in* and often is fitted with a brake for controlling speed when paying out wire.

REEM. A variant of *ream. See* REAM.

REEVE. To pass the end of a rope, chain, etc., through a hole or opening, as in a block, dead-eye, ring-bolt, or the like; as, *lanyards always are rove* (or *reeved*) *right-handed in dead-eyes.* Usually with *off,* to rig the necessary rope in a block, set of blocks, a sheave, etc., as, to *r. off* a guy-tackle; to *r. off* the signal halyards. To go through openings or spaces between rocks, floating ice, vessels, etc., in a cautionary sense; usually with *through,* as, "the cutter *reeved through* a score of dangerous passages among the reefs." (Past and past participle is *reeved* only, in this last-named sense) **Port r.,** *see* **P. warden** *in* PORT.

REEVING-LINE. Any rope temporarily *rove* in a block, set of blocks, bull's-eyes, etc., for a specific purpose; a *dummy gantline*; a small line bent to a rope of greater size for pulling the latter through a block, sheave-hole, etc. **R.-line bend,** method of joining two lines so that they will pass through an opening as a continuous rope. It is made by half-hitching and seizing the respective ends of each rope to the other's standing part.

REFERENCE LINE. A basic line, or line representing a *reference plane,* from which vertical or horizontal measurements are taken, as in laying off the structural dimensions in shipbuilding; a *tidal plane of reference (see* TIDAL). *Cf.* **Base l.** *in* LINE.[2]

REFIT. To prepare for further use; to recondition, restore, or repair, as a ship; to make necessary repairs, rig out, re-supply, and re-provision a vessel for another cruise or voyage. The act or process of refitting; as, *she is at the dockyard for r.*

REFLECTING CIRCLE. *See* CIRCLE.

REFLECTING QUADRANT. Early name for the quadrant; *see* QUADRANT.

REFRACTION. Bending of light rays in their passage through a medium of varying density; specifically, *atmospheric r.,* the change in direction *downward* of light rays emanating from a heavenly body whose altitude is other than 90°, or in the zenith. The *correction* applied to a body's apparent altitude in order to allow for this displacement of such celestial object; always *subtractive*. *R.* has a maximum value of about 35 minutes of arc in the horizon and decreases with increase of altitude to nil in the zenith. *Cf.* ALTITUDE. Tables of *mean r.*, or those values for any apparent altitude calculated for a standard barometric height and air temperature, are found in principal works on nautical astronomy and usually are accompanied with a tabular correction to be applied to the values in cases where atmospheric conditions depart from the standard and required precision demands it. *Bowditch* gives *mean r.* for a barometer height of 30.00 inches and Fahrenheit thermometer 50°. Due to hidden vagaries of density and thermal differences in surface and upper layers of the atmosphere, *r.* values should be considered approximate only for altitudes less than 10°,—their field for pitfalls for the unwary, particularly so in calm, cold weather, when the phenomenon of *terrestrial r.*, or displacement of the sea horizon, is also apt to add its quota to a veritable *r. complex. R.* accounts for the fact that at true sunset or sunrise an observer having his eyes at sea level would note that body's lower limb raised above the horizon by very nearly its semi-diameter; which leads us to a useful point to be noted in checking the compass by sunset or sunrise bearing: In normal atmospheric conditions, altitude of sun's lower limb will be 16' plus *dip* corresponding to observer's height of eye at *true sunrise* or *sunset*. Thus, with eye 50 feet above sea level, sun will be clear of the sea horizon by very nearly 24', or by very nearly three-fourths his diameter.

REFRIGERATED CARGO. Perishable commodities carried in holds or compartments the temperature of which is maintained as required for successful carriage of such goods. Generally, *r. cargo* consists of three classes: *frozen, chilled,* and *air-cooled;* the first-named embracing fresh meats, poultry, fish, butter, and egg products carried at 10 to 15° F. (*see* MEAT-CARRYING SHIP); *chilled cargo* being the term for mutton and beef carried at about 29°; and *air-cooled* products take in bacon, ham, fruits, (apples, pears, plums, etc.), milk, eggs, and fresh vegetables, at from 35 to 40°; *see* **Cargo c.** *in* COOLING; *also* FRUIT-CARRIER. Any ship equipped to transport *r. cargo* is termed a *refrigerated vessel*, whether capable of carrying whole or part cargoes of such goods. Commodities are said to be given *refrigerated stowage* when loaded as *r. cargo*.

REFUGE, Port of. See **H. of refuge** *in* HARBOR.

REFUSE STAYS. To miss stays, or fail to *come about*, in tacking; *see* MISS STAYS.

REGATTA. (*It.*)   Originally, a gondola race in Venice; now, a pulling or sailing race, or organized variety of such races, as at a yacht-meeting.

REGISTER. A written record or account; especially, an official book containing particulars of persons, property, transactions, ships, etc.; as, *r. of seamen; Lloyd's R.* A document serving as evidence of nationality and ownership of a vessel, also termed *certificate of registry,* issued by Collector of Customs at vessel's hailing port to her owners, who usually are required by law to be bona fide citizens of country concerned,—especially so in U.S.A. *R.* is issued in accordance with sworn particulars presented by builders and owners of ship concerned, which, generally, must have been built or rebuilt under certain conditions in, seized by, or forfeited to the government of, country in question; contains vessel's name, origin, date built, owner's name, port of registry, type, tonnage, power, principal dimensions, and other identifying information. In U.S., vessel is then said to be *documented*. The master's name must be endorsed on the *r.* before the Customs officer concerned or by a Consul at a foreign port. The document usually must be produced by ship's master in entering at customs at any port during course of a foreign voyage and in any transaction in which the fact of authorized title to ownership of vessel is required. In U.S., registration or documentation is denoted by three terms, *viz.,* vessels in foreign trade are *registered;* those in coastwise or inland trade are *enrolled;* those of smaller tonnage engaged in coastwise trade, whale fishery, cod fishery, etc., and yachts under certain conditions are *licensed.* A document combining the last two registration forms, termed *Certificate of License and Enrollment* may be granted certain domestic vessels. (*Cf. Documentation of Vessels* in *Navigation Laws of the United States*, issued by *U.S. Government Printing Office, Washington, D.C.*) **Lloyd's r.,** *see* LLOYD'S. **Navy r.,** *see* **N. publications** *in* NAVY.

REGISTERED. Officially certified and recorded, as certain data concerning a vessel appearing in the *certificate of registry* or the *tonnage certificate.* As qualifying the following-named measurements, *see* BREADTH; DEPTH; LENGTH; TONNAGE.

REGISTRY. Act of registering; enrollment; an official record or *register;* registration; an entry in a register. **Certificate of r.,** *see* REGISTER. **Port of r.,** *see* PORT.

REGULAR. Formed, arranged, or following a procedure, according to a specified or customary rule; as, *shackles and thimbles of r. type; channels now are marked with the r. buoys; vessel will berth in her r. turn.* Designating personnel of permanent status or standing, as distinguished from such in a volunteer or reserve capacity, rating, or rank; as, *"both regulars and reserves bent to the job with a* *will."* Thorough; typical; unmitigated; as, *seas were running like r. Cape Horners; she is a r. submarine, like most heavily laden tankers; it blew a r. gale.* **R.-lay rope,** right-handed or hawser-laid rope; *see* ROPE.

REGULATIONS FOR PREVENTING COLLISIONS AT SEA. The present International Rules consisting of 32 "articles" date from 1885, when the rules adopted by Great Britain in 1884 were adopted and amended by an act of U.S. Congress. *International Marine Conference* at Washington in 1889 made certain further amendments and the rules as drawn up by that body were included in U.S. statutes as of August 19, 1890, and have been in effect since that date. In 1897, the U.S. Congress passed "an act to adopt regulations for preventing collisions upon certain harbors, rivers, and inland waters of the United States." This act, which has been amended from time to time, contains the *Inland Rules* and provides that the Commandant, U.S. Coast Guard, is empowered to draw up additional rules relative to the navigation of certain domestic waters, in accordance with the authority for formulating such, as prescribed in *International Rules* (Article 30). Local rules for preventing collisions accordingly have been drawn up under the title of *Pilot Rules,* as follows: "Pilot Rules for certain inland waters of the Atlantic and Pacific Coasts and of the Gulf of Mexico"; "Pilot Rules for the Great Lakes and their connecting and tributary waters and the St. Mary's River"; "Pilot Rules for the Western Rivers and the Red River of the North."

The *International Conference on Safety at Sea, London, 1948,* revised present *International Regulations for Preventing Collisions at Sea* and invited the Government of the United Kingdom to fix the date on and after which revised regulations shall be applied, upon substantial unanimity being reached by the governments concerned as to their acceptance. The Conference requested the Government of the U.K. to give not less than one year's notice of such date to all States represented (34).

The regulations commonly are referred to as *Rules of the Road,* although properly only the *Steering and Sailing Rules,* included as numbered 17 to 27, are concerned with procedure in avoiding risk of collision.

"Substantial unanimity" having been reached, as announced by the U. K. on Dec. 19, 1952, the Regulations become effective on Jan. 1, 1954.

REGULATIONS FOR
PREVENTING COLLISIONS AT SEA
PART A.
PRELIMINARY AND DEFINITIONS
Rule 1

(*a*) These Rules shall be followed by all vessels and seaplanes upon the high seas and in all waters

connected therewith navigable by seagoing vessels, except as provided in Rule 30. Where, as a result of their special construction, it is not possible for seaplanes to comply fully with the provisions of Rules specifying the carrying of lights and shapes, these provisions shall be followed as closely as circumstances permit.

(*b*) The Rules concerning lights shall be complied with in all weathers from sunset to sunrise, and during such times no other lights shall be exhibited, except such lights as cannot be mistaken for the prescribed lights or impair their visibility or distinctive character, or interfere with the keeping of a proper look-out.

(*c*) In the following Rules, except where the context otherwise requires:—

   (i) the word "vessel" includes every description of water craft, other than a seaplane on the water, used or capable of being used as a means of transportation on water;

   (ii) the word "seaplane" includes a flying boat and any other aircraft designed to manœuvre on the water;

   (iii) the term "power-driven vessel" means any vessel propelled by machinery;

   (iv) every power-driven vessel which is under sail and not under power is to be considered a sailing vessel, and every vessel under power, whether under sail or not, is to be considered a power-driven vessel;

   (v) a vessel or seaplane on the water is "under way" when she is not at anchor, or made fast to the shore, or aground;

   (vi) the term "height above the hull" means height above the uppermost continuous deck;

   (vii) the length and breadth of a vessel shall be deemed to be the length and breadth appearing in her certificate of registry;

   (viii) the length and span of a seaplane shall be its maximum length and span as shown in its certificate of airworthiness, or as determined by measurement in the absence of such certificate;

   (ix) the word "visible," when applied to lights, means visible on a dark night with a clear atmosphere;

   (x) the term "short blast" means a blast of about one second's duration;

   (xi) the term "prolonged blast" means a blast of from four to six seconds' duration;

   (xii) the word "whistle" means whistle or siren;

   (xiii) the word "tons" means gross tons.

PART B.
LIGHTS AND SHAPES
Rule 2

(*a*) A power-driven vessel when under way shall carry:—

(i) On or in front of the foremast, or if a vessel without a foremast then in the fore part of the vessel, a bright white light so constructed as to show an unbroken light over an arc of the horizon of 20 points of the compass (225°); so fixed as to show the light 10 points (112½°) on each side of the vessel, that is, from right ahead to 2 points (22½°) abaft the beam on either side; and of such a character as to be visible at a distance of at least 5 miles.

(ii) Either forward of or abaft the white light mentioned in sub-section (i) a second white light similar in construction and character to that light. Vessels of less than 150 feet in length, and vessels engaged in towing, shall not be required to carry the second white light but may do so.

(iii) These two white lights shall be so placed in a line with and over the keel that one shall be at least 15 feet higher than the other and in such position that the lower light shall be forward of the upper one. The horizontal distance between the two lights shall be at least three times the vertical distance. The lower of these two white lights or, if only one is carried, then that light, shall be placed at a height above the hull of not less than 20 feet, and, if the breadth of the vessel exceeds 20 feet, then at a height above the hull not less than such breadth, so however that the light need not be placed at a greater height above the hull than 40 feet. In all circumstances the light or lights, as the case may be, shall be so placed as to be clear of and above all other lights and obstructing superstructures.

(iv) On the starboard side a green light so constructed as to show an unbroken light over an arc of the horizon of 10 points of the compass (112½°), so fixed as to show the light from right ahead to 2 points (22½°) abaft the beam on the starboard side, and of such a character as to be visible at a distance of at least 2 miles.

(v) On the port side a red light so constructed as to show an unbroken light over an arc of the horizon of 10 points of the compass (112½°), so fixed as to show the light from right ahead to 2 points (22½°) abaft the beam on the port side, and of such a character as to be visible at a distance of at least 2 miles.

(vi) The said green and red sidelights shall be fitted with inboard screens projecting at least 3 feet forward from the light, so as to prevent these lights from being seen across the bows.

(b) A seaplane under way on the water shall carry:—

(i) In the forepart amidships where it can best be seen a bright white light, so constructed as to show an unbroken light over an arc of the horizon of 220 degrees of the compass, so fixed as to show the light 110 degrees on each side of the seaplane, namely, from right ahead to 20 degrees abaft the beam on either side, and of such a character as to be visible at a distance of at least 3 miles.

(ii) On the right or starboard wing tip a green light, so constructed as to show an unbroken light over an arc of the horizon of 110 degrees of the compass, so fixed as to show the light from right ahead to 20 degrees abaft the beam on the starboard side, and of such a character as to be visible at a distance of at least 2 miles.

(iii) On the left or port wing tip a red light, so constructed as to show an unbroken light over an arc of the horizon of 110 degrees of the compass, so fixed as to show the light from right ahead to 20 degrees abaft the beam on the port side, and of such a character as to be visible at a distance of at least 2 miles.

Rule 3

(a) A power-driven vessel when towing or pushing another vessel shall, in addition to her sidelights, carry two bright white lights in a vertical line one over the other, not less than 6 feet apart, and when towing more than one vessel shall carry an additional bright white light 6 feet above or below such light, if the length of the tow, measuring from the stern of the towing vessel to the stern of the last vessel towed, exceeds 600 feet. Each of these lights shall be of the same construction and character and one of them shall be carried in the same position as the white light mentioned in Rule 2 (a) (i), except the additional light, which shall be carried at a height of not less than 14 feet above the hull. In a vessel with a single mast, such lights may be carried on the mast.

(b) The towing vessel shall also show either the stern light specified in Rule 10 or in lieu of that light a small white light abaft the funnel or after mast for the tow to steer by, but such light shall not be visible forward of the beam. The carriage of the white light specified in Rule 2 (a) (ii) is optional.

(c) A seaplane on the water, when towing one or more seaplanes or vessels, shall carry the lights prescribed in Rule 2 (b) (i), (ii), and (iii); and, in addition, she shall carry a second white light of the same construction and character as the white light mentioned in Rule 2 (b) (i), and in a vertical line at least 6 feet above or below such light.

Rule 4

(a) A vessel which is not under command shall carry, where they can best be seen, and, if a power-driven vessel, in lieu of the lights required by Rule 2 (a) (i) and (ii), two red lights in a vertical line one over the other not less than 6 feet apart, and of such a character as to be visible all round the horizon at a distance of at least 2 miles. By day she shall carry in a vertical line one over the other not less than 6 feet apart, where they can best be seen, two black balls or shapes each not less than 2 feet in diameter.

(b) A seaplane on the water which is not under command may carry, where they can best be seen, two red lights in a vertical line, one over the other, not less than 3 feet apart, and of such a character as to be visible all round the horizon at a distance of at least 2 miles, and may by day carry in a vertical line one over the other not less than 3 feet apart, where they can best be seen, two black balls or shapes, each not less than 2 feet in diameter.

(c) A vessel engaged in laying or in picking up a submarine cable or navigation mark, or a vessel engaged in surveying or underwater operations when from the nature of her work she is unable to get out of the way of approaching vessels, shall carry, in lieu of the lights specified in Rule 2 (a) (i) and (ii), three lights in a vertical line one over the other not less than 6 feet apart. The highest and lowest of these lights shall be red, and the middle light shall be white, and they shall be of such a character as to be visible all round the horizon at a distance of at least 2 miles. By day, she shall carry in a vertical line one over the other not less than 6 feet apart, where they can best be seen, three shapes each not less than 2 feet in diameter, of which the highest and lowest shall be globular in shape and red in colour, and the middle one diamond in shape and white.

(d) The vessels and seaplanes referred to in this Rule, when not making way through the water, shall not carry the coloured sidelights, but when making way they shall carry them.

(e) The lights and shapes required to be shown by this Rule are to be taken by other vessels and seaplanes as signals that the vessel or seaplane showing them is not under command and cannot therefore get out of the way.

(f) These signals are not signals of vessels in distress and requiring assistance. Such signals are contained in Rule 31.

Rule 5

(a) A sailing vessel under way and any vessel or seaplane being towed shall carry the same lights as are prescribed by Rule 2 for a power-driven vessel or a seaplane under way, respectively, with the exception of the white lights specified therein, which they shall never carry. They shall also carry stern lights as specified in Rule 10, provided that vessels towed, except the last vessel of a tow, may carry, in lieu of such stern light, a small white light as specified in Rule 3 (b).

(b) A vessel being pushed ahead shall carry, at the forward end, on the starboard side a green light and on the port side a red light, which shall have the same characteristics as the lights described in Rule 2 (a) (iv) and (v) and shall be screened as provided in Rule 2 (a) (vi), provided that any number of vessels pushed ahead in a group shall be lighted as one vessel.

Rule 6

(a) In small vessels, when it is not possible on account of bad weather or other sufficient cause to fix the green and red sidelights, these lights shall be kept at hand lighted and ready for immediate use, and shall, on the approach of or to other vessels, be exhibited on their respective sides in sufficient time to prevent collision, in such manner as to make them most visible, and so that the green light shall not be seen on the port side nor the red light on the starboard side, nor, if practicable, more than 2 points (22½ degrees) abaft the beam on their respective sides.

(b) To make the use of these portable lights more certain and easy, the lanterns containing them shall each be painted outside with the colour of the lights they respectively contain, and shall be provided with proper screens.

Rule 7

Power-driven vessels of less than 40 tons, vessels under oars or sails of less than 20 tons, and rowing boats, when under way shall not be required to carry the lights mentioned in Rule 2, but if they do not carry them they shall be provided with the following lights:—

(a) Power-driven vessels of less than 40 tons, except as provided in section (b), shall carry:—

(i) In the fore part of the vessel, where it can best be seen, and at a height above the gunwale of not less than 9 feet, a bright white light constructed and fixed as prescribed in Rule 2(a) (i) and of such a character as to be visible at a distance of at least 3 miles.

(ii) Green and red sidelights constructed and fixed as prescribed in Rule 2(a) (iv) and (v), and of such character as to be visible at a distance of at least 1 mile, or a combined lantern showing a green light and a red light from right ahead to 2 points (22½°) abaft the beam on their respective sides. Such lantern shall be carried not less than 3 feet below the white light.

(b) Small power-driven boats, such as are carried by sea-going vessels, may carry the white light at a less height than 9 feet above the gunwale, but it shall be carried above the sidelights or the combined lantern mentioned in sub-section (a) (ii).

(c) Vessels of less than 20 tons, under oars or sails, except as provided in section (d), shall, if they do not carry the sidelights, carry where it can best be seen a lantern showing a green light on one side and a red light on the other, of such a character as to be visible at a distance of at least 1 mile, and so fixed that the green light shall not be seen on the port side, nor the red light on the starboard side. Where it is not possible to fix this light, it shall be kept ready for immediate use and shall be exhibited in sufficient time to prevent collision and so that the green light shall not be seen on the port side nor the red light on the starboard side.

(d) Small rowing boats, whether under oars or sail, shall only be required to have ready at hand an electric torch or a lighted lantern showing a white light, which shall be exhibited in sufficient time to prevent collision.

(e) The vessels and boats referred to in this Rule shall not be required to carry the lights or shapes prescribed in Rules 4(a) and 11(e).

Rule 8

(a) (i) Sailing pilot-vessels, when engaged on their station on pilotage duty and not at anchor, shall not show the lights prescribed for other vessels, but shall carry a white light at the masthead visible all round the horizon at a distance of at least 3 miles, and shall also exhibit a flare-up light or flare-up lights at short intervals which shall never exceed 10 minutes.

(ii) On the near approach of or to other vessels they shall have their sidelights ready for use and shall flash or show them at short intervals to indicate the direction in which they are heading, but the green light shall not be shown on the port side, nor the red light on the starboard side.

(iii) A sailing pilot-vessel of such a class as to be obliged to go alongside of a vessel to put a pilot on board may show the white light instead of carrying it at the masthead and may, instead of the side lights above mentioned, have at hand ready for use a lantern with a green glass on the one side and a red glass on the other to be used as prescribed above.

(b) A power-driven pilot-vessel when engaged on her station on pilotage duty and not at anchor shall, in addition to the lights and flares required for sailing pilot-vessels, carry at a distance of 8 feet below her white masthead light a red light visible all round the horizon at a distance of at least 3 miles, and also the sidelights required to be carried by vessels when under way. A bright intermittent all round white light may be used in place of a flare.

(c) All pilot-vessels, when engaged on their stations on pilotage duty and at anchor, shall carry the lights and show the flares prescribed in sections (a) and (b), except that the sidelights shall not be shown. They shall also carry the anchor light or lights prescribed in Rule 11.

(d) All pilot-vessels, whether at anchor or not at anchor, shall, when not engaged on their stations on pilotage duty, carry the same lights as other vessels of their class and tonnage.

Rule 9

(a) Fishing vessels when not fishing shall show the lights or shapes prescribed for similar vessels of their tonnage. When fishing they shall show only the lights or shapes prescribed by this Rule, which lights or shapes, except as otherwise provided, shall be visible at a distance of at least 2 miles.

(b) Vessels fishing with trolling (towing) lines, shall show only the lights prescribed for a power-driven or sailing vessel under way as may be appropriate.

(c) Vessels fishing with nets or lines, except trolling (towing) lines, extending from the vessel not more than 500 feet horizontally into the seaway shall show, where it can best be seen, one all round white light and in addition, on approaching or being approached by another vessel, shall show a second white light at least 6 feet below the first light and at a horizontal distance of at least 10 feet away from it (6 feet in small open boats) in the direction in which the outlying gear is attached. By day such vessels shall indicate their occupation by displaying a basket where it can be seen; and if they have their gear out while at anchor, they shall, on the approach of other vessels, show the same signal in the direction from the anchor ball towards the net or gear.

(d) Vessels fishing with nets or lines, except trolling (towing) lines, extending from the vessel more than 500 feet horizontally into the seaway shall show, where they can best be seen, three white lights at least 3 feet apart in a vertical triangle visible all round the horizon. When making way through the water, such vessels shall show the proper coloured sidelights but when not making way they shall not show them. By day they shall show a basket in the forepart of the vessel as near the stem as possible not less than 10 feet above the rail; and, in addition, where it can best be seen, one black conical shape, apex upwards. If they have their gear out while at anchor they shall, on the approach of other vessels, show the basket in the direction from the anchor ball towards the net or gear.

(e) Vessels when engaged in trawling, by which is meant the dragging of a dredge net or other apparatus along or near the bottom of the sea, and not at anchor:—

(i) If power-driven vessels, shall show in the same position as the white light mentioned in Rule 2(a) (i) a tri-coloured lantern, so constructed and fixed as to show a white light from right ahead to 2 points (22½ degrees) on each bow, and a green light and a red light over an arc of the horizon from 2 points (22½ degrees) on each bow to 2 points (22½ degrees) abaft the beam on the starboard and port sides, respectively; and not less than 6 nor more than 12 feet below the tri-coloured lantern a white light in a lantern, so constructed as to show a clear, uniform, and unbroken light all round the horizon. They shall also show the stern light specified in Rule 10 (a)..

(ii) If sailing vessels, shall carry a white light in a lantern so constructed as to show a clear, uniform, and unbroken light all round the horizon, and shall also, on the approach of or to other vessels show, where it can best be seen, a white flare-up light in sufficient time to prevent collision.

(iii) By day, each of the foregoing vessels shall show, where it can best be seen, a basket.

(f) In addition to the lights which they are by this Rule required to show vessels fishing may, if necessary in order to attract attention of approaching vessels, show a flare-up light. They may also use working lights.

(g) Every vessel fishing, when at anchor, shall show the lights or shape specified in Rule 11 (a), (b) or (c); and shall, on the approach of another vessel or vessels, show an additional white light at least 6 feet below the forward anchor light and at a horizontal distance of at least 10 feet away from it in the direction of the outlying gear.

(h) If a vessel when fishing becomes fast by her gear to a rock or other obstruction she shall in daytime haul down the basket required by sections (c), (d) or (e) and show the signal specified in Rule 11 (c). By night she shall show the light or lights specified in Rule 11 (a) or (b). In fog, mist, falling snow, heavy rainstorms or any other condition similarly restricting visibility, whether by day or by night, she shall sound the signal prescribed by Rule 15 (c) (v), which signal shall also be used, on the near approach of another vessel, in good visibility.

NOTE.—*For fog signals for fishing vessels, see Rule 15 (c) (ix).*

Rule 10

(a) A vessel when under way shall carry at her stern a white light, so constructed that it shall show an unbroken light over an arc of the horizon of 12 points of the compass (135 degrees), so fixed as to show the light 6 points (67½ degrees) from right aft on each side of the vessel, and of such a character as to be visible at a distance of at least 2 miles. Such light shall be carried as nearly as practicable on the same level as the sidelights.

NOTE.—*For vessels engaged in towing or being towed, see Rules 3 (b) and 5.*

(b) In a small vessel, if it is not possible on account of bad weather or other sufficient cause for this light to be fixed, an electric torch or a lighted lantern shall be kept at hand ready for use and shall, on the approach of an overtaking vessel, be shown in sufficient time to prevent collision.

(c) A seaplane on the water when under way shall carry on her tail a white light, so constructed as to show an unbroken light over an arc of the horizon of 140 degrees of the compass, so fixed as to show the light 70 degrees from right aft on each side of the seaplane, and of such a character as to be visible at a distance of at least 2 miles.

Rule 11

(a) A vessel under 150 feet in length, when at anchor, shall carry in the forepart of the vessel, where it can best be seen, a white light in a lantern so constructed as to show a clear, uniform, and unbroken light visible all round the horizon at a distance of at least 2 miles.

(b) A vessel of 150 feet or upwards in length, when at anchor, shall carry in the fore part of the vessel, at a height of not less than 20 feet above the hull, one such light, and at or near the stern of the vessel and at such a height that it shall be not less than 15 feet lower than the forward light, another such light. Both these lights shall be visible all round the horizon at a distance of at least 3 miles.

(c) Between sunrise and sunset every vessel when at anchor shall carry in the fore part of the vessel, where it can best be seen, one black ball not less than 2 feet in diameter.

(d) A vessel engaged in laying or in picking up a submarine cable or navigation mark, or a vessel engaged in surveying or underwater operations, when at anchor, shall carry the lights or shapes prescribed in Rule 4(c) in addition to those prescribed in the appropriate preceding sections of this Rule.

(e) A vessel aground shall carry by night the light or lights prescribed in sections (a) or (b) and the two red lights prescribed in Rule 4(a). By day she shall carry, where they can best be seen, three black balls, each not less than 2 feet in diameter, placed in a vertical line one over the other, not less than 6 feet apart.

(f) A seaplane on the water under 150 feet in length, when at anchor, shall carry, where it can best be seen, a white light, visible all round the horizon at a distance of at least 2 miles.

(g) A seaplane on the water 150 feet or upwards in length, when at anchor, shall carry, where they can best be seen, a white light forward and a white light aft, both lights visible all round the horizon at a distance of at least 3 miles; and, in addition, if the seaplane is more than 150 feet in span, a white light on each side to indicate the maximum span, and visible, so far as practicable, all round the horizon at a distance of 1 mile.

(h) A seaplane aground shall carry an anchor light or lights as prescribed in sections (f) and (g), and in addition may carry two red lights in a vertical line, at least 3 feet apart, so placed as to be visible all round the horizon.

Rule 12

Every vessel or seaplane on the water may, if necessary in order to attract attention, in addition to the lights which she is by these Rules required to carry, show a flare-up light or use a detonating or other efficient sound signal that can not be mistaken for any signal authorized elsewhere under these Rules.

Rule 13

(a) Nothing in these Rules shall interfere with the operation of any special rules made by the Government of any nation with respect to additional station and signal lights for ships of war or vessels sailing under convoy, or for seaplanes on the water; or with the exhibition of recognition signals adopted by shipowners, which have been authorized by their respective Governments and duly registered and published.

(b) Whenever the Government concerned shall have determined that a naval or other military vessel or waterborne seaplane of special construction or purpose can not comply fully with the provisions of any of these Rules with respect to the number, position, range, or arc of visibility of lights or shapes, without interfering with the military function of the vessel or seaplane, such vessel or seaplane shall comply with such other provisions in regard to the number, position, range or arc of visibility of lights or shapes as her Government shall have determined to be the closest possible compliance with these Rules in respect of that vessel or seaplane.

Rule 14

A vessel proceeding under sail, when also being propelled by machinery, shall carry in the daytime forward where it can best be seen, one black conical shape, point upwards, not less than 2 feet in diameter at its base.

Rule 15

(a) A power-driven vessel shall be provided with an efficient whistle, sounded by steam or by some substitute for steam, so placed that the sound may not be intercepted by any obstruction, and with an efficient fog-horn, to be sounded by mechanical means, and also with an efficient bell. A sailing-vessel of 20 tons or upward shall be provided with a similar fog-horn and bell.

(b) All signals prescribed by this Rule for vessels under way shall be given:—

    (i) by power-driven vessels on the whistle;

    (ii) by sailing-vessels on the fog-horn;

    (iii) by vessels towed on the whistle or fog-horn.

(c) In fog, mist, falling snow, heavy rainstorms, or any other condition similarly restricting visibility, whether by day or night, the signals prescribed in this Rule shall be used as follows:—

(i) A power-driven vessel making way through the water shall sound at intervals of not more than 2 minutes a prolonged blast.

(ii) A power-driven vessel under way, but stopped and making no way through the water, shall sound at intervals of not more than 2 minutes two prolonged blasts, with an interval of about 1 second between them.

(iii) A sailing-vessel under way shall sound, at intervals of not more than 1 minute, when on the starboard tack one blast, when on the port tack two blasts in succession, and with the wind abaft the beam three blasts in succession.

(iv) A vessel when at anchor shall at intervals of not more than 1 minute ring the bell rapidly for about 5 seconds. In vessels of more than 350 feet in length the bell shall be sounded in the fore part of the vessel, and in addition there shall be sounded in the after part of the vessel, at intervals of not more than 1 minute for about 5 seconds, a gong or other instrument, the tone and sounding of which cannot be confused with that of the bell. Every vessel at anchor may in addition, in accordance with Rule 12, sound three blasts in succession, namely, one short, one prolonged, and one short blast, to give warning of her position and of the possibility of collision to an approaching vessel.

(v) A vessel when towing, a vessel engaged in laying or in picking up a submarine cable or navigation mark, and a vessel under way which is unable to get out of the way of an approaching vessel through being not under command or unable to manœuvre as required by these Rules shall, instead of the signals prescribed in subsections (i), (ii) and (iii) sound, at intervals of not more than 1 minute, three blasts in succession, namely, one prolonged blast followed by two short blasts.

(vi) A vessel towed, or, if more than one vessel is towed, only the last vessel of the tow, if manned, shall, at intervals of not more than 1 minute, sound four blasts in succession, namely, one prolonged blast followed by three short blasts. When practicable, this signal shall be made immediately after the signal made by the towing vessel.

(vii) A vessel aground shall give the signal prescribed in sub-section (iv) and shall, in addition, give three separate and distinct strokes on the bell immediately before and after each such signal.

(viii) A vessel of less than 20 tons, a rowing boat, or a seaplane on the water, shall not be obliged to give the above-mentioned signals, but if she does not, she shall make some other efficient sound signal at intervals of not more than 1 minute.

(ix) A vessel when fishing, if of 20 tons or upwards, shall at intervals of not more than 1 minute, sound a blast, such blast to be followed by ringing the bell; or she may sound, in lieu of these signals, a blast consisting of a series of several alternate notes of higher and lower pitch.

Rule 16

Speed to be moderate in fog, &c.

(a) Every vessel, or seaplane when taxi-ing on the water, shall, in fog, mist, falling snow, heavy rainstorms or any other condition similarly restricting visibility, go at a moderate speed, having careful regard to the existing circumstances and conditions.

(b) A power-driven vessel hearing, apparently forward of her beam, the fog-signal of a vessel the position of which is not ascertained, shall, so far as the circumstances of the case admit, stop her engines, and then navigate with caution until danger of collision is over.

PART C.

STEERING AND SAILING RULES

Preliminary

1. *In obeying and construing these Rules, any action taken should be positive, in ample time, and with due regard to the observance of good seamanship.*

2. *Risk of collision can, when circumstances permit, be ascertained by carefully watching the compass bearing of an approaching vessel. If the bearing does not appreciably change, such risk should be deemed to exist.*

3. *Mariners should bear in mind that seaplanes in the act of landing or taking off, or operating under adverse weather conditions, may be unable to change their intended action at the last moment.*

Rule 17

When two sailing vessels are approaching one another, so as to involve risk of collision, one of them shall keep out of the way of the other, as follows:—

(a) A vessel which is running free shall keep out of the way of a vessel which is close-hauled.

(b) A vessel which is close-hauled on the port tack shall keep out of the way of a vessel which is close-hauled on the starboard tack.

(c) When both are running free, with the wind on different sides, the vessel which has the wind on the port side shall keep out of the way of the other.

(d) When both are running free, with the wind on the same side, the vessel which is to

windward shall keep out of the way of the vessel which is to leeward.

(e) A vessel which has the wind aft shall keep out of the way of the other vessel.

Rule 18

(a) When two power-driven vessels are meeting end on, or nearly end on, so as to involve risk of collision, each shall alter her course to starboard, so that each may pass on the port side of the other. This Rule only applies to cases where vessels are meeting end on, or nearly end on, in such a manner as to involve risk of collision, and does not apply to two vessels which must, if both keep on their respective courses, pass clear of each other. The only cases to which it does apply are when each of two vessels is end on, or nearly end on, to the other; in other words, to cases in which, by day, each vessel sees the masts of the other in a line, or nearly in a line, with her own; and by night, to cases in which each vessel is in such position as to see both the sidelights of the other. It does not apply, by day, to cases in which a vessel sees another ahead crossing her own course; or, by night, to cases where the red light of one vessel is opposed to the red light of the other or where the green light of one vessel is opposed to the green light of the other or where a red light without a green light or a green light without a red light is seen ahead, or where both green and red lights are seen anywhere but ahead.

(b) For the purposes of this Rule and Rules 19 to 29 inclusive, except Rule 20 (b), a seaplane on the water shall be deemed to be a vessel, and the expression "power-driven vessel" shall be construed accordingly.

Rule 19

When two power-driven vessels are crossing, so as to involve risk of collision, the vessel which has the other on her own starboard side shall keep out of the way of the other.

Rule 20

(a) When a power-driven vessel and a sailing vessel are proceeding in such directions as to involve risk of collision, except as provided in Rules 24 and 26, the power-driven vessel shall keep out of the way of the sailing-vessel.

(b) A seaplane on the water shall, in general, keep well clear of all vessels and avoid impeding their navigation. In circumstances, however, where risk of collision exists, she shall comply with these Rules.

Rule 21

Where by any of these Rules one of two vessels is to keep out of the way, the other shall keep her course and speed. When, from any cause, the latter vessel finds herself so close that collision can not be avoided by the action of the giving-way vessel alone, she also shall take such action as will best aid to avert collision (see Rules 27 and 29).

Rule 22

Every vessel which is directed by these Rules to keep out of the way of another vessel shall, if the circumstances of the case admit, avoid crossing ahead of the other.

Rule 23

Every power-driven vessel which is directed by these Rules to keep out of the way of another vessel shall, on approaching her, if necessary, slacken her speed or stop or reverse.

Rule 24

(a) Notwithstanding anything contained in these Rules, every vessel overtaking any other shall keep out of the way of the overtaken vessel.

(b) Every vessel coming up with another vessel from any direction more than 2 points (22½°) abaft her beam, i.e., in such a position, with reference to the vessel which she is overtaking, that at night she would be unable to see either of that vessel's sidelights, shall be deemed to be an overtaking vessel; and no subsequent alteration of the bearing between the two vessels shall make the overtaking vessel a crossing vessel within the meaning of these Rules, or relieve her of the duty of keeping clear of the overtaken vessel, until she is finally past and clear.

(c) If the overtaking vessel can not determine with certainty whether she is forward of or abaft this direction from the other vessel, she shall assume that she is an overtaking vessel and keep out of the way.

Rule 25

(a) In a narrow channel every power-driven vessel when proceeding along the course of the channel shall, when it is safe and practicable, keep to that side of the fairway or mid-channel which lies on the starboard side of such vessel.

(b) Whenever a power-driven vessel is nearing a bend in a channel where a power-driven vessel approaching from the other direction can not be seen, such vessel, when she shall have arrived within one-half mile of the bend, shall give a signal by one prolonged blast of her whistle, which signal shall be answered by a similar blast given by any approaching power-driven vessel that may be within hearing around the bend. Regardless of whether an approaching vessel on the farther side of the bend is heard, such bend shall be rounded with alertness and caution.

Rule 26

All vessels not engaged in fishing shall, when under way, keep out of the way of any vessels fishing with nets or lines or trawls. This Rule shall not give to any vessel engaged in fishing the right of ob-structing a fairway used by vessels other than fishing vessels.

Rule 27

In obeying and construing these Rules due regard shall be had to all dangers of navigation and collision, and to any special circumstances, including the limitations of the craft involved, which may render a departure from the above Rules necessary in order to avoid immediate danger.

PART D.

MISCELLANEOUS

Rule 28

(a) When vessels are in sight of one another, a power-driven vessel under way, in taking any course authorized or required by these Rules, shall indicate that course by the following signals on her whistle, namely:—

One short blast to mean "I am altering my course to starboard."

Two short blasts to mean "I am altering my course to port."

Three short blasts to mean "My engines are going astern."

(b) Whenever a power-driven vessel which, under these Rules, is to keep her course and speed, is in sight of another vessel and is in doubt whether sufficient action is being taken by the other vessel to avert collision, she may indicate such doubt by giving at least five short and rapid blasts on the whistle. The giving of such a signal shall not relieve a vessel of her obligations under Rules 27 and 29 or any other Rule, or of her duty to indicate any action taken under these Rules by giving appropriate sound signals laid down in this Rule.

(c) Nothing in these Rules shall interfere with the operation of any special rules made by the Government of any nation with respect to the use of additional whistle signals between ships of war or vessels sailing under convoy.

Rule 29

Nothing in these Rules shall exonerate any vessel, or the owner, master or crew thereof, from the consequences of any neglect to carry lights or signals, or of any neglect to keep a proper look-out, or of the neglect of any precaution which may be required by the ordinary practice of seamen, or by the special circumstances of the case.

Rule 30

Reservation of Rules for
Harbours and Inland Navigation

Nothing in these Rules shall interfere with the operation of a special rule duly made by local authority relative to the navigation of any harbour, river, lake, or inland water, including a reserved seaplane area.

Rule 31

Distress Signals

When a vessel or seaplane on the water is in distress and requires assistance from other vessels or from the shore, the following shall be the signals to be used or displayed by her, either together or separately, namely:—

(a) A gun or other explosive signal fired at intervals of about a minute.

(b) A continuous sounding with any fog-signal apparatus.

(c) Rockets or shells, throwing red stars fired one at a time at short intervals.

(d) A signal made by radiotelegraphy or by any other signalling method consisting of the group ... — — — ... in the Morse Code.

(e) A signal sent by radiotelephony consisting of the spoken word "Mayday."

(f) The International Code Signal of distress indicated by N.C.

(g) A signal consisting of a square flag having above or below it a ball or anything resembling a ball.

(h) Flames on the vessel (as from a burning tar barrel, oil barrel, &c.).

(i) A rocket parachute flare showing a red light.

The use of any of the above signals, except for the purpose of indicating that a vessel or a seaplane is in distress, and the use of any signals which may be confused with any of the above signals, is prohibited.

NOTE.—*A radio signal has been provided for use by vessels in distress for the purpose of actuating the auto-alarms of other vessels and thus securing attention to distress calls or messages. The signal consists of a series of twelve dashes, sent in 1 minute, the duration of each dash being 4 seconds, and the duration of the interval between two consecutive dashes 1 second.*

Rule 32

All orders to helmsmen shall be given in the following sense: right rudder or starboard to mean "put the vessel's rudder to starboard"; left rudder or port to mean "put the vessel's rudder to port."

REGULATION LIGHTS. *See* **Navigation l's in** LIGHT.

REGULATOR. Chiefly in U.S., a shipyard employee who superintends adjustment of structural members in their correct positions during building of a vessel.

REGULUS. (*L. = a petty king or ruler*) *Cor Leonis*, or *a Leonis*, principal star in the group *Leo;* has a magnitude of 1.34; declination 12¼° N. and S.H.A. 208½°; *see* LEO.

RELATIVE. With respect or reference to something understood as a datum point or line; with relation or proportionate to a standard; comparative.

R. bearing, that of an object referred to ship's fore-and-aft line; thus, as in calibrating a radio direction-finder, one of 150° means the object or signal bears that number of degrees to the right of line of vessels' keel, observer looking forward, and so for any angle up to 360° or zero, the complete sweep of the horizon. Also expressed as a number of points or degrees *on* (or *off*) either *bow* or *quarter;* or with reference to ship's line of beam (right angles to fore-and-aft line); thus, *the light bears 2½ points* (or 28°) *on our port bow; land was last seen 3 points on the starboard quarter; a spanking breeze 2 points abaft the beam.* R. bearings usually are indicated in ordinary ship routine in points from right ahead or from right astern as on either *bow* or *quarter* up to 4 points; those between those limits are referred to the *beam;* thus, while it is proper to express the *r. bearing* as "4 points or *broad* on the port (or starboard) quarter," the phrase *"4 points abaft the beam"* should not be used. *"4½ points on the bow"* gives way to *"3½ points before the beam"; "5 points on the quarter"* to *"3 points abaft the beam,"* etc. **R. movement,** motion of a body with relation to another moving body. Resultant rate and direction at which one moving vessel approaches another; *e.g.,* in the case of a ship steering so as to take up a new station with relation to the *guide* in a fleet formation,—usually in the least possible time. **R. rank,** corresponding official grade or rank as that existing in positions held by officers in different branches of a government service; equivalent rank; *see* RANK. **R. wind,** also termed *apparent wind,* direction and force of wind as observed on a moving vessel. It is the resultant of two forces representing the respective directions and velocities of ship and surface wind; thus a *r. wind* observed as from N.E. at 14 miles per hour, course and speed of vessel being North, 10 knots, corresponds to a surface breeze from East at a velocity of 10 miles per hour.

RELEASING-GEAR. *See* GEAR.

RELIEF. Act of relieving or being released from a post or duty. One who takes his turn or *relieves* another; as a helmsman, lookout man, watchman, etc. A fresh replacement or relay of men in line of duty. Assistance in time of stress or war. **R. valve,** *see* VALVE.

RELIEVE. To replace or release, as by one man substituting another at a post or duty; familiar in the order "*R. the wheel and lookout!*" addressed to the *relief watch* mustered for next relay of duty. To bring reinforcements to, as in time of war. **Relieving-boards,** in cargo stowage, planks or boards laid across a lower tier or successive tiers of cases, drums, etc., for purpose of distributing the sustained weight of next or upper tiers. *Cf.* DUNNAGE. **Relieving tackle,** *see* TACKLE.

REMETALLING. Act of renewing the copper sheathing on bottom planking of a vessel. *Cf.* **C.-bottomed** *in* COPPER.

REMORA. (*L. = a hindrance*) A small fish of a family characterized by a suctorial oval disk along the top of the head. By means of this organ it firmly adheres to floating objects, sharks, sword-fish, etc., and even to ships, apparently for the sole purpose of obtaining free transportation, casting off or freeing itself as and when it pleases.

REND. Archaic term for a split in a plank or opening up of a planking seam, as from exposure to the sun.

RENDER. (Fr. *rendre,* to give up) To ease or lighten up a line through a block, sheave, dead-eye, thimble, etc.; to assist in slacking a rope, chain, etc., through or around an aperture or object; as, to *r.* the fall through a set of blocks; to *r.* turns around the capstan. In older usage, to coil or flake down a line for clear running, as a halyard or a brace. A line is said to *r.* when passing through a block, fairlead, etc., without obstruction; or, when under stress, is forced to pay out.

RENDEZVOUS. (Fr. *rendez vous,* render yourselves) An appointed meeting-place for two or more vessels; assembling place for a fleet. In old British navy days, a station to which the *press gang* brought recruits for the fleet; later, a place for enlistment.

REPEAT. To reiterate or reproduce a signal. **R. sign,** in Morse flashing or sound signalling, *IMI* (. . — — . .), made by receiving party, requests that message, or part of message indicated, be repeated. A *repeating-ship,* in former naval parlance, was one of the ships in a fleet detailed to *r.* all signals hoisted by the flagship; also, *repeater.*

REPEATER. One of the three pennants of *International Code of Signals,* called *first, second,* and *third substitutes,* which denote, respectively, that first, second, or third flag in a hoist is to be repeated. **R. compass,** *see* **Gyro c.** *in* COMPASS.

REPORT. To announce or indicate the passing or presence of a vessel, as to a coastal signal station, or vessel's position at sea, as to her owners by radio-telegraphy. Announcements concerning movements of vessels usually take the form of: "*Reported* off Hillsboro Light"; "*r'd* by Lloyd's as missing"; "*r'd* as having a heavy list to port"; etc. A written official account of facts, conditions observed, etc.; as, a *customs r.;* a *survey r.;* a *weather r.*

REPOSE, Angle of. *See* ANGLE.

REPRISAL. Act of retaliating by force with view of obtaining redress for an injury, as to a nation's shipping or commerce, by seizing property or subjects of the offending country. Such action may or may not establish a *casus belli,* but is not with intention of opening hostilities. *Cf.* **L. of marque** *in* LETTER. In older usage, a ship recaptured from an enemy.

REQUEST NOTE. In Great Britain, a special permit issued by the customs, upon formal application, authorizing the landing of perishable or other specially required commodities or goods before vessel has been entered and officially cleared.

REQUISITION. To commandeer or demand supplies, use of ships and their crews, piers, etc., as by a government in time of war. A written application for supplies, equipment, or other necessaries, as in preparation for a voyage.

RESCUE. The retaking of a prize by the persons captured with it. According to *International Law,* the term differs from *recapture* in that property involved, as a vessel and her cargo, is restored to its owner. It is also generally applied to recovery of a prize with outside help before the crew or other persons in charge of the property are overcome by the enemy. To free, release, or deliver from danger, violence, exposure to evil, etc.; as, "both ships with their cargoes were *rescued* from the menacing savages."

RESERVE. Having the quality of being *reserved,* or withheld, as an extra supply for a future or special use. **Naval r.,** *see* NAVAL. **R. bunker,** a compartment or tank containing an extra or stand-by supply of fuel for ship's boilers or engines. **R. buoyancy,** that volume of a vessel which is above water level and which can be made watertight. As a measure of seaworthiness in the load condition, it may be expressed as a percentage of vessel's total volume; or may be defined as the remaining force of buoyancy equal to vessel's *freeboard* in inches times the *tons per inch immersion* at load draft. **R. speed,** a U.S. navy term for highest speed of which ship's engines are capable.

RESHIP. To transfer, as cargo, to another vessel; to take on board the second time, as landed cargo; or to engage, or be engaged, as a crew or a crew member, for a next voyage.

RESIDUAL ERROR. A small error observed as remaining after adjustment of an instrument, as a compass, radio direction-finder, or a sextant. *Cf.* ERROR.

RESIDUE CARGO. A U.S. customs term for that part of ship's lading destined to a domestic port to which vessel is bound after landing of cargo manifested for port of first entry.

RESIN. *See* ROSIN.

RESISTANCE. A force tending to prevent or retard motion; specifically, that which is overcome in driving a vessel at a given speed through the water, usually divided into *frictional* or *skin r.,* that due to friction between water and ship's wetted surface; *eddy-making r.*, that due to making of eddies and dead water; and *wave r.*, or that attributed to formation of waves set up by the moving hull. **Center of lateral r.,** *see* CENTER. **Curve of r.,** *see* CURVES OF SHIP CALCULATIONS. **Lateral r.,** *see* **L. plane** *in* LATERAL. **Residuary r.,** in model experimental work aimed at separating the components of *total r.*, that quantity less *frictional r.*, or that assumed to be the sum of *eddy-making r.* and *wave-making r., wind r.* not considered. **R. welding,** fusion welding in which *r.* to an electric current supplies the required heat in the contacting parts of united material. **Tow-rope r.,** total *r.* as observed in ship model towing experiments, results of which serve as a basis for speed and power calculations and design of hull in proposed vessels. **Wake r.,** the favorable or abating element in slip of ship's propeller, due to that part of a vessel's wake which follows, or has a tendency to follow, the hull in a line with, and extending a short distance on either side of, vessel's midship fore-and-aft vertical plane. **Wind r.,** that due to wind pressure on the various above-water surfaces of a vessel, in considering the forces tending to retard motion through the water. Also termed *air r.*

RESPONDENTIA BOND. *See* BOTTOMRY.

RETAINED MAGNETISM. Transient magnetism received by induction from earth's magnetic field and temporarily retained in an iron or steel vessel while steering for some days in about one direction. Also, *retentive magnetism. See* GAUSSIN ERROR.

RETARDATION. Amount or extent to which anything is retarded; act of delaying or slowing. **R. of mean solar time,** correction by which an interval of *sidereal time* is reduced to one of *mean solar time.* Having a value of 3 min. 55.91 secs. of mean time corresponding to a sidereal day (24 hours), it is subtracted from the sidereal interval by the appropriate *pro rata* amount. **R. of the tides,** also termed *lagging of the tide; see* LAG.

RETIRING BOARD. *See* BOARD.

RETROGRADE. Moving in a backward direction. Astronomically, appearing to move from east to west; contrary to general planetary motion, whether apparent or real; decreasing in right ascension or celestial longitude; as, *r. motion.* Rotating in a reverse direction. To go, or appear to go, backward; as a planet in decreasing its right ascension, when it is said to be in *retrogradation.*

RETURN. An official written report or statement by an officer to a superior concerning certain required data; as, a *r.* of men unfit for duty; a *r.* of remaining supplies; etc. Designating a turning back or sharp change in direction; as, the *r.* voyage; the *r.* roll; an enemy's *r.* fire. **R.-block,** a snatch-block; *see* BLOCK. **R. list,** document signed by the master of a foreign-bound ship in which are indicated the names of any crew members who have failed to join the vessel upon her departure from berth. It is addressed to the shipping office and usually dispatched with the pilot.

REVENUE. Sum of customs duties, excise, fines, rents, taxes, etc., received by a government during a specified period; source or item of gross income, as *r.* from freight. **R. cutter,** an armed government vessel employed to enforce *r.* laws, prevent smuggling, looting of shipwrecked property, etc. In U.S., the term now is *Coast Guard cutter,* the former *Revenue Cutter Service* and *Life-saving Service* having been merged into one and called *U.S. Coast Guard,* January 28, 1915. **R. ensign,** *see* **U.S. Revenue e.** *in* ENSIGN. **R. ton,** *see* TONNAGE.

REVERSE. Opposite or contrary in position; as, a *r.* bar or frame. To turn or move in an opposite direction; as, to *r.* the engines. To turn end for end, as a tackle, anchor cable, etc. **R. bar,** also called *r. frame; see* **Built-up f.** *in* FRAME. **R. tiller,** a tiller extending abaft the rudder-head, commonly so fitted as a space-economizing measure.

REVERSIBLE. Capable of being reversed or of reversing; as, a *r.* capstan; *r.* current. **R. days,** the *lay days* thus designated in a charter-party, meaning that charterer has the option of using, up to total number of lay days, part of stipulated loading-time as additional discharging-time, or vice versa. Thus, if 3 days are agreed upon as loading-time and 3 days as discharging-time, the term implies that, in event of 4 days occupied for loading, only 2 days would remain for discharging. Also, in formal chartering usage, often *time reversible.* **R. screw,** *see* **Controllable pitch p.** *in* PROPELLER. **R. winch,** any hoisting-engine or winch which lowers or turns in *reverse* by the motivating power, as distinguished from one in which lowering is controlled entirely by braking.

REVERSING. Changing to an opposite or contrary motion or position. **R. current,** a tidal alternate ebb and flow in approximately opposite directions. **R. gear,** any arrangement of gears, slide-valve control, etc., for changing the turning direction of an engine. **R. thermometer,** *see* **Upsetting t.** *in* THERMOMETER.

REVETMENT. (Fr. *revêtir,* to line or reclothe) A facing of concrete, masonry, piling, stones, etc., to prevent erosion of a river-bank, edge of a channel, levee, etc.; a retaining-wall.

REVIEW. A formal inspection of naval forces by a superior officer, high government official, or a sovereign, for the purpose of noting state of discipline, condition of ships, and skill in maneuvering.

REVOLUTION. (L. *revolvere,* to revolve; from *re,* again; *volvere,* to turn or roll) A complete circuit made by one object about a central point, as that of a planet in its orbit. A body is said to make a *r.* when turning through 360° about an axis *outside of itself,* in which, strictly, a *r.* differs from a *rotation,* or a complete turn, as of a wheel, about an axis *within the body.* This apparent misuse of the word in referring to *revolutions of a propeller* is accepted practice on board ship. **R. counter,** an instrument showing a continuous record of *r's* made by an engine. In a marine plant, it is geared to a working part of the main engine or to the propeller-shaft and is used for determining engine output, while the *r. rate* taken therefrom commonly is employed also in determining vessel's speed. Also termed *r. recorder.* **R. indicator,** instrument connected electrically with a *r. counter* for showing on ship's navigating bridge the direction in which and number of *r's* per minute (usually abbrev. *r.p.m.*) the main engine or engines are turning. The term often is applied to a *r. counter* itself.

REVOLVER. In the procedure of finding a vessel's position by two horizontal angles measured between a central charted object and two others at either side of such object, or by what is called the *three-point problem,* the indeterminate condition, in which vessel is found to occupy a place afloat on any part of the circle passing through all three charted objects, is called a *revolver* Source of the term probably lies in the fact that the *station-pointer* may be "revolved" through the seaward arc of circle referred to, while its arms remain in coincidence with the selected objects. (A *r.* occurs only when middle object lies on the landward side of a line joining the other two) *See* **S.-pointer** *in* STATION.

REVOLVING. Turning round; making or constructed to make a revolution or rotation. **R. light;** *see* **Flashing l.** *in* LIGHT. **R. storm,** a tornado, typhoon, cyclone, or hurricane; *see* CYCLONE.

RHODING. Either of the bearings in which the journal of a pump-brake works.

RHUMB. (Gr. *rombos,* a magic wheel; a whirling motion) An old-fashioned term for one of the named 32 *points* (each of $11\frac{1}{4}°$) of the compass; as in the early reference, "*Afore an godlich winde we seyled an rhumb to north of east.*" A loxodrome, or loxodromic curve; *see* LOXODROME. **R. sailing,** act of sailing on a *loxodrome* or *rhumb line* which is represented on a Mercator's chart by a straight line; opposed to *great circle sailing.*

RIB. One of the transverse frames in a vessel or boat; the *timbers* or framing to which the outside planking or plating is secured.

RIBBAND. Any long, narrow strip of timber or plate; especially, in shipbuilding, such strip secured fore-and-aft along the frames to keep latter in position in early stage of construction. Also *ribbon.* A painted stripe or a small molding along the side of a vessel. To secure or provide with a *r.* or *r's,* as the frames erected in building a ship, stage-work posts, etc. **Launching r.,** hardwood strip secured as a flange along the outside edge of the standing ways to prevent lateral movement of the sliding ways during launching of a vessel. The strip is further secured by braces or *shores* the heels of which are strongly butted against piles or a specially raised step along sides of launching-slip; these are called *r.-shores.* **R. lines,** in the body and sheer plans, those showing intersections of *r's* with the frames; sometimes distinguished as *frame-r.* and *floor-r.* lines (the latter shown along ends of *floors*). **R. planking,** *see* PLANKING.

RIBBED. Formed, strengthened, or provided with ribs or ridges; as, a *r. plate; r. sand* on a shore.

RIBBON. (Etymologically same as *riband, ribband, rib-band*) A thin strip of wood or metal; a *rib-band.* A painted stripe, as of white on a dark-colored ground, along the sheer line or water line of a vessel's hull; also, *ribband.* A narrow strip or shred of cloth, bunting, etc.; as, a narrow *pennant;* sails torn to *r's.* **Blue r.,** *see* BLUE. **Irish r.,** *see* **Irish p.** *in* PENNANT. **R. fish,** any of a number of different fishes, so named from their compressed, elongated shape; as, the *oarfish, cutlass-fish, dealfish,* etc. **R. seal,** a North Pacific seal thus named from its stripes and bands of yellowish white.

RIDDLE MEASUREMENT. Another name for *New Measurement,* as referred to in remarks on MEASUREMENT.

RIDE. To lie fast to an anchor or to a single mooring. To float or move buoyantly on the surface, as a boat. To overlap or press upon, as *riding turns,* or those of a rope outside of other turns in a lashing, around a pair of bitts, etc. To sit upon or straddle a boom, yard, etc., as a sailor. To **r. aportlast,** old term meaning to *r.* at anchor with lower yards sent down and secured athwartships on ship's rails, as in heavy weather; also, *r. aportoise* (or *a-portoise;* pron. *a-portiz*). To **r. down a stay or backstay,** to slide down such stay or come down along it in a *bos'n's chair,* as in tarring, painting, serving, etc. To **r. down a halyard,** to· come down on it from aloft with one's weight, as in setting sail; to sway or bear down on such rope, as in setting it taut. To **r. down a sail,** as in bending a new sail, to haul taut the earings and stretch the head-rope by bearing down with one's weight on middle of the rope before finally setting up on the earings and passing the robands. To **r. easy,** to lie at anchor without straining on the cable or cables; opposed to *riding hard.* To **r. hard,** to strain heavily at the cables, as a vessel at anchor during bad weather. (A vessel is said to be *tide-rode* when she is at anchor and swinging to the tide current, regardless of wind direction; when swinging to, or heading into, the wind, she is *wind-rode*) To **r. out,** to successfully weather a gale while *at anchor* or *hove to;* as, *she rode out the hurricane.* To **r. the Spanish mare,** to punish an offender, as in former Dutch and English ships, by forcing him to get astride of and hold his own on a swinging boom in a seaway.

RIDER. A supplementary strengthening piece of timber or plate; as a *r. frame.* A doubling timber extending from keelson to a deck beam inside the ceiling and through-bolted to the main frame over which it is fitted. A tier of casks, barrels, etc., stowed over a ground or bottom tier. An extra clause or an amendment affixed to a supposedly complete document, as the articles of agreement, a charter-party, etc. **R. frame,** a frame welded or riveted to another for stiffening purposes. **R. keelson,** *see* **K.-capping** *in* KEELSON. **R. plate,** the capping, or continuous plate along the upper or inside edge of a keelson or a side-stringer. In composite-built vessels, or those having outside planking and iron or steel structural members, one of a series of diagonal plates secured to the outer surface of frames for longitudinal strength purposes. **Knee-r.,** *see* KNEE. **Keel-r.,** *see* KEEL.

RIDGE. A sharply defined elevation of the sea-bottom, or reef. Upper part of the narrowing portion of a whale's body, or that immediately forward of its tail. **R.-rope,** the backbone of an awning; also, a horizontally stretched rope to which a side of an awning is secured. A life-line along the sides of a bowsprit.

RIDING. Lying or pressing upon; as, *r.* turns of a lashing, cable, etc. Employed to ride with or upon; used in *riding.* Lying fast or swinging to an anchor or anchors only; lying-to or hove-to, usually with *out;* as, *the trawlers are r. out the gale.* **R. athwart,** said of a vessel at anchor when she is lying broadside to wind, while current is running against the latter, but not strong enough to tail vessel with it; also termed *r. between wind and tide.* **R. bitts,** used for securing the anchor-cable in older days before windlasses displaced the capstan and chain took the place of the hemp cable; sometimes applied to the only means of making fast the anchor-chain or rope in smaller craft. Also, *anchor bitts.* **R. boom,** *see* **Boat-b.** *and* **Guess-warp b.** *in* BOOM. **R.-buckler,** *see* BUCKLER. **R. chain,** length of chain cable, in a lay-out of permanent moorings, to which ship is connected. When a ship is moored, that chain to which she is *riding;* opposed to the *lee chain* (or *cable*). **R.-chocks,** heavy metal blocks fitted on deck between a windlass and hawse-pipes for taking stress of either cable from windlass, as when *riding* at anchor. Such chock is so shaped that alternate links of chain are guided in a groove in the vertical position as cable is hove in. This leaves the flat-lying link next inboard in position for being prevented from running out by forward side of chock, which, for allowing free passage of cable

in paying out, is provided with a lifting part worked by a lever at side of the chock. It also is provided with a pawl or other holding-down device as a means for preventing cable from jumping when seated in the chock. Also called *cable-stopper.* **R. hawse-fallen** or **hawse full,** *see* HAWSE. **R.-light,** the light or one of the lights required to be shown by a vessel at anchor; *see* REGULATIONS FOR PREVENTING COLLISIONS: *Rule 11.* **R.-sail,** a trysail or triangular sail set on the after mast and sheeted aft; chiefly used in fishing vessels to steady ship head to wind. **R. scope,** *see* SCOPE. **R. seizing,** a *round seizing; see* SEIZING. **R. stopper;** same as *R. chock, q.v.*

RIFT. A rocky or shallow area in a stream; a fording-place. A split or fissure, as in dry wood. The rippling wash on a beach from a breaking wave. To burst open; to cleave; to split; as logs or planks. **R.-sawed planking,** *see* **Q.-sawed** *in* QUARTER.

RIG. (Nor. *rigga,* to bandage; to put on sails; *rigg,* rigging) Distinctive arrangement of masts, rigging, and sails that indicates a type of vessel, regardless of size or form of hull; *the Mary is of barque r.,*—or, *is fitted with the barque r.; we have adopted the ketch r.* In describing a vessel, her *r.* is denoted in the combining word *rigged,* rather than *rig;* thus, a boat having a *Marconi r.* is *Marconi-rigged;* a *barque-rigged* vessel. Used, however, in a broad sense, or embracing a number of types in the two principal *rigs,* it is customary to refer to *fore-and-aft r.* and *square r.* thus: *Braces are used only in square r.; his experience is limited to fore-and-aft r.* Any hoisting-gear, derrick with its accessories, tackle, fishing-gear, etc. To fit a vessel's masts, yards, booms, etc., with rigging; to fit a boat with masts, sails, and necessary sailing-gear. With *out* or *in,* to place in position for use or re-stow; as, to *r. out,* or *r. in,* a jib-boom, a boat-boom, a sounding-boom, etc. To ship and make ready a pump brake, capstan bars, a messenger, etc.; as, to *r. the pumps;* to *r. the capstan;* to *r. a chain messenger.* To fit and set up or place a part or unit of rigging specified; as, to *r.* the topmast backstays; to *r.* the royal braces; to *r.* a hoisting-purchase. **Bermuda r.,** as used in small craft and yachts, a fore-and-aft *r.* characterized by lofty jib-headed sails throughout, with comparatively short length of foot; also, *Marconi r.* (*For other rigs, see:* DANDY; **F.-and-aft** *in* FORE; GUNTER; LUG; SPRIT; SQUARE)

RIGEL. Brightest star of the *Orion* group; has a magnitude of 0.34; declination $8\frac{1}{4}°$ S.; right ascension 5 hrs. 12 min. *See* ORION.

RIGGER. One whose occupation is to prepare, fit, and install the various pieces of rigging in a vessel; particularly, the fitting and setting up of stays, shrouds, backstays, and other *standing rigging* units; a *ship-rigger.* In a shipyard, an employee who oversees the hoisting into place of heavy structural parts or units, such as stern frame, stem-post, rudder, masts and booms, large ventilator cowls, machinery, boilers, etc. The term in Great Britain is applied to one of a number of men engaged in shifting vessels about a harbor at such times as a crew is not attached to the vessel thus handled. **Loft r.,** *see* LOFT. **R.'s horn,** also *slush-horn; see* HORN. **R.'s screw,** a vise-like clamping device for forcibly drawing together the end and standing parts of a wire or heavy fiber rope around a thimble, preparatory to putting in an eye-splice or seizing the parts. It is made in two forms—one for fiber rope, the other for wire. Also, *rigging-screw.*

RIGGING. Generally, the whole equipment of masts, spars, sails, and cordage in any way connected therewith. Properly, all cordage fitted to masts, yards, booms, etc., and to sails of a vessel; distinguished as *running r.,* or all ropes and chains that are used in making or taking in sail, hoisting or topping booms and yards, masthead tackles, etc., and worked or hauled upon in any way; and *standing r.,* the ropes, chains, turnbuckles, dead-eyes with their lanyards, generally covered in the *shrouds, stays,* and *backstays,* that constitute the system of staying and supporting the masts, bowsprit, and jib-boom, and also providing means for vessel's crew to climb and work with reasonable safety aloft. More particularly, as combined in such designations as *fore r., top-gallant r., main-topmast r.,* the term denotes the *shrouds* (standing r.) of, respectively, *fore lowermast, top-gallant mast,* and *main topmast;* but, often *all standing r.* on a particular mast is referred to as *fore r., main r., mizzen r.,* etc. **Broom in the r.,** *see* BROOM. **Eyes of the r.,** *see* EYE. **Head r.,** standing r. supporting bowsprit and jib-boom, including all stays leading from those spars to the foremast. **Lower r.,** shrouds supporting a lowermast. **Masthead r.,** that point on a masthead where the eyes of backstays, shrouds, and stays encircle or are shackled to an eye-band on the mast. To **rattle down the r.,** *see* RATLINE. **To ride down the r.,** *see* To r. down a stay *in* RIDE. **R. batten,** a rounded piece of wood seized along a stay or shroud for protection against chafing by certain gear in the vicinity; a *scotchman.* Any batten secured to the *r.;* especially, those sometimes taking the places of ratlines in lower *r.; cf.* RATLINE. **R. leather,** sewn around a stay or shroud for same purpose as that of *batten* above referred to; *chafing-leather; cf.* LEATHER. **R. loft,** *see* LOFT. **R. luff,** a special luff tackle used for setting up standing *r.;* also, a *two-fold purchase* for same purpose. The moving block is made fast to the *lanyard* and standing block to shroud or stay. **R. plan,** *see* Sail p. *in* PLAN. **R. screw,** a *turnbuckle* fixed at lower or inboard end of a shroud, backstay, stay, etc., for setting up such pieces of *standing r.* instead of using the *dead-eye and lanyard* system. Screws are fitted only to *r.* of *wire rope* and its recent substitute, *steel rods. Cf.* TURNBUCKLE. Also, same as *rigger's*

screw; see RIGGER. **R. stopper,** in the hemp *r.* days, a device for reinforcing a damaged shroud or stay resulting from gunfire in action. **Rod r.,** recently adopted substitute for wire rope as material for shrouds and stays, particularly in large sailing-yachts. In the latter, rods or bars, which are approximately of same size as wire rope ordinarily used, sometimes are made of stainless steel.

RIGHT. Straight; direct; not oblique; as, *r. ahead; r. ascension.* Toward the *r.* hand; as, *r. helm; r. bank of a river* (looking downstream or toward river's mouth). Proper; suitable; correct; as, *r. size of rope; r. whale* (so named because *r.* kind to hunt). A power, privilege, authority, or claim vested in a party or nation by law; as, *r. of search; r. of way.* To restore to a normal position; as, to *r. a vessel having a list.* To recover the natural position; as, *this boat, when capsized, will r. herself.* **Circle of r. ascension,** *see* CIRCLE. **R. ascension; r. ascension of the mean sun; r. ascension of the meridian;** *see* ASCENSION. **R. astern,** in a direction in line with the keel and astern of the vessel; as, *the yacht is r. astern of us.* **R.-handed screw,** *see* PROPELLER. **R.-hand lay,** cordage is said to have a *r.-hand lay,* or is laid *r.-handed,* when the strands advance obliquely *from left to right. Cf.* LAY *and* LAID. **R. handsomely!,** order to a helmsman to give ship an easy even swing toward the right, in sense of having turning effect of rudder under easy control. **R. of angary,** *see* ANGARIA. **R. of approach.** that granted by *International Law* to a war-vessel to draw near any merchant vessel for the purpose of verifying her flag and character. The vessel approached is not required to stop or heave to and her voyage may not be interfered with. **R. of convoy,** as agreed by treaty between most maritime nations, the exemption from *visit and search* of neutral vessels by a belligerent, when such vessels are protected by a warship of their own flag, as in convoy, and commanding officer of the latter has declared such vessel or vessels under his protection are carrying no contraband of war. **R. of mooring,** that by which vessels are permitted to anchor or moor in certain areas. Incidental to the *r. of navigation,* it is the privilege of only those vessels used in navigation and thus generally debars hulks, harbor lighters, rafts, and others from mooring in the areas specified by the port or local authority. **R. of navigation;** every vessel regardless of her nationality enjoys the common right or privilege of navigating anywhere on the high seas and, excepting in time of war, in the territorial waters of any nation. The right, however, allows a foreign vessel mooring or landing privileges only at such places or ports as are appropriate for such purpose, except in the event of peril or extreme necessity. **R. of pursuit,** internationally recognized *r.* of a state to pursue and bring back to port any vessel that is required to answer for a violation of the law while in territorial waters of such state.

The offending vessel may be thus placed under arrest anywhere on the high seas, as well as within the state's home waters, although exercise of the *r. of seizure* in connection with a serious law violation, generally is justified only within limits of state's jurisdiction. **R. rudder!,** order to a helmsman to put vessel's rudder to the *r.,* or starboard, side. *Cf.* **Rule 32,** REGULATIONS FOR PREVENTING COLLISIONS. **R. of visit and search,** internationally recognized *r.* of a nation's armed vessels, in time of war, to stop, visit, and examine the papers of a neutral merchant vessel in order to determine her true national status, character and destination of her cargo, and, generally, whether or not she is in any way assisting an enemy. Such visit and possible capture resulting may be conducted in the belligerent's home waters or upon the high seas. The *r.* also may be exercised in time of peace by war-vessels of every nation in the case of a vessel suspected of piratical activities. **R. of way,** privilege of a vessel to continue on her course or track without obligation to keep clear of another, as, *e.g.,* in certain rivers where a vessel proceeding downstream or with the current has *r.-of-way* over another crossing the stream in any direction. Where, however, a situation arises in which either of two vessels is required to keep out of the way of the other, and so becomes a "burdened" vessel, the other is then simply a "privileged" vessel in the ordinary course of events, and, properly, never may be said to have *r.-of-way.* As, in thick weather, when approaching vessels are hidden to each other's view, no question of *r.-of-way,* burden, or privilege exists, so, upon such vessels being sighted by each other, should action by the "burdened" craft prove insufficient to prevent collision, "privileged" one is obligated to "take such action as will best aid to avert collision." All questions of *r.-of-way* therefore disappear in the conditions noted and, perhaps, is sufficient basis for the accepted aphorism, *"No r.-of-way exists at sea."* Again, in obeying a code of collision prevention rules, it must be borne in mind that some unusual or unforeseen circumstances may arise in which a "burdened" vessel may find it impossible to take action as prescribed in such rules and thus is forced to transfer the *burden* of avoiding collision, partly or wholly, to the "privileged" ship by use of the appropriate signal provided for in the rules. *Cf.* **Rules 21** and **27,** REGULATIONS FOR PREVENTING COLLISIONS. **R.-of-way signal,** a flag, shape, or system of lights displayed from a station at entrance to a canal, harbor, or narrow channel, indicating that a certain vessel (or vessels) is free to proceed unhindered through such channel, etc. **R. the helm!,** obsolete command to put ship's rudder amidships, or in line with the keel; now, *Midship the helm!* or *Helm midships! See* HELM. **R. whale,** *see* WHALE. **R.-whale porpoise,** so called from having no dorsal fin, a porpoise of genus *Tursio; cf.* DOL-

PHIN *and* PORPOISE. **R.-whaling,** the hunting of *r.* *whales.*

RIGHTING. Act of returning or being restored to a natural or normal position; specifically, the act of returning, or return, by whatever means, of a heeled or listing vessel to her normal upright position. *See* COUPLE, RIGHTING; **Righting l.** *in* LEVER; **Righting m.** *in* MOMENT.

RIGIL KENTAURUS. (Ar. *al rijil al Kentaurus,* the Centaur's foot) *α Centauri,* or brightest star in the *Centaurus* group. Easily recognized as the brighter of a conspicuous couple 4½° apart called the *pointers,* because in line with about the middle of near-by *Crux,* the *Southern Cross,* to the westward. It is a binary star, or one of a pair revolving about a common center of gravity and appearing as a single star to the unaided eye. Astronomers now list this luminary's place as that of α² *Centauri,* which is somewhat brighter than his close-sticking brother α¹. *See* CENTAURUS.

RIGOL. Obsolete term for an *eye-brow* or *wriggle; see* **E.-brow** *in* EYE.

RIME. A rung or step of a ladder. To enlarge a grommet, cringle-strop, eyelet, etc., as by stretching with an inserted fid. Chiefly in British use, a variant of *ream; see* REAM. A *riming-stool,* such as is used by sailmakers for stretching cringle-strops, grommets, etc., is a circular hardwood block supported by legs and containing several holes of various sizes. The work is laid over an appropriate hole while fid is inserted and usually forced into such grommet, etc., by a mallet.

RIND. Older whaling term for skin of a whale; *whale-rind.*

RINE. A good quality of Russian hemp; usually called *Riga rine.*

RING. Piece of metal, wood, or other material, usually circular in shape and open, like a band or hoop; as, a *piston-r.;* a *gimbal r.* A grommet. A sail-hoop or *r.,* one of a number of such that confine a fore-and-aft sail to a mast. **Bishop's r.,** named for the person who explained the phenomenon, a dusky red *r.* of 20° radius around the sun caused by particles of volcanic dust in the atmosphere which was attributed to the great eruption of Krakatao in 1883. **Check r.,** also called *guard r.* and *safety r.,* any *r.* serving to prevent something from working out of place; as, a *stern tube check r.,* or flat metal *r.* tap-bolted to outer end of a stern tube as a guard against the *lignum vitæ* bearing strips from slipping out. **Junk r.,** any packing round a piston, or a *r.* for keeping same in place. **Mariner's r.,** also once called a *sea r.,* a later form of the *astrolabe,* which consisted of a brass *r.* or hoop graduated on half its inner surface. It was held suspended in a vertical plane parallel to direction of the sun while a ray from the latter, passing through a small hole on one side of the *r.* indicated on the inner and opposite, or graduated side, the sun's altitude. *Cf.* ASTROLABE. **R. net,** a fishing-net of Italian origin in many respects similar to a *purse seine,* excepting its inner *landing-bag* in which fish are entrapped (mackerel, menhaden, herring, sardines, etc.); also called *semi-purse seine* and *lampara.* **R.-plate,** a lug pad, pad-eye, or small plate having a forged eye through which a ring is fitted; often found on steel decks, bulwarks, and bulkheads for securing lashings, boom guys, etc. **R.-rope,** in older ships, a line used to haul the *anchor-r.* close up to the cathead after heaving anchor up to its approximate stowed position; also, a rope wound about an *anchor-r.* as a chafing protection for the hemp cable; sometimes, a lashing for securing end of cable in a *clinch,* when made fast to anchor; a *cable-bend.* **R'staff,** corrupted form of *wringstaff.* **R.-stopper,** *see* **C'head** and **C'head-stopper** *in* CAT. **R'tail,** also *ring-sail; see* SAIL. **R'tail boom,** *see* BOOM. **Shroud-r.,** a stern-tube check *r.; cf.* Check *r.* To **r. up the anchor,** to haul *anchor-r.* close up to cathead, as in securing for sea. (Also see *ring* as combining term in ANCHOR; BULL; CLINCH; KEY; LAP; LASHING; PACK; **R.-bolt** *in* BOLT; **R.-sail** *in* SAIL)

RINGING. Of ship's bell, a rapid to and fro motion made with its tongue as a fog-signal for a vessel at anchor or a mustering signal for fire-drill, etc.; opposed to *striking* the bell, or with its tongue giving single sharp blows, as in a lookout's signal or that indicating number of shots of anchor-cable hove in or payed out; or, also, in announcing time in which two distinct blows, or *strokes,* with a slight pause between each succeeding two (or one) are given, as in 7 *bells:* .. .. ..

RIP. Surface of water ruffled or made rough by opposing currents; rippling or roughening of sea surface over and in vicinity of a shoal, caused by more or less interference of the latter with tidal flow; often referred to as *tide-rips.* A small rapid in a stream. **R.-fishing,** *see* FISHING.

RIPARIAN. (L. *ripa,* a bank) Relating or pertaining to the bank of a river, lake, or sheltered tidewater; living on or frequenting the banks of streams, lakes, or other inland waters; as, *birds of r. habits.* **R. rights,** privileges of ownership of land bordering on a watercourse, according to law.

RIPE. Said of fish when nearing spawning-time or actually spawning when taken; as, *r. herring.*

RIPPER. West of England and Newfoundland dialectal term for a *fog-horn.* A fishing-jig.

RIPPING-IRON. Calker's rave-hook, reefing-iron, or clearing-iron; *see* **Calking-irons** *in* IRON; *also* **Rave-h.** *in* HOOK.

RIPPLE. Ruffled area of sea surface caused by light airs and breezes during generally calm weather; more or less roughened surface of a stream or a tidal current passing over a shallow rocky area or a shoal, or less pronounced current effect than seen in a *rip;* a rippling; a wavelet. Said of the sound of water running over a rough surface, small waves on a beach, against a boat's sides, etc.; as in, *the wavelets r. across her bows and the cable idly droops.*

RIPRAP. Stones, rocks, or concrete blocks thrown together or dumped to form a breakwater, protection of a river-bank against erosion by current or ice, etc.; such protecting work itself. To strengthen, support, or protect with a *r.*

RISE. To move upward or increase in elevation; as, to *r. from the forecastle; tide rises for six hours.* To come to the surface, as a submarine. An elevation of considerable area in the sea-bottom; opposed to a *deep.* **R. and fall,** tidal range on a given date at a certain locality, or sum of vertical movement of tide above and that below mean sea level. **R. and shine!,** familiar call to sailors to rise from sleep. **R. of bottom; r. of floor,** *see* DEADRISE. **R. of tide,** vertical distance of surface, at time of high water, above *tidal datum level.* **R. tacks and sheets!,** *see* RAISE.

RISER. One of the upright pieces in a stairway, extending from step to step. On board ship, an *open r.* stairway or *companionway* is one having no *r's* and usually is then termed a *ladder;* as, a companion-ladder, deck ladder, etc. In a vessel's bottom planking, one of the two or more strakes of heavy planking next to the *garboard strake.* In boat-building, stringer supporting ends of thwarts; more usually, *rising.* Part of a system of piping that extends vertically, as from one deck to another; *r.-pipe.*

RISING. Increasing in elevation; ascending; increasing in force; as, a *r. sea bottom;* a *r. gale.* Appearing above the horizon; *the r. land was still far off.* A stringer or stout batten secured to the frames, in the line of sheer of a boat, as a support for ends of the thwarts and, also, in larger craft, as an additional stiffener for upper sides of the boat. Any fore-and-aft timber serving as a support for beams of a deck; also, *r.-piece.* **R. floor,** same as *deep floor; see* FLOOR. **R. line,** in shipbuilding plans, a line indicating the locus of each *floor head* (or *end*); also, *line of floors.* **R. timbers,** floor timbers in the extreme forward and after ends of a wooden vessel; same as *r. floors.* **R. tide,** increasing depth of water or upward vertical movement of the surface during interval between low and high water; a daily increase of height of tide, as on the approach of full or new moon. **R. wood,** in wood-built ships, the filling-in timber above the keel at extreme ends of hull, or narrowing parts near and at junction of stem and stern posts with keel. **R. wood of keel,**

that portion of keel above the *rabbet,* or line of lower edge of garboard strake.

RISKS, MARINE. *See* **M. risk** *in* MARINE; *also,* **M.I. Policy** *in* INSURANCE, MARINE. Any special *r's* provided for are indicated in a rider clause attached to the standard insurance policy.

RIVER. A natural stream, larger than a brook, creek, or rivulet, flowing into a lake, sea, or other stream. When flowing into another *r.,* such stream is called an *affluent, branch,* or *tributary;* as, *the Missouri is a tributary of the Mississippi River. R's* of the world having greatest volume of flow in the order noted are: *Amazon* of Brazil, *Congo* of W. Africa, *La Plata* of Uruguay and Argentine,— fed by *Parana* and *Uruguay Rivers,* and *Mississippi* of the U.S.; a few of greatest length in statute miles are: *Nile,* 3930; *Amazon,* 4050; *Yangtze Kiang,* 3500; *Congo,* 2700; *Amur,* 2700; *Hwang Ho (Yellow R.),* 2700; *Mekong,* 2600; *Lena,* 2650; *Ob,* 2500; *Parana,* 2450; *Volga,* 2300. **Bed of a r.,** bottom of channel in which a *r.* flows. **R. gage,** a fixed vertical batten, timber, or the like, on a river-bank or pier for indicating the height of water surface above local low water datum level. It is appropriately marked, as with feet and inches, feet and quarter-feet, etc. **R. pilot,** one who pilots vessels on a *r.* or certain stretch of a *r.* **R. port,** a sea-port located on one or both sides of a *r.* **R. wall,** a breast-work, rip-rap, or other form of sustaining or retaining wall on a *r.-bank.* **Tidal r.,** a river in which tide ebbs and flows for a considerable distance inland from its mouth.

RIVET. One of the wrought iron or mild steel pins greatly used in shipbuilding for joining the various structural parts, securing deck, shell, and bulkhead plating to beams, frames, etc. *R's* usually are made with one finished end, called the *head,* the other, or the *point,* being burred or hammered into the shape desired, while in the heated state, over the work thus secured together. Parts connected by this process are said to be *riveted* together. *R's* are named for their shape, as, pan-head, snap, boiler-point, flush-point, countersunk, etc.; or from their various uses, as, *shell-plating r., keel-plate r., deck r.,* etc. In ordinary ship-riveting, *r.-holes* are punched from the faying surface which results in the hole being slightly enlarged at other side of the metal. For this reason, *r's* are made of increased diameter toward their heads to effectively fill the hole. *Diameter* of *r's* varies with thickness of material riveted; thus, in shell-plating, a ¾-inch *r.* usually is employed with ½-inch plates. *Spacing* of the *r's* also varies with kind of work in which used and generally is expressed as a number of times the diameter of *r.;* thus, in water-tight work a spacing of 3½ diameters may be required, while as much as 7 diameters might be called for in securing plates to frames or beams. The spacing, meas-ured from center to center of neighboring *r's,* is also termed the *pitch* of the *r's* in a series, as in a plating-seam, landing of a plate on a beam, etc. Small *r's,* such as used in joining thin metal, are "driven cold," *i.e.,* without being heated. **Bat r.,** one that has a cone-shaped head. **Boat r.,** *see* BOAT. **Boiler-point r.,** used in boiler-plating, said to be best holding *r.* because point is subjected to extra hammering in order to shape it like a broad cone. **Flush-head r.,** has its head countersunk and flush with surface of metal; *bullhead r.* **Lap-r.,** to connect lapping edges of plates by riveting. **Panhead r.,** named for its profile form, or that like an inverted *pan,* in shape like a frustum of a cone; most commonly used in shipbuilding. **Raised-head r.,** one that has a slightly raised head, but less so than a *snap-head r.* **R.-buster,** a pneumatic tool for cutting off heads of *r's,* as required in repair work or replacement of improperly driven work. **R.-holder,** man in a riveter's squad who holds a heavy hammer or *dolly* against head of *r.* while latter is being clinched at its point during riveting process. **R. shank,** body of a *r.* between its *head* and *point.* **R. snap,** a set tool used for shaping *r.* points in *snap,* or nearly hemispherical, form. **R. tool,** used for calking round heads and points of *r's* in the finished work; also, *r. set.* **R. weld,** *see* P. weld *in* PLUG. **Snap-head r.,** also *snap r.,* one having a nearly hemi-spherical head, chiefly for neat appearance; some-times, *cuphead, buttonhead,* and *roundhead r.* **Stern-post r.,** one of the *tap r's* fastening ends of shell-plating strakes to stern-post; *see* **Tap r.** **Straight-shank r.,** one of uniform diameter from head to point, used in *drilled r.-holes* only; also, *straight-neck r.* **Tack r.,** *see* **Q. rivet** *in* QUILTING. **Tap r.,** used in places where a through *r.* can not be fitted, as in securing hooded ends of shell-plating to a stem- or a stern-post. Its shank is threaded and screwed into a *tapped hole* in such structural member. Usually of *flush-head* pattern, a square central head is provided for using a spanner in screwing *r.* in place. The central head is cut off in completion of the work. Also, *stud r.* **Tapered-neck r.,** usual type of *r.* employed in work of over ½-inch thick-ness of plate, etc. Opposed to *straight-neck* (or *straight-shank)* type, its shank is slightly swelled or tapered immediately below the head and is used always with *punched holes.* Also called *swell-neck r.;* sometimes, *cone-neck r.*

RIVETER. One employed in riveting; a *rivet-machine,* especially one that closes up and shapes the points of rivets by pressure only; *cf.* **H. riveter** *in* HYDRAULIC. **R.'s squad,** detail of men employed in ship construction at riveting. In hand work, usually consists of 1 heater, 1 passer, 1 holder-up (rivet-holder), and 2 hammer-men (clinchers); the two first-named may be boys and sometimes one may perform both the *heating* and *passing* jobs, *i.e.,* heating of rivets by portable forge and delivering each as required to the actual *r's.* Where an automatic *riveting-hammer* is used, one man only clinches the rivet.

RIVETING.   Act or process of fastening metal together by means of *rivets.* A set or series of *rivets* connecting two or more parts of metal; as, *chain r.; zig-zag r.* Used in joining by rivets; as, a *r.-machine.* **Bull-r.,** act of pressing rivets into place with a hydraulic machine, or *bear.* **Butt-r.,** that of securing a covering-plate, or *butt-strap,* to the two butting ends of plates. **Chain r.,** rows of rivets lying parallel to each other with rivets in line abreast; used in butt-straps and plating seams where water-tight or oil-tight work is required. **Cold r.,** that done without heating rivets, as chiefly with use of small sizes of material. **Cross r.,** also called *zig-zag* and *staggered r.;* see **Zig-zag r.** **Double r.,** two rows of rivets; in butt-strap work, two on each side of butt, or *four* rows in all. **Lap-r.,** connecting of lapped joints by *r.* **Hydraulic r.,** that done by a *hydraulic riveter; see* HYDRAULIC. **Machine r.,** as done by steady pressure on both head and point of rivet, *r.* performed by hydraulic or pneumatic *r.-machine;* claimed by most modern shipbuilders to be more efficient and economical than *hand r.* **Oiltight r.,** calls for flawless coincidence of rivet-holes and *pitch* of rivets between 3 and 3½ diameters. **Pin r.,** that in which a headless heated piece of rivet material is clinched with applied steady pressure simultaneously at both ends by a *r.-machine.* Work performed by this method is claimed to be of highly efficient order. **Pneumatic r.,** that in which point of rivet is clinched by pneumatic hammer. Such means commonly is used with rivets up to 1¼-inch diameter. **R.-machine,** device for *r.* by steady pressure, as that using hydraulic power; a *bull-riveter, r.-ram,* or *bear.* Portable hydraulic machines are capable of applying a pressure of about 150 tons and, chiefly for that reason, rivets of large diameter generally are set with greater efficiency than is possible with the hammering method. **R. set,** *see* **R. tool** *in* RIVET. **Single r.,** that in which *one row* of rivets connects the parts; *two rows,* or one at each plate end, in a butt-strap. **Snap-r.,** work in which snap-headed points are formed on rivets, as by a die or swaging-tool, or, in *pin r.,* on both ends of rivets. **Staggered r.,** same as *zig-zag r., q.v.* **Triple r.,** three rows of *chain r.; six rows* at plate ends in a butt-strap. **Watertight r.,** that in joints which must be made watertight; pitch of rivets usually is 4 to 4½ diameters in such work, in order to secure efficient calking in the seams, etc. **Zig-zag r.,** arrangement of rows of rivets so that the latter are one-half the pitch ahead of those in next row; also, *cross r.; staggered r.*

R.M.S.   In British use, abbrev. *Royal Mail Steamer* (or *Ship*).

R.N.   Br. abbrev. *Royal Navy.*

R.N.R.   Br. abbrev. *Royal Naval Reserve.*

ROACH.   More or less cut-away part or curving upward of foot of a square sail, which provides necessary clearance between sail and a stay or the yard next below. Extent of such arching, as measured vertically at mid-point of a horizontal line from clew to clew of sail; as, *the royal has a 2-foot r.* The term sometimes is incorrectly applied to the *round,* or convexity given by sailmakers to luff and foot of jibs and staysails, and luff, head, and foot of gaff sails to meet stretching conditions in both bolt-rope and canvas, according to cut of sail. *R.* also should not be confused with *goring* of a sail, or triangular addition to a leech, as for purpose of giving a royal, lower topsail, or a course a widening sweep toward its clews; *cf.* GORE. *R.* of a mainsail or crossjack is provided by *goring* for about one-fifth length of its foot from clews; a square foresail usually has neither gore nor roach; upper topsails are given a small *r.* to clear sail from lower-topsail yard; top-gallant sails are *roached* to clear topmast stay; royals, to clear top-gallant stay.

ROAD.   Also, *roads; roadstead;* an anchorage; especially, a large partly protected area in which vessels may anchor. **Open r.,** usually *open roadstead,* such area protected from gales by near-by land only; a *r.* open to the sea. **Rules of the R.,** *see* REGULATIONS *for* PREVENTING COLLISIONS.

ROADSTER.   English name for a vessel or barge that navigates by means of fair tides or winds; as, a **Thames r.** Sometimes applied contemptuously, as to a ship; as, *this r. can do only six knots.*

ROARING FORTIES.   Originally applied by sailing-ship men to the southern round-the-world belt between 40th. and 50th. parallels of latitude in which an extremely generous supply of strong westerly winds, particularly in the winter season, was the secret of so many record performances in speed between Cape of Good Hope and Australia, or thence toward Cape Horn on the homeward run; now, general term for principal trade-route regions of North Atlantic and North Pacific oceans, or latitudes of the "brave west winds of poesy."

ROBALO.   (*Sp.*)   A pike-like fish of West Indies and tropical America habitat. Upwards of three feet in length and having two large dorsal fins, is considered valuable as food; also called *snook.* A smaller species is known as *robalito.*

ROBAND. (Orig. *raband;* from Ice. *ra,* spar or yard; *band,* band)   A short piece of rope-yarn, spunyarn, sennit, or the like, used for seizing each eyelet in the head or luff of a sail to a hank, hoop, or a jackstay, as in bending various sails; also, *robbin; roving.*

ROCK.   A concreted mass of stone or stony matter; especially, a cliff, promontory, or a single mass rising above or near the sea surface. In *plural,* a reef consisting largely of such matter; as, *Fowey Rocks.*

To move to and fro with a jerky roll, as a boat. **Half-tide r.,** one that is exposed at half-tide; a *r.* usually just awash. **R. cod,** a fish of the cod family that frequents rocky bottom areas; local name for several different cod-like fishes living about rocks or over rocky bottom; a *rock-fish.* **R'bound,** girt with *r's;* difficult of approach on that account, as a *r'bound coast;* rocky. **R'fish,** any of many fishes that live among *r's* or near rocky bottom; the *black r.* and *red r.* of the North Pacific coasts; a *grouper* of the Bahamas and Florida coasts; the *striped bass* of Atlantic and Pacific U.S. coasts; the *r. hind* of West Indies; etc. **R.-hopper;** a small penguin of southern latitudes; *see* PENGUIN. **R'ing shackle,** on a mooring-buoy, the shackle to which ship's cable or lines are secured. **R'ing shaft,** any shaft on an engine that oscillates instead of revolving in its bearings. **R.-nosing,** whalers' term for pursuing or seeking a catch near the shore while ship lies at anchor. **Sunken r.,** one whose summit lies below sea level and is dangerous to navigation.

ROCKER. A boat having a *rockered keel, i.e.* one with a slight upward curvature from amidships toward each end; *see* KEEL.

ROCKET. A projectile driven by liberated gases from a contained combustible. It may be a shell fired from a gun and assisted in maintaining its velocity by the means indicated, as a *r.-shell;* may be a means of carrying a line, as to a vessel in distress, when it is called a *line-throwing r.;* or used as a signal, in which case a part of the *r.* explodes aloft and throws stars of certain colors or simply bursts with a loud report or reports. Sometimes the term is applied to a shell-like signal of the last-named type which is projected by gunpowder from a mortar, or to the gun-thrown projectile that carries a line, as from a *line-throwing* gun. **Anchor r.,** *see* ANCHOR. **Harpoon r.,** also called *r. bomb, whaling-r.; see* **B.-harpoon** *in* BOMB. **Life r.,** a projectile or *r.* for carrying a life-line or line by which a hawser may be hauled in, as in the case of rescue operations involving a stranded vessel. **R. apparatus,** life-saving gear featuring the *rocket-thrown* line to a vessel in distress, as fired to a stranded ship by a shore life-saving crew. Although formerly such line was fired off to the vessel by *r.,* common practice now is to use a projectile fired from a *line-throwing gun* for the purpose, the term *r. apparatus,* however, being still often applied to the gear in question. Line is thrown to ship to supply the distressed crew means by which a hawser may be hauled off and made fast. Hawser is then set taut by shore crew and used as a traveler along which the breeches buoy is pulled in taking off persons from vessel; *see* **Breeches-b.** *in* BUOY. Also known as *breeches-buoy apparatus.* **R. gun,** firing-piece from which a *r.* is projected; a *whaling-gun.* **R. line,** that thrown by a *r.;* a line carried by any projectile.

R. signal, bursting of a *r.,* often throwing colored stars or streamers, such as a distress signal; a *signal-r.* **R.-socket,** a small gun-metal mortar, usually set in a wood rail or side of the deck, as on a navigating-bridge, for readiness in case of projecting a *r. signal,*—particularly, a distress signal.

ROCKS AND SHOALS. Colloquial U.S. navy term for the *"Articles for the Government of the Navy."*

ROD. A slender batten or bar of wood or metal; a measuring-strip or batten on which certain structural dimensions are indicated, as for use in ship construction. A connecting-rod in an engine. A pole for a fishing-line. **Half-breadth r.,** same as **Half-breadth staff;** *see* HALF. **R.-bolt,** a bolt made of a required length cut from a *r.* of metal. It is usually threaded at one end and fitted with a nut which serves as a driving head; *see* BOLT. **R. fender,** bundle of light *r's*—usually of cane—securely lashed together for service as a fender; sometimes called a *faggot fender.* **R. iron,** collective term for structural iron or steel in *rod* form. **R. rigging,** *see* RIGGING. (For *rod* as designated by the following combining words, see: FIT; GRAB; GUIDE; GUY; JACK; LIGHTNING; SOUNDING.)

RODE. Preterit of verb *to ride;* as, *the vessel r. at anchor for a week.* In New England and Eastern Canada, a fisherman's term for a boat's *anchor-rope.* **Tide-r.; wind-r.:** *see* RIDE.

RODGERS' ANCHOR. *See* ANCHOR.

ROGER, JOLLY. *See* JOLLY.

ROGUE'S YARN. *See* YARN.

ROLL. Movement of a vessel in *rolling* or oscillating from side to side; as, *a heavy r.; a r. to port of* 30°. To incline, as a vessel, from side to side in a rhythmic motion, though not necessarily to a constant angle from the upright. To advance, as a succession of heavy sea waves; as in, *"Off old Cape Stiff where seas r. mountains high."* Usually with *up,* to furl a square or gaff sail; as, to *r. up the mainsail.* A list of names of crew members often is called a *r.,* as in *muster r., pay r.* **Bending-r's,** machine by which plates and structural parts are given required curvature by being passed between two or more heavy steel cylinders in turning or *rolling* motion. **Double r.,** as distinguished from the *single r.,* lateral motion of a ship from her inclination to either side of upright to the opposite side and back to the former; as, from port to starboard and return to port. The single *r.* here is from port to starboard only. **Fire r.,** *see* FIRE. **Muster r.,** *see* MUSTER. **Period of r.,** *see* **Rolling p.** *in* PERIOD. **R.-cumulus,** *see* CLOUD. **R. template,** a pattern or mold for the correct amount of curvature to be given a curved plate in the *bending-rolls.* **Rope-r.,** a reel on which a rope is wound. **Weather r.,** that of a vessel from upright toward weather side in a beam sea.

ROLLER. A stout bar rotating on its longitudinal axis, often tapered to a minimum diameter at its mid-point, for protecting a hawser or other rope from friction wear, as at a mooring-chock. Any cylindrical piece of wood or metal on which anything *rolls.* One of a succession of long heavy swelling waves resulting from a recent gale or advancing from a distant storm; *e.g.,* the *Cape-Horners,* well-known *r's* of the South Atlantic, that have their origin in the roaring forties and fifties during winter season. **Blind r's,** a swell running over a submerged rock and breaking only during heavy weather; also, *blinders.* **Hatch r.,** *see* HATCH. **R. bearing,** *see* BEARING. **R. chock,** a mooring- or warping-chock provided with one or more vertical *r's* for reducing friction wear in a hawser; a fairlead in the form of a horizontal *r.,* as fitted on fishing craft for hauling in lines, etc.; a *r. fairlead.* **R. flag,** signal displayed at St. Helena and Ascension Islands, in the South Atlantic, to warn boats against attempting to land during prevalence of *r's.* **R. gear,** any of several reefing or stowing devices sometimes fitted to sails of smaller fore-and-aft rigged vessels, essentially consisting of a *rolling* boom for reefing, and either a rolling boom or stay for stowing. **R. handspike,** *see* HANDSPIKE. **R.-rule,** a parallel rule that is moved on a plane surface, such as a chart spread on a table, by means of *r's* or a single *r.* attached. **R. ship,** probably the strangest power-driven craft ever built, launched at Toronto, Canada, in 1897. Vessel was in the form of a cylinder 25 feet in diameter and 125 feet in length, but designed to *roll* over the water *broadside on.* Its single deck was mounted to maintain a horizontal position; a set of paddles was fitted to periphery of hull at midship point; navigating was done from a bridge at each end of the rotating hull, or extension of the stationary deck to platforms at both "sides" of the monster. From the last-named appendages were hung the two rudders required to steer the course as the vessel kept rolling along. At best a speed of 6 to 7 knots could be obtained in smooth water and, in short, the bold experiment resulted in complete failure. **Trawl-r.,** a *r. chock* fitted on a fishing-boat's gunwale; *see* **R. chock.**

ROLLING. Rotating or oscillating as on an axis; having an undulatory motion, as waves; roll or motion of a vessel from side to side. **R. chock,** also **r. cleat;** *see* B. keel *in* BILGE. **R. circle,** in a paddle-wheel, circle described by a point having same rotational speed as vessel's speed through the water; used in considerations of power and gearing. **R. down to St. Helena,** sailormen's term for sailing the East Indiaman's homeward-bound stretch between Cape of Good Hope and St. Helena, a part of the passage characterized by prevailing clear weather and steady S.E. trade winds. With squared yards before the breeze average ship maintained a continuous roll in the following sea. In more recent years it was customary to call at St. Helena for telegraphic orders from owners, often also a supply of fresh water and vegetables. The island lies directly in the homeward track about 1700 miles from the Cape. **R. hitch,** used where stress is parallel, or nearly so, with the spar, line, etc., to which a rope is thereby made fast; same as the *magnus hitch* in which, however, all turns lie flat in a stress at about right angles to spar, stay, etc. The term sometimes is applied also to a round turn and two half hitches, as in securing a line to a spar. **R. period,** *see* PERIOD. **R. reef,** as a substitute for reefing in the conventional reef-point system, a shortening of sail area by means of a *rolling boom,* or spar at foot of sail designed to roll in sail as required. It is found to be a handy system in smaller fore-and-aft rigged pleasure craft. For a square sail fitted with the *r. reef* system, *see* CUNNINGHAM PATENT REEF. **R. tackle,** a handy billy, watch tackle, or other small purchase set taut in steadying an object; especially, a tackle used to ease the parrel or crane of a heavy yard during heavy *r.* of vessel, by setting it up between the quarter of yard and the mast. **R. swell,** a long pronounced swell; a succession of *rollers.* **R. topsail,** *see* CUNNINGHAM PATENT REEF.

ROMBOWLINE. Old sea term for canvas and cordage that have been condemned as unfit for use except in chafing gear; *rumbowline.*

RONCADOR. (*Sp.* = *snorer*) Any of several fishes characterized by their croaking, drumming, or wheezing noises when taken from water, including the *croaker, drumfish, grunts,* and others of the American coasts.

ROOM. Extent or space; as, *sea r.; swinging-r.* Space enclosed by a bulkhead or partition; as, *radio r.; state r.* **Blubber-r.,** compartment in the hold of older whalers for temporarily stowing blubber. On outward cruise the space was filled with oil casks, firewood, etc. To **fill the blubber-r.,** whalemen's slang for eating a hearty meal. **R. and space,** a wood shipbuilding term for distance between side of one frame to corresponding side of the next, —*room* being width of frame and *space* the distance between sides of adjacent frames. **Ward-r.,** in larger passenger vessels, space in officers' living quarters used for social purposes and also sometimes as a dining-room. In warships, a similar room for use of the senior officers, including dining purposes. *Wardroom mess* is the group regularly served at meals in a *ward-r.* **Well-r.,** accessible recess in bottom of a boat for facilitating removal of bilge-water by a bailer. (Also see *room* as designated by the following in BOILER; CHART; ENGINE; FIRE; HEAD; LIGHT; SAIL; SEA)

ROOT. The shorter leg of a knee; especially, that of a knee cut from the natural-grained timber at foot of a tree-trunk; also, *root-leg.*

ROOVE. A *burr,* or small washer or ring, such as is used in clenching copper fastenings in boat-building. *Rooving* is the act of riveting or clenching the end of a copper (or other rust-resisting metal) nail or bolt over a *roove* or *burr. Cf.* BURR. (The word is a dialectal term in north of England and in Scotland for *rivet*) Also, and perhaps more correctly, *rove.*

ROPE. In marine use, general term for cordage composed of *strands* and, as a rule, larger than one inch in circumference. Smaller cordage, including boat-lacing, houseline, roundline, samsonline, wire lanyard, and aerial wire, though *rope* in the manufacturing sense, usually is covered by the term *small stuff.* Special *r.,* such as the left-hand-laid lead-line stuff, is always called *line. Fiber r.* is made from the fibers of many different plants, such as the *abaca* of which a high grade of cordage called *manila* is composed; *ambary,* an Indian hemp plant; *rine,* a Russian hemp; *flax;* and *cotton, Sisal* or *henequen,* from a Mexican plant, is a good second to *abaca* and often is blended with that fiber in the *manila* product. *Coir,* the fibrous matter of the coconut shell; *jute; nylon;* and the recent *orlon* also are employed in manufacture of *r. Wire r.,* of similar form to *fiber r.* usually is simply termed *wire; see* WIRE. Excepting the small *hemp* line used as permanent lashings, heaving-lines, ratlines, awning-roping, etc., to-day a vessel's cordage usually is limited to three-strand, or plain-laid, *manila,* and *wire* of six-strand type. Size of fiber *r.* is measured by its circumference in inches; *wire,* in U.S. generally, by its diameter in inches; in Great Britain by its circumference. *Cf.* HEMP; MANILA. In *r.-making,* the general principle of spinning the yarns comprising each strand in a direction contrary to their lay in the twisted strand, and the latter laid to form the *r.* with same twist as in the yarns, has been adhered to for centuries. While it is apparent that the twisted strands allow an uneven distribution of stress in a *r.,* in that the heart yarns bear the brunt of a pull before the outer yarns, this disadvantage is more than balanced by the generally desirable quality of flexibility, particularly when the *r.* is wet. Hence, *r.* having strands of straight fiber,—*i.e.,* not made up of a set of twisted yarns,—which has appeared on the market from time to time, undoubtedly has greater tensile strength than the conventional type, but, for the reason indicated, its use seems to have been limited to long pull duty, —chiefly in towing work. (For *lay* of *r., see* **Hard-l.; Hawser-l.; Shroud-l.;** etc. in LAID) *R.* may be named from material or fiber from which manufactured; as, *coir r.; flax r.; hemp r.; manila r.; nylon r.; sisal r.;* and from the number of strands it contains, as *3-strand r.; 4-strand r.; 6-strand wire;* etc. Many of the various *r's* have self-identifying names; as, *wheel-r.; tow r.; buoy r.; leech r.; bucket r.; bow r.* Others have special names of the traditional sort:

as, *monkey r.; bull r.; jack-r.* To *r.* a sail or an awning is to sew or marl the *roping* along its edges. **Back-handed r.,** also *back-laid* or *left-handed r.,* cordage in which the slope of the laid strands advances from right to left. Also, *see* BACKHANDED. **Bolt-r.,** the *r.* sewn to edges of sails, awnings, hatch-tents, etc.; a good quality of hemp especially made for *leech-r's, head-r's,* etc., of sails; sometimes, a served flexible *wire,* in which case it is *marled* to sail instead of sewn. **Callao r.,** named for the port at which much used, a hawser for use in a swell to hold cargo-carrying craft alongside ship. Consists of a length of wire at each end of a heavy coir hawser (which is sometimes doubled); coir part supplies the needed elasticity in absorbing the surge or run of lighter in a swell. **Check r.,** a breast or spring line used to *check* a moving vessel alongside a wharf, as in decreasing her way, cutting around a corner, bringing her closer alongside, etc.; *also see* CHECK. **Dip r.,** as used in *clearing hawse,* line dipped around the riding cable in the opposite direction and with same number of turns as the lee cable is turned round riding cable; its end is made fast to unshackled end of lee cable and hauled on from the deck; *see* **H.-rope** *in* HAWSE. **Gift r.,** a line given one boat by another as an obliging *tow r.;* sometimes, a *guess-warp.* **Hide-r.,** *see* HIDE-ROPE. To **know the r's,** to be familiar with names and uses of the various *r's* constituting ship's rigging; hence, to know the details of a business, organization, etc., or "tricks of the trade." **Lang-lay r.** *see* WIRE. **Left-handed r.,** *see* **Back-handed r. Regular-lay r.,** right-hand, or hawser-laid *r.;* also called *plain-laid r.;* cordage in which the strands advance in a left to right slope. **R. roll,** a drum on which a *r.* is wound; a *r.-reel.* **R.'s-end,** to flog with an end of a *r.,* once sometimes given additional weight by an overhand or a figure-eight knot; to administer the *cat.* **R's of Maui,** so termed by the Maoris, the apparent rays of the sun as often showing when that luminary is behind a cloud; the *sun's backstays.* Maui, at such times, is perhaps engaged in some deep-sea Pacific fishing; *see* MAUI. **R.-spinner,** one engaged in making *r.;* especially, in actual work of laying up the yarns and strands as in rope-walk activities, or *r.-spinning.* **R.-walk,** a long, covered space or building in which manufacture of *r.* is carried on; so named from the early days of *r.-making,* when *r.-makers* "walked" as they spun fiber into *yarns,* then yarns into *strands,* and finally strands into *ropes.* **R.-yarn,** a number of fibers twisted together to form one of the threads or units composing a *strand* of a *r.* **R.-yarn Sunday,** old term for a Wednesday afternoon in U.S. men-o'-war, when all but necessary work was suspended. Its purpose was to give the men an opportunity to attend to their personal sewing, washing, etc. **Twice-laid r.,** cordage made from yarns once used in a former *r.* **Water-laid r.,** composed of three or four plain-laid *r's* laid together to form one *r.* and thus having an opposite lay to such *r's.* Although having less cross-section material and consequently less tensile strength than a plain-laid *r.* of same size, is more elastic, more easily dried and coiled down, and so better suited in the large sizes to special heavy work, such as in towing, salvage, etc. This is *cable-laid r.* which formerly was made by wetting the fibers in spinning instead of using a lubricating oil, tallow, etc. *Lead-line* usually is of this type. **Weather r.,** hemp or flax *r.* treated with hot Stockholm or pine tar as protection against ravages of sea-water and weather, such as that used for roping sails, for rigging-lanyards, ratlines, foot-ropes, and shrouds. **White r.,** untarred *r.* **Wire r.,** *see* WIRE.

ROPING. Act of sewing or marling the bolt-rope to a sail; such rope itself, or that fixed to the edges of a sail. **R. needle,** *see* NEEDLE. **R. palm,** *see* PALM. **R. twine,** heavy twine of flax, hemp, or cotton, used for sewing the bolt-rope to sails; often substituted by 4, 6, or 8 parts of seaming twine, hand-twisted together and waxed.

RORQUAL. (Nor. *rörhval* = red whale, from the red streaks in its skin) Any of a genus of baleen whales, including some very large species, having a dorsal fin; a *finback.* See WHALE.

ROSE. A circular card or diagram, showing radiating lines; as, a *wind r.;* a *compass r.* A perforated metal box or strainer fitted over the end of a bilge-suction pipe, sea-water inlet, etc., to prevent entry of foreign matter in piping system; a *r.-box;* also, called a *strum.* **R. lashing,** or *r. seizing, see* LASHING.

ROSIN. Also, *resin;* the solid, usually amber-colored, substance that remains after distilling crude turpentine, or sap from various pine and fir trees. It is much used in marine varnishes, as an ingredient in marine glue, tarring compositions for hemp rope, wood structural parts and planking, etc. Equal parts of *r.* and asphalt (pitch) composed the material for paying caulked planking seams in older wooden ships.

ROSLYN YAWL. *See* YAWL.

ROSSEL CURRENT. That branch or continuation of the South Equatorial Current of the Pacific that flows from the Fiji Islands' vicinity toward New Guinea and Torres Strait. The other branch, known as *Australia Current,* sweeps southwestward to east coast of Australia, thence southward to about 35° latitude, and finally to southeastward to join the general westerly drift; *see remarks in* CURRENT.

ROSTRUM. (*L. = beak*) Carved beak or raised ornamented prow of an ancient war galley; *cf.* ACROSTERIUM. The name was given to the platform or stage in the Roman Forum, from its decoration with the prows or beaks of captured galleys.

ROT, DRY. Also, sap rot; *see* DRY.

ROTATOR, LOG. *See* LOG.

ROTORSHIP, FLETTNER'S. Named for her peculiar means of propulsion and her German inventor; also called *Flettner's sailless ship (circa 1920).* Vessel was fitted with two large vertical cylinders or "*rotors*" corresponding to masts and sails. Effective wind action on rotors was obtained by rotating them by electric motors in such direction that their after sides moved *with the wind.* This gave streamlining effect of a preponderance of flow, and consequent pressure of wind, on required driving surface of each cylinder, in sailing with a breeze at an angle with ship's fore-and-aft line. The experiment proved the craft's performance to at least equal a moderately speedy sailing-vessel, but appears to have been short-lived because of inability to compete with the steamer.

ROTTEN. Defective in solidity; decayed; unsound; as timber thus affected. **R. ice,** floating ice that is rendered unsound by honey-combing effect of sea-water action, or melting. **R. stops,** *see* STOP.

ROUGH. Stormy; tempestuous; as, a *r. sea;* a *r. voyage.* In an unfinished or crude state; as, *r. spar-timber.* **R. log,** *see* **Deck l.** in LOG.[2] **R. mast,** piece of timber *in the rough,* out of which a mast may be made. **R. sea,** turbulent or disturbed sea surface; state of sea in which waves have combing crests and in height measure, vertically from trough to crest, five to eight feet, and which is produced in open sea by winds of force 5 to force 7, or by a fresh breeze, a strong breeze, or a moderate gale. **R. side,** that side of an iron or steel bulkhead to which its stiffeners are riveted or welded. **R. timber,** trunks of trees ready for fashioning into spars, frames, planking, etc. **R.-tree rail,** in old wooden ships, the *main bulwark* rail, as distinguished from the *topgallant rail.* It was so called from its protection of rough *spar-timber* stowed for spare use immediately below it along the bulwark stanchions.

ROUND. Having a partly or wholly circular or globular form; as, *r. iron;* a *r. gunwale.* To sail about or around; as, to *r.* a cape. With *down, in,* or *up,* to haul on a specified slack rope, tackle, etc. With *to,* to turn vessel into the wind, as in reducing headway; to *heave to.* As opposed to *roach,* convex curvature given to the leech or other edge of a fore-and-aft sail; *cf.* ROACH. The rundle or rung in a ladder. To **go r. on her heel,** said of a square-rigged vessel when boxhauled; *see* BOXHAUL. To **haul r.,** also to *haul around; see* HAUL. To **heave r.,** *see* HEAVE. **R.-bar davit,** ordinary *rotating davit* in which a fair curve is given its upper part for purpose of swinging a boat, anchor, etc., clear of ship's side; *cf.* DAVIT. **R. charter,** a round-trip charter, or hire of a vessel for a complete voyage; *cf.* CHARTER. To **r. down,** to overhaul or haul down on the lower block of a slack-hanging tackle. **R'ed gunwale,** *see* GUNWALE. **R'house,** in old-time ships, a cabin under the forward projecting part of a poop, built in the midship section and often having its fore side rounded. Originally used by the poop guard or watchmen; later formed the entrance to poop quarters from the quarter-deck; more recently was a removable deck-house used as a galley. The term also has been applied to a deck-house built in way of the mainmast for use of petty officers, or what has been traditionally called the *half-deck* in British vessels, used partly or wholly as living quarters for apprentices. To **r. in,** to haul in the slack of a rope; especially, to take in the slack of a tackle, as a brace, sheet, etc. To *r. in* the weather braces also means to haul in those tackles as lee braces are eased off, particularly in the case of lower yards, when wind draws toward the beam, from the close-hauled position. **R'ing,** turns of old rope, strands, or small stuff laid around a heavier line as protection against chafing; any heavier type of service. **R'ing out,** arching or curving posture of a whale preparatory to making a dive; the animal's back *r's out,* or appears above the surface as dive is begun. **R'line,** small stuff of tarred hemp used for heavy service and seizings. It is composed of three strands, each having two yarns, and is laid right-handed; thus may be called the smallest hemp *rope.* **R. of angles,** as a check on accuracy of a sextant, a series of angles accurately measured between selected points in the plane of the horizon, so that, beginning from first object, the *r.* must equal 360°. **R. of beam,** arching or camber of beam; *see* CAMBER. **R. seam,** *see* SEAM. **R. seizing,** *see* SEIZING. **R. sennit,** *see* SENNIT. **R. stern,** an elliptical or rounded counter, as opposed to a *transom stern,* or counter presenting a flat surface. **R. the fleet,** in the British navy, a former punishment administered in the form of a series of floggings arranged so that each ship of an anchored fleet might witness the infliction and profit thereby. Culprit was carried in a boat, secured to one of its thwarts, and given the number of lashes prescribed alongside every ship in succession. **R. thimble,** another name for a cringle; *see* CRINGLE. A fiber-rope thimble; *see* THIMBLE. **R'top,** old term for the platform at a lowermasthead, or *top,* which often was more or less circular in shape. **R. to,** *see opening remarks in* ROUND. **R. turn,** a complete turn or encircling of a line about an object, as opposed to a single turn; always a means of providing holding power by friction and thus relieving stress on hitches, as in making fast a rope to a post, bar, etc. A *r. turn in the hawse* is an additional twist in ship's cables due to another 180° swing in wrong direction; *see* **Elbow in h.** *in* HAWSE. To **r. up,** to draw the blocks of a tackle together by hauling on its fall; to haul a slack line through its leading block, fairleader, etc.; also, to *r. in.*

ROUSE. To haul or pull with full concerted force; sometimes with *up;* as, to *r. up the topsail halyards;* to *r. up cable from the locker.* To wake from sleep,

often with *out;* as, to *r. out the watch.* A short, strong haul or pull; as, *give a r. on the main sheet.* **R.-about block,** *see* BLOCK. **R. and bitt!,** an equivalent of the familiar *"Rise and shine!";* see RISE.

ROVE. Past tense of verb *to reeve.* A metal ring or bur on which the head of a boat nail in clinched; a *roove;* see ROOVE. **R.-clinch nail,** *see* NAIL. **R. iron,** a punch having a cupped point for clinching ends of boat-nails over *roves* or *rooves;* also called *r.-punch. R.* is also the term for the long end or bight of a cargo-sling that is hooked to the fall.

ROVER. A roaming sea robber; a pirate or a pirate's vessel; a *sea-rover. (Archaic)*

ROVING. *See* ROBAND.

ROW. To propel a vessel or boat by means of oars. To transport in any craft propelled by oars; as, *cargo was rowed to shore in surf-boats.* The word generally is displaced by *pull* in nautical parlance; as in, *boat was pulled by four oars; cargo was pulled to shore; he pulls a long stroke; etc.* **Rowed of all!,** formerly, order to *cease pulling* given to boat's crew by a coxswain; the present *"Way enough!"* **R.-port,** *see* **O.-hole** *in* OAR. To **r. guard,** *see* GUARD.

ROWER. One who pulls an oar; an oarsman; especially, in *plural,* a crew manipulating heavy oars or sweeps, as in a barge, lighter, large river craft, or, as formerly, in the war galleys.

ROWLOCK. (Usually pron. *rollok*) Any device on side or gunwale of a boat serving as a fulcrum or pivot for an oar. Commonly in the form of a U-shaped swiveling crotch, also may be a single peg or pin to which oar is secured by a grommet, simply a grommet itself, or oar may be confined to its work by *thole-pins* or an *oar-hole* in the gunwale; *see* **O.-hole** *in* OAR. **Becket r.,** a grommet fixed in boat's gunwale and embracing the shaft of an oar. **Box r.,** an oar-hole, or U-shaped notch in upper side of boat; usually found in larger boats of naval ships; also, *sunken r.*

ROWSER-CHOCK. Variant of *rouser-chock; see* CHOCK.

ROYAL. In square rig, sail set on the *royal yard,* or cross-spar hoisted on the *royal-mast.* Next above the *topgallant-sail,* or *upper topgallant* where that sail is *doubled,* is sheeted to the topgallant yardarms and, being of lighter canvas, usually is set only in light to fresh breezes. *Royals* appear to have been first spread in about 1700, top place having been usurped since the days of "good Queen Bess" by the *top-gallant,* which itself had then not long been "gallantly set above the top-sayle," and, until clipper-ship style came in with its *skysail* and *moonraker,* remained loftiest canvas for perhaps 140 years. Naval ships seldom, if ever, arrived at the stage in sail development that raised any canvas above the "brave little royal." The term seems to have been given the sail because of its princely prominent place on the mainmast, as seen likewise in the 16th. century designation *poop royal; see* POOP. **R.-mast,** generally, that portion of the top-gallantmast extending above the eyes of the top-gallant rigging, or point at which topgallant-back-stays are secured to mast; *see* **Royal-m.** *in* MAST. **R. packet,** *see* PACKET. **R. salute,** *see* SALUTE. **R. pole,** in absence of a skysail yard, that portion of a *r.-mast* from eyes of *r.-backstays* to the *truck,* or extreme upper end of mast.

RUA.   Siamese word denoting a boat or small decked craft and appearing as a combining term in *r.-pet, r.-yayap,* etc., for various local rigs in Gulf of Siam, Indo-Chinese coast, etc.

R.P.M.   Abbrev. *revolutions per minute; also, r.p.m.*

RUBBER.   Piece of flat steel set in a handle for creasing or rubbing down turned in edges of canvas. Used by sailmakers preparatory to sewing a flat seam where the selvaged canvas can not be fitted. A *rubbing-piece,* or any piece of wood, metal, matting, etc., used to protect something from chafing; a *chafing-piece; cf.* CHAFING.

RUBBING.   Chafing or friction, as caused by one object bearing and working against another. **R.-batten,** vertical strip of wood on fore side of a lower-mast to prevent chafing by yards in sending the latter down or aloft; a *chafing-batten.* **R.-paunch,** *see* PAUNCH. **R.-piece,** a beading or rounded strip of wood, sometimes a stout rope, secured fore-and-aft along a boat's side, usually just below the gunwale, to serve as a fender when alongside a pier, vessel, etc.; also termed *rubber, rubbing-strake;* a *fender-guard; see* FENDER. **R.-plate,** *see* PLATE.

RUCHBAH.   (Ar. *rukbah,* knee)   Star of magnitude 2.80 in the group *Cassiopeia,* having a right ascension of 1 hr. 22½ min. and declination of very nearly 60° N. When near the meridian above the pole, it may be recognized as second from the easternmost star, *ε Cassiopeiæ.* It is within a minute of inferior transit when *Mizar,* second from end of the "handle" in the *Big Dipper* is on the meridian *above* the pole, and vice versa. *See* CASSIOPEIA. *Ruchbah* is catalogued as δ *Cassiopeiæ.*

RUCK.   To crease or wrinkle, as in taking in slack canvas when sewing it to a rope; to bunch together as canvas. To *r. a gaff-topsail* is to lower the gaff above which it is spread in order to take in the sail, as when its downhaul has been carried away. To *r. a jib* or a *staysail* is to lay its luff in orderly folds, beginning from the tack, preparatory to bending the sail.

RUDDER.   (A.S. *rother,* paddle; Ger. *ruder,* rudder)   The vertical flat piece or structure of wood or metal that is fitted at after end (in special cases also at *fore* end) of a vessel's immersed body as the means

by which she is steered. *R's* of modern vessels vary through about six different types, most common of which still is the old-fashioned blade hinged at its forward edge to the *rudder-post.* Whatever type is in use, effect of *rudder action,* or its turning effect, on an advancing vessel is that, upon *r.* being turned to one side of the fore-and-aft line, vessel's stern is slued toward the opposite side, ship's head accordingly swinging to same side as that to which *r.* is turned. It is found that actual pivoting of the hull, during a steady swing caused by *r.* action, takes place at a point between one-fourth and one-third of vessel's length from her stem. *Cf.* HELM. Maximum turning effort occurs when *r.* is placed at an angle with the fore-and-aft line of between 35 and 40 degrees. **Back piece of a r.,** in a wooden *r.,* a piece or one of the pieces fitted to after edge of main part of *r.* for purpose of increasing area of the latter. **Balanced r.,** one that is turned on a vertical axis passing through the approximate center of stream pressure, vessel going ahead. Due to the fact that maximum pressure on *r.* is forward of the blade's center of area, greater portion of *r.* area extends abaft the turning axis. However, for high-powered vessels that frequently are required to maneuver in the astern direction, such *r.* often is over-balanced, *i.e.,* its turning axis purposely is designed to pass a little *abaft* the actual balancing axis for the going-ahead condition. Advantage of *balanced r.* is that, compared with the ordinary *r.* hinged at its forward edge, power required in steering-engine is greatly reduced. Generally, 20 to 30 per cent of *r.* area lies forward of turning axis. Also called *balance r.* and *equipoise r.* **Bow r.,** *see* BOW.[2] **Bow of a r.,** *see* BOW. **Danube r.,** a temporary plate fitted to after edge of an ordinary *r.* for providing additional steering power, such as is required by regulation in certain narrow waters,—originally in the *Danube River* from which it is named; also, *Suez Canal r.;* a *salmon-tail.* **Double-plate r.,** *see* DOUBLE. **Drop r.,** as sometimes fitted to small flat-bottomed sailing-craft, a *r.* that may be lowered to extend beneath bottom of boat. It provides a measure of lateral resistance in addition to good steering qualities under sail. **Ease the r.,** *see* EASE. **Equipoise r.,** *see* **Balanced r.** **Full r.,** the hard over position, or maximum angle to which *r.* may be turned out of the fore-and-aft line. **Give her more r.!,** order to helmsman to increase angle of *r.* already applied. **Gulleting of a r.,** *see* GULLETING. **Horizontal r.,** *see* HORIZONTAL. **Jury r.,** an improvised *r.,* or any makeshift replacing a lost or damaged *r.; see* JURY. **Kick of r.,** *see* **Helm-k.** *in* KICK. **Left r.!,** order to helmsman to put vessel's *r.* to port or left side. **Mind your r.!,** *see* **Mind your h.!** *in* HELM. **Oertz r.,** named for its inventor, an early streamlined *r.* designed to smooth out the more or less confused flow of water from propeller and along ship's hull. Consists of a built *r.* having a convex rounded forward edge that is snugged into a concave rounding built to the *rudder-post*. Also built to rudder-post is the corresponding nosing on the forward side, the whole arrangement then becoming much like the airfoil pattern, in cross-section, followed in airplane design. It is claimed for this *tapering-tail r.*, as some have dubbed it, that it greatly improves both steering qualities and speed of vessels which have discarded the *single-plate r.* with its square rudder-post and open spaces in way of the hinging (gudgeons and pintles). **Pilot r.**, an auxiliary *r.* attached to after edge of a partly balanced *r.*, which, as in the *Flettner r.*, is designed to sheer main *r.* to either side at any required angle. Such *r.* may be moved by hand or a small steering-engine; however, its apparent economical advantages have failed to compensate for hazardous exposure of its mechanism to heavy seas, without considering its small braking effect on speed, and thus generally has not found favor in ocean vessels. **Plate r.**, ordinary hinged *r.* the blade of which is made of a single plate; a *single-plate r.* **Reversing r.**, *see* KITCHIN REVERSING RUDDER. **Right r.!**, *see* RIGHT. **Right (or left) 5, 10, etc. degrees of r.!**, in piloting, order to a helmsman to turn *r.* number of degrees indicated. **Right (or left) handsomely!**, order implying *r.* effect to produce an easy even swing to vessel; *see* RIGHT. **R. amidships!**, *see* **H. amidships!** *in* HELM. **R. arms**, in a hinged *r.*, forgings extending fore-and-aft as stiffeners across a single-plate *r.* or to which plating is fastened in a built or streamlined *r.* Each arm is secured to the *r.-stock* and part of it projects forward in the form of a heavy eye in which one of the several pintles is set. Also called *r.-band, r.-brace, r.-stay.* **R. area**, that of immersed surface of blade of *r.* at vessel's designed load draft, which value in naval surface ships averages .026 of draft times length; in merchant craft of all sizes, regardless of *r.* type, differs little from .016; while in harbor craft usually ranges between .03 and .04. **R. angle**, that of blade of *r.* with vessel's fore-and-aft line when *r.* is turned to a given position. When angle is *zero, r.* is amidships. **R.-band**, *see* **R. arms**. **R. bearding**, in a wooden or single-plate *r.*, line of timber or plate at its junction with *r.-stock.* **R.-bearer**, in larger vessels, an inboard fitting designed to carry weight of *r.* and resist radial thrust due to power applied in steering. Essentially consists of a heavy bearing seat that supports *r.* by a collar fitted about *r.-stock;* also, *r.-carrier*. **R. blade**, main portion of *r.* presented to water-flow in steering a vessel; the *r.* proper, excluding the *stock,* or heavy vertical member at fore end of a hinged *r.*, at leading edge of *blade*. **R. brake**, a friction-band about a rudderhead or a steering-quadrant that may be screwed up or otherwise compressed when required to control *r.*, as in event of damage to steering-gear, changing from hand to power control, damping heavy knocks by a high sea, etc. **R. breeching**, in oldtime ships, a

rope or tackle for taking weight of *r.* to ease pintles and gudgeons in a heavy head sea; later, a tackle used to set taut the rudderhead (upper end of *stock*) against side of *r.-casing*, as in steadying *r.* in a rough sea when at anchor or in a heavy swell when becalmed. **R. bushings**, brasses or bearing metal about pintles or in gudgeons of a *r.* **R.-carrier**, *see* **R.-bearer**. **R. casing**, the housing in which a *r.-stock* is confined. Its purpose is to provide water-tightness between vessel's shell and upper end of stock. **R. chain**, as found in wooden vessels, a chain leading from either quarter direct to the *horn,* or upper corner of *r. blade,* for securing *r.* in event of steering-gear damage or carrying away of *r.* itself. **R. chocks**, wedges serving to steady a *r.* in its casing, or for same use as *r. breeching; cf.* 2nd. part of **R. breeching.** Also, *r.-stops; r. stop-cleats; see* **R.-stops**. **R. clamp**, a temporary bracing of timbers or structural steel for firmly holding a *r.* during launching of vessel. **R.-coat**, in wooden vessels, tarred canvas tacked to lip of *r.-port* or to *r.-stock* close to deck for keeping water from splashing inboard through *r. casing.* **R. coupling**, in larger vessels, meeting flanged joint in *r.-stock* between the blade and *r.-port. R.-stock* may be uncoupled at that point to facilitate removal of *r.* and so avoid disturbing steering arrangement at *rudderhead*. **R.-fish**, any of several fishes that habitually follow vessels, some of which are attracted by the trailing log-rotator; also, *log-fish.* The pilot-fish; *see* PILOT. **R.-flange**, one of the flanges in the *r. coupling (q.v.)* **R. frame**, in a built *r.*, that to which plating on both sides is secured. **R. gland**, collar-ring holding the packing in a stuffing-box through which a *r.-stock* passes. **R'head**, upper or inboard end of *r.-stock* to which the tiller or the quadrant is fitted. **R. heel**, lowest part of *r.-blade*. **R.-heel-bearing**, *see* HEEL. **R.-hole**, the *r.-port,* or mouth of *r. casing,* through which *r.-stock* passes into vessel's hull; also, *r.-stock hole.* **R.-horn**, upper corner of trailing edge of *r.* in wooden ships; also the metal attachment for a *r. chain* at that point. **R. indicator**, *see* **H. indicator** *in* HELM. **R.-iron**, *see* IRON. **R.-lock**, device for preventing a *r.* from being lifted from its gudgeons, as in a heavy sea; usually takes the form of a *locking-pintle; see* PINTLE. **R.-nail**, *see* NAIL. **R. pendant**, *see* PENDANT. **R.-pintle**, *see* PINTLE. **R.-post**, in a sailing-vessel or a twin-screw powered vessel, the *stern-post,* or that on which a hinged *r.* swings; in a single-screw vessel, the after vertical *post* or member of the *stern frame,* but often also called *stern-post,* supporting the *r.* In latter case, forward vertical part of stern frame is termed the *propeller-* or *body-post.* **R.-port**, *see* PORT.² **R. pit**, a well in the deck of a dry-dock into which a ship's *r.* may be lowered for inspection or repairs; also called *r. well.* **R. quadrant**, *see* **Q. tiller** *in* QUADRANT. **R.-stock**, in the hinged type of ship's *r.*, vertical shaft at its leading edge which forms the main strength member of, and receives the torque applied in turning, the r. It extends upward and inboard, terminating at its connecting-point with steering-gear,—usually at a tiller or quadrant. **R. snug,** one of the several projections at leading edge of a hinged r. in which the pintles are set; also, a gudgeon in which a pintle works; a r. lug; see GUDGEON. **R.-stays,** see **R. arms. R. stops,** two or more chocks or cleats projecting from a r.-stock or from r.-post, or from both, for preventing r. from turning about 38° out of the fore-and-aft line; also, r. chocks; r. stop-cleats. **R. stuffing-box,** fitted about a r.-stock inside vessel's shell or at a deck for preventing passage of water. **R. telltale,** a helm indicator; see HELM. **R. trunk,** tubular enclosure housing a r.-stock; see **R. casing. R. vang,** see **R. chain. R. well,** see **R. pit. Shift the r.!,** same as **Shift the helm!,** see HELM. **Single-plate r.,** see **Plate r. Standard r.,** chiefly in naval usage, required angle of r. in performing certain maneuvers in ship formation. **Streamlined r.,** one built to present minimum resistance to stream-flow; cf. **Oertz r. Suez Canal r.,** see **Danube r. Underhung r.,** also called a spade r., one of balanced type supported and turned by a single shaft or stock at its upper edge only. A r. of partly underhung and partly hinged type, usually known as a semi-balanced r., to-day is commonly fitted to twin-screw vessels having cruiser sterns. Its stock is hinged to the short r.-post for about half-depth of the blade, while a lower portion of the latter extends forward and under the r.-post. Both types noted usually are streamlined in section, are normally entirely submerged, and are considered most efficient.

RULE. A regulation; a law; a method prescribed for determining a quantity or a desired result. A graduated strip of wood or metal for measuring distances, sometimes provided with scales for mathematical solutions in drawing, etc.; a ruler. **Danube r.,** so named from its adoption by the European Commission of the Danube, 1871, as that for determining deduction allowed from a powered vessel's gross tonnage to obtain her net registered tonnage. The r. was taken with some changes in phraseology from the British Merchant Shipping Act, 1854, with the additional proviso that deduction for propelling spaces be limited to 50% of gross tonnage. It requires that, in the case of screw vessels, 75% of space occupied by and included for working of boilers and machinery shall be added to that space, and in paddle-propelled vessels 50% to that space, as the deduction from gross tonnage. U.S. law (46 U.S.C. 77) gives a shipowner the option of using this rule for establishing his vessel's net registered tonnage. **Hague r's,** see HAGUE CONVENTION. **Moorsom's r.,** see remarks in MEASUREMENT. **R's of the Road,** see REGULATIONS FOR PREVENTING COLLISIONS. **Seven-tenths r.,** see TWO OR MORE BEARINGS WITH RUN BETWEEN. **Simpson's r's,** named for Thomas Simpson, English mathematician, 1710-

1761, certain r's for calculating areas of surfaces having one side of irregular curvature, commonly employed in measuring ships' internal spaces for tonnage. Use of Simpson's First Rule is required by U.S. law in admeasurement of vessels (46 U.S.C. 77). (See any good work on elementary ship construction) **Warsaw-Oxford r's,** those adopted by the International Law Association, 1931, with the view of establishing uniform practice in connection with cost, insurance, and freight contracts; cf. C.I.F. **York-Antwerp r's,** see AVERAGE.

RUMBO. Old term for grog; also, stolen rope or other ship's gear sold for drink-money.

RUMBOWLINE. See ROMBOWLINE. Also, grog of well fortified quality, often varied to rumbullion.

RUMMAGE. (Room-age) Thorough search for dutiable or contraband goods, as by customs officers; to make such search. In former usage, denoted room or space in a vessel for stowing cargo; the stowing of cargo; to arrange or stow cargo; and to prepare space for stowage of cargo by moving other goods. Also, one directing the stowage in a ship's hold was called a rummager.

RUN. Aftermost or narrowing part of vessel's hull. A trough for carrying water off a deck to the scuppers. Distance sailed; a track or route followed, as between two points. A school of migratory fish. A runway or long sloping gang-plank. Act of running; quantity loaded by chute, as coal, iron ore, etc., from a given number of railway cars, pockets, or an elevator. To go, move, travel, turn, or work; as, running gear, blocks, etc. To ply regularly to. To sail a vessel before the wind, especially during heavy weather. To flow, as a river or tidal current. To reeve, stretch out, pass, or carry, as a hawser, line, etc.; usually with through, along, out; as, the line is r. through a bow chock; a life-line must be r. along the deck; the warp was r. out to a near-by buoy. To advance or surge along; as, the sea runs mountains high. To pass through or by successfully; as, to r. a blockade. With up, to hoist or set; as, r. up the ensign!; we ran up our flying jib. **By the r.,** see BY. **Correction for r.,** see CORRECTION. **Cut and r.,** to suddenly leave a berth, cutting moorings in doing so; hence, to depart in haste. To **let go by the r.,** see LET. To **r. afoul of,** see AFOUL. To **r. ahead of one's reckoning,** see AHEAD. To **r. away,** in hauling on a line, to walk or r. with the rope along the deck, instead of making short pulls. To **r. deep,** to swim far under water, as a whale, a school of fish, etc. To **r. down,** to collide with and sink another vessel. To **r. down a coast,** to sail parallel with and along a coast as in approaching a port or in coastwise sailing. To **r. in with,** to sail close to, as the shore or another ship. **R. man,** formerly, in British navy, a deserter. To **r. the works,** in whaling, to render or try out blubber in the try-works. To **r. under,** to swim under water and near the surface, as a whale after being harpooned. To **r. (or pass) the net,** see NET.

RUNABOUT. A small speedy motorboat designed for short runs in sheltered waters, usually for pleasure.

RUNDLE. A round, rung, or step in a ladder. An older term for the drum of a capstan, or that part on which turns of a rope are wound in heaving.

RUNG. One of the projecting handles, or spokes, in a steering-wheel. A bar or step, round or rundle, of a ladder. Archaic term for a ship's floor-timber. Outer ends of floors in wooden ships were often called *r.-heads; see* **F. heads** *in* FLOOR.

RUNNER. In a purchase, such as a fish-tackle or one of the lower yard braces, a single rope rove in a fixed block and connected to the moving or hauling block of a tackle, its standing end and standing block of tackle terminating at a common point; such rig usually is termed a *r. and tackle.* Loosely, any whip or fall used as a working hoist. A vessel or person in charge of such that carries the catch of a fishing-fleet to market. A smuggler or a vessel engaged in smuggling; as, a *rum-r.* A person who solicits patronage of sailors at boarding-house he represents; one employed by a tailor, shop-keeper, etc., for a similar purpose. One of a number of men engaged as a crew for the *run,* or passage from one place to another only. Man who attends to ships' mooring-lines about a pier, wharf, set of dolphins, etc., as in landing a hawser by boat, making fast, or letting go as required. A carangoid fish, or one of the family including the *amber jack, cavalla, leather jack, moonfish,* etc., of warmer seas, so named from its swift swimming and leaping from the water; the *jurel* of U.S. Atlantic coast. *R.* of a trawl is its main line to which the snells or snoods bearing the hooks are made fast.

RUNNING. Designating something that travels, moves, or is movable; as, a *r. bowline; r. rigging;* a *r. bowsprit.* Continuous; as, a *r. fight;* successive; as, *r. days.* To flow or surge; as, *current is r. to the northward; a heavy sea is r.* A vessel is said to be *r.,* especially during heavy weather, when sailing or *driving* directly before the wind; also a whale when swimming away from its pursuers. **R. agreement,** articles of agreement that continue in force for two or more successive voyages and for a stipulated period; *see* ARTICLES. **R. block,** moving block in a tackle; *see* BLOCK. **R.-bowline,** *see* BOWLINE. **R. bowsprit,** a reefing-bowsprit; *see* BOWSPRIT; REEFING. **R. days,** consecutive days as distinguished from *working days;* a charter-party term used in stipulating number of days allowed for loading or discharging a cargo, in reckoning demurrage, duration of charter, etc.; *see* **L. days** *in* LAY; *also* DEMURRAGE. **R.-down clause,** also termed *collision clause,* provision in a marine insurance policy for payment of costs resulting from a collision in which insured vessel is at fault; *see* **C. damages** *in* COLLISION. **R. fight,** an engagement in which vessels concerned are making way through the water, as when pursued or in pursuit. **R. fix,** place of a ship as determined by the *position line* obtained from one observation brought forward on the chart, according to course and distance run, to time of a second observation. Point of crossing or intersection of first position line with second is the *fix.* **R. free,** *see remarks in* FREE. **R. gear,** same as *r. rigging.* **R. hitch,** a slip-knot; any hitch formed around standing part of a rope, allowing latter to slide or slip through it; also, *r. knot.* **R. large,** *see* **Running l.** *in* LARGE. **R. lights,** those required by *Regulations for Preventing Collisions* to be shown by vessels under way; also, *navigation lights; cf.* LIGHT. **R. part,** as distinguished from *standing part,* that portion of a rope in a tackle which is hauled upon or moves through a block or blocks. **R. rigging,** *see remarks in* RIGGING. **R. survey,** approximate or preliminary delineation of a coast-line obtained by observations from a moving vessel. Using course and distance sailed as a base-line, positions of prominent points or objects are plotted, in general, by triangulation method, or that in which intersection of two compass bearings of each object taken at different points in the base-line indicates location of object. **R. the easting down,** *see* EASTING.

RUSSIAN HEMP. An important grade of hemp used in manufacture of cordage. It is grown principally in the southwestern part of Russia. *Cf.* HEMP.

RUST. The reddish brown coating or scale (*iron oxide*) formed on iron and steel surfaces by oxidation; also, the deposit of such oxide accompanying dripping condensation (*sweat*) from, or slow leaks in, iron decks or other structural parts, often harmful to certain cargoes, producing ugly stains on cases, etc. *R.* accumulating between faying surfaces of iron is powerful enough to cause distortion of the metal and even bursting through of rivet-ends. Hence, in ship construction, the necessity for a substantial coating of anti-corrosive composition on all faying or lapping parts. **R. putty,** *see* PUTTY.

RUTTER. (Fr. *routier,* a track chart) Archaic term for a chart showing the track or route followed on a voyage; a *track chart.*

S

S. In freeboard, or Plimsoll, marks on ship's side, denotes summer season line or limit to which a sea-going vessel may be immersed in sea-water, or a lake or river vessel in fresh water. In ships' log-books and weather records, abbrev. for *snow* or *snowing; south; smooth sea*. International Code flag, "*Sugar,*" having a white ground with a central blue square about one-ninth of flag's area. Hoisted singly, flag *S* denotes "*My engines are going full speed astern*"; also, as a towing signal, displayed by *ship towed*, indicates "*Go astern*" and by *ship towing,* "*My engines are going astern,*" or may be indicated by flashing the Morse Code *S* (...) as such towing signal. **S.-bend,** double bend or curve in a river resembling letter *S*; also, *S-turn*.

SACCOLEVA. Originally, a Levantine vessel of barquentine-like rig, or having square sails on the foremast with small lateen main and mizzen; now, almost any two-masted vessel approaching the ketch rig, *i.e.,* having a large lug or lateen mainsail and a small mizzen at stern.

SADDLE. A block or timber having a rounded notch in which a boom or other spar may rest in the stowed position; a support for a rack on which a pinion works, as in some steering-gears; *see* **Q.-block** *in* QUADRANT. A hollowed block on a bowsprit serving as a rest for the heel of a jib-boom. A support for the jaws of a fore-and-aft sail's boom, usually in the form of a collar fitted around the mast. At inner end of a hoisting gaff and between its jaws, a vertical hinged block shaped to fit against and slide on the mast. In a coal-bunker hatch, a ridge shaped like an inverted V for diverting coal to each side of hatchway during coaling operations; also, *saddleback*. **Boiler s.,** *see* BOILER.

SAFETY. Freedom or security from danger; state of being safe or free from harm or loss; safeness; security. **Factor of s.,** ratio of breaking stress to working stress, as taken into account in using ropes, chain, hooks, shackles, etc. Thus, adopting a *s. factor* of 3 for a wire rope, stress applied to the rope should not exceed one-third the breaking stress. **S. angle,** approximate inclination or angle of roll

defining the limit beyond which vessel's righting power is dangerously reduced. **S. belt,** a life-jacket or life-preserver; any belt worn as a safeguard, such as that securing a leadsman in the chains. **S. car,** *see* **L.-car** *in* LIFE. **S. certificate,** that issued by a government authority to a passenger vessel engaged in an international voyage under provisions of *International Convention for the Safety of Life at Sea, 1948,* stating that ship has complied with Convention regulations regarding her structure, boilers and machinery, watertight subdivision arrangements, life-saving appliances, and radio-telegraph installations. **S. collar,** a clamped ring or strap fitted about a shaft or other part of an engine, winch, etc., to prevent sliding or starting movement of a particular part. **S. hook,** a cargo hook fitted with a *lip,* or piece hinged to the shank, which drops over mouth of hook, thus preventing fouling of hook with edge of hatch coaming or other obstacle; sometimes such lip is made to lock over point of hook; a *drop-lip hook; cf.* **Cargo h.** *in* HOOK. **S. keel,** *see* KEEL. **S. plug,** *see* **Fusible p.** *in* PLUG. **S. radio-telegraphy certificate,** as issued by a government authority to a vessel, states that the provisions of *International Convention for the Safety of Life at Sea, 1948,* have been complied with in the matter of radio-telegraphy equipment in cargo ships of over 500 tons (gross tonnage); a *s. radio-telephony certificate,* applicable to vessels of 500 tons upwards but less than 1600 tons, is of similar force and tenor, but only in cargo vessels of such tonnage not equipped with a radio-telegraph installation. Vessels here referred to are those engaged on international voyages. **S.-rail,** a guard-rail; *see* **L.-rail** *in* LIFE. **S. lamp,** *see* FLAME SAFETY LAMP. **S.-tackle,** a preventer purchase or tackle; an additional tackle rigged for extra security. **S. valve,** *see* VALVE.

SAG. To droop, sink, or bend downward in the middle or throughout the length, as a spar suspended at its ends or a vessel thus deformed through strain. To make excessive leeway, as a boat, due to wind, sea, or current; to fall or drop off to leeward, as in sailing. Amount or degree of downward bend, as in a timber or a vessel. *Sagging,* the converse of *hogging,* may be produced in a vessel by excessive preponderance of buoyancy forces at or toward ends of the hull, as when ship is burdened unwisely with a major weight of cargo at approximately her mid-length. In a seaway, as when vessel's course is at right angles to waves, a maximum *sagging moment* occurs when trough of sea arrives at or about amidships with each end supported by the adjacent waves. As a result, *compression* at upper part of structure takes place *longitudinally,* and *tension* at lower parts, or tendency is present to produce deformation or fracture above and below the neutral axis, particularly in the loaded condition referred to. *Cf.* HOGGING.

SAGITTARIUS. (*L. = an archer*) A southern constellation, through which the sun passes at about the winter solstice, lying next to and east of *Scorpio.* The group contains two bright navigational stars; *see* KAUS AUSTRALIS; *also,* NUNKI.

SAIC. (Turk. *shaiqa*) A kind of ketch-rigged vessel formerly common in the Levant.

SAIL. (A.S. *seglian,* to sail; *segel,* a sail) To make headway or be driven, as a boat, by wind pressure on a *s.* or *s's;* hence, by extension, to impel or be impelled, as a vessel, by means of steam or any other motive power. To depart, as a vessel on a voyage. To govern or direct a vessel; especially, by means of wind power; as, to *s. a schooner.* A short passage or excursion; as, *we enjoyed the s. down the bay.* Any unidentified sailing craft sighted at sea; as, *a s. hove in sight;* or, collectively, as, *a fleet of ten s.* In plural, customary sailing-ship short name for the *sailmaker.* A sheet of canvas or any textile fabric that is spread to impel a boat or vessel by action of wind pressure on its surface. *Sails* are of two general classes; *viz., fore-and-aft,* or those having the *luff* or forward edge attached to a stay or, either wholly or in part, to, or near, a mast; and *square,* or those spread from a *yard,* or spar lying at right angles to a mast. The former may be triangular in shape, as jibs, trysails, staysails, or jib-headed boom sails; or may be quadrilateral, usually with the after side *(leech)* of greater length than the other. Square *s's* take the name from their right-angled shape at the *head earings,* or points at which the *leeches* (vertical sides) meet the *head* at ends of the yard, rather than from their approximately rectilineal shape. Earliest *s.* used probably was of "square" pattern set only in fair winds, but the three-sided *lateen* with its long oblique hoisting yard apparently was foremost in utilizing the breezes for sailing *close-hauled.* The former is known to have been fitted to the roving Viking-ships, while the *lateen,* a favorite with the Venetians of the Middle Ages, was at least experimented with by the Phoenicians long before the Christian era. A combination of *square* and *lateen s's* appears to have been adopted

in larger vessels of the 15th. century, notably in the *caravel* of Columbus's time, but any kind of *topsail,* or *s.* above a *course,* as all lower *s's* once were called, was a rarity as late as A.D. 1400. Square topsails may be said to date from 1500; probably a century later in the Spanish *galleon* a *top-gallant s.* appeared above the topsail. Meanwhile the *lateen* seems to have been favored as an *after s.* and ships of western Europe retained that canvas well into the 17th. century. About 1700, the *royal* was first set above the *top-gallant* and continued as loftiest canvas until the days of the clippers; *see* ROYAL. Outside of the historical all-lateen rigs peculiar to the Mediterranean, the credit for building and rigging, in about 1840, first vessels having an entire spread of pure *fore-and-aft s's* (jibs and gaff *s's*) on two or more masts goes to these United States. Such rig is the *schooner* type. Parts of a *triangular s.* are the *luff,* or forward edge; *leech,* or upper after edge; *foot,* or lower edge; angle of juncture of leech and foot, the *clew;* upper angle is the *head;* and foremost or lowest point, the *tack.* A *quadrilateral fore-and-aft s.* has a *luff,* the fore side; *leech,* or after side; *head,* or upper edge usually spread along a *gaff; foot,* often spread on a *boom;* its *tack* is lower forward corner; *throat,* upper forward corner; the *peak* is its highest or upper after point; and *clew,* its lower after corner. A *square s.* is bent to its yard by its *head;* its *leeches* are the two outer edges; and *foot,* its lower side. The *head-earings* are its upper corners, secured to the *yard-arms; clews,* lower corners to which the *sheets* are attached. *Roping,* or the bolt-rope secured to a *s.* along its edges, is named for its position; as, *luff-, head-, leech-,* and *footrope.* In a fore-and-aft *s.,* the roping is on *port side* of the canvas; in a square *s.,* on the *after side.* In square-rig, the *foresail* and all *lower topsails* are heavy-weather canvas, the strongest on board; in fore-and-aft rig, usually all lower canvas but that on after mast, where three or more masts are present. Names given to *sails* are legion, particularly in smaller vessels and the yachting field, and no doubt a good-sized volume might be used in their description. With the trading-vessel in mind, however, principal canvas is named for the mast on which it is set or to which its boom or yard is attached; thus, in square rig, we have the *fores'l* set from the *fore yard,* which is slung from the *foremast* (or *fore-lowermost*); next above, the *lower* and *upper tops'ls* in way of the *topmast;* then the *topgallants'l* (sometimes also divided into *lower* and *upper*), fitted to its yard on the *topgallantmast;* and finally, the *royal* in way of the *royalmast,* if we omit, for the present, the lofty *skys'l* hoisted on the *skys'l pole. Stays'ls* take their name from the stays on which they are set; as, *fore stays'l; main-topmast stays'l;* and in this respect *jibs,* which are set on the *head stays,* also must be considered *stays'ls; see* JIB. In the fore-and-aft rig, all *gaff s's* are named for their respective masts, excepting the *spanker,* or aftermost *s.* on a *mizzen* or a *jigger* mast, and their surmounting *gaff-tops'ls* for topmasts on which set; thus, *fores'l; fore gaff-tops'l; spanker; mizzen gaff-tops'l.* *Cf.* FORE; MAIN; MAST. **Annie Oakley,** as spread in some larger yachts, a parachute spinnaker characterized by a series of holes down its middle for freeing it of dead cushioning air; *see* SPINNAKER. **Baby jib-tops'l,** yachting term for a small jib set well aloft on an outermost stay. **Bonaventure mizzen,** in old-time vessels, such as the *caravel,* a lateen *s.* set on the after mast. **Boom fores'l, boom mains'l,** a gaff *s.* on the foremast or mainmast, fitted with a boom. **Cap jib,** *see* JIB. **Course,** in more modern usage, *s.* spread on a lower yard in square-rigged vessels; as, the *fore course,* more commonly termed *fores'l.* Formerly, all principal lower canvas, including staysails, were called *courses.* **Drift-s.,** also sometimes, *sheer s.;* a drogue, sea-anchor, or *drag-s.; see* DRAG. **Duke of York,** as termed in British ships, a *spencer,* or former gaff *s.* serving as a *trys'l; see* SPENCER. **Flying s.,** any *s.* that is *set flying,* i.e., hoisted from the deck to its position while unattached to a stay, mast, etc. **Fores'l,** in square rig, lowermost *s.* on the foremast, or that bent to the fore yard; in a schooner, *s.* bent to and set abaft the foremast; in the ketch, yawl, and sloop rig, *s.* set on the fore stay, often called *stay fores'l* or simply the *stays'l.* **Full s.,** *see* FULL. **Plain s.,** *see* PLAIN. **Ring-tail,** a kind of *studding-s.* set between gaff and boom, abaft the leech, of a fore-and-aft *s.;* especially, such *s.* formerly fitted on clipper ships to the spanker; also, *ring-s.* **Ring-tail tops'l,** a jib-shaped *s.* set above a *leg-o'-mutton spanker.* Its luff hoists on the topmast, while its long leech and its foot meet at the clew which, in turn, is sheeted down to spanker-boom end. **S. area,** usually expressed in square feet, total surface measurement of vessel's sails. **S. batten,** one of several strips of light wood fitted in a *s.* at about right angles to the leech as a means of stiffening or flattening canvas to its work. Chiefly found in racing yachts. To **s. broad,** same as to *s. large; see* LARGE. **S.-burton,** a tackle used for hoisting a *s.* aloft for bending. **S.-carrying power,** measure of a vessel's power to stand up to pressure of wind with all plain *s.* set to a breeze,—generally taken as one of force 5 (about 26 knots) on the beam. Necessarily a question of dynamical stability, vessel's righting arm times her weight (displacement) should balance total wind pressure times distance of *center of effort* (center of gravity of *s.* area) from *center of lateral resistance* of hull (*cf.* CENTER). Thus, for boats or vessels of similar type, a comparison of amount of *heel* under wind conditions noted will indicate any adjustment required in weight or ballast distribution or amount of *s. area* with view of conforming to an adopted standard of stability, or *s.-carrying* capability. To **s. close to the wind,** to *s.* close-hauled; *see To* l.

close *in* LAY. **S.-cloth,** commonly flax, cotton, or hemp *canvas; nylon* is some small yachts. For years American choice has been *cotton* canvas in sailmaking, while the British have preferred *flax.* Merchant craft standard width of cotton canvas is 22 inches; Britain's flax, 24 inches. The former runs from number 00 to 12, but, generally, Nos. 0 to 5 only are used for sailmaking, heaviest being No. 0; *flax* is similarly designated. No. 00 cotton of 22-inch width weighs 20 ounces per lineal yard; No. 0, 19 ounces; No. 1, 18 ounces; each number thereafter decreasing by 1 ounce, No. 5 being 14 oz. Lighter grades of flax are sometimes referred to as *10-ounce duck; 12-oz. duck; etc.* Cloths are sewn together with a flat seam that varies in lap from 1½ inches in the heavier canvas to 1 inch in the lighter grades. *Hemp s.-cloth* is rough in texture and somewhat inferior to cotton and flax, but has been greatly used in smaller European and Indian trading-craft. **S.-cover,** *see* COVER. **S.-fish,** a close relative of the sword-fish; in length about 6 feet, has a large dorsal fin suggestive of a *s.;* also, the *basking shark.* **S.-fluke,** a marysole, smear dab, or whiff, as so called in various parts of British Isles; a king of flounder. **S.-grommet,** *see* EYELET. **S.-hank,** *see* HANK. **S. ho!,** traditional cry from the lookout or any man aloft upon sighting a vessel under *s.* Acknowledgment usually took the form of the question from the officer of the deck, *"Where away?";* and the reply, *"Three points on the lee bow,"* for example. **S.-hook,** a small sharp-pointed hook attached to a lanyard, used by sailmakers for holding canvas in position while sewing a seam. **S.-hoop,** *see* HOOP. To **s. large,** also to *s. broad; see* LARGE. **S. loft,** a spacious room or entire upper floor in a building used for sailmaking purposes. **S. moment,** vertical distance of *center of effort* from *center of lateral resistance* multiplied by total wind pressure on *s. area; see* **S.-carrying power. S. needle,** *see* NEEDLE. **S. plan,** *see* PLAN. **S. pressure,** in connection with *s.-carrying power,* total pressure of wind against all plain *s.* set at right angles to wind direction. Expressed in *pounds,* its value is, very nearly, *s. area* in sq. *ft. times* $.003\ V^2$, where $V =$ wind velocity in *knots.* **S. room,** enclosed space in a vessel for stowing sails, awnings, and other canvas fittings; a *s. locker.* **S. slide,** a variation of the common *hank;* it is made with an elongated bearing surface for sliding on forward side of a railway or track on a mast; *see* RAILWAY. **S.-tackle,** *see* **S.-burton. S.-track,** *see* RAILWAY. **S.-trimmer,** in sailing-navy days, one of a number of men detailed to trim or otherwise handle sail during an engagement. **S. twine,** cotton or flax sewing material made of two or three threads twisted together; specifically, such *twine* used in *seaming;* for *roping* work, a heavier twine is supplied. **Save-all,** a small *s.* temporarily set below or between regular sails for catching wind spilled from latter, as in lighter breezes;

termed a *water-s.* when set below a boom, as in a schooner; a *Jamie Green.* To **set a s.,** to spread it for use in sailing. To **set s.,** to spread vessel's canvas for sailing; hence, to depart on a voyage. **Tanned s.,** as often seen on fishing-boats, *s.* colored by an oak bark solution or the like for preservation of canvas against ravages of weather and sea-water. **Trinket,** originally, a small lateen sail above the fores'l in old-time ships prior to advent of square tops'ls; later, any small "kite" or light upper *s.,* as a *skys'l, topgallant stays'l,* etc. **Under s.,** said of a vessel when under way with sails set. **Wind s.,** a canvas ventilator; *see* VENTILATOR. **Working s.,** *plain s.,* or that most commonly in use; that used in sailing on various courses; as in working to windward in narrow waters, following a channel, etc. (*For other sail terms see:* BALLOON; BENTINCK; BERMUDA; CROSSJACK; DRAG; DRIVER; FLYING; FORE; GAFF; GUNTER; GRETA GARBO; HEAD; JAMIE GREEN; JIB; JIGGER; JOLLY; JUMBO; LATEEN; LEG; LIGHT[2]; LUG; MAINSAIL; MIDDLE; MILL; MIZZEN; PLAIN; QUEEN; RAFFE; RIDING; ROYAL; SETTEE; SHADOW; SKYSAIL; SMOKE; SPANKER; SPENCER; SPINNAKER; SPRITSAIL; SQUARESAIL; STAYSAIL; STORM; STUDDING; TOP-GALLANT; TOPSAIL; TRYSAIL. *Phraseology concerning sail may be found in* ABOUT; BACK; BEND; CLOSE; CROWD; CUT; DEPTH; DROP; FILL; FINE; FREE; FULL; HEAVE; LARGE; LINING; LOOSE; MAKE; POINT; PRESS; RIDE; SHORTEN; SKIN; STRIKE; TOUCH; TRIM; WIND.)

SAILAGE. Collectively, outfit of sails that a vessel may spread; sail area that is, or may be, spread.

SAILED. Furnished with, or having all sails; especially, having all sail bent and ready for sea.

SAILING. Act or art of navigating or maneuvering a vessel that is driven by sail-power; hence, by extension, art of directing; managing, and navigating a vessel propelled by any motive power; navigating; sea-going. In navigation, method followed in finding course to steer and distance from one point to another or resultant course and distance covered on several different courses, position arrived at, etc.; as, *great circle s.; plane s.; mercator s.* Act of departing, as a vessel from a port. **Circular s.,** older term for *great circle s.; spherical s. (q.v.)* **Composite s.,** *see* COMPOSITE. **Current s.,** method of shaping and steering a course that will counteract the effect of a current on ship's track; also includes determination of course and distance made good under given current conditions. **Great circle s.,** *see* GREAT. **Mercator s.,** method of shaping a course or determining course and distance between two points according to principles on which Mercator's chart is constructed; art of following a *rhumb* line, or *loxodrome,* which is shown as a straight line on Mercator's chart; *see* **Mercator's c.** *in* CHART. **Meridian s.,** *see* MERIDIAN. **Middle latitude s.,** so named from being based on the assumption that easting or westing (departure) on an oblique course is that made on the mid-latitude parallel, or that of the mean of respective latitudes of place left and place to which vessel is bound or has arrived at. Applicable only in latitudes of same name, it assumes area traversed to be a plane and for this reason is practicable only for distances up to about 500 miles. However, by applying a correction to the *middle latitude,* as given in *Bowditch,* course and distance calculated by this method agree very closely with the supposedly more rigorous *Mercator s.* For example, true course and distance from *Cape Race* to *Reykjavik,* using corrected mean of latitudes, are almost identical with *Mercator* method at *44° 48′, 1477 miles.* Without correcting the mid-latitude as noted, result is *45° 21′, 1491 miles.* Another example of close agreement of corrected *middle latitude* method with *Mercator s.:* True course from *East Cape, N.Z.,* to *Cape Horn* is identical by both methods at *103° 20′,* while distance is *4762 miles* by this sailing and *4761* by *Mercator.* Problems in *middle latitude s.* involving a few hundred miles are readily solved by means of the *Traverse Table* (see any good nautical tables, such as *Bowditch, Norie,* or *Raper*). The method is also called *mean latitude s.* **Oblique s.,** *see* OBLIQUE. **Order of s.,** *see* ORDER. **Parallel s.,** *see* PARALLEL. **Plane s.,** any navigational practice involving courses and distances which assumes the area concerned to be a plane, as in *traverse s.* **Rhumb s.,** method in which course shaped follows a *loxodrome* or *rhumb* line; *see* LOXODROME; RHUMB. An *oblique* course in all cases, it is longer than the *great circle* track by an amount that increases with the mid-latitude and longitude difference between points considered. In example noted under **Middle latitude s.,** by *rhumb s.,* or following *Mercator* track, *great circle* distance from *East Cape* to *Cape Horn* would be *4310 miles.* **Right s.,** archaic term for *s.* on any one of the four cardinal points; *i.e.,* so that either the latitude or longitude only changes. **S. board,** placed at a ship's gangway, a blackboard on which may be indicated date and time of *s.* **S. directions,** a publication, usually in book form, giving particulars of certain waters, detailed information regarding a coast, currents, recommended tracks, etc., for use of mariners; also called *Pilot,* as *North Sea Pilot, U.S. Atlantic Coast Pilot,* etc. **S.-ice,** *see* ICE. **S. master,** formerly an officer charged with the navigation in a war-vessel; now, only applied to one who manages, handles, and navigates a large yacht, a surveying-vessel, or a salvage ship under a usually accompanying superior. **S. on a bowline,** said of a square-rigged vessel that has her bowlines hauled taut, as when *s.* close-hauled or nearly so; when having sails rap full and *s.* near the wind, sometimes referred to as *s. on an easy bowline.* Cf. BOWLINE. **S. on her own bottom,** said of any trading or fishing vessel that is free of all financial encumbrance and hence inferring a successful career. **S. orders,** *see* ORDER. **S.**

trim, loaded or ballasted to a desirable trim for sailing or leaving port for sea; the appropriate set or position of sails for satisfactory sailing. **Spherical s.,** as distinguished from *plane s.,* that in which sphericity of the earth is taken into account; chiefly, *great circle s.* **Traverse s.,** process of determining resultant course and distance made good from two or more courses and distances *traversed,* or *sailed: plane s.* reckoned by means of a *traverse table.*

SAILMAKER. One whose occupation is the making of sails; one engaged or skilled in *sailmaking.* A petty officer in a sailing-ship who has charge of upkeep of sails and all canvas work, such as boat covers, skylight covers, windsails, and tarpaulins. To-day, the sailmaker's craft embraces not only designing, cutting, sewing, roping, etc., of the canvas in fitting a vessel with sails, but probably is more concerned with the making of awnings, tarpaulins, various covers (as for guns, machinery, etc.), and screens of that material. Also, much of the former *palm-and-needle* hand work in sewing now is done by machines and, like the seldom sighted "proud white wings," the master craftsman may be numbered with the "few and far between." (*For terms designated as* **Sailmaker's,** *see* HEAVER; MATE; NEEDLE; PALM; SPLICE)

SAILOR. A mariner; seafarer; seaman; especially, in nautical usage, one serving in the deck department and holding rating of *seaman, apprentice seaman, able seaman, ordinary seaman,* etc. **Flying-fish s.,** *see* FLYING. **S.'s chest,** as once customarily carried by sailors in merchant ships, traditional receptacle or box for personal belongings, which usually was supplemented by the no less important canvas bag for sea-boots, oilskins, and working clothes. The typical chest had a broad bottom, inward sloping sides, and fancy grommets serving as handles. Also, a painted design usually ornamented its cover, the latter often overlaid with canvas bearing a neatly fringed edge. **S.-monger,** chiefly in U.S., one who interested himself in the illicit practice of luring seamen away from their vessels, by fair means or foul, for *shanghaiing* purposes; *see* SHANGHAI; *also* CRIMP. **S.'s choice,** *see* P'fish *in* PIG. **S.-fisherman,** a deep-sea fisherman; a whaler or whaleman. **Sailors' home,** an institution that cares for and provides incapacitated and retired seamen with living accommodation; or, as found in many important ports, an establishment, usually under management of a benevolent society, at which seamen may obtain board and lodging at moderate cost. **S.'s knot,** the *square,* or *reef,* knot; often so termed when distinguished from the *granny; cf.* GRANNY; *also* R. knot *in* REEF. **Turnpike s.,** archaic English colloquialism for a highway mendicant who pretends to be a shipwrecked or destitute seaman.

SAILORIZING. Practice of sailing; *esp.* where the work of sewing canvas, splicing, seizing, rigging tackle and gear, etc., is included; following the vocation of a sailor.

SAILORMAN. A sailor in full sense of the name; as, *it takes a s. to rig a ship.*

SAINT ELMO'S FIRE. Also, *St. Elmo's light; see* CORPOSANT.

SAINT HELENA, Rolling down to. *See* ROLLING.

SAINT-HILAIRE METHOD. MARCQ ST. HILAIRE METHOD. *Cf.* INTERCEPT.

SAINT ULMO'S FIRE. Same as *St. Elmo's fire, q.v.*

SALINITY. As referred to sea water, degree of saltness, or, properly, percentage of mineral content in a given volume of the liquid. Average for all oceans and connecting seas is 3.50%, very nearly, of which sodium chloride, or common salt, predominates to the extent of 78%; hence the term *salt water.* Highest *s.* is that of the Red Sea, averaging about 4.2%; the Baltic, an exceptionally low average at about .7%; *cf. remarks in* OCEAN. **S. indicator,** an electrical device fitted to a boiler-feed system for indicating saline content of feed-water.

SALINOMETER. A hydrometer graduated to indicate proportion of saline content of water; a sea-water hydrometer; also, *salimeter. Cf.* HYDROMETER.

SALLY. (L. *salire,* to leap or spring) To rush or burst forth, as a body of men. **S.-port,** in sailing-navy days, a port on each quarter of a *fire-ship* for escape of men detailed to set the blaze. *Sallying* is the act of producing, or attempting to produce, a rolling motion to, and so assist in freeing, a stranded vessel or one caught in ice, by causing the crew to run or march in a body from side to side of the deck. The *sallies* should be timed to equal vessel's single period of roll; the men should consecutively occupy same interval in passing from one side to the other as vessel ordinarily would occupy in making a *single roll,* as from port to starboard. The maneuver is sometimes termed to *s. ship.*

SALMON. The much esteemed food fish, averaging about 15 pounds in weight, found along the European and North American Atlantic coasts, classified as *Salmo salar;* also, a related genus, *Oncorhynchus,* of Northern Pacific waters; both of which ascend rivers to spawn. The name also is locally applied to several different fishes having the pink or yellowish red flesh of the true *s.* The terms *parr, smolt,* and *grilse* designate the fish in distinct stages of its development. **Humpback s.,** *see* HUMPBACK. **Pacific s.,** any of several species of genus *Oncorhynchus,* among which perhaps the *quinnat s.,* averaging over 20 pounds, is the most important. All of this genus die after spawning. **S. tail,** an extension-piece fitted to after edge of a rudder-blade for purpose of increasing steering power in narrow waters; a Danube or Suez Canal rudder; *see* **Danube r.** *in* RUDDER.

SALOON. (Fr. *salon,* a reception hall or room) In cargo and smaller passenger vessels, the main cabin, or that serving as a dining-room, assembly room, etc.; in larger ships, any spacious room specially designated and appropriately furnished for comfort of passengers, such as *1st. class dining-s., 2nd. class s. lounge,* etc.; also, often for accommodation of officers, as, *officers' dining-s.,* or simply *s.* **S. deck,** as often termed in vessels carrying one class of cabin passengers, deck for use of, or on which accommodation for such, is located. **S. passenger,** as distinguished from a *steerage passenger,* one occupying best accommodation afforded by ship; *cf.* **Cabin p.** *in* PASSENGER. **S. stores,** articles or supplies for use of, or for sale on board to, passengers or crew. Such stores, according to U.S. law, are considered dutiable merchandise, if purchased at a foreign port.

SALT. *Sodium chloride,* the crystalline substance used in pickling beef, fish, etc., seasoning of foods, and manufacture of sodium compounds, etc. Pure *s.* content of sea water averages about 2.7% of total mineral deposit; *cf.* SALINITY. A sailor; especially one of long experience; a *tar.* Containing, or preserved in, *s.;* as, a *s. lake; s. pork.* Usually with *down,* to pickle or preserve in *s.;* as, to *s. down* a catch of fish, timbers in a wooden vessel, etc. **S. eel,** older sea term for a rope's end; hence, a *s.-eeling,* or a flogging. **S. fish,** cod, haddock, herring, etc., preserved by salting or pickled in brine; especially, that subsequently dried in the sun, chiefly *cod.* **S. horse,** sailors' usual term for *s. beef,* formerly pickled in casks for long voyages. **S. junk,** older term for partly dried pork pickled in brine; often applied to either *s. beef* or *s. pork; s. horse.* **S. provisions,** those preserved in or by *s.,* as for a lengthy voyage; *s.* beef, pork, fish, etc. *Cf.* LIME-JUICER. **S. stops,** in softwood-built vessels, short pieces of board perforated with small drip-holes, set horizontally between frame timbers at about light waterline level for holding coarse *s.* filled in frame spaces in process termed *salting,* or that in which spaces between ceiling and outer planking are filled up to the weather deck with *s.,* with the view of allowing moisture to produce brine which acts as a preservative in the wood. As *s.* melts away, it is replenished by way of the ceiling air-strake near the deck. **S.-water tailor,** U.S. local name for the *bluefish* or *skipjack.* **S.-water soap,** for use with sea water, a soap containing sodium and coconut or palm oil; also, *marine soap.*

SALUTE. Discharge of cannon, dipping of colors or sails, or other regulation or conventional token of honor or respect for a high personage, flag of a nation, a particular ship, a port visited, etc., as by a vessel; token of respect as executed in regulation form of salutation by the hand, or by held position of a rifle, sword, etc. A *s.* of a certain number of *guns* means such number of single rounds fired, regardless of number of pieces employed. To greet or honor, as with a *s.* **Consular s.,** in honor of a visiting consul, usually a *s.* of seven guns. **International s.,** *see* INTERNATIONAL. **National s.,** in U.S., in honor of the President, firing of 21 guns at 5-second intervals; also, same to flag of any country; sometimes, improperly, *s. to the nation.* **Personal s.,** in U.S., that honoring the President, 21 guns; or the Vice-President, Cabinet members, Supreme Court justices, Governors of States, foreign ambassadors, highest ranking Admiral, highest ranking General, 17 guns. **Presidential s.,** *see* **National s. Royal s.,** fired in honor of a sovereign, 21 guns, with colors of foreign country concerned flown at the fore; same as *National* and *International s.* **S. to the nation,** fired at noon, July 4, a gun for each state in the United States. **Saluting** by firing an *odd* number of guns dates from early in 17th. century. An *even* number then indicated a ship's master had died during the voyage.

SALVAGE. (Fr. = a saving; L. *salvare,* to save) Act of voluntarily saving (or *salving*) a vessel, her cargo or part thereof, or a wreck (and in some cases lives of persons on a distressed vessel) from a peril of the sea or other extraordinary danger. That part of property that is salved. Compensation allowed *salvors* of ship and/or cargo. To *salve* or *save* that which is in peril; as, *the goods were salvaged in time.* **Military s.,** restoration of a vessel or her cargo by recapture in time of war. **S. agreement,** formal document outlining remuneration for and conditions under which a salvor's services are accepted by master or owner of a distressed vessel. Lloyd's standard form of agreement is almost universally adopted and to-day any remuneration stipulated in this document must be considered, in general, a tentative arrangement, since *s.* awards of any importance are decided by arbitration between the parties in interest. "*No cure—no pay*" is the outstanding feature of this contract and, in actual *s.* operations, contractors may make reasonable use of ship's gear, but "shall not unnecessarily damage, abandon, or sacrifice the same or any other of the property." **S. association,** a body composed mainly of underwriters, merchants, and shipowners having for its aim the protection of its members and their connected interests in legal matters principally concerned with insurance contracts, wrecked or stranded vessels, and their cargoes. Also, a *s.* contracting company equipped to salve stranded vessels or cargoes of wrecked or sunken craft. **S. bond,** same as *S. agreement.* **S. clause,** that included in an insurance policy which stipulates proportion of *s.* compensation payable by insurers. **S.-dock,** a kind of catamaran-built vessel designed for raising sunken submarines. It is constructed of two similar hulls connected by deck bridges forward and aft, with a gantry amidships supporting a heavy-lift crane. **S. hawser,** see **Insurance h.** in HAWSER. **S. lien,** in maritime law, that existing upon a salved vessel or cargo for *s.* compensation,—always a lawful claim against property salved. **S. loss,** in the case of vessel and cargo salved under conditions in which total loss would have occurred in the absence of timely *s.* services, or a constructive total loss situation, difference between amount salved property brings on the market and that payable for *s.*, subtracted from original total value of property loss or value for which it was insured. **S. master,** person appointed by a *s.* company or contractor to assume charge of salving operations, as in raising or refloating a vessel; also called *wrecking master,* especially in U.S. **S. vessel,** one of moderate size and draft specially equipped to refloat stranded vessels, prepare requisite attached gear preparatory to raising sunken craft, supply and operate powerful pumps, make temporary hull repairs below or above the surface, remove obstructions such as rocks by explosives, etc.; also are capable of heavy long-distance towing and often are fitted with several fire-fighting nozzles connected to special pumps. Also termed *s. tug; wrecking-ship; s.-boat.* **S. value,** also, *salved value,* that of a vessel and/or cargo upon been taken to a place of safety by *salvors.* Such value is the basis on which *s.* compensation is awarded.

SALVOR. (*Lit.* = *savior*) One who voluntarily renders services in salving property or lives of persons in distress or peril; especially, one who skillfully and enterprisingly salves or assists in salving a vessel, her cargo, or lives of her people. Such services usually meet with a generous award, particularly in cases involving exposure of *s.* to personal danger or hardship and extreme difficulties in operation concerned, in order to encourage repetition of similar undertakings.

SAMPAN. (Chin. *san pan,* three planks) Common name for a plank-built, flat or rounded bottom, open boat of China, East Indies, Malaya, and Japan. It is propelled either by sculls or sail; often has a shelter or roofing over part or fore-and-aft, in which, particularly in China, a family usually permanently lives. Also, *sanpan.*

SAMSON. Combining term connoting quality of strength or weightiness. **S.-line,** three-strand, plain-laid, tarred hemp, usually 9-thread, or slightly larger than *round-line* (*see* ROUND), used for heavy seizings and service; sometimes, untarred and used for lacings and signal halyards, in which case usually called *s. cord.* **S.-post,** a king-post; *see* **Joggle-p.** *in* POST. Also, in older wooden ships, an upright timber or stanchion set on the keelson and supporting one or more deck-beams; a heavy post used in a rigging loft, as to secure end of a stay for stretching out, serving,

etc.; a single bollard or bitt at fore end of a small vessel for making fast a tow-rope, anchor cable, etc.; a windlass-bitt, towing-bitt, or other heavy post-like fitting for securing mooring-lines. A strengthening knee that backs such post as the last-named often is termed a *s.-knee.*

SAND. The fine grains or particles of crushed or worn rock of which the sea shore or a beach commonly is composed. A *s.-bank* or *s.-bar;* often in *pl.,* as *Goodwin Sands; shifting sands.* To sprinkle with *s.* or use *s.* as an abrasive; as for foothold purposes, for scouring a deck, etc. **S. anchor,** see ANCHOR. **S.-and-canvas,** to scour, remove old varnish, etc., from wood-work with a piece of canvas held in the hand and *s.* as an abrasive,—a common job on deep-water sailing-ships. In bygone navy days this treatment was forcibly applied to a shipmate whose lack of personal cleanliness became a source of annoyance. Though out of step with regulations, the process usually produced the desired effect. **S. ballast,** see BALLAST. **S.-bank,** a shoal or raised tract of *s.* formed by action of currents. **S. bar,** as formed at mouths of swift-flowing rivers by action of current against that of in-rolling swell or breakers, or along a coast by reaction of undertow from breakers, a ridge or bank of *s.* often varying in elevation with conditions and sometimes becoming an obstruction to navigation in absence of dredging operations. **S. bores,** ridges of *s.* forming a reef or shoal. **S. dunes,** hillocks or mounds formed by dry drifting *s.;* same word as *downs.* **S. ejector,** a heavy pump used to remove *s.* or silt from a river bottom and discharge it through a conduit to shore. **S. flounder,** also called *s. fluke,* a flounder that frequents sandy bottom; the *window-pane,* a species of American turbot. **S.-glass,** see GLASS. **S.-jack,** see JACK. **S. shark,** see SHARK. **S.-strake,** the garboard strake; *see* GARBOARD. **S.-sucker,** vessel equipped with powerful pumps for dredging, that either receives dredged matter into her hold or discharges it to shore through a pipe-line or conduit; a *suction-dredge.* **S. waves,** heavy wave-like ridges of *s.* formed on comparatively shallow sea-bottoms, notably in certain areas of the North Sea; there they are said to appear after a lengthy period of strong N. to N.E. winds.

SANDBAGGER. A former type of sloop yacht remarkable for her heavy spread of canvas and so named from her carriage of *sand ballast* in handy bags which were shifted as required to counteract excessive heel due to press of sail; any boat that uses sandbags for this purpose.

SANITARY TANK. *See* TANK.

SANTA ANA. A fresh to strong hot easterly wind of desert origin, occurring in summer on southern California coast.

SARDINE. The small popularly esteemed food fish of genus *Sardinella,* included in the herring family. Same as the *pilchard,* true or European *s.* (*Sardinella pilchardus*), is taken in great quantities on Atlantic coasts of France, Spain, and Portugal, also generally in Mediterranean waters. A closely allied species is found on the American Pacific coast and another in West Indies waters. Important competition in the *s.* industry of late years has arisen in the young of herring and the menhaden among other small fishes, also preserved in olive oil and commercially presented as *sardines.*

SARGASSO SEA. Extensive area of comparatively still water in the North Atlantic, so named from *sargassum,* or *gulf weed,* that abounds on the surface throughout the region. Vortex of the general clockwise circulation of surface waters north of the Equator, its limits and extent are subject to seasonal changes, a minimum area with less E. and W. expanse occurring in winter. Perhaps the most transparent sea water is here observed and, generally, light winds prevail. The Sea may be considered to lie between latitude of Bermuda and 25° N., from 40° to 65° W. in longitude. *Cf.* GULF WEED.

SATELLITE. (L. *satellitis,* an attendant) One of the "moons," or secondary planets, revolving about their *primaries* in the solar system. *Cf.* MOON. **S. depression,** a secondary area of low barometric pressure following in the wake of a primary one.

SATURN. A major planet, sixth in order from the sun and distant from the latter about 886 millions of miles (statute), remarkable for his system of encircling rings. Second to *Jupiter* in size, has a mean diameter of 72,000 miles which presents an angular measurement of 19½″ at his nearest approach to Earth. The planet's orbital plane lies at an inclination with the ecliptic of 2° 29½′; he completes a revolution about the sun in 29½ years; and is known to have at least 10 satellites. *Saturn* is one of the four so-termed navigational planets, the others being *Venus, Mars,* and *Jupiter.*

SAUCER. A socket for the. pivot of a capstan. A round flat caisson used in raising sunken vessels.

SAURY. Also called *skipper* and *bill-fish,* an edible slender long-beaked fish about 18 inches in length found in temperate waters on both sides of the North Atlantic. Swimming in large schools, the fish put up a good display of leaping from the water when pursued.

SAVE-ALL. A net stretched under a gangway or gang-plank to catch any article that may be dropped; a tarpaulin, old sail, awning, etc., in which odds and ends of cargo, hold-sweepings, small stores, or the like are gathered for hoisting; a *catch-all.* A *drip-pan* or receptacle for catching oil or water from a machine or a port-light. A *water-sail* or any sail spread between two others in light winds; *see* **Save-all** *in* SAIL.

SAW-FISH. An ugly member of the *ray* family, found in shallow tropical seas, chiefly in vicinity of river mouths. In length from 10 to 20 feet, has a shark-like appearance with addition of an elongated flat beak, toothed on each edge, from which it gets its name. *Cf.* RAY.

SAXBOARD. Old term for the uppermost plank in the side of an open boat.

SCAFF-NET. As used in some U.S. rivers, a large *scoop-net,* usually 10 to 12 feet square, stretched at each corner by the legs of two crossing bow-shaped pieces of wood, and dropped in horizontal position from a small boom or *lifting-pole.*

SCAFFOLDING. In shipbuilding, strong temporary framework built around, and at certain places attached to, a hull for supporting workmen and their tools. It usually is erected progressively with placing of shell plating, working from bilges upward.

SCALE. Incrustation on inside of a steam boiler, consisting of deposit of calcium, magnesium, and iron carbonates, calcium sulphate, among other impurities in fresh water. Black coating of oxide on surface of newly forged or rolled plates, etc.; usually called *mill s.;* sometimes, *forge s., hammer s.* An accumulation of rust (ferro oxide) on iron and steel surfaces, as on ships' plating. A graduated measure or rule; *see* GUNTER'S SCALE. Ratio of linear measurements on a chart, drawing, or model to actual dimensions of body or object that is represented; as, *natural s.* of a chart or plan is 1: 50,000; *s.* of ½ inch to a foot. A system of numbers indicating, progressively, force, intensity, or amount; as, a *wind s.; state of sea s.; cloud s.* A series of graded values; as, a *displacement s.; deadweight s.; tons per inch s.* To remove *s.,* as from an iron surface. **Chart s.,** on harbor plans and charts of small areas the *natural s.* and *distance s.* only are given, as a rule; on Mercator's charts, *s.* for distance is taken from latitude graduations at mid-latitude concerned; gnomonic charts usually give specific directions for distance measurement. In laying off a plane chart or plan to any adopted *s.* of latitude, length of a degree of longitude will be, without appreciable error, length of latitude degree times *cosine* of latitude of the vicinity; conversely, an adopted length of degree of longitude times *secant* of latitude concerned will give length of the latitude degree, or 60 nautical miles. (For other terms designating different *scales,* see BEAUFORT; CLOUD; DISPLACEMENT; **M. sky** *in* MACKEREL; PLANE; SEA; WIND)

SCALING. Act or process of removing scale from iron or steel plating, frames, etc. *S.-hammers,* or *chipping-hammers* are used for this purpose; *cf.* CHIPPING. Also, *s.-chisels* driven by electric and pneumatic hammers are employed.

SCALLOP. Any of a large number of species of world-wide distributed bivalve mollusks constituting the genus *Pecten* and allied genera of the *Pectinidæ* family, most of which are highly esteemed as food. The shallow disk-shaped shell is more or less ridged or radially ribbed and the *sea* or *giant s.* attains a diameter of 8 inches. Many New England fishing-draggers turn to taking *s's* during summer. The shells usually prefer shallow water, but sometimes a multitude may be taken from a single *bank* in 150 to 200 fathoms. The *sea s.* is termed *Pecten magellanicus.*

SCALP. Whaling term for the entire upper part of a whale's head.

SCAMPAVIA. (*It.*)   A swift war-vessel or galley used by Neapolitans and Sicilians circa 1800. Pulled by about 40 large oars or sweeps, they were rigged also with a large main lateen sail and a small mizzen of that type. They carried a gun forward and sometimes one or two aft. In length, were about 150 feet.

SCANDALIZE. To spill or reduce spread area of a fore-and-aft sail, as by dropping the peak and hauling up the tack or the clew of a gaff sail; to render any sail ineffective in such manner, especially in fore-and-aft rig.

SCANT. Said of the wind when blowing with such force or direction that vessel sailing close will barely lie her course; as, *the breeze is s. for a N.E. course;* also, when drawing to a less favorable point, so that vessel must be close-hauled to hold her course; as, *the wind is scanting.*

SCANTLING. In shipbuilding, sizes of structural parts, including frames, beams, girders, and plating, which must be adhered to according to specifications. Minimum *s.* are prescribed for the various types and sizes of vessels by classification societies. Also, generally, softwood timber measuring less than 5″ x 5″. **Full s. ship,** *see* FULL. **S. numeral** or **number,** in connection with classification or grading of vessels (*cf.* CLASSIFICATION), one of the tabulated numerals that govern minimum sizes of structural material and certain equipment contained in a ship. Such numerals are obtained from a devised formula that is based upon dimensions of a suitable standard type of vessel. Chiefly in the interests of seaworthiness, they are designed to provide the appropriate index for sizes of frames, plating, etc., consistent with departure of proposed vessel's dimensions from those of basic type vessel. *See* **L. numerals** *in* LLOYD's. **S. of frames,** *see* FRAME. **Scheme of s.,** specification or detailed description of sizes of material and method of construction in the various parts of a ship's hull.

SCARF. (Nor. *skarv;* Sw. *skarf,* a joint)   In older *whaling,* cut made in blubber of a carcase, as in marking out the width of a blanket-piece; *see* **B.-piece** *in* BLANKET; *also* BLUBBER. A *scarf-joint,* or connection of two ends of timber or structural metal by overlapping so that material forms a continuous piece of same cross-section. Ends are chamfered, notched, tapered, etc., fitted together, and through-bolted, riveted, or welded. Parts thus united are said to be *scarfed;* the operation, *scarfing.* Where the ends are cut across longer side of material, it is termed an *edge s.;* when cut across the shorter side, a *flat s.* Simplest forms are the *plain s.,* in which tapered ends are laid face to face; *box s.* or *half-and-half lap s.,* in which half of material in each piece is cut away straight across, both ends butted squarely; and *V-s.,* consisting of one end cut like a long wedge fitting into a corresponding cutting away in the other, as chiefly used in joining spars, the whole *s.* being secured by metal bands or hoops. With view of resisting tension, as in keels, keelsons, futtocks, stemposts, etc., the *hook s.* or *hook-and-butt* is a wooden shipbuilding favorite; *see* **H.-scarf** *in* HOOK. **Key s.,** also, *keyed s.,* in this type one or more square slots are cut across the joint in such manner that a *key* may be inserted and driven to set tightly on end, or prevent longitudinal movement of, both faying parts. **Locked s.,** any type of *s.* that is set up by a locking device, such as a key or cog driven through the joint. **S. weld,** ends of steel or iron structural parts shaped to meet in a *s.* and welded together. *Thin end* of either of scarfed parts is termed a *lip of the s.*

SCARIDÆ. A family of brightly colored fishes, typical of which is the *parrot-fish* or *parrot-wrasse,* found in warmer seas. In many respects greatly resembles the *Labridæ* (*q.v.*)

SCEND. Upward or vertical motion of a vessel in heaving or pitching. Surge or onward motion imparted by a heavy sea, as that part of leeway attributed to surge of sea waves termed *s. of the sea.* To be carried or lifted, as a vessel in a seaway. Also, *send.*

SCHEAT. (Pron. *shay-ăt*)   Probably of Arabic origin, name given the star marking N.W. corner of the *Square of Pegasus.* Listed by astronomers as *β Pegasi,* it is located about 13° due north of *Markab* (*a Pegasi*), S.W. member of the Square. A line joining these two, extended northward, passes close to *Polaris* at about 61° from *Scheat;* if extended southward, comes very near to *Fomalhaut* at 45° from *Markab.* The star has a magnitude of 2.61 and lies in declination 28° N., right ascension 23 hrs. Another name for it appears in older usage as *Menkib,* from Arabic *mankib,* meaning a *shoulder. Cf.* PEGASUS.

SCHEDAR. (Ar. word; pron. *shedd-ar*)   Also written *Schedir,* one of *Cassiopeia's* brighter stars, having a magnitude varying from 2.1 to 2.6 and southernmost member of the group. When on the meridian below the pole, it is easily recognized as second star from western end of this constellation, otherwise known as the *Lady's Chair*. It is listed as a *Cassiopeiæ*. Cf. CASSIOPEIA.

SCHNAPPER. An important food fish found in Australian and New Zealand waters. Of the *Sparidæ* family, it has a long thorny dorsal fin, attains a length of 1½ to 2 feet, generally pinkish in color, and in profile, from back to mouth appears as a well-defined arc of a circle.

SCHNÖRKEL. Original tubular "breathing" apparatus developed by the Germans for use by submarines while the craft was cruising entirely submerged. The term appears to have been adopted from a code word given the invention. Now called *snorkel* in U.S. navy and *snorter* by the British.

SCHOOL. Popular term for a *shoal* or large company of fishes, porpoises, or smaller sea mammals; sometimes applied to a *gam* or *herd* of whales. When grouping together in large numbers near the surface, fishes are said to be *schooling up*. This use of the word apparently is a confusion with *shoal; see* SHOAL. A naval institution for instruction of personnel in manufacture and use of guns, projectiles, etc.; as a *gunnery s.; torpedo s.* **Navigation s.,** a nautical college or *s.; see* NAVIGATION. **S. ship,** a training-ship, often a laid-up war-vessel, on board which boys or recruits are quartered and undergo a period of preliminary instruction and training for naval or merchant marine service.

SCHOOLMASTER. The leader of a shoal of fish, herd of walruses, gam of whales, etc. A species of *snapper,* habitat in West Indies and southern U.S. waters, noted for its skill in avoiding capture.

SCHOONER. Originally, a two-masted vessel characterized by the fore-and-aft rig of her principal sails, foresail being somewhat less in area than her mainsail and both *gaff sails,* but carrying square topsails and sometimes a top-gallantsail on the fore. This type of rig has continued in common use in trading vessels about the British Isles and western Europe until recent years. Spreading of gaff sails only on each mast appears to have originated as general custom in New England in the early 1800's. Says the *New Oxford Dictionary:* "The evidence of two or three old prints seems to prove that the type now called *schooner* existed in England in 17th. century, but apparently it first came into extensive use in New England." The accepted story that a vessel of some kind of *s.* rig was first to be named a *s.* from a bystander's exclamation, *"O, how she scoons!",* at her launching, Gloucester, Mass., 1713, bears the earmarks of an invention. It seems more likely that the word may be traced to the *skonnert,* a contemporary Norwegian production of the type. In America, between 1880 and turn of the century, the *s.* increased in size from the 3-master to 5- and 6-masters, and one, the *Thomas W. Lawson,* came out in 1902 with no less than 7 lowermasts and topmasts complete. (*See* MAST) The term also is applied to a type of yacht having two masts, entirely fore-and-aft rigged but having the mainsail only gaff sail aboard, all canvas between masts being *staysails*. Perhaps no other rig has suffered as many variations without disturbing the appellative *schooner*. **Baldhead s.,** any *s.* having no topmasts. **Bermuda-rigged s.,** *see* **Bermuda r.** *in* RIG; *also* BERMUDA. **Brig-s.,** *see* **Hermaphrodite b.** *in* BRIG. **Cat s.,** a two-masted *s.* having no head sails. **Main-topsail s.,** a two- or three-masted vessel of *jackass brig* or *jackass barque* type, so named from carrying square topsails on the *mainmast*. Cf. JACKASS. **S. bark,** a kind of jackass rig that appeared about 1920 on a few 5-masted vessels owned at Bremen, Germany. Foremast and mizzenmast were fitted with square rig, the other masts fore-and-aft rigged. The craft were equipped with auxiliary power. Called by Germans *schonerbark;* the British favored *five-masted topsail schooner* as more descriptive of the short-lived oddity. **S. guy,** *see* **G.-span** *in* GUY. **S.-rigged,** having the rig of a *s.;* especially, fitted with gaff sails and staysails only. In steam vessels, when yards were dispensed with, any ship having two or more masts was called a *s.-rigged* vessel. **S. smack,** a fishing vessel having two masts and all fore-and-aft sails, mainmast being loftier than foremast and carrying a larger gaff sail. The typical swift-sailing *Gloucester fisherman,* with her fine yacht-like lines, developed from the early *s. smack*. **Scow s.,** a broad-beamed, bluff-bowed vessel used for heavy lading in sheltered waters and rigged with gaff sails. **Square topsail s.,** *see* **Topsail s. Staysail s.,** a yachting rig in which two or more staysails are set between masts instead of a gaff sail with its topsail. **Steam s.,** type of lumber-carrying vessel used on Pacific coast of U.S., so named from the original pre-steam sailing rig and still greatly resembling the earlier *s.* in hull form. These capacious vessels are from 150 to 200 feet in length, are constructed to carry heavy deck cargoes, and usually in two-masted vessels a long forward deck space is provided by placing power spaces and bridge well aft. Three-masted craft of the type have a small hold abaft the engine-room. **Tern s.,** chiefly in "Downeast" usage, a three-masted trading *s.* **Topsail s.,** original *s.* rig in which square topsails and often a top-gallantsail were carried above a gaff-and-boom sail on the foremast. On mainmast and mizzenmast sails spread with boom and gaff are set and, usually, gaff topsails above. An early type carried square topsails on the main and was termed a *main-topsail s.* or *two-topsail s.* The latter, however, is also applied to an all-fore-and-aft *s.* carrying two topmasts and a gaff-topsail on each.

SCHUYT. (Du.; pron. *skoit*) A bluff-bowed sloop-rigged fishing or trading vessel of the Holland coast. Shallow draft and broad of beam she is provided with large lee-boards to hold her own in a side wind.

SCIROCCO. *See* SIROCCO.

SCOOP. The bucket or deep shovel of a dredge. A bailer of shovel-like form for removing water by hand from a boat. To dredge as with a *s.* To take in food, as a whale, with open mouth while swimming. With *out,* to bail or dip out water, as from a boat. **S.-net,** a hand net in the form of an open bag fixed at end of a long handle for lifting fish, as from a seine, pound, etc.; a *dip-net.* A type of trawl trailed along a river-bottom in capturing fish, crabs, shrimps, etc. **Wind s.,** a curved sheet of metal placed in an air-port open side to wind for *scooping* the breeze into a cabin or other compartment.

SCOOTER. Chiefly in U.S. and Canada, a strong, beamy boat having a sloping fore-foot and equipped with runners for sailing either in water or over ice as required.

SCOPE. Limited extent, length, room, or sweep through which anything may move or be operated; as, *s.* of cable; ship's *s.* in swinging. **Long s.,** a vessel is said to be riding to a *long s.* when length of anchor-cable payed out greatly exceeds that required to hold her in depth of water at her berth. Ordinary conditions call for length of cable, or *riding s.,* as measured from hawse-pipe to anchor, equal to five times the depth of water. **Radar s.,** short for the vision-field, or *oscilloscope,* in a radar installation; *see* RADAR.

SCORE. Groove cut in the shell of a block to receive the strop; around the sides of a dead-eye to seat the stay, shroud, etc.; grooved entrance to a sheave-hole in a spar. **Pintle s.,** *see* PINTLE.

SCORPIO. (*L.* = scorpion) A conspicuous southern constellation called by sailors the *Chain-hook* from its resemblance to that instrument. It extends from N.W. to S.E. between declinations 20 to 43 degrees and right ascension 16 to 17½ hours. The bright reddish *Antares* lies close to the *handle* and another bright member of the group, *Shaula* (λ *Scorpii*) marks the *point* of the *Hook* in 37° S. The sun passes through the northern part of this constellation during latter part of November. *Cf.* ANTARES.

SCOTCH BOILER. *See* BOILER.

SCOTCH PRIZE. *See* PRIZE.

SCOTCHMAN. A batten to resist chafing; *see* **R. batten** *in* RIGGING. Also, in older use, a ring suspended in an eye on a piece of metal, which latter was seized to a shroud or stay. It served as a fair-lead for a rope or for hooking on a block.

SCOTER. A large sea-duck of genus *Oidemia* found on northern coasts of America, Europe, and Asia. Commonly called the *surf duck* and characterized by its bill which is humped or swollen at the base, the bird nests near fresh-water pools and lakes, feeds on fish, mollusks and crustaceans. The more common species are *surf s.* and *white-winged s.* of America; *velvet s.* of Asia and Europe. It has generally dark plumage. The flesh is not valued as food.

SCOTTISH, SCOTCH. Pertaining to or originating in Scotland. **S. cut,** common arrangement of cloths in jibs and staysails in which canvas is laid parallel to both leech and foot of sail, meeting in a miter (*last*) at right angles to the *luff* and terminating in the *clew.* **S. rig,** as first applied to four-masted barques about 1885, a vessel carrying double top-gallant sails and usually a jiggermast with its topmast in one spar; opposed to *English rig* in which single topgallant sails remained the conservative feature. *Cf.* JUBILEE RIG.

SCOURING. Removal or clearing-out of silt in a channel by means of a strong current. **S. basin,** also termed *sluicing basin* or *pond,* in a tidal dock system, a bay or lock in which water is retained until about low tide and then released to *scour* or wash out the dock entrance with object of clearing channel of silt.

SCOUSE. An old sailing-ship dish of stewed preserved vegetables and sea-biscuit, sometimes with pieces of meat. *Bread s.* was its usual name when minus the meat, with biscuit predominating. *Cf.* LOBSCOUSE.

SCOUT. (*O.F. escoute,* spy) A fast vessel or an airplane sent on a reconnoitering mission, as to obtain information of movements, strength, position, etc., of an enemy. A person thus engaged. An English corruption of *schuyt;* see SCHUYT. **S. cruiser,** *see* CRUISER.

SCOW. (Du. *schouw*) Beamy flat-bottomed vessel or boat used in sheltered waters for freighting or lighterage purposes, often as a ferry or for carrying a pile-driver, dredging machinery, serving as a pontoon, etc. Of simple construction, usually is of rectangular cross-section with outward sloping ends and may be either completely decked over or open to weather. The craft bears many names according to locality in which employed; as, *bateau, flatboat, deal-scow, punt, square-ender,* etc. The term often is used contemptuously in referring to a vessel having marked shortcomings; as, *the old scow can not get out of her own way! She is an awkward s. to handle; etc.* To transport by *s.;* as, *all cargo was scowed to shore by puffing tugs.* **Bilge-board s.,** a smooth-water, *s.*-shaped, racing boat, usually sloop-rigged and fitted with starboard and port *bilge-boards* instead of a single *centerboard.* The lee bilge-board only is used when boat is sailing close to wind. **Deck s.,** one having a covering deck on which all cargo is carried. Such craft sometimes are used to dispose of garbage, dredged rocks, or other loose matter by simply turning them on their bilges with a thwartship pull on the towing-bridle; *e.g.,* the daily dumping of city refuse off entrance to Havana, Cuba, is effected by this method. **Dump s.,** partly decked *s.* with open lading compartments, the bottoms of which may be swung open downward to dispose of the load. Much used in carrying away mud dredgings to sea or a special dumping-ground. **House-s.,** one on which a house is erected, as for sheltering machinery, carrying cargo requiring protection from weather, etc. **Mud-s.,** *see* MUD. **New Zealand s.,** a former two- or three-masted schooner-rigged type of *s.* employed as a cargo-carrier between Australia and New Zealand and also in the domestic trade of latter country. The craft was equipped with two or more center-boards and an unusually large rudder area. **S.-house,** a house-boat or floating dwelling; *see* **H.-boat** *in* HOUSE. **S.-sling,** often called a *tray,* a kind of cargo sling in the form of a square or oblong wood or metal receptacle, such as is used for hoisting small packages, buckets, kegs, etc.; sometimes, simply *scow.*

SCOWBANKER. A crew member of a *scow;* hence, a former English name for a poor sailor; a worthless fellow.

SCOWING. Another term for lifting an anchor by its crown; *see* BECUEING.

SCRAG WHALE. Any small whale of lean or shrivelled appearance; especially, a poor specimen of a finback or a right whale.

SCRAPE BOTTOM, To. A vessel is said to *scrape bottom* when moving and touching the sea bottom, as in passing over a shoal; also, to *touch bottom.*

SCREEN. A partition, portable frame-work, sheet of metal, canvas, etc., placed or fitted as a separating, concealing, or shielding device; as, a *wind s.; light s.; fire s.* **Air-port s.,** circular *s.* of fine wire netting fitted in an open port-light for preventing entrance of insects. **Armor s.,** steel plate around breech of a gun for protecting its crew from flying splinters, etc.; a *gun-s.* **Clear-view s.,** circular piece of plate glass, or a rotating fan before a glass, that is turned at high speed by a motor as a means of clearing one's vision in rain, falling snow, etc. It is fixed on the forward side of a navigating bridge or in a pilot-house window. **Ladder s.,** *see* LADDER. **Light s.,** *see* **L.-board** *in* LIGHT. **Magazine s.,** *see* MAGAZINE. **S. bulkhead,** a light dust-proof metal partition between boiler and engine-room spaces; any light bulkhead serving as a protection from fire, heat, wind, spray, etc., or for shutting off the view. **Solar s.,** one of the colored shade glasses fitted on a sextant for dampening the glare in taking an observation of the sun. **Smoke s.,** *see* SMOKE.

SCREW. A screw propeller. Combining word designating a particular device that embodies the mechanical principle of the *s.* or is activated or controlled by means of one or more *screws.* Now rarely heard, a vessel having a given number of *s.* propellers; as, *single s.; twin s.; triple s.* **Auxiliary s.,** *see* AUXILIARY. **Feathering s.,** *see* FEATHERING. **Lag-s.,** a lag-bolt; *see* BOLT. **Left-handed s.,** same as *left-handed propeller.* **Packing-s.,** *see* PACKING. **Quadruple s.,** vessel propelled by four *screws; cf.* remarks in PROPELLER. **Rigger's s.,** *see* RIGGER. **Right-handed s.,** same as *right-handed propeller.* **S. anchor,** *see* **Screw-m.** *in* MOORING. **S. aperture,** opening or space between propeller-post and rudder-post in which a propeller works; *cf.* **P. arch** *in* PROPELLER. **S.-bolt,** also termed *nut-bolt,* a bolt threaded at one end for setting up by means of a nut; opposed to a *clinched bolt; see* BOLT. **S. boss,** *see* **P. boss** *in* PROPELLER. **S. current,** water column projected by motion of a propeller. **S. hoist,** an endless-chain tackle in which a *s.* worm turns an upper sheave by working in the toothed periphery of the latter; *cf.* **Chain-hoist b.** *in* BLOCK. **S'ing lighter,** a scow specially built for placing *s.* moorings, as for buoys in a harbor channel. It has a central well through which *s.* anchors are lowered and *screwed* into the mud or sand bottom. The craft is fitted with sheer legs and appropriate gear for handling such moorings. **S. mooring,** *see* **Screw-m.** *in* MOORING. **S.-post,** same as *propeller-post; see* PROPELLER. **S.-shackle,** one having its pin threaded as a *s.* **S. steering-gear,** *see* STEERING. **S. steamer,** a steam-vessel propelled by one or more *screws.* **Stretching-s.,** as fitted in lengthy steering-rods or wheel-chains, one of the turnbuckles or *rigging-screws* for taking up the slack due to wear and tear. **Tangent s.,** that fitted to the index arm of a sextant for making final small adjustments in angle measured; so named from shank of *s.* being tangential to instrument's arc. **Triple s.,** a vessel having three propellers, usually a right-handed *s.* on starboard side, a left-handed one on port side, and either a right- or left-handed one in midship line. **Twin s.,** vessel having a *s.* on each side of midship line, usually same as the arrangement in a *triple s.*

SCRIEVE BOARD. See **Scrive b.** *in* BOARD.

SCRIMSHAW. Archaic term, chiefly in American deep-water ships, for ornamental designs done by hand on shells, ivory, etc. Often creditable work, such as etching a ship, was turned out by whaling-men on the teeth of sperm whales, walrus tusks, etc. To do a piece of fine work; especially, to engrave and color a design in whalebone, ivory, shells, etc. *S. work* was done by *scrimshawing.* The word had a few variants, as *scrimshandy, scrimshon,* etc.

SCRIVE BOARD. See BOARD.

SCROLL HEAD. Ornamental termination of the cutwater in the form of a volute, taking the place of a figurehead. Also, in older ships, a similar carving on the end of a rail, balustrade, etc.

SCUD. (Nor. *skudda,* to push)   Scattered fragments of vapory cloud drifting with the wind; especially, the *fracto-nimbus; see No. 8 in* CLOUD. To run or drive before a gale with little or no canvas spread.

SCULL.   Short, light, spoon-bladed oar; especially, one of a pair pulled by one person. A racing boat propelled by one or two persons using *sculls* or short oars. English dialectal form of *school* or *shoal,* as of fish. To propel a boat with a single oar over the stern. Blade of oar is moved from side to side and turned obliquely at end of each stroke, so as to administer a thrust similar in effect to action of a screw propeller. Oar is worked either in a *sculling-notch,* as that cut in upper edge of a square-sterned boat, or in a *rowlock;* sometimes in a *becket.*

SCULP.   To *flense* or remove both skin and blubber from a seal. Among Newfoundland sealers, a broad-bladed clasp-knife used for this purpose is termed a *sculping-knife.*

SCUM-COCK.   Valve fitted on a boiler for blowing off impurities, grease, etc., from surface of the water; a *brine-cock; surface blow-off cock.*

SCUNNER.   In sealing vessels, an ice-master or one who directs vessel's course through floating ice. He is stationed in the fore top. Distinguished from the *barrel-man,* or lookout at a loftier perch; *cf.* BARREL. (Chiefly in Newfoundland usage)

SCUP.   Another name for the American *porgy. See* PORGY.

SCUPPER.   Any opening for carrying off water from a deck, either directly or through a *scupper-pipe.* Scupper-pipes and waste-pipes leading from decks below a weather deck, or from enclosed superstructures usually are led to ship's bilges, but where leading overboard, their outboard ends are above load waterline and fitted with *storm,* or non-return, *valves.* In *pl.,* the waterways at side of a weather deck or in way of the *scuppers.* **S.-grating,** *see* GRATING. **S.-hose,** a canvas tube fitted to outboard orifice of a *s.* to lead waste water clear of ship's side. **S.-nail,** *see* NAIL.

SCURVY.   A disease formerly common on long-voyage sailing-ships, as when crew was restricted to a limited range of nutrition, or diet of salt or preserved provisions over a period of considerable duration. Patients suffered general debility accompanied by sores and flabbiness of flesh in legs, spongy bleeding gums, and bleeding from mucous membranes. By U.S. law (*46 U.S.C. 666*) *anti-scorbutics,* or *s.* preventive, must be provided the crew within 10 days after salt provisions mainly have been served and so long as such diet continues: "Lime or lemon juice and sugar daily at the rate of half a pint per week for each member of the crew."

SCUTTLE.   A small opening in a deck or elsewhere usually fitted with a cover or lid, or a door, as for access to a compartment, or hatchway, etc., or a means of escape; a *port-hole.* To cut a hole in the bottom or otherwise allow entry of water for purpose of sinking a vessel. **Air-s.,** *see* **A.-port** *in* AIR. **Bunker s.,** small circular opening fitted with a cast-iron cover flush with the deck, such as is found in tugs and other coal-burning vessels for bunkering; also, *coal s.; deck s.* **Cap-s.,** *see* CAP. **Escape s.,** *see* **E.-hatch** *in* ESCAPE. **Gammoning-s.,** same as *g'ing hole; see* GAMMON. **S.-butt,** a cask fitted with a bilge opening and lid for use of a dipper, originally secured on deck near the galley for containing the daily supply of drinking and cooking water; said to have been named from its position, in older ships, in vicinity of the *galley s.* Hence, in modern usage, a drinking fountain for use of crew. From gossip exchanged at the *s.-butt,* galley news and general rumor often is referred to as *s.-butt;* as, *the s.-butt has it we call at Gib for orders.* **S.-frame,** metal rim or frame around a port-hole or a bull's eye.

S.D.   Abbrev. SEMIDIAMETER, *q.v.*

SEA.   The ocean in general; *see* OCEAN. Large body of salt water, less in area and generally forming an arm of an ocean; sometimes almost entirely land-locked; as, *Mediterranean, Black,* and *Red Seas.* An area bounded by or containing a number of islands; as, *Sea of Japan; Caribbean Sea.* Some large lakes having more or less salty content are called *seas;* as, *Caspian Sea; Dead Sea;* these, incidentally, being respectively 85 and 1290 feet *below* mean ocean level. A wind-driven wave; flow or course of waves; as, *vessel shipped a s.; a heavy s. is running.* The *sea* surface; as, *a smooth s.; a rough s.* In an adjectival sense, indicating something pertaining to the *sea* in compound terms; as, *s.-anchor; s.-boots; s.-serpent.* Descriptive of direction *toward* which waves are advancing relative to ship's fore-and-aft line, terms such as the following are used: *beam s.; following s.; head s.; quartering,* or *quarterly, s.;* direction *from,* as *a northerly s.; a S.W. s.* In log-books and weather records, *state of the sea* may be indicated according to the following generally accepted scale or designating letter:—

State of the Sea

0	Calm	*(height)*	B. Broken or irregular
1	Smooth	*less than 1 ft.*	C. Choppy, short, or cross
2	Slight	*1 to 3 ft.*	G. Ground swell
3	Moderate	*3 to 5 ft.*	H. Heavy swell
4	Rough	*5 to 8 ft.*	L. Long rolling
5	Very rough	*8 to 12 ft.*	M. Moderate
6	High	*12 to 20 ft.*	S. Smooth
7	Very high	*20 to 40 ft.*	T. Tide-rips
8	Precipitous	*Over 40 ft.*	
9	Confused		

Character of Swell

0 No swell	5 Moderate, long
1 Low, short or average	6 Heavy, short
2 Low, long	7 Heavy, average length
3 Moderate, short	8 Heavy, long
4 Moderate, average length	9 Confused swell

Arm of the s., *see* ARM. **At s.,** on the *s.;* attached to a vessel on a voyage, whether in port or on the high seas, as said of a crew member in legal parlance; on a passage from one port to another, said of a vessel. **Closed s.,** *see* MARE. **Cross s.,** *see* CROSS. **Deep-s.,** pertaining to or used in greater depths, as distinguished from coastal waters; as, *deep-s. soundings; see* DEEP. To **follow the s.,** to go to *s.;* to make a profession or vocation of going to *s.* **Four seas,** *see* FOUR. **Green s.,** *see* GREEN. **Half seas over,** half way across the *s.;* hence, well on the way to drunkenness. **High s.,** *see* HIGH. **Hollow s.,** a precipitous curling wave or continued series of waves that rise steeply in shoaling water or when meeting a current; dangerous state of *s.* for small craft, or that immediately prior to "breaking" or final stage in which wave crests fall over and forward of body of wave. To **kill the s.,** *see* KILL. **Ladies' s.,** *see* LADY. **Open s.,** *see* OPEN. **Perils of the s.,** *see* **M. risk** *in* MARINE. To **put to s.,** to leave port; *see* PUT. To **quarter the s.,** to steer such course as will bring the *s.* (waves) on vessel's quarter. **Rolling s.,** waves having small or no crests and advancing in pronounced regularity of form and size; properly, *rolling swell.* **Rough s.,** state of *s.* surface in which waves are from 5 to 8 feet in height, as measured vertically from trough to crest, or those driven by a fresh breeze. Such waves vary in length, measured from crest to crest of successive waves, from 30 to 50 feet. *See* WAVE. **S. anchor,** *see* ANCHOR; *also* DRAG. **S.-claw anchor,** *see* ANCHOR. **S. acorn,** *see* ACORN; *also* BARNACLES. **S. bag,** a duffle bag; cylindrical-shaped canvas receptacle used by sailors for carrying personal clothing. **S. bank,** a dike or breastwork to protect a shore-line from inroads of the *s.;* a *s.-wall.* **S. bass,** *see* BASS. **S. bear,** any fur-bearing seal; the sea-lion; the sea-elephant. A polar bear. **S. beef,** salt horse; flesh of whales, porpoises, etc. **S. bird,** any bird frequenting the ocean or its coasts; a *s.-fowl.* **S. biscuit,** *see* BISCUIT. **S.-bladder,** a Portuguese man-o'-war. **S.-boat,** boat or vessel adapted to open *s.* navigation; considered with reference to her behavior in a heavy *s.,* a vessel may be a *good s.-boat,* a *poor s.-boat,* etc. A light lifeboat kept in readiness for lowering in cases of emergency at sea. **S.-boots,** high waterproof boots worn by sailors. **S.-borne,** carried over the *s.;* as *s.-borne commerce.* **S.-bow,** a miniature rainbow often seen when sun shines through spray, as about ship's bows or crests of breaking waves; a *marine-bow; cf.* RAINBOW. **S.-bream,** *see* BREAM. **S. breeze,** *see* BREEZE. **S. buoy,** outermost buoy, or that marking the entrance to a fairway or a port. **S. calf,** the *s. dog* or harbor seal, a small species found close to shore and often ascending rivers; native to northern Atlantic and Pacific waters north of latitude 35°. It is named for its cry which resembles that of a calf. **S. canary,** among fishermen and whalers, the *beluga,* or white whale; *see* BELUGA. **S. card,** old term for a chart; also, the compass-card. **S. captain,** a shipmaster or person actively engaged as master of a merchantman. **S. catfish,** any of several *cats* chiefly inhabiting tropical seas; especially, the *gaff-topsail catfish,* so named from its high dorsal fin, found on southeastern and Gulf coasts of U.S. **S. chart,** a marine map or chart. **S.-chest,** a sailor's box or chest; *see* **S's chest** *in* SAILOR. Also, that part of an intake between ship's side and a *sea-valve.* **S.-cock,** a valve or cock controlling connection of a pipe with the sea; used with intake system for flooding ballast-tanks, sanitary circulation, etc. **S. connections,** such valves as control entry or discharge of water through ship's shell plating; especially those below ship's water-line, such as intakes for fire, ballast, and sanitary pumping systems, circulating pumps, boiler blow-downs, etc. **S. cow,** the manatee or the dugong; sometimes, the walrus; *see* DUGONG; *also* MANATEE. **S.-crow,** locally applied to various marine birds, perhaps through indifference to correct names for such; as, cormorant, gull, jaeger, skua, etc. **S.-delivery line,** *see* LINE. **S.-devil,** the devil-fish; a small voracious shark; *see* MANTA; ANGEL-FISH. **S.-dog,** an old sailor; a pirate; the *s. calf* or harbor seal; the dog-fish. **S.-dove,** the rotche or dovekie, a species of small *auk;* the black guillemot. **S.-eagle,** any of several eagles that feed chiefly on fish and live near the seacoast. Important species are the *white-tailed eagle* and *Kamchatkan s. eagle* of northern Europe and Asia; the osprey; also, sometimes, the *eagle ray.* **S.-eel,** *see* CONGER EEL. **S.-elephant,** largest of seals; *see* OTARY. **S.-fight,** a naval battle; armed conflict between vessels at sea. **S. floor,** bottom of the ocean or its contiguous waters. **S. fog,** low-lying fog along a seacoast, occurring during light off-shore winds or in calm weather when land is much colder than the *s.* **S.-fox,** the *fox-shark* or thrasher; also, *s.-ape; see* SHARK. **S.-gasket,** a fixed gasket or furling-line, such as is used at sea. **S.-gate,** outer or supplementary gate in a tidal dock system, use as a safeguard against a heavy sea; the main entrance to a tidal basin or dock system. **S.-going,** *see* SEAGOING. **S.-hog,** also, *s.-pig;* the porpoise. **S.-horse,** *see* HORSE. **S. ivory,** that obtained from marine animals, as from the walrus's tusks. **S. king,** title assumed by a Norse pirate chief upon starting out on a cruise (*Historical*); *cf.* VIKING. **S. kindly,** said of a vessel that behaves well in heavy weather, *i.e.,* with respect to rolling, pitching, and shipping water. **S.-ladder,** *see* LADDER. **S. laws,** *see* LAW. **S. lawyer,** a crew member of the argumentative, captious, or litigious type, ever ready to question orders rather than to obey them. **S. legs,** referred to one's ability to walk properly on the deck while ship rolls and pitches, a novice is said to have "found his *s. legs*"; hence, freedom from seasickness. **S. letter,** *see* LETTER. **S. level,** surface level at its mean position, half-tide level, or midway between mean high and mean low water levels. From this datum, land elevations, heights of lights, etc., are measured. Careful observations show that *mean s. level* undergoes a cycle of small changes through a period of 19 years. *Cf.* LEVEL. **S.-lion,** a large eared seal of Pacific waters, chief of which is the *Stella* of the Aleutian Islands region, a species attaining 12 feet in length and weight of 1400 pounds. A smaller genus, *Otaria jubata,* inhabits the west coast of South America; the *Californian s.-lion* is still smaller. Another small one is found on the south coast of Australia. The animal's coat is of coarse hair without the silky inner fur and so has little commercial value. **S. mark,** *see* MARK. **S.-mew,** *see* MEW. **S. mile,** the nautical or geographical mile; *see* MILE. **S. mule,** a scow-like tug designed to push or pull working-craft in sheltered waters. The boat usually is fitted with a propeller that may be raised or lowered according to depth of water present. **S.-needle,** a gar-fish; *see* GAR. **S.-otter,** *see* OTTER. **S.-ox,** the walrus. **S.-painter,** *see* PAINTER. **S. pass,** same as *s. letter.* **S. pay,** remuneration for one's services during a voyage or commissioned status of ship, as opposed to *port* or *shore pay,* or that earned while ship lies at a home port or is laid up. **S. pilot,** *see* PILOT. **S.-pig,** a *s.-hog;* a porpoise; a dolphin; a dugong. **S.-plane,** *see* SEAPLANE. **S. power,** a nation of great naval strength; a nation's striking capabilities in naval warfare. **S. puss,** also termed *s. purse,* a whirlpool-like undertow due to effect of breakers over uneven depths; an undertow along a beach. **S.-quake,** agitation of the sea, sometimes accompanied by shocks, due to a submarine earthquake. **S. rate,** *see* RATE. **S. reach,** *see* REACH. **S. ring,** old term for a type of astrolabe; or instrument for observing altitudes of the sun; *see* ASTROLABE. **S. risk,** in marine insurance, hazard of injury or loss attending carriage of goods by sea. **S.-room,** space at sea needed for maneuvering a vessel; especially, that required in weathering a storm. **S.-rover,** *see* ROVER. **S. scallop,** *see* SCALLOP. **S. service,** in naval usage, service at sea as distinguished from shore duty; a period of active duty aboard ship during a cruise or voyage; total experience at sea. **S. sled,** a type of high-speed, surface-skimming, small, powered craft having a square sloping fore end and usually an inverted V-shaped channel in the bottom center line. Purpose of such channel is to imprison air for cushioning effect and lessening resistance. **S.-snake,** any of several species of venomous serpents that live in and swim at surface of the sea, chiefly in tropical parts of the Pacific and in the Indian Ocean. They feed on fishes and gen-

erally are of 3 to 6 feet in length, although some of 10 and 12 have been reported. **S.-steps,** metal bars or plates fitted on sides of naval ships for boarding from boats, etc., at sea. **S. stock,** provisions or stores for use at sea; *s. stores.* **S.-train,** the various auxiliaries carrying ammunition, fuel, supplies, etc., also repair and hospital ships, attached to a long-range operating naval fleet. A ferry for transporting a train of railway cars; *see* **C.-ferry** *in* CAR. **S. wall,** an embankment or wall for protection against waves or tidal action along a shore or waterfront. **S. watches,** regular hours of duty at sea as distinguished from *anchor watches; see* WATCH. **S. water,** specific gravity is about 1.025; weight 64 lbs. per ft.^{3}; one ton of 2240 lbs. has a volume of 35 ft.^{3}; its pressure is very nearly equal to four-ninths the depth in feet, expressed in lbs. per in.^{2} *See remarks in* OCEAN. **S. waves,** *see* WAVE. **S.-wife,** a wrasse of European waters related to the *tautog.* **S.-wolf,** a viking; a pirate; the *s.-lion;* the *s.-elephant;* the European bass. **S.-wrack,** marine vegetation cast up on the shore; such as eelgrass, various weeds, etc., and, especially, *kelp.* **Seven seas,** the seven oceans, viz., *North* and *South Atlantic; North* and *South Pacific; Indian; Arctic; Antarctic.* **Short s.,** irregular, broken, or interrupted sea waves, such as often occur where a current sets against a stiff wind or waves from different directions cross each other, particularly in comparatively shallow water in both cases.

SEABOARD. The seacoast. That part of a country bordering on a seacoast. At, near, or bordering on the seacoast; as, a *s.* town.

SEACOAST. Shore of the sea or ocean; seaboard; seashore.

SEAFARING. Following the vocation of a mariner or *seafarer.*

SEAGOING. Designed or fitted for navigating the open sea or ocean, as distinguished from inland or sheltered-water sailing; as, a *seagoing vessel;* a *s. tug.* Seafaring.

SEAL. Any pinniped except the walrus; a carnivorous mammal of either of the families *Phocidæ* or *Itariidæ,* the true and eared seals, respectively. Expert swimmers and divers, they are noted adepts in capture of fish on which they chiefly feed. *Phocidæ* members differ from the *Otariidæ* in that the hind flipper-like limb is really the animal's tail, while in the otary two distinct flippers function as that member; also, no exterior ears are present in the former. Both have two forward flippers. Chiefly inhabiting colder coasts and floating ice, they are hunted for their fur, hide, and oil. The *fur seals* and sea-lions belong to the *Otariidæ; cf.* OTARY. **Elephant s.,** also, *sea-elephant,* largest of seals, habitat in Southern Hemisphere, so named from its lengthy snout. Males of the species are said to reach a length of 20 feet. Belongs to the otaries. **Fur s.,** any of several included in the *Otariidæ* and valuable for their silky fur beneath the usual coat of hair and thus distinguished from the *hair s.* Found in higher latitudes of both hemispheres, more important is the *Callorhinus alascanus* that breeds on Pribilof Islands, Alaska. Once hunted to near extinction, under present U.S. Fish and Wild Life protection the Pribilof *rookery* now is the basking home of some 3,800,000 fur-bearing seals. **Harp s.,** the common *Arctic* or *Greenland s.,* commonly found from coasts of Newfoundland to polar regions. Also called *hopper s.,* it is called a *harp* from the male's harp-shaped patch on each side of his light-colored body. This *hair s.* is taken in great numbers about April of each year by Newfoundland sealing vessels,—moderate sized composite ships,—that are restricted to one voyage for their annual catch from the thousands of animals congregating on the southward drifting ice-floes. In its second year the *harp s.* is known as a *Bedlamer;* in its third year, a *turner;* the young are called *bluesides;* and female is known as a *jennie-harp.* **S. fishery,** industry of taking seals; also, *sealery.*

SEALED ORDERS. *See* ORDER.

SEALER. Seal-hunting vessel; any craft used in taking seals. A member of a sealing-vessel's crew.

SEAM. Line of meeting or union, as that of edges or butts of two planks or plates, cloths of canvas, etc.; a fissure or crack in a plate. **Bight s.,** also termed *false* and *blind s.,* a doubling of the canvas in middle of cloth to form a *flat s.* **Butt s.,** line of union of butt ends of two planks or plates. **Cord s.,** in canvas, one in which edges of two cloths are laid together, curled over, and sewn to form a *rib* or *cord.* Used to stiffen the canvas, as in sides of a bag, a draw-bucket, etc. **Flat s.,** canvas *s.* in which edge of one cloth is laid flat on the other cloth and both edges stitched to opposite cloths, as in joining the material in a sail. **Gunning a s.,** act of forcing stop-leak putty, red lead, or the like into a *lap s.* in plating; *cf.* **Red-lead g.** *in* GUN. **Lap s.,** in plating, junction of edges in which plates overlap each other; any lapping *s.,* as in clinker-laid planking in a boat. **Monk s.,** *see* **M.-stitching** *in* MIDDLE. **Round s.,** one in which edges of canvas are sewn together without lapping. **S. composition,** *see* GLUE, MARINE. **S.-nail,** *see* NAIL. **S. strap,** piece of metal joining butt ends of plating; *see* **B.-strap** *in* BUTT.

SEAMAN. (A.S. *sæman*) A mariner; a sailor; a seafarer, as opposed to a landsman; "a man versed in the ways of the sea and ships." Generally, and in U.S. legal sense, a *s.* is any person engaged or employed in the navigation of a vessel in any capacity. Britain's *Merchant Shipping Act (1894)* defines a *s.* as "any person (except masters, pilots, and apprentices duly indentured and registered) employed or engaged in any capacity on board any ship."

Able s., usually abbrev. A.B. (*able-bodied*), one employed in the deck department, qualified by experience (usually three years' sea service on deck), and capable of performing all duties required in management, maintenance, and operation of his vessel; including proficiency in steering by compass, taking soundings with hand lead, keeping lookout, splicing rope, rigging cargo-gear, running deck machinery, and hoisting or lowering boats. **Merchant s.,** *see* MERCHANT. **Ordinary s.,** a deck hand having less experience than that required for rating or certificate of *able s.* Formerly, one who served as deck-boy for one year was eligible for rating as *O.S.* (as usually abbrev.); now, a beginner usually rates as O.S., or lowest rating carried. **S.-gunner,** one holding rating of *s.* while in training for proficiency in gunnery. Ordinarily, his next step is *gunner's mate.* (In U.S. navy, ratings corresponding to *A.B.* and *O.S.* of the merchant service are called *Seaman* and *Apprentice Seaman*).

SEAMANSHIP. Art of, or skill used in, navigating and maneuvering a vessel; skill of a good seaman. **Deck s.,** management, practical use, and maintenance of gear and equipment on the decks and exterior parts of a vessel; including handling and care of cargo gear, ground tackle, mooring-lines, sounding gear, life-saving equipment, and gangways. **Marline-spike s.,** craft of splicing, seizing, serving, fitting, etc., of fiber and wire rope, as practised among seamen.

SEAMEN'S LIEN. That of a seaman against a vessel for wages due. Classed as a *preferred maritime lien,* it ranks first in priority claims; *see* **Maritime l.** *in* LIEN.

SEAMEN'S RECORDS. U.S. Coast Guard maintains a record of all persons to whom documents have been issued authorizing them to serve as crew members of U.S. vessels of the *merchant marine;* also, all records of issues of licenses, suspensions and revocations of certificates of service and licenses, and current employment of merchant seamen. In Great Britain, the Registrar-General of Shipping and Seamen at London performs a similar national service.

SEAMING TWINE. Sail twine used in sewing seams; made of cotton or flax, its size depending on its number of threads, or the *ply.* For heavy canvas, 6- to 8-ply twine; for light work, a 4- to 5-ply; 6-ply being an all-round convenient size. Excepting for fine light work, the twine is doubled in sewing. It is always well waxed upon reeving it in the needle, as an anti-kinking measure, and a sewing length of about four feet is used.

SEAMLESS. Having no seam; especially, in something made of metal; as certain high grade piping or tubing. **S. boat,** a metal boat having a shell without seam. Such craft, usually the lifeboat type, are made of two single stamped plates riveted to the keel bar which latter is turned upward at each end to form the stem- and stern-posts. The framing, thwarts, etc., are fitted afterward.

SEAPLANE. An airplane designed to take off from and maneuver upon the water. *Rules for Preventing Collisions at Sea,* as drawn up at *International Convention for Safety of Life at Sea, 1948,* include provision for lights, fog-signals, steering rules, etc., for such craft. Meaning of the term as therein defined is "a flying-boat or any other aircraft designed to maneuver on the water."

SEARCH. To examine or explore with a specific object in view; as, to *s. for contraband;* to *s. a vessel* (as for stowaways, a piece of cargo, etc.) To exercise the **right of visit and s.;** *see* RIGHT. **S.-light,** *see* LIGHT.

SEARCHER. A revenue or customs officer who inspects or examines vessels, passengers' luggage, etc., for concealed dutiable goods. An instrument for examining large guns for possible defects in the bore.

SEASHORE. Coast of the sea; land adjacent to a sea or ocean. In a legal sense, the **foreshore;** *see* FORE. The seaside.

SEASONING. Process, either artificial or natural, in which timber parts with a major proportion of its moisture content, thereby increasing its life and adaptability for ship and boat construction. Timber *seasoned* in the open air, while consuming months and even years in the treatment, is found superior in every way to rapid kiln-dried product. **Water-s.,** the term for placing hardwood ship timber (logs) under water for several years, as was customary in old "wooden-wall" navy days. Oak timber thus treated was found more durable and less affected by warping than the dried material. **Weather-s.,** in former wooden vessel construction, where urgent demand for the launched hull was not present, the completely framed body was allowed to stand for several months completely exposed to the elements for *conditioning* before the outside planking work was begun.

SEATING. A bed or rest in which a more or less upright timber is butted or set; as the *floor s.* in wooden vessels, or that part of the deadwood in which a deep floor (or floors) is *seated* and faired. **Engine s.,** *see* **E. foundation** *in* ENGINE.

SEAWARD. In the direction of or toward the sea; as, *the stream flows s.* Out from the coast or toward the offing; as, *the boat stood s. on a long reach.*

SEAWATER. *See* **S. water** *in* SEA.

SEAWAY. Progress through the water at sea. Motion of sea waves. A vessel is said to be *in a s.* when pitching or rolling motion due to a rough sea is markedly present.

SEAWEED. Any of the many plants or grasses growing in all seas, either floating freely or attached to rocks or the sea-floor; specifically, those of the *Alga* group, as dulse, sea-lettuce, kelp, etc., and the *Sargassum* species of tropical waters. Most important of these is the *kelp.* *Cf.* GULF WEED; KELP; *also,* **S.-wrack** *in* SEA.

SEAWORTHINESS. State of being seaworthy; that reasonably safe and proper condition in which a vessel's hull and equipment, her cargo and stowage thereof, machinery, and complement of crew are deemed adequate to undertake a specified sea voyage or to be employed in a particular trade. **Certificate of s.,** *see* CERTIFICATE. A charterer, under a *bare boat* or *demise charter* agreement, generally is responsible for maintenance of vessel's *s.,* while in the case of a *voyage* or *time charter,* shipowner is the responsible party, faulty cargo stowage excepted.

SECOND.[1] Next in order of importance, place, or time; immediately following the *first;* secondary; subordinate. **S. assistant engineer,** in U.S. vessels, officer ranking third in the engine department and who usually is in charge of the 12 to 4 watch at sea. He is charged with the maintenance of all fire-room auxiliaries and proper functioning of boiler operations, taking in fuel, keeping account of fuel consumption, etc. Corresponding rank, with similar duties, is *third engineer* in British merchant ships; *see* ENGINEER. **S. difference,** in determining with precision the values of declination, right ascension, etc., of sun, moon, and planets corresponding to a given Greenwich Mean Time, as from the Nautical Almanac, the hourly difference or rate of change in a value that corresponds to instant of half interval between the even hour of G.M.T. and that given in problem concerned. **S. dog watch,** *see* WATCH. **S. hand,** in fishing vessels of Great Britain, a qualified seaman acting as "mate" or assistant to the skipper. **S. magnitude,** comparative brightness of a star; *see* MAGNITUDE. **S. numeral** or **number,** *see* **L. numerals** *in* LLOYD'S.

SECOND.[2] A measure of time equal to one-sixtieth of a minute. Also, a measure of arc, or in angular measure, equal to one-sixtieth of a minute and expressed by the symbol "; thus, two and one-quarter minutes $(2\frac{1}{4}')$ may be written $2'15''$. In the conversion of *arc* to *time,* as in expressing a difference of longitude as a time interval, $15''$ (arc) $= 1$ *sec.* (time), and $1'' = .067$ *sec.* An arc of $1''$ in a great circle on the earth's surface represents, very nearly, a distance of $101\frac{1}{2}$ feet. *Cf.* MINUTE.

SECONDARY. Subordinate; next in importance though functioning similarly to a primary; a satellite or moon. **S. circle,** a great circle passing through the poles of another and so having its plane perpendicular to the latter; thus, an *hour circle* is *s.* to the *equinoctial.* **S. low,** *see* LOW. **S. meridian,** *see*

MERIDIAN. **S. planet,** any satellite of a planet; *see* PLANET. **S. port,** as listed in Tide Tables, any port for which time and height of *high* (and sometimes *low*) *water* may be obtained by applying the constants given to time and height at a *standard port of reference.*

SECRET-BLOCK. *See* BLOCK.

SECTION. A drawing or representation of internal parts of a vessel, as would appear if cut through by an intersecting plane. **Areas of sections,** *see* AREA. **Midship s.,** *see* MIDSHIP. **S. modulus,** constant quantity that expresses the measure of longitudinal strength, or resistance to bending strain in a vessel's hull under unit conditions. It is equal to the *moment of inertia* about neutral axis of *midship s.* divided by distance of farthest stressed member above or below that axis.

SECTIONAL DOCK. *See* DOCK.

SECTOR. Arc of the horizon through which a light is designed to show in a particular color, or is not visible therein. On charts, it usually is indicated by lines representing its limiting bearings. **Danger s.,** that through which a light shows *red,* indicating presence of a danger, such as a rock or shoal, within such *s.* **Zenith s.,** *see* ZENITH.

SECUNNI. Also, *seacunny;* Anglo-Indian name for a lascar helmsman or quartermaster.

SECURE. To make fast, stow, or lash in place, as a boat, movable cargo, a spar, a gun, etc.

SEE A FOX, To. *See* FOX.

SEECATCH. (Russ. *syekach*) In Alaska, the adult male fur seal or sea-bear. Also, *seecatchie.*

SEEKING. Among pilots, act of sailing about off a port or coast in search of, or to intercept, any inward-bound vessels requiring services of a pilot. The practice to-day is greatly obviated due to the grouping of pilots at a single station or on board a pilot-vessel stationed at entrance of almost any principal port.

SEEL. Now almost obsolete term for the laboring of a vessel in a heavy sea; also, to roll or lurch; or heel to pressure of sail.

SEICHE. (*Fr.*) A remarkable fluctuation or oscillation of water level often occurring on lakes and land-locked seas, particularly where the land in the vicinity is mountainous. The phenomenon, not well understood, lasts from a few minutes to several hours and is thought to arise from a sudden local inequality in barometric pressure.

SEINE. A lengthy net used in the open sea or from the shore for capturing fish that swim near the surface in schools. It is set in vertical position by floats attached to its upper edge and sinkers at lower edge and is manipulated to encircle the fish as a school approaches. The *s.* has many varieties, ranging from a simple net to the bag-like drawstring arrangement for completely imprisoning the catch. Perhaps, for *boat-seining,* most common in use is the *purse* or *tuck s.* which is *pursed* or drawn together to envelop the catch as it is encircled. A *s.* hauled to shore is termed a *beach* or *shore s.,* sometimes a *long-haul s.;* among those worked from boats are the *capelin s., deep-sea s., drag s., drift s.,* and *purse s.* To catch fish with a *seine,* or engage in *seining.* To **boat a s.,** to haul a *s.* with its attached gear on board the *seiner* or *seining-boat* and stow it in such manner that it may be payed out *all clear* for setting. **S.-boat,** a *seiner,* or large boat used to carry a *s.* and crew engaged in *seining.* **S. float,** one of the supporting pieces of cork or light wood attached at intervals to the head of a *s.* The term is also given the required spherical or ellipsoidal blocks acting as supporting *floats* to each bight in a life-line, such as is fitted around a lifeboat's gunwale or sides of a life-raft. **S. gang,** group of fishermen working together in the operation of *seining.*

SEINER. A seine-boat; one engaged in *seining.*

SEISMIC WAVES. *See* WAVE.

SEIZE. To fasten or bind with turns of small cordage, as one rope to another, a block to a stay, etc.

SEIZING. The turns of marline, spunyarn, wire, or special cordage used to *seize* one object to another; act of fastening with turns of small cordage, or *seizing-stuff.* One of the pieces of small rope that secure, at intervals of several yards, the head of a *drift* net to its warp, which, in turn, is suspended parallel with the surface by buoy-ropes, or those attached to floats along the entire length of line of nets; *cf.* **D.-net** *in* DRIFT. **Cross s.,** turns of small stuff securing two ropes that cross each other; a *s.* in which the turns cross each other, as in securing a batten across shrouds. **End s.,** *see* END. **Flat s.,** a series of turns lying *flat,* as in securing two ropes to each other side by side; it is completed by two cross turns around the whole and between the ropes. **Racking s.,** *see* RACKING. **Rose s.,** *see* Rose l. *in* LASHING. **Round s.,** similar to a *flat s.* but with a second or riding layer of turns. **S. stuff,** marline, spunyarn, houseline, roundline, or such small cordage suitable for *seizing* work; also, galvanized wire strand one-sixteenth to one-fourth inch in diameter, having 7 to 19 threads. **Throat s.,** a *round s.* made on the parts forming an eye, at *throat of the eye,* for setting a thimble in a block-strop or for securing together the parts of a double stay at fore side of a mast.

SEIZURE. Arrest of a vessel and/or her cargo as by a writ of attachment with view of satisfying a lien or libel in admiralty; for violation of a public law, such as smuggling or carrying on an illicit trade; etc. *Cf.* **R. of pursuit** *in* RIGHT.

SELF. Prefix used in compound terms to denote that object named is itself the agent in its usually obvious purpose or use. **S.-bailing, s.-draining, s.-emptying,** as applied to a special lifeboat, cockpit in a small vessel, etc., indicates such is designed to free itself of water by gravity *via* scuppers fitted with non-return valves. **S.-closing door,** *see* **Watertight d.** *in* DOOR. **S.-igniting water light,** *see* **Water l.** *in* LIGHT. **S.-lubricating block,** a purchase-block fitted with an automatic device for lubricating its sheave-bearing arrangement. **S.-reefing topsail,** as fitted in some small European vessels, a square topsail having a *roller* on under side of its yard designed to *roll up* the sail in shortening canvas, and so obviate reefing by use of reef-points as in usual procedure. An early form of this rolling notion, in which the yard itself acted as the "roller," appeared about a century ago; *see* CUNNINGHAM PATENT REEF. **S.-righting boat,** a type of coastal lifeboat designed to quickly right herself upon being capsized. Her principal distinguishing features are high whaleback ends containing air-tanks and an unusually heavy metal keel. **S.-trimming hatchway,** *see* HATCH. **S.-trimming vessel,** so termed from her structural arrangement which allows a bulk cargo to require little or no trimming in the loading process. Hatches are usually wide and no 'tween decks interfere with flow of the grain, coal, ore, etc., taken in. A midship fore-and-aft bulkhead is provided and in some larger craft the upper outside corners are built up as *wing ballast tanks* of triangular section. **S.-unloading vessel,** as chiefly employed on the Great Lakes, one carrying an installation of elevators and conveyors for completely unloading a cargo in bulk without any assistance from shore.

SELVAGE. (Old Du. *selfegge; self,* self; *egge,* edge) Also, *selvedge;* edge of canvas or sail-cloth woven so as to prevent raveling. Side edges, or *guarding,* of a fishing-net, as distinguished from the head and foot.

SELVAGEE. A length of cordage consisting of parallel-laid rope-yarns marled together or a number of parallel wires bound as one with wire service. **S. strop,** a rope strop made like a hank or skein and marled *selvagee fashion.* Size for size, it is more pliable; takes a better grip on a stay, shroud, etc., in setting up with a tackle; and is stronger than the ordinary laid rope.

SEMAPHORE. (Gr. *sema,* sign; *phora,* motion) Apparatus by which distant signals are shown, as by a system of lights, flags, disks, or movable arms, for controlling traffic in a canal or other waterway; indicating depth of water in a fairway, dock entrance, or on a bar; announcing local ice and weather conditions; etc. The *International Code* or military system of signaling in which letters of the alphabet are represented by various positions of one's out-stretched arms,—usually with the addition of short-staffed hand-flags,—with relation to the body; or, mechanically, by wooden or metal arms set at various angles with a post or pole. Messages always are made in plain language by this means. U.S. Hydrographic Office publication *H.O. 87, International Code of Signals, Vol. I,* contains instructions in *s. signaling.*

SEMI. (*L.* = half) Prefix signifying *half;* sometimes *partly* or *incompletely.* It is usually unaccompanied by the *hyphen,* except before capitalized terms. **S'box beam,** *see* BEAM. **S'circle,** half a circle or an arc of 180°. Half a circular area, as divided by its *diameter;* specifically, the half-area of a cyclonic storm, or that on either side of storm's path or *line of progression; see* DANGEROUS SEMICIRCLE; *also* **N. semicircle** *in* NAVIGABLE. **S'circular deviation,** so called because waxing and waning throughout the compass *semicircle* in which a vessel is swung. In magnetic compass deviation analysis, it is that component of total deviation in an uncompensated compass which has a maximum value with ship's head on *E.* and *W.,* gradually disappearing to *nil* as ship is swung to *N.* or *S. by compass;* and also that component which attains greatest value on *N.* and *S.* by compass, waning to zero on *E.* and *W.* Value of the former on *E.* and *W.,* called *coefficient B,* is the mean of deviations observed on these points, with sign of that on *W.* reversed; while *coefficient C* is the mean of deviations observed on *N.* and *S.,* with sign of that observed on *S.* reversed. *See* DEVIATION. **S'diameter,** as given in *Nautical Almanacs* for correcting altitudes and angular distances of sun and moon observed by sextant, by reducing such values to the datum point of body's center, *half* the angular *diameter* of body's disk. **S.-Diesel engine,** *see* ENGINE. **S'diurnal tide,** *see* TIDE. **S'fixed ammunition,** *see* AMMUNITION.

SEND. *See* SCEND. To **s. down,** to lower an object to the deck from aloft; especially, an upper mast or a yard. To **s. up,** to hoist aloft, as a mast or yard to its proper position.

SENHOUSE SLIP. *See* **P. hook** *in* PELICAN.

SENNIT. Small cordage made by braiding or plaiting rope-yarns, spunyarn, or other *small stuff;* used for chafing-service, lanyards, lashings, robands, etc.; also, for valve or stuffing-box packing, manhole gaskets, etc. **Flat s.,** made by plaiting any number of strands greater than two; 5-yarn *s.* of this type is often called *English s.* **French s.,** *see* FRENCH. **Round s.,** made by braiding an even number of yarns or strands around a heart strand; or, by making a series of *crowns* with any number of yarns, with or without a heart strand. **Square s.,** made with 8 or 12 yarns, the finished product being roughly square in cross section; much used for packing.

SENSIBLE HORIZON. *See* HORIZON.

SENTRY. A sentinel or guard; a marine or sea-man stationed on guard duty. **S.-board,** a platform outside the *gangway* of old-time ships for a sentinel or sentry to stand on. (See older use of *gangway* in GANGWAY; also GANGBOARD) **Submarine s.,** see KITE.

SEPARATE CASE AMMUNITION. See **Semi-fixed a.** *in* AMMUNITION.

SEPARATE LOADING AMMUNITION. See AM-MUNITION.

SEPARATION CLOTH. See CLOTH.

SEPARATOR. Any machine, device, or apparatus for separating the constituent parts of a mixture. **Oil s.,** see OIL. **Steam s.,** device for removing water and impurities from steam before it reaches the engine; usually operated on the principle of giving steam an abrupt change of direction of flow; some-times by flowing steam through a perforated plate or plates; or a combination of both devices.

SERANG. (Pers. *sarhang*, a commander) Boat-swain of a lascar crew; skipper of a small East Indian vessel.

SERGEANT-FISH. The *cobia* or *snook*, an edible pelagic fish found off the warmer coasts of America and in both East and West Indies waters. About four feet in length, has a stout body; somewhat of mackerel proportions, tapering to head and tail; a high mid-dorsal fin with added fringe to tail on upper and lower sides; and has a conspicuous full-length dark stripe along each side. The name some-times is applied to the *robalo* (*q.v.*)

SERPENS. (L. = serpent) A small constellation N.W. of, and adjoining, *Ophiuchus*. Its brightest member is *Unuk* (a *Serpentis*) of magnitude 2.75 located in 6° 35′ N. declination and 15 hrs. 42 min. right ascension, or 20° almost due south of *Alphacca* of the *Northern Crown*.

SERVE. (L. *servare*, to protect or preserve) To wind marline, spunyarn, or other small stuff around a rope, keeping the turns close together, as protec-tion against weather and wear; to similarly apply a single thread of wire or seizing-wire about an eye-splice made in a wire rope for securing the splice, as in a hoisting-wire. Before the advent of galvan-ized iron and steel wire rope, all standing rigging of the bare metal was coated with paint or tar and protected by *serving*. A rope is *served* after being *wormed* and *parceled*; see PARCELING. The *serving* or *service* is applied by a tool made of hardwood called the *serving-mallet* in heavier work, or the *serving-board*, for smaller ropes. To **s. the cable,** in former usage, to wind old rope about the hemp an-chor cable for a few fathoms from the anchor as protection from chafing on a hard or rocky bottom.

SERVICE. Period of duty performed in one's oc-cupation; as, *two years' s. at sea.* A branch or kind of employment; as, *naval s.; Smith & Co.'s s.; tug-boat s.* A medium of supply; that which serves; as, *water s.; ship s.* The *serving*, or protecting turns of spunyarn or small stuff around a rope, stay, shroud, etc.; *cf.* SERVE. **Certificate of s.,** see CERTIFICATE. **Cus-toms s.,** see CUSTOM. **S. certificate,** as formerly re-quired of mates and masters of deep-water vessels, prior to present system of certificating and licensing merchant-ship personnel, a written statement by a shipowner stating that the holder performed satis-factory sea-going *s.* in his employe. Such document was duly authenticated by a collector of customs for use in granting clearance, etc. **S. force,** see **S.-train** in SEA. **S. speed,** a merchant service term for a ves-sel's mean sea speed on a series of voyages. Usually considered as speed at which vessel is most economi-cally driven, sometimes what is called a *s. horse-power* is preferred as representing vessel's per-formance from this view-point. **S. stripes,** see HASH-MARKS. **S. tank,** for providing a ready supply of oil or water, a working tank; such as one for fuel oil in way of the fire-room or engine-room space; a gravity tank for the domestic water supply; etc. **Shore s.,** naval term for duty on shore, as distin-guished from *sea s.,* or that performed on board a vessel in commission.

SET. To spread a sail to the wind. To flow or have motion in a given direction; as, *the current sets N.E.; vessel s. toward the rocks in a gale.* To dry or harden, as paint, pitch, concrete, etc. Usu-ally with *up* or *taut,* to draw or pull with stress; as, to *s. up the backstays;* to *s. taut on a tackle.* To ap-point, lay out, or place in order; as, to *s. the watches;* to *s. a course* (in steering); to *s. a net* (in fishing). Direction toward which a current flows; as, *a northerly s.* A complement or *suit;* as *a s. of sails.* A tool used in the completing stage of work; a punch; as, *a nail s.; a rivet s.* In shipyard work, a soft iron bar bent to the curve of a frame, as a pat-tern for use on the *bending-slab;* a *set-iron.* Ap-pearance, arrangement, or type; as, *by the s. of her sails, the sloop was close-hauled; she is a German by the s. of her spars.* **Frame s.,** see FRAME. **S.-bolt,** a punch or drift for sinking a bolt deeper in its hole or knocking it out altogether; a pin or bolt against which wedges are driven in fitting planks close to-gether. To **s. by the compass,** old term for noting a bearing by compass and thence vessel's position with relation to a point or landmark; to steer a course by compass. To **s. flying,** to set a sail from the deck by hoisting it into place *flying,* or not con-fined to a stay, yard, etc., as in the case of a loose jib or staysail, a studding-sail, Jamie Green, spin-naker, etc. **S.-hammer,** see FLATTER. **S.-line,** in fish-ing, a line having a series of baited hooks through-out its length; see **Small-line f.** *in* FISHING. **S.-net,** any fishing-net that is held in a stationary position, as distinguished from a trawl, seine, or other type that is moved about in the actual capture of fish.

S. piling, also termed *sett piling; see* PILE. To **s. sail,** *see* SAIL.

SETT. Same as *wring-staff (q.v.)*

SETTEE SAIL. As found in Arab and Mediterranean craft, a kind of quadrilateral sail of *lateen* type but less lofty in the peak and having a luff of about one-fifth the depth of its leech. It is reefed along the *foot. Cf.* LATEEN. Also, *setee, settie.*

SETTER. A set-hammer; *see* FLATTER. **Gaff-s.,** a boat-hook.

SETTING. Act of placing, fitting, or securing something; as, *s. sail; s. of planking; s. of a sextant.* Designating that which sets; as, *s.-maul; s.-pole; s. sun.* **S.-fid,** *see* FID. **S.-hammer,** a set-hammer; *see* FLATTER. **S.-maul,** or **s.mallet,** common mallet used in *making* or *setting* oakum in a seam in the work of calking wood planking; also termed *making-maul,—mallet.* **S.** *or* **s. to,** process of fitting or drawing timbers or planking together preparatory to securing them in position, as in ship-building practice. This is the improvising of leverage effect by ingenious use of wedges, bolts, the wring-bolt, and the wring-staff in the many varied situations in which curved planking and structural members require forcible *s.* in place. **S. up,** also termed *wedging up,* in preparations for launching a vessel, operation of gradually transferring weight of the hull from keel and bilge blocks to the *sliding ways* by driving long wedges between top side of the latter and the *launching-cradle. See* **L.-cradle** and **L. ways** *in* LAUNCHING.

SETTLE. To cause to subside or become free of disturbance; as, *a heavy rain will s. this choppy sea.* To ease or let down as by a tackle; as, to *s. the yard in its lifts.* Weather is said to be *settled* when remaining free of disturbance. To **s. the halyards,** to ease the halyards so as to lower a yard or a sail a few inches, as when a dry sail becomes wet by rain, or when the breeze freshens in a fair-wind trim. To **s. the land,** to cause the land to sink below the horizon by receding from it.

SETTLING TANK. *See* TANK.

SEVEN SEAS. The Seven Oceans; *see* SEA.

SEVEN-TENTHS RULE. *See* TWO OR MORE BEARINGS *with run between.*

SEVERAL FISHERY. *See* FISHERY.

SEW.[1] (Pron. *so*) To stitch together with palm, needle, and twine; as, to *s. canvas* (in sailmaking).

SEW.[2] (Pron. *su*) A corruption of *sue,* as in the expression *to be sewed up,* said of a grounded vessel; *see* SUE.

SEWGEE. Variant of *soogee.*

SEXTANT. (L. *sextus,* sixth) Optical instrument for measuring angular distances; especially, altitudes of heavenly bodies at sea. Named from the length of its *arc* or its shape, which, roughly is like that of a 60° sector of a circle, when in use it is held in the plane of a circle in which are situated the observer's eye and both points between which angle is measured. Angles up to about 120° may be observed by the instrument, or double of the arc indicated by position of the *radius* or *index bar,* due to the principle involved in its construction. In measuring an altitude of a celestial body, for example, observer directs *s.* toward the horizon immediately below body observed. With the index or radius arm at zero, he sees in the horizon glass, which is half clear and half silvered, equal portions of the horizon, direct and reflected, respectively. By moving forward the *index bar,* reflected horizon will disappear and body observed will show (sometimes with a little seeking manipulation) in the silvered portion of *horizon glass.* The final precise measurement is then effected by use of the *tangent* or *micrometer screw* at the arc end of index bar, where angle is then read off by *vernier* or *micrometer* attached. Thus a ray of light from the body has been reflected from the *index glass* at pivoting end of index arm or bar to the silvered portion of the *horizon glass,* thence to observer's eye. *Half the angle* (or altitude) then has been measured according to the principle in optics that "the angle between first and last reflection is twice that at which reflecting surfaces are set, when a ray suffers two reflections in a given plane." Hence, if the index bar is moved forward 40° from zero, an angle of 80° has been observed, and so indicated on the *limb* or *arc. Cf.* QUINTANT. **Adjustments of s.,** while it is impossible to eliminate errors in a *s.* due to faulty centering of the radius or the graduated arc, and want of parallelism in glasses or shades, all of which may be considered negligible in a well-made instrument, it is important that the observer should be familiar with the *four* following: (1) The *index glass* and (2) the *horizon glass* must be set perpendicular to the plane of the instrument; (3) telescope or sight *line of collimation* must be parallel to the plane of instrument; and (4) *index glass* and *horizon glass* must be parallel when index is set at *zero.* **Bubble s.,** has an attachment in which the horizon is indicated in a floating mark, or other arrangement. It is designed for use when the horizon is obscured. Original of this type had a leveling bubble; hence its name. **S. telescope,** screwed into its collar when needed, directs observer's sight to the horizon glass; may be *direct* or *inverting,* the latter often having cross-wires in the tube for accurate collimating. **Surveying s.,** a light handy *s.* or *quintant* specially made for taking horizontal angles in hydrographic surveying, as from a boat.

SHACK-BAIT. Nova Scotian and New England term for bait obtained at sea, as distinguished from a regular stock carried on board; *see* **Shack-f.** *in* FISHERMAN.

SHACKLE. Originally, a circular or oval-shaped ring fitted on inside of a gun-port or a scuttle for securing such at sea. Any of several metal fittings, commonly U-shaped, with a removable *pin* or bolt across its "mouth," for connecting chain, making fast a pendant, stay, guy, etc. In *pl.*, hand-cuffs, leg-irons, or manacles for confining prisoners. To secure by means of one or more *shackles,*—usually with *on;* as, to *s. on the cable.* **Anchor s.**, originally, the Jew's harp, or lyre-shaped *s.* which superseded the earlier *ring* of an anchor; *see* JEW'S HARP. Later, also the *bending s.* uniting end of chain cable to an anchor. Now, any *s.* having a *bow* of greater width than its *mouth,* or distance between its *lugs.* In modern larger vessels, a cable *s.* is always U-shaped, as, also, is the large *s.* fitted in lieu of the *anchor-ring.* **Bending s.**, the one connecting end of chain cable to an anchor. Always larger than a *s.* joining lengths of cable, it often has a pin that is keyed outside of, instead of through, one of the lugs. Also, *end s.* **Connecting s.**, *chain cable s.* uniting two lengths or *shots* of chain. American and British merchant ships have held to the 15-fathom length since chain cable displaced the old hemp cable, each successive length or *shot* terminating in the *connecting s.* Sometimes such *shot* is also termed a *s.;* as in *three shackles' scope of chain.* The *connecting s.* has an oval pin with flattened head, its end being flush with outside of lug, and is held in place by a small hardwood peg or key of lead driven through a hole in the lug and through a corresponding hole in the pin near its end. In U.S. navy and some modern vessels, the *Kenter s.* which is made in the form of a cable *link* has superseded the traditional *s. See* KENTER SHACKLE. **Joiner s.**, same as *connecting s.* **Mooring s.**, such as is used in uniting a wire and a fiber hawser, or eye of a heavy wire to the standing part in mooring, a large U-shaped *s.* having a screw pin with a large eye for facilitating turning by hand; *also see* **M. shackle** *in* MOORING. **Parts of s.**, the *bow* is its curved part; *lugs* or *eyes,* raised open parts for receiving the *pin;* its *mouth,* part opposite the *bow,* closed by inserting the pin. **S. of cable,** a length or shot of chain cable; *see* **Connecting s. Size of s.**, of types in general use on board ship is indicated by diameter of metal in the *pin,* this usually being greater than that in the *bow;* thus, a *one-inch s.* is one having *seven-eighths* inch diameter metal in its bow. Size of *anchor-cable s.* is referred to as diameter of metal in its *bow,* its pin being of same cross-section, but oval-shaped with major axis of section lying in direction of stress. **Span-s.**, *see* SPAN. **Strength of s.**, safe working load of a new steel *s.* is usually taken as *four times* the square of diameter of metal in *bow;* older

worn material as *three times* that figure; expressed in *long tons.*

SHAD. An important food fish of the herring family genus *Alosa,* found on North American coasts. *Common* or *white s.* grows to about two feet in length; has a deeper belly than his common herring cousin; lives in sea water and ascends rivers to spawn.

SHADE. One of the colored hinged glasses on a sextant for reducing the glare when taking a solar observation. **S. deck,** *see* DECK. **S.-deck vessel,** one having a continuous weather deck of light construction and more or less open between such deck and its next below.

SHADOW. A light-weather spinnaker having a *gaff-* instead of a *jib-head.*

SHADOW PIN. The *style,* or vertical pin fitted in an azimuth instrument or in center of a compass card for indicating the bearing of the sun by shadow thrown on rim of the card. Bearing observed is then equal to number of degrees coinciding with shadow *minus* 180°.

SHAFFLE. A variant of *snaffle.*

SHAFT. A bar that transmits motion in a machine; specifically, the heavy cylindrical steel bar or series of such bars joined on end and constituting the *shafting,* by which rotary motion is transmitted from engine to propeller or paddle-wheel. The main part, or *shank,* of an anchor. **Main s.**, the *shafting; see* above. **Paddle s.**, *see* PADDLE. **Propeller s.**, *see* PROPELLER. **Rocking s.**, *see* ROCK. **S. alley,** same as **S. tunnel. S. angle,** the inclination of center line of a *propeller s.* and vertical center plane of ship is the *horizontal angle;* that of center line of *s.* with either the base line or designed water-line plane is the *vertical angle.* **S. bearing,** part of *s.* in contact with one of its beds; also, a bed in which *s.* rotates. **S. bracket,** *see* **S. strut. S. coupling,** flanged ends and bolts constituting the connecting joint of two lengths of *shafting.* **S. horsepower,** abbrev. *SHP, see* HORSEPOWER. **S.-hole,** in a single-screw vessel, aperture in the *propeller-* or *body-post* through which aftermost section of *propeller s.* (*tail-end s.*) extends to the propeller. It is the entrance to the *stern tube* in which are housed the *lignum vitae* bearings supporting the *s.* **S. log,** in a wood-built screw vessel, the heavy timber connected to keel and deadwood and through which *tail-end s.* extends to propeller. **S.-pipe,** tubular housing in which *tail-end s.* works; *see* **S. tube** *in* STERN. **S. stools,** foundations for bearings in which propeller shafting is supported. **S. strut,** an exterior heavy two-legged bracket or frame containing at its apex the aftermost *s.* bearing where propeller is at either side of vessel's fore-and-aft center line, as in the case of twin screws. In lieu of *struts,* larger vessels have a bossing or rounded protuberance built to the hull and containing a *stern tube* similar to single-screw arrangement. Also called *s. bracket; s. stay; propeller strut.* **S.-tube,** same as **S.-pipe. S. tunnel,** watertight alley or passage housing propeller *shafting* and providing access to latter throughout its length from engine-room to *stern tube;* also, *s. alley.* **Spare s.,** extra *propeller* or *tail-end s.* required to be carried as a replacement in event of damage to *s.,* as by propeller striking an object, heavy weather, or through latent defect. **Tail s.,** or tail-end *s., see* **P. shaft** *in* PROPELLER. **Thrust s.,** that section of propeller shafting which rests in the *thrust bearings,* or *thrust block;* it is provided with two or more *collars* that take the axial *push* or *thrust* as screw turns ahead or a *pull* in going astern.

SHAG MAT. *See* **Thrum m.** *in* MAT.

SHAGREEN. Dried tubercled skin of certain sharks and rays used for rasping and polishing wood. **S. ray,** a small *skate* found off the British coast and other European waters, so named because yielding *s.*

SHAKE. A fissure or crack in timber, caused by rapid drying, frost, bending of tree in a gale, etc. (Planking and other ship timber is said to be *shaky,* when cracks, shakes, or splits are in evidence.) To shiver or flap about, as a sail when vessel lies too close to wind. Usually with *out* or *off,* to loose or open out; to rid one's self of; as, to *s. out a reef;* to *s. off the other ship,* i.e., by steering away from or out-distancing her.

SHAKEDOWN CRUISE. *See* CRUISE.

SHAKINGS. Short ends of rope-yarns, frayed cordage, waste pieces of canvas, etc. collected aboard ship; junk.

SHALLOP. (Prob. of East Indian origin) An archaic term for a small light two-masted vessel or a boat driven by either oars or sails. The term sometimes denotes a *shell,* or long narrow racing-boat driven by two or four oarsmen.

SHALLOW. Having little depth; shoal; as, *s. water.* Part of an area having shoal water; a shoal; sometimes in *pl.;* as, *tide-rips form on the shallows.* **S.-floored,** having floors of comparatively little depth; *cf.* FLOOR. **S.-waisted,** said of a vessel having little depression amidships, as one having a flush deck.

SHAM ABRAHAM, To. *See* ABRAHAM.

SHAMAL. A dry wind from north-west prevailing for months on end in the Persian Gulf.

SHAN. (*Scand.* origin) Old shipbuilders' term for a fibrous, gnarled, or knotty defect in a timber or spar.

SHANGHAI. To force or procure by any illicit means or to induce by false representations any person to ship as a seaman on board any vessel, usually with the object of securing an advance from the victim's wages or a premium ("blood money"). Although *crimps* made a business of procuring sailors by trickery, including inducement to ship by the aid of intoxicants and drugs, for many years subsequent to the recognized legal activities of the *press-gangs* in some European seaports, *shanghaiing* appears to have had its American beginning at New York in Civil War days, with San Francisco a close second and the scene of more daring in this nefarious traffic than perhaps is recorded of any other port. The successful exploits of noted *crimps* and *boarding-house masters* in supplying whole crews by the *s.* process have been the subject of many a dog-watch yarn in deep-water vessels since the practice was stamped out, about 1900. No specific legislation dealing with this felony appears to have been enacted in U.S. until 1906, in the form of a law against illegal shipment of seamen (*18 U.S.C. 144*).

SHANK. Main part or vertical shaft of an anchor; part of a tool between its handle and acting part, as that of a chisel, a chain-hook, etc.; part of a tackle- or hoisting-hook between its eye and curved portion. **S.-painter,** rope or chain securing an old-fashioned anchor's flukes in the stowed position.

SHANTY. *See* CHANTEY.

SHAPE. A ball, cone, or cylindrical drum, made of canvas or light metal, exhibited as a signal. A bar of structural metal having a curved or angular cross section, such as a *bulb-angle, channel,* or a *T-bar.* **Day s.,** as required in certain rules for harbor traffic, prevention of collisions, etc., a *s.* in a signal consisting of one or more balls, cones, or drums, to be shown by certain vessels. **To s. a course** is to determine the *compass course,* or course to steer, by applying any necessary correction to the *true course* as determined by calculation or taken from a chart; often with *for,* as, to *s. a course for St. Helena.* Also to lay a vessel's head in a direction with reference to a sighted point of land, a harbor entrance, etc.; as, to *s. a course to take us clear of the cape.* Also, to *set* or *lay a course.*

SHAPING. In shipbuilding, act of beveling plates, forming beveled flanges, joggling, etc., by means of various machines, such as the bulldozer, joggler, keel-bender, press brake, and shaper. **S. a course,** act or process of *laying* or *setting* a course to steer; *see* SHAPE.

SHARESMAN. Member of a fishing-vessel's crew who *shares* in profits of a voyage or season. He may be engaged on the "no catch—no pay" basis or may assume part of the capital risks involved. Also, *shareman.*

SHARK. Common name for a great variety of voracious sharp-toothed fishes found in all oceans, though most species prefer tropical waters. Largest of all fishes are included in the *s.* group and perhaps the *white* or *man-eating s.* leads with his length of over 30 feet and befitting ichthyological title *Carcharodon carcharias.* Sharks have a well-rounded body, usually grayish in color, generally proportionately lengthy, with upper part of tail markedly elongated. Some species are hunted for their valuable *liver oil,* rich in vitamin D, which in recent years has greatly supplemented *cod liver oil.* The *Greenland s.,* a ferocious 20- to 25-footer that will not hesitate to attack a full-sized whale, is a noted source of the oil. Like several others, including the *blue s.* and *tiger s.,* the *Greenland s.,* also called *ground, gurry,* or *nurse s.* and *sleeper,* shares in the man-eating reputation chiefly assigned to the more commonly encountered *white s.,* as the Norwegian fishermen pursuing the animal each summer at the head of Baffin Bay can amply assure us. The common fallacy that the ugly creatures must turn on one side or on their backs in order to sink their several rows of sharp triangular teeth into a floating morsel apparently is based on the fact that the protruding snout is some distance forward of the mouth. However, the observed truth is that Mr. *S.* simply lifts his head and takes his vicious bite. **Basking s.,** one of the largest known, named for its habit of basking at the surface; habitat in North Atlantic, has remarkably small teeth, feeds on minute animal life, and is harmless to man; killed for its yield of *liver oil,* often amounting to 8 or 10 barrels; also called *oil s.; sail-fish* and *sun-fish* (from its prominent dorsal fin); *homer* and *hoe-mother* (in the Orkneys); and *liver s.* **Blue s.,** man-eating species, active and voracious, from 20 to 25 feet in length; found in warmer and temperate seas. **Dog s.,** see **D.-fish** *in* DOG. Also called *hound s.* **Fox s.,** the *sea-fox, sea-ape, swingle-tail,* or *thrasher* (*Alopias vulpes*), found off the American and European coasts; 12 to 15 feet in length, about half of which is taken up with his remarkable tail that he uses to *thrash* the water in rounding up fish for an unsatiable appetite. **Greenland s.,** *see remarks above.* **Hammer-headed s.,** *see* HAMMER-HEAD. **Land s.,** *see* LAND. **Oil s.,** any of several species yielding *s. liver oil,* including the *basking s., Greenland s.,* and *tope.* **Tiger s.,** named for its irregular yellowish bands and spots, any of several man-eating sharks chiefly found in Indian Ocean and tropical Pacific. A leading member of this formidable species is *Stegostoma tigrinum.* **Tope,** a small species native to the British coasts and western Europe, called *miller-dog* and *penny-dog* in England. Generally classed with the *dog-fish* group, or smallest of *sharks,* the name is also applied to the *piked dog-fish* and *soup-fin s.* (Last-named is species from fins of which Chinese obtain the gelatin for a tasty soup) **Whale s.,** another name for the *basking s.*

SHARK-CHASER. Chemical consisting of 80% dye stuff and 20% copper acetate, a packet of which is issued to U.S. naval personnel on duty afloat during war, for discoloring and tainting sea water with view of repelling sharks in event of a swimming emergency.

SHARK'S MOUTH. In an awning, an opening or gap to fit around a mast, stay, ventilator, etc.

SHARP. Acute-angled; pointed; projecting; clean-cut. **S.-bilged,** said of a vessel or boat having a comparatively flat bottom and so a *sharply* curving bilge; sometimes, *hard-bilged.* **S.-bottomed,** having a more or less *V-shaped* bottom or marked rise of floor, or *deadrise.* **S. iron,** a caulker's *reaming-iron,* or tool used to open narrow seams in planking, preparatory to caulking process. **S. up,** position of the *lower yards* when a square-rigged vessel is sailing as close to wind as possible; when at anchor or in port, position of *all yards* braced parallel with *lower yards* as above, or that in which yards are said to be *pointed.*

SHARPIE. Originally used on the Connecticut shore, a lengthy flat-bottomed fishing or pleasure boat, rigged with two masts and leg-o'-mutton sails; fitted with a centerboard and usually rocker-keel built; clews of sails are extended by horizontal sprits, foot of former having considerable rise. Excepting some racing and pleasure variations of the rig and model, the *s.* has about disappeared in favor of the fisherman's motor-driven craft. Also, *sharpy.*

SHARPSHOOTER. A former fine-lined type of fishing schooner built on the New England coast. So called in the Bahamas, a sharp-sterned decked boat carrying a jib-headed sail.

SHAULA. (Ar. *al shaulah,* the sting) The star λ *Scorpii* marking the tip of the *Scorpion's tail,* or point of the *Chain-hook.* It is located in declination 37° S. and right ascension 17 hrs. 30 min.; magnitude 1.71; *see* SCORPIO.

SHEAR. (A.S., *sceran,* to cut, shear, or shave) Stress that causes or tends to cause contiguous parts of a structural member or of the whole structure, as concerned with shipbuilding, to slide relatively to each other in a lateral direction, or parallel to planes of contact of the parts; *shearing stress.* In *pl.,* a pair of heavy scissors, such as is used for cutting *sail-cloth, sheet metal,* etc.; a shipyard machine for cutting and trimming plates and other structural iron; a *shearing-machine; cf.* **A.-shears** *in* ANGLE. The term also is a variant of *sheer; see* SHEER.

SHEARING. Act of being subjected to, severed or deformed by, *shear.* Cutting by means of *shears.* **S.-machine,** see SHEAR. **S.-punch,** a machine for forming holes in plating, etc., by a punch that *shears* the metal before it; holes are punched *from the faying surface* of the metal.

SHEARWATER. (Ger. *wasserscherer*) A sea-bird of the family comprising the albatrosses, fulmars, and petrels (*cf.* PETREL), classified chiefly as of genus *Puffinus*. Varying in length from 10 to 18 inches, it is named for its habit of closely skimming the waves when in flight; has a lengthy wing-spread and usually dark-colored back with white under surface. The *Manx s., greater s.,* and *sooty s.* are Atlantic species; *Audubon's s.,* a small one of Florida coast and West Indian waters; several others live in the Pacific and Indian Oceans. Any of the North Atlantic species is commonly called a *hagdon*. The term also has been applied to upper part of a vessel's stem, especially that portion in a *clipper bow* curved under the bowsprit; *see* CUTWATER.

SHEATHBILL. A sea bird of a family constituting the *Chionididæ* and only genus *Chionis,* from the Greek word for *snow, chion*. Much resembling the pigeons in appearance, its entire plumage, however, being white, the bird is so called from its horny case or *sheath* over the base of upper side of its short bill. Habitat in high southern latitudes.

SHEATHE. (From an old Teutonic word meaning to *separate*) To cover a surface with thin protective material, such as copper sheets on a vessel's bottom planking or sheet metal on a bulkhead. A plated deck is said to be *sheathed* when covered by a layer of caulked deck planking.

SHEATHING. That which sheathes; a protective casing or layer of metal or wood. **Copper s.,** *see* **Composition m.** *in* METAL. **Creosoted s.,** thin planking treated with *creosote* laid over the underwater surface of barges, scows, etc., as protection from wood-borers and/or wear and tear. **S.-metal,** sheets of *copper* or *Muntz metal; see* COPPER *and* **Composition m.** *in* METAL. Also, sheets of thin galvanized iron for covering a partition or bulkhead, chiefly as protection against spread of fire. **S.-nail,** *see* NAIL. **S.-paper, s.-felt,** laid between metal *s.* and bottom of wood-planked vessels and usually saturated with coal tar, creosote, or such preservative.

SHEATH-KNIFE. A pointed knife or dagger, usually having a fixed handle, carried in a sheath or scabbard as a weapon. This type of knife is by law prohibited to be worn by any seaman on board ship (*46 U.S.C. 710*). *Also see* **Sheath-k.** *in* KNIFE.

SHEAVE. (M.E. *schive;* O. Du. *schijfe;* a disk or wheel. The earlier and more correct *shive* [pron. *shiv*] probably was corrupted by the Dutch pron.) A disk or wheel, grooved on its periphery, set in a tackle-block, mast, yard, or elsewhere as a "roller" over which a rope or chain travels; a pulley. A layer of the turns in a coil of new rope. To *s. a boat,* among Newfoundland fishermen, is to stop her by holding water with the oars or to stop and quickly turn a boat by use of oars. As designating its contained *sheaves,* a block often is referred to as *single-,* double-, treble-sheaved, etc., or simply *single, double,* etc.; *see* BLOCK. **Block s.,** may be *dummy* or *roller-bearing, i.e.,* provided with a simple bushing on which it bears on the *pin* in turning, or with a "patent" roller bushing. Hence the terms *dummy s.* and *patent s.* Size of *s.* is indicated by its outside diameter and thickness measurements; its groove should be about one-eighth inch wider than diameter of rope. Fiber rope should be worked on a *s.* measuring at least 3 times circumference of rope; thus, a suitable *s.* for a 3-inch manila is one of 9 inches diameter; for wire, at least 5 times circumference or 15 times diameter: a $\frac{3}{4}$-inch diameter wire requiring a *s.* of at least 11 inches in diameter. **Chain s.,** one having its circumference fashioned to nest and grip a chain, as by a series of *whelps* that engage each flat-lying link. **Dead s.,** *see* **D. sheave** *in* DEAD. Also, *dumb s.* **Dummy s.,** one having no roller bearings, as opposed to a *s.* fitted with such, or patent *s.* **S.-hole,** a slot or aperture in a mast, yard, bulwark stanchion, etc., in which a *s.* is fitted.

SHEEPSHANK. A kind of hitch or knot, of which there are several varieties, for shortening a rope: In its simplest form, consists of two bights laid side by side and a half-hitch taken over each bight's eye with rope's standing part. This method is a *toggled s.* when the bights mentioned are secured to standing part by toggles or seizings. For smaller ropes, the *knotted* or *man-o'-war s.,* a combination of an interlaced knot made with the parts and the half-hitches required, the latter automatically included.

SHEEPSHEAD. A food fish of U.S. Atlantic and Gulf coasts, included in the *Sparidæ* family with the sea breams, porgies, and scup. Has deep compressed body, about 15 inches in length, with black vertical bands and thorny dorsal fringe. Its blunt snout might be termed, more correctly, its *face*.

SHEER. Upward curvature of a vessel's upper lines from about amidships toward each end. In a timber, opposite of *camber;* a bowing or turning upward from the middle. Angle of fore-and-aft line with direction of current or a strong breeze when lying at single anchor, as effected by position of helm or trim of yards. A canting or heading away from the course, as by effect of a current in shallow water, or intentional, as by action of the helm. To turn off from the course; to swerve or swing from an original heading; as, *we sheered off to clear the buoy; vessel suddenly sheered toward the bank; s. alongside! s. off!* To **break s.,** *see* BREAK. **Hog s.,** an improper application of the term *s.* in denoting a *rising* amidships; *see* **H.-sheer** *in* HOG. **Plank-s.,** *see* PLANK. **Rank s.,** a sudden change in direction of ship's head caused by uneven depths in shallow water, an unexpected current, or displacing of water by a near-by passing vessel, resulting in temporary loss of control of steering. **S. batten,** a strip of wood or metal fastened to frames of a vessel in building to serve as a guide for laying plating or planking to follow s. line of hull according to plan. Also, a strong wood batten or metal rod fixed across lower ends of shrouds to secure dead-eyes or turnbuckles in place; a s.-pole. **S. draft,** see **Profile p.** in PLAN. **S.-hooks,** as formerly used to cut away an enemy's rigging, a set of hooks that were sharpened like sickles and mounted on a pole. **S.-hulk,** see HULK. **S.-legs,** spars constituting *sheers* (sometimes *shears*), or apparatus for lifting heavy weights. Two or more *legs* are lashed together with lower ends spread apart and set in erect position with their heads and feet secured. The hoisting-tackle is fixed to head of the arrangement. **S.-line,** that described by an upper deck line or rail; see **Sheer l.** in LINE. **S. mast,** see **Sheer m.** in MAST. **S. mold,** see MOLD. **S.-molding,** see MOLDING; also, sometimes *s.-rail*. **S. plan,** see **Profile p.** in PLAN. **S. plate,** any plate in a s. strake. **S.-pole,** a batten or metal rod seized to lower ends of standing rigging across the upper dead-eyes for securing latter in position; cf. **S. batten. S. rail,** the *s.-molding;* a *guard-* or *fender-rail* on small vessels. **S. ratline,** see RATLINE. **S. strake,** see STRAKE. **S. sail,** archaic term for a *drag* or *drogue;* especially one of the conical shaped type; see DRAG.

SHEERS. (Of uncertain origin; also, *shears*) See **S.-legs** *in* SHEER. Ordinarily, a single pair of sheer-legs constitute *sheers,* any necessary inclination given the spars being effected by means of guys. However, some permanent *s.,* such as are erected in a dockyard for lifting heavy guns, boilers, machinery, etc., consist of *three* legs, two of which are stepped at equal distances from the dockside, while the third, controlled by a special engine, acts as a guying leg in canting the sheer-heads outward over a ship alongside or as required. **Masting s.,** those rigged for placing masts in position or removing them from a vessel.

SHEET.[1] (A.S. *sceatline,* a rope for securing the *sceata,* or clew of a sail) A tackle, single rope, or chain leading from the clew (or either clew) of a sail, or to a boom near the clew, as in a boom-sail, for extending sail as required in setting. A *s.* is named for its sail, with the designating term indicated first in the case of square sails; thus, *weather topgallant s.; lee upper-topsail s.; port fore s.; starboard main-royal s.;* and in fore-and-aft sails, *flying-jib s.; main s.; mizzen-staysail s.;* etc. A sail is said to be *sheeted* to some point or in a named direction, according to the lead of its *s.* from the clew; thus, square sails above the courses are *sheeted* to yard-arms next below; a flying-jib is *sheeted* well aft. **Flowing s.,** see FLOW. **Fore-s. horse,** see HORSE. To **give her s.,** to ease off the *s.* or *sheets,* as of fore-and-aft sails when breeze is drawing aft, or in *taking a fisherman's reef* (see FISHERMAN). **Head s's,** those of the *head sails,* or those forward of foremast; as in, *Flatten in the head sheets! Ease off the head sheets!*

Lee s., in a square sail, *s.* attached to the *lee clew;* opposed to *weather s.,* or that on windward side of sail. To **pay with the topsail s.,** to leave behind an unpaid debt. **S. bend,** see BEND. **S. bitts,** in larger square-rigged vessels, bitts or bollards fitted on deck near the mast for making fast topsail and top-gallant sheets. To **s. home,** to haul a *s.* so as to flatten its sail to the wind; to haul *sheets* of a square sail out to yard-arms as in setting sail. **S.-traveler,** as fitted in fore-and-aft rig, a ring attached to a sheet-block and confined to a *horse;* see HORSE. **S. winch,** a small hand winch for hauling in on a *s.* **Short s.,** in the old studding-sail days, rope leading from inside clew of a topmast *stuns'l* into the top; thus distinguished from the *long s.,* or that from outer clew to *stuns'l boom-end.* **Weather s.,** in a square sail other than a course, *s.* on side of sail next the wind; opposed to *lee s.,* or that on lee side of sail.

SHEET.[2] A large broad piece of thin metal, distinguished from a plate by its thickness, usually taken as one-eighth inch or under. An expanse of cloud; as, *a s. of stratus.* Clear space amidst floating ice; as, *a s. of open water.* Space in a boat forward of abaft the thwarts,—usually in *pl.;* as, *fore sheets, stern sheets.* **S. ice,** see ICE. **S. metal,** brass, copper, iron, etc., rolled into *sheets;* in shipyard work, such material of one-eighth inch thickness or under. **S.-metal worker,** one who works with *s. metal* in making lockers, light tanks, smokestack casing, ventilator cowls; covering insulation in cooling chambers, fire-proofing bulkheads; etc. **Tube s.,** see TUBE.

SHEET ANCHOR. See ANCHOR.

SHELF. In wooden ship construction, line of timbers bridging, bolted to, and thus stiffening the frames, but chiefly for supporting the ends of deck-beams. In launching a large vessel, a row or series of lugs or brackets riveted to the narrowing and sloping sides of ship toward her ends for providing a means of butting the *heads* or upper ends of upright timbers of the launching cradle; cf. **L. cradle** *in* LAUNCHING. A ledge or submerged reef; a shoal or sand-bank; especially such having a deep-water approach. A coast or shore is said to be *shelfy* or *shelvy* when abounding with outlying irregular shallows, sand-banks, rocky ledges, or reefs. **Armor-s.,** see ARMOR. **Continental s.,** comparatively shallow zone extending along the coast of almost every continent. At about 100 fathoms, generally there is a marked descent of the ocean floor known as the *continental slope.* **S.-piece,** same as *shelf* in wooden ships; see remarks above. **S.-plate,** same as *armor-s.*

SHELL. Hard outer covering of a crustacean or a mollusk; a mollusk itself. Of a block, wood or metal casing containing the sheave or sheaves. A very light, long and narrow racing-boat driven by oars; a shallop. Outside covering of planking or plating forming surface of a vessel's hull; also, *skin.* A metal bullet-shaped projectile containing an explosive charge. Abbrev. *sh.* or *brkn sh* (also *bkn sh*) on charts indicates sea-bottom in that vicinity is more or less covered with *shells* or pieces of *shells,* as those from oysters, clams, etc. To bombard, or fire bombs or *shells* at, into, or upon; as, *ship was shelled by a shore battery.* **Acorn-s.,** *see* ACORN. **Boiler s.,** *see* BOILER. **Oil s.,** *see* OIL. **S.-boat,** a racing s.; *see above.* **S. boiler,** any boiler having a cylindrical body. **S.-bossing,** also termed *shaft-bossing,* rounded protuberance on the hull for carrying a propeller-shaft's tail-end tube, as built in twin- and quadruple-screw vessels. **S.-chocks,** *see* CHOCK. **S. doubling,** an extra thickness of plating fitted for local strength purposes in ship's *s.;* a *doubling-plate.* **S. expansion,** a drawing showing shapes, dimensions, weights, details of butts and connections, and other pertinent information concerning the plates constituting a ship's *s. plating,* as developed from a model on which the arrangement of strakes, butts, etc., has been laid off. **S.-flange,** *see* FLANGE. **S. ice,** that originally formed on a water surface but left unsupported by falling of such surface. **S. landings,** as showing a strake-line, points on ship's frames indicating position of edges of *s. plating.* **S. liners,** filling-pieces between frames and raised strakes of *s. plating;* same as frame-liner; *see* **F.-liner** *in* FRAME. **S. longitudinal,** in the *Isherwood* or longitudinal framing system, the fore-and-aft girders or stiffeners secured to inside of *s. plating. Cf. remarks in* FRAME. **S. lugs,** at the outer edge of a 'tween-deck stringer plate, the short pieces of angle-bar connecting that plate with *s. plating* between transverse frames. **S. plating,** that constituting ship's *skin* or outer surface of the hull. **S.-room,** in a war-vessel, a magazine for stowage of projectiles, such as *shells* and bombs.

SHELLBACK. A veteran of the seas; an old salt; a sea-dog.

SHELLMAN. Member of a gun's crew whose duty is to pass shells to the gun for loading.

SHELTER. That which affords protection from weather or sea, as a weather shore, a breakwater, a harbor. A protective house or other superstructural erection on a vessel, as a *wing s.* or "cab" at either end of a navigation bridge; sometimes, fore part of a pilot-house that extends to forward side of bridge. Also, main-deck space under a forward-projecting poop. A temporary screen, as a tarpaulin, set up as a wind-break. To take refuge or protection; as, *the brig sheltered in Southwest Harbor.* **S. deck,** a continuous deck above the principal or strength deck of the hull. As the name suggests, it may be regarded as a means of merely sheltering certain cargo, cattle, etc., since, in general, the space it covers must not be permanently closed to the weather in order to obviate the inclusion of its measurement in the *net tonnage,*—that on which almost all taxes and dues are imposed. A *s.-deck vessel* is allowed a lighter

standard of construction above the main or strength deck.

SHELVING COAST. A coast in which the bottom gradually and constantly slopes from the shore into deep water, as opposed to a *bold, bluff,* or *steep* shore or coast.

SHELVY. *See remarks under* SHELF.

SHERADIZING. *See* GALVANIZED.

SHERATAN. (*Ar.*) Star of magnitude 2.72 in *Aries,* lying about 4° S.W. of his brighter neighbor, *Hamal* (α *Arietis*). *See* HAMAL.

SHETLAND YAWL. *See* HAAF.

SHIELD. A steel screen or protecting plate about the breech of a gun, a conning-tower, etc. *Also see* MASK.

SHIFT. To change in direction or position; as, *the wind will s. to N.E.; s. the gaff-tops'l tack!; s. the helm!; a heavy roll caused cargo to s.* Act of shifting, as a vessel from one berth to another. A removal; change in direction or position; as, a *s.* of 10 feet; a *s.* of wind; a *s.* of the grain cargo. **S. of butts,** staggered disposition of butts in planking or plating in order that as few as possible will occur in alignment and so tend to preserve proper distribution of strength. **S. the helm!,** *see* HELM.

SHIFTING. Changeable; varying in position or direction; as, *s.* sands; a *s.* wind. Designating anything that is movable or may shift or move; as, *s.* ballast; a *s.* sand-bar. Charge made by a tug for towing or assisting in moving a vessel from one berth to another. **S.-backstay,** as used in fore-and-aft rig, especially in larger yachts, a topmast or lowermast backstay that may be slacked off when on the lee side and set taut when on weather side. Usually leading farther aft than permanent standing rigging of that name, it is so termed because it may be *shifted* or let go altogether when sail bellies against it in a breeze. Also, *running-backstay; preventer backstay.* **S.-ballast,** *see* BALLAST. **S.-beam,** a removable beam in a hatchway for supporting hatch-covers; *see remarks in* HATCH. **S.-boards,** heavy planks constituting a temporary longitudinal bulkhead erected in a vessel's center line (sometimes also at quarter-breadth) for prevention of the possible *shifting* of a bulk cargo. Some grain-carrying ships are fitted with permanent steel *shifting-bulkheads.* Especially in the case of grain cargoes, most maritime nations require by law the fitting of *s.-boards,* or portable grain bulkheads, as sometimes called; *cf.* GRAIN. **S. of cargo,** lateral displacing of a stowed cargo caused by heavy rolling, an extraordinary lurch, or listing of vessel. Particularly with bulk-grain laden ships, the danger of a permanent heavy list arises from this cause and prior to enactment of laws requiring *shifting-boards* and *feeders* in grain stowage, many a good ship had found her end by capsizing or foundering in a heavy sea. *Cf.* GRAIN *and* FEEDER. **S. sand,** a sandbank or bar consisting greatly of sand on which the depth of water frequently changes because of the varying effect of currents in the vicinity. **S.-stock anchor,** an all-metal anchor of the old-fashioned type so termed from its movable *stock* which may be unkeyed and laid alongside its *shank* in stowing. One end of stock is sharply curved to allow this without withdrawal from shank.

SHIM. A piece or thin layer of wood or metal inserted between structural parts, as for fairing a surface of planking or plating; a bed-plate, a bearing, etc. To fair or true up by inserting a *s.*

SHIN. To climb a spar, stay, rope, etc., by alternately gripping it with the hands and legs; usually with *up;* as, to *s.* up a pole. Also, *shinney up.*

SHINGLE. (Nor. *singling,* small rounded stones) Water-worn rounded stones, larger than those comprising gravel and up to a few inches in diameter, collectively forming the surface of a beach; sometimes, such stone-littered beach or shore itself. **S.-ballast,** as once much used by home-trade sailing vessels on the British coasts, coarse gravel or shingle carried for ballast. **S. trap,** line of piling or heavy stakes for preventing the washing away of *s.* or gravel from a beach.

SHINGLED. In older usage, a vessel or boat was said to be *shingled* if her planking strakes overlapped, *i.e., clinker-built.*

SHIP. (A.S. *scip;* of Old Teutonic origin) Generally, any decked vessel that is used in deep-water navigation. While the term usually denotes, for legal purposes, "any vessel transporting goods or passengers by sea," depending upon the particular legislation concerned, its meaning has been extended to cover almost every type of craft afloat, excepting boats propelled by oars or paddles; and a still broader application includes "boats, vessels, or any floating structure whatsoever" within the compass of jurisdictional matters *in admiralty,* particularly those involving salvage awards and claims. Among seamen, as denoting a *rig,* a square-rigged vessel having three or more masts, each of which carries square sails; although, in Britain, for some time after the earliest 4-masted barques appeared in the 1870's these also generally were called *ships.* The *s.* was referred to as *she* prior to the 14th. century; then seems to have changed gender to *he* well into the 17th., before her original femininity status was revived. An English record of Henry VI's vessels putting to sea (1425) states that *"eurie shyp wayed his anker."* (See VESSEL) A British naval training station is sometimes referred to as *His* (or *Her) Majesty's Ship;* as, *H.M.S. Excellent* (Whale Island) at Portsmouth, England; and there is a famous islet named *H.M.S. Diamond Rock* off Mar-

tinique, French West Indies, so honored since 1804 from the fact that 120 navy men with a few cannon there held out against the French for about 17 months until all ammunition was gone, when they honorably surrendered. The rock still is saluted by passing British war-vessels. To load or transport goods, live stock, or any cargo on a vessel; as, to *s.* apples to London. To engage for service on board a vessel; as, to *s.* a crew; or to attach one's self to a *s.* or any craft in a seaman's capacity; as, to *s.* on a tanker. To fix or set in position any removable part of equipment; to *s.* the rowlocks; gangway is *shipped* on the port side. A vessel is said to be *shipping water* when seas frequently break or splash aboard; to *s.* a sea is to take aboard part of a heavy wave, as in rough weather. **Arcform s.,** chiefly in connection with the comparatively recent longitudinal-framed, or *Isherwood,* cargo-carrying vessel, a form of hull in which no sharp turn of bilge is present because of vessel's sides curving in an *arc* from her floor-heads to a maximum breadth of hull at load water-line. It is claimed that the elimination of the broad flat bottom thus effected throughout the fuller body length gives greater propulsion efficiency in that a less disturbed flow presents itself to the propeller. **Belted s.,** a war-vessel having a *belt* of armor at and about her water-line. **Cartel s.,** a vessel sailing under a flag of truce for purpose of exchanging prisoners with, or bearing important communications, proposals, etc., to an enemy. Such ship usually flies the flags of both belligerent principals. **General refrigerated s.,** vessel capable of giving different kinds of cargo refrigerated stowage; *see* REFRIGERATED CARGO. **Line-of-battle s.,** formerly, a war-vessel of sufficient size and armament to take her place in the *line of battle;* usually, one superior to a frigate; a *three-decker;* also called *ship of the line.* **Light s.,** any vessel sailing in ballast or carrying little or no cargo. Also, a vessel built to conform with minimum standards required in her structural arrangement and parts. **Long-s.,** old term for a *viking s.* or long galley-like open boat or vessel of the Norsemen. To **sally s.,** *see* SALLY. **S.-biscuit,** *see* H.-tack *in* HARD. **S.-borer,** the toredo, or *s.-worm; see* **M. borer** *in* MARINE. **S. boy,** a lad serving on board *s.;* especially, one who assists the steward or cook in a small vessel. **S'breaker,** one who breaks up vessels unfit for further use and sells the material as scrap. **S. broker,** person or agent engaged in transacting business of chartering vessels or obtaining cargo space for shippers; procuring freight and passengers for shipping lines; or of representing a shipping firm at a foreign or outside port in all matters concerning ship's business with shore interests. Also, an agent who negotiates sale or purchase of vessels on a commission basis. **S. calculations,** *see* CURVES OF S. CALCULATIONS. **S. canal,** artificial waterway for seagoing vessels; as, the *Panama Canal.* **S. carpenter,** one whose occupation is to build or repair wooden vessels; also, one who lays wood decks, fits hold and spar ceiling, wooden hatch-covers, etc.; a shipwright. Not to be confused with *ship's carpenter, q.v.* **S. chandler,** one who furnishes vessels with supplies, including cordage, canvas, paints, blocks, lanterns, buckets, brooms, deck fittings, etc., and often all ordinary provisions, such as meats, canned goods, biscuit, flour, and vegetables. **S. channel,** a fairway or navigable passage; especially, one for deeper draft vessels; *see* FAIRWAY. **S. fever,** an old name for *typhus,* which also has been called *jail fever* and *spotted fever.* **S.-keeper,** a guard or watchman in charge of one or more vessels that have no crew on board; a custodian of one or more laid-up ships. In older whaling, a crew-member left in charge of ship while the master engages himself in the actual pursuit of a whale or whales. **S. money,** a tax imposed on seaports and towns in England for coastal defense purposes. It is said to have been in force during times of war from the year 1007 to 1640. **S. of the line,** *see* **Line-of-battle s.** To **s. on a lay,** to join a fishing-vessel, sealer, etc., under the condition that remuneration for one's services will be according to a stipulated percentage of the catch. *See remarks under* LAY. To **s. over,** in U.S. navy parlance, to re-enlist for another period (in regular Navy, generally six years, if age is over 21). **S. pendulum,** *see* CLINOMETER. **S. protest,** also called *marine* or *sea protest; see* PROTEST. **S.-rigged,** having all masts fitted with yards and square sails; rigged like a *s.* **S.-royal,** or **King's s.,** originally, in England, one built and maintained by the royal revenue in early navy days; later, a **s. of the line** or other important vessel of the *Royal Navy.* **S. stores,** provisions and supplies for use only on board ship. Not subject to duty, these usually are required to be manifested and provisions other than those for immediate consumption often are placed under seal by customs officers. Generally, heavy fines are imposed on a vessel in cases of illegal landing of stores. **S. time,** clock time on board ship. Former general practice at sea was to set clocks to *apparent solar time* corresponding to vessel's position at sun's upper transit, or *apparent noon,* time being advanced or retarded during the night or forenoon according to change of longitude. To-day the custom prevails, especially in passenger liners and naval vessels, of keeping *zone time,* or mean solar time corresponding to the nearest or most convenient even 15 degrees of longitude east or west of Greenwich, clocks being altered *one hour* at a single setting, accordingly. *See* **Zone t.** *in* TIME. **S.-worm,** the *toredo* or *s.-borer; see* **M. borer** *in* MARINE. **S.'s bells,** strokes of ship's bell announcing each half hour of a watch; *see* BELL. **S.'s business,** that carried on in administering affairs on board *s.;* specifically, keeping of crew's accounts, disbursement records, maintenance records, and official log; entering and clearing *s.* at customs; engaging and discharging crew; and all matters requiring attention of vessel's master in connection with cargo, passengers, surveys, etc. **S.'s carpenter,** *see* CARPENTER. **S.'s doctor,** also called *s.'s surgeon* and *medical officer,* a staff officer who is a qualified medical practitioner required by law on vessels carrying a specified minimum number of crew or passengers. U.S. requires a doctor on vessels carrying more than 50 steerage passengers. As general custom and recognized necessity, passenger lines appoint one or more physicians to each of their vessels and provide all medical and surgical supplies ordinarily used. **S.'s lantern,** a fixed or portable lamp for use aboard; especially, one from which a regulation light is shown, as a *stern light; see* LANTERN. **S.'s name,** *see* NAME BOARD. **S.'s stores and equipment,** as a legal term denotes all articles, materials, and supplies necessary for the navigation, propulsion, and maintenance of a vessel. **S.'s tackle** or **tackling,** legal term for the cordage, blocks, and working gear necessary for taking in or discharging cargo, as appears in charter agreements, insurance policies, mortgages, and other documents. **S.'s warrant,** in Great Britain, a document issued to a neutral vessel by the *Ministry of Shipping* upon satisfactory assurances by owners of such vessel that she will in no way carry on a trade which may benefit an enemy. It supplements the *navicert* of World War I; *see* NAVICERT. **S.'s writer,** formerly, in U.S. navy, an enlisted man holding this rating who performed ship's clerical work, including, chiefly, maintenance of the conduct book, making up of quarter, station, and watch bills, and assisting the paymaster. (As a combining word, *ship* or *ship's* occurring in other terms may be found under the following captions:—ABANDON; ABOUT; BLOCK; COMPANY; DAY; DRESS; DRILL; DRIVE; EQUIP; FAIR; FIGHTING; FIRE; FLAG; FOUR; FREE; GARE; GENERAL; GUARD; HOSPITAL; HUSBAND; JOINER; JUMP; LIGHT; LOG; MOTHER; NUMBER; OPTION; PAPERS; PENNANT; RAILWAY; RECEIVE; REEFER; REPEAT; SISTER; STORE; TWIN; VICTUALING; WIND²)

SHIPBUILDER. One who constructs vessels; a shipwright. In its broader sense, an administrative member of a partnership or a company engaged in the business of designing, building, powering, rigging, and fitting out a vessel for delivery to her owner in accordance with specifications drawn up in contract form.

SHIPBUILDING. Art or occupation of constructing vessels; marine architecture.

SHIPENTINE. An American term for a *four-masted barque,* following the pattern of *brigantine* and *barquentine,* upon the appearance of first vessels of that rig which were built in British yards in the 1870's. The name gradually died out in the '90's in favor of the more descriptive term. *See* BARK.

SHIPFITTER. In ship construction, one who makes templates for the various plates, etc., with markings thereon indicating rivet-holes, bevelings, and other data. Patterns may be taken from the mold-loft floor or from the hull itself. He also sees that the finished product is correctly shaped and set in place.

SHIPMAN. Archaic name for a mariner or sailor. The word appears as *scipmann* in Old English or Anglo-Saxon literature in the 13th. century and as *shipman* commonly was in use from 15th. to 17th. In English ports, a *s.*, as distinguished from a *quayman* or *dockman*, is a longshoreman or dock laborer who works on board a vessel at discharging or loading of cargo. **S.'s card,** old term for a chart or plan for mariners' use.

SHIPMASTER. The master or person in command of any vessel other than a warship; especially, a qualified and experienced master mariner commanding a merchant vessel. He usually is given the courtesy title of *captain*, which customarily is continued subsequent to active service as a *s.* **S.'s lien,** in maritime law, rightful claim by master of a ship against *freight money* earned by his vessel for his wages and any moneys advanced by him in interests of the ship. He has no lien on ship herself.

SHIPMATE. A fellow seaman; one who serves on same vessel with another.

SHIPMENT. A consignment of goods or merchandise taken on board for transportation. Act or process of shipping or dispatching goods from one port to another.

SHIP MORTGAGE ACT. Title of an act passed by *U.S. Congress, June 5, 1920,* governing the sale, conveyance, or mortgage of vessels of the United States, with particular provisions with respect to maritime liens involved.

SHIPOWNER. Owner of a ship or ships, or of one or more shares in a ship.

SHIPPED BILL OF LADING. *See* RECEIVE.

SHIPPER. One who ships goods or cargo; person who places merchandise in charge of a vessel, her owner, or her charterer for transportation. Also, *consignor*, as *consigning* goods to a *consignee.* **S.'s guarantee,** questionable practice of a *shipper* in guaranteeing immunity of a shipowner (or his agent the shipmaster and consequently the *ship*) in return for issuance of clean *bills of lading* for a cargo shipment, notwithstanding the fact of goods in question having been received on board in faulty condition. (Thus, *Mr. S.* stands with a clean slate; the *ship* gets blamed for bad handling of his goods by *consignee;*—and who can guess the other half of the transaction?) **S.'s manifest,** also termed *export declaration*, a list or manifest indicating weights, quantities, values, and other details of merchandise shipped to a foreign port or ports. It is required from all *shippers* by customs authorities and is chiefly for use in compiling statistics on country's export trade. **S.'s protest,** official complaint or *protest* made by a *s.* against refusal of a shipmaster or shipowner to sign clean bills of lading, or such showing no qualifying remarks or exceptions concerning condition or tally of merchandise shipped. (Such *protest* indicates shipowner or the master closes his door against the immunity proposition referred to in **S.'s guaranty!**)

SHIPPING. Vessels of all types, in a collective sense, as belonging to or frequenting a port, region, or country; vessels generally; commercial tonnage. Act or business of sending goods by ship (or other means of transportation) to a buyer or selling agent. Act or procedure of engaging seamen as members of a crew. Act of embarking or *taking ship,* as a passenger. **American Bureau of S.,** abbrev. A.B.S.; *see* BUREAU. **Merchant s. laws,** *see* MERCHANT. **S. agent,** a shipowner's representative at a foreign or outside port; one who receives goods for shipment and attends to business of dispatching them by ship. **S. articles,** *see* ARTICLES. **S. bill,** as required in British ports, document obtained by a shipper from customs house giving him permission to export certain goods. Presentation of *bill* to customs officer at dock authorizes shipment of the merchandise. **S. Board,** in U.S., a commission, set up by Act of Congress in 1916 and dissolved in 1933, that was charged with similar responsibilities to those of the subsequent *Maritime Commission* instituted in 1936 and which was absorbed by Department of Commerce in 1950. *See* **M. Commission** *in* MARITIME. **S. Commissioner,** official appointed by U.S. Coast Guard (under Treasury Department) for administration of procedure in engaging and discharging seamen of U.S. ships at principal U.S. ports, as required by law. Included in his duties is that of mediator in disputes between shipmasters or shipowners and crew members; especially, in questions regarding imposition of fines or other disciplinary action. He is responsible also for all riders or conditional clauses supplementing the standard form of *Articles of Agreement* which seamen must sign before him or his deputy upon engagement as crew members of vessels in the foreign trade. **S. documents,** forms or official papers in current use for transaction of business and compliance with statutory requirements, as between carrier, shipper, consignee, underwriters, consuls, and customs or other government authority. Also termed *shipper's papers; s. papers.* **S. laws,** *see* **M. shipping laws** *in* MERCHANT; **Maritime l.** *in* LAW. **S. master,** *in* Great Britain, official corresponding to the *U.S. Shipping Commissioner (see above)*; also, in U.S. ports, one who procures seamen for a *s.* concern or supplies vessels with crews. **S. note,** also called *s. permit,* a *s.* line's written authority given a shipper for delivery of goods to dock. It usually is in the form of a receipt in duplicate, one half of which is returned to shipper as a *dock receipt* for his shipment, the other, or *mate's receipt,* retained by the line for making out bills of lading according to quantities, marks, etc., indicated. **S. office,** in Great Britain, that of a *s. master,* or official having similar duties to those of the *U.S. Shipping Commissioner.* Under the *Ministry of Shipping,* such offices are located in each principal port; also, *mercantile marine office.* In U.S., often applied also to an office at which seamen are procured for a *s. line.* **S. permit,** *see* **S. note.** **S. pool,** *see* POOL. **S. ton,** *see* TON. **S. value,** marine insurance valuation of goods, also called *shipped value.* It is taken as the cost of cargo to the party insured, plus all expenses incurred in *s.* and insurance charges.

SHIPSHAPE. In a seamanlike or orderly manner, as desirable on board ship; hence, well arranged; trim; neat; as expressed in the old English phrase, *"In shipshape and Bristol fashion."*

SHIPSMITH. In older use, one who forges chains, davits, yard-bands, mast-hoops, chain-plates, etc., or repairs such fittings on board. In early days of iron fittings, larger men-o'-war carried a *ship's smith,* which rating later developed into that of *ship's armorer.*

SHIPWAY. Sometimes called a *slipway,* space in a shipyard occupied by the blocks on which a vessel rests while being built and subsequently by the extended *ways* on which she slides in being launched.

SHIPWRECK. Total or partial loss of a vessel, as by foundering, stranding, or driving against rocks, etc.; a wrecked vessel or a remaining part of such; wreckage. To suffer loss of one's ship; as, *we were s'd on the Goodwins;* having experienced *s.,* as a *s'd crew.*

SHIPWRIGHT. (A.S. *scipwyrhta*) An experienced ship carpenter who supervises the building and launching of wooden vessels. Also called *yard carpenter,* he usually is familiar with all wood-work details of steel ship construction, from laying of the keel-blocks to floating the finished product. Especially in some British yards, a *s.* is one who keeps the frames fair and set at their proper height by blocking, shoring, etc., during early stages of a vessel's construction; also supervises preparations for launching.

SHIPYARD. Also, shipbuilding yard; a place or enclosure in which vessels are constructed and fitted out. Sometimes the term is also applied to a *ship-repair yard,* in which vessels are dry-docked, painted, repaired, re-masted, etc.

SHIVER. To shake or flutter, as a sail pointing into the wind. A boat is said to be *shivering in the wind* when sailing too close or when headed into the breeze, as when taking way off in approaching a mooring.

SHOAL. A sand-bank, bar, or such elevation of the sea floor, usually so called when depth of water thereon is *six fathoms* or less. A throng or assembled multitude of fishes; as, a *s.* of mackerel. To cause the depth to lessen, as by sailing from a deep to a shallow area; as, *we are shoaling the water; "a change from blue to green tells us the water shoals."* Having a lesser depth; as, *shoaling* water. To throng or gather together in great numbers, as fishes. Of little depth; shallow. **Magnetic s.,** *see* MAGNETIC. **S.-mark,** a buoy or beacon indicating the edge or limit of a *s.* or reef.

SHOALER. A coasting-vessel; one who habitually sails in coasters.

SHOD. An anchor is said to be *shod* when its hold has been broken, or *comes home,* as in soft mud, owing to an accumulation on the buried fluke parting or sliding through that bottom deposit. Also, an anchor is *shod* or fitted with a *shoe,* or piece of heavy plank lashed across a fluke, to assist in holding when dropped in oozy or soft mud bottom. (*Archaic*)

SHOE. In a single-screw vessel's stern frame, lower part uniting propeller-post with rudder-post; continuation of keel at bottom of screw-race, often called *skeg* in smaller craft. A heavy block or bearing-piece of heavy plank in which the heel of a boom or sheer-leg is stepped; a sole-block. A false keel; *see* KEEL. A triangular piece of plate or heavy plank for enlarging area of an old-fashioned anchor's fluke; *cf.* SHOD. Runner-shaped piece of wood at lower side of a trawl or drag-net. **Anchor s.,** as once used in wooden ships, a rounded block temporarily fitted on the bill of an anchor-fluke to prevent injury to vessel's planking. **Beam s.,** a socket or support for end of a hatch-beam. **To s. an anchor,** *see* ANCHOR PHRASEOLOGY. **S. block,** *see* BLOCK. **S.-plate,** a false keel or rubbing-plate for protecting vessel's keel-plate against damage in grounding; *see* **False k.** *in* KEEL.

SHOLE. A sole-block or shoe; *see* **Sole-b.** *in* BLOCK.

SHOOKS. Cargo term for bundles of cask or barrel staves, heads, and hoops; also, sides of boxes or crates; shipped ready for putting together.

SHOOT. To forge ahead by force of motion, as a vessel by her own momentum; as, to *s. into the wind's eye.* To throw out or set a trawl or a fishing-net; to tow a fishing-line. A *chute* or conduit, as used in loading ships; a *grain-s.; coal-s.; ore-s.;* etc.; or a *garbage-s.; cf.* CHUTE. **Ash-s.,** *see* ASH. **S. anchor,** another name for the old *waist* or *sheet anchor; see* ANCHOR. **To s. the sun,** to observe sun's altitude by a sextant.

SHORE.[1] Land bordering a body of water; a coast. The *foreshore,* or beach; *see* **F'shore** *in* FORE. (In narrower rivers and streams, the bordering land usually is called *bank*) **In s.,** *see* INSHORE. **Lee s.,** *see* LEE. **On-s.,** in a direction toward the *s.;* moving toward the *s.;* as, *an on-s. breeze.* **S. boat,** one used for ferrying persons or carrying articles between ship and *s.;* a boat belonging to *s.,* as distinguished from one that is part of a ship's equipment. **S.-fast,** hawser or cable made fast to *s.;* especially, such rope or chain leading to *s.* from an anchored vessel. **S. fisheries,** fishing industry carried on from the *s.* in boats or small craft, as distinguished from *off-shore* or *pelagic* fisheries in which vessels stow the catch on board; also called *strand fisheries. Cf.* FISHERY. **S. grounds,** in-shore fishing grounds; opposed to *off-shore* grounds. **S. leave,** U.S. navy term for permission to remain on shore for a period exceeding usual *liberty* of 24 to 48 hours. **S.-line,** line of the water's edge along a *s.* **S. seine,** any type of net that is worked from the *s.,* as distinguished from a seine used in deep water by a vessel. **S. whaling,** hunting of whales in boats or small vessels attached to a land station. Captured whales are towed to the station for processing. Opposed to *ship-whaling.* **Weather s.,** coast or *s.* lying in the direction from which the wind is blowing; especially, such *s.* affording shelter from sea or wind.

SHORE.[2] A prop or timber placed on end against a structure for supporting or steadying it, such as employed in holding a ship upright in a graving-dock; any prop or supporting piece fitted to strengthen a damaged or strained structural part, as a deck, bulkhead, tank top, etc. To place or fit a *s.* or *shores,*—usually with *up;* as, to *s. up* a deck-beam. **Breast s.,** also called *side s.* and *wale s.,* one of the nearly horizontal *shores* placed against ship's side at about load water-line for holding vessel upright in a dry-dock; especially used in a *graving dock.* **Skeg s.,** a diagonal prop placed against the stern-post or the rudder-post for temporarily holding a vessel from sliding down the ways when keel-blocks have been knocked away preparatory to launching. **Spur s.,** a boom for breasting a vessel off from a quay or pier, as for providing space for a lighter between ship and quay. **Trip s.,** one of several upright *s's* placed under after end of keel of a large vessel for temporarily assisting in supporting the hull upon removal of keel-blocks, etc., in the preparatory stage of launching. Also called *tumble s.,* it is rounded at each end and falls as vessel begins moving on the ways. *Also see* **B. shore** *in* BILGE; **C.-shore** *in* CAP; DOG-SHORE; DRIVING-SHORE; **Launching-r.** *in* RIBBAND.

SHORING. Arrangement or system of props or shores, as that set up to support a vessel on the stocks or in a graving dock; shores collectively. Act of placing props or shores.

SHORT. Lacking in a specific requirement; not having a reasonable amount; as *s.* of a crew; *s.* of fuel. Having a lesser length than usual; as, a *s.* foremast. Not lengthy in distance or time; as, a *s.* tack; a *s.* voyage. **S. arm floor,** *see* **Long and short f's** *in* FLOOR. **S. blast,** in *Regulations for Preventing Collisions,* a blast of about *one second's duration* made on the whistle or foghorn. **S. bridge,** a bridge deck so called when about three-twentieths of vessel's over-all length or under; *see* **Bridge d.** *in* DECK. **S. forecastle,** raised forecastle having a length of less than one-fifth the vessel's over-all length. **S.-landed,** said of cargo when quantity discharged is tallied as less than that shown in cargo manifest or bill of lading. **S. sea,** *see* SEA. **S. sheet,** *see* SHEET. **S.-shipped,** said of goods billed for shipment but *shut out,* as it is often termed, *i.e.,* not loaded through lack of space or other unforeseen cause. Also, of goods lacking in quantity indicated in bill of lading. **S. splice,** *see* SPLICE. **S. stay,** *see* ASTAY. **S. ton,** a weight of 2000 pounds; *see* TON. **S. up,** said of anchor-cable when hove in to a *s.* stay; *see* ASTAY; also, *To* **h. short** *in* HEAVE.

SHORTEN. To reduce in length or extent; as to *s.* the tow-rope; often with *in,* as, to *s. in* a sheet, etc. To **s. sail,** to take in sail or reduce spread of canvas, as by reefing.

SHORT-LONG FLASHING. Abbrev. *S-L. Fl.;* a light having the characteristic phase of a *short flash* of about 0.4 second and a *long flash* of 4 times that duration, such group repeated about 8 times a minute. *Cf.* LIGHT.[1]

SHOT. A projectile or round of ammunition fired from a gun. A section of an extended drift-net. A single cast of a net or set of nets. A single haul or catch of fish. Whale shot; the waxy solid obtained from oil of sperm whales; spermaceti. A length of chain cable,—usually 15 fathoms. **Case-s.,** *see* CASE. **Cross-bar s.,** as formerly used for cutting up an enemy's rigging, etc., a projectile that expanded on leaving the gun into the form of a cross, with one quarter of the ball at each arm. **Chain-s.,** *see* CHAIN. **Fresh-s.,** *see* FRESH. **S.-garland,** *see* GARLAND. **S.-ladle,** a device once used to extract a ball or shell from a muzzle-loading gun. **S. locker,** a room for stowing cannon-balls or empty shells; sometimes, a *magazine* for live shells.

SHOULDER. An abrupt projection or offset in a structure, timber, machinery part, etc.; as, the prominent piling protection on an outer corner of a wharf or pier; a protuberance in a shaft; the butting part at base of a portable stanchion, at head of a tenon, etc. Any projecting part affording support or limiting motion of something. Prominent convex portion of a frame, timber, etc. In former usage, bulging part of vessel's hull about her water-line,—a prominent feature in the old sailing man-o'-war; *see* **Tumble h.** *in* HOME. **S.-block,** a tackle-block having a projection at one side of its *swallow* to provide a clear entrance for a rope, as when block rests on edge against a spar, etc. **S. gun,** *see* **Line-throwing g.** *in* GUN. **S.-of-mutton sail,** *see* **L.-o'-mutton sail** *in* LEG. **S.-strap,** originally, a detachable flap fitted to shoulders of horsemen's jackets for keeping the cord, strap, etc., of a bag in place; now, the stiffened pieces of cloth worn on each *shoulder* of officers' uniforms. Also called *s.-boards* and, loosely, *epaulets,* they serve to display the wearer's ranking insignia or *s.-marks* borne thereon,—usually gold stripes on a blue ground. Admirals in most navies have all-gold *s.-straps,* with stars, etc.

SHOVE.   To push or urge along by force. The downstream movement of an ice-jam, as in the St. Lawrence River at spring-time break-up of the ice. To **s. off,** to push or thrust away a boat from a landing-place, pier, gangway, etc., as with a boat-hook or oar. Hence, to leave or get under way; or depart, as a vessel or person.

SHOVELHEAD.   A kind of shark; *see* HAMMERHEAD.

SHOWELL.   An older shipyard term for an extension of each *sliding way* that serves the purpose of *skeg-shores* (*see* SHORE). It is fastened securely to the *sliding ways* to prevent ship from starting before the appropriate time during launching preparations.

SHRIMP.   Any of several crustaceans, usually not more than a few inches in length and in appearance not unlike the *sea crayfish.* Related to the *lobster* and *prawn,* it is found in tropical and temperate regions in both fresh and sea water, and, generally, is considered excellent food. The *s.* fishery of S.E. Atlantic coast of U.S. and Gulf of Mexico is an important one. Taken by a *drag-net* or *trawl,* they are pursued by *s.-draggers* or *s.-trawlers* in shallower coastal waters.

SHRINK ON, To.   To fit and cause a metal part to firmly grip another by expanding it by heating, so that it neatly unites with such other part; then contraction due to cooling fixes the connection. In this way, for example, a steering quadrant is *shrunk on* a rudder-stock (also *keyed* for additional security); a jacket on a cannon; and a brass bearing surface on a propeller-shaft. A connection of this type is referred to as a *shrinkage fit.*

SHROUD.   (Ice. *skruth,* rigging or furniture) Ropes, today chiefly of wire, constituting that part of a vessel's *standing rigging* which laterally supports a lowermast and a bowsprit, or serves as a means of climbing aloft (with attached *ratlines*), as in the case of topmast or topgallant rigging. Excepting some sailing-yachts with their *diamond s's*

(*cf.* **D.-rig** *in* DIAMOND), *mast-shrouds* give support to lowermasts only, the *backstays* carrying the burden of the upper masts, although in hemp-rigging days, *topmast s's* set up to sides of the wider *tops* of the day perhaps afforded *some* lateral stiffening to such spar. In the square-rigger, *lowermast s's* partook of backstaying power to a great extent in that a foremost *s.* was set about perpendicular to ship's keel, which meant that, in the case of *raking* masts, foremost *s.* on each side always led to rail *abaft* foot of mast. Thus, remaining *s's,* from 4 to 6 in number on each side, increased in their aftward slope until aftermost one or two contributed to mast's support more in the *backstay* function than that of lateral staying effect, particularly so in the clipper's raking rig. No such effective backstaying efficiency is obtainable in the lower rigging of the schooner or fore-and-aft rig, however, for the chief reason that a similar *aftward lead* of *s's* would interfere with vessel's sail spread, especially in fair winds. Actually, the weight of boom, gaff, and sail in the schooner provides the major portion of pull against mast's tendency to lean forward under head-sail pressure or in plunging in a head sea. The *s.* arrangement in this rig, it also may be noted, must have proportionately greater ,strength than is required in square rig, due to lengthy span and consequent small angle rigging lies with mast. In *machinery,* the term *s.* or *shrouding* is given an enclosing or limiting plate, ring, or part of a casting; as, the disk end of a gear-wheel; a close-fitting ring outside of tips of blades in a turbine casing; etc. **Lower s.,** one of the *s's* comprising the *lower rigging; see* RIGGING. **Preventer s.,** a *s.* temporarily rigged to assist or relieve stress on regular *s.* or *s's;* such *s.* is often fitted on sailing yachts for setting up on weather side in a beam breeze. **S.-band,** a hoop or band around a mast for securing upper ends of *s's.* It is fitted with the required *eyes* for shackling on each *s.;* fitted to steel masts in powered vessels; also, *s.-hoop.* **S.-cap,** a watertight cover, such as tarred canvas, a cylindrical-shaped lid of copper or lead, etc., fitted over the turned-up ends of *s's,* where the latter are not *spliced* to the dead-eyes or solid thimbles. **S. knot,** *see* **F. shroud knot** *in* FRENCH. **S.-laid rope,** *see* LAID. Also see *shroud* as a combining term with the captioned word in BENTINCK; BOWSPRIT; FUTTOCK; HAMMOCK; PAD; TRUCK.

SHROUDED PROPELLER.   *See* PROPELLER.

SHUT.   To close or bar a passage, as a dock-gate or a canal-lock. To obscure or close to view; usually with *out* or *in;* as *the point shuts out* (or *in*) *the river's mouth.* To **s. in the land,** *see* LAND. **S.-out cargo,** *see* **S.-shipped** *in* SHORT.

SHUTTER STRAKE.   *See* STRAKE.

SHY.   Scant, or falling short; *see* SCANT. A shipyard carpenter's word for a deficiency, as in a timber dimension; thus, *this plank is about ½-inch shy of the width.*

SICK. Defective; needing repairs; unsound. A vessel is said to be *s. for* (or *of*) *paint* when badly in need of a new coat; *gear-s.,* when having old or unsound rigging, cargo falls, etc.; or *sail-s.,* if her canvas is greatly in need of repairs or renewals. **Land-s.,** *see* **L'sick** *in* LAND. **S. bay,** space on board ship for treatment of sick or injured seamen or passengers; *see* HOSPITAL. **S. list,** on a warship or large liner, a report or *list* of persons that are ill or otherwise incapacitated or unfit for duty, as submitted to the commanding officer by ship's surgeon or senior medical officer. **S. seam,** a sailmaker's term for a worn-out condition of the stitches in a seam.

SIDE. General term for entire outer surface of a vessel's hull appearing above water-line, on either hand, looking forward, divided into *starboard s.* and *port s.* That portion extending above the upper deck often is termed *topside.* To **s. a timber,** as in shipyard work, is to trim it to a required width and, also, to smoothen the sides of a timber, as by planing. To measure *siding* of a timber, stern-post, etc.; *see* SIDING. **Lee s.,** that *s.* sheltered or away from the wind; opposed to *weather s.* To **man the s.,** as customary in naval ships, to place a line of men standing at attention along the rail, in turrets, etc., as a salute to a high official, at a celebration, etc. **Over the s.,** *see* OVER. To **pipe the s.,** *see* PIPE. **S.-arms,** *see* ARMS. **S.-bar keel,** *see* **Center-plate k.** *in* KEEL. **S. bitt** (of a windlass), either of the bitts supporting the barrel ends of an old-style *windlass.* The slack turns of the idle cable are thrown over one bitt while other cable is in use. **S.-boy,** *see* To **p. the side** *in* PIPE. **S. bunker,** a coal-bunker in a 'tween deck in way of the engine-room or fire-room casing; an oil-fuel tank at *s.* of a fire-room, extending from double-bottom tank-top to next deck above. **S.-coaming,** one of the fore-and-aft coamings of a hatchway. **S. curtain,** as a protection from wind or spray, canvas spread along ship's side in way of an open deck, as in passenger vessels; any similar protecting canvas, such as a downward extension to an awning at vessel's side. **S. girder,** also called **s. intercostal keelson,** *q.v. in* KEELSON. **S. intercostal stringer,** *see* **I. stringer** *in* INTERCOSTAL. **S. keelson,** *see* KEELSON. **S.-light,** *see* LIGHT. **S. launching,** *see* remarks in LAUNCHING. **S.-light screens,** *see* **L.-board** *in* LIGHT. **S.-light towers,** *see* **B.-lighthouses** *in* BOW.[2] **S. plating,** that area of shell plating extending from turn of bilges to upper limit of the hull. **S.-plate rudder,** *see* **D.-plate rudder** *in* DOUBLE. **S. scuttle,** any small opening or port in ship's *s.* **S.-shore,** *see* **Breast s.** *in* SHORE.[2] **S. steps,** *see* **Sea-l.** (*2nd. def.*) *in* LADDER. **S. stringer,** *see* STRINGER. **S.-wheeler,** a paddle-wheel steam-boat. **Weather s.,** the *s.* toward the wind; opposed to *lee s.*

SIDEREAL. (L. *sidus,* a star) Relating to the stars; measured by apparent motion of a star or a fixed point in the heavens; as, a *s. year.* **S. chronometer,** a precision-made clock that indicates *s. time* at a given place, or that corresponding to a given meridian. Formerly some ships carried a *s. chronometer,* but to-day such clock generally is limited to astronomical observatory use. *See* **Sidereal t.** *in* TIME. **S. day,** interval that elapses between two successive upper transits of a star at any place; more correctly, the interval between such transits of the *vernal equinoctial point.* As with the mean solar day, it has 24 hours, each containing 60 minutes of 60 seconds each, but is *shorter* than the *mean solar day* by 3 min. 55.91 secs. of *mean solar time.* **S. hour angle,** arc of the celestial equator, measured *westward,* from the vernal equinox (*First Point of Aries*) to the hour circle passing through a heavenly body or to a given meridian. In the current *Nautical Almanac* it is used to indicate the places of *stars,* in lieu of the formerly employed *right ascension* and is given in degrees, etc., of arc. The right ascension of a star may be found by subtracting the *s. hour angle* (abbrev. *S.H.A.*) from 360° and converting the result into time; thus, if the S.H.A. is 215°, star's right ascension is 9 hours 40 minutes. *Cf.* **H. angle** *in* HOUR. **S. noon,** *see* NOON. **S. period,** time in which a planet or satellite makes a complete revolution about its primary with reference to the stars, as viewed from the primary; thus, our Moon's *s. period,* or *s. revolution* as it also is termed, is 27d. 7h. 43m. 11.5s. of *mean solar time,* or the interval occupied by her orbital travel from a star in her path back to the same star. **S. time,** *see* TIME. **S. year,** *see* YEAR.

SIDING. Act of trimming or smoothing the *sides* of a timber to a required breadth or thickness. Measure of thickness or breadth of a timber, stern-post, etc., as taken at right angles to plane in which such member lies; thus, *s.* of a frame-timber is its *fore-and-aft* dimension, while that of a stern-post is *athwartship* measurement.

SIGHT. Sextant observation of a heavenly body; as, a *s.* of the sun. A device for setting an instrument in a desired direction of alignment by the eye, as a *pelorus* or a *gun.* To observe or view, either with naked eye or as by a telescope; as, to *s.* the land, a whale, a boat, etc. To direct or lay a gun at required elevation, etc., as by *sights.* **Back s.,** *see* **Back o.** *in* OBSERVATION. To **heave in s.,** *see* HEAVE. To **s. an anchor,** to temporarily heave it to the surface for inspection as to whether it is clear of fouling turns of cable, as occasionally done when lying at anchor for days on end. **S. edge,** *see* EDGE. **S. hood,** *see* **S.-hood** *in* SIGHTING. **S.-vane,** as attached to a pelorus, bearing-plate, or an azimuth circle, either of two vertical metal pieces that are lined up as *sights* in direction of object observed. The *object-vane,* or taller one, usually is provided with a fine wire set in a central opening and the *eye-vane,* or one nearer the observer, has a peep-hole or slit. Line of *s.* through eye-vane to vertical wire in object-vane, as object is brought in coincidence with wire, gives direction required. For convenience and accuracy in taking bearings, object-vane of some instruments is fitted with a reflecting prism in which a small arc of compass-card or plate in vicinity of the bearing is seen at base of wire. **Time s.,** *see* TIME.

SIGHTING. Act of observing or first bringing into view; as, *s.* a light; or of aiming, as a gun. **S.-hood,** rounded armored protection over breech of a gun, so called from its *sight-holes* through which aiming of gun may be directed and shots observed. **S.-shot,** a round fired to ascertain the correct range, or to determine any necessary degree of change in elevation or side aim in order to strike the target.

SIGN. An indication, as of an approaching change in weather, a decreasing depth of water, etc. A representation of a letter or number, or a symbol denoting a certain procedure, as in signaling by semaphore, Morse code, etc.; as, the *J s.; call s.; repeat s.;* etc. A mathematical symbol; as, *minus s.* A conspicuous lettered board, notice on a bulkhead, etc.; as, that marked *"Keep clear of Propellers"; "Fire Hydrant No. 10";* etc. To write one's name as a token of obligation or assent. **Bridge s.,** *see* BRIDGE. **S's of the zodiac;** *see* ZODIAC. To **s. on,** to attach one's name to the *articles of agreement; see* ARTICLES. To **s. off,** to signify one's assent to discharge from, or release of obligation to, a vessel (or her master) by signing the *articles,* as at termination of a voyage.

SIGNAL. Any pre-arranged sign,—as by a special flag or flags; by the position or consecutive positions of a semaphore arm or arms; by display of colored lights or rockets; flashing of a light; by sounds or sounding of a horn, whistle, or bell; or detonation of an explosive,—for conveying information. To communicate by *signals* or announce specific information by a *s.;* as, to *s.* a ship; to *s.* approach of a gale. **Blinker s.,** *see* BLINKER. **Compass s.,** *see* COMPASS. **Coston s.,** *see* **Coston l.** *in* LIGHT. **Danger s.,** *see* DANGER. **Distant s.,** also *distance s.,* as visual *s.* hoisted in lieu of flags where colors in these would be impossible to distinguish owing to distance or adverse visibility conditions. Usually in the form of one or more shapes, as balls, drums, or cones, or a combination of such, it is displayed at a prominent point or station to indicate ice or weather conditions, depth of water on a bar, navigation status of a channel, etc. An international *distant s.* code adopted by some maritime nations for merchant shipping coastal communications appears to have been abandoned about the turn of this century. The system used numbers 1 to 4 for repre-

senting a phrase or word; thus, *1 3 2 4* was signaled by a hoist consisting of a *cone point upward,* a *ball,* a *cone point downward,* and a *drum,* in downward vertical order. **Distress s's,** *see* **Rule 31** *in* REGULATIONS FOR PREVENTING COLLISIONS. **Engine Bell s's,** or *bell-pull s's,* as used in American tugs and coastal trading craft, the following are given to engine room by the *pull-wire* system:—

When engine is stopped	1 bell means	Slow ahead
Running full ahead	1 bell	Slow
Running slow ahead	1 bell	Stop
Running slow ahead	Jingle	Full ahead
When engine is stopped	2 bells	Slow astern
Running astern	Jingle	Full astern
Running astern	1 bell	Stop
Running full ahead	4 bells	Full astern
Running slow ahead	3 bells	Full astern

Fog s., *see* FOG. **Harbor s's,** *see* **P. signals** *in* PORT. **International Code of s's,** *see* CODE. (The Code is published in two volumes as *H.O. No. 87* by U.S. Navy Hydrographic Office, Washington, D.C.) **Information s.,** *see* INFORMATION SIGNAL. **Meal s.,** *see* **Meal p.** *in* PENNANT. **Pilot s's,** as included in the *International Code,* displayed together or separately the following "shall be deemed signals for a pilot": *In the Daytime,* (1) the flag *G,* signifying "I require a pilot"; (2) the signal *P T,* signifying "I require a pilot"; (3) the Pilot Jack hoisted at the fore. *At Night:* (1) the pyrotechnic light, commonly known as a *blue light,* every 15 minutes; (2) a bright *white light,* flashed or shown above the bulwarks at short or frequent intervals for about a minute at a time; (3) the signal *P T* by flashing light. **Pyrotechnic s's,** *see* PYROTECHNIC. **Semaphore s's,** those made in a semaphore system; *see* SEMAPHORE. The old 4-armed fixed semaphore formerly used in *distant signaling* as an alternative to the system employing a ball, cone, drum, and sometimes a *weft,* and in which the position of each arm indicated a number, officially was abandoned, with all so-called *distant s's,* at the *International Radiotelegraph Conference* held at Washington, 1927; *cf.* **Distant s.** **S. code,** *see* CODE. **S. flag,** any burgee, square flag, or pennant displayed as a *s.,* either by itself or with one or more other flags, or with one or more *shapes.* **S. flags** are either of a single color or have a design showing two or three *distinctive* colors. As best suited for marine use these generally are limited to black, blue, red, yellow, and white. **S. halyards,** *see* HALYARD. **S.-lamp, -lantern, -light,** *see* **Signal-l.** *in* LANTERN. **S. letters,** the four letters, denoted by *International Code* flags, which have been assigned each vessel at her registration. They are for identifying vessel by a single *hoist* in which first one or two flags indicate her nationality; also, the *radio call sign* of vessel, which is identical with letters thus signified. *See* NATIONALITY MARK *and* NUMBER. **S.-pistol,** *see* PISTOL. **S. station,** a coast station, often at site of a lighthouse, for sending and receiving messages to and from vessels. *Cf.* **L. signal stations** *in* LLOYD'S. **S. tower,** in a warship, a raised armored station for use and protection of signalmen. **S. yard,** a cross-spar on a mast for displaying *s's*. Halyards are rove at each yard-arm and sometimes, on longer yards, at two or more other points on the spar. **S. yeoman,** also *yeoman of s's, see* YEOMAN. **Storm s's,** *see* **W. signals** *in* WEATHER. **Submarine sound s's,** those sent out as *fog s's* by a submarine *bell* or *oscillator,* as from a lightship. Since the present system of radiobeacons was instituted, usefulness of these *s's* now practically belongs to the past. However, a few stations have retained the device in connection with a method of *distance-finding* provided for use of vessels equipped with a *submarine-s. receiving apparatus.* This consists of two telephone receivers connected to a diaphragm receiver below water-line on each bow of ship. Relative intensity of audibility determines general direction from which *s's* arrive; thus, with both receivers to his ears, a navigator compares sounds from either side of ship by use of a two-way switch; if *s's* of equal intensity are heard, sending-station lies ahead. *See* OSCILLATOR *and* **R. distance-finding stations** *in* RADIO. **Time s.,** *see* TIME. **Very's s's,** *see* VERY'S. **Weather s.,** *see* WEATHER; also, INFORMATION SIGNAL. **Whistle s's,** those given by a steam-vessel or other powered craft in the form of one or more separate *blasts;* specifically, the prescribed blast or blasts to be made on the steam whistle or siren in a powered vessel, as when in fog, or in any situation involving risk of collision, according to rules set forth in REGULATIONS FOR PREVENTING COLLISIONS.

SIGNALING. The sending, receiving, and interpreting of messages conveyed by a system of signals; of or pertaining to a signal or a system of signals; as, *Morse s.;* semaphore *s.;* a *s. class; s. apparatus.* **S. mirror,** a flat piece of stainless steel or other metal having a polished surface of not less than 20 in.,^{2} for flashing or directing sun's reflection as a signal of distress, Two of such mirrors were required lifeboat equipment by U.S. Coast Guard regulations during World War II, chiefly with view of providing means for attracting attention of rescuing aircraft.

SIGNALMAN. A former U.S. navy rating now absorbed in that of *Quartermaster (1948),* or a present rating in the British navy, designating one who sends and receives signals, particularly those by flag, flashing-light, and semaphore. Any person whose duties chiefly are concerned with *signaling,* as at a coastal station; a *signal man* stationed at a hatchway to give signals for hoisting, lowering, etc., of drafts of cargo; also, *hatch man.*

SILK-ROOM. Specially constructed space, usually in a 'tween deck, for stowage of silk, as in vessels

regularly engaged in the Far East trade. Such space or room isolates contents from all other cargo, is wood lined and thoroughly insulated against harmful condensation of moisture due to sudden changes of air temperature.

SILL. (Ice. *syll,* a foundation timber) Concrete or timber at bottom of a canal lock, dock basin entrance, etc., against or on which the gates abut or rest in closing. Lower part of a side-port or door frame; foundation timber of a deck-house, poop bulkhead, etc. A lip, or projecting piece of curved metal or leather, acting as a spout to throw drippings clear of ship's side at outer end of a scupper-pipe. **Dock s.,** *see* DOCK.

SILT. (Prob. of *Old Teutonic* source, akin to *salt*) Mud or earthy substance suspended in, or deposited by, water; a deposit of such substance; especially, that at bottom, sides, or mouth of a river. To **s. up,** choke or obstruct with *s.;* as, *the bar silts up at neap tides.*

SILVER. Combining term designating certain fishes of more or less *silvery* appearance. **S. eel,** the *cutlass-fish (q.v.);* a pale variety of the common eel. **S. gar,** one of the *Belonidæ* family; *see* GAR. **S. hake,** *see* HAKE. **S. king,** the tarpon. **S. moonfish,** the *Selene vomer; see* **M.-fish** *in* MOON. **S. salmon,** a small species of the *Pacific s.; see* SALMON. **S. whiting,** *see* WHITING.

SILVERY GULL. The herring-gull; *see* GULL.

SIMOOM. (Ar. *samum;* from *samm,* to poison) A hot, dry, dust-laden, almost suffocating wind of short duration that occasionally blows from the Arabian, Sahara, and Syrian deserts. Also written *simoon.*

SIMPSON'S RULES. *See* RULE.

SIMULTANEOUS ALTITUDES. Those of two or more celestial bodies observed at same instant, or reduced to their respective values at a common instant, for determining ship's position. Objects having a wide difference in azimuth are selected with the view of obtaining a definite intersection of at least two of the *lines of position* resulting from such observations.

SINGING. Distinctly audible vibratory sounds emitted by a taut towing-wire cutting through the water, rigging in a siff breeze, blades of a moving propeller, etc. A *s. propeller* is one that gives out a constant note when turning at a certain rate at constant depth. The sound apparently is amplified in the interposed medium of vessel's shell plating in vicinity of screw. **S. fish,** a toadfish, also called *midshipman,* capable of making a humming sound; *see* MIDSHIPMAN.

SINGLE. To reduce two or more parts in a tackle, lashing, mooring, etc., to one in number; usually with *up,* as to take in all bights of mooring-lines and reduce all moorings to a minimum, preparatory to casting off, in leaving a pier or wharf. In one piece; one only; unaccompanied; individual. Opposed to *double,* as denoting some knots; *e.g., s. carrick bend, s. wall, s. diamond;* or as applied to sails, as *s. topsail, s. topgallants'l.* **S.-banked,** said of a boat having an oarsman handling one oar on each thwart. **S. block,** one having a *s.* sheave. **S.-bottom,** having no inner bottom; as, a *s.-bottom vessel.* **S. burton,** a purchase having two *s. blocks;* especially, a *s. Spanish burton; see* BURTON. **S. decker,** also *s.-decked vessel,* any type of craft having one continuous deck that marks upper limit of the hull. **S.-ended boiler,** one that is fired at one end only. **S. fastening,** *see* FASTENING. **S.-plate keelson,** *see* KEELSON. **S.-plate rudder,** *see* **Plate r.** *in* RUDDER. **S.-ply canvas,** that having single threads constituting the weft or woof; usually applied to sail cloth of the lighter grades, or *No. 3* and above. **S. purchase,** *see* PURCHASE. **S. riveting,** connection of edges and ends of plates or sheets by a *single row* of rivets, as in lighter work. **S. spar,** *see* **Pole m.** *in* MAST. **S.-sticker,** a one-masted vessel; a sloop or cutter. **S. topsail,** in square rig, sail set between a lower yard and a topgallants'l and hoisted on a topmast. Since about 1853 the sail gave way to *double tops'ls,* or what amounted to a halving of the *s. tops'l* spread; *see* TOPSAIL. **S.-tree mast,** a lowermast made of a *s.* tree trunk; opposed to a *built mast.* **S.-way launching,** *see remarks in* LAUNCHING.

SINK. To founder or fall beneath the surface, as a lost vessel; to swim deeper, as a school of fishes in passing below a net. To further immerse by a certain degree or amount; as, *ship will s. five feet in loading.* To cause to descend below the surface; as, to *s.* a vessel. To set in position in the ground; as, to *s.* a mooring post or anchor. To cause the land, by sailing away from it, to descend below the intervening horizon; as, *by morning we had sunk the coast.* To **s. without trace,** to torpedo, blow up, or otherwise utterly destroy a vessel and annihilate her crew, with the view of leaving no evidence of their fate. *Sinkage* is an increase of mean draft due to additional weight placed on board. *Sinking-ballast* is heavy material occupying little space, such as pig iron, sand, stone, etc., and employed to both materially increase vessel's draft and lower the center of gravity.

SINKER. A weight, as a piece of lead or iron, used to sink a sounding-wire, a fishing line or net, a lobster pot, etc.

SIREN. Sound-producing instrument used as a whistle on many powered vessels and as a fog-signal at some coast stations. Whistling effect is produced from rapid interruption of steam or compressed air passing through a perforated disk that rotates over a fixed plate similarly perforated. Disk is activated by pressure flow against slanting surfaces of the holes or perforations, the pitch of note rising with increase of pressure and consequent acceleration of disk's rotating speed. A ship's *s.* is fitted with a trumpet fixed to throw the instrument's penetrating note forward and, to this end, often is placed on the foremast. Also written *syren.* The term is said to have its source in the Greek word *seiren,* denoting a *sea nymph,* or one of a number of quasi-humans of the gentler sex said to have lived somewhere off the coasts of southern Italy. These were noted for their capability of luring sailors to destruction on the rocks by their beauty and sweet singing. Indeed, it is also alleged that the famed *Odysseus* escaped the treacherous ladies' tricks by lashing himself to his vessel's mast and filling his sailors' ears with wax!

SIRENIAN. Of or pertaining to the *Sirenia,* an order of large, aquatic, herbivorous mammals, including the dugong, manatee, and sea cow. Any of the *Sirenia.*

SIRIUS. (Gr. *seirios,* scorching) Brightest star in the heavens, of the group *Canis Major,* easily located just S.E. of *Orion.* With *Betelgeuse* (α Orionis), reddish member a few degrees north of the *Belt* (three stars close in line), and bright *Procyon* (α Canis Minoris) to the N.E., *Sirius* stands at the southern corner of an equilateral triangle formed by lines joining all three. Classified as α *Canis Majoris,* its magnitude is given as —1.58; sidereal hour angle 259¼°; and declination as 16° 39′ S.

SIRMARK. *See* SURMARK.

SIROCCO. (*It.*) Also, *scirocco;* a hot dust-laden S.E. wind that occasionally blows from the Libyan Desert toward Sicily and southern Italy during summer. On the North African coast it is excessively dry and parching, but becomes humid and oppressive after passing over the Mediterranean waters. The term also is applied generally to any hot wind originating in dry heated regions, as the *harmattan* of West Africa, *khamsin* of Egypt, *leste* of Canary Islands, *leveche* of Spain, etc.

SISAL HEMP. (From *Sisal,* a port on north coast of Yucatan) The white fiber of several agaves originally cultivated in Mexico and Central America for making mats, cordage, etc.; especially, that from the *henequen,* which ranks next to manila in rope manufacture. *See* ROPE *and* IXTLE.

SISTER. Resembling another object in form or size; of the same type in size and design; as, *s. ships.* **S.-block,** a tackle-block having two sheaves, both of which lie in the same plane, either with one above the other, when it also is called *long-tail block* and *tandem block,* or with one abreast the other, when it is also termed a *sheet block.* **S.-hooks,** a pair of close-fitting hooks that form an eye when clasped together as in hooking on to a cringle, eye-bolt, etc.

Also called *clasp-, clip-, clove-,* and *match-hooks,* they are used for securing pendants, clew-garnet blocks, and other smaller gear where neatness and elimination of chafing by a shackle or pointed hook is desirable. **S. keelson,** *see* **Assistant k.** *in* KEELSON.

SKAG. A heavy chain used when necessary in close waters as a drag for steadying a towed barge that has a tendency to sheer about.

SKATE. One of many fishes constituting the genus *Raja* and related genera of the *ray* family, several of which are considered excellent food; *see* RAY. The term also denotes one of two curved skids temporarily hooked to the keel and secured in a vertical position to the gunwale of a ship's lifeboat. The *skates* serve as runners or slides that hold boat clear of a listing vessel's side and thus allow her to descend steadily in lowering to water.

SKAW. (Ice. *skaga,* to jut out) A promontory or headland.

SKEET. A flat wooden scoop or bailer, such as used for removing water from a dory or other flat-bottomed boat. Formerly, it was a long-handled scoop used to throw water against ship's sides, as in washing down in port.

SKEG. (Ice. *skaga,* to project or jut out) Aftermost and deepest part of the deadwood, or that next the stern-post; projecting end of keel on which the rudder is stepped, as in smaller powered craft; the *sole-piece* or horizontal part of stern frame below the propeller in a single-screw vessel. **S. shore,** *see* SHORE.[2]

SKELETON. A vessel's principal frame-work fitted together without plating or planking, as in early stage of construction. Having the leading features only, or bare necessities; as, a *s. deck,* or platform deck having planks spaced an inch or two apart; a *s. rig,* or that of a *s.-rigged* vessel, in which all light yards, upper masts, etc., have been removed. **S. crew,** a temporary crew, considerably fewer in number than vessel's regular complement, such as that engaged in shifting a vessel in sheltered waters or for a short coastwise run not included in a voyage. **S. floor,** *see* **Bracket f.** *in* FLOOR.

SKERRY. (Ice. *sker,* a rock or reef) Chiefly in north and west of Scotland, an outlying reef of rocks; a rocky islet.

SKEW-BACK BLADES. In some merchant vessels, blades of the propeller set with an inclination aftward instead of usual arrangement in which they lie at right angles to axis of shaft. Properly, those having their center lines *curved* as viewed from either side are *skewed,* while those having a *straight* center line are said to be *raked.* Certain advantages are claimed for such set of the blades, chief of which are that tip clearance from the hull is thereby increased and so thrown farther clear of hull eddies, and that each blade is spread over a greater sector of the propeller disk. This latter feature tends to reduce thrust fluctuations resulting from irregular flow in wake of propeller-post or bossings.

SKID. (Ice. *skidh,* a billet of wood) One of two or more parallel pieces of timber, structural iron, etc., supporting a heavy object or objects, as a spar or a water-tank on deck; such timbers, etc., used as runners for sliding or moving over rollers any weighty object, such as a piece of machinery. A number of planks fixed edge to edge to serve as a runway over which cargo is hauled or trucked between ship and shore, as through a side-port; a similar set of planks hung against ship's side as a fender or protection against blows and scratches from drafts of cargo during loading or discharging. **Boat s's,** a pair of thwartship timbers or beams of structural iron often extending from side to side of, and supported by stanchions above, a weather deck. Primarily for raising boats clear of deck, usually a platform of open planks is laid fore-and-aft on the structure which also provides space for stowage of spars and other gear. Usually referred to as *the skids, forward s's, after s's, poop s's,* etc. The term sometimes denotes the thwartships foundation-pieces on which *boat-chocks* are mounted. **Landing-s.,** a plank runway from ship to shore serving as a gangway for transferring cargo, baggage, etc. **S. fins,** another name for *rolling-chocks; see* **B. keel** *in* BILGE.

SKIFF. (Old Ger. *skif*) Any open boat that is propelled by oars, sail, or motor and used for any purpose. Many different types of *skiffs* are named for places at which a particular build or size of craft is popular, especially in the fisherman's field.

SKIMMER. So called from its skimming over the water with its long and flat lower mandible immersed for catching its food, a long-winged bird allied to the *terns.* The *black s. (Rhynchops nigra),* commonly found on southern U.S. coasts, grows to about 18 inches in length; has a dark back and white belly, with red and black bill.

SKIMMING-DISH. Old-fashioned local term for a broad-beamed, light-draft sailing yacht fitted with a centerboard; an American yachtsman's appellative for a centerboard sloop, as distinguishing in a derisive sense such craft from a *cutter.*

SKIMMINGS. Referred to damaged cargo, denotes the spoiled portion of a bagged commodity, such as coffee and cacao beans, lentils, peas, etc., separated from the unharmed and marketable goods.

SKIN. Plating or planking constituting the *shell* or outer surface of a hull; also sometimes applied to the *ceiling (see* **I. skin** *in* INNER). In furling or stowing a sail, especially in a *harbor furl,* last and clearest stretch of canvas turned over and covering the whole; *see* FURL. **S. area,** in matters concerning *s. frictional resistance,* extent of the immersed surface of a hull; ship's *wetted surface.* In vessels of ordinary form, its value in *square feet* is, very nearly, 15.8 times the square root of the product of displacement *(in tons)* and water-line length *(in feet).* **S.-boat,** as found chiefly in Arctic regions, native-made craft in which the shell consists of animal skins,—principally walrus-hide in larger boats, as in the *oomiak,* and seal skins, as in the *kayak.* *See* BAIDAR; OOMIAK; KAYAK. **S. plating,** *see* **Shell p.** *in* PLATING. **S. resistance,** that set up by friction of water against vessel's immersed surface when moving through the water. Its value depends upon area and degree of roughness of *s. area* and, of course, speed of vessel, being proportionately greater as a component of total resistance, or aggregate of *eddy-making, wave-making,* and *s. resistance,* at low speeds than at greater. For a vessel of normally smooth surface, expressed in *pounds* it amounts to, very nearly, one-hundredth of the product of ship's wetted surface (in *square feet*) times speed (in *knots*) to the 1.86th. power. *Cf.* RESISTANCE. To **s. up a sail,** to top off with a clear stretch of canvas to present a smooth surface in *furling* a sail; *see remarks above.*

SKIP. A loading-tray; *see* TRAY.

SKIPJACK. A large broad-beamed, clipper-bowed, decked boat of V-bottom build once common on the U.S. Atlantic coast and much used in fishing, oystering, etc., especially in more sheltered areas. Usually fitted with a centerboard, the craft's main feature is that of being straight-framed throughout, with a sharp turn of bilge or common meeting-line of sides and oblique-planked bottom. Generally, carries a single mast with leg-o'-mutton sail and jib, but formerly often yawl or schooner-rigged. Also, any of various fishes that habitually jump from or play about the water's surface, as the bluefish, bonito, butterfish, cavalla, leather-jack, moonfish, saury, etc.; often, *skipper.*

SKIPPER. (Du. *schipper;* from *schip,* ship) In Great Britain, the official title of a certificated mariner in command of a fishing vessel of over 25 tons gross. Colloquially, the master of any merchant or fishing vessel, especially one of smaller tonnage. **S.'s daughters,** white-caps or white-crested waves, such as appear in a fresh to strong breeze.

SKRIMSHAW. *See* SCRIMSHAW.

SKUA. (Ice. *skufr*) Also called *skua gull;* a *jaeger* or large gull-like sea-bird of North Atlantic coasts, especially northwestern Norway. Allied species are found in higher southern latitudes. *See* JAEGER.

SKY. (Of *Scand.* origin) The heavens or the apparent blue canopy above us; meteorologically, the region of the clouds. A specific cloud formation; as, an *overcast s.;* a *woolly s.* **Mackerel s.,** that in which the *cirro-stratus cloud* is prominent; *see* CLOUD. **S. pilot,** a chaplain, often so named in the armed forces. **S.-scraper,** a skysail or any sail set above all others in square rig; a moonraker. *Cf.* **F. kites** *in* FLYING. **Water s.,** *see* WATER.

SKYLIGHT. A deck erection fitted with framed glass covers or windows for admission of light and often serving as a ventilator, as above a cabin, crew's quarters, engine-room, etc. **S. cover,** protective canvas made to cover a *s.,* as in bad weather. **S. gear,** the mechanical arrangement of cranks, screw-rods, etc., used to lift and lower heavy *s.* tops from a position below, as commonly found with *engine-room s's.* **S. grating,** a series of brass rods serving as a guard over windows of a *cabin s.*

SKYSAIL. Square sail set above a royal on the *s. pole,* as carried in the clippers of last mid-century. A kind of staysail set between the topmasts on a racing schooner-rigged yacht. **S.-mast,** *see* MAST.

SLAB. A bulky hanging part of a sail, as that of a course before hauling taut the buntlines in taking in the canvas. Any bulky piece of material having a more or less flat surface; as a *s. of plate,* a *s. of wood.* **Bending s.,** in a shipbuilding yard, a solid floor or level surface made of cast-iron blocks or layers of heavy plate for facilitating the *bending* of frames and other structural members to a desired shape, in connection with furnace-heating of the material. It is provided with round or square holes of about 1½-inch diameter or side, 4 to 6 inches apart, for inserting bolts and dogs in the process of securing a frame, etc., as it is bent to curvature required, which usually is indicated by chalk-line on the *slab.* Thus fastened to slab, the structural part is then left to cool. Also termed *bending-block, -floor, -platform, -table; furnace slab; leveling-block.* **Keel s.,** narrow stiffening bar or plate on each side of vertical plate extending below ship's bottom to form a *side-bar keel; see* **Center-plate k.** *in* KEEL. **S. keel,** *see* KEEL. **S. line,** on a large square mainsail or a crossjack, one of the lines leading from each quarter of the yard and sometimes from its middle, direct to foot of, and abaft, the sail. It was used to either simply raise sail's foot, as in a light following breeze to give a clear view ahead (from the poop), or to assist the buntlines in taking in the sail. Also, *slap line.* **S. reef,** the single and sometimes double reef in the old-time quadruple-reefing square topsail; *see* **F. reef** *in* FRENCH.

SLACK. Loose; not taut or tense; as, a *s. chain.* Weak; slow in motion; as, a *s. current.* Loose part of canvas, cordage, etc.; idle end of a rope; as, *s. of a sail; s. of a tackle.* To ease off or loose, as a rope; to *slacken;* usually with *away, off,* or *up;* as, S. *away the sheet!;* S. *off the lee braces!;* to *s.* up a hawser. **S. cloth,** *see* CLOTH. **S. in stays,** said of a vessel that is slow or difficult to *bring about, i.e.,* in tacking. To **s. out,** to *s. away,* as a mooring-line, cable, etc., from ship's bitts, windlass, etc. To **take in the s.,** to haul in or round up slack rope or chain, as that in a tackle, slackness in a hawser, etc. **S. water,** in tidal waters, period or state between ebb and flood when there is no appreciable horizontal movement of surface waters.

SLACKEN. To become slack or less tense, as a rope. To slack away, off, out, or up; *see* SLACK. To decrease in speed or motion; as, *the ebb current is slackening.*

SLACKNESS. Referred to a vessel's sailing qualities, tendency to *fall off* from the wind, indicating the *center of effort* is too far forward of that of lateral resistance; opposed to *ardency; cf.* ARDENT.

SLAMMING. Another word for *pounding,* the *slam* of ship's bottom near the stem in a heavy head sea; *s.* or *pounding damage* is that suffered by bottom plating, etc., from such cause; *see* POUNDING.

SLANT. A pleasing or satisfactory period or occasion; as, a *fine-weather s. through the trades.* **S. of wind,** a duration of favorable wind; an opportune breeze.

SLAT. To flap or slap, as a loose sail or awning, or slack ropes beating against a mast, in a breeze. To flap about, as sails in a calm when vessel is rolling in a swell. A thin flat piece of wood or metal, such as one of those in a jalousie door or shutter. A deposit of silt that hardens on being exposed at low water; also, *slatt.*

SLATCH. Archaic word for a *slant* of wind or weather; *see* SLANT. Also, the idle or slack end of a rope.

SLATE, LOG. *See* LOG.²

SLAVE. S. jib, a working jib, or one seldom taken in, as so termed by some yachtsmen. **S. ship,** a slaver, or former carrier of *s's* picked up chiefly from tropical Africa. **S. station,** *see* LORAN.

SLEEPER. One of the knees that connect the transom to timbers in a wooden vessel's counter. In a slipway or building berth, one of the heavy timbers forming the foundation for sustaining a vessel's weight, or that on which the *cribbing* is placed. A water-logged piece of timber, pile, etc., floating almost entirely submerged. The Greenland shark; *see* SHARK. **Engine s's,** *see* E. **foundation** *in* ENGINE.

SLEEVE. Tubular piece of metal into which a rod or pipe is fitted or which encloses butting ends of two rods or pipes, as in an expansion joint or in an iron deck-rail; any tubular part fitting about or forming a socket for some other part. **Clean s.,** in U.S. navy, not wanting in good conduct marks on one's uniform sleeve. Satisfactory service is indicated by *having a clean s.* **S. weld,** joint of butting

ends of rods or piping made by welding a *s.* to cover both parts in vicinity of the butt. The *Sleeve* was an old British navy name for the English Channel.

SLEIGH. Among former New England whalemen, the upper jaw-bone of a sperm whale. **Nantucket sleigh-ride,** *see same.*

SLEW. See SLUE.

SLICE. A shipyard term for one of the long hardwood wedges that are driven between *sliding ways* and sill of *cradle* to raise a vessel, preparatory to launching, clear of keel and building blocks and so bring ship's weight on the ways; also, *launching-wedge.* A chisel-pointed bar with a long handle for various uses, such as stripping a vessel's bottom of old metal sheathing, etc.; *slicing* or cutting up a coal fire in stoking; cutting blubber from a whale's carcase; and the like. A *s.-bar* or *fire-s.;* a *cutting-spade* (whaling); also, *slicer.*

SLICK. A glossy smooth area on the water's surface, as from a filmy spread of oil or the slue of a vessel in turning under hard over helm. **Oil-s.,** *see* OIL.

SLIDE. To move by slipping or gliding, as an object on a bearing surface; as, to *s. down the ways;* to *launch.* Having a sliding motion; as, a *s.-valve.* **Louver s.,** *see* LOUVER. **Rapson's s.,** *see* RAPSON'S SLIDE. **S. block,** as found in some sailing yachts, a piece of metal fitted in fore end of a gaff for confining the spar to a *railway* along after side of mast, thus dispensing with *jaws* on gaff. Chiefly found in sailing yachts, *s.* may be *T-shaped* where railway is of the channel type; or may be a *claw* to fit over a rail of *T section.* **S. knot,** a bend or knot made by two half hitches over standing part of rope, so that second hitch lies next to object to which line is thus made fast. Knot is *slided* against object and thus is secure from coming adrift. Also called *back hitch* and *studding-sail-tack bend,*—the latter from its use with the old *stuns'ls.*

SLIDING. Designating that which slips or glides; pertaining to or used in the act of *sliding.* **S. balk** or **baulk,** an older name for one of the heavy dressed timbers constituting the *standing ways* on which a vessel slides in *launching;* also, *s. plank.* **S. bowsprit,** same as *running bowsprit; see* BOWSPRIT. **S. gunter,** *see* GUNTER. **S. keel,** *see* CENTERBOARD. **S. limb,** *see* LIMB. **S. ways,** also, *bilgeways,* launching-ways that travel with ship in the operation of *launching; s. planks.*

SLIGHT SEA. *See scale of* **State of the Sea** *in* SEA.

SLING. A rope strop or special chain that is secured to and takes the weight of a draft or piece of cargo, machinery, etc., when connected to a hoisting fall or tackle; any of several devices for holding together or otherwise securing one or more pieces of cargo, etc. for lifting; as, a *chain s., net s.,* *platform s., can-hooks* (for casks), *bridle* (for rod iron, piping, etc.), etc. In *pl.*, a four-legged bridle, such as is used for lifting an automobile, truck, heavy boat, or the like. Middle portion of a yard, especially a lower one, so called from the chain or chains supporting yard to the mast. To secure a lift or draft of cargo or other goods in a *s.* for hoisting; to suspend by a *s.* **Canvas s.,** one having a piece of strong canvas between the parts for providing a wide bearing surface in lifting bagged goods, such as flour, sugar, and seeds. **Chain s.,** a bridle or single length of short-link chain adapted to slinging iron rods, piping, castings, etc. **Flour s.,** same as *canvas s.* **Platform s.,** used for lifting a draft of similar small packages, a wood or metal board or *tray* slung by a four-legged bridle. To **s. a hammock,** *see* HAMMOCK. To **s. a yard,** to secure a hoisting yard independently of its halyards or lifts by a lashing about its middle to the mast, as was customary in former naval vessels in preparation for an engagement. **S.-band,** a hoop or band around middle of a lower yard for taking stress of the supporting chains or chain called the *slings.* **S.-cleat,** a becket fixed on outer side of a shroud for holding a slack rope, as a weather sheet of a course; a *thumb-cleat.* **Web s.,** another name for a *canvas s.*

SLIP. To let run overboard, as a cable, in sense of speeding ship's departure; as, to *s. and run.* To release and let run out, as a mooring, a towing-hawser, etc. A device for releasing a hook. In *U.S.,* area of water between two wharves; a *ferry-s.* Inclined plane on which vessels are built; a *slip-way;* place where vessels are hauled up for repairs; a *marine railway.* Difference between distance actually made through water and that as reckoned by revolutions of a paddle or a propeller (*cf.* PITCH²); usually expressed as a *percentage of engine distance,* or that by revolutions. (This is *true·s.* In navigational practice *s.* is calculated regardless of presence of a current and thus may have a *minus value* where vessel has made good a distance *greater* than that indicated by shaft revolutions, in which case difference referred to is termed *negative·s.* In usual case of greater run according to engines, it is called *positive s.*) **Building s.,** berth where vessels are built and launched. **Patent s.,** older British name for a *marine railway; see* **Slip d.** *in* DOCK. **S. angle,** that between a vessel's fore-and-aft line and plane of face of a propeller-blade at point of mean effective effort. To **s. a cable,** *see* CABLE. **S.-dock,** *see* DOCK. **S.-hook,** *see* **P. hook** *in* PELICAN. **S.-iron,** a plating-liner; see LINER. **S. knot,** a hitch or knot that slides or *slips* along the standing part of rope on which it is made; a slide-knot; a running bowline (*see* **Running-b.** *in* BOWLINE). Any knot that may be loosed by a smart jerk on end of rope; especially, a *s. reef knot* in which second half knot is made with an end and a bight; *see* **R. knot** *in* REEF. Not to be

confused with a **s. hitch,** or that made on a cleat or a belaying-pin, as for quickly letting go a halyard or sheet in a boat, by laying rope's bight under the completing turn, so that a sharp pull immediately releases rope. **S.-rope,** a line that, at a distance, may be detached from an object, as, for example, one that temporarily secures a boat or vessel to ring of a buoy, both ends of rope being on board. Short end is let go and rope hauled through ring and aboard. **S.-stopper,** a short chain or rope secured to the deck forward of the windlass for temporarily relieving the latter of anchor cable stress, or for additional security in holding anchor in stowed position at sea. So called because fitted with a *s.-hook* for ready release. It often is provided with a turnbuckle for setting up in securing an anchor. **S. tender,** one employed to make fast and let go ferry-boats' lines in a *s.* **Wet s.,** in connection with a shipyard, area between two wharves or piers where dock trials of propulsion plant and final outfitting of new vessels are carried out. In U.S., sometimes also called *wet dock.*

SLIPWAY. The prepared and usually re-enforced inclined surface on which *keel-* and *bilge-blocks* are laid for supporting a vessel under construction; a *building slip.* Also, a *patent s.* or *marine* railway; *see* **Slip d.** *in* DOCK.

SLIVER. A slice or launching-wedge; *see* SLICE. Side of a small fish cut off in one piece for baiting hooks in catching cod, halibut, or other fishes by line.

SLOB ICE. *See* ICE.

SLOOP. One masted fore-and-aft rigged vessel, usually carrying a fore staysail and one or more jibs and, also, in heavier craft a gaff topsail (formerly a *square* topsail). Of similar rig to that of the *cutter,* difference between the two is more of a yachting distinction than designation of a type. Actually, a *cutter* is a deep-keeled or narrow-beamed *sloop,* the original name for the rig, although attempts have been made to distinguish the two by crediting a cutter with a larger spread of canvas, particularly in the head sails. A popular distinction in the smaller craft field is that a *s.* is broader beamed, carries a centerboard, and is intended for smooth-water sailing. *Cf.* CUTTER. Formerly, a *s.-of-war,* or naval vessel of ship, brig, topsail-schooner, or almost any rig, carrying guns on her upper or weather deck only; later, in early days of steam propulsion, a British vessel carrying guns on one deck; *see* **P. sloop** *in* PADDLE. **S.-rigged,** having the rig of a *s.;* as, a *s.-rigged yacht.*

SLOPE. Deviation from the horizontal. **Continental s.,** *see* **Continental s.** *in* SHELF. **S. oar,** *see* OAR.

SLOPS. (Ice. *sloppr,* a loose garment) The loose trousers or "breeches" extending just below the knee, worn by British navy sailors in 17th. and 18th. centuries. Also, originally in England, bedding and clothes furnished by the Admiralty to seamen of the Royal Navy; now, clothing, small stores, etc., supplied at cost. **Slop book,** official record of clothing, tobacco, and small stores issued to crew members. **Slop chest,** supply of personal necessities kept on board for sale to members of the crew, as required by law in American and British merchant ships engaged on a foreign voyage. U.S. law requires that such supply shall include boots or shoes, hats or caps, underclothing and outer clothing, oiled clothing, and everything necessary for the wear of a seaman; also a full supply of tobacco and blankets; and these shall be sold to seamen for their own use at a profit not exceeding 10% of reasonable wholesale value at the port at which voyage commences (*46 U.S.C. 670–671*). **S.-chute,** *see* **Garbage-c.** *in* CHUTE.

SLOT LINK. *See* **Slot l.** *in* LINK.

SLOUSE. (Newfoundland dialectal) To sail with a wet deck, *i.e.,* with vessel shipping water continuously. Also, usually with *along,* to sail *full and by* under easy sail; to sail in a general direction, as in following a coastline.

SLUDGE. Mire; soft mud; wet snow; slush. **S. boat,** specially constructed tank vessel for disposing of residue of a sewage plant. **S.-hole,** *see* **M.-hole** *in* MUD. **S. ice,** *see* ICE.

SLUE. To turn or twist about a weighty object; especially, a boom, mast, etc., in its seat or pivoting point; also *slew.* To sheer or yaw from side to side, as a vessel at single anchor in a breeze or a helmless barge being towed. Chiefly in U.S., a secondary or side channel, as at a river's mouth or in a strait; a wide inlet from a river. **S.-rope,** a guy or line attached to an object for turning it around or checking its tendency to turn, as that made fast to a bulky piece of cargo suspended in transfer to or from a vessel; a wire rope at foot of a crane or derrick for *sluing* purposes; sometimes, a *boom guy.*

SLUER. In older whalemen's parlance, helmsman or boat-steerer; probably so called from his customary *sluing* strokes of the steering-oar.

SLUICE. Opening at foot of a bulkhead, usually in the form of a gate-valve, called *s.-cock* or *s.-valve,* for permitting flow of oil or water from one compartment to another. Valve is controlled by a rod leading to a deck or decks above. A flood-gate in a canal or locking system for conducting water to a lower level. **S.-master,** officer having charge of raising and lowering of vessels in a lockage system, as at a tidal dock entrance, by manipulation of the *s's.* **S. keel,** as built in some smaller powered craft, principally tug-boats, to facilitate short turning in maneuvering, a keel that is deepened to form a partly

opened *skeg,* or after deadwood, for reducing lateral resistance consequent to such turning.

SLUMGULLION. In older whaling, *lipperings* or mixture of blood, oil, and sea-water issuing from blubber as it is hoisted aboard from carcase alongside; gurry; offal. *Cf.* GURRY; LIPPER; OFFAL. (*Chiefly U.S.*)

SLUSH. Wet or half-melted snow, especially when under foot; sludge; mushy floating ice. Refuse fat from ship's galley, formerly always collected in the *s.-barrel* for greasing down masts; when mixed with tar for applying to parceling before serving a rope; lubricating sheaves; etc. Mixture of white lead and tallow for coating wire rigging, machinery parts, etc. Any greasy mixture used as a lubricant or preservative. To daub with *s.;* with *down,* to apply *s.* to a wood mast, working downward; as, to *s. down the topmast.* **S. fund,** money derived from sale of *s.* and other refuse material in a warship and used, at direction of commanding officer, for small luxuries for crew, target prizes, etc. **S.-horn,** a *rigger's horn; see* HORN. **S.-lamp,** in its early form, a receptacle containing *s.* and fitted with a cotton wick or piece of tow, used as a light below deck. More recently, in ships not provided with electric lighting, colza oil lamps of this sort commonly were employed in engine-rooms, coal bunkers, and fire-rooms. *Cf. remarks in* LAMP.

SLUSHY. An old lower-deck name for the ship's cook.

SMACK. (Du. *smak*) Chiefly in Great Britain, a small decked sailing-vessel of any fore-and-aft rig engaged in trawling or in the coasting trade. The name sometimes is used on U.S. Atlantic coast for any licensed sailing-vessel or partly decked boat engaged in fishing, but especially to one having a *well* in which the catch is kept alive, or a *well s.* **Schooner s.,** *see* SCHOONER. With present-day use of powered vessels and boats in the fisheries, the word, generally, is falling into obsolescence.

SMALL. Little in size; of comparatively little extent or magnitude; petty; of minor consequence. **S. arms,** cutlasses, pistols, rifles, bayonets, etc. **S.-arms ammunition,** *see* AMMUNITION. **S. circle,** *see* CIRCLE. **S. craft,** boats and *s.* vessels generally. **S. Damage Club,** organization of shipowners that insures its members against minor damage to ship or cargo; *see* **Mutual i.** *in* INSURANCE. **S. helm,** rudder turned to a *s.* angle with keel; as, *this ship steers with s. helm.* **S.-line fishing,** *see* FISHING. **S. of an anchor,** *see* ANCHOR PHRASEOLOGY. **S. sail,** collective term for loftier or lighter canvas, in old-fashioned usage; as, *Take in all s. sail!;* also, *light sail; cf.* SAIL. To **steer s.,** to use *s.* angles of helm in steering; see **S. helm. S. stuff,** general term for *s.* cordage used for light lashings or stops, seizings, service, etc., such as marline, houseline, spunyarn, roundline, or other tarred hemp line up to 15-thread *ratline stuff,* or any un-tarred line up to *point-line,* in size.

SMART. Neat and shipshape in appearance; speedy in sailing or maneuvering. A vessel is said to be *s.* (also *lively*) *in stays* when she ordinarily comes about quickly, as in *tacking.* **S. money,** in British navy, an allowance for injury suffered in the service, usually as an increase of pension.

SMELLING THE BOTTOM. Also, *feeling the bottom, smelling the ground;* decreasing speed with more or less erratic steering observed as a vessel enters shallow water. This is attributed to restriction of displacement flow about ship's hull and so, in the steering, as the phrase more particularly refers to, unevenness of water's depth often bringing about unbalanced pressures on the hull which may result in vessel taking a broad and possibly dangerous sheer.

SMELT. Small edible fish of similar habits as, and allied to, the *salmon* and *trout.* Widely known in temperate and colder latitudes, lives along coasts and ascends rivers to spawn. Has small silvery scales, with greenish translucent appearance along its back; generally attains maximum length of 10 inches.

SMITH, ANGLE. *See* ANGLE.

SMITH'S ANCHOR. *See* ANCHOR.

SMITING LINE. *See* LINE. (English use)

SMOKE. The common cloudlike gaseous product of burning material, often among seamen extended to a dusty haze, such as that coming off shore prior to the *harmattan* on west coast of Africa. The land is said to be *smoky* when slightly obscured by a haziness that often appears in light off-shore winds or in calms during warm weather; also, a *smoky horizon* is a poorly defined one, such as interferes with taking accurate altitude observations of celestial bodies. **S. box,** part of a steam boiler in which *s.* is collected before passing to atmosphere. A receptacle in which phosphorus or other *s.*-producing chemical is ignited for laying down a *s. screen.* **S. cover,** protection of light close-fitting canvas about a mast, furled sail, yard, etc., that is situated abaft the smokestack and so usually in contact with *s.* therefrom. **S. pipe-line,** one of the pipes leading from the various compartments to a glass-fronted cabinet usually located in pilot house. An uptake draft is produced by a motor-driven fan and any consequent issue of *s.* immediately announces presence of fire in compartment indicated. **S. sail,** piece of canvas hoisted like a sail just forward of galley funnel for carrying *s.* clear of ship's hull during a head wind. (Older use) **S. screen,** cloud of low-lying *s.* laid down by a vessel or vessels for purpose of confusing an enemy's fire, obscuring maneuvers, etc. **S'stack,** also called *funnel* and, chiefly in American ships, *stack,* the large prominent tubular erection for carrying off *s.* and combustion gases from coal or oil-burning furnaces of ship's boilers, or one of much smaller cross-section for exhaust gases of internal combustion engines. First-named type consists of an inner and outer area of light plate with an air-space of several inches between; *see* **Funnel-c.** *in* CASING. **S'stack guys,** same as **funnel guys;** *see* FUNNEL.

SMOOTH. Having an even surface; not rough; as, a *s. sea; s. bottom.* A comparative lull or moderation in height of heavy sea waves. To *dub* or dress a wood surface, as with an adze or plane; *see* DUB. **S. full,** said of sails filled out by the wind; *rap full.* **S. log,** as distinguished from the *scrap* or *rough log,* in merchant vessels, the *chief officer's* or the *chief engineer's log,* a neatly prepared copy of daily happenings as taken from *rough log,* together with any additional data for information of owners of vessel concerned. A similar official journal or log is required of naval vessels for use of headquarters ashore. **S.-planked,** said of a boat built with planking set edge to edge and thus presenting a *s.* surface; carvel-built; *see* CARVEL.

SMOTHERING. Act or method of extinguishing fire aboard ship by exclusion of oxygen to flames or source of threatening combustion by blanketing with carbon dioxide gas (CO_2), foam, fog-foam, or steam. **S. line,** pipe in a *s.-line system* for conveying steam or other *smothering* agent to a compartment in event of fire.

SMUG BOAT. *See* BOAT.

SMUGGLER. A person who brings in merchandise or takes it out of a country contrary to law, or with intent of fraudulently avoiding payment of customs duties; also, a vessel used for smuggling purposes.

SNACK LOCKER. *See* LOCKER.

SNAKE. To pass a *snaking* or line about two parallel ropes in zig-zag fashion; to finish off a flat seizing with zig-zag turns extending from each outside turn of such, called a *snaking-seizing,* and usually one of wire. To flake down a rope or chain, as for clear running, in a continuous series of zig-zag turns. **S.-boat,** the long dugout of southern China, Indo-China, and Thailand called *pambanmanche* (literally, *three-plank boat* in Annamese) used on rivers and sheltered waters. **S.-line,** also *s. lashing,* a small line used for securing a heavy block or other part of running gear to a shroud or backstay, as when such is hanging idle; also *see* **Snake-l.** *in* LINE.[1] **S. piece,** old shipbuilding term for a *pointer,* or cant timber in vessel's counter; *see last definition under* POINTER. **S. wire,** a long steel wire, usually flat in section, for thrusting into waste and scupper pipes, drains, etc., in process of clearing such of clogging matter. To *worm* is sometimes used for to *s.; see* WORM.

SNAP. To break or sever sharply and suddenly, as a hawser under excessive tension. A cup-shaped rivet *set;* a *rivet-s.* A securing catch, latch, lip, or the like that is held in position by a spring or springy action, such as that for closing a hook, a locker door, etc. **S. block,** same as snatch-block; *see* BLOCK. **S. hook,** *see* HOOK. **S. rivet,** *see* **Snap-head r.** *in* RIVET. **S.-riveting,** *see* RIVETING.

SNAPPER. A fish of the large bass-like family *Lutianidæ,* found generally in all warmer seas, first in importance of which, as valuable food fishes, are the *red s.,* abundant in Gulf of Mexico and caught along American Atlantic coast from 40° N. to 30° S. and the *gray s.,* found in Bahamas, on Florida coast, and as far north as Nantucket Island. These are named for their colors and attain a length of nearly two feet. A snapping turtle. The schnapper. Also, in local usage, young of the bluefish, red grouper, rosefish, sea bass, etc.

SNATCH. To temporarily place the bight of a rope over a bitt, cleat, etc., for purpose of securing a clear lead, as to a winch. A *s.-block* or *s.-cleat.* **S.-block,** *see* BLOCK; also called *notch-block.* **S.-cleat,** a curved chock or cleat about which a rope may be led; a *thumb-cleat; see* CLEAT.

SNEAK-BOAT. *See* BOAT.

SNELL. *Same as* SNOOD.

SNIB. (Variant of *snub*) A fastening or catch; especially, one of the clamps or *dogs* for securing a bulkhead door. *Cf.* DOG.

SNIPE. (Variant of *snip*) In older wood shipbuilding, to reduce the molding or depth of end of a beam, stiffener, stringer, etc., by cutting away sharply or beveling. The part thus treated.

SNOOD. (A.S. *snod,* a small cord) Short piece of thin wire, gut, horsehair, etc., to which the hook is attached on a fishing-line; *esp.,* one of those attached at intervals along a *trawl line* and sometimes fitted with a cork for floating it clear of bottom. Also called *leader* and *snell; cf.* GANGING; **Great line f.** *and* **Small line f.** *in* FISHING. To fasten a hook with a *s.*

SNORKEL. U.S. navy's adopted version of the German term *schnörkel,* meaning a recent tubular device that permits a submarine when navigating below the surface to "breathe," or take in air from surrounding water by a certain filtering process. The word appears to have received official sanction in 1946, while British navy chose *snorter* for the same device. While using the *s.,* a submarine is said to be *snorkeling,* the corresponding word in British usage being *snorting.*

SNORTER. Chiefly among American seamen, a heavy gale at sea; *esp.,* one occurring in winter in the North Atlantic. The word also is a variant of *snotter.*

SNOTTER. Piece of flexible wire or fiber rope, having an eye at each end, used as a handy means of slinging bundles of rods, piping, machinery parts, etc., by taking a round turn and passing one eye through the other before *hooking on.* One or more wire slings of *s.* type are much preferred by stevedores for lifting a heavy piece of cargo. Any small *strop* for a special use, such as on a mast for supporting the heel of a sprit, or on a lug-sail yard for attaching the halyard. In old-time navy usage, in connection with the snappy evolution of sending down royal and topgallant yards, a *s.* was a piece of flat sennit fitting under the yard-arm brace-and-lift band and having an eye facing *inboard.* Upon raising the yard with the yard-rope, the spar was tilted and its lower end was quickly divested of its brace and lift by a tripping-line previously made fast to the *s.* Upper end of yard was easily taken care of as it was being lowered.

SNOW. (Du. *snaauw*) A *brig* having her spanker hooped to a trysail mast fitted close abaft the mainmast, instead of the former conventional rig of hoisting that sail on the lowermast itself; also, early term for a vessel of *barque* rig that departed from the customary rig in having her square-rigged masts of equal height and, excepting the courses, same square sails of equal size.

SNUB. To check a vessel's headway by an anchor with short scope of cable or a forward line made fast to a pier, dolphin, etc., as in sharply turning ship in a direction desired when coming to a berth, shifting along, around, or toward a wharf, etc. To check or hold an anchor cable or line that is paying out by use of the windlass brake, by taking an extra turn on bitts, bollard, cleat, etc., in use. Act or result of *snubbing.* **S.-line** or **snubbing-line,** *see* **Check-l.** *in* LINE. **Snubbing-post,** a pile or mooring-post at a corner of a pier, entrance to a lock, or other appropriate position for making fast a *check-* or *snubbing-line;* a billet-head, bollard, or loggerhead, such as that fitted in bow of a whaling-boat.

SNUG. Tidy; compact; fitting exactly; as rigging or sails. With *alongside, together,* or *up,* lying close against, as ship to ship, a vessel to a wharf, etc. Secure against wind and tide; as, a *s.* berth; a *s.* harbor. **Rudder s.,** a gudgeon; *see* **R. snug** *in* RUDDER. To **s. down,** old phrase meaning to reduce top hamper in preparation for bad weather by sending down upper masts and yards, close-reefing topsails, etc., and to secure all movables alow and aloft.

SNY. (Of Scand. origin; prob. Ice. *snua,* to turn) Upward curving in a timber or plank; *esp.,* that in each strake of outside planking toward each end of a vessel. Measure of this edge curvature from selected points in a straight line over a given distance is called *spiling. Snying* is the area of *snyed* planking on either bow or quarter; also, the process of forging and fitting one of several *plates* at or near extreme ends of hull which must be given both edgewise and convex curvature.

SOCKET. (Dim. of *sock*) A hole, sleeve, hollow part, or recess into which a fitting or part of anything may be inserted and securely held or connected; a coupling; as a *stanchion s.; a rail s.* **Rocket-s.,** *see* **R.-socket** *in* ROCKET. **S. signal,** a rocket or detonating signal discharged from a *rocket-s.* **Wire-rope s.,** the so-called *patent eye* that dispenses with the usual *eye splice; see* **Patent e.** *in* EYE; also termed *s.-eye.*

SOFT. Opposed to *hard;* as, *s. bottom; s. ice.* Yielding; flexible; loose; as, *s. mud; s. wire; s. seams* (also *sick seams*). **S.-laid,** said of rope having qualities opposed to those of *hard-laid* cordage; *cf.* **Hard-l.** *in* LAID. **S. patch,** *see* remarks *in* PATCH. **S. sky,** appearance of cloud formation, colors seen at sunset or sunrise in the sky, glare of sun, etc., foreboding mild temperatures and gentle winds. **S.-tack,** baked leavened bread; *s. tommy;* shore bread; as distinguished from *hard-tack, q.v. in* HARD. **S'wood built,** said of a vessel whose planking and timbers consist of such woods as spruce, fir, the softer pines, etc.; having frames, keelsons, beams, and planking of *softwood.*

SOGER. (Var. of *soldier*) Old sailors' name for a *hang-back,* or one displaying little enthusiasm in his attitude toward his duties; a shirker; or, in more recent verbiage, a *gold-bricker.* Also, one of a number of wooden pins fitted at intervals along a fishing-vessel's rail for belaying the hand-lines in fishing from the deck. (*Chiefly New England use*)

SOLAN GOOSE. The common gannet; *see* GANNET.

SOLANO. (*Sp.*) A warm, oppressive, south-easterly wind, often beginning in a violent squall charged with fine dust from its source on the heated North African deserts, blowing on east coast of Spain for short periods during summer.

SOLAR. (L. *solaris;* from *sol,* the sun) Pertaining to or measured by the sun. **Mean s. day; mean s. time;** *see* MEAN. **S. day,** as distinguished from *lunar* and *sidereal* day, interval between two successive transits of the apparent sun over the meridian of a given place. Also referred to as *apparent solar day,* its length is dependent on rate of earth's orbital motion, variations of which result in a maximum difference of such length of about 51 seconds. Hence the necessity for the fictitious *mean sun* by which our clocks may be regulated to hours of constant length in the *mean s. day.* **S. eclipse,** *see* ECLIPSE. **S. parallax,** *see* **Horizontal p.** *in* PARALLAX. **S. system,** the sun and group of bodies revolving about him, consisting of 9 *planets* with *moons* or *satellites* (*see* PLANET), the *Asteroids,* and 22 known *comets.* **S. time,** that reckoned by the sun; *apparent time,* or that shown by a sun dial; *see* **S. day. S. tide,** component of the tide wave attributed to sun's attraction; a daily tide occurring in some tropical partly land-locked seas, also from same cause. **S. winds,** another name for *land and sea breezes; see* BREEZE. **S. year,** *see* YEAR.

SOLDIER'S WIND. A steady beam wind; so called because little skill and less work are required in sailing with such wind; also, the older *soger's* breeze; *cf.* SOGER.

SOLE. The sill or *poppet-board* on which a launching-poppet's uprights are stepped; also, *s. piece; see* POPPET. That part of a clinker-built boat's plank that is overlapped by, or overlaps, next strake; the overlapping joint or seam is termed *soleing.* An old name for the deck or "floor" of a cabin. Any of several small flatfishes of the *Soleidæ* family, many of which, *esp.,* the *common* or *European s.,* are considered excellent as food; also, the local name for certain small *flounders.* Bottom edge of a rudder. **S.-block,** a shoe or shole; *see* BLOCK. **S. piece,** in a stern frame, lowest or bridging part between *propeller-* and *rudder-posts,* also sometimes called *heel piece;* projecting part from after end of keel for supporting a rudder; a *skeg.* In a wooden vessel, fore-and-aft piece of timber on lower edge of rudder to increase depth of latter to that of the false keel. In preparations for launching, a timber or plate bolted to inshore end of each *sliding way* and *ground way* for securing vessel against starting. When all is ready, *s. piece* is cut through and vessel is free to move. A timber so used sometimes is called a *tie-plank;* a plate, *sole-plate.* A filling or uniting piece between stem and keel in a wooden boat also is termed a *s. piece* and also *stem heel.* **S. plate,** a *bed-plate* on which an engine, winch, capstan, etc., rests and is secured; *see* FOUNDATION PLATE.

SOLENOID. (Gr. *solen,* channel, conduit) A helical coil of wire in one or more layers through which an electric current is passed to produce a magnetic field. A piece of soft iron temporarily magnetized within such field is used in various devices, such as those for controlling different types of brakes on electric winches, any of which commonly is called a *s. brake.* Generally, these brakes are of such construction as to automatically set by some mechanical means when power is shut off the winch or engine. They are released by means of the electro-magnetic pull of the *s.* immediately upon applying the power. **S. valve,** one that is controlled by a *s.*

SOLID. Of one substance; having no break in continuity of form; opposed to *skeleton* or *lightened,* as a *s. floor;* not hollow or tubular, as a *s. hold pillar;* cast or fashioned in one piece, as a *s. rudder frame,* a *s. thimble,* a *s. pintle.* **S. bulkhead,** a timbered and planked permanent partition in a wooden vessel's hold. It is usually calked and made watertight. **S. floor,** *see* FLOOR. **S. frame,** *see* FRAME. **S. propeller,** *see* PROPELLER. **S. spar,** one made from a tree trunk, as distinguished from a *built spar; cf.* BUILT.

SOLSTICE. (Fr.; from L. *sol,* sun; *sistere,* to cause to stand) Also called *solstitial point,* either of two diametrically opposed points in the *ecliptic* at which the sun attains his highest declination, 23° 27' nearly. On about June 21 and December 22, respectively, the *summer s.* and *winter s.* occur, coincident with sun's arrival in each case at right ascension 6 hrs. 00 min. 00 sec. and 18 hrs. 00 min. 00 sec. The *solstitial colure* is the *hour circle* passing through both solstitial points.

SONAR. (Coined from *SO* in *sound; N* in *navigation; A* in *and;* and *R* in *ranging*) The submarine-detecting system developed in *World War II* by American and British scientific experiments which resulted in reducing the German U-boat menace to a satisfactory minimum. *S.* includes all types of underwater devices used for depth indicating, listening, echo-ranging, and locating of objects. If we say that *radar* gives eyes to the ship, *s.* provides her with *ears* and a *voice* beneath the surface, and so of chief importance is its echo-ranging capabilities or determining of bearing and distance of an enemy submarine. This is done by sending out bursts of highly intense sound energy in a slowly revolving cone-shaped underwater beam and receiving of a return echo as outgoing sound strikes target. In the target-searching process thus the direction from which echo returns is determined and time required for echo to arrive indicates distance of the object. The instrument that sends out the "pings" or sounds is termed the *transducer.* It is claimed for *s.* that the device can spot a submarine up to 2500 yards distance off.

SONIC DEPTH FINDER. A bathometer, depthometer, or fathometer; see FATHOMETER.

SOOGEE. (Short for *soogee-moogee;* of uncertain origin) A solution of washing soda, soap powder, soft soap, or the like, used for washing paint. To wash or scrub paintwork, decks, etc., with *s.* Also spelled *sewgee, suegee, suji, sujee, sugee.*

SOUL-AND-BODY LASHING. See LASHING.

SOUND.[1] (A.S. *sund,* a narrow sea; water; swimming. Ice. *sund,* swimming; strait; prob. because one might swim across it) An inlet of the sea; a passage connecting two larger bodies of water and usually of greater extent than a *strait.* Also, the *air-* or *swimming-bladder* of a fish.

SOUND.[2] (A.S. *gesund;* prob. from L. *sanus,* sound or healthy) Free of defect or decay; undamaged; as, *she's s. in every timber;* a *s.* cargo. To examine the condition of something by appropriate test; as, to *s.* a vessel's spars or timbers.

SOUND.[3] (L. *sonus,* sound or noise) Sensation perceived through the ear, as the noise of a horn, report of a gun, etc. Any distinctive or characteristic noise; as, *s.* of a bell; *s.* of breakers. Distance or range of audibility; as, *within s. of the Cape Race horn; beyond s. of the surf.* To cause to make a *s.* by striking a bell, blowing a ship's whistle, etc.; as, *the liner sounded 3 blasts on her siren.* Giving forth a *s.;* as, *bell and whistle buoys s. by action of the waves.* Characterized by *s.;* as, a *s. signal.* Under average conditions, *velocity* of *s.* in *air* of 32°F. is close to 1090 feet per second, thereafter increasing 1.15 ft. for each degree rise in temperature. Its speed through *sea-water* may be taken as 4800 feet per second. Varying atmospheric pressure, humidity, and salinity affect these values to some extent; but, for navigational purposes, 1100 ft. per sec. in air and 4800 ft. in sea-water are considered to be sufficiently accurate. *Cf.* **R. distance-finding stations** *in* RADIO.

SOUND.[4] (O. Fr. *sonder,* to measure a depth) To measure the depth of water, as with a *lead-line* or a *fathometer;* with a *rod* or a *plumb-bob,* as in a tank, etc.; to fathom. To suddenly dive toward bottom, as a fish or whale; *esp.,* upon being hooked or harpooned. **S.-line,** older name for a harpoon-line. To **s. a line;** to **s. all line;** *see* LINE.[1]

SOUNDER. A machine or apparatus for *sounding,* or measuring depth of water in which ship is navigated; an early name for the *sounding-machine, esp.,* the apparatus devised by *Sir William Thomson (later, Lord Kelvin; 1824–1907)* and called by its first users the *flying s.,* from its capability of obtaining depths up to 100 fathoms while vessel travels at any speed up to *16 knots.* Later known as *Lord Kelvin's s.* or *sounding-machine,* determination of depth by its means is based on a recording of water pressure at the sea floor, either by distance a piston is depressed in a cylinder or by the measure of air compressed in a tube sealed at one end. In the former means, a marker indicates position of piston, and thus the depth, on a graduated scale on the cylinder, attained by the attached *sinker;* in the *tube* method, (generally using a glass tube of 1/8-inch bore and 24 inches in length) the column of imprisoned air that was compressed by the sea-water, when measured by a special scale gives depth in fathoms as defined by discoloration of a chemical coating marking rise of water in tube (in accordance with *Boyle's law* of compression of gases: *"pressure times volume is constant"*). Other instruments that register depth by means of a *rotator* acting through its vertical travel to bottom, such as *Massey's, Walker's,* and *Wigzell's* patents, appeared on the market about same time or subsequent to the Kelvin invention. **Sonic s.,** *see* ECHO SOUNDING.

SOUNDING. Measurement of depth of water by a *lead-line* or *sounder;* a depth thus ascertained. Act of measuring depth; *see* SOUND[4]. In *pl.,* recorded depths; *esp.,* those indicated on charts at positions where determined. American and British charts show depths of water in *fathoms* or, in the case of harbor plans and special local charts, in *feet,* datum surface or *plane of reference* being, generally, that of *mean low water* or of *lowest low water* ordinarily observed in locality considered; *cf.* CHART; DATUM. *Soundings* are indicated in *meters* (3.281 feet) on modern charts published by Austria, Belgium, Chile, France, Germany, Holland, Italy, Norway, Portugal, Spain, and Sweden. Japan uses the *fathom* (6 feet). Older Dutch charts show the *vadem* of 5.9 feet; Danish and Norwegian, the *favn* of 6.18 feet; Swedish, the *famn* of 5.84 feet; and Spanish, the old *braza* of 5½ feet. **Bearing and s.,** *see* BEARING. **Echo s.,** *see* ECHO SOUNDING. To **get on** or **off s's,** to steer in such direction as will bring vessel into or away from an area in which *s's* may be obtained (usually 100 fathoms or less). **Off s's,** having a depth of water at sea of over 100 fathoms; outside the *100-fathom curve* shown on a chart; *cf.* **F.-line** *in* FATHOM. **On s's,** as opposed to *off s's,* said of a vessel navigating in an area having less than 100 fathoms depth; also, sometimes, *in s's.* To make a port, pass through a strait, etc., *on s's* is to navigate by *s., i.e.,* by shaping and checking the course or courses according to bottom information given on chart, as in thick weather. **S.-boom,** a small spar rigged out perpendicular to ship's side at a handy location for taking *s's* with a *s.-machine.* Its purpose is to keep the *sinker* and *depth-recording device* clear of ship's side during the operation of *s.* and to this end, the *s.-wire lead-block* is rigged to slide out to boom's end or in to the rail as required. **S.-bottle,** in deep-sea exploration *s.,* a strong metal container fitted with non-return valves for taking samples of water at great depths. Valves are set to open at pressure corresponding to approximate depth. (Sea-water pressure varies directly as depth and, expressed in *lbs. per in.*^{2}, is .444 times depth in *feet*) **S.-lead,** *see* LEAD.[1] **S.-line,** *see* **L.-line** *in* LEAD.[1] **S.-machine,** essentially consists of a hand- or motor-operated reel on which a special galvanized steel wire, usually about 300 fathoms in length, is wound. It is fitted with a brake for controlling speed of the *sinker,* between which and end of wire is secured the recording device. Weight of sinker varies with speed of ship, from 25 to 40 lbs. In U.S. powered vessels of more that 500 gross tonnage, a *s.-machine,* or *deep-sea s. apparatus,* as it is officially termed, is required as navigational equipment. *Cf.* SOUNDER. **S.-pipe,** a tube or pipe leading to a deck above from a tank, well, or bilge as a conduit for a rod and line in *s.* the contents of such space. It is fitted with a screwcap. **S.-pole,** a graduated batten or pole used for measuring depths in shallow water, as in hydrographic surveying operations; any lengthy stick or batten for ascertaining depth of water. **S.-rod,** short piece of brass or iron rod, usually graduated in inches, attached to a line for *s.* bilges, tanks, etc. It

is sometimes jointed at each 6-inch mark for use in curved *s.-pipes.* **S. sextant,** a light handy sextant used for measuring horizontal and vertical angles in a *s. survey* of a harbor, river, etc. **S. tube,** a glass tube of accurate bore used as a recorder of depth attained by the sinker in *s.; esp.,* that used with the *Lord Kelvin s.-machine; see* SOUNDER. In taking a *s.,* it is placed sealed end up in a *sheath* or holder which is secured at end of *s.-wire* and above *sinker.* As depth increases sea water rises in tube and discolors the chromate of silver coating therein, thus leaving a salmon-colored portion at upper or sealed end of tube. Length of this portion, according to the scale supplied with the apparatus, indicates *s.* in fathoms; thus, a 20-inch tube will show a one-inch column in which air has been compressed at 100 fathoms to 266.7 lbs. per in.^{2}, plus original air pressure in tube of about 14.7 lbs. per in.^{2}, or a total of close to 281 lbs. A correction for height of barometer above 29.50" must be *added* to depth obtained, since greater pressure of air correspondingly withstands rise of water in tube with consequent indication of *lesser* depth. The correction is given on the reading scale provided. Tubes of larger bore and made of *ground glass* are also used, the mark of water's rise in the dry tube showing without use of chemical coating. However, those of accurate bore of about one-eighth inch are more dependable in that the water mark usually is clear cut (with chemical coat) which often is not the case with the free surface of water in the greater-diameter ground glass substitute. **S.-tube holder,** the sheath or case in which a *s. tube* is placed in taking a *s.* with the *s.-machine.* To **strike s's,** to find bottom with the *deep-sea lead, s.-machine,* or fathometer, as in approaching a coast; to *get on s's.*

SOUSE. To steep in pickle, as fish or meat. To drench or plunge into water; to suffer damage by heavy rain, spray, etc.; as, *all baggage was soused in the driving sleet.* A *sousing* is a thorough wetting; as, *the boys got a s. in a boarding sea.*

SOUTH. (Of *Old Teutonic* origin, signifying *side toward the sun*) In the direction opposite to, or 180° from, *north;* point of the compass usually designated by S. Coming from the *s.;* as, a *s. wind;* flowing or heading toward *s.;* as, *current is setting s.; on port tack* steering S. Lying toward or facing the *s.;* as, the *s. coast; s. entrance to the port.* **S. Equatorial Current,** *see* CURRENT. **S. Sea,** the Pacific Ocean,—so called by *Vasco Nunez de Balboa,* Spanish governor of Darien, who first sighted it as expanding toward the *s.* from the Panama Isthmus *(1513).* **S. temperate zone,** *see* ZONE. (For compass points partly denoted by *S,* see **Points of the c.** in COMPASS.)

SOUTHEAST TRADES. *See* TRADE.

SOUTHEASTER. Strong wind, gale, or storm from a southeasterly direction.

SOUTHERLY BUSTER. *See* BRICKFIELDER.

SOUTHERN. Pertaining to or situated in the *south*. **S. Cross,** *see* CRUX. **S. hemisphere,** *see* HEMISPHERE. **S. lights,** *see* AURORA. **S. Triangle,** a small southern constellation usually listed by its Latin name *Triangulum Australe.* Its brightest star, *α Trianguli Australis,* has a magnitude of 1.88 and lies at eastern end of the base of a conspicuous isosceles triangle easily located just southeast of the *Centaurs* or "pointers" to the *Southern Cross.*

SOUTHING. Distance made to southward of point of departure, as measured on a meridian; opposite to *northing.*

SOUTHWARD. Toward the *south;* in direction, nearer to *S.* than to *E.* or *W.* Extending, facing, or situated in a southerly direction. (Usually pron. "*sutherd*" by seamen)

SOUTHWEST MONSOON. *See* MONSOON.

SOUTHWESTER. Commonly, "*sou'wester*"; a hat of waterproof material, having a broad rim at the back for shedding water from wearer's neck in bad weather. A gale or strong wind from a southwesterly direction.

SPACE. A designated portion of a vessel's enclosed volume or a particular area on board; as, *hold s.; propelling-power s.; crew s.; passenger-deck s. Cf.* EXEMPTED SPACE.

SPACING. The setting of certain structural parts in their allotted positions with relation to each other, as expressed in units of distance. **Frame s.,** *see* FRAME. **S. of beams,** *see* BEAM. **S. of rivets,** *see* RIVET.

SPADE. A cutting instrument, shaped like a broad chisel, used for removing blubber, etc., from a whale. *Cf.* FLENSE. To hamstring an attacked whale, as in former practice, with a *s.; see* HAMSTRING. **Head-s.,** *see* HEAD. **Pot-s.,** *see* POT. **S. rudder,** *see* **Underhung r.** *in* RUDDER.

SPALE. Also, *spaling, spall; see* **C.-spale** *in* CROSS.

SPALL. In ship construction, one of the cross members in a staging, on which the planks rest. To set the frames at their proper distance apart, as by use of *cross-spales. Cf.* **C.-spale** *in* CROSS.

SPAN. A rope extended between two points, as from mast to mast, so that a hoisting-tackle may be secured to its bight. A connecting-rope between two uprights, as davit heads, ship's funnel and a mast, etc. Short length of rope, single or double, fixed horizontally in the rigging and fitted with *bull's eyes* or *fairleaders* for halyards, buntlines, etc. Distance or spacing apart of similar members; as. *s.* of the frames. Length of a given portion of a member between supports; as, *s.* of a deck-girder between pillars. A *whale* is aid to *s.* when swimming in one general direction and surfacing to breathe

at more or less regular intervals. **Davit-s.,** *see* DAVIT. **Guy-s.,** *see* GUY. **Peak s.,** *see* **P. pendant** *in* PEAK. **S.-block,** a hoisting-block secured in the bight of a *s.;* also, a block at the end of a short *s.* or pendant at a masthead, such as is used for a gantline or, formerly, studding-sail halyards. **S.-shackle,** in older use, a heavy square or triangular *s.* secured to a forecastle deck-beam for receiving the heel of the fish-davit; now, any type of shackle fitted to an eyebolt in the deck, serving to take the turns of a lashing, as in securing boats, gear-boxes, spars, etc. **Yard-s.,** the heavy forging, usually bow-shaped, fitted on after side of a lower yard at the slings. It forms that part of the *truss* which holds yard well forward of mast and in which is fitted the pivoting arrangement for swinging or topping the yard. Also termed *truss-bow* and *truss-yoke.*

SPANISH. Of or pertaining to Spain; according to usage by Spanish seamen, as indicated in the early adoption of the word as a combining term by English sailors, as in *S. burton; S. bowline; S. windlass;* etc. **S. mackerel,** a large species of the *Scombridæ* family, allied to the *common mackerel,* found off the American coast from Cape Cod to Brazil. The name often is given to several other members of same family, including the *Monterey mackerel* of the Californian coast; the *cero* and *pintado,* close cousins, caught in West Indies and U.S. Atlantic coastal waters. *Cf.* CERO and MACKEREL. **S. Main,** the northern South American coast from the Panama Isthmus to the Orinoco River; so called from its original exploration and possession by the Spaniards in the 16th. century. To **ride the S. mare,** *see* RIDE. (Also see *Spanish* as a combining term under the following: BURTON; FOX; REEF; WINDLASS)

SPANK. To beat, pound, or slap the water, as a boat in sailing into a head sea.

SPANKER. Lowest and aftermost sail on a brig, barquentine, barque, ship, 3-, 4-, or 5-masted schooner, and that on the 5th. mast of a schooner having more than 5 masts. In each case it is a fore-and-aft sail, usually fitted with both gaff and boom, but sometimes, in the barque and ship rig, of jib-headed, or triangular, shape when it is called a *storm* or *mutton s.* Also was sometimes termed the *driver* in barques and ships and, in older use, the *mizzen* in any 3-masted vessel. Often, especially in British square-rigged types, *s.* was the *brailing-in* kind, or that set by hauling out its head on a *standing gaff* and stretching aft its clew on a *boom,* while stowed against the mast by *brails. (Cf.* BRAIL) **S. gaff,** *see* GAFF. **S.-mast,** *see remarks in* MAST.

SPANKING BREEZE. A steady fresh or strong breeze favorable for sailing.

SPAR. *(Scand. origin)* General term for a boom, mast, yard, stout pole, etc. Usually round in section and made from the trunk of a suitable tree, also may be *built* of several longitudinal parts of wood or of steel plating in tubular form. (*Cf.* BUILT) To furnish or equip a vessel with her requisite *spars*. (*Cf.* **O'sparred** *in* OVER *and* **U'sparred** *in* UNDER) In *sparmaking,* suitable pieces of timber from which a *s.* of certain dimensions might be fashioned formerly were designated by such names as *barling, boat, boom, cant, middling,* etc., according to length in *feet* and greatest circumference in *hands* of 4 inches. Especially in Great Britain, a *s.* in the timber trade is a straight tree trunk, free of branches, and measuring 8 inches or *less* in diameter; thus distinguished from a *mast,* which *exceeds* 8 inches. **Awning s.,** a pole or piece of timber for supporting or securing an awning; sometimes called a *ridge s.* when sustaining the raised middle of a tent-shaped awning. **Boat s.,** also called *boat-boom, pudding boom, rolling s.,* a round piece of timber secured fore-and-aft to the davits as a means of steadying a boat in the swung-out position. It is fitted with a pudding at its middle, so that boat may be snugged taut against it without injury to her planking. **Built s.,** one that is made by fitting together several sections of timber as longitudinal components of its body; distinguished thus from a *cut s.* or a *grown s.,* as one fashioned from a balk of timber and one from a smoothed tree-trunk respectively are termed. **Foot s.,** a *stretcher,* or piece of wood fitted athwartships in a boat, serving as a bracing foothold for an oarsman. **Fender s.,** a heavy boom or log made fast floating alongside a quay or wharf for holding a vessel clear of the structure; *see* CAMEL. **Grown s.,** *see* **Built s. Hollow s.,** a *built s.* of tubular form, usually having an *inside* diameter of three-fifths the *outside* diameter; chiefly found in larger sailing yachts as a weight-saving measure in masts and booms. **Monkey s.,** *see* MONKEY. **Rolling s.,** same as **Boat s. Rough s.,** a tree-trunk that may be fashioned into a *s.;* also, *rough-tree s.* **Single-s. mast,** *see* **Pole m.** *in* MAST. **Solid s.,** as distinguished from a *built s.* or a *tubular s.,* one consisting of solid timber; *esp.,* as made from a trunk of a tree. **S. and boom gear,** old term for arrangement in which a boom is guyed to plumb the hatch and a second one over the side, as when the falls leading from each connect to a common hook in working cargo; also, *hoist and yard-arm.* **S. buoy,** a wooden or steel spar-shaped buoy moored at one end so that it floats more or less upright. *S. buoys* are widely used as channel markers at points of lesser importance than those occupied by buoys of the lighted, bell, whistle, etc., types. **S. ceiling,** the battens, collectively, that are fitted across inside surfaces of a steel vessel's frames to protect packaged cargo from contact with both shell plating and framing, while also providing air courses at sides of cargo as required for ventilation. Usually fitted for easy removal, the wood is about 2 by 6 inches in size and spaced about 10 inches apart. **S. deck,** originally, the weather or main deck extending from poop to forecastle; now, a weather or upper deck above the *main* or *strength* deck. **S.-deck vessel,** as so designated in ship classification, is a type having two or more complete decks and of lighter construction than a *full-scantling* vessel, but heavier than the *awning-* or *shelter-deck* type. To **s. down** preparatory to *rattling down* (*see* remarks *in* RATLINE), to lash battens, small *spars,* oars, etc., about 4 feet apart across the shrouds for holding the latter at their proper distances apart and providing means for the man or men to stand while fitting and seizing on the ratlines. **Steel s.,** a tubular *s.* made of steel plating riveted or welded together. Smaller types are sometimes of steel tubing. **Towing s.,** known also as a *fog-buoy, position-buoy,* and *fog s.,* a small *s.* towed by vessels in convoy or fleet formation during fog or darkness as an aid to ship next astern in column in keeping station; sometimes substituted by a keg or small drum. **Water s.,** a piece of timber or small *s.* used as a derrick in drawing water aboard by hand, as in sailing-vessels. Bucket-rope was led through a block at head of *s.* and usually two men were employed at keeping a tub or cask filled by this means when washing down the decks.

SPARMAKER. One who specializes in making *spars* and providing them with the necessary fittings; a *mastmaker.*

SPARE. Designating an item of reserve equipment carried as an emergency replacement; as in *s. boom, s. foresail, s. oars, s. propeller, s. yards,* etc. That which is held in reserve; as, two compasses and a *s.* **S. bunker,** a compartment that may be used for either fuel or cargo; a *reserve bunker; see* RESERVE. **S. mast,** *see* MAST. **S. pump-handle,** an extra crew member, or one not required in ship's complement. Also, a *hangback,* or one not over-enthusiastic in line of duty; *see* SOGER.

SPARKS. Familiar name for a radio operator of a merchant vessel.

SPARRING. Another term for the *spar ceiling; see* SPAR.

SPEAK. To hail and communicate with by voice, as a passing vessel; as, to *s.* a ship. Prior to general use of radio at sea, it was customary for arriving vessels to report all such communications, or "vessels spoken," upon entering at customs. A typical entry in ship's log reads, for example: *"10.30—42° 10' S. 105° 15' E.—Spoke barque CLARENDON bound for Melbourne; all well."* **S'ing trumpet,** *see* MEGAPHONE. **S'ing tube,** also called *voice-pipe* and *voice-tube,* a pipe or tube, usually made of brass, for conveying the voice from one part of ship to another, as from the bridge to crow's nest, engine-room, etc. In U.S. vessels, such tube providing communication between the pilot-house and engine-room, an emergency steering station, steering-engine room, or the radio room may not exceed

125 feet in length; must be at least 2 inches in diameter if not over 75 feet in length; and at least 2½ inches if over 75 feet. Telephone equipment may be installed in all cases in lieu of *speaking-tubes.*

SPEAR-FISH. Any of several ocean fishes of the genus *Tetrapturus.* A close relative of the *sail-fish,* has a beak much like that of the *sword-fish,* and grows to a length of 5 to 7 feet.

SPECIAL. Combining term denoting the characteristic of particular importance; extraordinary; as, *s. signals; s. service.* **S. cargo,** goods that require unusual care in stowage and/or security from theft; *esp.,* such valuable items as furs, laces, jewelry, shoes, bottled wines and spirits, toilet articles, and more expensive wearing apparel. Also, valuable merchandise of a fragile nature; dangerous, explosive, or foul-smelling goods demanding *special stowage* or protection, often are included in this category. **S. survey,** *see* SURVEY.

SPECIFIC. S. duty, *see* DUTY. **S. gravity,** *see* GRAVITY.

SPECIFICATIONS. As part of the written contract for the building of, or extensive repairs to, a vessel, a description in detail of kind, quality, and sizes of structural material, fittings, and equipment to be provided, methods or systems to be followed in the work, and all pertinent information supplementing or confirming that given in the plans or drawings. For a new vessel the document opens with owners' requirements as to size, tonnage, draft, propulsion plant, classification supervision, and other initial procedure details, with the view of clearly indicating just what is expected of the builders in fulfillment of contract.

SPECK. (Du. *spek,* fat) Blubber of whales and other marine mammals. **S.-block,** in former whaling, the block fixed on the *blubber-guy (see* BLUBBER) for receiving the *s.-fall,* or hoisting-rope by which blubber was taken aboard from a whale secured alongside.

SPECKSIONEER. In older whaling, the chief *harponeer,* whose duties also included supervision of the work of *flensing,* or cutting and removing blubber from a whale. Also, *spectioneer.*

SPECTACLE. Combining term designating a fitting the shape of which suggests a pair of *spectacles.* **S. frame,** *see* FRAME. **S.-iron,** *see* IRON. **S. plate,** a piece of flat metal having a hole at each end, such as that serving as a connecting link between span and guy on a round-bar davit head; also *s. eye.*

SPEED. Rate of motion; velocity. In sea-going vessels, *s.* is indicated in *knots,* whether considered as *through the water* or *over the ground. Average s.* is that *made good,* as determined by distance sailed in nautical miles between two points on a track followed, divided by number of hours occupied in covering such distance; this also being expressed in *knots,* rather than *miles per hour.* **Economical s.,** that of a merchant vessel with respect to profitable operation. In determining this value, several factors necessarily are taken into consideration, including increasing cost of fuel with higher speeds; that of crew wages, maintenance, insurance, etc., with lower speeds; current demand for tonnage; and particular requirements of the trade concerned. **Engine s.,** rate at which a propeller or paddle-wheel is turned by ship's engines. It usually is expressed in *revolutions per minute,* but may be indicated in *knots* or *miles per hour* as that *s.,* sometimes called *s. of advance,* at which vessel would be driven through the water in the absence of any *slip.* Cf. PITCH[2]; SLIP. **Full s.,** in merchant vessels, that corresponding to propeller revolutions required to maintain an *average s.* desired on a given passage; often, the normal *engine s.,* expressed in revolutions, determined by the master as that producing ship's *economical s.* under conditions prevailing. In naval usage, the term usually occurs in orders given by an officer commanding a group of vessels proceeding in formation and indicates a *s. through the water* of one-fourth greater than the *standard,* or *cruising, s.* as set by the flagship or guide. On individual ships, generally, *s.* is set by and expressed in propeller revolutions, the term *reserve* or *top s.* being used for maximum effort of engines. It is the navigator's duty to determine *s. of vessel* corresponding to shaft revolutions considered. **Half s.,** in merchant vessels, an *engine s.* of approximately three-fourths of *full s.* In naval ships, usually a *s. through the water* of one-fourth less than *standard s.; cf.* **Full s. Moderate s.,** *see* MODERATE. **Reserve s.,** also *top s.,* highest *s.* of which ship's engines normally are capable (U.S. navy). **Slow s.,** in merchant ships, an *engine s.* of about one-half less than *full s.* In naval maneuvering usage, as in fleet formation, one-half less than *standard s.,* or that set as *s. through water* by flagship or guide. **S. cone,** a black canvas cone hoisted at a yard-arm of the guide or flagship of a group or squadron of naval vessels as a *speed signal.* With apex upward it indicates ahead movement, while its relative hoist denotes *full, standard, half,* or *slow, full s.* being highest position. Usually, a special pennant is flown as an answering or repeating signal by each ship at the position corresponding to that of the *cone.* **S.-length ratio,** as used in model experiments in connection with resistance and powering of vessels, the ratio of *s.* in *knots* to square root of length of waterline in *feet.* **S. of advance,** *see* **Engine s. S. of light,** *see* LIGHT.[1] **S. of sound,** *see* SOUND.[3] **Standard s.,** also *cruising s.,* that at which a fleet in formation normally adheres to, as ordered by flagship or guide. Thus indicated it is *s. of vessels through the water. Engine s.* in revolutions per minute corresponding to above then is determined by each individual vessel and also termed *standard s.*

SPELL. A period occupied or turn taken at any duty or work; relief of one person by another in the line of continuous duty; as, a *s.* at the helm. A rest period, as from a job demanding constant physical effort: indicated in the order "*Spell-O!*", as when men are heaving on a hand-winch, pumping bilges, etc. To relieve or take a turn of duty for a time; as, to *s.* one another at the pumps.

SPENCER. (From the short jacket of that name worn in England and called for Earl *Spencer,* circa 1800) A kind of trysail formerly set abaft the fore lowermast in brigs and brigantines and abaft fore and main lowermasts in the barque, barquentine, and ship rig. It was the gaff type, loose-footed, and, when hoisted, was hooped to an auxiliary mast, the *s.-mast,* fitted close to the lowermast. In some larger vessels, the sail had a standing gaff, in which case it was taken in by brails and stowed against the lowermast. The sail disappeared in favor of lower and topmast staysails, last vessels observed setting *fore* and *main spencers* being a few Italian barques in 1900. In British ships, a *fore s.* was called a *Duke of York.*

SPEND. To incur the loss or carrying away of a part of ship's equipment; as, "In getting under way we were forced to *s.* an anchor." "In a great tempest was our foremast *spent* complete." A vessel is said to be in a *spent* condition when, nearing the end of a voyage, with no cargo aboard, her fuel and stores are exhausted or nearly so.

SPERM. Short for *spermaceti;* also, sometimes for *s. oil,* the valuable pale yellowish oil taken from the head cavities of the *s. whale* and the *dolphin.* **S. whale,** *see* WHALE. (Also called *trunk whale*) **S.-whale porpoise,** the *beaked* or *bottlenose* whale.

SPERMACETI. (L. *sperma,* seed, sperm; *cetus,* whale) A waxy, yellowish to white substance extracted from the oil found in the *case,* or head cavity, and in lesser quantity from certain parts of the back, of the *sperm whale.* Also, a similar substance taken from the *bottle-nose whale* or *dolphin.* Consisting of the esters of fatty acids, when purified it is white, brittle, translucent, and odorless, and is used for making candles, cosmetics, and ointments. **S. whale,** the *cachalot* or *sperm whale; see* WHALE.

SPERON. (It. *sperone,* spur) Obsolete term for the beak, prow, or more or less ornamented cutwater at upper part of vessel's stem.

SPEW OAKUM, To. *See* OAKUM.

SPET. A small barracuda; *esp.,* a species about 2½ feet in length found on southern coasts of Europe; *cf.* BARRACUDA.

SPHERE. (Gr. *sphaira,* ball or sphere) A ball or globe; a body or space bounded by a curved surface all points of which are equally distant from a point within called its *center;* any globular body; one of the heavenly bodies: *esp.,* one in the solar system. **Celestial s.,** the "heavenly dome" or apparent surface of the heavens which, in nautical astronomy, is assumed to be a true *s.,* its center coinciding with that of the earth. The various great circles of reference, such as the meridian, prime vertical, rational horizon, hour circles, equinoctial, and ecliptic, and also the apparent diurnal paths of the heavenly bodies, are conceived to be drawn on this great concave we commonly call the *sky.* **Quadrantal s.,** *see* **Q. correctors** *in* QUADRANTAL. **Terrestrial s.,** the earth.

SPHERICAL. Of or pertaining to a sphere; having the form of a sphere; globular. **S. angle,** *see* ANGLE. **S. buoy,** one showing a dome-like or hemispherical surface above water. In the British navigational buoyage system, such buoys mark the ends of middle grounds in a fairway or an isolated danger. **S. sailing,** *see* SAILING. **S. triangle,** figure on surface of a sphere formed by arcs of three intersecting great circles. **S. trigonometry,** that branch of mathematics which treats of the relations of sides and angles in the solution of those values in *s. triangles; esp.,* as applied in navigation, those involved in great circle sailing and determination of altitudes, azimuths, and hour angles of the heavenly bodies.

SPHEROID. A globular figure or mass not truly spherical, such as our Earth, which is described as an *oblate s.* or *ellipsoid,* her polar diameter being 26.7 statute miles less than that of the equator. (*Cf.* EARTH) This means that in the plane of the equator she is *circular* in shape, while her girth figure in that of the meridian is *elliptical. Geoid* is another geometrical term for the Mother-Earth model.

SPICA. Principal star in the group *Virgo* and listed in Nautical Almanac as *α Virginis.* Has a magnitude of 1.21; right ascension, 13h. 22m.; and declination, 11° S. It may be located by continuing the curve of the *Big Dipper's* handle through *Arcturus,* which star lies at half-way mark between tail of *Dipper* and *Spica.* The star lies in line with the gaff of the *Cutter's Mainsail,* or sail-shaped constellation *Corvus,* at about 11° northeastward of the latter.

SPIDER. A two- or three-legged metal fitting projecting from a mast, vessel's side, etc., for holding a block clear of such surface; a *strut.* **S.-band,** metal band around a mast a few feet above the deck for holding belaying-pins to which ropes, etc., leading aloft are secured. Also, a *futtock-band; see* FUTTOCK. **S. batten,** piece of wood, such as one of those in the *spar ceiling,* that is held in position by *s. dogs.* **S. dog,** piece of flat metal bent at a right angle for securing a bar or batten in position; *esp.,* when the latter lies in a curved line, as the battens comprising *spar ceiling* in a vessel's hold, or a frame-bar being set to shape on a *bending-slab*. **S.-hoop,** same as *s.-band*.

SPIKE. Any large *nail* of square section and, usually, of greater length than 3½ inches; also called *s.-nail;* loosely, any nail-like piece of pointed metal. In building vessels and larger boats, *spikes* of galvanized iron or a non-corrosive metal are used chiefly for fastening planking. Also, are greatly employed in wharf and other waterfront construction. A handy bar or lever; a *handspike;* also, short for *marline-spike*. A projecting thorny spine, as in the fins of some fishes. A young mackerel. To fasten with *spikes,* as planking to a ship's timbers. To disable a cannon by driving a *s.* or such piece of metal into the vent, or, in more modern usage, by removing part of the breech mechanism; hence, to frustrate one's activities or aggressive intentions, as in *to s. one's guns*. The word appears as a variant of *speck* in *s.-tackle, s.-tub,* etc.; *see* SPECK. **S. iron,** *see* **Calking-irons** *in* IRON. **S.-plank,** in the old auxiliary steam vessels on Arctic voyages, a bridge built forward of the mizzenmast for conning purposes in navigating through ice.

SPIKEFISH. *See* **S.-fish** *in* SAIL.

SPILE. A wooden plug for a vent in a cask, or serving as a spigot. A pin or plug driven in the hole left by a withdrawn bolt, spike, etc.; also, in this sense, a *spill*. A heavy stake driven into the ground; a *pile; see* PILE. **S.-driver,** a pile-driver; *see* PILE. **S.-worm,** the ship-worm or teredo; *see* **M. borer** *in* MARINE.

SPILING. Piles; piling collectively. The edge-curve in a strake of planking or plating. In *pl.,* dimensions of off-sets taken from a straight-edge in laying off curvature of a structural part, as edge of a plate, beam, etc., or other rounding or bellying shape in plating, framing, etc. **S.-batten,** a light straight-edged rod or batten from which *spilings* are measured.

SPILL. A *spile,* or plug for stopping a hole in a cask. An overflow of a liquid through a tank top or hatchway on to the deck, as when a compartment in an oil-tank vessel is filled to excess. To shake or throw the wind out of a sail by slacking off its sheet, brailing in, or partly gathering it in by buntlines, leechlines, etc., in order to ease pressure on the sail, to reef it, or take it in; *cf.* **Spilling-l.** *in* LINE. **S.-pipe,** *see* **C.-locker pipe** *in* CHAIN.

SPILLER. The long stout line with many hooks attached at intervals throughout greater part of its length, as used in *spillet-* or *spilliard-fishing*. (*S.W. England and S. Ireland*) The compartment in a pound-net, sometimes fitted as a narrow-mouthed annex to the *pot,* from which the catch is lifted; *see* POUND. In New England mackerel fishing, a kind of seine spread out alongside the vessel for tempo-

rarily securing part of the catch; also, a small seine used to take the fish that are imprisoned in a larger one.

SPILLING-LINE. Any line used for gathering in a sail (*see* SPILL); a brail; *esp.,* such rope on a square sail; *see* LINE.

SPIN. To fish with a troll having a *spinner,* or device for alluring the fish by rapidly rotating the hook or hooks as the line is towed. To **s. a yarn,** to tell a story of the "long-winded" entertaining sort. To **s. foxes,** to lay up two or three lengths of marline, spunyarn, etc., by a *spinning-jenny; see* FOX.

SPINDLE. In a built mast, the main or central piece; also called the *heart*. The stout vertical axle on which a *capstan* pivots. A spar-shaped *beacon* usually surmounted by a cage, ball, or other day-mark and sometimes a lantern.

SPINDRIFT. Fine spray and foam swept by the wind from crests of the waves, or the resulting foamy streaks lying in the direction of the wind; also, *spoondrift*. Scud, or broken vapory clouds driven before the wind; *see* SCUD.

SPINE. One of the thorn-like rays in fins of certain fishes. The heart-wood, or *duramen,* in a mast or other spar, timber, etc., that has been fashioned from the trunk of a tree; *see* DURAMEN.

SPINNAKER. A large, light, jib-headed sail set on side opposite the mainsail in larger sloop-rigged yachts when sailing before the wind. Its foot is extended by a *s.-boom,* with sheet secured on deck forward of mast. The boom is stepped at foot of mast and set in position by a *topping-lift* leading to the masthead and a *guy* to the quarter. The sail is set "flying," or hoisted while lightly stopped at intervals along the leech, its tack hauled out to boom's end, the sheet then hauled aboard, stops carrying away in the last-named phase of the operation. **Parachute s.,** a more recent type, sometimes called a *double s.* and, in American yachting circles, a *Mae West,* that hoists forward of all head stays and is sheeted to an outrigged boom on each side. This huge bellying sail usually takes the place of all other canvas when yacht is steering directly with the breeze. A variation of the type is the *twin s.,* which, in effect, is the *parachute* cut down its middle to allow a flatter set by sheeting it to each bow and so abaft and clear of the head stays.

SPINNER. *See* SPIN. A spinning-jenny.

SPINNING-JENNY. Hand spinning-machine once commonly used in European ships for making *foxes* or small stranded stuff by twisting and laying together two or three parts of marline, rope-yarn, spunyarn, etc. (*Cf.* FOX) The device consists of a frame or stand on which is fitted a central toothed wheel operated by a crank and geared to three pinions set at equal distances apart, all turning in a common vertical plane. The parts of marline, etc., are secured to an eye at center of each pinion and so twisted by the turning motion. As that process continues, the parts naturally *lay* together in a direction opposite to that of the administered twist; thus, a *left-hand twist* given the parts results in a *right-hand lay.* The man controlling the desired lay moves a cone-shaped block, or *set,* held between all parts at the appropriate rate along the line in the making and away from the *jenny.*

SPIRIT COMPASS. *See* **Fluid, liquid,** or **oil c.** *in* COMPASS.

SPIRKET. An old shipbuilding term for a space between floor-timbers.

SPIRKETING. In older shipbuilding, first strake or strakes of inside planking next to the waterways or above beam ends and reaching the gun-port sills; these often were included in what was called the *quick-work; see* QUICK. **S. plate,** chiefly in composite and older iron construction, a narrow plate riveted to the frames immediately above and along the line of beams in a lower deck or along the line of hold beams. In many vessels, the short bulwark-plate or plating at either side of the stem, usually tapered downward at its after end; also called *bow-chock plate* and *apron-plate; see* APRON.

SPIT. A long point of low-lying land or a narrow shoal extending from a coast or shore-line.

SPITFIRE JIB. *See* JIB.

SPLICE. (Old Du. *splissen,* to split) A joining of two rope ends, or an end with any part of the same or another rope, by interweaving the strands. To unite two pieces of cordage, a rope to a chain, etc., by *splicing;* often with *in, esp.* when a rope is thus secured to some fitting; as, to *s. in* a hook, thimble, etc. **Back s.,** a substitute for a *whipping* on a rope's end. Strands are *crowned* (*see* CROWN) and their ends interwoven, or *tucked over one and under one,* into body of rope. **Bight s.,** *see* BIGHT. **Chain s.,** *see* CHAIN. To **draw a s.,** to undo or withdraw the strands in a *s.,* as in disconnecting two ropes thus joined. **Draw s.,** so called because it may be easily *drawn,* a *short s.* made with unusually lengthy unlayed strands in joining ends of large-sized fiber rope. It is completed by neatly laying along and seizing the strand ends to body of rope. **Eye s.,** *see* EYE. **Flemish eye-s.,** *see* EYE. **Horseshoe s.,** *see* HORSESHOE. **Irish s.,** *see* IRISH. **Long s.,** so called from the lengthy space it occupies in the rope, a *s.* in which rope thus united is not increased in size, as required for passing through a block or for neat appearance. Strands of each end are unlaid for a distance of 6 to 8 times circumference of rope and *married;* then one strand is further unlaid and its pairing mate in the other end is laid **in its** place; this is repeated with each pair, so that con-

necting ends of each pair lie at separate points along the rope. The several pairs of strands are *tucked* or turned about each other *with the lay* and tapered as desired. There are thus the same number of uniting places as there are strands in the rope. Also called *round s.* **Mariner's s.,** joining of cable-laid hawser ends, either by *short splices* in each rope at nine separate intervals in the hawser or *long splices* extending over a common space. (Each rope in this type of hawser corresponds to a *strand* in ordinary rope) This is the *s.* of all *s's* and only a thorough *sailorman* can make a job of it. **Round s.** = *long s.* **Sailmaker's s.,** so named for its use in bolt-rope work of sails, any *s.* in which the strand formation in the rope is not disturbed, *i.e.,* each strand end always is turned or *tucked* round only one strand of the rope. **Short s.,** in this strong but bulky *s.,* strands of each rope are unlaid for about the distance in feet as there are inches in rope's diameter, then married and strands tucked *over one and under one* until 3 or 4 *tucks* are completed. Handiest method to begin the *s.* is to form a half-knot in each meeting pair of strands and draw all taut; this provides the first *tuck.* **Span s.,** = *horseshoe s.* To **s. the main brace,** to administer a drink of spirits to the crew or group of men on an occasion of extraordinary exertion, exposure, etc.; also, in celebration of an event of mutual interest. Hence, to join with one in taking a drink; to drink to excess. **Tail s.,** joining of a piece of fiber rope as a *tail* to the end of a wire. A difficult *s.* to put in, it has many variations, but generally follows *long s.* procedure, two strands of the wire pairing with one of the fiber strands and tapered in final tucks according to choice. The entire *s.* usually is *served* on completion.

SPLICING-FID. *See* **Hand f.** *in* FID. **Splicing-vise,** same as *rigger's screw; see* RIGGER.

SPLINE. In shipbuilding drawings, a long flexible strip of rubber, steel, or wood for fairing curved lines. A thin strip of wood fitted in a planking-seam and smoothed flush with surface, as sometimes found in larger yachts. **S.-planking** is the term for deck- or side-planking finished in this manner, or by *splining.*

SPLINTER. A thin piece rent or split from a plank, timber, etc. To split or be riven into slivers or fragments, as wood or metal fittings or parts of a ship by gun-fire, a mast by lightning, etc. **S.-bulkhead,** *see* BULKHEAD. **S.-netting,** *see* NETTING. **S.-screen,** an armor- or gun-screen; *see* SCREEN.

SPLIT. To part or cleave lengthwise, as a timber in direction of the grain. To burst or be rent asunder; often with *apart* or *open;* as, *ship s. apart on the rocks; the casks s. open.* Cleft; divided; separated. **S. fall,** in cargo hoisting, one of two separate falls, as distinguished from the usual *double whip,* or two falls connecting to a common hook. **S. fish,**

mackerel, herring, etc., that have been cut open and cleaned preparatory to salting or curing. **S. jigger,** *see* JIGGER. **S. link,** chain link cut in matching longitudinal halves and capable of being riveted together after being inserted in the chain. **S. lug,** *see* **L. rig** *in* LUG. **S. spirit,** a wishbone gaff; *see* WISHBONE RIG. **S. tacks,** *see* To **s. or break t's** *in* TACK.

SPLITTER. A tool used to partly split or open the edges of lapped plating preparatory to calking. One of the crew in a fishing-vessel who splits fish for cleaning.

SPOIL GROUND. *See* GROUND.

SPOKE. One of the projecting radial parts in a steering-wheel. Hence, a change in rudder angle; as, *a s. or two of right helm; "Right—just a s.!"* **Midship s.,** also *king s., see* MIDSHIP. **S. sheave,** a block-sheave having radial pieces, or *spokes,* as distinguished from a solid or *disk sheave.*

SPONGE. The porous elastic mass constituting the skeleton of certain invertebrate sea-water animals that fix themselves to rocks, coral bottom, etc. Remarkable for its rapid absorbent qualities, the *s.* is much used in washing, bathing, etc. Most important *s.* fishing is carried on in the Mediterranean, the Caribbean, and Gulf of Mexico, chief producing countries being Bahama Islands, Cuba, Egypt, Tunisia, Turkey, and United States. World's largest *s.* market is at Tarpon Springs, Florida. To clean or dry off water from a surface; as, to *s. the brightwork.* To swab out a cannon, as in cleaning after discharge. **Loofah s.,** the fibrous interior of a gourd from a tropical plant of the genus *Luffa.* It is used in filtering impurities from the feed-water supply to steam boilers.

SPONSON. In older naval construction, a gun-platform projecting from ship's side to provide a greater arc of fire. Projecting structural timbers, etc., supporting each paddle-box in a side-wheeler. **S.-beam,** in a paddle-wheel vessel, fore-and-aft timber or girder supporting outer bearing of paddle-shaft and the paddle-box structure; also, *spring beam.* **S. deck,** platform forward or abaft a paddle-box, usually triangular in shape, or having its outer edge sloping from ship's side to outside limit of paddle-box. It is laid on the diagonal bracing timbers of the *s.,* or the *sponsing,* as sometimes called.

SPONSOR. The person who names or *christens* a vessel at the launching ceremony; *see* CHRISTEN.

SPONTANEOUS COMBUSTION. A danger always present in coal cargoes and bunker coal and, under certain conditions, apt to arise in many other substances. It may be defined as the gradual heating and igniting of a substance by chemical action of constituents of the substance itself, or of a combination of substances. *Cf.* COAL.

SPOOM. To scud, drive, or sail swiftly before a strong wind and rough sea; also, to *spoon.* (Now probably obsolete)

SPOON. In trolling, a piece of bright metal resembling the bowl of a spoon used as a lure. The device is set between the hook or hooks and end of line and usually is designed to revolve as line is towed. A *trolling-s.* Resembling or suggesting the form of a *s.* **S. bow,** *see* BOW. **S. fashion,** said of the stowage of boats in which one *nests* inside the other; *see* NEST. **S. oar,** *see* OAR. **S. stern,** one having a *s.-like* bulge above water.

SPOONDRIFT. *See* SPINDRIFT.

SPOT. To place in a desired position, as a sling of cargo being lowered, a vessel alongside a pier, ship's gangway, etc. At hand and ready for use, shipment, etc.; as, a *s. ship; s. cargo.* An edible fish, resembling and of same family as the *drumfish,* found on the U.S. Atlantic coast; averaging nine inches in length, the fish bears a remarkable black *spot* about two inches behind each eye and has 15 diagonal dark stripes across its back. *Cf.* DRUMFISH. **S. weld,** to join metal parts by welding only at certain points, as distinguished from connecting in a continuous weld.

SPOUT. To eject or forcibly throw out, as water or vapor; said of a whale or other cetacean; to blow from the *blow-hole* or *s.* A trough or tubular conduit through which grain is loaded from an elevator. A waterspout.

SPOUTER. Old-fashioned slang term for a whaling-vessel or her master.

SPRAT. Local name for several different species of small fishes; the European *Pomolobus sprattus,* a small herring related to the common herring; a *garvie herring.*

SPRAY. (Du. *spreiden,* to spread or scatter) Water thrown and scattered by the wind, as from crests of waves, sea dashing against ship's side, etc. A vessel is said to be *spraying* when more or less continuously taking *s.* aboard, as in a rough sea. **Buffalo s.-board,** *see* BUFFALO. **S.-board,** a screen or board raised above a boat's gunwale for protection against *s.;* a *s.-screen.* **S.-hood,** a canopy or covering, usually made of canvas, for shielding persons or the engine in a motor-boat from rain or *s.;* a hood over a companionway; *cf.* HOOD.

SPREAD. Extent, expanse, area; as, *a heavy s. of canvas.* In a square sail, length of the *head* or thwartship dimension, as distinguished from *depth* or *hoist,* the vertical distance from head to foot; in a fore-and-aft sail, distance from mast to leech. To set or stretch out, as a sail, an awning, tarpaulin, etc. To **s. fires,** in a boiler furnace, to disperse a coal-banked fire over the entire grate surface and add more fuel, as in getting up steam.

SPREADER. Any bar, small spar, batten, etc., fitted to spread one or more stays, as an outrigger for leading a rope, to hold apart a bridle sling in lifting a vehicle, etc.

SPRING. A mooring- or warping-line leading in a fore-and-aft or diagonal direction from ship's side; such line used to *spring ship,* or draw her alongside by the thwartship component of force exerted as when line is in tension and vessel in motion; also, *s.-line.* One of a number of heavy moorings, usually consisting of a length of large-sized coir or manila, to which a ship's wire hawser is secured, as installed on a pier to secure vessels in a commonly prevailing swell. A crack, fissure, or other weakening deformation occurring in a mast or other spar, the spar being then referred to as *sprung.* The *sheer,* or rise from amidships toward either end, in a vessel's fore-and-aft lines; gradual upward curvature of the rail or deck from amidships. To haul, or cause a vessel to swing or cant, by means of a *s.-line.* To bend, crack, split, or otherwise strain or weaken, as a spar, timber, plank, etc.; as, *we sprung the main yard in coming about.* To become bent, twisted, warped, etc., from a straight line or surface, as a plank, which then is said to be *sprung.* To bend by force, so as to fit in place, as a plank, timber, etc.; often with *down, in,* or *out.* To **s. a butt,** *see* BUTT. To **s. a leak,** *see* LEAK. **S. beam,** *see* **S.-beam** *in* SPONSON. **S. bearings,** older name for the *shaft bearings,* or those mounted on the *pillow-* or *plummer-blocks* which at intervals support the *line-shaft* between engine and propeller. **S. block,** *see* BLOCK. **S. buffer,** *see* BUFFER. To **s. her luff,** *see* LUFF. **S. herring,** the *alewife* or *gaspereau; see* ALEWIFE. **S. hook,** same as *Snap-h. in* HOOK. **S. lay rope,** a more recent type of cable-laid flexible wire rope made up of six small ropes having alternate strands of wire and fiber, the whole being laid around a heavy hemp core. This arrangement of fiber and steel supplies elasticity desirable in mooring-lines and such cordage subjected to sudden stress. If not kept thoroughly lubricated, however, the rope will fast deteriorate because of its moisture-absorbing tendency; *"sea-water has no love for steel."* **S. log,** *see* LOG. **S. stay,** *see* STAY. **S. tide,** *see* TIDE. **S. tiller,** *see* TILLER.

SPRIT. (A.S. *spreot,* pole, spear; Du. *spriet,* bowsprit) A small spar or pole for spreading or extending something; a spreader; an outrigger; short for *bowsprit.* Specifically, the spar spreading a *spritsail,* or that extends from mast at or near foot of sail to peak of the latter. **S. rig,** a handy, economical rig used in fishing-boats, barges, etc., so named from the one or more *spritsails* carried.

SPRITSAIL. A fore-and-aft quadrilateral sail of similar shape to that of a gaff sail and spread in same position as the latter in some boats and small vessels. Its peak is extended by a *sprit* that is secured by a *snotter* or *stirrup* to the mast, usually a foot or two above the tack. The throat of sail may be hoisted and *sprit* pushed up in place by hand, as in small boats, or its luff may be permanently secured to the mast. In larger craft, it is sometimes rigged with brails by which both sail and sprit are gathered in against the mast in stowing. In any case, a boat-sail of this type can be taken in very quickly by hand, *i.e.,* without brails, in same fashion. Setting the sail, when sprit has not been disturbed, then amounts to little more than drawing aft its sheet. In old-time ships, a *s.* was a square sail spread on a yard crossed under the then high-rising *bowsprit;* sometimes above this sail a *top s.* of similar shape was set from a yard mounted on an auxiliary mast; and, in larger vessels, a *top-gallant s.* spread below the outer end of bowsprit. These constituted a ship's *head sails* prior to the comparatively recent advent of *jibs* and *staysails.* **Levantine s.,** of nearly square shape at its head and having a standing sprit, a brailing-in *s.* that is hanked to its topping-lift. **S.-sheet knot,** kind of stopper-knot made with the strands of both ends of a small piece of rope, once commonly set as a clew-strop in a sail. The bight forms an eye to which sheet of sail is secured. Knot consists of a *double wall* and *double crown,* or same as a *manrope knot,* but with twice the number of strands. **S. topsail,** also called *lug topsail,* a quadrilateral *gaff-topsail* of similar shape to a *lug,* so named for the *yard* or *sprit* spreading its head. **S. yard,** spar slung across the bowsprit for setting the old-time *s., top s.,* or *top-gallant s.* To **s.-yard a shark,** in the old sailing-ship diversion, to hook and capture a shark, jam a stick of wood vertically between his open jaws, and then set him adrift. The fish then drowns or is voraciously set upon by his fellows.

SPRUNG. *See remarks in* SPRING.

SPUD. (Dan. *spyd,* a spear) An armor-pointed vertical pile or post that may be dropped or lifted on end from a scow, dredge, etc., to serve as an anchor. Larger vessels of scow type having construction or dredging *plant* aboard usually are equipped with a *spud* at each corner of the hull.

SPUN-YARN. Soft right- or left-hand laid hemp *small stuff* of 2, 3, or 4 yarns. Used for seizings and service, it is described as 2-yarn s., 3-yarn s., etc. **S. Sunday,** same as *Rope-yarn Sunday; see* ROPE. **S. winch,** a *spinning-jenny.*

SPUR. Part of a deck-beam that is interrupted by a hatchway, etc.; a half-beam; any projecting structural part serving as a support or a stiffener. A shore fitted vertically between launching-ways and an overhanging part of ship's side preparatory to the launching. A *breast shore;* a *spur shore; see* SHORE. One of the projections on the arms or crown of a stockless anchor for catching the bottom, and so canting both flukes downward, upon the initial horizontal pull of the cable. The ram of older war-vessels. One of the "spikes" in a heavy boot worn by whalemen when standing on a carcase in the work of *flensing*, or stripping off blubber, as in older whaling; also, the *sole* of a boot thus armed for slippery treading. An auxiliary projection from a pier or wharf; a small jetty or mole built of stone, rocks, etc. **S.-beam,** in a paddle vessel, diagonal timber extending from each end of the *sponson-beam* to ship's side, serving as a brace or stiffener to the sponson structure, and forming outer edge of *sponson deck;* any diagonal timber constituting the *sponsing; see* SPONSON. **S. gear,** meshing toothed or "spurred" wheels or pinions, such as found in steam winches. A *s.* is synonymous with *tooth,* which may be *straight,* or at right angles to plane of wheel; or may be of *herring-bone* type, or V-shaped. **S. grommet,** as fitted in heavier sails, a brass grommet having small inner projections that grip into a sewn-in grommet as the fitting is set in place; *see* GROMMET. **S.-shore,** *see* SHORE.[2]

SPURLING.   An old English word for flowing; running or turning, as a rope in a block. **S. gate,** *see* **C.-locker pipe** *in* CHAIN. **S.-line,** *see* LINE.[1]

SPURNWATER.   A V-shaped breakwater at fore end of a flush-deck vessel; *see* BREAKWATER.

SPY-GLASS.   A handy telescope for navigating-bridge use.

SQUADRON.   Division of a fleet, usually under command of a flag officer; also, two or more ships attached to a common station or service. **Flying s.,** group of war-vessels capable of, and detailed for cruising at, high speed. **Red, White,** and **Blue S's,** former three divisions of the British fleet, named, respectively, for the color of each commanding admiral's flag. *Admiral of the Red* was the naval designation for such officer in command of the *Red S.,* and so on. **White S.,** popular title for the ships of the U.S.N. when *white* was the adopted peace-time color of hull.

SQUALL. (Sw. *sqvala,* to gush out)   A suddenly rising strong wind, or sudden increase of wind, of short duration, usually followed immediately by rain or snow; a gust of wind. Sudden blasts or *squalls* greatly vary in force and extent, from those representing the *bursting* of a monsoon, occupying several hundred miles of advancing front, to the single gust or puff from the summer cloud. They occur with greatest frequency in vicinity of islands in tropical latitudes and near the dividing line of areas having considerable differences in sea-water temperature; are most violent under conditions in which heavier cold winds break through prevailing warm breezes or an area of calms and light variable winds such as is found in the region of the equator. Heavy *s's* prevail at the front of an advancing tropical cyclone; often with a heavy *line s.*

the trade wind shifts a whole eight points in direction, as from N.E. to S.E., in vicinity of the equator; violent gusts sweep down the ravines and valleys of mountainous coasts, as those of Greenland and the Magellan Straits; while the fine weather *rain s.,* occurring in both tropic and temperate latitudes, may amount to little more than a strong breeze of a few minutes' duration. **Arched s.,** so called from its first indication of approach, or arch-like formation of dark cloud appearing above the horizon and broadening with its ascent into the zenith. The wind bursts forth as the *arch* reaches nearly overhead. This type commonly accompanies a change of wind direction, as from S.W. to N.W. in the North Atlantic, a gale usually ensuing,—particularly during winter if lightning appears in the latter quarter,—from that point of the compass at which the *arch* arises. **Black s.,** one accompanied by heavy dark clouds, or a single dark cloud. **Bull's-eye s.,** one in which an isolated small white cloud indicates the vortex of disturbance. Usually of a violent character, it is the *white s.* of the South and West African coasts. **Leeward s.,** so termed in the South Pacific, a *s.* occurring on lee side of a small island and characterized by shift of wind direction from that of prevailing trades or monsoon. **Line s.,** one marked by a front of dark cloud sometimes extending several hundred miles. Often attended with a shower of rain or snow, it is a front of cool air displacing the lighter warmer atmosphere of a region of some extent. It sometimes blows with extreme violence in which case a sudden drop of temperature occurs with its passage, which lasts only a few minutes. **White s.,** a kind of whirlwind or tornado appearing as a disturbance of the sea surface immediately below a single cumulo-nimbus cloud. Actually a *waterspout* in embryo, it properly falls without the category of *s.,* yet there is a belief among seamen of the old school that many a good ship met with disaster through being struck by "a raging tempest with nary a cloud in sight!" The *white s.,* then, is a traditional blast that gives warning of its approach only by a turbulence arising on the surface, while accompanied by a clear sky. **Look out for s's,** *see* LOOK.

SQUALLY.   Characterized by frequent squalls; gusty; as, *s. weather was met with off the Cape.* In weather records and ships' deck logs, usual *abbrev.* for such conditions is *Q* or *q.*

SQUAM.   Local Down-East name for a fisherman's sou'wester; *see* SOUTHWESTER.

SQUARE.   At right angles with the fore-and-aft line and with the masts,—said of a vessel's yards when so braced, or *squared.* To line up or fair; often with *up;* as, to *s.* (or *s. up*) the ratlines, a tier of cargo, etc.; to *s. up* the deck, or replace gear, ropes, etc. To brace the yards at right angles to the keel; as in "*S. the main yards!*" Area of deck in passenger quarters at foot of a stairway. A block of cargo in tier. **Gunner's s.,** a device for setting the old-time cannon at proper elevation. **Naval s.,** as commonly painted on the poop deck in sailing-navy days, a diagram indicating the fore-and-aft, beam, and quarter lines. It was used to facilitate observation of relative bearings, particularly in maneuvers. To **s. away,** to alter ship's course in a leeward direction, at same time bracing in the yards accordingly; often with *for,* as in *we squared away for the Windward Passage.* **S. body,** that part of the hull below water-line which has a constant cross-sectional form. **S.-body frames,** *see* FRAME. **S. cloths,** in sailmaking, those cloths which terminate at right angles, as when meeting the head or foot of sail. **S. frame,** *see* FRAME. **S. knot,** *see* **R. knot** *in* REEF.[1] **S. mark,** piece of marline, twine, or the like, tucked in the strands of the hauling part of a brace or a topping-lift for indicating a yard is *trimmed s.* when such *mark* lies at the belaying-pin. **S. of an anchor,** in an old-fashioned anchor, part of its shank that is *s.* in cross section and about which the wooden stock was fitted. The later iron stock is set in a hole through shank at the *s.* **S. of Pegasus,** *see* PEGASUS. **S. of the hatch,** area of hold immediately below a hatchway; sometimes also, area extending from a 'tween-deck hatchway to ship's sides. **S.-rigged,** having some principal sails of *s.* shape and spread on yards; as said of a brig, brigantine, barque, barquentine, or ship. In nautical usage, the presence of one or more masts carrying the *s. rig* distinguishes a vessel as *s.-rigged,* regardless of the number bearing the *fore-and-aft rig.* **S.-rigger,** a *s.-rigged* vessel; *esp.,* one having two or more masts carrying only *s.-rig.* **S. sail,** *see* SAIL. **S. stations,** in the sheer plan of a ship, vertical lines at equally spaced distances between stem and stern; also often shown on the half-deck plan, they are numbered and indicate the peripheries of cross-sectional areas of the hull; also called *sections.* **S. stern,** also called *flat* and *transom stern,* as opposed to a round or elliptical form of stern, one having a more or less flat surface, usually sloping upward, and in effect constituting vessel's *counter.* It is generally confined to sailing vessels of wooden construction. **S. yards,** a vessel is said to have *s. yards* when having unusually lengthy upper yards, as in the jubilee rig; *see* JUBILEE RIG.

SQUAT. Depression of after end of a vessel, or change of trim by the stern, due to motion through the water. Actually, in the case of ships having a *speed-length ratio* of less than about 1.0, upon speed becoming great enough to produce wave-making, the hull sinks bodily with little change of trim. With higher speed-length ratios, however, *squat* appears under same conditions and in shallow water may increase to the undesirable extent of contact of the hull with the sea-bottom. A good example of degree of *s.* is seen in the marked depres-

sion of a destroyer's after end when the vessel is proceeding at high speed.

SQUEEGEE. A piece of wood having a straight edge shod with leather or rubber and fitted with a handle for wiping or scraping off all water from a surface, as in drying a deck; also, *squilgee.*

SQUID. *See* CALAMARY. **S.-jigger** or **s.-jig,** a device for catching *s.* commonly used by fishermen on American northeastern coasts. Consists of a number of hooks radially set on a lead sinker that it attached to a line. It is *jigged* or *jerked* continuously with the objective of hooking the *s.* by any means without use of bait. The *s.* is greatly used for baiting cod-lines, etc.

SQUILGEE. In the old studding-sail days, a strop or becket fitted with a toggle for holding the *stun's'l* together as it was hoisted into position. When all was ready for spreading, at the order *"Out s.!",* sail was loosed by a jerk of the toggle. An older term for any small tripping-line, guy, or other short temporary slip-rope, strop, etc.; also older form of *squeegee.* (*Squillagee* is a variant of the word)

SQUIRM. A curly spiral formed in a rope due to heavy stress when turned about a capstan, winch end, drum, etc.

STABBER. Sailmaker's pricker or small marline-spike; often has a triangular shape in section. *Cf.* PRICKER.

STABILITY. (L. *stabilis;* from *stare,* to stand) State or quality of being in equilibrium; tendency of a vessel to return to her original position upon being inclined therefrom. In order that the upright position may be maintained, *s.* conditions demand that ship's *center of gravity* lie vertically below her *center of buoyancy,* and, in general, great *transverse s.* obtains, or vessel is said to be *"stiff,"* when the points indicated are comparatively greatly separated; *"tender"* or *"crank,"* when comparatively close. *Cf.* **Righting l.** *in* LEVER; *also* METACENTER. **Curve of s.,** *see* CURVES OF SHIP CALCULATIONS. **Dynamical s.,** work done in inclining a vessel from the upright to a given angle of heel. Expressed in foot-tons, it is equal to the *displacement* times length of the *righting arm.* (*See* **Righting l.** *in* LEVER) In considerations of sail-carrying power, such value also equals the product of total wind pressure times distance of *center of effort* from *center of lateral resistance.* (*See* these terms in CENTER) **Initial s.,** that measured by resistance of ship to heeling, up to angles of about 12°. Also called *metacentric s.,* from the fact that the *metacenter* remains a fixed point throughout the range of such inclination. A *s. test* necessarily involves determination of vessel's *initial s.* (*Cf.* **Metacentric height** *in* METACENTER) **Range of s.,** as usually indicated in a *curve of statical s.,* angle through which a vessel may be inclined from the upright before reaching the vanishing point of righting power. **S. test,** that for *initial s.,* as determined by heeling effect produced by shifting a known weight a given distance in a transverse direction on board. Since weight times distance moved, divided by displacement, gives shift of vessel's *center of gravity,* the value of *GM,* or *metacentric height,* is equal to such shift (in feet) times *cotangent of angle of heel.* This, in principle, is the method generally used, although a more elaborate procedure is favored in which deflection of a long plumb-line is measured with the view of more precisely determining the heel angle. **Statical s.,** moment of the force with which a floating body tends to return to a position of equilibrium upon being inclined from such position. (*Cf.* **C. of statical stability** *in* CURVES OF SHIP CALCULATIONS) **Transverse s.,** that commonly considered as the measure of a vessel's tendency to return to the upright upon being inclined to port or starboard, as distinguished from *longitudinal s.,* or that concerned with questions of trim, pitching, etc., particularly in naval architecture.

STABILIZER. *See* **G.-stabilizer** *in* GYRO.

STABLE FLOTATION. *See* FLOTATION.

STACK. *See* **S'stack** *in* SMOKE. **S.-hook,** *see* HOOK.

STADIMETER. (Gr. *stadion,* ancient measure of about 600 feet; E. *meter*) An instrument for determining distance off an object of known height by observing the angle subtended by such height at the eye. It is a modified form of the sextant, principally used as a range-finder in station-keeping and in coastal sounding-survey work.

STAFF. (Of *Teutonic* origin) A graduated measuring-batten, stick, rod, rule, etc., such as that commonly used by shipwrights; a handspike, lever, or the like, provided with a long handle. Pole for displaying a flag; *see* **F'staff** *in* FLAG. Short for the *cross-staff* or the *back-staff; see* BACKSTAFF *and* **C.-staff** *in* CROSS. The body of officers detailed as direct assistants to a commanding officer of a naval establishment, fleet, or squadron; complement of officers in a merchant ship; *ship's s.* **Almucantar-s.,** or **astronomer's s.;** *see* ALMUCANTAR. **Fore-s.,** *see* FORE. **Futtock-s.,** *see* FUTTOCK. **Half-breadth s.,** *see* HALF. **Half s.,** *see* HALF. **Jacob's s.,** old name for the *cross-s.* **Long-s.,** *see* LONG. **Overcast s.,** a graduated rod or measure used by shipwrights to determine differences of curvature in a vessel's frame timbers. **Ship's s.,** in a merchant vessel, the officers in each department; usually includes deck and engine-room licensed officers, purser, surgeon, chief steward, and chief radio operator. **Spiling s.,** *see* **S.-batten** *in* SPILING. **S. captain,** in larger ocean passenger ships, officer next in rank to the master. In addition to his duties as master's assistant, he usually is charged with carrying out all fire, bulkhead-door, and boat drills, and has general supervision of all safety appliances, life-boats, fire-fighting apparatus, etc. **S. commander,** a British naval officer, usually holding rank as *commander,* who is in charge of hydrographic surveying work and directly responsible to the Admiralty. **S. officer,** in U.S. merchant vessels, an officer in the *s. department,* or that defined as "a separate and independent department composed of a medical division and a purser's division." (*Title 46, C.F.R. 10.25–5*) *S. officers* are registered by U.S. Coast Guard in the grades of *chief purser; purser; senior assistant purser; junior assistant purser; junior assistant purser and pharmacist's mate; surgeon.* **Tide s.,** a graduated pole or batten erected as a tide gauge or indicator of height of water level above the tidal datum plane. **Wring-s.,** in shipbuilding, a strong piece of wood used in the ring of a *wring-bolt* for drawing planking against frames on curved parts of the structure; also, *wrain-s.*

STAGE. A platform or scaffold, such as that suspended over, or built from the ground against, ship's sides, to accommodate seamen or workmen engaged in painting, caulking, riveting, etc. An arrangement of stages is termed *staging.* Given state or degree of progression of the *tide;* as, *half-flood s.; slack s.* Short for **landing-s.;** *see* LANDING. **S. lashing,** shipyard term for soft-laid cordage,—usually tarred hemp, used only for lashing or securing purposes. In older *whaling,* blubber was stripped from a carcass lying alongside as the men stood on the *cutting-s.; see* CUTTING-FALL.

STAGGER. To zig-zag or arrange alternately on each side of a median line, as rivets, bolts or butts in planking, etc. A vessel is said to *s. under a press of sail* when spreading an area of canvas that is excessive for the prevailing force of wind.

STAITH. In Great Britain, a landing-stage or wharf from which railway carloads of coal, ore, or other bulk are transshipped into vessels, often by raising each car and dumping contents into a loading-chute.

STAKE. A slender post or pointed piece of wood driven in the bottom and appearing above surface as a marker for a channel, dredging work, survey, etc., or for spreading a fish-net, in sheltered waters. **S.-boat,** a mark-boat; *see* **M.-boat** *in* MARK. Also, local term for an anchored scow serving as a make-up station for river tows in the port of New York. Harbor tugs leave their up-river bound barges, etc., at the *s.-boat;* thence the river tug takes her complete tow.

STANCH. Also *staunch.* Seaworthy, tight, and sound; said of a vessel with respect to her fitness for carrying a prospective cargo.

STANCHION. (O. Fr. *estance,* a stay) An upright bar, post, prop, or pillar for supporting a deck, rail, awning-spar, bulwark, skids, etc. Usually named according to its use or position; as, *beam-s., bulwark-*

s., deck-s., hold-s. **Hatch s.,** *see* HATCH. **Quarter s.,** *see* **Q. pillar** *in* QUARTER. **Rail s.,** *see* RAIL.

STAND. To maintain a relative position; as, the barometer *stands* at 30.05 inches; the river now *stands* at high level. To sail in a specified direction; to hold a course; as, to *s.* to the north-east; often with *in, off,* or *on,* as, to *s. in* for the land; to *s. off* from the point; to *s. on* the port tack. To be or get ready to perform a specified duty,—usually with *by;* as, to *s. by* to let go anchor; to *s. by* the fore sheet; to *s. by* a vessel. To perform or be occupied in a certain duty; as, to *s. watch;* to *s. a trick* at the wheel. A vessel is said to *s. up* to a press of sail when not excessively heeling to a beam breeze. **Compass s.,** also *binnacle s.,* usually for facilitating azimuth observations, a raised platform on which a binnacle is erected. To **s. clear,** to move from, or remain out of the way of, a danger; to direct the course away from, or to clear, an object or position of danger. To **s. off and on,** to sail on alternate tacks toward and away from shore. **S, of a chronometer,** old term for the *error* of chronometer, *i.e.,* the interval it is fast or slow of Greenwich civil time, or of Greenwich sidereal time if a sidereal chronometer, at a given date. **S. of the tide,** *see* TIDE. **S.-on vessel,** the privileged vessel, or one required to hold her course and speed as prescribed by *Rules for Prevention of Collisions.* To **s. to sea,** to sail away from the land.

STANDARD.[1] A large flag or pennant containing the coat-of-arms or emblem of a ruler, displayed at the main when such dignitary is on board. In wooden ships, an inverted knee timber, such as one placed above a deck-beam instead of under it; a *standing knee.* A pillar, stanchion, or the like, for supporting some fitting, piece of machinery, etc.; such as that serving as a bearer for a lower tops'l yard; the upright bar, or *bell s.,* on which ship's bell is mounted, as on the forecastle head; a *boat-chock s.,* or one of the props on which some boat-chocks are raised; etc. In the adjectival comparative sense, according to, following, or gauged by established authority, custom, model, or prescribed method; as, *s. time; s. quarantine procedure; s. ship; s. sheer; s. riveting.* **S. compass,** *see* COMPASS. **S. patch,** *see* PATCH. **S. port of reference,** as included in *Tide Tables,* a port for which times and heights of high water (also, often for *low* water) are given for each day. To these data, constants indicated are applied to determine time and height of tide at secondary ports therein listed. **S. rudder,** *see* RUDDER. **S. speed,** *see* SPEED.

STANDARD.[2] A shipping timber measure of which there are several values, differing according to local usage. The *Petrograd s.* of the Baltic and White Sea trade is, perhaps, the most widely used for sawn deals. Notably at some Scandinavian and Baltic ports, however, the *s.* varies with the kind of timber; as, for example, the *Drontheim s.*

of sawn deals equal to 198 cu. ft.; that of square timber, 163½ cu. ft.; while the *s.* of round timber is 144 cu. ft. **Christiania s.,** 120 pieces of 1¼" x 9" x 11' = 1237½ board ft. or 103 cu. ft. **London or Irish s.,** 120 pcs. of 3" x 9" x 12' = 3240 board ft. or 270 cu. ft. **Petrograd s.,** 120 pcs. of 1½" x 11" x 12' = 1980 board ft. or 165 cu. ft. **Quebec s.,** 100 pcs. of 2½" x 11" x 12' = 2750 board ft. or 292 cu. ft.

STANDING. Fixed; not movable; established; as, *s. gaff; s. block; s. orders.* **S. block,** a fixed block in a purchase, as distinguished from a *running* or *moving* block. **S. bowsprit,** as opposed to a *running* or *reefing* bowsprit, one that is permanently fitted. **S. gaff,** *see remarks under* GAFF. **S. jib,** in older square-rigged ships, a large jib set next forward of the fore topmast stays'l; later displaced by *inner* and *outer jibs; see* JIB. Also, in some smaller fore-and-aft rigged vessels carrying three head sails, the jib next forward of the fore stays'l (or *jumbo*), or abaft the flying jib; sometimes, simply an *inner jib.* **S. knee,** *see remarks in* STANDARD. **S. lug,** *see* **L. rig** *in* LUG. **S. orders,** *see* **Standing o's** *in* ORDER. **S. part,** main part of a rope, as distinguished from its end or bight in making it fast to something; *see* PART. In a tackle, the fixed part of the fall; opposed to the *hauling part.* Of a hook, the *shank* or part opposite the *point.* **S. rigging,** *see remarks in* RIGGING. **S. topsail,** another name for a *gaff topsail.* **S. ways,** *see* **L. ways** *in* LAUNCHING.

STAPLE. A U-shaped bolt, dog, or slender piece of metal used for various purposes. **Mooring-s.,** *see* MOORING. **S.-angle,** also *stapling; see* **A.-staples** *in* ANGLE. **S. knee,** a kind of double beam-knee fitted with one arm below a beam and another above a beam of deck next below, part between being bolted to a frame timber. Now probably obsolete, it was made of iron and built in wooden vessels; also sometimes called *yoke-knee.*

STAR. Any of the self-luminous bodies in the heavens, other than the sun or a comet; often, in common usage, also a *planet.* The various groups of stars, or constellations, as distinguished by astronomers to-day retain the names given them by the ancients. (*See* CONSTELLATION) Also, many of the brighter individual stars still bear their original ancient Greek or medieval Arabic proper names. The present system of distinguishing each member of a group in the order of its magnitude by a Greek letter appears to have been instituted about A.D. 1600. This has been further developed in the use of Roman letters and even numbers, as many additional luminaries that are useful to the astronomer have been located by the modern telescope. *Navigational stars,* or those used in sextant observations, include those of brightness up to 3rd. magnitude (*see* MAGNITUDE). It will be noted that the Latin genitive form of the constellation's name is given in indicating a *star* by Greek letter, etc.; thus, *Regu-*

lus, chief in the group *Leo*, is catalogued as *α Leonis*; a less important member as *ε Leonis*; etc. In older usage, a principal *star* sometimes was designated by the word *Cor* (Latin = *heart*); thus, *Regulus* = *Cor Leonis*; *Aldebaran* = *Cor Tauri*; etc. **Binary s.**, a double *s.*, usually appearing to the unaided eye as one, but consisting of two stars that revolve about a common center of gravity. Examples are *Acrab* and *Castor*, positions of which are given in Nautical Almanacs for the brighter, or *β²* *Scorpii* and *α² Geminorum*, respectively. There are about 70 of such having greater brightness than the 3rd. magnitude in the *Nautical Almanac* catalogue. **Clock s.**, *see* CLOCK. **Dog s.**, *see* DOG. **Lunar s.**, *see* LUNAR. **Morning s.. evening s.;** any of the planets *Mercury, Venus, Mars, Jupiter*, or *Saturn* appearing shortly before sunrise or after sunset: *esp.*, the brighter *Venus* and *Jupiter*. To **s. a shoal,** to sound depth of water on a shoal by covering the ground in a starlike pattern; *i.e.*, by proceeding on recrossing lines suggestive, when charted, of a *s.* **S. boat,** a popular type of racing yacht of the smaller class. About 22 feet in length, is rigged with a single jib and jib-headed mainsail. **S. chart,** map or chart indicating positions of *stars* in either a part of or the entire heavens. **S.-finder,** any of several devices for indicating relative positions of *stars* or recognizing a particular *s.;* a *s.* chart. **S. time,** sidereal time, or that determined by observation of transit or altitude of a *s.; see* TIME. **Three-s. problem,** determination of ship's position by intersection of plotted *lines of position* obtained from altitude observations of three *stars* situated roughly equi-distant in azimuth.

Navigational Stars: Apparent Places, July, 1953.

Special Name	Constell. Name		Mag.	S.H.A.	Dec.
Achernar	α	Eridani	0.6	336° 00'	57° 28' S.
Acrab	β¹	Scorpii	2.8	119° 19'	19° 41' S.
Acrux	α	Crucis	1.0	174° 00'	62° 51' S.
Adhara	ε	Canis Majoris	1.6	255° 48'	28° 54' S.
Agena (= Hadar)	β	Centauri	0.9	149° 52'	60° 09' S.
Aldebaran	α	Tauri	1.1	291° 41'	16° 25' N.
Alderamin	α	Cephei	2.6	40° 37'	62° 23' N.
Algeiba	γ¹	Leonis	2.6	205° 39'	20° 05' N.
Algol	β	Persei	var.	313° 43'	40° 47' N.
Alhena	γ	Geminorum	1.9	261° 15'	16° 26' N.
Alioth	ε	Ursæ Majoris	1.7	167° 00'	56° 13' N.
Alkaid (= Benetnasch)	η	Ursæ Majoris	1.9	153° 34'	49° 33' N.
Almach (or Almak)	γ	Andromedæ	2.2	329° 44'	42° 06' N.
Alnilam	ε	Orionis	1.8	276° 32'	1° 14' S.
Alphard	α	Hydræ	2.2	218° 40'	8° 27' S.
Alphecca	α	Coronæ Borealis	2.3	126° 49'	26° 52' N.
Alpheratz	α	Andromedæ	2.1	358° 30'	28° 50' N.
Al Suhail	* λ	Argûs	2.2	223° 26'	43° 15' S.
Al Na'ir	α	Gruis	2.2	28° 40'	47° 11' S.
Altair	α	Aquilæ	0.9	62° 52'	8° 45' N.
Ankaa (= Nair-al-Zaurak)	α	Phœnicis	2.4	354° 00'	42° 33' S.
Antares	α	Scorpii	1.2	113° 21'	26° 20' S.
Arcturus	α	Bootis	0.2	146° 37'	19° 25' N.
Arided (= Deneb)	α	Cygni	1.3	50° 02'	45° 07' N.
Bellatrix	γ	Orionis	1.7	279° 20'	6° 19' N.
Benetnasch (= Alkaid)	η	Ursæ Majoris	1.9	153° 34'	49° 33' N.
Betelgeuse (Betelgeux)	α	Orionis	var.	271° 50'	7° 24' N.
Canopus	* α	Argûs	−0.9	264° 17'	52° 40' S.
Capella	α	Aurigæ	0.2	281° 41'	45° 57' N.
Caph	β	Cassiopeiæ	2.4	358° 19'	58° 54' N.
Castor	α²	Geminorum	1.6	247° 05'	32° 00' N.
Deneb	α	Cygni	1.3	50° 02'	45° 07' N.
Deneb Kaitos (= Diphda)	β	Ceti	2.2	349° 41'	18° 14' S.
Denebola	β	Leonis	2.2	183° 19'	14° 50' N.
Diphda (= Deneb Kaitos)	β	Ceti	2.2	349° 41'	18° 14' S.
Dschubba	δ	Scorpii	2.5	120° 36'	22° 30' S.
Dubhe	α	Ursæ Majoris	1.9	194° 47'	62° 00' N.

Duhr (= Zosma)	δ	Leonis	2.6	192° 05′	20° 47′ N.
El Nath	β	Tauri	1.8	279° 10′	28° 34′ N.
Eltanin (or Etamin)	γ	Draconis	2.4	91° 06′	51° 30′ N.
Enif	ε	Pegasi	2.5	34° 31′	9° 40′ N.
Fomalhaut	α	Piscis Australis	1.3	16° 13′	29° 52′ S.
Hadar (= Agena)	β	Centauri	0.9	149° 52′	60° 09′ S.
Hamal	α	Arietis	2.2	328° 52′	23° 15′ N.
Kaus Australis	ε	Sagittarii	1.9	84° 43′	34° 25′ S.
Kiffa Australis	α²	Libræ	2.9	137° 55′	15° 51′ S.
Kiffa Borealis	β	Libræ	2.7	131° 22′	9° 13′ S.
Kochab	β	Ursæ Minoris	2.2	137° 17′	74° 21′ N.
Markab	α	Pegasi	2.6	14° 23′	14° 57′ N.
Menkalinan	β	Aurigæ	2.1	270° 58′	44° 57′ N.
Menkar	α	Ceti	2.8	315° 02′	3° 55′ N.
Merak	β	Ursæ Majoris	2.4	195° 14′	56° 38′ N.
Miaplacidus *	β	Argûs	1.8	221° 50′	69° 32′ S.
Mirach	β	Andromedæ	2.4	343° 13′	35° 23′ N.
Mirfak	α	Persei	1.9	309° 45′	49° 42′ N.
Mizar	ζ¹	Ursæ Majoris	2.2	159° 29′	55° 10′ N.
Murzim	β	Canis Majoris	2.0	264° 50′	17° 56′ S.
Nair-al-Zaurak (= Ankaa)	α	Phœnicis	2.4	354° 00′	42° 33′ S.
Naos *	ζ	Argûs	2.3	239° 31′	39° 52′ S.
Nunki	σ	Sagittarii	2.1	76° 54′	26° 21′ S.
Peacock	α	Pavonis	2.1	54° 29′	56° 53′ S.
Phecda	γ	Ursæ Majoris	2.5	182° 09′	53° 57′ N.
Phact	α	Columbæ	2.8	275° 31′	34° 06′ S.
Polaris	α	Ursæ Minoris	2.1	varying	89° 03′ N.
Pollux	β	Geminorum	1.2	244° 23′	28° 08′ N.
Ras-al-hague	α	Ophiuchi	2.1	96° 48′	12° 36′ N.
Regulus	α	Leonis	1.3	208° 31′	12° 12′ N.
Rigel	β	Orionis	0.3	281° 55′	8° 15′ S.
Rigil Kentaurus	α	Centauri	0.1	140° 53′	60° 39′ S.
Ruchbah	δ	Cassiopeiæ	2.8	339° 18′	60° 00′ N.
Schedar	α	Cassiopeiæ	2.5	350° 32′	56° 17′ N.
Shaula	λ	Scorpii	1.7	97° 23′	37° 04′ S.
Sheratan	β	Arietis	2.7	331° 59′	20° 35′ N.
Sirius	α	Canis Majoris	−1.6	259° 14′	16° 39′ S.
Spica	α	Virginis	1.2	159° 19′	10° 55′ S.
Unuk	α	Serpentis	2.8	124° 30′	6° 34′ N.
Vega	α	Lyræ	0.1	81° 09′	38° 44′ N.
Wezen	δ	Canis Majoris	2.0	253° 23′	26° 19′ S.
Zosma	δ	Leonis	2.6	192° 05′	20° 47′ N.

(* *See* ARGO)

STARBOARD. (A.S. *steorbord: steor* = helm or rudder; *bord* = side; so called because in early ships the rudder was slung from that side) Pertaining to, situated on, or toward the right-hand side of a vessel, looking forward; opposed to *port;* as, a *s. list; s. braces; s. beam.* To **have her s. sheets aft,** said of a square-rigged vessel having her port side presented to the wind. To **have s. tacks aboard,** *see* ABOARD. **S. bower,** *see* BOWER. **S. helm,** *see* HELM. **S. tack,** *see* TACK. **S. watch,** *see* WATCH.

STARBOWLINES. In old navy parlance, men of the *starboard watch; see* WATCH.

STARFISH. Member of a large class of echinoderms, the *Asteroidea,* so named from its star-shaped body of strong radially disposed arms,—usually five in number. The animal feeds chiefly on mollusks and displays a destructive fondness for the oyster, especially.

STARGAZER. Another name for a *moonsail; see* MOONRAKER. A small spiny-rayed marine fish of the family *Uranoscopidæ,* so named from the position of its eyes which are on top of the head and apparently look directly upward.

START. To open and begin drawing the contents from; as, to *s. a cask of beer, rum, etc.* To loosen or spring a plank, bolt, or other fixture; as, to *s. a seam* (and so *spring a leak*). To ease a rope or piece of gear under stress; as, to *s. a sheet*. The signal given for *s.* of a yacht race, as the dipping of a flag, sound of a gun, whistle, etc. A vessel is said to be *started* when any mechanical means of giving her a *starting push* has been resorted to in launching. To **s. a ship from the stump,** *see* STUMP.

STARTING TUB. A tub having a hose led from its bottom by which, the device being set in a hatchway, fresh-water casks in a hold formerly were filled from the deck. The tub was similarly used in loading molasses, as at some West Indies ports.

STATE OF SEA. *See* SEA.

STATEROOM. A private room or cabin in a passenger-vessel.

STATICAL STABILITY. *See* STABILITY.

STATION. Place to which a crew member is assigned; *esp.,* in an emergency, as at handling a lifeboat, fire-fighting, closing a bulkhead door, etc. Place or region in which a naval or other government vessel is assigned for duty. Position allotted a vessel in a convoy or squadron. Office or place occupied by government or harbor authority, coast patrol, etc., on shore; as, *life-saving s.; naval s.; quarantine s.; radio-compass s.; signal s.* In ship design, one of a number of vertical transverse planes, at right angles and perpendicular to the keel, laid off at equidistant intervals between stem and stern for reference and measurement purposes; also called *transverse sections* and *ordinates.* To place or assign to a specified duty or post; as, to *s. a lookout.* At the command "*Stations!*" in American and British vessels, particularly those of the liner type, officers and men take up their assigned posts preparatory to docking or mooring ship and leaving port. **Boarding s.,** place at which customs and immigration officers board incoming vessels, as at entrance to a port. **Boat s.,** post assigned a crew member at launching of a lifeboat. **Coast s.,** a radio-telegraph or *signal s.* established on a coast; *esp.,* for ship communication purposes. **Fire s.,** post assigned a crew member at *fire drill; see* FIRE. **Life-saving s.,** place on a coast at which a lifeboat and her crew, line-throwing gun, breeches buoy apparatus, and other life-saving equipment are held in readiness to assist persons in landing from a stranded vessel; *cf.* **L.-saving Service** *in* LIFE. **Lloyd's signal s.,** *see* LLOYD'S. **Naval s.,** *see* NAVAL. **Pilot s.,** place or local area at which pilots are furnished or landed from vessels. **Quarantine s.,** *see* QUARANTINE. **Radio-compass s.,** *see* RADIO. **Signal s.,** *see* SIGNAL. **S. bill,** a posted list showing places assigned to and duties required of each member of ship's company at exercise of boat, fire, and water-tight-door drills, including accompanying requirements, such as mustering passengers, providing

blankets, life-belts, etc. **S. buoy,** an auxiliary buoy moored near a lightship, an important buoy, or a surveying vessel, to serve as a marker in event of removal or breaking adrift of its primary. Many coastal lightships have at least two such buoys. **S. pointer,** the *three-arm protractor,* or instrument for indicating an observer's position on a coastal chart in connection with measurement by sextant of two adjacent horizontal angles subtended by three *recognized* and *charted* objects. Consists of a graduated disk or circle from center of which three ruler-like arms project. One of these, the *zero arm,* is fixed; the others movable. The latter are set and clamped at, respectively, angles observed between left and middle, right and middle, objects. Then, with instrument laid on chart, zero arm is placed to coincide with middle shore object, while the other arms are moved to coincide with both right and left objects. Center of graduated circle, as usually indicated by a pencil dot, then is observer's position. Since the observer's position lies at the intersection of two circles that may be drawn through such position, the right and middle objects, and left and middle objects, respectively, the *s. pointer* method is susceptible of great accuracy where the objects observed are selected with the view of obtaining a well-defined "cut" of the circles. **Whaling s.,** *see* WHALING.

STATUTE MILE. *See* MILE.

STATUTORY DECK LINE. Datum line from which a vessel's *freeboard* is measured. It is painted black on a light ground or white on a dark ground on each side of the hull, at mid-distance between stem and stern, as a horizontal stripe 12 inches long by 1 inch in width, the upper edge of which indicates the exposed surface of freeboard deck plating or planking at vessel's side. *See* FREEBOARD *and* **Freeboard d.** *in* DECK.

STAUNCH. *See* STANCH.

STAVE. One of the pieces of wood constituting the sides of a cask, tub, etc. As designated in the timber trade, *staves* are pieces of softwood 3 to 4 feet in length and of varied widths and thicknesses. Usually with *in,* to crush or break in, as the bilge of a cask, a boat's planking, etc. A vessel's planking or plating that is seriously crushed or burst inward is said to be *staved in* or *stove in.*

STAY. (A.S. *stæg;* Du., Ger., Scand. *stag.* Of Teutonic origin) One of the ropes, now usually of wire, in the arrangement of *standing rigging* for supporting or stiffening a mast in the fore-and-aft direction. It leads aft and upward to a masthead from a bowsprit, jib-boom, the hull, or from another mast; as, *fore s., main-topmast s., mizzen-royal s.,* etc. In rigging a vessel, a mast is first secured against swaying aft, or *stayed, i.e.,* by setting up its *s.* or *stays.* (*Cf.* BACKSTAY) Hence, generally, any supporting or steadying rope, as a *guy* or the like; a stiffening or strengthening bar or rod, as a *bulwark s.*, a *boiler s.*; or any bar, pipe, plate, etc., functioning as a stiffener or support against racking, bending, etc. It is also an old term for the *stud*, or transverse piece, in a chain-cable link. To steady or support by means of a *s.*; as, to *s. a topmast.* To tack, or come about, as in sailing. **At a long s.; at a short s.**; *see* ASTAY. **Belly-s.**, or *belly-guy, see* BELLY. **Fresh-water s.**, an old deep-water square-rig sailor's term for a *triatic s., q.v.* **Head s's**, the ropes (usually *wire*), collectively, that lead aft and upward from fore part of vessel, bowsprit, and jib-boom, or that part of the standing rigging which *stays* the foremast and its topmast, topgallantmast, etc. On some or all of these the *head sails* (jibs, foretopmast stays'l, fore stays'l, etc.) are set. To **heave in s's**, to head into the wind, as in taking way off a sailing-vessel; *see* HEAVE. **In s's**, said of a vessel when her head sails are shaking, as in turning into the wind in "staying," or "coming about" from one tack to another. **Main s., main-topmast s., main-topgallant s., main-royal s., main-skysail s.**, as named for the masthead at which each terminates, *stays* leading aft and upward from the deck or from an appropriate point on the foremast. **Mizzen s., mizzen-topmast s.**, etc., those *staying* the mizzenmast arrangement; *cf.* **Main s.**, etc. To **ride down a s.** or **backstay**, *see* RIDE. **Rudder s.**, *see* **R. arms** *in* RUDDER. **Slack in s's**, slow in coming about; *see* SLACK. **Spring s.**, in the schooner rig, *s.* leading from lowermast cap to same point on the mast next in order; in effect, it is a continuation of the *fore s.*, which leads from vessel's stem to foremasthead. **S.-hole**, in a stays'l or a jib, one of the small eyelets or grommets at intervals along its luff. The hanks for confining sail to its *s.* are seized to the sail through the *s.-holes.* **S. light**, a lantern hoisted on or secured to a *s.*, as an anchor-light on a *fore s.* **S.-tackle**, a purchase used for setting up a *s.*; a hoisting-tackle suspended from a *s.* **Storm s.**, a temporary *s.* for setting a storm stays'l, storm jib, etc. **Triatic s.**, in the schooner rig, one leading from a topmasthead aft and downward to the lowermast cap of mast next in order; chiefly found in two-masted vessels. It functions as a backstay in stiffening the topmast from which it leads. Also, *fresh-water s.* (Also see *stay* in connection with caption words BOILER; BULWARK; FORE; GUSSET; JACK; JIB; JUMPER; MARTINGALE; MISS STAYS.

STAYSAIL. Properly, any fore-and-aft sail of triangular shape, excepting *jibs*, spread from a *stay.* Especially in small craft usage, however, the term also designates a fore-and-aft sail, either of triangular or quadrilateral pattern, that is set "flying" and in no way connected with a stay; *cf.* **Fisherman's s.** *in* FISHERMAN. In square-rigged vessels, *lower s's*, as those set on a main or a mizzen stay, and the *fore-topmast s.* usually are designed for heavy weather, the former often being called *storm s's.* Formerly, *lower s's* were called *courses*, in common with the square foresail, mainsail, crossjack, etc.; *cf.* COURSE (*sail*). Staysails are named for the stays to which they are secured; as, *main-topmast s., main-topgallant s., mizzen s., jigger s.* **Middle s.**, *see* MIDDLE. **Queen s.**, *see* QUEEN.

STAYSHIP. The *remora*, a sucking fish once believed capable of stopping a ship; *see* REMORA.

STEADY. Constant; undeviating; as, a *s. course; a s. breeze.* A vessel is said to be *s.* when rolling or pitching comparatively little in the existing seaway. A *steadying* sail or sails, in small powered craft, often are set to offset rolling or to assist in steering by means of wind pressure during rough weather. **Steady!**, order given a helmsman to keep ship on a present heading; *esp.*, upon completing an alteration of course; also, *Steady so!; S. as you go!*

STEALER. In the shell plating toward the ends of a vessel, a plate or strake introduced as a single continuation of two tapering strakes. Two strakes are thus merged into one by the *s.* in the necessarily reduced area of plating as stem or stern is approached. *Cf.* **D.-strake** *in* DROP.

STEAM. Water in the vaporous state; the invisible gaseous form into which water is converted when heated to boiling point; commonly, visible vapor. To move by the agency of *s.*; as, *the liner steamed into harbor.* To apply *s.* or expose to the action of *s.*; as, to *s. a plank* (for bending). Operated by *s.* power; as, *s. engine; s. vessel; s. pump.* **Mixed s.**, blend of saturated and superheated *s.* for the purpose of drying the former and so improving its efficiency. **Saturated s.**, *s.* having the same temperature and pressure as the water from which generated. Its density or moisture content is constant for any given pressure. **S. chest**, chamber from which *s.* is distributed to a cylinder; also, *valve-chest; valve-box.* **S. coal**, or **steamboat coal**, is coal suitable for use in *s. boilers.* **S.-cock**, any small valve or cock by means of which *s.* is supplied or cut off. **S. coils**, piping arranged in a spread-out series of coils, as at bottom of an oiltank, through which *s.* is passed for heating the liquid to increase its fluidity and so facilitate pumping operations. Often, *s.-heating coils* or *pipes.* **S. cutter**, *see* CUTTER. **S. ejector**, *see* EJECTOR. **S. engine**, *see* ENGINE. **S. frigate**, *see remarks in* FRIGATE. **S.-jacket**, *see* JACKET. **S. lighter**, *see* LIGHTER. **S. navvy**, a dredging machine operated by *s.* **S.-port**, in a reciprocating engine, channel through which *s.* enters a cylinder from the *s. chest.* **S.-pressure test**, that of determining efficiency and tightness of a boiler, coils, tubing, etc., by subjecting such to a pressure of *s.* **S.-reducing valve**, a self-acting valve placed in a *s.-line* to supply *s.* at a lower pressure than that entering such line. **S. schooner**, *see* SCHOONER. **S. separator**, *see* SEPARATOR. **S. smother-**

ing system, arrangement of piping for conveying *s.* to the various compartments for fire extinguishing or gas-freeing purposes; *see* SMOTHERING. **S.-steering gear,** apparatus for turning ship's rudder by means of a *s. engine* that is operated at will by means of the helmsman's steering-wheel. **S. tiller,** a steering-gear arrangement in which the operating engine is mounted on and moves with the tiller. The engine (*steering-engine*) drives the tiller by means of a pinion working on a bow-shaped rack, **or** fixed *quadrant,* fitted on the deck. **S. trap,** a self-acting device by which water is drained from passing or contained *s.,* as in a·pipe or vessel. **S. trawler,** *see* TRAWLER. **S. vessel,** a vessel propelled by *s.;* a *steamer* or *steamship.* **S. whistle,** the instrument sounded by *s.* and commonly used in *s. vessels* for giving required signals in fog, steering signals, etc. It usually is mounted on the fore side of ship's funnel, or forward funnel, if more than one fitted. **S. winch,** a hoisting or warping engine operated by *s.* **S. waste-pipe** or **escape-pipe,** means whereby the escaping *s.* from a safety valve of a boiler or boilers is conducted to the atmosphere. It usually is fitted on and reaches same height as after side of ship's funnel or funnels. **Super-heated s.,** boiler or saturated *s.* that is heated above its initial temperature in a *superheater,* or special apparatus for the purpose. Drier and lighter than *saturated s.,* it thus more closely approaches the perfect gas state and, accordingly, is more efficient in an engine.

STEAMBOAT. A boat or vessel propelled by steam power; more commonly applied to coasting or inland-water craft; a *steam vessel* or *steamship.* **S'ing,** occupation of running or working on board a *s.;* among longshoremen, act of carrying cargo on one's back.

STEAMER. General term for a vessel propelled by steam power, as distinguished from a sailing-vessel; often still applied to a comparatively large power-driven vessel of any type, as a *motor-ship.* Earliest ocean *s.,* or, properly, auxiliary *s.,* was the American ship-rigged, paddle-wheeled *Savannah* which crossed the Atlantic in 1819. Next to perform that crossing was the Canadian three-masted topsail schooner *Royal William,* also fitted with paddles, in 1833. First Atlantic crossings under steam power alone were made by the British paddle-wheelers *Sirius* and *Great Western* in 1837. Last *paddle s.* built for trans-Atlantic service was the Cunard liner *Scotia* in 1861; she continued until 1874. First *screw s.* on the same run was the *Great Britain* of British registry in 1845; and, as probably the first vessel propelled by both paddles and a propeller, the *Great Eastern,* noted for her work in the early days of the trans-oceanic telegraph cable, made the crossing in 1860. **Lake-type s.,** the Great Lakes type of cargo *s.,* or one characterized by a lengthy continuous weather deck with respective locations of pilot-house and engine-room at her extreme forward and after ends. **Mail s.,** *see* MAIL. **Paddle s.,** one propelled by paddle-wheels; a side-wheeler; *cf.* **P. wheel** in PADDLE. **Pig s.,** *see* **P. boat** in PIG. **Screw s.,** one driven by a screw propeller as distinguished from a *paddle s.* **Stern-wheel s.,** one propelled by a paddle-wheel fitted across the stern, as commonly found in river navigation; a *stern-wheeler.* **S.-chair,** *see* CHAIR. **Tramp s.,** as distinguished from a cargo *liner,* the *tramp,* or one not engaged in a steady trade, but taking cargo, as advantageously offering, to any port. **Twin-screw s.,** one propelled by two screws, one at each side of the fore-and-aft center line.

STEAMING. Operation of cleaning the inside surfaces of a tank that has contained oil, molasses, chemicals, etc., by the agency of *steam.* The *steaming out* process is applied to oil-tanks, etc., for the purpose also of expelling obnoxious or dangerous gases from such compartments or receptacles. *Cf.* BUTTERWORTH SYSTEM. A vessel often is said to be *s.* when proceeding under engine power, regardless of type of propulsion in use. **S. time,** as recorded in ships' log-books, total time in which vessel's propelling plant has been in use in a given day, in the duration of a passage, or on an entire voyage. *S. time* customarily begins at a specified point clear of port of departure and ends with arrival at such point or position off port of destination. **S.-out system,** *see* **S. smothering system** in STEAM. **S. range,** *see* CRUISING RADIUS.

STEAMSHIP. A large vessel propelled by steam power; *esp.,* one designed for ocean voyages; a *steam-vessel.*

STEEL. Essentially an alloy of iron and carbon, hardness and ductility of the metal is governed principally by percentage content of the latter constituent. *Ship s.,* the ordinary *mild* quality made for plating, frames, etc., contains from .18 to .25% of carbon, about 5% manganese, and .04% respectively of phosphorus and sulphur. It has a tensile strength of from 25 to 35 tons per square inch and will stretch about 20% of its length before breaking. *S.* of the *high tensile* variety, having a strength of 35 to 40 tons per sq. in., is used in shipbuilding for principal longitudinal strength members, such as sheer strakes and upper deck of the hull. Various *steels* contain certain extra elements for giving the metal special properties to meet its intended use. Among these are *chrome s.,* containing about 2% chromium, for machinery gears, armor plate, and other uses demanding a high elastic limit and resistance to shocks; *manganese s.,* having 10% to 14% manganese, of the required hardness for castings; *nickel s.,* with 2¼% to 4½% of nickel, for armor plate, propeller shafting, special castings, noted for its qualities of hardness, toughness, and strength; *tungsten s.,* having 3% to 10% of that alloy, remarkable for hardness and ability to withstand heat as "high-speed" metal tool material and for its quality of retaining magnetism above all other steels. **Angle-s.**, angle-bars of *s.* in a collective sense; see **A.-bar** *in* ANGLE.

STEEP-TO. Said of a cliff, coast, or shore-line rising sharply from a navigable depth or having considerable depth of water close to it.

STEER. To guide or point a moving vessel in a desired direction; as, to *s. a course.* To control or govern a vessel's heading, as by means of the helm; as, to *s. by compass;* to *s. for the buoy.* To obey the helm or be directed or governed; as, *the craft steers well.* To **s. a trick,** to take one's turn at the helm. To **s. clear of,** to direct the course to pass clear of a specified object or peril; hence, to keep away from danger. To **s. small,** or **with a small helm,** said of a vessel when requiring little movement of the rudder in steering a course. **S'ed course,** a compass course; see COURSE. **S'staff** and **S'tree** formerly designated a *tiller.*

STEERAGE. Originally, the underdeck after part of a vessel used as passenger space; now, an inferior grade of passenger accommodation located on a lower deck; see **Steerage p.** *in* PASSENGER. Also, formerly in naval ships that part of the berth deck, usually forward of the wardroom, used as quarters for clerks and junior officers; now known as *junior officers' quarters.* Effect of the helm; steering qualities of or manner in which a vessel is affected by action of her helm; act of steering. **S. mess,** *see* MESS.

STEERAGEWAY. A rate of headway that is sufficient to make a vessel answer her helm. **Bare s.** is understood generally to mean the lowest speed at which a vessel, in the circumstances, is propelled toward her destination.

STEERING. Act of pointing or turning a vessel toward a desired direction by action of the helm or other means. Combining term denoting something pertaining to the guiding or directing of a boat or vessel through the water. **S. compass,** *see* COMPASS. **S.-engine,** apparatus or engine that operates ship's rudder by remote control, as from the pilot-house. It may be a steam, electric, or hydraulic type, or a combination of the last two. **S.-gear,** arrangement of engine, tackles, rods, chains, etc., by which vessel's rudder is controlled and turned. It usually is named from its source of operating power; as, *electric s.-gear,* in which an electric motor or motors is the working agent; *electro-hydraulic* gear (*see* ELECTRO-HYDRAULIC); *pneumatic,* in which compressed air works the *s.-engine; screw* gear, operated either by hand or power, featuring use of a left-handed and a right-handed screw-shaft connected to opposite sides of a cross-head tiller; *hand s.-gear (see* HAND). *Also see* **E.-steering-gear** *in* EMERGENCY. **S.-gear flat,** in larger ships, a special deck or platform

on which the *s.-engine* is installed; as, for example, that immediately above a balanced rudder. **S. light,** a small white light fixed abaft the funnel or after mast of a towing-vessel for vessel towed to steer by; also, a small dimmed light set on a *s.-pole* in vessels having a pilot-house well forward; *see* **S.-pole. S.-oar,** *see* OAR. **S.-pole,** particularly in the Lake-type of steamer, or one in which the distance from pilot-house to the bows is comparatively small, a pole rigged bowsprit fashion from the stem to provide a mark representing ship's head for steering and piloting purposes. Sometimes the *jack-staff* is made to hinge at its foot and so serve for a *s.-pole* as required. By night, a small light (*s.-light*), visible only in direction of pilot-house, is set on the pole end. **S.-quadrant,** *see* **Q. tiller** *in* QUADRANT. **S.-sail,** obsolete name for a *studding-sail.* **S.-telegraph,** *see* TELEGRAPH. **S.-wheel,** hand-wheel used by the helmsman in *s.* Usually made of wood and varying in size from about five feet in diameter in *hand s.-gear* (in some larger sailing-ships and for *emergency hand s.-gear* in some powered vessels, double wheels, or twin wheels mounted on same spindle, of this type are carried) to about 1½ feet in *powered s.* installations, its spokes project beyond the rim for providing convenient leverage grips for the helmsman. A departure from this pattern, however, now is seen in the all-metal wheel in which projecting spokes are done away with as consistent with the small effort required in controlling the power in use for *s.*

STEERMAN. Also, *steersman;* one who steers a boat or vessel; helmsman. In early ships, a *s.* was second in command or one of the master's assistants, corresponding to our present *mate.* The word for such officer still appears in the Norwegian *styrmann* (Old Nor. *styra,* to steer).

STEERSMANSHIP. The art of, or skill in, steering; also, *steermanship.*

STEEVE. Angle a bowsprit makes with the keel or the horizontal; also called *steeving.* To point upward from the horizontal, as a spar; especially said of the bowsprit; as, *her bowsprit steeves high.* A spar temporarily rigged as a derrick in stowing bales in tier, as cotton, hemp, etc. A jack-screw used to force bales of fiber, etc., into place during stowage in a vessel's hold; to stow cargo by such means.

STELLAR. (L. *stella,* star) Of, pertaining to, or resembling a star or the stars. S. month = sidereal month; *see* **S. period** *in* SIDEREAL. **S. observation,** *see* **To work an o.** *in* OBSERVATION. **S. parallax** = annual or holiocentric parallax; *see* PARALLAX.

STEM. (Old Teutonic origin) The piece of timber, bar, or post at which a vessel's outside planking or plating terminates at her fore end; the more or less upright continuation of the keel at extreme forward end of the hull; a vessel's *bow* or *prow.* To make headway against, as in sailing in a contrary current; to head into or against, as breakers, ice, a tidal current, a stream; to force vessel's *s.* against a pier, etc., as in turning short around. In England, chiefly in the coal trade, to load or agree to load a vessel within a specified period of time or on a particular date; as, *shipper stemmed the vessel for June 5.* **Bar s.,** also termed *s.-post,* the forged or cast steel *s.* or upward continuation of vessel's keel at fore end. **Clipper s.,** the raking or forward curving *s.,* including the cutwater, of a *clipper bow; see* **Clipper b.** *in* BOW.[2] **False s.,** *see* FALSE. **Fashion-plate s.,** also *fabricated, plated,* or *soft-nose s.; see* FASHION. **Free s.,** *see* **Stemming l.** *in* LIST. **From s. to stern,** from one end of the ship to the other; hence, covering thoroughly or completely affecting, as in *she was swept by breaking seas from s. to stern; vessel was given a s.-to-stern overhauling.* **Raking s.,** a straight *s.* having a forward rake,—a feature generally followed in more recent shipbuilding; *see remarks in* RAKE. **S. anchor,** in large vessels carrying three *bower anchors,* the *center bower,* or anchor that is stowed in the *s.* or *middle hawse-pipe.* **S.-band,** in wooden boats, a protective and strengthening piece of iron or other metal fitted on fore edge of the *s.* It terminates on the keel just abaft junction of the latter with *s.;* also, *s.-iron.* **S. cap,** a small plate or an ornamental top on a boat's *s.* **S. fender,** *see* **Bow f.** *in* FENDER. **S. foot,** junction of *s.* and *keel;* the *fore foot.* **S. head,** upper part or end of the *s.* **S. knee,** in boatbuilding, a knee fitted as a strengthening piece at union of *s.* and keel. In wooden vessels, it is another name for the *stemson.* **S. net,** in drift-net fishing, the one nearest the vessel in a line of nets. (Vessel "rides" or lies head on to line of nets at its *lee* end) **S. note,** *see* **N. of readiness** *in* NOTICE. **S.-piece,** in wooden vessels lower part of *knee of the head* which is bolted to the *s.; see* **K. of the head** *in* KNEE; also, one of the filling-pieces or timbers fitted between the *s.* and knightheads. **S. winder,** a saltwater sailor's term for a Lake-type steamer, from the pilot-house being at her extreme forward end.

STEMMING LIST. *See* LIST.[2]

STEMSON. In larger wooden ships, curved timber forming the innermost member of the *stem* arrangement. Scarfed to the keelson and usually continued to the upper deck, its purpose is to fortify the scarfs in the *apron. Cf.* APRON.

STEP. A socket, shoe, block, framing, or platform on which a mast, stanchion, pillar, etc., rests in its erect position; as, a *mast-s.* for receiving the heel of a mast. To place in the erect position, as a mast in such fitting. **To s. off,** to measure a distance, as on a chart, by *steps* of the dividers, the latter being set at a convenient unit of cables, miles, etc. **Side-steps,** *see* **Sea-l.** *in* LADDER.

STEPPING-LINE. *See remarks in* BEARDING. *Cf.* **Stepping-p.** *in* POINT.

STERN. (Ice. *stjorn,* a steering; A.S. *steoran,* to steer) Extreme after end of a vessel; that portion above the counter and abaft the stern-post. Obsolete term for the helm; also, an old English form of *steer.* A contraction of *astern,* meaning to *back water,* as in rowing, which occurs in the order *'Stern all!* (The old New Bedford whalers' *'Starn all*) To **bring down by the s.,** to trim the vessel so that her draft will be greater at after end than at her stem; to trim by the *s. Brought down by the s.,* in former usage, indicated ship carried too many officers in proportion to total number of crew, the phrase suggesting such influence on vessel's trim being due to the fact that all officers were quartered *aft.* **By the s.,** said of a vessel when floating deeper aft than forward; having a greater draft at the *s.* than at the stem; trimmed by the *s.,* as often indicated in feet and/or inches, thus, *ship is 2 ft. 3 in. by the s.,* i.e., she is floating deeper by that amount at her *stern* than at her fore end or *stem.* **Cruiser s.,** one with no overhang, or *counter,* above load water-line level and usually having considerable *tumble home,* or inward slope from water-line to ship's deck; so called from its first adoption in naval ships. **Elliptical s.,** one in which the projecting counter terminates at the deck in a rounded or *elliptical* pattern. **Lute s.,** an open-work extension built abaft the *transom s.* in small craft for the purpose of breaking up a sea as boat is beached head on. Commonly found on fishing-boats of south coast of England. To **make s.-board;** to **make a s. board,** a going or falling sternwise, *esp.* as in missing stays or in boxhauling; to force a vessel to make sternway by means of sails, oars, or engines. *Cf.* To **make stern-b.** *in* BOARD. **Round s.,** *see* ROUND. **S. anchor,** an anchor having its cable or mooring-line leading to the *s.;* any anchor carried at a vessel's after end. **S'board** = sternway; making way *s.* first; also written *s. board* and *s.-board.* **S. bushing,** bearing in which a propeller-shaft is set at vessel's stern; *esp.,* the friction-resisting material on which the shaft works at after end of the *s. tube,* or housing for the shaft in the propeller-post of a single-screw vessel. Also termed *s.-tube bearing; s.-tube bushing.* **S. casting,** the *s. frame* as made of a steel casting; *see* **S. frame.** **S. chase,** act of a vessel pursuing another, both steering approximately same course; also, former term for a gun at after end of vessel for defense in event of a *s. chase. See* CHASE. **S. chaser,** a chase *gun* mounted aft. **S'fast,** a rope or other mooring used for securing after end of a small vessel or boat. **S. frame,** heavy strength member in single or triple screw vessels, combining the *rudder-post* on which ship's rudder is hung and the *propeller-post* through which propeller-shaft passes. Space between rudder- and propeller-posts, or that in which the screw works, is called the *race.* **S. gland,** movable ring that secures or compresses packing in the stuffing-box at fore or inner end of a *stern tube;* also, *s.*

tube gland. Cf. **S. tube. S. hook,** one of the strengthening timbers, more or less curved, fitted horizontally across fore side of *s.-post* and extending over several frames on each side thereof. **S. knee,** in wooden vessel, the heavy knee connecting after end of *keel* to the *s.-post;* also called *heel knee.* **S. light,** *see Rule 10 in* REGULATIONS FOR PREVENTING COLLISIONS. **S. line,** a rope leading from the *s.,* such as is used in securing a vessel or boat to a pier, to another vessel, etc.; a *s.-rope;* a *s'fast.* **S. molding,** finishing or ornamental work, such as rounded battens, often representing a rope, fitted on or around the *s.* **S. on,** having the *s.* foremost; lying with, or presenting, the *s.* in a direction indicated; as, *she docked s. on; a barque moored s. on to the mole; our boat was running s. on to a heavy sea.* **S. pipe,** a hawse-pipe fitted at the *s.* for use with a *s. anchor; cf.* **H.-pipe** *in* HAWSE. **S. pointer,** *see* POINTER. **S. port,** a door or other opening in the *s.,* such as that used for loading or discharging lengthy timber; a gun port in the *s.* **S.-post,** generally, the heavy upright timber or bar at after extremity of the keel. The rudder is hung on this member which frequently is also called *rudder-post.* The entire *s. frame,* as fitted to accommodate a propeller, often is termed the *s.-post,* while the forward member of such frame, commonly called the *propeller-* or *body-post,* also is sometimes known as *s.-post. See* **Inner p.** *in* POST; *also* **F. stern-post** *in* FALSE. **S. sheets,** *see* SHEET.[2] **S. tube,** cylindrical casting through which a propeller-shaft emerges from the hull. It contains the aftermost shaft bearing which usually is lubricated by sea-water entering its after end. Tube is always housed in the after peak tank in single-screw vessels and in a small specially built tank in the case of wing propellers (as *twin screws*). Forward end of tube is fitted with a *stuffing-box* in the tank bulkhead. Also called *shaft pipe* and *shaft tube.* **S'way,** motion in a *s. foremost* direction; opposed to *headway.* **S.-wheeler,** vessel propelled by a single paddle-wheel mounted athwartship at her *s.* Such craft, essentially for smooth-water navigation, are found in almost all large rivers of the world. **S. window,** one of two or more square openings in the *s.* of older vessels of high-built *square-s.* type. Such *window,* fitted with a storm shutter for heavy weather, afforded admission of light and ventilation to captain's or officers' quarters below the poop. **Torpedo** or **torpedo-boat s.,** so named from its original use in torpedo-boat construction, a flat broad *s.,* built to lessen the *squat,* or increase of vessel's after draft, when running at high speed. **Transom s.,** *see* TRANSOM. **Tunnel s.,** in some vessels of shallow-draft design, designates an after body having a *tunnel* shape above and some distance forward of the propeller. As engines turn ahead, water rises in tunnel and completely immerses propeller.

STERNAGE. Obsolete term for a vessel's *steering* qualities; *esp.,* with regard to making a good course by compass.

STERNSMAN. Old-time word for a pilot or helmsman; a *steerman* or *steersman. Cf.* STEERMAN.

STERNSON. In wooden construction, the shaped timber forming a continuation of keelson or upper part of deadwood and bolted to *stern-post.* Also, *sternson-knee.*

STERNWAY. *See* **S'way** *in* STERN.

STEVEDORE. (Sp. *estivador,* a packer or stower) One whose occupation is unloading or loading vessels; a longshoreman. To load or discharge a cargo or cargoes as by a number of *s's,* or under the direction of a superintending *s.* **Contract s.,** person or firm that undertakes to load and stow, or discharge, a cargo or cargoes according to terms of an agreement, usually in writing. **S's hook,** an iron hook having a wood T-handle, used by longshoremen in moving bales, boxes, etc., by hand; also, *bale hook; box hook; cotton hook.*

STEVEDORING. Operation of loading or unloading ship cargoes. The term generally is limited to *loading* of goods from shore, another vessel, or any vehicle within reach of ship's "tackles" and proper stowage of the goods in vessel concerned; and *unloading,* to a landing place on shore, aboard a vessel alongside, or into any vehicle also reached directly by ship's gear.

STEVENSON LINK or STEPHENSON LINK. *See* **D.-link** *in* DRAG; *also* **L. motion** *in* LINK.

STEWARD. Member of crew whose duty is the catering to domestic requirements of crew and/or passengers. He is variously named according to his specific assignment; as, in naval ships, *cabin s., wardroom s., warrant officers' s., commissary s.;* in passenger vessels, *bedroom s., deck s., glory-hole s.,* or, as in charge of accommodation and catering to passengers of different classes, *2nd. Class s., 3rd. Class s.;* and, in cargo vessels, as chief of the catering department and often assisted by the *2nd. S.,* usually is called *The Steward* or *chief s.* **Chief s.,** responsible head of the *steward's department* in merchant vessels. His duties include supervision of cooking, proper supply and care of provisions, and attention to comfort and safety of passengers. In some passenger lines he is under the direct supervision of *ship's purser.*

STEWARDESS. A woman serving as a steward; *esp.,* one who waits upon female passengers on board ship.

STICK. A pole, spar, or mast; any piece of timber out of which a spar may be fashioned; in *plural,* the spars collectively, as in *her sticks were carried away.* **Creasing-s.,** *see* CREASING-STICK. **Gob-s.,** *see*

GOB-STICK. **Head-s.,** see **H.-stick** in HEAD. **Packing-s.,** see PACKING. **Tally-s.,** see TALLY.

STIFF. Consistently strong and constant in motion; as, a *s. breeze*, a *s. current*. Quality of possessing comparatively great initial stability, or resistance to inclining by an external force other than the sea, as under pressure of sail; opposed to *crank*. *Cf.* CRANKY, CRANK. **S. leg,** see *remarks in* LEG.

STIFFENER. Angle-bar or stringer fastened to a surface, as a plated bulkhead, for increasing rigidity; also, *stiffening-bar*. **Bulkhead s.,** see BULKHEAD.

STIFFENING. Any heavy substance, as ballast or cargo, taken on board for the purpose of increasing vessel's initial stability. The term usually connotes temporary adjustment of or precaution against the *crank* condition, as in moving ship in port or in sheltered waters. Permanent ballast or kentledge is sometimes known as *s.; see* BALLAST *and* KENTLEDGE. **S.-booms,** heavy logs or spars hung just afloat along each side of a vessel for keeping her upright in lieu of ballast, etc.; also, *s.-spars*. **S. side,** that side of a bulkhead to which the *stiffeners* are secured; also, *rough side*.

STILL WATER LEVEL. Mean level, or that to which water surface would subside if wave action ceased.

STING RAY. One of the *ray* fishes so called from its capability of inflicting a painful wound with its whip-like tail; *se* RAY.

STIRRUP. One of the short ropes that hang from a yard or boom to support the *foot-rope* and so lessen depth of the rope's bight under a man's weight. **S.-plate,** a clamp or connecting-plate uniting keel and stern-post in wooden boats and smaller vessels.

STOCK. (A.S. *stocc,* a stick, post, or tree-trunk) An anchor-stock; *see remarks and* **A.-stock** *in* ANCHOR. A rudder-stock; *see* **R.-stock** *in* RUDDER. Net value of a catch of fish (New England). In *plural,* shores, blocks, and timbers or frames on which a vessel rests in the process of being built. **Sea s.,** provisions or stores for use at sea; *sea stores*. **S. of the bowsprit,** its housed or inboard end; that part in way of the chocking-bits; *bowsprit heel* or *step*. **S. tackle** or **s.-and-bill tackle,** as used in stowing an old-fashioned anchor, handy purchase (usually *two-fold*) for attaching to the *s.* and/or one of the *bills* (end of either fluke).

STOCKADE. A row of piling acting as a breakwater for a pier, wharf, etc.

STOCKHOLM TAR. See TAR.

STOCKLESS ANCHOR. A so-called *patent anchor,* or one without a *stock; see* **Patent a.** *in* ANCHOR.

STOCKS. See STOCK.

STOKEHOLD. Space in a steam vessel's boiler-room provided for tending the fires; also, *fire-room*. In earlier days of steam, *stokehole* was the term for such space; also for the opening in a boiler through which fuel was passed to the furnace. **S. bulkhead,** watertight partition separating the boiler-room from an adjoining compartment.

STOKER. A fireman, or one whose duties, under the engineer in charge, chiefly are concerned with feeding fuel to and cleaning boiler furnace fires on board ship. The term is not commonly in use outside the British navy. **Mechanical s.,** a contrivance by which coal is automatically fed to a boiler furnace. Valuable as a labor-saving device, it also has the advantage of obviating loss of heat due to inrush of air that occurs with each opening of the fire-door in boilers not thus fitted.

STOMACH PIECE. See APRON.

STOOL. A chock or built support for a shaft, piping, a winch, pump, etc.; a bearer. **Backstay s.,** see BACKSTAY. **Boiler s.,** see **B. saddles** in BOILER. **Derrick s.,** see **D.-table** in DERRICK. **Riming s.,** see RIME.

STOP. A projection on a mast or spar serving as a support or a preventer to some fixture or fitting; any contrivance for arresting action of, or securing, a movable part or object; a piece of small stuff, etc., for securing a sail, rope, or other gear. To halt or check the progress of; as, to *s.* the engines; to *s.* a ship by signal. To obstruct or prevent entrance or loss of a liquid; as, to *s.* a leak in ship's planking; from a cask; etc. To temporarily seize, as by a small line, rope-yarn, etc., or other *s.* **Keel s.,** a fitting to which the after end of keel of a ship's boat is butted in locating boat in correct position for securing in the chocks. **Rotten s's,** chiefly in yachting, pieces of light twine, weak yarns, etc., used to hold a sail (spinnaker, flying jib, etc.) in the furled state when sent aloft for setting. **Rudder s's,** see RUDDER. **Salt s's,** see SALT. **S.-seine,** a short seining-net for completing the encirclement of fish by hauling it across the mouth of a *main seine*. **S.-valve,** see VALVE. **S.-water,** see STOPWATER.

STOPPER. A short length of rope or chain, or any contrivance, used temporarily to take the stress on a hawser, chain cable, halyard, etc. It is named for its location or for its particular use; as, *bitt-s., cable s., cathead s., clamp s., stern-line s., deck s*. To *s.* off a line, chain cable, etc., is to affix the appropriate *s.* to such. **S.-bolt,** an eye- or ring-bolt to which a *deck s.* may be secured. **S.-knot,** any knot made at the end of a rope for preventing the latter from reeving, as through a block, a dead-eye, stanchion eye, etc.; a man-rope knot, a Matthew Walker or lanyard knot. **Shroud-s.,** also called *fighting-s.* and *rigging-s.,* in former hemp-rigging days, a contrivance for quickly securing and setting up any standing rigging severed in battle. It consisted mainly of two dead-eyes rove with a lanyard. (For various *stoppers,* as designated by the following prefixed caption words, see BITT; BLOCK; CABLE; CAT; CHAIN; CHECK; DOG; LEAK; RIGGING; RING; SLIP; WING)

STOPWATER. Any contrivance for *stopping* a leak: *specif.,* in *wooden* vessels, a softwood dowel or treenail driven across a scarph seam, as in the keel, close to the garboard strake, to prevent seepage of water into the hull, which likely would occur due to impracticability of satisfactorily caulking a butt or seam in heavier timbers; in *steel* construction, in lieu of caulking, any device for making faying parts water- or oil-tight, as by insertion of canvas soaked in oil, red-lead putty, felt, stranded cotton, heavy asphalt, etc., where usual caulking procedure is impossible due to inaccessibility of structural parts concerned. Any device for retarding motion of a boat or vessel; as a *sea-anchor* or *drag.*

STORAGE. As differentiated from *stowage,* or the secure and orderly placing or *stowing* of goods on board a vessel for carriage, the act of *storing* or state of goods being *stored,* as cargo deposited in a warehouse for safe-keeping prior to shipment or immediately upon being landed.

STORES. The supplies of provisions, clothing, cordage, necessary articles and gear for use on board ship. In *singular,* place in which certain *s.* are kept; as, *boatswain's store; steward's s.;* the ship's *slop chest.* A *marine store* is a shop or other etablishment at which paints, cordage, deck fittings, etc., are sold. **Bill of s.,** a list of ship's *s.* certified by U.S. customs as allowed to be carried duty free. **Naval s.,** supplies for war-vessels; now generally a commercial term only, denoting resin, tar, turpentine, pitch, and other resinous products. **Sea s.,** provisions and supplies for use on a sea voyage. **Small s.,** general term for articles of small value intended for use of ship's crew: brushes, buttons, needles, thread, soap, tobacco, razors, etc.; also, such articles for ship's use as brooms, twine, buckets, small stuff, thimbles, shackles, paint-brushes, etc. **Store-ship,** a naval or other government vessel used to carry merchandise and supplies to a fleet, garrison, or station. **Ship s.,** see SHIP.

STOREKEEPER. Member of a vessel's crew who is charged with the custody and issuance of ship's stores; as, *deck s.; engine s.; steward's s.* An official in charge of public stores; as, a *naval s.; ordnance s.*

STOREROOM. Compartment or room in which ship's supplies or stores are kept; often called *store;* as, *boatswain's store.*

STORM. (From Old Teutonic source; akin to Du. *storen,* to disturb) A wind of force 11: see BEAUFORT SCALE. The strong wind that circulates about an area of low barometric pressure; a cyclone. Although often accompanied by hail, lightning, rain,

sleet, or snow, a *s.* at sea rarely is termed a *hailstorm, rainstorm,* etc. **Anticyclonic s.,** a strong wind generated by the outflow from the center of an area of high barometric pressure; *see* ANTICYCLONE. **Cyclonic s.,** *see* CYCLONE. **Electric s.,** violent disturbance of the earth's electro-magnetic conditions, or those of a locality, characterized by interruption of radio waves and often interference of north-seeking properties of the magnetic compass. Heavy thunder and lightning, whether or not accompanied by strong winds. **Extra-tropical s.,** cyclonic disturbance with winds of gale force originating outside the tropics. **Eye of the s.,** center or vortex of a cyclone; *see* CYCLONE. **High-area s.,** *see* HIGH. **Law of s's,** *see* LAW. **Line-s.,** *see* LINE.² **Low-area s.,** *see* LOW. **Magnetic s.,** *see* MAGNETIC. **Revolving s.,** one having the characteristics of a cyclone; *see* CYCLONE. **S. area,** that over which a *s.* extends or which apparently will be covered by the advancing *s.* **S. axis,** line joining the points of lowest barometric pressure in a cyclone. It usually coincides with the *line of progression,* or path, of the *s.* **S. belt,** general area covered by paths of *s's; espec.,* that traversed by tropical cyclones. **S.-bound,** said of a vessel when obstructed by the path of a *s.* or of one delayed in harbor by bad weather. **S.-breeder,** a heavy cloud-bank presaging bad weather; *s.-cloud.* **S. canvas,** special heavy-weather sails or close-reefed sails, such as are set in winds of whole-gale force: *s.* staysails, trysails, double-reefed foresail, reefed topsails, etc. **S. card,** a small card or chart depicting the general circular motion of wind in a cyclonic *s.,* from which, by observing changes in wind direction and/or changes in barometer readings, the mariner deduces his position with relation to center of *s.* and its *line of progression,* or path along which *s.* is advancing. **S. center,** generally, point at which barometer attains its lowest reading in a *s.* area; vortex or small area around which the wind circulates in a cyclone. At sea, such area may be 5 to 15 miles in diameter and is characterized by clear weather, light variable winds, and a heavy confused swell. **S.-cloud,** threatening bank of cloud on the horizon; *cirrus* or *mares' tails; cirro-cumulus* or *mackerel sky* cloud formation. **S.-cone,** a signal shaped like a cone formerly used at coastal stations to indicate approach of a *s.* or winds of gale force. **S. cover,** canvas secured over a skylight, ventilator shaft, etc., sheet-iron cover over a fiddley, or other protective covering used in bad weather. **S.-current,** see CURRENT. **S.-drum,** a signal-shape formerly used with the *s.-cone, q.v.* **S.-flag,** a signal-flag displayed as a *s. warning;* a small ensign or other flag flown in bad weather in lieu of a larger one commonly used. **S. jib,** *see* Spitfire j. *in* JIB. **S.-kite,** *see* Life-k. *in* KITE. **S. mizzen,** *see* S. spanker. **S. oil,** also called *sea-quelling oil,* is carried by most vessels for emergency use in keeping down a breaking sea, as when ship is hove to in the heavy laden condition, hoisting and launching boats, taking a disabled vessel in tow, boarding a wreck, etc. Vegetable and animal oils are more effective than the mineral product in that the necessary *slick* or film spreads much more rapidly and is not hindered to same extent by the congealing effect of colder sea temperatures. U.S. merchant vessels are required, if power-driven and over 200 gross tonnage, to carry 30 gallons of *s. oil;* if 5000 tons or over, 100 gallons; oil to be accessible and available at all times and effective means provided for its distribution. **S. petrel,** also called *stormy petrel; see* PETREL. **S.-rail,** as a means affording a hand-grip during rolling motion of the vessel, a wooden or metal railing fitted about waist high along the sides of a deck-house, in a passageway, etc. **S. sail,** any of a number of sails, small in area and strongly made, that are bent and set during heavy weather; a *s. trysail.* **S.-scud,** the *fracto-nimbus* cloud formation, or that often observed as broken-up rain-cloud rapidly driven across an overcast sky during a gale; *see* **No. 8** *in* CLOUD. **S. signal,** one or more flags or lights displayed at a coastal station as a warning of approaching winds of gale force. **S. spanker,** also termed *s. mizzen* in 3-masted square-rigged vessels, a triangular sail set on the after mast of 3- and 4-masted barques and ships in lieu of the gaff-headed *spanker* during heavy weather or when such may be expected on short notice. **S. stay,** *see* STAY. **S. staysail,** a heavy-weather triangular sail usually bent on a *main* or a *mizzen* stay; *cf.* STAYSAIL. **S. track,** path or line of progression of a cyclone; also, a *s. lane,* or narrow belt through which cyclonic *s's* pass with more or less frequency and regularity; path of a *s.* **S. trysail,** a strongly made gaff-headed, loose-footed sail or one of triangular shape with comparatively short luff set abaft a mast in heavy weather. It is primarily intended for use when vessel is *hove to.* **S.-valve,** *see* VALVE. **S. waves,** heavy sea or swell coming from a *s.* area; high waves driven before a gale. **S. zone,** belt or area occupied by an advancing *s.;* belt through which certain *s's* travel; a *s. lane.*

STORMY PETREL. *See* PETREL.

STOVE-BOLT. *See* BOLT.

STOVE IN. *See* STAVE.

STOW. (From Old Teutonic source, meaning *to place*) To pack away, lash in place, or otherwise secure something in position aboard ship; to place compactly and without loss of space, as cargo in a vessel's hold; as, to *s.* an anchor; to *s.* lumber on deck, in 'tween decks, etc. To roll up and secure a fore-and-aft sail; in older usage, to send down an upper mast or yard and secure it on deck. With *down,* in whaling, to place away in casks or tanks the oil obtained from a whale or whales; as, *we stowed down 100 barrels;* such yield being termed a *stowdown.* **S.-net,** funnel-shaped net anchored in

a tideway for capture of small fishes. It may be more than 20 feet in diameter at its mouth and over 100 feet in length, with meshes diminishing in size toward its tail or closed end. **S.-wood,** pieces of wood used to chock or secure cargo as required in *stowing; dunnage.*

STOWAGE. Act or process of *stowing* goods, merchandise, or stores, gear, etc., on board a vessel. State of being *stowed;* as, *space economy demands compact s.* That which is *stowed;* as, *the s. consists entirely of bagged grain.* Money paid for *stowing* goods. Supports, chocks, lashings, special fittings, etc., collectively, for securing any or part of ship's equipment or gear; such as those for *stowing* spare anchors, boats, rafts, spars, and the like. **Ammunition s.,** *see* AMMUNITION. **Boat s.,** *see* BOAT. **Boom s.,** *see* BOOM. **Broken s.,** that resulting in broken up and unoccupied space in vessel's hold, such as is caused by bulky irregular-shaped units of cargo; also, small packages, pieces, etc., used to fill in such unoccupied space. **Candy s.,** a stevedore's term for stowed cargo that is perishable by heat. **Deep s.,** state of being *stowed* to an unusual height, as goods in a deep compartment; empty barrels, certain cased or bagged merchandise, bales, etc., the bottom tiers of which may not suffer crushing damage by *deep s.* **Overstowage,** *see* O'stowage *in* OVER. **Short s.,** in the lumber trade, short or small pieces included in a shipment with the view of reducing waste of space to a minimum in the *s.* Often shipper is required by charter agreement to supply a stipulated percentage of short lengths for this purpose. **Small s.,** collectively, suitable small packages or pieces for filling in any spaces that otherwise would be wasted in the *s.* of cargo; *broken s.* **S. certificate,** in the interests of safety and insurance, document signed by a port warden, surveyor of cargoes, or other authorized person, stating that a vessel's lading is properly secured and/or *stowed* preparatory to proceeding to sea. **S. factor,** volume, usually expressed in cubic feet, occupied by a ton (2240 lbs.) of cargo properly dunnaged and stowed. *Cf.* **M. cargo** *in* MEASUREMENT. **S. plan,** that showing the disposition of cargo throughout the vessel. Its purpose is to indicate the comparative volumes occupied by different lots of goods and, where more than one port of discharge are concerned, destination of each consignment. **S. space,** entire volume taken up by a container in which goods are shipped. Space in a vessel available for *s.* of cargo.

STOWAWAY. One who conceals himself in a vessel for the purpose of obtaining a free or an unauthorized passage.

STOWDOWN. *See remarks in* STOW.

STRAGGLER. Crew member who has overstayed his leave of absence; vessel that has dropped astern from her assigned position in a convoy, as from lack of steaming power or breakdown of engines.

STRAGGLING-MONEY. *See* MONEY.

STRAIGHT. Not crooked or curved; unbroken; as, a *s. course to the cape;* a *s. coastline.* Unmodified; free of complications; as, a *s. bill of lading.* **S. bill,** *see* **B. of lading** *in* BILL. **S. deck,** as opposed to one following the curve of ship's side, a deck in which all planking is laid parallel to the fore-and-aft center line. **S.-framed,** denoting an economical type of construction in which main body of vessel is practically free of curvature, such as that found in cargo ships built during World Wars I and II. **S. of breadth,** *see* BREADTH. **S.-shank rivet,** *see* RIVET. **S. stem,** as opposed to a *clipper* stem or *bow,* one having no curvature above water-line. **S. timbers,** those in wooden shipbuilding having little or no curvature, such as structural material for keel, keelsons, stern-post, etc.

STRAIN. (O.Fr. *estraindre,* from L. *stringere,* to bind or draw tight) Distortion or deformation caused by excessive tension, bending, or pressure, as in a ship's cable, plating, etc.; loosely, stress; as, *s. on a hawser.* To sustain heavy and varied stresses, as a vessel laboring in a high sea, *straining* at her moorings in a gale, etc. To exert a striving effort; as to *s. at the oars.* **S.-band,** a strengthening cloth or band on a sail. **Panting s's,** *see* PANTING.

STRAINER. A rose-box or strum; *see* ROSE.

STRAIT. A comparatively narrow stretch of water connecting two seas or large areas; a passage between a coast-line and an island or between two areas of land; often in *pl.,* as *Magellan Straits.* **S's oil,** *see* OIL.

STRAKE. (M.E. *streke,* a stroke or drawn line. Properly, a variant of *streak*) One of the rows or strips of planking or plating that constitute the outside surface, decks, sides of deck-houses, or bulkheads in a vessel. In shipbuilding, *strakes* are distinguished by letters, each plate in a *s.* being numbered; thus, in shell plating, second *s.* from the keel and tenth from stern-post (or from stem) is designated *B-10;* midship *s.* in a deck is composed of plates *M-1, M-2,* etc.; while port or starboard *s's* often are marked *P-A, P-B,* etc., starting from midship or *M s.,* with individual plates indicated as *PA-1, PB-2, SA-1, SB-1,* etc. A similar system is carried on in the preparation of *s's* for deck erections and bulkheads. **Air s.,** *see* AIR. **Bead-s.,** a beading representing the continuation of bulwark rail in side planking or plating, where ship's sides are carried to a higher deck such as a raised forecastle or a poop; also, *beading-s.* **Bilge s.,** *see* BILGE. **Binding s.,** in a wood deck, either of *s's* of heavy planking running next to and along the line of hatches; also called *bolt s.* In boat-building, usually third *s.* of planking from the gunwale and first of side-planks fitted in a carvel-built boat. Any *s.* of planking of greater strength than others in a series, as for structural reasons. **Bolt s.,** in wooden ships, a *s.* through which the beam-knee fastenings pass. **Broad s.,** one of the heavy *s's* next to the *garboard;* usually three in number, they gradually decrease in thickness to that of ordinary bottom planking. **Closing s.,** in welded shell-plating, *s.* at turn of the bilge; so called because last to be fitted in place. **Gore s.,** another term for a *drop s.; see* DROP. **Inner s.,** in the *in-and-out* system of plating, the *sunken s.,* or that faying against frames; opposed to *outer s.,* or that usually called *raised s.* **Knuckle s.,** that at a sharp turn upward in vessel's side, as planking along the *knuckle* or turn of the counter. **Nib s.,** *see* Nibbing-plank *in* NIB. **Outer s.,** the *raised s.* in the *in-and-out* system of plating, or that also called the *raised-and-sunken* system; also, *outside* or *overlapping s.* **Paint s.,** also *black s.,* in old wooden ships, *s.* just above the wales; so named because it formed the lower limit of topside painting. This *s.* and those below it were coated with tar or pitch. **Passing s.,** *s.* of plating lying between two butts of adjacent *s's* at a given frame space. **Rubbing s.,** *see* R.-piece *in* RUBBING. **Sand s.,** the *garboard s.,* or that next the keel; so called in older boat-building. **Sheer s.,** so named from its upper edge marking ship's line of sheer curvature, *s.* of shell-plating or outside planking in way of main or strength deck. Considered an important longitudinal strength member, its material is considerably heavier than the ordinary side *s's.* Also, upper side *s.* in way of a raised deck; as, *bridge sheer-s., shelter-deck sheer-s., poop sheer-s.,* etc. **Shutter s.,** also *closing s.,* in a wooden hull, the completing *s.* in work of planking ship's hull. It is chosen as such that requires little or no twisting in fitting it in place. **S. book,** in shipbuilding, record of required dimensions of each plate in the various *s's.* **Thick s.,** one of greater thickness than its neighboring planks or plates; *esp.,* in wooden vessels, heavier ceiling planking laid over ends of futtocks and floor-heads for greater strength. **Topside s.,** uppermost range of ordinary side-plating, or *s.* next below the *sheer-s.* **Wash s.,** in an open boat, a thin plank fitted above the gunwale for keeping off spray or increasing the freeboard. (Also see *Strake* as compounded with the prefixed terms BLACK; BOTTOM: CLAMP; CLINKER; DIMINISHING; DROP; GARBOARD; IN-AND-OUT; LANDING; LIMBERS; LOCK; STEALER)

STRAND.[1] (A.S. *strand,* shore) Shore or beach of the ocean, a sea, or any arm of a sea; rarely, a bank of a river. (*Chiefly poetic*) To run aground; to be driven or to drift ashore; as, the ship *stranded* on a shoal. To run, or cause to run, a vessel aground; as, ship was *stranded* to avoid collision.

STRAND.[2] (Old Nor.-Fr. *estran,* rope) In cordage, one of several twisted yarns or threads, or groups of such, which are laid up or twisted together to form a rope; *see* ROPE. In rope-making, to lay the prepared *s's* to complete the manufactured product.

(A *s.* in plain-laid cordage is called a *ready*) A rope is said to be *stranded* when one of its *s's* carries away. **S. of a cable-laid rope,** one of the ropes forming *s's* (usually three) of such rope or hawser. **S'ed wire,** wire rope.

STRANDING. In maritime law, action of a vessel in running aground and being stuck fast in such predicament for a time. *S.* may be accidental or purposely done to avoid a worse impending peril, such as collision or foundering, in which latter case the term *voluntary s.* is applied.

STRAP. (A.S. *stropp,* a thong or band. Variant of *strop*) Narrow strip of flexible material, *esp.* leather, usually fitted with a buckle, for temporarily holding together or securing something; a band of flexible metal, rope, etc., used to tightly secure a bale, case, etc., of cargo; a narrow strip of any material; a *strop* (*see* STROP); a foreganger (*see* **F'ganger** *in* FORE). **Belly-s.,** *see* BELLY. **Butt-s.,** *see* BUTT. **Eccentric-s.,** band securing the journal at head of eccentric-rod in a reciprocating engine. **Seam s.,** same as *butt-s.* **Shoulder s.,** *see* SHOULDER. **S. adze,** *see* ADZ. **S.-brake,** also called *band-brake,* as fitted to a windlass, wire-reel, winch, etc., the flexible metal band controlling paying-out motion by tightening as required. **S.-laid,** *see* LAID. **S.-plate,** or *strapping,* in later wooden construction, long narrow steel plates secured diagonally across inner surfaces of ship's frames for additional strengthening, chiefly in way of standing rigging.

STRATEGY, NAVAL. See NAVAL.

STRATO-CUMULUS. See CLOUD.

STRATUS. See CLOUD.

STRAY LINE. See *stray-line mark* in LINE.[1]

STREAK. A painted stripe, as that along a vessel's waterline or, in some small craft, a *sheer-stripe* or *sheer-streak* marking the line of sheer, just below the bulwarks. Same word as *strake,* but to-day not commonly used in that sense; *see* STRAKE. **Wind-s's,** spindrift on the sea surface; *see* SPINDRIFT. Also, "mares' tails," the feathery or ribbon-like appearance of *cirrus* cloud; *see* CLOUD.

STREAM. Any course or current of water flowing on the earth's surface; as, a river; an ocean current, as *Gulf S.* To put in use or operation outside the vessel; as, to *s.* an anchor-buoy or a patent log. Among tugboatmen, chiefly in U.S. ports, the operation of, or charges for, *streaming* is that of assisting a ship away from a wharf, pier, etc., and into the fairway. **Back-s.,** *see* BACK. **Down-s.,** *see* DOWN. **In the s.,** as opposed to *alongside,* or fast in berth at a pier, quay, etc., said of a vessel when at anchor, *esp.,* when in a tideway or channel. **Land-s.,** *see* LAND. **S. anchor,** *see* ANCHOR. **S. cable,** chain or wire hawser for use with a *s. anchor;* American Bureau of Shipping rules require, for example, a powered

vessel of 7850 *equipment tonnage* (approximately the *gross tonnage*) to carry 105 fathoms of a choice of 1⅝-inch wrought iron stud-link chain, 1 7/16-inch short-link chain, or 1½-inch steel wire (6-strand, 24-thread). (*Bower cable* required is 270 fathoms of 2¼-inch wrought iron stud-link chain in such vessel) **S.-current,** *see* CURRENT. **Tail of a s.,** *see* TAIL. To **tail with the s.,** *see* TAIL.

STREAMLINED. Having a contour offering little resistance to the lines of flow, or *streamlines,* of air or water, as in modern hull and superstructure design, particularly in that of faster vessels. **S. rudder,** *see* RUDDER.

STRENGTH. Quality of a material or a structure by which it withstands the application of force without yielding or injury; as *tensile s.* of a rope, *longitudinal s.* of a ship, etc. Enduring quality or toughness; power to resist force; as, spars of unusual *s.* Intensity or force; as, *s.* of a magnetic field. **S. deck,** uppermost continuous deck or that upon which ship's hull is chiefly dependent for *longitudinal s.;* the main deck. **S. of manila** and **wire rope,** *see* MANILA *and* WIRE. **Tensile s.,** measure of a material's ability to endure a pulling stress without deformation or rupture. It usually is given in pounds or tons per square inch of cross section.

STRESS. (O.F. *estrecier,* to restrain. Considered by some authorities as abbrev. from *distress*) Resistance to a force tending to deformity of a material or a structure; as, *breaking s.* of a rope; *tensile, compression,* or *shearing s.,* or a combination of these, to which a vessel is subjected, as in dry-docking, during launching, carrying heavy cargo, laboring in a seaway, etc. A constraining or delaying force; hindering pressure; as, *s.* of weather; *s.* of circumstances. **Curves of longitudinal shearing s's** and **loads,** *see* CURVE. **Hogging s.,** a force or combination of forces tending to create the hogging condition in a ship's hull; *cf.* **H. moment** *in* HOGGING. **Racking s.,** also termed *lateral* and *transverse,* that in a vessel resulting from sidewise force or pressure, as, for example, during heavy rolling in a beam sea. **Working s. for ropes,** *see* WORKING.

STRETCH. (A.S. *streccan,* to extend) Elongation or strain produced by a tensile stress; as, *s.* of a rope or a sail. A *reach* or straight portion of a river or a buoyed channel; indicated extent of a shore or coastline. In older usage, distance sailed on one tack, when vessel was said to *s.* or *reach.* **S. out!,** order to oarsmen to pull hard and strong.

STRETCHER. In a boat, a thwartship piece of wood against which an oarsman braces his feet. A bar or cross-piece of wood for holding apart the legs of a bridle-sling; *cf.* SPREADER. A temporary thwartship piece in a boat to prevent the gunwales from being crushed inward, as in belly-slinging; a stiffener.

STRETCHING-POST. One of a pair of posts or stanchions between which bolt-rope is stretched in a sail-loft.

STRETCHING-SCREW. *See* SCREW.

STRIKE. To collide with; as, to *s.* a rock; to *s.* the pier; to strand or run aground. To sound a bell by strokes or blows, as with its tongue; as, to *s.* eight bells. To harpoon a whale. To lower down, as a flag, upper masts, sail, etc.; as, to *s.* the top-gallant masts; to lower the ensign as a salute or to signify surrender to an enemy. With *below,* to lower an object into a vessel's hold; as, to *s.* ammunition, stores, cargo, etc. *below.* With *down,* to pack or stow away, as fish, whale-oil, etc.; as, we *struck down 500 barrels;* to stow down. With *out,* to transfer cargo or stores from ship's hold to dock or elsewhere; as, to *s. out* all lower hold cargo. To **s. amain,** *see* AMAIN. **S. clause,** that written in bills of lading and affreightment contracts by which ship is held to be "not responsible for any damage, loss, or delay caused by, or that in any way may be due to, stoppage of loading or discharging as a result of labor *strikes* or disturbances." **S. hull,** *see* HULL. **S. mast,** *see* **Knuckle m.** *in* MAST. To **s. sail,** in older use, to lower one or more sails suddenly, as in a sharp maneuver, approach of a squall, or in token of surrender; also, as a salute to a superior ship, a sovereign, etc. To **s. soundings,** *see* SOUNDING. To **s. the bottom,** to touch or slide over the sea-bottom as in a small area of shallow water; to *touch and go.*

STRIKER. One who uses a harpoon, as in whaling, sword-fishing, etc. A shipwright's helper. A man-helper, or pole to which a brush may be attached, as where arm's-length painting is impracticable; a *paint-s.* Occupant or person in charge of a *s.-boat,* or drive-boat, used in certain seine-fishing for frightening the schools toward the nets, as by splashing with oars, shouting, throwing pebbles, etc. **Dolphin-s.,** same as *martingale boom; see* BOOM.

STRING. In wooden ships, highest strake of ceiling-planking in the hold, usually through-fastened to the sheer-strake; also, in old ships, strake of planking between the rail and upper-edge line of the gun-ports. **Lock-s.,** *see* LOCK. To **s. out,** to extend along the deck, as a group of men when hauling on a rope. **S.-piece,** horizontal squared timber extending along edge of a wharf and bolted to piling as a strengthening girder to the whole structure.

STRINGER. An inside longitudinal girder or stiffener bridging the beams or the frames in the transverse framing system. Depending on its location, may be called a *bilge s., side s.,* etc. A *deck-s.,* or *deck s.-plate,* often is referred to as simply a *s.; see* DECK. Also, a *side keelson* sometimes is known as a *bottom s.* Any unit in the structure that ties or bridges frames in a longitudinal direction; the *shelf,*

in wooden vessels; a *poppet ribband (see* POPPET). **Beam s.,** *see* BEAM. **Central s.,** also, *stanchion s.* and *midship s.,* a girder fitted in center line of vessel under the deckbeams for receiving upper ends of pillars or stanchions. **Gunwale s.,** *see* **G.-plate** *in* GUNWALE. **Intercostal s.,** *see* INTERCOSTAL. **Panting-s.,** *see* PANTING. **S.-plate,** *see* PLATE. **Web s.,** *see* WEB.

STRIP. A long narrow piece of wood or metal; as, a *s.* of planking. To remove or send down sails and running gear; to dismantle or divest vessel of portable working equipment; to unrig or *s. down.* **Rubbing-s.,** *see* **R.-piece** *in* RUBBING. **S. planking,** *see* PLANKING. **S'ping line,** auxiliary pipe-line from a *s'ping pump* used in oil-tank vessels for completing discharge from tanks upon main pumps becoming more or less ineffective and so relieving the latter of much wear and tear. To **s. to a gantline,** to completely unrig a mast, leaving only the gantline last used. Hence, to dismantle or remove all gear from a part specified or from the whole ship; to plunder or deprive a vessel of her gear or equipment; to thoroughly divest one of his possessions.

STROKE. Complete motion given an oar as manipulated by the rower or *oarsman,* or that consisting of the *pulling s.* and the *recovery s.* Rate or manner of rowing; as, a *fast s.;* a *long s.;* the *feathering s. at 30 per minute.* A certain style adopted in pulling (or rowing); as, the *galley s.; gig s.;* etc. To row at a specified rate; as, *boat's crew stroked at 26 per minute. Cf.* ROW. To **keep s.,** to move the oars in unison; to maintain a constant rhythmic sweep in pulling. **S. oar,** that nearest the stern, or the oar setting the rate of *s.* Person handling this oar is called *s.-oarsman* or simply *stroke;* often is referred to as *pulling s.*

STRONG. Sturdy; forceful; capable of withstanding pressure or tension; moving with rapidity or force; as, *s.* timbers; *s.* rope; a *s.* current. **S.-beam,** same as *trolley-beam; see* BEAM. **S. breeze,** *see* BEAUFORT SCALE. **S. gale,** *see* BEAUFORT SCALE. **S.-room,** special compartment for valuable cargo, specie, etc.

STRONGBACK. A boom or spar against which a boat is secured in the swung-out position; *cf.* **Boat s.** *in* SPAR. A hatch-beam or any portable timber or metal beam supporting the hatch-covers; a *shifting-beam (see* SHIFTING) Any bar to which a cargo-port, manhole cover, etc., is secured in the closed position. A fore-and-aft spar serving as a raised spreader for a boat cover; a ridge-pole or middle spar over which an awning is spread. In older ships, timber or iron beam to which chain cable might be triced up clear of the windlass. **Deck s.,** *see* DECK.

STROP. (A.S. *stropp,* a thong or band) Piece of rope or band of metal fitted around a block, deadeye, bull's eye, etc., for taking the stress and securing such in place; a rope grommet; metal frame inside the shell of a block for supporting the sheave-pin and conveying applied stress to the hook or shackle independent of shell itself. A length of rope having its ends spliced together for slinging cargo, etc.; a rope sling; short piece of rope similarly spliced for use in hooking a tackle to a hawser, etc. Also *strap, esp.* in U.S. **Bow s.,** a grommet or ring of rope passed through a boat's stem for attaching the painter. **Jaw-s.,** *see* JAWS. **Kicking-s.,** *see* KICK. **Parting-s.,** a sling or rope *s.* that is weaker than the rope or tackle used with it, so that in event of extraordinary stress it will be first to *part.* **Quarter s.,** *see* QUARTER. **Selvagee s.,** *see* SELVAGEE.

STRUCTURAL MAST. *See* MAST.

STRUM. A rose-box or strainer; *see* ROSE.

STRUT. Bar of metal or a timber for resisting pressure or compression, as opposed to a *tie* or a *stay;* sometimes for resisting both pressure and tension (*cf.* **S. strut** *in* SHAFT) **S.-stay,** lateral stiffening stay on a sailing-yacht's mast; *see* **J.-stay** *in* JACK.

STUD. Piece of cast iron or steel set inside each link of a chain. Fitted across major axis of link at mid-length, its use is to prevent deformation of the link under heavy stress and also provides prevention against kinking of the chain; also, *cable s.* or *stay pin.* A bolt threaded at both ends, one end being screwed into a tapped hole while a nut is fitted to the projecting end for drawing or securing parts together; also termed *s.-bolt.* **S. link** or **studded link,** *see* LINK. A *long s. link* is found at anchor end of some cables to take the *Jew's harp,* or shackle connecting cable to anchor. This extra long link has its *s.* fitted at about one-third length, thus allowing room for passing the shackle. **S.-link chain,** *see* CHAIN. **S. rivet,** also called *screw rivet, see* **Tap r.** *in* RIVET.

STUDDING. Vertical timbers constituting the framing of a wooden deck-house, cattle pens, etc.

STUDDING-SAIL. Usually contracted to *stuns'l,* a light sail set in fair winds as a side extension to a square sail or sails and named accordingly; as, *fore-royal s.-s.; main-topmast s.-s.; main lower s.-s.* In earlier use called a *steering-sail, s.-s's* appear to have developed their full spread in the clippers of the 1860–1870's, thence gradually disappeared with increase in size of iron vessels and corresponding proportional decrease in complement of crew carried. Uppermost one was the *royal s.-s.,* head of which was spread by a *s.-s. yard,* or portable sliding spar forming an extension to the *royal yard.* Foot of each *s.-s.* was extended by a similar spar called a *s.-s. boom,* to which also was bent the head of *s.-s.* next below. Thus, the *royal-s.-s. boom* formed a continuation of the *topgallant yard; topgallant s.-s.* was clewed to its boom extending from *upper-topsail yard* (or topsail yard before the advent of double topsails); and *topmast-s.-s. boom* extended from the

lower (fore or main) *yard.* Sometimes a *lower s.-s.* was set from the *topmast-s.-s. boom* and clewed out to a boom outrigged from ship's rail, but often such sail was triangular in shape and sheeted home to clew of the course, so dispensing with a lower boom. *S.-s's* were limited, as a rule, to 3-masted ships and barques and were spread on the appropriate side of both foremast and mainmast. **S.-s.-halyard bend,** as formerly used in sending a *s.-s.* aloft, a bend or hitch made by passing a round turn with end of halyard, then round the standing part and under all parts, thence tucked once or twice between the latter. It is similar in effect to the *timber hitch,* but more readily released. **S.-s.-tack bend,** as secured to *tack-cringle* of a *s.-s.,* made by passing end through cringle and forming a *clove hitch,* with end on cringle side, over standing part. Also called *buntline hitch* and *back hitch,* it is easily released while its security increases with stress on the line.

STUDSAIL. Chiefly in sailing-yachts and smaller craft, a *bonnet,* or extension-piece of canvas for increasing area of sail, temporarily attached to foot of a jib or other fore-and-aft sail.

STUFF. Mixture of tallow, pine tar, resin, turpentine, or any similar concoction used as a preservative on masts, spars, deck and outside planking, etc.; *slush* (*see* SLUSH) Material for certain work; as, *caulking s.; seizing s.; planking s.* **Small s.,** *see* SMALL.

STUFFING-BOX. *See* BOX. **Rudder s.-b.,** *see* RUDDER. **S.-b. bulkhead,** after peak bulkhead, so called because *propeller-shaft s.-b.* is fitted through it. It usually extends upward to main deck. **S.-b. recess,** another name for the *tunnel recess,* or space at after end of shaft-tunnel for manipulating tail section of propeller-shaft in withdrawing or shipping.

STUMP. Standing part of a mast, jib-boom, etc., where such spar has been broken or carried away. A short heavy post used for mooring; *see* **M.-stump** *in* MOORING. To **start a ship from the s.,** to build an entirely new vessel, as distinguished from repairing one existing; hence, to construct and equip a vessel completely. **S.-mast,** *see* MAST; also *cf.* JUBILEE RIG.

STUMPY. Having unusually short masts; of heavy short appearance, as a *s. bowsprit.* In England, a *Thames barge* having neither bowsprit nor topmast; *see* BARGE.

STUNS'L. *See* STUDDING-SAIL.

STURGEON. A food fish of the genus *Acipenser,* often attaining a length of 8 feet, found in seas and rivers of the north temperate zone. Of the *ganoid* or thick-scaled fishes, it has a tough skin and further protection by 5 rows of prominent bony plates; has an elongated upper jaw and a shark-like tail. Roe of the *s.* produces *caviar* and its bladder is made into *isinglass.* The fish common to European and North American Atlantic coasts is classified as *Acipenser sturio.*

STYLE. Also, *stile; see* SHADOW PIN.

SUBAQUEOUS. (L. *aqua,* water; *sub,* under or below) Formed or occurring under water; as, *s. weeds.* Adapted for use beneath the water's surface; submarine; as, a *s. helmet;* a *s. suit.*

SUBCHARTER. An agreement made by a charterer whereby he hires all or part of vessel to another party. Usually authorized by shipowner to thus sublet, original charterer enters such contract independently of charter-party signed by owner.

SUBDIVISION FACTOR. *See* **Floodable l.** *in* LENGTH.

SUBMARINE. Living, growing, or used beneath the sea surface; subaqueous; as, *s. plants; s. shell-fish; s. armor; s. cable.* A *s. boat,* or naval vessel specially designed for rapid submersion and emersion, as well as for continued operation entirely below the surface. (*Cf.* SNORKEL) Latest *s's* are capable of making 15 to 20 knots when submerged; 20 to 25 when surfaced. Chief use of *s.* is for torpedo attack on larger vessels; also carries two or more guns for surface use, anti-aircraft protection, etc. Crew numbers from 50 to 70 officers and men. In U.S. navy the vessels are named after fishes; as, *Hake; Trout; Tarpon;* etc. **S. armor,** *see* DIVING-DRESS. **S. bell,** *see* **Submarine sound s.** *in* SIGNAL. **S. cable,** special insulated and protected wire laid on sea bottom for conducting messages by telephone or telegraph. First one in America was laid from Cape Tormentine, New Brunswick, to Cape Traverse, Prince Edward Island, a distance of 9 miles, in 1852. *Cf.* GREAT EASTERN. **S. chaser,** a small naval vessel designed for pursuit and destruction of enemy *submarines.* **S. current,** one flowing at a considerable depth and independent of any surface current in the vicinity. **S. earthquake,** violent movement of earth's crust at the sea bottom, often resulting in a corresponding disturbance on the surface, such as dangerous *tidal waves,* so called, and *rollers.* **S. mine,** *see* MINE. **S. oscillator,** *see* OSCILLATOR. **S. sentry,** *see* KITE. **S. sound s's,** *see* SIGNAL.

SUBMERGED. (L. *submersum;* from *sub,* under; *mergere,* to plunge) Buried, covered, or hidden in a liquid; lying beneath the sea surface; as, a *s. rock;* a *s. wreck.* **S. needle,** a sharp pinnacle of rock on the sea bottom. **S. screw-log,** device for indicating vessel's speed and distance covered by a rotating screw set in a fitting protruding from ship's bottom; *see* **Pitometer l.** *in* LOG.[1]

SUBMERSIBLE PUMP. *See* PUMP.

SUBPERMANENT MAGNETISM. That magnetic property in a steel vessel caused by induction from earth's magnetic field and rendered more or less permanent by the hammering, etc., to which the hull is subjected during construction; *see* INDUCED MAGNETISM.

SUBPOLAR. Pertaining to, or lying at, a point below the elevated pole of the heavens; as, *s. culmination of a star.* Located near the terrestrial pole; as, *northern s. latitudes.* A heavenly body is said to be *s.* when above the horizon at *lower transit (transit sub polo),* i.e., when observer's latitude is greater than 90°—body's declination, or its *polar distance.*

SUBSIDY. Grant of funds, property, or free use of property by a government to mercantile marine interests with the view of encouraging pursuit of commerce especially valuable to the public weal and maintaining an adequate and efficient merchant fleet, considered as an important asset to the nation in time of war. In the U.S., such a *s.,* bounty, or subvention, as it is variously termed, is granted under certain conditions to shipbuilders, shipowners, and ship operators or charterers, as, for example, *construction s., navigation s., operating differential s. See* **Mail s.** *in* MAIL; **Navigation s.** *in* NAVIGATION; *and* OPERATING DIFFERENTIAL SUBSIDY.

SUBSISTENCE. Extra money paid a ship's crew member in lieu of customary provisions to which he is entitled, or in event of no food being served on board or elsewhere by the vessel.

SUB-SOLAR. (L. *sub,* under; *sol,* the sun) Having the sun in the zenith; beneath the sun; hence, *tropical.* **S.-s. point,** that vertically under the sun, or point on the earth's surface having the sun in the zenith at a given instant; point at which local sidereal time and latitude are identical with sun's apparent right ascension and declination, respectively. In navigational theory, it is the center of a **circle of equal altitude** of the sun; *see* CIRCLE.

SUBSTITUTE. In International Code flag signaling, one of the three repeating flags; *see* REPEATER. A crew member engaged to take the place of one who has failed to join his vessel at time and/or place specified in the *articles of agreement.* An item of rations supplied in lieu of that customarily provided.

SUCK. To draw in air when the liquid is low or a valve is in bad order: said of a *pump.* To **s. the monkey,** same as to **tap the admiral;** *see* ADMIRAL.

SUCKER. Any of various fishes having a special organ or a *sucking* mouth for attaching themselves to a rock, other fish, etc., at will; a *s.-fish* or *sucking-fish;* a hagfish; the remora, or *shark-s.; see* LAMPREY; REMORA. A baby whale or other cetacean. A suction-dredger; *see* **S.-sucker** *in* SAND.

SUCTION. A *s.-pipe; see* **B.-suction pipe** *in* BILGE. Term denoting loosely the effect on a vessel's steering or maneuvering from a current or eddying flow set up, *esp.* in narrow and shallower waters, by (1) advance of a passing vessel; (2) indraft toward ship's screw or paddles, whether vessel is at rest or otherwise. First or more important of these calls for prompt preventive action against possible dangerous effect of indraft toward the stern of a large vessel in narrow channels. The peculiar hydraulic phenomenon of a moving vessel tending to sheer away from a nearer river-bank is analogous to (1) in that returning displaced water flowing in greater volume from the offshore side throws predominating pressure on that quarter of vessel, and so slues her stern toward the bank, with similar effect to that of ordinary rudder action. Any indraft or sheering effect commonly is called *s.* by pilots; also, *s.* often denotes *sticking* of a vessel on a shoal, mud, etc., as when rising tide fails to refloat her owing to water not gaining admittance between hull and the ground; *cf.* SMELLING THE BOTTOM. **S.-box,** *see* ROSE. **S.-dredger,** *see* **S.-sucker** *in* SAND. (*Also see* INTERACTION)

SUED. (M.E. dialectal *sew* or *sue,* to drain, as a pond, field, etc.) Said of a vessel that has grounded, having reference to a later depth of water, *esp.* that occurring at a lower stage of tide; as, *ship is s.* (or *s. up*) *more than 3 feet, i.e.,* water must rise at least that amount in order to refloat her. *Cf.* SEW.[2]

SUEGEE. *See* SOOGEE.

SUEZ CANAL. Named for the isthmus through which it cuts in connecting the Mediterranean with the Red Sea, was opened to traffic, November 17, 1869. Having a total length of 104.5 statute miles, its minimum width is 196 feet with a maximum draft for ships passing through of 34 feet. Primarily constructed for shortening steaming distance from Europe to the Far East, compared with passage via Cape of Good Hope the canal effects a saving of about 3600 miles from Atlantic European ports to Calcutta; 2800 miles to China (via Sunda Strait); and 1200 to Australia. **S.C. rudder,** *see* RUDDER. **S.C. tonnage,** *see* TONNAGE.

SUFFERANCE. Chiefly in England, written permission given a vessel by customs authority for shipment of goods; *esp.,* such as were already landed; a *bill of s.* **S. wharf,** pier, quay, etc., at which landed cargo may be kept and re-shipped duty free.

SUGG. (Prob. an old form of *surge*) To heave and bump heavily on the bottom by action of the sea, as a vessel when stranded.

SUJI-MUJI. *See* SOOGEE.

SUIT. A group, complement, or set; *esp.,* as indicating a spread of canvas; as, a new *s.* of sails (or canvas) was bent; an old *s.* of jibs; a heavy-weather *s.* of topsails; a new *s.* for the mainmast; etc. Sometimes synonymous with a *set;* as, a *s.* (or *set*) of awnings, tarpaulins, flags, etc.

SULPHUR-BOTTOM. The blue whale, or finback; *see* **B. whale** *in* BLUE.

SUMATRA. A sudden heavy squall blowing from about southwest from the island of Sumatra during the S.W. monsoon. (China Sea)

SUMMER. Pertaining to, or occurring during, the summer season. **S. freeboard,** *see* **Summer f.** *in* FREEBOARD. **S. monsoon,** *see* MONSOON. **S. tanks,** *see* TANK.

SUMNER LINE. Named for its discoverer, *Thomas H. Sumner,* an American shipmaster, the *line of position* resulting from an altitude observation of a heavenly body, chief feature of which is that ship's position lies at some point on such line. (*Cf.* **L. of position** *in* LINE[2]) Sumner's accidental discovery took place during a rough passage from Charleston, S.C., to Greenock, Scotland, on December 18, 1837. In his own words: "At about 10 a.m. an altitude of the sun was observed and chronometer time noted; but, having run so far without observations, it was plain the latitude by dead reckoning was liable to error. Longitude by chronometer was determined using this uncertain latitude and it was found to be 15′ E. of the D.R. position; a second latitude was then assumed 10′ N. of that by D.R., which gave a position 27 miles E.N.E. of former position; a third latitude was assumed still 10′ farther north, which gave another position 27 miles E.N.E. of the second. Plotting the three positions, they were seen to lie in a straight line, and this line extended passed through *Smalls* light (S.W. coast of Wales). It thus was apparent that the altitude observed must have happened at all three plotted points, at ship's position, and at *Smalls* light at the same instant." Concluding that the ship was somewhere on the line referred to, she was kept on E.N.E., the course steered since preceding midnight, and "in less than an hour *Smalls* light was made nearly ahead and close aboard." *See* **C. of equal altitude** *in* CIRCLE. **S's method,** determination of ship's position by plotting the *lines of position* obtained (1) from two observations of a heavenly body, second observation being taken when body has changed in azimuth by at least two points, or (2) from altitudes taken of two different bodies at same instant (*see* SIMULTANEOUS ALTITUDES). Principles of Sumner's discovery applied in each case, place of ship is indicated at intersection of the position lines resulting from each altitude observation. The cumbersome calculations involved in *Sumner's* original determination of his *line of position* by using two or three different latitudes to find the corresponding longitudes, however, soon was replaced by assuming a single latitude (usually that by *dead reckoning*), since it was noted that the position line lies in a direction 90° from the observed body's azimuth. The line, therefore, may be more readily and with equal accuracy laid off through the longitude corresponding to *one* assumed latitude. *S's method* has been also called the *double altitude* problem, particularly in British usage.

SUMP. A small depression or well for facilitating drainage to a suction-pipe, as in bilges, a corner of a deck in a compartment, etc.

SUN. Central and controlling body of our *solar system,* or luminary around which Earth and the several planets revolve, has a diameter of 864,392 statute miles, or 31' 59.26" angular measurement at a mean distance from this planet of 92,897,416 statute miles, and has a horizontal parallax of 8.80". The *sun* as actually seen in the heavens is called the *apparent s.* and *apparent right ascension* and *declination* given in Nautical Almanacs refer to that of *apparent sun's center. Apparent* distinguishes from *true* in that, because of *aberration* of light, sun's *true* position in the ecliptic averages 20½ seconds of arc eastward of its *apparent* place; in other words, we observe "old Sol" in the position he occupied 8 *min.* 18.7 *secs.,* very nearly, *prior* to any given instant. In the matter of keeping accurate *solar* time, since the apparent (or the true) sun varies in his rate of continuous eastward advance in the ecliptic, astronomers have recourse to what is called *mean solar time,* divisions of which have a constant durational value throughout the year; *see* **M. solar day** *in* MEAN. **Against the s.,** in a counter-clockwise direction; opposed to *with the s.;* a right-hand laid rope is coiled down *with the s.,* left-hand cordage *against the s.: see* AGAINST. **From s. to s.,** from sunrise to sunset; for duration of sunlight hours. **Land of the midnight s.,** northern region of Norway in which *s.* is above the horizon for the entire 24 hours during midsummer. **Land of the rising s.,** Japan. **Mean s.,** *see* MEAN. **Midnight s.,** *see* MIDNIGHT. **Right ascension of the mean s.,** *see* ASCENSION. To **shoot the s.,** also to *take the s.,* to measure the *s's* altitude, as with a sextant; originally, to observe *s's meridian altitude:* hence, to obtain the latitude. **S'bow,** a rainbow formed by *s's* rays, as opposed to a *lunar bow; esp.,* such a bow seen in flying spray. **S. deck,** an uppermost deck for recreation purposes, sports, etc., as found in larger passenger vessels. A shade deck; *see* **Shade d.** *in* DECK. **S. dog,** *see* PARHELION. **S. drawing water,** appearance of shaded rays from the *s.* when he is behind a cloud; such ray-like phenomenon is called *s's backstays; see* **R's of Maui** *in* ROPE. **S.-fish,** an oddly shaped fish found in all temperate and tropical seas. Often 4 to 5 feet in length, has a single deep ventral fin vertically below one high dorsal fin, and a kind of fringed tail fin extending up and down its abruptly terminating, or truncated, body. It swims lazily near the surface, usually with dorsal fin exposed. Both skin and flesh are tough and the fish is considered of no food value. The name is also given to several other species, including the *basking shark, cobbler, moon-fish,* and the *opah* (see these terms); and also to any large *jelly-fish.* **S. over the fore yard,** usual introductory phrase to a forenoon tot of grog. The expression dates from 17th.

century East Indiamen's usage and signifies a well-earned relaxation from constant necessary lookout for rocks, shoals, etc., with the *s.* bearing nearly ahead, so hindering good surface vision in the morning hours, as in steering eastward over the then poorly charted far eastern waters. **S's lower** (and **upper**) **limb,** *see* LIMB. **S.-valve,** as fitted in some unattended or unwatched lighthouses, buoys, etc., device that controls supply of the luminant by contraction and expansion effect of daylight and darkness. **S.-wake,** glare or reflected rays of the *s.* on the sea surface shortly before *sunset.* A "narrow" wake presages good weather and a "broad" wake bad weather on day following. **With the s.,** right-handed, or in same direction as motion of the hands of a clock; clockwise, *cf.* **Against the s. S'downer,** among junior officers and midshipmen in former U.S. navy days, a captain noted for strictly requiring those on leave to return on board before sunset; hence, a rigid disciplinarian.

SUNK. Designating a portion of a vessel's structure lying partly below a deck-line; as, a *s. bridge; s. forecastle; s. poop; see* BRIDGE; FORECASTLE; POOP.

SUNKEN. Lying beneath or below a reference plane or line; lying on the bottom; submerged; as, a *s. manhole;* a *s. wreck.* **S. rock,** *see* ROCK. **S. rowlock,** *see* **Box r.** *in* ROWLOCK.

SUPERCARGO. (Sp. *sobrecargo,* one in charge of cargo) Originally, an officer who superintended care of cargo, arranged for its sale at foreign ports, and managed all commercial business attending a merchant vessel's voyage. Now, one appointed by a charterer or shipper to supervise care of cargo with view of effecting sound and proper delivery of goods, live stock, etc. Also, in some cargo liners, a *freight clerk,* whose duties require arrangement and supervision of stowage and attention to all clerical matters connected with receipt and delivery of cargo at the several ports of call.

SUPERHEATER. As commonly installed with boilers in modern steam-driven vessels, a contrivance, usually consisting of an enclosed system of coils in which steam is further heated and consequently deprived of most of its moisture content before passing into the engine. *See* **Superheated s.** *in* STEAM.

SUPERINTENDENT. **S. engineer,** *see* PORT ENGINEER. **Marine s.,** *see* MARINE; *cf.* **O'looker** *in* OVER.

SUPERIOR. Of higher rank; as, a *s. officer.* Greater in size, magnitude, position, etc. **S. conjunction,** *see* CONJUNCTION. **S. planet,** *see* PLANET. **S. tide,** *see* TIDE.

SUPERSONIC ECHO-SOUNDER. More recent echo-sounding apparatus characterized by use of inaudible electrically transmitted high-frequency waves that are more or less restricted to a "beam" than is the case with the ordinary echo-sounder; *cf.* ECHO SOUNDING; FATHOMETER.

SUPERSTRUCTURE. Any raised portion of a vessel's hull above an uppermost continuous deck, such as a poop, bridge house, or a topgallant forecastle, and extending from side to side of the vessel. **S. deck,** that laid over a *s.;* as, *poop deck, bridge deck, raised quarter-deck.* Among shipbuilders, the term often designates the deck upon which the *s.* or *s's* are built; *esp.,* an *awning* or a *shelter* deck.

SUPPLEMENT. Measure of that angle or arc by which a given angle or arc is less than 180°; a supplementary angle or arc. *Supplemental* or *supplementary* angles or arcs are those whose sum = 180°.

SUPPLY SHIP. Same as *store-ship; see* STORES.

SUPPORTER. In older wooden vessels, a knee under a cathead; also, a *bibb,* or bracket supporting the trestle-trees *(see* BIBB).

SURF. Breaking swell or waves on a shore or shelving beach; *breakers,* collectively. **S.-board,** as used in the sport of *s.-riding,* a broad 6- to 9-foot board on which one stands and is carried to shore by the surging crest of a sea. **S.-boat,** rowed or sometimes powered boat specially designed for passing through heavy *s.* Usually built with great sheer and flat floors, its construction varies according to local conditions under which operated. May be used as a coastal life-boat, or for carriage of cargo or passengers. **S. days,** those in which it is impracticable to load or discharge cargo from a vessel lying in a roadstead because of rough state of sea or a surf prevailing. **S.-fish,** any species of fishes that swim in a *s.* **S. scoter,** *see* SCOTER. **S. whiting,** the silver whiting; *see* WHITING.

SURFACE CURRENT. *See* CURRENT.

SURGE. Onward motion of, or that caused by, a swell or wave; sudden slipping of a rope under stress, as when turned round the bitts, etc. A vessel is said to be *surging* when pitching in a rough sea while at anchor. To ease the turns of a rope on a capstan, winch, bitts, etc., as in reducing or maintaining the tension. To **s. the capstan,** *see* CAPSTAN.

SURGEON. In a passenger vessel, the ship's "doctor" or medical officer; in U.S. navy, a medical officer ranking as lieutenant-commander, commander, or captain. **Fleet s.,** *see* **F.-captain,** etc., *in* FLEET. **S.-general,** chief of Bureau of Medicine and Surgery in U.S. navy. Usually holds rank of rear-admiral. **S.-fish,** a small deep-bellied fish having lengthy spiny dorsal and anal fringes; probably so called from its one or two lance-like movable spines at each side near the tail. Also called *barber-fish* and *tang,* it is found in most tropical seas; *see* HANDSAW FISH.

SURMARK. Also, *sirmark;* an indicating mark on a frame mold, plank, timber, etc., to show where beveling is required.

SURMULLET. The red mullet or goatfish; any mullet of the *Mullidæ* family. *See* GOATFISH; MULLET.

SURVEY. An official examination or inspection to determine the condition of a vessel, her cargo, stores, engines, equipment, etc., or extent and appraisal of damage suffered by any of these, a pier, wharf, etc., often, also, with the view of fixing responsibility for such loss. To conduct such *s.,* as by one or more appointed experts or *surveyors.* Procedure of ascertaining and delineating the contour, elevations and depths, correct geographical position, etc., of a portion of the earth's surface. To conduct and map or chart such area, as a harbor, coastline, or any expanse of land or water. *See* COAST AND GEODETIC SURVEY. **Damage s.,** *see* DAMAGE. **Harbor s.,** *see* HARBOR. **Hydrographic s.,** *see* HYDROGRAPHIC. **Periodical s.,** *see* PERIODIC. **Running s.,** *see* RUNNING. **Special s.,** *see* **P. survey** *in* PERIODIC. **S. report,** document signed by one or more surveyors concerned stating the nature, extent, and cause of damage sustained, as by a vessel or her cargo, or both. It usually concludes with recommendations for repairs, disposal of damaged cargo, etc., and, where applicable, indicates responsibility for damage or loss in question as attributable to the vessel, nature of cargo, or to faulty stowage or other action of certain persons. **S'ing vessel,** *see* VESSEL.

SURVEYOR. One who *surveys* or, in older usage, superintends or oversees the work of others. **Landing s.,** *see* LANDING. **Marine s.,** *see* MARINE. **S. of the port,** U.S. customs official who inspects incoming vessels and their lading and supervises inspectors, weighers, etc., at a principal port.

SUSPECTED BILL OF HEALTH. *See* **B. of health** *in* BILL.

SWAB. (Older word, *swabber;* from Du. *zwabber,* one who mops up) A mop; piece of rope or canvas teased out to form a mop, often fitted with a handle, as for drying up decks or cleaning out a heavy gun. Slang term for an officer's epaulet. A lout; a clumsy fellow; a lubber. To mop or clean up with a *s.* **Fire-s.,** *see* FIRE.

SWAGE. (O.F. *souage*) A swage-block; *see* BLOCK. Also, *swedge.*

SWALLOW. Aperture in a block through which the rope passes. **S.-tail,** a flag or streamer having a forked fly; a burgee. To **s. the anchor,** to retire from a sea career or take up a shore position.

SWAMP. To capsize, sink, or cause to become filled or partly filled with water; as, a heavy sea *swamped* our boat. To become filled with water; to sink; to be wrecked; as, "Take in the mainsail lest we *s.!*"

SWAN-NECK. A fitting, *esp.* a rod or pipe, having a curve suggesting the neck of a swan; a gooseneck. **S. davit,** *see* DAVIT. **S. ventilator,** an air-shaft or vent-pipe terminating in a 180° curve; also, *goose-neck ventilator.*

SWASH. (Emphatic form of *wash,* or probably imitative of rushing or splashing sound of water) Action or noise of water dashing against something, as rocks, a breakwater, etc.; also, the water thus in motion; as, *s.* of waves on a shore; *s.* of the propeller. A channel between sand-banks or one between a bank and shore. A bar or ledge over which the sea washes. To splash, dash, or noisily wash about or over; as *swashing* waves. To cause an agitation or splashing; as, the whale *swashed* violently with his tail. **S.-bank,** a protective shoal or ledge, or a *revetment,* over which a tidal current flows or the sea breaks. **S.-bucket,** a scullery bucket; a slush or slop-pail or bucket. **S.-channel,** tidal waterway between a reef or bank and shore; also, a *swash* or *swashway.* **S.-plate,** vertical plate fitted longitudinally in a tank for reducing movement of liquid, as oil or water, when tank is partially filled. As in a *deep tank,* where such plate or plates extend to some height, it is termed a *s. bulkhead;* also, *wash-plate.*

SWAY. (Scand. origin) To throw one's weight laterally on a rope, as a halyard, in an effort to further set up on a sail, etc. Usually with *up,* to raise an upper mast, yard, sail, etc., preparatory to releasing it for sending down; with *away* or *aloft,* to hoist a yard, topmast, sail, etc., into position. To **s. on end,** to hoist in a vertical position, as a spar. To **s. across,** to guy or heave a yard in a horizontal position; also, to stretch out a square sail sent aloft for bending; to *cross* a yard.

SWEAL. (M.E. *swelen,* to singe, scorch, or burn slowly) To bream, or rid a vessel's bottom of barnacles by burning or singeing, as once customary in older days of wooden ships; *cf.* BREAMING.

SWEAT. Condensation of moisture in beads or drops on interior surfaces of a vessel due to sudden change of air temperature, as when passing from warm to cooler waters or vice versa. In the absence of ample ventilation or an installation for stabilizing temperatures in holds or other compartments, damage to cargo, baggage, stores, etc., by *s.* drippings from structural parts of ship (chiefly steel decks) may amount to considerable loss. *Cf.* **C. paint** *in* CORK. Usually with *up* or *in,* to haul, hoist, set up, or stretch out as taut as possible, as by extra pulls on a halyard, tackle, earing, or the like; as, to *s. up* on the tops'l halyards; to *s. in* (or *flatten in*) a jib sheet.

SWEEP. Track on which a quadrant or tiller travels. A long broad-bladed oar used either in steering or propelling a boat or small vessel. Range or motion of oars; as, to pull with a long *s.; s.* of the oars. Any lengthy arc of curvature in a vessel's structure; as, *s.* of the counter; downward *s.* of stem. Any curved line in a plan of a vessel. Curve or catenary in a hawser, cable, etc. Range or radius covered by a vessel in swinging at single anchor. A wire drag, such as is used to discover presence of sharp elevations in the sea bottom or to bring moored mines to surface; *see* **Wire d.** *in* DRAG *and* **M.-sweeper** *in* MINE. Effect of a rushing volume of water over the deck, *esp.* of a damaging nature; as, breaking seas made a clean *s.* of her fore deck. To flow or rush over, as waves on a deck, pier, shore, etc. With *away,* to carry off by violence, as an object before the strength of a current, waves, etc. To madly thresh the flukes up and down, said of a wounded whale. To move strongly or rapidly as a tidal current, a bore, torrent, etc. To drag the bottom with a wire, as in search of mines, rocky pinnacles, a lost anchor, etc. To draw a seine or such net around a shoal of fish; to fish with a *s.-net* or *s.-seine.* **Back-s.,** *see* BACK. To **s. the deck,** *see* DECK. To **s. the seas,** to drive off, sink, or capture all enemies, pirates, and dangerous competitors, as referred to Dutch 17th. century maritime activities. Certain of that nation's ships engaged in the East Indian trade are said to have displayed a broom at the masthead in token of their aggressive program. To **s. for an anchor,** *see* ANCHOR PHRASEOLOGY.

SWEEPER, MINE. *See* **M.-sweeper** *in* MINE.

SWEEPINGS. Marketable remnants of a bulk cargo, such as grain, or spillage from broken bags or other faulty or damaged containers left in a vessel's hold; also called *spillage.*

SWELL. Unbroken undulation of the sea surface; succession of long rolling non-crested waves, as that continuing after a gale. To rise or spread as a river during freshets or heavy rains. **Cross s.,** *see* CROSS. **Ground s.,** *see* GROUND. **S. damage,** that suffered by waterfront property or moored craft from a *s.* or series of waves set up by a passing vessel. Such damage may be considerable, particularly in the case of a larger-sized vessel moving at only moderate speed. **S.-fish,** a puffer or globe-fish; *see* **G.-fish** *in* GLOBE. (See also ROLLER)

SWEPT PLANKING. Also, *spring* planking; *see* PLANKING.

SWIFTER. A piece of rope used for *bousing,* or drawing together the parts of a lashing, shrouds, etc., as in tautening; *see* BOUSE. A single *shroud,* or rope supporting a lowermast; an old term for a *bowsprit shroud* or a *jib-boom guy.* A stout rope tightly encircling a boat just below the gunwale for strengthening or chafing purposes. Usually with *in,* to tauten slack rigging, etc., by bousing or frapping; as, to *s. in* the lee shrouds. **Head s's,** bowsprit shrouds, jib-boom guys, and martingale back-ropes, collectively. **To s. a lashing,** to insert a handspike between the parts and twist them, thus setting taut the whole. **To s. the capstan,** *see* CAPSTAN.

SWIG. (Ice. *sveigja,* to bend or sway) With *off,* to sway or pull with a jerk at right angles on a rope, as in tautening or further setting up. Usually with *in,* to pull laterally on a belayed rope, as in tautening a halyard or a sheet, thence giving in the slack thus obtained for re-belaying: as, to *s. in* a jib sheet; *cf.* SWAY. With *up,* to further set up on a tackle, a sail, etc.; as, to *s. up* the royal halyards; to *s. up* the flying jib. Act of *swigging off, in,* or *up; as, Take a s. on the spanker sheet!* Old name for a tackle or purchase the falls of which run at a considerable angle, as one consisting of a standing double block and a pair of separated single blocks.

SWING. To turn about a pivotal point, as a vessel at single anchor upon change of tide; as, to *s.* to the ebb stream. To change smartly the direction of ship's head, as by rudder action; as, to *s.* three points to eastward; to *s.* into the wind. To hang or suspend, as a hammock, a door, a ship's rudder, etc. To swig off; to sway; as in setting up a line tackle, etc. Act of turning on a pivot; as, *s.* of the main yard; *s.* of a boom. A vessel's maneuver in turning; as, a *s.* to port. **To s. clear,** to turn within a certain radius without fouling other craft, the shore, etc.; said of a vessel at anchor. **To s. out,** to move to a position over and outside ship's rail, as a sling of cargo suspended from a boom or a boat from davits, an anchor by means of a crane or davit, etc., ready for lowering. **To s. ship,** in ascertaining compass errors or deviations on various headings, to bring ship's head successively on a number of equi-distant compass points. Observation by bearings of the sun, a distant landmark, a range, etc., is made as vessel is steadied on each pre-determined heading. Vessel also may be *swung* for compass adjustment. *Cf.* **C. adjustment** *in* COMPASS; *also* DEVIATION.

SWINGING. **S. basin** or **s. berth,** a space in a dock system used for *s.* or turning vessels toward or away from their allotted berths upon entering or leaving. **S. boom,** *see* BOOM. **S. buoy,** *see* **Swinging b's** *in* BUOY; *cf.* **Swinging m.** *in* MOORING. **S. space,** necessary room or area for turning, as that required by an anchored vessel; also, *s. room.* **S. the lead,** sailors' expression designative of one's tactics in the shirking of responsibility or evading work.

SWIVEL. (A.S. *swifan,* to move swiftly) A fitting that turns axially on a bolt or pin; a chain-link having a *swiveling* eye at one end for releasing any twist set up in the chain; a *mooring-s. Cf.* **M. shackle** *in* MOORING. **Chain-s.,** *see* CHAIN. **Mooring-s.,** *see* MOORING. **Oar s.,** *see* OAR. **S.-anchor,** as used in some small craft, an anchor fitted with a turning or *swiveling ring.* **S.-block,** one fitted with a *s.-hook* so that its shell is free to turn in any direction; also, in older usage, a block made of two shells one over the other and connected with a *s.* **S.-gun,** a small cannon mounted on a *s.* **S.-hook,** *see* HOOK.

SWORDFISH. So named from its rigid long sword-like beak, large widely distributed pelagic fish highly valued as food. Of a single distinct family, the *Xiphiidæ,* has a high dorsal and deeply forked cercal fins; may attain a length of 8 feet and weight of 5- to 6-hundred pounds. The name has been extended also to the *cutlass-fish* and the *gar pike.*

SWORD MAT. *See* MAT.

SYNCHRONISM. State of being synchronous, or concurring at same instant; *specif.,* in naval architecture, the heavy rolling of a vessel in a beam sea (or nearly abeam) caused by her *rolling period* and the *wave period* having approximately equal values, or by vessel's period being about *half* that of the waves. Such condition may be controlled temporarily by a substantial change of course and/or speed. *Cf.* **Rolling p.** *and* **Wave p.** *in* PERIOD.

SYNODIC MONTH. A complete *lunation* or period of time elapsing between two successive occurrences of new moon; *see remarks in* MOON. The period usually is concurrent with a complete cycle, at a given place, of the twice-daily arrival of the *lunar tide-wave. Cf.* HARMONIC ANALYSIS.

SYNOPTIC CHART. *See* CHART.

SYPHERING. The overlapping of chamfered edges of planking, so presenting a flush surface, as in construction of a bulkhead, a deck-house, etc.

SYREN. *See* SIREN.

SYZYGY. (L. *syzygia,* a joining or conjunction) Point in a planet's orbit at which the body is nearest a straight line with earth and sun, *i.e.,* when in *conjunction* or *opposition,* as our *moon* at the phases of *new* and *full.* **S. tide,** a *spring tide,* or that corresponding to the direct combined effect of respective attractions of sun and moon, as occurs at *new* and at *full* moon. Depending on geographical position, a given place is visited by such tide, ordinarily of maximum range, from one-half to $2\frac{1}{2}$ days after *s.* takes place. **The syzygies,** times of new and full moon.

T

T. As an abbreviation, $t = time$ or local hour angle, *thunder, ton* or *tons;* T = *tropical* in vessels' load-line marks; *true,* as in distinguishing a *true* from a compass or magnetic course or bearing; also = *time,* as in G. C. T. (Greenwich civil time). The letter is denoted by International Code flag "tare," showing red, white, and blue equal vertical divisions. Flown singly, it signifies *"Do not pass ahead of me"*; as a towing signal, by ship *towing,* means *"I am increasing speed"* and by ship *towed,* *"Increase speed,"* or flashing Morse code *T* which is a single *dash* (−). **T-bar, T-beam, T-bulb-bar, T-iron,** etc., are common terms for such structural metal having a *T-shaped* cross-section.

TABERNACLE. *See* **M.-trunk** *in* MAST.

TABLE. To turn in a broad hem along the edges of a sail before attaching the bolt-roping. Part so doubled is called *tabling;* as, *head-tabling, leech-tabling,* etc. Outside portion of a keel, stem, or a stern-post, beyond surface of planking. **Bending t.,** *see* **Bending s.** *in* SLAB. **Boom t.,** *see* BOOM. **Chart t.,** that forming covering surface of a cabinet or chest of drawers, for spreading out a chart or charts, as in a chart-room. **Mast t.,** stool or raised platform supporting the heels of booms; *see* **D.-table** *in* DERRICK. **Plane t.,** *see* PLANE.

TABLES, NAUTICAL. Arrangement of mathematical values or other information in condensed tabular form for use of navigators in concisely determining ship's position by observation, as from *altitude t.;* a heavenly body's true bearing, as from *azimuth t.;* position arrived at in sailing given courses and distances, as from *traverse t.;* information on tides and currents, as from *tide t.* and *current t.;* etc.

TABLING. *See* TABLE.

TACHOMETER. (Gr. *takhos,* speed; *metron,* a measure) Mechanical device for indicating number of revolutions turned by a paddle- or a propeller-shaft; a revolution-counter. Also, *tachymeter.*

TACK. Lower forward corner of a fore-and-aft sail; weather clew of a course, or rope or tackle

holding down such clew, as when sailing on or close to the wind; any rope or fastening that secures a sail's forward or weather lower corner, excepting a *studding-sail t.,* which hauls out the lower *outboard* corner of such sail. In sailing, direction of ship's head with relation to that from which wind is blowing; thus, according to whether wind direction is on, or forward of, starboard or port beam, vessel is said to be on the *starboard t.* or on the *port t.,* respectively; hence, distance or duration sailed on either is called a *t.* Also, the act of *going about* when sailing close-hauled, so as to bring wind on opposite side; as, *we made a t. to clear the berg.* Short piece of line attached to lower end of the hoist of a flag to provide necessary space between flags as in signaling; also, *tack-line.* To change from one *t.* to another by *coming about,* or turning vessel into the wind and bringing latter on the other side, sail being trimmed or hauled about accordingly; *cf.* ABOUT; to *t. ship.* **False t.,** act of turning into the wind and then filling away on same *t.;* an unsuccessful *t.,* or one attempted, but vessel loses way and falls back on original heading; *see* MISS STAYS. To **break** or **split t's with,** to sail on opposite *t's* to those of another boat or vessel, as in racing. **Hard t.,** sea-biscuit; *see* HARD. To **haul t's aboard,** *see* ABOARD. To **have the starboard t.** (or **port t.) aboard,** *see* ABOARD. To **hold t's with,** to sail on same *t's* for same duration as an opposing vessel, as in racing. **Lazy t.,** stout single rope attached to each clew of a course (square fores'l, mains'l, etc.) for temporarily holding down the *t.* (weather clew) until *t.-tackle* is set up; also, for keeping control of a gaff-tops'l when set flying, a sliding bight made fast to *t.* of sail and around a topmast backstay. **Main t.,** weather clew of a square mainsail or its tackle; forward lower corner of the *mains'l* in fore-and-aft rig; also *mains'l t.* To **make a t.,** to sail close-hauled in one direction for a certain time or distance; also, to *come about* or *t.* **Midship t.,** *see* MIDSHIP. To **raise t's and sheets,** *see* RAISE. **Soft t.,** *see* SOFT. **Split t's,** opposite *t's* sailed by two vessels, as in racing to windward. **T. and t.,** as by a series of equal *t's;* said of a vessel working dead to windward, or toward direction from which wind is blowing. **T. and half t.,** a long *t.* followed by a short one. **T.-block,** that used in a tackle or single whip for securing the *t.* of a square or a lateen sail. **T. bumpkin,** *see* BUMPKIN. **T. cringle,** grommet, eyelet, or metal ring through which the *t.-lashing* is passed in a fore-and-aft sail; *cf.* CRINGLE. **T. earing** or **t.-lashing,** piece of rope used to secure the *t.* of a fore-and-aft sail. **T.-pin,** old name for a belaying-pin; the pin to which *t.* of a square, lug, or a lateen sail is secured. **T. rivet,** *see* **Q. rivet** *in* QUILTING. **T.-tackle,** purchase used to heave down the *t.* of a course (fores'l, mains'l, or crossjack in square rig). **T. tricing-line,** as fitted on a loose-footed fore-and-aft gaff sail, line for hauling up the *t.* and so spilling the sail instead of lowering it or settling its halyards. **T. welding,** *see* WELDING.

TACKLE. (Du. *takel*) A purchase, or set of blocks (usually two) in which a rope or chain is rove for obtaining a mechanical advantage in hoisting or pulling; *see* PURCHASE, *also* **P. ratio** *in* POWER. In a collective sense, gear or equipment, *esp.* blocks, cordage, hooks, etc.; as, *ship's t.* or *tackling; cargo t.; fishing t.* (As the term for a purchase, usually pron. "*tay-kel*"; otherwise, "*tak-kel*") *Also see* BURTON. **Boom t.,** a purchase used to guy out a boom of a fore-and-aft sail; also called *boom-guy t.* **Cutting t.,** *see* CUTTING-FALL. **Gun t.,** *see* **Gun-tackle p.** *in* PURCHASE. **Lifting power of a t.,** *see* **P. ratio** *in* POWER. **Mast t.,** *see* **M.-tackle** *in* MAST. To **overhaul a t.,** *see* O'haul *in* OVER. **Relieving t.,** as a means of providing frictional resistance to heavy jerks on the steering-gear during rough sea conditions, a *t.* consisting usually of four double-sheaved blocks each pair of which forms a separate *t.* on either side of tiller or quadrant. Its fall is rove as a purchase securing one side of tiller, thence is carried across and similarly rove on other side. Thus a jerk or surge is frictionally dissipated in the eight sheaves ordinarily contained in the device. **T.-board,** in rope-making, frame at one end of rope-walk that holds the *whirls* for the yarns. **Tack-t.,** *see* TACK. **Tail t.,** a handy purchase with its moving block fitted with a tail, or short piece of rope, for making fast to a hawser, stay, etc.; *cf.* **H. billy** *in* HANDY. **Watch t.,** a small two-fold purchase used for setting up various gear, such as halyards, rigging lanyards, sheets, etc.; so called from its use by the watch on deck only. A *handy billy.* (For many other terms compounded with *Tackle,* see CAT; DECK; FISH; GROUND; etc.)

TACKLINE. A 6-foot length of line used to separate groups or hoists of signal flags displayed on same halyard; *also see remarks in* TACK.

TACKLING. *See 2nd. definition in* TACKLE.

TACTICAL DIAMETER. *See* DIAMETER.

TACTICS. (Gr. *taktika,* arrangements) Art of effectively using a fighting force, as in battle. **Naval t.,** art or skillful operation of bringing to bear, as by maneuvering, the battling strength of a squadron or group of vessels against an enemy. *Cf.* **N. strategy** *in* NAVAL.

TAFFRAIL. (Properly, corrupted form of *taffarel* or *tafferel,* from Du. *tafereel,* dim. of table) In older wooden ships, upper part of the stern, often ornamentally carved and flat, thus suggestive of a *table.* Rail around a vessel's poop or stern. **T. log,** *see* LOG.[1]

TAG-BOAT. *See* BOAT.

TAIL. Short piece of rope attached to a block, larger rope, chain, etc. Rear end; inferior or diminishing end or limiting portion of anything; as, *t.* of a shaft, of a bank, of a gale, of a tidal stream, etc. To lie, as a vessel at anchor, with stern toward a certain direction or object; as, ship *tails* to the bank, up stream, down channel, etc. With *on,* to lay hold of a line, as a number of men in hauling; as, to *t.* on to the main brace; also, to *tally on.* To attach a block or tackle to something by its *t.* **Cat-t.,** *see* CAT. **Monkey t.,** *see* MONKEY. **Rat t.,** **rat-t. splice,** *see* RAT. **Salmon t.,** *see* SALMON. **T.-bay,** portion of a canal lock in way of the lower gates. **T.-block,** *see* BLOCK. **T. gate,** lower level entrance to a canal lock. **T. of a stream,** diminishing flow of a tidal current, as that nearing slack water or turn of tide; *t.* of the *ebb* or *flood.* **T. plate,** *see* **H. plate** *in* HORSESHOE. **T. shaft, t.-end shaft,** *see* **P. shaft** *in* PROPELLER. **T.-splice,** *see* SPLICE. **T.-strop,** handy piece of rope having a cringle or thimble spliced in one end; *see* **Snake-l.** *in* LINE[1]; *also* LIZARD. **T.-tackle,** *see* TACKLE. To **t. with the stream,** to lie head on to and parallel with direction of flow of current, as a ship at anchor; to *t.* to the tide.

TAIL of a fish. *See* HOMOCERCAL.

TAKE. To ascertain or determine something; as, to *t.* soundings; *t.* an observation. To put in use, adopt, appropriate; as, to *t.* the northern track; *t.* a long tack; *t.* fish; *t.* rank with; *t.* ship. To lay hold of or manipulate; as, to *t.* a turn with a rope; *t.* a pull; *t.* an oar; *t.* the helm; usually with *in,* as to *t. in* sail; *t. in* the slack; *t. in* cargo; *t. in* the lines; with *up on,* as to *t. up on* a halyard, sheet, etc. To ship or receive aboard; as, to *t.* water, fuel, etc. To touch or rest upon; as, to *t.* the ground (stranding); to *t.* the blocks (in dry-docking). Amount of fish captured in a haul; as, the *t.* was 10 barrels. To **t. a departure,** *see* DEPARTURE. To **t. a turn,** to pass a line around a belaying-pin, cleat, bitt, etc., as in securing or checking it. To **take care of the lee hitch,** *see* LEE. To **t. in water,** to leak, as a boat; to ship water. To **t. up** (or **in**) **the slack,** to haul in the loose or relaxed part of a rope, parts of a tackle fall, etc. To **t. up on a rope, stay, tackle,** etc., to tauten or set up such rigging or gear; to haul in the slack.

To **t. water,** to ship water, as a vessel in a rough or heavy sea; *also see.* To **m. water** *in* MAKE.

TAKEN ABACK. *See* ABACK.

TALLY. An account or record of the number of packages, sometimes including identifying marks on such, loaded or discharged as cargo. To keep such account or record; as, to *t.* a shipment of goods. Old term meaning to haul in on the sheets of a course. With *on,* to lay hold of a rope, as a group of men, and haul; as, *T. on to the tops'l halyards!* **Hand t.,** a small watch-like counting device that continuously registers total number of pieces *tallied.* Each piece of cargo, etc., is accounted for by simply pressing an attachment with the thumb. **T.-board,** as attached to the tail-block of breeches-buoy gear for taking persons off a stranded vessel, a tablet of wood on which is printed in French and English directions for making fast the life-saving gear, etc., as follows: "Make the tail of the block fast to the lowermast, well up. If the masts are gone, then to the best place you can find. *Cast off shot-line, see that the rope in the block runs free,* and show signal to the shore." (*Cf.* **Breeches b.** *in* BUOY) **T.-sticks,** one of the small pieces of split bamboo used by Chinese in *tallying* cargo. One *stick* representing one piece of cargo, each is passed by shore *tallyman* to ship's *tallyman,* or vice versa, as goods are loaded or discharged. Total *sticks* thus given or received determine number of packages transferred to or from ship.

TAMARACK. *See* HACKMATACK.

TAMPION. A canvas cover, plug, or stopper over the mouth of a cannon not in use. Also, *tompion.*

TAN. To apply a preservative or hardener to boat-sails or fish-nets, as by soaking in an oak bark or other solution. **Tan-and-oiler,** fishing-boat spreading sails colored by tanning process. (*Newfoundland local*)

TANCHORD ANGLE. *See* ANGLE.

TANG. A pad-hook, or one of several broad hooks on a mast-band, fitted aloft for receiving the eye of a shroud, stay, or backstay. Found on yachts and some smaller sailing-vessels. Also, another name for the surgeon-fish; *see* **S.-fish** *in* SURGEON.

TANGENT SCREW. *See* SCREW.

TANGENCY, Point of. *See* POINT.

TANK. Compartment in a vessel for carrying liquid cargo, fuel oil, or fresh water. One of the subdivisions of a ship's double-bottom space used for water ballast, fuel oil, boiler-feed water, etc. Any cistern for collecting or storing a liquid. Large receptacle, usually of iron or steel, for the storing of provisions or fresh water. **Ballast t.,** space or compartment for carrying water ballast; also, *bilge t.; see remarks in* BALLAST. **Boat t's,** airtight *t's* fitted along the sides in a lifeboat for providing buoyancy in event of boat being flooded through damage or taking seas aboard; also, the regulation *t's* for protection of provisions in a ship's boat. **Cantilever t's,** *see* **G.-tanks** *in* GUNWALE. **Deep t.,** *see* DEEP. **Expansion t.,** an overflow chamber that provides for expansion and replenishment of a liquid, as in a cargo *t.;* a *t.* fitted with an *expansion trunk; see* TRUNK. **Free t.,** one partially filled, thus entailing a *free surface; see* FREE. **Gunwale t.,** same as *cantilever t.* **Holy water t.,** one containing the fresh water used in the circulating system for cooling cylinders of a Diesel engine. (*Slang*) **McIntyre t.,** early ballast *t.* similar in construction to present cellular double-bottom *t's* but laid *on top* of ship's floors. **Oil t.,** one for storing or carrying oil; short for *oil tanker,* or vessel fitted with *t's* for carriage of oil. **Oil-service t.,** *see* **O. service pump** *in* OIL. **Peak t.,** one at either extreme end of the hull, as *fore peak t.* or *after peak t.* **Receiving t.,** *see* RECEIVE. **Sanitary t.,** one that provides sea-water for flushing toilets, etc. It is fixed in an elevated position and kept supplied by the *sanitary pump.* **Settling t.,** in vessels using oil fuel, *t.* in which oil is heated preparatory to use and let stand for a time until any water content *settles* to bottom. Water is then drained or pumped off. **Side t's,** in some vessels built for carrying heavy bulk cargoes, a continuation of the double-bottom *t's* up each side, usually extending to the first deck. Also, *twin t's,* or those opening to the weather deck, at each side of a tween deck, used for cargo or water ballast. A *cantilever* or other type of *wing t.* **Summer t's,** those built at either side of the expansion trunk in a *t. vessel;* so named from their use for additional cargo to that carried in *main t's* during *summer,* as provided for in load-line regulations. **T.-gauge,** a measuring-stick or rod for ascertaining the *ullage* or distance from surface of the liquid in a *t.* to the *t. top* or *cover;* also, *ullage-stick.* **T. barge,** *t.* vessel without means of propulsion and thus towed as required. May be of scow-like build, as for supplying bunker fuel in harbor, or of sea-going type, but in either case fitted with a pumping plant. **T. lid,** steel hinged cover of a *t.,* or *t. hatch-cover.* It is fitted with *dogs* for screwing down securely. **T'ship** = *t.* vessel. **T. top,** inner bottom, or plating constituting top of double-bottom *t's.* Top or upper surface of any *t.* **T. vessel,** one specially constructed for carriage of bulk liquids, including petroleum and its products, whale oil, molasses, and wine. Also called *tanker,* vessel's cargo space is subdivided into separate *t's* by fore-and-aft and thwartship bulkheads, such *t's* commonly holding over 500 tons in an *oil-tanker.* A complete pumping system is installed with pipe-line extending to every *t.* in the hull. Ship's propulsion plant is confined to after end of hull and usually is separated, and so protected from an inflammable cargo, from cargo *t's* by a *cofferdam.* **T. water-ballast,** *see* BALLAST. **Trimming t.,** one near the end of a vessel, often a *peak t.,* used for regulating ship's *trim,* or required difference of draft of water at stem and stern. **Wing t's,** *see* **Side t's.**

TANKAGE. Capacity of a tank or tanks.

TANKER. A tank vessel; *see* TANK.

TANKERMAN. In U.S., a person qualified to perform all duties included in the handling of bulk liquid cargoes, *esp.* petroleum and its products, with competent knowledge of fire-fighting equipment and its use in connection therewith. Such person is certificated upon passing examination by Coast Guard authority. Colloquially, any seaman who, customarily or preferably, sails on tank vessels.

TANNED SAILS. *See* SAIL.

TAP. A tool for *tapping,* or cutting threads on inside of a hole bored in a metal, to receive a correspondingly threaded screw-bolt, stud, etc. A spigot; plug or spile to stop a hole or a vent, as in a cask; a cock, faucet, or small valve. **T.-bolt,** *see* BOLT. **T. rivet,** *see* RIVET; also called *stud rivet.* To **t. the admiral,** *see* ADMIRAL.

TAPER. To decrease in diameter, width, thickness, etc., toward one end, as in a plank, rope, a spar. Such diminution in size of an object; a *tapering.* **T'ed liner,** *see* LINER. **T'ed planking,** etc., *see* DIMINISHING PLANKING. **T'ed-neck rivet,** *see* RIVET. To **t. off,** to cause to gradually decrease in size; hence, to gradually lessen in intensity, as a gale or a current; to cease little by little.

TAR. (A.S. *teru,* pitch or resin from a tree, *treow*) A viscous dark-colored liquid obtained by distillation of resinous woods, coal, peat, bituminous shale, etc., and used as a preservative on wood, cordage, and iron; often named for its source, as *pine t., vegetal t., coal t., petroleum t.,* etc. *Cf.* PITCH.[1] A sailor, so named from his association with the *tar-pot* in old hemp-rigging days. **Coal t.** was used extensively on ships' bottom planking both prior to and following the advent of copper sheathing; also, mixed with a resin and often called *black varnish,* was applied to hemp or served wire shrouds and backstays. Equal parts of *pine* and *coal t's* were considered good treatment for any hemp rigging,- footropes, runners, ratlines, etc. **Stockholm t.,** a good quality of *pine t.,* mixed with fish or linseed oil, often by boiling, has long been a favorite for preserving and waterproofing tarpaulins. To **t. down,** to coat standing rigging with *t.* or a mixture containing *t.* **T.-pot,** receptacle for *t.* (usually a mixture of *t.* and grease) in riggers' and sailors' work; also, *t.-bucket.*

TARPAULIN. (Pron. *tar-pôlin;* from *tar* plus *palling,* a covering) A sheet of stout waterproofed canvas, usually jute or hemp, for covering a hatch, cargo, etc. Generally, three *t's* are placed on weath-

er-deck hatches. *Cf.* **Stockholm t.** *in* TAR; also, **To b. down the hatches** *in* BATTEN. Also spelled *tarpauling.* **T. muster,** *see* MUSTER.

TARPON. A noted game fish found in West Indies waters, on coasts of Florida and Georgia, and in Gulf of Mexico. Attains a length of six feet; has large silvery scales, elongate body with compressed sides, three ventral fins, one dorsal, and large homocercal fin. It is considered a poor food fish.

TARRED STUFF. General term for hemp cordage treated with a pine tar; *esp.,* small line such as ratline, houseline, marline, spunyarn, etc. *Cf.* **H. rope** *in* HEMP.

TARTAN. Also, *tartana;* a Mediterranean coasting vessel rigged with one mast and a bowsprit; spreads a large lateen sail with a forestaysail and a jib. A *tartanella* (Ital. dim. of *tartan*) is a small fishing-vessel of similar rig.

TAUNT. Old word for *tall* and *well stayed;* as *t. masts. See* ATAUNT.

TAURUS. (L. = bull) A northern zodiacal constellation which the sun passes during June. Located north and west of *Orion,* it contains the bright reddish star *Aldebaran,* of magnitude 1.1, and a closely grouped cluster known as the *Pleiades* or *Seven Sisters. See* ALDEBARAN.

TAUT. Hauled tight; tensely stretched; not slack; as a rope, sail, chain cable, etc.; *e.g.,* hand *t.;* to heave *t.;* set *t.;* a *t.* sheet. To **hold a t. hand,** to enforce strict discipline; said of an officer. **T. hand,** a rigid disciplinarian (*Archaic*). **T. helm,** continuous weather helm, as carried when vessel tends to lay toward the wind in sailing. *See* ARDENT.

TAUTOG. (Am. Indian) An edible fish of the Labridæ family found on Atlantic coast of North America. Also called *blackfish* from its color, averages about 10 inches in length; has a blunt nose, long dorsal fringe, and lobeless tail. *Cf.* LABRIDÆ.

TEA CLIPPER. *See* CLIPPER.

TEAK. (Port. *teca;* from Tamil *tekku*) A yellowish brown, hard, close-grained, durable, shipbuilding wood obtained from a tree of same name native to southern India, Burma, and Thailand. It contains a resinous oil that provides valuable resistance to the *teredo* or ship-worm and is used extensively for ships' side and deck planking, rails, skylights, deck-houses, winch beds, doors, companion-ladders, etc. Best grade and hardest is known as *Burma t.* Original supply of this excellent timber having been exhausted, it is now grown in planted forests and for the first time in America, seeds of the tree were brought from Ceylon and planted in the Panama Canal Zone, April, 1926. Progress of this venture and subsequent plantings is said to have proven satisfactory. Also, *teakwood.*

TEE. Something shaped like a *T;* having the form of a *T.* **T.-bar; T.-beam;** etc., *see* T.

TEHUANTEPECER. A strong wind from north to north-east on the Pacific coasts of Guatemala and Nicaragua, more frequently occurring during winter. It is regarded as the overflow of a high-pressure area in Gulf of Mexico, or that restricted to the comparatively narrow *Tehuantepec* pass, and hence often attaining gale force. *Cf.* PAPAGAYO; NORTHER.

TELEGRAPH. Instrument or apparatus for transmitting signals or messages; *specif.,* that used aboard ship for issuing and repeating orders from and to the navigating bridge; as, *engine-room t.* **Docking t.,** used for orders to officer in charge of handling mooring-lines at either end of ship; signals include such orders as *"Heave in," "Let go," "All clear?",* etc. **Engine-room t.,** or **engine t.,** for orders to engineer-in-charge regarding movements or speed of main engines; as, *"Full speed," "Slow," "Half astern," "Stop,"* etc. **Steering t.,** for orders to emergency steering station at after end of ship; sometimes combined with *docking t.,* usually indicates position of rudder in both bridge and emergency station instruments. **T.-block,** *see* BLOCK. **T.-chain,** *see* CHAIN. **Wireless t.** = radiotelegraph.

TELEMOTOR. (Gr. *tele,* far off; + *motor*) Hydraulic device for operating a steering-engine from the navigating bridge or pilot-house. As steering-wheel is turned, working fluid is compressed by a piston in one of two cylinders, which in turn transmits pressure to receiving piston and thence control-valve system of steering-engine is acted upon. Also, an electrically operated system for same use.

TELEPHONE. **Docking t.,** means of speaking communication between navigating bridge and either end of vessel in connection with docking, mooring, etc. **Marine t.,** *see* MARINE.

TELEPHONY, WIRELESS. *See* RADIO.

TELESCOPE. (Gr. *teleskopos,* seeing afar) The well-known *spy-glass,* designed to magnify and clarify distant objects to the eye; often called *"the glass"* by ships' officers. As used aboard ship, the instrument usually is the direct refracting or Galilean type, in which light rays are converged to a focus through the large *object lens,* thence magnified by the *eye-piece* at inner end of smaller tube, or part fitted to slide into the outer or object tube, as focal adjustment is made accordingly. For astronomical use, both *refracting* and *reflecting t's* are in use. In principle, this latter type reflects the rays by a large mirror to another of concave surface design at outer end of tube, thence rays are brought to focus through a central hole in large mirror and magnified by the eye-piece. For *reflecting t's,* less perfect glass is required than that in a *refractor* and hence commonly are of greater diameter than the latter. The 200-inch *reflecting t.* of the California Institute of Technology at Mount Palomar, set up in June, 1948, is largest known of this type. *T's* may be *direct* or *inverting,* according to arrangement of lenses. Those for ship use are direct type, *i.e.,* objects are seen right side up, as opposed to inverting instruments. **Sextant t.,** *see* SEXTANT. **T. mast,** *see* MAST.

TELLTALE. An indicator, such as a pointer, for showing functional position or motion of a machinery part, etc.; any audible or visual device for warning, indicating, etc. **Rudder t.,** a *helm indicator; see* HELM. **T. compass,** mariner's compass usually suspended from deckhead in captain's cabin. It is fitted with a glass bottom so that ship's course may be checked from a position below the instrument. A cabin compass.

TEMPERATE ZONES. *See* ZONE.

TEMPERATURE, OCEAN. Sea *surface t.* varies from 27° F. in polar latitudes to 96° in the Persian Gulf during summer. 80° to 88° is ordinary range in the tropics, but annual variations are greater in the temperate zones with probably a 25° maximum range. At 45° N. and 45° W., in the North Atlantic trade-route zone, a minimum of about 45° F. occurs in February against a maximum of 60° in September. Generally, *t.* becomes more equable at a lower figure with increase of distance below the surface, a difference of 30° from surface water making a nearly constant 50° F. at 100 fathoms in tropical latitudes. A variation of only 15° at 800 fathoms is found between latitudes 60° N. and 60° S. Mean average *t.* of ocean water, all depths considered, is very nearly 40° F.

TEMPLATE. Often spelled *templet,* a pattern, model, or mold, usually made of thin wood or stiff paper, shaped to exact size and dimensions of a piece of work to be laid out, as in shipbuilding. Either of two heavy wedges that set up a *keel-block* in a slipway or dry-dock; usually *templet* in this case. **To lift a t.,** to construct a pattern or mold from the actual form or dimensions of a structural part, as of a vessel.

TEMPLET. *See* TEMPLATE.

TEND. Short for *attend;* to watch, stand by to manipulate, keep clear for running, etc., as a rope. **To t. ship,** in older phraseology meant to take any measure necessary to prevent a moored vessel from fouling her cables by swinging in a wrong direction to change of tide. *Cf.* GROW.

TENDER.[1] Said of a vessel having small initial stability; same as *crank. See* CRANKY; STABILITY.

TENDER.[2] A small vessel used to attend on large vessels, as in supplying provisions, landing passengers, mails; any vessel serving as an auxiliary to a fishing fleet; a despatch-boat; etc. **Hatch t.,** *see* HATCH. **Lighthouse t.,** *see* LIGHTHOUSE. **Slip t.,** *see* SLIP. **Water-t.,** *see* WATER.

TENDER CLAUSE.   Stipulation in a marine insurance policy that entitles insurer to decide port or repair-yard at which damage to vessel is to be repaired and, where appropriate, to require *tenders* taken for repair of such damage.

TENSILE STRENGTH.   See STRENGTH.

TENT.   Hatch t., see HATCH. To **t. an awning,** to secure its sides down to the deck as a security measure against strong winds or for purpose of collecting rain-water.

TEREDO. (Gr. *teredon,* worm that gnaws wood and clothing)   Genus of mollusks containing the *marine borers* or *ship-worms, esp., T. navalis.* See **M. borer** *in* MARINE.

TERM.   In older ships, a piece of carved work fitted under each end of the poop rail; also, *term-piece.* A timber forming the limit of a square counter at each side.

TERMINAL.   *Esp.* so called in U.S., a point of interchange between land and water carriers, as a pier, wharf, etc., or group of such, equipped with facilities for care and handling of cargo and/or passengers.

TERN.   Any of several gull-like sea birds constituting a sub-family called *Sterninæ.* Generally smaller, swifter and more graceful in flight than the true gulls, usually have a straight slender bill and deeply forked tail, from which latter they have been called *sea swallows.* Most *t's* are white with more or less dark-shaded tops. The *Arctic t.* is said to hold the distinction of living in more daylight hours than any bird because of its habit of migrating to high southern latitudes as Arctic winter approaches and vice versa. He breeds on seacoasts from New England to Greenland and on Arctic islands in the northern summer.

TERN SCHOONER.   "Down-East" term for a three-masted schooner; *see* SCHOONER.

TERRESTRIAL.   Pertaining to the earth; earthly; opposed to *celestial; as, t. equator; t. meridian.* **T. sphere** = the earth.

TERRITORIAL.   Pertaining to territory, or a region of land; *esp.,* that considered as part of a national domain; as, *t. limits.* **Admiralty t. jurisdiction,** see ADMIRALTY. **T. waters,** see **M. belt** *in* MARINE.

TERTIARY MERIDIAN.   See MERIDIAN.

TEST.   Examination, trial, or decisive experiment; a proving of effectiveness, efficiency, or quality of anything; as, a *pressure t.* on a tank. Hence, the means of such proof or trial; as, a *hose t.;* a *boring t.* **Drilling t.,** see DRILLING TEST. **Hose t.,** see HOSE. **Hydraulic t.,** see HYDRAULIC. **Percussive t.,** also termed *drop t.;* as applied to cast steel anchors by authority or direction of a classification society, usually consists of dropping the anchor from a height of 12 feet, both end on and side on, to a steel or iron slab. If this *t.* is satisfactory, anchor then is suspended and hammered all over with a sledge, so that if metal gives a "clear ring" it is considered free of either original flaws or any developed by the *drop t's.* **T. cock,** see COCK. **T. head,** for *t.* of a double bottom, etc., *see* HEAD.

TEXAS.   In western U.S., structure on uppermost deck of a river steamboat containing officers' cabins and pilot-house; also, short for *t. deck,* such uppermost deck itself, *esp.* so termed in Great Lakes vessels.

THALWEG. (Ger. *thal,* valley; *weg,* way) Line following deepest course of a river or other waterway; *esp.,* that constituting a boundary between nations or states.

THAMES BARGE.   See BARGE.

THAMES TONNAGE.   See TONNAGE.

THERMOMETER.   See CENTIGRADE; FAHRENHEIT.

THERMOSTATIC ALARM.   In an automatic fire-detection installation, sounding of a gong or bell upon an abnormal increase of temperature in a compartment indicated.

THERMOTANK SYSTEM.   Air-conditioning or mechanical ventilation installation commonly found in larger passenger vessels. Outside air is heated or cooled to required temperature in one or more tanks by a system of piping coils through which steam or cooled brine passes; thence the conditioned air, circulated in ducts by power-driven fans, is distributed throughout accommodation, living quarters, etc. A similar system frequently is employed also in maintaining cargo holds at constant temperature and hygrometric atmospheric content.

THICK.   Of relatively great depth between opposite surfaces; as, a *t. plank;* opposed to *thin,* as a *t. coat of tar.* Descriptive of atmospheric conditions in which distance of visibility is markedly shortened by fog, smoke, mist, falling snow, rain, or sleet; as, *t. weather;* a *t. squall.* **T.-and-thin block,** see BLOCK. **T. strake,** see STRAKE. **T. stuff,** old shipbuilding general term for all plank more than four and less than twelve inches in thickness.

THIEF.   A bung-dipper or drinking-can, usually made of tin and in elongate cylindrical form, so weighted that it tilts and fills upon reaching surface of liquid, as in a cask. An auxiliary net for catching fish that drop out of a main net while latter is hauled aboard, as in drift-net fishing; a *t.-net.*

THIMBLE.   A round or oval-shaped fitting of non-corrosive metal, galvanized iron, etc. and U-shaped in cross-section, set in an eye of a rope as protection against damaging effect of shackle-pins, hooks, etc. Depending on its use, however, *t.* may be of several different patterns. Generally, for smaller fiber ropes it is circular-shaped, while for all wire ropes and larger fiber cordage it is of oval or *horse-collar* form. *Cf.* CRINGLE. **Lanyard-t.,** *see* LANYARD. **Round t.** = cringle. **Solid t.,** as distinguished from the usual open type, one made in a single casting of iron or steel with a hole for a shackle-pin. Usually oval-shaped, sometimes of half-round form, it is used in lower eyes of stays, shrouds, and backstays, or where *t.* must endure severe compression stresses. **T.-eye,** the chub mackerel, *q.v.*

THOLE. Pin of wood or metal set in a boat's gunwale to serve as a fulcrum for an oar. Oar is confined to *t.* by a strop or grommet. Also, *t.-pin.* **T.-board,** short flat piece of wood on topside of a boat for strengthening or deepening the parts into which rowlocks or *t.-pins* are inserted.

THOROUGHFOOT. To lessen the tautened twist in a fiber rope, or condition in which rope easily develops kinks, by coiling down *against the lay* and bringing lower end up through coil; thence coiling down *with the lay.* Repeat the operation, if necessary. (When the lay has grown *long,* as when rope is frequently coiled or worked in a tackle *with the lay,* reverse above procedure) *With the lay,* for *right-hand* laid cordage, means in same direction as hands of a clock move; for *left-hand* laid cordage, the converse of this. A *tackle* is said to be *t.* when in the tangled state of having one or more blocks turned over and dipped through parts of the fall.

THRASH. To sail a vessel close-hauled under a press of canvas into a choppy or lively sea; as, to *t.* the lugger to windward. Vessel is said to be *thrashing* to windward in such case.

THRASHER. Also *thresher; see* **Fox s.** *in* SHARK. **T.-whale,** the grampus.

THREAD. A single string or filament of fiber or wire in a rope; a number of such units spun together to make a *rope-yarn,* a number of which twisted together in turn constitute a *strand. T.,* as a rope-yarn, is used as a designating unit in sizes of certain small stranded cordage; as, *15-t. manila; 21-t. ratline stuff* (indicating 3 strands of 5 and 7 yarns respectively). *See* **M. rope** *in* MANILA. Strands of wire rope often are described as containing a certain number of *t's; e.g.,* a 6 × 19 wire also may be referred to as one having 6 *19-t.* strands. **T. herring,** so named from its single long thin ray at rear of the dorsal fin, species of herring found in West Indian and U.S. east coast waters.

THREE. Characterized by, or possessing, similar features *three* in number; as in *t.-sheave block; t.-skysail-yarder.* **T.-arm protractor,** or **t.-armed p.,** *see* **S. pointer** *in* STATION. **T.-decker,** a vessel having *t.* decks; *esp.,* the former *ship of the line* or *line-of-battle ship* carrying guns on *t.* decks. **T.-fathom line,** *see* **F.-line** *in* FATHOM. **T.-island vessel,** one having

superstructures consisting of a forecastle, bridge, and poop, as commonly found in general cargo ships; *cf.* SUPERSTRUCTURE. **T.-leg mooring,** *see* MOORING. **T. L's,** *see* L. **T.-masted,** having *t.* masts; as, a *t.-masted schooner, barque,* etc. A vessel thus equipped often is called a *t.-master.* **T.-mile limit,** *see* **M. belt** *in* MARINE. **T.-point problem,** that of determining observer's position from measurement of two adjacent angles subtended by *t.* charted landmarks on or near a coastline, *i.e.,* angles subtended by a middle object and objects on its right and left, respectively. *See* **S. pointer** *in* STATION; also *cf.* REVOLVER. **T.-skys'l-yarder,** a *t.-masted* ship that carries a skysail on each mast; hence, in old sailors' cant, a vessel completely ship-rigged; a full-rigged ship. **T.-star problem,** *see* STAR.

THREEFOLD BLOCK. A tackle-block having three sheaves; called also *treble block.* Two such blocks with fall working in all sheaves is a *threefold purchase; see* PURCHASE.

THRESHER. *See* THRASHER.

THROAT. Upper forward corner, or *nock,* of a quadrilateral fore-and-aft sail. End of a gaff next the mast; *esp.,* where such spar is fitted with *jaws* for partially embracing the mast. The *turn,* or heaviest part of a knee timber or a breast-hook. In an old-fashioned anchor, curved part of either *arm* where it joins the *shank.* Part of a block through which the fall is rove; also, *swallow.* In a floor timber, midship part, or that of greatest depth, in way of the keel. The part of an eye in a rope next the splice; also, *point of the eye.* **T.-bolt,** in a hoisting gaff, eye-bolt to which the *t. halyard* is attached. **T. brail,** *see* BRAIL. **T. downhaul,** *see* DOWNHAUL. **T. halyard,** rope or purchase for hoisting *t.* of a gaff; *cf.* HALYARD. **T. seizing,** a *round* or a *flat* seizing by which both parts of a block-strop, shroud about a dead-eye, double stay around a masthead, an eye in a hawser, etc., are drawn taut together for strength or snugness, or both; *cf.* SEIZING.

THROTTLE. (Dim. of *throat*) Short for *throttle-valve, -lever, -wheel, -governor,* etc., or means of controlling or regulating flow of steam, gas, etc., to an engine. To stop or reduce speed of an engine by such means.

THROUGH. **T. bill of lading,** *see* BILL. **T. fastenings,** *see* FASTENING. **T. rate,** *see* RATE. **T. the cabin windows; t. the hawse-pipes,** *see* **To come in t. the hawse-pipes,** etc., *in* HAWSE.

THRUM (Older form, *thrumb*) The small pieces used in making a *t.,* or *shag, mat* for prevention of chafing of sails, ropes, etc. To cover with shag or small pieces of rope-yarn, as canvas in making a *t. mat;* to *t.* canvas; *see* **Thrum m.** *in* MAT.

THRUST. (Ice. *thrysta,* to thrust, force, press, or compel) Measured effort delivered by an impelling force; *specif.*, the impulsion or push exerted by a propeller in driving a vessel. *Cf.* **Thrust hp** *in* HORSEPOWER. **T. bearing,** *see* BEARING; also called *t. block,* its common and earlier form is the *horseshoe* type, so named from the horseshoe-shaped bearing pieces that receive the axial drive or *t.* pressure from several *collars* forged on the shaft. Later patents are the *Kingsbury* (U.S.) and the *Mitchell* (British); *see* KINGSBURY THRUST BEARING. **T.-block,** *see* BLOCK. **T. collar,** raised part or ring on the *t.-shaft* that rotates against *t.-bearing;* shaft may be forged with several collars, as in *horseshoe bearing* type, or with a single heavy one, as in *Kingsbury* patent. **T. recess,** *see* **Tunnel r.** *in* RECESS. **T.-shaft,** *see* SHAFT. **T. sheave,** same as *t. collar.* **T. shoes,** the horseshoe-shaped bearings referred to in **T. bearing.**

THUMB CLEAT. *See* CLEAT.

THUNDER-CLOUD. Also called *thunder-head; see* **Cumulo-nimbus** *in* CLOUD.

THURROCK. (A.S. *thurruc,* a ship's hold) Obsolete term for the bottom part of a vessel's hull. Also *thorrocke.*

THWART. One of the planks that extend crosswise in an open boat for lateral stiffening and as seats for the oarsmen. In larger boats, a stanchion usually is fitted at mid-length of *t.;* also, for seating passengers, as in life-boats, *lower t's* sometimes are fitted at a lesser height and alternating with usual *t's.* In staging erected along vessels' sides, as in shipyard work, one of the cross pieces supporting the horizontally laid planks. As an aphetic form of *athwart, see* ATHWART. **Mast t.,** a *t.* through which a mast passes or is stiffened by a clamp secured thereto. Where a mast is stepped between *t's,* what is termed a *gangboard* or *mast carling* is laid fore-and-aft, fastened to *t's,* and provided with a hole through which mast is passed and so fixed in position for spreading sail.

THWARTSHIP. Extending, leading, or lying in, or nearly in, a horizontal plane at right angles to the fore-and-aft line; as, *t.* bulkhead; *t.* bunker; *t.* alley. Same as *athwartship.*

TICKET. Seamen's colloquialism for a personal license or a certificate; as, an *able seaman's t.* Especially among British merchant marine officers, a certificate of competency; as, a *master's t.; chief's t.* (that of a *1st. class engineer*); etc.

TICKLER. On the coast of Labrador, a narrow passage or entrance to a harbor; a deep narrow-mouthed inlet.

TIDAL. Of or pertaining to a tide or tides; having a periodical flow and ebb or rise and fall, as a *t. river;* caused by the tide, as a *t. current; t. action.* **T. alarm,** a warning signal, such as a whistle or a horn, indicating approach of a *bore;* a whistle blown by flow of tide, as on a buoy, serving as a thick-weather warning to vessels. **T. basin,** an en-

closed dock or system of docks in which a constant depth of water may be maintained by means of floodgates. Usually found in principal sea-ports at which the *t. range* is comparatively great, as, *e.g.,* Liverpool, England. **T. bore,** *see* BORE. **T. breeze,** a light wind caused by horizontal movement of the tide, as in a gulf or bay area during fair settled weather. **T. clock,** a time-piece showing height of tide at any hour and times of high and low water. **T. constant,** for obtaining time and height of tide at a secondary port or place, number of minutes or feet to be added to or subtracted from time and height given for each day at a standard port of reference, as indicated in published *t. tables.* **T. crack,** rift in ice resulting from change in tide level, as along and near the shore of a bay or harbor. **T. current,** horizontal movement of waters due to advance or recession of the tide wave over comparatively shallow or constricted areas; *see* CURRENT. Also called *t. stream, esp.* in a strait or channel. **T. current chart,** *see* CHART. **T. curve,** *see* MARIGRAPH. **T. datum,** *see* DATUM. **T. day,** *see* **T. day** *in* TIDE. **T. difference,** same as *t. constant,* q.v. **T. eddy,** whirlpool or turning in a contrary direction of a *t. stream,* as from meeting streams or a sharp turn or bend in a coastline. **T. fall,** decrease of depth of water from time of high water to that of the following low water. **T. friction,** *see* FRICTION. **T. harbor,** a port or haven in which the tide flows and ebbs; a natural harbor. *See* HARBOR. **T. interval,** average elapsed time between successive high waters; that of the common semidiurnal tide has a mean value of nearly 12 hours 25 minutes. **T. lights,** as exhibited at a harbor entrance, a river bar, dock gate, etc., those of a system of signals for indicating present depth of water and, in some cases, also direction of local *t. stream.* **T. loop,** cotidal line or curve, roughly parabolic, indicating advance of the tide wave by joining all points at which high water simultaneously occurs. In comparatively narrow waters, as, *e.g.,* the English Channel, apex of *loop* lies offshore in deep water. *Cf.* COTIDAL. **T. plane of reference,** *t.* level from which height of tide is measured. Soundings on coastal charts indicate depth of water below such *plane* or level, which, depending upon peculiarities of *t. range* in a given region, usually is that corresponding to average depth at lowest state of tide. Thus, where inequalities in *t. range* are small, *low water* at ordinary spring tides (*L.W.O.S.*) generally is adopted as reference level; where conditions are otherwise, mean of lower low waters (*L.L.W.*) may be taken. *See also* INDIAN TIDE-PLANE; *also,* **M. low water** *in* MEAN. **T. range,** mean value of differences between high and low water levels, as usually established from observations covering at least one lunar month. *Mean spring range* is difference observed between successive high water and low water levels at time of spring tides at a given place. *Ratio of ranges* is that of a secondary port's *t. range* to the range at a standard port of reference; *cf.* **S. port of reference** *in* STANDARD.[1] **T. rise,** height of a given high water level above chart *datum* or plane of reference; same as *height of tide*. **T. river,** one in which the tide and/or its influence on depth of water extend for a considerable distance upstream or inland. **T. stream,** *see* **T. current. T. velocity,** rate of surface motion of a *t. current,* usually expressed in *knots.* Maximum velocity generally coincides with half tide, or midtime between high and low water. **T. waters,** all waters that are in any way connected with the sea and therefore subject to the recurring flow and ebb of tides or are influenced thereby in a consequential rise or fall of surface level. **T. wave,** distinct from the *bore* of shallow waters, a heavy sea wave or roller, often of destructive proportions upon reaching shore, due to either a seismic disturbance or the driving force of a violent storm. It is thus popularly named from its tide-like inundating effect on a coast. Notable examples of such destructive waves are those attending the Galveston hurricane disaster, Sept. 8, 1900, in which 6000 lives were lost, and the eruption of Krakatoa, volcano off Java, Aug. 27, 1883, resulting in a loss of 35,000.

TIDE. (A.S. *tid,* time, an occasion, a season) Alternate rise and fall of the ocean's surface and that of its arms and connecting waters due to the more or less joint attraction of sun and moon. *T.* may be considered as mainly the result of attraction by the latter body, since her influence amounts to nearly 2.3 times that of the sun. At times of new and full moon, combined attraction of these bodies causes highest, or *spring, t's;* as sun and moon draw toward quadrature (1st. and 3rd. quarters of moon) height of *t's* diminishes to what are termed *neap t's.* Marked differences in height of the *t. wave* are due to Moon's varying distance from Earth, greatest lunar influence being at *perigee,* least at *apogee;* also, to great and opposite declinations of Sun and Moon, such as occur at *full moon* near the summer and winter solstices. We have, therefore, a complicated source of varying tidal heights lying in the ever-changing relative positions of Sun, Moon, and Earth, to which must be added the interrupting effect of large bodies of land on the east-west advance of the *t. wave* around or over the globe and, also, the braking or restricting element occasioned by shallower and narrower parts of the oceans, its bordering gulfs, bays, straits, etc. Thus, to simply and clearly present or describe what actually gives rise to the great natural phenomenon, *ebb and flow of t.,* with its many variations from month to month, is to attempt the impossible. Indeed, it is doubtful if a satisfactorily lucid explanation ever has been given regarding the prime source of the *t. wave,* respect due the theories of gravitational effect of Sun and Moon combined with centrifugal force of Earth's rotatory motion, notwithstanding. The *flood* and *ebb* streams or currents, or regularly reversing horizontal motion of waters in channels, harbors, etc., are also called **tides. Acceleration of t's,** also called *priming of the t's; see* **A. of the tides** *in* ACCELERATION, *also* **L. of the tides** *in* LAG. **Age of the t.,** *see* AGE OF THE TIDE. **Falling t.,** stage of the *t.* in which its height diminishes, or interval between high water and next low water. **Half t.,** *see* HALF. **Harmonic analysis of t's,** *see* HARMONIC ANALYSIS. **Lagging of the t.,** *see* LAG. **Lee t.** or **leeward t.,** *see* LEE. **Mean of the t's,** *see* MEAN. **Mean range of t.,** *see* MEAN. **Meteorological t.,** general term for a time or height of high water markedly affected by direction and force of strong winds, abnormal local barometric pressure, or both. **Mixed t.,** as chiefly found on both shores of the Pacific, one of usual semidiurnal type but having irregular successive heights which occur during periods of higher declination of Moon, markedly so when that body is at *perigee* or a day or two thereafter. **Neap t.,** *see* NEAP. **Priming of the t's,** *see* **L. of the t's** *in* LAG. **Perigean t.,** one of increased range attributed to Moon's position in *perigee.* **Range of t.,** *see* **T. range** *in* TIDAL. **Retardation of t's,** *see* **L. of the t's** *in* LAG. **Rip t.,** surface current showing agitated or rippling water; *see* RIP. **Rise of t.,** *see* **T. rise** *in* TIDAL. **Rising t.,** state of *t.* when growing in height toward its maximum rise; the *flood t.;* opposed to a *falling t.* **Solar t.,** *see* SOLAR. **Semidiurnal t.,** one having an average interval between successive high or low waters of about 12 hours 25 minutes. Its main features are regularity of recurrence, maximum height shortly after new and full moon, and minimum height at about 1st. and 3rd. quarter. **Spring t.,** one of semidiurnal type that attains a comparatively great height (as measured above *tidal datum*) twice in a lunar month. Usually reaches maximum rise at 1 to 2½ days after times of full and new moon; opposed to *neap t.;* called also *syzygy t.* **Stand of the t.,** period in which *t.* remains stationary in height, as at or near the end of flood or ebb. Also, *slack water,* or interval between flow and ebb or ebb and flow during which no perceptible horizontal surface motion occurs. Times of *high* and *low water* at some localities differ from those of *slack water,* particularly in long arms of the sea and tidal rivers, by as much as 1 to 2 hours, and the flood stream actually may be coincident with a *falling t.* or vice versa. **Superior t.,** also, *direct t.,* the *t.* resulting from passage of Moon over observer's *upper,* or *superior, meridian;* opposed to *inferior,* or *opposite, t.* **To tail to the t.,** *see* **To t. with the stream** *in* TAIL. **T. and half-t.,** also called *double high water,* that occurring in some deep inlets on a coast along which flow tidal streams of considerable magnitude. A typical example is the *t.* in the Solent and Southampton Water on south coast of England. First high water level recedes for about an hour, then rises for about 1¼ hours to its former level or higher. This is due to the ebb stream now turning westward along the coast, entering the wider-mouthed Spithead and holding back *t. fall* in waters referred to until free ebb conditions arrive. Where interval between high waters in such cases is somewhat less, or about 1½ hours, *t. and quarter-t.* obtains. **T. ball,** a globe-shaped signal indicating time of high or low *t.,* appropriate time for entering or leaving a tidal basin, etc. **T. barge,** vessel having no propelling power and so depending on the *t.* for moving in a river or sheltered tidal waters. **T'bound,** said of a vessel detained because of insufficient depth of water at low stage of *t.* **T.-crack,** *see* **T.-cack** *in* TIDAL. **T. day,** about 24 hours 50 minutes, or interval between two successive arrivals of the *t. wave,* or average interval between high waters corresponding thereto, as considered chiefly in connection with *t's* of semidiurnal type; also, *tidal day.* **T. gage** (or **gauge**), *see* GAUGE. **T.-gate,** *see* GATE. **T. harbor,** also *tidal harbor, see* HARBOR. **T. indicator,** a *t.-clock* or other device for showing depth of water or height of *t.* at any hour; a *t.-gauge.* **T'land** (or **t.-land**), *see* LAND. **T. lock,** *see* **Guard-l.** *in* LOCK. **T.-mark,** designated or indicated limit of high or low water on a shore, wharf, etc.; a watermark; *see* MARK. **T.-net,** a fish-net set to take a catch during ebb of *t.,* as in a river or creek; sometimes fixed bow-fashion, with convex side seaward, on a shore. **T.-pole,** vertical stake or pole driven in shoal water and marked to serve as an indicator of height of *t.* **T. predictor,** an instrument by means of which a summation of the harmonic constituent values involved mechanically predicts both times and heights of *t's* at a given place. *Cf.* HARMONIC ANALYSIS. **T. race,** *see* RACE. **T.-rips,** ruffled or agitated surface, such as is caused by *t. current* passing over a shoal or by conflicting currents; *cf.* RIP. **T. rock,** *see* **Half-tide r.** *in* ROCK. **T.-rode,** said of a vessel riding at anchor head on to *t.;* opposed to *wind-rode,* or heading into the wind regardless of current or *t.* **T. tables,** *see* TABLES, NAUTICAL. **T'water,** area of water affected by ebb and flow of *t.; esp.,* that portion of a river so affected. **T.-water glacier,** *see* GLACIER. **T.-walker,** *see* **P. inspector** *in* PROPELLER. **T'way,** path or channel followed by a *t. current;* flow or ebb of *t.* in such channel or region. **T's work,** calking or repairing of a vessel's bottom, work on sides of a pier, etc., during low stage of *t.* Progress made in sailing with a current during favorable *t.* **Tropic t.,** one of diurnal type, *i.e.,* having one *t.* each day, during period of Moon's greatest declination, changing to semidiurnal type as such declination approaches zero. So named from its prevalence in tropical latitudes. **True t.,** as opposed to that part of *t. current* or advancing *t. wave* which follows abrupt turns in a coastline, main *t.* itself which sets in a general steady direction with relation to the coast. **Turn of the t.,** time flood *t.*

commences after cessation of ebb stream, or converse of this. **Weather t.,** tidal stream or current flowing against the wind; one that is favorable in sailing close-hauled; also, *windward t.*

TIE. (A.S. *tiegan;* from *teag,* a rope) To fasten or join together the end or ends of a rope; to unite, as beams by a plank or a plate. Usually with *up,* to make fast or secure, as a vessel alongside a pier by means of mooring-lines, a boat alongside a vessel, etc. A *tye,* or part of hoisting gear secured to a yard; *see* TYE. **T.-block,** *see* **Tye-b.** *in* BLOCK. **T. plank,** one of several heavy planks or timbers securing *sliding ways* to *ground ways* in order to hold ship in place after keel-blocks are removed prior to launching. **T. plate,** single plate laid fore-and-aft or diagonally over deck-beams under a wood deck for extra strength, as in way of a line of stanchions, along a hatch coaming, under a deck-house sill, etc.; *see also* **D. tie-plate** *in* DIAGONAL. **T. rod,** a bolt, bar, or rod fitted to *t.* or unite opposite parts. **Tie-tie,** one of several pieces of cord or other small stuff attached to a hammock for use in stowing in lieu of a lashing.

TIER. A row or layer, as of similar pieces of cargo stowed in ship's hold; series of fakes of a hawser or chain cable as coiled down or ranged clear for running. Vessels are said to *lie in t.* when made fast or moored close alongside each other in ranks or rows, as a laid-up fleet. **Cable-t.,** *see* CABLE. **Ground t.,** *see* GROUND. **To t. a cable,** to fake down clear by laying cable in long lengths snugged side by side in successive layers.

TIERCE. (Fr. *tiers,* a third part) A cask having a capacity about midway between a *barrel* and a *hogshead,* or one-third of a *pipe,* formerly commonly used as packing container for salt beef, the *salt horse* of long-voyage provisions. Weight of a *t.* of beef, from 300 to 330 pounds; capacity, 42 Imperial or 50 U.S. gallons.

TIERER. Formerly, one of a number of men detailed to stow the anchor-cable clear for running, or faked down in tiers; now, one who assists in stowing the submarine cable in a cable-ship.

TIGER SHARK. *See* SHARK.

TIGER-WOOD. *See* ITAKA WOOD.

TIGHT. Taut; not slack or loose; as, *t. lashings.* Not leaky; staunch and sound; water-*tight;* as, a *t. vessel;* a *t. cask.* Difficult to accomplish or maintain; as, a *t. schedule;* a *t. run.*

TILEFISH. A deep-bellied pelagic food fish of the North Atlantic. Attains a length of 3 feet; has a protruding lower jaw; is covered with large round yellowish spots; and has a deep dorsal fringe extending almost full length of body.

TILLER. Arm or lever fitted to the *rudder-stock,* or *rudder-head,* for turning rudder as required in steering; the *helm,* as often termed in smaller craft. **Quadrant t.,** *see* QUADRANT. **Spring t.,** one connected to a quadrant by shock-absorbing springs. **Reverse t.,** *see* REVERSE. **T.-comb,** as often fitted in small sailing craft, a fixed curved rack in which a knife-edged iron on under side of *t.* may be set, thus holding *t.* at any desired angle. **T. head,** free end of *t.,* or that to which *steering-ropes* or *-chains* may be attached. **T.-ropes** or **-chains,** those leading from *t. head* to steering-wheel or steering-engine; *steering-ropes* or *-chains.* **T. telltale,** a helm indicator, or device for showing position of *t.,* and so the angle of rudder, at all times.

TIMBER. In wood shipbuilding, any principal piece of wood in the structure; *esp.,* one of the ribs or frames to which the outside planking is fastened; *see* FRAME. **T. carrier,** vessel specially designed for carrying *t.;* a lumber-carrier. Usually of single-deck type, has unusually large hatchway area and hold is to a great extent free of obstructions to block stowage, such as pillars or stanchions, deep knees, girders, web frames, and other inward projecting structural parts. Vessel is provided with ample water-ballast capacity in view of counteracting weight of deck-loads with that of rain and sea-water commonly absorbed by the exposed cargo. **T. head,** upper end of a *frame-t.* rising above weather deck and serving as one of the *bulwark stanchions;* when extended above ship's rail for making fast ropes, etc., it is called a *kevel head (see* KEVEL); a wooden *bitt.* **T. load-line,** freeboard or Plimsoll marks assigned to vessels considered capable of carrying *t. deck-loads.* Excepting mark indicated by *W N A* (Winter North Atlantic), such load-line gives a greater allowance of draft, or lesser freeboard, than ordinary marks assigned. To distinguish *t. load-line marks* from the latter, letter *L* is prefixed; thus *W* becomes *L W; S* becomes *L S;* etc. *Cf.* FREEBOARD. **Top t.,** uppermost piece in a frame *t.,* or that above a *futtock* in larger wooden vessels; also, *top piece.* (Also see *t.* as designated by the following captions: BOLLARD; CANT; COUNTER; FASHION; FLITCH; FLOOR; FUTTOCK; GROUND; HALF; HAWSE; HORN; KNEE; KNUCKLE; LONG; MIDDLE; MIXED; RISING)

TIME. Measured or measurable duration; as, *steaming t.; elapsed t.* A system by which days, hours, etc., are reckoned or computed; as, *apparent t.; lunar t.* Instant of occurrence of an event; as, *t. of observation; arrival t.* Hour of day as indicated by a clock, watch, or other means; as, *chronometer t.; ship t.* To-day it is usually customary to indicate *t.* of day aboard ship by the 24-hour system, instead of the former use of a.m. and p.m.; thus *0030* takes the place of 12.30 a.m.; *1230* for 0.30 or 12.30 p.m.; *2210* for 10.10 p.m.; etc. In nautical astronomy, *t.* in almost all calculations is a most essential element and involves use of one or more of the three systems, *apparent solar t., mean solar t.,* and *sidereal t.*

Apparent solar t., usually shortened to *apparent t.* and abbrev. *A.T.; see* S. **day** *in* SOLAR. **Astronomical t.,** *sidereal t.; see* ASTRONOMICAL. **Chronometer t.,** that indicated by a chronometer; *cf.* CHRONOMETER. **Civil t.,** local clock *t.* used in every-day life. It is *mean solar t.* corresponding to the meridian of place considered or that of an adopted standard meridian in the region. **Corrected t.,** that occupied by a sailing-yacht in covering the course in a race, less her *t. allowance* or *handicap.* **Equation of t.,** number of minutes and seconds constituting difference between *mean solar t.* and *apparent solar t.,* as given in nautical almanacs. **Greenwich civil t.,** also called *universal t.,* mean solar *t.* of longitude 0° 0′ 0″, or the Meridian of Greenwich, England; *see G.C.T.* **Longitude in t.,** hours, minutes, and seconds corresponding to longitude of a place; *see remarks on* LONGITUDE. **Mean solar t.,** usually termed *mean t.; see* M. **solar day** *in* MEAN. **Retardation of mean solar t.,** *see* RETARDATION. **Sidereal t.,** westerly hour angle of vernal equinoctial point, expressed from 0 to 24 hours; *see* **Right a. of meridian** *in* ASCENSION. **Solar t.,** *see* SOLAR. **Star t.,** same as *sidereal t.* **T. azimuth,** a heavenly body's true bearing determination of which depends upon *t.* of observation, body's declination and observer's latitude being known; distinguished from *altitude azimuth* in which altitude, declination, and latitude are the elements involved. **T. ball,** a globe-shaped signal dropped from a prominent pole or signal yard in a seaport for the purpose of indicating an even hour of *Greenwich mean t.* Prior to present general use of *radio t. signals,* it provided a convenient means for checking ships' chronometers. **T. charter,** *see* CHARTER. **T. of flight,** *see* FLIGHT. **T. policy,** *see* POLICY. **T. reversible,** *see* REVERSIBLE. **T. sight,** observation of the altitude of a celestial body for purpose of determining solar or sidereal *t.* at place of observer. Also, such observation in connection with determination of longitude and also called *longitude by chronometer; cf.* LONGITUDE. **T. signal,** chiefly for providing ships with correct Greenwich mean *t., radio t. signals* now to a great extent have displaced the *t. ball, t. gun,* etc.; *see* **R. time signal** *in* RADIO. Also, in flag-signaling by International Code, a hoist of 5 flags of which the uppermost is *T,* denoting signal indicates hours and minutes of clock *t.; as, T2145* (24-hour system). **T. triangle,** in nautical astronomy, spherical triangle formed by polar distance and zenith distance of body observed, with colatitude of observer as measured on the meridian. So named from its use in determining body's *hour angle,* or that at the *pole,* given the three sides referred to. **True t.,** that indicated by the hour angle of a celestial body other than the moon at a given place; *apparent solar t.,* or that shown on a sun dial. **Universal t.,** chiefly among astronomers, identical with *Greenwich civil t.,* or *Greenwich mean t.; cf.* G.C.T. **Zone t.,** mean solar *t.* of standard meridians 15°, or 1 hour of longitude, apart, with *Greenwich meridian* taken as zero. As local civil *t.*, its use extends as nearly as practicable 7½° east and west of each standard meridian and is expressed from 0 to 24 hours, midnight to midnight, with identifying number of *zone* concerned. Thus, an entry in ship's log noting an occurrence at 7.15 p.m. in longitude 50° W. is written *1915* (+ *3*), or at 9.20 a.m. in longitude 130° E., as *0920* (− *9*). Within 7½° east and west of Greenwich meridian, zone is indicated as −*0* and +*0*, respectively. Advantage of *zone t.* as standard use in a group or fleet of ships has led to its adoption by most navies and also by many trans-oceanic merchant vessels; *esp.* since its practical value, chiefly in that of uniformity, was shown experimentally in convoy and naval tactics during World War II.

TIMENOGUY. (Pron. ti-men'-o-guy) A piece of rope or small line set taut between two points for preventing running gear from fouling or coming in contact with other parts in ship's rigging. A *crane-line* or *traveling lizard* in a purchase; *see last definition of* **Crane-l.** *in* LINE.[1]

TINDAL. (East Indies origin) In a lascar crew, a boatswain's mate or assistant to the deck *serang; cf.* SERANG. Also, *tendal.*

TIP. The point, extremity, or end part; as, *t.* of a propeller-blade; *t.* of a headland; *t.* of a nozzle (in an oil-burner of a boiler-furnace). *Esp.* in Great Britain, a hoisting-scaffold by which a railway wagon is raised and dumped of its contents into a chute leading to a vessel's hold, as in loading coal. Also called *staith*. Usually in *pl.*, an elevated runway equipped with chutes or other arrangement for dumping cars as above. Amount of *change of trim;* as a *t.* of 7 inches; *see* TRIM. To tilt or cant; to cause to fall by upsetting. To cause a difference in forward and after drafts of a vessel, as by a change in disposition of cargo or ballast in the fore-and-aft line. **T. clearance,** distance by which propeller-blade *tips* clear vessel's hull or stern frame in revolving. To **t. over,** to upset or capsize, as a boat. To **t. the grampus,** to administer a sousing or ducking to a lookout man guilty of falling asleep on duty. (Archaic)

TIPPING. Tilting or canting. **T. brackets,** same as *tripping brackets; see* TRIPPING. **T. center,** that about which vessel *tips* in a change of trim. It is the center of gravity of water surface plane corresponding to a given draft, or roughly, mid-point between ship's perpendiculars, the midship point. **T. damage,** in shipbuilding, that resulting from faulty launching calculations, usually in the matter of an improper water level, which allows vessel's after end to sink deeper than required, thus bringing about a *t.* or tilting effect and consequent abnormal local stress in the hull. Such damage, of the bot-

tom-crushing type, always occurs forward of vessel's longitudinal center of gravity (in the usual stern-first launching) for the reason that lack of buoyancy in hull's after end fails in its supporting and lifting effects, and so an even and easy departure from the *ways,*—supreme requisites in a successful launching. **T. scale,** tabulated information giving number of inches of change in vessel's draft due to filling or emptying each ballast tank, fuel tank, boiler, etc.; also that due to loading or discharging a unit weight of cargo (usually 100 tons) in or from the various holds or compartments. Generally takes the following form: *Filling No. 1 D.B. Tank, sinks 10 inches Forward, rises 2 inches Aft,* etc. *Cf.* TRIM.

TITANIC. White Star trans-Atlantic passenger liner which foundered after collision with an iceberg, April 15, 1912, on her maiden voyage, from Southampton toward New York. Out of passengers and crew numbering 2,207, resulting loss of life was 1,517. Vessel was largest of her time, 882 feet in length and triple-screw driven by wing reciprocating and midship direct turbine engines. This notable disaster gave rise to the International *Convention for Safety of Life at Sea* first held at London, England, in 1914, for the purpose of taking steps toward the prevention of a recurrence of such catastrophe; *see* **I. Convention for Safety of Life at Sea** *in* INTERNATIONAL.

TOADFISH. Kind of non-edible fish having a broad flat head, wide mouth, large vertical fins at entrance to head, and both dorsal and ventral fringes. More commonly found along U.S. Atlantic coast, a species of the family also is found on the southwest Pacific coast and called *midshipman; see* MIDSHIPMAN.

TOAD'S BACK. In older square-rigged vessels, an iron step or socket in which a *trysail-mast* was stepped in its place close to and abaft a lowermast.

TOE. Extreme edge of the flange of a structural part, such as a beam, stringer, angle-bar, etc. Point of the palm, or fluke, of an anchor. **T.-cleat,** piece of wood serving as a step for holding lower end of a rowlock in place, as in a boat. **T. link,** in the *chains* of older ships, lowest link, which was secured to both planking and a frame-timber by the chain-bolt; *see* **C.-plate** *in* CHAIN.

TOGGLE. Piece of wood or metal fitted crosswise in end of a rope or a chain for purpose of quickly engaging or disengaging with a link, ring, or an eye; any small button, pin, knotted end of a rope, etc., serving such purpose, as that in a *becket* for holding a coil of rope clear of the deck, for connecting flags, etc. A movable barb in a harpoon for engaging the flesh and so preventing withdrawal of instrument from victim's body. **Blubber-t.,** *see* **Blubber-f.** *in* FID. **T.-bolt,** also *t.-pin,* a bolt or pin fitted with a movable inset piece of metal, or *t.,* at or near its inserted end. *T.* serves as a T-shaped locking device for securing bolt in place. **T.-hook,** a grab-hook fitted with a securing pin across or through both toes, or points; *see* **Grab-h.** *in* HOOK. **T.-iron,** a harpoon having a hingèd or movable barb; *see above remarks.* **T.-lanyard,** line in which a *t.* is fitted at its end or one in which an eye engages a *t.; a becket.* **T.-pin,** *see* **T.-bolt. T'd sheepshank,** *see* SHEEPSHANK.

TOLERANCE. Allowed variation from exact conformity to specified weight, dimensions, standard, etc., as provided in naval regulations concerning stores and supplies, fittings, machinery parts, etc.

TOLL. A charge or due paid by owner of merchandise carried or handled via a canal, dock, wharf, etc., or a lighter. Charge or charges levied on a vessel for passage through a canal, such being payable according to schedule authorized by government of country or states concerned, *e.g.,* whether vessel is cargo-laden or light, is carrying passengers or not, is naval or merchant type, etc. To scatter *bait* on the surface as a lure for capture of fish, as with use of *t.-bait,* or *tolling.*

TOLLAGE. Charge or due made as a *toll;* the toll itself.

TOM. In shipbuilding, a short *shore* or distance-piece, such as that set between frames during their erection. Piece of timber fitted as a brace or chock for securing a boiler, heavy machinery, etc., or a block of cargo against shifting due to motion of vessel in a seaway. **Long t.,** *see* LONG. **To t. down,** to hold down or secure a piece, tier, or block of cargo by use of *toms* fitted to extend from such cargo to a deck-beam, beam-stringer, etc.

TOMAHAWK. Kind of hammer used in smoothing off or finishing a rivet head in heavier watertight work. To finish and make a rivet watertight as by use of a *t.*

TOMCOD. Small gadoid edible fish found in northern latitudes of Pacific and Atlantic. Classified as of genus *Microgadus* (= small cod) greatly resembles the common *cod,* except in size.

TOMPION. *See* TAMPION.

TON. (Var. of *tun,* from A.S. *tunne,* a ton) Unit of *tonnage,* which may be that of weight, as in *deadweight* tonnage, or *burden,* and *displacement;* or that of capacity, as in *gross* and *net* tonnage. In the former, it is equal to *2240 lbs.;* in the latter, *100 cubic feet; cf.* BURDEN; DEADWEIGHT; TONNAGE. **Freight t.,** *see* **M. cargo** *and* **M. ton** *in* MEASUREMENT. **Long t.** = 2240 lbs. (avoirdupois) **Revenue t.,** *see* TONNAGE. **Shipping t.,** same as *freight t.* **Short t.** = 2000 lbs.; chiefly a local marketing unit, as in U.S. and Canada. **T's per inch immersion,** usually abbrev. *T.P.I.,* number of *tons* weight which, when

taken aboard, will increase vessel's *mean draft* by one inch. Also referred to as *t's per inch sinkage* and *t's per inch.*

TONGUE. A block of hardwood fitted in the throat of a gaff to bear the thrust of latter against mast. In old hemp-rigging days, piece of rope spliced into a shroud or backstay to form a strop or eye for hooking on a block. Upper part or piece of a mast composed of several pieces or scarfed lengths. Raised section in a propeller- or stern-post for connecting with a vertical-plate keel. A long narrow point projecting from a coastline.

TONNAGE. Whole amount of shipping of a nation, a line, a port, etc., passing through a canal, engaged in whaling, etc. Weight of cargo carried in a vessel, expressed in *tons. T.* of war-vessels is given in *displacement tons; see* DISPLACEMENT. Merchant vessels are described as being of certain *deadweight* capacity, or *tons burden* in older use, which means that craft in question is capable of carrying a load of a certain number of tons of 2240 lbs. as limited by allowed depth of immersion, or her authorized *load-line;* also, as having a certain *gross t.,* or a total internal cubic measurement of a given number of *tons,* or units of 100 cubic feet, *less* such space or spaces in which no fuel, cargo, or stores is carried. From the official *gross t.,* or *gross registered t.,* the *net registered t.* is arrived at by deducting certain spaces, including crew's quarters, storerooms, chart-room, wheel-house, superstructures for use of passengers, and a generous allowance for propulsion-plant according to internationally recognized rules governing ship measurement for *t.* Net registered *t.* is that upon which dues or taxes are charged, as a general rule, and also is a ready basis for estimating vessel's available cargo space or bulk capacity. The older word *tunnage* appears to have been in use in the 16th. century for indicating a ship's hold capacity for carrying *tunnes* (later *tuns*) of wine. The *tun,* or cask of 252 old English wine gallons, with its contents, closely approximated the *long ton* weight, 2240 lbs., and it occupied a space of nearly 40 cubic feet. Hence the relation of the *ton burden* and the *shipping ton.* **Panama Canal t.,** as that determined by the Canal authorities, similar to *Suez Canal t.;* resulting *net t.* is about 25% more than vessel's *net registered t.; see* **Suez Canal t. Registered t.,** official *gross* and *net t.* as shown in vessel's certificate of registry. **Revenue t.,** chiefly in use in U.S.A., a more or less arbitrary commercial unit which varies with different ports, types of cargo handled, trade concerned, and with different carriers. It may, however, be adopted as standard measurement or weight by carriers at a particular port engaged in handling similar commodities in the same trade. Generally, it may be termed a variation of the *shipping ton.* **Suez Canal t.,** that on which dues for passage through this waterway are determined. The *Moorsom* system of *t.* measurement, or that in which 100 cubic feet = 1 ton, is used but with certain differences in deductions from *gross t.* which give a *net t.* of about 30% greater than the internationally recognized *registered t.* appearing in a vessel's *register* or *certificate of registry* (the ship's title deed). **Thames t.,** that adopted by the Royal Thames Yacht Club in 1855, and to a certain extent still in use; equal to the product of *length minus breadth* x *breadth* x ½ *breadth* divided by *94.* **T. certificate,** *see* CERTIFICATE. **T. breadth,** that taken at each of the several stations designated for *t.* measurement. It is the horizontal distance between inside faces of opposite *frames* or, where present, those of opposite *ceiling battens;* or, in wooden vessels, between inner surfaces of *ceiling.* **T. deck,** that below which *under deck t.* is measured. It is second deck from below in vessels having two or more continuous decks. **T. depth,** *see* DEPTH. **T. duty,** taxes or dues levied on a vessel for maintenance of buoys, dredged channels, docks, etc., at a particular port. A tax levied by customs authorities on a foreign-built vessel upon changing her flag to that of country concerned. **T. length,** inside clear measurement along center fore-and-aft line of upper surface of *t. deck.* **T. opening,** for purpose of securing exemption from measurement for *t.,* a hatchway or other opening provided with non-watertight temporary means for closing, such as a bridge-deck entrance partly fitted with removable planks or a shelter deck hatchway with wooden covers only. **T. plan,** for reference purposes in calculating vessel's *t., body plan,* usually accompanied by the *sheer plan,* with all necessary dimensions and areas. **T. scale,** tabulated values of *deadweight* or *displacement t.,* or both, corresponding to all drafts between *light* and *load* lines. **Tween-deck t.,** aggregate space between decks above the *t. deck.* **Under-deck t.,** vessel's cubic capacity below *t. deck.*

TOOLS, NON-SPARKING. As required in oil-tank vessels, hammers, wrenches, etc., used in opening and closing tank covers, iron doors, etc., connecting transfer hose, and in other work in vicinity of or connected with the petroleum cargo. Usually made of bronze or beryllium copper, they will not give off sparks when knocked against steel, thus providing a safety measure against ignition of explosive gases.

TOOTHED WHALES. *See* WHALE.

TOP. In square-rigged vessels, a platform at a lowermasthead, usually semicircular in shape with curved side forward, fixed on the *trestle-trees,* or approximately at same height as eyes of the shrouds. Serves to spread topmast shrouds and as a working floor for men engaged at rigging repairs, splicing, etc. Formerly, in naval ships a *t.* also was used as a

place of vantage for sharpshooters and, as steam power displaced the sail, it developed into the *fighting top* in which at least one gun was mounted, the platform itself being circular and protected all round by an iron or steel bulwark. Designating something fixed, lying above or over, or covering, an object; as, *t.-mark* (of a buoy); *t. tier; t. timber; tank t.* To raise a boom or a yard at one end; usually with *up,* as, to *t. up the main yard.* To complete or finish by placing a final tier of cargo, by carefully running a liquid into a tank, etc.; usually with *off,* as, to *t. off* bulk grain with bagged cargo; to *t. off* a tank of oil (in loading). **Fighting t.,** *see above remarks.* **Half t.,** *see* HALF. **Tank t.,** *see* TANK. **T.-and-butt planking,** *see* **Anchor-stock p.** *in* PLANKING. **T. and topgallant,** in full rig or complete array. *(Archaic)* **T.-armor,** protective railing of metal, canvas, or netting around or across after side of a *t.* **T.-block,** large single block placed at lowermast cap for leading the mast-rope (or *t.-rope*) from sheave in heel of topmast when *striking,* or sending down, that spar. Upper part of a propeller-shaft bearing. **T.-burton,** *see* BURTON. **T.-chain,** *see* CHAIN. **T.-cloth,** canvas cover over the hammocks formerly placed in a *t.* as protection for men there stationed in action. **T.-gun,** a rapid-fire, or quick-firing, gun mounted in a war-vessel's *t.;* a *fighting-t. gun.* **T. hamper,** *see* HAMPER. **T. keel,** upper timber in a keel composed of two lengths, one above the other. Both timbers are through-bolted together and butts of each staggered for continuity of strength. **T.-light,** *see* LIGHT[1]. **T.-lining,** a chafing-cloth sewed on after surface of a topsail for protection against wear and tear of sail against rim of the *t.* **T.-mark,** conspicuous shape or identifying marker surmounting a beacon or a buoy, such as a ball, cage, diamond, cone, triangle, etc. **T.-netting,** same as *t.-armor, q.v.* **T. pendant,** same as *masthead pendant; see* PENDANT. **T. piece,** also called *t. timber; see* TIMBER. **T.-rail,** a guard-rail, usually consisting of a stout iron rod or bar, parcelled and tarred, extending across after end of a *t.* in larger vessels. **T.-rope,** same as *mast-rope; see* MAST. **T. tackle,** same as *t. burton; see* BURTON.

TOPE. *See* **Oil s.** *and* **Tope** *in* SHARK.

TOPGALLANT. (A.S. *top,* top; M.E. *galante,* noble, stately, lofty) Originally and prior to use of mast of that name, *top galante,* or top of a second mast (*topmast*) which appeared above the *top castel,* or fighting-top at upper extremity of the single mast, in larger ships of the 16th. century. Hence, the word's later meaning of making a brave or gallant show or attaining the highest pitch or summit, as in "the very top-gallant of all our glory" (1666). In a square-rigged vessel, mast, sail, rigging, or yard next above the *upper topsail* or the *topmast;* also written *top-gallant;* as, *t.-mast; t.-sheet; t.-brace; t.-stay;* etc. Designating a part of greater height; as, *t. forecastle*; *t. bulwarks*. **Top and t.**, *see* TOP. **T. rail,** in sailing-vessels, the main bulwark rail which caps the *t. bulwark,* or that portion of bulwarks above the *pin-rail.* (See *Topgallant* as a prefixed term under following captions: BREEZE; BULWARK; FORECASTLE; GALE; MAST; RIGGING; SAIL; SHROUD)

TOPHEAVY. (Also written *top-heavy*)   *See* HEAVY.

TOPMAN. A sailor or a marine stationed in one of the *tops;* a *fore t., main t.,* or a *mizzen t. (Older naval usage)* Also, *topsman.*

TOPMAST. Mast extending above a lowermast; second mast above deck; *see* MAST. **Telescoping t.,** *see* **Telescope m.** *in* MAST. **T. hounding,** *see* HOUNDING. **T. shrouds,** standing rigging leading from each side of a *top* to the *topmasthead* in square rig, or from the cross-trees in fore-and-aft rig. In some smaller sailing craft, they are spread by long cross-trees or a single cross-tree and set up at vessel's rail, thus providing stiffening for the *t.* In the old sailing-navy days, *t. shrouds,* of which there were usually four in number on each side, were set up as stiffeners for the *t.,* as well as affording means, with their ratlines, for climbing aloft. In merchant ships, however, the latter use only was considered, since the staying power of shrouds spread from the customary comparatively narrow *top* was a negligible quantity. *See* SHROUD. *Cf.* BACKSTAY.

TOPPING. Act of lifting, supporting, or tilting a boom or a yard at one end; *see* TOP. Usually with *off,* act of completing a vessel's lading, as when full cargo can not be taken in because of limited depth of water, ship being moved to a deeper berth in order to finish loading; *also see remarks in* TOP. **Boom t.-lift,** *see* LIFT. **Boot-t.,** *see* BOOT-TOPPING. **T.-lift,** *see* LIFT.

TOPSAIL. Sail set on a *topmast;* that next above a *course,* in square rig, as *fore lower t.;* or one set above a gaff sail, in fore-and-aft rig, as *main-gaff t.* Original centuries-old *t.* was hoisted on the topmast and spread between lower yard and the *t'gallants'l.* It was called a *single t.* subsequent to its division into *double t's,* as distinguishing it from the latter spread. To an American shipmaster goes the credit of displacing the old *single t.* with an *upper* and a *lower t. (double-t. rig),* the former bent to a hoisting yard, latter to a stationary one. He was Frederick Howes of Brewster, Massachusetts, who thus rigged his vessel, the ship *Climax* of Boston, in 1853. Chief advantages of Howes' innovation were a saving of time and labor in reefing,—an operation notoriously frequent with the old *t's,* whose cumbersome area and usual quadruplicate array of reef-points demanded the maintenance of a heavy crew, especially so in the "driving" seamanship displayed by the clippers in their subsequent speed competition with the growing

steam tonnage on ocean routes. By simply taking in an *upper t.,* canvas thus was reduced to a *double-reefed t.,* now represented in the *lower t. Cf.* SAIL. **Club t.,** a *gaff t.* fitted with a light spar, or *club,* extending a few feet along upper part of the luff for purpose of increasing hoist of the sail above the truck. **Gaff t.,** *see* GAFF. **Jack t.,** *see* JACK. **Jib t.,** *see* JIB. **To pay with the t. sheet,** to leave an unpaid debt behind upon one's discharge from a vessel. **Rolling t.,** *see* CUNNINGHAM PATENT REEF. **T. haul!,** *see* **Mains'l haul!** *in* MAINSAIL. **T. schooner,** *see* SCHOONER. **T. yard,** spar spreading the head of a square *t.* It is a hoisting yard when bearing a *single t.* With *double t's,* either an *upper t.* or a *lower t.* yard, the former being hoisted in setting sail, the latter stationary.

TOPSIDE. On or above a weather deck or a superstructural deck. Usually in *pl.,* portion of vessel's outer surface above waterline. **T. plating,** that constituting outer skin or surface between ship's load-line and upper extremity of the hull. **T. strake,** *see* STRAKE. **T. tanks,** *see* **Side t's** *in* TANK.

TOPTAIL. To turn the tail up and out of water, as a whale in making a quick dive upon being attacked.

TORNADO. On West African coast, a violent squall from shore, followed by heavy rain. Occurs in March to June and October to November. Any *cyclone* of small diameter and of most violent character.

TORPEDO. A genus of the *ray* family of fishes containing the *electric,* or *t., ray; see* RAY. The high-speed, self-propelled, underwater explosive dirigible projected from a war-vessel against an enemy. **Otter-t.,** *see* OTTER. **T.-tube,** *see* **L.-tube** *in* LAUNCHING. (Also see *torpedo* as a combining term in OFFICER; RAFT; STERN)

TORRID ZONE. *See* ZONE.

TORSION-METER. An instrument for determining *shaft horsepower* developed by an engine; *see* **Shaft hp** *in* HORSEPOWER. Also called *torsimeter, torsiometer.*

TOSS. *Cf.* **To toss oars** *in* OAR.

TOTAL. (L.L. *totalis,* all, entire)   Complete; absolute. **T. eclipse;** *see* ECLIPSE. **T. loss,** *see* LOSS.

TOUCH. Widest part of a plank in *top-and-butt* or *anchor-stock* system of side-planking; *cf.* **Anchor-stock p.** *in* PLANKING. Angle of turn of curved or knuckled timbers in a vessel's stern or counter. To steer close enough to the wind as to shake the weather leech of a sail; as, to *keep the royal touching.* To graze or temporarily come in contact with the sea-bottom, as a vessel in sailing; to collide lightly with a wharf, another ship, etc., as in moving vessel in harbor. To make a comparatively brief call at a port, as for bunkering, taking on passengers, or discharging a small amount of cargo; usually with *at*, as, *we t'd at Gibraltar.* To **t. and go, in** sailing, to graze or lightly contact bottom without appreciable lessening of speed; also referred to as *scraping the bottom.* To **t. and trade,** as usually limited to licensed fishing-craft, to carry cargo to or from a foreign port or ports while en route to or from the fishing grounds. U.S. navigation laws require that a vessel intending to engage in such activity shall obtain permission from the collector of customs of district vessel departs from. *(R.S. 4364)* **T'd bill of health,** same as *suspected bill; see* **B. of health** *in* BILL. To **t. up a sail,** to stretch and make the head of a square sail snugger in appearance, by taking in on the earings and renewing robands, as necessary; to tauten the gaskets on a furled or stowed sail; to *snug up* a sail. To **t. the wind,** to sail as close to wind as possible without unduly shaking the canvas spread.

TOURIST CLASS PASSENGER. *See* PASSENGER.

TOW.[1] (A.S. *togian,* to drag or pull) To draw along through the water, as a vessel pulling a barge, raft, another vessel, etc. That which is *towed;* as, *we picked up a t.* Act or condition of being *towed;* as, *barges taken in tow.* A *t.* or craft taken *in t.* has been extended to denote also a number of barges, scows, etc., being *pushed* by a powered vessel or *tug,* as is common practice on rivers and in sheltered waters, *esp.* in U.S.A. Generally where liability for collision damage is in question, the *towing* vessel with her *t.* is considered a single vessel. **T.-boat,** powered boat or vessel designed for *towing* work; a *tug* or *tugboat;* usually written *towboat.* **T.-hook,** *see* **T.-hook** *in* TOWING. **T.-iron,** *see* IRON. **T.-line,** same as **t.-rope. T. mast,** *see* MAST. **T'path,** track or path traveled by horses or men in *towing* canal boats; also *towing-path.* **T.-rope,** also *t'rope,* hawser or line used in *towing* a vessel or vessels; *cf.* **Insurance h.** *in* HAWSER. Also *t.-line* or *t'line.*

TOW.[2] Short coarse or broken fibers separated from the better material through the hackling process in the initial stage of flax or hemp rope manufacture. *Cf.* OAKUM; HACKLE.

TOWAGE. Act of *towing,* which includes assisting vessels in berthing, turning, shifting, etc., in harbor; also, the *towing* of a vessel in or out of port, through a narrow or dangerous passage, etc., in expediting her voyage, as opposed to *salvage.* Fee or charges made for such service; *t. dues.*

TOWER. T. crane, *see* CRANE. **T. mast,** *see* MAST.

TOWING. Act of one who, or that which, *tows;* towage. **T. bridle,** consists of two parts, or legs, of chain or hawser attached to end of *towline,* each secured to bitts on either quarter of *t. vessel* or either bow of *vessel towed. Cf.* BRIDLE. **T. bitts,** see BITT. **T. buoy,** also **t. spar;** *see* SPAR. **T. hook,** as more commonly used by towboats in Europe, heavy steel

hook to which the towline is secured. It usually is fitted to turn on a vertical axis, is provided with a shock-absorbing compressive spring, and may be disengaged from towline by knocking up its securing *tripper* or *keeper* which holds point of hook in working position, thus allowing it to drop or open by its hinged shank. Also called *tow-hook.* **T. lights,** *see Rule 3,* REGULATIONS FOR PREVENTING COLLISIONS. **T. machine,** also *t. winch,* as used in heavy long-distance *t.* at sea, a winch, usually steam-driven, to which a wire *t.-hawser* is attached. It automatically takes care of increasing and decreasing stresses in the *towline* consequent to surging or heaving of the sea by easing out line as a certain maximum tension is reached, recovering such length of line as tension relaxes, so that length of hawser in use is as little interfered with as possible. A later type of the machine is known as the *automatic tension engine,* in which a practically constant tension is maintained in the *t.* hawser with additional advantage of employing a wire of about one-half the strength and one-third the length of hawser required in an ordinary *t. machine.* **T.-net,** or *tow-net,* a fine-meshed net bridled to a towline, such as is used by naturalists in capturing surface specimens of plant and animal life. **T.-rail,** also *t.-beam; see* RAIL. **T. signals,** those listed in International Code for use between a *vessel towing* and a vessel being *towed;* any pre-arranged system of signaling adopted by a *towboat* and her *tow.* **T.-timber,** a kevel head, or timber rising above deck, used for making fast a *towline;* a *t.-bitt; see* **T. head** *in* TIMBER.

TOWROPE RESISTANCE. *See* RESISTANCE.

T. R. Abbrev. *tons registered;* as, a *ship of 1700 t.r.*

TRACK. Path or course of a vessel as indicated on a chart; wake of a vessel. A rail on which hanks of a sail travel, as on a gaff or a mast; *see* RAILWAY, *also remarks in* RAIL. To delineate, as on a chart, the path of a ship or of a hurricane, a stretch of submarine cable, or a line of soundings. **Bottle-t.,** as indicated on a chart, path followed by a drifting bottle thrown overboard for purpose of estimating set and drift of surface current or currents. *Cf.* BOTTLE PAPERS. **Hurricane t.,** *see* HURRICANE. **Sail-t.,** *see* RAILWAY. **Storm t.,** *see* STORM. **T.-boat,** a barge or other inland water craft that is towed from the bank of a canal or river. **T. chart,** a small-scale general chart on which is drawn the path or *t.* followed on a voyage; also, a blank, or *skeleton,* chart used for same purpose. **T.-road,** a towpath; *see* TOW.

TRADE. (From Old Teut. source, meaning a path, track, or step) Waterborne commerce; exchange of merchandise by one country or port with another; carriage of goods by ship to or from a designated country, region, or port; as, *China t.; Mediterranean t.; Calcutta t.* To exchange or barter with; to engage in purchase and/or sale of goods; as, *our* *ships t. with the natives; U.S. trades extensively with Britain.* **Coasting t.,** *see* COASTING. **Colonial t.,** commerce between a nation and her colonies overseas. The term often is applied to that between Great Britain and Australia or New Zealand, or both. **Domestic t.,** *see* DOMESTIC TRADE. **Foreign t.,** *see* FOREIGN. **Home t.,** *see* HOME. **T. route,** sea lane or track customarily followed by merchant vessels. **T. winds,** commonly called *the trades,* those blowing from an approximately constant direction, (*trade* formerly meant *track* or *path*) or *track-winds,* found over several extensive oceanic regions; *esp.,* the *Northeast* and the *Southeast t. winds* of tropical and subtropical latitudes in the Atlantic and Pacific and, also, the South Indian Ocean's *Southeast t's.* These result from flow of cool surface air toward the equator, Earth's rotation accounting for the easterly element in their direction. Off the Portuguese coast a wind having a constant northerly direction and often reaching a moderate gale force prevails during summer. It is called the *Portuguese t.* Also, the prevailing westerly winds of higher latitudes,—often called *roaring forties* in this connection,—particularly those of the southern hemisphere, have been termed *t. winds, brave west winds, mollyhawk t's, easting bullies,* etc., by sailing-ship men experienced in those regions.

TRADER. A vessel engaged on a *trading voyage;* a merchantman; as, a *West Coast t.*

TRADES, The. *See* **T. winds** *in* TRADE.

TRAFFIC SIGNALS. Flags, shapes, lights, etc., displayed at a canal or dock entrance, in a harbor, or other place frequented by shipping, in accordance with a recognized code or system, for purposes of directing vessels with respect to entering a lock, berthing, opening bridges, anchoring in special areas, and the like; control signals or specially marked buoys, etc.

TRAIL. (M.E. *trailen,* to draw or drag; to tow) **T.-board,** in older sailing-vessels, an ornamented plank on either side of the cutwater, serving as a brace or stiffener for the figure-head. **T.-knee,** one of a pair of knees on either side of the cutwater for stiffening or laterally supporting the latter. (*Older wooden vessels*) **T.-line,** also *trailing-line; see* LINE.[1] **T.-net,** a drag-net; last net in a fleet of *drift-nets; see* NET.[2] To **t. oars,** *see* OAR.

TRAIN. To bring to bear; to direct or aim; as, to *t.* a heavy gun (*esp.* in azimuth); to *t.* a telescope toward a distant object. The repair and supply ships, oil-tank vessels, hospital ships, etc., constituting the sustaining force of a naval fleet; *sea-t.; see* **S.-train** *in* SEA. **T. ferry,** *see* **C.-ferry** *in* CAR. **T. oil,** *see* OIL. **T.-tackle,** a purchase for running out and training guns, as in former war-vessels; also *training-tackle; training-rope; t.-rope.*

TRAINER. In U.S. navy, member of a gun's crew who directs the *training* of the weapon.

TRAINING. Act of one who, or that which, directs or *trains.* **T.-ship,** a school-ship; *see* SCHOOL. **T.-tackle,** *see* **T.-tackle** *in* TRAIN. **T.-wall,** a jetty, wingdam, pier of masonry or dumped stone, etc., for deflecting the current, as in a river or harbor; *cf.* **Training-j.** *in* JETTY; REVETMENT.

TRAMMEL. (Fr. *trémail,* a net) A fixed gill-net, loosely mounted for entangling fish; *esp.,* a set of three parallel nets, middle one of which is fine-meshed and loosely hung, the others coarse-meshed and stretched out. Fish entering from either side push fine-mesh middle net into one of the larger meshes of outer net and thus become entangled in the bight of fine-meshed netting.

TRAMONTANA. (It.) A cold, dry, violent wind blowing down the Adriatic Sea from the Alpine country. Frequently occurring in winter, it appears as a southerly extension of the *Bora,* or wind of gale force from N. to N.E. in the Gulf of Venice region. Also called *gli Secchi* (dry winds) on eastern Italian shore.

TRAMP. Short for *tramp steamer;* a powered cargo vessel that engages in any trade or run for which freight is offering; distinguished from a *cargo-liner,* or vessel plying a regular run. Often called *ocean t.,* such vessel's occupation is termed *tramping.*

TRANSATLANTIC. (L. *trans,* across, over; *Atlantic Ocean*) Lying or belonging beyond the Atlantic; extending across or crossing the Atlantic; as, a *t. telegraph cable;* a *t. liner.* In popular usage, the latter term usually is limited to a passenger vessel plying between principal ports of North America and Europe.

TRANSFER. Chiefly in naval tactical terminology, distance made to right or left of original course after helm has been put hard over (35° rudder angle) and vessel has swung 8 point, or 90°, in making a turn. A local train-ferry, barge, or car-float for conveying railway cars or trucks, as across a river, etc. The loading or discharging of cargo, as from or to a wharf, etc.

TRANSHIP. Var. of *transship.*

TRANSIRE. (L. = to pass; to pass through or across) A customs document issued at a port of entry to coasting vessels for entry and clearance uses. It describes the cargo, its consignors and consignees, port of destination, etc. In effect its authorizes removal of dutiable goods from port of entry to another port or place.

TRANSIT. (L. *transitus,* a crossing; from *transire,* to pass through or across) Passage across, through, or over; as, *t.,* culmination, or meridian passage of a heavenly body; Panama Canal *t.; t.* of a star over the field of a telescope. A surveying instrument for precisely measuring horizontal angles in localities of varying elevation; also, the astronomer's *t. instrument,* or telescope mounted in the plane of the meridian, by which the exact time of culmination or meridian passage of a heavenly body is observed and hence determination of precise clock time. *Merchandise* is said to be *in t.* during the period commencing with delivery to *carrier* and ending with final delivery to *consignee.* Range lights, or other leading marks are said to be *in t.* when *in range,* or exactly in line; *cf.* **R. light** *in* RANGE. **Lower t.,** meridian passage of a heavenly body either *below the pole* or across that part or continuation of the meridian lying below observer's horizon; opposed to *upper t.,* or passage over that part of meridian *above the pole* containing observer's zenith. Interval between lower and upper *t's,* in the case of a fixed star, expressed in *mean solar time,* is 11 hrs. 58 min. 02 secs., very nearly. **T. cargo,** that remaining aboard for discharge at another port. **T. circle,** *see* **M. circle** *in* MERIDIAN. **T. duty,** charge levied on goods by a country through which they are routed for delivery in another. **T. port,** one at which cargo is transferred to another vessel, barges, etc., for final transportation to destination; a *transshipment port.* **Upper t.,** also called *superior t.* as opposed to *inferior t.* or lower culmination; *see* **Lower t.**

TRANSMITTER, RANGE. *See* RANGE.

TRANSOM. (M.E. *traunsum;* from L. *transtrum,* a cross-piece) The rib or frame unit, constituting aftermost transverse strength member of the hull proper and to which are secured the various timbers or structural members forming vessel's *counter,* or part projecting or overhanging abaft her stern-post; also called *t. frame.* Any transverse structural member attached to the stern-post. In smaller wooden vessels, upper part of a projecting stern often is called the *t.,* and space below deck abaft the stern-post referred to as *the t.* A long seat or couch in a cabin, usually fitted with drawers beneath; a *settee.* **Deck t.,** also called *t. beam,* any deck beam connecting the *t. frames* or fitted athwartship in the *t. space,* or that abaft vessel's stern-post; in square-sterned wooden craft, aftermost beam or that supporting after ends of deck planking. **Main t.,** *t. beam* connecting the *t. frames* in way of the stern-post. The deck-planking is secured to this beam. Any thwartship structural member supporting the deck, however, in whatever arrangement of framing, etc., in the structure abaft stern-post, is termed a **t. beam.** In the conventional overhanging counter of smaller steel vessels, the *cant-beams* extend radially from the *main t.* to meet the *cant-frames,* while forming deck-plating support. **T. board,** that forming the stern of a "square-ended" boat; a back-rest across the after seat or *stern sheets* in a boat. **T. floor,** one of the deep floor-plates at after end of the main

body; *esp.,* that floor which is secured to the stern-post; *see* **Transom f.** *in* FLOOR. **T. frame,** in steel vessels, aftermost frame in the main body, or that secured to head of the stern-post; generally, the unit composed of *t. frame, t. beam,* and *t. floor.* (*See opening remarks re t.*) In wooden craft, horizontal timber secured to head of the stern-post and serving as a butting base for the smaller fashion timbers or frames which shape the stern and counter. **T. knee,** one of the knees connecting a *t. beam* to a side frame timber. **T. plate,** same as *t. floor.* **T. stern,** the "square" or "flat" stern or counter, usually sloping outward from the stern-post, as distinguished from a *sharp* or *rounded* stern. **Wing t.,** in wooden vessels, as distinguished from a *deck t.,* the *t. frame,* q.v.

TRANSPORT. (L. *trans,* across; *portare,* to carry) A vessel employed by a government in carrying troops, military equipment, stores, etc.; a *troopship;* as, an *army t.;* a *naval t.* To convey from one place to another, as goods or persons by ship. **Ministry of T.,** in Great Britain, that government department concerned with matters pertaining to the country's *merchant marine,* including certificating of personnel, classification and periodical survey of ships, government assignment of tonnage, etc. It supplants, in general, the former Marine Department of the Board of Trade and is headed by the *Minister of T.*

TRANSPORTATION. Act of transporting; conveyance; state of being transported. The charge for such conveyance; a ticket or pass authorizing one to travel, as by ship. **Military Sea T. Service,** established Oct. 1, 1949, under U.S. navy control, for providing, as carrying agent, *ocean t.* for all personnel and materiel of the Department of Defense. It supplants the *Naval T. Service* and that part of *Army T. Corps* concerned with ocean shipping.

TRANSSHIPMENT. Act of *transshipping* or transferring cargo from one vessel to another for further transportation, in accordance with practice customary in the particular trade or with procedure stipulated in the contract of affreightment.

TRANSVERSE. (L. *trans,* across; *vertere,* to turn) Lying at right angles with the fore-and-aft line; crosswise; athwart; as opposed to *longitudinal* or *fore-and-aft, esp.* in structural terminology. **T. framing,** in shipbuilding, system of framing in which pairs of ribs, or *frames,* laterally extend from vessel's keel outward and thence upward to form contour of ship's bottom and sides. A *t. frame* unit essentially consists of a pair of "ribs" meeting and joined to the keel and, at their upper ends connected by a deck-beam, plane of the whole set-up being at a right angle with ship's keel. *See* FRAME. **T. bulkhead,** *see* BULKHEAD. **T. metacenter,** *see* METACENTER. **T. numeral,** *see* **L. numerals** *in* LLOYD'S. **T. stability,** *see* STABILITY. **T. stresses,** those to which a vessel is subjected in a sidewise or thwartship direction; *see* **Racking s.** *in* STRESS.

TRAP. Any device or structure that automatically snares, confines, or subdues something; short for a *fish-t.* or a *t.-net.* **Shingle-t.,** *see* SHINGLE. **Steam-t.,** *see* STEAM. **T.-net,** a pound or other enclosure set for capturing fish; a *fish-t.; see* **P.-net** *in* POUND. **Wave-t.,** *see* WAVE.

TRASH ICE. Also called *land trash,* broken-up ice on or along the shore in Arctic regions.

TRAVELER. Also *traveller;* a metal ring, hank, thimble, or the like that moves on a bar, boom, track, stay, etc., such as that for confining a sheet of a fore-and-aft sail to a *t.-iron* or *horse.* **Gaff-t's,** *see* GAFF. **Jib-t.,** also called *tack-ring; see* **Jib-i.** *in* IRON. **T.-iron,** *see* IRON.

TRAVELING. Also, *travelling;* sliding or running, as on a *traveler.* **T. backstays,** *see* BACKSTAY. **T.-guy,** *see* GUY.

TRAVERSE. (Fr. *traverser,* to turn) A number of different courses sailed, considered as a resultant single course, as in the determination of a vessel's progress against contrary winds; a compound course; motion or act of crossing back and forth, as a vessel across a given line of direction or course. In older usage, to swivel or turn a gun to right or left, as in aiming or training; to lay something crosswise; to thwart, in the sense of being contrary, as a *t. wind;* to cross and recross, as a boat or vessel making a sounding survey, as, to *t. a shoal.* To **cast a t.,** *see* CAST. **Tom Cox's t.,** old-time facetious term meaning to shirk work or responsibility by pretending to be otherwise busy; as, to *work Tom Cox's t.* To **t. a yard,** in former usage, to brace or lay a yard fore-and-aft or nearly so. **T. board,** old-time device for recording courses sailed during a watch of 4 hours. Consisted of a wooden tablet on which was inscribed a compass-card diagram with peg-holes at each point. A peg was inserted at the point representing ship's course for each half hour. **T.-circle,** track on which a gun is turned in training or pointing on the target. **T. sailing,** *see* SAILING. **T. tables,** values, in tabulated form, of *difference of latitude* and *departure* made when sailing on a given *course* for a given *distance* (in nautical miles). Present-day *t. tables* in navigational use give such values for distances up to 600 miles. Principally used in *plane sailing,* the tables also may be used as a convenient means of determining the missing elements of a right-angled triangle, any two being given. **T. wind,** an obstructing or contrary wind; *esp.,* one that hinders vessel from steering a necessary course, as through a channel. (*Older usage*) To **work** (or **solve**) **a t.,** to calculate *course and distance made good* or position arrived at, given the several courses and distances sailed from a certain point. *Cf.* **D. reckoning** *in* DEAD.

TRAWL. (Fr. *trôler,* to drag about; prob. of Teutonic origin) A large conical-shaped bag-net towed or dragged near or along the sea-bottom, extensively used in capturing fish. Varies in size from about 10 feet wide at mouth and 20 feet in length, in the case of a *shrimp-t.,* to over 100 feet by 200 feet or more for cod, flounder, halibut, etc.; also called *drag-net* and *ground-net.* Also, a lengthy fishing-line having hooks attached to *snoods* spaced at regular intervals throughout its length; a boulter; *see* **Great-line f.** *and* **Small-line f.** *in* FISHING. To capture fish by means of a *t.;* to engage in *trawling.* **Beam-t.,** a *t.-net* so named from its *beam* which serves to spread mouth of net; *see* **T.-beam.** Use of *beam-t.* is limited to small powered trawlers and sailing smacks. Its maximum beam-spread is about 45 feet, with a length of net, from beam to *cod end,* or tip, of about 100 feet. **Otter t.,** as distinguished from a *beam-t.,* one in which mouth of net is spread by the sheering effect of a pair of *otter-boards,* as vessel drags the apparatus along. Usually supplied with two wire *warps,* each of these is attached to an otter-board in such manner that boards present a slanting surface to line of advance of 25 to 30 degrees. With this arrangement, net is towed clear of bottom and may be made much larger than the *beam-t.* **Runner of a t.,** *see* RUNNER. To **set,** or **shoot, a t.,** to bait and lay out a *t.-line;* also, to *throw a t.* To **strip a t.,** to take fish from hooks of a *t.-line.* **T.-anchor,** *see* **Sand-a.** *in* ANCHOR. **T.-beam,** the spreader or piece of wood to which upper leading edge of *t.-net* is secured in a *beam t.* Raised about 3 feet above sea-bottom by an iron frame or runner at each end, called *t.-heads,* the tow-line or *t.-warp* is attached to these by a bridle. *T.-beam* thus lies horizontally and at right angles with the *t.-warp,* mouth of net opening out below the beam and so dragged over the bottom. **T.-boat,** small boat employed in setting, stripping, or taking in *t.-lines,* as in long-line fishing. (*Chiefly U.S.*) **T.-fish,** such fish as are captured by *t.-lines.* **T. fisherman,** one who engages in taking fish by *t.-net;* a trawlerman; a *trawler,* or vessel employed in fishing by *t.-net.* **T.-head,** one of the supports or runner-like frames that keep a *t.-beam* clear of sea-bottom; *cf.* **T.-beam. T.-buoy,** *see* **K.-buoy** *in* KEG. **T.-killick,** *see* KILLICK. **T.-line,** *see remarks in* TRAWL. **T.-net,** *see remarks in* TRAWL. **T.-roller,** *see* ROLLER. **T.-smack,** in Great Britain, a ketch-rigged vessel employed in beam-trawling; now greatly superseded by powered craft. **T.-warp,** tow-line or drag-rope of a *t.-net.* With a *beam-t.,* it is a single rope; *otter-t's* usually employ two.

TRAWLER. Vessel designed for capturing fish by means of a drag-net or *trawl;* also called *dragger.* Sailing *t's,* usually ketch-rigged vessels of from 50 to 75 feet in length, formerly were found operating in large numbers off European coasts only,—chiefly in the North Sea,—until inroduction of *steam t's* in early years of present century. This took the *t.* farther afield and in deeper water than the sailer's maximum of 20 fathoms. To-day the heavily built powered vessel leaves European ports for the fishing grounds off Iceland, Lapland, Labrador and on or near the Grand Bank of Newfoundland, operating in depths up to 200 fathoms or more. Chief of the *trawler's catch* are the cod, haddock, halibut, fluke, and herring. *Sailing t's* and smaller powered *t's* employ the *beam-t.;* larger craft driven by steam or Diesel power use the *otter-t.* (*see* TRAWL) and modern vessels of the latter type attain a length of 250 feet. **Line t.,** boat employed in trawl-line fishing. *Cf.* TRAWL. **Side-set t.,** an *otter-t.* in which the *t.* is set and hauled in from vessel's side, as distinguished from one rigged for the operation over the stern. **T.-drifter,** vessel fitted out for both *trawling* and *drift-net* fishing, as principally found in the moderate-sized North Sea type thus equipped to quickly change to the comparatively short herring season's demand for the drift-net method.

TRAY. A rectangular, low-sided, box-shaped sling for transferring small cases or packages in loading or discharging cargo; also called a scow, skip, pallet, and platform-sling. *Cf.* SLING.

TREAD. One of the steps in a *companion-* or *deck-ladder.* The entire length of a vessel's *keel.*

TREATY PORT. *See* PORT.[1]

TREBLE. Threefold; triple; consisting of three similar parts. **T. block,** also *threefold* or *triple-sheaved block,* a purchase-block having three sheaves of same diameter. **T. planking,** *see* PLANKING. **T. purchase,** also *threefold purchase, q.v.* in PURCHASE.

TREBLING. Additional planking on a vessel's bows as protection against wear and tear or pressure of ice; also *ice-doubling, ice-lining.*

TREENAIL. (*Tree* + *nail*) Usually pron. "*trennil.*" A round wooden pin used for fastening planking and timbers in wood-built vessels. Made from a tough hard wood, such as elm, locust, oak, maple, teak. Depending upon character of timber and particular work involved, *t's* may be exactly cylindrical or slightly tapered. Generally, the former type is more commonly used, the hole in which *t.* is driven being made about one-sixteenth inch smaller in diameter than *t.* itself. In securing side-planking by *t's,* the pins are alternated with metal bolts (copper, galvanized iron, etc.) both of which are driven through plank, frame, and ceiling. *T.* is sawed off flush with plank surface and each end expanded by driving in a small pointed piece of hardwood called a **t.-wedge.** Also spelled *trenail.*

TREND. Tendency toward, or inclination in, a given direction; as, *northerly t. of a coast.* Relative direction or angle with the fore-and-aft line in which ship's cable leads when swinging at single anchor. In an old-fashioned anchor, enlarged part of *shank* where it approaches and forms junction with the *arms.* To run, tend, or lead in direction; as, *the land t's to the eastward.*

TRESTLETREES. On a mast, bars or strong pieces of wood fixed fore-and-aft at each side as a foundation for *crosstrees* and so the *top* in a square-rigged vessel. The *fid,* which holds up a topmast or a topgallantmast, rests across forward ends of *t.* Also *trestle-trees* and *trestles.*

TRIACONTER. *See remarks in* GALLEY.

TRIAL. The testing or trying out of a vessel's speed and/or engine performance, as over a *measured mile* or other exactly known distance; a *trial-trip.* *Progressive t's* denote a series of such testings run at different engine speeds under similar conditions of sea, weather, draft, and trim. **T. basin,** also called *t. tank; see* **Model b.** *in* BASIN *and* MODEL. **T. range,** same as *measured mile* or *course.*

TRIANGLE. A tripodal arrangement of spars set up as a derrick for hoisting a heavy weight; *three-legged sheers.* **Time t.,** *see* TIME. *Cf.* **A. triangle** *in* ASTRONOMICAL. **Southern T.,** *see* SOUTHERN.

TRIATIC STAY. *See* STAY.

TRICE. (Du. *trijsen,* to hoist; of Scand. origin) Usually with *up,* to lift or haul up by means of a line; to pull or lash up, in the sense of lifting an object clear of something; to hoist, as by a *topping-lift* or a *tricing-line.* Old name for a *windlass.* In smaller vessels, a *tricing-stay* is a rope set up parallel to and on after side of a mast for securing the luff of a *trysail,* similarly to that function of a *jib stay.*

TRICK. A spell or turn of duty; as, to steer a *t.* at the helm; a 5-minute *t.* at the pumps.

TRI-COLORED LANTERN. As required by power-driven *trawlers,* a signal-light described in *Rule 9 (e),* REGULATIONS FOR PREVENTING COLLISIONS.

TRIGGER. In older launching procedure, one of several blocks (or a single block on each side of ship in the case of small vessels) securing the ends of dogshores. When knocked away, dogshores are released and vessel is free to move down ways. *Cf.* DOGSHORE, *also* **L. ways** *in* LAUNCHING. **T.-bar,** *see* BAR; also called *tumbler.* **T. fish,** member of a family of deep-bodied and oddly colored fishes called the *Balistidæ.* It usually inhabits warmer seas, averages about 12 inches in length, and, of its many species, several are good food fishes.

TRIGONOMETRY. (Gr. *trigonon,* triangle; *metron,* measure) This branch of mathematics is employed in the solution of problems in navigation and nautical astronomy and in prepared tabulated values for facilitating such work. Navigational tables usually include both natural and logarithmic trigonometric functions (sines, tangents, secants, etc.) amongst other valuable data for determining a required element in both *plane* and *spherical t*. **Plane t.** is used in problems in *traverse, parallel, middle latitude,* and *Mercator sailings*. **Spherical t.** is involved in the solution of astronomical values, such as *azimuths, altitudes,* and *hour angles* of heavenly bodies; also in determining courses, distances, and track-points in *great circle sailing* and in *composite sailing*. It is believed that we are indebted to the Bithynian astronomer, *Hipparchus,* who lived circa 130 B.C., for the invention of *t.;* but the builders of the Egyptian pyramids, centuries before that gentleman's time, apparently possessed a basic working knowledge of the subject.

TRIM. (A.S. *trymman,* to strengthen or set in order) State or condition of a vessel with respect to disposition in stowage of her cargo, fitness for sailing, arrangement of rigging or deck gear, etc.; as, *the collier was in good t. alow and aloft*. Difference in a vessel's forward and after drafts; as, *a t. of 18 inches by the stern, i.e.,* a deeper draft by that amount at after end. To adjust or arrange the sails or yards as may be required in sailing; as in *"all sail t'd to a stiff beam wind."* To adjust vessel's floating position, as by moving ballast or loading more cargo at one end, so that hull is upright or desired difference in forward and after drafts is obtained; as, to *t. ship upright;* to *t. her 2 feet by the stern*. To make ready or put in condition for use; as, to *t. the binnacle-lamp;* to *t. a piece of timber,* as in shipbuilding; to *put ship in fighting t., sailing t.,* etc. **Change of t.,** number of inches by which the difference in forward and after drafts is increased or diminished due to a change in disposition of weights, as of cargo or ballast, on board. It is determined by dividing the *inch-t. moment* into product of weight moved by distance moved in the fore-and-aft line; or, if weight or weights are loaded or removed from vessel, *inch-t. moment* divided into product of total weight times distance from *tipping-center,* or *center of flotation* (approximately *mid-point* of plane bounded by ship's waterline). *Change of t.* being, *e.g.,* 10 inches, due to weight placed *forward* of tipping-center, vessel's draft will increase 5 inches forward and decrease 5 inches aft. *Cf.* **Inch-trim m.** *in* MOMENT; this value usually is given for each foot of draft on vessel's *deadweight scale*. (In *t.* calculations, weights are expressed in *long tons* (2240 lbs.); distances in *feet*) **T. moment** = *inch-t. moment.* **T. of masts,** *see* MAST. To **t. the yards sharp up, square, forward a point,** etc., to brace yards for sailing close-hauled, for a following wind, for a quarterly breeze, etc.

TRIMMER. *See* C.-passer *in* COAL; a fireman's helper, called *coal-t.* in British steam-vessels, although firemen in medium-sized and smaller ships often are engaged as *"fireman and t."* One of a number of men employed in *trimming,* or evenly distributing, a bulk cargo, such as coal, in vessel's hold during loading. **Sail-t.,** *see* SAIL. **Self-t.,** short for *self-trimming vessel; see* SELF.

TRIMMING. Act or operation of evenly distributing or stowing bulk grain, coal, etc., as it piles up in a hatchway during loading into vessel's hold. Act of adjusting floating position of a vessel; *see* TRIM. **T. charge,** that payable by a vessel for work done by *trimmers* during loading operations, as with a cargo of coal, grain, ore, etc. **T. hatch,** *see* HATCH; sometimes also called *t. hole*. **T.-in bunkers,** additional charge for bunker coal, representing cost of *t.* fuel in bunker compartments. **T.-tank,** *see* TANK.

TRINCOMALI-WOOD. *See* HALMALILLE.

TRINITY HOUSE. A corporation chartered by Henry VIII in 1514 for advancement of commerce and navigation. Under authority of certain acts of Parliament, it is especially concerned with establishment and maintenance of navigational aids on coasts of England and Wales and efficiency of pilot service at certain principal ports. *T. H.* pilots are those licensed by the corporation, as, *e.g., Thames pilots* who are required to hold a certificate of competency as master mariner before acceptance into such service. Under the *Master,* the *Elder Brethren of the T. H.* act in advisory capacity and as assessors in higher courts in connection with important actions involving collisions, damage losses, salvage, etc.

TRINKET. *See* SAIL.

TRIP. A voyage or journey; an excursion. A pawl or detent, as in a capstan. To break out an anchor from the bottom. To lift a yard to a perpendicular position, preparatory to sending it down, for repairs to yard-arm, etc. To raise a topmast or topgallantmast enough to withdraw the *fid,* as in housing or sending down. To let go a chain lashing, such as that securing an anchor on a bill-board or hanging to a cathead, or a deck-load securing-chain, by throwing out a tumbler, releasing a slip-hook, etc. A girder, floor-plate, beam, etc., is said to *t.* or be *t'd* when bowed or otherwise strained out of its normal shape or alignment. **Anchor-t.,** *see* ANCHOR. **Jonah t.,** a voyage or passage characterized by dire and disastrous experiences by the crew; *see* JONAH. **Maiden t.,** *see* MAIDEN VOYAGE. **Round t.,** a complete voyage, or one terminating with return to its starting point. **Trial t.,** *see* TRIAL. **T.-book,** *see* BOOK. **T. charter,** same as *voyage charter; see* CHARTER. **T.-hook,** a slip-hook; *see* **P. hook** *in* PELICAN. **T.-shore,** *see* SHORE.[2] To **t. an anchor,** *see* ANCHOR PHRASEOLOGY.

TRIPLE. Consisting of three similar parts, rows, objects, etc.; threefold; treble; three times repeated. **T.-banked,** said of an arrangement of oars; *see* BANK. **T.-expansion engine,** *see* **Multiple-expansion e.** *in*

ENGINE. **T. riveting,** *see* RIVETING. **T.-screw ship,** *see* SCREW. **T.-tail,** an edible deep-bodied fish of warmer latitudes in the Atlantic, including the south and southeastern coasts of U.S., so named from its long dorsal and anal fins extending backward and giving the appearance of a three-lobed tail. It is classified as *Lobotes surinamensis.* The fish averages about 18 inches in length.

TRIPOD MAST. A mast supported or stiffened by two smaller *masts* or *legs* in lieu of shrouds or back-stays, so named from its tripod-like appearance. Found in some war-vessels, dredges, and vessels specially rigged for handling extra heavy lifts.

TRIPPING. (Verbal noun form of *trip*) Act of something that *trips*. The buckling or straining out of the perpendicular or alignment of a structural part, such as a floor-plate, a girder, a beam, or the like. *Cf.* TRIP. **T. brackets,** small knees or brackets serving as stiffening at intervals along a girder or other structural part to withstand possible *t.* **T.-line,** *see* LINE[1]; *also* **A.-trip** in ANCHOR. **T.-link,** ring or keeper securing a slip-hook; sometimes applied to a *slip-hook* itself; *cf.* **P. hook** in PELICAN. **T.-palms,** *see* ANCHOR PHRASEOLOGY.

TRIREME. (L. *tri,* three; *remus,* oar) Ancient galley having three banks of oars. *Cf.* GALLEY.

TROCHOIDAL WAVE. *See* WAVE.

TROLLEY BEAM. *See* BEAM.

TROLLING. (Not to be confused with *trawling,* although closely related etymologically) Act of fishing by means of one or more *trolls* or *t.-lines,* which operation consists of trailing the latter from a moving boat. Lines are from 40 to 60 feet in length and vary in number from one in a rowing boat to about 6, separated by outrigged poles, in powered craft. Hook is baited or fitted with a bright or colored lure and attached to end of line. Also called *shooting* and *whiffing,* such fishes as albacore, bonito, blue-fish, tarpon, tuna, mackerel, and salmon are captured by *t.* Boats engaged in *t.* are called *trollers.* The lure attached to hook is called a *troll* also.

TROOPSHIP. A vessel engaged in, or designed for, carriage of troops; a trooper; a transport.

TROPIC. (Gr. *tropikos,* pertaining to the turning of the sun at each solstice; *trope,* a turning) On both celestial and terrestrial spheres, either of two small circles parallel to and equi-distant N. and S. of the equator about 23° 27′. The northern circle is called *t. of Cancer;* the southern one, *t. of Capricorn.* On the earth these mark the N. and S. limits of the *tropics,* or *torrid zone* or *belt,* extending between latitudes 23° 27′ N. and S., within which, at any time of year at some place the sun passes through the zenith. **T. bird,** a beautiful tern-like bird found chiefly in tropical seas, often at great distances from shore. Has a satin-like fine plumage of white with dark-shaded upper sides of wings and back. Its tail terminates in two forked elongated feathers equal in length to that of its body. Constituting the genus *Phaethon,* three important species are the *red-billed, red-tailed,* and the *yellow-billed t.* birds. **T. tides,** *see* TIDE.

TROPICAL. Of or pertaining to the *tropics;* as, *t. latitudes.* **T. disturbance,** a cyclonic wind system of such threatening appearance or character that its development into a hurricane, typhoon, or cyclone may occur; a stormy condition in *t.* latitudes. **T. year,** *see* YEAR.

TROT. One of the short lines (*leaders* or *snoods*) to which each hook is attached in a *t.-line;* a trawl- or *t.-line* itself. *See remarks in* TRAWL.

TROTMAN'S ANCHOR. *See* ANCHOR.

TROUGH. An elongated area of low barometric pressure; a lengthy sudden depression on the sea floor; the hollow between waves.

TROUT. Any of certain fishes of the *salmon* family, highly valued as food and by anglers for their remarkable gameness. Most *t.* live in clear cold fresh water, but some ascend rivers from the sea only to spawn. Beautifully colored and usually mottled or speckled on sides and back, they generally attain a length of from 10 to 15 inches.

TROW. An old-fashioned ketch-rigged barge-like vessel used for river and short coastwise work in Great Britain. A fishing-boat having an open well for carrying fish alive.

TRUCK. A circular disk or flattened globular cap fixed over the upper end of a flag-staff or a mast. It usually has a pair of holes through which flag-halyards are rove. *Cf.* **M. truck** in MAST. Also, a fair-leader for several parts of running rigging; *see* **F.-lead** in FAIR; a *leading-t.* or *shroud t.* **Block t.,** *see* BLOCK. **Parrel t.,** *see* PARREL. **T.-plate,** on a stern-post, a vertical piece of plate or heavy flange to which the strake ends of shell plating are riveted.

TRUE. Correct; exact; in accord with fact or reality; not false; as, *t. azimuth; t. horizon; t. time; t. vertical.* Designating a corrected apparent or observed value; as, a *t. altitude;* a *t. course; t. bearing; t. place of a star; t. wind.*

TRU-LAY WIRE. Trade name for *preformed wire rope; see* WIRE.

TRUNDLE-HEAD. Landsman's term for the *drumhead* of a capstan.

TRUNK. A casing or shaft entirely enclosing a hatchway between two or more decks; a *t.-hatch* or *t. hatchway.* A trunkway, passage, or conductor; a ventilating-shaft or air-duct. Upper part of a cabin extending above deck in a small vessel. **Centerboard t.,** *see* CENTERBOARD. **Coaling-t.,** a trunkway in a bunkering-hatch; *see* **Coaling-h.** in HATCH. **Escape**

t., as required by law and usually leading from after end of a shaft-tunnel, a trunkway through which a ladder is fitted as an emergency exit to weather deck. **Expansion t.,** upper portion of a cargo tank or that narrowed into the form of a *t.* Its purpose is to allow rise and fall of contained liquid's surface due to temperature expansion and contraction of the bulk, while main part of tank remains filled to capacity and so protected against development of a free liquid surface therein. **Mast-t.,** *see* MAST. **Rudder t.,** *see* **R. casing** *in* RUDDER. **T. bulkhead,** *see* BULKHEAD. **T. buoy,** usually of cylindrical form, a *mooring-buoy* having a hawse-hole or *t.* through which the mooring-pendant or cable passes. The latter holds buoy in position when not in use. *Cf.* **Hong Kong mooring-b.** *in* BUOY. **T. cabin,** as found in smaller vessels, a cabin having its sides extending partially above deck. **T. deck,** that covering the *t.* in a *t.-deck vessel.* It usually is given a small lateral bracket-supported extension in order to provide additional working space around hatches and winches. **T.-deck vessel,** powered cargo vessel characterized by a raised longitudinal *t.* extending along the upper deck, flush with forecastle, bridge, and poop erections. *T.* has a breadth of about five-twelfths vessel's midship beam throughout its length. Specially built for bulk-cargo trade, vessel is thus provided with a permanent *feeder,* as required with grain cargoes. The *t*'s covering deck is called *t. deck (q.v.)* **T. engine,** *see* ENGINE. **T. hatch,** see opening remarks under TRUNK. **T. whale,** the sperm whale. **T. ventilator,** large air-duct or ventilating shaft, cylindrical or rectangular in cross-section; *ventilating-t.*

TRUNKFISH. Member of a family of small tropical fishes, characterized by its rigid tortoise-like covering of bony plates which allow only its jaws, tail, fins, and eyes to move. Has a flat belly and humped body, the latter being either quadrilateral or triangular in cross section. Several species are known; *see* COW-FISH.

TRUSS. Strong iron pivoting device by which the middle of a lower yard is confined to the mast, while allowing it to be braced or topped up as required. Usually it is assisted in sustaining weight of yard by a single piece of heavy chain, secured to mast and top of yard, called a *sling.* The *t.-bow* or *t.-yoke* is a forging in the *t.* arrangement which projects the yard far enough forward of mast to clear the rigging when braced at any angle required. *T.-bands* or *t.-hoops* secure *t.* to mast and yard. **Hog-t.,** *see* **H.-frame** *in* HOG.

TRY. To *lie to* in heavy weather with storm canvas set. (*Archaic*) Usually with *out,* to render or melt out whale oil from the blubber. To *lie a-try* (or *atry*), *see* ᴀɪRY. **T.-pot,** in whaling, large pot for *trying out* the oil from blubber; *see* **Try-p.** *in* POT. **T.-works,** furnaces and appurtenances for melting

out, or *trying out,* whale-blubber, either on board a whaler or on shore.

TRYSAIL. Triangular or quadrilateral shaped sail set abaft and having its luff attached to a lower mast. In larger vessels used as a heavy-weather sail in lying to, but in smaller craft, often set on an after mast, also for keeping vessel headed into the wind, as when fishing while at anchor or attached to nets. A riding-sail; a spencer. *Cf.* **R.-sail** *in* RIDING; *also* SPENCER. **Gaff t.,** one having a loose foot and a gaff at its head; a *spencer,* in former larger vessels. **Storm t.,** *see* STORM. **T. mast,** *see* MAST. **T. rig,** in small yachting craft, kind of sailing rig featuring triangular fore and main lower canvas spread by a *wishbone,* or double sprit.

T.S.S. Abbrev. *twin-screw steamer.* **Tr. S.S.** = *triple-screw steamer* (or *ship*).

TUB. A sawed-off portion of a cask, or a vessel of like form ready made, used for washing clothing, for stowing fishing-lines, for steeping salt meat, etc.; as, a *wash-deck t.;* a *faking t.;* a *steep t.* A cylindrical band or sleeve confining a gaff or a yard to a mast; as, a *t.-parrel;* a *gaff-t.* A rack-block, or timber fitted with sheaves and serving as the lower block in a tops'l-halyard purchase of older ships; *see remarks under* RACK.[1] In a disparaging sense, a heavy, bluff-bowed vessel or boat, or craft that has seen better days. In long-line or trawl-line fishing, a section of the line that stows in a *t.* (usually a cut-down flour barrel), in length about 300 fathoms in the case of a *cod trawl,* for example. **Ballast t.,** heavy barrel-shaped receptacle fitted with a sling and used for hoisting in or discharging ballast, as in smaller vessels. **Faking-t.,** *see* FAKING-BOX. **Fall t.,** box, crate, or tub-shaped receptacle in which lifeboat falls are coiled down ready for running. **Line t.,** *t.*-shaped receptacle in which a harpoon-line, shot-line, fishing-line, etc., is faked or coiled down for compact stowage and clear running. **Spike t.,** a wooden *t.* for holding blubber in readiness for trying out, as in older whaling-ships; properly, *speck t.; cf.* SPECK. **T. oar,** in a whaling boat, oar in way of the *line-tub* pulled by the *t. oarsman.* It was fourth oar from forward or, usually, that forward of *stroke oar.* Also short for *t. oarsman* who saw that *harpoon-line* ran clear from *t.* and coiled it down in the receptacle as required. **T. trawling,** long-line, trawl-line, or trot-line fishing; line-fishing in which a *t.* is used for stowing the line. **Wash-deck t.,** one usually made by sawing a cask in two, for use in washing down decks by broom and bucket. As a reservoir for a supply of sea-water, in larger sailing-ships it was kept filled by the man or men detailed to handle one or more draw-buckets over the rail.

TUBE. A pipe; a hollow cylinder serving as a conduit; a tubular or terete fitting or housing for a working part; as, a *boiler t.; speaking-t.;* a *stern t.* **Boiler t.,** *see* BOILER. **Fire t.,** one of the *t's* through which combustion gases pass in a *fire-t.* boiler. *Cf.* **F.-tube boiler** *in* FIRE. **Shaft t.,** *see* SHAFT. **Sounding-t.,** *see* SOUNDING. **Stern t.,** *see* STERN. **T.-plate,** also *t.-sheet,* in a boiler, plate or sheet perforated with holes for reception of *t's.* **Voice t.,** a *speaking-t.,* or pipe through which one's voice is carried, as in communication between pilot-house and engine-room. By U.S. law, a vessel using *bell signals* for required engine movements must be fitted with a *t.* for carrying the sound of such signals from engine-room to pilot-house or navigating-bridge. This *t.* often is used for oral communication also.

TUBULAR. (L. *tubulus,* dim. of *tubus,* a pipe or tube) Having the form of a pipe or *tube;* made of a *tube* or system of *tubes;* as, a *t.* spar; a *t.* boiler. **T. booms, masts,** or other spars are made either of a single solid-drawn *t.* or of two or more sections of large steel *tubing.* The latter are joined, in heavier spars, by shrinking a heated end over a cool one in the forging process. *Welding* often is resorted to in the case of smaller spars.

TUCANA. Also, *Toucan;* a small southern constellation located nearly on opposite side of the pole to *Southern Cross* and having about same position in declination. Its brightest star is α *Tucanæ,* of magnitude 2.91; right ascension 22 hrs. 15 min.; declination $60\frac{1}{2}°$ S.

TUCK. Point or line of meeting of vessel's port and starboard outside planking or plating strakes under the counter. A *t.-net* or *t.-seine.* Act of inserting a strand of a rope between other strands, as in splicing; the joint thus made, or, collectively, a single *t.* made by each strand, designated *first t., second t.,* etc. **Square t.,** denoting the "square-cut" planking ends in a boat having a more or less vertical transom stern. **T.-net,** a *purse-seine* or net of similar construction and use; *see* SEINE. An auxiliary *purse-net* for taking fish from within a large one. **T.-plate,** same as *oxter-plate, q.v. in* PLATE. **T.-rail,** timber to which after ends of planking are butted in square-sterned vessels; also, *t.-timber.* It serves as a finishing-piece at the knuckle or turn of the counter. **T.-seine,** a small deep-bunted seine used to take fish rounded up in a larger seine. (*Chiefly British*)

TUG. (M.E. *toggen,* to draw; from Ice. *tog,* a tow-rope) Strongly built powered vessel of small tonnage specially designed for towing; a *tug-boat* or *towboat. Cf.* TOW. There are two types, generally considered: the *harbor* or *river t.* and the *sea-going t.* **Wrecking t.,** large *t.* carrying necessary gear and equipment for rendering assistance to vessels stranded, damaged by collision, etc.; a *salvage-t.*

TUMBLE HOME. *See* HOME.

TUMBLER. A trip, detent, or pawl, as in a capstan or a windlass. A device for tripping, or smartly

releasing a lashing, etc.; *specif.,* the *tripping-gear* formerly much in use for letting go an anchor from a *billboard,* which consisted of a horizontal bar fitted with two horns for engaging the chain-lashing ends. By turning bar on its axis by means of a fixed lever, lashings were set taut; sudden release of lever allowed bar to turn outward, freeing its horns from the lashings as anchor slipped overboard. It was also called *anchor-tripper* and *trigger-bar.* Also, a *clapper,* or bearing-block between jaws of a hoisting gaff; *see* CLAPPER.

TUN. A large cask originally used as the common unit in shipments of wine. Its weight with contents was nearly a *long ton;* hence the source of our present *ton; see* TONNAGE.

TUNA. *See* TUNNY. **T. clipper,** local name for a Californian powered vessel designed for taking *t.* (or *tunny*) along the west coast of U.S. and often as far south as the equator.

TUNNEL. Short for *shaft-tunnel; see* SHAFT. In a pound-net, the narrowing entrance to the *pot; see* **P.-net** *in* POUND. **Pipe t.,** *see* PIPE. **T. escape,** a trunk-way or emergency exit leading to weather deck from after end of *shaft-t.;* an *escape trunk; see* TRUNK. **T. frames,** those supporting the plating of a *t.* or a *t. escape.* (*Shaft-t.* frames and plating usually are curved to form a rounded or dome-shaped top on the *t.*) **T. platform,** a wooden walk or working platform extending along one side of the propeller shafting in a *t.* **T. recess,** *see* RECESS. **T. stern,** *see* STERN. **T. well,** *see* WELL.

TUNNY. Large oceanic fish of the *mackerel* family, generally found in warmer latitudes. Usually called *horse mackerel* on the American Atlantic coast; *tuna* on the Pacific side; or, more widely known as the *common,* or *great, t.,* representing the principal of several species. The *little t.* of the North Atlantic and Mediterranean and the *long-finned t.,* or *albacore,* seldom attain a greater weight than 60 lbs., but the *great t.* is known to have reached 14 feet in length and a weight of 1500 lbs. Extensive *t. fishing* is carried on in Pacific waters by hook and line; in the Mediterranean and near-by Atlantic also by heavy fixed nets extending 1 to 2 miles from shore. Largest *t.* are captured in the latter region. The fish travel in schools, thrashing and jumping about as if continually in play. Its flesh is canned on a large scale on the U.S. Pacific coast.

TURBINE ENGINE. *See* ENGINE. The term usually is shortened to *turbine.* **Exhaust t.,** *see* EXHAUST. **Geared t.,** *see* **Geared e.** *in* ENGINE.

TURBO. (L. = a whirling or that which spins round) Combining term meaning *turbine.* **T.-electric drive,** ship propulsion system essentially consisting of a *turbine-driven* generator which supplies electric power to a motor directly coupled to propeller shaft. **T.-generator,** combination consisting of a high-speed steam *turbine* and an electric generator working on a common shaft; power thus produced is used for motor-driven pumps, winches, etc., for lighting ship, or for driving propeller in *t.-electric drive* installations. **T.-reciprocating drive,** system in which exhaust steam from a triple- or a quadruple-expansion reciprocating engine is further utilized in a *turbine; see* **E.-turbine** *in* EXHAUST. In triple-screw vessels, both *wing engines* are reciprocating and exhaust into turbine which drives midship propeller. Reversing is done by wing screws only.

TURBOT. A large *flounder* of European coastal waters, greatly valued as a food fish. Attains a weight of 30 to 40 pounds. The name also designates several flounders or flatfishes similar in appearance to the true *t.; e.g.,* the American *plaice* or *summer flounder,* New Zealand *halibut,* Californian *halibut,* and European *brill. Cf.* FLOUNDER; HALIBUT.

TURK'S HEAD. Kind of weaved knot made by working one or more pieces of small line around a cylindrical object. In appearance like a turban, it is used as a finishing trim on ends of cross-pointing work, as on a stanchion or hand-rail, as a grip-knot on a man-rope, foot-rope, etc.; and is designated according to its number of strands, which are worked over and under each other; as *3-strand t. h.* (its simplest form); *4-strand t. h.;* etc.

TURN. A change in direction; as, in naval tactical maneuvers, one of 90° from original course; the reversal of tidal flow from ebb to flood or vice versa, or *t. of the tide;* a bend or turning-point in a channel. A single wind or bight of a rope, etc., laid around a belaying-pin, post, bollard, or the like; as, to *take a t. on the bitts.* A spell of duty; as, one's *t. at the gangway.* Authorized place in sequence, according to local custom or regulation, given a particular vessel that awaits with others to move into a loading or discharging berth. In Great Britain, also called *stem; cf.* **Stemming 1.** *in* LIST.² More or less sudden curvature in vessel's structure; as, *t. of the bilge; t. of the counter.* To execute a *t.,* as in naval tactical maneuvering; to abruptly change course; as, to *t. to port;* to *t. into the wind;* to *t. about.* With *in,* to secure a shroud, stay, or other rope to a dead-eye, bee, cringle, etc., by passing the end around and seizing it to its standing part; opposed to *splicing in;* as, to *t. in a dead-eye,* etc.; also, to *put a turning in a dead-eye,* etc. **Round t.,** see ROUND. **T. about,** also *t. around,* period elapsing between time of a vessel's arrival at and departure from a port,—*esp.,* a terminal port of a regular run. To **t. flukes,** *see* FLUKE. To **t. in,** to lie down in one's berth for rest or sleep. To **t. in all standing,** to go to bed without removing one's clothing, as in preparedness for an emergency call. To **t. turtle,** to completely overturn; to capsize, as a boat.

TURNBUCKLE. Mechanical device for setting up shrouds, stays, deck-load lashings, steering-chains, etc. Consists of either a long open link or cylindrical box having a screw-thread at one end and a swivel at the other, or a right-hand screw-thread at one end and a left-hand one at the other. It is connected to the appropriate threaded attachments (eye-bolts, fork-bolts, etc.) at end or ends of the rope or chain concerned and set up by wrench or lever. Fixed *t's* usually are fitted at lower ends of shrouds and back-stays, at ends of awning ridge-ropes, and other standing gear that requires tension adjustment from time to time.

TURNER. In Newfoundland sealers' cant, a seal in its third year; a *t. harp;* a *t. hood. Cf.* **Harp s.** *in* SEAL; **H. seal** *in* HOOD.

TURNING. Act or course of anything that turns. **T. basin,** same as *swinging basin, q.v. in* SWINGING. **T. circle,** nearly circular path made by a powered vessel with helm hard over and engines turning at constant speed. (Usually full or cruising speed) Diameter of circle, which is very little affected in a wide variation of vessel's speed, is about 6 times the length of a single-screw ship and about 4 times a twin-screw vessel's length. **T. gear,** device for *t.* ship's main engines as may be required in making repairs, etc., when engines are dead or lying idle; usually takes the form of a *t. engine* in larger vessels; also called *jacking gear;* a *jacking engine; see* **Turning e.** *in* ENGINE. Also, the rack and pinion gear, turned by a hand-crank, for moving a large ventilator-cowl about its axis. **T. in a dead-eye,** act of securing a shroud or stay around a dead-eye, bee, thimble, etc.; *see remarks under* TURN.

TURNPIKE SAILOR. See SAILOR.

TURNTABLE. A platform mounted on a pivot at the stern of a seining vessel for facilitating stowage of nets thereon.

TURRET. (O.F. *tourete,* dim. of *tour,* a tower; from L. *turris*) In a *warship,* a flat tower-like structure protecting the breeches and loading mechanism of one or more heavy guns. It is designed to revolve as required in training the guns. Modern battleships are equipped with two or more *t's,* heavily armor-plated and containing as many as three 12- to 16-inch guns. In the now apparently obsolete *t. steamer,* the narrow raised *trunk* extending fore-and-aft in midship center line. **T. captain,** in U.S. navy, a first-class petty officer in charge of a *t. crew* and ranking next to officer commanding while in the *t.* **T. deck,** that laid over the *trunk* or *t.* in a *t. vessel.* **T.-gun,** heavy gun protected by a *t.* **T. ship,** war vessel characterized by one or more *t's* protecting her heaviest guns. (*Older usage*) **T.-steamer,** type of cargo vessel of 2,000 to 7,500 gross tonnage having a raised trunk of about half her beam in breadth extending fore-and-aft. Built with no sheer, usually had forecastle, poop, and bridge erections on t. deck. Designed to lessen tonnage under Suez Canal system of measurement; in effect a whaleback vessel in which the *harbor deck* curved upward to form sides of *trunk* or t. Now obsolete, superseded by a modification of the type known as a *trunk vessel*. (*See* TRUNK)

TURRETED CLOUDS. See *Cumulo-nimbus* class in CLOUD.

TURTLE. A *tortoise*, in a broad sense; any reptile of the order *Chelonia*, comprising land, sea, and fresh-water *turtles. Sea t's*, of which there are many species, inhabit warmer waters. Largest are the widely distributed *leatherback, loggerhead,* and *green t's*, the first-named attaining a weight of over 1,000 pounds. *Green t.* provides the much canned *t. meat* and excellent soup of that name. Unlike the majority, it is strictly herbivorous. Best *tortoise shell* is taken from the small, also widely known *hawksbill t.* All *t's* are oviparous and usually bury their eggs in sand banks and beaches, the young left to dig out and fend for themselves. *T's* grow slowly and most live to as long as 50 years. **T.** or **t.-back deck,** *see* DECK. **T.-peg,** a sharp-pointed single-barbed spear or harpoon fitted on the end of a long shaft. When t. is "pegged," shaft is withdrawn and captive hauled in by a line made fast to the *peg;* also, *t.-spear*. To **turn t.,** *see* TURN.

TURTLEBACK. A whaleback, or vessel having wings of her weather deck rounded off. A *t. deck*.

TWEEN DECK. Contraction of *between deck;* often written *'tween deck*, and, connoting an indefinite space on such deck, *'tween decks*. Located in, or pertaining to, a *t. d.* or *t. d's;* as, *t.-d. hatch; t.-d. bunker; t.-d. tank; t.-d. tonnage*.

TWICE-LAID. Laid a second time, as yarns from old cordage in making rope or teased-out junk in spinning small stuff; as, *t.-l. rope; t.-l. spunyarn*.

TWIDDLING-LINE. *See* LINE.[1] Also, *twiggling-line*.

TWIN. Double; twofold; consisting of two distinct members of identical form; as, *t. screws; t. ships*. **T.-boat,** small steamboat having two separate hulls side by side and a propelling paddle between them; a *catamaran*. **T.-screw vessel,** one driven by *t. screws,* one on each side of the fore-and-aft center line. **T.-bulkhead tanker,** modern tank-vessel which is fast displacing the older type,—or that having a single through center-line bulkhead with summer tanks in the wings outside of the expansion-trunk, —so named from its two longitudinal bulkheads equi-distant from midship center line, thus dividing the cargo space between transverse bulkheads into *three* compartments or *tanks* instead of *two* as in the older type, and also dispensing with summer tanks and expansion trunk.

TWINE. Strong thread or string of fiber composed of a number of smaller threads twisted together, such as that used in sail-making, for light seizings, whippings, etc. It is usually designated as *3-ply, 5-ply*, etc., meaning its component threads or strands number 3, 5, etc. **Roping t.,** *see* ROPING. **Sail t.,** *see* SAIL. **Seaming t.,** *see* SEAMING T.

TWINS, The. *See* CASTOR and POLLUX; GEMINI.

TWISTED-THREAD CANVAS. Also, *double-thread c.,* kind of heavy sail-cloth in which the warp and weft, or the warp only, are made of doubled threads twisted together.

TWISTER. A *Spanish windlass*. A waterspout or tornado.

TWO. Having the essential feature of a group of *two;* as, a *t.-master;* a *t.-arm mooring*. **T. blocks,** *chock-a-block* or *block-and-block,* position of blocks in a tackle when they are hauled close together, thus stopping further use of tackle. **T.-compartment ship,** one so subdivided that, in the event of any two compartments being flooded, vessel will not founder or capsize. *Cf.* **Floodable l.** *in* LENGTH. **T.-decker,** old-time naval ship having a complete outfit of guns on two continuous decks. **T. half hitches,** rope's end turned around standing part of line and passed through the bight, this being repeated. The whole snugly drawn is same as the *clove hitch*. **T.-leg mooring,** *see* **Three-leg m.** *in* MOORING. **T.-tops'l schooner,** *see* **Topsail s.** *in* SCHOONER.

TWO OR MORE BEARINGS WITH RUN BETWEEN. Determination of a vessel's distance from or position off shore, as from a lighthouse, headland, radio-beacon, etc., commonly is effected by "doubling the angle on the bow," *i.e.,* by observing the object's *relative bearing,* or angle from ship's fore-and-aft line, thereafter noting vessel's distance run up to the instant at which such bearing is observed to have *doubled*. Distance run in such interval then is equal to ship's distance off object *at time of second bearing,* since, as may be shown graphically, *distance run (over the ground)* and *distance off* form the two equal sides of an isosceles triangle. In the simplest and most popular **Four-point bearing,** doubling of 4 points, or 45°, as first bearing gives vessel's distance off when *abeam,* or 8 points, or 90° from the bow. When, however, as is often required, the navigator wishes to check beforehand the distance he *will* pass object observed on the beam bearing, a lesser angle on bow is doubled and, by use of a simple rule or a multiplying factor, the *beam passing* distance is found from that obtained by "doubling the angle." Thus, by what is known as the **Seven-tenths rule,** a *2-and-4-point* observation giving 5 miles off when object bears 4 points on bow, vessel will pass *abeam* of object 5 x .7 = 3.5 miles. Here, the hypotenuse of a right-angled isosceles triangle being known as

5 miles in length, we are multiplying that value by the sine of 45°, shortened to the practical .7, from .70711. Navigation tables include factors for multiplying a distance run between two consecutive bearings, *whether doubled or not,* to obtain both distance off at time of second bearing and that at which ship will pass object abeam. A simple well-known method of finding distance off vessel will pass when abeam is the **Twenty-six and a half and four points** rule: "Distance run from instant object bears 26½° on bow until it bears 4 points, or 45°, on bow is equal to distance off vessel will pass object abeam." Again using 26½°, vessel's distance off object when abeam is equal to distance run in the interval between instant of object's bearing 26½° *before the beam* and that of its bearing 26½° *abaft the beam.* Also, distance run from time object bears *one point* (11¼°) *before the beam* until it is exactly abeam, multiplied by 5, gives the beam distance off, very nearly. The two methods last noted may be found convenient during poor visibility conditions, or when shore object may be obscured at lesser angles on the bow.

TWOFOLD PURCHASE. *See* PURCHASE.

TYE. (Older form of *tie*) In the gear used for setting a square hoisting sail, such as an upper tops'l, a single topgallants'l, or a royal, a chain attached to middle of yard and leading through a sheave in the mast (sometimes through a *tye-block*), thence to the halyard arrangement abaft the mast. *See remarks in* HALYARD. **Peak t.,** supporting chain or wire secured to the peak of a *standing gaff* and the lower masthead; also, *peak span.*

TYFON HORN. Patented sound-signal device used as a navigational aid during fog or poor visibility conditions at a lighthouse or coastal station. May be operated by steam or compressed air which produces the required blast by vibratory action of a special diaphragm.

TYPHOON. (Gr. *tuphon,* a great whirlwind) A cyclone so named in the China Sea, Philippines, and Japan; *see* CYCLONE.

TYZACK'S ANCHOR. *See* ANCHOR.

U

U. Abbrev. in the form (U) denotes, on charts and in Light Lists, that light indicated is *unwatched* or *unattended,* thus warning the navigator of possible failure of such light; as *u* in log-books and meteorological records, signifies *ugly, threatening appearance* of weather. In International Code of signals, *U* is a square flag showing two white and two red squares of equal size, alternately set. This flag, hoisted singly, denotes *"You are standing into danger,"* which signal also may be given by Morse Code flashing as - - -, or two dots and a dash, the symbol for *U.* Having resemblance in shape to letter *U;* as, *U-bar; U-bolt; U-clip; U-section:* etc. **U boat,** short for German *unterseeboot,* or submarine.

ULLAGE. (O.F. *eullage,* complete filling of a cask) Inside measurement from surface of a liquid to the top or limit of space in a cask or tank; quantity of liquid by which containing vessel lacks of being full; deficiency, as of contents of a cask of liquor. In tank-vessels, *u.* is measured to inside of tank cover by an *u.-stick, u.-rod,* or *u.-gauge,* through the circular *u.-hole* which is about 10 inches in diameter and provided with an *u.-plug* capable of being closed airtight.

UMBRA. (L. = shadow) Conical shadow projected from a planet or satellite, within which the sun is totally obscured to an observer. For example, in a partial or a total eclipse of the moon, that part or the whole of her surface which is completely darkened is said to have *entered the u. Cf.* PENUMBRA. A deep-bodied fish of temperate seas having dark diagonal stripes over its entire body. From 12 to 16 inches in length, its several species are regarded as good food fishes, *esp.* that found in Mediterranean waters, distinguished as *Umbrina cirrhosa.*

UMBRELLA. A *bonnet* or *hood* fitted around the *funnel* or smokestack of some vessels as a protection against rain, etc. It slopes from top of funnel so as to cover space between casing and funnel proper; hence the name. *Cf.* **Funnel-c.** *in* CASING.

UMIAK. *See* OOMIAK.

UNA BOAT. English name for a *catboat,* so called from the name of first boat of that rig taken to England; also, *Una-boat.*

UNBEND. To detach or remove from a secured position; as an anchor from its cable; a rope that is hitched or knotted to something; a sail from its yard, stay, mast, etc.; gear from a mast or spar; the turns of a lashing; etc.

UNBITT. To remove the turns of a rope or chain from a bollard or bitts.

UNDECKED. Having no deck; open to the weather, as a boat.

UNDER. Below or beneath in place or position; as, *u.-deck; u.-steward.* Beneath, in the sense of being hidden; as, *u'current; u. water; u. the lee of the land; u. the counter.* Lacking in fitness or falling short of a standard; as, *u'manned; u'masted.* Sustaining, in the sense of carrying, being equipped with, or possessing; as, *u. sail; u. arms; u. bare poles.* **U'bowing a tide,** sailing close to wind with set of current against vessel's lee bow, thus holding up or *sheering* her to windward. **U'canvassed,** said of a vessel fitted with an area of sail too small for her size of hull. **U.-deck** tonnage, *see* TONNAGE. **U'foot,** said of an anchor when lying immediately below ship's *fore-foot,* or vertically below the stem. **U. hack,** said of an officer who is confined to his quarters for a minor infraction of discipline. **U. hatches,** *see* HATCH. **U'hauled,** said of a vessel at anchor when lying more or less across the channel or direction of normal tidal stream through being affected by an *u.-current.* **U'hung rudder,** *see* RUDDER. **U'manned,** having an insufficient number of men for proper handling or safe navigation of; said of a vessel. **U'masted,** said of sailing craft that are fitted with masts either too light or too short, and therefore incapable of spreading an area of canvas which apparently would produce greater speed results, as consistent with size and lines of hull concerned. **U'run,** to haul a boat under and along a hawser, chain, trawl, net, etc., as for examination or repairs to such; as, to *u'run a hawser,* etc. To *u'run a hose* is to raise it and pass it through the hands while walking along its length for the purpose of expelling all contained water. To *u'run a tackle*, to lay all its parts clear and in order for use; to *clear a tackle*, as by dipping a capsized block through its parts. **U'running a trawl** is the act of hauling a boat along the line while taking fish therefrom and re-baiting the hooks. **U. sail**, said of a vessel under way with sails set. (A vessel under way propelled by both sail and machinery is called a *powered vessel* in *Rules of the Road;* when such craft is *u. sail* only, she is a *sailing vessel*) **U'sailed**, lacking a full equipment of sails or having an insufficient sail area. **U'set**, a current below the surface; *esp.*, one flowing in a direction contrary to that occurring on the surface; an *u'current*. **U'sparred**, having size, length, or number of masts, yards, booms, etc., below standard for class of vessel concerned. **U. the lee**, sheltered or protected from wind or sea, or both; as, *u. the lee of the cape;* on or off the sheltered or lee side; as, *another ship u. the lee*. **U'tow**, on a shelving beach, seaward flow below the surface or receding water from the breaking waves; an *u'set*. **U'water body**, also *u'body,* immersed portion of vessel's hull; *specif.*, that portion below the waterline when vessel is in the *light* condition. **U. way**, a vessel is said to be *u. way* when not at anchor, or aground, or *made fast* to the shore. (Often erroneously written "*underway*")

UNDER BELOW! Same as *Look out below!* Shout of warning to persons near or in way of anything about to fall, be dropped, or be lowered, as from aloft or through a hatchway.

UNDERWRITER. (A.S. *underwritan,* to sign) Person or corporation that *underwrites* or subscribes an insurance policy; an insurer; as, a *marine u.; see* INSURANCE, MARINE; *also* LLOYD'S. *Cf.* **H. policy** *in* HULL.

UNEQUIPPED PORT. See PORT.[1]

UNION. (Fr.; from L. *unio,* unity) Colors or emblem representing the confederacy or oneness of a number of states, countries, etc., comprising a nation, often occupying the whole field in a *flag*, or, in certain flags, set usually in the upper inside corner, as in the U.S. and the British ensigns. *Cf.* **Union j.** *in* JACK; ENSIGN. **U. down**, reversed or upside-down position of ship's ensign as displayed for a distress signal or with accompanying two-flag International Code signal *N C*, meaning "*I am in distress and require immediate assistance.*" **U. gear**, cargo-hoisting arrangement in which the *yard-arm* or *overside fall* and *midship* or *hatch fall* are connected to a common hook. It is sometimes called *double-fall system* and *burton tackle*.

UNIREME. (L. *unus,* one; *remus,* oar) Ancient galley having one bank or tier of oars. *Cf.* GALLEY.

UNIVALVE. Any mollusk with a shell consisting of a single piece, as a *conch* or a *snail;* any *gastropod*.

UNIVERSAL. Unlimited; general; all-embracing. **U. joint,** device serving as a joint which allows rotary motion in both parts of a shaft lying obliquely to each other, as, *e.g.,* that in a rod leading to a steering-engine control-valve. **U. time,** *see* G.C.T.; *also* TIME.

UNKINKABLE ROPE. Cordage in which the yarns in each strand are laid in same direction as the strands themselves. Rope of this type, while having the advantage of keeping free of *kinks* under ordinary conditions of weather and use, its *dead lay* or lack of compactness in unity of the strands and consequent failure under continuous work render it generally unsatisfactory, *esp.* where lengthy parts of such cordage are employed. Its use, therefore, is confined to lifeboat tackles and such gear held in readiness for emergencies or special occasions.

UNLAY. To separate or untwist the strands of a rope. To *u. a strand* is to remove it from the rope. Strand or strands thus handled are said to be *unlaid*.

UNLOAD. To discharge, as ballast or cargo from a vessel; to withdraw the charge from a gun.

UNMOOR. To loose from or take in the principal moorings preparatory to leaving a berth; as a vessel reducing to single anchor from the moored condition, or "singling up" her lines at a dock.

UNNEUTRAL SERVICE. That rendered to an enemy by a merchant vessel of a neutral nation, such as delivery of supplies to naval ships at sea, landing contraband at an enemy port or via a friendly port for use of the belligerent, running a blockade, or in any way assisting or abetting the enemy.

UNREEVE. To withdraw or haul out a rope or chain from a block, dead-eye, thimble, etc. To *u. a tackle* is to remove its rope from the blocks.

UNRIG. To remove or strip a vessel's rigging; *esp.*, her running gear. To strip a cargo-boom, accommodation-ladder, sounding-boom, etc., of its working gear, as for housing.

UNSEAWORTHINESS. The converse of *seaworthiness*. Where question of such state or condition arises, as in the marine insurance field, unless a particular case evinces a flagrant disregard of requirements and responsibilities of the insured in maintaining a seaworthy vessel, it is recognized that *u.* in fact is difficult to establish in a court of law. Generally, the presumption is held that vessel was or is *seaworthy* until the contrary is proved, onus of proof being with the insurer. *Cf.* SEAWORTHINESS.

UNSHIP. To remove or detach, as a boat's rudder, a gangway-stanchion, a deck-ladder, etc., from its working position or connection.

UNSTEP. To remove from its *step,* as a mast. *Cf.* **M.-step** *in* MAST.

UNSTOWED. Not stowed; lying loose or in disorder, as pieces of cargo or working gear.

UNVALUED POLICY. See **O. policy** *in* OPEN.

UNWATCHED. *See* U.

UP. In many instances used in nautical phraseology in an adverbial sense, as in *clew up; lie up; heave up; send up; set up; shore up;* as a preposition in *sail up the bay; climb up the rigging; leading up the foremast;* etc.; and in a verbal sense in such shortened commands as *Up anchor!* (for *Heave up anchor!*); *Up helm!* (for *Put the helm up!*); *Up behind!* (for *Come up behind!*). **Up behind!,** *see* **To c. up behind** *in* COME. **Up oars!,** *see* OAR. **Up tacks and sheets!,** or *Tacks and sheets!,* for *Raise tacks and sheets!,* see remarks under RAISE.

UP-AND-DOWN. Lying or leading in a vertical line. An anchor-cable is said to be *up-and-down* while hanging from the hawse-pipe by its own weight, as when ship is lying in slack water; or when anchor lies directly beneath the fore foot, *esp.,* while being *broken out,* or just prior to being *aweigh.* **U.-and-d. fall,** midship or hatch fall; *see* **U. gear** *in* UNION. **U.-and-d. the mast,** probably with reference to the air stirred up by flapping of sails as vessel heaves in a swell during a calm, descriptive of such home-made wind; *see* PADDY'S HURRICANE.

UPHROE. See EUPHROE.

UPPER. Farther up or higher in place or position; relatively loftier; as, *u. berth; u. tween deck; u. strakes; u. staysail.* **U. deck,** *see* DECK. **U. topsail,** *see* TOPSAIL. **U. transit,** *see* **Lower t.** *in* TRANSIT. **U. works,** collectively, erections comprising a vessel's superstructure; *see* SUPERSTRUCTURE. In older usage, all parts of the hull above load water-line; also called *deadworks.* **U. yards,** all yards fitted on the *u. masts; tops'l, t'gallant, royal,* and *skys'l* yards.

UPRIGHT. A piece of timber, angle-bar, etc., set in a vertical position for supporting or strengthening something; such as is fitted in a temporary bulkhead or partition, or in a shipyard staging erected alongside a vessel. A ship is said to be *u.* when floating with no list or inclination to either side.

UPSET. To overturn or capsize, as a boat. To swage or thicken by hammering, as a heated cable-shackle pin; to burr the end of a metal rod, as in making a bolt. **U. shackle,** one in which the curved end, or *bow,* is fixed, as in a block, or at lower end of a shroud or stay; a *set shackle.*

UPSETTING MOMENT. Also, *capsizing moment,* or converse of *righting moment; see* MOMENT. *Cf.* **Upsetting l.** *in* LEVER.

UPTAKE. In a ventilating system, a shaft or pipe through which vitiated air, obnoxious gases, etc., are expelled. The *breeching* or sheet-metal conduit that conveys smoke and combustion gases from a boiler-furnace into ship's funnel; usually consists of two walls separated by an air space of about 3 inches for reducing heat radiation. Swinging dampers are fitted in the *u.* for controlling fires.

URANUS. Seventh planet from the sun from which it is distant approximately 1,780,000,000 statute miles. Has a diameter of 30,878 miles; is attended by four satellites; and revolves round the sun once in a period of about 84 of our years. The planet is too faint for use in practical navigation.

URSA MAJOR. (L. = greater she-bear) A conspicuous northern constellation also known as the *Great Bear, Dipper, Plough,* and *Charles' Wain* or *Charlie's Wagon,* easily recognized by the dipper-like formation of its seven principal stars. The two stars marking the outer limit of the "bowl" are called the *Pointers* for their use in locating *Polaris,* or *Pole Star.* Line of the Pointers extended 28°, or about the length of *Great Bear* itself, comes close to *Polaris;* and when the tail star, or end of the *Dipper's* handle, is directly below or above *Polaris,* the latter bears very nearly *true north,* or has arrived at upper or lower culmination. Pointers are named *Dubhe* and *Merak,* or α (alpha) and β (beta) *Ursæ Majoris,* respectively, the former marking the lip of the dipper-bowl. Tail-end star is *Alkaid* or *Benetnasch* (η *Ursæ Majoris*).

URSA MINOR. (L. = little bear) Also called *Little Dipper; see* DIPPER.

USEFUL LOAD. Weight of cargo and necessary fuel, water, and stores that a vessel carries when floating at her load-line marks; also termed *net capacity.* *Cf.* **F. and down** *in* FULL.

U. S. N. Abbrev. *United States Navy.*

U. S. N. R. Abbrev. *United States Naval Reserve.*

UVROU. Var. of *euphroe; see* EUPHROE.

V. In the International Code of Signals, square flag having a white ground with an oblique or diagonal red cross; code-name = *victor*. Hoisted singly or flashed in Morse by 3 dots and a dash (. . . –) denotes "*I require assistance*"; as a towing signal, by ship towing, means "*Set sails*" and by ship towed, "*I will set sails*." As a symbol in weather records, *v* = variable, usually in describing winds. **V-shaped,** having the form of a *V*; as *V-thread; V-bottom; V-scarf; V-stern*.

VALEMAN. In a drifter, crew member who keeps the nets in proper order and repair. (*Chiefly British*)

VALUATION, CERTIFICATE OF. See CERTIFICATE.

VALUED POLICY. In marine insurance, one in which a *fixed value* is agreed upon as payable by insurer in event of partial or total loss of subject matter insured; opposed to an *unvalued* or *open policy*. *Cf.* **O. policy** *in* OPEN.

VALVE. (L. *valva,* leaf or fold in a folding door) A distinct part of a shell, as either of the two pieces comprising the shell of *bivalve* mollusks,—the oyster, mussel, clam, etc. One of the many mechanical devices for controlling the flow or, in certain cases, the pressure of a fluid, gas, or loose material in a pipe or conduit; a cock, faucet, or tap. **Alarm v.,** any valve that operates an alarm, as by pressure in an indicator or by a float which makes an electric contact and rings a bell as warning that a fuel tank is nearly filled; a small *safety v.* on a boiler, set to open at a pressure of 5 to 10 pounds less than at which regular *safety v.* opens. **Blow-off v.,** one used to discharge contents of a boiler, evaporator, etc.; a *blow v.* A *surface blow v.* is for discharging scum or grease from surface of water in a boiler. **By-pass v.,** also called *pilot v.,* used to equalize pressure on both sides of a large *v.* before latter is opened, as in a high-pressure steam line. **Check v.,** a *non-return v.,* or one permitting flow in one direction only, as in a boiler-feed line; *storm* and *scupper v's* are simple forms of this *v.* **Delivery v.,** that controlling discharge overboard of water circulating in a condenser; *overboard discharge v.* **Dew v.,** one automatically draining a cylinder of water, as in deck machinery. **Escape v.,** a *relief v.,* or one designed to open in event of excessive pressure in an engine, boiler, etc. **Gate v.,** so named from its *gate* or disk, usually wedge-shaped, which is raised or lowered in opening and closing, giving a straight passage of flow the full diameter of pipe. Main line connections in tank-vessels usually are fitted with *gate v's.* **Kingston v.,** *see* KINGSTON VALVE. **Maneuvering v.,** special *v.* in a turbine used for increasing and decreasing speed as required during *maneuvering* of ship. **Pet v.,** a pet cock; *see* COCK. **Relief v.,** *see* REDUCER. **Safety v.,** automatic *escape* or *relief v.* that is set to open at a predetermined pressure; *esp.,* such *v.* as required by law to be fitted on a ship's boiler. **Sea v.,** one for closing or opening the intake below ship's water-line that supplies sea-water to ship's fire pumps, sanitary system, for filling ballast-tanks, etc. **Steam-reducing v.,** *see* STEAM. **Stop v.,** cuts off supply of steam from boilers to main engines. Where more than one boiler is present, a *boiler stop v.* controls steam flow from each individual boiler to *main steam line* and that controlling steam flow in the last-named is termed *main stop v.* In the *feed line* between *feed-pump* and boiler a *feed stop v.* is fitted. **Storm v.,** a simple form of *non-return* or *check v.* at outer end of a scupper-pipe. Also called *clack v., clapper v., flap v.,* and *scupper v.,* it allows waste water to escape overboard while preventing ingress of sea-water. **Throttle v.,** *see* THROTTLE. **Wheel v.,** any *v.* that is opened or closed by means of a *hand-wheel,* as distinguished from one operated by a lever, spring, or other device. **Whistle v.,** as usually fitted to whistles sounded by steam or compressed air in order to overcome the strong pull otherwise required to open such *v.;* also called *balanced whistle-v.* Pull on *v.-lever* opens a small port which allows the steam or air to pass to atmospheric side of *v.* or to an extension thereof. This balances pressure on either side of *v.* and permits complete opening of *v.* possible with an easy pull. Whistles operated by electric control usually are of this type.

VALVE CHEST. See MANIFOLD.

VAN. (Abbrev. *vanguard*) Foremost division or squadron; leading line of ships in formation, as in naval maneuvers.

VANE. Device fitted on the truck of a mast for indicating direction of wind, as an arrow of sheet metal, a long slender cone of light canvas or bunting, etc., free to swing about on a vertical spindle. **V. propeller,** also, *v. wheel,* a kind of screw-propeller used in some shallow-draft river vessels. It is only partially immersed (the boss barely immersed when vessel is deepest laden) and has large flat-surfaced blades, each of which is joined to the boss by two strong arms. **Sight v.,** *see* SIGHT.

VANG. Either of the guys leading from each side of the peak end of a *standing gaff;* a cargo-boom guy. Usually consists of a pendant with a *luff* or *two-fold tackle* at its lower end.

VAPOR-PIPE. A vent-pipe providing means for escape of gas from a tank, as in a tank-vessel.

VARIABLE. Shifting or changeable in direction or force; as, *v. winds; v. currents.* Characterized by a varying feature; as, a *v. curvature; v. pitch.* A *v. wind* itself. In *pl.,* ocean region in which changeable winds prevail; *esp.,* that between outer limits of N.E. and S.E. trade winds, or, roughly, between latitudes 30° and 40°; *the variables.* **V.-delivery pump,** one in which delivery of fluid may be adjusted as required; a *v.-stroke pump.* Used to supply necessary varying pressure to cylinders of hydraulic steering-gear and in hydro-electric windlasses or winches. **V.-pitch propeller,** screw in which the pitch of blades, or angle surface of blade makes with the fore-and-aft line, varies from boss to tips, usually decreasing in that order. **V. stars,** those changing in magnitude, usually during more or less regular periods. The navigational star *Algol* (β *Persei*) is one of this type, its magnitude having a range from 2.2 to 3.5 which is believed to be the result of an eclipsing satellite.

VARIATION. Amount or rate of change; as, *v. of the compass; v. in altitude.* In nautical almanacs, abbrev. *var.;* as, *var. in 1 hour.* Declination or angle *magnetic meridian* makes with the *true* or *geographical meridian; see* **M. declination** *in* MAGNETIC; **D. of compass needle** *in* DECLINATION; *also remarks in* COMPASS. **Line of no v.,** *see* **Agonic l.** *in* LINE.[2] **Lines of equal v.,** *see* **I. lines** *in* ISOGONIC.

VAST. Contraction of *avast;* as, *vast heaving!* Cf. AVAST.

V-BOTTOM BOAT. Also called *straight-framed boat* and *deadrise boat,* small craft having a bottom of broad *V-shaped* cross-section, with sharp turn of bilge. The boat has straight frames and floors throughout.

VECTOR, RADIUS. *See* RADIUS.

VEER. To pay out, slack off, or allow to run, as a chain cable or a hawser; often with *away* or *out;* as, to *v. away* (or *out*) *more cable.* In older usage, to *wear,* or turn ship away from the wind and bring it on the other side, in lieu of *coming about* or *tacking;* also, usually with *off,* to steer farther from direction of wind. Use of the word to denote a shift in wind direction to-day may be considered obsolete. In referring to such "veering" or changing of wind relative to a vessel's course, a breeze is said to *draw forward* or *aft,* while shift of its *compass direction* to the right, or clockwise, is called *hauling* and to the left, *backing.* To **v. and haul,** to pay out and haul in alternately, or at same time on different parts, as of a hawser, purchase, etc.

VEERING TRIM, In. As formerly used by *whalers,* said of their vessel when shortened down to handy canvas for prompt and quick maneuvering among, or in the vicinity of, floating ice.

VEGA. Brightest star in the northern heavens, excepting, sometimes, the variable *Betelgeux* in *Orion; see* LYRA.

VELIC POINT. Also, *center-velic;* same as **center of effort;** *see* CENTER.

VENDAVALE. A strong southwest wind, usually accompanied by rain, frequently occurring in winter in the western Mediterranean. Also, a series of thunder-squalls frequently arising from the westward on east coast of Mexico. Also spelled *vendaval.*

VENT. An outlet or pipe for releasing air or a gas under pressure, or for supplying air, or for both purposes, as that fitted to a *cargo-* or a *ballast-tank;* a small hole in a cask, usually fitted with a plug, for such purpose.

VENTILATING. Act of supplying, or used in a system of, ventilation. **Ammunition v.,** *see* AMMUNITION. **V.-funnel,** *see* FUNNEL. **V.-trunk,** *see* **T. ventilator** *in* TRUNK.

VENTILATION. System or process of providing, by allowing free entry of, or forcing or inducing fresh air into, a compartment or group of compartments or spaces in a vessel, thereby also expelling vitiated air, either by natural draft through one or more conduits or *ventilators,* or by artificial means, as in an arrangement of fans or blowers. **Exhaust v.,** *see* EXHAUST. **Mechanical v.,** *see* MECHANICAL. **Natural v.,** that in which circulation is induced by the naturally ascending warm air, by the wind, or by currents of air due to vessel's onward motion. **Supply v.,** system in which fresh air is forced mechanically into ship's spaces, displaced foul or vitiated air thence being drawn off by uptake vents or exhausted through doors, stairways, etc. This system lends itself to temperature control, or preheating of delivered air as required in crew or passenger spaces, etc.

VENTILATOR. Any opening, conduit, pipe, or the like through which fresh air is introduced or vitiated air, gases, etc., escape; any contrivance for expelling foul or stagnant air or for supplying fresh air, as from or to a cabin, hold, etc. **Bell-mouthed** or **cowl v.**, an air conduit, usually tubular in form, terminating above a weather deck in a vertical *cowl,* at top of which a 90° elbow opens out in an enlarged bell-shaped mouth. Cowls vary in size from about 6 inches in diameter to as much as four feet, depending on magnitude of space they serve. They are mounted on that part of *v. trunk* extending above deck and so fitted as to allow "trimming" in any direction, *i.e.,* free turning toward or away from the wind or air-current prevailing. As a general rule in *natural ventilation,* a *v.* leading from a weather side or end of a hold or tween-deck space is an *uptake* and its cowl should be turned *back* to apparent direction of wind, while a *lee v.* is a *downtake* and should be trimmed to *face* direction of wind; the reason for this is that draft below decks has a natural tendency to flow in a direction contrary to the *apparent direction* of wind. **Canvas v.,** a large portable canvas tube having an opening near its top end with wings or broad flaps for catching wind. It is hoisted over a hatchway, tank top, or other opening for forcing a supply of fresh air into a hold, tank, etc.; more commonly called a *wind-sail.* **Gooseneck** or **swan-neck v.,** as often fitted to serve a cabin, store-room, bunker space, etc., below a superstructural deck, small tubular *v.* having its upper end curved downward through 180°. Usually placed at side of deck with mouth on its after side. Some are made with a hinged cover, which may be secured by a butterfly nut, for preventing entrance of water. **Mushroom v.,** named for the shape of its top, tubular fitting in which is mounted a vertical screw-spindle that is fixed to center of a hemispherical or *mushroom-shaped* cover. The *v.* is closed or opened by simply turning cover as required. **Trunk v.,** *see* TRUNK. **V. coaming,** that part of trunk of a *v.* extending above a weather deck and to which the *v. cowl* is fitted. Where removal of *cowl* is necessary for safety reasons during heavy weather, *coaming* is covered with a wooden cap or plug and a canvas *hood.* **V. turning-gear,** for moving a large *v. cowl* about its vertical axis, consists of a pinion turned by a hand-wheel or crank and working in a rack encircling cowl. It is chiefly fitted to *stokehold* and *engine-room v's,* which are trimmed by this means from below.

VENUS. (L.) Second planet from the sun, moving in an orbit between Mercury and Earth, and most brilliant of all planets when at or near greatest elongation. Her mean distance from Sun is approximately 67,196,000 statute miles and from Earth at nearest approach, about 25,702,000 miles. Has a diameter of 7,575 miles, or nearly .97 that of Earth. Her *semidiameter* in arc varies from a little less than 5" to 30½". The planet never attains a greater angular distance from Sun than about 46½°; and as *Morning Star,* or when rising *before* Old Sol, was called *Lucifer* by the ancients and *Hesperus* when appearing in the western sky as *Evening Star.*

VERIFICATION OF FLAG. Internationally recognized right of a war-vessel to force any craft on the high seas to heave to and produce satisfactory proof of her nationality and ownership, when such craft is suspected of sailing under false colors, or of concealing her identity in any way.

VERNAL EQUINOX. *See* EQUINOX.

VERNIER. (Named for its inventor, *Pierre Vernier, 1580–1637*) An auxiliary scale fitted to slide along the measuring scale of an instrument, as on the limb of a sextant, arc of a theodolite, or on a mercurial barometer, for taking accurate readings when index mark lies between divisions on the main scale. Its principle may be illustrated as follows: A number of consecutive divisions on the scale are equal in length to the vernier, which is graduated in a number of divisions totaling *one more* than those on the scale. Then, in the case of 9 divisions on scale being equal in length to 10 on the *v.,* coincidence of 1st. mark from zero on *v.* with 1st. mark on scale indicates a value of one-tenth the scale subdivision must be added to next less subdivision, or that just passed by the index or zero mark on *v.* Thus, if index lies between 20° 30' and 20° 40', as in a sextant, with division 1 of *v.* coinciding with a division mark on the limb, reading is 20° 30' plus 1', or 20° 31'; and so on.

VERTEX. Apex; highest point; zenith. Sun's or moon's *upper limb.* In a *great circle,* either of its diametrically opposite points lying nearest the pole; tangential point at which such circle meets with a latitude parallel,—always 90°, or 5400 nautical miles, from the circle's intersection with the equator.

VERTICAL. Pertaining to the *vertex.* Plumb; upright; perpendicular to a horizontal base or plane of the horizon. A *v.* line or plane. **Angle of the v.,** *see* ANGLE. **V. angle,** *see* **A. of elevation** *in* ANGLE. **V.-cut sail,** as opposed to the cross-cut sail favored by racing yachtsmen, a gaff-, boom-, lug-, or lateen sail in which the cloths run parallel with the leech. **V. danger angle,** *see* **D. angle** *in* DANGER. **V. force,** in magnetism, *v.* component of the earth's total intensity at a given place, as measured by *dip* of a magnetic needle; *see* **D. of the needle** *in* DIP. **V. iron,** in connection with magnetic-compass compensation or adjustment, the various structural parts of an iron or steel vessel that lie more or less in the *v.* and thus must be considered in correcting that part of the deviation due to magnetic induction in such iron, or *coefficient B* in the rectangular method of compass compensation; *see* DEVIATION. (See also

Vertical as a combining term under CIRCLE; ENGINE; KEEL; LIMB)

VERY'S NIGHT SIGNALS. (Named for their inventor, *Lieut. Samuel W. Very, U.S.N., 1877*) A former naval code of pyrotechnic signaling in which colored stars were fired from a special pistol (*Very's pistol*). Green, red, and white stars were projected in various sequences and numbers from cartridges thus prepared to meet requirements of the code or regulation signals.

VESSEL. (O.F. *vaissel;* F. *vaisseau;* L. *vascellum,* dim. of *vas,* a vessel) As generally used among seamen, the term "vessel" means any craft that is protected from entrance of sea-water by a continuous deck and is used for purposes of navigation; hence the difference between such craft and a "boat." In legal usage, however, the broader definition of *v.,* *esp.* where admiralty jurisdiction is concerned, may be stated as including "every description of water craft or other contrivance used, or capable of being used, as a means of transportation in water." *Cf.* BOAT; SHIP. **Auxiliary v.,** *see* AUXILIARY. **Awning-deck v.,** *see* AWNING. **Burdened v.,** as prescribed in *Rules of the Road* for two approaching *v's,* one that must keep out of the way of the other. **Cantilever-framed v.,** single-deck *v.* of the bulk-cargo carrying, self-trimming type, characterized by a bridge-like structural arrangement of transverse framing in which frames turn inward several feet below the deck and connect with a fore-and-aft girder on either side of the line of hatchways. Lighter framing continues upward from the *knuckle* or turn of main frames, thus forming a triangular-section space or corner below outer extremities of deck. This space often is turned to use as wing ballast-tanks. *Cf.* **S.-trimming v.** *in* SELF. **Cargo v.,** one primarily designed for carriage of cargo. She becomes a *passenger v.* when carrying more than 12 passengers on an international voyage (foreign trade) according to regulations of International Conference on Safety of Life at Sea, 1948. In U.S. coasting trade, such *v.* may not carry more than 16 passengers and not more than 12 in intercoastal trade, or that between Atlantic and Pacific ports. **Certified v.,** one built in a foreign country and owned in U.S.A. Such *v.* once was provided with a sea letter to certify her neutrality; *see* **Sea l.** *in* LETTER. **Concrete v.,** one built of concrete reinforced by steel rods, chiefly with the view of overcoming shortage of material for all-steel construction in World War I. Hulls up to 400 feet in length have been built of concrete, which is about the limit of practicability, owing to amount of steel rods required to withstand the greater longitudinal stresses in a lengthy *v.* Weight of material, as compared with a steel hull, is from $2\frac{1}{2}$ to 3 times greater, with consequent loss of deadweight carrying capacity. Excepting a few lighters, storage hulks, etc., the *concrete v.* is almost forgotten. **Classification and inspection of v's,** *see* CLASSIFICATION. **Coasting v.,** generally, one engaged in trading between ports on a coast; a coaster. However, such *v.,* in accordance with navigation laws or custom, may be a coastal trader only within certain specified limits. *Cf.* **C. trade** *in* COASTING. **Combination v.,** *see* **I. ship** *in* INTERMEDIATE. **Corrugated v.,** so called from the hull's two longitudinal rounded ridges in the shell plating between load-line and turn of bilge, a patented type that appeared about 1920 with the claim of economy in propulsive power and increase in carrying capacity. The experiment appears to have been short-lived, chief objection being its high cost of construction. **Flush decked v.,** *see* FLUSH. **Interaction of passing v's,** *see* INTERACTION; *cf.* SUCTION. **Longitudinal-framed v.,** *see remarks in* FRAME. **Meeting v.,** *see* MEETING VESSELS. **Over-taking v.,** *see* OVER. **Packet v.,** *see* PACKET. **Partial awning-deck v.,** one having an awning or shelter deck for a portion of her length; usually of the **raised quarterdeck** type; *see* RAISED. **Passenger v.,** = passenger ship. **Privileged v.,** one of two approaching *v's* directed by *Rules of the Road* to hold course and speed; the *stand-on v.* (*Cf. contra* **Burdened v.**) **Reinforced concrete v.,** *see* **Concrete v. Self-trimming v., self-unloading v.;** *see* SELF. **Shade-deck v.,** *see* SHADE. **Single-decked v.,** *see* **S. decker** *in* SINGLE. **Spar-deck v.,** *see* SPAR. **Stand-on v.,** *see* **Privileged v. Tank v.,** *see* TANK. **Surveying v.,** as usually attached to a navy or other governmental authority, *v.* specially equipped for carrying out hydrographic surveys preparatory to publication of charts, tidal data, and sailing directions. Included in equipment are powered boats appropriately fitted for sounding and plotting depths of water over shoals and comparatively shallow areas, laying out marker-buoys, station-flags, etc., also observing directions and velocities of tidal streams. **Trunk-deck v.,** *see* TRUNK. **V.'s numbers,** *see* NUMBER.

VIBRATING NEEDLE. As used in connection with compensating a vessel's magnetic compass, a small delicately pivoted magnetic needle by means of which the intensity of its directive power, as observed on shore free of any local attraction and at site of ship's compass, determines relative magnitude of horizontal component of vessel's magnetic field.

VIBRATING PERIOD. Also, *oscillating period;* time, measured in seconds, occupied by a single oscillation or "swing" of the card of a magnetic compass upon being deflected through an arc of about 30° and instantly freed. Such observation being made as a test of card's comparative efficiency, period necessarily is a criterion of its directive power which depends upon the horizontal intensity of magnetic field, moment of inertia of card, and magnetic moment of card's needles.

VICE-ADMIRAL. *See* ADMIRAL.

VICTORY SHIP. In U.S., either of two types, *AP2* and *AP3*, of standard single-screw cargo vessels built in the war emergency program, from 1942, by the Maritime Commission (now *Federal Maritime Board*). An improvement on the *Liberty ship* in speed and cargo-carrying efficiency, hulls of both *Victory* types are identical in shape but greater in length by 20 feet and in beam by 5 feet than the *Liberty*, with a deadweight capacity of 10,700 tons and load displacement 15,200 tons on a load draft of 28 ft. 6 in. Speed of *AP2*, 15 knots; *AP3*, 16 knots. *Cf.* **L. ship** *in* LIBERTY.

VICTUALING. Providing or storing with food; the supplying of provisions, as to a ship. **V. bill,** a list of all bonded stores taken on board a merchant vessel for use as provisions. When authorized by customs authority, it becomes one of vessel's clearance papers. **V. department,** or **v. office,** authority or office directing supply of provisions and stores to the navy. (*British*) **V. scale,** in merchant vessels, list of minimum provisions to be served each member of crew on each day of the week, as prescribed in *Articles of Agreement,* or *Shipping Articles.* According to navigation laws of most countries, a copy of such agreement is required to be posted in crew's quarters. *Cf.* To **sign a's** *in* ARTICLES; *also* POUND AND PINT. **V. ship,** a vessel that conveys provisions to a naval fleet or to another vessel; a *victualer.* **V. yard,** place for storing provisions and supplies for naval ships; also a yard from or at which food and stores are delivered to the vessels. (*British*)

VIGIA. (Sp. = lookout; watch) Word formerly placed on most charts to warn the mariner of a reported danger such as a rock pinnacle, shoal, or a reef, exact position of which has not been determined or verified. Now found only on Spanish charts and perhaps a few others, American and British usage indicates such warning alongside of the danger reported by initials *P.D.* (= *position doubtful*), or by the rarer *E.D.* (= *existence doubtful*) *Cf.* P.D.; E.D.

VIKING. (Ice. *vikingr,* pirate) Member of a crew of the hardy Northmen or Scandinavians who, as freebooters, rovers, or pirates, plundered the coasts of Europe in the 8th. to 10th. centuries. Several typical *v. ships,* or craft in which the *v's* put to sea, have been recovered in a remarkably good state of preservation on the Norwegian coasts. The vessels were pointed at each end, with high-rising stem- and stern-posts ornamentally carved at their top ends,— in larger craft, with the view of presenting vessel's appearance as a living monster, stem-post bearing the figure of an animal's head and stern-post terminating in a form resembling a tail, as of a fish or whale. They had a low freeboard, open waist, and usually a single tent for a cabin at after end. A single square sail was spread and they carried a single bank of oars, numbering 10 to 20 on each side. Each man's shield was placed facing outward along the gunwale, which custom afforded greater protection against a rough sea in addition to giving the craft a formidable appearance. The master, or commander of a crew of *v's,* if connected with one of the many royal families among Norsemen of the period, was called a *sea king.*

VIOL. A stout rope formerly used as a *messenger* for heaving in a hemp anchor-cable; also *voyal; voyol.* **V.-block,** a heavy *snatch-block* formerly used in leading a *v.* to the capstan; any large snatch-block.

VIRGO. (L. = virgin) A constellation through which the celestial equator passes and the sun enters at the autumnal equinox. It lies directly south of the *Dipper's handle* and contains a navigational star of magnitude 1.21 known as *Spica; see* SPICA.

VISA. (Fr. = official signature) Endorsement made by a consul or other representative of a foreign country on a passport, indicating that bearer of the document is permitted to enter such country. Signature of approval of a signal message, telegram, orders, etc., as by a superior officer. Also, *visé,* from Fr. *viser,* to authenticate by signature. To authorize, approve, or authenticate by a *v.*

VISIBILITY. Quality or state of being visible or apparent to the eye; distance at which an object may be seen under given conditions, as a light, the sea horizon, etc. **Arc of v.,** *see* ARC.

Scale of v.—

0	Dense fog.	Objects not *v.* at 50 yards.		
1	Thick fog.	Do.	do.	200 do.
2	Fog.	Do.	do.	500 do.
3	Moderate fog.	Do.	do.	½ mile.
4	Thin fog.	Do.	do.	1 do.
5	Poor *v.*	Do.	do.	2 miles.
6	Moderate *v.*	Do.	do.	5 do.
7	Good *v.*	Do.	do.	10 do.
8	Very good *v.*	Do.	do.	30 do.
9	Excellent *v.*	Do.	*v.* at over 30 miles.	

VISIBLE HORIZON. *See* HORIZON.

VISIT. Act of a naval officer in boarding a neutral vessel, or in causing her master or person delegated to come aboard war-vessel concerned, in exercise of the **right of v. and search;** *see* RIGHT.

VISOR. Small sloping awning over one or more windows or port-lights for protection against sun-glare, rain, etc., as on fore side of a pilot-house, public-rooms in passenger quarters, etc.

VISUAL HORIZON. Same as *visible horizon.*

VOICE TUBE. *See* TUBE.

VOITH-SCHNEIDER PROPELLER. *See* PROPELLER.

VOLUME. Measure of space occupied, expressed in cubic feet, inches, meters, etc.; amount of space in any magnitude of three dimensions; mass; bulk;

capacity. **V. coefficient,** as taken into account in bulk liquid cargoes, change in *v.* caused by a change of one degree in temperature of the mass. (The standard temperature of 60° (*Fahrenheit*) usually is taken in petroleum handling) Thus, *v. coefficient* .004 for crude oil indicates a change in bulk of about 40 barrels with a change of temperature of 1° in a cargo of 100,000 barrels. Where a liquid bulk cargo will be exposed to a rise in temperature *en voyage,* sufficient *ullage* must be allowed in order to avoid possible overflow of tanks. **V. of displacement,** *see* DISPLACEMENT.

VOLUNTARY LOSS. In connection with a *general average act,* such property as is sacrificed or expenditure incurred in the interests of common safety of ship, cargo, and freight. *See* **General a.** *in* AVERAGE.

VOYAGE. (M.E. *viage;* O. Fr. *viage, voiage;* Fr. *voyage*) Among seamen generally, a complete journey by sea from a home port to a foreign port or ports and return to home port or one within the region or country of departure. (A coastwise "voyage" usually is called a *trip;* a single leg of a *v.* is a *passage; see* PASSAGE) A sea-going expedition or enterprise, as a *whaling v.;* a cruise. In marine insurance and the legal world, a *v.* may be defined according to circumstances and purposes in view. It may be, for example, a single passage beginning with date at which loading commences and ending upon completion of discharge at port of destination; or, from time of sailing until return to dock or anchorage at the home port. From the shipowner's standpoint, his vessel may complete several *v's* between foreign ports during a single *v.* thus covered for his records. Ships engaged on a regular run usually consider a *v. ended* either upon arrival at dock or upon the completion of discharge of inward cargo, and *begun* immediately after such event. In general, a *v.* for which a merchant seaman is engaged *begins* with date specified in the *articles of agreement* and *ends* with his vessel's arrival at place of final discharge of cargo. **Bon v.,** a wish of welfare meaning "*Have a pleasant v.*" From the French = good *v.* (to you). **Broken v.,** an unprofitable cruise, as in whaling. **Dance v.,** slang term for an unsuccessful fishing trip. **Maiden v.,** *see* MAIDEN VOYAGE. **V. policy,** insurance policy covering property concerned only for *v.* stipulated.

VOYAL. Variant of *viol.*

V SCARF. *See* SCARF.

VULGAR ESTABLISHMENT. *See* ESTABLISHMENT OF THE PORT.

W

W. As an abbrev., stands for compass point *West;* also *Winter,* in freeboard or load-line markings. In log-books and weather records, *w* = heavy dew. In International Code of Signals, the square flag "*William*," having a central red square set in a larger white square with an all-round blue border. Hoisted singly, flag *W* denotes "*I require medical assistance*," which signal also may be used by flashing the Morse code *dot-dash-dash* (. — —). As a *towing* signal, *W* denotes by flag or flashing light "*I am paying out the towing hawser.*" This may be used by either *vessel towing* or *vessel towed.*

WACK. Variant of *whack.*

WAD. Bunch of old rope-yarns, tow, or the like formerly rammed down on the charge in muzzle-loading cannon.

WAFT. (Old past tense and past participle of verb *to wave,* as a flag) A signal made by a pennant with its fly made fast to the halyard, by a pennant with an overhand knot in it, or by any flag with a stop around its middle. The first-named formerly was used as a distant signal in the International Code. In Great Britain, displayed in harbor in any of its forms denotes the request that a customs officer board and issue an allowance of sealed tobacco for use of ship's crew. Also *weft; wheft.*

WAGER POLICY. Also called *honor policy;* in marine insurance, a policy under which assured party may recover without proof of his insurable interest, in event of loss; or, one in which actual possession of the document is sufficient proof of interest in property insured. Such policy contains the words, or their equivalent, "Interest or no interest," "This policy to be deemed sufficient proof of interest," etc. Cf. p.p.i.

WAGES. Seamen's remuneration for services rendered in merchant vessels, as recognized generally by all maritime nations, is secured by a *lien* on both ship and freight earned on voyage in question; such lien ranks first in priority, excepting, in certain cases, a lien for salvage. According to U.S. navigation laws, a seaman's right to *w.* shall not be dependent upon freight earned by his vessel and, whether or not freight is earned, seaman is entitled to claim and recover his *w.* from the master or owner *in personam.* "But in all cases of wreck or loss of vessel, proof that any seaman has not exerted himself to the utmost to save vessel, cargo, and stores shall bar such claim." *R.S. 4525 (46 U.S.C. 592)* No seaman shall forfeit his lien upon the ship by any agreement, or be deprived of any remedy for recovery of his *w.,* and "every stipulation by which any seaman consents to abandon his right to his *w.* in the case of loss of ship, or to abandon any right which he may have or obtain in the nature of salvage, shall be wholly inoperative." *R.S. 4535 (46 U.S.C. 600)* If discharged before vessel sails on a voyage, without fault and his consent, or before he has earned a month's *w.,* seaman is entitled to *w.* earned with an additional month's *w.* If vessel is wrecked, *w.* end, but seamen are entitled to transportation to port of shipment as "destitute seamen" provided for in *R.S. 4578 (46 U.S.C. 679)* When a vessel is sold at a foreign port, besides payment of *w.* master must provide adequate employment on board some other vessel bound to the port at which seaman was originally shipped, or to such other port as may be agreed upon, or provide him passage home, or deposit with U.S. consul such sum of money as is sufficient to defray such expense. *R.S. 4582 (46 U.S.C. 684)* Upon discharge of a seaman at a foreign port because of a *justifiable complaint,* master must pay *w.,* plus one month's *w.,* and provide transportation as above. *R.S. 4583 (46 U.S.C. 685)*

WAIF. In older whaling, a large shape, such as a cone, drum, or a disk fashioned by canvas spread that part of weather or upper deck between quarter on one or more hoops, hoisted at the fore or main truck as a signal to vessel's absent boats. Also, a buoy or float made fast to the end of a harpoon-line as a marker or claim to whale attached, or a flag on the end of a pike or sharp stick marking the carcase of a whale. Also, *weft* and sometimes *waft.*

WAIN, The. Constellation *Ursa Major;* Charlie's Wain; *see* ursa major.

WAIST. Midship or widest part of the upper deck; *esp.*, in a vessel having no midship superstructure, deck or poop and forecastle; middle part of the ship. **W. anchor,** a *sheet anchor* formerly stowed in the *w.* **W.-board,** planking temporarily fitted on the rail of old-time *low-waisted* vessels for added protection against a rough sea; a board or plank for same purpose in a small vessel or open boat. **W.-boat,** in whaling, boat stowed in the *w.* and usually commanded by the 2nd. mate who was called the *w.-boater.* **W.-cloth,** canvas covering for the hammocks stowed in hammock-nettings or the *hammock-berthing* along the bulwarks in ship's *w.;* also, *hammock-cloth.* (*Older naval usage*) **W.-plate,** at break of a forecastle, bridge, or poop deck, a shell plate that meets the bulwarks or rail of deck next below. It usually is curved downward in its upper edge to present a finished appearance. **W.-tree,** a spare spar lashed on the rail in the *w.* of old-time ships. Its idle time thus was profitably utilized in increasing vessel's bulwark protection against the sea.

WAISTER. Formerly, a green hand or an old or physically handicapped sailor whose duties were confined to the *waist, esp.* on board a *whaler;* also, an old seaman in the naval service who has made little or no advancement in rating.

WAIVER CLAUSE. Conventional point of agreement in marine insurance policies, indicating that either insurer or insured may take such action or incur such necessary expense as will lessen loss to property insured, without disturbing the rights of either party under the insurance contract.

WAKE. Disturbed water following, or track left by, a moving ship, an iceberg, a storm, etc. As considered in dealing with propeller design and powering of different hulls, *wake current* is implied in the term. This may be explained as follows: As vessel moves ahead, the particles of water next her hull are given a forward motion which increases in velocity as the stern is approached, so that propeller actually works in water moving with the vessel. This *w.* or forward motion decidedly has the advantage of increasing propeller efficiency, chiefly in that the *slip* thus naturally is reduced to at least reasonable bounds. *W. current* is greatest at the surface and close to hull. However, the *w.* as denoting the disturbed column of water astern of ship, following her with different diminishing velocities, is principally due to wave-action set up by the moving hull, to stream-line flow around vessel's quarters, and to increased thickness and velocity of the hull's frictional belt of water as stern is approached, which, in the case of a very full-lined underbody, actually becomes a forward drag of water close to the stern. **In the w. of,** in line with; having the same direction, in the sense of following; as, *the cruiser proceeded in the w. of two*

destroyers; following behind. Sometimes incorrectly used to denote *in the way of,* which means *at* or *near* or *close at hand.* **Sun-w.,** *see* SUN. **W. resistance,** *see* RESISTANCE.

WALE. Uppermost strake of planking in an open boat; more correctly, *gunwale.* In older wooden shipbuilding, certain broad heavy strakes of planking, also called *bends,* in vessel's sides above waterline; *see* BEND. A *wale-piece,* or timber bolted along a row of piles, as on the side of a wharf, or fixed to side of a stone pier or quay, as a fending-piece or bearer for taking the impact and distributing pressure of ships' hulls. **Foot w's,** old name for strakes of ceiling-planking in ship's hold; *esp.,* those extending across the floor timbers. **Main w's,** in former armed vessels, strakes of outside planking between water-line and lowest deck carrying guns. **W.-shore,** *see* **Breast s.** *in* SHORE.[2] **Wing w's,** planking on outside of a paddle-wheel box. (*Archaic*)

WALK. A ropewalk; *see* **R.-walk** *in* ROPE. A catwalk; *see* CATWALK. **Admiral's w.,** *see* ADMIRAL. **Captain's w.,** *see* CAPTAIN. To **w. away,** *see* **To r. away** *in* RUN. To **w. back,** to release or ease the stress on a rope by reversing the capstan or winch in use; to hold on to a line that has been hauled upon, while easing it by walking toward its lead or a belaying-pin, bollard, etc. To **w. the plank,** *see* PLANK.

WALKING. A powered vessel is said to be *walking* when, at cruising speed, a vibration is set up in the hull, or a marked change takes place in usual vibration observed, upon entering shallow water. Also termed *taking a walk, feeling* or *smelling the bottom,* it is the effect of restriction of displacement flow about the hull; *see* SMELLING THE BOTTOM. In this connection, a timely warning is given the mariner in the phenomenon of a sudden increase of the angle which the *displacement wave* makes with vessel's fore-and-aft line, *esp.* marked in smooth water, as shallowing depths are entered. Larger vessels produce a more noticeable wave in this respect: By actual observation, a vessel of 3000 tons displacement, entering a depth of 10 fathoms from a surrounding region of 40 to 100 fathoms, at a speed of 9½ knots created a more pronounced displacement wave which broadened to an angle with ship's course of about double that produced in 40 fathoms' depth. The vessel began *taking a walk,* or *walking,* upon reaching 8 fathoms. **W.-beam,** lever or beam that transfers power to driving shaft in a **beam engine;** *see* ENGINE. **W.-scow,** any sheltered-water craft moved by heaving on a line or tackle attached to movable *spuds,* or sharp-ended piles, driven into the bottom at will. Such vessel is used in dredging, laying a line of pipe, pile-driving, etc., *esp.* in swift-running currents. Also, *w.-boat.*

WALKWAY. A catwalk; *see* CATWALK.

WALL. Earthwork or structure of stone, brick, or other material enclosing a tidal dock or basin; face of a pier or quay, *esp.,* one of masonry; a *dock wall.* A temporary *stop-knot* made by turning the strands of a rope's end about each other; a *single w.* becomes a *double w.* when strands of the former are followed round a second time. A *double w.* is sometimes employed as a *lanyard knot* in smaller *lanyards* (ropes rove through *dead-eyes* for setting up shrouds, etc.) The combination *double w.* and *double crown* on a rope's end is a *manrope knot.* To *w.* a rope means to put in a *w. knot* at its end, as for preventing reeving through a block or for temporarily securing strands against unlaying. **Cold w.,** well-defined bounding line of cold water or northwestern edge of the Gulf Stream, generally extending from about Lat. 40° N. and Long. 60° W. along American coast to about latitude of Cape Hatteras. The "cold" water is that of the slow southwestward flowing branch of the *Arctic* or *Labrador current.* (*See* **A. current** *in* ARCTIC) In smooth weather, *cold w.* may be seen as a distinct dividing line between the dark green water of that cold current and the deep blue of the northeastward flowing Gulf Stream. **River w.,** *see* RIVER. **Sea w.,** *see* SEA. **Training w.,** *see* TRAINING; *cf.* REVETMENT. **W.-sided,** having perpendicular sides, or nearly so; said of a vessel built with no *tumble home;* opposed to *bank-sided,* the older term for *tumble home.*

WALRUS. (Scand. origin; Nor. *hvalros;* literally, *whale horse*) Large mammal allied to the seals, found only in Arctic and contiguous waters. Often weighing more than a ton, the male has very heavy neck and shoulders, with two large tusks extending downward from his upper jaws. The female, much less weighty, has fine slender tusks, which, as also in the male, are a high-grade quality of ivory. *W.* hide produces a valuable leather and the blubber yields an oil of similar quality to that from seals. The *w.* of Alaskan and Siberian northern coasts is a larger species than his cousin of Greenland, Spitzbergen, etc.

WAPP. (M.E. *wappen,* to wrap) Old name for a fair-leader set in the rigging. Also, a handy lanyard kept ready in the lower rigging for use as a *shroud-stopper;* for bousing or frapping the hemp shrouds, as in temporarily setting them taut; and for similar purposes about the rigging. Also, *wop.*

WAR. Act of w., a hostile act which may be pronounced as sufficient cause for a nation to prosecute her rights in question; *see* **A. of hostility** *in* ACT. **Contraband of w.,** *see* CONTRABAND. **W. head,** detachable explosive end of a torpedo; *w.-nose.*

WARDROOM. *See* ROOM. Also, *ward-room.* (The old-time quarters of the officers who kept the *warde,* or watch)

WARM-SIDED. Navy descriptive term for a ship mounting guns of heavy caliber; as, a *warm-sided wagon* (= warship).

WARP. (Teut. origin; Ice. *varp,* a throwing or casting; Sw. *varp,* drawing of a net; Dan. *varp,* a towline) A *rope* or hawser used in mooring or shifting a vessel, as by making fast its end to a post, buoy, or other fixed object, and heaving with a winch or capstan; a *hauling-line.* In *canvas,* the threads running lengthwise, across which the *woof* or *weft* is woven. It is always stronger than the *woof,* to the extent of containing double the material in heavier sail-cloth. **Fire w.,** *see* FIRE. **Guess-w.,** *see* GUESS-WARP. **Herring-w.,** rope by which the end of a line of nets is secured to the *drifter.* Cf. **D.-net** *in* DRIFT. **Trawl-w.,** *see* TRAWL. **W.-laid rope,** *cable-* or *water-laid* cordage having a *short* lay, *i.e.,* both primary strands and finished rope are twisted and laid up harder than commonly required in working rope; *cf.* **C.-laid** *in* CABLE. To **w. ship,** to haul or heave vessel by a *w.* or *w's;* to *haul ship in, ahead, astern, across,* etc., by means of one or more *w's.*

WARPAGE. Former term for harbor dues, wharfage, moorage, etc., in smaller ports. (*Chiefly British*) Charges for *warping* a vessel.

WARPING. Act of moving a vessel by means of warps; *see* To **w. ship** *in* WARP. **W. bridge,** *see* BRIDGE. **W. buoy,** a moored buoy to which may be made fast a *warp* or *hauling-line* in shifting ship by *w.;* a *mooring-buoy.* **W.-chock,** a mooring-chock; *see remarks in* CHOCK. **W.-cone,** a powered *capstan* shaped like a frustum of a cone. Used for heaving on *w.-lines,* large passenger ships usually are fitted at each end with two or more such *cones,* and, *esp.* in some European ports, often are used at a tidal dock entrance for assisting vessels through the lock or locks. Also called *gipsy, gypsy, gypsey. Cf.* GYPSY. **W.-line,** a hauling-line, or small hawser used in *w.* a vessel. **W.-post,** as fixed on a pier, wharf, etc., a wood post or pile, metal bollard, etc.,—sometimes an old cannon,—for attaching *w.-lines.* **W.-winch,** an electric- or steam-engine installed on a weather deck for *mooring* or *w.* purposes. In merchant vessels, it is usually of a type that may be used for both *w.* and hoisting cargo; also, such winch fitted at after end of ship often is constructed to handle the emergency steering tackles, in event of break-down of steering-engine. Also called *mooring-winch,* when adapted to heavy work and generally found only on larger vessels.

WARRANT. A document that authorizes, sanctions, or vouches for a certain action; a certificate of rank or appointment issued by naval authority to one inferior to a commissioned officer. **Dock w.,** *see* DOCK. **W. officer,** *see* OFFICER.

WARRANTY. In marine insurance, a condition or fact implied or expressed in the policy as *warranted* by insured party to exist or become existent, or that some act relative thereto has been, or shall be, done. Since such *w.* is *per se* a condition that establishes validity of the insurance agreement, policy becomes void if *w.* is literally untrue or unfulfilled. *W.* is an *implied* one where, from custom or general usage, it becomes unnecessary to write it in the policy; *e.g.,* a *w. of seaworthiness;* or *w's of legality* and *neutrality* with respect to trade in which the insured is engaged or will be engaged, etc. An *express w.* must be written in, or incorporated with, the policy; *e.g.,* a *loading w.* in which the insured agrees to take on board no goods of a specified character, or that no more than a certain quantity of such goods shall be carried.

WARSAW. The fish *black grouper* of the U.S. southern coasts; the *jewfish. Cf.* GROUPER; JEW-FISH.

WARSAW-OXFORD RULES. *See* RULE.

WARSHIP. Also, *war-vessel; see* MAN-OF-WAR.

WASH. Disturbed water caused by action of a propeller, paddles, oars, etc. *Rush* or *flow* of breaking waves, as over rocks; *sweep* or *rush* of waves or breakers on a beach, or the noise thus made; *swash* or *surge* of one or more waves set in motion by a passing vessel, as along a river-bank. Shallow part of a river or arm of the sea that occasionally or periodically is left dry by a falling tide; a marshy region of such character. The *blade* of an oar. To move with a rushing or swashing sound, as waves on a beach. With *down,* to scrub and rinse off with water; as, to *w. down* decks, a hold, etc. With *away, overboard, off, out,* etc., to dislodge and carry off by the action or force of sea-waves, strong current, tidal rise, etc.: "The gig was *w'd away;* ship's cat *w'd off* the skylight; the cook *w'd overboard;* with our fo'c'sle suffering the cleanest *w'ing out* it ever had!" *Cf.* SWASH. **Dry w.,** *see* DRY. **Land-w.,** *see* LAND. **Oil-w.,** *see* OIL. **W.-board,** a broad plank, fixed or removable, fitted vertically along the *gunwale* or around a cockpit in a boat for protection against entrance of water in a rough sea or when boat suddenly heels, as in a squall; one or more horizontal strakes of planking fitted over and inboard from an open boat's gunwale, often having a raised inboard edge, or coaming; also, one or more broad planks, or *weather-boards,* temporarily fitted across a *doorway* or, in former usage, across a lower-deck *gunport* for similar protection. **W. bulkhead,** a **swash bulkhead;** *see* BULKHEAD. **W.-deck gear,** *see* GEAR. **W.-plate,** also **swash-plate;** *see* SWASH. **W.-port,** a **freeing port;** *see* PORT.[2] **W.-strake,** a vertical *w.-board; see* STRAKE.

WASTE. That which is rejected; refuse; leakage; overflow. Fiber remnants, as from cotton, wool, flax, or the like, used for cleaning and wiping machinery parts, etc.; old rags. **W.-board,** a corruption of *waist-board; a wash-board; see* WAIST; WASH. **W.-heat boiler,** *see* BOILER. **W.-pipe,** often simply *waste,* a *drain-* or *scupper-pipe;* any conduit for releasing or ejecting *w.* matter overboard. **W. steam,** that allowed to escape without being utilized; *exhaust*

steam. **W.-water,** sea-water discharged overboard after circulating in a condenser, sanitary system, etc.

WATCH. (A.S. *wacian,* to be awake, to watch, be vigilant) To be alert, attentive, vigilant, "wide awake"; as, *W. out!; W.-ho, w.!* (Older significance of the word connotes *continuing without sleep, keeping vigil, continually being on one's guard*) A *buoy* is said to *w.* when remaining in its place and floating properly. A *period of duty,* usually four hours, to which a division of ship's crew, or a specified number of men, is assigned. Excepting many naval vessels, the former *two-w.* system, or that in which one-half the crew or half those assigned to *w.* duty stood alternate *w's* at sea, has been displaced to a great exten_ by the *3-watch system,* in which, generally, a *w.* of four hours is succeeded by an off-duty period of eight hours. By law, enacted March 4, 1915, all U.S. merchant vessels of gross tonnage over 100, excepting those exclusively navigating rivers, harbors, bays, sounds, bayous, canals, and lakes (other than the Great Lakes), shall divide the deck and engine departments of the crew into at least *three w's* while vessel is at sea. Following are the traditional names for each *w.* period in American and British vessels. It will be noted that, under the *two-w.,* or *w. and w.,* system, the *dog w's* (between 4 p.m. and 8 p.m.) provide the means of alternating *w. hours* each day. The more modern *3-w. system* knows no *dog w.,* the 4 p.m. to 8 p.m. period usually being known as *evening w.*

Afternoon w.	Noon to 4 p.m.
First dog w.	4 p.m. to 6 p.m.
Second dog w.	6 p.m. to 8 p.m.
First w.	8 p.m. to midnight
Middle w.	Midnight to 4 a.m.
Morning w.	4 a.m. to 8 a.m.
Forenoon w.	8 a.m. to Noon.

In the *two-w.* division of crew, particularly in larger sailing-ships, *w's* were distinguished as *starboard* and *port,* the former being the *captain's w.* (or *2nd. mate's w.*) and *port w.,* the chief *mate's.* The force of men constituting that portion of crew detailed as *w.-keepers* is divided, in any system of *w's,* into the *w. on deck,* or *w. on duty,* and *w. below,* or *w. off duty,* at a given time. Any group having same *w.* duty usually is referred to as *the w.* **Admiral's w.,** *see* ADMIRAL. **Coolashi w's,** a sailing-ship term for general duty performed by all hands, with no regular *w's* set, as when working ship through narrow waters; also, *calashee, kalashi.* (Prob. of East Indian origin) **Graveyard w.,** the *middle w.,* or period from midnight to 4 a.m., so called from the drear stillness commonly prevailing on board during those hours. **Officer of the w.,** abbrev. *O.O.W.,* officer in charge of the *w.* and responsible for navigation of the vessel in absence of the master or commanding officer. Often called *officer on w.* when he is only officer on duty; otherwise, senior officer is *officer of the w*. **Throttle w.,** an engineer's *w.* so called from constant attendance at the *throttle* to minimize racing of propeller when vessel is pitching heavily. **W. and w.,** the *two-w.* system; "toe-and-heel" *w's; see opening remarks in* WATCH. **W. bells,** strokes of ship's bell announcing clock time throughout a *w.; see remarks in* BELL. **W. bill,** posted list of persons comprising ship's company, as divided into *w's*. **W.-box,** in old-time men-of-war, a box or shelter for a sentry or guard; sentry-box. **W. buoy,** a marker buoy; *see* **S. buoy** *in* STATION. **W.-cap,** a knitted, dark blue, close-fitting cap worn by enlisted men in U.S. naval vessels during cold weather. A cover of sheet metal or canvas placed over ship's smokestack when she is laid up; *funnel or stack cover*. **W.-coat,** a heavy cloth coat or *reefer*, such as that worn by an officer in cold or bad weather. **W.-mark,** in war-vessels, a mark worn on the sleeve by a seaman to indicate the *w*. to which he belongs. In the *w. and w.* system, usually a piece of white tape on a blue jacket or black tape on a white jacket, on right sleeve signifying *starboard w.*, left sleeve the *port w*. **W. on deck,** the *w. on duty*, as distinguished from the *w. below; see remarks under* WATCH. (For the following terms having *watch* as a *suffix*, see ANCHOR; HACK; HARBOR; MATE; NIGHT; QUARTER; RADIO; SEA. Also, for terms having the *prefix, watch,* see LIGHT[1]; NUMBER; OFFICER; TACKLE)

WATER. Pure *fresh w.* consists in volume of two parts *hydrogen* and one of *oxygen*, as signified in its symbol H_2O. It freezes at a temperature of 32° *Fahr.* and boils at 212°; attains its maximum density at 39°, when its weight is 1000 ounces (nearly) or 62½ lbs. per cubic foot, a long ton (2240 lbs.) occupying a volume of 35.84 *cu. ft. Sea w.* freezes at 27° *Fahr.* and weighs 64 lbs. per *cu. ft.*, or a ton of 2240 lbs. = 35 *cu. ft. Cf.* **S. water** *in* SEA; *also,* ICE. **Broken w.,** an area of ripples, wavelets, or eddies, as caused by a current over a shoal or shallowing *w.*, or by a school of fish, *esp.* observable during light winds. **Cold-w. test,** same as *hydraulic test; see* **H. test** *in* HYDRAULIC. **Indian springs low w.,** *see* INDIAN TIDE-PLANE. **Territorial w's,** *see* **M. belt** *in* MARINE. **True w.,** depth of *w.* corrected for tidal rise to that indicated on chart. (*For other terms having* **water** *as a suffix, see* ALL; BILGE; CHOW-CHOW; DEAD; DEEP; FEED; FOUL; FRESH; HIGH; HOLD; INJECTION; LAND; LIGHT[2]; LOW; MAKE; MEAN; NORTH; OPEN; PILOT; PUBLIC; QUICK; SEA; SLACK; TAKE; TIDAL; TIDE) **W. anchor,** same as *sea anchor; see* ANCHOR. **W. bailiff,** a customs officer whose duty includes searching of vessels. (*Chiefly British*) Formerly, in Great Britain, an official having certain jurisdiction over shipping and waterfront activities, including enforcement of port regulations, fishing, and, in some cases, collection of custom duties. **W. ballast,** sea *w.* carried in various compartments for ballasting purposes, as in *double-bottom* and *deep* tanks. **W.-boat,**

a lighter or vessel used for supplying vessels in harbor with fresh water. **W.-board,** a *weather-* or *waist-board* set on the gunwale of a boat for keeping out splashing *w.* **W.-borne,** lifted on or floated by the *w.;* supported by the *w.* only, as opposed to resting on ground, as a vessel. Carried or transported by ship or boat, as merchandise; *waterborne.* **W.-borne commerce,** traffic or trade as carried on by transportation of goods on lakes, rivers, and the high seas. **W.-butt,** a large cask in which *fresh w.* is carried on board ship for domestic purposes; now generally displaced by iron tanks. **W. clerk,** person employed by a shipping concern or agency to transact business directly connected with interests of vessels in port, including aid to shipmasters with customs formalities, obtaining fuel and sea stores, clearing manifests at consulates, etc. Formerly, a *w. clerk* negotiated chartering of vessels for a broker. **W.-course,** one of the holes in floor-plates or floor-timbers to allow passage of *w.;* a *limber-hole; see* LIMBERS. **W. craft,** vessels and boats collectively. **W.-finder,** device by which the depth of water, if any, lying at bottom of oil in a tank is determined. Also called *thief-sampler,* it usually consists of a vertical strip of chemically-treated paper fixed to the sounder or gauge. *W.* discolors paper and so marks its depth. **W.-front,** region along a line of docks; land or street fronting a body of *w., esp.* a harbor. **W. guard,** in Britain, an officer of the customs who guards landed dutiable goods and prevents unauthorized landing of imported merchandise; a *customs guard.* **W. indicator,** a gauge showing surface-level of *w.* in a tank or boiler; a gauge-glass. Sometimes the device is fitted with an automatic alarm which sounds upon *w.* falling to a certain level, as in a boiler. **W.-laid,** *see* **Water-laid r.** *in* ROPE. **W.-line model,** *see* MODEL. **W.-logged,** heavy, log-like, barely afloat or manageable, as a wooden vessel making *w.* badly and saturated therewith to the extent that she is kept afloat wholly or partly by buoyancy of her cargo; *w.-soaked,* as a timber or pile. **W.-mark,** *w.-line* of a boat; a *tidal mark,* or that indicating height to which *w.-level* has risen or level of low *w.* **W. monkey,** a *chatty,* or globular receptacle having a long narrow mouth and made of porous clay, formerly used for *drinking-w.* on board ship in the tropics. Condensation of *w.* seepage keeps contents reasonably cool. (Of East Indian origin, the word is from Tamil, *shati,* a cooling-pot) **W. prism,** in engineering, a canal, river, etc., or a portion of such, considered as a prism of mid-channel length and cross-section bounded by contour of bottom and surface level. **W.-sail,** *see* **Save-all** *in* SAIL. **W. sky,** as seen in an ice-covered area at sea, dark or dull appearing patches or streaks in the sky near the horizon caused by reflection of, and thus indicating, open *w.* **W.-sprinkling system,** as required by law on U.S. vessels carrying passengers and which also carry freight upon a main deck that is accessible to passengers and crew while being navigated, an arrangement of piping on the deckhead by means of which *w.* under pressure may be sprinkled from jets, in case of fire, over entire area of deck below. Such system must also be installed in sleeping compartments, unless bed-frames, etc., are made of fire-resisting material. **W. tender,** a petty officer or leading fireman who is responsible to engineer of the watch for proper supply of *w.* and maintenance of required steam pressure in boilers, which generally includes the necessary attention to *w. feed* system and supervision of the boiler firing. In merchant vessels, he is required to hold a certificate as *w. tender* issued by the Coast Guard. (*U.S.*) **W. whip,** old term for a purchase, usually a single whip, rigged from a lower yard-arm for hoisting in moderate weights. So called from its use in taking in casks of fresh water. **White w.,** an area of breaking waves, as over a shallow bank; so called from its whitish appearance. A whale is said to *w.-water* when beating the *w.* with its flukes, as when attacked. (*Whaling*) (Other compound terms containing the prefix **water** are given under BOILER; BREAKER; LEVEL; LIGHT[1]; LINE[2]; PLANE; SEASONING; SPAR.

WATERAGE. Archaic English term for carriage of merchandise or goods by water, or charges for such service.

WATERCOURSE. Bed or channel formed or followed by a river or other stream in its flow toward another body of water. Also, *see* **W.-course** *in* WATER.

WATERMAN. One who manages or plies small vessels or boats for hire in sheltered waters; a ferryman or boatman; a *line-runner,* or man who runs or carries out warping-lines in a small boat, as in berthing or warping vessels. **W.'s knot,** a clove hitch, or two half-hitches laid over a post, etc., as in making fast the painter or bowfast of a boat.

WATERSHED. A projecting piece of wood or plate fitted slantwise over an outside doorway or window to prevent entrance of water from above, rain, etc.; an *eye-brow* or *wriggle.*

WATERSPOUT. One of the most remarkable phenomena observed at sea, the peculiarities of which have not yet been thoroughly understood. Although also not unknown in larger rivers and lakes, it is said the *w.* occurs more frequently in the Atlantic than in any other ocean and it appears to be limited to neither latitude, season, nor weather conditions. Primarily caused by an agitation in a cloud (which may suddenly come into existence or may already have been formed) due to sudden temperature changes, the "spout" first appears as a whirling inverted-cone-shaped mass reaching downward, as if alive, with an elongated trunk or column to meet a corresponding whirling disturbance on the surface. And of particular note is the fact that

this latter agitation takes place *before* the monster's "trunk" actually is seen to connect with it. The completed column then travels along at almost any speed and in often an unpredictable direction, sometimes changing in form from a vertical or slanting position to a curve into the horizontal. In the whirling process volumes of water are carried into the clouds. Although usually appearing singly, groups of three or four have been observed to take shape out of the same cloud or near-by clouds. The *w.,* minus the *water,* practically may be considered a replica of the *tornado,* many of the larger type attaining a diameter comparable to that of the "twister." Average diameter of the column varies from 50 to 150 feet and its height or length may be 1000 to 3000 feet. In a lengthy discussion of the phenomenon, Mr. W. E. Hurd of *U.S. Weather Bureau* concludes with the following: "*Waterspouts* spring into their brief existence under all manners and combinations of weather circumstances over warm water and cold water, though most frequently over warm. They are found to occur in weather settled and unsettled; in cyclones and in anticyclones; in calms, light winds, and gales; under all sky conditions from cloudiness to overcast; in warm weather and in cold; at all seasons of the year. They are found to rotate in either sense, regardless of their low-pressure centers; to set their courses directly or at angles with or against the prevailing surface winds; to drop from the clouds and rise from the water; to exhibit moderate to terrific forces; to acquire many varieties of shapes and appearances from the ordinary to the grotesque, and to vary in size from small excrescences in the cloud, or mere whirls or protuberances on the water, to cloud-and-sea-spanning creations of monstrous diameter or length."

WATERTIGHT. Impervious to passage of water. Combining term denoting such quality; as in *w. flat* (or partial *deck*). As prefixed word compounded with the following, see BULKHEAD; COMPARTMENT; DOOR; FLOOR; HATCH; RIVETING.

WATERWALL. Arrangement of tubes in the walls and floors of a boiler-furnace through which boiler-water circulates. Installed as a means of increasing heating surface while also reducing to a minimum the heat radiation from furnace walls.

WATERWAY. In *steel* vessels, a gutter or channel along the outer edge of a wood deck for receiving water drainage off deck, thence delivering it overboard through scuppers. In *wooden* construction, two or more strakes of heavy planking at sides of a deck, an inner or middle strake being let down into the deck-beams and called *locking-strake. W's* are longitudinal strength members corresponding to the *deck stringer-plate* in steel ships. *Cf.* GUTTER WATERWAY. A body of navigable water; a fairway; canal. **International w.,** *see* INTERNATIONAL. **W. bar,** a *deck-stringer* inner angle-bar; *see* DECK.

WATT. (Named for *James Watt,* Scottish inventor) An electrical measure denoting the rate of work represented by a current of one *ampere* under a pressure of one *volt,* which amounts to, very nearly, 44.23 foot-pounds per minute; also, *volt-ampere.* One *horsepower* closely approximates 746 *w's.* The *kilowatt* is 1000 *w's.* **W.-meter,** an instrument for measuring electrical power.

WAVE. Undulation or moving ridge or swell on the sea surface, having a distinct forward or translatory movement apart from any oscillatory motion in the particles composing it. Little or no onward movement of the water composing *w.* itself is observed in deep-water *w's,* but, upon reaching shallow depths, base of the *w.-body* being more or less retarded, its crest rushes on and eventually topples over in the form of a *breaker.* For ocean *storm-w's,* probably a fair average is 35 feet in height, with a span of about 1000 feet between crests, these figures depending upon force and duration of wind producing such undulations, as well as upon the magnitude of expanse over which *w's* are born and driven. Highest and longest *w's* are found in winter in high southern latitudes where, before the prevailing westerly gales, a formidable array of mountainous "green seas" is driven, unhindered by any intervening land, clear around the world. **Bow w's,** those produced by passage of a vessel through the water. They lead from the bows at an angle with the fore-and-aft line depending upon vessel's speed, underbody form, displacement, and depth of water. The *bow w.* angle being connected directly with *hull resistance,* in model-basin trials comparison of such *w's* is given consideration in questions of suitable powering for hulls of different designs. *Cf. remarks in* WALKING. **Sand w's,** *see* SAND. **Seismic w's,** sea disturbance caused by an earthquake on the sea floor. Usually appears as one or two heavy *rollers* followed by a long gradually subsiding swell. Such *w's,* upon reaching comparatively shallow water, become dangerously steep and in many instances as *breakers* have swept a coast with devastating fury. They commonly are called *tidal w's; see* **T. wave** *in* TIDAL. **Storm w's,** *see* STORM. **Tidal w.,** *see* TIDAL. **Trochoidal w. theory,** generally accepted theory of *w.* formation, or that in which contour of a cross-section of successive *w's* describes a *trochoid, i.e.,* path of a point on the circumference of a circle which is conceived to roll along on underside of mean sea surface level, but contrary in direction to that of the advancing *w.* A succession of diminishing trochoids continues downward until still *w.* is reached, which may be, in the case of larger *w's,* at a depth of several fathoms. It is noteworthy that each particle of water in the *w.-forming* process has a fixed circular orbit around which it completes a turn in a time equal to the *w. period.* **W. length,** distance in feet measured perpendicularly between two successive *w. crests;* horizontal distance from crest to crest. **W. period,** time in seconds occupied between passage of two successive *w. crests* over a fixed point. **W. profile,** in still water, actual outline of the surface as viewed against vessel's hull when she is moving at a given speed. It is considered in naval architecture in connection with longitudinal strength requirements in different hulls. **W. trap,** an arrangement of piling, etc., so as to narrow a dock entrance, or locally widen space between wharves or piers, for allowing incoming *w's* to spread and abate. **W.-trough,** hollow between two *w's;* line of greatest depression between *w's.* **W. velocity,** rate of onward motion of a *w. crest,* as passing a fixed point, or that equal to the *w. length* divided by *w. period.* Large *w's* of the deep-sea type are driven at about half the velocity of the wind causing them; thus a continuing *strong breeze,* which blows at 30 knots, will set up a *w. velocity* of close to 25 feet per second.

WAVESON. Of historical note as the term in early English law for *flotsam,* or wreckage, cargo, etc., left floating after loss of a vessel. *Cf.* FLOTSAM.

WAY. Motion through the water. A vessel is said to *gather w.* when her speed is increasing or when starting to move ahead or astern; she *loses w.* when her speed is diminishing; and is *under w.* when proceeding from one place toward another, whether actually in motion through the water or not. *(Cf.* **U. way** *in* UNDER) She has *headway* when moving ahead; *sternway* when moving stern first; in both cases always with relation to the water only, since the craft may have neither headway nor sternway while being carried in any direction by a current. In *pl.,* timbers on which a vessel slides while being launched; *see* **L.-ways** *in* LAUNCHING. **Feeling the w.,** *see* FEEL. **Fresh w.,** *see* FRESH. **To freshen the w.,** to increase speed, as by spreading additional sail. **To give w.,** *see* GIVE. **To keep her w.,** *see* KEEP. **W. enough!,** command to cease rowing, as when approaching boat's destination. Usually, without further orders, crew tosses and boats oars and, also, unships rowlocks.

W — C. (*W minus C*) Same as C — W, *q.v.*

WEAKFISH. A food fish of the genus *Cynoscion,* so named from its tender flesh. The *common w.,* also called *sea trout* and *squeteague,* is found on the U.S. Atlantic coast south of Cape Cod, as far as the Mississippi; the *white w.* (*white trout* or *silver squeteague*) and *spotted w.* (also *spotted sea trout, spotted squeteague, salmon*) are caught on the east coast south of Cape Hatteras and on the Gulf coasts. The fish is from 15 to 20 inches in length, has graceful lines, and is not unlike the common trout, excepting its additional lengthy dorsal fin just forward of the tail.

WEAR. To bring a vessel on the other tack, when sailing close-hauled, by turning away from the wind instead of *tacking,* or *coming about,* by heading into it. *Wearing* usually must be resorted to when vessel is under shortened canvas as in heavy weather, or when wind is too light to allow of holding her way in the tacking maneuver, which commonly is the case in square rig. In the former situation, as ship lays off from the wind, after yards are braced in to gain the benefit of wind-pressure leverage on head sails in turning. Wind now drawing aft, all after yards are braced for the new tack and head yards gradually hauled around as vessel is steered up to her next course on the other tack. What is termed *turning ship on her heel* is performed when light winds render *tacking* impossible. Vessel is *wore* by first turning her by helm as far into the wind as she will go; then head yards are braced *abox*, or to bring sails flat *aback;* this throws ship's head off and gives her a little sternway; helm being used accordingly, vessel now swings away from wind until head sails shiver; then head yards are hauled around and, as she gathers headway, *wearing ship* is completed as in the former case. In the uncommon instance of *w'g* a fore-and-aft rigged vessel, the maneuver becomes a dangerous one in strong winds due to necessary *gybing* involved, in which point the square-rigger scores a 100% advantage over the schooner. The *turning ship on her heel*, also *going round on her heel*, referred to was called *boxhauling*, in the sense of getting ship on the other tack where room for *wearing* under continuous headway was limited or insufficient; for which reason, also the possibility of *missing stays* might be obviated under such conditions. *Cf.* BOX-HAUL.

WEATHER. Atmospheric conditions with respect to temperature, barometric pressure, wind force and direction, humidity, precipitation, degree of cloudiness, visibility, etc., existing at a certain place or region at a given time; existing meteorological conditions noted by an observer. State of *w.* and related phenomena are noted in *log-books* and *w. reports* by the following or like symbols: b = blue sky, whether clear or hazy; c = clouds (detached); d = drizzling rain; f = fog; g = gloomy; h = hail; l = lightning; m = misty; o = overcast; p = passing showers; q = squally; r = rain; s = snow; t = thunder; u = ugly, threatening; w = dew. To pass to windward of, *esp.* in the sense of safely clearing, an object; as, *the vessel w'ed Cape Horn in a howling gale.* To successfully pass through, or make headway in, unfavorable conditions, a storm, etc.; as, *the missing boats failed to w. the gale.* As opposed to *lee,* toward or lying in the direction from which the wind blows; windward; as, *w. side; w. yard-arm;* or from which a current or tidal stream is setting; as, *w. anchor; w. ship* (of a group at anchor); *w. buoy.* **Bad w.,** that characterized by winds of gale force accompanied by a heavy sea; a rain- or snow-storm. With respect to cargo-handling, such inclement *w.* as would cause damage to goods if ex-

posed thereto; or, on account of rough sea conditions or heavy swell, loading or discharging *via* lighters is deemed hazardous; or, any state of *w.* or sea detrimental to safe handling or transfer of cargo. To **keep one's w. eye open,** *see* EYE. To **make bad w. of it;** to **make good w. of it,** *see* MAKE. **Stress of w.,** constraint or delaying force of or by the elements; sustained violence imposed by gales and high seas; as, *vessel put in for repairs due to stress of w.* **Thick w.,** *see* THICK. **W.-beaten,** seasoned, worn, or toughened by exposure to the *w.; w.-worn; w.-bitten.* **W.-bitt,** old-fashioned term meaning to lay a second turn of cable round the bitts; a second or third turn of cable (former hemp *anchor-cable*) on the *bitt-head* or *bitts.* **W.-board,** windward or *w.* side of ship (*archaic*); *see* **W.-board** *in* WASH. **W.-bound,** delayed in port by bad *w.;* wind-bound; also, *w.-fast.* **W. bow,** that facing the wind, or nearly so; opposed to *lee bow.* **W. brace,** one leading from a *w.* yard-arm; as, *w. fore brace; see* BRACE. **W. breeder,** an unusually clear state of the atmosphere often occurring before a gale or cyclone. **W. Bureau,** in U.S., a division of the Department of Agriculture charged with keeping *w. report* statistics and daily forecasting of *w.* throughout the nation. **W. chart,** map of a region showing by lines and symbols the meteorological conditions existing at a given hour. These include precipitation, force and direction of wind, temperature, humidity, barometric pressure, and appearance of sky, together with the isobars and isotherms derived from such information, as reported by the stations distributed throughout region concerned. **W.-cloth,** *see* CLOTH. **W. deck,** as distinguished from a *'tween deck* or other deck below another, one wholly exposed to the elements. **W.-driven,** tossed or driven by strong winds or gales, as a disabled or unseaworthy vessel. **W.-fast,** *see* **W.-bound. W.-flag,** a pennant or square flag displayed as a *w.* signal or warning. **W.-gall,** *see* GALL. **W. gauge,** *see remarks in* GAUGE. **W.-glass,** a barometer; *see* GLASS. **W. helm,** *see* To **carry a lee,** or **a weather h.** *in* HELM. **W. leech,** *see* **Lee l.** *in* LEECH. **W. lurch,** a sudden roll to windward, as when sailing in a cross sea. **W. main and lee cro'jack braces!,** order to man and haul on the braces named in the maneuver of *wearing ship,* in a vessel of *3-masted ship* rig. In a *4-masted barque,* **W. main and cro'jack braces!** In a *4-masted ship,* **W. main cro'jack, and lee jigger braces!** *Cf.* WEAR. **W. map,** *see* **W. chart. W. observation,** recorded particulars of meteorological conditions at a given place or position at sea. Result of such is often sent by radio from certain selected or commissioned vessels to headquarters concerned. To **w. out,** to pass through or encounter successfully, but with considerable difficulty; as, to *w. out* the gale. **W. quarter,** *see* QUARTER. **W. report,** result of a *w. observation* as sent in by telegraph, radio, etc., in the form of a report. **W. roll,** a vessel's roll to windward, as in a heavy beam sea.

W. permitting clause, stipulation in a charter-party stating that any day or part of a day during which transfer of cargo is not carried on because of bad *w.* is not to be included in the counted *lay days. Cf.* **L. days** *in* LAY; *also,* DEMURRAGE. **W.-rope,** *see* ROPE. **W. sheet,** *see* SHEET.[1] **W. ship,** one of the government vessels stationed as required at sea primarily for the purpose of reporting existing *w.* conditions for the benefit of aviators. As agreed upon by the *International Civic Aviation Organization,* there were, in July, 1950, made available for continuous duty at 10 stations, widely scattered to meet requirements of trans-Atlantic air traffic, 25 vessels. Of these, the United States supplied 14 (all U.S. Coast Guard); Great Britain 4; France, Holland, and Norway 2 each; Canada 1; with Belgium and Denmark contributing $10,000 each per year, Portugal and Ireland $4,000 each, toward operating costs. In addition to routine *w.* reports, the ships relay radio communications from aircraft and surface vessels as required, and have proved most useful in sending out advice to vessels regarding aircraft in distress, as well as in rescue services made possible by their own immediately available assistance. **W. shore,** *see* SHORE.[1] **W. signal,** one giving information on expected *w.,* esp. that displayed at a coast signal station. **W. tide,** *see* TIDE.

WEATHERLINESS. Quality of being *weatherly,* or capable of sailing close to the wind while making comparatively little leeway; *esp.,* in a rough sea; said of sailing-craft. Having qualities of a good sea-boat.

WEATHERMOST. Farthest to windward; as, *the w. vessel.*

WEB. The main portion of a beam, girder, frame, or the like, or that distinct from any attached angle-bars, flanges, or connections with another structural member. **W. frame,** *see* FRAME. **W. framing,** in shipbuilding, system in which ordinary transverse frames are reduced in size, consequent deficiency in strength being compensated for by fitting *w. frames* of 3 to 4 times the depth, or molding, and in lieu of, every 5th. to 7th. ordinary frame. A vessel thus constructed is called a *w.-framed ship.* **W. stringer,** a wide bridging and stiffening girder fitted horizontally between *w. frames,* as in a deep hold, or in an engine space where compensation is necessary for loss of transverse strength due to absence of beams. **W. plate,** the wide plate, or *w.,* in a girder, stringer, frame, etc. **W. sling,** as used in hoisting bagged cargo, a broad rope-enforced canvas sling or, sometimes, one in the form of a small rope net. A heavy canvas *w. sling* is used, belly-band fashion, in hoisting aboard or landing live animals; also, *animal-sling.*

WEDGE. (A.S. *wecg*) Triangular piece of wood or metal tapering to a thin edge like an elongated *V.* As extensively used in shipyard work for setting up keel-blocks, shores, etc., *w's* usually are made of hard wood such as oak, maple, beech, birch, etc. Lifting, splitting, or *wedging* power of this simple machine is employed to actually raise a vessel from her position on keel- and bilge-blocks to that of resting in the *launching-cradle,* superimposed on the *sliding ways.* (*Cf.* LAUNCHING) Since the raising power of an 18-inch *w.* having a 3-inch depth of butt is 6 times that of the blow administered by the *w. ram,* or piece of timber swung end on to *ram* or *butt* each *w.,* it is simply a matter of employing a sufficient number of such *w's* to lift any hull on the stocks. *Power of w.* is equal to length of its face times force of blow divided by depth of *w.* (between faces at butt end). In naval architectural calculations in stability, rolling, etc., the **emerged w.** is that *w.-shaped* portion of ship's volume bounded by the water-surface plane and vessel's raised waterline plane, when she is heeled, or transversely inclined, with no change in displacement occurring. It is the opposite of **immersed w.,** or that correspondingly formed at vessel's low side. **Hatch w.,** *see* HATCH. **Launching w.,** special long *w.* used in the operation of *wedging up* the *launching cradle* so as to remove vessel's weight from the blocks to the *sliding ways.* (*See opening remarks in* WEDGE) Such *w's* also are called *adjusting w's.* **Mast w.,** *see* MAST. **Treenail w.,** *see* TREENAIL.

WEEP. To show signs of a slight leak, as from a cask or through a plank seam in a boat. A *weeping* joint, seam, crack, etc., is one from which water or other liquid slowly leaks or oozes.

WEFT. (A.S. *wefan,* to weave) In canvas, the cross-threads, or *woof,* which are woven through the *warp,* or threads running lengthwise. The *width* measurement of sail-cloth. The word is a variant of *waft* and also of *waif; see* WAFT; WAIF.

WEIGH. (A.S. *wegan,* to bear, carry, or move) To raise or lift vessel's anchor from the bottom; *esp.* in the sense of departing from an anchorage, as in *we weighed for sea; the skipper intends to w.* (or *w. anchor*) *at dawn. Cf.* AWEIGH. See To **weigh a.,** etc., *in* ANCHOR PHRASEOLOGY. (*W.* as a corruption of *way* sometimes is met with in the erroneous phrase *under weigh*) **W'ing line,** same as **anchor-trip;** *see* ANCHOR.

WEIR. A fence of stakes, brushwood, stones, etc., fixed in a tideway, river, or sheltered tidal water, for taking fish; a *fish-weir.* Where set in a tideway, often is V-shaped, with apex toward, or facing, the flood stream; when set along a shore, with apex outward. Any net spread on stakes for taking fish at high water or ebb stage of tide; *esp.,* in localities having a large tidal range. A *w.* is also that portion of a canal bank, dam, or other embankment containing gates for release of waste water; sometimes termed a *waste w.* **W.-fishing,** industry or practice of capturing fish by means of *weirs.*

WELD. To forge into permanent union, as two bars of iron, while metal is softened by heat of such intensity as to promote fusion of the contacting surfaces; also, to unite or form by a fusing heat, with or without pressure, as in *electric* and *oxyacetylene welding.* A union or joint formed by *welding;* as, a *butt w., lap w., scarf w., split w.*

WELDING. Any of the various methods or processes of uniting metals, *esp.* iron and steel parts, in which, necessarily, cohesion of the molecules is effected by heating the parts to a very high temperature. *W.* of the direct *fusion* type has greatly displaced the older *forging* in present-day shipbuilding practice and, also to a large extent, has superseded the former all-riveted work because of its great saving of material and labor. **Butt w.,** that in which two pieces are united butt to butt. Essentially consists of fusing of the contacting metal while the parts are forced together under pressure. **Electric w.,** fusion of metal in this commonly practiced method is effected by passage of an electric current through the junction of parts or by heating the latter to fusion by an electric arc. What is termed *carbon-arc w.* is that in which the *filler-rod,* or *metal filling,* required remains outside the electrical circuit; in *metal-arc w.,* the filler-rod is used as one of the poles of the arc. The latter process is popular in ship construction and marine engineering. Also, *electric-arc w.* **Flash w.,** an improvement on the *butt w.* process above mentioned, so named from the practice of producing an electric arc between the parts as they approach each other. The quickly fusing units are then, with suitable equipment, forced together under heavy pressure. **Forge w.,** art or practice of uniting metal by subjecting it to blows of a hammer while it is softened by heating. **Fusion w.,** as distinguished from *forge w.,* uniting of metals by a fusing heat, as produced by an *oxyacetylene* torch, *electric* current, or by the *thermite* process. **Resistance w.,** that in which the parts in contact are heated by an electric current; so called from the heat-producing resistance to current flow. **Spot w.,** type of *resistance w.* in which overlapping parts are joined at regular *spots.* It replaces riveting, as of lapping plates, etc. **Tack w.,** procedure of *tacking,* or temporarily holding the parts in position by short light *welds* along a line of *w.,* preparatory to making the permanent weld; also that of *w.* small attached parts which bear comparatively little stress. **Thermite w.,** process employed in repairing large castings and heavy forgings which depends upon a supply of liquid metal (*thermite*) being brought into contact with the fracture (or scarf) to be *welded.* A mold is built around the junction and into this is poured from a crucible a mixture of powdered aluminum and iron oxide which, when ignited, violently combine, produce intense heat, and form a steel in liquid state. The uniting surfaces thus exposed to such heat, with the molten metal, completely knit together, or fuse, in the finished *weld.*

WELDWOOD. Trade name for high-grade *plywood* specially fabricated for use in boat-building. *Cf.* PLYWOOD.

WELIN DAVIT. *See* **Quadrant d.** *in* DAVIT.

WELL. A chamber or inclosure into which *bilge-water* drains for facilitating use of the *pumps.* In large vessels, it takes the form of a double-bottom cofferdam extending one or two frame or floor spaces and from side to side, between two double-bottom tanks. In a fishing vessel, a *compartment* into which sea-water is allowed to freely circulate through holes in the craft's bottom for the purpose of keeping fish alive for marketing. A *shaft* in which a propeller is raised or lowered in shipping or unshipping, as in heavy ice conditions. In wooden vessels, an inclosure built around the *bilge-pumps* for their protection and to facilitate inspection of suction-box, etc. Portion of a *weather deck* having bulwarks and extending between a raised forecastle or a poop and a midship or bridge erection; as, a *forward w.; after w.;* a *w. deck.* A sunken space near the fo'c's'le head in old-fashioned war-vessels for stowing an *anchor;* an *anchor w.* In *marine insurance,* a vessel is said to be *w.* as warranted or authentically reported *safe* or unharmed at a given date and place. In the Pentland Firth and vicinity, a dangerous eddy or whirlpool. (*Local, north of Scotland*) **Centerboard w.,** *see* **C.-casing** *in* CENTERBOARD. **Drain w.,** *see opening text in* WELL. **Rudder-w.,** *see* **R. pit** *in* RUDDER. **Tunnel w.,** a *drain w.* at after end of a *shaft tunnel* for receiving leakage from stern tube and water used in cooling shaft bearings. (See *well* as a combining term under ANCHOR; BILGE; FISH; PROPELLER; PUMP; DECK; ROOM)

WELT. A strip of wood fastened over a flush joint or seam for strengthening purposes, as on inside of planking in a carvel-built boat; a seam-batten.

WEST. (A.S.; of Aryan origin) Point of the compass lying on one's left hand when facing north; point on the horizon at which the sun *sets* at the equinoxes; opposite of *east.* Portion of a country lying toward the sunset; the *Occident, New World,* or the *West,* as indicating the Western Hemisphere from the European's homeland. Emanating from the *w.;* as, a *w. wind.* **W. by N.,** point of the compass $11\frac{1}{4}°$ *north* of *west.* **W. by S.,** $11\frac{1}{4}°$ or one point *south* of *w.* **W.N.W.,** $22\frac{1}{2}°$ or two points *north* of *w.* **W.S.W.,** $22\frac{1}{2}°$ or two points *south* of *w.* **Magnetic W.,** the point *W.* indicated by a correct *magnetic* compass. **True W.,** geographical *w.;* point in the celestial horizon diametrically opposite *true East,* or intersecting point of the equinoctial, horizon, and prime vertical at any place other than at either geographical pole. **W.-country whipping,** *see* WHIPPING.

WESTERLY. Having a direction toward the *west:* proceeding toward *west;* as, a *w. set of current;* a *w. drift.* Facing the *west;* toward the *west* in situation; as, *the w. shore; the two w. buoys.* Coming from the *west;* as, a *w. breeze.* Westward; toward the *west,* in an adverbial sense; as, *the stream runs w.* **Westerlies** are the prevailing winds of the temperate zones, generally north and south of Lat. 30° in either region.

WESTERN OCEAN. Ancient name for the *Atlantic,* the vast expanse lying west of the once only-known world. The term still is used among sailors, *esp.* to denote the principal America-Europe trade-route zone, or region of the *North Atlantic* between Latitudes 40° and 60°.

WESTING. Distance made good to the *westward:* departure in miles from a given meridian toward the *west;* distance traveled on a *true west* course.

WESTWARD. Lying or facing toward the *west:* westerly; as, *the w. cape.* In a westerly direction; as, *ten ships of the line headed w.* (WEST recalls the old riddle offered a green hand by the veteran salt:
*"The wind was West and West steered we
With flowing sheet; how could that be?"*)

WET. Covered, soaked, or splashed with, or containing. water or other liquid. Rainy; characterized by an above-average rain-fall; drizzly; as, the *w. season; w. monsoon.* To splash or cover with water; as, to *w. the decks; wetted fore-and-aft with spray.* To **row w.,** to *pull w.,* or splash with one's oar in rowing. **W. basin,** a tidal dock or *basin; see* TIDAL. **W. boat,** vessel or boat that easily ships water or throws an unusual amount of spray from her weather bow in sailing. **W. cargo,** in a miscellaneous, or *general,* cargo, distinguishing term for goods which may give off sufficient moisture, or suffer leakage, which may cause damage to *dry cargo,* either by absorption or direct contact with leakage. Examples of *w. cargo* are: barreled beef, fish, etc. in brine; **casks** of beer, syrup, or other liquids; green hides; oils in tins; wood pulp. **W. dock,** *see* DOCK. **W. fish,** fresh fish, such as cod, haddock, herring, halibut, etc., as distinguished from any shellfish. *(Chiefly British)* **W. monsoon,** *see* MONSOON. **W. provisions,** *see* PROVISION. **W. slip,** *see* SLIP. **W. smack,** also *well smack; see* SMACK.

WETTED SURFACE. Measured outside area of that portion of vessel's hull below the waterline, including bilge keels, propeller-bossing, and rudder. A close approximation to *w. surface* of ordinary ship forms, expressed in *square feet,* may be found from the formula: $S = 15.8$ *times square root of product of Displacement (in tons) and Length of waterline (in feet).* The value is taken into account chiefly in connection with determination of resistance and powering of vessels.

WHACK. A portion; an allowance or share; *esp.,* that indicated in the *victualling scale; see* POUND AND PINT.

WHALE. (A.S. *hwael;* M.E. *whal*) Any marine mammal of the order *Cetacea; esp.,* one of large size, as distinct from the dolphin, porpoise, grampus, etc. It has a hairless smooth skin of dark color generally; two paddle-like limbs, or *flippers,* about one-third its length from the head; a broad fish-like tail, but with lobes (or *flukes*) spread horizontally; and a single blow-hole, or a pair of such, through which it *blows* or *spouts* (exhales) and takes in air upon surfacing. *W's* generally are classified as *toothed* and *whalebone* or *baleen,* the latter so called from the plates of baleen suspended from its upper jaw. *(See* BALEEN) The *blubber,* or layer of oil-yielding fat next the animal's skin, serves as protection against cold; hence, heavier *w's* in this respect are taken in high latitudes. A large *w.* yields from 100 to 180 barrels of oil. *(Also cf.* SPERM; SPERMACETI) In addition to whalebone and oil, today large quantities of *whale-meat* are taken and put to use for table consumption. Long so used in Japan, it has more recently grown popular in western Europe, *esp.* in Norway and Britain. It is said there are about 2½ tons of prime cuts in a large *w.* and whalemen customarily partake of a fresh *w. steak* when pursuing their vocation. The meat is somewhat coarser and darker than beef. Most important *whaling-grounds* are in or near the Antarctic, *esp.,* in vicinity of the Ross Sea (due south of New Zealand); in the region of the Azores; off southern Korea; and Alaskan waters. *W's* vary greatly in size from the 20-foot *caaing w.* or *pilot w.* and *bottle-nose* (a larger cousin of the *dolphin*) to the *Blue* or *Sulphur-bottom,* a species attaining 80 to 90 feet in length. Some confusion exists in the identifying names given the animal; as, *e.g.,* the *Arctic right w.* or *Bowhead* becomes a *Nordcaper* off the Norwegian coast and a *Greenland w.* in northwestern Atlantic waters; the *Sulphur-bottom* also is known as *Blue w.* and *Finback,* while these names often denote separate members of the cetacean order. However, the *rorquals* seem to comprise some of the largest *w's,* including the *finners,* or finbacks, *Blue w., Common Finback* or *Jupiter w.,*—all 50- to 80-footers,—but not the heavy flippered *Humpback,* although it also has a small dorsal *fin.* Excepting the *Caaing w.* (also known as *Pilot w.* and *Blackfish*) and *Bottlenose,* all these are *baleen* or *whalebone w's.* The large *Cachalot* or *Sperm w.,*—a 60- to 70-foot member,—and its pygmy relative *(see* KOGIA) belong to the purely *toothed* class. The U.S. *Whaling Treaty Act,* May 1, 1936, in accordance with international agreement, provides for protection of *w's* and regulations governing their capture. Section 4 of the Act prescribes: "That for the purposes of this act, *right whales* shall be deemed to include North Atlantic or North

Cape whales, Greenland or Bowhead whales, and Pacific right whales; calves or suckling whales shall be deemed to include whales having a length less than the following dimensions: Blue or sulphur-bottom, 60 feet; finbacks, 50 feet; and humpbacks, 35 feet." (*16 U.S.C. 904*) **Gray w.,** *see* GRAY WHALE. **Little piked w.** or **piked w.,** *see* PIKED WHALE. **W'boat,** the sharp-sterned open boat, about 25 feet in length, manned by 5 oarsmen and an officer, formerly used in hunting *w's;* also, a similar craft, proportionately narrower, sometimes fitted with a propelling engine and used as a lifeboat in warships. The latter often is called a *whaler.* **W. catcher,** one of several small strongly-built, quick-turning, speedy, powered vessels equipped for hunting *w's* in co-operation with a mother-ship, or *w.-oil factory vessel,* in modern whaling practice; in length about 130 feet; speed, 12 to 16 knots. From 4 to 8 of such *catchers* work with the parent vessel. **W.-fin,** baleen or whalebone; *see* BALEEN. **W. fishery,** *see* FISHERY. **W.-iron,** a hand harpoon; a toggle-iron; *see* TOGGLE. **W.-lance,** *see* LANCE. **W.-line,** strong, carefully made manila rope, 4 to 6 inches in circumference, used in hunting *w's* or towing; also, *w.-rope.* As used on a *w. catcher,* the elasticity of such line is assisted in withstanding the shocks or jerks from a struggling *w.* or heave of the sea while heavy stress is on the harpoon by an arrangement of lead-blocks and springs. **W.-oil,** *see* OIL; *also,* **Try-p.** *in* POT; has a specific gravity of .92 to .93; solidifies at 30° Fahrenheit; occupies 38.8 cubic feet per ton weight, or 2240 lbs. **W.'s bone,** an old name for *ivory,* so called from the former belief that teeth of the *sperm w.* were the main source of that material. **W.-shark,** another name for *basking shark; see* SHARK. **W.-shot,** older whalemen's term for *spermaceti,* from its granular appearance; *see* SPERMACETI.

WHALEBACK.   A rounded deck or *hood; see* Turtle or **turtle-back d.** *in* DECK. Also, a type of bulk-carrying steamer having a rounded-off weather deck fore-and-aft, with deck erections supported on stanchions or turrets. Also called *pig-boat* from the *nose,* or snout-like termination of her spoon bow, with its two hawse-pipes suggesting the nostrils, and *cigar-boat* from her tubular and pointed shape, the odd-lined craft was a Great Lakes production of about 1890 and was used for a time on ocean voyages. Became obsolete soon after turn of the century, chiefly on account of being unsuited to heavy weather, particularly in heading into a high sea.

WHALEBOAT HAT.   The *cocked hat,* or full-dress *fore-and-after,* worn by naval officers on special occasions. (*U.S. navy*)

WHALEBONE.   Chiefly obtained from the Arctic and Antarctic *right whales* (so named by whalers because it is the *right* animal to pursue) the stringy bony substance taken from the mouths of *baleen whales; see* BALEEN. **W. whales,** *see* WHALE.

WHALEMAN.   A man employed in the whale fishery; a *whaler,* or one who hunts whales. In older usage, a *whalingman.*

WHALER.   A vessel or a person engaged in the capture of whales; a *whaleman.* Navy term for a *whaleboat* carried in ship's equipment; *cf.* **W'boat** *in* WHALE. A *shore* or any steel or wooden brace for temporarily supporting a bulkhead, a section of a deck, etc. **Right w.,** a vessel engaged in the capture of the valuable *right whale,* or *Arctic, Greenland,* or *Bowhead w.* of Arctic waters and the *Southern Right w.* of the Antarctic and south temperate latitudes,—both "fish" of 50 to 70 feet in length, with huge jaws and enormous head, and greatest producers of whalebone.

WHALING.   The industry or occupation of hunting whales, which also generally includes the operation of extracting oil from the captured animals' *blubber,* separating *spermaceti* from *sperm oil* taken from the *sperm whale,* and preparing *whalebone* for the market. The former individual sailing or auxiliary-propelled *w.-vessel* has given place to the *factory ship* of past quarter century, with her attending *whale catchers* which quickly dispatch each quarry by means of a deadly missile from the *harpoon-gun,* inflate the carcase by an air-pump, and tow it to the mother vessel. A modern factory ship is capable of processing more than 20 large whales in a day, as compared with the old sailing whaler's two or three,—an improvement chiefly due to the operation of hauling the carcase bodily through a slipway at vessel's stern. The *whale-oil factory ship* also is called a *w. tanker,* from her similarity of construction and hold arrangement to an oil-tank vessel. *Cf.* **W. catcher** *in* WHALE; *also* FACTORY SHIP. **Pelagic w.,** as opposed to *shore w.,* that pursued by a vessel on board of which oil is extracted from blubber, etc., as in a factory ship; also, *ship w.* **Right w.,** pursuit and capture of *right whales; see* **Right w.** *in* WHALER. **Shore w.,** *see* SHORE.[1] **Sperm w.,** pursuit of the *sperm whale* for its exceedingly valuable oil, a lubricant of .87 to .88 specific gravity which will not mix with ordinary *whale oil.* (*Cf.* **W. Oil** *in* WHALE) Hunting the *sperm* has been considered the most hazardous type of *w.* on account of the creature's extreme ferocity, its huge jaws and teeth having ground to pieces many an attacking boat in older *w.* history. It roams about in packs with a belligerent "bull" in the lead and will attack any obstacle in its path. Found in all warm seas, feeds almost entirely on an octopus-like squid. **W.-gun,** a breech- or muzzle-loading gun of about 3½-inch bore used for firing a harpoon or other type of projectile at whales. **W. master,** one having charge of a *w.-station* or the master of a whaler. **W.-rocket,** explosive shell or rocket attached to a harpoon or a lance fired at a whale. **W.-station,** a shore establishment to which whales are taken for processing, etc. *Cf.* **S. whaling,** *in* SHORE.[1]

WHARF. (A.S. *hwearf,* a dam, a bank or shore of a river) A waterside structure of wood, masonry, etc., at which vessels may be berthed for landing or taking in cargo, passengers, etc.; a large jetty; a pier. *Cf.* QUAY. *Pl.* is *wharfs* or *wharves.* **Careening w.,** jetty, pier, or other waterfront berth at which vessels were careened; a *careenage. Cf.* CAREEN. **Sufferance w.,** *see* SUFFERANCE. **W.-boat,** a rowed or powered boat used about wharves, as for running warping-lines. A decked barge, scow, or the like, moored for use as a landing, or *w.,* and connected to a river-bank, levee, etc., by a bridge or ramp at a place in which tidal range or change of water-level renders use of a pier or *w.* impracticable. *Cf.* **L.-stage** *in* LANDING. **W. demurrage,** charge for cargo left on a *w.,* pier, or quay, upon expiration of a certain time (usually 24 hours) since its discharge from ship. It is payable each day at a certain rate per ton. (*U.S.*) **W. rat,** a person having little or no apparent means of subsistence who loiters about wharves or a waterfront, usually with intent to steal from ships and warehouses as opportunity offers. **W.-spike,** a long heavy spike-nail, such as is used to fasten timbers in a *w.;* also, *dock-spike.*

WHARFAGE. A charge per ton of cargo landed or loaded, per unit of registered tonnage, according to ship's length, etc., or a fee per day, for privilege of using a *w.; pierage; quayage. Wharves* of a port, collectively; accommodation or berthing at a wharf or wharves.

WHARFINGER. Formerly, *wharfager.* Owner or manager of a *wharf;* one who has charge of a waterfront warehouse in which landed cargo or goods awaiting shipment are stored; *esp.,* such space on, or adjoining, a *wharf* or pier. In British usage, one who represents a shipowner or a charterer in superintending details of checking, loading, and discharging cargoes. Also, *wharfmaster.*

WHARFMAN. One who is employed on a wharf or pier, or on a number of these, to assist with handling of ships' mooring-lines, placing and removing of passenger gangways, camels, propeller-booms, etc.; a *dockman* or *pierman.*

WHARFMASTER. A wharfinger, or person in charge of one or more docks or wharves; a wharf superintendent.

WHEEL. *See* **S.-wheel** *in* STEERING. A propeller or paddle-wheel. To swing or turn in changing direction, as a squadron in line abreast. **Cable w.,** *see* **C.-lifter** *in* CABLE. **Kick of w.,** *see* **Helm-k.** *in* KICK. **Side w.,** a *paddle-w.; see* PADDLE. **W.-boat,** a boat equipped with removable *w's* to facilitate its carriage over land. **W.-chain,** also called *steering-* and *tiller-chain,* one of the two chains connecting a

steering-w. or a *steering-engine* with the *tiller.* **W.-house,** a wholly or partially inclosed deck erection for protection of helmsman and steering-gear. In larger vessels it is located on the navigation-bridge and also shelters the various instruments and equipment employed in vessel's navigation and general management. Also, *pilot-house.* **W.-rod,** piece of iron or steel rod taking the place of a portion of a lengthy *w.-chain;* also, *steering-rod.* **W.-rope,** in smaller vessels, a rope, usually of flexible wire, used in lieu of a *w.-chain.* (Also see *Wheel* combined with following caption words in BEVEL; FEATHERING; LEE; MONKEY; PADDLE; STERN)

WHEELSMAN. A helmsman or steersman; one who steers by means of the *wheel,* so commonly called in vessels on the Great Lakes and U.S. inland waters, where *wheeling* also ordinarily denotes steering.

WHEFT. A variant of *waft.*

WHELK. A gastropod commonly found on the sea-coasts of North America and Europe; much used as food in the latter country, commonly for baiting trawl-lines on the American coasts.

WHELP. One of the longitudinal ridges on the barrel of a capstan or on a drumhead of a mooring-winch for providing a grip for a heavy rope or hawser when heaving. On a *wildcat,* as in a windlass, one of the inward projecting pieces that engage each second or flat-lying link of the chain cable; also, *grab; grip.*

WHERE AWAY? *See* **S. ho!** *in* SAIL. (Also, similarly, *Land ho!; Ice ho!*)

WHERRY. A boat propelled by sails or oars, having no characteristic rig or build but so called in many localities both on the British coasts and in New England. Appears to have been so named originally in England where, generally, it was a lengthy light pulling boat used for carrying passengers in sheltered waters, or a larger sailing-barge or fishing-boat usually rigged with a single mast and a sprit-sail or loose-footed gaff-sail and called *Thames w., Norfolk w.,* etc., according to locality in which built or operated. Such terms as *Portsmouth w., Ryde w., Southampton w.,* with the craft themselves now belong to the past. A scull or racing-boat pulled by one person often is called a *w.* and in U.S. navy, a light handy row-boat of 12 to 14 feet in length, principally for officers' use, also is so called.

WHIFFING. *See* TROLLING.

WHIFFLING BREEZE. A light variable or baffling wind.

WHIP. (Du. *wippen,* to shake, to move up and down) A rope rove in a single block, as for hoisting use. Called a *single w.* when block is fixed; *double w.* when block moves with object hauled upon or hoisted. The *gun-tackle,* although commonly called *double w.* regardless of which of its blocks is the moving one, properly becomes a *double w.* only when the fixed block is that one to which standing end of fall is secured. Thus, a *double w.* has a mechanical advantage of 1 to 2; a *single w.* has none. *Cf.* PURCHASE. *Whip* formerly was applied loosely to any tackle used for hoisting moderate weights, serving in this respect to designate use of a rig rather than the method of reeving it; *e.g.,* a *hatch-w.,mast-w.,* etc., might be a *gun-tackle, luff,* or other simple purchase. **W. and pendant,** a *w.* rove in a block at hauling end of a *runner* or *pendant;* also, *w. and runner.* Has a practical purchase power of nearly 1:4,—once commonly used for *tops'l-yard braces* in square rig. To **w. a rope,** to secure a rope's end against fagging or unlaying by a number of turns of twine around it. *Cf.* WHIPPING. **W. on w.,** old term for the rig consisting of one handy tackle hooked to the fall of another; as, *luff on luff.* **W.-staff,** now probably obsolete name for a boat's tiller, or an extension to it. (Also see *Whip* as combined with following in ASH; BUNT; COACH; DOUBLE; HATCH; MAST; WATER; YARD)

WHIPPING. The turns of twine or small stuff laid around a rope close to its end for security against unlaying or fagging. Small cordage is *whipped* with twine; larger, with marline, roundline, samsonline, etc.; wire rope, with wire. By an old sailors' rule, *w.* should extend along rope to a width equal to rope's diameter, beginning at a distance of half that measure from rope's end. In a *plain w.* ends of the *w.* are covered or tucked under first and last 3 or 4 turns. A **sailmaker's w.** is completed by one or two crossing turns over the whole at each hollow between strands of rope, using a palm and needle. Marline, roundline, etc., similarly is worked with a marline-spike. The **West-country w.,** a relic of old "Bristol fashion," is made by using both ends of the twine, etc., to form a series of overhand knots on alternate sides of the rope. The ends are either joined in a square knot or tucked away between strands of the rope.

WHIRLPOOL. A vortex or eddy caused by meeting of opposing currents, or by flow of water through a channel of sharply irregular depth or curvature; any agitation from such causes, whether whirling or not. *Cf.* CHARYBDIS; MAELSTROM.

WHIRLWIND. A mass or column of air rotating about a vertical or slightly inclined axis with high velocity, while usually moving bodily over the surface at a rate varying from a very few to a score of miles an hour; a tornado; a *waterspout* in its early stage; a *windspout.*

WHISKERS. In older sailing-ships, the long horizontal spars set at right angles to, and at the end of, the bowsprit for spreading the jib-boom guys and so laterally stiffening the lengthy jib-boom. Each usually was steadied down by a *whisker-jumper,* or guy, leading from outer end of spar to the cutwater. With later reduction in jib-boom length and resulting elimination of former elaborate head rigging, *w.* or *whisker-booms* gave way to *spreaders,* much shorter, often of iron, and also often called *out-riggers.*

WHISTLE. (A.S. *hwistle,* pipe or flute; a hissing sound) Instrument which produces a sound by passage of steam or air under pressure into a cavity or against a thin edge, or a combination of both. A *ship's w.* is considered efficient when its sound can be clearly heard in still weather at a distance of two miles and, by U.S. law, is required to be placed at least 6 feet above the pilot-house. Its sound should be unobstructed over at least 20 points of the compass, or from right ahead to two points or more abaft either beam. **Boatswain's w.,** *see* **B.'s pipe** *in* BOATSWAIN. **Chime w.,** a combination of two or more *w's* that sound in harmony, usually with a deep musical tone. One or two of these commonly are installed in large passenger liners. **Mess w.,** *see* MESS. **W. buoy,** or **whistling-buoy,** *see* BUOY. **W. control,** electrical contrivance by which ship's *w.* is sounded from the navigation bridge or wheelhouse. By turning a small lever, *w.* is blown at will or may be set to sound a regular recurring blast, as in thick weather. To **w. for a breeze,** to coax a breeze, or engage in the superstitious practice among sailors in sailing-ship days of plaintively entreating the winds for a breeze by whistling with the lips in a variety of soft continuous notes, while facing direction from which it was desired that the wind would increase or spring up. Earlier custom required that a group of men occupy a more prominent position, such as the poop, when thus engaged; *esp.,* during a lengthy spell of light airs and calms. **W.-pull,** a cord or lanyard used to sound vessel's *w.,* as from the bridge or pilot-house; a *w.-lanyard.* **W. signals,** *see* SIGNAL.

WHITE. Distinguished by the color of clean snow or pure sunlight; opposite of *black.* Hence, light-colored; having a whitish appearance; as, a *w. light; w. water.* **W'caps,** foam-crested waves, such as those set up by a fresh breeze; once often familiarly called "the skipper's daughters," from their usual accompanying and often desirable sailing breeze; also, *w. horses* and *horses' manes, esp.,* waves of the steep breaking type, as those occurring in shallower waters in a weather tide. **W'fish,** the *menhaden;* the *whiting.* The *w. whale; see* BELUGA. **W. horse,** tough, sinewy substance in the head of a sperm whale; also, that part of the head, just above the upper jaw, in which the substance occurs. In *pl., see* **W'caps. W. light,** as distinguished from a colored light, *esp.* from a red or a green one, a natural light, or one having the color of pure sunlight and protected by, or shining through, none other than an uncolored glass or lens. The masthead, anchor, and stern lights required by *Regulations for Prevention of Colli-sions, e.g.,* are *w. lights.* A lantern or lamp, as on a buoy or in a lighthouse, showing an uncolored light. **W. rainbow,** a fog-bow; *see* RAINBOW. **W.-water,** *see* WATER. **W. whale,** *see* BELUGA. (Also see under following captions terms having the prefix *White:* ENSIGN; LEAD[1]; LINE[1]; OAK; OAKUM; PINE; ROPE; SHARK; SQUADRON; SQUALL; WATER)

WHITING. The *silver hake; see* HAKE.

WHOLE GALE. A wind of force 10; *see* BEAUFORT SCALE.

WIDE BERTH. *See* To **give a wide b. to** *in* BERTH.

WIDOW'S MAN. Formerly, in the British navy, one of a class of fictitious seamen whose pay contributed to a benefit fund for widows of service men.

WIGWAG. A now obsolete method of signaling by waving a long-staffed hand-flag or a lantern with short and long strokes from the high or vertical position. Usually following the Morse code, a short to-and-fro wave or stroke represented the *dot;* a long one, the *dash.*

WILD. Not easily controlled; going "wide of the mark"; as, *the vessel steers w.; w. navigation.* Unchecked or uncontrolled; as, *the cable ran w.; she took a w. Bay-of-Fundy sheer; "scud running w. across a stormy sky."*

WILDCAT. Chain-grab, cable-holder, or drum on a *windlass* shaped to receive each engaged link of *chain cable* in passage of the latter to or from the hawse-pipe. It nests each horizontal link while each vertical one is held between *whelps.* On larger war and passenger vessels, it often works on a vertical shaft operated, in heaving, by an engine on deck below. In the latter case, *w.* itself usually is called *windlass* in naval vessels. When paying out cable, as in anchoring, *w.* may be released from engine control and its motion checked or stopped by a brake.

WILLIWAW. Violent cold-air squall coming off a mountainous coast, such as is frequently met with at all seasons in the Magellan Strait, Alaskan coast, etc. Also, *willywaw.*

WILLY-WILLY. Heavy windstorm accompanied by rain occurring on N.W. coast of Australia. Also, *willie-willie.*

WINCH. (A.S. *wince,* a bent handle or crank; a reel) Machine or engine used for hoisting or heaving on board ship. Named from its use, as *boat w., brace w., cargo w., mooring w., trawl w.;* or according to operating power, as *hand w., electric w., hydraulic w., motor w., steam w.* **Boat w.,** one, usually powered by electricity, installed for handling a single lifeboat or a group of boats. In the former case, boat-fall winds on a barrel and *w.* is fitted with one or more brakes for lowering; in the latter, *w.* is used only for lifting boats from water. **Brace**

w., as installed in larger sailing-ships, one having three barrels on which are wound, respectively, the lower-yard, lower-tops'l, and upper-tops'l braces. Starboard and port braces of each yard are wound in opposite directions on same barrel; so that same amount of rope is payed out as is hove in. It is operated by hand, fitted with a brake for controlling swing of yards, as when ship is brought about (*tacking*), and *wire* braces always used. **Cargo w.,** any *w.* used for hoisting cargo. Modern ships usually have at least two *w's* at each hatchway,—commonly placed near either end of hatch. Such *w's* are fitted with a *barrel,* on which a hoisting-fall may be wound, and two or more drumheads for use in hoisting or heaving, capstan fashion. **Crab w.,** a small *hand w.,* often of portable type, chiefly used for hoisting cargo or ballast in smaller sailing-vessels; a *dolly-w.* or *gypsy; see* DOLLY; GYPSY. (Prob. a corruption of *grab w.,* once applied to a small capstan that sometimes was used for heaving on a chain cable) **Dolly w.,** *see* **Crab w. Mast w.,** *see* MAST. **Spunyarn w.,** a *spinning-jenny, q.v.* **W. end,** the drumhead or gypsy of a powered *w.; see* GYPSY. **W'man,** one who operates a powered *w.; esp.,* member of a gang of longshoremen who is detailed to that work in loading or discharging cargo. **W. partners,** timbers, girders, or angle-bars fitted between deck-beams for stiffening and strengthening the deck in way of a *w.* or *w's,* or immediately below a *w. bed.* **W. platform,** also *w.-table,* a raised platform or large mast-table on which one or two *cargo w's* are installed.

WIND.[1] Horizontal movement of air; local surface motion of the atmosphere, or that generally attributed to flow from a relatively high barometric pressure area toward one of lesser pressure. *W.* velocity on the broad ocean increases with sharpness of the barometric gradient, *i.e.,* with increase of difference in atmospheric pressure of adjacent regions. A marked increase occurs in straits or other narrowing connecting waters, *esp.* those having high or mountainous shores, due to the congesting "funnel effect" on passage of the breeze. Strong *w's* swoop down mountain valleys to the sea, as falling currents of cold air, in the *willywaw* or the persistent *bora.* Howling *typhoon* or *hurricane* whirls spirally toward a vortex of low pressure and squalls roll on along the surface in a downward-upward screaming flow. *Land* and *sea* breezes often occur with a remarkable regularity; the seasonal *monsoons* have their appointed times; and the *trades* blow out their unending steady freshness. Our restless atmosphere, due to wide thermal variations and resulting barometric changes, thus keeps on the move toward an equilibrium unattainable. Local *w's* appear to have been first named in the Mediterranean. Genoese sailors, following their compass-point designations, probably should be credited with such appellatives as *Levante* (East wind), *Scirocco* (S.E.), *Mezzogiorno* (S.), *Libeccio* (S.W.), *Ponente* (W.), *Mistrale* (N.W.) *Cf.* ANTI-TRADES; CYCLONE; HURRICANE; MONSOON; SQUALL; TYPHOON; **T. winds** *in* TRADE. **All in the w.,** sailing too close to the *w.;* all sail shaking, as when pointed into the *w.* or when *w.* suddenly draws ahead; hence, in a state of confusion. **Bare w.,** one which narrowly allows vessel to lay her course while sailing close-hauled; a *scant w.* **Before the w.,** with the *w.;* having a *following w.,* as when sailing with *squared* yards. **Between w. and water,** *see* BE-TWEEN. **Brave west w's,** *see* ROARING FORTIES. **Cap-ful of w.,** a light squall; a gust of *w.* **Catabatic w.,** heavy cold *w.* or air-current from a high to a low level, as that flowing down a mountain valley or glacier. **To eat the w. out of,** *see* EAT. **Eye of the w.,** *see* EYE. **Flower of the w's,** on old charts, cus-tomary elaborate figure of the compass-card with, in those drawn or engraved in England, picture of a *rose* in its center; hence, the present-day term *compass-rose; see* COMPASS. **To fly to, up in,** or **up into, the w.,** *see* FLY. **To gain the w.,** *see* GAIN; also, to *get the w. of* (another vessel). **To haul the w.,** *see* HAUL. **Head to w.,** heading or pointing toward the *w., i.e.,* in direction from which *w.* is blowing. **To hold a close w.** or **good w.,** in sailing, to make little leeway when close-hauled. **To hold the w.,** or **a w.,** to sail close-hauled without being obliged to *go about,* or *tack;* to sail on course desired when close-hauled, or nearly so; also, in a square-rigged ves-sel, to have all canvas drawing, as distinguished from the less favorable condition of sailing with *squared yards,* or directly *before the w.* **In the w.'s eye,** in same direction from which *w.* is blowing; "in the teeth of the gale." **To jam a vessel into the w.,** *see* JAM. **Kona w's,** stormy southwest *w's* over the Hawaiian Islands. **Land w.,** one blowing off the land; *land breeze; see* BREEZE. **On the w.,** a vessel is said to be sailing *on the w.* when having the *w.* abeam or nearly so. **Periodic w.,** one prevailing at regular recurring periods or seasons; a monsoon. To **sail close to the w.,** *see* To **l. close** *in* LAY. **Sea w.,** a breeze from the sea; *see* **Land and sea b's** *in* BREEZE. To **take the w. out of one's sails,** to sail close to windward of another vessel, thus more or less cutting off her supply of *w.,* as in racing; hence, to render one's words or position ineffective or humiliatingly helpless. **Three sheets in the w.,** in an intoxicated condition; "half-seas over." To **touch the w.,** *see* TOUCH. **W. arrow,** on a pilot chart or weather map, symbol for direction of *w.* Usually the number of its barbs or feather-ends indicates *force* of *w.* **W.-bound,** said of a vessel when delayed at anchor or in harbor by contrary *w's.* **W. chart,** map or chart showing direction and force of *w.* or *w's* prevailing in a given region at a specified time, period, or season; a weather map. **W.-dodger,** a can-vas shield for protection against *w.,* as on a ship's bridge; *see* DODGER. **W. dog,** a broken rainbow seen near or on a detached cloud; also, *water gall;* often appears in sunny breezy weather and usually pre-sages continued fresh or strong *w's. Cf.* GALL. **W.-gauge,** instrument for measuring *w.* velocity; an *anemometer.* **W.-rode,** as opposed to *tide-rode,* a vessel is said to be *w.-rode* when lying at anchor and heading into the *w.;* esp., when force of *w.* is such that a weather tide fails to swing her from that heading. **W. rose,** on a pilot chart or a seasonal weather map, small diagram indicating direction and force of *w's* observed in region or locality con-cerned. **W.-sail,** *see* **Canvas v.** *in* VENTILATOR. **W. scale,** a system of numbers or names indicating pro-gressively the velocity and comparative force or in-tensity of the *w.* Of the several systems devised for mariners' use in log-books and weather-observation reports, that of *Admiral Beaufort* of the British navy *(1805)* apparently still is the most widely em-ployed; *see* BEAUFORT SCALE. **W.-scoop,** a portable device for catching and deflecting *w.* into a cabin, crew's quarters, etc. Usually is a sheet of metal bent to form a channel and fitted to project from an air-port. Also *w.-catcher.* **W.-spout,** or **windspout,** a wa-terspout in its early stage of formation. It is simi-lar to the *sand spout* or swirling column occurring on hot deserts. (See under the following captions for additional terms involving *Wind:* BACKING; BEAM; BEAT; DOWN; FAIR; FALL; GLACIER; HOME; HUG; IN THE WIND; JUNK; LADY; LEADING; PASSAGE; PINCH; PUNA; SLANT; SOLDIER'S; STORM; TEHUANTEPECER; TRAVERSE.

WIND.[2] (Pron. *wynd*)   To turn a vessel end for end while fast to a pier, wharf, etc., by means of warping-lines. To cause a vessel being towed or as-sisted in maneuvering to turn sharply, either by pulling on a line leading from her bow or her quarter or by pushing the vessel near either end, as in pointing a large ship into a slip in docking; often with *into* or *round;* as, *liner was wound into her berth by 10 tugs; our tug will w.* (or *w. round) the barges before reaching the slip.* **To w. in** a wire hawser or a chain cable is to round up the slack wire on a reel, or slack cable by capstan or wind-lass. **To w. off** means to haul away a wire from its reel, or any line stowed on a reel. **To w. up,** to reel up or stow a wire, etc., on its reel. An important standing order or rule is to *w. ship's chronometers* at a certain hour each day. This usually is done by *navigating officer* at 8 a.m.

WINDAGE.   Surface of a vessel exposed to the wind. What is termed *wind drag* is force exerted by wind pressure against a vessel lying at anchor with head to wind, or stress borne by the anchor-cable due to such force, which depends upon vessel's *w.*

WINDING.   In older usage, act of hauling or heav-ing by means of a capstan, winch, or windlass. A *call* made on the boatswain's whistle. **W. pendant; w. tackle;** *see* PENDANT. (Pron. *wynding)*

WINDJAMMER. A sailing-vessel, or a sailor who habitually ships on such vessel; originally so called derisively by seamen engaging on early steam-vessels.

WINDLASS. (M.E. *windas*. Corrupted by influence of now obsolete *windlass*, to turn about; to perplex; a roundabout course) A winch or capstan of special design for heaving in an anchor-cable (*chain*); an anchor winch. It usually is installed on the forecastle head, so that cables of both *bower anchors* lead straight over their respective *wildcats* from hawse-pipes to chain-locker; *see* WILDCAT. In larger passenger vessels and warships, a vertical or *capstan w.* shows only its *wildcat* above deck, operating engine being housed below. The former type is provided with a gypsy or drum at each side for heaving on warping-lines, etc., axes on which wildcat and drum rotate lying horizontal and athwartships. In its simplest and early form, *w.* consists of a rotating barrel mounted at each end on a strong vertical timber which also served as a *bitt*. By means of a handspike inserted in one of several holes in projecting end of barrel, the machine usually was operated by two men. A suitable arrangement of *pawls* held barrel from "walking back," as when leverage applied was momentarily interrupted or when *w.* was required to "hold its own" in the rest position. Such *w.* still is used on smaller vessels both for anchor work and heaving on a warping-line. **Chinese** or **differential w.,** as in the *capstan* of this name, *w.* having two barrels of different diameters on same axis. It is an example of an ancient method of employing differential motion; *see* **Chinese c.** *in* CAPSTAN. **Pumping w.,** hand-operated *w.* used in sailing-ships since the advent of chain anchor-cable, and so named from the up-and-down motion of thwartship *w.-brakes* or *w.-levers* in its operation. The levers alternately raise and lower two stout fore-and-aft arms, each fitted with a pawl, that engage either of two racks on periphery of *w.* barrel. At mid-point of barrel, master-pawls continuously drop into place as levers are worked. Depending on its size, *w.* is manned by from 2 to 8 hands. **Spanish w.,** as chiefly employed in lieu of a *rigger's screw*, an improvised purchase for drawing two parts of a rope together, consisting of a greased piece of line placed round the work with a round turn, its ends laid round a bar or roller and each spike-hitched on a *marline-spike*. The spikes are used as levers in heaving line around the roller. **W.-capstan,** as commonly used in larger sailing-ships, a *top-gallant-fo'c'sle* capstan which is geared to the ordinary horizontal *w.* housed below that deck. When required for heaving anchor, its spindle is connected to a worm gear turning in a toothed rack around middle of *w. barrel*.

WINDLIFT. An obsolete name for a *windlass*.

WINDLOP. State of water surface as disturbed by short, choppy, lopping waves; *esp.*, those set up in a current or tideway running against the wind, as over shallows, in a river, etc. *Cf.* LOP.

WINDOW-PANE. A species of American *turbot*, so called from its translucent thin body. *Cf.* TURBOT.

WINDSAIL. *See* **Canvas v.** *in* VENTILATOR.

WINDWARD. (Pron. *winderd* by seamen) In the direction from which the wind is blowing; toward the wind; as, a *w. shore; current sets to w.; she sailed to w. of the island.* As an adjective, in some instances synonymous with *weather;* as, a *w.* (or *weather*) *channel, ebb, flood, island, passage, tide, vessel;* but *weather* for more than a century past has superseded *w.* in terms designating something *on board ship;* thus, the older *w. braces* now is *weather braces;* the *w. side, weather side; w. ports,* now *weather ports;* etc. To **cast,** or **lay, an anchor to w.,** to provide for an emergency; to plan for the future. To **get to w. of,** to obtain an advantage over (another person or a situation). To **work to w.,** to sail on frequent tacks in order to make progress against an unfavorable wind. The navigation involved is called *w. sailing.* **W. great-circle sailing,** branch of navigation that takes into account the proper *tack* on which, during adverse winds, a vessel should sail in order to make constant progress toward point of destination, *i.e.*, by deviating as little as possible from the *great circle track*.

WING. That part of a hold or any lower-deck space which is nearest either of ship's sides. Projecting platform at forward and after ends of a steamer's paddle-box; *see* **P. wing** *in* PADDLE. Division of a fleet at extreme right or left of line of advance; as *right w.* Outer forward part on either side of an otter-trawl. Usually with *out,* to shift or extend weights toward ship's sides, as cargo or ballast, with view of increasing the rolling period, or of trimming vessel upright; as, to *w. out* an ore cargo. **W. and w.,** set of a schooner's sails when running directly or nearly before the wind,—*fores'l* boomed out on one side and *mains'l* on the other. Also formerly applied to the square-rigged vessel's spread of *stuns'ls* on both sides, under similar conditions. **W.-boards,** arrangement of planks extending downward at an angle from a hatchway to prevent bulk cargo, such as coal, from shifting into the *w.* corners of the hold. **W.-bracket,** *see* **M. bracket** *in* MARGIN. **W. compartment,** *see* COMPARTMENT. **W. deck,** *see* DECK. **W.-feeder,** *see* FEEDER. **W. house,** small deck-house at side of weather deck, such as is used for deckstores, as a lamp-room, paintlocker, etc. **W.-passage,** a corridor or alleyway along the side of a 'tween deck, passengers' quarters, etc. **W. stopper,** rope for securing the old hemp cable in ship's hold; named for its place, in the *w.* **W. tanks,** *see* **Side t.** *in* TANK. **W. transom,** *see* TRANSOM. **W. wales,** *see* WALE.

WINTER. Abbrev. *W* in load-lines of vessels having a gross tonnage of 150 and over (all sailing vessels and any powered vessel less than 330 feet in length, *W N A = Winter North Atlantic*) The following are the seasonal limits in which minimum freeboard marked *W* is allowed, according to U.S. law, in conformity with *International Load Line Convention, 1930:*—16th. October to 15th. April, in the *North Atlantic* between Longitudes 15° and 50°, north of Latitude 45°, and north of Lat. 60° from Long. 15° to coast of Norway; elsewhere in N. Atlantic, north of Lat. 35°, from 1st. November to 31st. March. In *Mediterranean* and *Black Seas,* 16th. December to 15th. March. In *North Pacific,* north of parallel of 35° and a rhumb line from Lat. 35° and Long. 150° W. to a point on Vancouver Island, B.C., in Lat. 50°, from 16th. October to 15th. April. In *South Pacific,* south of Lat. 33° and the New Zealand and Australian coasts; *South Indian Ocean,* south of a rhumb line from Lat. 30° on S. African coast to Lat. 35° on southwestern Australian coast; in *South Atlantic,* south of Lat. 34°; 16th. April to 15th. October. **W. ice,** *see* ICE. **W. monsoon,** *see* MONSOON. **W. solstice,** point in the ecliptic at which sun is farthest north or south of the equinoctial; day of the year in which *Sol* attains his minimum altitude in the meridian of an observer at any place outside the tropics. Our *summer solstice* thus becomes the *w. solstice* (about June 21) to those living in the southern hemisphere. *Cf.* SOLSTICE.

WIPER. Member of the crew who assists in general work in ship's engine department, so named from being commonly occupied at cleaning machinery, etc.

WIRE. A slender thread, lengthy rod of small diameter, or strand composed of several threads of metal. Usually round in section, a single thread of *w.* ordinarily becomes a *rod* if greater than three-sixteenths inch in diameter and, depending upon its use, may be made with a diameter as small as .004 inch. A *w. rope* of any size usually is called a *w.* **W. brush,** commonly used for cleaning steel surfaces preparatory to painting, a brush or broom having steel wire bristles and usually made to be fixed on a long handle, if so required. **W. drag,** *see* DRAG. **W.-mesh bulkhead,** *see* BULKHEAD. **W.-net sling,** cargo-sling made of *w. rope* in the form of a net about 8 to 10 feet square, having from 5 to 8-inch meshes. It is used for handling small heavy packages. *Cf.* **C.-net** *in* CARGO. **W.-reel,** *see* REEL. **W. seizing-stuff,** *see* **S. stuff** *in* SEIZING. **W. stopper,** a vise-like *nipper* or clamp for holding a *w. rope* used as a hawser. *Cf.* **H.-clamp** *in* HAWSER.

WIRELESS. *See* RADIO.

WIRE ROPE. Usually consists of 6 strands, similarly laid as in manufacture of fiber cordage, threads of *wire* taking the place of *rope-yarns.* Size of *w.* rope in U.S. generally is that of its *diameter,* expressed in inches; British custom, that of its *circumference.* *W. rope,* or simply *wire* among seamen, is described as having a certain number of *strands,* each having so many *threads;* thus, a 6 x 12 wire has 6 strands each containing 12 small wires or threads. For the purpose of giving flexibility to working rope and also serving as a reservoir for the lubricant, a *hemp core* of about same size as that of each strand is set in the *w.,* and where an extra flexible quality is required, a core is set in each strand also. Standing rigging *w.* may have a core of iron *w.,* more frequently one of hemp, and such rope has fewer and larger threads per strand. Generally, a wire's flexibility increases with number of threads in each strand; thus, a 6 x 37 *w.* is suitable for use in a purchase, while the comparatively rigid 6 x 7 is adapted only for shrouds, stays, etc. Strength of *w.* compared with that of good *manila rope* of same size varies from 8 times greater in the case of high-grade uncoated 6 x 19 *plow steel w.* to about 3 times for 6 x 19 *phosphor bronze w.* Plow steel, cast steel, wrought iron, and phosphor bronze *w.,*—the kinds found aboard ship,—vary in strength in the order noted, their respective *breaking stresses,* in long tons, being approximately 40, 30, 22, and 16 *times rope's diameter squared.* The process of galvanizing *steel w.* diminishes its tensile strength by about one-tenth. Common galvanized steel *hoisting w.,* usually 6 x 19 type, may be considered as capable of withstanding a steady tension of 20 times its diameter squared. **Lang-lay,** or **Lang's lay, w.,** named for *John Lang,* manager of a British cordage manufacturing concern, Dixon Corbitt, Ltd., Newcastle-on-Tyne, a branch of which was set up at Birkenhead for production of 2500 miles of submarine cable for the trans-Atlantic project via the "Great Eastern." (*Cf.* GREAT EASTERN) The rope's strands have the same twist as lay of the strands in rope itself, instead of the usual *contrary* twist in stranded cordage. It is claimed the *w.* gives longer service than one of ordinary lay under same conditions of use, for the reason that less friction or denting takes place in such arrangement and a greater proportion of surface is exposed to wear than in standard lay. Its disadvantage is chiefly in handling. Ends of *w.* must always be well secured, or unstranding will result; hence its use, *esp.* in larger sizes, is confined to winding or a straight pull in great lengths. **Preformed-lay w.,** in this type, the threads and strands are given the shape, prior to assembly of the finished product, that they would assume if forcibly twisted as in ordinary *w.-rope* manufacture. It is said that the rope possesses higher bending resistance qualities, compared with ordinary *w.* It requires no precaution against unlaying when cut, since no "spring" is present in the lay, due to the natural "nesting" of all units in the rope; and, on that account, it has a much less tendency to kink than the commonly laid *w*. **W.-rope lay** is, at least in *w's* used on board ship, almost always *right-handed, i.e.,* the strands slope onward from left to right, or, facing the rope, "from your port nostril to your starboard eyebrow." **W.-rope clips,** U-shaped clamps used to secure the end of a *w*. to the standing part, as in turning in a temporary eye. **W.-rope socket,** also called *socket-eye,* a cone-shaped socket into which the end of a *w*. is inserted and spread as a substitute for an eye-splice, the socket being a fixed part of the eye; *see* **Patent e.** *in* EYE.

WISHBONE RIG. A sailing-yacht rig thus named from its double gaff or *sprit* being suggestive of a *wishbone.* Also called *main-trysail rig,* a jib-headed mainsail having a raised clew is thus fitted; the *w*. lies at an upward angle from mast and sail is hoisted or set between its arms or halves. The *w*. pivots on mast and from that point divides in two streamlined bowed parts which are connected at their after ends by a cross-piece, clew of sail being hauled out and secured to the latter. It is claimed that a fore-and-aft sail is spread to better advantage with this arrangement than with the conventional boom-and-gaff or loose-footed sail, under any trim of canvas. As fitted to a staysail, the sheet is relieved of much of its stress, or that component of the pull due to bellying of sail, which is borne as a *thrust* by the *w*.

WITH THE SUN. *See* SUN.

WITHE. A crance or boom-iron; also, *wythe. See* CRANCE.

W/M Abbrev. *Weight or Measurement,* usually appearing in the phrase: *W/M at ship's option. See* **M. cargo; M. rate; M. ton** *in* MEASUREMENT.

W N A. Abbrev. *Winter North Atlantic.* Letters in freeboard or load-line marks indicating minimum freeboard allowed a vessel navigated in the N. Atlantic during *winter.* For *sailing-ships,* it is the only mark providing an increase of freeboard,—in this case 3 inches,—above the normal minimum, or that marked by the line passing through center of load-line disk. For *powered* vessels not exceeding 330 feet in length (*between perpendiculars*) it is shown 2 inches below the mark *W* (= *Winter*); for those of greater length than 330 feet, it is the *W* mark. *Cf.* WINTER.

WOLF-FISH. A ferocious member of the *blenny* family inhabiting the N. Atlantic and N. Pacific. Has a blunt nose and strong ugly teeth; a dorsal fringe extending full length of body, which tapers to a small unforked tail; usually bluish or gray with dark cross-bars on back, or, as in the Pacific species, wholly brown. It attains a length of 4 to 6 feet.

WOODLOCK. In wooden vessels, a piece of hardwood fitted on fore side of rudder-stock in way of a *pintle,* so that it will keep rudder from rising, as in heavy weather, by butting against a *gudgeon.* Also, *wood-lock. Cf.* **Locking-p.** *in* PINTLE.

WOOF. *See* WEFT.

WOOLPACK. Alto-cumulus clouds. The *big w*. is a cumulus cloud, or a number of such, collectively. *See* CLOUD.

WOOLD. To take a number of close-fitting turns around a spar, as with a rope or chain, in the process of *fishing* it or strengthening it in way of a scarf; to wrap or wind turns about, as in lashing two spars together. The turns taken, *esp.,* in the former, are referred to as the *woolding* and each turn is hove taut by a stout stick termed a *woolder,* or *woolding-stick. (Archaic)*

WOP. Variant of *wapp.*

WORK. To strain or labor, as structural parts under stress; a vessel is said to *w*. when her timbers, planking, etc., "groan" or evince loss of rigidity, as in a seaway; also said of a cargo, *esp.,* case goods stowed in tier, from pitching or rolling motion of ship. To handle or operate; as, to *w*. *cargo;* to *w*. *ship to windward* (as by *tacking*); to *w*. *the lines* (in *warping ship*). To perform a specific task or duty; as, to *w*. *a sight* (or an *observation*); to *w*. *one's passage;* often with *in,* as, to *w*. *in a grommet, splice,* etc.; to *w*. *in the harbor* (by sailing or tide). That which is accomplished; as, a *day's w.;* a *tide's w*. In *pl.,* structural arrangement; as, *upper w's; see* UPPER. To **run the w's,** *see* RUN. To **w. a traverse,** *see* TRAVERSE. To **w. double tides,** to accomplish the *w*. of two days in one. To **w. one's passage,** to perform duty as a crew member in payment for transportation. To **w. up,** to assign to needless arduous or distasteful tasks; to exact punishment by requiring extra hours of duty or labor; as, to *w*. *up* the crew. (Also see *Work* as compounded with the following prefixes in BREAST; CHART; DAY'S; QUICK; TIDE)

WORKAWAY. One who works on board ship in payment for a passage; *esp.,* in a foreign-going vessel, a person repatriated by a consul, such as a distressed seaman, who nominally becomes a member of the crew upon signing of ship's articles, as formally required.

WORKING. In sailing, act of making progress in a given direction; *esp.* under adverse conditions; as, *w*. *to windward, to the northward, up a channel, into harbor,* etc. Operating; moving; as, *w*. *gear; w*. *parts of a tackle.* Relating to, or occupied by, *work;* as, a *w*. *day;* a *w*. *party.* Ordinarily in use, as distinguished from a special adaptation; as, *w*. *anchor; w*. *chart; w*. *gangway; w*. *sails.* **W. buoyancy,** *see* BUOYANCY. **W. canvas,** in a collective sense, sails in ordinary use, or those exclusive of storm canvas, fine-weather kites, etc.; plain sail. *Cf.* **W. sails** *in* SAIL. **W. days,** a charter-party term meaning days in which cargo ordinarily is worked at port concerned, Sundays and holidays excepted. Often referred to as simply *days.* **W. lights,** those for illuminating purposes, as in transfer of cargo at night;

esp., as distinguished from the regulation signal lights displayed by *fishing-vessels*, those used during sorting of fish, handling gear, etc., in the hours of darkness. **W. lines,** *see* LINE.[1] **W. log,** book in which is recorded the work performed each day; as, *deck w. log*; also, *work log*. **W. loose,** a bolt, chock, key, shore, rivet, plank end, etc., is said to be *w. loose* (or *work loose*) when giving way or becoming slack or movable because of vibration effect, strain, or other cause. **W. party,** a group of seamen detailed to some special work, either ashore or afloat. (*Naval usage*) **W. pool,** *see* POOL. **W. sails,** *see* **W. canvas.** **W. stress for rope, chain,** etc., maximum tension to which such should be subjected in ordinary use. It may be expressed as the *breaking stress* divided by *safety factor* adopted. (*Cf.* **Factor of s.** *in* SAFETY). Thus, breaking stress of *cast steel wire* being 30d², in long tons, a safety factor of 5 gives *w. stress* as 6 tons in the case of a 1″ diameter wire. *W. stress*, or *safe working load*, as often called, of good *manila rope* up to 5 inches in *circumference* may be stated as $C^2 \div 6$; larger sizes, $C^2 \div 7$, in *long tons*. Where d = diameter of metal, *safe w. load* for *steel chain* = 8d²; for a *steel hook* = two-thirds d² (diameter at lower quarter of hook); for a *steel shackle* = 3d² (dia. of pin); and a *steel ring-bolt* = 2d².

WORM. The spiral threaded section of a shaft which engages a toothed wheel, such as that in a capstan-spindle for turning a windless. To lay spun-yarn or other small stuff in the *contlines,* or hollows between strands, of a rope, for the purpose of making a smooth surface preparatory to *serving;* such small stuff thus used is called *worming. Cf.* **L.-rooming** *in* LINK. **Packing w.,** *see* **P'ing screw** *in* PACK. **Ship-w.,** *see* **M. borer** *in* MARINE. **W.-eaten,** condition of a vessel's timbers or outside planking when more or less damaged by the *ship-w.* or *marine borer.* A ship thus damaged also is said to be *w.-eaten.*

WORMLINE. Marline, spunyarn, roundline, or the like used for *worming* a rope; the *worming; see* WORM.

WRACK. (Doublet of *wreck*) Vegetation cast up on a beach, as various algæ, eel-grass, kelp, and the like. A variant of *rack,* the *scud,* or wind-driven *fracto-nimbus* or *fracto-stratus* cloud; *see* RACK².

WRAIN. Variant of *wring,* appearing in *w.-bolt, w.-staff; see* WRING.

WRASSE. A member of the *Labridæ* family of fishes, most of which are brilliantly colored and almost all species considered good food. Found chiefly in warmer seas, *esp.* in the Indian Ocean and tropical Pacific, but a few species inhabit temperate Atlantic latitudes and the Mediterranean, as the *rainbow w.* or *peacock fish, black w.,* and *green w.* The *tautog* or *blackfish* and the *cunner, nibbler,* or *sea-wife,* found on U.S. Atlantic coast, also belong to the *w.* family. *Cf.* LABRIDÆ.

WRECK. (Ice. *rek,* a thing drifted ashore; of Scand. origin) Partial or total destruction of a vessel, as by stranding, collision, or force of the elements; shipwreck; a badly damaged vessel or remains of such vessel; property washed up on a shore, such as fragments of a ship or some of her cargo; shipwrecked property; flotsam, jetsam, or lagan; wreckage. To cause to suffer damage to, disable, or destroy a vessel, as by driving her, or causing her to drive, on the rocks, or by causing her to founder; to engage in *wrecking,* whether for plunder or for rescue or salvage purposes, as in boarding a *w.* According to U.S. law, a *w.* or wreckage washed ashore becomes, in general, the property of person owning the shore, if not reclaimed by its original owner. In Great Britain, such material or goods, including *flotsam, jetsam,* and *lagan,* is forfeited to the crown, but may be recovered by the owner within a year, upon payment of certain charges, such as salvage or storage. **W. buoy,** a *green-painted* buoy marking a sunken *w.* When placed in a fairway or entrance to a port, if to be left on starboard hand of a vessel entering from sea (or, in Great Britain, going in the direction of the *flood stream*) it is conical in shape, or a *nun buoy;* if to be left on port hand, it is flat-topped, or a *can buoy;* and if to be passed on either side, spherical. The last-named, in U.S. buoyage, may be colored with *red and black* horizontal bands or stripes, as an *obstruction buoy.* Where necessary, such buoy may exhibit a light which always is *green* in color and usually a flashing one. Sometimes a *w.-marking vessel* or *boat* may be placed in lieu of a buoy. Particulars of position of sunken *w's* and the means installed for marking such are given in *Notices to Mariners, Hydrographic Bulletin,* and like informative sources. **W. chart,** coastal chart of a region indicating positions of *w's.* **W. commissioner,** or **commissioner of w's,** in Great Britain, person who holds a preliminary inquiry into circumstances of a shipping casualty, assisted by two or more nautical assessors. Result of such inquiry may lead to a formal investigation by *Ministry of Transport* authorities. **W.-free,** free of requirement to forfeit goods from a *w.,* a privilege granted by Edward I of England to the *Cinque Ports.* (*Historical*) **W. master,** officer taking charge of wrecked property; *see* RECEIVER OF WRECK. A person having charge of a *w.* or goods washed ashore in the interests of salvors or owner of such property. **W.-wood,** fragmentary pieces of wood found floating or washed up on a beach, as from a *w.*

WRECKAGE. Goods or parts of a wrecked vessel washed ashore or afloat; remains of a *wreck;* that which has been *wrecked; wreck.*

WRECKER. One who causes a vessel to be wrecked; a plunderer of a wreck or wreckage. One engaged in the salvage of goods or cargo from a stranded **vessel**, or of vessel herself; also, a ship employed in such service.

WRECKING. Occupation or procedure of salving wrecked or diabled vessels or their cargoes. Act of feloniously disabling or destroying a vessel; *esp.*, that of causing the stranding of any craft for plunder. In addition to prescribing punishment for the crime of *w.*, or plundering a wrecked vessel, *Title 18 U.S. Code, 488,* states that "whoever willfully obstructs the escape of any person endeavoring to save his life from such vessel, or the wreck thereof; or whoever holds out or shows any false light, or extinguishes any true light, with intent to bring any vessel sailing upon the sea into danger, or distress, or shipwreck, shall be imprisoned not less than ten years and may be imprisoned for life." *Cf.* JIBBER THE KIBBER. **W. blocks,** *see* BLOCK. **W.-cable,** *see* CABLE. **W. master,** also *wreck master, see* MASTER. **W.-pump,** as commonly included in equipment for salvage operations, any powerful pump for removing water from damaged or sunken vessels. **W. tug,** *see* **S. vessel** *in* SALVAGE. (For other terms connected with *w.* in the sense of *salving,* see under SALVAGE)

WRIGGLE. A rigol, watershed, or eyebrow; *see* **E.-brow** *in* EYE.

WRING. To bend, twist, or strain a spar out of line or from its normal position; as, *overmuch tension on jib stays will w. the topmast; our royalmast was wrung to port.* (*Archaic*) **W.-bolt,** in wooden shipbuilding, a kind of adjustable ring-bolt used in *setting* or working the strakes of outside planking into place in the procedure of securing them to the frames, *esp.,* where planking must be bent or twisted, as at vessel's forward end or at turn of the counter. Shank of *w.-bolt* is fitted in a piece of wood or metal laid across inner surfaces of two adjacent frames and is supplied with forelock or toggle-pin holes for adjusting to working length required. The bolt being fixed in position desired, its ring is used as a fulcrum for the *w.-staff* (also called *wrain-staff, wrain-stave,* and *sett*) or handy hardwood lever, in *wringing,* or *setting,* the plank into place. Each plank is thus treated progressively, by working along its length as it is secured to each frame.

WRINKLING. Corrugations or any irregular bending in a metal plate due to excessive compression or shearing stress.

WRITER. *See* **S.'s writer** *in* SHIP.

WRONG. Now probably obsolete equivalent of *to blanket,* or take the wind from, another vessel, as in racing; *see* BLANKET.

W. T. Abbrev. *watertight;* also, W/T; as in *W.T. Door, W/T Flat, w.t. bulkhead,* etc.

WYE. A fitting similar in shape to the letter *Y;* a *Y bend; Y branch.*

WYTHE. *See* WITHE.

X. Square flag "X-ray" of the International Code, showing a white ground with a blue Greek cross extending full breadth and length of flag. Flown uppermost in a 4-flag hoist, it signifies a *true bearing* that is indicated by the other 3 flags; as, *X 0 0 5; X 3 5 0;* or, respectively, true bearings 5° and 350°. Hoisted singly, it means "*Stop carrying out your intentions and watch for my signals.*" As a *towing signal,* hoisted or otherwise exhibited singly, by *ship towing* signifies "*Get spare towing-hawser ready*"; by *ship towed,* "*Spare towing-hawser is ready.*"

XEBEC. (Pron. *zebek* or *ksebek*) (Sp. *jabeque* or *xabeque;* prob. from Turkish, *sumbeki,* a kind of boat) A small Mediterranean trading vessel, lateen-rigged and usually having three masts; the Spanish *jabeque,* French *chebec,* and *sciabecco* of the Italians, once known as *mistico* in Sicily and nearby African shores. The historical and probably original *x.,* however, was the much larger 3-masted vessel of war mounting 15 to 24 guns, notably such craft manned by Algerine corsairs,—a motley mob composed of Arabs, Berbers, Moors, Negroes, Turks, and others,—in the 18th. and 19th. centuries. Low-waisted with projecting stern and raking stem, vessel was a remarkably fast sailer and carried an enormous spread of canvas. She was square-rigged on foremast, had lateen sails on main and mizzen, and it is said that the craft was capable of setting a lateen on the foremast and dispensing with all square canvas during head winds or adverse heavy weather. Whatever the character of her crew of 300 or more, it appears the *x.* of the corsairs was admirably handled in any circumstances, including the showing of "a clean pair of heels to the King's frigates." Sometimes written *zebec.*

XIPHIAS. (L. = swordfish) The genus comprising the common swordfish, or that constituting the *Xiphiidæ; see* SWORDFISH. Another name for the small constellation *Dorado,* also called the *Swordfish; see* DORADO.

Y

Y. In the International Code of Signals, denoted by square flag *"yoke,"* which has a series of diagonal alternating yellow and red bars of equal width, having an upward slant at a 45° angle with the hoist. Displayed singly, it denotes *"I am carrying mails."* As a towing signal, the flag, or its Morse code equivalent by flashing light *dash-dot-dash-dash* (– . – –), signifies *"I can not carry out your order,"* as sent by either *vessel towing* or *vessel towed.* Having the shape of, or suggesting, the letter Y; as, a *Y-bend;* a *Y-branch* (in a pipe); a *wye.* **Y-gun,** *see* GUN.

YACHT. (Du. *jaght,* short for *jaghtschip,* a vessel for chasing; from *jagen,* to hunt or chase) Vessel or boat specially built for racing, or one used for pleasure only; a vessel, often more or less luxuriously fitted out, for conveyance of distinguished persons, for pleasure cruising, for sport of fishing, etc.; any craft, other than a fishing- or a trading-vessel, used for private or official trips, or for racing. According to *Lloyd's* classification rules, a *y.* is a pleasure-boat over 30 feet in length and driven by either sail or mechanical power. U.S. navigation laws require every *y.* of over 15 gross tonnage and *any y.* having dutiable goods on board to make due entry at customs house at port to which such *y.* returns from visiting a foreign country; otherwise, in general, a *y.* is free to travel from port to port without entering and clearing at customs in any place within U.S. territory. This privilege also applies to foreign *y's,* as and when similar reciprocal courtesy is extended by their governments to U.S.-owned craft. All U.S. powered *y's* are subject to requirements of vessel inspection regulations by the Coast Guard and cruising *y's* mentioned above are required to be *enrolled* and *licensed.* *Y's* often are designated from their rig or powering; as, *cutter y.; ketch y.; schooner y.; sloop y.; gasoline y.; motor y.; oil y.; steam y.* **Auxiliary y.,** a *sailing-y.* having an engine and propeller to supplement her sail power; *see* AUXILIARY. **Barge y.,** shallow-draft *sailing-y.* having a flat bottom and fitted with a centerboard or lee-boards for lateral resistance. **Cruising y.,** one designed and equipped for covering long distances, *esp.* in open waters. Chief requisite in such vessel is reasonably good behavior in heavy weather, while of such hull design that sacrifice of speed in attaining this quality is brought to a minimum. **Y.-built,** having the graceful lines of a *y.;* marked with the elegance of a well-appointed *y.* **Y. club,** an association of yachtsmen for the promotion of good fellowship and their common interests. **Y. ensign,** a modified form of a national ensign authorized for display on *y's; see* **Yacht e.** *in* ENSIGN. **Y. marline,** *see* MARLINE. **Y. measurement,** an adopted formula or rule according to which a *y.* is measured for tonnage and classified, or *rated,* accordingly for purposes of entry in a race or series of races. Also called *y. rating,* usual criteria are length, sail area, and displacement. *Cf.* HANDICAP. **Y. stern,** the lengthy graceful overhanging stern or counter-found on larger first-class *y's;* stern of a boat or vessel likened to such.

YACHTING. Act of cruising, racing, or sailing in a *yacht;* sailing for pleasure in a *yacht,* as on a *y.-trip* or *y. cruise.*

YACHTSMAN. One who owns or sails a *yacht* for pleasure, or is actively engaged in yacht-racing, or in *yachtsmanship,* which may be defined as the art of managing a yacht.

YACHTY. Of yacht-like appearance; trim and neat; said of a vessel.

YARD.[1] (A.S. *gyrd,* a stick or rod) A cross-spar for spreading the head of a *square,* a *lateen,* or a *lug* sail; also, such spar for carrying two or more sets of halyards for hoisting flags, shapes, or lights as signals; a *signal-y.* **Y.** of a square sail is secured to its mast at its middle and may be fitted to pivot horizontally on a fixed point (its *truss* or *crane*), as a *lower y.* (that of a *course,* or foresail, mainsail, etc.), a *lower-tops'l y.,* or a *lower-topgallant y.;* or may be rigged also for hoisting in setting sail, as an *upper-tops'l y.,* an *upper-topgallant y.,* or a *royal y.* An exception to these is the small spar extending the head of an uppermost studding-sail, as the *main-royal-stuns'l y.* All *y's* crossing the square-rigger's masts are tapered toward each end, or *y.-arm,* from their greatest diameter at the *slings,* or part in way of the mast. Heavier *y's* in more recent years were either *built* wooden spars or of the steel tubular type. A *lateen-sail y.,* comparatively lengthy, is confined to the mast on which hoisted at about one-fourth its length from the forward end. It slopes aft and upward at a sharp angle; *see* LATEEN. *Y.* of a *lug sail* usually is slung by its halyards at about one-third its length from forward and may slope upward at almost any angle, depending upon cut of sail concerned. *Cf.* **L. rig** *in* LUG; *also* **J.-yard** *in* JACK. To **back a y.,** *see* To **b. a sail** *in* BACK. **Head y's,** in a vessel square-rigged on two or more masts, those on the foremast; opposed to *after y's,* or those abaft a mainmast. To **lay a y. aback,** to brace a *y.* so that wind strikes fore side of its sail; as, to *lay the head y's aback.* To **man the y's,** *see* MAN. **Monkey y.,** *see* **M. spar** *in* MONKEY. To **point the y's,** *see* POINT. **Quarter of a y.,** that portion extending from the *slings,* or middle portion, to about half-way out from the mast, on either side; outside or beyond the *q.* is the *y.-arm.* **Spare y.,** one kept available as a replacement for another *y.* **Y.-arm,** either extremity of the *y.* of a square sail, usually considered as extending one-quarter of length of *y.* from either end. As distinguished from the *hatch-boom,* which is guyed to plumb a hatchway in the two-boom system of transferring cargo, the boom guyed outward beyond ship's side to plumb the pier, a vessel alongside, etc. **Y.-arm cleat,** fitting on a *y.-arm* for receiving turns of the *head-* or the *reef-earing,* as in stretching out a square sail in bending or reefing; *cf.* EARING. **Y.-arm hoop,** iron band round a *y.-arm.* It is fitted with the necessary eyes for connecting the brace, lift, foot-rope, and reef-tackle. **Y.-arm to y.-arm,** said of vessels lying or sailing close alongside each other; *esp.,* in describing older combat of the hand-to-hand order. **Y.-becket,** *see* **Hand-b's** *in* BECKET. **Y.-rope,** gantline for sending up or down an upper *y.* **Y.-tackle,** a purchase used in hoisting a heavy weight when employing a *lower y.* as a derrick. Also, a purchase for sending aloft or lowering to the deck a *lower* or a *topsail y.* **Y.-whip,** a hoisting-rope rove through a block on a *y.;* also, a light tackle attached to a *lower y.* for hoisting purposes; *see* WHIP. The fall used on a *y.-arm* (cargo boom) for lifting from or landing goods on a wharf, lighter, etc.; *see* **Y.-arm.** (Also see terms combined or connected with *Yard* in the following: AFTER; CRANE; CROSSJACK; FORE; JACK; LOWER; PARREL; ROYAL; SIGNAL; SLING; SPRITSAIL; TOPGALLANT; TOPSAIL; TRAVERSE; TRIM; TRUSS)

YARD.[2] Short for *dockyard, navy yard, repair yard, shipyard, victualling yard,* etc. **Y. master,** superintendent or overseer of general operations in a *shipyard; esp.,* the moving of material by cranes, railway cars, etc., about the *y.*

YARE. An old English word meaning lively, active, easily worked or manageable, as descriptive of a vessel.

YARN. A *rope-yarn,* or number of lengthy fiber threads twisted together; *see* **R.-yarn** *in* ROPE; *also,* SPUNYARN. An entertaining story, or tale of adventure, deftly "spun" as the narrator progresses. To tell stories; to swop "yarns"; *see* To **s. a yarn** *in* SPIN. **Heart y.,** *see* HEART. **Rogue's y.,** as a mark for identifying ownership or maker of cordage, originally adopted by the British navy, a *rope-y.* of different twist, material, or color from the others laid in one or more strands of a rope; so named for its use in tracing stolen cordage. **Warp y's,** threads in sail-cloth running lengthwise; *see* WARP. **Weft y's,** threads running crosswise in canvas; also, *woof y's; woof threads; see* WEFT.

YARROW BOILER. See BOILER.

YAW. (Old Teutonic origin) To swing temporarily from the course by the action of a following or quarterly sea, as commonly occurs with smaller vessels, markedly so in heavy weather. While such deviation to either side of the course takes place independently of the steering, it may be greatly reduced by an alert experienced helmsman, who naturally will anticipate the "swing" or *yaw, esp.,* in a quarterly sea, with a generous amount of counteracting rudder, as vessel's stern lifts to each oncoming "sweeper." To steer wildly, or run off the course alternately from side to side, from whatever cause. Such deviation or swing from the course (not to be confused with *sheer; see* SHEER) as, a *y.* of 10 degrees. Act of *yawing* may be defined as an oscillatory movement of a vessel about a vertical axis passing through her center of gravity, or nearly so.

YAWL. (Du. *jol,* a skiff or yawl) A two-masted fore-and-aft rigged vessel or boat having her after mast,—called *jigger, mizzen,* or *dandy,* and less than half the height of her mainmast,—stepped abaft the stern-post. Mainmast is stepped farther forward than in the *sloop* rig but spreads similar canvas. An outrigger over the stern takes care of sheeting out the mizzen. *Cf.* DANDY. Also, a ship's small working boat, or *jolly-boat;* in Great Britain, a boat or light vessel, usually having a sharp stern, rigged with two or three lug sails; a moderate-sized rowing or sailing boat included in equipment of a British war-vessel; any small boat attached to a fishing-vessel, lightship, yacht, dredge, etc.; a dinghy. (Older form, *yaul*) **Cat y.,** a *catboat* carrying a small mizzen, as in the *y.* rig; *see* CATBOAT. **Roslyn y.,** a *sharpie* carrying one or two jibs and a small mizzen or jigger; named for Roslyn, Long Island, home of the original. *Cf.* SHARPIE. **Shetland y.,** *see* HAAF. **Y.-rigged,** having the masts and sails characteristic of a *y.,* as indicated in initial remarks under YAWL.

YEAR. Period occupied by the sun in making his apparent circuit in the ecliptic, or completing his path through the heavens, as measured from one *vernal equinox* to the next; period in which the earth makes a complete revolution around the sun, or that elapsing between two successive passages of the sun's center through the vernal equinoctial point. Called the *astronomical, equinoctial, natural, solar,* or *tropical y.,* it is equal to 365 days, 5 hours, 48 minutes, 45.51 seconds of *mean solar time* (*see* **E. year** *in* EQUINOCTIAL) and is the basis for our reckoning of time by the calendar. **Lunar y.,** *see* LUNAR. **Sidereal y.,** this is the *true* measure of the period occupied by the earth in her orbital circuit. It is the time elapsing between two successive arrivals of "*Old Sol*" at a given point amongst the fixed stars, and is equal to 365 days, 6 hours, 9 minutes, 8.97 seconds of *mean solar time,* a difference of 20 minutes, 23.46 seconds, *longer* than the *astronomical y.;* also called *astral y.*

YELLOW. Of the color yellow; having a yellowish tint or color. **Y. flag,** the quarantine or pratique flag; *see* Q; **Q. signals** *in* QUARANTINE; *and* PRATIQUE. **Y. jack,** *see* JACK. **Y. metal,** Muntz or marine metal; *see* **Composition m.** *in* METAL. **Y. pine,** *see* PINE. **Y.-tailed shad,** the fish *menhaden*. **Y.-tailed snapper,** kind of snapper found in West Indies and Caribbean waters; *see* SNAPPER.

YEOMAN. A petty officer who performs clerical duties in one of the departments on a naval vessel; sometimes, a purser's clerk on a passenger liner. **Signal y.,** in the British navy, a warrant officer or 1st. class petty officer in charge of flag or flashing signaling procedure; also, *y. of signals.*

YIELD POINT. In testing strength of new material, *e.g.,* tensile strength of steel plate, the stress at which permanent deformation, strain, or *set* is produced in a test-piece, or that exceeding the *elastic limit* of the material.

YOKE. In lieu of a *tiller,* a cross-piece fixed to the rudder-head in smaller craft. A pair of *y.-lines,* or *y.-ropes,* are fitted to its ends for steering by hand. Where a steering-wheel is in use, the *tiller-* or *wheel-ropes* (or *chains*) replace the *y.-lines.* Cf. **B.-yoke** *in* BOAT. **Mast-y.,** *see* MAST. **Truss-y.,** *see* TRUSS.

YORK-ANTWERP RULES. See AVERAGE.

YOUNG ICE. See ICE.

Z

Z. International Code square flag *"zebra,"* consisting of four colored isosceles triangles of equal area having their apexes meeting at flag's center, *black* triangle being at the hoist; *blue,* at the fly; *yellow,* at top; and *red* one at bottom. Flown singly, the flag indicates *"I wish to address,* or *am addressing, a shore station"*; or its equivalent may be indicated by flashing the Z character in Morse code, *dash-dash-dot-dot* (– – . .) As a *towing signal,* hoisted or otherwise displayed singly by *ship towing,* Z-flag denotes *"I am commencing to tow"*; by *ship towed,* *"Commence towing."* Morse code Z by flashing also may be used for these signals. As an *abbrev.,* Z = *azimuth* (*see* AZIMUTH); z = *zenith distance* and, in weather recording, *hazy.* Resembling the letter Z in form; as, *Z-crank; Z-iron; Z-beam. Cf.* **Z-bar** *in* BAR; **Z-frame** *in* FRAME.

ZEBEC. Variant of *Xebec.*

ZENITH. Point in the heavens directly above one's head, or that indicated by projection or extension of the *plumb-line;* central and highest point of the celestial dome; opposite to *nadir.* **Z. distance,** angular distance from center of a heavenly body to the z.; complement of the *true altitude* of body's center. **Z. telescope,** an astronomical instrument for accurately determining the *latitude* of a place by observing z. *distances* of two stars that culminate as close as possible in time, and at nearly same altitude on opposite sides of the z. Mean of latitudes thus obtained is the *true latitude. Cf.* LATITUDE.

ZEPHYR. (Gr. *Zephyrus,* god of the west wind) A soft gentle breeze; *esp.,* one from the southwest or west. (*Chiefly poetic*)

ZIGZAG. A line or path containing sharp angles or turns from side to side throughout its course. Having short turns or angles in its onward path; as, a z. *course* or *track.* To proceed on a course characterized by short turns or "legs" from side to side of the mean heading, as in *zigzagging* for protection against, or confusing, an enemy submarine. **Z. bulkhead,** a partition or bulkhead having two or more angles or corners in its extent. **Z. clock,** a time-piece that may be set to sound an alarm at

each instant ship's course must be changed, in accordance with a given z. plan, in order to assure maintenance of the required *mean course,* or course to be *made good;* also, z. *control.* **Z. riveting,** *see* RIVETING.

ZINCS. Plates or pieces of zinc fitted inside or outside a ship's hull as a means of protecting the steel against corrosive effect of galvanic action, or electrolysis, as in way of propeller-blades, stern tubes, sea-valves, pipe-lines, etc., or other parts known to suffer such attack. Also called *anodes,* from their use as positive electrodes or entering poles of the generated current; *see* ELECTROLYSIS.

ZODIAC. (Gr. *zodiakos,* a circle of animals) Imaginary belt in the heavens following and extending about 8° on each side of the *ecliptic,* while embracing also the orbits of our Moon and principal planets. What are called the *12 signs of the z.* take their names from the constellations through which the Sun successively passes in his apparent perennial path. These are, beginning with Sun's arrival at the *vernal equinox, Pisces,* or Latin word for *fishes; Aries* = ram; *Taurus* = bull; *Gemini* = twins; *Cancer* = crab; *Leo* = lion; *Virgo* = virgin; *Libra* = balance; *Scorpio* = scorpion; *Sagittarius* = archer; *Capricornus* = goat; *Aquarius* = water-bearer. *Cf.* ECLIPTIC.

ZODIACAL. Pertaining to, or within, the *zodiac;* as, z. *stars.* **Z. light,** a nebulous light or faint luminous area in the sky appearing shortly before dawn in the east and after twilight in the west. Of elongated triangular form, having its base in the horizon and its apex in the ecliptic, it reaches to varying altitudes according to greater or lesser extent of its base. It is most clearly and frequently seen in tropical and sub-tropical latitudes. The phenomenon is said to be produced by reflected light from thousands of meteors that revolve about the Sun in or nearly in the plane of the ecliptic.

ZONDA. (Native name) A hot dry wind blowing from W. to N.W. over the Argentine pampas, particularly in summer.

ZONE. (Gr. = a girdle or belt)   An area or region of definite limits or generally distinct from an adjoining or surrounding region; as, *Canal Z.; danger z.; ice z.; z. of operations.* An encircling belt of a sphere; *specif.,* any of the great climatic-latitude divisions of the Earth, *viz.,* the *Torrid z.,* extending between the *Tropics of Cancer* (23° 27′ N.) and *Capricorn* (23° 27′ S.); *North Temperate z.,* between 23° 27′ N. and *Arctic circle* (66° 33′ N.); *North Frigid z.,* or entire region poleward of last-named; *South Temperate z.,* between 23° 27′ S. and *Antarctic circle* (66° 33′ S.); *South Frigid z.,* or entire region south of last-named limit. **Freeboard z.,** *see* FREEBOARD. **Littoral z.,** *see* LITTORAL. **Storm z.,** *see* STORM. **Z. time,** *see* TIME.